C# FOR EXPERIENCED PROGRAMMERS

DEITEL™ DEVELOPER SERIES

Deitel™ Books, Cyber Classrooms, Complete Tra
published by

DEITEL™ *Developer* Series

C#: A Programmer's Introduction

C# for Experienced Programmers

Java™ Web Services for Experienced Programmers

Visual Basic® .NET for Experienced Programmers

Visual C++® .NET: A Managed Code Approach
   For Experienced Programmers

Web Services: A Technical Introduction

Java 2 Micro Edition for Experienced Programmers (Spring 2003)

Java 2 Enterprise Edition for Experienced Programmers (Spring 2003)

ASP .NET and Web Services with Visual Basic® .NET for Experienced
   Programmers (Fall 2002)

ASP .NET and Web Services with C# for Experienced Programmers
   (Spring 2003)

How to Program Series

Advanced Java™ 2 Platform How to
   Program
C How to Program, 3/E
C++ How to Program, 3/E
C# How to Program
e-Business and e-Commerce How to
   Program
Internet and World Wide Web How to
   Program, 2/E
Java™ How to Program, 4/E
Perl How to Program
Python How to Program
Visual Basic® 6 How to Program
Visual Basic® .NET How to
   Program, 2/E
Wireless Internet & Mobile Business
   How to Program
XML How to Program

.NET How to Program Series

C# How to Program
Visual Basic® .NET How to Program, 2/E

Visual Studio® Series

C# How to Program
Visual Basic® .NET How to Program, 2/E
Getting Started with Microsoft® Visual
   C++™ 6 with an Introduction to
   MFC
Visual Basic® 6 How to Program

For Managers Series

e-Business and e-Commerce for
   Managers

Coming Soon

e-books and e-whitepapers
Premium CourseCompass, WebCT and
   Blackboard Multimedia Cyber
   Classroom versions

ining Courses and Web-Based Training Courses
Prentice Hall

Multimedia Cyber Classroom and Web-Based Training Series

(For information regarding Deitel™ Web-based training visit **www.ptgtraining.com**)

C++ Multimedia Cyber Classroom, 3/E

C# Multimedia Cyber Classroom

e-Business and e-Commerce Multimedia Cyber Classroom

Internet and World Wide Web Multimedia Cyber Classroom, 2/E

Java™ 2 Multimedia Cyber Classroom, 4/E

Perl Multimedia Cyber Classroom

Python Multimedia Cyber Classroom

Visual Basic® 6 Multimedia Cyber Classroom

Visual Basic® .NET Multimedia Cyber Classroom, 2/E

Wireless Internet & Mobile Business Programming Multimedia Cyber Classroom

XML Multimedia Cyber Classroom

The Complete Training Course Series

The Complete C++ Training Course, 3/E

The Complete C# Training Course

The Complete e-Business and e-Commerce Programming Training Course

The Complete Internet and World Wide Web Programming Training Course, 2/E

The Complete Java™ 2 Training Course, 4/E

The Complete Perl Training Course

The Complete Python Training Course

The Complete Visual Basic® 6 Training Course

The Complete Visual Basic® .NET Training Course, 2/E

The Complete Wireless Internet & Mobile Business Programming Training Course

The Complete XML Programming Training Course

To follow the Deitel publishing program, please register at

www.deitel.com/newsletter/subscribe.html

for the *DEITEL™ BUZZ ONLINE* e-mail newsletter.

To communicate with the authors, send e-mail to:

deitel@deitel.com

For information on corporate on-site seminars and public seminars offered by Deitel & Associates, Inc. worldwide, visit:

www.deitel.com

For continuing updates on Prentice Hall and Deitel publications visit:

www.deitel.com,
www.prenhall.com/deitel or
www.InformIT.com/deitel

C# FOR EXPERIENCED PROGRAMMERS

PROGRAMMERS

DEITEL™ DEVELOPER SERIES

H. M. Deitel
Deitel & Associates, Inc.

P. J. Deitel
Deitel & Associates, Inc.

J. A. Listfield

T. R. Nieto
Deitel & Associates, Inc.

C. H. Yaeger
Deitel & Associates, Inc.

M. Zlatkina

Prentice
Hall

PRENTICE HALL, Upper Saddle River, New Jersey 07458

Library of Congress Cataloging-in-Publication Data

On file

Acquisitions Editor: *Karen McLean*
Project Manager: *Mike Ruel*
Executive Managing Editor: *Vince O'Brien*
Formatters: *Chirag Thakkar, John Lovell*
Director of Creative Services: *Paul Belfanti*
Art Editor: *Xiaohong Zhu*
Creative Director: *Carole Anson*
Design Technical Support: *John Christiana*
Chapter Opener and Cover Designers: *Dr. Harvey M. Deitel, Laura Treibick and Tamara L. Newnam*
Manufacturing Manager: *Trudy Pisciotti*
Manufacturing Buyer: *Lisa McDowell*
Marketing Manager: *Kate Hargett*
Marketing Assistant: *Corrine Mitchell*

© 2003 Pearson Education, Inc.
Upper Saddle River, New Jersey 07458

Printed in the United States of America

Cover photo: Michael Howell/Index Stock Imagery, Inc.

10 9 8 7 6

ISBN 0-13-046133-4

Pearson Education Ltd., *London*
Pearson Education Australia Pty. Ltd., *Sydney*
Pearson Education Singapore, Pte. Ltd.
Pearson Education North Asia Ltd., *Hong Kong*
Pearson Education Canada, Inc., *Toronto*
Pearson Educacion de Mexico, S.A. de C.V.
Pearson Education–Japan, *Tokyo*
Pearson Education Malaysia, Pte. Ltd.
Pearson Education, Inc., *Upper Saddle River, New Jersey*

To Karen McLean, Editor of the *Deitel™ Developer Series*:

It is a privilege to work with you—a consummate professional and our friend—on this very special publishing program.

Harvey and Paul Deitel

To Will O'Brien, Piotr Dollar, Andrew Fleming and Adam Ross:

For all the good times we have shared over the last four years.

Jeff

In loving memory of Grandpa Foster.

Tem R. Nieto

To my brother Lowell:

You are the funniest and most caring person I know.

Cheryl

To the special person in my life, Igor Levit:

Who has been there to provide support and encouragement when I needed it most. Thank you for being the person you are.

Love, *Marina*

Trademarks

Contents

Preface   xxxix

Introduction to .NET and C#   1
1.1   Introduction   2
1.2   History of the Internet and World Wide Web   2
1.3   World Wide Web Consortium (W3C)   4
1.4   Extensible Markup Language (XML)   4
1.5   Key Software Trend: Object Technology   5
1.6   Introduction to Microsoft .NET   7
1.7   C#   9
1.8   .NET Framework and the Common Language Runtime   9
1.9   Tour of the Book   10
1.10 Summary   19
1.11 Internet and World Wide Web Resources   21

**2   Introduction to the Visual Studio .NET IDE and
C# Programming**   22
2.1   Introduction   23
2.2   Visual Studio .NET Integrated Development Environment (IDE) Overview   24
2.3   Menu Bar and Toolbar   27
2.4   Visual Studio .NET Windows   29
       2.4.1   **Solution Explorer**   29
       2.4.2   **Toolbox**   30
       2.4.3   **Properties** Window   31
2.5   Using Help   33
2.6   Simple Program: Displaying Text and an Image   34
2.7   Simple Program: Printing a Line of Text   43
2.8   Arithmetic   52

| 2.9 | Decision Making: Equality and Relational Operators | 53 |
| 2.10 | Summary | 58 |

3 **Control Structures** **60**

3.1	Introduction	61
3.2	Control Structures	61
3.3	**if** Selection Structure	63
3.4	**if/else** Selection Structure	63
3.5	**while** Repetition Structure	64
3.6	Assignment Operators	67
3.7	Increment and Decrement Operators	67
3.8	**for** Repetition Structure	69
3.9	Example: Using the **for** Structure to Compute Compound Interest	71
3.10	**switch** Multiple-Selection Structure	76
3.11	**do/while** Repetition Structure	80
3.12	Statements **break** and **continue**	81
3.13	Logical and Conditional Operators	84
3.14	Introduction to Windows Application Programming	88
3.15	Summary	95

4 **Methods and Arrays** **97**

4.1	Introduction	98
4.2	Methods in C#	99
4.3	Method Definitions	99
4.4	Argument Promotion	106
4.5	C# Namespaces	108
4.6	Value Types and Reference Types	109
4.7	Passing Arguments: Pass-by-Value vs. Pass-by-Reference	110
4.8	Scope Rules	114
4.9	Recursion	117
4.10	Method Overloading	119
4.11	Arrays	122
4.12	Declaring and Allocating Arrays	123
4.13	Passing Arrays to Methods	126
4.14	Passing Arrays by Value and by Reference	126
4.15	Multiple-Subscripted Arrays	130
4.16	**foreach** Repetition Structure	135
4.17	Summary	136

5 **Object-Based Programming** **137**

5.1	Introduction	138
5.2	Implementing a Time Abstract Data Type with a Class	139
5.3	Class Scope	147
5.4	Controlling Access to Members	147
5.5	Initializing Class Objects: Constructors	149
5.6	Using Overloaded Constructors	150
5.7	Properties	154

5.8	Composition: Objects References as Instance Variables of Other Classes	161
5.9	Using the **this** Reference	165
5.10	Garbage Collection	167
5.11	**static** Class Members	168
5.12	**const** and **readonly** Members	173
5.13	Indexers	175
5.14	Data Abstraction and Information Hiding	181
5.15	Software Reusability	183
5.16	Namespaces and Assemblies	183
5.17	**Class View** and **Object Browser**	189
5.18	Summary	191

6 Object-Oriented Programming: Inheritance   192

6.1	Introduction	193
6.2	Base Classes and Derived Classes	194
6.3	**protected** and **internal** Members	197
6.4	Relationship between Base Classes and Derived Classes	197
6.5	Case Study: Three-Level Inheritance Hierarchy	218
6.6	Constructors and Destructors in Derived Classes	221
6.7	Software Engineering with Inheritance	227
6.8	Summary	228

7 Object-Oriented Programming: Polymorphism   229

7.1	Introduction	230
7.2	Derived-Class-Object to Base-Class-Object Conversion	230
7.3	Type Fields and **switch** Statements	237
7.4	Polymorphism Examples	238
7.5	Abstract Classes and Methods	239
7.6	Example: Inheriting Interface and Implementation	241
7.7	**sealed** Classes and Methods	249
7.8	Example: Payroll System Using Polymorphism	250
7.9	Example: Creating and Using Interfaces	260
7.10	Delegates	272
7.11	Operator Overloading	277
7.12	Summary	282

8 Exception Handling   284

8.1	Introduction	285
8.2	Exception Handling Overview	286
8.3	Example: **DivideByZeroException**	289
8.4	.NET **Exception** Hierarchy	294
8.5	**finally** Block	295
8.6	**Exception** Properties	303
8.7	Programmer-Defined Exception Classes	308
8.8	Handling Overflows with Operators **checked** and **unchecked**	312
8.9	Summary	314

9   Graphical User Interface Concepts: Part 1   316

9.1   Introduction   317
9.2   Windows Forms   318
9.3   Event-Handling Model   321
      9.3.1   Basic Event Handling   322
9.4   Control Properties and Layout   326
9.5   **Label**s, **TextBox**es and **Button**s   330
9.6   **GroupBox**es and **Panel**s   337
9.7   **CheckBox**es and **RadioButton**s   340
9.8   **PictureBox**es   349
9.9   Mouse Event Handling   351
9.10 Keyboard Event Handling   353
9.11 Summary   357

10   Graphical User Interface Concepts: Part 2   358

10.1 Introduction   359
10.2 Menus   359
10.3 **LinkLabel**s   368
10.4 **ListBox**es and **CheckedListBox**es   372
      10.4.1   **ListBox**es   375
      10.4.2   **CheckedListBox**es   377
10.5 **ComboBox**es   380
10.6 **TreeView**s   385
10.7 **ListView**s   391
10.8 Tab Control   398
10.9 Multiple-Document-Interface (MDI) Windows   403
10.10 Visual Inheritance   412
10.11 User-Defined Controls   416
10.12 Summary   421

11   Multithreading   423

11.1 Introduction   424
11.2 Thread States: Life Cycle of a Thread   425
11.3 Thread Priorities and Thread Scheduling   427
11.4 Thread Synchronization and Class **Monitor**   432
11.5 Producer/Consumer Relationship without Thread Synchronization   434
11.6 Producer/Consumer Relationship with Thread Synchronization   440
11.7 Producer/Consumer Relationship: Circular Buffer   449
11.8 Summary   460

12   Strings, Characters and Regular Expressions   462

12.1 Introduction   463
12.2 Fundamentals of Characters and Strings   463
12.3 **String** Constructors   465
12.4 **String** Indexer, **Length** Property and **CopyTo** Method   466
12.5 Comparing **String**s   468

12.6	**String** Method **GetHashCode**	472
12.7	Locating Characters and Substrings in **String**s	473
12.8	Extracting Substrings from **String**s	476
12.9	Concatenating **String**s	477
12.10	Miscellaneous **String** Methods	478
12.11	Class **StringBuilder**	480
12.12	**StringBuilder** Indexer, **Length** and **Capacity** Properties, and **EnsureCapacity** Method	482
12.13	**StringBuilder Append** and **AppendFormat** Methods	484
12.14	**StringBuilder Insert**, **Remove** and **Replace** Methods	488
12.15	**Char** Methods	491
12.16	Card Shuffling and Dealing Simulation	494
12.17	Regular Expressions and Class **Regex**	498
12.18	Summary	509

13   Graphics and Multimedia   510

13.1	Introduction	511
13.2	Graphics Contexts and Graphics Objects	513
13.3	Color Control	514
13.4	Font Control	522
13.5	Drawing Lines, Rectangles and Ovals	527
13.6	Drawing Arcs	530
13.7	Drawing Polygons and Polylines	533
13.8	Advanced Graphics Capabilities	537
13.9	Introduction to Multimedia	543
13.10	Loading, Displaying and Scaling Images	544
13.11	Animating a Series of Images	546
13.12	Windows Media Player	559
13.13	Microsoft Agent	562
13.14	Summary	576

14   Files and Streams   578

14.1	Introduction	579
14.2	Data Hierarchy	579
14.3	Files and Streams	581
14.4	Classes **File** and **Directory**	583
14.5	Creating a Sequential-Access File	593
14.6	Reading Data from a Sequential-Access File	605
14.7	Random-Access Files	616
14.8	Creating a Random-Access File	620
14.9	Writing Data Randomly to a Random-Access File	624
14.10	Reading Data Sequentially from a Random-Access File	629
14.11	Case Study: A Transaction-Processing Program	634
14.12	Summary	654

15   Extensible Markup Language (XML)   656

15.1	Introduction	657

15.2   XML Documents   657
15.3   XML Namespaces   662
15.4   Document Object Model (DOM)   665
15.5   Document Type Definitions (DTDs), Schemas and Validation   683
        15.5.1   Document Type Definitions   684
        15.5.2   Microsoft XML Schemas   687
        15.5.3   W3C XML Schema   690
        15.5.4   Schema Validation in C#   691
15.6   Extensible Stylesheet Language and **XslTransform**   695
15.7   Microsoft BizTalk™   702
15.8   Summary   705
15.9   Internet and World Wide Web Resources   707

16   Database, SQL and ADO .NET   709
16.1   Introduction   710
16.2   Relational Database Model   711
16.3   Relational Database Overview: **Books** Database   712
16.4   Structured Query Language (SQL)   719
        16.4.1   Basic **SELECT** Query   719
        16.4.2   **WHERE** Clause   720
        16.4.3   **ORDER BY** Clause   723
        16.4.4   Merging Data from Multiple Tables: **INNER JOIN**   726
        16.4.5   Joining Data from Tables **Authors**, **AuthorISBN**,
                  Titles and **Publishers**   728
        16.4.6   **INSERT** Statement   731
        16.4.7   **UPDATE** Statement   732
        16.4.8   **DELETE** Statement   733
16.5   ADO .NET Object Model   734
16.6   Programming with ADO .NET: Extracting Information from a Database 735
        16.6.1   Connecting to and Querying an Access Data Source   735
        16.6.2   Querying the **Books** Database   742
16.7   Programming with ADO.NET: Modifying a Database   744
16.8   Reading and Writing XML Files   752
16.9   Summary   755

17   ASP .NET, Web Forms and Web Controls   757
17.1   Introduction   758
17.2   Simple HTTP Transaction   759
17.3   System Architecture   761
17.4   Creating and Running a Simple Web Form Example   762
17.5   Web Controls   775
        17.5.1   Text and Graphics Controls   776
        17.5.2   **AdRotator** Control   780
        17.5.3   Validation Controls   785
17.6   Session Tracking   796
        17.6.1   Cookies   797
        17.6.2   Session Tracking with **HttpSessionState**   806

17.7   Case Study: Online Guest Book   815
17.8   Case Study: Connecting to a Database in ASP .NET   822
17.9   Tracing   836
17.10   Summary   838
17.11   Internet and Web Resources   840

18   ASP .NET and Web Services   842
18.1   Introduction   843
18.2   Web Services   844
18.3   Simple Object Access Protocol (SOAP) and Web Services   847
18.4   Publishing and Consuming Web Services   849
18.5   Session Tracking in Web Services   864
18.6   Using Web Forms and Web Services   877
18.7   Case Study: Temperature Information Application   883
18.8   User-Defined Types in Web Services   893
18.9   Summary   903

19   Networking: Streams-Based Sockets and Datagrams   905
19.1   Introduction   906
19.2   Establishing a Simple Server (Using Stream Sockets)   907
19.3   Establishing a Simple Client (Using Stream Sockets)   909
19.4   Client/Server Interaction with Stream-Socket Connections   910
19.5   Connectionless Client/Server Interaction with Datagrams   919
19.6   Client/Server Tic-Tac-Toe Using a Multithreaded Server   924
19.7   Summary   939

20   Data Structures and Collections   941
20.1   Introduction   942
20.2   Self-Referential Classes   942
20.3   Linked Lists   944
20.4   Stacks   956
20.5   Queues   961
20.6   Trees   964
        20.6.1   Binary Search Tree of Integer Values   966
        20.6.2   Binary Search Tree of **IComparable** Objects   973
20.7   Collection Classes   981
        20.7.1   Class **Array**   981
        20.7.2   Class **ArrayList**   984
        20.7.3   Class **Stack**   990
        20.7.4   Class **Hashtable**   994
20.8   Summary   1000

21   Accessibility   1002
21.1   Introduction   1003
21.2   Regulations and Resources   1004
21.3   Web Accessibility Initiative   1006

21.4   Providing Alternatives for Images   1006
21.5   Maximizing Readability by Focusing on Structure   1008
21.6   Accessibility in Visual Studio .NET   1008
        21.6.1   Enlarging Toolbar Icons   1009
        21.6.2   Enlarging the Text   1010
        21.6.3   Modifying the **Toolbox**   1011
        21.6.4   Modifying the Keyboard   1011
        21.6.5   Rearranging Windows   1012
21.7   Accessibility in C#   1014
21.8   Accessibility in XHTML Tables   1020
21.9   Accessibility in XHTML Frames   1024
21.10   Accessibility in XML   1025
21.11   Using Voice Synthesis and Recognition with VoiceXML™   1025
21.12   CallXML™   1033
21.13   JAWS® for Windows   1038
21.14   Other Accessibility Tools   1039
21.15   Accessibility in Microsoft® Windows® 2000   1041
        21.15.1   Tools for People with Visual Impairments   1042
        21.15.2   Tools for People with Hearing Impairments   1044
        21.15.3   Tools for Users Who Have Difficulty Using the Keyboard   1045
        21.15.4   Microsoft Narrator   1048
        21.15.5   Microsoft On-Screen Keyboard   1051
        21.15.6   Accessibility Features in Microsoft Internet Explorer 6.0 1052
21.16   Summary   1053
21.17   Internet and Web Resources   1054

22   Mobile Internet Toolkit   1057
22.1   Introduction   1058
22.2   Mobile Internet Toolkit Client Devices   1058
22.3   Introduction to the Mobile Internet Toolkit and Mobile Web Forms   1060
22.4   Advanced Mobile Web Forms Controls   1075
22.5   Example: Deitel Wireless Portal   1083
22.6   Device-Independent Web Design Using Style Sheets and Templates   1088
22.7   Consuming a Web Service from a Mobile Application   1101
22.8   Summary   1107
22.9   Internet and World Wide Web Resources   1108

A   Operator Precedence Chart   1109

B   Number Systems   1111
B.1   Introduction   1112
B.2   Abbreviating Binary Numbers as Octal Numbers and Hexadecimal
        Numbers   1115
B.3   Converting Octal Numbers and Hexadecimal Numbers to Binary Numbers 1117
B.4   Converting from Binary, Octal or Hexadecimal to Decimal   1117
B.5   Converting from Decimal to Binary, Octal or Hexadecimal   1118

B.6   Negative Binary Numbers: Two's Complement Notation   1119
B.7   Summary   1120

C   Career Opportunities   1122
C.1   Introduction   1123
C.2   Resources for the Job Seeker   1124
C.3   Online Opportunities for Employers   1125
         C.3.1   Posting Jobs Online   1127
         C.3.2   Problems with Recruiting on the Web   1129
         C.3.3   Diversity in the Workplace   1129
C.4   Recruiting Services   1130
C.5   Career Sites   1131
         C.5.1   Comprehensive Career Sites   1131
         C.5.2   Technical Positions   1132
         C.5.3   Wireless Positions   1132
         C.5.4   Contracting Online   1133
         C.5.5   Executive Positions   1134
         C.5.6   Students and Young Professionals   1135
         C.5.7   Other Online Career Services   1135
C.6   Summary   1136
C.7   Internet and World Wide Web Resources   1137

D   Visual Studio .NET Debugger   1142
D.1   Introduction   1143
D.2   Breakpoints   1144
D.3   Examining Data   1146
D.4   Program Control   1149
D.5   Additional Method Debugging Capabilities   1153
D.6   Additional Class Debugging Capabilities   1155
D.7   Summary   1158

E   Generating Documentation in Visual Studio .NET   1160
E.1   Introduction   1161
E.2   Documentation Comments   1161
E.3   Documenting C# Source Code   1162
E.4   Creating Comment Web Pages   1170
E.5   Creating XML Documentation Files   1172
E.6   Summary   1177

F   ASCII Character Set   1179

G   Unicode®   1180
G.1   Introduction   1181
G.2   Unicode Transformation Formats   1182
G.3   Characters and Glyphs   1183
G.4   Advantages and Disadvantages of Unicode   1184

G.5   Unicode Consortium's Web Site   1184
G.6   Using Unicode   1185
G.7   Character Ranges   1188
G.8   Summary   1189

H   COM Integration   1191
H.1   Introduction   1191
H.2   ActiveX Integration   1192
H.3   DLL Integration   1196
H.4   Summary   1200
H.5   Internet and World Wide Web Resources   1201

I   Introduction to HyperText Markup Language 4:
Part 1   1202
I.1   Introduction   1203
I.2   Markup Languages   1203
I.3   Editing HTML   1204
I.4   Common Elements   1204
I.5   Headers   1207
I.6   Linking   1208
I.7   Images   1210
I.8   Special Characters and More Line Breaks   1214
I.9   Unordered Lists   1216
I.10   Nested and Ordered Lists   1217
I.11   Summary   1220
I.12   Internet and World Wide Web Resources   1221

J   Introduction to HyperText Markup Language 4:
Part 2   1222
J.1   Introduction   1223
J.2   Basic HTML Tables   1223
J.3   Intermediate HTML Tables and Formatting   1225
J.4   Basic HTML Forms   1228
J.5   More Complex HTML Forms   1231
J.6   Internal Linking   1238
J.7   Creating and Using Image Maps   1241
J.8   `<meta>` Tags   1243
J.9   `frameset` Element   1245
J.10   Nested `frameset`s   1247
J.11   Summary   1249
J.12   Internet and World Wide Web Resources   1251

K   Introduction to XHTML: Part 1   1252
K.1   Introduction   1253
K.2   Editing XHTML   1253
K.3   First XHTML Example   1254

K.4   W3C XHTML Validation Service   1257
K.5   Headers   1258
K.6   Linking   1260
K.7   Images   1263
K.8   Special Characters and More Line Breaks   1267
K.9   Unordered Lists   1269
K.10 Nested and Ordered Lists   1270
K.11 Summary   1273
K.12 Internet and World Wide Web Resources   1274

L   Introduction to XHTML: Part 2   1275
L.1   Introduction   1276
L.2   Basic XHTML Tables   1276
L.3   Intermediate XHTML Tables and Formatting   1279
L.4   Basic XHTML Forms   1281
L.5   More Complex XHTML Forms   1284
L.6   Internal Linking   1292
L.7   Creating and Using Image Maps   1295
L.8   **meta** Elements   1297
L.9   **frameset** Element   1298
L.10 Nested **frameset**s   1302
L.11 Summary   1304
L.12 Internet and World Wide Web Resources   1305

M   HTML/XHTML Special Characters   1307

N   HTML/XHTML Colors   1308

O   Bit Manipulation   1311
O.1   Introduction   1312
O.2   Bit Manipulation and the Bitwise Operators   1312
O.3   Class **BitArray**   1324
O.4   Summary   1327

P   Crystal Reports® for Visual Studio .NET   1328
P.1   Introduction   1328
P.2   Crystal Reports Web Site Resources   1328
P.3   Crystal Reports and Visual Studio .NET   1329
      P.3.1   Crystal Reports in Web Applications   1332
      P.3.2   Crystal Reports and Web Services   1332

Bibliography   1334

Index   1338

Illustrations

1   Introduction to .NET and C#   1

1.1   .NET Languages (tabular information from Microsoft Web site,
       www.microsoft.com.).   7

**2   Introduction to the Visual Studio .NET IDE and
C# Programming**   22

2.1   **Start Page** in Visual Studio .NET.   24
2.2   **New Project** dialog.   26
2.3   Visual Studio .NET environment after a new project has been created.   26
2.4   Visual Studio .NET menu bar.   27
2.5   Visual Studio .NET menu bar summary.   27
2.6   Visual Studio .NET toolbar.   28
2.7   Tool-tip demonstration.   28
2.8   Toolbar icons for various Visual Studio .NET windows.   29
2.9   **Solution Explorer** window.   29
2.10   **Toolbox** window.   30
2.11   Demonstrating window auto-hide.   31
2.12   **Properties** window.   32
2.13   **Dynamic Help** window.   33
2.14   Simple program as it executes.   34
2.15   Creating a new Windows application.   35
2.16   Setting the project location.   35
2.17   Setting the form's **Text** property.   36
2.18   Form with sizing handles.   36
2.19   Changing property **BackColor**.   37
2.20   Adding a new label to the form.   38
2.21   Label in position, with its **Text** property set.   38
2.22   **Properties** window displaying the label's properties.   39

2.23   **Font** window for selecting fonts, styles and sizes.   39
2.24   Centering the text in the label.   39
2.25   Inserting and aligning the picture box.   40
2.26   **Image** property of the picture box.   40
2.27   Selecting an image for the picture box.   41
2.28   Picture box after the image has been inserted.   41
2.29   IDE in run mode, with the running application in the foreground.   42
2.30   Our first program in C#.   43
2.31   Visual Studio .NET-generated console application.   46
2.32   Execution of the **Welcome1** program.   47
2.33   Displaying multiple lines in a dialog.   48
2.34   Some common escape sequences.   48
2.35   Adding a reference to an assembly in Visual Studio .NET.   50
2.36   Internet Explorer's GUI.   51
2.37   Dialog displayed by calling **MessageBox.Show**.   51
2.38   Arithmetic operators.   52
2.39   Precedence of arithmetic operators.   53
2.40   Equality and relational operators.   53
2.41   Using equality and relational operators.   54
2.42   Precedence and associativity of operators discussed in this chapter.   58

3   **Control Structures**   **60**
3.1   C# keywords.   62
3.2   C# program for examination-results problem.   65
3.3   Arithmetic assignment operators.   67
3.4   Increment and decrement operators.   68
3.5   Precedence and associativity of the operators discussed thus far in this book. 68
3.6   Counter-controlled repetition with the **for** structure.   69
3.7   Calculating compound interest, using the **for** structure.   72
3.8   Buttons for message dialogs.   73
3.9   Icons for message dialogs.   74
3.10   Numeric formatting characters.   76
3.11   Using the **switch** multiple-selection structure.   77
3.12   Using the **do/while** repetition structure.   80
3.13   Using the **break** statement in a **for** structure.   81
3.14   Using the **continue** statement in a **for** structure.   83
3.15   Conditional and logical operators.   86
3.16   Precedence and associativity of the operators discussed so far.   87
3.17   IDE showing code for the program in Fig. 2.14.   89
3.18   Windows Form Designer–generated code when expanded.   90
3.19   Code generated by the IDE for **welcomeLabel**.   91
3.20   Using the **Properties** window to set a property value.   92
3.21   Windows Form Designer-generated code reflecting new property values.   92
3.22   Changing a property in the code-view editor.   93
3.23   New **Text** property value reflected in design mode.   94
3.24   Method **ASimpleProgram_Load**.   94

3.25   IntelliSense feature of Visual Studio .NET.   94
3.26   The result of changing a property value at execution time.   95

4   Methods and Arrays   97
4.1   Using programmer-defined method **Square**.   100
4.2   C# built-in data types.   106
4.3   Allowed implicit conversions.   107
4.4   Namespaces in the Framework Class Library.   108
4.5   Demonstrating **ref** and **out** parameters.   110
4.6   Scoping.   115
4.7   Calculating factorials with a recursive method.   118
4.8   Using overloaded methods.   120
4.9   Syntax error generated from overloaded methods with identical parameter
       lists and different return types.   122
4.10   Precedence and associativity of the operators discussed so far.   123
4.11   Initializing arrays in three different ways.   124
4.12   Passing an array reference by value and by reference.   127
4.13   Double-subscripted rectangular array with three rows and four columns. 131
4.14   Initializing multidimensional arrays.   133
4.15   Using the **foreach** structure with an array.   135

5   Object-Based Programming   137
5.1   **Time1** abstract data type represents the time in 24-hour format.   140
5.2   Using an abstract data type.   144
5.3   Accessing **private** class members from client code generates syntax errors. 148
5.4   Overloaded constructors provide flexible object-initialization options. 150
5.5   Overloaded constructor demonstration.   152
5.6   Properties provide controlled access to an object's data.   155
5.7   Properties demonstration for class **Time3**.   158
5.8   **Date** class encapsulates day, month and year information.   162
5.9   **Employee** class encapsulates employee name, birthday and hire date. 163
5.10   Composition demonstration.   164
5.11   **this** reference used implicitly and explicitly to enable an object to
       manipulate its own data and invoke its own methods.   166
5.12   **this** reference demonstration.   167
5.13   **static** members are accessible to all objects of a class.   170
5.14   **static** member demonstration.   171
5.15   **const** and **readonly** class member demonstration.   174
5.16   Indexers provide subscripted access to an object's members.   176
5.17   Assembly **TimeLibrary** contains class **Time3**.   184
5.18   Simple class library.   188
5.19   Assembly **TimeLibrary** used from class **AssemblyTest**.   188
5.20   **Class View** of class **Time1** (Fig. 5.1) and class **TimeTest** (Fig. 5.2). 190
5.21   **Object Browser** when user selects **Object** from **Time1.cs**.   190

6   Object-Oriented Programming: Inheritance   192
6.1   Inheritance examples.   195

6.2   Inheritance hierarchy for university **CommunityMember**s.   196
6.3   Portion of a **Shape** class hierarchy.   197
6.4   **Point** class represents an *x-y* coordinate pair.   198
6.5   **PointTest** class demonstrates class **Point** functionality.   200
6.6   **Circle** class contains an *x-y* coordinate and a radius.   201
6.7   **CircleTest** demonstrates class **Circle** functionality.   204
6.8   **Circle2** class that inherits from class **Point**.   205
6.9   **Point2** class represents an *x-y* coordinate pair as **protected** data. 207
6.10   **Circle3** class that inherits from class **Point2**.   209
6.11   **CircleTest3** demonstrates class **Circle3** functionality.   210
6.12   **Point3** class uses properties to manipulate its **private** data. 212
6.13   **Circle4** class that inherits from class **Point3**, which does not
        provide **protected** data.   214
6.14   **CircleTest4** demonstrates class **Circle4** functionality.   216
6.15   **Cylinder** class inherits from class **Circle4** and overrides method **Area**. 218
6.16   Testing class **Cylinder**.   220
6.17   **Point4** base class contains constructors and finalizer.   222
6.18   **Circle5** class inherits from class **Point4** and overrides a finalizer method. 224
6.19   Order in which constructors and destructors are called.   226

7   Object-Oriented Programming: Polymorphism   229
7.1   **Point** class represents an *x-y* coordinate pair.   231
7.2   **Circle** class that inherits from class **Point**.   232
7.3   Assigning derived-class references to base-class references.   234
7.4   Abstract **Shape** base class.   241
7.5   **Point2** class inherits from **abstract** class **Shape**.   242
7.6   **Circle2** class that inherits from class **Point2**.   244
7.7   **Cylinder2** class inherits from class **Circle2**.   245
7.8   **AbstractShapesTest** demonstrates polymorphism in
        Point-Circle-Cylinder hierarchy.   247
7.9   **abstract** class **Employee** definition.   251
7.10   **Boss** class inherits from class **Employee**.   252
7.11   **CommissionWorker** class inherits from class **Employee**.   253
7.12   **PieceWorker** class inherits from class **Employee**.   255
7.13   **HourlyWorker** class inherits from class **Employee**.   257
7.14   **EmployeesTest** class tests the **Employee** class hierarchy.   259
7.15   Interface for returning age of objects of disparate classes.   262
7.16   **Person** class implements **IAge** interface.   262
7.17   **Tree** class implements **IAge** interface.   263
7.18   Demonstrating polymorphism on objects of disparate classes.   264
7.19   **IShape** interface provides methods **Area** and **Volume** and property **Name**. 266
7.20   **Point3** class implements interface **IShape**.   267
7.21   **Circle3** class inherits from class **Point3**.   268
7.22   **Cylinder3** class inherits from class **Circle3**.   270
7.23   **Interfaces2Test** uses interfaces to demonstrate polymorphism in
        Point-Circle-Cylinder hierarchy.   271
7.24   Bubble sort using delegates.   273

7.25   Bubble-sort **Form** application.   274
7.26   Overloading operators for complex numbers.   277
7.27   Using operator overloading.   280

8   Exception Handling   284
8.1   Exception handlers for **FormatException** and
        DivideByZeroException.   289
8.2   Demonstrating that **finally** blocks always execute regardless of
        whether an exception occurs.   298
8.3   **Exception** properties and stack unwinding.   304
8.4   **ApplicationException** subclass thrown when a program performs
        illegal operations on negative numbers.   309
8.5   **SquareRootTest** class throws an exception if error occurs when
        calculating the square root.   310
8.6   Operators **checked** and **unchecked** and the handling of arithmetic
        overflow.   313

9   Graphical User Interface Concepts: Part 1   316
9.1   Sample Internet Explorer window with GUI components.   318
9.2   Some basic GUI components .   318
9.3   Components and controls for Windows Forms.   319
9.4   Common **Form** properties and events.   320
9.5   Event-handling model using delegates.   321
9.6   Events section of the **Properties** window.   322
9.7   Simple event-handling example using visual programming.   323
9.8   List of **Form** events.   324
9.9   Details of **Click** event.   325
9.10   Class **Control** properties and methods.   327
9.11   Anchoring demonstration.   328
9.12   Manipulating the **Anchor** property of a control.   329
9.13   Docking demonstration.   329
9.14   Class **Control** layout properties.   329
9.15   **Label** properties.   331
9.16   **TextBox** properties and events.   331
9.17   **Button** properties and events.   332
9.18   Program to display hidden text in a password box.   332
9.19   **GroupBox** properties.   337
9.20   **Panel** properties.   337
9.21   Creating a **Panel** with scrollbars.   338
9.22   Using **GroupBox**es and **Panel**s to arrange **Button**s.   338
9.23   **CheckBox** properties and events.   340
9.24   Using **CheckBox**es to change font styles.   341
9.25   **RadioButton** properties and events.   344
9.26   Using **RadioButton**s to set message-window options.   344
9.27   **PictureBox** properties and events.   349
9.28   Using a **PictureBox** to display images.   349
9.29   Mouse events, delegates and event arguments.   351

9.30   Using the mouse to draw on a form.   352
9.31   Keyboard events, delegates and event arguments.   354
9.32   Demonstrating keyboard events.   355

10   **Graphical User Interface Concepts: Part 2**   **358**
10.1   Expanded and checked menus.   360
10.2   Visual Studio .NET **Menu Designer**.   361
10.3   **MainMenu** and **MenuItem** properties and events.   362
10.4   Menus for changing text font and color.   363
10.5   **LinkLabel** control in running program.   369
10.6   **LinkLabel** properties and events.   369
10.7   **LinkLabel**s used to link to a folder, a Web page and an application.   370
10.8   **ListBox** and **CheckedListBox** on a form.   373
10.9   **ListBox** properties, methods and events.   373
10.10   **String Collection Editor**.   375
10.11   **ListBox** used in a program to add, remove and clear items.   375
10.12   **CheckedListBox** properties, methods and events.   378
10.13   **CheckedListBox** and **ListBox** used in a program to display a
        user selection.   379
10.14   **ComboBox** demonstration.   381
10.15   **ComboBox** properties and events.   381
10.16   **ComboBox** used to draw a selected shape.   382
10.17   **TreeView** displaying a sample tree.   386
10.18   **TreeView** properties and events.   386
10.19   **TreeNode** properties and methods.   387
10.20   **TreeNode Editor**.   388
10.21   **TreeView** used to display directories.   388
10.22   **ListView** properties and events.   391
10.23   **Image Collection Editor** window for an **ImageList** component. 392
10.24   **ListView** displaying files and folders.   393
10.25   Tabbed pages in Visual Studio .NET.   398
10.26   **TabControl** with **TabPage**s example.   399
10.27   **TabPage**s added to a **TabControl**.   399
10.28   **TabControl** properties and events.   399
10.29   **TabControl** used to display various font settings.   400
10.30   MDI parent window and MDI child windows.   404
10.31   SDI and MDI forms.   404
10.32   MDI parent and MDI child events and properties.   405
10.33   Minimized and maximized child windows.   406
10.34   **MenuItem** property **MdiList** example.   407
10.35   **MdiLayout** enumeration values.   408
10.36   MDI parent-window class.   409
10.37   **Child** class for MDI demonstration.   412
10.38   Class **VisualInheritance**, which inherits from class **Form**, contains
        a button (**Learn More**).   413
10.39   Visual Inheritance through the Form Designer.   415

10.40   Class **VisualInheritanceTest**, which inherits from class
        VisualInheritance.VisualInheritance, contains an
        additional button.   415
10.41   Custom control creation.   417
10.42   Programmer-defined control that displays the current time.   418
10.43   Custom-control creation.   420
10.44   Project properties dialog.   420
10.45   Custom control added to the **ToolBox**.   420
10.46   Custom control added to a **Form**.   421

11 Multithreading   **423**

11.1   Thread life cycle.   426
11.2   Thread-priority scheduling.   429
11.3   Threads sleeping and printing.   429
11.4   Producer and consumer threads accessing a shared object without
        synchronization.   435
11.5   Producer and consumer threads accessing a shared object with
        synchronization.   440
11.6   Producer and consumer threads accessing a circular buffer.   450

12 Strings, Characters and Regular Expressions   **462**

12.1   **String** constructors.   465
12.2   **String** indexer, **Length** property and **CopyTo** method.   466
12.3   **String** test to determine equality.   469
12.4   **StartsWith** and **EndsWith** methods.   471
12.5   **GetHashCode** method demonstration.   472
12.6   Searching for characters and substrings in **string**s.   473
12.7   Substrings generated from **string**s.   476
12.8   **Concat static** method.   478
12.9   **String** methods **Replace**, **ToLower**, **ToUpper**, **Trim** and **ToString**.   479
12.10   **StringBuilder** class constructors.   481
12.11   **StringBuilder** size manipulation.   483
12.12   **Append** methods of **StringBuilder**.   485
12.13   **StringBuilder**'s **AppendFormat** method.   486
12.14   **StringBuilder** text insertion and removal.   488
12.15   **StringBuilder** text replacement.   489
12.16   **Char**'s **static** character-testing methods and case-conversion methods.   491
12.17   **Card** class.   494
12.18   Card dealing and shuffling simulation.   495
12.19   Character classes.   499
12.20   Regular expressions checking birthdays.   499
12.21   Quantifiers used in regular expressions.   502
12.22   Validating user information using regular expressions.   502
12.23   **Regex** methods **Replace** and **Split**.   507

13 Graphics and Multimedia   **510**

13.1   **System.Drawing** namespace's classes and structures.   512

13.2   GDI+ coordinate system. Units are measured in pixels.   513
13.3   **Color** structure **static** constants and their RGB values.   515
13.4   **Color** structure members.   515
13.5   Classes that derive from class **Brush**.   516
13.6   Color value and alpha demonstration.   516
13.7   **ColorDialog** used to change background and text color.   519
13.8   **Font** class read-only properties.   522
13.9   **Font**s and **FontStyle**s.   523
13.10   An illustration of font metrics.   525
13.11   **FontFamily** methods that return font-metric information.   525
13.12   **FontFamily** class used to obtain font-metric information.   525
13.13   **Graphics** methods that draw lines, rectangles and ovals.   528
13.14   Demonstration of methods that draw lines, rectangles and ellipses.   528
13.15   Ellipse bounded by a rectangle.   530
13.16   Positive and negative arc angles.   531
13.17   **Graphics** methods for drawing arcs.   531
13.18   Arc-method demonstration.   531
13.19   **Graphics** methods for drawing polygons.   534
13.20   Polygon-drawing demonstration.   534
13.21   Shapes drawn on a form.   538
13.22   Paths used to draw stars on a form.   541
13.23   Image resizing.   544
13.24   Animation of a series of images.   546
13.25   Container class for chess pieces.   549
13.26   Chess-game code.   551
13.27   Windows Media Player demonstration.   559
13.28   Peedy introducing himself when the window opens.   563
13.29   Peedy's *Pleased* animation.   564
13.30   Peedy's reaction when he is clicked.   564
13.31   Peedy flying animation.   565
13.32   Peedy waiting for speech input.   566
13.33   Peedy repeating the user's request for Seattle-style pizza.   566
13.34   Peedy repeating the user's request for anchovies as an additional topping. 567
13.35   Peedy recounting the order.   567
13.36   Peedy calculating the total.   568
13.37   Microsoft Agent demonstration.   568

14   Files and Streams   **578**
14.1   Data hierarchy.   581
14.2   C#'s view of an *n-byte* file.   582
14.3   **File** class methods (partial list).   583
14.4   **Directory** class methods (partial list).   584
14.5   Testing classes **File** and **Directory**.   584
14.6   Regular expression used to determine file types.   588
14.7   Base class for GUIs in our file-processing applications.   594
14.8   Record for sequential-access file-processing applications.   596
14.9   Create and write to a sequential-access file.   599

14.10 Sample data for the program of Fig. 14.9.   605
14.11 Reading sequential-access files.   606
14.12 Credit-inquiry program.   610
14.13 Random-access file with fixed-length records.   617
14.14 Record for random-access file-processing applications.   617
14.15 Creating files for random-access file-processing applications.   621
14.16 Writing records to random-access files.   624
14.17 Reading records from random-access files sequentially.   629
14.18 Record-transaction class for the transaction-processor case study.   634
14.19 **TransactionProcessorForm** class runs the
       transaction-processor application.   638
14.20 **StartDialogForm** class enables users to access dialog boxes
       associated with various transactions.   639
14.21 **UpdateDialogForm** class enables users to update records in
       transaction-processor case study.   644
14.22 **NewDialogForm** class enables users to create records in
       transaction-processor case study.   649
14.23 **DeleteDialogForm** class enables users to remove records from files in
       transaction-processor case study.   652

15 Extensible Markup Language (XML)   656

15.1   XML used to mark up an article.   657
15.2   **article.xml** displayed by Internet Explorer.   660
15.3   XML to mark up a business letter.   660
15.4   XML namespaces demonstration.   662
15.5   Default namespace demonstration.   664
15.6   Tree structure for Fig. 15.1.   665
15.7   **XmlNodeReader** used to iterate through an XML document.   666
15.8   DOM structure of an XML document illustrated by a class.   669
15.9   **XPathNavigator** class used to navigate selected nodes.   676
15.10 XML document that describes various sports.   682
15.11 XPath expressions and descriptions.   683
15.12 Document Type Definition (DTD) for a business letter.   684
15.13 XML document referencing its associated DTD.   685
15.14 XML Validator validates an XML document against a DTD.   687
15.15 XML Validator displaying an error message.   688
15.16 XML document that conforms to a Microsoft Schema document.   688
15.17 Microsoft Schema file that contains structure to which **bookxdr.xml**
       conforms.   689
15.18 XML document that conforms to W3C XML Schema.   690
15.19 XSD Schema document to which **bookxsd.xml** conforms.   690
15.20 Schema-validation example.   692
15.21 XML document that does not conform to the XSD schema of Fig. 15.19.   694
15.22 XML file that does not conform to the Schema in Fig. 15.17.   694
15.23 XML document containing book information.   696
15.24 XSL document that transforms **sorting.xml** (Fig. 15.23) into XHTML. 697
15.25 XSL style sheet applied to an XML document.   700

15.26   BizTalk terminology.   703
15.27   BizTalk markup using an offer Schema.   703

16   Database, SQL and ADO .NET   709

16.1   Relational-database structure of an **Employee** table.   711
16.2   Result set formed by selecting **Department** and **Location** data
        from the **Employee** table.   712
16.3   **Authors** table from **Books**.   712
16.4   Data from the **Authors** table of **Books**.   713
16.5   **Publishers** table from **Books**.   713
16.6   Data from the **Publishers** table of **Books**.   714
16.7   **AuthorISBN** table from **Books**.   714
16.8   Data from **AuthorISBN** table in **Books**.   714
16.9   **Titles** table from **Books**.   715
16.10   Data from the **Titles** table of **Books**.   715
16.11   Table relationships in **Books**.   718
16.12   SQL query keywords.   719
16.13   **authorID** and **lastName** from the **Authors** table.   720
16.14   Titles with copyrights after 1999 from table **Titles**.   721
16.15   Authors from the **Authors** table whose last names start with **D**.   722
16.16   Authors from table **Authors** whose last names contain **i** as the
        second letter.   723
16.17   Authors from table **Authors** in ascending order by **lastName**.   723
16.18   Authors from table **Authors** in descending order by **lastName**.   724
16.19   Authors from table **Authors** in ascending order by **lastName** and
        by **firstName**.   725
16.20   Books from table **Titles** whose titles end with **How to Program**
        in ascending order by **title**.   726
16.21   Authors from table **Authors** and ISBN numbers of the authors' books,
        sorted in ascending order by **lastName** and **firstName**.   727
16.22   **TitleAuthor** query of **Books** database.   728
16.23   Portion of the result set produced by the query in Fig. 16.22.   729
16.24   **Authors** after an **INSERT** operation to add a record.   731
16.25   Table **Authors** after an **UPDATE** operation to change a record.   733
16.26   Table **Authors** after a **DELETE** operation to remove a record.   734
16.27   Accessing and displaying a database's data.   735
16.28   Execute SQL statements on a database.   742
16.29   Modifying a database.   744
16.30   Application that writes **DataSet** XML representation to a file.   752
16.31   XML document generated from **DataSet** in **DatabaseXMLWriter**.   754

17   ASP .NET, Web Forms and Web Controls   757

17.1   Web server/client interaction. Step 1: The **GET** request, **GET**
        /books/downloads.htm HTTP/1.1.   760
17.2   Client interacting with Web server. Step 2: The HTTP response,
        HTTP/1.1 200 OK.   760
17.3   Three-tier architecture.   761

17.4   ASPX page that displays the Web server's time.   762
17.5   Code-behind file for a page that displays the Web server's time.   764
17.6   HTML response when the browser requests **WebTime.aspx**.   767
17.7   Creating an **ASP.NET Web Application** in Visual Studio.   769
17.8   Visual Studio creating and linking a virtual directory for the **WebTime**
       project folder.   770
17.9   **Solution Explorer** window for project **WebTime**.   770
17.10 **Web Forms** menu in the **Toolbox**.   771
17.11 **Design** mode of Web Form designer.   771
17.12 **HTML** mode of Web Form designer.   772
17.13 Code-behind file for **WebForm1.aspx** generated by Visual Studio .NET.   773
17.14 **GridLayout** and **FlowLayout** illustration.   774
17.15 **WebForm.aspx** after adding two **Label**s and setting their properties.   774
17.16 Web controls commonly used in ASP.NET applications.   775
17.17 Web controls demonstration.   776
17.18 **AdRotator** class demonstrated on a Web form.   781
17.19 Code-behind file for page demonstrating the **AdRotator** class.   782
17.20 **AdvertisementFile** used in **AdRotator** example.   783
17.21 Validators used in a Web Form that generates possible letter combinations
       from a phone number.   786
17.22 Code-behind file for the word-generator page.   788
17.23 HTML and ECMAScript sent to the client browser.   793
17.24 ASPX file that presents a list of programming languages.   798
17.25 Code-behind file that writes cookies to the client.   800
17.26 ASPX page that displays book information.   803
17.27 Cookies being read from a client in an ASP .NET application. 804
17.28 **HttpCookie** properties.   806
17.29 Options supplied on an ASPX page.   806
17.30 Sessions are created for each user in an ASP .NET Web application.   808
17.31 **HttpSessionState** properties.   812
17.32 Session information displayed in a **ListBox**.   812
17.33 Session data read by an ASP .NET Web application to provide
       recommendations for the user.   813
17.34 Guest-book application GUI.   816
17.35 ASPX file for the guest book application.   816
17.36 Code-behind file for the guest book application.   818
17.37 Log-in Web Form.   822
17.38 ASCX code for the header.   824
17.39 Code-behind file for the log-in page of authors application. 825
17.40 ASPX file that allows a user to select an author from a drop-down list.   830
17.41 Database information input into a **DataGrid**.   832
17.42 ASPX page with tracing turned off.   837
17.43 Tracing enabled on a page.   838
17.44 Tracing information for a project.   838

18   ASP .NET and Web Services   842
18.1   ASMX file rendered in Internet Explorer.   845

18.2   Service description for a Web service.   846
18.3   Invoking a method of a Web service from a Web browser.   847
18.4   Results of invoking a Web-service method from a Web browser.   847
18.5   SOAP request for the **HugeInteger** Web service.   848
18.6   **HugeInteger** Web service.   849
18.7   Design view of a Web service.   856
18.8   Adding a Web service reference to a project.   857
18.9   Web reference selection and description.   858
18.10   **Solution Explorer** after adding a Web reference to a project.   859
18.11   Using the **HugeInteger** Web service.   859
18.12   **Blackjack** Web service.   865
18.13   Blackjack game that uses **Blackjack** Web service.   869
18.14   Airline reservation Web service.   878
18.15   Airline Web Service in design view.   880
18.16   ASPX file that takes reservation information.   880
18.17   Code-behind file for the reservation page.   881
18.18   **TemperatureServer** Web service.   884
18.19   Class that stores weather information about a city.   887
18.20   Receiving temperature and weather data from a Web service.   889
18.21   Class that stores equation information.   895
18.22   Web service that generates random equations.   897
18.23   Returning an object from a Web-service method.   899
18.24   Math tutor application.   900

19 Networking: Streams-Based Sockets and Datagrams 905

19.1   Server portion of a client/server stream-socket connection.   910
19.2   Client portion of a client/server stream-socket connection.   913
19.3   Server-side portion of connectionless client/server computing.   919
19.4   Client portion of connectionless client/server computing.   921
19.5   Server side of client/server Tic-Tac-Toe program.   925
19.6   Client side of client/server Tic-Tac-Toe program.   931
19.7   Class **Square**.   938

20 Data Structures and Collections 941

20.1   Sample self-referential **Node** class definition.   943
20.2   Two self-referential class objects linked together.   944
20.3   A graphical representation of a linked list.   945
20.4   Definitions of classes **ListNode**, **List** and **EmptyListException**. 947
20.5   Demonstrating the linked list.   951
20.6   A graphical representation of the **InsertAtFront** operation.   954
20.7   A graphical representation of the **InsertAtBack** operation.   954
20.8   A graphical representation of the **RemoveFromFront** operation.   955
20.9   A graphical representation of the **RemoveFromBack** operation.   956
20.10   **StackInheritance** extends class **List**.   957
20.11   Using class **StackInheritance**.   958
20.12   **StackComposition** class encapsulates functionality of class **List**. 960
20.13   **QueueInheritance** extends class **List**.   962

20.14   Using inheritance to create a queue.   963
20.15   A graphical representation of a binary tree.   965
20.16   A binary search tree containing 12 values.   965
20.17   Definitions of **TreeNode** and **Tree** for a binary search tree.   966
20.18   Creating and traversing a binary tree.   970
20.19   A binary search tree.   972
20.20   Definitions of class **TreeNode** and **Tree** for manipulating
        IComparable objects.   974
20.21   Demonstrating class **Tree** with **IComparable** objects.   978
20.22   Program that demonstrates class **Array**.   982
20.23   Some methods of class **ArrayList**.   985
20.24   Demonstrating the **ArrayList** class.   985
20.25   Using the **Stack** class.   991
20.26   Using the **Hashtable** class.   996

21   Accessibility   1002

21.1   Acts designed to improve Internet and computer accessibility for people
        with disabilities.   1004
21.2   We Media's home page.   1005
21.3   Enlarging icons using the **Customize** feature.   1009
21.4   Enlarged icons in the development window.   1009
21.5   Text Editor before modifying the font size.   1010
21.6   Enlarging text in the **Options** window.   1010
21.7   Text Editor after the font size is modified.   1011
21.8   Adding tabs to the **Toolbox**.   1012
21.9   Shortcut key creation.   1013
21.10   Removing tabs from Visual Studio environment.   1013
21.11   Console windows with tabs and without tabs.   1014
21.12   Properties of class **Control** related to accessibility.   1015
21.13   Application with accessibility features.   1016
21.14   XHTML table without accessibility modifications.   1021
21.15   Table optimized for screen reading, using attribute **headers**.   1022
21.16   Home page written in VoiceXML.   1026
21.17   Publication page of Deitel and Associates' VoiceXML page.   1028
21.18   VoiceXML tags.   1032
21.19   **Hello World** CallXML example.   1033
21.20   CallXML example that reads three ISBN values.   1035
21.21   CallXML elements.   1038
21.22   **Display Settings** dialog.   1041
21.23   **Accessibility Wizard** initialization options.   1042
21.24   Scroll Bar and Window Border Size dialog.   1042
21.25   Adjusting window-element sizes.   1043
21.26   **Display Color Settings** options.   1043
21.27   **Accessibility Wizard** mouse cursor adjustment tool.   1044
21.28   **SoundSentry** dialog.   1044
21.29   **ShowSounds** dialog.   1045
21.30   **StickyKeys** window.   1045

21.31 **BounceKeys** dialog.   1046
21.32 **ToggleKeys** window.   1046
21.33 **Extra Keyboard Help** dialog.   1047
21.34 **MouseKeys** window.   1047
21.35 **Mouse Button Settings** window.   1048
21.36 **Mouse Speed** dialog.   1049
21.37 **Set Automatic Timeouts** dialog.   1049
21.38 Saving new accessibility settings.   1050
21.39 **Narrator** window.   1050
21.40 **Voice-settings** window.   1051
21.41 **Narrator** reading **Notepad** text.   1051
21.42 Microsoft **On-Screen Keyboard**.   1052
21.43 Microsoft Internet Explorer 6.0's accessibility options.   1052
21.44 Advanced accessibility settings in Microsoft Internet Explorer 6.0. 1053

22 Mobile Internet Toolkit   1057

22.1   Multiple forms in a mobile Web Form page.   1060
22.2   Code-behind file for the mobile application.   1062
22.3   Creating a **Mobile Web Application** in Visual Studio .NET.   1065
22.4   Visual Studio .NET creating and linking a virtual directory for the
       Welcome project folder.   1065
22.5   **Solution Explorer** window for project **Welcome**.   1066
22.6   Design mode of the Mobile Web Form Designer.   1066
22.7   HTML mode of Mobile Web Form Designer.   1067
22.8   Code-behind file for **MobileWebForm1.aspx** generated by Visual
       Studio .NET.   1068
22.9   **Mobile Web Forms** group in the **Toolbox**.   1069
22.10 **Welcome.aspx** after adding two **Label**s and setting their properties. 1070
22.11 Web Form with embedded C# code.   1071
22.12 Section of **machine.config** file.   1075
22.13 ASPX page for mobile Craps program.   1075
22.14 Code-behind file for craps application.   1077
22.15 Demonstrating **List**s and **Link**s.   1083
22.16 Style sheets and templates in a mobile Web Form.   1088
22.17 **Web.config** file used for **Portal2.aspx**.   1093
22.18 **AdBanners.xml** file used for **Portal2.aspx**.   1095
22.19 Code-behind file for the Deitel Wireless Portal.   1097
22.20 ASPX page that allows a mobile device to access a Web service.   1102
22.21 Code-behind file for mobile Web application that access a Web Service. 1103

A Operator Precedence Chart   1109

A.1   Operator precedence chart.   1109

B Number Systems   1111

B.1   Digits of the binary, octal, decimal and hexadecimal number systems. 1113
B.2   Comparison of the binary, octal, decimal and hexadecimal number systems. 1114

B.3	Positional values in the decimal number system.	1114
B.4	Positional values in the binary number system.	1114
B.5	Positional values in the octal number system.	1115
B.6	Positional values in the hexadecimal number system.	1115
B.7	Decimal, binary, octal and hexadecimal equivalents.	1115
B.8	Converting a binary number to decimal.	1117
B.9	Converting an octal number to decimal.	1117
B.10	Converting a hexadecimal number to decimal.	1118

C Career Opportunities 1122

C.1	**Monster.com** home page.	1125
C.2	**FlipDog.com** job search.	1126
C.3	List of a job seeker's criteria.	1128
C.4	Advantage Hiring, Inc.'s Net-Interview™ service.	1131
C.5	**eLance.com** request for proposal (RFP) example.	1134

D Visual Studio .NET Debugger 1142

D.1	Syntax error.	1143
D.2	Debug sample program.	1144
D.3	Setting a breakpoint.	1145
D.4	Debug configuration setting.	1146
D.5	Console application suspended for debugging.	1146
D.6	Execution suspended at a breakpoint.	1147
D.7	**Watch** window.	1147
D.8	**Autos**, **Locals** and **This** windows.	1148
D.9	**Immediate** window.	1150
D.10	**Debug** toolbar icons.	1150
D.11	**Breakpoints** window.	1150
D.12	Disabled breakpoint.	1151
D.13	**New Breakpoint** dialog.	1152
D.14	**Breakpoint Hit Count** dialog.	1152
D.15	**Breakpoint Condition** dialog.	1152
D.16	Debugging methods.	1153
D.17	**Call Stack** window.	1154
D.18	IDE displaying a method's calling point.	1154
D.19	Debug program control features.	1155
D.20	Using the **Immediate** window to debug methods.	1155
D.21	Object debugging example.	1156
D.22	Breakpoint location for class debugging.	1157
D.23	Expanded class in **Watch** window.	1158
D.24	Expanded array in **Watch** window.	1158

E Generating Documentation in Visual Studio .NET 1160

E.1	**Point** marked up with XML comments.	1162
E.2	**Circle** class marked up with XML comments.	1164
E.3	**CircleTest** class marked up with XML comments.	1167
E.4	Selecting the **Build Comment Web Pages** from **Tools** menu.	1170

E.5   Saving a document to a file.   1171
E.6   HTML documentation of class **Circle**.   1171
E.7   HTML documentation of method **Area** method of class **Circle**. 1172
E.8   XML documentation generated by Visual Studio .NET.   1172

F   ASCII Character Set   1179
F.1   ASCII character set.   1179

G   Unicode®   1180
G.1   Correlation between the three encoding forms.   1183
G.2   Various glyphs of the character A.   1183
G.3   Unicode values for multiple languages.   1185
G.4   Some character ranges.   1188

H   COM Integration   1191
H.1   ActiveX control registration.   1192
H.2   **Customize Toolbox** dialog with an ActiveX control selected. 1193
H.3   IDE's toolbox and **LabelScrollbar** properties.   1194
H.4   ActiveX COM control integration in C#.   1194
H.5   **Add Reference** dialog DLL Selection.   1197
H.6   COM DLL component in C#.   1198

I   Introduction to HyperText Markup Language 4: Part 1   1202
I.1   Basic HTML file.   1205
I.2   Header elements **h1** through **h6**.   1207
I.3   Linking to other Web pages.   1208
I.4   Linking to an e-mail address.   1209
I.5   Placing images in HTML files. (Courtesy of Prentice Hall, Inc.) 1210
I.6   Using images as link anchors.   1212
I.7   Inserting special characters into HTML.   1214
I.8   Unordered lists in HTML.   1216
I.9   Nested and ordered lists in HTML.   1217

J   Introduction to HyperText Markup Language 4: Part 2   1222
J.1   HTML table.   1223
J.2   Complex HTML table.   1226
J.3   Simple form with hidden fields and a text box.   1228
J.4   Form including textareas, password boxes and checkboxes.   1231
J.5   Form including radio buttons and pulldown lists.   1234
J.6   Using internal hyperlinks to make your pages more navigable.   1238
J.7   Picture with links anchored to an image map.   1241
J.8   Using **meta** to provide keywords and a description.   1243
J.9   Web site using two frames—navigation and content.   1245
J.10   Framed Web site with a nested frameset.   1248

K   Introduction to XHTML: Part 1   1252
K.1   First XHTML example.   1254
K.2   Validating an XHTML document.   1257
K.3   XHTML validation results.   1258
K.4   Header elements **h1** through **h6**.   1259
K.5   Linking to other Web pages.   1260
K.6   Linking to an e-mail address.   1262
K.7   Placing images in XHTML files.   1263
K.8   Using images as link anchors.   1265
K.9   Inserting special characters into XHTML.   1267
K.10   Unordered lists in XHTML.   1269
K.11   Nested and ordered lists in XHTML.   1270

L   Introduction to XHTML: Part 2   1275
L.1   XHTML table.   1276
L.2   Complex XHTML table.   1279
L.3   Simple form with hidden fields and a textbox.   1282
L.4   Form with textareas, password boxes and checkboxes.   1285
L.5   Form including radio buttons and drop-down lists.   1288
L.6   Using internal hyperlinks to make pages more easily navigable.   1292
L.7   Image with links anchored to an image map.   1295
L.8   Using **meta** to provide keywords and a description.   1297
L.9   Web document containing two frames—navigation and content.   1299
L.10   XHTML document displayed in the left frame of Fig. L.9.   1301
L.11   Framed Web site with a nested frameset.   1303

M   HTML/XHTML Special Characters   1307
M.1   HTML/XHTML special characters.   1307

N   HTML/XHTML Colors   1308
N.1   HTML/XHTML standard colors and hexadecimal RGB values.   1308
N.2   HTML/XHTML extended colors and hexadecimal RGB values.   1309

O   Bit Manipulation   1311
O.1   Bitwise operators.   1313
O.2   Results of combining two bits with the bitwise AND operator (&).   1313
O.3   Results of combining two bits with the bitwise inclusive OR operator (|). 1313
O.4   Results of combining two bits with the bitwise exclusive OR operator (^). 1314
O.5   Displaying the bit representation of an integer.   1314
O.6   Demonstrating the bitwise AND, bitwise inclusive OR, bitwise exclusive
       OR and bitwise complement operators.   1317
O.7   Using the bitshift operators.   1321
O.8   Bitwise assignment operators.   1323
O.9   Sieve of Eratosthenes.   1324

P   Crystal Reports® for Visual Studio .NET   1328
P.1   Crystal Report sample in PDF form.   1329

P.2   Report expert choices.   1330
P.3   Expert formatting menu choices.   1330
P.4   Crystal Reports designer interface.   1331
P.5   Crystal Report being published as Web service. 1332

Preface

Live in fragments no longer. Only connect.
Edward Morgan Forster

We wove a web in childhood,
A web of sunny air.
Charlotte Brontë

Welcome to C# and the world of Windows, Internet and World-Wide-Web programming with Visual Studio .NET and the .NET platform! This book is the second in the new *Deitel™ Developer Series*, which presents leading-edge computing technologies to software developers and IT professionals.

C# (pronounced "C-sharp") was developed by Microsoft expressly for its .NET platform. C# provides the features that are most important to programmers, such as object-oriented programming, graphics, graphical-user-interface (GUI) components, exception handling, multithreading, multimedia (audio, images, animation and video), file processing, prepackaged data structures, database processing, Internet and World-Wide-Web-based multi-tier application development, networking, Web services and distributed computing. The language is appropriate for implementing Internet- and World-Wide-Web-based applications that integrate seamlessly with Windows-based applications.

The .NET platform offers powerful capabilities for software development and deployment, including language and platform independence. For example, developers writing code in any (or several) of the .NET languages (such as C#, Visual Basic .NET and Visual C++ .NET) can contribute components to the same software product. In addition to providing language independence, .NET extends program portability by enabling .NET applications to reside on, and communicate across, multiple platforms. This facilitates the creation and use of *Web services*, which are applications that expose functionality to clients over the Internet.

The .NET platform enables Web-based applications to be distributed to consumer-electronic devices, such as wireless phones and personal digital assistants (PDAs), as well as to desktop computers. The capabilities that Microsoft has incorporated into the .NET platform increase programmer productivity and decrease development time.

Who Should Read This Book

Deitel & Associates, Inc. has several C# publications, intended for different audiences. We provide information on **www.deitel.com**, here and inside this book's back cover to help you determine which publication is best for you.

Our first C# book, *C# How to Program*, was published as part of our *How to Program Series*, for college and university students. It provides a comprehensive treatment of C# and includes learning aids and extensive ancillary support. *C# How to Program* assumes that the reader has little or no programming experience. Early chapters focus on fundamental programming principles. The book builds on this to create increasingly complex and sophisticated programs that demonstrate how to use C# to create graphical user interfaces, networking applications, multithreaded applications, Web-based applications and more. We encourage professors and professionals to consider the *The Complete C# Training Course*. This package includes *C# How to Program* as well as the *C# Multimedia Cyber Classroom*, an interactive multimedia CD-ROM that provides extensive e-Learning features. *The Complete C# Training Course* and *C# Multimedia Cyber Classroom* are discussed in detail later in this Preface.

C#: A Programmer's Introduction, is part of the new *Deitel™ Developer Series*, intended for professional software developers—from novices through experienced programmers. *C#: A Programmer's Introduction* is a part of the *A Programmer's Introduction* subseries, which is designed for programmers with little (or no) programming experience. The book begins with C# programming fundamentals. The core of *C#: A Programmer's Introduction* emphasizes achieving program clarity through the proven techniques of *structured programming*, *object-based programming*, *object-oriented programming (OOP)* and *event-driven programming*. The book provides a rigorous introduction to programming principles in general and to C# fundamentals, in particular. It continues with brief introductions to upper-level topics such as ASP .NET, ADO .NET and Web services. Unlike the *How to Program Series* books, the *Deitel™ Developer Series* books do not include the extensive pedagogic features and ancillary support materials required for academic courses.

This book, *C# for Experienced Programmers*, is also part of the *Deitel™ Developer Series*. This publication is a part of the *For Experienced Programmers* subseries, designed for the experienced software developer who wants a deep treatment of a new technology with minimal, if any, introductory material. *C# for Experienced Programmers* delves deeply into the more sophisticated topics that are introduced briefly in *C#: A Programmer's Introduction*. There is considerable overlap between these books.

A fourth publication, *ASP .NET with C# for Experienced Programmers*, is forthcoming. This book was originally titled *Advanced C# for Experienced Programmers*.

Each of our C# books presents many complete, working C# programs and depicts their inputs and outputs in actual screen shots of running programs. This is our signature *LIVE-CODE™ approach*—we present concepts in the context of complete working programs. Each book's source code is available free for download at **www.deitel.com**.

Please examine both the *Deitel™ Developer Series* professional books and the *How to Program Series* textbooks to determine which best suits your needs. *C#: A Programmer's Introduction* and *C# for Experienced Programmers* are both derived from *C# How to Program*. Depending on your particular needs, you should purchase either one or both of these *Deitel™ Developer Series* books, or *C# How to Program*.

The C# books in the *Deitel™ Developer Series* were written after the first edition of *C# How to Program*. We added to each of these *Deitel™ Developer Series* books a chapter on the new Microsoft Mobile Internet Toolkit for our readers who wish to develop wireless Internet applications for wireless phones, pagers and PDAs. This material will be added to the second edition of *C# How to Program*.

For a detailed listing of Deitel™ products and services, please see the "advertorial" pages at the back of this book and visit **www.deitel.com**. Readers may also want to register for our new *Deitel™ Buzz Online* e-mail newsletter (**www.deitel.net/newsletter/subscribe.html**), which provides information about our publications, company announcements, links to informative technical articles, programming tips, teaching tips, challenges and anecdotes.

As you proceed, if you would like to communicate with us, please send an e-mail to **deitel@deitel.com**—we always respond promptly. Please check our Web sites, **www.deitel.com**, **www.prenhall.com/deitel** and **www.InformIT.com/deitel** for frequent updates, errata, FAQs, etc. When sending an e-mail, please include the book's title and edition number. We sincerely hope that you enjoy learning C# with our publications.

Features of *C# for Experienced Programmers*

This edition contains many features, including:

- *Syntax Highlighting.* This book uses five-way syntax highlighting to emphasize C# programming elements in a manner similar to that of Visual Studio .NET. Our syntax-highlighting conventions are as follows:

  ```
  comments
  keywords
  literal values
  errors and ASP .NET directives
  text, class, method and variable names
  ```

- *"Code Washing."* This is our term for the process we use to format the book's programs so that they have a carefully commented, open layout. The code is grouped into small, well-documented pieces. This greatly improves code readability—an especially important goal for us, considering that this book contains approximately 26,000 lines of code in 230 complete LIVE-CODE™ programs.

- *Web Forms, Web Controls and ASP .NET.* The .NET platform enables developers to create robust, scalable Web-based applications. Microsoft's .NET server-side technology, Active Server Pages (ASP) .NET, allows programmers to build Web documents that respond to client requests. To enable interactive Web pages, server-side programs process information users input into HTML forms. ASP .NET is a significant departure from ASP 3.0, allowing developers to program Web-based applications using .NET's powerful object-oriented languages such as C# and Visual Basic .NET, rather than using only scripting languages. ASP .NET also provides enhanced visual programming capabilities, similar to those used in building Windows forms for desktop programs. Programmers can create Web pages visually, by dragging and dropping Web controls onto Web forms. Chapter 17, ASP .NET, Web Forms and Web Controls, introduces these powerful technologies.

- **Web Services and ASP .NET.** Microsoft's .NET strategy embraces the Internet and Web as integral to software development and deployment. Web services technology enables information sharing, e-commerce and other interactions using standard Internet protocols and technologies, such as Hypertext Transfer Protocol (HTTP), Extensible Markup Language (XML) and Simple Object Access Protocol (SOAP). Web services enable programmers to package application functionality in a manner that turns the Web into a library of reusable software components. In Chapter 18, ASP .NET and Web Services, we present a Web service that allows users to manipulate "huge integers"—integers too large to be contained in C#'s built-in data types. In this example, a user enters two huge integers and presses buttons to invoke Web services that add, subtract and compare the two integers. We also present information related to Web services in Appendix P, Crystal Reports® for Visual Studio .NET, which discusses a popular reporting program for database-intensive applications. Crystal Reports, which is integrated into Visual Studio .NET, provides the ability to expose a report as a Web service. The appendix provides introductory information and directs readers to a walk-through of this process on the Crystal Decisions Web site, **www.crystalde-cisions.com/netzone**.

- **Object-Oriented Programming.** Object-oriented programming is the most widely employed technique for developing robust, reusable software. This text offers a rich treatment of C#'s object-oriented programming features. Chapter 5, Object-Based Programming, introduces how to create classes and objects. These concepts are extended in Chapter 6, Object-Oriented Programming: Inheritance, which discusses how programmers can create powerful new classes quickly by "absorbing" the capabilities of existing classes. Chapter 7, Object-Oriented Programming: Polymorphism, familiarizes the reader with the crucial concepts of polymorphism, abstract classes, concrete classes and interfaces, which facilitate powerful manipulations among objects belonging to an inheritance hierarchy.

- **XML.** Use of Extensible Markup Language (XML) is exploding in the software-development industry, in the e-business and e-commerce communities, and is pervasive throughout the .NET platform. Because XML is a platform-independent technology for describing data and for creating markup languages, XML's data portability integrates well with C#-based portable applications and services. Chapter 15, Extensible Markup Language (XML), introduces XML. In this chapter, we introduce basic XML markup and discuss the technologies such as DTDs and Schema, which are used to validate XML documents' contents. We also explain how to manipulate XML documents programmatically using the Document Object Model (DOM™) and how to transform XML documents into other types of documents via Extensible Stylesheet Language Transformations (XSLT).

- *Multithreading.* Computers enable programmers to perform many tasks in parallel (i.e., concurrently), such as printing documents, downloading files from a network and surfing the Web. Multithreading is the technology through which programmers can develop applications that perform concurrent tasks. Historically, a computer has contained a single, expensive processor, which its operating system would share among all applications. Today, processors are becoming increasingly inexpensive, making it possible to build affordable computers with many processors working in parallel—such computers are called multiprocessors. Multithreading is effective on both single-processor and multiprocessor systems. .NET's multithreading capabilities make the platform and its related technologies better prepared to handle today's sophisticated multimedia-intensive, database-intensive, network-based, multiprocessor-based, distributed applications. Chapter 11, Multithreading, introduces this powerful capability.

- *ADO .NET.* Databases store vast amounts of information that individuals and organizations must access to conduct business. As an evolution of Microsoft's ActiveX Data Objects (ADO) technology, ADO .NET represents a new approach for building applications that interact with databases. ADO .NET uses XML and an enhanced object model to provide developers with the tools they need to access and manipulate databases for large-scale, extensible, mission-critical multi-tier applications. Chapter 16, Database, SQL and ADO .NET, introduces the capabilities of ADO .NET and the Structured Query Language (SQL) to manipulate databases.

- *Wireless Development.* By some estimates, about a billion people worldwide are using mobile devices, such as wireless phones and PDAs, and this number is increasing rapidly. To simplify the creation of Web content for mobile devices, Microsoft provides the Mobile Internet Toolkit (MIT). The MIT, which is built on ASP .NET, allows wireless content to be created using Visual Studio .NET's object-oriented languages. One program can be created that will be compatible with a variety of devices and able to display different content based on the type of device (e.g., a wireless phone versus a PDA). Chapter 22, Mobile Internet Toolkit, introduces wireless Web application development.

- *Visual Studio .NET Debugger.* Debuggers help programmers find and correct logic errors in program code. In Appendix D, Visual Studio .NET Debugger, we explain how to use key debugger features, such as setting "breakpoints" and "watches," stepping into and out of methods, and examining the method call stack.

- *COM (Component Object Model) Integration.* Prior to the introduction of .NET, many organizations spent tremendous amounts of time and money creating reusable software components called COM components, which include ActiveX$^{®}$ controls and ActiveX DLLs (dynamic link libraries) for Windows applications. In Appendix H, COM Integration, we discuss some of the tools available in Visual Studio .NET for integrating these legacy components into .NET applications. This integration allows programmers to use existing sets of COM-based controls with .NET components.

- *XML Documentation.* Documenting program code is crucial for software development, because different programmers often work on an application during the software's lifecycle, which usually includes multiple versions and can span many years. If programmers document software code and methods, other programmers working on the application can learn and understand the logic underlying the code, thus saving time and avoiding misunderstandings. To automate documenting programs, Visual Studio .NET provides an XML tool for C# programmers. Appendix E, XML Documentation, explains how a programmer can insert comments in the code, which produces a separate file providing the code documentation.

- *Career Opportunities.* Appendix C, Career Opportunities, introduces career services available on the Internet. We explore online career services from both the employer's and employee's perspectives. We list many Web sites where readers can submit applications, search for jobs and review applicants. We also review services that build recruiting pages directly into e-businesses. One of our reviewers told us that he had used the Internet as a primary tool in a recent job search, and that this appendix would have helped him dramatically expand his search.

- *Unicode®.* As computer systems evolved worldwide, computer vendors developed numeric representations of character sets and special symbols for the local languages spoken in different countries. In some cases, different representations were developed for the same languages. Such disparate character sets hindered communication among computer systems. C# supports the *Unicode Standard* (maintained by a non-profit organization called the *Unicode Consortium*), which maintains a single character set that specifies unique numeric values for characters and special symbols in most of the world's languages. Appendix G, Unicode®, discusses the standard, overviews the Unicode Consortium Web site, **www.unicode.org** and presents a C# application that displays "Welcome to Unicode!" in several languages.

- *XHTML.* The World Wide Web Consortium (W3C) has declared HTML to be a legacy technology that will undergo no further development. HTML is being replaced by the Extensible Hypertext Markup Language (XHTML)—an XML-based technology that is rapidly becoming the standard for describing Web content. We use XHTML in Chapter 15, Extensible Markup Language (XML), and offer an introduction to the technology in Appendix K, Introduction to XHTML: Part 1, and Appendix L, Introduction to XHTML: Part 2. These appendices overview headers, images, lists, image maps and other features of this emerging markup language. (We also present a treatment of HTML in Appendices I and J, because ASP .NET, used in Chapters 17 and 18, generates HTML content).

- *Accessibility.* Although the World Wide Web has become an important part of many people's lives, the medium currently presents many challenges to people with disabilities. Individuals with hearing and visual impairments, in particular, have difficulty accessing multimedia-rich Web sites. In an attempt to improve this situation, the World Wide Web Consortium (W3C) launched the Web Accessibility Initiative (WAI), which provides guidelines for making Web sites accessible to people with disabilities. Chapter 21, Accessibility, describes these guidelines and highlights various products and services designed to improve the Web-browsing experiences of individuals with disabilities. For example, the chapter introduces VoiceXML™ and CallXML™—two XML-based technologies for increasing the accessibility of Web-based content for people with visual impairments.

- **Bit Manipulation.** Computers work with data in the form of binary digits, or bits, which can assume the values 1 or 0. Computer circuitry performs various simple bit manipulations, such as examining the value of a bit, setting the value of a bit and reversing a bit (from 1 to 0 or from 0 to 1). Operating systems, test-equipment, networking software and many other kinds of software require that programs communicate "directly with the hardware" by using bit manipulation. Appendix O, Bit Manipulation, overviews the bit manipulation capabilities that the .NET Framework provides.

Pedagogic Approach

C# for Experienced Programmers contains a rich collection of examples that have been tested on Windows 2000 and Windows XP. The book concentrates on the principles of good software engineering and stresses program clarity. We are educators who teach edge-of-the-practice topics in industry classrooms worldwide. We avoid arcane terminology and syntax specifications in favor of teaching by example. The text emphasizes good pedagogy.

We use fonts to distinguish between Visual Studio .NET's Integrated Development Environment (IDE) features (such as menu names and menu items) and other elements that appear in the IDE. Our convention is to emphasize IDE features in a sans-serif bold Helvetica font (e.g., **Project** menu) and to emphasize program text in a serif bold Courier font (e.g., **bool x = true;**).

LIVE-CODE™ Teaching Approach

C# for Experienced Programmers is loaded with numerous LIVE-CODE™ examples. This style exemplifies the way we teach and write about programming and is the focus of our multimedia *Cyber Classrooms* and Web-based training courses as well. Each new concept is presented in the context of a complete, working example that is followed by one or more windows showing the program's input/output dialog. We call this method of teaching and writing the ***LIVE-CODE™ Approach**. We use programming languages to teach programming languages.* Reading the examples in the text is much like entering and running them on a computer. Readers have the option of downloading all of the book's code examples from **www.deitel.com**, under the **Downloads/Resources** link. Other links provide errata and answers to frequently asked questions.

World Wide Web Access

All of the source code for the examples in *C# for Experienced Programmers* (and our other publications) is available on the Internet as downloads from the following Web sites:

> **www.deitel.com**
> **www.prenhall.com/deitel**

Registration is quick and easy and these downloads are free. We suggest downloading all the examples, then running each program as you read the corresponding portion of the book. Make changes to the examples and immediately see the effects of those changes—this is a great way to improve your programming skills. Any instructions for running the examples assumes that the user is running Windows 2000 or Windows XP and is using Microsoft's Internet Information Services (IIS). Additional setup instructions for IIS and other software can be found at our Web sites along with the examples. [*Note:* This is copyrighted material. Feel free to use it as you study, but you may not republish any portion of it in any form without explicit permission from Prentice Hall and the authors.]

Visual Studio .NET belongs to a family of products that are available for purchase and download from Microsoft. Visual Studio .NET, which includes C#, comes in four different editions—Academic, Professional, Enterprise Developer and Enterprise Architect. Visual Studio .NET Academic contains Visual Studio .NET Professional's features in addition to features designed for students and professors (e.g., an Assignment Manager that documents assignment submission, Application Publishing Tools that aid in the notification of assignments, code samples and more).

Microsoft also offers stand-alone products (Visual C# .NET Standard, Visual C++ .NET Standard and Visual Basic .NET Standard) for various .NET-languages. Each product provides an integrated development environment (similar to Visual Studio .NET) and a compiler. Visit **msdn.microsoft.com/vstudio/howtobuy** for descriptions and ordering information.

Objectives

Each chapter begins with objectives that inform readers of what to expect and gives them an opportunity, after reading the chapter, to determine whether they have met the intended goals.

Quotations

The chapter objectives are followed by sets of quotations. Some are humorous, some are philosophical and some offer interesting insights. We have found that readers enjoy relating the quotations to the chapter material. Many of the quotations are worth a "second look" *after* you read each chapter.

Outline

The chapter outline enables readers to approach the material in top-down fashion. Along with the chapter objectives, the outline helps users anticipate topics and set a comfortable and effective learning pace.

Approximately 26,000 Lines of Code in 230 Example Programs (with Program Outputs)

We present C# features in the context of complete, working C# programs. The programs range in size from just a few lines of code to substantial examples containing hundreds of lines of code. All examples are available as downloads from our Web site, **www.deitel.com**.

665 Illustrations/Figures

An abundance of charts, line drawings and program outputs is included.

402 Programming Tips

We have included programming tips to help readers focus on important aspects of program development. We highlight hundreds of these tips in the form of *Good Programming Practices*, *Common Programming Errors*, *Testing and Debugging Tips*, *Performance Tips*, *Portability Tips*, *Software Engineering Observations* and *Look-and-Feel Observations*. These tips and practices represent the best the authors have gleaned from many decades of programming and teaching experience. One of our customers—a mathematics major—told us that she feels this approach is like the highlighting of axioms, theorems and corollaries in mathematics books; it provides a foundation on which to build good software.

52 Good Programming Practices

Good Programming Practices *are tips that call attention to techniques that will help developers produce programs that are clearer, more understandable and more maintainable.*

131 Common Programming Errors

Developers learning a language tend to make certain kinds of errors frequently. Pointing out these Common Programming Errors *reduces the likelihood that readers will make the same mistakes.*

33 Testing and Debugging Tips

When we first designed this "tip type," we thought the tips would contain suggestions strictly for exposing bugs and removing them from programs. In fact, many of the tips describe aspects of C# that prevent "bugs" from getting into programs in the first place, thus simplifying the testing and debugging processes.

46 Performance Tips

Developers like to "turbo charge" their programs. We have included 46 Performance Tips *that highlight opportunities for improving program performance—making programs run faster or minimizing the amount of memory that they occupy.*

15 Portability Tips

We include Portability Tips *to help developers write portable code and to provide insights on how C# achieves its high degree of portability.*

96 Software Engineering Observations

The object-oriented programming paradigm necessitates a complete rethinking of the way we build software systems. C# is an effective language for achieving good software engineering. The Software Engineering Observations *highlight architectural and design issues that affect the construction of software systems, especially large-scale systems.*

25 Look-and-Feel Observations

We provide Look-and-Feel Observations *to highlight graphical-user-interface conventions. These observations help developers design attractive, user-friendly graphical user interfaces that conform to industry norms.*

Summary
Each chapter ends with a summary that helps readers review and reinforce key concepts.

Approximately 4,800 Index Entries (with approximately 6,150 Page References)
We have included an extensive Index. This resource enables readers to search for any term or concept by keyword. The Index is especially useful to practicing programmers who use the book as a reference.

"Double Indexing" of All C# LIVE-CODE™ Examples
C# for Experienced Programmers has 230 LIVE-CODE™ examples, which we have "double indexed." For every C# source-code program in the book, we took the file name with the `.cs` extension, such as **ShowColors.cs**, and indexed it both alphabetically (in this case, under "S") and as a subindex item under "Examples." This makes it easier to find examples using particular features.

C# Multimedia Cyber Classroom and The Complete C# Training Course

We have prepared an interactive, CD-ROM-based, software version of *C# How to Program,* called the *C# Multimedia Cyber Classroom.* This resource, ideal for corporate training and college courses, is loaded with interactive e-learning features. The *Cyber Classroom* is packaged with the *C# How to Program* textbook at a discount in *The Complete C# Training Course.* If you already have that book and would like to purchase the *C# Multimedia Cyber Classroom* separately, please visit **www.InformIT.com/cyber-classrooms**. The ISBN number for the *C# Multimedia Cyber Classroom* is 0-13-064587-7. Many Deitel™ *Cyber Classrooms* are available in CD-ROM and Web-based training formats.

The CD-ROM provides an introduction in which the authors overview the *Cyber Classroom*'s features. The textbook's 204 LIVE-CODE™ example C# programs truly "come alive" in the *Cyber Classroom.* If you are viewing a program and want to execute it, you simply click the lightning-bolt icon, and the program will run. You immediately will see—and hear, when working with audio-based multimedia programs—the program's output. Click the audio icon, and one of the authors will discuss the program and "walk you through" the code.

The *Cyber Classroom* also provides navigational aids, including extensive hyperlinking. The *Cyber Classroom* is browser based, so it remembers sections that you have visited recently and allows you to move forward or backward among those sections. The thousands of index entries are hyperlinked to their text occurrences. Furthermore, when you key in a term using the "find" feature, the *Cyber Classroom* will locate occurrences of that term throughout the text. The Table of Contents entries are "hot," so clicking a chapter name takes you immediately to that chapter.

Readers like the fact that solutions to approximately half the exercises in *C# How to Program* are included with the *Cyber Classroom.* Studying and running these extra programs is a great way for readers to enhance their learning experience.

Professionals and student users of our *Cyber Classrooms* tell us that they like the interactivity and that the *Cyber Classroom* is an effective reference due to its extensive hyperlinking and other navigational features. We received an e-mail from a reader who said he lives "in the boonies" and cannot attend a live course at a university, so the *Cyber Classroom* provided an ideal solution to his educational needs.

Professors tell us that their students enjoy using the *Cyber Classroom* and spend more time on the courses and master more of the material than in textbook-only courses. For a complete list of the available and forthcoming *Cyber Classrooms* and *Complete Training Courses,* see the *Deitel™ Series* page at the beginning of this book, the product listing and ordering information at the end of this book or visit **www.deitel.com, www.prenhall.com/deitel** or **www.InformIT.com/deitel**.

Deitel e-Learning Initiatives

e-Books and Support for Wireless Devices

Wireless devices will play an enormous role in the future of the Internet. Given recent bandwidth enhancements and the emergence of 2.5 and 3G wireless technologies, it is projected that, within two years, more people will access the Internet through wireless devices than through desktop computers. Deitel & Associates, Inc., is committed to wireless accessibility and has recently published *Wireless Internet & Mobile Business How to Program*. To fulfill the needs of a wide range of customers, we are developing our content in traditional print formats and in new electronic formats, such as e-books, so that readers can access content virtually anytime, anywhere. Visit `www.deitel.com` for periodic updates on all Deitel technology initiatives.

e-Matter

Deitel & Associates, Inc., is partnering with Prentice Hall's parent company, Pearson PLC, and its information technology Web site, `InformIT.com`, to launch the Deitel e-Matter series at `www.InformIT.com/deitel` in Fall 2002. The Deitel e-Matter series will provide professionals with an additional source of information on specific programming topics at modest prices. e-Matter consists of stand-alone sections taken from published texts, forthcoming texts or pieces written during the Deitel research-and-development process. Developing e-Matter based on pre-publication manuscripts allows us to offer significant amounts of the material well before our books are published.

Course Management Systems: WebCT, Blackboard, CourseCompass and Premium CourseCompass

We are working with Prentice Hall to integrate our *How to Program Series* courseware into four series of Course Management Systems-based products: WebCT, Blackboard™, CourseCompass and Premium CourseCompass. These enable instructors to create, manage and use sophisticated Web-based educational programs. Course Management Systems feature course customization (such as posting contact information, policies, syllabi, announcements, assignments, grades, performance evaluations and progress tracking), class and student management tools, a grade book, reporting tools, communication tools (such as chat rooms), a whiteboard, document sharing, bulletin boards and more. Instructors can use these products to communicate with their students, create online quizzes and exams from questions directly linked to the text and efficiently grade and track test results. For more information about these upcoming products, visit `www.prenhall.com/cms`. For demonstrations of existing WebCT, Blackboard and CourseCompass course materials, visit `cms.prenhall.com/webct`, `cms.prenhall.com/blackboard` and `cms.prenhall.com/coursecompass`, respectively.

Deitel and InformIT Newsletters

Deitel Column in the InformIT Newsletters

Deitel & Associates, Inc., contributes articles to the free *InformIT* weekly e-mail newsletter, subscribed to by more than 750,000 IT professionals worldwide. For registration information, visit `www.InformIT.com` and click the **MyInformIT** tab.

Deitel™ Buzz Online Newsletter

Our own free newsletter, the *Deitel™ Buzz Online*, includes commentary on industry trends and developments, links to articles and resources from our published books and upcoming publications, product-release schedules, challenges, anecdotes and more. For registration information, visit `www.deitel.com/newsletter/subscribe.html`.

The Deitel™ Developer Series

Deitel & Associates, Inc., is making a major commitment to .NET programming through the launch of our *Deitel™ Developer Series*. *C#: A Programmer's Introduction*, *C# for Experienced Programmers*, *Visual Basic .NET for Experienced Programmers* and *Visual C++ .NET for Experienced Programmers* are the first .NET books in this new series. These will be followed by several advanced books, beginning with *ASP .NET with C# for Experienced Programmers* and *ASP .NET with Visual Basic .NET for Experienced Programmers*.

The *Deitel™ Developer Series* is divided into three subseries. The *A Technical Introduction* subseries provides IT managers and developers with detailed overviews of emerging technologies. The *A Programmer's Introduction* subseries is designed to teach the fundamentals of new languages and software technologies to developers from the ground up. These books discuss programming fundamentals, followed by brief introductions to more sophisticated topics. Finally, the *For Experienced Programmers* subseries is designed for seasoned developers seeking to learn new programming languages and technologies without the encumbrance of introductory material. The books in this subseries move quickly to in-depth coverage of the intermediate features of the programming languages and software technologies being covered.

ASP .NET with C# for Experienced Programmers

Our forthcoming publication *ASP .NET with C# for Experienced Programmers* (available in 2003) is geared toward experienced .NET developers. This new book will cover enterprise-level Web-programming topics, including: Creating multi-tier, database intensive ASP .NET applications using ADO .NET and XML; constructing custom Web controls and developing Web services. This book also will include configuration and security topics. Updates on the status of this publication are posted at **www.deitel.com**. Before reading this book you should be familiar with C# at the level of either *C# How to Program* or *C# for Experienced Programmers*.

Acknowledgments

One of the great pleasures of writing a book is acknowledging the efforts of many people whose names may not appear on the cover, but whose hard work, cooperation, friendship and understanding were crucial to the production of the book. Because this publication has been derived from *C# How to Program*, we would like to acknowledge those who have helped us with both publications.

Many other people at Deitel & Associates, Inc., devoted long hours to this project. Below is a list of our full-time employees who contributed to this publication:

Sean E. Santry
Matthew R. Kowalewski
Jonathan Gadzik
Kyle Lomelí
Lauren Trees
Rashmi Jayaprakash
Laura Treibick

Betsy DuWaldt
Barbara Deitel
Abbey Deitel

We would also like to thank the participants in the Deitel & Associates, Inc., College Internship Program who contributed to this publication.[1]

Jeffrey Hamm (Northeastern)
Kalid Azad (Princeton)
Christopher Cassa (Massachusetts Institute of Technology)
David Tuttle (Harvard)
Thiago Lucas da Silva (Northeastern)
Ori Schwartz (Boston University)
Elizabeth Rockett (Princeton)
Barbara Strauss (Brandeis)
Christina Carney (Framingham State)
Brian Foster (Northeastern)
Mike Preshman (Northeastern)

We are fortunate to have been able to work with the talented and dedicated team of publishing professionals at Prentice Hall. We especially appreciate the extraordinary efforts of our editors, Petra Recter and Karen McLean of Prentice Hall and PH/PTR, respectively and Michael Ruel, who managed the extraordinary review processes for our *Deitel™ Developer Series* C# publications. We would also like to thank Mark L. Taub, Editor-in-Chief for computer publications at PH/PTR, for conceptualizing the *Deitel™ Developer Series*. He provided the necessary environment and resources to help us generate the many books in this series. A special note of appreciation goes to Marcia Horton, Editor-in-Chief of Engineering and Computer Science at Prentice Hall. Marcia has been our mentor and our friend for 18 years at Prentice Hall. She is responsible for all aspects of Deitel publications at all Pearson divisions including Prentice Hall, PH/PTR and Pearson International.

Laura Treibick, the Director of Multimedia at Deitel & Associates, Inc., designed the cover. Tamara Newnam (**smart_art@earthlink.net**) carried the cover through to completion, and produced the art work for our programming-tip icons.

We wish to acknowledge the efforts of our first- and second-round reviewers. Adhering to a tight time schedule, these reviewers scrutinized the text and the programs, providing countless suggestions for improving the accuracy and completeness of the presentation. We sincerely appreciate the time these people took from their busy professional schedules to help us ensure the quality, accuracy and timeliness of this book.

---

1. The *Deitel & Associates, Inc. College Internship Program* offers a limited number of salaried positions to Boston-area college students majoring in Computer Science, Information Technology, Marketing, Management and English. Students work at our corporate headquarters in Maynard, Massachusetts full-time in the summers and (for those attending college in the Boston area) part-time during the academic year. We also offer full-time internship positions for students interested in taking a semester off from school to gain industry experience. Regular full-time positions are available to college graduates. For more information about this competitive program, please contact Abbey Deitel at **deitel@deitel.com** and visit **www.deitel.com**.

Merged reviewer list from *C# How to Program* **and** *C# for Experienced Programmers*:

Hussein Abuthuraya (Microsoft)
Lars Bergstrom (Microsoft)
Indira Dhingra (Microsoft)
Eric Gunnerson (Microsoft)
Peter Hallam (Microsoft)
Habib Hegdarian (Microsoft)
Anson Horton (Microsoft)
Willis Johnson (Microsoft)
Latha Lakshminarayanan (Microsoft)
Kerry Loynd (Microsoft)
Tom McDade (Microsoft)
Syed Mehdi (Microsoft)
Shanku Niyogi (Microsoft)
Cosmin Radu (Microsoft)
Ratta Rakshminarayana (Microsoft)
Paul Randal (Microsoft)
Imtiaz Syed (Microsoft)
Ed Thornburg (Microsoft)
Richard Van Fossen (Microsoft)
Rishabh Agarwal (Delteq Systems Pte. Ltd.)
José Antonio González Seco (Sadiel S.A.)
Paul Bohman (WebAIM)
Alex Bondarev (SureFire Commerce, Inc.)
Ron Braithwaite (Nutriware)
Filip Bulovic (Objectronics PTY Ltd.)
Mark Burhop (University of Cincinnati)
Carl Burnham (Southpoint)
Matt Butler (Oakscape Inc.)
Andrew Chau (Rich Solutions, Inc.)
Dharmesh Chauhan (Microsoft Consultant, Singapore)
Shyam Chebrolu (SAIC Broadway & Seymour Group)
Kunal Cheda (DotNetExtreme.com)
Edmund Chou (MIT Student, www.devhood.com project, Microsoft Intern)
James Chegwidden (Tarrant County College)
Vijay Cinnakonda (University of Toledo)
Michael Colynuck (Sierra Systems)
Jay Cook (Canon Development Americas)
Jeff Cowan (Magenic Technologies)
Robert Dombroski (AccessOnTime)
Shaun Eagan ((Eagan Consulting)
Brian Erwin (Extreme Logic)
Hamilton Fong (Montag & Caldwell, Inc.)
Gnanavel Gnana Arun Ganesh (Arun Microsystems)
Sam Gentile (Consultant)
Sam Gill (San Francisco State University)

John Godel (TJX)
David Haglin (Minnesota State University in Mankato)
Ric Heishmann (Northern Virginia Community College)
Jeff Isom (WebAIM)
Rex Jaeschke (Consultant)
Amit Kalani (MobiCast)
Priti Kalani (Consultant)
Yashavant Kanetkar
Bryan Keller (csharphelp.com)
Patrick Lam (EdgeNet Communications)
Yi-Fung Lin (MIT Student, www.devhood.com project, Microsoft Intern)
Maxim Loukianov (SoloMio Corporation)
Gaurav Mantro (EDS PLM Solutions)
Jaimon Mathew (Osprey Software Technology)
Robert Meagher (Compuware NuMega Lab)
John Mueller
Arun Nair (iSpan Technologies)
Saurabh Nandu (Mastercsharp.com)
Simon North (Synopsys)
Jibin Pan (csharpcorner.com)
Graham Parker (VBUG)
Bryan Plaster (Valtech)
Chris Rausch (Sheridan Press)
Debbie Reid (Santa Fe Community College)
Bryn Rhodes (Softwise, Inc.)
Craig Schofding (C.A.S. Training)
Rahul Sharma (Maxutil Software)
Devan Shepherd (XMaLpha Technologies)
Srinivasa Sivakumar (Equity Office)
David Talbot (Reallinx, Inc.)
Satish Talim (Pune-Csharp)
Pavel Tsekov (Consultant)
John Varghese (UBS Warburg)
Peter Weng (MIT Student, www.devhood.com project, Microsoft Intern)
Jesse Wilkins (Metalinear Media)
Warren Wiltsie (Fairleigh Dickinson University/Seton Hall University)
Phil Wright (Crownwood Consulting Ltd.)
Norimasa Yoshida (MIT Graduate Student)

We would sincerely appreciate your comments, criticisms, corrections and suggestions for improving the book. Please address all correspondence to:

deitel@deitel.com

We will respond promptly.

Well, that's it for now. Welcome to the exciting world of C# programming. We hope you enjoy this look at Microsoft's premier .NET language. Good luck!

Dr. Harvey M. Deitel
Paul J. Deitel
Jeff Listfield
Tem R. Nieto
Cheryl H. Yaeger
Marina Zlatkina

About the Authors

Dr. Harvey M. Deitel, Chairman and Chief Strategy Officer of Deitel & Associates, Inc., has 41 years experience in the computing field, including extensive industry and academic experience. Dr. Deitel earned B.S. and M.S. degrees from the Massachusetts Institute of Technology and a Ph.D. from Boston University. He worked on the pioneering virtual-memory operating-systems projects at IBM and MIT that developed techniques now widely implemented in systems such as Unix, Linux™ and Windows XP. He has 20 years of college teaching experience, including earning tenure and serving as the Chairman of the Computer Science Department at Boston College before founding Deitel & Associates, Inc., with his son, Paul J. Deitel. He is the author or co-author of several dozen books and multimedia packages and is writing many more. With translations published in Japanese, Russian, Spanish, Traditional Chinese, Simplified Chinese, Korean, French, Polish, Italian, Portuguese and Greek, Dr. Deitel's texts have earned international recognition. Dr. Deitel has delivered professional seminars to major corporations, and to government organizations and various branches of the military.

Paul J. Deitel, CEO and Chief Technical Officer of Deitel & Associates, Inc., is a graduate of the Massachusetts Institute of Technology's Sloan School of Management, where he studied Information Technology. Through Deitel & Associates, Inc., he has delivered Java, C, C++ and Internet and World Wide Web programming courses to industry clients including Compaq, Sun Microsystems, White Sands Missile Range, Rogue Wave Software, Boeing, Dell, Stratus, Fidelity, Cambridge Technology Partners, Open Environment Corporation, One Wave, Hyperion Software, Lucent Technologies, Adra Systems, Entergy, CableData Systems, NASA at the Kennedy Space Center, the National Severe Storms Laboratory, IBM and many other organizations. He has lectured on C++ and Java for the Boston Chapter of the Association for Computing Machinery and has taught satellite-based Java courses through a cooperative venture of Deitel & Associates, Inc., Prentice Hall and the Technology Education Network. He and his father, Dr. Harvey M. Deitel, are the world's best-selling programming language textbook authors.

Tem R. Nieto, Director of Product Development of Deitel & Associates, Inc., is a graduate of the Massachusetts Institute of Technology, where he studied engineering and computing. Through Deitel & Associates, Inc., he has delivered courses for industry clients including Sun Microsystems, Compaq, EMC, Stratus, Fidelity, NASDAQ, Art Technology, Progress Software, Toys "R" Us, Operational Support Facility of the National Oceanographic and Atmospheric Administration, Jet Propulsion Laboratory, Nynex, Motorola, Federal Reserve Bank of Chicago, Banyan, Schlumberger, University of Notre Dame, NASA, Hewlett-Packard, various military installations and many others. He has co-authored numerous books and multimedia packages with the Deitels and has contributed to virtually every Deitel & Associates, Inc., publication.

Cheryl H. Yaeger, Director of Microsoft Software Publications with Deitel & Associates, Inc., graduated from Boston University in three years with a bachelor's degree in Computer Science. Cheryl has co-authored various Deitel & Associates publications, including *C# How to Program, C# A Programmer's Introduction, C# for Experienced Programmers* and *Visual Basic .NET for Experienced Programmers* as well as contributed to other Deitel publications including *Perl How to Program, Wireless Internet & Mobile Business How to Program, Internet and World Wide Web How to Program, Second Edition* and *Visual Basic .NET How to Program, Second Edition.*

Marina Zlatkina graduated from Brandeis University in three years with degrees in Computer Science and Mathematics, and in her fourth year earned a Master of Arts in Computer Science. During her Brandeis career, she conducted research in databases and has been a teaching assistant. Marina co-authored *C# How to Program, C#: A Programmer's Introduction* and *C# for Experienced Programmers*, and contributed to another Deitel publication, *e-Business & e-Commerce for Managers.*

Jeff A. Listfield is a Computer Science graduate of Harvard College. His coursework included classes in computer graphics, networks and computational theory and he has programming experience in C, C++, Java, Perl and Lisp. Jeff has co-authored *C# How to Program, C#: A Programmer's Introduction* and *C# for Experienced Programmers*, and contributed to *Perl How to Program.*

About Deitel & Associates, Inc.

Deitel & Associates, Inc., is an internationally recognized corporate instructor-led training and content-creation organization specializing in Internet/World Wide Web software technology, e-business/e-commerce software technology, object technology and computer programming languages education. The company provides courses in Internet and World Wide Web programming, wireless Internet programming, Web services (in both Java and .NET languages), object technology, and major programming languages and platforms, such as Visual Basic .NET, C#, Visual C++ .NET, Java, Advanced Java, C, C++, XML, Perl, Python, ASP .NET, ADO .NET and more. Deitel & Associates, Inc., was founded by Dr. Harvey M. Deitel and Paul J. Deitel, the world's leading programming-language textbook authors. The company's clients include many of the largest computer companies, government agencies, branches of the military and business organizations. Through its 25-year publishing partnership with Prentice Hall, Deitel & Associates, Inc., publishes leading-edge programming textbooks, professional books, interactive CD-ROM-based multimedia *Cyber Classrooms, Complete Training Courses*, e-books, e-matter, Web-based training courses and course management systems e-content. Deitel & Associates, Inc., and the authors can be reached via e-mail at:

> `deitel@deitel.com`

To learn more about Deitel & Associates, Inc., its publications and its worldwide corporate on-site curriculum, see the last few pages of this book or visit:

> `www.deitel.com`

Individuals wishing to purchase Deitel books, *Cyber Classrooms, Complete Training Courses* and Web-based training courses can do so through bookstores, online booksellers and:

> `www.deitel.com`

```
www.prenhall.com/deitel
www.InformIT.com/deitel
www.InformIT.com/cyberclassrooms
```

Bulk orders by corporations and academic institutions should be placed directly with Prentice Hall. See the last few pages of this book for worldwide ordering details. To follow the Deitel publishing program, please register at

```
www.deitel.com/newsletter/subscribe.html.
```

The World Wide Web Consortium (W3C)

 Deitel & Associates, Inc., is a member of the *World Wide Web Consortium (W3C)*. The W3C was founded in 1994 "to develop common protocols for the evolution of the World Wide Web." As a W3C member, Deitel & Associates, Inc., holds a seat on the W3C Advisory Committee (the company's representative is our CEO and Chief Technology Officer, Paul Deitel). Advisory Committee members help provide "strategic direction" to the W3C through meetings held around the world. Member organizations also help develop standards recommendations for Web technologies (such as XHTML, XML and many others) through participation in W3C activities and groups. Membership in the W3C is intended for companies and large organizations. To obtain information on becoming a member of the W3C visit **www.w3.org/ Consortium/Prospectus/Joining**.

Introduction to .NET and C#

Objectives

- To learn the history of the Internet and the World Wide Web.
- To become familiar with the World Wide Web Consortium (W3C).
- To learn what the Extensible Markup Language (XML) is and why it is an important technology.
- To understand the impact of object technology on software development.
- To understand the Microsoft® .NET initiative.
- To preview the remaining chapters of the book.

Things are always at their best in their beginning.
Blaise Pascal

High thoughts must have high language.
Aristophanes

Our life is frittered away by detail...Simplify, simplify.
Henry David Thoreau

Before beginning, plan carefully....
Marcus Tullius Cicero

Look with favor upon a bold beginning.
Virgil

I think I'm beginning to learn something about it.
Auguste Renoir

Outline

1.1   Introduction
1.2   History of the Internet and World Wide Web
1.3   World Wide Web Consortium (W3C)
1.4   Extensible Markup Language (XML)
1.5   Key Software Trend: Object Technology
1.6   Introduction to Microsoft .NET
1.7   C#
1.8   .NET Framework and the Common Language Runtime
1.9   Tour of the Book
1.10   Summary
1.11   Internet and World Wide Web Resources

1.1 Introduction

Welcome to C#! We have worked hard to provide programmers with the most accurate and complete information regarding the C# language and the .NET platform. We hope that this book will provide an informative, entertaining and challenging learning experience for you. In this chapter, we present the history of the Internet and World Wide Web and introduce Microsoft's .NET initiative. The chapter concludes by touring the remainder of the book.

1.2 History of the Internet and World Wide Web

In the late 1960s, at a conference at the University of Illinois Urbana-Champaign, ARPA—the Advanced Research Projects Agency of the Department of Defense—rolled out the blueprints for networking the main computer systems of approximately a dozen ARPA-funded universities and research institutions. The computers were to be connected with communications lines operating at a then-stunning 56 Kbps (1 Kbps is equal to 1,024 bits per second), at a time when most people (of the few who had access to networking technologies) were connecting over telephone lines to computers at a rate of 110 bits per second. Researchers at Harvard talked about communicating with the Univac 1108 "supercomputer," which was located across the country at the University of Utah, to handle calculations related to their computer graphics research. Many other intriguing possibilities were discussed. Academic research was about to take a giant leap forward. Shortly after this conference, ARPA proceeded to implement what quickly became called the *ARPAnet*, the grandparent of today's *Internet*.

Things worked out differently from the original plan. Although the ARPAnet did enable researchers to network their computers, its chief benefit proved to be its capability for quick and easy communication via what came to be known as *electronic mail* (*e-mail*). This is true even on today's Internet, with e-mail, instant messaging and file transfer facilitating communications among hundreds of millions of people worldwide.

The network was designed to operate without centralized control. This meant that if a portion of the network should fail, the remaining working portions would still be able to route data packets from senders to receivers over alternative paths.

The protocol (i.e., set of rules) for communicating over the ARPAnet became known as the *Transmission Control Protocol (TCP)*. TCP ensured that messages were routed properly from sender to receiver and that those messages arrived intact.

In parallel with the early evolution of the Internet, organizations worldwide were implementing their own networks to facilitate both intra-organization (i.e., within the organization) and inter-organization (i.e., between organizations) communication. A huge variety of networking hardware and software appeared. One challenge was to enable these diverse products to communicate with each other. ARPA accomplished this by developing the *Internet Protocol (IP)*, which created a true "network of networks," the current architecture of the Internet. The combined set of protocols is now commonly called *TCP/IP*.

Initially, the use of the Internet was limited to universities and research institutions; later, the military adopted the technology. Eventually, the government decided to allow access to the Internet for commercial purposes. When this decision was made, there was resentment among the research and military communities—it was felt that response times would become poor as "the Net" became saturated with so many users.

In fact, the opposite has occurred. Businesses rapidly realized that, by making effective use of the Internet, they could refine their operations and offer new and better services to their clients. Companies started spending vast amounts of money to develop and enhance their Internet presence. This generated fierce competition among communications carriers and hardware and software suppliers to meet the increased infrastructure demand. The result is that *bandwidth* (i.e., the information-carrying capacity of communications lines) on the Internet has increased tremendously, while hardware costs have plummeted. The Internet has played a significant role in the economic growth that many industrialized nations experienced over the last decade.

The *World Wide Web* allows computer users to locate and view multimedia-based documents (i.e., documents with text, graphics, animations, audios or videos) on almost any subject. Even though the Internet was developed more than three decades ago, the introduction of the World Wide Web (WWW) was a relatively recent event. In 1989, Tim Berners-Lee of CERN (the European Organization for Nuclear Research) began to develop a technology for sharing information via hyperlinked text documents. Basing the new language on the well-established *Standard Generalized Markup Language (SGML)*—a standard for business data interchange—Berners-Lee called his invention the *HyperText Markup Language (HTML)*. He also wrote communication protocols to form the backbone of his new hypertext information system, which he referred to as the World Wide Web.

Surely, historians will list the Internet and the World Wide Web among the most important and profound creations of humankind. In the past, most computer applications ran on "stand-alone" computers (computers that were not connected to one another). Today's applications can be written to communicate among the world's hundreds of millions of computers. The Internet and World Wide Web merge computing and communications technologies, expediting and simplifying our work. They make information instantly and conveniently accessible to large numbers of people. They enable individuals and small businesses to achieve worldwide exposure. They are changing the way we do business and conduct our personal lives.

1.3 World Wide Web Consortium (W3C)

In October 1994, Tim Berners-Lee founded an organization, called the *World Wide Web Consortium (W3C)*, that is devoted to developing nonproprietary, interoperable technologies for the World Wide Web. One of the W3C's primary goals is to make the Web universally accessible—regardless of its users' disabilities, languages or cultures.

The W3C is also a standardization organization and is composed of three *hosts*—the Massachusetts Institute of Technology (MIT), France's INRIA (Institut National de Recherche en Informatique et Automatique) and Keio University of Japan—and over 400 members, including Deitel & Associates, Inc. Members provide the primary financing for the W3C and help set the strategic direction of the Consortium. To learn more about the W3C, visit **www.w3.org**.

Web technologies standardized by the W3C are called *Recommendations*. Current W3C Recommendations include *Extensible HyperText Markup Language (XHTML™)* for marking up content for the Web, *Cascading Style Sheets (CSS™)* for describing how content is formatted and the *Extensible Markup Language (XML)* for creating markup languages. Recommendations are not actual software products, but documents that specify the role, syntax and rules of a technology. Before becoming a W3C Recommendation, a document passes through three major phases: *Working Draft*, which, as its name implies, specifies an evolving draft; *Candidate Recommendation,* a stable version of the document that industry can begin to implement; and *Proposed Recommendation*, a Candidate Recommendation that is considered mature (i.e., has been implemented and tested over a period of time) and is ready to be considered for W3C Recommendation status. For detailed information about the W3C Recommendation track, see "6.2 The W3C Recommendation track" at

```
www.w3.org/Consortium/Process/Process-19991111/
process.html#RecsCR
```

1.4 Extensible Markup Language (XML)

As the popularity of the Web exploded, HTML's limitations became apparent. HTML's lack of *extensibility* (the ability to change or add features) frustrated developers, and its ambiguous definition allowed erroneous HTML to proliferate. In response to these problems, the W3C added limited extensibility to HTML. This was, however, only a temporary solution—the need for a standardized, fully extensible and structurally strict language was apparent. As a result, XML was developed by the W3C. XML combines the power and extensibility of its parent language, Standard Generalized Markup Language (SGML), with the simplicity that the Web community demands.

Data independence, the separation of content from its presentation, is an essential characteristic of XML. Since an XML document describes data, any application conceivably can process such a document. Recognizing this, software developers are integrating XML into their applications to improve Web functionality and interoperability. XML's flexibility and power make it perfect for the middle tier of client/server systems, which must interact with a wide variety of clients. Much of the processing that was once limited to server computers now can be performed by client computers, because XML's semantic and structural information enables it to be manipulated by any application that can process text. This reduces server loads and network traffic, resulting in a faster, more efficient Web.

XML is not limited to Web applications. Increasingly, XML is being employed in databases—the structure of an XML document enables it to be integrated easily with database applications. As applications become more Web enabled, it seems likely that XML will become the universal technology for data representation. All applications employing XML will be able to communicate, provided that they can understand each other's XML markup, or *vocabulary*.

Simple Object Access Protocol (SOAP) is a technology for the distribution of data (marked up as XML) over the Internet. Developed initially by Microsoft and Develop-Mentor, SOAP is a W3C Working Draft that provides a framework for expressing application semantics, encoding data and packaging data. Microsoft .NET (discussed in Sections 1.6 and 1.7) uses XML and SOAP to mark up and transfer data over the Internet. XML and SOAP are at the core of .NET—they allow software components to interoperate (i.e., communicate easily with one another). SOAP is supported by many platforms, because of its foundations in XML and HTTP. We discuss XML in Chapter 15, Extensible Markup Language (XML), and SOAP in Chapter 18, ASP .NET and Web Services.

1.5 Key Software Trend: Object Technology

What are objects, and why are they special? Object technology is a packaging scheme that facilitates the creation of meaningful software units. These units are large and focused on particular application areas. There are date objects, time objects, paycheck objects, invoice objects, audio objects, video objects, file objects, record objects and so on. In fact, almost any noun can be represented as a software object. Objects have *properties* (i.e., *attributes*, such as color, size and weight) and perform *actions* (i.e., *behaviors*, such as moving, sleeping and drawing). Classes represent groups of related objects. For example, all cars belong to the "car" class, even though individual cars vary in make, model, color and options packages. A class specifies the general format of its objects; the properties and actions available to an object depend on its class.

We live in a world of objects. Just look around you—there are cars, planes, people, animals, buildings, traffic lights, elevators and so on. Before object-oriented languages appeared, *procedural programming languages* (such as Fortran, Pascal, BASIC and C) focused on actions (verbs) rather than things or objects (nouns). We live in a world of objects, but earlier programming languages forced individuals to program primarily with verbs. This paradigm shift made writing programs a bit awkward. However, with the advent of popular object-oriented languages, such as C++, Java and C#, programmers can program in an object-oriented manner that reflects the way in which they perceive the world. This process, which seems more natural than procedural programming, has resulted in significant productivity gains.

One of the key problems with procedural programming is that the program units created do not mirror real-world entities effectively and therefore are difficult to reuse. Programmers often write and rewrite similar software for various projects. This wastes precious time and money as programmers repeatedly "reinvent the wheel." With object technology, properly designed software entities (called objects) can be reused on future projects. Using libraries of reusable componentry can reduce the amount of effort required to implement certain kinds of systems (compared with the effort that would be required to reinvent these capabilities in new projects). C# programmers use the .NET Framework Class Library (known commonly as the FCL), which is introduced in Section 1.8.

Some organizations report that software reusability is not, in fact, the key benefit of object-oriented programming. Rather, they indicate that object-oriented programming tends to produce software that is more understandable because it is better organized and has fewer maintenance requirements. As much as 80 percent of software costs are not associated with the original efforts to develop the software, but instead are related to the continued evolution and maintenance of that software throughout its lifetime. Object orientation allows programmers to abstract the details of software and focus on the "big picture." Rather than worrying about minute details, the programmer can focus on the behaviors and interactions of objects. A roadmap that showed every tree, house and driveway would be difficult, if not impossible, to read. When such details are removed and only the essential information (roads) remains, the map becomes easier to understand. In the same way, a program that is divided into objects is easy to understand, modify and update because it hides much of the detail. It is clear that object-oriented programming will be the key programming methodology for at least the next decade.

Software Engineering Observation 1.1

Use a building-block approach to create programs. By using existing pieces in new projects, programmers avoid reinventing the wheel. This is called software reuse, *and it is central to object-oriented programming.*

[*Note*: We will include many of these *Software Engineering Observations* throughout the book to explain concepts that affect and improve the overall architecture and quality of a software system and, particularly, of large software systems. We also will highlight *Good Programming Practices* (practices that can help programmers write programs that are clearer, more understandable, more maintainable and easier to test and debug), *Common Programming Errors* (problems we highlight to ensure that programmers avoid the most common errors), *Performance Tips* (techniques that will help programmers write programs that run faster and use less memory), *Portability Tips* (techniques that will help programmers write programs that can run, with little or no modification, on a variety of computers), *Testing and Debugging Tips* (techniques that will help programmers remove bugs from their programs and, more importantly, write bug-free programs in the first place) and *Look-and-Feel Observations* (techniques that will help programmers design the "look and feel" of their graphical user interfaces for appearance and ease of use). Many of these techniques and practices are only guidelines; you will, no doubt, develop your own preferred programming style.]

The advantage of writing your own code is that you will know exactly how it works. The code will be yours to examine, modify and improve. The disadvantage is the time and effort that goes into designing, developing and testing new code.

Performance Tip 1.1

Reusing proven code components instead of writing your own versions can improve program performance, because these components normally are written to perform efficiently.

Software Engineering Observation 1.2

Extensive class libraries of reusable software components are available over the Internet and the World Wide Web; many are offered free of charge.

1.6 Introduction to Microsoft .NET

In June 2000, Microsoft announced its *.NET* (pronounced "dot-net") *initiative*. The *.NET platform* is one that provides significant enhancements to earlier developer platforms. .NET offers a new software-development model that allows applications created in disparate programming languages to communicate with each other. The platform also allows developers to create Web-based applications that can be distributed to a great variety of devices (even wireless phones) and to desktop computers.

Microsoft's .NET initiative is a broad new vision for embracing the Internet and the Web in the development, engineering and use of software. One key aspect of the .NET strategy is its independence from a specific language or platform. Rather than requiring programmers to use a single programming language, developers can create a .NET application by using any combination of .NET-compatible languages (Fig. 1.1). Programmers can contribute to the same software project, writing code in the .NET languages (such as C#, Visual C++ .NET, Visual Basic .NET and many others) in which they are most proficient. Part of the initiative includes Microsoft's *Active Server Pages (ASP) .NET* technology, which allows programmers to create applications for the Web. With ASP .NET, developers can create Web-based, database-intensive applications quickly by harnessing the power of .NET's object-oriented languages. Developers can use ASP .NET to develop powerful and robust Web applications, taking advantage of ASP .NET's optimizations for performance, testing and security.

A key component of the .NET architecture is *Web services* , which are applications that expose (i.e., make available) functionality to clients via the Internet. Clients and other applications can use these Web services as reusable building blocks. One example of a Web service is Dollar Rent a Car's reservation system, known as Quick Keys.[1] Dollar wanted to expose the functionality of its mainframe-based system, so that other companies could provide customers with the ability to make rental-car reservations. Dollar could have created individual, proprietary solutions for its business partners. To expose its functionality in a reusable way, Dollar implemented its solution using Web services. The results have been phenomenal. Through the newly created Web service, airlines and hotels can use Dollar's reservation system to reserve cars for their clients. Dollar's business partners do not need to use the same platform as Dollar uses, nor do they need to understand how the reservation system is implemented. Reimplementing its application as a Web service has provided Dollar with millions of dollars of additional revenue, as well as thousands of new customers.

Programming Languages	
APL	Oberon
C#	Oz

Fig. 1.1   .NET Languages (tabular information from Microsoft Web site, **www.microsoft.com**.). (Part 1 of 2.)

1. Microsoft Corporation, "Dollar Rent A Car Breathes New Life Into Legacy Systems Using .NET Connected Software," 15 March 2002 **<www.microsoft.com/business/casestudies/b2c/dollarrentacar.asp>**.

Programming Languages (Cont.)	
COBOL	Pascal
Component Pascal	Perl
Curriculum	Python
Eiffel	RPG
Fortran	Scheme
Haskell	Smalltalk
J#	Standard ML
JScript .NET	Visual Basic .NET
Mercury	Visual C++ .NET

Fig. 1.1   .NET Languages (tabular information from Microsoft Web site,
www.microsoft.com.). (Part 2 of 2.)

Web services extend the concept of software reuse by allowing programmers to concentrate on their specialties without having to implement every component of every application. Instead, companies can buy Web services and devote their time and energy to developing their products. Visual programming (discussed in Chapter 2) has become popular, because it enables programmers to create applications easily, using such prepackaged components as buttons, textboxes and labels. Similarly, programmers may create an application using Web services for databases, security, authentication, data storage and language translation without having to know the internal details of those components.

When companies link their products via Web services, a new user experience emerges. For example, a single application could manage bill payments, tax refunds, loans and investments, using Web services from various companies. An online merchant could buy Web services for online credit-card payments, user authentication, network security and inventory databases to create an e-commerce Web site.

The keys to this interaction are XML and SOAP, which enable Web services to communicate. XML gives meaning to data, and SOAP is the protocol that allows Web services to communicate easily with one another. XML and SOAP act as the "glue" that combines various Web services to form applications.

Universal data access is another essential .NET concept. If two copies of a file exist (e.g., on a personal and a company computer), the oldest version must be updated constantly—this is called file *synchronization*. If the files are different, they are *unsynchronized*, a situation that could lead to errors. With .NET, data can reside in one central location rather than on separate systems. Any Internet-connected device can access the data (under tight control, of course), which would then be formatted appropriately for use or display on the accessing device. Thus, the same document could be seen and edited on a desktop PC, a PDA, a wireless phone or some other device. Users would not need to synchronize the information, because it would be fully up-to-date in a central location.

.NET is an immense undertaking. We discuss various aspects of .NET throughout this book. Additional information is available at **www.microsoft.com/net**.

1.7 C#

The *C#* (pronounced "C-Sharp") programming language, developed at Microsoft by a team led by Anders Hejlsberg and Scott Wiltamuth, was designed specifically for the .NET platform as a language that would enable programmers to migrate to .NET. This migration is easy for a large base of programmers because C# has roots in C, C++ and Java, adapting the best features of each and adding new features of its own. The C# Language Specification is available for download at **msdn.microsoft.com/vstudio/techinfo/ articles/upgrade/Csharpdownload.asp**.

C# is an event-driven, fully object-oriented, visual programming language in which programs are created using an *Integrated Development Environment* (*IDE*). With the IDE, a programmer can create, run, test and debug C# programs conveniently, thereby reducing the time it takes to produce a working program to a fraction of the time it would have taken without using the IDE. The process of creating an application rapidly using an IDE is referred to as *Rapid Application Development (RAD)*.

1.8 .NET Framework and the Common Language Runtime

The *.NET Framework* is at the heart of .NET. This framework manages and executes applications, contains a class library (called the *Framework Class Library*, or *FCL*), enforces security and provides many other programming capabilities. The details of the .NET Framework are found in the *Common Language Specification* (*CLS*), which contains information about the storage of objects and other information. The CLS has been submitted for standardization to ECMA (the European Computer Manufacturers Association). This allows independent software vendors to create the .NET Framework for other platforms. The .NET Framework exists only for the Windows platform, but is being developed for other platforms, as well, such as Microsoft's *Shared Source CLI* (*Common Language Infrastructure*). The Shared Source CLI is an archive of source code that provides a subset of the Microsoft .NET Framework for both Windows XP and the FreeBSD[2] operating systems.[3] For more information in the Shared Source CLI, visit **msdn.microsoft.com/library/ default.asp?url=/library/en-us/dndotnet/html/mssharsource- cli.asp**.

The *Common Language Runtime (CLR)* is another central part of the .NET Framework—it executes C# programs. Programs are compiled into machine-specific instructions in two steps. First, the program is compiled into *Microsoft Intermediate Language (MSIL)*, which defines instructions for the CLR. Code converted into MSIL from other languages and sources is woven together by the CLR. Then, another compiler in the CLR compiles the MSIL into machine code (for a particular platform), creating a single application.

Why bother having the extra step of converting from C# to MSIL, instead of compiling directly into machine language? The key reasons are portability between operating systems, interoperability between languages and execution-management features such as memory management and security.

---

2. The FreeBSD project provides a freely available and open-source UNIX-like operating system that is based on UC Berkeley's *Berkeley System Distribution* (*BSD*). For more information on BSD, visit **www.freebsd.org**.
3. Microsoft Corporation, "The Microsoft Shared Source CLI Implementation," March 2002, **<msdn.microsoft.com/library/en-us/Dndotnet/html/mssharsource- cli.asp>**.

If the .NET Framework exists (and is installed) for a platform, that platform can run any .NET program. The ability of a program to run (without modification) across multiple platforms is known as *platform independence*. Code written once can be used on another machine without modification, saving both time and money. In addition, software can target a wider audience—previously, companies had to decide whether converting (sometimes called *porting*) their programs to different platforms was worth the cost. With .NET, porting is simplified.

The .NET Framework also provides a high level of *language interoperability*. Programs written in different languages are all compiled into MSIL—the different parts can be combined to create a single, unified program. MSIL allows the .NET Framework to be *language independent*, because MSIL is not tied to a particular programming language. Any language that can be compiled into MSIL is called a *.NET-compliant language*.

Language interoperability offers many benefits to software companies. C#, Visual Basic .NET and Visual C++ .NET developers, for example, can work side-by-side on the same project without having to learn another programming language—all their code is compiled into MSIL and linked together to form one program. In addition, the .NET Framework can package preexisting components (i.e., components created using tools that predate .NET) and .NET components to work together. This allows companies to reuse the code that they have spent years developing and integrate it with the .NET code that they write. Integration is crucial, because companies cannot migrate easily to .NET unless they can stay productive, using their existing developers and software.

Another benefit of the .NET Framework is the CLR's execution-management features. The CLR manages memory, security and other features, relieving the programmer of these responsibilities. With languages like C++, programmers must manage their own memory. This leads to problems if programmers request memory and never release it—programs could consume all available memory, which would prevent applications from running. By managing the program's memory, the .NET Framework allows programmers to concentrate on program logic.

The .NET Framework also provides programmers with a huge library of reusable classes. This library, called the Framework Class Library (FCL), can be used by any .NET language.

This book explains how to develop .NET software with C# and the FCL. Steve Ballmer, Microsoft's CEO, stated in May 2001 that Microsoft was "betting the company" on .NET. Such a dramatic commitment surely indicates a bright future for C# and its community of developers.

1.9 Tour of the Book

In this section, we tour the chapters and appendices of *C# for Experienced Programmers*. In addition to the topics presented in each chapter, several of the chapters contain an Internet and Web Resources section that lists additional sources from which readers can enhance their knowledge of C# programming.

Chapter 1—Introduction to .NET and C#

The first chapter presents the history of the Internet, World Wide Web and various technologies (such as XML and SOAP) that have led to advances in computing. We introduce the Microsoft .NET initiative and the C# programming language, including Web services. We explore the impact of .NET on software development and software reusability. The chapter concludes with a tour of the book.

Chapter 2—Introduction to the Visual Studio® .NET IDE and C# Programming

Chapter 2 introduces Visual Studio .NET, an *integrated development environment* (*IDE*) that allows programmers to create C# programs. Visual Studio .NET enables *visual programming*, in which *controls* (such as buttons and text boxes) are "dragged" and "dropped" into place, rather than added by typing code. Visual programming increases software-development productivity by eliminating many tedious programming tasks. For example, a graphical user interface's (GUI's) properties (information such as size and color) can be modified through the Visual Studio .NET IDE, allowing changes to be made quickly and causing the results to appear immediately on the screen. Rather than having to guess how the GUI will appear while they are writing a program, programmers view the GUI exactly as it will appear when the finished program runs. Visual Studio .NET also contains tools for debugging, documenting and writing code. The chapter presents features of Visual Studio .NET, including its key windows, and shows how to compile and run programs. We use the capabilities of Visual Studio .NET to create a simple Windows application without typing a single line of code. The chapter also introduces readers to non-visual programming in C#. Every concept is presented in the context of a complete working C# program and is followed by one or more screen shots showing actual inputs and outputs as the program executes. This is our LIVE-CODE™ approach. We discuss fundamental tasks, such as how a program inputs data from its users and how to write arithmetic expressions. This chapter also demonstrates displaying text in a window called a **MessageBox**.

Chapter 3—Control Structures

This chapter introduces the principles of structured programming, a set of techniques that will help the reader develop clear, understandable and maintainable programs. The chapter then introduces the use of control structures that affect the sequence in which statements are executed. Control structures produce programs that are easily understood, debugged and maintained. We discuss the three forms of program control—sequence, selection and repetition—focusing on the **if/else**, **while**, **for**, **do/while** and **switch** structures. We explain the **break** and **continue** statements and the logical operators. We build on information presented in the previous chapter to create programs that are interactive (i.e., they change their behavior to suit user-supplied inputs). We present an example that combines visual and non-visual programming techniques. This example builds upon the first example presented in Chapter 2.

Chapter 4—Methods and Arrays

A *method* allows the programmer to create a block of code that can be called upon from various points in a program. Larger programs can be divided into interacting classes, each consisting of methods—this is sometimes called the "divide and conquer" strategy. Programs are divided into simple components that interact in straightforward ways. We discuss how to create our own methods that can take inputs, perform calculations and return outputs. *Recursive* methods (methods that call themselves) and method overloading, which allows multiple methods to have the same name, are introduced. We demonstrate overloading by creating two **Square** methods that each take an integer (i.e., a whole number) and a floating-point number (i.e., a number with a decimal point), respectively. This chapter also introduces arrays, our first data structure. Data structures are crucial to storing, sorting, searching and manipulating large amounts of information. *Arrays* are groups of related data items that allow the programmer to access any element directly. Rather than creating 100 separate variables that are all related in some way, the programmer can create an array of 100 elements and access these elements by their location in the array. We discuss how to declare and allocate arrays, and we build on the techniques of the previous chapter by passing arrays to methods. Chapter 3 provides essential background for the discussion of arrays, because repetition structures are used to iterate through elements in the array. The combination of these concepts helps the reader create highly structured and well-organized programs. We discuss multidimensional arrays (both rectangular and jagged), which can be used to store tables of data. We introduce the **foreach** structure, which iterates through arrays.

Chapter 5—Object-Based Programming

Chapter 5 introduces objects and classes. Object technology has led to considerable improvements in software development, allowing programmers to create reusable software components. Objects allow programs to be organized in natural and intuitive ways. This chapter presents the fundamentals of object-based programming, such as encapsulation, data abstraction and abstract data types (ADTs). These techniques hide the details of components so that the programmer can concentrate on the "big picture." We create a **Time** class, which displays the time in standard and universal formats. We show how to create reusable software components with assemblies, namespaces and dynamic link library (DLL) files. We create classes and namespaces, and discuss properties and the **readonly** and **const** keywords. This chapter lays the groundwork for the next two chapters, which introduce object-oriented programming.

Chapter 6—Object-Oriented Programming: Inheritance

In this chapter, we discuss inheritance—a form of software reusability in which classes (called *derived classes*) are created by absorbing attributes and methods of existing classes (called *base classes*). The inherited class (i.e., the derived class) can contain additional attributes and methods. We show how finding the commonality between classes of objects can reduce the amount of work it takes to build large software systems. A detailed case study demonstrates software reuse and good programming techniques by finding the commonality among a three-level inheritance hierarchy: the **Point**, **Circle** and **Cylinder** classes. We discuss the software engineering benefits of object-oriented programming. Crucial object-oriented programming concepts, such as creating and extending classes, are presented in this chapter.

Chapter 7—Object-Oriented Programming: Polymorphism

Chapter 7 continues our presentation of object-oriented programming. We discuss polymorphic programming and its advantages. *Polymorphism* permits classes to be treated in a general manner, allowing the same method call to act differently depending on context (e.g., "move" messages sent to a bird and a fish result in dramatically different types of action—a bird flies and a fish swims). In addition to treating existing classes in a general manner, polymorphism allows new classes to be added to a system easily. We identify situations in which polymorphism is useful. A payroll system case study demonstrates polymorphism—the system determines the wages for each employee differently to suit the type of employee (bosses, paid fixed salaries; hourly workers, paid by the hour; commission workers, who receive a base salary plus commission; and piece workers, who are paid per item produced). These programming techniques and those of the previous chapter allow the programmer to create extensible and reusable software components.

Chapter 8—Exception Handling
Exception handling is one of the most important topics in C# from the standpoint of building mission-critical and business-critical applications. Users can enter incorrect data, data can be corrupted and clients can try to access records that do not exist or are restricted. A simple division-by-zero error may cause a calculator program to crash, but what if such an error occurs in the navigation system of an airplane while it is in flight? In some cases, the results of program failure could be disastrous. Programmers need to know how to recognize the errors (*exceptions*) that could occur in software components and handle those exceptions effectively, allowing programs to deal with problems and continue executing instead of "crashing." Programmers who construct software systems from reusable components built by other programmers must deal with the exceptions that those components may "throw." This chapter covers the details of C# exception handling, the termination model of exception handling, throwing and catching exceptions and FCL class **Exception**.

Chapter 9—Graphical User Interface Concepts: Part 1
Chapter 9 explains how to add sophisticated GUIs to programs. By using the techniques of rapid application development (RAD), programmers can create GUIs from reusable components, rather than explicitly programming every detail. The Visual Studio .NET IDE makes developing GUIs even easier by allowing the programmer to position components in a window through so-called visual programming. We discuss how to construct user interfaces with *Windows Forms controls* such as labels, buttons, textboxes and picture boxes. We also introduce *events*, which are messages sent by a program to signal to an object or a set of objects that an action has occurred. Events most commonly signal user interactions with GUI controls, but also can signal internal actions in a program. We overview event handling and discuss how to handle events specific to controls, the mouse and the keyboard.

Chapter 10—Graphical User Interface Concepts: Part 2
Chapter 10 introduces more complex GUI components, including menus, link labels, panels, list boxes, combo boxes and tab controls. *Multiple Document Interface (MDI)* programming is presented, which allows multiple documents (i.e., forms) to be open simultaneously in a single GUI. We conclude with an introduction to visual inheritance, which enables programmers to combine the GUI concepts presented in this chapter with the object-oriented concepts presented in Chapter 6 to create user interfaces that can be used and extended by other programmers. Tips are included throughout the chapter to help the programmer create visually appealing, well-organized and consistent GUIs.

Chapter 11—Multithreading
Users have come to expect much from applications. Users want to download files from the Internet, listen to music, print documents and browse the Web—all at the same time! To do this, programmers need a feature called *multithreading*, which allows applications to perform multiple activities concurrently. The .NET Framework includes built-in capabilities to enable multithreaded applications while shielding programmers from complex details. The .NET languages are better equipped to deal with more sophisticated multimedia, net-

work-based and multiprocessor-based applications than languages that do not have multi-threading features. This chapter introduces the FCL's threading classes and covers threads, thread life-cycles, time-slicing, scheduling and priorities. We analyze the producer-consumer relationship, thread synchronization and circular buffers. This chapter lays the foundation for creating the multithreaded programs that clients demand.

Chapter 12—Strings, Characters and Regular Expressions

In this chapter, we discuss the processing of words, sentences, characters and groups of characters. In C#, **string**s (groups of characters) are objects. This is yet another benefit of C#'s emphasis on object-oriented programming. Objects of type **string** contain methods that can copy, search, extract substrings and concatenate strings with one another. We introduce class **StringBuilder**, which defines string-like objects that can be modified after initialization. As an interesting example of strings, we create a card shuffling-and-dealing simulation. We discuss regular expressions, a powerful tool for searching and manipulating text.

Chapter 13—Graphics and Multimedia

In this chapter, we discuss *GDI+* (an extension of the *Graphics Device Interface—GDI*), the Windows service that provides the graphical features used by .NET applications. The extensive graphical capabilities of GDI+ can make programs more visual and fun to create and use. We discuss C#'s treatment of graphics objects and color control. We also discuss how to draw arcs, polygons and other shapes. This chapter also demonstrates how to use various pens and brushes to create color effects and includes an example that demonstrates gradient fills and textures. We also introduce techniques for turning text-only applications into exciting, aesthetically pleasing programs that even novice programmers can write with ease. The second half of the chapter focuses on audio, video and speech technology. We discuss adding sound, video and animated characters to programs (primarily via existing audio and video clips). You will see how easy it is to incorporate multimedia into C# applications. This chapter introduces an exciting technology called *Microsoft Agent* for adding *interactive animated characters* to a program. Each character allows users to interact with the application, using more natural human communication techniques, such as speech. The agent characters respond to mouse and keyboard events, speak and hear (i.e., they support speech synthesis and speech recognition). With these capabilities, your applications can speak to users and actually respond to their voice commands!

Chapter 14—Files and Streams

Imagine a program that could not save data to a file. Once the program is closed, all the work performed by the program is lost forever. For this reason, this chapter is one of the most important for programmers who will be developing commercial applications. We introduce FCL classes for inputting and outputting data. A detailed example demonstrates these concepts by allowing users to read and write bank account information to and from files. We introduce the FCL classes and methods that help perform input and output conveniently—they demonstrate the power of object-oriented programming and reusable classes. We discuss benefits of sequential files, random-access files and buffering. This chapter lays the groundwork for the material presented in Chapter 19, Networking: Streams-Based Sockets and Datagrams.

Chapter 15—Extensible Markup Language (XML)

The Extensible Markup Language (XML) derives from SGML (Standard Generalized Markup Language), which became an industry standard in 1986. Although SGML is employed in publishing applications worldwide, it has not been incorporated into the mainstream programming community because of its sheer size and complexity. XML is an effort to make SGML-like technology available to a much broader community. XML, created by the World Wide Web Consortium (W3C), describes data in a portable format. XML differs in concept from markup languages such as HTML, which only describes how information is rendered in a browser. XML is a technology for creating markup languages for virtually any type of information. Document authors use XML to create entirely new markup languages to describe specific types of data, including mathematical formulas, chemical molecular structures, music, recipes and much more. Markup languages created with XML include XHTML (Extensible HyperText Markup Language, for Web content), MathML (for mathematics), VoiceXML™ (for speech), SMIL™ (Synchronized Multimedia Integration Language, for multimedia presentations), CML (Chemical Markup Language, for chemistry) and XBRL (Extensible Business Reporting Language, for financial data exchange). The extensibility of XML has made it one of the most important technologies in industry today and is being integrated into almost every field. Companies and individuals constantly are finding new and innovative uses for XML. In this chapter, we present examples that illustrate the basics of marking up data with XML. We demonstrate several XML-derived markup languages, such as *XML Schema* (for checking an XML document's grammar), *XSLT (Extensible Stylesheet Language Transformations,* for transforming an XML document's data into another text-based format such as XHTML) and Microsoft's *BizTalk™* (for marking up business transactions). (For readers who are unfamiliar with XHTML, we provide Appendices K and L, which provide a detailed introduction to XHTML.)

Chapter 16—Database, SQL and ADO .NET

Data storage and access are integral to creating powerful software applications. This chapter discusses .NET support for database manipulation. Today's most popular database systems are relational databases. In this chapter, we introduce the Structured Query Language (SQL) for performing queries on relational databases. We also introduce *ActiveX Data Objects* ADO .NET—an extension of ADO that enables .NET applications to access and manipulate databases. ADO .NET allows data to be exported as XML, which enables applications that use ADO .NET to communicate with a variety of programs that understand XML. We show the reader how to create database connections, using tools provided in Visual Studio .NET, and how to use ADO .NET classes to query a database.

Chapter 17—ASP .NET, Web Forms and Web Controls

Previous chapters demonstrated how to create applications that execute locally on the user's computer. In this chapter and Chapters 18 and 22, we discuss how to create Web-based applications using *Active Server Pages (ASP) .NET*. This is a crucial aspect of .NET and of Microsoft's vision of how software should be developed and deployed on the Internet. ASP .NET is an integral technology for creating dynamic Web content marked up as HTML. (For readers who are unfamiliar with HTML, we provide a detailed introduction in Appendices I and J.) *Web Forms* provide GUIs for ASP .NET pages and can contain *Web controls*, such as labels, buttons and textboxes with which users interact. Like Windows Forms, Web Forms are designed using visual programming. This chapter presents many interesting examples, which include an online guest book application and a multi-tier, database-intensive application that allows users to query a database for a list of publications by a specific author. Debugging Web Forms using the **Trace** property also is discussed.

Chapter 18—ASP .NET and Web Services

Chapter 18 continues our discussion of ASP .NET. In this chapter, we introduce *Web services*, which are programs that "expose" services (i.e., methods) to clients over the Internet, intranets and extranets. Web services offer increased software reusability by allowing services on disparate platforms to interact with each other seamlessly. This chapter presents several interesting examples that include Web services for manipulating huge numbers (up to 100 digits), simulating the card game of blackjack and implementing an airline reservation system. One particularly interesting example is our temperature server, a Web service that gathers weather information for dozens of cities in the United States.

Chapter 19—Networking: Streams-Based Sockets and Datagrams

Chapter 19 introduces the fundamental techniques of streams-based networking. We demonstrate how streams-based *sockets* allow programmers to hide many networking details. With sockets, networking is as simple as if the programmer were reading from and writing to a file. We also introduce *datagrams,* in which packets of information are sent between programs. Each packet is addressed to its recipient and sent out to the network, which routes the packet to its destination. The examples in this chapter focus on communication between applications. One example demonstrates using streams-based sockets to communicate between two C# programs. Another, similar example sends datagrams between applications. We also show how to create a multithreaded-server application that can communicate with multiple clients in parallel. In this client/server tic-tac-toe game, the server maintains the status of the game, and two clients communicate with the server to play the game.

Chapter 20—Data Structures and Collections

This chapter discusses arranging data into aggregations such as linked lists, stacks, queues and trees. Each data structure has properties that are useful in a wide variety of applications, from sorting elements to keeping track of method calls. We discuss how to build each of these data structures. This is also a valuable experience in crafting useful classes. In addition, we cover pre-built collection classes in the FCL. These classes store sets, or collections, of data and provide functionality that allow the developer to sort, insert, delete and retrieve data items. Different collection classes store data in different ways. This chapter focuses on classes **Array**, **ArrayList**, **Stack** and **Hashtable**, discussing the details of each. When possible, C# programmers should use the FCL to find appropriate data structures, rather than implementing these data structures themselves. This chapter reinforces much of the object technology discussed in Chapters 5–7, including classes, inheritance and composition.

Chapter 21—Accessibility

The World Wide Web presents challenges to individuals with disabilities. Multimedia-rich Web sites are difficult for text readers and other programs to interpret; thus, users with hearing and visual impairments may have difficulty browsing such sites. To help rectify this situation, the World Wide Web Consortium (W3C) launched the *Web Accessibility Initiative* (*WAI*), which provides guidelines for making Web sites accessible to people with disabilities. This chapter provides a description of these guidelines, such as the use of the **headers** element to make tables more accessible to page readers, the **alt** attribute of the **img** element to describe images and the combination of XHTML and Cascading Style Sheets (CSS) to ensure that a page can be viewed on almost any type of display or reader. We illustrate key accessibility features of Visual Studio .NET, Internet Explorer and Windows 2000. We also introduce *VoiceXML™* and *CallXML™*, two technologies for increasing the accessibility of Web-based content. VoiceXML helps people with visual impairments to access Web content via speech synthesis and speech recognition. CallXML allows users with visual impairments to access Web-based content through a telephone.

Chapter 22—Mobile Internet Toolkit

The demand for wireless applications is growing rapidly. Within the next two years, the number of people browsing the Web from wireless devices will exceed the number browsing from desktop computers. The *Mobile Internet Toolkit (MIT)* extends Visual Studio .NET by providing a set of FCL classes for creating Web applications for mobile devices. We introduce mobile Web controls and mobile Web Forms that can be used to create ASP .NET applications that target a wide range of mobile devices. Furthermore, mobile Web applications created using the MIT can be designed to determine the type of device making the request and generate markup appropriate for that specific device. For example, a personal digital assistant and mobile phone can request the same page, but receive different markup. This is known as device-specific rendering, a process demonstrated in this chapter. Finally, we demonstrate how to consume a Web service from a mobile Web application. In this example, we show how similar it is to access a Web service from a mobile application, as it is to access a Web service from a Windows application.

Appendix A—Operator precedence chart

This appendix lists C# operators and their precedence.

Appendix B—Number Systems

This appendix explains the binary, octal, decimal and hexadecimal number systems. It also reviews the conversion of numbers among these bases and illustrates mathematical operations in each base.

Appendix C—Career Opportunities

This appendix provides career resources for C# programmers.

Appendix D—Visual Studio .NET Debugger

This appendix introduces the Visual Studio .NET debugger for locating logic errors in programs. Key features include setting "breakpoints," stepping through programs line-by-line and "watching" variable values.

Appendix E—Generating Documentation in Visual Studio .NET

Appendix E discusses how to use documentation comments within C# programs. Programmers can use Visual Studio .NET's documentation tool to generate XML- or HTML-formatted documentation.

Appendix F—ASCII Character Set

This appendix contains a table of the 128 ASCII (American Standard Code for Information Interchange) alphanumeric symbols and their corresponding integer values.

Appendix G—Unicode®
This appendix introduces the Unicode Standard, an encoding scheme that assigns unique numeric values to the characters of most of the world's languages. We include a Windows application that uses Unicode encoding to print welcome messages in several languages.

Appendix H—COM Integration
Prior to .NET, COM (Component Object Model) was critical for specifying how different Windows programming languages communicate at the binary level. For example, COM components such as ActiveX controls and ActiveX DLLs often were written in Microsoft Visual C++, but used in other Windows programs. The .NET platform does not directly support COM components, but Microsoft provides tools for the integration of COM components with .NET applications. In this appendix, we explore some of these tools by integrating an ActiveX control and an ActiveX DLL into C# applications.

Appendices I and J—Introduction to HyperText Markup Language 4: 1 & 2
These appendices provide an introduction to HTML—a markup language for describing the elements of a Web page so that a browser, such as Microsoft's Internet Explorer, can render that page. The reader should be familiar with the contents of these appendices before studying Chapter 17, ASP .NET, Web Forms and Web Controls. No C# programming is presented in these appendices. Some key topics covered in Appendix I include incorporating text and images in an HTML document, linking to other HTML documents on the Web, incorporating special characters (such as copyright and trademark symbols) into an HTML document and separating parts of an HTML document with horizontal lines (called *horizontal rules*). In Appendix J, we discuss more substantial HTML elements and features. We demonstrate how to present information in lists and tables. We discuss how to collect information from users browsing a site. We explain how to use internal linking and image maps to make Web pages easier to navigate. We also discuss how to use frames to display multiple documents in the browser window.

Appendices K and L—Introduction to XHTML: Parts 1 & 2
In these appendices, we introduce the Extensible HyperText Markup Language (XHTML), an emerging W3C technology designed to replace HTML as the primary means of describing Web content. As an XML-based language, XHTML is more robust and extensible than HTML. XHTML incorporates most of HTML's elements and attributes—the focus of these appendices. Appendices K and L are included for our readers who do not know XHTML or who would like a review of XHTML before studying Chapter 15, Extensible Markup Language (XML) and Chapter 21, Accessibility.

Appendix M—HTML/XHTML Special Characters
This appendix provides many commonly used HTML/XHTML special characters, called *character entity references*.

Appendix N—HTML/XHTML Colors
This appendix lists commonly used HTML/XHTML color names and their corresponding hexadecimal values.

Appendix O—Bit Manipulation

This appendix discusses C#'s powerful bit-manipulation capabilities. This helps programs process bit strings, set individual bits on or off and store information more compactly. Such capabilities—inherited from C—are characteristic of low-level assembly languages and are valued by programmers writing systems software, such as operating system and networking software.

Appendix P—Crystal Reports

Visual Studio .NET integrates a special edition of *Crystal Reports*®—a Windows-based report generator. This appendix presents the resources that Crystal Decisions, the company that produces Crystal Reports, offers on its Web site and overviews Crystal Report's unique functionality and features in Visual Studio .NET.

1.10 Summary

In the late 1960s, at a conference at the University of Illinois Urbana-Champaign, ARPA—the Advanced Research Projects Agency of the Department of Defense—rolled out the blueprints for networking the main computer systems of approximately a dozen ARPA-funded universities and research institutions. Shortly after this conference, ARPA proceeded to implement the ARPAnet, the grandparent of today's Internet.

Although the ARPAnet did enable researchers to network their computers, its chief benefit proved to be its capability for quick and easy communication via what came to be known as electronic mail (e-mail). This is true even on today's Internet, with e-mail, instant messaging and file transfer facilitating communications among hundreds of millions of people worldwide.

The protocol (i.e., set of rules) for communicating over the ARPAnet became known as the Transmission Control Protocol (TCP). TCP ensured that messages were routed properly from sender to receiver and that those messages arrived intact. ARPA developed the Internet Protocol (IP), which created a true "network of networks," the current architecture of the Internet. The combined set of protocols is now commonly called TCP/IP.

The World Wide Web allows computer users to locate and view multimedia-based documents (i.e., documents with text, graphics, animations, audios or videos) on almost any subject. In 1989, Tim Berners-Lee of CERN (the European Organization for Nuclear Research) began to develop a technology for sharing information via hyperlinked text documents. Berners-Lee called his invention the HyperText Markup Language (HTML). He also wrote communication protocols to form the backbone of his new hypertext information system, which he referred to as the World Wide Web.

In October 1994, Berners-Lee founded an organization, called the World Wide Web Consortium (W3C), that is devoted to developing nonproprietary, interoperable technologies for the World Wide Web. One of the W3C's primary goals is to make the Web universally accessible—regardless of an individual's disabilities, language or culture.

The Extensible Markup Language (XML) combines the power and extensibility of its parent language, Standard Generalized Markup Language, with the simplicity that the Web community demands. Data independence, the separation of content from its presentation, is an essential characteristic of XML. Because an XML document describes data, any application conceivably can process such a document. XML's flexibility and power make it perfect for client/server systems, which must interact with a wide variety of clients.

Simple Object Access Protocol (SOAP) is a technology for the distribution of objects (marked up as XML) over the Internet. Developed initially by Microsoft and Develop-Mentor, SOAP is a W3C Working Draft that provides a framework for expressing application semantics, encoding data and packaging data. Microsoft .NET uses XML and SOAP to mark up and transfer data over the Internet. XML and SOAP are at the core of .NET—they allow software components to communicate easily with one another.

Object technology is a packaging scheme that facilitates the creation of meaningful software units. Objects have properties (i.e., attributes, such as color, size and weight) and perform actions (i.e., behaviors, such as moving, sleeping or drawing). Classes represent groups of related objects.

With the advent of popular object-oriented languages, such as C++, Java and C#, programmers can program in an object-oriented manner that reflects the way in which they perceive the world. This process, which seems more natural than procedural programming, has resulted in significant productivity gains.

With object technology, properly designed software entities (called objects) can be reused on future projects. Using libraries of reusable componentry can reduce the amount of effort required to implement certain kinds of systems (as compared to the effort that would be required to reinvent these capabilities in new projects). C# programmers use the .NET Framework Class Library (known commonly as the FCL).

In June 2000, Microsoft announced its .NET initiative. The .NET platform is one that provides significant enhancements to earlier developer platforms. .NET offers a new software-development model that allows applications created in disparate programming languages to communicate with each other. The platform also allows developers to create Web-based applications that can be distributed to a great variety of devices (even wireless phones) and to desktop computers.

One key aspect of the .NET strategy is its independence from a specific language or platform. Rather than requiring programmers to use a single programming language, developers can create a .NET application by using any combination of .NET-compatible languages. Programmers can contribute to the same software project, writing code in the .NET languages in which they are most proficient. Part of the initiative includes Microsoft's Active Server Pages (ASP) .NET technology, which allows programmers to create applications for the Web.

A key component of the .NET architecture is Web services, which are applications that expose functionality to clients via the Internet. Clients and other applications can use these Web services as reusable building blocks.

Universal data access is another essential .NET concept. With .NET, data can reside in one central location rather than on separate systems. Any Internet-connected device can access the data (under tight control, of course), which would then be formatted appropriately for use or display on the accessing device.

C# is an event-driven, fully object-oriented, visual programming language in which programs are created using an Integrated Development Environment (IDE). With the IDE, a programmer can create, run, test and debug C# programs conveniently, thereby reducing the time it takes to produce a working program to a fraction of the time it would have taken without using the IDE.

The .NET Framework is at the heart of .NET. This framework manages and executes applications, contains the FCL, enforces security and provides many other programming capabilities. The details of the .NET Framework are found in the Common Language Specification (CLS), which contains information about the storage of data types, objects and so on.

The Common Language Runtime (CLR) is another central part of the .NET Framework—it executes C# programs. Programs are compiled into machine-specific instructions in two steps. First, the program is compiled into Microsoft Intermediate Language (MSIL), which defines instructions for the CLR. Code converted into MSIL from other languages and sources is woven together by the CLR. Then, another compiler in the CLR compiles the MSIL into machine code (for a particular platform), creating a single application.

1.11 Internet and World Wide Web Resources

www.deitel.com
This is the official Deitel & Associates, Inc. Web site. Here you will find updates, corrections, downloads and additional resources for all Deitel publications. In addition, this site provides information about Deitel & Associates, Inc., downloads and resources related to our publications, information on international translations and much more.

www.deitel.com/newsletter/subscribe.html
You can register here to receive the *DEITEL™ BUZZ ONLINE* e-mail newsletter. This free monthly newsletter updates readers on our publishing program, instructor-led corporate training courses, hottest industry trends and topics, and much more. The newsletter is available in full-color HTML and plain-text formats.

www.prenhall.com/deitel
This is Prentice Hall's Web site for Deitel publications, which contains information about our products and publications, downloads, Deitel curriculum, and author information.

www.InformIT.com/deitel
This is the Deitel & Associates, Inc. page on Pearson's InformIT Web site. (Pearson owns our publisher Prentice Hall.) InformIT is a comprehensive resource for IT professionals providing articles, electronic publications and other resources for today's hottest information technologies. The Deitel kiosk at **InformIT.com** provides two or three free articles per week and for-purchase electronic publications. All Deitel publications can be purchased at this site.

www.w3.org
The World Wide Web Consortium (W3C) is an organization that develops and recommends technologies for the Internet and World Wide Web. This site includes links to W3C technologies, news, mission statements and frequently asked questions (FAQs). Deitel and Associates, Inc. is a member of the W3C.

www.netvalley.com/intval.html
This site presents the history of the Internet and the World Wide Web.

www.microsoft.com
The Microsoft Corporation Web site provides information and technical resources for all Microsoft products, including .NET, enterprise software and the Windows operating system.

www.microsoft.com/net
The .NET home page provides downloads, news and events, certification information, and subscription information.

Introduction to the Visual Studio .NET IDE and C# Programming

Objectives

- To become familiar with the Visual Studio .NET integrated development environment (IDE).
- To use the commands contained in the IDE's menus and toolbars.
- To understand the various kinds of windows in Visual Studio .NET.
- To use the features provided by the toolbars.
- To understand Visual Studio .NET's help features.
- To create, compile and execute a simple C# program.
- To use input and output statements.
- To become familiar with primitive data types.
- To use arithmetic operators.
- To write decision-making statements.
- To use relational and equality operators.

Seeing is believing.
Proverb

Form ever follows function.
Louis Henri Sullivan

Intelligence… is the faculty of making artificial objects, especially tools to make tools.
Henri-Louis Bergson

Outline

2.1   Introduction

2.2   Visual Studio .NET Integrated Development Environment (IDE) Overview

2.3   Menu Bar and Toolbar

2.4   Visual Studio .NET Windows

    2.4.1   Solution Explorer

    2.4.2   Toolbox

    2.4.3   Properties Window

2.5   Using Help

2.6   Simple Program: Displaying Text and an Image

2.7   Simple Program: Printing a Line of Text

2.8   Arithmetic

2.9   Decision Making: Equality and Relational Operators

2.10   Summary

2.1 Introduction

Visual Studio .NET is Microsoft's integrated development environment (IDE) for creating, documenting, running and debugging programs written in a variety of .NET programming languages. Visual Studio .NET also offers editing tools for manipulating several types of files. Visual Studio .NET is a powerful and sophisticated tool for creating business-critical and mission-critical applications. In this chapter, we provide an overview of the Visual Studio .NET features needed to create a simple C# program. We introduce additional IDE features throughout the book.

This chapter also introduces C# programming and presents examples that illustrate several important features of the language. Examples are analyzed one line at a time. In this chapter, we create *console applications*—applications that contain output consisting predominantly of text. There are several types of projects that programmers can create in C#; the console application is one of the basic types. Text output in a console application is displayed in a *console window* (also called a *command window*). On Microsoft Windows 95/98, the console window is the **MS-DOS prompt**. On Microsoft Windows NT/2000/XP, the console window is called the **command prompt**.

With C#, a program can be created to have multiple types of output (windows, dialogs and so on). These programs are called *Windows applications* and provide graphical user interfaces. This chapter provides a brief overview of the creation of both Windows and console applications in C#. In the next chapter, we provide a detailed treatment of *program development* and *program control* in C#.

2.2 Visual Studio .NET Integrated Development Environment (IDE) Overview

When Visual Studio .NET is executed for the first time, the *Start Page* is displayed (Fig. 2.1). This page contains helpful links, which appear on the left side. Users can click the name of a section (such as **Get Started**) to browse its contents. We refer to single-clicking with the left mouse button as *selecting* or *clicking* and to clicking twice with the left mouse button as *double-clicking*. [*Note*: The user should be aware that there are slight differences in the way Visual Studio .NET appears, depending on the version being used.]

When clicked, the *Get Started* section loads a page containing links to recently opened projects (such as **WindowsApplication1** in Fig. 2.1), along with the dates that the projects were last modified. Alternatively, the user can select **Recent Projects** from the **File** menu. The first time Visual Studio .NET is loaded, this section will be empty. Notice the two *buttons* on the page: *Open Project* and *New Project*.

Fig. 2.1   **Start Page** in Visual Studio .NET.

We now provide a brief overview of the other **Start Page** links,[1] shown in Fig. 2.1. The **What's New** section displays new features and updates for Visual Studio .NET, including downloads for code samples and new programming tools. The **Online Community** section includes ways to contact other software developers, using newsgroups, Web pages and other online resources. The **Headlines** section provides a way to browse news, articles and how-to guides. The **Search Online** section allows the user to browse through the *MSDN* (*Microsoft Developer Network*) online library. The MSDN site includes numerous articles, downloads and tutorials for a variety of technologies. The **Downloads** section allows the user to obtain updates and code samples. The **XML Web Services** section provides programmers with information about *Web services*, which are reusable pieces of software accessible over the Internet. We discuss this technology in Chapter 18, ASP .NET and Web Services. **Web Hosting** provides information for developers who wish to post their software (such as Web services) online for public use. The **My Profile** page allows users to customize Visual Studio .NET, such as by setting keyboard and window layout preferences. Users also can customize Visual Studio .NET by selecting **Options...** or **Customize...** from the **Tools** menu. [*Note*: From this point forward, we use the **>** character to indicate the selection of a menu command. For example, we use the notation **Tools > Options...** and **Tools > Customize...** to indicate the selection of the **Options...** and **Customize...** commands from the **Tools** menu.]

Visual Studio .NET can even browse the Web—the Internet Explorer Web browser is part of the IDE. To access a Web page, type its address into the location bar (see Fig. 2.1) and press the *Enter* key. Several other windows appear in the IDE in addition to the **Start Page**. We discuss these windows in the upcoming sections.

To create a new C# program, click the **New Project** button in the **Get Started** section. This action displays the *dialog* shown in Fig. 2.2. Visual Studio .NET organizes programs into *projects* and *solutions*. A project is a group of related files, such as C# code, images and documentation. A solution is a group of projects that represents a complete application or a set of related applications. Each project in the solution may perform a different task. In this chapter, we create a single-project solution.

Visual Studio .NET allows programmers to create projects in a variety of programming languages. This book focuses on C#, so select the **Visual C# Projects** folder in the **New Project** dialog (Fig. 2.2). There is a variety of project types from which to choose, several of which are used throughout this book. In this case, we will create a *Windows application*. Windows applications are programs that execute inside the Windows operating system, like Microsoft Word, Internet Explorer and Visual Studio .NET. Typically, such programs contain *controls*—graphical elements, such as buttons and labels—with which users interact.

By default, Visual Studio .NET assigns the name `WindowsApplication1` to the project and to the solution (Fig. 2.2). The default location for storing related files is the folder where the last project was created. The first time Visual Studio .NET executes, the default folder is the **Visual Studio Projects** folder in the **My Documents** folder. Users can change both the name and the location of the folder in which to save the project. After selecting a name and location for the project, click **OK** in the **New Project** dialog. The IDE will change its appearance, as shown in Fig. 2.3.

---

1. Many links on the **Start Page** require that the computer be connected to the Internet.

Visual C# **Projects** folder   C# **Windows application** (selected)

Description of selected project

Project location   Project name

Fig. 2.2   New Project dialog.

Tabs   Menu   Toolbar   Title bar   Menu bar   **Solution Explorer**

Form (Windows application)   Active tab   **Properties** window

Fig. 2.3   Visual Studio .NET environment after a new project has been created.

In this figure, the large gray box represents the window for our application. This box is called the *form*. We discuss how to add controls to the form later in this chapter. The form and controls are the *graphical user interface* (*GUI*) of the program. That is, they are the graphical components through which users interact with the program. Users enter data (*inputs*) into the program by entering information from the keyboard and by clicking the mouse buttons. The program displays instructions and other information (*outputs*) for users to read in the GUI.

The top of the IDE window (the *title bar* in Fig. 2.3) displays the text **Windows-Application1 - Microsoft Visual C# .NET [design] - Form1.cs [Design]**. This title provides the name of the project (**WindowsApplication1**), the programming language (**Microsoft Visual C# .NET**), the *mode of the IDE* (**design** mode), the file being viewed (**Form1.cs**) and the mode of the file being viewed (**Design** mode). The file name **Form1.cs** is the default for C# Windows applications. We discuss the various modes in Section 2.6.

Notice how a tab appears for each open document (Fig. 2.3). In our case, the documents are the **Start Page** and **Form1.cs [Design]**. To view a tabbed document, click the tab with the name of the document you wish to view. Tabbing saves space and allows easy access to multiple documents.

2.3 Menu Bar and Toolbar

Commands for managing the IDE and for developing, maintaining and executing programs are contained in the menus. Figure 2.4 shows the menus displayed on the Visual Studio .NET menu bar. *Menus* contain groups of related commands that, when selected, cause the IDE to perform various actions (e.g., opening a window). For example, new projects can be created by selecting **File > New > Project...** from the menu bar. The contents of the menus shown in Fig. 2.4 are summarized in Fig. 2.5. Visual Studio .NET provides different modes in which the user can work. One of these modes is the design mode, which will be discussed in Section 2.6. Certain menu items appear only in specific IDE modes.

| File | Edit | View | Project | Build | Debug | Data | Format | Tools | Window | Help |

Fig. 2.4 Visual Studio .NET menu bar.

Menu	Description
File	Contains commands for opening projects, closing projects, printing projects, etc.
Edit	Contains commands such as cut, paste, find, undo, etc.
View	Contains commands for displaying IDE windows and toolbars.
Project	Contains commands for adding features, such as forms, to the project.
Build	Contains commands for compiling a program.
Debug	Contains commands for debugging and executing a program.

Fig. 2.5 Visual Studio .NET menu bar summary. (Part 1 of 2.)

Menu	Description
Data	Contains commands for interacting with databases.
Format	Contains commands for arranging a form's controls.
Tools	Contains commands for additional IDE tools and options for customizing the environment.
Window	Contains commands for arranging and displaying windows.
Help	Contains commands for getting help with Visual Studio .NET.

Fig. 2.5   Visual Studio .NET menu bar summary. (Part 2 of 2.)

Rather than having to navigate the menus for certain commonly used commands, the programmer can access the commands from the *toolbar* (Fig. 2.6). The toolbar contains icons that represent commands. To execute a command, click its icon. Click the *down arrow* beside an icon to display related options. Figure 2.6 shows the standard (default) toolbar and an icon that has a down arrow next to it.

Positioning the mouse pointer over an icon highlights that icon and, after a few seconds, displays a description called a *tooltip* (Fig. 2.7). Tooltips help novice programmers become familiar with the IDE' features.

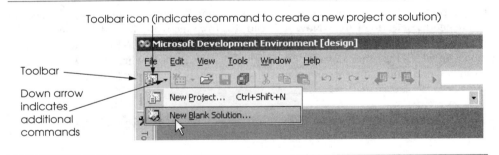

Fig. 2.6   Visual Studio .NET toolbar.

Fig. 2.7   Tooltip demonstration.

2.4 Visual Studio .NET Windows

Visual Studio .NET provides programmers with windows for exploring files and customizing controls. In this section, we discuss the windows that are essential for developing C# applications. These windows can be accessed using the toolbar icons below the menu bar and on the right edge of the toolbar (Fig. 2.8) or by selecting the name of the desired window from the **View** menu.

2.4.1 Solution Explorer

The **Solution Explorer** window (Fig. 2.9) lists all the files in the solution. When Visual Studio .NET is first loaded (right portion of Fig. 2.9), the **Solution Explorer** is empty—there are no files to display. After a new project has been created or an existing project has been loaded, the **Solution Explorer** displays that project's contents (left portion of Fig. 2.9).

The *start-up project* of the solution is the project that runs when the solution is executed. It appears in bold text in the **Solution Explorer**. For our single-project solution, the start-up project, **WindowsApplication1**, is the only project. The C# file is **Form1.cs**; it contains the program's code. We discuss the other files and folders later in the book.

Fig. 2.8   Toolbar icons for various Visual Studio .NET windows.

Fig. 2.9   Solution Explorer window.

The plus and minus boxes to the left of the **Solution Explorer** elements expand and collapse the elements (or trees), respectively (similar to those in Windows Explorer). Click a plus box to display more options; click a minus box to collapse a tree that already is expanded. Users also can expand or collapse a tree by double-clicking the name of the folder. Many other Visual Studio .NET windows also use the plus-and-minus convention.

The **Solution Explorer** contains a toolbar. One icon on the toolbar reloads the files in the solution (refreshes), and another icon displays all files in the solution (including hidden files, or files that are located in the project's directory, but are not generally viewed as part of the project). The number of icons in the toolbar changes, depending on the type of file selected. We discuss these icons later in the book.

2.4.2 Toolbox

The **Toolbox** (Fig. 2.10) contains reusable software components (or controls) that can be used to customize applications. Using *visual programming*, programmers can "drag and drop" controls onto a form instead of writing code themselves. Just as people do not need to know how to build an engine to drive a car, programmers do not need to know how to build a control to use it. This allows them to concentrate on the big picture, rather than the complex details of every control. The wide variety of tools available to programmers is a powerful feature of C#. We demonstrate the power of the controls later in the chapter when we create our own C# program visually.

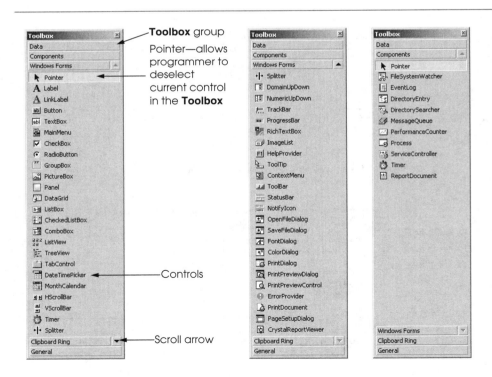

Fig. 2.10   **Toolbox** window.

The **Toolbox** (Fig. 2.10) contains groups of related components (e.g., **Data**, **Components** and **Windows Forms**). Expand the members of a group by clicking the name of the group. Users can scroll through the individual items by using the black scroll arrows on the right side of the **Toolbox**.

Selecting a control name enables programmers to add that control to their application. They can either double-click the control to add it to their application or select the item (by clicking it once) and use the mouse pointer to drag it onto their application. The first control in the group is not a control—it is the mouse pointer (the selected item in Fig. 2.10). Clicking this name allows the user to deselect the current control in the **Toolbox**, thus restoring the normal uses of the mouse pointer. Note that there are no tooltips, because the **Toolbox** icons already are labeled with the names of the controls. In later chapters, we discuss many of these controls.

Initially, the **Toolbox** may be hidden, with a **Toolbox** tab showing on the side of the IDE (Fig. 2.11). Moving the mouse pointer over a hidden window name opens the associated window. Moving the mouse pointer outside the window hides the window. This feature is known as *auto-hide*. To "pin down" the **Toolbox** (i.e., disable auto-hide), click the *pin icon* in the upper right corner of the window (see Fig. 2.11). If the window is not hidden (i.e., auto-hide is disabled), the pin icon will appear to be standing up. To enable auto-hide (if it has been disabled), click the pin icon again. Notice that when auto-hide is enabled, the pin icon appears on its side, as is shown in Fig. 2.11.

2.4.3 Properties Window

The **Properties** window (Fig. 2.12) allows manipulation of the *properties* of a form or control. Properties specify information about a control, such as its size, color and position. Each control has its own set of properties. The bottom of the **Properties** window contains a description of the selected property.

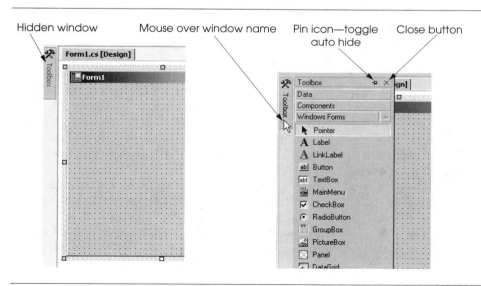

Hidden window   Mouse over window name   Pin icon—toggle auto hide   Close button

Fig. 2.11   Demonstrating window auto-hide.

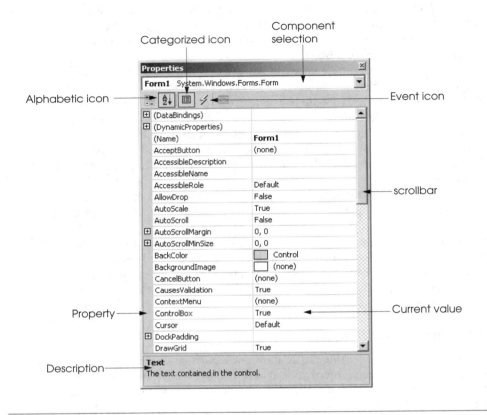

Fig. 2.12 Properties window.

The left column of the **Properties** window lists the control's properties (a form in Fig. 2.12). The column on the right displays their current values. The leftmost two icons on the toolbar sort the properties either alphabetically (by clicking the *alphabetic icon*) or categorically (by clicking the *categorized icon*), meaning that the properties are organized into groups based on their purpose. Users can scroll through the list of properties by *dragging* the scrollbar up or down (i.e., holding down the left mouse button while the mouse cursor is over the scrollbar, moving the mouse up or down, and releasing the mouse button). The *event icon* allows the control or form to respond to certain user actions. We discuss events in Chapter 9, Graphical User Interface Concepts: Part 1. We show how to set individual properties later in this chapter and throughout the book.

The **Properties** window also is important to visual programming. Controls are usually customized after they are created from the **Toolbox**. The **Properties** window allows programmers to modify controls visually (i.e., without writing code). This setup has a number of benefits. First, the programmer can see which properties are available for modification and what the possible values are; the programmer does not have to look up or remember what settings a particular property can have. Second, the window displays a brief description of each property, allowing the programmer to understand each property's purpose. Third, a property's value can be set quickly using the window; only a single click is required, and no code need be written. All these features are designed to help software developers program without performing many repetitive tasks.

At the top of the **Properties** window is a drop-down list, or a control containing a down arrow, which, when clicked, displays a list of options. This drop-down list is called the *component selection*. The first line in the list shows the component that is currently being altered. The programmer can use the list to choose which component to edit. For example, if a GUI contains several buttons, the programmer can select the name of a specific button to configure.

2.5 Using Help

Visual Studio .NET has an extensive help mechanism. The ***Help*** *menu* contains a variety of options. The ***Contents*** *menu item* displays a categorized table of contents of available help topics. Menu item ***Index*** displays an alphabetical index that users can browse. The **Search** feature allows users to find particular help articles, based on a few search words. In each case, a subset of available topics, or filter, can narrow the search to articles related only to C#.

Dynamic help (Fig. 2.13) provides a list of articles, based on the current content (i.e., the items around the location of the mouse cursor). To open dynamic help (if it is not already open), select **Help > Dynamic Help**. After you click an object in Visual Studio .NET, relevant help articles will appear in the **Dynamic Help** window. The window lists relevant help entries, samples and "Getting Started" information, in addition to providing a toolbar for the regular help features. Dynamic help is an excellent way to get information about the features of Visual Studio .NET. Note, however, that **Dynamic Help** may slow down Visual Studio.NET.

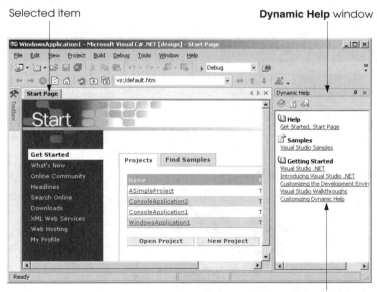

Selected item   **Dynamic Help** window

Relevant help articles for selected item (**Start Page**)

Fig. 2.13   **Dynamic Help** window.

Performance Tip 2.1

If you experience slow response times from Visual Studio .NET, you can disable (i.e., close) **Dynamic Help** *by clicking the* **X** *in the upper right corner of the window.*

In addition to dynamic help, Visual Studio .NET provides *context-sensitive help*. Context-sensitive help is similar to dynamic help, except that context-sensitive help immediately brings up a relevant help article rather than presenting a list. To use context-sensitive help, select an item and press the *F1* key. Help can appear either *internally* or *externally*. With external help, a relevant article immediately pops up in a separate window, outside the IDE. With internal help, a help article appears as a tabbed window inside Visual Studio .NET. The help options can be set from the **My Profile** section of the **Start Page**.

2.6 Simple Program: Displaying Text and an Image

In this section, we create a program that displays the text "**Welcome to C#!**" and an image of the cover art from our book *C# How to Program*. The program consists of a single form that uses a label to display text and a picture box to display an image. Figure 2.14 shows what the program looks like as it executes. The example illustrated here (as well as the image file used in the example) is available on our Web Site (**www.deitel.com**) under the **Downloads/Resources** link.

In creating the program, we do not write a single line of program code. Instead, we use the techniques of visual programming. Various programmer *gestures* (such as using the mouse for pointing, clicking, dragging and dropping) provide Visual Studio .NET with sufficient information for it to generate all or a major portion of the program code. Later in this chapter, we begin our discussion of writing program code, and throughout the book, we produce increasingly substantial and more powerful programs. Visual C# programming usually involves a combination of writing a portion of the program code and having Visual Studio .NET generate the remaining code.

To create, run and terminate this first program, perform the following steps:

Fig. 2.14   Simple program as it executes.

1. *Create the new project.* If a project is already open, close it by selecting **File > Close Solution**. A dialog asking whether to save the current solution may appear; to keep any unsaved changes, save the solution. Next, create a new Windows application for the program by opening Visual Studio .NET and selecting **File > New > Project... > Visual C# Projects > Windows Application** (Fig. 2.15). Name the project **ASimpleProject**, and select a directory in which to save the project. To do the latter, click the **Browse...** button, which opens a **Project Location** dialog (Fig. 2.16). Navigate through the directories, find one in which to place the project and select **OK**. This selection returns you to the **New Project** dialog; the selected folder appears in the **Location** text field. When you are satisfied with the location of the project, click **OK**. Visual Studio .NET will load the new solution, and a form labeled **Form1** will appear. We have already seen an example of this form in Fig. 2.3.

Fig. 2.15   Creating a new Windows application.

Fig. 2.16   Setting the project location.

2. *Set the text of the form's title bar.* First, set the text that appears in the title bar. This text is determined by the form's *Text* property (Fig. 2.17). If the form's **Properties** window is not open, click the **Properties** icon in the toolbar or select the **View** menu's **Properties Window** command. Use the mouse to select the form; the **Properties** window shows information about the currently selected item. In the window, click in the box to the right of the **Text** property's box. To set a value for the **Text** property, type the desired value into the box. In this case, type **A Simple Program**, as in Fig. 2.17. When you have finished, press the *Enter* key to update the form's title bar in the design area.

3. *Resize the form.* Click and drag one of the form's enabled *sizing handles* (the small squares around the form shown in Fig. 2.18) to change the size of the form. Enabled sizing handles are white. The mouse cursor changes appearance when it is over an enabled sizing handle. Disabled sizing handles are gray. The grid on the background of the form is used to align controls and does not appear when the program executes.

Fig. 2.17 Setting the form's **Text** property.

Fig. 2.18 Form with sizing handles.

4. *Change the form's background color.* The **BackColor** property specifies a form's or control's background color. Clicking **BackColor** in the **Properties** window causes a down-arrow button to appear next to the property value (Fig. 2.19). When clicked, the down arrow drops down to display other options. (The options vary, depending on the property.) In this case, it displays the tabs **System** (the default), **Web** and **Custom**. Click the **Custom** tab to display the *palette* (a selection box of colors). Select the box that represents yellow. The palette will disappear, and the form's background color will change to yellow.

5. *Add a label control to the form.* Double-click the **Label** control in the **Toolbox**. This action creates a label with sizing handles in the upper left corner of the form (Fig. 2.20). Double-clicking any **Toolbox** control places that control on the form. Alternatively, programmers can drag controls from the **Toolbox** to the form. Labels display text; our label displays **label1** by default. Notice that our label is the same color as the form's background color, because the form's background color is also the default background color for controls added to the form.

6. *Set the label's text.* Select the label so that its properties appear in the **Properties** window. The label's **Text** property determines the text (if any) that the label displays. The form and label each have their own **Text** property. Forms and controls can have the same types of properties without conflict. We will see that many controls have property names in common. Set the **Text** property of the label to **Welcome to C#!** (Fig. 2.21). Resize the label (using the sizing handles) if the text does not fit. Move the label to the top center of the form by dragging it or using the arrow keys. Alternatively, you can move the label by selecting **Format > Center In Form > Horizontally** from the menu bar.

Fig. 2.19 Changing property **BackColor**.

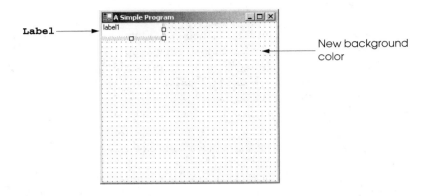

Label ——→

New background
color

Fig. 2.20   Adding a new label to the form.

Label centered
with updated
Text property

Fig. 2.21   Label in position, with its **Text** property set.

7. *Set the label's font size and align the label's text.* Clicking the **Font** property value causes an *ellipsis* button (**...**) to appear next to the value, as in Fig. 2.22. The ellipsis button indicates that a dialog will appear when the programmer clicks the button. When the button is clicked, the **Font** *window* shown in Fig. 2.23 is displayed. Users can select the font name (**Microsoft Sans Serif**, **Arial**, etc.), font style (**Regular**, **Bold**, etc.) and font size (**8**, **10**, etc.) in this window. The text in the **Sample** *area* displays the selected font. Under the **Size** category, select **24**, and click **OK**. If the text does not fit on a single line, it will wrap to the next line. Resize the label if it is not large enough to hold the text. Next, select the label's **TextAlign** property, which determines how the text is aligned within the label. A three-by-three grid of alignment choices is displayed, corresponding to where the text appears in the label (Fig. 2.24). Select the top center grid item, so that the text will appear at the top center of the label.

Fig. 2.22   Properties window displaying the label's properties.

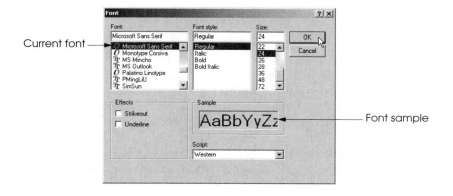

Fig. 2.23   Font window for selecting fonts, styles and sizes.

Fig. 2.24   Centering the text in the label.

8. *Add a picture box to the form.* The picture-box control displays images. This step is similar to Step 5. Find the picture box in the toolbox and add it to the form. Move it underneath the label, by either dragging it or using the arrow keys (Fig. 2.25).

New picture box

Updated label

Fig. 2.25 Inserting and aligning the picture box.

9. *Insert an image.* Click the picture box to load its properties in the **Properties** window, and find the *Image property*. The **Image** property shows a preview of the current picture. No picture has been assigned, so the **Image** property displays **(none)** (Fig. 2.26). Click the ellipsis button to display an **Open** dialog (Fig. 2.27). Browse for a picture to insert, select the picture and press the *Enter* key. The image formats include PNG (Portable Network Graphics), GIF (Graphics Interchange Format) and JPEG (Joint Photographic Experts Group). Each of these file formats is supported on the Internet. To create a new picture, it is necessary to use image-editing software, such as Jasc Paint Shop Pro, Adobe Photoshop Elements or Microsoft Paint. We use the picture **ASimpleProgram-Image.png**, which is located with this example on our Web site (**www.deitel.com**). After the image has been inserted, the picture box displays as much of the picture as it can (depending on size), and the **Image** property shows a small preview. To display the entire image, resize the picture box by dragging the picture box's sizing handles (Fig. 2.28).

Image property value (no image selected)

Fig. 2.26 **Image** property of the picture box.

Fig. 2.27   Selecting an image for the picture box.

Newly inserted image (after the picture box has been resized)

Fig. 2.28   Picture box after the image has been inserted.

10. *Save the project*. Select **File > Save All** to save the entire solution. To save an individual file, select it in the **Solution Explorer**, and select **File > Save**. The created program stores the source code in the C# file **Form1.cs**. The project file contains the names and locations of all the files in the project. Choosing **Save All** saves both the project and the C# file.

11. *Run the project*. Prior to this step, we have been working in the IDE *design mode* (i.e., the program being created is not executing). This mode is indicated by the text **Microsoft Visual C# .NET [design]** in the title bar. While in design mode, programmers have access to all the environment windows (i.e., **Toolbox** and **Properties**), menus, toolbars and so on. While in *run mode*, however, the program is executing, and users can interact with only a few IDE features. Features that are not available are disabled or grayed out. The text **Form1.cs [Design]** in the title bar means that we are designing the form visually, rather than programming it using code. If we had been writing code, the title bar would have contained only the text **Form1.cs**. To execute or run our program, we first need to compile

it, which is accomplished by clicking the **Build Solution** option in the **Build menu** (or by pressing *Ctrl + Shift + B*). The program can then be executed by clicking the **Start** button (the blue triangle), selecting **Debug > Start** command or pressing the *F5* key. Figure 2.29 shows the IDE in run mode. Note that the IDE title bar displays **[run]** and that many toolbar icons are disabled.

12. *Terminate execution.* To terminate the program, click the running application's **Close** button (the **x** in the top right corner). Alternatively, click the **End** button (the blue square) in the toolbar or enter *Shift + F5*. Either action stops program execution and puts the IDE into design mode.

Software Engineering Observation 2.1

Visual programming can be simpler and faster than writing code.

Software Engineering Observation 2.2

The creation of most programs requires more than visual programming. In such programs, some code must be written by the programmer. Examples include applications that use event handlers (used to respond to the user's actions), databases, security, networking, text editing, graphics and multimedia.

Start button   End button   Run mode   Design form

Form design (with grid)   Running application

Fig. 2.29   IDE in run mode, with the running application in the foreground.

2.7 Simple Program: Printing a Line of Text

We now turn our discussion towards nonvisual, or conventional, programming; here, we will demonstrate the creation of programs by only writing code. As we will see throughout the text, C# programming is a mixture of two styles: Visual programming allows programmers to develop a GUI and avoid tedious tasks, while conventional programming specifies the program's behavior.

We begin by considering a program that displays a line of text. The program and it's output are shown in Fig. 2.30. When executed, this program outputs text to a console window.

This program illustrates several important features of C#. Line 10 in Fig. 2.30 does the "real work" of the program, displaying the phrase **Welcome to C# Programming!**.

Line 1 begins with **//**, indicating that the remainder of the line is a *comment*. A comment that begins with **//** is called a *single-line comment*, because the comment terminates at the end of the line. There is also a syntax for writing *multiple-line comments*. A multiple-line comment, such as

```
/* This is a multiple-line
   comment. It can be
   split over many lines */
```

begins with *delimiter* **/*** and ends with *delimiter* ***/**. All text between these delimiters is treated as a comment and is ignored by the compiler. In the Visual Studio .NET IDE, all comment text appears in green.

Software Engineering Observation 2.3

Visual Studio.NET will often catch syntax errors as you are creating the program, even before the program is compiled. A syntax error occurs when the compiler cannot recognize a statement. Look out for jagged red lines that appear directly below a syntax error.

C# uses the same syntax as that employed by the C programming language for multiple-line comments (**/*...*/**) and the same syntax as that employed by C++ for single-line comments (**//**). C# programmers generally use C++-style single-line comments, instead of C-style comments. Throughout this book, we primarily use C++-style single-line comments.

```
1   // Fig. 2.30: Welcome1.cs
2   // A first program in C#.
3
4   using System;
5
6   class Welcome1
7   {
8      static void Main( string[] args )
9      {
10         Console.WriteLine( "Welcome to C# Programming!" );
11     }
12  }
```

```
Welcome to C# Programming!
```

Fig. 2.30 Our first program in C#.

Line 4 (known as a **using** *directive*) is added to our code by the Visual Studio.NET IDE and declares that the program uses features in the **System** *namespace*. A *namespace* groups various C# features into related categories. One of the great strengths of C# is that programmers can use the rich set of namespaces provided by the .NET framework. These namespaces contain code that programmers can reuse, rather than "reinventing the wheel," thereby making programming easier and faster. The namespaces that are defined in the .NET Framework contain preexisting code known as the *.NET Framework Class Library*. An example of one of the features in namespace **System** is **Console**, which we discuss momentarily. The various features are organized into namespaces that enable programmers to locate them easily. We discuss many namespaces and their features throughout the book.

Lines 6–12 define our first *class* (these lines collectively are called a *class definition*). C# programs consist of pieces called *classes*, which are logical groupings of members (e.g., *methods*) that simplify program organization. These methods (which are like functions in procedural programming languages) perform tasks and return information when the tasks are completed. A C# program consists of classes and methods created by the programmer and of preexisting classes found in the Framework Class Library. Throughout this book, we demonstrate how to use both types of classes in programs.

Every program in C# consists of at least one class definition that the programmer defines. These classes are known as *programmer-defined classes*. In Chapter 5, Object-Based Programming, we discuss programs that contain multiple programmer-defined classes. The **class** *keyword* begins a class definition in C# and is followed immediately by the *class name* (**Welcome1** in this example). Keywords (or *reserved words*) are reserved for use by C# and always consist of lowercase letters. (A complete table of C# keywords is presented in the next chapter.) By convention, each word in a class name begins with an uppercase letter and has an uppercase letter to begin each additional word in the class name (e.g., **Sample-ClassName**). The name of the class is known as an *identifier*, which is a series of characters consisting of letters, digits, underscores (_) and "at" symbols (**@**). Identifiers cannot begin with a digit and cannot contain spaces. Examples of valid identifiers are **Welcome1**, **_value**, **m_input5Field** and **button7**. The name **7button** is not a valid identifier, because it begins with a digit, and the name **input field** is not a valid identifier, because it contains a space. The "at" character (**@**) can be used only as the first character in an identifier. C# is *case sensitive*—that is, uppercase and lowercase letters are considered different letters—so **a1** and **A1**, for example, are different identifiers.

 Good Programming Practice 2.1

Always begin a class name with an uppercase first letter. This practice makes class names easier to identify.

The *left brace* (**{**) in line 7 begins the *body of the class definition*. The corresponding *right brace* (**}**) in line 12 ends the class definition. Notice that lines 8–11 in the body of the class are indented.

Line 8 is present in all C# console and Windows applications. These applications begin executing at **Main**, which is known as the *entry point* of the program. The parentheses after **Main** indicate that **Main** is a program building block, called a *method*. C# class definitions normally contain one or more methods, and C# applications contain one or more classes. For a C# console or Windows application, exactly one of the methods must be called **Main**, and it must be defined as shown on line 8; otherwise, the program is not executable.

The left brace (**{**) in line 9 begins the *body of the method definition* (the code that will be executed as a part of our program). A corresponding right brace (**}**) terminates the method definition's body (line 11). Notice that the line in the body of the method is indented between these braces (as a matter of good style).

Good Programming Practice 2.2

*Indent the entire body of each method definition one "level" of indentation between the left brace (**{**) and the right brace (**}**) that define the method body. This layout makes the structure of the method stand out, improving the method definition's readability.*

Line 10 instructs the computer to perform an *action*, namely, to output the series of characters contained between the double quotation marks. Characters delimited in this manner are called *strings*, *character strings* or *string literals*. We refer to characters between double quotation marks generically as *strings*. Whitespace characters in strings are significant—the compiler does not ignore these characters when they appear in strings.

The **Console** *class* enables programs to output information to the computer's *standard output*, normally the screen. Class **Console** also provides methods that allow C# programs to display strings and other types of information at the console window.

Method **Console.WriteLine** displays (or *prints*) a line of text in the console window. When **Console.WriteLine** completes its task, it positions the *output cursor* (the location where the next character will be displayed) at the beginning of the next line in the console window.

All of line 10, including **Console.WriteLine**, its *argument* in the parentheses (**"Welcome to C# Programming!"**) and the *semicolon* (**;**), is called a *statement*. Every statement must end with a semicolon. When this statement executes, it displays the message **Welcome to C# Programming!** in the console window (Fig. 2.30).

In C# statements, we normally precede each class name with its namespace name and a period. For example, line 10 normally would be written as

```
System.Console.WriteLine( "Welcome to C# Programming!" );
```

for the program to run correctly. However, the **using** directive on line 4 eliminates the need to specify explicitly the namespace **System** when using classes in that namespace. This practice can save time and eliminate confusion for programmers.

Common Programming Error 2.1

Omitting the semicolon at the end of a statement is a syntax error.

Testing and Debugging Tip 2.1

When the compiler reports a syntax error, the error might not be on the line indicated by the error message. First, check the line where the error was reported. If that line does not contain syntax errors, check the lines that precede the one reported.

Now that we have presented this program to you, let us provide a step-by-step explanation of how to create and run it in Visual Studio .NET:

1. *Create the console application.* Go to the **File** menu, and choose **New > Project...**. A dialog will appear. In the left pane, choose **Visual C# Projects**;

in the right pane, choose **Console Application**. It is possible to specify other information about the project in the bottom portion of this dialog (i.e., the name and location of the project). After entering all the necessary information, click **OK** to create the project. The project is then created, and the code window is opened for editing. The new application is shown in Fig. 2.31. Note that we created our earlier application in the same way, except that now we have chosen to create a console application instead of a Windows application.

This application can be built (compiled) and executed, but will not do anything until we add more code (which is done in Step 3). Let us briefly look at the code generated for us by the IDE.

Notice that this code contains features that we have not yet discussed. We have not yet explained these features for both display and clarity reasons; at this point in the book, this code is neither required nor relevant to the discussion of this program. Much of the extra code that the IDE provides is used either for documentation or to help create graphical user interfaces. One of the things that the reader will no doubt notice is that we do not show the lines directly above and below the class definition. These lines are used to create namespaces, a topic that will be discussed in Chapter 5, Object-Based Programming. [*Note*: Several times early in this text, we ask the reader to mimic certain C# features that we introduce. We do this especially when it is not yet important to know all the details of a feature to use that feature in C#. Programmers often learn how to program by mimicking what other programmers have done. For each detail we ask the reader to mimic, we indicate where the full discussion will be presented later in the text.] The code for all examples in the book is available on our Web site, **www.deitel.com**, under the **Downloads/Resources** link.

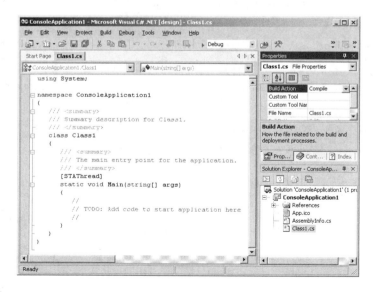

Fig. 2.31   Visual Studio .NET-generated console application.

2. *Change the name of the code file.* For the programs in this book, we usually change the name of the code file. By default, the file is named **Class1.cs**. This name can be changed by right-clicking the name of the file in the **Solution Explorer** window and selecting **Rename** from the list of options. The reader can then enter a new name for the file, provided that the name ends in **.cs** (the file extension for C# code files).

3. *Complete the code.* In the text editor, replace the comment

```
//
// TODO: Add code to start application here
//
```

which is located within method **Main**, with line 10 from Fig. 2.30 (this comment is no longer necessary, for we are adding code to the program).

4. *Run the program.* We are now ready to compile and execute our program. To do so, we simply follow the same steps that we executed for the example in the earlier part of this chapter. To compile the program, go to the **Build** menu and select **Build Solution**. If the program contains no syntax errors, the preceding command creates a new file called **Welcome1.exe**, which contains the Microsoft Intermediate Language (MSIL) code for our application. To execute this program, choose option **Start Without Debugging**[2] in the **Debug** menu.

Program execution begins with method **Main**, which is the entry point to the program. Next, the statement at line 10 of **Main** displays **Welcome to C# Programming!** Figure 2.32 shows the result of executing the program.

Although the previous program displays output at the command prompt, most C# applications use windows, or *dialogs*, to display output. The .NET Framework Class Library includes class **MessageBox** for creating dialogs. Class **MessageBox** is defined in namespace **System.Windows.Forms**. The program in Fig. 2.33 displays the same string shown in Fig. 2.30, but in a message dialog, using class **MessageBox**.

Fig. 2.32   Execution of the **Welcome1** program.

2. Selecting **Debug > Start Without Debugging** causes the command window to prompt the user to press a key after the program terminates, allowing the user to observe the program's output. In contrast, if we run this program by using **Debug > Start**, as we did for the Windows application in the earlier part of this chapter, a command window opens, the program displays the message **Welcome to C# Programming!**, and the command window closes immediately thereafter.

```
1   // Fig. 2.33: Welcome2.cs
2   // Printing multiple lines in a dialog.
3
4   using System;
5   using System.Windows.Forms;
6
7   class Welcome2
8   {
9      static void Main( string[] args )
10     {
11         MessageBox.Show( "Welcome\nto\nC#\nprogramming!" );
12     }
13  }
```

Fig. 2.33   Displaying multiple lines in a dialog.

In this example, each word is placed on a separate line. Line 11 produces the four separate lines of text in the dialog. Normally, the characters in a string are displayed exactly as they appear between the double quotes. However, notice that the two characters "\" and "**n**" do not appear on the screen. The *backslash* (\) is called an *escape character*. It indicates that a "special" character is to be output. When a backslash is encountered in a string of characters, the next character is combined with the backslash to form an *escape sequence*. The escape sequence \n is the *newline character*. It causes the *cursor* (i.e., the indicator of the current screen position) to move to the beginning of the next line in the console window. Some common escape sequences are listed in Fig. 2.34.

Escape sequence	Description
\n	Newline. Position the screen cursor to the beginning of the next line.
\t	Horizontal tab. Move the screen cursor to the next tab stop.
\r	Carriage return. Position the screen cursor to the beginning of the current line; do not advance to the next line. Any characters output after the carriage return overwrite the previous characters output on that line.

Fig. 2.34   Some common escape sequences. (Part 1 of 2.)

Escape sequence	Description
\ \	Backslash. Print a backslash character.
\ "	Double quote. Print a double-quote (**"**) character.

Fig. 2.34   Some common escape sequences. (Part 2 of 2.)

Many compiled classes in C# (including **MessageBox**) need to be referenced, or specified as a part of the project, before they can be used in a program. Depending on the type of application we create, classes may be compiled into files with a *.exe* (*executable*) extension, a *.dll* (or *dynamic link library*) extension or one of several other extensions. Such files are called *assemblies* and are the packaging units for code in C#. [*Note*: Assemblies can be composed of many files of several different types.] Namespaces group related *classes* together; the assembly is a package containing the MSIL code into which a project has been compiled, plus any other information that is needed for these classes. The assembly that we need to reference can be found in the Visual Studio .NET documentation (also called the *MSDN Documentation*) for the class we wish to use. The easiest way to access this information is to go to the **Help** menu in Visual Studio.NET, and choose **Index**. Then type in the name of the class for which documentation is desired. Class **MessageBox** is located in assembly **System.Windows.Forms.dll**. We must add a reference to this assembly to use class **MessageBox** in our program. We now discuss an example of adding a reference to **System.Windows.Forms** within the IDE.

Common Programming Error 2.2

*Including a namespace with the **using** directive, but not adding a reference to the proper assembly, results in a compilation error.*

To begin, make sure you have an application open. Select the ***Add Reference...*** option from the **Project** menu, or right-click the **References** folder in the **Solution Explorer** and select **Add Reference...** from the pop-up menu that appears. This selection opens the **Add Reference** dialog (Fig. 2.35). Double-click **System.Windows.Forms.dll** to add this file to the **Selected Components** list at the bottom of the dialog. Then click **OK**. Notice that **System.Windows.Forms** now appears in the **References** folder of the **Solution Explorer** (Fig. 2.35).

After referencing the appropriate assembly and providing a **using** directive for the corresponding namespace (line 5), we can use the classes in that namespace (such as **MessageBox**).

The reader may notice that we did not add any references to our previous programs. Visual Studio .NET adds a few references when a project is created. Also, by default, some assemblies do not require references. Class **Console**, for instance, is located in the assembly **mscorlib.dll**, but a reference to this assembly is not required to use it.

The **System.Windows.Forms** namespace contains many classes that help C# programmers define graphical user interfaces (GUIs) for their applications. *GUI components* (e.g., buttons) facilitate both data entry by the user and the formatting or presentation of data outputs to the user. For example, Fig. 2.36 is an Internet Explorer window with a bar containing menus (**File**, **Edit**, **View**, etc.). Below the menu bar is a set of buttons, each with a defined task in Internet Explorer. Below the buttons is a *combo box* in which the user can type the location of a Web site to visit. To the left of the combo box is a *label* that indicates the purpose of the combo box. The menus, buttons, combo boxes and labels are part of Internet Explorer's GUI. They enable users to interact with Internet Explorer. C# contains classes that create the GUI components described here. Other classes that create GUI components are described in Chapters 9 and 10, Graphical User Interface Concepts: Part 1 and Graphical User Interface Concepts: Part 2, respectively.

In **Main** (Fig. 2.33), line 11 calls method *Show* of class **MessageBox**. This method takes a string as an argument and displays it to the user in a message dialog. Method **Show** is called a *static method*. Such methods are called by using their class name (in this case, **MessageBox**) followed by the *dot operator* (**.**) and the method name (in this case, **Show**). We discuss static methods in Chapter 5, Object-Based Programming.

Fig. 2.35   Adding a reference to an assembly in Visual Studio .NET.

Label   Button   Menu   Combo box   Menu bar

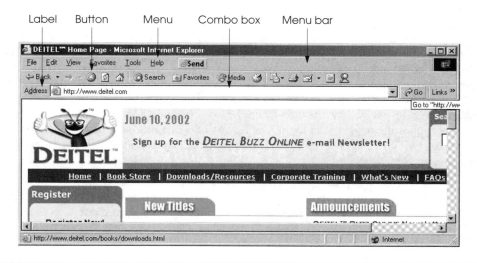

Fig. 2.36   Internet Explorer's GUI.

Line 11 displays the dialog shown in Fig. 2.37. The dialog includes an **OK** button that allows the user to *dismiss* (*close*) the dialog.

C# allows large statements to be split over many lines. For example, we could have split the statement on line 11 into the following two lines:

```
MessageBox.Show(
    "Welcome\nto\nC#\nprogramming!" );
```

All statements end with a semicolon (**;**), so the compiler recognizes that these two lines represent only one statement. However, you cannot split a statement in the middle of an identifier (e.g., the class name) or a string.

 Common Programming Error 2.3

Splitting a statement in the middle of an identifier or a string is a syntax error.

The user can close the dialog by clicking the **OK** button or the close box. Once this action occurs, the program terminates, because the **Main** method terminates.

OK button allows the user   Close box
to dismiss the dialog   Dialog is sized to
                                 accommodate its
                                 contents
                                 Mouse cursor

Fig. 2.37   Dialog displayed by calling **MessageBox.Show**.

2.8 Arithmetic

Most programs perform arithmetic calculations. Figure 2.38 summarizes the *arithmetic operators* used in programs. Note the use of various special symbols not used in algebra. The *asterisk* (*****) indicates multiplication, and the *percent sign* (**%**) represents the *modulus operator*, which is discussed shortly. The arithmetic operators in Fig. 2.38 are binary operators, because they each require two operands. For example, the expression **sum + value** contains the binary operator **+** and the two operands **sum** and **value**.

C# applies the operators in arithmetic expressions in a precise sequence, determined by the following *rules of operator precedence*, which are generally the same as those followed in algebra:

1. Operators in expressions contained within pairs of parentheses are evaluated first. Thus, *parentheses may be used to force the order of evaluation to occur in any sequence desired by the programmer.* Parentheses are at the highest level of precedence. With *nested* (or *embedded*) parentheses, the operators in the innermost pair of parentheses are applied first.

2. Multiplication, division and modulus operations are applied next. If an expression contains several multiplication, division and modulus operations, operators are applied from left to right. Multiplication, division and modulus are said to have the same level of precedence.

3. Addition and subtraction operations are applied last. If an expression contains several addition and subtraction operations, operators are applied from left to right. Addition and subtraction have the same level of precedence.

The rules of operator precedence enable C# to apply operators in the correct order. When we say that operators are applied from left to right, we are referring to the *associativity* of the operators. If there are multiple operators, each with the same precedence, the associativity determines the order in which the operators are applied. Later, we will see that some operators associate from right to left. Figure 2.39 summarizes the rules of operator precedence. This table will expand as we introduce additional C# operators in subsequent chapters. See Appendix A for a complete operator-precedence chart.

C# operation	Arithmetic operator	Algebraic expression	C# expression
Addition	+	$f + 7$	**f + 7**
Subtraction	–	$p - c$	**p – c**
Multiplication	*	bm	**b * m**
Division	/	x / y or $\frac{x}{y}$ or $x \div y$	**x / y**
Modulus	%	$r \bmod s$	**r % s**

Fig. 2.38 Arithmetic operators.

Operator(s)	Operation	Order of evaluation (precedence)
( )	Parentheses	Evaluated first. If the parentheses are nested, the expression in the innermost pair is evaluated first. If there are several pairs of parentheses on the same level (i.e., not nested), they are evaluated from left to right.
*, / or %	Multiplication Division Modulus	Evaluated second. If there are several such operators, they are evaluated from left to right.
+ or –	Addition Subtraction	Evaluated last. If there are several such operators, they are evaluated from left to right.

Fig. 2.39   Precedence of arithmetic operators.

2.9 Decision Making: Equality and Relational Operators

This section introduces C#'s **if** structure, which allows a program to make a decision based on the truth or falsity of some *condition*. If the condition is met (i.e., the condition is *true*), the statement in the body of the **if** structure executes. If the condition is not met (i.e., the condition is *false*), the body statement does not execute. Conditions in **if** structures can be formed by using the *equality operators* and *relational operators*, summarized in Fig. 2.40. The relational operators all have the same level of precedence and associate from left to right. The equality operators both have the same level of precedence, which is lower than the precedence of the relational operators. The equality operators also associate from left to right.

Common Programming Error 2.4

It is a syntax error if the operators ==, !=, >= and <= contain spaces between their symbols (as in = =, ! =, > =, and < =, respectively).

Standard algebraic equality operator or relational operator	C# equality or relational operator	Example of C# condition	Meaning of C# condition
Equality operators			
=	==	x == y	x is equal to y
≠	!=	x != y	x is not equal to y
Relational operators			
>	>	x > y	x is greater than y
<	<	x < y	x is less than y
≥	>=	x >= y	x is greater than or equal to y
≤	<=	x <= y	x is less than or equal to y

Fig. 2.40   Equality and relational operators.

Common Programming Error 2.5

Reversing the operators != , >= *and* <= *(as in* =! , => *and* =< *respectively) is a syntax error.*

Common Programming Error 2.6

Confusing the equality operator (== *) with the assignment operator (* = *) is a logic error. The equality operator should be read "is equal to," and the assignment operator should be read as "gets" or "gets the value of." Some people prefer to read the equality operator as "double equals" or "equals equals."*

The next example uses six **if** statements to compare two numbers input into a program by the user. If the condition in any of the **if** statements is true, then the assignment statement associated with that **if** statement executes. The user inputs values that the program converts to integers and stores in variables **number1** and **number2**. The program compares the numbers and displays the results of the comparison in the console window. The program and some sample outputs are shown in Fig. 2.41.

```
1   // Fig. 2.41: Comparison.cs
2   // Using if statements, relational operators and equality
3   // operators.
4
5   using System;
6
7   class Comparison
8   {
9      static void Main( string[] args )
10     {
11        int number1,          // first number to compare
12            number2;          // second number to compare
13
14        // read in first number from user
15        Console.Write( "Please enter first integer: " );
16        number1 = Int32.Parse( Console.ReadLine() );
17
18        // read in second number from user
19        Console.Write( "\nPlease enter second integer: " );
20        number2 = Int32.Parse( Console.ReadLine() );
21
22        if ( number1 == number2 )
23           Console.WriteLine( number1 + " == " + number2 );
24
25        if ( number1 != number2 )
26           Console.WriteLine( number1 + " != " + number2 );
27
28        if ( number1 < number2 )
29           Console.WriteLine( number1 + " < " + number2 );
30
31        if ( number1 > number2 )
32           Console.WriteLine( number1 + " > " +  number2 );
33
```

Fig. 2.41   Using equality and relational operators. (Part 1 of 2.)

```
34              if ( number1 <= number2 )
35                  Console.WriteLine( number1 + " <= " + number2 );
36
37              if ( number1 >= number2 )
38                  Console.WriteLine( number1 + " >= " + number2 );
39
40          } // end method Main
41
42      } // end class Comparison
```

```
Please enter first integer: 2000

Please enter second integer: 1000
2000 != 1000
2000 > 1000
2000 >= 1000
```

```
Please enter first integer: 1000

Please enter second integer: 2000
1000 != 2000
1000 < 2000
1000 <= 2000
```

```
Please enter first integer: 1000

Please enter second integer: 1000
1000 == 1000
1000 <= 1000
1000 >= 1000
```

Fig. 2.41   Using equality and relational operators. (Part 2 of 2.)

As stated previously, every C# program consists of at least one class definition. Line 7 begins the definition of class **Comparison**. Lines 8–42 define the body of the class. The program begins execution with method **Main** on line 9. Lines 11–12 are a *declaration*. The words **number1** and **number2** are the names of *variables*. A variable is a location in the computer's memory where a value can be stored for use by a program. All variables must be declared with a name and a data type before they can be used in a program. This declaration specifies that the variables **number1** and **number2** are data of type *int*, which means that these variables will hold *integer* values (i.e., whole numbers such as –11, 7, 0 and 319145). There are certain data types already defined in the .NET Framework, known as *built-in data types*, or *primitive data types*. Types such as **string**, **int**, **double** and **char** are examples of primitive data types. Primitive-type names are keywords. The 15 primitive types are summarized in Chapter 4, Methods and Arrays.

A variable name can be any valid identifier. Declarations end with a semicolon (**;**) and can be split over several lines for readability, with each variable in the declaration separated by a comma (i.e., a *comma-separated list* of variable names). Several variables of the same type may be declared in one or in multiple declarations. In this example, we could have written two declarations, one for each variable, but the declaration we used is more concise.

Lines 15–16 prompt the user to input an integer and read from the user a **string** representing the first of the two integers that the program will add. Variables of type ***string*** store strings of characters. The message on line 15 is called a *prompt*, because it directs the user to take a specific action. The prompt is displayed using **Console** method ***Write***. Unlike method **WriteLine**, **Write** does not position the output cursor at the beginning of the next line in the console window after displaying its string; rather, the output cursor is positioned immediately after the last character displayed with **Write**. Thus, the user will enter integer values directly after the prompt.

Method ***ReadLine*** (line 16) causes the program to pause and wait for user input. The user inputs characters from the keyboard and, when finished, presses the *Enter* key to return the string to the program. Unfortunately, the .NET Framework does not provide a simple input dialog. For this reason, the examples in these early chapters receive user input through the console window.

Technically, the user can send anything to the program as input. For this program, if the user types a noninteger value, a *runtime logic error* (an error that has its effect at execution time) occurs. Chapter 8, Exception Handling, discusses how to make your programs more robust by handling such errors.

When the user types in a number and presses *Enter*, the program returns the string representation of this number, now provided as an argument to method **Int32.Parse**. Method ***Int32.Parse*** (a static method of class **Int32**) converts its **string** argument to an integer. Class **Int32** is part of the **System** namespace. Line 16 assigns the integer that **Int32.Parse** returns to variable **number1** by using the *assignment operator (=)*. The **=** operator is a *binary operator*, because it has two *operands*—**number1** and the result of applying method **Int32.Parse**. The entire statement is an *assignment statement*, because it assigns a value to a variable. In an assignment statement, the right side of the assignment is evaluated first; then the result is assigned to the variable on the left side of the assignment.

Any subsequent references to **number1** in the program use this value. Line 20 inputs another value that is converted to an **int** and assigned to **number2**. Any subsequent references to **number2** in the program use this value. We have converted the values entered into integers because arithmetic, relational and equality operators cannot be used with strings.

The **if** structure in lines 22–23 compares the values of the variables **number1** and **number2** for equality. If the values are equal, the program outputs the value of **number1 + " == " + number2**. Notice that this expression uses the operator **+** to "add" (or combine) numbers and strings. This version of the **+** operator is used for ***string*** *concatenation*. Concatenation is the process that enables a **string** and a value of another data type (including another **string**) to be combined to form a new **string**.

If **number1** contains the value **1000** and **number2** contains the value **1000**, the expression evaluates as follows: C# determines that the operands of the **+** operator are of different types and that one of them is a **string** (i.e., both **number1** and **number2** are **int**s, but **" == "** is a **string**). Next, **number1** and **number2** are converted to a **string** and concatenated with **" == "**. At this point, the **string**, namely, **"1000 == 1000"**, is sent to method **Console.WriteLine** to be output. As the program proceeds through the **if** structures, more **string**s will be output by these **Console.WriteLine** statements. For example, given the value **1000** for both **number1** and **number2**, the **if** conditions at lines 34 (**<=**) and 37 (**>=**) will also be true. Thus, the output displayed will be

```
1000 == 1000
1000 <= 1000
1000 >= 1000
```

The third output window of Fig. 2.41 demonstrates this case.

Common Programming Error 2.7

*Confusing the **+** operator used for string concatenation with the **+** operator used for addition can lead to strange results. For example, assuming that integer variable **y** has the value **5**, the expression **"y + 2 = " + y + 2** results in the string **"y + 2 = 52"**, not **"y + 2 = 7"**. First, the value of **y** (**5**) is concatenated with the string **"y + 2 = "**; then the value **2** is concatenated with the new, larger string **"y + 2 = 5"**. The expression **"y + 2 = " + (y + 2)** would produce the desired result.*

Common Programming Error 2.8

*Replacing operator **==** in the condition of an **if** structure, such as **if (x == 1)**, with operator **=**, as in **if (x = 1)**, is a syntax error.*

Common Programming Error 2.9

*Forgetting the left and right parentheses around the condition in an **if** structure is a syntax error. The parentheses are required.*

There is no semicolon (**;**) at the end of the first line of each **if** structure in Fig. 2.41. Such a semicolon would result in a logic error at execution time. For example,

```
if ( number1 == number2 );
    Console.WriteLine( number1 + " == " + number2 );
```

would actually be treated by C# as

```
if ( number1 == number2 )
    ;
Console.WriteLine( number1 + " == " + number2 );
```

where the semicolon on the line by itself—called the *empty statement*—is the statement to execute if the condition is true. When the empty statement executes, no task is performed. The program continues with the **Console.WriteLine** statement, which executes regardless of whether the condition is true or false; this outcome is, of course, incorrect.

Notice the use of spacing in Fig. 2.41. Remember that the compiler normally ignores whitespace characters, such as tabs, newlines and spaces. Thus, statements may be split over several lines and may be spaced according to the programmer's preferences without affecting the meaning of a program. However, it is incorrect to split identifiers and string literals. Ideally, statements should be kept small, but it is not always possible to do so.

Good Programming Practice 2.3

A lengthy statement may be spread over several lines. If a single statement must be split across lines, choose breaking points that make sense, such as after a comma in a comma-separated list or after an operator in a lengthy expression. If a statement is split across two or more lines, indent all subsequent lines with one level of indentation to show clearly that the continuation line(s) is (are) part of the same statement.

The chart in Fig. 2.42 shows the precedence of the operators introduced in this chapter. The operators are displayed from top to bottom in decreasing order of precedence. Notice that all these operators, with the exception of the assignment operator (**=**), associate from left to right. Addition is left associative, so an expression such as **x + y + z** is evaluated as if it were written as **(x + y) + z**. The assignment operator is right associative, so an expression such as **x = y = 0** is evaluated as if it were written as **x = (y = 0)**. The latter expression, **x = (y = 0)**, first assigns the value **0** to variable **y**; it then assigns the result of that assignment, **0**, to **x**. This method is a concise way to assign the same value to several variables.

Good Programming Practice 2.4

*Refer to the operator-precedence chart when writing expressions containing many operators. Confirm that the operators in the expression are performed in the expected order. If you are uncertain about the order of evaluation in a complex expression, use parentheses to force the order, as you would do in an algebraic expression. Remember that some operators, such as the assignment operator (**=**), associate from right to left rather than from left to right.*

In this chapter, we have introduced important features of Visual Studio .NET and the various tools provided by this IDE. Important features of C# also have been introduced, including those for displaying data on the screen, inputting data from the keyboard, performing calculations and making decisions. The next chapter demonstrates many similar techniques, as we reintroduce C# Windows applications (applications that provide a graphical user interface) and introduce C#'s control structures.

2.10 Summary

The Visual Studio .NET integrated development environment (IDE) is the environment used for creating, documenting, running and debugging programs. There are various windows used in Visual Studio .NET. These windows include the **Solution Explorer**, which lists all the files in a solution; the **Toolbox**, which contains controls that customize forms; and the **Properties** window, which displays a control's characteristics (e.g., colors and fonts). Visual Studio .NET provides several help features, including context-sensitive and dynamic help.

Most C# programs are constructed using a combination of visual and nonvisual programming. Programming console applications—i.e., applications that predominantly write text to the command prompt are a form of nonvisual programming.

Operators	Associativity	Type
( )	left to right	parentheses
* / %	left to right	multiplicative
+ -	left to right	additive
< <= > >=	left to right	relational
== !=	left to right	equality
=	right to left	assignment

Fig. 2.42 Precedence and associativity of operators discussed in this chapter.

There are various pieces that make up C# programs, such as namespaces, classes and methods. All C# programs contain one or more classes, exactly one of which must contain method **Main**, known as the entry point of the program. Methods can perform tasks and return information when their tasks are completed. Data can be passed to a method, if such data are necessary for the method to complete its task.

The .NET Framework Class Library provides many namespaces, one of which includes the class that contains the method which displays a message dialog. Namespaces need to be referenced before they can be used. Developers can add a reference to their project via **Project > Add Reference…**.

C# provides arithmetic, equality and relational operators for manipulating values in a program. Oftentimes, values will need to be input by the user. Data can be read from the user via method **ReadLine**.

Control Structures

Objectives

- To use the **if** and **if/else** selection structures to choose among alternative actions.
- To use the **while** repetition structure to execute statements in a program repeatedly.
- To use the increment, decrement and assignment operators.
- To use the **for** and **do/while** repetition structures to execute statements in a program repeatedly.
- To understand multiple selection as facilitated by the **switch** selection structure.
- To use the **break** and **continue** program-control statements.
- To use the logical operators.

Let's all move one place on.
Lewis Carroll

The wheel is come full circle.
William Shakespeare

How many apples fell on Newton's head before he took the hint?
Robert Frost

Who can control his fate?
William Shakespeare

Outline

3.1   Introduction
3.2   Control Structures
3.3   `if` Selection Structure
3.4   `if/else` Selection Structure
3.5   `while` Repetition Structure
3.6   Assignment Operators
3.7   Increment and Decrement Operators
3.8   `for` Repetition Structure
3.9   Example: Using the `for` Structure to Compute Compound Interest
3.10   `switch` Multiple-Selection Structure
3.11   `do/while` Repetition Structure
3.12   Statements `break` and `continue`
3.13   Logical and Conditional Operators
3.14   Introduction to Windows Application Programming
3.15   Summary

3.1 Introduction

In this chapter, we present control structures that enable programmers to control the order of execution. C#'s sequence, selection and repetition structures are used to select and repeat various statements, thereby enabling the execution of complex algorithms. In the process of presenting these structures, we introduce commonly used shorthand operators, which allow the programmer to calculate and assign new values to variables quickly. When we study object-based programming in depth in Chapter 5, we will see that control structures are helpful in building and manipulating objects.

3.2 Control Structures

Normally, statements in a program execute one after the other in the order in which they appear in the program. This process is called *sequential execution*. Various C# statements, however, enable the programmer to specify that the next statement to execute may not be the next one in sequence. A *transfer of control* occurs when a statement other than the next one in the program executes.

C# provides three types of selection structures. The **if** selection structure performs (selects) an action if a condition is true or skips the action if the condition is false. The **if/else** selection structure performs an action if a condition is true and performs a different action if the condition is false. The **switch** selection structure performs one of many actions, depending on the value of an expression.

The **if** structure is called a *single-selection structure*, because it selects or ignores a single action (or a single group of actions). The **if/else** structure is called a *double-selection structure*, because it selects between two different actions (or groups of actions). The **switch** structure is called a *multiple-selection structure*, because it selects among many different actions (or groups of actions).

C# provides four repetition structures: **while**, **do/while**, **for** and **foreach**. (**foreach** is covered in Chapter 4, Methods and Arrays.) Each of the words **if**, **else**, **switch**, **while**, **do**, **for** and **foreach** are C# keywords. Figure 3.1 lists the complete set of C# keywords. We discuss the vast majority of C# keywords throughout this book.

C# has only eight control structures—one sequence structure, three types of selection structure and four types of repetition structure. Each program is formed by combining as many of each type of control structure as is necessary.

Single-entry/single-exit control structures make it easy to build programs; the control structures are attached to one another by connecting the exit point of one control structure to the entry point of the next. This construction is similar to the stacking of building blocks; thus, we call it *control-structure stacking*. There is only one other way in which control structures may be connected, and that is through *control-structure nesting*, where one control structure can be placed inside another. Thus, algorithms in C# programs are constructed from only eight different types of control structures, combined in only two ways.

C# Keywords				
abstract	as	base	bool	break
byte	case	catch	char	checked
class	const	continue	decimal	default
delegate	do	double	else	enum
event	explicit	extern	false	finally
fixed	float	for	foreach	goto
if	implicit	in	int	interface
internal	is	lock	long	namespace
new	null	object	operator	out
override	params	private	protected	public
readonly	ref	return	sbyte	sealed
short	sizeof	stackalloc	static	string
struct	switch	this	throw	true
try	typeof	uint	ulong	unchecked
unsafe	ushort	using	virtual	void
volatile	while			

Fig. 3.1   C# keywords.

3.3 `if` Selection Structure

In a program, a selection structure chooses among alternative courses of action. For example, suppose that the passing grade on an examination is 60 (out of 100). Then the *pseudocode* statement

> *If student's grade is greater than or equal to 60*
>> *Print "Passed"*

determines if the condition "student's grade is greater than or equal to 60" is true or false. Pseudocode is an artificial and informal language that helps programmers develop algorithms. Pseudocode is similar to everyday English; it is convenient and user friendly, and it is not an actual computer programming language. Pseudocode helps the programmer "think out" a program before attempting to write it in a programming language, such as C#.

If the condition is true, then *Passed* is printed, and the next pseudocode statement in order is "performed." If the condition is false, then the *Print* statement is ignored, and the next pseudocode statement in order is performed. The preceding pseudocode *If* statement may be written in C# as

```
if ( studentGrade >= 60 )
   Console.WriteLine( "Passed" );
```

Notice that the C# code corresponds closely to the pseudocode, demonstrating how pseudocode can be useful as a program development tool. The statement in the body of the **if** structure outputs the character string **"Passed"** in the console window. The decision is made based on the condition. A decision can be based on any expression that evaluates to a value of C#'s *bool* type (i.e., any expression that evaluates to **true** or **false**).

3.4 `if/else` Selection Structure

The **if** selection structure performs an indicated action only when the condition evaluates to true; otherwise, the action is skipped. The **if/else** selection structure allows the programmer to specify different actions to perform when the condition is true and when the condition is false. For example, the pseudocode statement

> *If student's grade is greater than or equal to 60*
>> *Print "Passed"*
> *Else*
>> *Print "Failed"*

prints *Passed* if the student's grade is greater than or equal to 60 and prints *Failed* if the student's grade is less than *60*. In either case, after printing occurs, the next pseudocode statement in sequence is "performed."

The preceding pseudocode *If/Else* structure may be written in C# as

```
if ( studentGrade >= 60 )
   Console.WriteLine( "Passed" );
else
   Console.WriteLine( "Failed" );
```

The *conditional operator* (`?:`) is related closely to the **if/else** structure. The `?:` is C#'s only *ternary operator*—it takes three operands. The operands and the `?:` form a *con-*

ditional expression. The first operand is a *condition* (i.e., an expression that evaluates to a `bool` value); the second is the value for the conditional expression if the condition evaluates to true; and the third is the value for the conditional expression if the condition evaluates to false. For example, the output statement

```
Console.WriteLine( studentGrade >= 60 ? "Passed" : "Failed" );
```

contains a conditional expression that evaluates to the string **"Passed"** if the condition **studentGrade >= 60** is true and evaluates to the string **"Failed"** if the condition is false.

The statement with the conditional operator performs in the same manner as the preceding `if`/`else` statement. The precedence of the conditional operator is low, so the entire conditional expression normally is placed in parentheses. Conditional operators can be used in some situations where `if`/`else` statements cannot, such as in the argument to the **WriteLine** method shown earlier.

The `if` selection structure normally can have only one statement in its body. To include several statements in the body of an `if` structure, enclose the statements in braces (`{` and `}`). A set of statements contained in a pair of braces is called a *block*. A block may contain declarations. The declarations in a block commonly are placed first in the block, before any action statements, but declarations may be intermixed with action statements as well.

3.5 `while` Repetition Structure

A *repetition structure* allows the programmer to specify that an action is to be repeated while a condition remains true. The pseudocode statement

> *While there are more items on my shopping list*
> *Purchase next item and cross it off my list*

describes the repetition that occurs during a shopping trip. The condition "there are more items on my shopping list" may be true or false. If it is true, then the action "Purchase next item and cross it off my list" is performed. This action executes repeatedly while the condition remains true. The one or more statements contained in the *While* repetition structure constitute the body of the *While*. The *While* structure's body may be a single statement or a block. Eventually, the condition becomes false (in this case, when the last item on the shopping list has been purchased and crossed off the list). At this point, the repetition terminates, and the first statement after the repetition structure executes.

As an example of a **while** structure, consider a program segment designed to find the first power of 2 larger than 1000. Suppose that **int** variable **product** contains the value **2**. When the following **while** structure finishes executing, **product** contains the result:

```
int product = 2;

while ( product <= 1000 )
   product = 2 * product;
```

When the **while** structure begins executing, **product** is 2. Variable **product** is repeatedly multiplied by 2, successively taking on the values 4, 8, 16, 32, 64, 128, 256, 512 and 1024. When **product** becomes 1024, the condition **product <= 1000** in the **while** structure becomes false. The repetition then terminates, with 1024 as **product**'s final value. Execution continues with the next statement after the **while** structure. [*Note*: If a **while** structure's condition is initially false, the body statement(s) will never be executed.]

We provide a sample program to demonstrate the **while** structure in Fig. 3.2. This program was created to solve the following problem:

> *A college offers a course that prepares students for the state licensing examination for real-estate brokers. Last year, several of the students who completed this course took the licensing examination. The college wants to know how well its students did on the exam. You have been asked to write a program to summarize the results, which consists of a list of the 10 students. Next to each name is written a 1 if the student passed the exam and a 2 if the student failed the exam.*

> *Your program should analyze the results of the exam as follows:*

> *1. Input each test result (i.e., a 1 or a 2). Display the message "Enter result" on the screen each time the program requests another test result.*

> *2. Count the number of test results of each type.*

> *3. Display a summary of the test results, indicating the number of students who passed and the number of students who failed the exam.*

> *If more than eight students passed the exam, print the message "Raise tuition."*

```
1   // Fig. 3.2: Analysis.cs
2   // Analysis of examination results.
3
4   using System;
5
6   class Analysis
7   {
8      static void Main( string[] args )
9      {
10        int passes = 0,              // number of passes
11            failures = 0,            // number of failures
12            student = 1,             // student counter
13            result;                  // one exam result
14
15        // process 10 students
16        while ( student <= 10 )
17        {
18           Console.Write( "Enter result (1=pass, 2=fail): " );
19           result = Int32.Parse( Console.ReadLine() );
20
21           if ( result == 1 )
22              passes = passes + 1;
23
24           else
25              failures = failures + 1;
26
27           student = student + 1;
28        }
29
```

Fig. 3.2   C# program for examination-results problem. (Part 1 of 2.)

```
30            // termination phase
31            Console.WriteLine();
32            Console.WriteLine( "Passed: " + passes );
33            Console.WriteLine( "Failed: " + failures );
34
35            if ( passes > 8 )
36                Console.WriteLine( "Raise Tuition\n" );
37
38        } // end of method Main
39
40    } // end of class Analysis
```

```
Enter result (1=pass, 2=fail): 1
Enter result (1=pass, 2=fail): 2
Enter result (1=pass, 2=fail): 1
Enter result (1=pass, 2=fail): 1
Enter result (1=pass, 2=fail): 1
Enter result (1=pass, 2=fail): 1
Enter result (1=pass, 2=fail): 1
Enter result (1=pass, 2=fail): 1
Enter result (1=pass, 2=fail): 1
Enter result (1=pass, 2=fail): 1

Passed: 9
Failed: 1
Raise Tuition
```

```
Enter result (1=pass, 2=fail): 1
Enter result (1=pass, 2=fail): 2
Enter result (1=pass, 2=fail): 2
Enter result (1=pass, 2=fail): 2
Enter result (1=pass, 2=fail): 2
Enter result (1=pass, 2=fail): 2
Enter result (1=pass, 2=fail): 1
Enter result (1=pass, 2=fail): 1
Enter result (1=pass, 2=fail): 1
Enter result (1=pass, 2=fail): 1

Passed: 5
Failed: 5
```

Fig. 3.2   C# program for examination-results problem. (Part 2 of 2.)

Lines 10–13 declare the variables used in **Main** to process the examination results. We have taken advantage of a C# feature that incorporates variable initialization into declarations (**passes** is assigned **0**, **failures** is assigned **0** and **student** is assigned **1**). Programs that contain repetition may require initialization at the beginning of each repetition; such initialization normally occurs in assignment statements.

Lines 16–28 define a **while** structure that should repeat as long as the value of **student** is less than or equal to 10. Notice the use of the nested **if/else** structure (lines 21–25) in the **while** structure's body.

3.6 Assignment Operators

C# provides several assignment operators for abbreviating assignment expressions. For example, the statement

```
c = c + 3;
```

can be abbreviated with the *addition assignment operator* (**+=**) as

```
c += 3;
```

The **+=** operator adds the value of the expression on the right of the operator to the value of the variable on the left of the operator and stores the result in the variable on the left of the operator. Any statement of the form

    variable **=** *variable* *operator* *expression***;**

where *operator* is one of the binary operators **+**, **-**, *****, **/** or **%** (or others we will discuss later in the book), can be written in the form

    variable *operator***=** *expression***;**

Figure 3.3 lists the arithmetic assignment operators, provides sample expressions that use these operators and give an explanation of the meaning of each sample expression.

 Common Programming Error 3.1

Placing a space character between the symbols that compose an arithmetic assignment operator is a syntax error.

3.7 Increment and Decrement Operators

C# provides the unary *increment operator*, **++**, and the unary *decrement operator*, **--**, the definitions of which are summarized in Fig. 3.4. A program can use the increment operator to increment the value of a variable called **c** by 1, rather than using the expression **c = c + 1** or **c += 1**. If an increment or decrement operator is placed before a variable, it is referred to as the *preincrement* or *predecrement operator*, respectively. If an increment or decrement operator is placed after a variable, it is referred to as the *postincrement* or *postdecrement operator*, respectively.

Assignment operator	Sample expression	Explanation	Assigns
Assume: **int** c = 3, d = 5, e = 4, f = 6, g = 12;			
+=	c += 7	c = c + 7	10 to c
-=	d -= 4	d = d - 4	1 to d
*=	e *= 5	e = e * 5	20 to e
/=	f /= 3	f = f / 3	2 to f
%=	g %= 9	g = g % 9	3 to g

Fig. 3.3   Arithmetic assignment operators.

Operator	Called	Sample expression	Explanation
++	preincrement	++a	Increment **a** by 1; then use the new value of **a** in the expression in which **a** resides.
++	postincrement	a++	Use the current value of **a** in the expression in which **a** resides; then increment **a** by 1.
--	predecrement	--b	Decrement **b** by 1; then use the new value of **b** in the expression in which **b** resides.
--	postdecrement	b--	Use the current value of **b** in the expression in which **b** resides; then decrement **b** by 1.

Fig. 3.4   Increment and decrement operators.

 Common Programming Error 3.2

*Attempting to use the increment or decrement operator on an expression other than a variable reference is a syntax error. A variable reference is a variable or expression that can appear on the left side of an assignment operation. For example, writing **++(x + 1)** is a syntax error, because **(x + 1)** is not a variable reference.*[1]

The chart in Fig. 3.5 shows the precedence and associativity of the operators that have been introduced thus far. The operators are shown from top to bottom in decreasing order of precedence. The second column describes the associativity of the operators at each level of precedence. Notice that the conditional operator (**?** **:**), the unary increment (**++**) and decrement (**--**) operators, the plus (**+**) operator, the minus (**-**) operator and the assignment operators (**=**, **+=**, **-=**, ***=**, **/=** and **%=**) associate from right to left. All other operators in the operator precedence chart in Fig. 3.5 associate from left to right. The third column names the groups of operators.

Operators	Associativity	Type
( )	left to right	parentheses
++ --	right to left	unary postfix
++ -- + -	right to left	unary prefix
* / %	left to right	multiplicative
+ -	left to right	additive
< <= > >=	left to right	relational
== !=	left to right	equality

Fig. 3.5   Precedence and associativity of the operators discussed thus far in this book. (Part 1 of 2.)

1. The term *variable reference* is equivalent to the term *lvalue* ("left value"), which is popular among C and C++ programmers.

Operators	Associativity	Type
? :	right to left	conditional
= += -= *= /= %=	right to left	assignment

Fig. 3.5   Precedence and associativity of the operators discussed thus far in this book. (Part 2 of 2.)

3.8 `for` Repetition Structure

The **for** repetition structure handles the details of *counter-controlled repetition*, where a counter is used to control the number of times a set of statements will execute. We illustrate the power of the **for** structure in Fig. 3.6. Method **Main** (lines 8–14) operates as follows: When the **for** structure (lines 12–13) begins executing, the program initializes the control variable **counter** to **1**. Next, the program tests the loop-continuation condition, **counter <= 5**. The initial value of **counter** is **1**; thus, the condition is true, so line 13 outputs **counter**'s value. Then the program increments variable **counter** in the expression **counter++**, and the loop begins again with the loop-continuation test. The control variable is now equal to **2**. This value does not exceed the final value, so the program performs the body statement again (i.e., performs the next *iteration*, or execution, of the loop). This process continues until the control variable **counter** becomes **6**, causing the loop-continuation test to fail and repetition to terminate. The program continues by performing the first statement after the **for** structure. (In this case, method **Main** terminates, because the program reaches the end of **Main**'s body.)

```
1   // Fig. 3.6: ForCounter.cs
2   // Counter-controlled repetition with the for structure.
3
4   using System;
5
6   class ForCounter
7   {
8      static void Main( string[] args )
9      {
10         // initialization, repetition condition and incrementing
11         // are all included in the for structure
12         for ( int counter = 1; counter <= 5; counter++ )
13            Console.WriteLine( counter );
14      }
15   }
```

```
1
2
3
4
5
```

Fig. 3.6   Counter-controlled repetition with the **for** structure.

The first line of the **for** structure (including the keyword **for** and everything in parentheses after **for**) sometimes is called the *for structure header*. Notice that the **for** structure specifies each of the items needed for counter-controlled repetition with a control variable. If there is more than one statement in the body of the **for** structure, braces (**{** and **}**) are required to define the loop's body.

Figure 3.6 uses the loop-continuation condition **counter <= 5**. If the programmer incorrectly writes **counter < 5** instead, the loop executes only four times. This common logic error is called an *off-by-one error*.

The general format of the **for** structure is

> **for** (*expression1*; *expression2*; *expression3*)
>   *statement*;

where *expression1* names the loop's control variable and provides its initial value, *expression2* is the loop-continuation condition and *expression3* increments or decrements the control variable.

In C#, programmers may declare the control variable in *expression1* of the **for** structure header (i.e., the control variable's type is specified before the variable name), rather than earlier in the code. When this approach is taken, the control variable can be used only in the body of the **for** structure (i.e., the name of the control variable will be unknown outside the **for** structure). Such a restriction on the use of a control variable's name defines the variable's *scope*, or where that variable can be used in a program. Scope is discussed in detail in Chapter 4, Methods and Arrays.

 Common Programming Error 3.3

*When a control variable is declared in the initialization section of a **for** structure header, using that control variable after the **for** structure's body is a compiler error.*

Expression1 and *expression3* in a **for** structure also can be comma-separated lists of expressions, which enables the programmer to use multiple initialization expressions and/or multiple increment or decrement expressions. For example, there may be several control variables in a single **for** structure that must be initialized and incremented or decremented.

 Good Programming Practice 3.1

*Place only expressions involving control variables in the initialization and increment or decrement sections of a **for** structure. Manipulations of other variables should appear either before the loop (if they execute only once, like initialization statements) or in the body of the loop body (if they execute once per iteration of the loop, like incrementing or decrementing statements).*

The three expressions in the **for** structure are optional. If *expression2* is omitted, C# assumes that the loop-continuation condition is always true, thus creating an infinite loop. A programmer might omit *Expression1* if the program initializes the control variable before the loop. *expression3* might be omitted if statements in the body of the **for** structure perform the incrementation or decrementation themselves, or if no incrementation or decrementation is necessary. The increment (or decrement) expression in the **for** structure acts as if it were a stand-alone statement at the end of the body of the **for** structure. Therefore, the expressions

```
counter = counter + 1
counter += 1
++counter
counter++
```

are equivalent when used in *expression3*. Some programmers prefer the form **counter++**, because it causes the control variable to be incremented after the body of the loop executes. For this reason, the postincrementing (or postdecrementing) form, in which the variable is incremented after it is used, seems more natural. However, because the variable being either incremented or decremented does not appear in a larger expression, preincrementing (or predecrementing) and postincrementing (or postdecrementing) the variable have the same effect. The two semicolons in the **for** structure are required.

Common Programming Error 3.4

*Using commas in a **for** structure header instead of the two required semicolons is a syntax error.*

Common Programming Error 3.5

*Placing a semicolon immediately to the right of a **for** structure header's right parenthesis makes the body of that **for** structure an empty statement. This is normally a logic error.*

The initialization, loop-continuation condition, and increment or decrement portions of a **for** structure can contain arithmetic expressions. For example, assume that **x = 2** and **y = 10**. If **x** and **y** are not modified in the body of the loops, then the statement

```
for ( int j = x; j <= 4 * x * y; j += y / x )
```

is equivalent to the statement

```
for ( int j = 2; j <= 80; j += 5 )
```

The increment of a **for** structure may be negative, in which case it is really a decrement, and the loop actually counts downward.

3.9 Example: Using the **for** Structure to Compute Compound Interest

Our next example demonstrates a simple application of the **for** repetition structure. The program in Fig. 3.7 uses the **for** structure to solve the following problem:

> *A person invests $1000.00 in a savings account that yields 5% interest annually. Assuming that all interest is left on deposit, calculate and print the amount of money in the account at the end of each year for 10 years. To determine these amounts, use the formula*
>
> $$a = p (1 + r)^n$$
>
> *where*
>
>   *p is the original amount invested (i.e., the principal)*
>   *r is the annual interest rate*
>   *n is the number of years*
>   *a is the amount on deposit at the end of the nth year.*

This problem involves a loop that performs the indicated calculation for each of the 10 years that the money remains on deposit.

```
1   // Fig. 3.7: Interest.cs
2   // Calculating compound interest.
3
4   using System;
5   using System.Windows.Forms;
6
7   class Interest
8   {
9      static void Main( string[] args )
10     {
11        decimal amount, principal = ( decimal ) 1000.00;
12        double rate = .05;
13        string output = "Year\tAmount on deposit\n";
14
15        for ( int year = 1; year <= 10; year++ )
16        {
17           amount = principal *
18              ( decimal ) Math.Pow( 1.0 + rate, year );
19
20           output += year + "\t" +
21              String.Format( "{0:C}", amount ) + "\n";
22        }
23
24        MessageBox.Show( output, "Compound Interest",
25           MessageBoxButtons.OK, MessageBoxIcon.Information );
26
27     } // end method Main
28
29  } // end class Interest
```

Argument 4:
MessageBox
icon (optional)

Argument 2: Title-bar
string (optional)

Argument 3: **OK**
dialog button
(optional)

Argument 1:
Message to display

Compound Interest

Year	Amount on deposit
1	$1,050.00
2	$1,102.50
3	$1,157.63
4	$1,215.51
5	$1,276.28
6	$1,340.10
7	$1,407.10
8	$1,477.46
9	$1,551.33
10	$1,628.89

OK

Fig. 3.7   Calculating compound interest, using the **for** structure.

C# allows several methods in a class to be defined with the same name. Programmers often use this technique, known as *method overloading*, to define several methods that perform similar actions, but take a different set of arguments. One example of an overloaded method is method **MessageBox.Show**. In the past, we have provided only one argument to this method—a **string** to be displayed in a message dialog. The program in Fig. 3.7; however, uses a version of method **MessageBox.Show** (lines 24–25) that takes four arguments. The dialog in the output of Fig. 3.7 illustrates the four arguments. The first argument is the message to display. The second argument is the string to display in the dialog's title bar. The third argument is a value indicating which button(s) to display. The fourth argument indicates which icon to display to the left of the message. Figures 3.8 and 3.9 provide a listing of the **MessageBoxButtons** and **MessageBoxIcon** choices. Information about other versions of method **MessageBox.Show** can be found in the MSDN documentation provided with Visual Studio .NET. We discuss method overloading in more detail in Chapter 4, Methods and Arrays.

Line 11 in method **Main** declares two *decimal* variables—**amount** and **principal**—and initializes **principal** to **1000.00**. The type **decimal** is a primitive data type used for monetary calculations. The .NET Framework also provides primitive data types *float* and *double* for storing real numbers (i.e., floating-point numbers, or numbers with decimal points, such as 3.4, 0.0 and –11.19). By default, C# treats such constants as the **1000.00** in Fig. 3.7 as type **double**, while whole-number constants, like 7 and –22, are treated as type **int**. Unfortunately, the imprecision of floating-point numbers can cause errors that may result in incorrect monetary values. Type **decimal** is available for performing monetary calculations properly, so the value **1000.00** needs to be converted from type **double** to type **decimal**. C# provides two types of conversion—*implicit conversion* and *explicit conversion*. Implicit conversion, also known as *promotion*, is the process in which C# converts (or *promotes*) the type of a value to another type so that a particular statement will execute properly. Implicit conversions are handled by C# and are not explicitly specified in the code. We have already seen an example of implicit conversion in Fig. 2.41, where several integers were implicitly converted into strings on lines 23, 26, 29, 32, 35 and 38.

MessageBox Buttons	Description
MessageBoxButtons.OK	Specifies that the dialog should include an **OK** button.
MessageBoxButtons.OKCancel	Specifies that the dialog should include **OK** and **Cancel** buttons. The dialog informs the user about some condition and allows the user either to continue or to cancel an operation.
MessageBoxButtons. YesNo	Specifies that the dialog should contain **Yes** and **No** buttons. Used to ask the user a question.
MessageBoxButtons. YesNoCancel	Specifies that the dialog should contain **Yes**, **No** and **Cancel** buttons. Typically used to ask the user a question, but still allows the user to cancel the operation.
MessageBoxButtons. RetryCancel	Specifies that the dialog should contain **Retry** and **Cancel** buttons. Typically used to inform a user about a failed operation and to allow the user to retry or cancel the operation.

Fig. 3.8   Buttons for message dialogs. (Part 1 of 2.)

MessageBox Buttons	Description
`MessageBoxButtons.AbortRetry-Ignore`	Specifies that the dialog should contain **Abort**, **Retry** and **Ignore** buttons. Typically used to inform the user that one of a series of operations has failed and to allow the user to abort the series of operations, retry the failed operation, or ignore the failed operation and continue.

Fig. 3.8   Buttons for message dialogs. (Part 2 of 2.)

MessageBox Icons	Icon	Description
`MessageBoxIcon.Exclamation`		Specifies an exclamation-point icon. Typically used to caution the user against potential problems.
`MessageBoxIcon.Information`		Specifies that the dialog contains an informational message for the user.
`MessageBoxIcon.Question`		Specifies a question-mark icon. Typically used in dialogs that ask the user a question.
`MessageBoxIcon.Error`		Specifies a dialog with an ∞ in a red circle. Alerts the user of errors or important messages.

Fig. 3.9   Icons for message dialogs.

Unfortunately, C# does not perform implicit conversion from type **double** to type **decimal**, because such a conversion may incur a loss of data (due to rounding errors), or the **double** value may be too large to be represented by type **decimal**. We instead use explicit conversion, where the code explicitly specifies that the conversion is to take place. Explicit conversion can be carried out in a few ways. In this example, we use the *cast operator*. This operator takes one operand and creates a temporary value of that operand in the desired type. The cast operator is known as a *unary operator* (i.e., an operator that takes only one operand) and is formed by placing parentheses around the name of the desired data type of the resulting value. On line 11, we use the cast operator to convert the **double** value **1000.00** to type **decimal**. It also is possible to specify that a constant is of type **decimal** by appending the letter **m** to the constant, as in **1000.0m**. Line 12 declares **double** variable **rate**, which we initialize to **.05**. Note that type **int** cannot represent real numbers, because fractions are not integers.

The **for** structure (lines 15–22) executes its body 10 times, varying control variable **year** from **1** to **10** in increments of **1**. Note that **year** represents n in the statement of the problem. C# does not have an exponentiation operator, so we use static method **Pow** in class **Math** for this purpose. **Math.Pow(x, y)** calculates the value of **x** raised to the **y**th power. Method **Math.Pow** takes two arguments of type **double** and returns a **double** value. Notice that we again use the cast operator—in this case, to convert the result of method **Math.Pow** to a **decimal** value. Lines 17–18 perform the calculation from the statement of the problem—that is,

$$a = p \, (1 + r) \, n$$

where *a* is **amount**, *p* is **principal**, *r* is **rate** and *n* is **year**. Note that the calculation **1.0 + rate** appears in the body of the **for** statement. The calculation produces the same result each time through the loop, so repeating the calculation is unnecessary.

Performance Tip 3.1

Avoid placing expressions containing values that do not change inside a loop. Such expressions should be evaluated only once before the loop. Most compilers will prevent redundant evaluations with a process that compilers perform called optimization.

Lines 20–21 append additional text to the end of the string **output**. The text includes the current value of **year**, a tab character to position to the second column, the result of the **String.Format("{0:C}", amount)** method call and a newline character to position to the next line. The call to method **String.Format** converts **amount** to a **string** and formats this **string** so that it will be displayed with two decimal places. [*Note*: Method **Format** uses .NET's string formatting characters to represent numeric and monetary values according to the user's *localization settings*.[2] For example, U. S. dollars are represented as **$634,307.08**, while Malaysian ringgits are represented as **R634.307,08**.] The first argument to method **String.Format** is the format string, while the second argument specifies the value to be formatted. Notice that format strings begin with an opening curly brace (**{**) and end with a closing curly brace (**}**). Within the braces are two values separated by a colon (**:**). The first value is a number indicating which argument is to be formatted, where **0** represents the first argument found after the format string, **1** represents the second argument and so on. In this example we have specified **0**, indicating that we wish to format the first argument after our format string (variable **amount**). The argument found after the colon specifies the formatting of the argument and is referred to as the *formatting character*, or *format specifier*. In this case, we are using formatting character **C** (for "currency"), which indicates that the string should be displayed as a monetary amount with two digits after the decimal point. There are several other formatting characters as well. These codes are explained in the MSDN documentation. Figure 3.10 describes the *numeric formatting characters*—the formatting characters used for string representations of numeric values.

---

2. Localization is the customization of software (e.g., an operating system) to display information via the customs and languages of a particular geographical region. Localization settings can be customized through the Start Menu by selecting **Control Panel > Regional and Language Options > Regional Options** in Windows XP or **Control Panel > Regional Options** in Windows 2000.

Formatting Characters	Description
C or c	Formats the string as currency. Precedes the number with an appropriate currency symbol ($ for U.S. settings). Separates digits with an appropriate separator character (comma for U.S. settings) and sets the number of decimal places to two by default.
D or d	Formats the string as a decimal.
N or n	Formats the string with comma separator characters and two decimal places.
E or e	Formats the string in scientific notation with a default of six decimal places (e.g., the value 27,900,000 becomes 2.790000E+007).
F or f	Formats the string with a fixed number of decimal places (two by default).
G or g	Formats the string as decimal, using the E or F format character, whichever provides the most compact result.
P or p	Formats the string as a percentage. By default, the value is multiplied by 100, and a percent sign is appended to it.
R or r	Ensures that a value converted to string can be converted back without loss of precision or data.
X or x	Formats the string as hexadecimal.

Fig. 3.10 Numeric formatting characters.

3.10 switch Multiple-Selection Structure

Occasionally, an algorithm contains a series of decisions in which the algorithm tests a variable or expression separately for each *constant integral expression* or *constant string expression* the variable or expression may assume. A constant integral expression is any expression involving character and integer constants that evaluates to an integer value (e.g., values of type **int** or **char**). A constant string expression is any expression composed of string literals that always results in the same **string**. The algorithm then takes different actions, based on those values. C# provides the ***switch*** *multiple-selection structure* to handle such decision making.

In the next example (Fig. 3.11), let us assume that a class of 10 students took an exam and that each student received a letter grade of A, B, C, D or F. The program will input the letter grades and summarize the results by using the **switch** structure to count the number of occurrences of each letter grade. Line 10 declares variable **grade** as type **char**. This variable stores the user's input for each letter grade. Lines 11–15 define counter variables that the program uses to count each letter grade. Line 17 begins a **for** structure that loops 10 times. At each iteration, line 19 prompts the user for the next grade, and line 20 invokes **Char** method **Parse** to read the user input as a **char**. Nested in the body of the **for** structure is a **switch** structure (lines 22–55) that processes the letter grades. The **switch** structure consists of a series of ***case*** *labels* and an optional ***default*** *case*.

When the flow of control reaches the **switch** structure (line 22), the program evaluates the *controlling expression* (**grade** in this example) in the parentheses following keyword **switch**. The value of this expression is compared with each **case** label until a match occurs. For example, assume that the user entered the letter **B** as the grade. **B** is then compared with each **case** in the **switch** structure, until a match occurs at line 29 (**case 'B':**). At this point, the statements for that **case** execute. For the letter **B**, lines 31–32 increment the number of **B** grades stored in variable **bCount**, and the **switch** structure exits immediately with the *break* statement. The **break** statement causes program control to proceed with the first statement after the **switch** structure. In this case, we reach the end of the **for** structure's body, so control flows to the control-variable increment expression in the **for** structure header. Then the counter variable in the **for** structure is incremented, and the loop-continuation condition is evaluated to determine whether another iteration of the loop is necessary.

```csharp
1   // Fig. 3.11: SwitchTest.cs
2   // Counting letter grades.
3
4   using System;
5
6   class SwitchTest
7   {
8      static void Main( string[] args )
9      {
10         char grade;      // one grade
11         int aCount = 0,   // number of As
12             bCount = 0,   // number of Bs
13             cCount = 0,   // number of Cs
14             dCount = 0,   // number of Ds
15             fCount = 0;   // number of Fs
16
17         for ( int i = 1; i <= 10; i++ )
18         {
19            Console.Write( "Enter a letter grade: " );
20            grade = Char.Parse( Console.ReadLine() );
21
22            switch ( grade )
23            {
24               case 'A':   // grade is uppercase A
25               case 'a':   // or lowercase a
26                  ++aCount;
27                  break;
28
29               case 'B':   // grade is uppercase B
30               case 'b':   // or lowercase b
31                  ++bCount;
32                  break;
33
34               case 'C':   // grade is uppercase C
35               case 'c':   // or lowercase c
36                  ++cCount;
37                  break;
38
```

Fig. 3.11 Using the **switch** multiple-selection structure. (Part 1 of 2.)

```
39              case 'D':    // grade is uppercase D
40              case 'd':    // or lowercase d
41                  ++dCount;
42                  break;
43
44              case 'F':    // grade is uppercase F
45              case 'f':    // or lowercase f
46                  ++fCount;
47                  break;
48
49              default:     // processes all other characters
50                  Console.WriteLine(
51                      "Incorrect letter grade entered." +
52                      "\nGrade not added to totals." );
53                  break;
54
55          } // end switch
56
57      } // end for
58
59      Console.WriteLine(
60          "\nTotals for each letter grade are:\nA: {0}" +
61          "\nB: {1}\nC: {2}\nD: {3}\nF: {4}", aCount, bCount,
62          cCount, dCount, fCount );
63
64  } // end method Main
65
66  } // end class SwitchTest
```

```
Enter a letter grade: a
Enter a letter grade: A
Enter a letter grade: c
Enter a letter grade: F
Enter a letter grade: z
Incorrect letter grade entered.
Grade not added to totals.
Enter a letter grade: D
Enter a letter grade: d
Enter a letter grade: B
Enter a letter grade: a
Enter a letter grade: C

Totals for each letter grade are:
A: 3
B: 1
C: 2
D: 2
F: 1
```

Fig. 3.11 Using the **switch** multiple-selection structure. (Part 2 of 2.)

 Good Programming Practice 3.2

*Indent the body statements of each **case** in a **switch** structure.*

If no match occurs between the controlling expression's value and any **case** label, the **default** case (line 49) executes. In this example, lines 50–52 display an error message. Note that the **default** case is optional in the **switch** structure. If the controlling expression does not match a **case** and there is no **default** case, program control proceeds to the next statement after the **switch** structure. Note that only the statements for one **case** can be executed in a **switch** statement; once those statements have been executed, the **break** statement for the current **case** will be reached, causing immediate exit from the structure.

Each **case** can contain one action, multiple actions or no actions at all. A **case** with no statements is considered an *empty* **case** and can omit the **break** statement. The **break** statement is required for each **case** (including the **default** case) that contains statements. The last **case** in a **switch** structure cannot be an empty **case**. If the controlling expression matches an empty **case**, the statements in the next nonempty case will be executed. This behavior is known as *fall-through*. It provides the programmer with a way to specify that certain statements are to be executed for several **case**s. Figure 3.11 demonstrates fall-through. For instance, lines 26–27 execute when the grade entered is either **A** or **a**, and lines 31–32 execute when the grade entered is either **B** or **b**.

Common Programming Error 3.6

*Not including a **break** statement at the end of each **case** in a **switch** structure is a syntax error. The exception to this rule is the empty **case**, for which **break** can be omitted.*

Common Programming Error 3.7

*Be sure to check all possible values when creating **case**s to confirm that no two **case**s in a **switch** statement are for the same integral value. If any values are the same, a compilation error will occur.*

Finally, it is important to notice that the **switch** structure is different than other structures in that braces are not required around multiple actions in a **case**.

Good Programming Practice 3.3

*Provide a **default** case in every **switch** structure. Cases not explicitly tested in a **switch** structure that lacks a **default** case are ignored. Including a **default** case focuses the programmer on processing exceptional conditions. There are situations, however, in which no **default** processing is required.*

Good Programming Practice 3.4

*Although the **case**s in a **switch** structure can occur in any order, it is considered good programming practice to place the **default** case last.*

When using the **switch** structure, remember that the expression after each **case** in a particular **switch** structure must be either an integral value or a string. A *character constant* is represented as a specific character in single quotes (such as **'A'**). An integer constant is simply an integer value. The expression after each **case** can also be a *constant*— a variable which contains a value that does not change throughout the entire program. Such a variable is declared with keyword *const* (discussed in Chapter 4, Methods and Arrays).

Chapter 7, Object-Oriented Programming: Polymorphism, presents a more elegant way of implementing **switch** logic. In that chapter, we use a technique called *polymorphism* to create programs that are clearer and easier to maintain and extend than programs that use **switch** logic.

3.11 do/while Repetition Structure

The *do/while* repetition structure is similar to the **while** structure. In the **while** structure, the test of the loop-continuation condition occurs at the beginning of the loop, before the body of the loop executes, while the **do/while** structure tests the loop-continuation condition *after* the body of the loop executes; therefore, the loop body always executes at least once with the **do/while** structure. When a **do/while** structure terminates, execution continues with the statement after the **while** clause. The program in Fig. 3.12 uses a **do/while** structure to output the values 1–5.

Lines 12–15 demonstrate the **do/while** structure. When program execution reaches this **do/while** structure, the program executes line 14, which displays the value of **counter** (at this point, **1**). Then the program evaluates the condition on line 15. The condition on line 15 increments the value of **counter**, after which it tests whether the new value is less than or equal to **5**. At this point, variable **counter** has a value of **2**, which is less than or equal to **5**, so the **do/while** structure's body executes again. The fifth time the structure executes, line 14 outputs the value **5**, and line 15 increments **counter** to **6**. Then the condition on line 15 evaluates to false, and the **do/while** structure exits.

Note that it is not necessary to use braces in the **do/while** structure if there is only one statement in the body. However, the braces normally are included to avoid confusion between the **while** and **do/while** structures. For example,

```
while ( condition )
```

typically is the header for a **while** structure. A **do/while** structure with no braces around a single-statement body appears as

```
do
    statement;
while ( condition );
```

```
1   // Fig. 3.12: DoWhileLoop.cs
2   // The do/while repetition structure.
3
4   using System;
5
6   class DoWhileLoop
7   {
8      static void Main( string[] args )
9      {
10        int counter = 1;
11
12        do
13        {
14           Console.WriteLine( counter );
15        } while ( ++counter <= 5 );
16
17     } // end method Main
18
19  } // end class DoWhileLoop
```

Fig. 3.12 Using the **do/while** repetition structure. (Part 1 of 2.)

```
1
2
3
4
5
```

Fig. 3.12   Using the **do/while** repetition structure. (Part 2 of 2.)

which can be confusing. The last line—**while(** *condition* **);**—might be misinterpreted by the reader as a **while** structure containing an empty statement (the semicolon by itself). Thus, the **do/while** structure with a single statement body often is written as follows, to avoid confusion:

```
do
{
    statement;
} while ( condition );
```

 Good Programming Practice 3.5

Some programmers always include braces in a do/while structure, even when the braces are unnecessary. This practice helps eliminate ambiguity between a while structure and a do/while structure that contains only one statement.

3.12 Statements break and continue

The **break** and **continue** statements alter the flow of control. The **break** statement, when executed in a **while**, **for**, **do/while** or **switch** structure, causes immediate exit from the structure. Execution continues with the first statement that follows the structure. Common uses of the **break** statement are to exit prematurely from a loop or to exit a **switch** structure (as in Fig. 3.11). Figure 3.13 demonstrates use of the **break** statement in a **for** repetition structure.

When the **if** structure in line 16 detects that **count** is **5**, the **break** statement is executed. This action terminates the **for** structure, and the program proceeds to line 24 (the line immediately after the **for** structure). This statement in line 24 concatenates the string **"\nBroke out of loop at count = "** with the value of **count**. Notice that if we had defined variable **count** in our **for** structure, it would be inaccessible here. The string-concatenation statement produces the string that is displayed in the message dialog in lines 26–27. The loop executes its body only four times.

```
1   // Fig. 3.13: BreakTest.cs
2   // Using the break statement in a for structure.
3
4   using System;
5   using System.Windows.Forms;
6
7   class BreakTest
8   {
```

Fig. 3.13   Using the **break** statement in a **for** structure. (Part 1 of 2.)

```
 9      static void Main( string[] args )
10      {
11         string output = "";
12         int count;
13
14         for ( count = 1; count <= 10; count++ )
15         {
16            if ( count == 5 )
17               break;              // skip remaining code in loop
18                                   // if count == 5
19
20            output += count + " ";
21
22         } // end for loop
23
24         output += "\nBroke out of loop at count = " + count;
25
26         MessageBox.Show( output, "Demonstrating the break statement",
27            MessageBoxButtons.OK, MessageBoxIcon.Information );
28
29      } // end method Main
30
31   } // end class BreakTest
```

Fig. 3.13   Using the **break** statement in a **for** structure. (Part 2 of 2.)

The **continue** statement, when executed in a **while**, **for** or **do/while** structure, skips the remaining statements in the body of that structure and proceeds with the next iteration of the loop. In **while** and **do/while** structures, the loop-continuation condition evaluates immediately after the **continue** statement executes. In a **for** structure, the increment or decrement expression executes; then the loop-continuation test evaluates.

We have stated previously that the **while** structure can replace the **for** structure in most cases. One exception occurs when the increment or decrement expression in the **while** structure follows the **continue** statement. In this case, the increment or decrement expression does not execute before the repetition-continuation condition is tested, and the **while** structure thus does not execute in the same manner as the **for** structure.

Figure 3.14 uses the **continue** statement in a **for** structure to skip the string-concatenation statement on line 19 when the **if** structure (line 15) determines that the value of **count** is **5**. When the **continue** statement executes, program control continues with the increment of the control variable in the **for** structure.

Performance Tip 3.2

*When used properly, the **break** and **continue** statements perform faster than their corresponding structured-programming techniques.*

```
1    // Fig. 3.14: ContinueTest.cs
2    // Using the continue statement in a for structure.
3
4    using System;
5    using System.Windows.Forms;
6
7    class ContinueTest
8    {
9       static void Main( string[] args )
10      {
11         string output = "";
12
13         for ( int count = 1; count <= 10; count++ )
14         {
15            if ( count == 5 )
16               continue;          // skip remaining code in loop
17                                  // only if count == 5
18
19            output += count + " ";
20         }
21
22         output += "\nUsed continue to skip printing 5";
23
24         MessageBox.Show( output, "Using the continue statement",
25            MessageBoxButtons.OK, MessageBoxIcon.Information );
26
27      } // end method Main
28
29   } // end class ContinueTest
```

Fig. 3.14 Using the **continue** statement in a **for** structure.

Good Programming Practice 3.6

*Some programmers believe that the **break** and **continue** statement violate the concept of structured programming. As the effects of these statements can be achieved by structured-programming techniques, these programmers simply avoid using **break** and **continue**.*

Software Engineering Observation 3.1

There is a debate between achieving quality software engineering and achieving the best-performing software. Often, one of these goals is achieved at the expense of the other. For all but the most performance-intensive situations, apply the following rule of thumb: First, make your code simple and correct; then make it fast and small, but only if necessary.

3.13 Logical and Conditional Operators

C# provides several *logical and conditional operators* that may be used to form complex conditions by combining simple conditions. The operators are **&&** (*conditional AND*), **&** (*logical AND*), **||** (*conditional OR*), **|** (*logical OR*), **^** (*logical exclusive OR, or logical XOR*) and **!** (*logical NOT*, or *logical negation*). In this section, we consider examples that use each of these operators.

> **Common Programming Error 3.8**
>
> *Placing a space between the characters of the **&&** and **||** operators is a syntax error.*

Suppose we wish to ensure that two conditions are *both* true in a program before we choose a certain path of execution. In this case, we can use the conditional **&&** operator as follows:

```
if ( gender == 1 && age >= 65 )
   ++seniorFemales;
```

This **if** statement contains two simple conditions. The condition **gender == 1** might be evaluated to determine whether a person is female. The condition **age >= 65** is evaluated to determine whether a person is a senior citizen. The two simple conditions are evaluated first, because the precedences of **==** and **>=** are both higher than the precedence of **&&**. The **if** statement then considers the combined condition

```
gender == 1 && age >= 65
```

This condition is true *if and only if* both of the simple conditions are true. Finally, if this combined condition is true, the body statement increments the count of **seniorFemales** by **1**. If either or both of the simple conditions are false, the program skips the incrementation step and proceeds to the statement that follows the **if** structure.

Now let us consider the **||** (conditional OR) operator. Suppose we wish to ensure that either *or* both of two conditions are true before we choose a certain path of execution. In this case, we use the **||** operator as follows:

```
if ( semesterAverage >= 90 || finalExam >= 90 )
   Console.WriteLine( "Student grade is A" );
```

This **if** statement also contains two simple conditions. The condition **semesterAverage >= 90** determines whether the student deserves an "A" in the course because of a solid performance throughout the semester. The condition **finalExam >= 90** determines whether the student deserves an "A" in the course because of an outstanding performance on the final exam. The **if** statement then considers the combined condition

```
semesterAverage >= 90 || finalExam >= 90
```

and awards the student an "A" if either or both of the simple conditions are true. Note that the message "**Student grade is A**" prints unless *both* of the simple conditions are false.

The **&&** operator has a higher precedence than the **||** operator. Both operators associate from left to right. An expression containing **&&** or **||** operators is evaluated only until truth or falsity is known. Thus, evaluation of the expression

```
gender == 1 && age >= 65
```

stops immediately if **gender** is not equal to **1** (i.e., if one condition is false, then the entire expression is false) and continues if **gender** is equal to **1** (i.e., the entire expression could still be true if the condition **age >= 65** is true). This performance feature for the evaluation of conditional AND and conditional OR expressions is called *short-circuit evaluation*.

Performance Tip 3.3

*In expressions using operator **&&**, if the separate conditions are independent of one another, then make the condition most likely to be false the leftmost condition. In expressions using operator | |, make the condition most likely to be true the leftmost condition. This use of short-circuit evaluation can reduce a program's execution time.*

The *logical AND* (**&**) and *logical OR* (|) operators are similar to the conditional AND and conditional OR operators, respectively, with one exception: The logical operators always evaluate both of their operands (i.e., there is no short-circuit evaluation). Therefore, the expression

```
gender == 1 & age >= 65
```

evaluates **age >= 65**, regardless of whether **gender** is equal to **1**. This feature is useful if the right operand of the logical AND or logical OR operator includes a needed *side effect*—a modification of a variable's value. For example, the expression

```
birthday == true & Console.WriteLine( age )
```

guarantees that variable **age** is printed in the preceding expression, regardless of whether the overall expression is true or false. Likewise, if we want the condition in the right operand to be the result of a mathematical operation, and we want the operation to execute in any case, then we can use the | operator.

Common Programming Error 3.9

Avoid using expressions with side effects in conditions. The side effects might look clever, but they often cause subtle errors and can be confusing to other programmer who read or maintain your code.

A condition containing the *logical exclusive OR* (^) operator (sometimes known as the *logical XOR* operator) is true *if and only if one of its operands results in a true value and one results in a false value*. If both operands are true or both are false, the result of the entire condition is false. This operator evaluates both of its operands (i.e., there is no short-circuit evaluation).

C# provides the **!** (logical negation) operator to enable a programmer to "reverse" the meaning of a condition. Unlike the operators **&&**, **&**, | |, | and ^, which combine two conditions (and thus are binary operators), the logical negation operator has only a single condition as an operand (and thus is a unary operator). The logical negation operator is placed before a condition to choose a path of execution if the original condition (without the logical negation operator) is false. Note that the logical negation operator has a higher precedence than the equality operator.

The console application in Fig. 3.15 demonstrates all the conditional and logical operators by displaying their truth tables in a label.

```
1    // Fig. 3.15: LogicalOperators.cs
2    // Demonstrating the logical operators.
3
4    using System;
5
6    class LogicalOperators
7    {
8       // main entry point for application
9       static void Main( string[] args )
10      {
11         // testing conditional AND operator (&&)
12         Console.WriteLine( "Conditional AND (&&)" +
13            "\nfalse && false: " + ( false && false ) +
14            "\nfalse && true:  " + ( false && true ) +
15            "\ntrue && false:  " + ( true && false ) +
16            "\ntrue && true:   " + ( true && true ) );
17
18         // testing conditional OR operator (||)
19         Console.WriteLine( "\nConditional OR (||)" +
20            "\nfalse || false: " + ( false || false ) +
21            "\nfalse || true:  " + ( false || true ) +
22            "\ntrue || false:  " + ( true || false ) +
23            "\ntrue || true:   " + ( true || true ) );
24
25         // testing logical AND operator (&)
26         Console.WriteLine( "\nLogical AND (&)" +
27            "\nfalse & false: " + ( false & false ) +
28            "\nfalse & true:  " + ( false & true ) +
29            "\ntrue & false:  " + ( true & false ) +
30            "\ntrue & true:   " + ( true & true ) );
31
32         // testing logical OR operator (|)
33         Console.WriteLine( "\nLogical OR (|)" +
34            "\nfalse | false: " + ( false | false ) +
35            "\nfalse | true:  " + ( false | true ) +
36            "\ntrue | false:  " + ( true | false ) +
37            "\ntrue | true:   " + ( true | true ) );
38
39         // testing logical exclusive OR operator (^)
40         Console.WriteLine( "\nLogical exclusive OR (^)" +
41            "\nfalse ^ false: " + ( false ^ false ) +
42            "\nfalse ^ true:  " + ( false ^ true ) +
43            "\ntrue ^ false:  " + ( true ^ false ) +
44            "\ntrue ^ true:   " + ( true ^ true ) );
45
46         // testing logical NOT operator (!)
47         Console.WriteLine( "\nLogical NOT (!)" +
48            "\n!false: " + ( !false ) +
49            "\n!true:  " + ( !true ) );
50
51      } // end method Main
52
53   } // end class LogicalOperators
```

Fig. 3.15   Conditional and logical operators. (Part 1 of 2.)

```
Conditional AND (&&)
false && false: False
false && true:  False
true && false:  False
true && true:   True

Conditional OR (||)
false || false: False
false || true:  True
true || false:  True
true || true:   True

Logical AND (&)
false & false: False
false & true:  False
true & false:  False
true & true:   True

Logical OR (|)
false | false: False
false | true:  True
true | false:  True
true | true:   True

Logical exclusive OR (^)
false ^ false: False
false ^ true:  True
true ^ false:  True
true ^ true:   False

Logical NOT (!)
!false: True
!true:  False
```

Fig. 3.15   Conditional and logical operators. (Part 2 of 2.)

On line 6, we begin class **LogicalOperators**. Method **Main** (lines 9–51) contains the code for this program. Lines 12–16 demonstrate the **&&** operator; lines 26–30 demonstrate the **&** operator. The remainder of **Main** demonstrates the **||**, **|**, **^** and **!** operators.

When a **bool** value is concatenated to a **string**, C# converts that **bool** value to its string representation, which will be either **"False"** or **"True"**.

Figure 3.16 shows the precedence and associativity of the C# operators that have been introduced thus far. The operators are shown from top to bottom in decreasing order of precedence.

Operators	Associativity	Type
()	left to right	parentheses
++ --	right to left	unary postfix

Fig. 3.16   Precedence and associativity of the operators discussed so far. (Part 1 of 2.)

Operators	Associativity	Type
++ -- + - ! (*type*)	right to left	unary prefix
* / %	left to right	multiplicative
+ -	left to right	additive
< <= > >=	left to right	relational
== !=	left to right	equality
&	left to right	logical AND
^	left to right	logical exclusive OR (XOR)
|	left to right	logical inclusive OR
&&	left to right	conditional AND
||	left to right	conditional OR
?:	right to left	conditional
= += -= *= /= %=	right to left	assignment

Fig. 3.16   Precedence and associativity of the operators discussed so far. (Part 2 of 2.)

3.14 Introduction to Windows Application Programming

Today, users demand software with rich graphical user interfaces (GUIs) that allow them to click buttons, select items from menus and much more. In this chapter and the previous chapters, we have created console applications. However, most C# programs used in industry are Windows applications with GUIs. For this reason, we now introduce Windows applications, although doing so this early in the book exposes some concepts that we do not explain fully until later chapters.

In Chapter 2, we introduced the concept of visual programming, which allows programmers to create GUIs without writing any programming code. In this section, we combine visual programming with the conventional programming techniques introduced in this chapter and the previous chapter. Through this combination, we can considerably enhance the Windows application introduced in Chapter 2.

Load the project **ASimpleProject** from Chapter 2 into the IDE. To identify the form and its controls easily in the program code, change the **Name** properties of the form, label and picture box to **ASimpleProgram**, **welcomeLabel** and **bugPictureBox**, respectively. [*Note*: This property may appear as **(Name)** in the **Properties** window.] To change a GUI component's properties, select the component (by clicking it) in the design window; then find the property you desire to change in the **Properties** window. Click the box to the right of the property's name to input a new value; press the *Enter* key when you are finished.

With visual programming, the IDE generates the program code that creates the GUI. This code contains instructions for the creation of the form and every control on it. Unlike a console application, a Windows application's program code is not displayed initially in the editor window. Once the program's project (e.g., **ASimpleProgram**) is opened in the IDE, the program code can be viewed by selecting **View > Code**. Figure 3.17 shows the code editor displaying the program code.

Collapsed comment

Collapsed code

Plus boxes

Fig. 3.17   IDE showing code for the program in Fig. 2.14.

Every Windows application consists of at least one class that *inherits* from class **Form** (which represents a form) in the .NET Framework Class Library's **System.Windows.Forms** namespace. The keyword **class** begins a class definition and is followed immediately by the class name (**ASimpleProgram**). Recall that the form's name is set using the **Name** property. A colon (**:**) indicates that the class **ASimpleProgram** inherits existing pieces from another class. The class from which **ASimpleProgram** inherits— here, **System.Windows.Forms.Form**—appears to the right of the colon. In this inheritance relationship, **Form** is called the *base class* (or *superclass*), and **ASimpleProgram** is called the *derived class* (or *subclass*). With inheritance, **ASimpleProgram**'s class definition has the *attributes* (data) and *behaviors* (methods) of class **Form**. We discuss the significance of the keyword **public** in Chapter 5. [*Note*: Changing a control's name in the **Properties** window may not change all occurrences of the control's name in the code. The reader should search the code and replace names that were not changed by the IDE. For example, the original form name (and class name) was **Form1**. Search the code for **Form1**, and change any remaining instances to **ASimpleProgram**.]

A key benefit of inheriting from class **Form** is that someone else has previously defined "what it means to be a form." The Windows operating system expects every window (e.g., a form) to have certain attributes and behaviors. However, because class **Form** already provides those capabilities, programmers do not need to "reinvent the wheel" by defining all those capabilities themselves. In fact, class **Form** already has hundreds of methods! In our programs up to this point, we have used only one method (i.e., **Main**), so you can imagine how much work went into creating class **Form**. The use of the colon to extend from class **Form** enables programmers to create forms quickly.

In the editor window (Fig. 3.17), notice that portions of text are enclosed in small rectangles with small plus boxes to their left. The plus box indicates that this section of code is *collapsed*. Although collapsed code is not visible, it is still part of the program. Code collapsing allows programmers to hide code in the editor, so that they can focus on smaller (and perhaps more important) code segments. Clicking the plus box expands the code (i.e., displays the entire segment of code). A small minus box to the left of expanded code can be clicked in order to collapse that portion of code. If programmers wish to view collapsed code quickly, they can place the cursor over the rectangle for that portion of code. Doing so will display the code in a small window.

The appearance of collapsed code differs depending on the nature of the code. Figure 3.17 demonstrates that collapsed comments appear as **/**/** within a rectangle, while collapsed statements appear as an ellipsis (**...**) within a rectangle. Finally, *regions* of code can be created in a C# program. A region is a portion of code entered between the tags **#region** and **#endregion**. These tags specify the text that appears in the rectangle when the code is collapsed. One such region is shown at the bottom of Fig. 3.17, as the rectangle containing the text **Windows Form Designer generated code**. The description in the rectangle indicates that the collapsed code was created by the *Windows Form Designer* (i.e., the part of the IDE that creates the code for the GUI). This collapsed code contains the code created by the IDE for the form and its controls, as well as code that enables the program to run. We will describe how this region was created shortly.

Upon initial inspection, the *expanded code* (Fig. 3.18) looks complex. This code is created by the IDE and normally is not edited by the programmer. Such code is present in every Windows application. Allowing the IDE to create this code saves the programmer considerable development time. If the IDE did not provide the code, the programmer would have to write it, which would require a considerable amount of time. The vast majority of the code shown has not been introduced yet, so you are not expected to understand how it works. However, certain programming constructs, such as comments and control structures, should be familiar. As you continue to study C#, especially in Chapters 5–10, the purpose of IDE-generated code will become clearer.

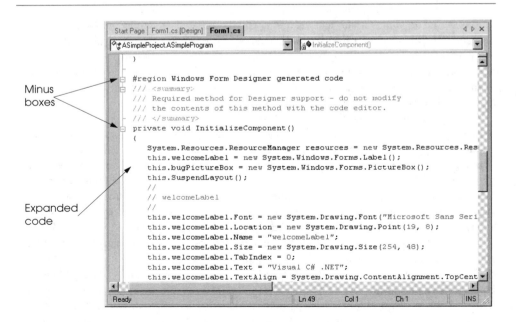

Fig. 3.18 Windows Form Designer–generated code when expanded.

Towards the top of Fig. 3.18, we see the text **#region**. This text indicates the beginning of a collapsible region of code. After **#region**, we see the text that will be displayed when the region is collapsed. This region ends when the text **#endregion** is encountered, after the end of method **InitializeComponent**.

When we created this application in Chapter 2, we used the **Properties** window to set properties for the form, label and picture box. Once a property was set, the form or control was updated immediately. Forms and controls contain a set of *default properties*, which are displayed initially in the **Properties** window when a form or control is selected. These default properties provide the initial characteristics of a form or control when it is created. When a control, such as a label, is placed on the form, the IDE adds code to the class (e.g., **ASimpleProgram**) that creates the control and sets some of the control's property values, such as the name of the control and its location on the form. Figure 3.19 shows a portion of the code generated by the IDE for setting the label's (in this case, **welcomeLabel**'s) properties. Properties set include the label's **Font, Location, Name, Text** and **TextAlign** properties. Recall from Chapter 2 that we explicitly set values for the label's **Name, Text** and **TextAlign** properties in the **Properties** window. Other properties, such as **Location**, are set only when the label is placed on the form.

The values assigned to the properties are based on the values specified in the **Properties** window. We now demonstrate how the IDE updates the Windows Form Designer–generated code when a property value in the **Properties** window changes. During this process, programmers must switch between code view and design view. To switch views, select the corresponding tabs—**Form1.cs*** for code view and **Form1.cs* [Design]** for design view. [*Note*: The asterisk following the file name indicates that the file has been modified and therefore needs to be saved.] Alternatively, select **View > Code** or **View > Designer**, respectively. Perform the following steps:

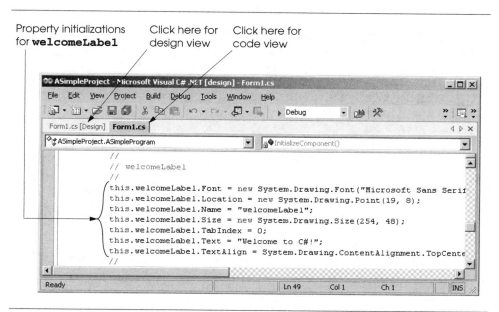

Fig. 3.19   Code generated by the IDE for **welcomeLabel**.

1. *Modify the label control's* **Text** *property, using the* **Properties** *window.* Recall that properties can be changed in design view by clicking a form or control to select it and modifying the appropriate property in the **Properties** window. Change the **Text** property of the label to "**Deitel**" (Fig. 3.20).

2. *Examine the changes in code view.* Switch to code view (**View > Code**), and examine the code. Notice that the label's **Text** property is now assigned the text that we entered in the **Properties** window (Fig. 3.21). When a property is changed in design mode, the Windows Form Designer updates the appropriate line of code in the class to reflect the new value.

Text
property

Fig. 3.20   Using the **Properties** window to set a property value.

Fig. 3.21   Windows Form Designer-generated code reflecting new property values.

3. *Modify a property value in code view.* In the code-view editor, find the three lines of comments indicating the initialization for **welcomeLabel**, and change the **string** assigned to **this.welcomeLabel.Text** from **Deitel** to **Visual C# .NET** (Fig. 3.22). Now, switch to design mode (**View > Designer**). The label now displays the updated text, and the **Properties** window for **welcomeLabel** displays the new **Text** value (Fig. 3.23). [*Note*: Property values should not be set using the techniques presented in this step. Here, we modify the property value in the IDE-generated code only as a demonstration of the relationship between program code and the Windows Form Designer.]

4. *Change the label's **Text** property at execution time.* In the previous steps, we set properties at design time. Often, however, it is necessary to modify a property while a program is running. For example, to display the result of a calculation, a label's text can be assigned a **string** containing the result. In console applications, such code is located in **Main**. In Windows applications, we must create a method that executes when the form is loaded into memory during program execution. Like **Main**, this method is invoked when the program is run. Double-clicking the form in design view adds a method named ***ASimpleProgram_Load*** to the class (Fig. 3.24). The cursor is placed in the body of the **ASimpleProgram_Load** method definition. Notice that **ASimpleProgram_Load** is not part of the Windows Form Designer–generated code. Add the statement **welcomeLabel.Text = "C#";** in the body of the method definition (Fig. 3.24). In C#, properties are accessed by placing the property name (i.e., **Text**) after the object name (i.e., **welcomeLabel**), separated by a dot operator. This syntax is similar to that used when accessing object methods. Notice that the *IntelliSense* feature displays the **Text** property in the member list after the class name and dot operator have been typed (Fig. 3.25). In Chapter 5, Object-Based Programming, we discuss how programmers can create their own properties.

Fig. 3.22   Changing a property in the code-view editor.

Text property value

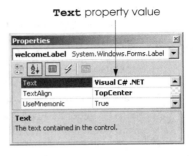

Fig. 3.23 New **Text** property value reflected in design mode.

ASimpleProgram_Load method

Fig. 3.24 Method **ASimpleProgram_Load**.

IntelliSense feature

Tooltip provides information about property chosen

Fig. 3.25 IntelliSense feature of Visual Studio .NET.

5. *Examine the results of the* **ASimpleProgram_Load** *method.* Notice that the text in the label looks the same as it did in Fig. 3.23. Note also that the **Properties** window still displays the value "**Visual C# .NET**" as the label's **Text** property and that the IDE-generated code has not changed either. Select **Build > Build** followed by **Debug > Start** to run the program. Once the form is displayed, the text in the label will reflect the assignment in **ASimpleProgram_Load** (Fig. 3.26).

6. *Terminate program execution.* Click the close button to terminate program execution. Once again, notice that both the label and the label's **Text** property contain the text **Visual C# .NET**. The IDE-generated code also contains the text **Visual C# .NET**, which is assigned to the label's **Text** property.

This chapter has discussed how to compose programs from control structures that contain actions and decisions. In Chapter 4, Methods and Arrays, we introduce another program-structuring unit called the *method*. We will learn to compose large programs by combining methods that are composed of control structures. We also discuss how methods promote software reusability. In Chapter 5, Object-Based Programming, we discuss in more detail another C# program-structuring unit called the *class*. We then create objects from classes and proceed with our treatment of object-oriented programming—a key focus of this book.

3.15 Summary

Program control is important in any programming language, as it specifies the order in which statements execute in a computer program. Normally, statements in a program execute one after the other in the order in which they appear. This process is called sequential execution. There are several control structures that enable the programmer to specify that the next statement to execute may be other than the next one in sequence. This technique is called transfer of control.

Fig. 3.26   The result of changing a property value at execution time.

The **if** and **if/else** selection structures are used to select actions to perform, based on the truth or falsity of a condition. These structures are known as the single-selection and double-selection structures, respectively. The **switch** structure, known as a multiple-selection structure, selects among several actions.

Repetition structures repeat actions, based on the truth or falsity of a condition. C#'s repetition structures include the **while**, **for** and **do/while** repetition structures.

The **break** statement is used to perform an immediate exit from a structure, while the **continue** statement is used to perform the next iteration in a repetition structure.

The unary increment and decrement operators add or subtract **1** from a variable. The conditional and logical operators are used to form complex conditions by combining simple conditions.

Developers normally combine visual programming with conventional programming when creating applications. This combination allows applications to be interactive and provide a rich graphical user interface. Visual Studio .NET enables developers to perform tasks (such as changing a property's value) in both a programmatic and visual manner.

Methods and Arrays

Objectives

- To construct programs modularly from methods.
- To be introduced to the common math methods available in the Framework Class Library.
- To understand the mechanisms for passing information between methods.
- To understand how the visibility of identifiers is limited to specific regions of programs.
- To be introduced to the array data structure.
- To understand how to declare an array, initialize an array and refer to individual elements of an array.
- To declare and manipulate multiple-subscripted arrays.

Form ever follows function.
Louis Henri Sullivan

E pluribus unum.
(One composed of many.)
Virgil

Now go, write it before them in a table,
and note it in a book.
Isaiah 30:8

When you call me that, smile.
Owen Wister

Outline

4.1	Introduction
4.2	Methods in C#
4.3	Method Definitions
4.4	Argument Promotion
4.5	C# Namespaces
4.6	Value Types and Reference Types
4.7	Passing Arguments: Pass-by-Value vs. Pass-by-Reference
4.8	Scope Rules
4.9	Recursion
4.10	Method Overloading
4.11	Arrays
4.12	Declaring and Allocating Arrays
4.13	Passing Arrays to Methods
4.14	Passing Arrays by Value and by Reference
4.15	Multiple-Subscripted Arrays
4.16	`foreach` Repetition Structure
4.17	Summary

4.1 Introduction

Most computer programs that solve real problems are much larger than the programs presented in the first few chapters of this text. Experience has shown that the best way to develop and maintain a large program is to construct it from small, simple pieces. This technique is known as *divide and conquer*. In the previous chapters, we called various methods to perform specific tasks. We also defined our own **Main** methods, specifying the actions to occur in our program. This chapter investigates methods in depth, describing many key features of the C# language that facilitate the design, implementation, operation and maintenance of large programs.

The chapter also introduces data structures. *Arrays* are data structures consisting of data items of the same type. Arrays are "static" entities, which means that they remain the same size once they are created. In this chapter, we show how to create and access arrays; we then use that knowledge to begin more complex array manipulations, including powerful searching and sorting techniques. Next, we demonstrate how to create more sophisticated arrays that have multiple dimensions. Chapter 20, Data Structures and Collections, introduces dynamic data structures, such as lists, queues, stacks and trees that can grow and shrink during program execution. In that chapter, we also introduce C#'s predefined data structures that enable the programmer to use existing data structures for lists, queues, stacks and trees, rather than having to "reinvent the wheel."

4.2 Methods in C#

C# programs are written by combining new methods and classes that the programmer writes with "prepackaged" methods and classes available in the *.NET Framework Class Library* *(FCL)*. In this chapter, we concentrate on methods. We discuss classes in detail in Chapter 5, Object-Based Programming.

The FCL provides a rich collection of classes and methods for performing common mathematical calculations, string manipulations, character manipulations, input/output operations, error checking and many other useful operations. This set of preexisting code makes the programmer's job easier by providing many of the capabilities that programmers need. The FCL methods are part of the .NET Framework, which includes FCL classes **Console** and **MessageBox** used in earlier examples.

Software Engineering Observation 4.1

Familiarize yourself with the rich collection of classes and methods in the FCL.

Software Engineering Observation 4.2

When possible, use the .NET Framework classes and methods instead of writing new classes and methods. This practice reduces both program development time and errors.

The programmer can write methods to define specific tasks that may be used at many points in a program. Such methods are known as *programmer-defined* (or *user-defined*) *methods.* The actual statements defining the method are written only once and are hidden from other methods.

A method is *invoked* (i.e., made to perform its designated task) by a *method call.* The method call specifies the name of the method and may provide information (as *arguments*) that the called method requires to perform its task. When the method call completes, the method either returns a result to the *calling method* (or *caller*) or simply returns control to the calling method. The calling method does not "know" *how* the called method performs its designated tasks; in particular, the called method may call other methods, and the calling method will be "unaware" of these calls. We will see how this "hiding" of implementation details promotes good software engineering.

Methods are called by writing the name of the method, followed by a left parenthesis, the *argument* (or a comma-separated list of arguments) of the method and a right parenthesis. The parentheses may be empty if the called method needs no arguments.

Variables declared in method definitions are *local variables*—only the method that defines them "knows" they exist. Most methods have a list of *parameters* that enable method calls to communicate information between methods. A method's parameters are also local variables to that method and are not visible in any other methods.

4.3 Method Definitions

The programs that have been presented thus far have each contained at least one method definition (such as **Main**) that called existing FCL methods to accomplish the program's tasks. We now consider how to write customized methods.

Consider the Windows application in Fig. 4.1, which uses a method called **Square** to calculate the squares of the integers from 1 to 10. Note that, in this example, we show all of the code that the Windows Form Designer generates. Throughout the remainder of the book, we omit portions of the generated code that are not relevant to our discussions. In programs with omitted code, we place a comment that indicates where the Visual Studio .NET–generated code appears in the original source file. The full examples can be downloaded from **www.deitel.com** via the **Downloads/Resources** link; they can then be compiled and executed to produce the same results we show in our screen shots. We do not discuss code generated by Visual Studio .NET in this example. Rather, we leave this discussion for Chapter 9, Graphical User Interface Concepts: Part 1, after the reader has learned all the concepts presented in the chapters on object-oriented programming (Chapters 5, 6 and 7).

Until now, our programs have used methods of class **Console** to obtain user input from the console window. These programs have output their results either to the console window or in **MessageBox**es. Although these approaches are valid ways to receive input from a user and display output, they are fairly limited in their capabilities: The console window can obtain only one value at a time from the user, and a message dialog can display only one message. It is much more common for programs to read multiple inputs simultaneously (e.g., when the user enters name and address information) or to display many pieces of data at once (such as the squares of the integers from 1 to 10 in this example). To introduce more elaborate user interfaces, the program in Fig. 4.1 illustrates two GUI concepts—attaching multiple GUI components to an application and *event handling*.

```
1   // Fig. 4.1: SquareInt.cs
2   // Demonstrates a programmer-defined Square method.
3
4   using System;
5   using System.Drawing;
6   using System.Collections;
7   using System.ComponentModel;
8   using System.Windows.Forms;
9   using System.Data;
10
11  namespace SquareInt
12  {
13     /// <summary>
14     /// Summary description for SquareInt.
15     /// </summary>
16     public class SquareInt : System.Windows.Forms.Form
17     {
18        private System.Windows.Forms.Button calculateButton;
19        private System.Windows.Forms.Label outputLabel;
20        /// <summary>
21        /// Required designer variable.
22        /// </summary>
23        private System.ComponentModel.Container components = null;
24
25        public SquareInt()
26        {
27           //
28           // Required for Windows Form Designer support
29           //
```

Fig. 4.1   Using programmer-defined method **Square**. (Part 1 of 4.)

```
30              InitializeComponent();
31          }
32
33          /// <summary>
34          /// Clean up any resources being used.
35          /// </summary>
36          protected override void Dispose( bool disposing )
37          {
38              if ( disposing )
39              {
40                  if ( components != null )
41                  {
42                      components.Dispose();
43                  }
44              }
45              base.Dispose( disposing );
46          }
47
48          #region Windows Form Designer generated code
49          /// <summary>
50          /// Required method for Designer support - do not modify
51          /// the contents of this method with the code editor.
52          /// </summary>
53          private void InitializeComponent()
54          {
55              this.calculateButton =
56                  new System.Windows.Forms.Button();
57              this.outputLabel = new System.Windows.Forms.Label();
58              this.SuspendLayout();
59              //
60              // calculateButton
61              //
62              this.calculateButton.Location =
63                  new System.Drawing.Point(32, 8);
64              this.calculateButton.Name = "calculateButton";
65              this.calculateButton.Size =
66                  new System.Drawing.Size(120, 23);
67              this.calculateButton.TabIndex = 0;
68              this.calculateButton.Text = "Calculate Squares";
69              this.calculateButton.Click +=
70                  new System.EventHandler(
71                      this.calculateButton_Click);
72              //
73              // outputLabel
74              //
75              this.outputLabel.Location =
76                  new System.Drawing.Point(16, 48);
77              this.outputLabel.Name = "outputLabel";
78              this.outputLabel.Size =
79                  new System.Drawing.Size(152, 144);
80              this.outputLabel.TabIndex = 1;
81              //
82              // SquareInt
```

Fig. 4.1   Using programmer-defined method **Square**. (Part 2 of 4.)

```
83               //
84               this.AutoScaleBaseSize =
85                  new System.Drawing.Size(5, 13);
86               this.ClientSize =
87                  new System.Drawing.Size(184, 197);
88               this.Controls.AddRange(
89                  new System.Windows.Forms.Control[] {
90                     this.outputLabel,
91                     this.calculateButton});
92               this.Name = "SquareInt";
93               this.Text = "SquareInt";
94               this.ResumeLayout(false);
95
96            }
97            #endregion
98
99            /// <summary>
100           /// The main entry point for the application.
101           /// </summary>
102           [STAThread]
103           static void Main()
104           {
105              Application.Run( new SquareInt() );
106           }
107
108           // Square method definition
109           int Square( int y )
110           {
111              return y * y; // return square of y
112
113           } // end method Square
114
115           private void calculateButton_Click(
116              object sender, System.EventArgs e )
117           {
118              outputLabel.Text = "";
119
120              // loop 10 times
121              for ( int counter = 1; counter <= 10; counter++ )
122              {
123                 // calculate square of counter and store in result
124                 int result = Square( counter );
125
126                 // append result to outputLabel
127                 outputLabel.Text += "The square of " + counter +
128                    " is " + result + "\n";
129              }
130
131           } // end method calculateButton_Click
132
133        } // end class SquareInt
134
135 } // end namespace SquareInt
```

Fig. 4.1   Using programmer-defined method **Square**. (Part 3 of 4.)

Fig. 4.1 Using programmer-defined method **Square**. (Part 4 of 4.)

To create the graphical user interface for this program, drag the appropriate components (a **Button** and a **Label**) from the **Toolbox** onto the **Form** in the Windows Form Designer. We demonstrated how to do this operation in Section 2.6. Arrange the components as shown in the screen capture of Fig. 4.1, and set the **Text** properties for the **Label** and **Button**. The program invokes a special method known as an *event handler* when the user clicks the **Calculate Squares** button. An event handler is a method that performs some action in response to an *event*. Events occur when certain actions take place in a graphical user interface, such as when the user clicks a button. Using GUI-component objects and events together allows programmers to create applications that interact with users in more sophisticated ways than we have seen previously. In Visual Studio .NET's Windows Form Designer, double clicking a GUI-component object causes Visual Studio .NET to generate an empty event-handler method. The event-handler method's name defaults to the GUI component's name, followed by an underscore and the name of the event. The programmer then can fill the event-handler method with code that performs an appropriate task when that event occurs. Fill in this empty event handler with the code shown on lines 118–129. Line 124 invokes our **Square** method to determine the square of a specified integer.

In Fig. 4.1, method **calculateButton_Click** (lines 115–131) is an event-handler method for **calculateButton**'s **Click** event (i.e., the event that occurs when the user clicks the button). This event handler begins by assigning the empty string (**" "**) to **outputLabel**'s **Text** property on line 118. This assignment ensures that the output does not scroll off the form if the user presses the **Calculate Squares** button more than once. Lines 121–129 repeatedly invoke method **Square** (lines 109–113) to calculate the squares of the integers from 1 to 10. Line 124 invokes the **Square** method and passes the variable **counter** as an argument. The result of each square calculation is stored in variable **result**. Lines 127–128 concatenate each result to the **Text** property of **outputLabel**. The property stores the text that will be displayed in this label. At the end of the loop, the **Label** contains the results of squaring the integers from 1 to 10. Notice that the property is accessed using the dot (**.**) operator.

Let us look more closely at how method **Square** is invoked on line 124. The parentheses, **()**, after **Square** represent the *method-call operator*, which has high precedence. At this point, the program makes a copy of the value of **counter** (the argument to the method call), and program control transfers to method **Square** (defined at lines 109–113). Method **Square** receives the copy of the value of **counter** in the *parameter* **y**. Then **Square** calculates **y * y** (line 111). Method **Square** uses a *return* statement to return the result of the calculation to the statement that invoked **Square** (located in line 124). Line 124 then assigns the returned value to variable **result**. Lines 127–128 concatenate **"The square of"**, the value of **counter**, **" is "**, the value of **result** and a newline character to the end of **outputLabel**'s **Text** property. The **for** repetition structure repeats this process 10 times.

The definition of method **Square** (line 109) shows (inside the parentheses) that **Square** expects an integer parameter **y**. Parameter **y** is the variable that holds the value passed to **Square** as an argument. The parameter name provides access to the value of the argument, so that code in the body of the method can use that value. Keyword **int**, which precedes the method name, indicates that method **Square** returns an integer result. The **return** statement in **Square** (line 111) passes the result of the calculation **y * y** back to the calling statement (line 124). Note that the entire method definition appears inside the braces of class **SquareInt**. All methods must be defined inside a class definition.

Good Programming Practice 4.1

Place a blank line between adjacent method definitions to separate the methods and enhance program readability.

Common Programming Error 4.1

Defining a method outside the braces of a class definition is a syntax error.

The format of a method definition is

```
return-value-type   method-name ( parameter-list )
{
    declarations and statements
}
```

The first line is sometimes known as the *method header*. The *method-name* is any valid identifier. The *return-value-type* is the data type of the result that the method returns to its caller. The *return-value-type* **void** indicates that a method does not return a value. Methods can return at most one value.

Common Programming Error 4.2

Omitting the return-value-type *in a method definition is a syntax error. If a method does not return a value, the method's* return-value-type *must be* **void***.*

Common Programming Error 4.3

Forgetting to return a value from a method that is supposed to return a value is a syntax error. If a return-value-type *other than* **void** *is specified, the method must contain a* **return** *statement that returns a value.*

Common Programming Error 4.4

Returning a value from a method whose return type has been declared **void** *is a syntax error.*

The *parameter-list* is a comma-separated list in which the method declares each parameter's type and name. The method call must specify one argument for each parameter in the method definition, and the arguments must appear in the same order as the parameters in the method definition. Each argument also must be compatible with its corresponding parameter's type. For example, a parameter of type **double** could receive values of **7.35**,

22 or **-.03546**, but not a value of **"hello"**, because a **string** cannot be implicitly converted into a **double**. If a method does not receive any values, the parameter list is empty (i.e., the method name is followed by an empty pair of parentheses). Each parameter in a method's parameter list must have a data type; otherwise, a syntax error occurs.

Common Programming Error 4.5
Using one type declaration for multiple method parameters of the same type, as in **float x, y** *instead of* **float x, float y***, is a syntax error, because a type is required for each parameter in the parameter list.*

Common Programming Error 4.6
Placing a semicolon after the right parenthesis enclosing the parameter list of a method definition is a syntax error.

Common Programming Error 4.7
Redefining a method parameter in the method's body is a compilation error.

Common Programming Error 4.8
Passing to a method an argument that is not compatible with the corresponding parameter's type is a syntax error. If the argument is not of the same type as its corresponding parameter, the argument's type must be one that can be implicitly converted to the type of the corresponding parameter.

The declarations and statements within braces form the *method body*. The method body also is referred to as a *block*. As discussed previously, a block is a set of statements enclosed in curly braces. Variables can be declared in any block, and blocks can be nested.

Common Programming Error 4.9
Defining a method inside another method is a syntax error (i.e., methods cannot be nested).

Software Engineering Observation 4.3
The number, type and order of arguments in a method call must exactly match those of the parameters in the corresponding method header.

There are three ways to return control to the point at which a method was invoked. If the method does not return a result (i.e., the method has a **void** return type), control returns when the program reaches the method-ending right brace or when the statement

　　　return;

executes. If the method does return a result, the statement

　　　return *expression***;**

returns the value of *expression* to the caller. When a **return** statement executes, control returns immediately to the point at which the method was invoked.

Notice the syntax that invokes method **Square** in Fig. 4.1—we use the method name, followed by the arguments to the method in parentheses. Methods in a class definition are allowed to invoke all other methods in the same class definition by using this syntax (an exception to this rule is discussed in Chapter 5, Object-Based Programming). We now have seen three ways to call a method with arguments—by using a method name by itself (such as **Square(x)**), by using a reference to an object followed by the dot (**.**) operator and the method name (such as **string1.CompareTo(string2)**), and by using a class name followed by a method name (such as **Math.Sqrt(9.0)**, where we want to call method **Sqrt** of class **Math**, located in the **System** namespace). This last syntax is for calling the *static* methods of a class; we discuss these methods in detail in Chapter 5, Object-Based Programming.

4.4 Argument Promotion

Another important feature of method definitions is the *coercion of arguments* (i.e., forcing arguments to the appropriate type). This process commonly is referred to as *implicit conversion* (discussed briefly in Chapter 3), because a copy of the variable's value is converted to a different type without an explicit cast. Explicit conversion (also introduced in Chapter 3) occurs when an explicit cast specifies that conversion is to occur. Such conversions also can be done with class **Convert** in namespace **System**. C# supports both widening and narrowing conversions. *Widening conversion* occurs when a type is converted to another type (usually a type that can hold more data) without losing data, and *narrowing conversion* occurs when data may be lost through a conversion (usually to types that hold a smaller amount of data). Figure 4.2 provides size information for the various built-in types of C#, and Fig. 4.3 shows the allowable implicit conversions.

Type	Size in bits	Values	Standard
bool	8	**true** or **false**	
char	16	**'\u0000'** to **'\uFFFF'**	(Unicode® character set)
byte	8	0 to 255	(unsigned)
sbyte	8	−128 to +127	
short	16	−32,768 to +32,767	
ushort	16	0 to 65,535	(unsigned)
int	32	−2,147,483,648 to 2,147,483,647	
uint	32	0 to 4,294,967,295	(unsigned)
long	64	−9,223,372,036,854,775,808 to +9,223,372,036,854,775,807	
ulong	64	0 to 18,446,744,073,709,551,615	(unsigned)
decimal	128	1.0×10^{-28} to 7.9×10^{28}	
float	32	$\pm 1.5 \times 10^{-45}$ to $\pm 3.4 \times 10^{38}$	(IEEE 754 floating point)
double	64	$\pm 5.0 \times 10^{-324}$ to $\pm 1.7 \times 10^{308}$	(IEEE 754 floating point)
object			
string			(Unicode® character set)

Fig. 4.2   C# built-in data types.

Type	Can be Converted to Type(s)
bool	object
byte	decimal, double, float, int, uint, long, ulong, short, ushort or object
sbyte	decimal, double, float, int, long, short or object
char	decimal, double, float, int, uint, long, ulong, ushort or object
decimal	object
double	object
float	double or object
int	decimal, double, float, long or object
uint	decimal, double, float, long, ulong or object
long	decimal, double, float or object
ulong	decimal, double, float or object
short	decimal, double, float, int, long or object
ushort	decimal, double, float, int, uint, long, ulong or object

Fig. 4.3   Allowed implicit conversions.

For example, the **Math** class method **Sqrt** can be called with an integer argument, even though the method is defined in class **Math** to receive a **double** argument. The statement

```
Console.WriteLine( Math.Sqrt( 4 ) );
```

correctly evaluates **Math.Sqrt(4)** and displays the value **2**. C# implicitly converts the **int** value **4** to the **double** value **4.0** before passing the value to **Math.Sqrt**. In many cases, C# applies implicit conversions to argument values that do not correspond precisely to the parameter types in the method definition. In some cases, however, attempting these conversions leads to compilation errors, because the conversion violates the rules C# uses to determine when a widening conversion can occur. In our previous **Math.Sqrt** example, C# converts an **int** to a **double** without changing the argument's value. However, converting a **double** to an **int** truncates the fractional part of the **double** value. Converting large integer types to small integer types (e.g., **long** to **int**) also can result in changed values. Such narrowing conversions can lose data; C# does not allow narrowing conversions to occur without an explicit cast operation.

C#'s conversion rules apply to expressions containing values of two or more data types (also referred to as *mixed-type expressions*) and to primitive data-type values passed as arguments to methods. C# converts the type of each value in a mixed-type expression to the "highest" type in the expression. To do so, C# creates a temporary copy of each converted value and uses it in the expression; the original values remain unchanged. A method argument's type can be promoted to any "higher" type. The table of Fig. 4.3 can be used to determine the highest type in an expression. For each type in the left column, the corresponding types in the right column are considered to be of a higher type. For instance, types **decimal**, **double**, **float**, **long** and **object** are higher than type **int**.

Converting values to lower types can result in data loss. In cases where information could be lost through conversion, the compiler requires the programmer to use a cast to force the conversion to occur. For example, to pass our **Square** method (Fig. 4.1), the **double** variable **y**, the method call would be written as

```
int result = Square( ( int ) y );
```

This statement explicitly casts (converts) a copy of the value of **y** to an integer for use in method **Square**. Thus, if **y**'s value is **4.5**, method **Square** returns **16**, not **20.25**.

Common Programming Error 4.10

*When performing a narrowing conversion (e.g., **double** to **int**), converting a primitive-data-type value to another primitive data type may result in loss of data.*

4.5 C# Namespaces

As we have seen, C# contains many predefined classes that are grouped into namespaces. We refer to this preexisting code collectively as the Framework Class Library. The actual code for the classes is located in **.dll** files called assemblies.

In C#, **using** statements specify the namespaces we use in each program. For example, a program includes the statement

```
using System;
```

to tell the compiler that it uses the **System** namespace. This **using** statement allows us to write **Console.WriteLine** rather than **System.Console.WriteLine** throughout the program. To use a class in a particular namespace, we must add a reference to the appropriate assembly (the procedure for which is demonstrated in Section 2.7). Assembly references for namespace **System** are added by Visual Studio .NET—other assemblies must be added explicitly.

We use a large number of the FCL classes in this book. Figure 4.4 lists a subset of the many namespaces in the FCL and provides a brief description of each. We use classes from these and other namespaces throughout the book.

Namespace	Description
System	Contains essential classes and data types (such as *int*, *double* and *char*). Implicitly referenced by all C# programs.
System.Data	Contains classes that form ADO .NET, used for database access and manipulation.
System.Drawing	Contains classes used for drawing and graphics.
System.IO	Contains classes for the input and output of data, such as with files.
System.Threading	Contains classes for multithreading, used to specify that multiple actions can occur concurrently.

Fig. 4.4   Namespaces in the Framework Class Library. (Part 1 of 2.)

Namespace	Description
`System.Windows.Forms`	Contains classes used to create graphical user interfaces.
`System.Xml`	Contains classes used to process XML data.

Fig. 4.4   Namespaces in the Framework Class Library. (Part 2 of 2.)

The set of namespaces available in the FCL is quite large (at the time of this book's publication, there were approximately 100 namespaces, including hundreds of classes). In addition to the namespaces summarized in Fig. 4.4, the FCL includes namespaces for complex graphics, advanced graphical user interfaces, printing, advanced networking, security, multimedia and accessibility (for people with disabilities), among many others. For an overview of the namespaces in the FCL, look up "Class Library" in the **Help** index.

4.6 Value Types and Reference Types

In the next section, we will discuss the passing of arguments to methods by value and by reference. To understand those processes, we first need to make a distinction between data types that are *value types* and data types that are *reference types*. A variable of a value type contains data of that type. A variable of a reference type, in contrast, contains the address of the location in memory where the data for that variable are stored. Value types normally represent single pieces of data, such as **int** or **bool** values. Reference types, on the other hand, refer to objects, which can contain many individual pieces of data. We discuss objects in detail in Chapters 5, 6 and 7.

C# includes built-in value types and reference types. The built-in value types are the *integral types* (**sbyte**, **byte**, **char**, **short**, **ushort**, **int**, **uint**, **long** and **ulong**), the *floating-point types* (**float** and **double**), and the types **decimal** and **bool**. The built-in reference types are **string** and **object**. Programmers can create new value types and reference types; such reference types include classes (Chapter 5), interfaces (Chapter 7) and delegates (Chapter 7).

The table in Fig. 4.2 lists the primitive data types; these data types are often used as building blocks for more complicated types. C#, like its predecessor languages C and C++, requires all variables to have a type before they can be used in a program. For this reason, C# is referred to as a *strongly typed language*.

In C and C++ programs, programmers frequently must write separate program versions to support different computer platforms, because the primitive data types are not guaranteed to be identical from computer to computer. For example, an **int** value on one computer might occupy 16 bits (two bytes) of memory, whereas an **int** value on another computer might occupy 32 bits (four bytes) of memory. In C#, **int** values are always 32 bits (four bytes).

Portability Tip 4.1

Primitive data types in C# are portable across all platforms that support C#.

Each data type in the table in Fig. 4.2 is listed with its size in bits (there are eight bits to a byte) and its range of values. The designers of C# wanted code to be portable; therefore, they chose to use internationally recognized standards for both character formats (Unicode®) and floating-point numbers (IEEE 754). Unicode® is discussed more in Appendix G.

4.7 Passing Arguments: Pass-by-Value vs. Pass-by-Reference

Two ways to pass arguments to methods in many programming languages are *pass-by-value* and *pass-by-reference*. When an argument is passed by value, the called method receives a *copy* of the argument's value.

Testing and Debugging Tip 4.1

With pass-by-value, changes to the called method's copy of the value do not affect the original variable's value. This condition prevents the occurrence of some possible side effects that hinder the development of correct and reliable software systems.

When an argument is passed using pass-by-reference, the caller gives the method the ability to access and modify the caller's original data directly. Pass-by-reference can improve performance, because it eliminates the overhead of copying large data items such as objects; however, pass-by-reference can weaken security, because the called method can modify the caller's data.

Software Engineering Observation 4.4

*When returning information from a method via a **return** statement, value-type variables always are returned by value (i.e., a copy is returned), and reference-type variables are always returned by reference (i.e., a reference to the object is returned).*

To pass an object reference into a method, simply specify the reference name in the method call. Then, in the method body, use the parameter name to reference the object. This name refers to the original object in memory, which allows the called method to access the original object in the caller directly.

In Section 4.6, we discussed the difference between value types and reference types. At this point, the reader can understand one of the major differences between the two data types: Value-type variables are passed to methods by value, whereas reference-type variables are passed to methods by reference. What if the programmer would like to pass a value type by reference? To enable such programming, C# provides the **ref** and **out** *keywords*. The **ref** keyword specifies that a value-type argument should be passed by reference, which enables the called method to modify the original variable. This keyword is used for variables that already have been initialized. The **out** keyword specifies an output parameter, which is an argument to which the called method will assign a value. Normally, when a method receives an uninitialized value, the compiler generates an error. Preceding the parameter with keyword **out** specifies that the called method will initialize the variable and prevents the compiler from generating an error message for the uninitialized variable. Figure 4.5 demonstrates the use of the **ref** and **out** keywords to manipulate integer values.[1]

```
1   // Fig. 4.5: RefOutTest.cs
2   // Demonstrating ref and out parameters.
```

Fig. 4.5   Demonstrating **ref** and **out** parameters. (Part 1 of 4.)

---

1. In Section 4.14, we discuss passing reference-type arguments both by value and by reference.

```
3
4    using System;
5    using System.Drawing;
6    using System.Collections;
7    using System.ComponentModel;
8    using System.Windows.Forms;
9    using System.Data;
10
11   public class RefOutTest : System.Windows.Forms.Form
12   {
13      private System.Windows.Forms.Button showOutputButton;
14      private System.Windows.Forms.Label outputLabel;
15
16      // Visual Studio .NET generated code
17
18      // main entry point for application
19      [STAThread]
20      static void Main()
21      {
22         Application.Run( new RefOutTest() );
23      }
24
25      // x passed in by value and method cannot modify
26      // original variable's value
27      void Square( int x )
28      {
29         x = x * x;
30
31         outputLabel.Text +=
32            "Value of variable within Square, " +
33            "after calculation: " + x + "\n";
34      }
35
36      // x passed in by reference and method modifies
37      // original variable's value
38      void SquareRef( ref int x )
39      {
40         x = x * x;
41
42         outputLabel.Text +=
43            "Value of variable within SquareRef, " +
44            "after calculation: " + x + "\n";
45      }
46
47      // x passed in as out parameter and method initializes
48      // and modifies original variable's value
49      void SquareOut( out int x )
50      {
51         x = 6;       // initialize
52         x = x * x;   // modify
53
```

Fig. 4.5   Demonstrating **ref** and **out** parameters. (Part 2 of 4.)

```
54          outputLabel.Text +=
55             "Value of variable within SquareOut, " +
56             "after calculation: " + x + "\n";
57       }
58
59       private void showOutputButton_Click(
60          object sender, System.EventArgs e )
61       {
62          int y = 5; // create new int and initialize to 5
63          int z;     // declare z, but do not initialize it
64
65          // display original value of y
66          outputLabel.Text =
67             "Value of y before calling SquareRef: " + y + "\n";
68
69          // use ref keyword to pass y by reference
70          SquareRef( ref y );
71          outputLabel.Text +=
72             "Value of y after exiting SquareRef: " + y + "\n";
73
74          // display original value of z
75          outputLabel.Text +=
76             "\nValue of z before calling SquareOut: " +
77             "uninitialized\n";
78
79          // z not yet initialized; must use
80          // out keyword to pass z by reference
81          SquareOut( out z );
82          outputLabel.Text +=
83             "Value of z after exiting SquareOut: " + z + "\n";
84
85          outputLabel.Text +=
86             "_____\n\n";
87
88          // display value of y
89          outputLabel.Text +=
90             "Value of y before calling Square: " + y + "\n";
91
92          // pass y by value
93          Square( y );
94          outputLabel.Text +=
95             "Value of y after exiting Square: " + y + "\n";
96
97          // display value of z
98          outputLabel.Text +=
99             "\nValue of z before calling Square: " + z + "\n";
100
101         // pass z by value
102         Square( z );
103         outputLabel.Text +=
104            "Value of z after exiting Square: " + z + "\n";
105
106      } // end method showOutputButton_Click
```

Fig. 4.5   Demonstrating **ref** and **out** parameters. (Part 3 of 4.)

107
108 } // end class RefOutTest

Fig. 4.5   Demonstrating **ref** and **out** parameters. (Part 4 of 4.)

This program contains three methods to calculate the square of an integer. Method **Square**, defined on lines 27–34, multiplies its argument by itself and assigns that new value to **x**. The original value passed is a value-type integer and is therefore unchanged after the method executes. Method **SquareRef**, defined on lines 38–45, performs the same action. **SquareRef** receives its argument as a **ref int**, specifying that **x** is an integer that is passed by reference to the method. As a result, the assignment on line 40 modifies the original argument's value in the caller, rather than a copy of that value. Method **SquareOut** (defined on lines 49–57) also calculates the square of an integer, but initializes **x** to **6** on line 51. **SquareOut** receives its argument as an **out int**, which indicates that **x** is an integer variable that is to be passed by reference and that may be passed to the method in an uninitialized state.

Method **showOutputButton_Click** (lines 59–106) is an event handler that invokes methods **SquareRef**, **SquareOut** and **Square** when the user clicks the **Show Output** button. This method begins by initializing **y** to **5** and declaring (but not initializing) **z**. Lines 70 and 81 call methods **SquareRef** and **SquareOut**. Notice the syntax used for passing **y** and **z**; in each case, we precede the argument either with **ref** or with **out**, as specified in the method header. If the proper keyword is left out, a syntax error occurs. Notice that **y** has been changed to **25** and **z** has been set to **36**. On lines 93 and 102, we call method **Square**, passing values **y** (**25**) and **z** (**36**). Arguments **y** and **z** both are passed by value—that is, only copies of their values are passed to the method. As a result, the values of **y** and **z** remain **25** and **36** after the method call. The output displays the values of **y** and **z** before, during and after each method call.

Common Programming Error 4.11

*The **ref** and **out** arguments in a method call must match those specified in the method definition; otherwise, a syntax error occurs.*

Software Engineering Observation 4.5

By default, C# does not allow the programmer to choose whether to pass each argument by value or by reference. Value-type variables are passed by value. Objects themselves are not passed to methods; rather, references to objects are passed to methods. The references themselves are passed by value. When a method receives a reference to an object, the method can manipulate the object directly, but the reference value cannot be changed (e.g., to refer to a new object).

4.8 Scope Rules

The *scope* (sometimes called *declaration space*) of an identifier for a variable, reference or method is the portion of the program in which the identifier can be accessed. A local variable declared in a block can be used only in that block or in blocks nested within that block. We define the possible scopes for an identifier as *class scope* and *block scope*.

Members of a class have class scope and are visible in what is known as the *declaration space of a class*. Class scope begins at the opening left brace ({) of the class definition and terminates at the closing right brace (}). Class scope enables methods of a class to access all members defined in that class. In Chapter 5, Object-Based Programming, we see that static members are an exception to this rule. In a sense, all instance variables and methods of a class are *global* to the methods of the class in which they are defined (i.e., the methods can modify the instance variables directly and invoke other methods of the class).

Identifiers declared inside a block have block scope (*local-variable declaration space*). Block scope begins at the identifier's declaration and ends at the block's terminating right brace (}). Local variables of a method have block scope, as do method parameters, which are local variables of the method. Any block may contain variable declarations. When blocks are nested in a method's body, and a variable declared in an outer block has the same name as a variable declared in an inner block, an error is generated. On the other hand, if a local variable in a method has the same name as an instance variable, the value in the calling method (main program) is "hidden" until the method terminates execution. In Chapter 5, we discuss how to access such "hidden" instance variables. The reader should note that block scope also applies to methods and **for** structures. With **for** structures, any variable declared in the initialization portion of the **for** header will be in scope only within that **for** structure.

Testing and Debugging Tip 4.2

Avoid using local-variable names that hide instance-variable names.

The program in Fig. 4.6 demonstrates various scoping scenarios with instance variables and local variables. Instance variable **x** (line 16) is initialized to **1**. This instance variable is hidden in any block (or method) that declares a local variable named **x**. The **showOutputButton_Click** event handler (lines 48–64) declares a local variable **x** and initializes it to **5** (line 51). Lines 53–54 display the value of this local variable to show that instance variable **x** (with value **1**) is "hidden" in method **showOutputButton_Click**.

The program defines two other methods—**MethodA** and **MethodB**—that take no arguments and return nothing. The program calls each method twice from method

Scoping. MethodA defines local variable **x** (line 22) and initializes it to **25**. Each call to **MethodA** displays the variable's value in **outputLabel**, increments the variable and displays it again before exiting the method. Each call to **MethodA** recreates local variable **x** and initializes it to **25**. Method **MethodB** does not declare any variables. Therefore, when it refers to variable **x**, the instance variable **x** is used. Each call to **MethodB** displays the instance variable in **outputLabel**, multiplies it by **10** (line 41) and displays it again before exiting the method. Thus, the next time method **MethodB** is called, the instance variable's initial value is its modified value, **10**. After the calls to **MethodA** and **MethodB**, the program again displays the local variable **x** in method **showOutputButton_Click**, to show that none of the method calls modified this particular variable **x**, as the methods all referred to variables in other scopes.

```
1   // Fig. 4.6: Scoping.cs
2   // Demonstrating scope of local and instance variables.
3
4   using System;
5   using System.Drawing;
6   using System.Collections;
7   using System.ComponentModel;
8   using System.Windows.Forms;
9   using System.Data;
10
11  public class Scoping : System.Windows.Forms.Form
12  {
13     private System.Windows.Forms.Label outputLabel;
14     private System.Windows.Forms.Button showOutputButton;
15
16     public int x = 1; // instance variable
17
18     // Visual Studio .NET generated code
19
20     public void MethodA()
21     {
22        int x = 25;     // initialized each time MethodA is called
23
24        outputLabel.Text = outputLabel.Text +
25           "\n\nlocal x in MethodA is " + x +
26           " after entering MethodA";
27
28        ++x; // increment local variable x
29
30        outputLabel.Text = outputLabel.Text +
31           "\nlocal x in MethodA is " + x +
32           " before exiting MethodA";
33     }
34
35     public void MethodB()
36     {
37        outputLabel.Text = outputLabel.Text +
38           "\n\ninstance variable x is " + x +
39           " on entering MethodB";
```

Fig. 4.6   Scoping. (Part 1 of 2.)

```
40
41          x *= 10;
42
43          outputLabel.Text = outputLabel.Text +
44              "\ninstance varable x is " + x +
45              " on exiting MethodB";
46      }
47
48      private void showOutputButton_Click(
49          object sender, System.EventArgs e )
50      {
51          int x = 5; // local x in method showOutputButton_Click
52
53          outputLabel.Text =
54              "local x in method showOutputButton_Click is " + x;
55
56          MethodA();      // MethodA has local variable x;
57          MethodB();      // MethodB uses instance variable x
58          MethodA();      // MethodA creates new local variable x
59          MethodB();      // instance variable x retains its value
60
61          outputLabel.Text = outputLabel.Text + "\n\n" +
62              "local x in method showOutputButton_Click is " + x;
63
64      } // end method showOutputButton_Click
65
66      // main entry point for the application
67      [STAThread]
68      static void Main()
69      {
70          Application.Run( new Scoping() );
71      }
72
73  } // end class Scoping
```

Fig. 4.6   Scoping. (Part 2 of 2.)

4.9 Recursion

The programs we have discussed thus far generally have been structured as methods that call one another in a hierarchical manner. For some problems, it is useful to have a method actually call itself. A *recursive method* is a method that calls itself, either directly or indirectly through another method. In this section, we consider recursion conceptually first; then we examine a program containing a simple recursive method.

Recursive problem-solving approaches have a number of elements in common. A recursive method actually "knows" how to solve only the simplest case(s), or *base case(s)*. If the method is called with a base case, the method returns a result. If the method is called with a more complex problem, the method divides the problem into two conceptual pieces—a piece that the method knows how to perform (the base case) and a piece that the method does not know how to perform. To make recursion feasible, the latter piece must resemble the original problem, but be a slightly simpler or smaller version of it. The method invokes (calls) a fresh copy of itself to work on the smaller problem; this event is referred to as a *recursive call*, or a *recursion step*. The recursion step also normally includes the keyword **return**, because its result will be combined with the portion of the problem that the method knew how to solve. Such a combination will form a result that will be passed back to the original caller.

The recursion step executes while the original call to the method is still "open" (i.e., it has not finished executing). The recursion step may result in many more recursive calls, as the method divides each new subproblem into two conceptual pieces. Each time the method calls itself with a slightly simpler version of the original problem, the sequence of smaller and smaller problems must converge on the base case, so that the recursion eventually can terminate. At that point, the method recognizes the base case and returns a result to the previous copy of the method. A sequence of returns ensues up the line until the original method call returns the final result to the caller. As an example of these concepts, let us write a recursive program to perform a popular mathematical calculation.

The factorial of a nonnegative integer n, written $n!$ (and pronounced "n factorial"), is the product

$$n \cdot (n - 1) \cdot (n - 2) \cdot \ldots \cdot 1$$

where 1! is equal to 1 and 0! is defined as 1. For example, 5! is the product $5 \cdot 4 \cdot 3 \cdot 2 \cdot 1$, which is equal to 120.

The factorial of an integer **number** greater than or equal to **0** can be calculated *iteratively* (nonrecursively) using a **for** structure as follows:

```
factorial = 1;
for ( int counter = number; counter >= 1; counter-- )
   factorial *= counter;
```

We arrive at a recursive definition of the factorial method with the following relationship:

$$n! = n \cdot (n - 1)!$$

For example, 5! is equal to 5 • 4!, as shown by the following calculations:

$$5! = 5 \cdot 4 \cdot 3 \cdot 2 \cdot 1$$
$$5! = 5 \cdot (4 \cdot 3 \cdot 2 \cdot 1)$$
$$5! = 5 \cdot (4!)$$

Figure 4.7 uses recursion to calculate and print the factorials of the integers 0–10. The recursive method **Factorial** (lines 17–24) first determines whether its terminating condition is **true** (i.e., whether **number** is less than or equal to **1**). If **number** is less than or equal to **1**, **factorial** returns **1**, no further recursion is necessary and the method returns. If **number** is greater than **1**, line 23 expresses the problem as the product of **number** and a recursive call to **Factorial**, evaluating the factorial of **number - 1**. Note that **Factorial(number - 1)** is a slightly simpler problem than the original calculation **Factorial(number)**.

Method **Factorial** receives a parameter of type **long** and returns a result of type **long**. As seen in Fig. 4.7, factorial values become large quickly. We choose data type **long** so the program can calculate factorials greater than 20!. Unfortunately, the **Factorial** method produces large values so quickly that even **long** does not help us print many more factorial values before the size of even the **long** variable is exceeded.

Calculating factorials of larger numbers requires the program to use **float** and **double** variables. This condition points to a weakness in most programming languages, namely, that the languages are not extended easily to handle the unique requirements of various applications. As we will see in our treatment of object-oriented programming, beginning in Chapter 5, C# is an extensible language; programmers with unique requirements can extend the language with new data types (called *classes*). A programmer could create a **HugeInteger** class, for example, that would enable a program to calculate the factorials of arbitrarily large numbers.

Common Programming Error 4.12

Forgetting to return a value from a recursive method can result in syntax or logic errors.

```
1   // Fig. 4.7: FactorialTest.cs
2   // Calculating factorials with recursion.
3   using System;
4   using System.Drawing;
5   using System.Collections;
6   using System.ComponentModel;
7   using System.Windows.Forms;
8   using System.Data;
9
10  public class FactorialTest : System.Windows.Forms.Form
11  {
12     private System.Windows.Forms.Button showFactorialsButton;
13     private System.Windows.Forms.Label outputLabel;
14
15     // Visual Studio .NET generated code
16
17     public long Factorial( long number )
18     {
19        if ( number <= 1 )         // base case
20           return 1;
21
22        else
23           return number * Factorial( number - 1 );
24     }
25
```

Fig. 4.7   Calculating factorials with a recursive method. (Part 1 of 2.)

```
26      // main entry point for application
27      [STAThread]
28      static void Main()
29      {
30          Application.Run( new FactorialTest());
31      }
32
33      private void showFactorialsButton_Click( object sender,
34          System.EventArgs e )
35      {
36          outputLabel.Text = "";
37
38          for ( long i = 0; i <= 10; i++ )
39              outputLabel.Text += i + "! = " +
40                  Factorial( i ) + "\n";
41      }
42
43  } // end class FactorialTest
```

Fig. 4.7   Calculating factorials with a recursive method. (Part 2 of 2.)

 Common Programming Error 4.13

Omitting the base case or writing the recursion step so that it does not converge on the base case will cause infinite recursion, eventually exhausting memory. Infinite recursion is analogous to the problem of an infinite loop in an iterative (nonrecursive) solution.

Most programming books introduce recursion much later than we have done here. We feel that recursion is a sufficiently rich and complex topic that it is better to introduce it earlier and spread examples of it over the remainder of the text. Other examples of recursion in this book can be found in Figures 10.21, 14.6, 17.22, 20.17 and 20.20.

4.10 Method Overloading

C# enables several methods of the same name to be defined in the same class, as long as the methods have different sets of parameters (in terms of the number of parameters, types of parameters or order of the parameters). This concept is called *method overloading*. When an overloaded method is called, the C# compiler selects the proper method by examining the number, types and order of the call's arguments. Method overloading commonly is used to create several methods with the same name that perform similar tasks, but on different data types. Figure 4.8 uses overloaded method **Square** to calculate the square of an **int** and a **double**.

Good Programming Practice 4.2

Overloading methods that perform closely related tasks can make programs more readable and understandable.

The compiler distinguishes overloaded methods by their *signatures*. A method's signature is a combination of the method's name and parameters. If the compiler were to look only at method names during compilation, the code in Fig. 4.8 would be ambiguous; the compiler would be unable to distinguish the two **Square** methods. The compiler uses *overload resolution* to determine which method to call. This process first searches for all the methods that *can* be used in the context, based on the number and type of arguments that are present. It might seem that only one method would match, but recall that C# can convert variable values to other data types implicitly. Once all matching methods are found, the closest match is chosen. This match is based on a "best-fit" algorithm, which analyzes the implicit conversions that will take place.

```
1   // Fig. 4.8: MethodOverload.cs
2   // Using overloaded methods.
3
4   using System;
5   using System.Drawing;
6   using System.Collections;
7   using System.ComponentModel;
8   using System.Windows.Forms;
9   using System.Data;
10
11  public class MethodOverload : System.Windows.Forms.Form
12  {
13     private System.Windows.Forms.Button showOutputButton;
14     private System.Windows.Forms.Label outputLabel;
15
16     // Visual Studio .NET generated code
17
18     // first version, takes one integer
19     public int Square( int x )
20     {
21        return x * x;
22     }
23
24     // second version, takes one double
25     public double Square( double y )
26     {
27        return y * y;
28     }
29  }
```

Fig. 4.8   Using overloaded methods. (Part 1 of 2.)

```
30      // main entry point for application
31      [STAThread]
32      static void Main()
33      {
34          Application.Run( new MethodOverload() );
35      }
36
37      private void showOutputButton_Click(
38          object sender, System.EventArgs e )
39      {
40          // call both versions of Square
41          outputLabel.Text =
42              "The square of integer 7 is " + Square( 7 ) +
43              "\nThe square of double 7.5 is " + Square( 7.5 );
44      }
45
46  } // end class MethodOverload
```

Fig. 4.8   Using overloaded methods. (Part 2 of 2.)

Let us look at an example. In Fig. 4.8, the compiler might use the logical name
"**Square** of **int**" for the **Square** method that specifies an **int** parameter (line 19) and
"**Square** of **double**" for the **Square** method that specifies a **double** parameter (line
25). If a method **Foo**'s definition begins as

```
void Foo( int a, float b )
```

the compiler might use the logical name "**Foo** of **int** and **float**." If the parameters are
specified as

```
void Foo( float a, int b )
```

the compiler might use the logical name "**Foo** of **float** and **int**." The order of the parameters is important to the compiler; it considers the preceding two **Foo** methods distinct.

So far, the logical names of methods that have been used by the compiler have not
mentioned the methods' return types. This is because method calls cannot be distinguished
by return type. The program in Fig. 4.9 illustrates the syntax error that is generated when
two methods have the same signature and different return types. Overloaded methods with
different parameter lists can have different return types. Overloaded methods need not have
the same number of parameters.

Common Programming Error 4.14

*Creating overloaded methods with identical parameter lists and different return types is a
syntax error.*

```
1   // Fig. 4.9: InvalidMethodOverload.cs
2   // Demonstrating incorrect method overloading.
3
4   public class InvalidMethodOverload
5   {
6      public int Square( double x )
7      {
8         return x * x;
9      }
10
11     // ERROR! Second Square method takes same number, order
12     // and types of arguments, but has different return type
13     public double Square( double y )
14     {
15        return y * y;
16     }
17  }
```

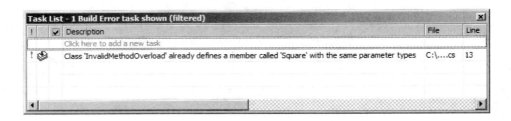

Fig. 4.9   Syntax error generated from overloaded methods with identical parameter lists and different return types.

4.11 Arrays

An array is a group of memory locations that all have the same name and type. A program can refer to any *element* of an array by giving the name of the array followed by the *position number* (a value that indicates a specific location within the array) of the element in square brackets ([ ]). The first element in every array is the *zeroth element*. The position number in square brackets is more formally called a *subscript* (or an *index*). A subscript must be an integer or an integer expression. If a program uses an integer expression as a subscript, the program evaluates the expression first to determine the subscript.

The brackets that enclose the subscript of an array are operators. Brackets have the same level of precedence as parentheses. The chart in Fig. 4.10 shows the precedence and associativity of the operators introduced thus far in the text. They are displayed from top to bottom in decreasing order of precedence, with their associativity and type. The reader should note that the ++ and -- operators in the first row represent the postincrement and postdecrement operators, respectively, while the ++ and -- operators in the second row represent the preincrement and predecrement operators, respectively. Also, notice that, in the first row, the associativity is actually mixed. This is because the associativity of the postincrement and postdecrement operators is from right to left, while the associativity of the other operators is from left to right.

Operators	Associativity	Type
( ) [ ] . ++ --	left to right	highest (unary postfix)
++ -- + - ! (*type*)	right to left	unary (unary prefix)
* / %	left to right	multiplicative
+ -	left to right	additive
< <= > >=	left to right	relational
== !=	left to right	equality
&	left to right	logical AND
^	left to right	logical exclusive OR
|	left to right	logical inclusive OR
&&	left to right	conditional AND
||	left to right	conditional OR
? :	right to left	conditional
= += -= *= /= %=	right to left	assignment

Fig. 4.10   Precedence and associativity of the operators discussed so far.

4.12 Declaring and Allocating Arrays

Arrays occupy space in memory. The programmer specifies the type of the elements and uses operator **new** to allocate dynamically the number of elements required by each array. Arrays are allocated with **new** because arrays are objects, and all objects must be created with **new**. However, we will see an exception to this rule shortly.

The declaration

```
int[] c = new int[ 12 ];
```

allocates 12 elements for integer array **c**. The preceding statement also can be performed in two steps as follows:

```
// declare array reference
int[] c;

// allocate space for array; set reference to that space
c = new int[ 12 ];
```

When arrays are allocated, the elements are initialized to zero for numeric primitive-data-type variables, to **false** for **bool** variables and to **null** for reference types.

 Common Programming Error 4.15

Unlike in C or C++, the number of elements in arrays in C# is never specified in square brackets after the array name. For example, the declaration int c[12]; causes a syntax error. Be sure to use the int[] c = new int[12]; syntax.

A single declaration may be used to reserve memory for several arrays. The following declaration reserves 100 elements for **string** array **b** and 27 elements for **string** array **x**:

```
string[] b = new string[ 100 ], x = new string[ 27 ];
```

Similarly, the following declaration reserves 10 elements for **array1** and 20 elements for **array2** (both of type **double**):

```
double[] array1 = new double[ 10 ],
         array2 = new double[ 20 ];
```

Arrays may be declared to contain any data type. In an array of value types, every element of the array contains one value of the declared type. For example, every element of an **int** array is an **int** value.

In an array of reference types, every element of the array is a reference to an object of the data type of the array. For example, every element of a **string** array is a reference to a **string**; each of the **string** references has the value **null** by default.

The next example demonstrates declaration, allocation, initialization and manipulation of array elements. Figure 4.11 creates three 10-element integer arrays and displays those arrays in tabular format. The program demonstrates several techniques for declaring and initializing arrays.

```
1   // Fig. 4.11: InitArray.cs
2   // Different ways of initializing arrays.
3
4   using System;
5   using System.Windows.Forms;
6
7   class InitArray
8   {
9      // main entry point for application
10     static void Main( string[] args )
11     {
12        string output = "";
13
14        int[] x;              // declare reference to an array
15        x = new int[ 10 ];    // dynamically allocate array and set
16                              // default values
17
18        // initializer list specifies number of elements
19        // and value of each element
20        int[] y = { 32, 27, 64, 18, 95, 14, 90, 70, 60, 37 };
21
22        const int ARRAY_SIZE = 10; // named constant
23        int[] z;                   // reference to int array
24
25        // allocate array of ARRAY_SIZE (i.e., 10) elements
26        z = new int[ ARRAY_SIZE ];
27
28        // set values in array
29        for ( int i = 0; i < z.Length; i++ )
30           z[ i ] = 2 + 2 * i;
31
32        output += "Subscript\tArray x\tArray y\tArray z\n";
33
```

Fig. 4.11   Initializing arrays in three different ways. (Part 1 of 2.)

```
34          // output values for each array
35          for ( int i = 0; i < ARRAY_SIZE; i++ )
36             output += i + "\t" + x[ i ] + "\t" + y[ i ] +
37                "\t" + z[ i ] + "\n";
38
39          MessageBox.Show( output,
40             "Initializing an array of int values",
41             MessageBoxButtons.OK, MessageBoxIcon.Information );
42
43       } // end Main
44
45    } // end class InitArray
```

Fig. 4.11   Initializing arrays in three different ways. (Part 2 of 2.)

Line 14 declares **x** as a reference to an array of integers. The variable **x** is of type
int[], which denotes an array whose elements are of type **int**. Line 15 allocates the 10
elements of the array with **new** and assigns the array to reference **x**. Each element of this
array has the default value **0**.

Line 20 creates another **int** array and initializes each element using an *initializer list*.
In this case, the number of elements in the initializer list determines the array's size. For
example, line 20 creates a 10-element array with the indices **0–9** and the values **32, 27,
64** and so on. Note that this declaration does not require the **new** operator to create the
array object; the compiler allocates memory for the object when it encounters an array declaration that includes an initializer list.

On line 22, we create constant integer **ARRAY_SIZE**, using keyword **const**. A constant must be initialized in the same statement where it is declared and cannot be modified
thereafter. If an attempt is made to modify a **const** variable after it is declared, the compiler issues a syntax error.

Constants also are called *named constants*. They often are used to make a program
more readable and usually are denoted with variable names in all capital letters.

Common Programming Error 4.16

*Assigning a value to a **const** after the variable has been initialized is a compiler error.*

On lines 23 and 26, we create integer array **z** of length **10**, using the **ARRAY_SIZE**
named constant. The **for** structure in lines 29–30 initializes each element in array **z**. The

expression **z.Length;** returns the length of the array. The element values are generated by multiplying each successive value of the loop counter by **2** and adding **2** to the product. After this initialization, array **z** contains the even integers **2, 4, 6, …, 20**. The **for** structure in lines 35–37 uses the values in arrays **x**, **y** and **z** to build an output string, which will be displayed in a **MessageBox**. Zero-based counting (remember, array subscripts start at zero) allows the loop to access every element of the array. The constant **ARRAY_SIZE** in the **for** structure's condition (line 35) is the length of each of the arrays.

4.13 Passing Arrays to Methods

To pass an array argument to a method, specify the name of the array without using brackets. For example, if array **hourlyTemperatures** is declared as

```
int[] hourlyTemperatures = new int[ 24 ];
```

then the method call

```
ModifyArray( hourlyTemperatures );
```

passes array **hourlyTemperatures** to method **ModifyArray**. Every array object "knows" its own size (via the **Length** property), so when we pass an array object into a method, we do not pass the size of the array as an additional argument.

Although entire arrays are passed by reference, individual array elements of primitive data types are passed by value, the same as simple variables. (The objects referred to by individual elements of a non-primitive-type array are passed by reference.) Such simple single pieces of data are sometimes called *scalars* or *scalar quantities*. To pass an array element to a method, use the subscripted name of the array element as an argument in the method call; for example, the zeroth element of array **scores** is passed as **scores[0]**.

For a method to receive an array through a method call, the method's parameter list must specify that an array will be received. For example, the method header for method **ModifyArray** might be written as

```
public void ModifyArray( int[] b )
```

indicating that **ModifyArray** expects to receive an integer array in parameter **b**. Arrays are passed by reference; when the called method uses the array parameter name **b**, it refers to the actual array in the caller.

4.14 Passing Arrays by Value and by Reference

In C#, a variable that stores an object, such as an array, actually stores only a reference to the object. The distinction between reference variables and primitive-data-type variables raises some subtle issues that programmers must understand to create secure, stable programs.

When a program passes an argument by value to a method, the called method receives a copy of that argument's value. Changes to the local copy do not affect the value of the original variable that the program passed to the method. If the argument is of a reference type, the method makes a local copy of the reference itself, not a copy of the actual object to which the reference refers. The local copy of the reference still refers to the original object in the caller's memory. Thus, reference types are always passed by reference, which means that changes to those objects in called methods affect the original objects in memory.

Performance Tip 4.1

Passing arrays and other objects by reference makes sense for performance reasons. If arrays were passed by value, a copy of each element would be passed. For large, frequently passed arrays, this procedure would waste time and would consume considerable amounts of memory in storing the copies of the arrays, causing poor performance.

C# also allows methods to pass references with keyword **ref**. This capability is subtle and, if misused, can lead to problems. For instance, when a reference-type object like an array is passed with **ref**, the called method actually gains control over the passed reference itself, allowing the called method to replace the original reference in the caller with a different object or even with **null**. Such behavior can lead to unpredictable effects, which can be disastrous in business-critical and mission-critical applications. The program in Fig. 4.12 demonstrates the subtle difference between passing a reference by value and passing a reference with keyword **ref**.

```
1   // Fig. 4.12: ArrayReferenceTest.cs
2   // Testing the effects of passing array references
3   // by value and by reference.
4
5   using System;
6   using System.Drawing;
7   using System.Collections;
8   using System.ComponentModel;
9   using System.Windows.Forms;
10  using System.Data;
11
12  public class ArrayReferenceTest : System.Windows.Forms.Form
13  {
14      private System.Windows.Forms.Label outputLabel;
15      private System.Windows.Forms.Button showOutputButton;
16
17      [STAThread]
18      static void Main()
19      {
20          Application.Run( new ArrayReferenceTest() );
21      }
22
23      private void showOutputButton_Click(
24          object sender, System.EventArgs e )
25      {
26          // create and initialize firstArray
27          int[] firstArray = { 1, 2, 3 };
28
29          // copy firstArray reference (but not array itself)
30          int[] firstArrayCopy = firstArray;
31
32          outputLabel.Text =
33              "Test passing firstArray reference by value";
```

Fig. 4.12   Passing an array reference by value and by reference. (Part 1 of 3.)

```
34
35       outputLabel.Text += "\n\nContents of firstArray " +
36          "before calling FirstDouble:\n\t";
37
38       // print contents of firstArray
39       for ( int i = 0; i < firstArray.Length; i++ )
40          outputLabel.Text += firstArray[ i ] + " ";
41
42       // pass reference firstArray by value to FirstDouble
43       FirstDouble( firstArray );
44
45       outputLabel.Text += "\n\nContents of firstArray after " +
46          "calling FirstDouble\n\t";
47
48       // print contents of firstArray
49       for ( int i = 0; i < firstArray.Length; i++ )
50          outputLabel.Text += firstArray[ i ] + " ";
51
52       // test whether reference was changed by FirstDouble
53       if ( firstArray == firstArrayCopy )
54          outputLabel.Text +=
55             "\n\nThe references refer to the same array\n";
56       else
57          outputLabel.Text +=
58             "\n\nThe references refer to different arrays\n";
59
60       // create and initialize secondArray
61       int[] secondArray = { 1, 2, 3 };
62
63       // copy secondArray reference
64       int[] secondArrayCopy = secondArray;
65
66       outputLabel.Text += "\nTest passing secondArray " +
67          "reference by reference";
68
69       outputLabel.Text += "\n\nContents of secondArray " +
70          "before calling SecondDouble:\n\t";
71
72       // print contents of secondArray before method call
73       for ( int i = 0; i < secondArray.Length; i++ )
74          outputLabel.Text += secondArray[ i ] + " ";
75
76       SecondDouble( ref secondArray );
77
78       outputLabel.Text += "\n\nContents of secondArray " +
79          "after calling SecondDouble:\n\t";
80
81       // print contents of secondArray after method call
82       for ( int i = 0; i < secondArray.Length; i++ )
83          outputLabel.Text += secondArray[ i ] + " ";
84
```

Fig. 4.12   Passing an array reference by value and by reference. (Part 2 of 3.)

```
85          // test whether reference was changed by SecondDouble
86          if ( secondArray == secondArrayCopy )
87             outputLabel.Text +=
88                "\n\nThe references refer to the same array\n";
89          else
90             outputLabel.Text +=
91                "\n\nThe references refer to different arrays\n";
92
93       } // end method showOutputButton_Click
94
95       // modify elements of array and attempt to modify
96       // reference
97       void FirstDouble( int[] array )
98       {
99          // double each element's value
100         for ( int i = 0; i < array.Length; i++ )
101            array[ i ] *= 2;
102
103         // create new reference and assign it to array
104         array = new int[] { 11, 12, 13 };
105      }
106
107      // modify elements of array and change reference array
108      // to refer to new array
109      void SecondDouble( ref int[] array )
110      {
111         // double each element's value
112         for ( int i = 0; i < array.Length; i++ )
113            array[ i ] *= 2;
114
115         // create new reference and assign it to array
116         array = new int[] { 11, 12, 13 };
117      }
118
119 } // end class ArrayReferenceTest
```

Fig. 4.12   Passing an array reference by value and by reference. (Part 3 of 3.)

Lines 27 and 30 declare two integer array variables, **firstArray** and **firstArrayCopy** (we make the copy so that we can determine whether reference **firstArray** gets overwritten). Line 27 initializes **firstArray** with the values **1**, **2** and **3**. The assignment statement on line 30 copies reference **firstArray** to variable **firstArrayCopy**, causing these variables to reference the same array object in memory. The **for** structure on lines 39–40 prints the contents of **firstArray** before it is passed to method **FirstDouble** (line 43) so we can verify that this array is passed by reference (i.e., the called method indeed changes the array's contents).

The **for** structure in method **FirstDouble** (lines 100–101) multiplies the values of all the elements in the array by **2**. Line 104 allocates a new array containing the values **11**, **12** and **13**; the reference for this array then is assigned to parameter **array** (in an attempt to overwrite reference **firstArray**—this, of course, will not happen, because the reference itself was passed by value). After method **FirstDouble** executes, the **for** structure on lines 49–50 prints the contents of **firstArray**, demonstrating that the values of the elements have been changed by the method (and confirming that, in C#, arrays are always passed by reference). The **if/else** structure on lines 53–58 compares references **firstArray** (which we just attempted to overwrite) and **firstArrayCopy**. The expression on line 53 evaluates to **true** if the operands to binary operator **==** indeed reference the same object. In this case, the object represented is the array allocated in line 27—not the array allocated in method **FirstDouble** (line 104).

Lines 61–91 perform similar tests, using array variables **secondArray** and **secondArrayCopy** and method **SecondDouble** (lines 109–117). Method **SecondDouble** performs the same operations as **FirstDouble**, but receives its array argument via keyword **ref**. In this case, the reference stored in **secondArray** after the method call is a reference to the array allocated on line 116 of **SecondDouble**, demonstrating that a reference passed with keyword **ref** can be modified by the called method so that the reference in the caller actually points to a different object—in this case, an array allocated in method **SecondDouble**. The **if/else** structure in lines 86–91 demonstrates that **secondArray** and **secondArrayCopy** no longer refer to the same array.

Software Engineering Observation 4.6

*When a method receives a reference-type object parameter by value, the object itself is not passed by value—the object is still passed by reference. Rather, the object's reference is passed by value. This arrangement prevents a method from overwriting references passed to it. In the vast majority of cases, protecting the caller's reference from modification is the desired behavior. In the rare situations where you truly want the called method to modify the caller's reference, pass the reference via keyword **ref**.*

Software Engineering Observation 4.7

In C#, reference-type objects (including arrays) are always passed by reference. So, a called method receiving a reference to an object in a caller can change the caller's object.

4.15 Multiple-Subscripted Arrays

So far we have studied *single-subscripted* (or *one-dimensional*) arrays—i.e., arrays that contain single lists of values. In this section, we introduce *multiple-subscripted* (often called *multidimensional*) arrays. Such arrays require two or more subscripts to identify particular elements. There are two types of multiple-subscripted arrays—*rectangular* and *jagged*. Rectangular arrays often represent *tables* of values, while jagged arrays store arrays of arrays.

Arrays that require two subscripts to identify a particular element commonly are called *double-subscripted arrays*. In this section, we concentrate on double-subscripted arrays (often called *two-dimensional arrays*). Rectangular arrays with two subscripts often represent tables of values consisting of information arranged in *rows* and *columns*, where each row is the same size and each column is the same size. An array with *m* rows and *n* columns is called an *m-by-n array*. To identify a particular table element, we must specify the two subscripts; by convention, the first subscript identifies the element's row, and the second subscript identifies the element's column. Figure 4.13 illustrates a double-subscripted rectangular array **a** that contains three rows and four columns (i.e., a three-by-four array).

Every element in array **a** is identified in Fig. 4.13 by an element name of the form **a[i , j]**, in which **a** is the name of the array and **i** and **j** are the subscripts that uniquely identify the row and column, respectively, of each element in **a**. Notice that the names of the elements in the first row all have a first subscript of **0**; the names of the elements in the fourth column all have a second subscript of **3**.

Multiple-subscripted arrays can be initialized in declarations in the same way as are single-subscripted arrays. A double-subscripted array **b** with two rows and two columns could be declared and initialized with

```
int[,] b = new int[ 2, 2 ];

b[ 0, 0 ] = 1;
b[ 0, 1 ] = 2;
b[ 1, 0 ] = 3;
b[ 1, 1 ] = 4;
```

or the declaration can be written on one line, using an *initializer list*, as follows:

```
int[,] b = { { 1, 2 }, { 3, 4 } };
```

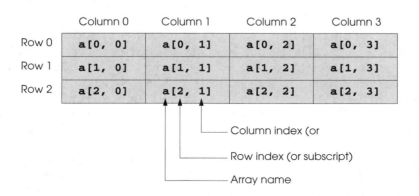

Fig. 4.13   Double-subscripted rectangular array with three rows and four columns.

The values are grouped by row in braces. Thus, **1** and **2** initialize **b[0 , 0]** and **b[0 , 1]**, respectively, and **3** and **4** initialize **b[1 , 0]** and **b[1 , 1]**, respectively. The compiler determines the number of rows by counting the number of subinitializer lists (represented by sets of braces) in the main initializer list. The compiler determines the number of columns in each row by counting the number of initializer values in the subinitializer list for that row. Method **GetLength** returns the length of a particular array dimension. In the preceding example, **b.GetLength(0)** returns the length of the zeroth dimension of **b**, or row zero.

We now demonstrate the creation of jagged arrays. Recall that jagged arrays are maintained as arrays of arrays. Unlike with rectangular arrays, the arrays that compose jagged arrays can be of different lengths. The declaration

```
int[][] c = new int[ 2 ][];  // allocate 2 rows

// allocate and initialize array for row 0
c[ 0 ] = new int[] { 1, 2, 3 };
// allocate and initialize array for row 1
c[ 1 ] = new int[] { 3, 4, 5 };
```

creates integer array **c** with row **0** (which is an array itself) containing three elements (**1**, **2** and **3**), and row **1** (another array) containing three elements (**3**, **4** and **5**). Each element of array **c** is an array itself, so jagged arrays can use property **Length** to determine the length of each subarray, without the need for method **GetLength**. For the jagged array **c**, the size of the zeroth subarray is **c[0].Length**, or **3**. To determine the number of subarray in a jagged array, we can use the **Length** property with the jagged array itself, as in **c.Length** (which would evaluate to **2** in this example).

The application in Fig. 4.14 demonstrates the initialization of double-subscripted arrays in declarations and the use of nested **for** loops to traverse the arrays (i.e., to manipulate each array element).

The declaration of **array1** (line 28) provides six initializers in two sublists. The first sublist initializes the first row of the array to the values **1**, **2** and **3**. The second sublist initializes the second row of the array to the values **4**, **5** and **6**. The declaration of **array2** (line 31) creates a jagged array of three arrays (specified by the **3** in the square brackets). Lines 32–34 initialize each subarray so that the first subarray contains the values **1** and **2**, the second contains the value **3** and the third contains the values **4**, **5** and **6**.

The **for** structure on lines 39–45 appends the elements of **array1** to **string output**. Note the use of nested **for** structures to output the rows of each double-subscripted array. In the nested **for** structures for **array1**, we use method **GetLength** to determine the number of elements in each dimension of the array. Line 39 determines the number of rows in the array by invoking **array1.GetLength(0)**, and line 41 determines the number of columns in the array by invoking **array1.GetLength(1)**. Arrays with additional dimensions would require more deeply nested **for** structures to process.

The nested **for** structures on lines 50–56 output the elements of jagged array **array2**. Recall that a jagged array is essentially an array that contains additional arrays as its elements. Line 50 uses the **Length** property of **array2** to determine the number of rows in the jagged array. Line 52 determines the **Length** of each subarray (i.e., row) with the expression **array2[i].Length**.

```
1    // Fig. 4.14: TwoDimensionalArrays.cs
2    // Initializing two-dimensional arrays.
3
4    using System;
5    using System.Drawing;
6    using System.Collections;
7    using System.ComponentModel;
8    using System.Windows.Forms;
9    using System.Data;
10
11   public class TwoDimensionalArrays : System.Windows.Forms.Form
12   {
13      private System.Windows.Forms.Button showOutputButton;
14      private System.Windows.Forms.Label outputLabel;
15
16      // Visual Studio .NET generated code
17
18      [STAThread]
19      static void Main()
20      {
21         Application.Run( new TwoDimensionalArrays() );
22      }
23
24      private void showOutputButton_Click(
25         object sender, System.EventArgs e )
26      {
27         // declaration and initialization of rectangular array
28         int[,] array1 = new int[,] { { 1, 2, 3 }, { 4, 5, 6 } };
29
30         // declaration and initialization of jagged array
31         int[][] array2 = new int[ 3 ][];
32         array2[ 0 ] = new int[] { 1, 2 };
33         array2[ 1 ] = new int[] { 3 };
34         array2[ 2 ] = new int[] { 4, 5, 6 };
35
36         outputLabel.Text = "Values in array1 by row are\n";
37
38         // output values in array1
39         for ( int i = 0; i < array1.GetLength( 0 ); i++ )
40         {
41            for ( int j = 0; j < array1.GetLength( 1 ); j++ )
42               outputLabel.Text += array1[ i, j ] + "   ";
43
44            outputLabel.Text += "\n";
45         }
46
47         outputLabel.Text += "\nValues in array2 by row are\n";
48
49         // output values in array2
50         for ( int i = 0; i < array2.Length; i++ )
51         {
52            for ( int j = 0; j < array2[ i ].Length; j++ )
53               outputLabel.Text += array2[ i ][ j ] + "   ";
```

Fig. 4.14 Initializing multidimensional arrays. (Part 1 of 2.)

```
54
55              outputLabel.Text += "\n";
56         }
57
58    } // end method showOutputButton_Click
59
60 } // end class TwoDimensionalArrays
```

Fig. 4.14   Initializing multidimensional arrays. (Part 2 of 2.)

Many common array manipulations use **for** repetition structures. For the remainder of this section, we will focus on manipulations of jagged arrays. Imagine a jagged array **a** that contains three rows, or arrays. The following **for** structure sets all the elements in the third row of array **a** to **0**:

```
for ( int col = 0; col < a[ 2 ].Length; col++ )
   a[ 2 ][ col ] = 0;
```

We specified the *third* row; therefore, we know that the first subscript is always **2**. (**0** is the first row and **1** is the second row.) The **for** loop varies only the second subscript (i.e., the column subscript). Notice the use of **a[2].Length** in the **for** structure's conditional expression. Each row of **a** is an array itself, and therefore the program can access a typical array's properties, including **Length**. This ability was demonstrated on line 52 of Fig. 4.14. Assuming that the length of array **a[2]** is **4**, the preceding **for** structure is equivalent to the assignment statements

```
a[ 2 ][ 0 ] = 0;
a[ 2 ][ 1 ] = 0;
a[ 2 ][ 2 ] = 0;
a[ 2 ][ 3 ] = 0;
```

The following nested **for** structures determine the total of all the elements in array **a**:

```
int total = 0;

for ( int row = 0; row < a.Length; row++ )

   for ( int col = 0; col < a[ row ].Length; col++ )
      total += a[ row ][ col ];
```

We use **a.Length** in the conditional expression of the outer **for** structure to determine the number of rows in **a**—in this case, three. The **for** structures total the elements of the array one row at a time. The outer **for** structure begins by setting the **row** subscript to **0**, so that the elements of the first row may be totaled by the inner **for** structure. Then the outer **for** structure increments **row** to **1**, so that the second row can be totaled. Finally, the outer **for** structure increments **row** to **2**, so that the third row can be totaled. The result can be displayed when the nested **for** structures terminate.

4.16 `foreach` Repetition Structure

C# provides the **foreach** repetition structure for iterating through values in data structures, such as arrays. When used with one-dimensional arrays, **foreach** behaves like a **for** structure that iterates through the range of indices from **0** to one less than the array's **Length**. Instead of using the array name subscripted by a counter, **foreach** uses a variable to represent the value of each element. The program in Fig. 4.15 uses the **foreach** structure to determine the minimum value in a two-dimensional array of grades.

The header of the **foreach** structure (line 16) specifies a variable, **grade**, and an array, **gradeArray**. The **foreach** structure iterates through all elements in **grade-Array**, sequentially assigning each value to variable **grade**. Line 18 compares each value with variable **lowGrade**, and if a particular value is less than **lowGrade**, line 19 replaces **lowGrade** with that value.

```
1   // Fig. 4.15: UsingForeach.cs
2   // Demonstrating the foreach structure.
3
4   using System;
5
6   class UsingForeach
7   {
8      // main entry point for application
9      static void Main( string[] args )
10     {
11        int[,] gradeArray = { { 77, 68, 86, 73 },
12           { 98, 87, 89, 81 }, { 70, 90, 86, 81 } };
13
14        int lowGrade = 100;
15
16        foreach ( int grade in gradeArray )
17        {
18           if ( grade < lowGrade )
19              lowGrade = grade;
20        }
21
22        Console.WriteLine( "The minimum grade is: " + lowGrade );
23     }
24  }
```

```
The minimum grade is: 68
```

Fig. 4.15 Using the **foreach** structure with an array.

For rectangular arrays, the repetition of the **foreach** structure begins with the element whose indices are all zero and iterates through all possible combinations of indices, incrementing the rightmost index first. When the rightmost index reaches its upper bound, it is reset to zero, and the index to the left of it is incremented by one. In this case, **grade** takes on the values as they are ordered in the initializer list in lines 11–12. When all the grades have been processed, **lowGrade** is displayed (line 22).

Although many array calculations are handled best with a counter, the **foreach** structure is useful when the indices of the elements are not important. The **foreach** structure is useful for looping through arrays of objects, as we discuss in Chapter 7, Object-Oriented Programming: Polymorphism.

4.17 Summary

The best way to develop and maintain a large program is to construct it from reusable pieces, such as methods and classes. This technique is called divide and conquer. Programs are written by combining new methods and classes that the programmer writes with prepackaged methods and classes in the .NET Framework Class Library (FCL) and in various other class libraries. The FCL provides a rich collection of classes and methods for performing common mathematical calculations, string manipulations, character manipulations, input/output, error checking and other useful operations. The programmer can write methods to define specific tasks that may be used at many points in a program. These methods are referred to as programmer-defined methods. The general format of a method definition enables the programmer to specify return types and parameter lists.

The scope of a variable is the portion of a program where that variable can be referenced. An identifier's duration (its lifetime) is the period during which the identifier exists in memory.

Recursion is a powerful problem-solving technique wherein methods can call themselves to solve a problem. With method overloading, several methods in a class can be defined with the same name, as long as they have different sets of parameters.

Arrays are groups of memory locations that all have the same name and type. Arrays group lists of logically related data together. Each piece of data, or element, can be accessed using a subscript, a numeric value placed within square brackets after the name of the array. The number in square brackets determines which element in the array is accessed.

C# also allows the creation of multidimensional arrays, or arrays that contain two or more subscripts. There are two types of such multiple-subscripted arrays—rectangular and jagged. Rectangular arrays with two subscripts often represent tables of values consisting of information arranged in rows and columns, where each row is the same size and each column is the same size. Jagged arrays are maintained as arrays of arrays. Unlike with rectangular arrays, rows in jagged arrays can be of different lengths.

C# provides one final repetition structure—the **foreach** structure. This structure is similar to the **for** structure, but provides a more natural way of iterating through arrays and other array-like structures that are discussed in later chapters.

Object-Based
Programming

Objectives

- To understand encapsulation and data hiding.
- To understand the concepts of data abstraction and abstract data types (ADTs).
- To create, use and destroy objects.
- To control access to object instance variables and methods.
- To use properties to keep objects in consistent states.
- To understand the use of the **this** reference.
- To understand namespaces and assemblies.
- To use the **Class View** and **Object Browser**.

My object all sublime
I shall achieve in time.
W. S. Gilbert

Is it a world to hide virtues in?
William Shakespeare

Your public servants serve you right.
Adlai Stevenson

Classes struggle, some classes triumph, others are eliminated.
Mao Zedong

This above all: to thine own self be true.
William Shakespeare

Outline

5.1   Introduction
5.2   Implementing a Time Abstract Data Type with a Class
5.3   Class Scope
5.4   Controlling Access to Members
5.5   Initializing Class Objects: Constructors
5.6   Using Overloaded Constructors
5.7   Properties
5.8   Composition: Objects References as Instance Variables of Other Classes
5.9   Using the `this` Reference
5.10   Garbage Collection
5.11   `static` Class Members
5.12   `const` and `readonly` Members
5.13   Indexers
5.14   Data Abstraction and Information Hiding
5.15   Software Reusability
5.16   Namespaces and Assemblies
5.17   Class View and Object Browser
5.18   Summary

5.1 Introduction

In this chapter, we investigate object orientation in C#. Some readers might ask, why have we deferred this topic until now? There are several reasons. First, the objects we build in this chapter are composed partially of structured program pieces. In order to explain the organization of objects, we needed to establish a basis in structured programming with control structures. We also wanted to discuss methods in detail before introducing object orientation. Finally, we wanted to familiarize readers with arrays, which are C# objects.

In our discussions of object-oriented programs in Chapters 1–4, we introduced many basic concepts (i.e., "object think") and terminology (i.e., "object speak") that relate to C# object-oriented programming. We also discussed our program-development methodology. We analyzed typical problems that required programs to be built and determined what classes from the .NET Framework Class Library were needed to implement each program. We then selected appropriate instance variables and methods for each program and specified the manner in which an object of our class collaborated with objects from the .NET Framework classes to accomplish the program's overall goals.

Let us briefly review some key concepts and terminology of object orientation. Object orientation uses classes to *encapsulate* (i.e., wrap together) data (*attributes*) and methods (*behaviors*). Objects have the ability to hide their implementation from other objects (this principle is called *information hiding*). Although some objects can communicate with one another across well-defined *interfaces* (just as the driver's interface to a car includes a steering wheel, accelerator pedal, brake pedal and gear shift), objects are unaware of how other objects are implemented (just as the driver is unaware of how the steering, engine, brake and transmission mechanisms are implemented). Normally, implementation details are hidden within the objects themselves. Surely, it is possible to drive a car effectively without knowing the details of how engines, transmissions and exhaust systems work. Later, we will see why information hiding is so crucial to good software engineering.

In *procedural programming languages,* like C, programming tends to be *action oriented.* C# programming, however, is *object oriented.* In C, the unit of programming is the *function* (functions are called *methods* in C#). In C#, the unit of programming is the *class.* Objects eventually are *instantiated* (i.e., created) from these classes, and functions are encapsulated within the "boundaries" of classes as methods.

C programmers concentrate on writing functions. They group actions that perform some task into a function; they then group functions to form a program. Data are certainly important in C, but they exist primarily to support the actions that functions perform. The *verbs* in a system-requirements document describing the requirements for a new application help a C programmer determine the set of functions that will work together to implement the system.

By contrast, C# programmers concentrate on creating their own *user-defined types,* called *classes.* We also refer to classes as *programmer-defined types.* Each class contains both data and a set of methods that manipulate the data. The data components, or *data members,* of a class are called *member variables,* or *instance variables* (many C# programmers prefer the term *fields*).[1] Just as we call an instance of a built-in type—such as **int**—a *variable,* we call an instance of a user-defined type (i.e., a class) an *object.* In C#, attention is focused on classes, rather than on methods. The *nouns* in a system-requirements document help the C# programmer determine an initial set of classes with which to begin the design process. Programmers use these classes to instantiate objects that work together to implement the system.

This chapter explains how to create and use classes and objects, a subject known as *object-based programming* (*OBP*). Chapters 6 and 7 introduce *inheritance* and *polymorphism*—key technologies that enable *object-oriented programming* (*OOP*). Although we do not discuss inheritance in detail until Chapter 6, it is part of several class definitions in this chapter and has been used in several examples previously. For example, in the program discussed in Section 3.14 (and in several subsequent programs), we inherited a class from **System.Windows.Forms.Form** to create an application that executes in its own window.

Software Engineering Observation 5.1

All C# objects are passed by reference.

5.2 Implementing a Time Abstract Data Type with a Class

Classes in C# facilitate the creation of *abstract data types* (*ADT*), which hide their implementation from clients (or users of the class object). A problem in procedural programming

---

1. We sometimes use industry-standard terminology, such as *data members* and *instance members,* rather than C# terms such as *fields.* For a listing of C#-specific terminology, please see the C# Language Specification, which can be downloaded from **msdn.microsoft.com/vstudio/ nextgen/technology/csharpdownload.asp**.

languages is that client code often is dependent on implementation details of the data used in the code. This dependency might necessitate rewriting the client code if the data implementation changes. ADTs eliminate this problem by providing implementation-independent *interfaces* to their clients. With such interfaces, the creator of a class can change the internal implementation of that class without affecting the class's clients.

Software Engineering Observation 5.2

It is important to write programs that are understandable and easy to maintain. Change is the rule, rather than the exception: Programmers should anticipate that their code will be modified. As we will see, classes facilitate program modifiability.

The first example in this chapter (and subsequent examples) will require multiple class definitions in the same project. To add a class to a project, select **Add Class...** from the **Project** menu. In the **Add New Item** dialog box that appears, enter the new class name in the **Name** text box, and click the **Open** button. Note that the file name (ending with the `.cs` file extension) appears in the **Solution Explorer** below the project name.

Our first example consists of classes **Time1** (Fig. 5.1) and **TimeTest1** (Fig. 5.2). Class **Time1** contains the time of day in 24-hour clock format. Class **TimeTest1** contains method **Main**, which creates an instance of class **Time1** and demonstrates the features of that class.

```
1    // Fig. 5.1: Time1.cs
2    // Class Time1 maintains time in 24-hour format.
3
4    using System;
5
6    // Time1 class definition
7    public class Time1 : Object
8    {
9       private int hour;      // 0-23
10      private int minute;    // 0-59
11      private int second;    // 0-59
12
13      // Time1 constructor initializes instance variables to
14      // zero to set default time to midnight
15      public Time1()
16      {
17         SetTime( 0, 0, 0 );
18      }
19
20      // Set new time value in 24-hour format. Perform validity
21      // checks on the data. Set invalid values to zero.
22      public void SetTime(
23         int hourValue, int minuteValue, int secondValue )
24      {
25         hour = ( hourValue >= 0 && hourValue < 24 ) ?
26            hourValue : 0;
27         minute = ( minuteValue >= 0 && minuteValue < 60 ) ?
28            minuteValue : 0;
```

Fig. 5.1   **Time1** abstract data type represents the time in 24-hour format. (Part 1 of 2.)

```
29          second = ( secondValue >= 0 && secondValue < 60 ) ?
30             secondValue : 0;
31
32       } // end method SetTime
33
34       // convert time to universal-time (24 hour) format string
35       public string ToUniversalString()
36       {
37          return String.Format(
38             "{0:D2}:{1:D2}:{2:D2}", hour, minute, second );
39       }
40
41       // convert time to standard-time (12 hour) format string
42       public string ToStandardString()
43       {
44          return String.Format( "{0}:{1:D2}:{2:D2} {3}",
45             ( ( hour == 12 || hour == 0 ) ? 12 : hour % 12 ),
46             minute, second, ( hour < 12 ? "AM" : "PM" ) );
47       }
48
49    } // end class Time1
```

Fig. 5.1 **Time1** abstract data type represents the time in 24-hour format. (Part 2 of 2.)

In Fig. 5.1, line 7 begins the **Time1** class definition, indicating that class **Time1** inherits from class *Object* (of namespace **System**). C# programmers use *inheritance* to create classes from existing classes. In fact, every class in C# (except **Object**) inherits from an existing class definition. On line 7, the **:** followed by class name **Object** indicates that class **Time1** inherits existing pieces of class **Object**. If a new class definition does not specify a **:** and class name to the right of the new class name, the new class implicitly inherits from class **Object**. It is not necessary to understand inheritance to learn the concepts and understand the programs presented in this chapter. We explore inheritance and class **Object** in detail in Chapter 6.

The opening left brace (**{**) on line 8 and closing right brace (**}**) on line 49 delimit the *body* of class **Time1**. Any information that we place in this body is said to be *encapsulated* (i.e., wrapped) in the class. For example, lines 9–11 of class **Time1** declare three **int** variables—**hour**, **minute** and **second**—that represent the time of day in *universal-time format* (*24-hour clock format*). Variables declared in a class definition, but not inside a method definition, are called *instance variables*; each instance (object) of the class contains its own separate copy of the class's instance variables.

Keywords *public* and *private* are *member access modifiers*. In this example, instance variables or methods with member access modifier **public** are accessible wherever the program has a reference to a **Time1** object. However, instance variables or methods declared with member access modifier **private** are accessible only in that class definition. A class's **public** members and **private** members can be intermixed.

Good Programming Practice 5.1

*Every instance variable or method definition should be preceded by a member access modifier. The default access modifier for class members is **private**.*

Lines 9–11 declare each of the three **int** instance variables—**hour**, **minute** and **second**—with member access modifier **private**, indicating that these instance variables of the class are accessible only to members of the class; this practice is known as *data hiding*. When an object of the class encapsulates such instance variables, only methods of that object's class can access the variables. Normally, instance variables are declared as **private** and methods are declared as **public**. However, it is possible to have **private** methods and **public** instance variables, as we will see later. Often, **private** methods are called *utility methods*, or *helper methods*, because they can be called only by other methods of the **private** method's class. The purpose of utility methods is to support the operation of a class's other methods. Using **public** data in a class is an uncommon and dangerous programming practice. Providing such access to data members is unsafe: Foreign code (i.e., code in other classes) could set **public** data members to invalid values, producing potentially disastrous results.

Good Programming Practice 5.2

We prefer to list instance variables of a class first, so that, when reading the code, programmers see the name and type of each instance variable before it is used in the methods of the class.

Good Programming Practice 5.3

*Even though **private** and **public** members can be intermixed, list all the **private** members of a class first in one group; then list all the **public** members in another group.*

Software Engineering Observation 5.3

*Declare all instance variables of a class as **private**. The architecture of accessing **private** data through **public** properties that first validate the data allows the developer to ensure that an object's data remain in a consistent state.*

Software Engineering Observation 5.4

*Make a class member **private** if there is no reason for that member to be accessed directly outside of the class definition.*

Classes often include *access methods* that can read or display data. Another common use for access methods is to test the truth of conditions; when used in this manner, such methods often are called *predicate methods*. For example, we could design predicate method **IsEmpty** for a *container class*—a class capable of holding many objects, such as a linked list, a stack or a queue. (These data structures are discussed in detail in Chapter 20, Data Structures and Collections.) **IsEmpty** would return **true** if the container is empty and **false** otherwise. A program might test **IsEmpty** before attempting to read another item from the container object. Similarly, a program might test another predicate method (e.g., **IsFull**) before attempting to insert an item into a container object.

Class **Time1** contains constructor **Time1** (lines 15–18) and methods **SetTime** (lines 22–32), **ToUniversalString** (lines 35–39) and **ToStandardString** (lines 42–47). These methods are the ***public** methods* (also called the ***public** services* or the ***public** interface*) of the class. *Clients* of class **Time1**, such as class **TimeTest1** (Fig. 5.2), use **Time1**'s **public** methods to manipulate the data stored in **Time1** objects or to cause class **Time1** to perform some service.

Lines 15–18 define the *constructor* of class **Time1**. A class's constructor initializes objects of that class. When a program creates an object of class **Time1** with operator **new**, the constructor is called to initialize the object. Class **Time1**'s constructor calls method

SetTime (lines 22–32) to initialize instance variables **hour, minute** and **second** to **0** (representing midnight). Constructors can take arguments, but cannot return values. As we will see, a class can have overloaded constructors. An important difference between constructors and other methods is that constructors cannot specify a return type. Generally, constructors are declared as **public**. Note that the constructor name must be the same as the class name.

Common Programming Error 5.1

Attempting to **return** *a value from a constructor is a syntax error.*

Method **SetTime** (lines 22–32) is a **public** method that receives three **int** parameters and uses them to set the time. A conditional expression tests each argument to determine whether the value is in a specified range. For example, the **hour** value must be greater than or equal to 0 and less than 24, because universal-time format represents hours as integers from 0 to 23. Similarly, both the **minute** and **second** values must be greater than or equal to 0 and less than 60. Any values outside these ranges are invalid values and cause the parameters to be set to zero by default. Setting invalid values to zero ensures that a **Time1** object always contains valid data (because, in this example, zero is a valid value for **hour, minute** and **second**). When users supply invalid data to **SetTime**, the program might want to indicate that the given time was invalid. In Chapter 8, we discuss exception handling, which can be used to indicate invalid initialization values.

Software Engineering Observation 5.5

Always define a class so that each of its instance variables always contains valid values.

Method **ToUniversalString** (lines 35–39) takes no arguments and returns a **string** in universal-time format, consisting of six digits—two for the hour, two for the minute and two for the second. For example, if the time were 1:30:07 PM, method **ToUniversalString** would return **13:30:07**. Lines 37–38 use **String** method **Format** to configure the universal time string. Line 37 passes to **Format** the *format string* **"{0:D2}:{1:D2}:{2:D2}"**, which contains several *format specifications* indicating that arguments **0, 1** and **2** (the first three arguments after the format-string argument) should each have the format **D2** (a two-digit, base-10, decimal-number format) for display purposes. The **D2** format specification causes single-digit values to appear as two digits with a leading **0** (e.g., **8** would be represented as **08**). The two colons that separate the curly braces **}** and **{** are the colons that separate the hour from the minute and the minute from the second in the resulting **string**.

Method **ToStandardString** (lines 42–47) takes no arguments and returns a **string** in standard-time format, consisting of the **hour, minute** and **second** values separated by colons and followed by an AM or a PM indicator (e.g., **1:27:06 PM**). Like method **ToUniversalString**, method **ToStandardString** uses **String** method **Format** to format the **minute** and **second** parameters as two-digit values with leading zeros if necessary. Line 45 determines the value for **hour** in the **string**: If the **hour** is **0** or **12** (AM or PM), it appears as **12**; otherwise, it appears as a value from **1–11**.

After defining the class, we can use it as a type in declarations such as

```
Time1 sunset;   // reference to a Time1 object
```

The class name (**Time1**) is a type name. A class can yield many objects, just as a primitive data type, such as **int**, can yield many variables. Programmers can create class types as needed; this capability is one reason that C# is known as an *extensible language*.

Class **TimeTest1** (Fig. 5.2) uses an instance of class **Time1**. Method **Main** (lines 11–40) declares and initializes **Time1** instance **time** (line 13). When the object is instantiated, *operator **new*** allocates the memory in which the **Time1** object will be stored; it then calls the **Time1** constructor (lines 15–18 of Fig. 5.1) to initialize the instance variables of the **Time1** object. As mentioned before, this constructor invokes method **SetTime** of class **Time1** to initialize each **private** instance variable to **0**. Operator **new** (line 13 of Fig. 5.2) then returns a reference to the newly created object; this reference is assigned to **time**.

Software Engineering Observation 5.6

*Note the relationship between operator **new** and the constructor of a class. When operator **new** creates an object of a class, that class's constructor is called to initialize the object's instance variables.*

```
1    // Fig. 5.2: TimeTest1.cs
2    // Demonstrating class Time1.
3
4    using System;
5    using System.Windows.Forms;
6
7    // TimeTest1 creates and uses a Time1 object
8    class TimeTest1
9    {
10       // main entry point for application
11       static void Main( string[] args )
12       {
13          Time1 time = new Time1();   // calls Time1 constructor
14          string output;
15
16          // assign string representation of time to output
17          output = "Initial universal time is: " +
18             time.ToUniversalString() +
19             "\nInitial standard time is: " +
20             time.ToStandardString();
21
22          // attempt valid time settings
23          time.SetTime( 13, 27, 6 );
24
25          // append new string representations of time to output
26          output += "\n\nUniversal time after SetTime is: " +
27             time.ToUniversalString() +
28             "\nStandard time after SetTime is: " +
29             time.ToStandardString();
30
31          // attempt invalid time settings
32          time.SetTime( 99, 99, 99 );
33
```

Fig. 5.2   Using an abstract data type. (Part 1 of 2.)

```
34              output += "\n\nAfter attempting invalid settings: " +
35                  "\nUniversal time: " + time.ToUniversalString() +
36                  "\nStandard time: " + time.ToStandardString();
37
38          MessageBox.Show( output, "Testing Class Time1" );
39
40      } // end method Main
41
42  } // end class TimeTest1
```

Fig. 5.2   Using an abstract data type. (Part 2 of 2.)

Note that the **TimeTest1.cs** file does not use keyword **using** to import the namespace that contains class **Time1**. If a class is in the same namespace as the class that uses it, the **using** statement is not required. Every class in C# is part of a namespace. If a programmer does not specify a namespace for a class, the class is placed in the *default namespace*, which includes all compiled classes in the current directory that do not reside in a namespace. In Visual Studio.NET, the current directory is the directory in which the current project resides. We must specify **using** statements for classes from the .NET Framework, because they are defined outside the namespace of each new application we create. Note that **using** statements are not required if the program fully qualifies the name of each class by preceding the class name with its namespace name and a dot operator. For example, a program can invoke class **MessageBox**'s **Show** method as follows:

System.Windows.Forms.MessageBox.Show("Your message here");

However, such lengthy names can be cumbersome.

Line 14 declares **string** reference **output** to store the **string** containing the results, which later will be displayed in a **MessageBox**. Lines 17–20 assign to **output** the time in universal-time format (by invoking method **ToUniversalString** of the **Time1** object) and standard-time format (by invoking method **ToStandardString** of the **Time1** object). Note the syntax of the method call in each case—the reference **time** is followed by the member access operator (**.**), followed by the method name. The reference name specifies the object that will receive the method call.

Line 23 sets the time for the **Time1** object to which **time** refers by passing valid **hour**, **minute** and **second** arguments to **Time1** method **SetTime**. Lines 26–29 append to **output** the new time in both universal and standard formats to confirm that the time was set correctly.

To illustrate that method **SetTime** validates the values passed to it, line 32 passes invalid time arguments to method **SetTime**. Lines 34–36 append to **output** the new time in both formats. All three values passed to **SetTime** are invalid, so instance variables **hour**, **minute** and **second** are set to **0**. Line 38 displays a **MessageBox** with the results of our program. Notice in the last two lines of the output window that the time was indeed set to midnight when invalid arguments were passed to **SetTime**.

Time1 is our first example of a class that does not contain method **Main**. Thus, class **Time1** cannot be used to begin program execution. Class **TimeTest1** defines a **Main** method, so class **TimeTest1** can be used to begin program execution. A class containing method **Main** also is known as the *entry point* into the program.

Note that the program declares instance variables **hour**, **minute** and **second** as **private**. Such instance variables are not accessible outside the class in which they are defined. A class's clients should not take account of the data representation of that class. Clients of a class should deal only with the services provided by that class. For example, the class could represent the time internally as the number of seconds that have elapsed since the previous midnight. Suppose that the data representation then changes. Clients still are able to use the same **public** methods and obtain the same results without being aware of the change in internal representation. In this sense, the implementation of a class is said to be *hidden* from its clients.

Software Engineering Observation 5.7

Information hiding promotes program modifiability and simplifies the client's perception of a class.

Software Engineering Observation 5.8

Clients of a class can (and should) use the class without knowing the internal details of how the class is implemented. If the class implementation changes (to improve performance, for example), but the class interface remains constant, the client's source code need not change. This practice makes it much easier to modify systems.

In this program, the **Time1** constructor initializes the instance variables to **0** (the universal-time equivalent of 12 AM) to ensure that the object is created in a *consistent state*—i.e., that all instance variables have valid values. The instance variables of a **Time1** object cannot store invalid values, because the constructor, which calls **Set-Time**, is called to initialize the instance variables when the **Time1** object is created. Method **SetTime** scrutinizes subsequent attempts by a client to modify the instance variables.

Normally, the instance variables of a class are initialized in that class's constructor, but they also can be initialized when they are declared in the class's body. If a programmer does not initialize instance variables explicitly, the compiler implicitly initializes them. In such situations, the compiler sets primitive numeric variables to **0**, **bool** values to **false** and references to **null**.

Methods **ToUniversalString** and **ToStandardString** take no arguments, because, by default, these methods manipulate the instance variables of the particular **Time1** object on which they are invoked. This condition often makes method calls more concise than conventional function calls in procedural programming languages. It also reduces the likelihood of passing wrong arguments, wrong types of arguments or a wrong number of arguments.

Software Engineering Observation 5.9

The use of an object-oriented programming approach often simplifies method calls by reducing the number of parameters that must be passed. This benefit of object-oriented programming derives from the fact that encapsulation of instance variables and methods within an object gives the object's methods the right to access the object's instance variables.

Classes simplify programming, because the client need take account only of with the **public** operations encapsulated in the object. Usually, such operations are designed to be client oriented, rather than implementation oriented. Clients are neither aware of, nor involved in, a class's implementation. Interfaces change less frequently than do implementations. When an implementation changes, implementation-dependent code must change accordingly. By hiding the implementation, we eliminate the possibility that other program parts will become dependent on the class-implementation details.

Often, programmers do not have to create classes from scratch. Rather, they can derive classes from other classes that provide behaviors required by the new classes. Classes also can include references to objects of other classes as members. Such *software reuse* can greatly enhance programmer productivity. Chapter 6 discusses *inheritance*—the process by which new classes are derived from existing classes. Section 5.8 discusses *composition* (or *aggregation*), in which classes include as members references to objects of other classes.

5.3 Class Scope

In Section 4.8, we discussed method scope; now we discuss class *scope*. A class's instance variables and methods belong to that class's scope. Within a class's scope, class members are immediately accessible to all of that class's methods and can be referenced by name. Outside a class's scope, class members cannot be referenced directly by name. Those class members that are visible (such as **public** members) can be accessed only through a "handle" (i.e., members can be referenced via the format *referenceName.memberName*).

If a variable is defined in a method, only that method can access the variable (i.e., the variable is a local variable of that method). Such variables are said to have *block scope*. If a method defines a variable that has the same name as a variable with class scope (i.e., an instance variable), the method-scope variable hides the class-scope variable in that method's scope. A hidden instance variable can be accessed in a method by preceding its name with the keyword **this** and the dot operator, as in **this.hour**. We discuss keyword **this** in Section 5.9.

5.4 Controlling Access to Members

The member access modifiers **public** and **private** control access to a class's data and methods. (In Chapter 6, we introduce the additional access modifiers **protected** and **internal**.)

As previously stated, **public** methods present to the class's clients a view of the *services* that the class provides (i.e., the **public** interface of the class). Previously, we mentioned the merits of writing methods that perform only one task. If a method must execute other tasks to calculate its final result, these tasks should be performed by a helper method. A client does not need to call these helper methods, nor does it need to be concerned with take account of how the class uses its helper methods. For these reasons, helper methods are declared as **private** members of a class.

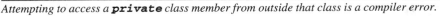

Common Programming Error 5.2

*Attempting to access a **private** class member from outside that class is a compiler error.*

The application of Fig. 5.3 (which uses the **Time1** class from Fig. 5.1) demonstrates that **private** class members are not accessible outside the class. Lines 12–14 attempt to access the **private** instance variables **hour, minute** and **second** of the **Time1** object to which **time** refers. When this program is compiled, the compiler generates errors stating that the **private** members **hour, minute** and **second** are not accessible.

Access to **private** data should be controlled carefully by a class's methods. To allow clients to read the values of **private** data, the class can define a *property* that enables client code to access the **private** data safely. Properties, which we discuss in detail in Section 5.7, contain *accessor methods* that handle the details of modifying and returning data. A property definition can contain a ***get** accessor*, a ***set** accessor* or both. A **get** accessor enables a client to read a **private** data value; a **set** accessor enables the client to modify that value. Such modification would seem to violate the notion of **private** data. However, a **set** accessor can provide data-validation capabilities (such as range checking) to ensure that the value is set properly. A **set** accessor also can translate between the format of the data used in the interface and the format used in the underlying implementation. Similarly, a **get** accessor need not expose the data in raw format; rather, the **get** accessor can edit the data and limit the client's view of them.

```
1   // Fig. 5.3: RestrictedAccess.cs
2   // Demonstrate compiler errors from attempt to access
3   // private class members.
4
5   class RestrictedAccess
6   {
7      // main entry point for application
8      static void Main( string[] args )
9      {
10        Time1 time = new Time1();
11
12        time.hour = 7;
13        time.minute = 15;
14        time.second = 30;
15     }
16
17   } // end class RestrictedAccess
```

Fig. 5.3   Accessing **private** class members from client code generates syntax errors.

Software Engineering Observation 5.10

*Class designers need not provide **set** or **get** accessors for each **private** data member; these capabilities should be provided only when doing so makes sense.*

Software Engineering Observation 5.11

*Declaring the instance variables of a class as **private** and the methods and properties (discussed in Section 5.7) of the class as **public** facilitates debugging, because problems with data manipulations are localized to the class methods that manipulate the data.*

5.5 Initializing Class Objects: Constructors

When a program creates an instance of a class, the program invokes the class's constructor to initialize the class's instance variables (data members). A class can contain overloaded constructors to provide multiple ways to initialize objects of that class. Instance variables can be initialized either by a constructor or when they are declared in the body of the class. Regardless of whether instance variables receive explicit initialization values, the instance variables always are initialized. In cases where no explicit initialization values are provided, instance variables receive their default values (**0** for primitive numeric-type variables, **false** for **bool** variables and **null** for references).

Software Engineering Observation 5.12

When appropriate, provide a constructor which ensures that every object is initialized with meaningful values.

When creating an object of a class, the programmer can provide *initializers* in parentheses to the right of the class name. The initializers are the arguments to the constructor. In general, declarations take the form

> *ClassName objectReference* = **new** *ClassName* (*arguments*);

where *objectReference* is a reference of the appropriate data type, **new** indicates that an object is being created, *ClassName* indicates the type of the new object (and the name of the constructor being called) and *arguments* specifies a comma-separated list of the values used by the constructor to initialize the object. Figure 5.4 demonstrates the use of initializers and overloaded constructors.

If a class does not define any constructors, the compiler provides a *default (no-argument) constructor*. The compiler-provided default constructor contains no code (i.e., the constructor has an empty body) and takes no parameters. The programmer also can provide a default constructor, as we demonstrated in class **Time1** (Fig. 5.1). Programmer-provided default constructors can have code in their bodies.

Common Programming Error 5.3

*If a class has constructors, but none of the **public** constructors is a default constructor, and a program attempts to call a no-argument constructor to initialize an object of the class, a compilation error occurs. A constructor can be called with no arguments only if there are no constructors for the class (in which case the compiler-provided default constructor is called) or if the class defines a **public** no-argument constructor.*

5.6 Using Overloaded Constructors

Like methods, constructors of a class can be overloaded. The **Time1** constructor in Fig. 5.1 initialized **hour**, **minute** and **second** to **0** (i.e., 12 midnight in standard time) via a call to the class **SetTime** method. However, class **Time2** (Fig. 5.4) overloads the constructor to provide a variety of ways to initialize **Time2** objects. Each constructor calls **Time2** method **SetTime**, which ensures that the object begins in a consistent state by setting out-of-range values to zero. C# invokes the appropriate constructor by matching the number, types and order of the arguments specified in the constructor call with the number, types and order of the parameters specified in each constructor definition.

```csharp
1   // Fig. 5.4: Time2.cs
2   // Class Time2 provides overloaded constructors.
3
4   using System;
5
6   // Time2 class definition
7   public class Time2
8   {
9      private int hour;     // 0-23
10     private int minute;   // 0-59
11     private int second;   // 0-59
12
13     // Time2 constructor initializes instance variables to
14     // zero to set default time to midnight
15     public Time2()
16     {
17        SetTime( 0, 0, 0 );
18     }
19
20     // Time2 constructor: hour supplied, minute and second
21     // defaulted to 0
22     public Time2( int hour )
23     {
24        SetTime( hour, 0, 0 );
25     }
26
27     // Time2 constructor: hour and minute supplied, second
28     // defaulted to 0
29     public Time2( int hour, int minute )
30     {
31        SetTime( hour, minute, 0 );
32     }
33
34     // Time2 constructor: hour, minute and second supplied
35     public Time2( int hour, int minute, int second )
36     {
37        SetTime( hour, minute, second );
38     }
39
```

Fig. 5.4   Overloaded constructors provide flexible object-initialization options. (Part 1 of 2.)

```
40        // Time2 constructor: initialize using another Time2 object
41        public Time2( Time2 time )
42        {
43           SetTime( time.hour, time.minute, time.second );
44        }
45
46        // Set new time value in 24-hour format. Perform validity
47        // checks on the data. Set invalid values to zero.
48        public void SetTime(
49           int hourValue, int minuteValue, int secondValue )
50        {
51           hour = ( hourValue >= 0 && hourValue < 24 ) ?
52              hourValue : 0;
53           minute = ( minuteValue >= 0 && minuteValue < 60 ) ?
54              minuteValue : 0;
55           second = ( secondValue >= 0 && secondValue < 60 ) ?
56              secondValue : 0;
57        }
58
59        // convert time to universal-time (24 hour) format string
60        public string ToUniversalString()
61        {
62           return String.Format(
63              "{0:D2}:{1:D2}:{2:D2}", hour, minute, second );
64        }
65
66        // convert time to standard-time (12 hour) format string
67        public string ToStandardString()
68        {
69           return String.Format( "{0}:{1:D2}:{2:D2} {3}",
70              ( ( hour == 12 || hour == 0 ) ? 12 : hour % 12 ),
71              minute, second, ( hour < 12 ? "AM" : "PM" ) );
72        }
73
74     } // end class Time2
```

Fig. 5.4   Overloaded constructors provide flexible object-initialization options. (Part 2 of 2.)

Because most of the code in class **Time2** is identical to that in class **Time1**, this discussion concentrates only on the overloaded constructors. Lines 15–18 define the no-argument constructor that sets the time to midnight. Lines 22–25 define a **Time2** constructor that receives a single **int** argument representing the **hour** and sets the time, using the specified **hour** value and **0** for the **minute** and **second**. Lines 29–32 define a **Time2** constructor that receives two **int** arguments representing the **hour** and **minute** and sets the time, using those values and **0** for the **second**. Lines 35–38 define a **Time2** constructor that receives three **int** arguments representing the **hour**, **minute** and **second** and uses those values to set the time. Lines 41–44 define a **Time2** constructor that receives a reference to another **Time2** object. When this last constructor is called, the values from the **Time2** argument are used to initialize the **hour**, **minute** and **second** values of the new **Time2** object. Even though class **Time2** declares **hour**, **minute** and **second** as **private** (lines 9–11), the **Time2** constructor can access these values in its **Time2** argument directly, using the expressions **time.hour**, **time.minute** and **time.second**, respectively.

Software Engineering Observation 5.13

*When one object of a class has a reference to another object of the same class, the first object can access all the second object's data and methods (including those that are **private**).*

Notice that the second, third and fourth constructors (lines 22, 29 and 35) have some arguments in common and that those arguments are kept in the same order. For instance, the constructor that begins on line 29 has as its two arguments an integer representing the hour and an integer representing the minute. The constructor on line 35 has these same two arguments in the same order, followed by its last argument (an integer representing the second).

Good Programming Practice 5.4

When defining overloaded constructors, keep the order of arguments as similar as possible; this practice makes client programming easier.

Constructors do not specify return types; doing so results in syntax errors. Also, notice that each constructor receives a different number or different types of arguments. Even though only two of the constructors receive values for each of the **hour**, **minute** and **second**, each constructor calls **SetTime** with values for **hour**, **minute** and **second**, using zeros for the missing values to satisfy **SetTime**'s requirement of three arguments.

Class **TimeTest2** (Fig. 5.5) starts the application that demonstrates the use of overloaded constructors (Fig. 5.4). Lines 15–20 create six **Time2** objects that invoke various constructors of the class. Line 15 invokes the no-argument constructor by placing an empty set of parentheses after the class name. Lines 16–20 invoke the **Time2** constructors that receive arguments. To invoke the appropriate constructor, we pass the proper number, types and order of arguments (specified by the constructor's definition) to that constructor. For example, line 16 invokes the constructor that is defined on lines 22–25 of Fig. 5.4. Lines 22–47 invoke methods **ToUniversalString** and **ToStandardString** for each **Time2** object to demonstrate that the constructors initialize the objects correctly.

```
1   // Fig. 5.5: TimeTest2.cs
2   // Using overloaded constructors.
3
4   using System;
5   using System.Windows.Forms;
6
7   // TimeTest2 demonstrates constructors of class Time2
8   class TimeTest2
9   {
10      // main entry point for application
11      static void Main( string[] args )
12      {
13         Time2 time1, time2, time3, time4, time5, time6;
14
15         time1 = new Time2();                 // 00:00:00
16         time2 = new Time2( 2 );              // 02:00:00
17         time3 = new Time2( 21, 34 );         // 21:34:00
18         time4 = new Time2( 12, 25, 42 );     // 12:25:42
19         time5 = new Time2( 27, 74, 99 );     // 00:00:00
20         time6 = new Time2( time4 );          // 12:25:42
```

Fig. 5.5   Overloaded constructor demonstration. (Part 1 of 2.)

```
21
22          String output = "Constructed with: " +
23             "\ntime1: all arguments defaulted" +
24             "\n\t" + time1.ToUniversalString() +
25             "\n\t" + time1.ToStandardString();
26
27          output += "\ntime2: hour specified; minute and " +
28             "second defaulted" +
29             "\n\t" + time2.ToUniversalString() +
30             "\n\t" + time2.ToStandardString();
31
32          output += "\ntime3: hour and minute specified; " +
33             "second defaulted" +
34             "\n\t" + time3.ToUniversalString() +
35             "\n\t" + time3.ToStandardString();
36
37          output += "\ntime4: hour, minute, and second specified" +
38             "\n\t" + time4.ToUniversalString() +
39             "\n\t" + time4.ToStandardString();
40
41          output += "\ntime5: all invalid values specified" +
42             "\n\t" + time5.ToUniversalString() +
43             "\n\t" + time5.ToStandardString();
44
45          output += "\ntime6: Time2 object time4 specified" +
46             "\n\t" + time6.ToUniversalString() +
47             "\n\t" + time6.ToStandardString();
48
49          MessageBox.Show( output,
50             "Demonstrating Overloaded Constructors" );
51
52       } // end method Main
53
54    } // end class TimeTest2
```

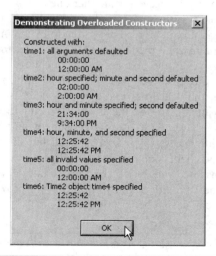

Fig. 5.5   Overloaded constructor demonstration. (Part 2 of 2.)

Each **Time2** constructor can also be written to include a copy of the appropriate statements from method **SetTime**. This approach might be slightly more efficient, because it eliminates the extra call to **SetTime**. However, consider what would happen if, for example, the programmer were to change the representation of the time from three **int** values (requiring 12 bytes of memory) to a single **int** value representing the total number of seconds that have elapsed in the day (requiring 4 bytes of memory). Placing identical code in the **Time2** constructors and method **SetTime** makes such a change in the class definition more difficult, because every constructor's body would require modifications to manipulate the data as a single **int** rather than three **int**s. If the **Time2** constructors call **SetTime** directly, on the other hand, any changes to the implementation of **SetTime** must be made only once, in the body of **SetTime**. This approach reduces the likelihood of introducing a programming error when altering the implementation, because we make only one change in the class, rather than changing every constructor and method **SetTime**.

Software Engineering Observation 5.14

If a method of a class provides functionality required by a constructor (or other method) of the class, call that method from the constructor (or other method). This practice simplifies the maintenance of the code and reduces the likelihood of introducing errors into the code.

5.7 Properties

Methods of a class can manipulate that class's **private** instance variables. A typical manipulation might be the adjustment of a customer's bank balance—a **private** instance variable of a class **BankAccount**—by a **ComputeInterest** method.

Classes often provide **public** *properties* to allow clients to *set* (i.e., assign values to) or *get* (i.e., obtain the values of) **private** instance variables. For example, in Fig. 5.6, we create three properties, **Hour**, **Minute** and **Second**, that access variables **hour**, **minute** and **second**, respectively. Each property contains a *get accessor* (to retrieve the field value) and a *set accessor* (to modify the field value).

Providing **set** and **get** capabilities appears to be the same as making the instance variables **public**. However, this aspect is another one of C#'s subtleties that makes the language so attractive from a software-engineering standpoint. If an instance variable is **public**, the instance variable can be read or written to by any method in the program. If an instance variable is **private**, a **public get** accessor seems to allow other methods to read the data at will. However, the **get** accessor can control the formatting and display of the data. Similarly, a **public set** accessor can scrutinize attempts to modify the instance variable's value, thus ensuring that the new value is appropriate for that data member. For example, an attempt to **set** the day of the month to 37 would be rejected, and an attempt to **set** a person's weight to a negative value would be rejected. So, **set** and **get** accessors can provide access to **private** data, but the implementation of these accessors controls what the client code can do to the data.

The declaration of instance variables as **private** does not guarantee the variables' integrity. Programmers must provide validity checking; C# provides only the framework with which programmers can design better programs.

Testing and Debugging Tip 5.1

*Methods that set the values of **private** data should verify that the intended new values are valid; if they are not, the **set** accessors should place the **private** instance variables into an appropriate consistent state.*

The **set** accessors of a property cannot return values indicating a failed attempt to assign invalid data to objects of the class. Such return values could be useful to a client of a class when handling errors. The client could take appropriate actions if the objects occupy invalid states. Chapter 8 presents exception handling—a mechanism that can be used to indicate attempts to set an object's members to invalid values.

Figure 5.6 enhances our **Time** class, now called **Time3**, to include properties for the **private** instance variables **hour**, **minute** and **second**. The **set** accessors of these properties strictly control the setting of the instance variables to valid values. An attempt to set any instance variable to an incorrect value causes the instance variable to be set to zero (thus leaving the instance variable in a consistent state). Each **get** accessor returns the appropriate instance variable's value. This application also introduces enhanced GUI event-handling techniques, as we define a GUI (Fig. 5.7) that includes several buttons the user can click to manipulate the time stored in a **Time3** object.

Lines 57–69, 72–84 and 87–99 define **Time3** properties **Hour**, **Minute** and **Second**, respectively. Each property begins with a declaration line that includes the property's access modifier (**public**), type (**int**) and name (**Hour**, **Minute** or **Second**).

```
1   // Fig. 5.6: Time3.cs
2   // Class Time3 demonstrates properties.
3
4   using System;
5
6   // Time3 class definition
7   public class Time3
8   {
9      private int hour;      // 0-23
10     private int minute;    // 0-59
11     private int second;    // 0-59
12
13     // Time3 constructor initializes instance variables to
14     // zero to set default time to midnight
15     public Time3()
16     {
17        SetTime( 0, 0, 0 );
18     }
19
20     // Time3 constructor: hour supplied, minute and second
21     // defaulted to 0
22     public Time3( int hour )
23     {
24        SetTime( hour, 0, 0 );
25     }
26
27     // Time3 constructor: hour and minute supplied, second
28     // defaulted to 0
29     public Time3( int hour, int minute )
30     {
31        SetTime( hour, minute, 0 );
32     }
33
```

Fig. 5.6   Properties provide controlled access to an object's data. (Part 1 of 3.)

```
34        // Time3 constructor: hour, minute and second supplied
35        public Time3( int hour, int minute, int second )
36        {
37            SetTime( hour, minute, second );
38        }
39
40        // Time3 constructor: initialize using another Time3 object
41        public Time3( Time3 time )
42        {
43            SetTime( time.Hour, time.Minute, time.Second );
44        }
45
46        // Set new time value in 24-hour format. Perform validity
47        // checks on the data. Set invalid values to zero.
48        public void SetTime(
49            int hourValue, int minuteValue, int secondValue )
50        {
51            Hour = hourValue;         // invoke Hour property set
52            Minute = minuteValue;     // invoke Minute property set
53            Second = secondValue;     // invoke Second property set
54        }
55
56        // property Hour
57        public int Hour
58        {
59            get
60            {
61                return hour;
62            }
63
64            set
65            {
66                hour = ( ( value >= 0 && value < 24 ) ? value : 0 );
67            }
68
69        } // end property Hour
70
71        // property Minute
72        public int Minute
73        {
74            get
75            {
76                return minute;
77            }
78
79            set
80            {
81                minute = ( ( value >= 0 && value < 60 ) ? value : 0 );
82            }
83
84        } // end property Minute
85
```

Fig. 5.6   Properties provide controlled access to an object's data. (Part 2 of 3.)

```
86      // property Second
87      public int Second
88      {
89         get
90         {
91            return second;
92         }
93
94         set
95         {
96            second = ( ( value >= 0 && value < 60 ) ? value : 0 );
97         }
98
99      } // end property Second
100
101     // convert time to universal-time (24 hour) format string
102     public string ToUniversalString()
103     {
104        return String.Format(
105           "{0:D2}:{1:D2}:{2:D2}", Hour, Minute, Second );
106     }
107
108     // convert time to standard-time (12 hour) format string
109     public string ToStandardString()
110     {
111        return String.Format( "{0}:{1:D2}:{2:D2} {3}",
112           ( ( Hour == 12 || Hour == 0 ) ? 12 : Hour % 12 ),
113           Minute, Second, ( Hour < 12 ? "AM" : "PM" ) );
114     }
115
116  } // end class Time3
```

Fig. 5.6   Properties provide controlled access to an object's data. (Part 3 of 3.)

The body of each property contains **get** and **set** accessors, which are declared using the reserved words **get** and **set**. The **get** accessor declarations are on lines 59–62, 74–77 and 89–92. These accessors return the **hour**, **minute** and **second** instance-variable values, respectively, that objects request. The **set** accessors are declared on lines 64–67, 79–82 and 94–97. The body of each **set** accessor performs the same conditional statement that was previously performed by method **SetTime** to set the **hour**, **minute** or **second**.

Method **SetTime** (lines 48–54) now uses properties **Hour**, **Minute** and **Second** to ensure that instance variables **hour**, **minute** and **second**, respectively, have valid values. After we define a property, we can use it in the same way that we use a variable. We assign values to properties by using the **=** (assignment) operator. When such an assignment occurs, the code in the **set** accessor for that property executes. The reserved word **value** represents the argument to the **set** accessor. Similarly, methods **ToUniversalString** (102–106) and **ToStandardString** (109–114) now use properties **Hour**, **Minute** and **Second** to obtain the values of instance variables **hour**, **minute** and **second**, respectively. Referencing a particular property executes the **get** accessor for that property.

When we use **set** and **get** accessor methods throughout the constructors and other methods of class **Time3**, we minimize the number of changes that we must make to the class definition in the event that we alter the data representation from **hour, minute** and **second** to another representation (such as total number of elapsed seconds in the day). When such changes are made, we must provide only new **set** and **get** accessor bodies. Using this technique also enables programmers to change the implementation of a class without affecting the clients of the class (as long as all the **public** methods of the class still are called in the same way).

Software Engineering Observation 5.15

*Accessing **private** data through **set** and **get** accessors not only protects the instance variables from receiving invalid values, but also hides the internal representation of the instance variables from the class's clients. Thus, if representation of the data changes (typically, to reduce the amount of required storage or to improve performance), only the method implementations need to change; the client implementations need not change, as long as the interface provided by the methods is preserved.*

Class **TimeTest3** (Fig. 5.7) defines an application with a GUI for manipulating an object of class **Time3**. [*Note*: We do not show Visual Studio.NET's *Windows Form Designer*-generated code. Instead, line 45 provides a comment to indicate where the generated code appears in the source-code file. You can download this code from the **Downloads/Resources** page of our Web site (**www.deitel.com**).]

```
1   // Fig. 5.7: TimeTest3.cs
2   // Demonstrating Time3 properties Hour, Minute and Second.
3
4   using System;
5   using System.Drawing;
6   using System.Collections;
7   using System.ComponentModel;
8   using System.Windows.Forms;
9   using System.Data;
10
11  // TimeTest3 class definition
12  public class TimeTest3 : System.Windows.Forms.Form
13  {
14     private System.Windows.Forms.Label hourLabel;
15     private System.Windows.Forms.TextBox hourTextBox;
16     private System.Windows.Forms.Button hourButton;
17
18     private System.Windows.Forms.Label minuteLabel;
19     private System.Windows.Forms.TextBox minuteTextBox;
20     private System.Windows.Forms.Button minuteButton;
21
22     private System.Windows.Forms.Label secondLabel;
23     private System.Windows.Forms.TextBox secondTextBox;
24     private System.Windows.Forms.Button secondButton;
25
26     private System.Windows.Forms.Button addButton;
27
28     private System.Windows.Forms.Label displayLabel1;
29     private System.Windows.Forms.Label displayLabel2;
30
```

Fig. 5.7   Properties demonstration for class **Time3**. (Part 1 of 4.)

```
31      // required designer variable
32      private System.ComponentModel.Container components = null;
33
34      private Time3 time;
35
36      public TimeTest3()
37      {
38          // Required for Windows Form Designer support
39          InitializeComponent();
40
41          time = new Time3();
42          UpdateDisplay();
43      }
44
45      // Visual Studio .NET generated code
46
47      // main entry point for application
48      [STAThread]
49      static void Main()
50      {
51          Application.Run( new TimeTest3() );
52      }
53
54      // update display labels
55      public void UpdateDisplay()
56      {
57          displayLabel1.Text = "Hour: " + time.Hour +
58              "; Minute: " + time.Minute +
59              "; Second: " + time.Second;
60          displayLabel2.Text = "Standard time: " +
61              time.ToStandardString() + "\nUniversal time: " +
62              time.ToUniversalString();
63      }
64
65      // set Hour property when hourButton pressed
66      private void hourButton_Click(
67          object sender, System.EventArgs e )
68      {
69          time.Hour = Int32.Parse( hourTextBox.Text );
70          hourTextBox.Text = "";
71          UpdateDisplay();
72      }
73
74      // set Minute property when minuteButton pressed
75      private void minuteButton_Click(
76          object sender, System.EventArgs e )
77      {
78          time.Minute = Int32.Parse( minuteTextBox.Text );
79          minuteTextBox.Text = "";
80          UpdateDisplay();
81      }
82
```

Fig. 5.7   Properties demonstration for class **Time3**. (Part 2 of 4.)

```
83        // set Second property when secondButton pressed
84        private void secondButton_Click(
85           object sender, System.EventArgs e )
86        {
87           time.Second = Int32.Parse( secondTextBox.Text );
88           secondTextBox.Text = "";
89           UpdateDisplay();
90        }
91
92        // add one to Second when addButton pressed
93        private void addButton_Click(
94           object sender, System.EventArgs e )
95        {
96           time.Second = ( time.Second + 1 ) % 60;
97
98           if ( time.Second == 0 )
99           {
100             time.Minute = ( time.Minute + 1 ) % 60;
101
102             if ( time.Minute == 0 )
103                time.Hour = ( time.Hour + 1 ) % 24;
104          }
105
106          UpdateDisplay();
107
108       } // end method addButton_Click
109
110    } // end class TimeTest3
```

Fig. 5.7   Properties demonstration for class **Time3**. (Part 3 of 4.)

Fig. 5.7   Properties demonstration for class **Time3**. (Part 4 of 4.)

Line 34 declares **Time3** reference **time**. Line 41 in the constructor creates an object of class **Time3** and assigns it to **time**. The GUI contains three text fields in which the user can input values for the **Time3** object's **hour**, **minute** and **second** variables, respectively. Next to each text field is a button the user can click to set the value of a particular **Time3** property. Lines 66–90 declare three event-handling methods for the buttons' **Click** events. Each event handler alters the value of a **Time3** property (**Hour**, **Minute** or **Second**). The GUI also contains a button that enables the user to increment the **second** value by **1**. Using the **Time3** object's properties, method **addButton_Click** (lines 93–108) determines and sets the new time. For example, **23:59:59** becomes **00:00:00** when the user presses the button. Each modification of the time results in a call to **UpdateDisplay**, which uses the **Time3** properties to display the **hour**, **minute** and **second** values, as well as the universal- and standard-time representations.

Properties are not limited to accessing **private** data; properties also can be used to calculate values associated with an object. For example, consider a **student** object with a property representing the student's GPA (called **GPA**). Programmers can either provide code that calculates the student's GPA in the **get** accessor for this property simply return a **private** variable containing the calculated GPA, called **gpa**. (The value in this variable will need to be calculated in some other way, such as using a **CalculateGPA** method.) The programmer can use either technique, but we recommend by using a property that calculates the GPA. Remember that client code should not be required to tell the **student** object when to calculate the GPA. The client code simply should use the **GPA** property. The underlying implementation should be hidden from the client.

5.8 Composition: Objects References as Instance Variables of Other Classes

In many situations, it is more convenient to reference existing objects than to rewrite the objects' code for new classes in new projects. Suppose we were to implement an **Alarm-Clock** object that needs to know when to sound its alarm. In this case, it would be easier to reference an existing **Time** object (like those from earlier examples in this chapter) than to write a new **Time** object. The use of references to objects of preexisting classes as members of new objects is called *composition* (or *aggregation*).

Software Engineering Observation 5.16

One form of software reuse is composition, in which a class has members that reference objects of other classes.

The application of Fig. 5.8, Fig. 5.9 and Fig. 5.10 demonstrates composition. The program contains three classes. Class **Date** (Fig. 5.8) encapsulates information relating to a specific date. Class **Employee** (Fig. 5.9) encapsulates the name of an employee and two **Date** objects representing the employee's birthday and hire date. Class **CompositionTest** (Fig. 5.10) creates an object of class **Employee** to demonstrate composition.

Class **Date** declares **int** instance variables **month**, **day** and **year** (lines 9–11). Lines 16–32 define the constructor, which receives values for **month**, **day** and **year** as arguments and assigns these values to the instance variables after ensuring that the values are in a consistent state. Note that lines 25–26 print an error message if the constructor receives an invalid **month** value. Ordinarily, rather than printing error messages, constructors "throw an exception." We discuss exceptions in Chapter 8, Exception Handling. Method **ToDateString** (lines 58–61) returns the string representation of a **Date**.

Class **Employee** (Fig. 5.9) encapsulates information relating to an employee's birthday and hire date (lines 10–13), using instance variables **firstName**, **lastName**, **birthDate** and **hireDate**. Members **birthDate** and **hireDate** are references to **Date** objects, each of which contains instance variables **month**, **day** and **year**. In this example, class **Employee** is *composed of* two references of type **string** and two references of class **Date**. The **Employee** constructor (lines 16–27) takes eight arguments (**first**, **last**, **birthMonth**, **birthDay**, **birthYear**, **hireMonth**, **hireDay** and **hireYear**). Line 24 passes arguments **birthMonth**, **birthDay** and **birthYear** to the **Date** constructor to create the **birthDate** object. Similarly, line 25 passes arguments **hireMonth**, **hireDay** and **hireYear** to the **Date** constructor to create the **hireDate** object. Method **ToEmployeeString** (lines 30–35) returns a **string** containing the name of the **Employee** and the string representations of the **Employee**'s **birthDate** and **hireDate**.

```
1   // Fig. 5.8: Date.cs
2   // Date class definition encapsulates month, day and year.
3
4   using System;
5
6   // Date class definition
7   public class Date
8   {
9      private int month;   // 1-12
10     private int day;     // 1-31 based on month
11     private int year;    // any year
12
13     // constructor confirms proper value for month;
14     // call method CheckDay to confirm proper
15     // value for day
16     public Date( int theMonth, int theDay, int theYear )
17     {
18        // validate month
19        if ( theMonth > 0 && theMonth <= 12 )
20           month = theMonth;
21
```

Fig. 5.8   **Date** class encapsulates day, month and year information. (Part 1 of 2.)

```
22            else
23            {
24                month = 1;
25                Console.WriteLine(
26                    "Month {0} invalid. Set to month 1.", theMonth );
27            }
28
29            year = theYear;              // could validate year
30            day = CheckDay( theDay );    // validate day
31
32        } // end Date constructor
33
34        // utility method confirms proper day value
35        // based on month and year
36        private int CheckDay( int testDay )
37        {
38            int[] daysPerMonth =
39                { 0, 31, 28, 31, 30, 31, 30, 31, 31, 30, 31, 30, 31 };
40
41            // check if day in range for month
42            if ( testDay > 0 && testDay <= daysPerMonth[ month ] )
43                return testDay;
44
45            // check for leap year
46            if ( month == 2 && testDay == 29 &&
47                ( year % 400 == 0 ||
48                    ( year % 4 == 0 && year % 100 != 0 ) ) )
49                return testDay;
50
51            Console.WriteLine(
52                "Day {0} invalid. Set to day 1.", testDay );
53
54            return 1;  // leave object in consistent state
55        }
56
57        // return date string as month/day/year
58        public string ToDateString()
59        {
60            return month + "/" + day + "/" + year;
61        }
62
63    }  // end class Date
```

Fig. 5.8   **Date** class encapsulates day, month and year information. (Part 2 of 2.)

Class **CompositionTest** (Fig. 5.10) runs the application with method **Main**. Lines 13–14 instantiate an **Employee** object, and lines 16–17 display the string representation of the **Employee** to the user.

```
1    // Fig. 5.9: Employee.cs
2    // Employee class definition encapsulates employee's first name,
```

Fig. 5.9   **Employee** class encapsulates employee name, birthday and hire date. (Part 1 of 2.)

```
 3    // last name, birth date and hire date.
 4
 5    using System;
 6
 7    // Employee class definition
 8    public class Employee
 9    {
10       private string firstName;
11       private string lastName;
12       private Date birthDate;   // reference to a Date object
13       private Date hireDate;    // reference to a Date object
14
15       // constructor initializes name, birth date and hire date
16       public Employee( string first, string last,
17          int birthMonth, int birthDay, int birthYear,
18          int hireMonth, int hireDay, int hireYear )
19       {
20          firstName = first;
21          lastName = last;
22
23          // create new Date objects
24          birthDate = new Date( birthMonth, birthDay, birthYear );
25          hireDate = new Date( hireMonth, hireDay, hireYear );
26
27       } // end Employee constructor
28
29       // convert Employee to String format
30       public string ToEmployeeString()
31       {
32          return lastName + ", " + firstName +
33             "  Hired: " + hireDate.ToDateString() +
34             "  Birthday: " + birthDate.ToDateString();
35       }
36
37    } // end class Employee
```

Fig. 5.9   **Employee** class encapsulates employee name, birthday and hire date. (Part 2 of 2.)

```
 1    // Fig. 5.10: CompositionTest.cs
 2    // Demonstrate an object with member object reference.
 3
 4    using System;
 5    using System.Windows.Forms;
 6
 7    // Composition class definition
 8    class CompositionTest
 9    {
10       // main entry point for application
11       static void Main( string[] args )
12       {
```

Fig. 5.10   Composition demonstration. (Part 1 of 2.)

```
13          Employee e =
14              new Employee( "Bob", "Jones", 7, 24, 1949, 3, 12, 1988 );
15
16          MessageBox.Show( e.ToEmployeeString(),
17              "Testing Class Employee" );
18
19      } // end method Main
20
21  } // end class CompositionTest
```

Fig. 5.10   Composition demonstration. (Part 2 of 2.)

5.9 Using the `this` Reference

Every object can access a reference to itself, called the ***this*** *reference*. The **this** reference can refer implicitly to the instance variables, properties and methods of an object. Keyword **this** is commonly used within methods, where **this** is a reference to the object on which the method is performing operations. In the Windows application in Fig. 4.1, there are several uses of **this** in method **InitializeComponent**. The application uses the **this** keyword to reference the form that is being initialized. Every form has an **InitializeComponent** method, so the **this** reference provides us with an easy way to access the information in the current object. Additional examples of **this** appear in Chapters 9 and 10.

We now demonstrate implicit and explicit use of the **this** reference to display the **private** data of a **Time4** object. Class **Time4** (Fig. 5.11) defines three **private** instance variables—**hour**, **minute** and **second** (lines 9–11). The constructor (lines 14–19) receives three **int** arguments to initialize a **Time4** object. Note that, for this example, we have made the parameter names for the constructor (line 14) identical to the instance-variable names for the class (lines 9–11). We do this to illustrate explicit use of the **this** reference. If a method contains a local variable with the same name as an instance variable of the method's class, the method will refer to the local variable, rather than to the instance variable (i.e., the local variable hides the instance variable in the method's scope). However, the method can use the **this** reference to refer to the hidden instance variables explicitly (lines 16–18).

Method **BuildString** (lines 22–27) returns a **string** created by a statement that uses the **this** reference explicitly and implicitly. Line 25 uses the **this** reference explicitly to call method **ToStandardString**, whereas line 26 uses the **this** reference implicitly to call the same method. Note that both lines perform the same task. Therefore, programmers usually do not use the **this** reference explicitly to reference methods within the current object.

Testing and Debugging Tip 5.2

Avoid using method-parameter names (or local-variable names) that conflict with instance-variable names to prevent subtle, hard-to-trace bugs.

```
1   // Fig. 5.11: Time4.cs
2   // Class Time4 demonstrates the this reference.
3
4   using System;
5
6   // Time4 class definition
7   public class Time4
8   {
9      private int hour;      // 0-23
10     private int minute;    // 0-59
11     private int second;    // 0-59
12
13     // constructor
14     public Time4( int hour, int minute, int second )
15     {
16        this.hour = hour;
17        this.minute = minute;
18        this.second = second;
19     }
20
21     // create string using this and implicit references
22     public string BuildString()
23     {
24        return "this.ToStandardString(): " +
25           this.ToStandardString() +
26           "\nToStandardString(): " + ToStandardString();
27     }
28
29     // convert time to standard-time (12-hour) format string
30     public string ToStandardString()
31     {
32        return String.Format( "{0}:{1:D2}:{2:D2} {3}",
33           ( ( this.hour == 12 || this.hour == 0 ) ? 12 :
34           this.hour % 12 ), this.minute, this.second,
35           ( this.hour < 12 ? "AM" : "PM" ) );
36     }
37
38  } // end class Time4
```

Fig. 5.11   `this` reference used implicitly and explicitly to enable an object to manipulate its own data and invoke its own methods.

Common Programming Error 5.4

*For a method in which a parameter (or local variable) has the same name as an instance variable, use reference **this** if you wish to access the instance variable; otherwise, the method parameter (or local variable) will be referenced.*

Class **ThisTest** (Fig. 5.12) runs the application that demonstrates explicit use of the **this** reference. Line 13 instantiates an instance of class **Time4**. Lines 15–16 invoke method **BuildString** of the **Time4** object and display the results to the user in a **MessageBox**.

Good Programming Practice 5.5

*The explicit use of the **this** reference can increase program clarity in some contexts where using **this** is optional.*

The problem of parameters (or local variables) hiding instance variables can be solved by using properties. If we have a property **Hour** that accesses the **hour** instance variable, then we do not need to use **this.hour** to distinguish between a parameter (or local variable) **hour** and the instance variable **hour**; we simply assign **hour** to **Hour**.

5.10 Garbage Collection

In previous examples, we have seen how a constructor initializes data in an object of a class after the object is created. Operator **new** allocates memory for the object, after which it calls that object's constructor. The constructor might subsequently acquire other system resources, such as network connections and databases or files.

Objects must have a disciplined way to return memory and release resources after the program no longer uses the objects. Failure to release such resources causes *resource leaks*, potentially exhausting the pool of available resources that programs might need to continue executing.

Unlike C and C++, in which programmers must manage memory explicitly, C# performs memory management internally. The .NET Framework performs *garbage collection* of memory to return to the system memory that is no longer needed. When the *garbage collector* executes, it identifies objects for which the application has no references. Such objects can be collected at that time or during a subsequent execution of the garbage collector. Therefore, the *memory leaks* that are common in such languages as C and C++, for which memory is not reclaimed by the runtime, are rare in C#.

```
1   // Fig. 5.12: ThisTest.cs
2   // Using the this reference.
3
4   using System;
5   using System.Windows.Forms;
6
7   // ThisTest class definition
8   class ThisTest
9   {
10      // main entry point for application
11      static void Main( string[] args )
12      {
13         Time4 time = new Time4( 12, 30, 19 );
14
15         MessageBox.Show( time.BuildString(),
16            "Demonstrating the \"this\" Reference" );
17      }
18   }
```

Fig. 5.12 **this** reference demonstration.

Allocation and deallocation of other resources, such as network connections, database connections and files, must be handled explicitly by the programmer. One technique employed to handle these resources (in conjunction with the garbage collector) is to define a *destructor* (sometimes known as a *finalizer*) that returns resources to the system. The garbage collector calls an object's destructor to perform *termination housekeeping* on that object just before the garbage collector reclaims the object's memory (a step called *finalization*).

Each class can contain only one destructor. The name of a destructor is formed by preceding the class name with the ~ character. For example, the destructor for class **Time** would be **~Time()**. Destructors do not receive arguments, so destructors cannot be overloaded. When the garbage collector is removing an object from memory, the garbage collector first invokes that object's destructor to clean up resources used by the class. However, we cannot determine exactly when the destructor is called, because we cannot determine exactly when garbage collection occurs. At program termination, any objects for which garbage collection has not previously occurred will receive destructor calls.

5.11 static Class Members

Each object of a class has its own copy of all the instance variables of the class. However, in certain cases, all class objects should share only one copy of a particular variable. Such variables are called **static** *variables*. A program contains only one copy of each of a class's **static** variables in memory, no matter how many objects of the class have been instantiated. A **static** variable represents *classwide information*; all of a class's objects share the same **static** data item.

The declaration of a **static** member begins with the keyword **static**. A **static** variable can be initialized in its declaration by following the variable name with an **=** and an initial value. In cases where a **static** variable requires more complex initialization, programmers can define a **static** *constructor* to initialize only the **static** members. Such constructors are optional and must be declared with the **static** keyword, followed by the name of the class. **static** constructors are called before any **static** members are used and before any class objects are instantiated.

We now consider a video-game example that justifies the need for **static** classwide data. Suppose that we have a video game involving **Martian**s and other space creatures. Each **Martian** tends to be brave and willing to attack other space creatures when the **Martian** is aware that there are at least four other **Martian**s present. If there are fewer than five **Martian**s present, each **Martian** becomes cowardly. For this reason, each **Martian** must know the **martianCount**. We could endow class **Martian** with **martianCount** as instance data. However, if we were to do this, then every **Martian** would have a separate copy of the instance data, and every time we create a **Martian**, we would have to update the instance variable **martianCount** in every **Martian**. The redundant copies waste space, and updating those copies is time consuming. Instead, we declare **martianCount** to be **static**, so that **martianCount** is classwide data. Each **Martian** can see the **martianCount** as if it were instance data of that **Martian**, but C# maintains only one copy of the **static** variable **martianCount**, which saves space. This technique also saves time; because there is only one copy, we do not have to increment separate copies of **martianCount** for each **Martian** object.

Performance Tip 5.1

When a single copy of a piece of data will suffice, use **static** *variables to save storage space.*

Although **static** variables might seem like *global variables* (variables that can be referenced anywhere in a program) in other programming languages, **static** variables need not be globally accessible; **static** variables have class scope.

The **public static** data members of a class can be accessed through the class name, using the dot operator (e.g., **Math.PI**). The **private static** members can be accessed only through methods or properties of the class. **static** members are available as soon as the class is loaded into memory at execution time, and they exist for the duration of program execution, even when no objects of that class exist. In order to enable a program to access a **private static** member when no objects of the class exist, the class must provide a **public static** method or property.

A **static** method cannot access instance (non-**static**) members. Unlike instance methods, a **static** method has no **this** reference, because **static** variables and **static** methods exist independently of any class objects, even when the class has no objects.

Common Programming Error 5.5

Using the **this** *reference in a* **static** *method or* **static** *property is a compilation error.*

Common Programming Error 5.6

A call to an instance method or an attempt to access an instance variable from a **static** *method is a compilation error.*

Class **Employee** (Fig. 5.13) demonstrates a **public static** property that enables a program to obtain the value of a **private static** variable. The **static** variable **count** (line 11) is not initialized explicitly, so it receives the value **0** by default. Class variable **count** maintains a count of the number of objects of class **Employee** that have been instantiated, including those objects that have already been marked for garbage collection, but have not yet been reclaimed by the garbage collector.

When objects of class **Employee** exist, **static** member **count** can be used in any method of an **Employee** object; in this example, the constructor (lines 14–23) increments **count**, and the destructor (lines 26–32) decrements **count**. If no objects of class **Employee** exist, the value of member **count** can be obtained through **static** property **Count** (lines 53–59); this technique also works when there are **Employee** objects in memory.

Class **StaticTest** (Fig. 5.14) runs the application that demonstrates the **static** members of class **Employee** (Fig. 5.13). Lines 12–13 use the **static** property **Count** of class **Employee** to obtain the current **count** value before the program creates **Employee** objects. Notice that the syntax used to access a **static** member is

ClassName.*StaticMember*

On line 13, *ClassName* is **Employee** and *StaticMember* is **Count**. Recall that we used this syntax in prior examples to call the **static** methods of class **Math** (e.g., **Math.Pow** and **Math.Abs**) and other methods, such as **Int32.Parse** and **MessageBox.Show**.

```
1    // Fig. 5.13: Employee.cs
2    // Employee class contains static data and a static method.
3
4    using System;
5
6    // Employee class definition
7    public class Employee
8    {
9       private string firstName;
10      private string lastName;
11      private static int count;   // Employee objects in memory
12
13      // constructor increments static Employee count
14      public Employee( string fName, string lName )
15      {
16         firstName = fName;
17         lastName = lName;
18
19         ++count;
20
21         Console.WriteLine( "Employee object constructor: " +
22            firstName + " " + lastName + "; count = " + Count );
23      }
24
25      // destructor decrements static Employee count
26      ~Employee()
27      {
28         --count;
29
30         Console.WriteLine( "Employee object destructor: " +
31            firstName + " " + lastName + "; count = " + Count );
32      }
33
34      // FirstName property
35      public string FirstName
36      {
37         get
38         {
39            return firstName;
40         }
41      }
42
43      // LastName property
44      public string LastName
45      {
46         get
47         {
48            return lastName;
49         }
50      }
51
```

Fig. 5.13 **static** members are accessible to all objects of a class. (Part 1 of 2.)

```
52      // static Count property
53      public static int Count
54      {
55         get
56         {
57            return count;
58         }
59      }
60
61   } // end class Employee
```

Fig. 5.13 **static** members are accessible to all objects of a class. (Part 2 of 2.)

Next, lines 16–17 instantiate two **Employee** objects and assign them to references **employee1** and **employee2**. Each call to the **Employee** constructor increments the value of **count** by one. Lines 19–26 display the value of **Count** as well as the names of the two employees. Lines 30–31 set references **employee1** and **employee2** to **null**, so they no longer refer to the **Employee** objects. Because these references were the only references in the program to the **Employee** objects, garbage collection can now be applied to those objects.

```
1   // Fig. 5.14: StaticTest.cs
2   // Demonstrating static class members.
3
4   using System;
5
6   // StaticTest class definition
7   class StaticTest
8   {
9      // main entry point for application
10     static void Main( string[] args )
11     {
12        Console.WriteLine( "Employees before instantiation: " +
13           Employee.Count + "\n" );
14
15        // create two Employees
16        Employee employee1 = new Employee( "Susan", "Baker" );
17        Employee employee2 = new Employee( "Bob", "Jones" );
18
19        Console.WriteLine( "\nEmployees after instantiation: " +
20           "Employee.Count = " + Employee.Count + "\n" );
21
22        // display the Employees
23        Console.WriteLine( "Employee 1: " +
24           employee1.FirstName + " " + employee1.LastName +
25           "\nEmployee 2: " + employee2.FirstName +
26           " " + employee2.LastName + "\n" );
27
28        // remove references to objects to indicate that
29        // objects can be garbage collected
30        employee1 = null;
```

Fig. 5.14 **static** member demonstration. (Part 1 of 2.)

```
31              employee2 = null;
32
33              // force garbage collection
34              System.GC.Collect();
35
36              // wait until collection completes
37              System.GC.WaitForPendingFinalizers();
38
39              Console.WriteLine(
40                  "\nEmployees after garbage collection: " +
41                  Employee.Count );
42      }
43  }
```

```
Employees before instantiation: 0

Employee object constructor: Susan Baker; count = 1
Employee object constructor: Bob Jones; count = 2

Employees after instantiation: Employee.Count = 2

Employee 1: Susan Baker
Employee 2: Bob Jones

Employee object destructor: Bob Jones; count = 1
Employee object destructor: Susan Baker; count = 0

Employees after garbage collection: 0
```

Fig. 5.14 **static** member demonstration. (Part 2 of 2.)

The garbage collector is not invoked directly by the program. Either the garbage collector reclaims the memory for objects when the runtime determines garbage collection is appropriate, or the operating system recovers the memory when the program terminates. However, it is possible to request that the garbage collector attempt to collect available objects. Line 34 uses **public static** method *Collect* from class *GC* (namespace **System**) to make this request. The garbage collector is not guaranteed to collect all objects that are currently available for collection. If the garbage collector decides to collect objects, it first invokes the destructor of each object. It is important to understand that the garbage collector executes as an independent entity called a *thread*. (Threads are discussed in Chapter 11, Multithreading.) It is possible for multiple threads to execute in parallel on a multiprocessor system or to share a processor on a single-processor system. Thus, a program could run in parallel with garbage collection. For this reason, we call **static** method *WaitForPendingFinalizers* of class **GC** (line 37), which forces the program to wait until the garbage collector invokes the destructors for all objects that are ready for collection and reclaims those objects. When the program reaches lines 41, we are assured that both destructor calls completed and that the value of **count** has been decremented accordingly.

In this example, the output shows that the destructor was called for each **Employee**, which causes the value of **count** to be decremented by two (once per **Employee** being collected). Lines 39–41 use property **Count** to obtain the value of **count** after invoking the garbage collector. If the objects had not been collected, the value of **count** would have been greater than zero.

Toward the end of the output, notice that the **Employee** object for **Bob Jones** was finalized before the **Employee** object for **Susan Baker**. However, the output of this program as run on your system could differ from the output we obtained, because the garbage collector is not guaranteed to collect objects in a specific order.

5.12 **const** and **readonly** Members

C# allows programmers to create *constants* whose values cannot change during program execution.

Testing and Debugging Tip 5.3

If the value of a variable should never change, make the variable a constant. This practice helps eliminate errors that might occur if the value of the variable were indeed to change.

To create a constant data member of a class, declare that member with either the **const** or the **readonly** keyword. Data members declared as **const** implicitly are **static** and must be initialized in their declaration. Data members declared as **readonly** can be initialized in their declaration or in their class's constructor. Neither **const** nor **readonly** values can be modified once they are initialized, although **readonly** variables can be assigned values in several constructors (only one of which will be called when an object is initialized).

Common Programming Error 5.7

*Declaring a class data member as **const**, but failing to initialize it in that class's declaration is a syntax error.*

Common Programming Error 5.8

*Assigning a value to a **const** variable after that variable is initialized is a compilation error.*

Common Programming Error 5.9

*The declaration of a **const** member as **static** is a syntax error, because a **const** member implicitly is **static**.*

Common Programming Error 5.10

*Declaring a class data member as **readonly** and attempting to use it before it is initialized is a logic error.*

Members that are declared as **const** must be assigned values at compile time. Therefore, **const** members can be initialized only with other constant values, such as integers, string literals, characters and other **const** members. Constant members with values that cannot be determined at compile time must be declared with keyword **readonly**. We mentioned previously that a **readonly** member can be assigned a value only once, either when it is declared or within the constructor of the class. When initializing a **static readonly** member in a constructor, a **static** constructor must be used.

Figure 5.15 demonstrates constants. The program consists of two classes: Class **Constants** (lines 8–22) defines two constants, and class **UsingConstAndReadonly** (lines 25–43) demonstrates the constants in class **Constants**.

```csharp
1   // Fig. 5.15: UsingConstAndReadOnly.cs
2   // Demonstrating constant values with const and readonly.
3
4   using System;
5   using System.Windows.Forms;
6
7   // Constants class definition
8   public class Constants
9   {
10      // create constant PI
11      public const double PI = 3.14159;
12
13      // radius is a constant
14      // that is uninitialized
15      public readonly int radius;
16
17      public Constants( int radiusValue )
18      {
19         radius = radiusValue;
20      }
21
22   } // end class Constants
23
24   // UsingConstAndReadOnly class definition
25   public class UsingConstAndReadonly
26   {
27      // method Main creates Constants
28      // object and displays its values
29      static void Main( string[] args )
30      {
31         Random random = new Random();
32
33         Constants constantValues =
34            new Constants( random.Next( 1, 20 ) );
35
36         MessageBox.Show( "Radius = " + constantValues.radius +
37            "\nCircumference = " +
38            2 * Constants.PI * constantValues.radius,
39            "Circumference" );
40
41      } // end method Main
42
43   } // end class UsingConstAndReadOnly
```

Fig. 5.15   **const** and **readonly** class member demonstration.

Line 11 in class **Constants** creates constant **PI**, using keyword **const**, and initializes **PI** with the **double** value **3.14159**—an approximation of π that the program uses to calculate the circumferences of circles. Note that we could have used the predefined constant **PI** of class **Math** (**Math.PI**) as the value, but we wanted to demonstrate how to define a **const** variable explicitly. The compiler must be able to determine a **const** variable's value at compile time; otherwise, a compilation error will occur. For example, if line 11 has initialized **PI** with the expression

```
Double.Parse( "3.14159" )
```

the compiler would have generated an error. Although the expression uses **string** literal **"3.14159"** (a constant value) as an argument, the compiler cannot evaluate the method call **Double.Parse** at compile time.

Variables declared as **readonly** can be initialized at execution time. Line 15 declares **readonly** variable **radius**, but does not initialize it. The **Constants** constructor (lines 17–20) receives an **int** value and assigns it to **radius** when the program creates a **Constants** object. Note that radius can also be initialized with a more complex expression, such as a method call that returns an **int**.

Class **UsingConstAndReadonly** (lines 25–43) uses the **const** and **readonly** variables of class **Constants**. Lines 33–34 use a **Random** object to generate a random **int** between **1** and **20** (using method **Next** of class **Random**) that corresponds to a circle's **radius**, and pass that value to the **Constants** constructor to initialize the **readonly** variable **radius**. Lines 36–39 output the radius and circumference of a circle in a **MessageBox**. Line 36 uses **Constants**'s reference **contantValues** to access **readonly** variable **radius**. Line 38 computes the circle's circumference, using **const** variable **Constants.PI** and **readonly** variable **radius**. Note that we use **static** syntax to access **const** variable **PI**, because **const** variables implicitly are **static**.

5.13 Indexers

Sometimes a class encapsulates data that a program can manipulate as a list of elements. Such a class can define special properties called *indexers* that allow array-style indexed access to lists of elements. With "conventional" C# arrays, the subscript number must be an integer value. A benefit of indexers is that the programmer can define both integer subscripts and noninteger subscripts. For example, a programmer could allow client code to manipulate data by using **string**s as subscripts that represent the data items' names or descriptions. Also, when manipulating "conventional" C# array elements, the array-subscript operator always returns the same data type—i.e., the type of the array. Indexers are more flexible: They can return any data type, even one that is different from the type of the data in the list of elements.

 Common Programming Error 5.11

*Declaring indexers as **static** is a syntax error.*

Although an indexer's subscript operator is used like an array-subscript operator, indexers are defined as properties in a class. Unlike normal properties, for which the programmer can choose an appropriate property name, indexers must be defined with keyword **this**. Indexers have the general form

```
accessModifier  returnType  this[  IndexType1 name1,  IndexType2 name2, ...  ]
{
   get
   {
      // use name1, name2, ... here to get data
   }

   set
   {
      // use name1, name2, ... here to set data
   }
}
```

The *IndexType* parameters specified in the brackets (**[]**) are accessible to the **get** and **set** accessors. These accessors define how to use the index (or indices) to select or modify the appropriate data member. As with properties, **get** must **return** a value of type *return-Type*, and **set** can use the **value** keyword to reference the value that should be assigned to the data member.

The program in Fig. 5.16 contains two classes: Class **Box** (lines 14–74) represents a box with a length, a width and a height, and class **IndexerTest** (lines 77–177) demonstrates class **Box**'s indexers.

```
1    // Fig. 5.16: IndexerTest.cs
2    // Indexers provide access to an object's members via a
3    // subscript operator.
4
5    using System;
6    using System.Drawing;
7    using System.Collections;
8    using System.ComponentModel;
9    using System.Windows.Forms;
10   using System.Data;
11
12   // Box class definition represents a box with length,
13   // width and height dimensions
14   public class Box
15   {
16      private string[] names = { "length", "width", "height" };
17      private double[] dimensions = new double[ 3 ];
18
19      // constructor
20      public Box( double length, double width, double height )
21      {
22         dimensions[ 0 ] = length;
23         dimensions[ 1 ] = width;
24         dimensions[ 2 ] = height;
25      }
26
27      // access dimensions by integer index number
28      public double this[ int index ]
29      {
```

Fig. 5.16 Indexers provide subscripted access to an object's members. (Part 1 of 5.)

```
30            get
31            {
32               return ( index < 0 || index >= dimensions.Length ) ?
33                  -1 : dimensions[ index ];
34            }
35
36            set
37            {
38               if ( index >= 0 && index < dimensions.Length )
39                  dimensions[ index ] = value;
40            }
41
42         } // end numeric indexer
43
44         // access dimensions by their string names
45         public double this[ string name ]
46         {
47            get
48            {
49               // locate element to get
50               int i = 0;
51
52               while ( i < names.Length &&
53                  name.ToLower() != names[ i ] )
54                  i++;
55
56               return ( i == names.Length ) ? -1.0 : dimensions[ i ];
57            }
58
59            set
60            {
61               // locate element to set
62               int i = 0;
63
64               while ( i < names.Length &&
65                  name.ToLower() != names[ i ] )
66                  i++;
67
68               if ( i != names.Length )
69                  dimensions[ i ] = value;
70            }
71
72         } // end indexer
73
74      } // end class Box
75
76      // Class IndexerTest
77      public class IndexerTest : System.Windows.Forms.Form
78      {
79         private System.Windows.Forms.Label indexLabel;
80         private System.Windows.Forms.Label nameLabel;
81
82         private System.Windows.Forms.TextBox indexTextBox;
```

Fig. 5.16 Indexers provide subscripted access to an object's members. (Part 2 of 5.)

```
83          private System.Windows.Forms.TextBox valueTextBox;
84
85          private System.Windows.Forms.Button nameSetButton;
86          private System.Windows.Forms.Button nameGetButton;
87
88          private System.Windows.Forms.Button intSetButton;
89          private System.Windows.Forms.Button intGetButton;
90
91          private System.Windows.Forms.TextBox resultTextBox;
92
93          // required designer variable
94          private System.ComponentModel.Container components = null;
95
96          private Box box;
97
98          // constructor
99          public IndexerTest()
100         {
101            // required for Windows Form Designer support
102            InitializeComponent();
103
104            // create block
105            box = new Box( 0.0, 0.0, 0.0 );
106         }
107
108         // Visual Studio .NET generated code
109
110         // main entry point for application
111         [STAThread]
112         static void Main()
113         {
114            Application.Run( new IndexerTest() );
115         }
116
117         // display value at specified index number
118         private void ShowValueAtIndex( string prefix, int index )
119         {
120            resultTextBox.Text =
121               prefix + "box[ " + index + " ] = " + box[ index ];
122         }
123
124         // display value with specified name
125         private void ShowValueAtIndex( string prefix, string name )
126         {
127            resultTextBox.Text =
128               prefix + "box[ " + name + " ] = " + box[ name ];
129         }
130
131         // clear indexTextBox and valueTextBox
132         private void ClearTextBoxes()
133         {
```

Fig. 5.16 Indexers provide subscripted access to an object's members. (Part 3 of 5.)

```
134          indexTextBox.Text = "";
135          valueTextBox.Text = "";
136       }
137
138       // get value at specified index
139       private void intGetButton_Click(
140          object sender, System.EventArgs e )
141       {
142          ShowValueAtIndex(
143             "get: ", Int32.Parse( indexTextBox.Text ) );
144          ClearTextBoxes();
145       }
146
147       // set value at specified index
148       private void intSetButton_Click(
149          object sender, System.EventArgs e )
150       {
151          int index = Int32.Parse( indexTextBox.Text );
152          box[ index ] = Double.Parse( valueTextBox.Text );
153
154          ShowValueAtIndex( "set: ", index );
155          ClearTextBoxes();
156       }
157
158       // get value with specified name
159       private void nameGetButton_Click(
160          object sender, System.EventArgs e )
161       {
162          ShowValueAtIndex( "get: ", indexTextBox.Text );
163          ClearTextBoxes();
164       }
165
166       // set value with specified name
167       private void nameSetButton_Click(
168          object sender, System.EventArgs e )
169       {
170          box[ indexTextBox.Text ] =
171             Double.Parse( valueTextBox.Text );
172
173          ShowValueAtIndex( "set: ", indexTextBox.Text );
174          ClearTextBoxes();
175       }
176
177    } // end class IndexerTest
```

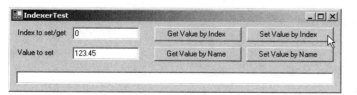

Before setting value
by index number

Fig. 5.16 Indexers provide subscripted access to an object's members. (Part 4 of 5.)

Fig. 5.16 Indexers provide subscripted access to an object's members. (Part 5 of 5.)

The **private** data members of class **Box** are **string** array **names** (line 16), which contains the names (i.e., **"length"**, **"width"** and **"height"**) for the dimensions of a **Box**, and **double** array **dimensions** (line 17), which contains the size of each dimension. Each element in array **names** corresponds to an element in array **dimensions** (e.g., **dimensions[2]** contains the height of the **Box**).

Box defines two indexers (lines 28–42 and lines 45–72) that each **return** a **double** value representing the size of the dimension specified by the indexer's parameter. Indexers can be overloaded like methods. The first indexer uses an **int** subscript to manipulate an element in the **dimensions** array. The second indexer uses a **string** subscript representing the name of the dimension to manipulate an element in the **dimensions** array. Each indexer returns a value of **-1.0** if its **get** accessor encounters an invalid subscript. Each indexer's **set** accessor assigns **value** to the appropriate element of **dimensions** only if the index is valid. Normally, the programmer would have an indexer throw an exception if the indexer received an invalid index. We discuss how to throw exceptions in Chapter 8, Exception Handling.

Notice that the **string** indexer uses a **while** structure to search for a matching **string** in the **names** array (lines 64–66). If a match is found, the indexer manipulates the corresponding element in array **dimensions** (line 69).

Class **IndexerTest** is a **System.Windows.Forms.Form** that manipulates the **private** data members of class **Box** through **Box**'s indexers. Instance variable **box** is declared on line 96 and initialized in the constructor on line 105 with dimension values of **0.0**. The event handler for button **Get Value by Index** (lines 139–145) invokes method **ShowValueAtIndex** (lines 118–122) to retrieve the value at the index number specified in **indexTextBox**. The event handler for button **Set Value by Index** (lines 148–156) assigns the value in **valueTextBox** to the location specified in **indexTextBox**. The event handler for button **Get Value by Name** (159–164) invokes the overloaded method **ShowValueAtIndex** (lines 125–129) to retrieve the value with the name specified in **valueTextBox**. The event handler for button **Set Value by Name** (lines 167–175) assigns the value in **valueTextBox** to the location with the name specified in **index-TextBox**.

5.14 Data Abstraction and Information Hiding

As we pointed out at the beginning of this chapter, classes normally hide the details of their implementation from their clients. This practice is called *information hiding*. As an example of information hiding, let us consider a data structure called a *stack*.

Readers can think of a stack as analogous to a pile of dishes. When a dish is placed on the pile, it is always placed at the top (a process referred to as *pushing* the dish onto the stack). Similarly, when a dish is removed from the pile, it is always removed from the top (a process referred to as *popping* the dish off the stack). Stacks are known as *last-in, first-out (LIFO) data structures*; the last item pushed (inserted) on the stack is the first item popped (removed) from the stack.

Stacks can be implemented with arrays and with other data structures, such as linked lists. (We discuss stacks and linked lists in Chapter 20, Data Structures and Collections.) A client of a stack class need not take account of the stack's implementation. The client knows only that when data items are placed in the stack, these items will be recalled in last-in, first-out order. The client takes account of *what* functionality a stack offers, but not of *how* that functionality is implemented. This concept is referred to as *data abstraction*. Although programmers might know the details of a class's implementation, they should not write code that depends on these details. This practice enables a particular class (such as one that implements a stack and its operations, *push* and *pop*) to be replaced with another version without affecting the rest of the system. As long as the **public** services of the class do not change (i.e., every method still has the same name, return type and parameter list in the new class definition), the rest of the system is not affected.

Most programming languages emphasize actions. In these languages, data exist to support the actions that programs must take; data are "less interesting" than actions and are considered crude. Only a few built-in data types exist in such languages, and it is difficult for programmers to create their own data types. C# and the object-oriented style of programming elevate the importance of data. The primary activities of object-oriented programming in C# are the creation of data types (i.e., classes) and the expression of the interactions among objects of those data types. To create languages that emphasize data, the programming-languages community needed to formalize some notions about data. The formalization we consider here is the notion of *abstract data types (ADTs)*. ADTs receive as much attention today as structured programming did decades earlier. ADTs, however, do not replace structured programming. Rather, they provide an additional formalization to improve the program-development process.

Consider built-in type **int**, which most people would associate with an integer in mathematics. Rather, an **int** is an abstract representation of an integer. Unlike mathematical integers, computer **int**s are fixed in size. For example, type **int** in .NET is limited approximately to the range –2 billion to +2 billion. If the result of a calculation falls outside this range, an error occurs, and the computer responds in some machine-dependent manner. It might, for example, "quietly" produce an incorrect result. Mathematical integers do not have this problem. Therefore, the notion of a computer **int** is only an approximation of the notion of a real-world integer. The same is true of **float** and other built-in types.

We have taken the notion of **int** for granted until this point, but we now consider it from a new perspective. Types like **int**, **float** and **char** are all examples of abstract data types. These types are representations of real-world notions to some satisfactory level of precision within a computer system.

An ADT actually captures two notions—a *data representation* and the *operations* that can be performed on the data. For example, in C#, an **int** contains an integer value (data) and provides addition, subtraction, multiplication, division and modulus operations; however, division by zero is undefined. C# programmers use classes to implement abstract data types.

Software Engineering Observation 5.17

Programmers can create types through the use of the class mechanism. New types can be designed so that they are as convenient to use as the built-in types. This feature marks C# as an extensible language. Although the language is easy to extend via new types, the programmer cannot alter the base language itself.

Another abstract data type we discuss is a *queue*, which is similar to a waiting line. Computer systems use many queues internally. A queue offers well-understood behavior to its clients: Clients place items in a queue one at a time via an *enqueue* operation, and get the items back one at a time via a *dequeue* operation. A queue returns items in *first-in, first-out (FIFO)* order, which means that the first item inserted in a queue is the first item removed. Conceptually, a queue can become infinitely long, but real queues are finite.

The queue hides an internal data representation that keeps track of the items currently waiting in line, and it offers a set of operations to its clients (*enqueue* and *dequeue*). The clients do not take account of the implementation of the queue; clients simply depend upon the queue to operate "as advertised." When a client enqueues an item, the queue should accept that item and place it in some kind of internal FIFO data structure. Similarly, when the client wants the next item from the front of the queue, the queue should remove the item from its internal representation and deliver the item in FIFO order (i.e., the item that has been in the queue the longest should be the next one returned by the next dequeue operation).

The queue ADT guarantees the integrity of its internal data structure. Clients cannot manipulate this data structure directly—only the queue ADT has access to its internal data. Clients are able to perform only allowable operations on the data representation; the ADT rejects operations that its public interface does not provide.

5.15 Software Reusability

C# programmers concentrate both on crafting new classes and on reusing classes from the Framework Class Library (FCL), which contains thousands of predefined classes. Developers construct software by combining programmer-defined classes with well-defined, carefully tested, well-documented, portable and widely available FCL classes. This kind of software reusability speeds the development of powerful, high-quality software. *Rapid applications development* (*RAD*) is of great interest today.

The FCL allows C# programmers to achieve software reusability across platforms that support .NET and rapid applications development. C# programmers focus on the high-level programming issues and leave the low-level implementation details to classes in the FCL. For example, a C# programmer who writes a graphics program does not need to know the details of every .NET-platform graphics capability. Instead, C# programmers concentrate on learning and using the FCL's graphics classes.

The FCL enables C# developers to build applications faster by reusing preexisting, extensively tested classes. In addition to reducing development time, FCL classes also improve programmers' abilities to debug and maintain applications, because proven software components are being used. For programmers to take advantage of the FCL's classes, they must familiarize themselves with the FCL's rich set of capabilities.

Software reuse is not limited to Windows-application development. The FCL also includes classes for creating *Web services*, which are applications packaged as services that clients can access via the Internet. Any C# application is a potential Web service, so C# programmers can reuse existing applications as building blocks to form larger, more sophisticated, Web-enabled applications.

Many people believe that Web services represent the next phase in the evolution of software development, in which the Web provides a library of functionality from which developers can build applications in a platform-independent manner. As Microsoft's premier .NET language, C# provides all the features necessary for creating scalable, robust Web services. We formally introduce Web Services in Chapter 18, ASP .NET and Web Services.

5.16 Namespaces and Assemblies

As we have seen in almost every example in the text, classes from preexisting libraries, such as the .NET Framework, must be imported into a C# program by adding a reference to the appropriate libraries (a process we demonstrated in Section 2.7). Remember that each class in the Framework Class Library belongs to a specific namespace. The preexisting code in the FCL facilitates software reuse.

Programmers should concentrate on making the software components they create reusable. However, doing so often results in *naming collisions*. For example, two classes defined by different programmers can have the same name. If a program needs both of those classes, the program must have a way to distinguish between the two classes in the code.

Common Programming Error 5.12

Attempting to compile code that contains naming collisions will generate compilation errors.

Namespaces help minimize this problem by providing a convention for *unique class names*. No two classes in a given namespace can have the same name, but different namespaces can contain classes of the same name. With hundreds of thousands of people writing C# programs, there is a good chance that the names that one programmer chooses to describe classes will conflict with the names that other programmers choose for their classes.

We begin our discussion of reusing existing class definitions in Fig. 5.17, which provides the code for class **Time3** (originally defined in Fig. 5.6). When reusing class definitions between programs, programmers create class libraries that can be imported for use in a program via a **using** statement. Only **public** classes can be reused from class libraries. Non-**public** classes can be used only by other classes in the same assembly.

The only difference between class **Time3** in this example and the version in Fig. 5.6 is that we show the **namespace**—i.e., **TimeLibrary**—in which **Time3** is defined. Each class library is defined in a **namespace** that contains all the classes in the library. We will demonstrate momentarily how to package class **Time3** into **TimeLibrary.dll**—the *dynamic link library* that we create for reuse in other programs. Programs can load dynamic link libraries at execution time to access common functionality that can be shared among many programs. A dynamic link library represents an assembly. When a project uses a class library, the project must contain a reference to the assembly that defines the class library.

```
1   // Fig. 5.17: TimeLibrary.cs
2   // Placing class Time3 in an assembly for reuse.
3
4   using System;
5
6   namespace TimeLibrary    // specifies namespace for class Time3
7   {
8      // Time3 class definition
9      public class Time3
10     {
11        private int hour;      // 0-23
12        private int minute;    // 0-59
13        private int second;    // 0-59
14
```

Fig. 5.17 Assembly **TimeLibrary** contains class **Time3**. (Part 1 of 3.)

```
15      // Time3 constructor initializes instance variables to
16      // zero to set default time to midnight
17      public Time3()
18      {
19         SetTime( 0, 0, 0 );
20      }
21
22      // Time3 constructor: hour supplied, minute and second
23      // defaulted to 0
24      public Time3( int hour )
25      {
26         SetTime( hour, 0, 0 );
27      }
28
29      // Time3 constructor: hour and minute supplied, second
30      // defaulted to 0
31      public Time3( int hour, int minute )
32      {
33         SetTime( hour, minute, 0 );
34      }
35
36      // Time3 constructor: hour, minute and second supplied
37      public Time3( int hour, int minute, int second )
38      {
39         SetTime( hour, minute, second );
40      }
41
42      // Time3 constructor: initialize using another Time3 object
43      public Time3( Time3 time )
44      {
45         SetTime( time.Hour, time.Minute, time.Second );
46      }
47
48      // Set new time value in 24-hour format. Perform validity
49      // checks on the data. Set invalid values to zero.
50      public void SetTime(
51         int hourValue, int minuteValue, int secondValue )
52      {
53         Hour = hourValue;
54         Minute = minuteValue;
55         Second = secondValue;
56      }
57
58      // property Hour
59      public int Hour
60      {
61         get
62         {
63            return hour;
64         }
65
```

Fig. 5.17 Assembly **TimeLibrary** contains class **Time3**. (Part 2 of 3.)

```
66              set
67              {
68                  hour = ( ( value >= 0 && value < 24 ) ? value : 0 );
69              }
70
71          } // end property Hour
72
73          // property Minute
74          public int Minute
75          {
76              get
77              {
78                  return minute;
79              }
80
81              set
82              {
83                  minute = ( ( value >= 0 && value < 60 ) ? value : 0 );
84              }
85
86          } // end property Minute
87
88          // property Second
89          public int Second
90          {
91              get
92              {
93                  return second;
94              }
95
96              set
97              {
98                  second = ( ( value >= 0 && value < 60 ) ? value : 0 );
99              }
100
101         } // end property Second
102
103         // convert time to universal-time (24 hour) format string
104         public string ToUniversalString()
105         {
106             return String.Format(
107                 "{0:D2}:{1:D2}:{2:D2}", Hour, Minute, Second );
108         }
109
110         // convert time to standard-time (12 hour) format string
111         public string ToStandardString()
112         {
113             return String.Format( "{0}:{1:D2}:{2:D2} {3}",
114                 ( ( Hour == 12 || Hour == 0 ) ? 12 : Hour % 12 ),
115                 Minute, Second, ( Hour < 12 ? "AM" : "PM" ) );
116         }
117     } // end class Time3
118 }
```

Fig. 5.17 Assembly **TimeLibrary** contains class **Time3**. (Part 3 of 3.)

We now describe, step by step, how to create the class library **TimeLibrary**, which contains class **Time3**:

1. *Create a class-library project.* From the **File** menu, choose option **New**, followed by **Project....** In the **New Project** dialog, ensure that **C# Projects** is selected in the **Project Types** section, and click **Class Library**. Name the project **TimeLibrary**, and choose the directory in which you would like to store the project. A simple class library will be created, as shown in Fig. 5.18. There are two important points to note about the generated code. The first is that the class does not contain a **Main** method. This condition indicates that the class in the class library cannot be used to begin the execution of an application. This class is designed to be used by other programs. Also notice that **Class1** is created as a **public** class. If another project uses this library, only the library's **public** classes are accessible. We created class **Time3** as **public** (line 9 of Fig. 5.17) for this purpose. Class **Time3** was created simply by renaming **Class1** (created by Visual Studio.NET as part of the project) as **Time3**. In the **Solution Explorer**, we also renamed the **Class1.cs** file as **Time3.cs**.

2. *Add the code for class **Time3**.* Delete the code for the **Class1** constructor. Then copy the remainder of the **Time3** code (lines 11–116) from Fig. 5.17 (you can find this file in the set of examples that can be downloaded from our Web site), and paste the code in the body of the class definition shown in Fig. 5.18.

3. *Compile the code.* From the **Build** menu, choose option **Build Solution**. The code should compile successfully. Remember that this code cannot be executed— there is no entry point into the program. In fact, if you try running the program by selecting the **Debug** menu and choosing **Start**, Visual Studio .NET displays an error message.

Compiling the project creates an assembly (a dynamic link library) that represents the new class library. This assembly can be found in the **bin\Debug** directory of the project. By default, the assembly name will include the namespace name. (In this case, the assembly name will be **TimeLibrary.dll**.) The assembly file contains class **Time3**, which other projects can use. Assembly files, which have file extensions **.dll** and **.exe**, are integral to C#. The Windows operating system uses executable files (**.exe**) to run applications, whereas it uses library files (**.dll**, which stands for *dynamic link library*) to represent code libraries that can be loaded dynamically by many applications and shared among those applications.

Next, we define a console application project containing class **AssemblyTest** (Fig. 5.19), which uses class **Time3** in assembly **TimeLibrary.dll** to create a **Time3** object and display its standard-time and universal-time string formats.

Before class **AssemblyTest** can use class **Time3**, the project containing class **AssemblyTest** must have a reference to the **TimeLibrary** assembly. To add the reference, select **Add Reference** from the **Project** menu. Using the **Browse** button, select **TimeLibrary.dll** (located in the **bin\Debug** directory of the **TimeLibrary** project), and click **OK** to add the resource to the project. After adding the reference, use keyword **using** to inform the compiler that we will use classes from namespace **Time-Library** (line 5 in Fig. 5.19).

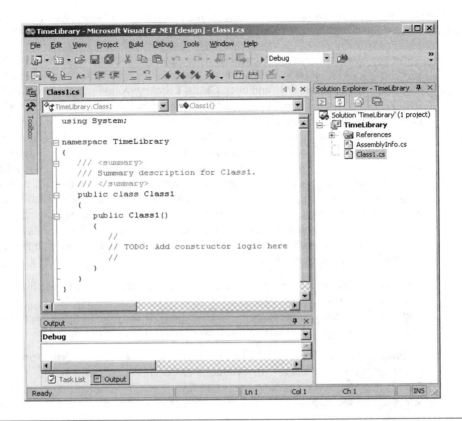

Fig. 5.18 Simple class library.

```
1   // Fig. 5.19: AssemblyTest.cs
2   // Using class Time3 from assembly TimeLibrary.
3
4   using System;
5   using TimeLibrary;
6
7   // AssemblyTest class definition
8   class AssemblyTest
9   {
10     // main entry point for application
11     static void Main( string[] args )
12     {
13        Time3 time = new Time3( 13, 27, 6 );
14
15        Console.WriteLine(
16           "Standard time: {0}\nUniversal time: {1}\n",
17           time.ToStandardString(), time.ToUniversalString() );
18     }
19  }
```

Fig. 5.19 Assembly **TimeLibrary** used from class **AssemblyTest**. (Part 1 of 2.)

```
Standard time: 1:27:06 PM
Universal time: 13:27:06
```

Fig. 5.19 Assembly **TimeLibrary** used from class **AssemblyTest**. (Part 2 of 2.)

5.17 Class View and Object Browser

Now that we have introduced key concepts of object-based programming, we present two features that Visual Studio .NET provides to facilitate the design of object-oriented applications: **Class View** and **Object Browser**.

The **Class View** displays the variables and methods for all classes in a project. To access this feature, select **Class View** from the **View** menu. Figure 5.20 shows the **Class View** for the **TimeTest1** project of Fig. 5.1 and Fig. 5.2 (class **Time1** and class **TimeTest1**). The view follows a hierarchical structure, positioning the project name (**TimeTest1**) as the root and including a series of nodes (e.g., classes, variables and methods). If a plus sign (**+**) appears to the left of a node, that node can be expanded to show other nodes. By contrast, if a minus sign (**-**) appears to the left of a node, that node has been expanded (and can be collapsed). According to the **Class View**, project **TimeTest1** contains class **Time1** and class **TimeTest1** as *children*. Class **Time1** contains methods **SetTime**, **Time1**, **ToStandardString** and **ToUniversalString** (indicated by purple boxes) and instance variables **hour**, **minute** and **second** (indicated by blue boxes). The lock icons, placed to the left of the blue-box icons for the instance variables, specify that the variables are **private**. Class **TimeTest1** contains method **Main**. Note that both class **Time1** and class **TimeTest1** contain the **Bases and Interfaces** node. If you expand this node, you will see class **Object** in each case, because each class inherits from class **System.Object** (discussed in Chapter 6, Object-Oriented Programming: Inheritance).

Visual Studio .NET's **Object Browser** lists all classes included in this project. Developers use the **Object Browser** to learn about the functionality provided by a specific class. To open the **Object Browser**, right click any built-in .NET class or method in the code editor and select **Go To Definition**. Figure 5.21 depicts the **Object Browser** when the user right clicks the class name **Object** in the code editor. Note that the **Object Browser** lists all methods provided by class **Object** in the **Members of 'Object'** window; this window offers developers instant access to information regarding the functionality of various objects. Note also that the **Object Browser** lists in the **Objects** window all classes in the FCL. The **Object Browser** can be used for quickly learning about a class or method of a class. Remember that you can view the complete description of a class or method in the online documentation available through the **Help** menu in Visual Studio .NET.

This chapter is the first in a series of three chapters that cover the fundamentals of object-based and object-oriented programming. In this chapter, we have discussed how to create proper class definitions, how to control access to class members and several features commonly used to craft valuable classes for reuse by other programmers. Chapter 6 focuses on *inheritance*. In that chapter, you will learn how to build classes that inherit data and functionality from existing class definitions. You also will learn about other C# features that are specific to the inheritance relationship between classes. These features serve as the basis for the object-oriented programming concept called *polymorphism* that we present in Chapter 7, Object-Based Programming: Polymorphism.

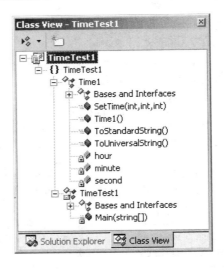

Fig. 5.20   **Class View** of class **Time1** (Fig. 5.1) and class **TimeTest** (Fig. 5.2).

Fig. 5.21   **Object Browser** when user selects **Object** from **Time1.cs**. (Part 1 of 2.)

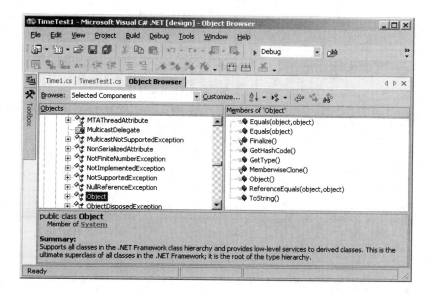

Fig. 5.21   **Object Browser** when user selects **Object** from **Time1.cs**. (Part 2 of 2.)

5.18 Summary

Instance variables and methods that are declared with member access modifier **public** are accessible wherever the program has a reference to an object of the class in which the **public** members are defined. Instance variables and methods that are declared with member access modifier **private** are accessible only to methods of the class in which the **private** members are defined.

A class's constructor is called when an object of that class is instantiated. Constructors initialize an object's instance variables and can be overloaded. If no constructors are defined for a class, a default constructor is provided by the compiler. The default constructor takes no parameters and has an empty body.

To allow clients to manipulate the value of **private** data, the class can provide a property definition. Property definitions contain accessor methods that handle the details of modifying and returning data. A property definition can contain a **set** accessor, a **get** accessor or both. A **get** accessor enables the client to read the field's value, and the **set** accessor enables the client to modify the field's value.

A class also can define indexers to provide subscripted access to the data in an object of that class. Indexers can be defined to use any data type as the subscript. Each indexer can define a **get** and **set** accessor.

The .NET Framework performs automatic garbage collection. Every class in C# can have a destructor that typically returns resources to the system. The destructor for an object is guaranteed to be called to perform termination housekeeping on the object just before the garbage collector reclaims the memory for the object.

Each class in the .NET Framework belongs to a specific namespace (or library) that contains a group of related classes and interfaces. Programmers can create their own namespaces to avoid naming collisions with identifiers in other programmer-defined libraries.

Object-Oriented Programming: Inheritance

Objectives

- To understand inheritance and software reusability.
- To understand the concepts of base classes and derived classes.
- To understand member access modifier **protected** and **internal**.
- To use the **base** reference to access base-class members.
- To understand the use of constructors and destructors in base classes and derived classes.
- To present a case study that demonstrates the mechanics of inheritance.

Say not you know another entirely, till you have divided an inheritance with him.
Johann Kasper Lavater

This method is to define as the number of a class the class of all classes similar to the given class.
Bertrand Russell

Good as it is to inherit a library, it is better to collect one.
Augustine Birrell

Outline

6.1	Introduction
6.2	Base Classes and Derived Classes
6.3	`protected` and `internal` Members
6.4	Relationship between Base Classes and Derived Classes
6.5	Case Study: Three-Level Inheritance Hierarchy
6.6	Constructors and Destructors in Derived Classes
6.7	Software Engineering with Inheritance
6.8	Summary

6.1 Introduction

In this chapter, we begin our discussion of object-oriented programming (OOP) by introducing one of its main features—*inheritance*. Inheritance is a form of software reusability in which classes are created by absorbing an existing class's data and behaviors and embellishing them with new capabilities. Software reusability saves time during program development. It also encourages the reuse of proven and debugged high-quality software, which increases the likelihood that a system will be implemented effectively.

When creating a class, instead of writing completely new instance variables and methods, the programmer can designate that the new class should *inherit* the class variables, properties and methods of another class. The previously defined class is called the *base class*, and the new class is referred to as the *derived class*. (Other programming languages, such as Java, refer to the base class as the *superclass*, and the derived class as the *subclass*.) Once created, each derived class can become the base class for future derived classes. A derived class, to which unique class variables, properties and methods normally are added, is often larger than its base class. Therefore, a derived class is more specific than its base class and represents a more specialized group of objects. Typically, the derived class contains the behaviors of its base class and additional behaviors. The *direct base class* is the base class from which the derived class explicitly inherits. An *indirect base class* is inherited from two or more levels up the *class hierarchy*. In the case of *single inheritance,* a class is derived from one base class. C#, unlike C++, does not support *multiple inheritance* (which occurs when a class is derived from more than one direct base class). (We explain in Chapter 7 how C# can use interfaces to realize many of the benefits of multiple inheritance while avoiding the associated problems.)

Every object of a derived class is also an object of that derived class's base class. However, base-class objects are not objects of their derived classes. For example, all cars are vehicles, but not all vehicles are cars. As we continue our study of object-oriented programming in Chapters 6 and 7, we take advantage of this relationship to perform some interesting manipulations.

Experience in building software systems indicates that significant amounts of code deal with closely related special cases. When programmers are preoccupied with special cases, the details can obscure the "big picture." With object-oriented programming, programmers focus on the commonalities among objects in the system, rather than on the special cases. This process is called *abstraction*.

We distinguish between the *"is-a" relationship* and the *"has-a" relationship*. "Is-a" represents inheritance. In an "is-a" relationship, an object of a derived class also can be treated as an object of its base class. For example, a car *is a* vehicle. By contrast, "has-a" stands for composition (composition is discussed in Chapter 5). In a "has-a" relationship, a class object contains one or more object references as members. For example, a car *has a* steering wheel.

Derived-class methods might require access to their base-class instance variables, properties and methods. A derived class can access the non-**private** members of its base class. Base-class members that should not be accessible to properties or methods of a class derived from that base class via inheritance are declared **private** in the base class. A derived class can effect state changes in **private** base-class members, but only through non-**private** methods and properties provided in the base class and inherited into the derived class.

Software Engineering Observation 6.1

*Properties and methods of a derived class cannot directly access **private** members of their base class.*

Software Engineering Observation 6.2

*Hiding **private** members helps programmers test, debug and correctly modify systems. If a derived class could access its base class's **private** members, classes that inherit from that derived class could access that data as well. This would propagate access to what should be **private** data, and the benefits of information hiding would be lost.*

One problem with inheritance is that a derived class can inherit properties and methods it does not need or should not have. It is the class designer's responsibility to ensure that the capabilities provided by a class are appropriate for future derived classes. Even when a base-class property or method is appropriate for a derived class, that derived class often requires the property or method to perform its task in a manner specific to the derived class. In such cases, the base-class property or method can be *overridden* (redefined) in the derived class with an appropriate implementation.

New classes can inherit from abundant *class libraries*. Organizations develop their own class libraries and can take advantage of other libraries available worldwide. Someday, the vast majority of new software likely will be constructed from *standardized reusable components*, as most hardware is constructed today. This will facilitate the development of more powerful and abundant software.

6.2 Base Classes and Derived Classes

Often, an object of one class "is an" object of another class, as well. For example, a rectangle *is a* quadrilateral (as are squares, parallelograms and trapezoids). Thus, class **Rectangle** can be said to *inherit* from class **Quadrilateral**. In this context, class **Quadrilateral** is a base class, and class **Rectangle** is a derived class. A rectangle *is a* specific type of quadrilateral, but it is incorrect to claim that a quadrilateral *is a* rectangle—the quadrilateral could be a parallelogram or some other type of **Quadrilateral**. Figure 6.1 lists several simple examples of base classes and derived classes.

Base class	Derived classes
Student	GraduateStudent UndergraduateStudent
Shape	Circle Triangle Rectangle
Loan	CarLoan HomeImprovementLoan MortgageLoan
Employee	FacultyMember StaffMember
Account	CheckingAccount SavingsAccount

Fig. 6.1   Inheritance examples.

Every derived-class object "is an" object of its base class, and one base class can have many derived classes; therefore, the set of objects represented by a base class typically is larger than the set of objects represented by any of its derived classes. For example, the base class **Vehicle** represents all vehicles, including cars, trucks, boats, bicycles and so on. By contrast, derived-class **Car** represents only a small subset of all **Vehicle**s.

Inheritance relationships form tree-like hierarchical structures. A class exists in a hierarchical relationship with its derived classes. Although classes can exist independently, once they are employed in inheritance arrangements, they become affiliated with other classes. A class becomes either a base class, supplying data and behaviors to other classes, or a derived class, inheriting its data and behaviors from other classes.

Let us develop a simple inheritance hierarchy. A university community has thousands of members. These members consist of employees, students and alumni. Employees are either faculty members or staff members. Faculty members are either administrators (such as deans and department chairpersons) or teachers. This organizational structure yields the inheritance hierarchy, depicted in Fig. 6.2. Note that the inheritance hierarchy could contain many other classes. For example, students can be graduate or undergraduate students. Undergraduate students can be freshmen, sophomores, juniors and seniors. Each arrow in the hierarchy represents an "is-a" relationship. For example, as we follow the arrows in this class hierarchy, we can state, "an **Employee** *is a* **CommunityMember**" and "a **Teacher** *is a* **Faculty** member." **CommunityMember** is the *direct base class* of **Employee**, **Student** and **Alumnus**. In addition, **CommunityMember** is an *indirect base class* of all the other classes in the hierarchy diagram.

Starting from the bottom of the diagram, the reader can follow the arrows and apply the *is-a* relationship to the topmost base class. For example, an **Administrator** *is a* **Faculty** member, *is an* **Employee** and *is a* **CommunityMember**. In C#, an **Administrator** also *is an* **Object**, because all classes in C# have **Object** as either a direct or indirect base class. Thus, all classes in C# are connected via a hierarchical relationship in which they share the eight methods defined by class **Object**. We discuss some of these methods inherited from **Object** throughout the text.

Another inheritance hierarchy is the **Shape** hierarchy of Fig. 6.3. To specify that class **TwoDimensionalShape** is derived from (or inherits from) class **Shape**, class **TwoDimensionalShape** could be defined in C# as follows:

```
class TwoDimensionalShape : Shape
```

In Chapter 5, we briefly discussed *has-a* relationships, in which classes have as members references to objects of other classes. Such relationships create classes by *composition* of existing classes. For example, given the classes **Employee**, **BirthDate** and **TelephoneNumber**, it is improper to say that an **Employee** *is a* **BirthDate** or that an **Employee** *is a* **TelephoneNumber**. However, it is appropriate to say that an **Employee** *has a* **BirthDate** and that an **Employee** *has a* **TelephoneNumber**.

With inheritance, **private** members of a base class are not accessible directly from that class's derived classes, but these **private** base-class members are still inherited. All other base-class members retain their original member access when they become members of the derived class (e.g., **public** members of the base class become **public** members of the derived class, and, as we will soon see, **protected** members of the base class become **protected** members of the derived class). Through these inherited base-class members, the derived class can manipulate **private** members of the base class (if these inherited members provide such functionality in the base class).

It is possible to treat base-class objects and derived-class objects similarly; their commonalities are expressed in the member variables, properties and methods of the base class. Objects of all classes derived from a common base class can be treated as objects of that base class. In Chapter 7, Object-Oriented Programming: Polymorphism we consider many examples that take advantage of this relationship.

Software Engineering Observation 6.3

Constructors never are inherited—they are specific to the class in which they are defined.

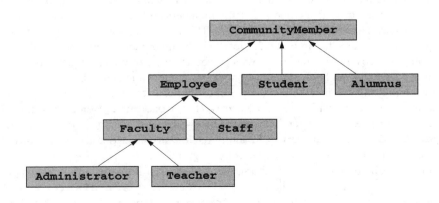

Fig. 6.2   Inheritance hierarchy for university **CommunityMember**s.

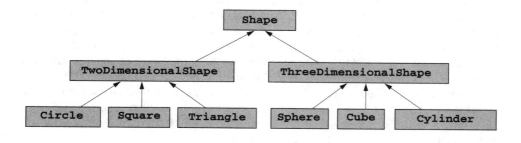

Fig. 6.3   Portion of a **Shape** class hierarchy.

6.3 `protected` and `internal` Members

Chapter 5 discussed **public** and **private** member access modifiers. A base class's non-**static public** members are accessible anywhere that the program has a reference to an object of that base class or one of its derived classes. A base class's **private** members are accessible only within the body of that base class. In this section, we introduce two additional member access modifiers, *protected* and *internal*.

Using **protected** access offers an intermediate level of protection between **public** and **private** access. A base class's **protected** members can be accessed only in that base class or in any classes derived from that base class.

Another intermediate level of access is known as **internal** access. A base class's **internal** members can be accessed only by objects declared in the same assembly. Note that an **internal** member is accessible in any part of the assembly in which that **internal** member is declared.

Derived-class methods normally can refer to **public**, **protected** and **internal** members of the base class simply by using the member names. When a derived-class method overrides a base-class member, the base-class member can be accessed from the derived class by preceding the base-class member name with keyword *base*, followed by the dot operator (**.**). We discuss keyword **base** in Section 6.4.

6.4 Relationship between Base Classes and Derived Classes

In this section, we use a point-circle hierarchy[1] to discuss the relationship between a base class and a derived class. We divide our discussion of the point-circle relationship into several parts. First, we create class **Point**, which directly inherits from class **System.Object** and contains as **private** data an *x-y* coordinate pair. Then, we create class **Circle**, which also directly inherits from class **System.Object** and contains as **private** data an *x-y* coordinate pair (representing the location of the center of the circle) and a radius. We do not use inheritance to create class **Circle**; rather, we construct the class by writing every line of code the class requires. Next, we create a separate **Circle2** class,

---

1. The point-circle relationship may seem unnatural when we discuss it in the context of a circle "is a" point. This example teaches what is sometimes called *structural inheritance*; the example focuses on the "mechanics" of inheritance and how a base class and a derived class relate to one another. In Chapter 7, we present more natural inheritance examples.

which directly inherits from class **Point** (i.e., class **Circle2** "is a" **Point** but also contains a radius) and attempts to use the **Point private** members—this results in compilation errors, because the derived class does not have access to the base-class's **private** data. We then show that if **Point**'s data is declared as **protected**, a **Circle3** class that inherits from class **Point** can access that data. Both the inherited and non-inherited **Circle** classes contain identical functionality, but we show how the inherited **Circle3** class is easier to create and manage. After discussing the merits of using **protected** data, we set the **Point** data back to **private** (to enforce good software engineering), then show how a separate **Circle4** class (which also inherits from class **Point**) can use **Point** methods to manipulate **Point**'s **private** data.

Let us first examine the **Point** (Fig. 6.4) class definition. The **public** services of class **Point** include two **Point** constructors (lines 13–24), properties **X** and **Y** (lines 27–54) and method **ToString** (lines 57–60). The instance variables **x** and **y** of **Point** are specified as **private** (line 10), so objects of other classes cannot access **x** and **y** directly. Technically, even if **Point**'s variables **x** and **y** were made **public**, **Point** can never maintain an inconsistent state, because the *x-y* coordinate plane is infinite in both directions, so **x** and **y** can hold any **int** value. In general, however, declaring data as **private**, while providing non-**private** properties to manipulate and perform validation checking on that data, enforces good software engineering.

We mentioned in Section 6.2 that constructors are not inherited. Therefore, class **Point** does not inherit class **Object**'s constructor. However, class **Point**'s constructors (lines 13–24) call class **Object**'s constructor implicitly. In fact, the first task of any derived-class constructor is to call its direct base class's constructor, either implicitly or explicitly. (The syntax for calling a base-class constructor is discussed later in this section.) If the code does not include an explicit call to the base-class constructor, an implicit call is made to the base class's default (no-argument) constructor. The comments in lines 15 and 21 indicate where the implicit calls to the base-class **Object**'s default constructor occur.

```
1   // Fig. 6.4: Point.cs
2   // Point class represents an x-y coordinate pair.
3
4   using System;
5
6   // Point class definition implicitly inherits from Object
7   public class Point
8   {
9      // point coordinates
10     private int x, y;
11
12     // default (no-argument) constructor
13     public Point()
14     {
15        // implicit call to Object constructor occurs here
16     }
17
18     // constructor
19     public Point( int xValue, int yValue )
20     {
```

Fig. 6.4   **Point** class represents an *x-y* coordinate pair. (Part 1 of 2.)

```
21          // implicit call to Object constructor occurs here
22          X = xValue;
23          Y = yValue;
24       }
25
26       // property X
27       public int X
28       {
29          get
30          {
31             return x;
32          }
33
34          set
35          {
36             x = value; // no need for validation
37          }
38
39       } // end property X
40
41       // property Y
42       public int Y
43       {
44          get
45          {
46             return y;
47          }
48
49          set
50          {
51             y = value; // no need for validation
52          }
53
54       } // end property Y
55
56       // return string representation of Point
57       public override string ToString()
58       {
59          return "[" + x + ", " + y + "]";
60       }
61
62    } // end class Point
```

Fig. 6.4   **Point** class represents an *x-y* coordinate pair. (Part 2 of 2.)

Note that method **ToString** (lines 57–60) contains the keyword *override* in its declaration. Every class in C# (such as class **Point**) inherits either directly or indirectly from class **System.Object**, which is the root of the class hierarchy. As we mentioned previously, this means that every class inherits the eight methods defined by class **Object**. One of these methods is *ToString*, which returns a **string** containing the object's type preceded by its namespace—this method obtains an object's **string** representation and sometimes is called implicitly by the program (such as when an object is concatenated to a **string**). Method **ToString** of class **Point** *overrides* the original **ToString** from class **Object**—when invoked, method **ToString** of class **Point** returns a **string** containing an ordered pair of the values **x** and **y** (line 59), instead of returning a **string** containing the object's class and namespace. To override a base-class method definition, a derived class must specify that the derived-class method overrides the base-class method with keyword **override** in the method header.

Software Engineering Observation 6.4

The C# compiler sets the base class of a derived class to **Object** *when the program does not specify a base class explicitly.*

In C#, a base-class method must be declared **virtual** if that method is to be overridden in a derived class. Method **ToString** of class **Object** is, in fact, declared **virtual**, which enables derived class **Point** to override this method. To view the method header for **ToString**, select **Help > Index...**, and enter **Object.ToString method** (filtered by .**Net Framework SDK**) in the search text box. The page displayed contains a description of method **ToString**, which includes the following header:

```
public virtual string ToString();
```

Keyword **virtual** allows programmers to specify those methods that a derived class can override—a method that has not been declared **virtual** cannot be overridden. We use this later in this section to enable certain methods in our base classes to be overridden.

Common Programming Error 6.1

A derived class attempting to override (using keyword **override***) a method that has not been declared* **virtual** *is a syntax error.*

Class **PointTest** (Fig. 6.5) tests class **Point**. Line 14 instantiates an object of class **Point** and assigns **72** as the x-coordinate value and **115** as the y-coordinate value. Lines 17–18 use properties **X** and **Y** to retrieve these values, then append the values to **string output**. Lines 20–21 change the values of properties **X** and **Y** (implicitly invoking their **set** accessors), and line 24 calls **Point**'s **ToString** method implicitly to obtain the **Point**'s **string** representation.

```
1   // Fig. 6.5: PointTest.cs
2   // Testing class Point.
3
4   using System;
5   using System.Windows.Forms;
6
7   // PointTest class definition
8   class PointTest
9   {
10      // main entry point for application
11      static void Main( string[] args )
12      {
13         // instantiate Point object
14         Point point = new Point( 72, 115 );
15
```

Fig. 6.5   **PointTest** class demonstrates class **Point** functionality. (Part 1 of 2.)

```
16          // display point coordinates via X and Y properties
17          string output = "X coordinate is " + point.X +
18             "\n" + "Y coordinate is " + point.Y;
19
20          point.X = 10; // set x-coordinate via X property
21          point.Y = 10; // set y-coordinate via Y property
22
23          // display new point value
24          output += "\n\nThe new location of point is " + point;
25
26          MessageBox.Show( output, "Demonstrating Class Point" );
27
28       } // end method Main
29
30    } // end class PointTest
```

Fig. 6.5   `PointTest` class demonstrates class `Point` functionality. (Part 2 of 2.)

We now discuss the second part of our introduction to inheritance by creating and testing (a completely new) class **Circle** (Fig. 6.6), which directly inherits from class **System.Object** and represents an *x-y* coordinate pair (representing the center of the circle) and a radius. Lines 9–10 declare the instance variables **x, y** and **radius** as **private** data. The **public** services of class **Circle** include two **Circle** constructors (lines 13–25), properties **X, Y** and **Radius** (lines 28–71), methods **Diameter** (lines 74–77), **Circumference** (lines 80–83), **Area** (lines 86–89) and **ToString** (lines 92–96). These properties and methods encapsulate all necessary features (i.e., the "analytic geometry") of a circle; in the next section, we show how this encapsulation enables us to reuse and extend this class.

```
1    // Fig. 6.6: Circle.cs
2    // Circle class contains x-y coordinate pair and radius.
3
4    using System;
5
6    // Circle class definition implicitly inherits from Object
7    public class Circle
8    {
9       private int x, y;       // coordinates of Circle's center
10      private double radius; // Circle's radius
11
```

Fig. 6.6   `Circle` class contains an *x-y* coordinate and a radius. (Part 1 of 3.)

```
12        // default constructor
13        public Circle()
14        {
15           // implicit call to Object constructor occurs here
16        }
17
18        // constructor
19        public Circle( int xValue, int yValue, double radiusValue )
20        {
21           // implicit call to Object constructor occurs here
22           x = xValue;
23           y = yValue;
24           radius = radiusValue;
25        }
26
27        // property X
28        public int X
29        {
30           get
31           {
32              return x;
33           }
34
35           set
36           {
37              x = value;   // no need for validation
38           }
39
40        } // end property X
41
42        // property Y
43        public int Y
44        {
45           get
46           {
47              return y;
48           }
49
50           set
51           {
52              y = value;   // no need for validation
53           }
54
55        } // end property Y
56
57        // property Radius
58        public double Radius
59        {
60           get
61           {
62              return radius;
63           }
64
```

Fig. 6.6   **Circle** class contains an *x-y* coordinate and a radius. (Part 2 of 3.)

```
65              set
66              {
67                  if ( value >= 0 )      // validation needed
68                      radius = value;
69              }
70
71          } // end property Radius
72
73          // calculate Circle diameter
74          public double Diameter()
75          {
76              return radius * 2;
77          }
78
79          // calculate Circle circumference
80          public double Circumference()
81          {
82              return Math.PI * Diameter();
83          }
84
85          // calculate Circle area
86          public double Area()
87          {
88              return Math.PI * Math.Pow( radius, 2 );
89          }
90
91          // return string representation of Circle
92          public override string ToString()
93          {
94              return "Center = [" + x + ", " + y + "]" +
95                  "; Radius = " + radius;
96          }
97
98  } // end class Circle
```

Fig. 6.6   **Circle** class contains an *x-y* coordinate and a radius. (Part 3 of 3.)

Class **CircleTest** (Fig. 6.7) tests class **Circle**. Line 14 instantiates an object of class **Circle**, assigning **37** as the *x*-coordinate value, **43** as the *y*-coordinate value and **2.5** as the radius value. Lines 17–19 use properties **X**, **Y** and **Radius** to retrieve these values, then concatenate the values to **string output**. Lines 22–24 use **Circle**'s **X**, **Y** and **Radius** properties to change the *x-y* coordinates and the radius, respectively. Property **Radius** ensures that member variable **radius** cannot be assigned a negative value. Line 28 calls **Circle**'s **ToString** method implicitly to obtain the **Circle**'s **string** representation, and lines 32–40 call **Circle**'s **Diameter**, **Circumference** and **Area** methods.

After writing all the code for class **Circle** (Fig. 6.6), we note that a major portion of the code in this class is similar, if not identical, to much of the code in class **Point**. For example, the declaration in **Circle** of **private** variables **x** and **y** and properties **X** and **Y** are identical to those of class **Point**. In addition, the class **Circle** constructors and method **ToString** are almost identical to those of class **Point**, except that they also supply **radius** information. The only other additions to class **Circle** are **private** member variable **radius**, property **Radius** and methods **Diameter**, **Circumference** and **Area**.

It appears that we literally copied code from class **Point**, pasted this code in the code from class **Circle**, then modified class **Circle** to include a radius. This "copy-and-paste" approach is often error-prone and time-consuming. Worse yet, it can result in many physical copies of the code existing throughout a system, creating a code-maintenance "nightmare." Is there a way to "absorb" the attributes and behaviors of one class in a way that makes them part of other classes without duplicating code?

```csharp
1   // Fig. 6.7: CircleTest.cs
2   // Testing class Circle.
3
4   using System;
5   using System.Windows.Forms;
6
7   // CircleTest class definition
8   class CircleTest
9   {
10      // main entry point for application.
11      static void Main( string[] args )
12      {
13          // instantiate Circle
14          Circle circle = new Circle( 37, 43, 2.5 );
15
16          // get Circle's initial x-y coordinates and radius
17          string output = "X coordinate is " + circle.X +
18              "\nY coordinate is " + circle.Y + "\nRadius is " +
19              circle.Radius;
20
21          // set Circle's x-y coordinates and radius to new values
22          circle.X = 2;
23          circle.Y = 2;
24          circle.Radius = 4.25;
25
26          // display Circle's string representation
27          output += "\n\nThe new location and radius of " +
28              "circle are \n" + circle + "\n";
29
30          // display Circle's diameter
31          output += "Diameter is " +
32              String.Format( "{0:F}", circle.Diameter() ) + "\n";
33
34          // display Circle's circumference
35          output += "Circumference is " +
36              String.Format( "{0:F}", circle.Circumference() ) + "\n";
37
38          // display Circle's area
39          output += "Area is " +
40              String.Format( "{0:F}", circle.Area() );
41
42          MessageBox.Show( output, "Demonstrating Class Circle" );
43
44      } // end method Main
```

Fig. 6.7   **CircleTest** demonstrates class **Circle** functionality. (Part 1 of 2.)

```
45
46   } // end class CircleTest
```

Fig. 6.7　`CircleTest` demonstrates class **Circle** functionality. (Part 2 of 2.)

In the next examples we answer that question, we use a more elegant class construction approach emphasizing the benefits of inheritance. Now, we create and test a class **Circle2** (Fig. 6.8) that inherits variables **x** and **y** and properties **X** and **Y** from class **Point** (Fig. 6.4). This class **Circle2** "is a" **Point** (because inheritance absorbs the capabilities of class **Point**), but also contains **radius** (line 9). The colon (**:**) symbol in the class declaration (line 7) indicates inheritance. As a derived class, **Circle2** inherits all the members of class **Point**, except for the constructors. Thus, the **public** services to **Circle2** include the two **Circle2** constructors (lines 12–24); the **public** methods inherited from class **Point**; property **Radius** (lines 27–40); and the **Circle2** methods **Diameter**, **Circumference**, **Area** and **ToString** (lines 43–65). We declare method **Area** as **virtual**, so that derived classes (such as class **Cylinder**, as we will see in Section 6.5) can override this method to provide a more appropriate implementation.

```
1    // Fig. 6.8: Circle2.cs
2    // Circle2 class that inherits from class Point.
3
4    using System;
5
6    // Circle2 class definition inherits from Point
7    class Circle2 : Point
8    {
9       private double radius; // Circle2's radius
10
11      // default constructor
12      public Circle2()
13      {
14         // implicit call to Point constructor occurs here
15      }
16
```

Fig. 6.8　**Circle2** class that inherits from class **Point**. (Part 1 of 3.)

```
17       // constructor
18       public Circle2( int xValue, int yValue, double radiusValue )
19       {
20          // implicit call to Point constructor occurs here
21          x = xValue;
22          y = yValue;
23          Radius = radiusValue;
24       }
25
26       // property Radius
27       public double Radius
28       {
29          get
30          {
31             return radius;
32          }
33
34          set
35          {
36             if ( value >= 0 )
37                radius = value;
38          }
39
40       } // end property Radius
41
42       // calculate Circle diameter
43       public double Diameter()
44       {
45          return radius * 2;
46       }
47
48       // calculate Circle circumference
49       public double Circumference()
50       {
51          return Math.PI * Diameter();
52       }
53
54       // calculate Circle area
55       public virtual double Area()
56       {
57          return Math.PI * Math.Pow( radius, 2 );
58       }
59
60       // return string representation Circle
61       public override string ToString()
62       {
63          return "Center = [" + x + ", " + y + "]" +
64             "; Radius = " + radius;
65       }
66
67    } // end class Circle2
```

Fig. 6.8   **Circle2** class that inherits from class **Point**. (Part 2 of 3.)

Fig. 6.8   **Circle2** class that inherits from class **Point**. (Part 3 of 3.)

Lines 14 and 20 in the **Circle2** constructors (lines 12–24) invoke the default **Point** constructor implicitly to initialize the base-class portion (variables **x** and **y**, inherited from class **Point**) of a **Circle2** object to **0**. However, because the parameterized constructor (lines 18–24) should set the *x-y* coordinate to a specific value, lines 21–22 attempt to assign argument values to **x** and **y** directly. Even though lines 21–22 attempt to set **x** and **y** values explicitly, line 20 first calls the **Point** default constructor to initialize these variables to their default values. The compiler generates syntax errors for lines 21 and 22 (and line 63, where **Circle2**'s method **ToString** attempts to use the values of **x** and **y** directly), because the derived class **Circle2** is not allowed to access the base class **Point**'s **private** members **x** and **y**. [*Note:* The line numbers in the output of Fig. 6.8 are slightly different than the line numbers we have mentioned, because the code that appears in the book is slightly modified from the actual program code.] C# rigidly enforces restriction on accessing **private** data members, so that even a derived class (i.e., which is closely related to its base class) cannot access base-class **private** data.

To enable class **Circle2** to access **Point** member variables **x** and **y** directly, we can declare those variables as **protected**. As we discussed in Section 6.3, a base class's **protected** members can be accessed only in that base class or in any classes derived from that base class. Class **Point2** (Fig. 6.9) modifies class **Point** (Fig. 6.4) to declare variables **x** and **y** as **protected** (line 10) instead of **private**.

```
1   // Fig. 6.9: Point2.cs
2   // Point2 class contains an x-y coordinate pair as protected data.
3
4   using System;
5
6   // Point2 class definition implicitly inherits from Object
7   public class Point2
8   {
9      // point coordinate
10     protected int x, y;
11
12     // default constructor
13     public Point2()
14     {
15        // implicit call to Object constructor occurs here
16     }
17
```

Fig. 6.9   **Point2** class represents an *x-y* coordinate pair as **protected** data. (Part 1 of 2.)

```
18        // constructor
19        public Point2( int xValue, int yValue )
20        {
21            // implicit call to Object constructor occurs here
22            X = xValue;
23            Y = yValue;
24        }
25
26        // property X
27        public int X
28        {
29            get
30            {
31                return x;
32            }
33
34            set
35            {
36                x = value; // no need for validation
37            }
38
39        } // end property X
40
41        // property Y
42        public int Y
43        {
44            get
45            {
46                return y;
47            }
48
49            set
50            {
51                y = value; // no need for validation
52            }
53
54        } // end property Y
55
56        // return string representation of Point2
57        public override string ToString()
58        {
59            return "[" + x + ", " + y + "]";
60        }
61
62    } // end class Point2
```

Fig. 6.9   **Point2** class represents an *x-y* coordinate pair as **protected** data.
(Part 2 of 2.)

Class **Circle3** (Fig. 6.10) modifies class **Circle2** (Fig. 6.8) to inherit from class **Point2** rather than inheriting from class **Point**. Because class **Circle3** is a class derived from class **Point2**, class **Circle3** can access class **Point2**'s **protected** member variables **x** and **y** directly, and the compiler does not generate errors when compiling Fig. 6.10. This shows the special privileges that a derived class is granted to access

protected base-class data members. A derived class also can access **protected** methods in any of that derived class's base classes.

```csharp
1   // Fig. 6.10: Circle3.cs
2   // Circle2 class that inherits from class Point2.
3
4   using System;
5
6   // Circle3 class definition inherits from Point2
7   public class Circle3 : Point2
8   {
9      private double radius; // Circle's radius
10
11     // default constructor
12     public Circle3()
13     {
14        // implicit call to Point2 constructor occurs here
15     }
16
17     // constructor
18     public Circle3(
19        int xValue, int yValue, double radiusValue )
20     {
21        // implicit call to Point2 constructor occurs here
22        x = xValue;
23        y = yValue;
24        Radius = radiusValue;
25     }
26
27     // property Radius
28     public double Radius
29     {
30        get
31        {
32           return radius;
33        }
34
35        set
36        {
37           if ( value >= 0 )
38              radius = value;
39        }
40
41     } // end property Radius
42
43     // calculate Circle diameter
44     public double Diameter()
45     {
46        return radius * 2;
47     }
48
```

Fig. 6.10 **Circle3** class that inherits from class **Point2**. (Part 1 of 2.)

```
49      // calculate circumference
50      public double Circumference()
51      {
52         return Math.PI * Diameter();
53      }
54
55      // calculate Circle area
56      public virtual double Area()
57      {
58         return Math.PI * Math.Pow( radius, 2 );
59      }
60
61      // return string representation of Circle3
62      public override string ToString()
63      {
64         return "Center = [" + x + ", " + y + "]" +
65            "; Radius = " + radius;
66      }
67
68   } // end class Circle3
```

Fig. 6.10 `Circle3` class that inherits from class **Point2**. (Part 2 of 2.)

Class **CircleTest3** (Fig. 6.11) performs identical tests on class **Circle3** as class **CircleTest** (Fig. 6.7) performed on class **Circle** (Fig. 6.6). Note that the outputs of the two programs are identical. We created class **Circle** without using inheritance and created class **Circle3** using inheritance; however, both classes provide the same functionality. However, observe that the code listing for class **Circle3**, which is 68 lines, is considerably shorter than the code listing for class **Circle**, which is 98 lines, because class **Circle3** absorbs part of its functionality from **Point2**, whereas class **Circle** does not. Also, there is now only one copy of the point functionality.

```
1    // Fig. 6.11: CircleTest3.cs
2    // Testing class Circle3.
3
4    using System;
5    using System.Windows.Forms;
6
7    // CircleTest3 class definition
8    class CircleTest3
9    {
10      // main entry point for application
11      static void Main( string[] args )
12      {
13         // instantiate Circle3
14         Circle3 circle = new Circle3( 37, 43, 2.5 );
15
16         // get Circle3's initial x-y coordinates and radius
17         string output = "X coordinate is " + circle.X + "\n" +
18            "Y coordinate is " + circle.Y + "\nRadius is " +
19            circle.Radius;
```

Fig. 6.11 `CircleTest3` demonstrates class `Circle3` functionality. (Part 1 of 2.)

```
20
21          // set Circle3's x-y coordinates and radius to new values
22          circle.X = 2;
23          circle.Y = 2;
24          circle.Radius = 4.25;
25
26          // display Circle3's string representation
27          output += "\n\n" +
28             "The new location and radius of circle are " +
29             "\n" + circle + "\n";
30
31          // display Circle3's Diameter
32          output += "Diameter is " +
33             String.Format( "{0:F}", circle.Diameter() ) + "\n";
34
35          // display Circle3's Circumference
36          output += "Circumference is " +
37             String.Format( "{0:F}", circle.Circumference() ) + "\n";
38
39          // display Circle3's area
40          output += "Area is " +
41             String.Format( "{0:F}", circle.Area() );
42
43          MessageBox.Show( output, "Demonstrating Class Circle3" );
44
45       } // end method Main
46
47    } // end class CircleTest3
```

Fig. 6.11 `CircleTest3` demonstrates class **`Circle3`** functionality. (Part 2 of 2.)

In the previous example, we declared the base-class instance variables as **protected**, so that a derived class could modify their values directly. The use of **protected** variables allows for a slight increase in performance, because we avoid incurring the overhead of a method call to a property's **set** or **get** accessor. However, in most C# applications, in which user interaction comprises a large part of the execution time, the optimization offered through the use of **protected** variables is negligible.

Using **protected** instance variables creates two major problems. First, the derived-class object does not have to use a property to set the value of the base-class's **protected** data. Therefore, a derived-class object can easily assign an illegal value to the **protected** data, thus leaving the object in an inconsistent state. For example, if we were to declare **Circle3**'s variable **radius** as **protected**, a derived-class object (e.g., **Cylinder**), could then assign a negative value to **radius**. The second problem with using **protected** data is that derived-class methods are more likely to be written to depend on base-class implementation. In practice, derived classes should depend only on the base-class services (i.e., non-**private** methods and properties) and not on base-class implementation. With **protected** data in the base class, if the base-class implementation changes, we may need to modify all derived classes of that base class. For example, if for some reason we were to change the names of variables **x** and **y** to **xCoordinate** and **yCoordinate**, then we would have to do so for all occurrences in which a derived class references these base-class variables directly. In such a case, the software is said to be *fragile* or *brittle*. The programmer should be able to change the base-class implementation freely, while still providing the same services to derived classes. (Of course, if the base class services change, we must reimplement our derived classes, but good object-oriented design attempts to prevent this.)

Software Engineering Observation 6.5

*The most appropriate time to use the **protected** access modifier is when a base class should provide a service only to its derived classes (i.e., the base class should not provide the service to other clients).*

Software Engineering Observation 6.6

*Declaring base-class instance variables **private** (as opposed to declaring them **protected**) enables programmers to change base-class implementation without having to change derived-class implementation.*

Testing and Debugging Tip 6.1

*When possible, avoid including **protected** data in a base class. Rather, include non-**private** properties and methods that access **private** data, ensuring that the object maintains a consistent state.*

We reexamine our point-circle hierarchy example once more; this time, attempting to use the best software engineering. We use **Point3** (Fig. 6.12), which declares variables **x** and **y** as **private** and uses properties in method **ToString** to access these values. We show how derived class **Circle4** (Fig. 6.13) can invoke non-**private** base-class methods and properties to manipulate these variables.

```
1   // Fig. 6.12: Point3.cs
2   // Point3 class represents an x-y coordinate pair.
3
4   using System;
5
6   // Point3 class definition implicitly inherits from Object
7   public class Point3
8   {
9      // point coordinate
10     private int x, y;
11
```

Fig. 6.12 **Point3** class uses properties to manipulate its **private** data. (Part 1 of 2.)

```
12      // default constructor
13      public Point3()
14      {
15         // implicit call to Object constructor occurs here
16      }
17
18      // constructor
19      public Point3( int xValue, int yValue )
20      {
21         // implicit call to Object constructor occurs here
22         X = xValue;    // use property X
23         Y = yValue;    // use property Y
24      }
25
26      // property X
27      public int X
28      {
29         get
30         {
31            return x;
32         }
33
34         set
35         {
36            x = value; // no need for validation
37         }
38
39      } // end property X
40
41      // property Y
42      public int Y
43      {
44         get
45         {
46            return y;
47         }
48
49         set
50         {
51            y = value; // no need for validation
52         }
53
54      } // end property Y
55
56      // return string representation of Point3
57      public override string ToString()
58      {
59         return "[" + X + ", " + Y + "]";
60      }
61
62   } // end class Point3
```

Fig. 6.12   Point3 class uses properties to manipulate its **private** data. (Part 2 of 2.)

```
1   // Fig. 6.13: Circle4.cs
2   // Circle4 class that inherits from class Point3.
3
4   using System;
5
6   // Circle4 class definition inherits from Point3
7   public class Circle4 : Point3
8   {
9      private double radius;
10
11      // default constructor
12      public Circle4()
13      {
14         // implicit call to Point3 constructor occurs here
15      }
16
17      // constructor
18      public Circle4( int xValue, int yValue, double radiusValue )
19         : base( xValue, yValue )
20      {
21         Radius = radiusValue;
22      }
23
24      // property Radius
25      public double Radius
26      {
27         get
28         {
29            return radius;
30         }
31
32         set
33         {
34            if ( value >= 0 )    // validation needed
35               radius = value;
36         }
37
38      } // end property Radius
39
40      // calculate Circle diameter
41      public double Diameter()
42      {
43         return Radius * 2;      // use property Radius
44      }
45
46      // calculate Circle circumference
47      public double Circumference()
48      {
49         return Math.PI * Diameter();
50      }
51
```

Fig. 6.13 **Circle4** class that inherits from class **Point3**, which does not provide **protected** data. (Part 1 of 2.)

```
52       // calculate Circle area
53       public virtual double Area()
54       {
55           return Math.PI * Math.Pow( Radius, 2 );   // use property
56       }
57
58       // return string representation of Circle4
59       public override string ToString()
60       {
61           // use base reference to return Point string representation
62           return "Center= " + base.ToString() +
63               "; Radius = " + Radius;   // use property Radius
64       }
65
66   } // end class Circle4
```

Fig. 6.13   Circle4 class that inherits from class **Point3**, which does not provide **protected** data. (Part 2 of 2.)

Software Engineering Observation 6.7

*When possible, use properties to alter and obtain the values of member variables, even if those values can be modified directly. A property's **set** accessor can prevent attempts to assign an inappropriate value to that member variable, and a property's **get** accessor can help control the presentation of the data to clients.*

Performance Tip 6.1

Using a property to access a variable's value is slightly slower than accessing the data directly. However, attempting to optimize programs by referencing data directly often is unnecessary, because the compiler optimizes the programs implicitly. [Today's so-called "optimizing compilers" are carefully designed to perform many optimizations implicitly, even if the programmer does not write what appears to be the most optimal code. A good rule is, "Do not second-guess the compiler."]

For the purpose of this example, to demonstrate both explicit and implicit calls to base-class constructors, we include a second constructor that calls the base-class constructor explicitly. Lines 18–22 declare the **Circle4** constructor that invokes the second **Point3** constructor explicitly (line 19) using the *base-class constructor-call syntax* (i.e., reference **base** followed by a set of parentheses containing the arguments to the base-class constructor). In this case, **xValue** and **yValue** are passed to initialize the **private** base-class members **x** and **y**. The colon symbol (**:**) followed by the **base** keyword accesses the base-class version of that method explicitly (line 19). By making this call, we can initialize **x** and **y** in the base class to specific values, rather than to **0**.

Common Programming Error 6.2

*It is a syntax error if a derived class uses **base** to call its base-class constructor with arguments that do not match exactly the number and types of parameters specified in one of the base-class constructor definitions.*

Class **Circle4**'s **ToString** method (line 59–64) overrides class **Point3**'s **ToString** method (lines 57–60 of Fig. 6.12). As we discussed earlier, overriding this method is possible, because method **ToString** of class **System.Object** (class

Point3's base class) is declared **virtual**. Method **ToString** of class **Circle4** displays the **private** instance variables **x** and **y** of class **Point3** by calling the base class's **ToString** method (in this case, **Point3**'s **ToString** method). The call is made in line 62 via the expression **base.ToString()** and causes the values of **x** and **y** to become part of the **Circle4**'s **string** representation. Using this approach is a good software engineering practice—recall that if an object's method performs the actions needed by another object, the programmer should call that method rather than duplicate its code body. Duplicate code creates code-maintenance problems. By having **Circle4**'s **ToString** method use the formatting provided by **Point3**'s **ToString** method, we avoid duplicating code. Also, **Point3**'s **ToString** method performs part of the task of **Circle4**'s **ToString** method, so we call **Point3**'s **ToString** method from class **Circle4** with the expression **base.ToString()**.

Common Programming Error 6.3

*When a base-class method is overridden in a derived class, the derived-class version often calls the base-class version to do additional work. Failure to use the **base** reference when referencing the base class's method causes infinite recursion, because the derived-class method would then call itself.*

Common Programming Error 6.4

*The use of "chained" **base** references to refer to a member (a method, property or variable) several levels up the hierarchy (as in **base.base.mX**) is a syntax error.*

Software Engineering Observation 6.8

A redefinition in a derived class of a base-class method that uses a different signature than that of the base-class method is method overloading rather than method overriding.

Software Engineering Observation 6.9

*Although method **ToString** certainly could be overridden to perform arbitrary actions, the general understanding in the C# .NET community is that method **ToString** should be overridden to obtain an object's **string** representation.*

Class **CircleTest4** (Fig. 6.14) performs identical manipulations on class **Circle4** as did classes **CircleTest** (Fig. 6.7) and **CircleTest3** (Fig. 6.11). Note that the outputs of all three modules are identical. Therefore, although each "circle" class appears to behave identically, class **Circle4** is the most properly engineered. Using inheritance, we have efficiently and effectively constructed a well-engineered class.

```
1   // Fig. 6.14: CircleTest4.cs
2   // Testing class Circle4.
3
4   using System;
5   using System.Windows.Forms;
6
7   // CircleTest4 class definition
8   class CircleTest4
9   {
```

Fig. 6.14   **CircleTest4** demonstrates class **Circle4** functionality. (Part 1 of 2.)

```
10      // main entry point for application
11      static void Main( string[] args )
12      {
13         // instantiate Circle4
14         Circle4 circle = new Circle4( 37, 43, 2.5 );
15
16         // get Circle4's initial x-y coordinates and radius
17         string output = "X coordinate is " + circle.X + "\n" +
18            "Y coordinate is " + circle.Y + "\n" +
19            "Radius is " + circle.Radius;
20
21         // set Circle4's x-y coordinates and radius to new values
22         circle.X = 2;
23         circle.Y = 2;
24         circle.Radius = 4.25;
25
26         // display Circle4's string representation
27         output += "\n\n" +
28            "The new location and radius of circle are " +
29            "\n" + circle + "\n";
30
31         // display Circle4's Diameter
32         output += "Diameter is " +
33            String.Format( "{0:F}", circle.Diameter() ) + "\n";
34
35         // display Circle4's Circumference
36         output += "Circumference is " +
37            String.Format( "{0:F}", circle.Circumference() ) + "\n";
38
39         // display Circle4's area
40         output += "Area is " +
41            String.Format( "{0:F}", circle.Area() );
42
43         MessageBox.Show( output, "Demonstrating Class Circle4" );
44
45      } // end method Main
46
47   } // end class CircleTest4
```

Fig. 6.14 **CircleTest4** demonstrates class **Circle4** functionality. (Part 2 of 2.)

6.5 Case Study: Three-Level Inheritance Hierarchy

Let us consider a more substantial inheritance example involving a three-level point-circle-cylinder hierarchy. In Section 6.4, we developed classes **Point3** (Fig. 6.12) and **Circle4** (Fig. 6.13). Now, we present an example in which we derive class **Cylinder** from class **Circle4**.

The first class that we use in our case study is class **Point3** (Fig. 6.12). We declared **Point3**'s instance variables as **private**. Class **Point3** also contains properties **X** and **Y** for accessing **x** and **y** and method **ToString** (which **Point3** overrides from class **Object**) for obtaining a **string** representation of the *x-y* coordinate pair.

We also created class **Circle4** (Fig. 6.13), which inherits from class **Point3**. Class **Circle4** contains the **Point3** functionality, in addition to providing property **Radius**, which ensures that the **radius** member variable cannot hold a negative value, and methods **Diameter**, **Circumference**, **Area** and **ToString**. Recall that method **Area** was declared **virtual** (line 53). As we discussed in Section 6.4, this keyword enables derived classes to override a base-class method. Derived classes of class **Circle4** (such as class **Cylinder**, which we introduce momentarily) can override these methods and provide specific implementations. A circle has an area that is calculated by the formula, πr^2, in which r represents the circle's radius. However, a cylinder has a surface area that is calculated by the formula, $(2\pi r^2) + (2\pi rh)$, in which r represents the cylinder's radius and h represents the cylinder's height. Therefore, class **Cylinder** must override method **Area** to include this calculation, so we declared class **Circle4**'s method **Area** as **virtual**.

Figure 6.15 presents class **Cylinder**, which inherits from class **Circle4** (line 7). Class **Cylinder**'s **public** services include the inherited **Circle4** methods **Diameter**, **Circumference**, **Area** and **ToString**; the inherited **Circle4** property **Radius**; the indirectly inherited **Point3** properties **X** and **Y**; the **Cylinder** constructor, property **Height** and method **Volume**. Method **Area** (lines 41–44) overrides method **Area** of class **Circle4**. Note that, if class **Cylinder** were to attempt to override **Circle4**'s methods **Diameter** and **Circumference**, syntax errors would occur, because class **Circle4** did not declare these methods **virtual**. Method **ToString** (lines 53–56) overrides method **ToString** of class **Circle4** to obtain a **string** representation for the cylinder. Class **Cylinder** also includes method **Volume** (lines 47–50) to calculate the cylinder's volume. Because we do not declare method **Volume** as **virtual**, no derived class of class **Cylinder** can override this method.

```
1   // Fig. 6.15: Cylinder.cs
2   // Cylinder class inherits from class Circle4.
3
4   using System;
5
6   // Cylinder class definition inherits from Circle4
7   public class Cylinder : Circle4
8   {
9       private double height;
10
```

Fig. 6.15   **Cylinder** class inherits from class **Circle4** and overrides method **Area**. (Part 1 of 2.)

```
11      // default constructor
12      public Cylinder()
13      {
14          // implicit call to Circle4 constructor occurs here
15      }
16
17      // four-argument constructor
18      public Cylinder( int xValue, int yValue, double radiusValue,
19          double heightValue ) : base( xValue, yValue, radiusValue )
20      {
21          Height = heightValue; // set Cylinder height
22      }
23
24      // property Height
25      public double Height
26      {
27          get
28          {
29              return height;
30          }
31
32          set
33          {
34              if ( value >= 0 ) // validate height
35                  height = value;
36          }
37
38      } // end property Height
39
40      // override Circle4 method Area to calculate Cylinder area
41      public override double Area()
42      {
43          return 2 * base.Area() + base.Circumference() * Height;
44      }
45
46      // calculate Cylinder volume
47      public double Volume()
48      {
49          return base.Area() * Height;
50      }
51
52      // convert Cylinder to string
53      public override string ToString()
54      {
55          return base.ToString() + "; Height = " + Height;
56      }
57
58  } // end class Cylinder
```

Fig. 6.15 **Cylinder** class inherits from class **Circle4** and overrides method **Area**. (Part 2 of 2.)

Figure 6.16 is a **CylinderTest** application that tests the **Cylinder** class. Line 14 instantiates an object of class **Cylinder**. Lines 17–19 use properties **X**, **Y**, **Radius** and

Height to obtain information about the **Cylinder** object, because **CylinderTest** cannot reference the **private** data of class **Cylinder** directly. Lines 22–25 use properties **X**, **Y**, **Radius** and **Height** to reset the **Cylinder**'s *x-y* coordinates (we assume the cylinder's *x-y* coordinates specify its position on the *x-y* plane), radius and height. Class **Cylinder** can use class **Point3**'s **X** and **Y** properties, because class **Cylinder** inherits them indirectly from class **Point3**—Class **Cylinder** inherits properties **X** and **Y** directly from class **Circle4**, which inherited them directly from class **Point3**. Line 29 invokes method **ToString** implicitly to obtain the **string** representation of the **Cylinder** object. Lines 33–37 invoke methods **Diameter** and **Circumference** of the **Cylinder** object—because class **Cylinder** inherits these methods from class **Circle4** and cannot override them, these methods, exactly as listed in **Circle4**, are invoked. Lines 41–45 invoke methods **Area** and **Volume**.

Using the point-circle-cylinder example, we have shown the use and benefits of inheritance. We were able to develop classes **Circle4** and **Cylinder** using inheritance much faster than if we had developed these classes "from scratch." Inheritance avoids duplicating code and the associated code-maintenance problems.

```
1   // Fig. 6.16: CylinderTest.cs
2   // Tests class Cylinder.
3
4   using System;
5   using System.Windows.Forms;
6
7   // CylinderTest class definition
8   class CylinderTest
9   {
10      // main entry point for application
11      static void Main( string[] args )
12      {
13         // instantiate object of class Cylinder
14         Cylinder cylinder = new Cylinder(12, 23, 2.5, 5.7);
15
16         // properties get initial x-y coordinate, radius and height
17         string output = "X coordinate is " + cylinder.X + "\n" +
18            "Y coordinate is " + cylinder.Y + "\nRadius is " +
19            cylinder.Radius + "\n" + "Height is " + cylinder.Height;
20
21         // properties set new x-y coordinate, radius and height
22         cylinder.X = 2;
23         cylinder.Y = 2;
24         cylinder.Radius = 4.25;
25         cylinder.Height = 10;
26
27         // get new x-y coordinate and radius
28         output += "\n\nThe new location, radius and height of " +
29            "cylinder are\n" + cylinder + "\n\n";
30
31         // display Cylinder's Diameter
32         output += "Diameter is " +
33            String.Format( "{0:F}", cylinder.Diameter() ) + "\n";
```

Fig. 6.16 Testing class **Cylinder**. (Part 1 of 2.)

```
34
35          // display Cylinder's Circumference
36          output += "Circumference is " +
37             String.Format( "{0:F}", cylinder.Circumference() ) + "\n";
38
39          // display Cylinder's area
40          output += "Area is " +
41             String.Format( "{0:F}", cylinder.Area() ) + "\n";
42
43          // display Cylinder's Volume
44          output += "Volume is " +
45             String.Format( "{0:F}", cylinder.Volume() );
46
47          MessageBox.Show( output, "Demonstrating Class Cylinder" );
48
49       } // end method Main
50
51    } // end class CylinderTest
```

Fig. 6.16 Testing class **Cylinder**. (Part 2 of 2.)

6.6 Constructors and Destructors in Derived Classes

As we explained in the previous section, instantiating a derived-class object begins a chain of constructor calls in which the derived-class constructor, before performing its own tasks, invokes the base-class constructor either explicitly or implicitly. Similarly, if the base-class was derived from another class, the base-class constructor must invoke the constructor of the next class up in the hierarchy, and so on. The last constructor called in the chain is class **Object**'s constructor whose body actually finishes executing first—the original derived class's body finishes executing last. Each base-class constructor initializes the base-class instance variables that the derived-class object inherits. For example, consider the **Point3/Circle4** hierarchy from Fig. 6.12 and Fig. 6.13. When a program creates a **Circle4** object, one of the **Circle4** constructors is called. That constructor calls class **Point3**'s constructor, which in turn calls class **Object**'s constructor. When class **Object**'s constructor completes execution, it returns control to class **Point3**'s constructor, which initializes the x-y coordinates of **Circle4**. When class **Point3**'s constructor completes execution, it returns control to class **Circle4**'s constructor, which initializes the **Circle4**'s radius.

Software Engineering Observation 6.10

When a program creates a derived-class object, the derived-class constructor immediately calls the base-class constructor, the base-class constructor's body executes, then the derived-class constructor's body executes.

When the garbage collector removes a derived-class object from memory, the garbage collector calls that object's destructor. This begins a chain of destructor calls in which the derived-class destructor and the destructors of the direct and indirect base classes execute in the reverse order of the order in which the constructors executed. Executing the destructors should free all the resources the object acquired before the garbage collector reclaims the memory for that object. When the garbage collector calls a derived-class object's destructor, the destructor performs its task, then invokes the destructor of the base class. This process repeats until class **Object**'s destructor is called.

C# actually implements destructors using class **Object**'s *Finalize* method (one of the eight methods that every C# class inherits). When compiling a class definition that contains a destructor, the compiler translates a destructor definition into a **Finalize** method that performs the destructor's tasks, then invokes the base class **Finalize** method as the last statement in the derived-class **Finalize** method. As mentioned in Chapter 5, we cannot determine exactly when the destructor call will occur, because we cannot determine exactly when garbage collection occurs. However, by defining a destructor, we can specify code to execute before the garbage collector removes an object from memory.

Our next example revisits the point-circle hierarchy by defining class **Point4** (Fig. 6.17) and class **Circle5** (Fig. 6.18) that contain constructors *and* destructors, each of which prints a message when it runs.

Class **Point4** (Fig. 6.17) contains the features shown in Fig. 6.4. We modified the constructors (lines 13–17 and 20–26) to output a line of text when they are called and added a destructor (lines 29–32) that also outputs a line of text when it is called. Each output statement (lines 16, 25 and 31) adds reference **this** to the output string. This implicitly invokes the class's **ToString** method to obtain the **string** representation of **Point4**'s coordinates.

```
1   // Fig. 6.17: Point4.cs
2   // Point4 class represents an x-y coordinate pair.
3
4   using System;
5
6   // Point4 class definition
7   public class Point4
8   {
9      // point coordinate
10     private int x, y;
11
12     // default constructor
13     public Point4()
14     {
15        // implicit call to Object constructor occurs here
16        Console.WriteLine( "Point4 constructor: {0}", this );
17     }
```

Fig. 6.17 **Point4** base class contains constructors and finalizer. (Part 1 of 2.)

```
18
19      // constructor
20      public Point4( int xValue, int yValue )
21      {
22         // implicit call to Object constructor occurs here
23         X = xValue;
24         Y = yValue;
25         Console.WriteLine( "Point4 constructor: {0}", this );
26      }
27
28      // destructor
29      ~Point4()
30      {
31         Console.WriteLine( "Point4 destructor: {0}", this );
32      }
33
34      // property X
35      public int X
36      {
37         get
38         {
39            return x;
40         }
41
42         set
43         {
44            x = value; // no need for validation
45         }
46
47      } // end property X
48
49      // property Y
50      public int Y
51      {
52         get
53         {
54            return y;
55         }
56
57         set
58         {
59            y = value; // no need for validation
60         }
61
62      } // end property Y
63
64      // return string representation of Point4
65      public override string ToString()
66      {
67         return "[" + x + ", " + y + "]";
68      }
69
70   } // end class Point4
```

Fig. 6.17　Point4 base class contains constructors and finalizer. (Part 2 of 2.)

Class **Circle5** (Fig. 6.18) contains the features in Fig. 6.13, and we modified the two constructors (lines 12–16 and 19–24) to output a line of text when they are called. We also added a destructor (lines 27–30) that also outputs a line of text when it is called. Each output statement (lines 15, 23 and 29) adds reference **this** to the output string. This implicitly invokes the **Circle5**'s **ToString** method to obtain the **string** representation of **Circle5**'s coordinates and radius.

Class **ConstructorAndFinalizer** (Fig. 6.19) demonstrates the order in which constructors and finalizers are called for objects of classes that are part of an inheritance class hierarchy. Method **Main** (lines 11–28) begins by instantiating an object of class **Circle5**, then assigns it to reference **circle1** (line 16). This invokes the **Circle5** constructor, which invokes the **Point4** constructor immediately. Then, the **Point4** constructor invokes the **Object** constructor. When the **Object** constructor (which does not print anything) returns control to the **Point4** constructor, the **Point4** constructor initializes the *x-y* coordinates, then outputs a **string** indicating that the **Point4** constructor was called. The output statement also calls method **ToString** implicitly (using reference **this**) to obtain the **string** representation of the object being constructed. Then, control returns to the **Circle5** constructor, which initializes the radius and outputs the **Circle5**'s *x-y* coordinates and radius by calling method **ToString** implicitly.

```
1   // Fig. 6.18: Circle5.cs
2   // Circle5 class that inherits from class Point4.
3
4   using System;
5
6   // Circle5 class definition inherits from Point4
7   public class Circle5 : Point4
8   {
9      private double radius;
10
11     // default constructor
12     public Circle5()
13     {
14        // implicit call to Point4 constructor occurs here
15        Console.WriteLine( "Circle5 constructor: {0}", this );
16     }
17
18     // constructor
19     public Circle5( int xValue, int yValue, double radiusValue )
20        : base( xValue, yValue )
21     {
22        Radius = radiusValue;
23        Console.WriteLine( "Circle5 constructor: {0}", this );
24     }
25
26     // destructor overrides version in class Point4
27     ~Circle5()
28     {
29        Console.WriteLine( "Circle5 destructor: {0}", this );
30     }
```

Fig. 6.18 **Circle5** class inherits from class **Point4** and overrides a finalizer method. (Part 1 of 2.)

```
31
32      // property Radius
33      public double Radius
34      {
35         get
36         {
37            return radius;
38         }
39
40         set
41         {
42            if ( value >= 0 )
43               radius = value;
44         }
45
46      } // end property Radius
47
48      // calculate Circle5 diameter
49      public double Diameter()
50      {
51         return Radius * 2;
52      }
53
54      // calculate Circle5 circumference
55      public double Circumference()
56      {
57         return Math.PI * Diameter();
58      }
59
60      // calculate Circle5 area
61      public virtual double Area()
62      {
63         return Math.PI * Math.Pow( Radius, 2 );
64      }
65
66      // return string representation of Circle5
67      public override string ToString()
68      {
69         // use base reference to return Point3 string
70         return "Center = " + base.ToString() +
71            "; Radius = " + Radius;
72      }
73
74   } // end class Circle5
```

Fig. 6.18 **Circle5** class inherits from class **Point4** and overrides a finalizer method. (Part 2 of 2.)

Notice that the first two lines of the output from this program contain values for the *x*-*y* coordinates and the radius of **Circle5** object **circle1**. When constructing a **Circle5** object, the **this** reference used in the body of both the **Circle5** and **Point4** constructors refers to the **Circle5** object being constructed. When a program invokes method **ToString** on an object, the version of **ToString** that executes is always the version defined in that object's class. Because reference **this** refers to the current

Circle5 object being constructed, **Circle5**'s **ToString** method executes even when **ToString** is invoked from the body of class **Point4**'s constructor. [*Note*: This would not be the case if the **Point4** constructor were called to initialize an object that was actually a new **Point4** object.] When the **Point4** constructor invokes method **ToString** for the **Circle5** being constructed, the program displays **0** for the **radius** value, because the **Circle5** constructor's body has not yet initialized the **radius**. Remember that **0** is the default value of a **double** variable. The second line of output shows the proper **radius** value (**4.5**), because that line is output after the **radius** is initialized.

```
1   // Fig. 6.19: ConstructorAndDestructor.cs
2   // Display order in which base-class and derived-class constructors
3   // and destructors are called.
4
5   using System;
6
7   // ConstructorAndDestructor class definition
8   class ConstructorAndDestructor
9   {
10     // main entry point for application.
11     static void Main( string[] args )
12     {
13        Circle5 circle1, circle2;
14
15        // instantiate objects
16        circle1 = new Circle5( 72, 29, 4.5 );
17        circle2 = new Circle5( 5, 5, 10 );
18
19        Console.WriteLine();
20
21        // mark objects for garbage collection
22        circle1 = null;
23        circle2 = null;
24
25        // inform garbage collector to execute
26        System.GC.Collect();
27
28     } // end method Main
29
30  } // end class ConstructorAndDestructor
```

```
Point4 constructor: Center = [72, 29]; Radius = 0
Circle5 constructor: Center = [72, 29]; Radius = 4.5
Point4 constructor: Center = [5, 5]; Radius = 0
Circle5 constructor: Center = [5, 5]; Radius = 10

Circle5 destructor: Center = [5, 5]; Radius = 10
Point4 destructor: Center = [5, 5]; Radius = 10
Circle5 destructor: Center = [72, 29]; Radius = 4.5
Point4 destructor: Center = [72, 29]; Radius = 4.5
```

Fig. 6.19 Order in which constructors and destructors are called.

Line 17 instantiates another object of class **Circle5**, then assigns it to reference **circle2**. Again, this begins the chain of constructor calls in which the **Circle5** constructor, the **Point4** constructor and the **Object** constructor are called. In the output, notice that the body of the **Point4** constructor executes before the body of the **Circle5** constructor. This demonstrates that objects are constructed "inside out" (i.e., the base-class constructor is called first).

Lines 22–23 set references **circle1** and **circle2** to **null**. This removes the only references to these **Circle5** objects in the program. Thus, the garbage collector can release the memory that these objects occupy. Remember that we cannot guarantee when the garbage collector will execute, nor can we guarantee that it will collect all available objects when it does execute. To demonstrate the destructor invocations for the two **Circle5** objects, line 26 invokes class **GC**'s method **Collect** to request the garbage collector to run. Notice that each **Circle5** object's destructor outputs information before calling class **Point4**'s destructor. Objects are destroyed "outside in" (i.e., the derived-class destructor completes its tasks before invoking the base-class destructor).

6.7 Software Engineering with Inheritance

In this section, we discuss the use of inheritance to customize existing software. When we use inheritance to create a new class from an existing one, the new class inherits the member variables, properties and methods of the existing class. We can customize the new class to meet our needs by including additional member variables, properties and methods, and by overriding base-class members.

Sometimes, it is difficult to appreciate the scope of problems faced by designers who work on large-scale software projects in industry. People experienced with such projects say that effective software reuse improves the software-development process. Object-oriented programming facilitates software reuse, thus shortening development times.

C# encourages software reuse by providing the .NET Framework Class Library (FCL), which delivers the maximum benefits of software reuse through inheritance. As interest in C# grows, interest in the FCL class libraries also increases. There is a worldwide commitment to the continued evolution of the FCL class libraries for a wide variety of applications. The FCL will grow as the .NET world grows explosively.

Software Engineering Observation 6.11

At the design stage in an object-oriented system, the designer often determines that certain classes are closely related. The designer should "factor out" common attributes and behaviors and place these in a base class. Then, use inheritance to form derived classes, endowing them with capabilities beyond those inherited from the base class.

Software Engineering Observation 6.12

The creation of a derived class does not affect its base class's source code. Inheritance preserves the integrity of a base class.

Software Engineering Observation 6.13

Just as designers of non-object-oriented systems should avoid proliferation of functions, designers of object-oriented systems should avoid proliferation of classes. Proliferation of classes creates management problems and can hinder software reusability, because it becomes difficult for a client to locate the most appropriate class of a huge class library. The alternative is to create fewer classes, in which each provides more substantial functionality, but such classes might provide too much functionality.

Performance Tip 6.2

If classes produced through inheritance are larger than they need to be (i.e., contain too much functionality), memory and processing resources might be wasted. Inherit from the class whose functionality is "closest" to what is needed.

Reading derived-class definitions can be confusing, because inherited members are not shown physically in the derived class, but nevertheless are present in the derived classes. A similar problem exists when documenting derived class members.

In this chapter, we introduced inheritance—the ability to create classes by absorbing an existing class's data members and behaviors and embellishing these with new capabilities. In Chapter 7, we build upon our discussion of inheritance by introducing *polymorphism*—an object-oriented technique that enables us to write programs that handle, in a more general manner, a wide variety of classes related by inheritance. After studying Chapter 7, you will be familiar with encapsulation, inheritance and polymorphism—the most crucial aspects of object-oriented programming.

6.8 Summary

Inheritance is the process by which one class "absorbs" the capabilities of an existing class. A new class that is created by inheriting from an existing class is called a derived class. The class from which the derived class inherits is called the base class.

Because derived classes can include their own instance variables, properties and methods, derived classes are often larger than their base classes. A derived class is more specific than its base class and represents a smaller group of objects.

Inheritance is an "is-a" relationship; that is, an object of a derived class also can be treated as an object of its base class. However, base-class objects are not objects of that class's derived classes. Composition is a "has-a" relationship; that is, a class object has references to one or more objects of other classes as members.

A base class's non-**static public** members are accessible anywhere that the program has a reference to an object of that base class or to an object of one of that base class's derived classes. A base class's **private** members are accessible only within the definition of that base class. A base class's **protected** members have an intermediate level of protection between **public** and **private** access. A base class's **protected** members can be accessed only in that base class or in any classes derived from that base class. A base class's **internal** members can be accessed only by objects in the same assembly.

When a base-class method is inappropriate for a derived class, that member can be overridden (redefined) in the derived class via an appropriate implementation. When a method that is overridden in a derived class is called on a derived-class object, the derived-class version (not the base-class version) is called.

When an object of a derived class is instantiated, the base class's constructor is called immediately (either explicitly or implicitly) to do any necessary initialization of the base-class instance variables in the derived-class object (before the derived class's instance variable are initialized). Base-class constructors and destructors are not inherited by derived classes.

7

Object-Oriented Programming: Polymorphism

Objectives

- To understand the concept of polymorphism.
- To understand how polymorphism makes systems extensible and maintainable.
- To understand the distinction between abstract classes and concrete classes.
- To learn how to create **sealed** classes, interfaces and delegates.

One Ring to rule them all, One Ring to find them,
One Ring to bring them all and in the darkness bind them.
John Ronald Reuel Tolkien

General propositions do not decide concrete cases.
Oliver Wendell Holmes

A philosopher of imposing stature doesn't think in a vacuum.
Even his most abstract ideas are, to some extent, conditioned
by what is or is not known in the time when he lives.
Alfred North Whitehead

Outline

7.1	Introduction
7.2	Derived-Class-Object to Base-Class-Object Conversion
7.3	Type Fields and `switch` Statements
7.4	Polymorphism Examples
7.5	Abstract Classes and Methods
7.6	Example: Inheriting Interface and Implementation
7.7	`sealed` Classes and Methods
7.8	Example: Payroll System Using Polymorphism
7.9	Example: Creating and Using Interfaces
7.10	Delegates
7.11	Operator Overloading
7.12	Summary

7.1 Introduction

The previous chapter's object-oriented programming (OOP) discussion focused on one of OOP's key component technologies, inheritance. In this chapter, we continue our study of OOP *polymorphism*. Both inheritance and polymorphism are crucial technologies in the development of complex software. Polymorphism enables us to write programs that handle a wide variety of related classes in a generic manner and facilitates adding new classes and capabilities to a system.

With polymorphism, it is possible to design and implement systems that are easily extensible. Programs can process objects of all classes in a class hierarchy generically as objects of a common base class. Furthermore, new classes can be added with little or no modification to the generic portions of the program, as long as those classes are part of the inheritance hierarchy that the program processes generically. The only parts of a program that must be altered to accommodate new classes are those program components that require direct knowledge of the new classes that the programmer adds to the hierarchy. In this chapter, we demonstrate two substantial class hierarchies and manipulate objects from those hierarchies polymorphically.

7.2 Derived-Class-Object to Base-Class-Object Conversion

Section 6.4 created a point-circle class hierarchy, in which class **Circle** inherited from class **Point**. The programs that manipulated objects of these classes always used **Point** references to refer to **Point** objects and **Circle** references to refer to **Circle** objects. In this section, we discuss the relationships between classes in a hierarchy that enable programs to assign derived-class objects to base-class references—a fundamental part of programs that process objects polymorphically. This section also discusses explicit casting between types in a class hierarchy.

An object of a derived class can be treated as an object of its base class. This enables various interesting manipulations. For example, a program can create an array of base-class references that refer to objects of many derived-class types. This is allowed despite the fact that the derived-class objects are of different data types. However, the reverse is not true— a base-class object is not an object of any of its derived classes. For example, a **Point** is not a **Circle** in the hierarchy defined in Chapter 6. If a base-class reference refers to a derived-class object, it is possible to convert the base-class reference to the object's actual data type and manipulate the object as that type.

The example in Fig. 7.1–Fig. 7.3 demonstrates assigning derived-class objects to base-class references and casting base-class references to derived-class references. Class **Point** (Fig. 7.1), which we discussed in Chapter 6, represents an *x-y* coordinate pair. Class **Circle** (Fig. 7.2), which we also discussed in Chapter 6, represents a circle and inherits from class **Point**. Each **Circle** object "is a" **Point** and also has a radius (represented via property **Radius**). We declare method **Area** as **virtual**, so that a derived class (such as class **Cylinder**) can override method **Area** to calculate the derived-class object's area. Class **PointCircleTest** (Fig. 7.3) demonstrates the assignment and cast operations.

```
1   // Fig. 7.1: Point.cs
2   // Point class represents an x-y coordinate pair.
3
4   using System;
5
6   // Point class definition implicitly inherits from Object
7   public class Point
8   {
9      // point coordinate
10     private int x, y;
11
12     // default constructor
13     public Point()
14     {
15        // implicit call to Object constructor occurs here
16     }
17
18     // constructor
19     public Point( int xValue, int yValue )
20     {
21        // implicit call to Object constructor occurs here
22        X = xValue;
23        Y = yValue;
24     }
25
26     // property X
27     public int X
28     {
29        get
30        {
31           return x;
32        }
33
```

Fig. 7.1   **Point** class represents an *x-y* coordinate pair. (Part 1 of 2.)

```
34              set
35              {
36                  x = value;   // no need for validation
37              }
38
39          } // end property X
40
41          // property Y
42          public int Y
43          {
44              get
45              {
46                  return y;
47              }
48
49              set
50              {
51                  y = value;   // no need for validation
52              }
53
54          } // end property Y
55
56          // return string representation of Point
57          public override string ToString()
58          {
59              return "[" + X + ", " + Y + "]";
60          }
61
62      } // end class Point
```

Fig. 7.1   **Point** class represents an *x-y* coordinate pair. (Part 2 of 2.)

```
1   // Fig. 7.2: Circle.cs
2   // Circle class that inherits from class Point.
3
4   using System;
5
6   // Circle class definition inherits from Point
7   public class Circle : Point
8   {
9       private double radius; // circle's radius
10
11      // default constructor
12      public Circle()
13      {
14          // implicit call to Point constructor occurs here
15      }
16
17      // constructor
18      public Circle( int xValue, int yValue, double radiusValue )
19          : base( xValue, yValue )
20      {
```

Fig. 7.2   **Circle** class that inherits from class **Point**. (Part 1 of 2.)

```
21              Radius = radiusValue;
22         }
23
24         // property Radius
25         public double Radius
26         {
27            get
28            {
29               return radius;
30            }
31
32            set
33            {
34               if ( value >= 0 ) // validate radius
35                  radius = value;
36            }
37
38         } // end property Radius
39
40         // calculate Circle diameter
41         public double Diameter()
42         {
43            return Radius * 2;
44         }
45
46         // calculate Circle circumference
47         public double Circumference()
48         {
49            return Math.PI * Diameter();
50         }
51
52         // calculate Circle area
53         public virtual double Area()
54         {
55            return Math.PI * Math.Pow( Radius, 2 );
56         }
57
58         // return string representation of Circle
59         public override string ToString()
60         {
61            return "Center = " + base.ToString() +
62               "; Radius = " + Radius;
63         }
64
65   } // end class Circle
```

Fig. 7.2   **Circle** class that inherits from class **Point**. (Part 2 of 2.)

Class **PointCircleTest** (Fig. 7.3) demonstrates assigning derived-class references to base-class references and casting base-class references to derived-class references. Lines 13–14 declare a **Point** reference (**point1**) and a **Circle** reference (**circle1**). Lines 16–17 append **string** representations of each object to **string output** to show the values used to initialize these objects. Because **point1** is reference to a **Point** object, method **ToString** of **point1** prints the object as a **Point**. Similarly, because **circle1** is reference to a **Circle** object, method **ToString** of **circle1** prints the object as a **Circle**.

```
1   // Fig. 7.3: PointCircleTest.cs
2   // Demonstrating inheritance and polymorphism.
3
4   using System;
5   using System.Windows.Forms;
6
7   // PointCircleTest class definition
8   class PointCircleTest
9   {
10     // main entry point for application.
11     static void Main( string[] args )
12     {
13        Point point1 = new Point( 30, 50 );
14        Circle circle1 = new Circle( 120, 89, 2.7 );
15
16        string output = "Point point1: " + point1.ToString() +
17           "\nCircle circle1: " + circle1.ToString();
18
19        // use 'is a' relationship to assign
20        // Circle circle1 to Point reference
21        Point point2 = circle1;
22
23        output += "\n\nCircle circle1 (via point2): " +
24           point2.ToString();
25
26        // downcast (cast base-class reference to derived-class
27        // data type) point2 to Circle circle2
28        Circle circle2 = ( Circle ) point2;
29
30        output += "\n\nCircle circle1 (via circle2): " +
31           circle2.ToString();
32
33        output += "\nArea of circle1 (via circle2): " +
34           circle2.Area().ToString( "F" );
35
36        // attempt to assign point1 object to Circle reference
37        if ( point1 is Circle )
38        {
39           circle2 = ( Circle ) point1;
40           output += "\n\ncast successful";
41        }
42        else
43        {
44           output += "\n\npoint1 does not refer to a Circle";
45        }
46
47        MessageBox.Show( output,
48           "Demonstrating the 'is a' relationship" );
```

Fig. 7.3   Assigning derived-class references to base-class references. (Part 1 of 2.)

```
49
50      } // end method Main
51
52   } // end class PointCircleTest
```

Fig. 7.3   Assigning derived-class references to base-class references. (Part 2 of 2.)

Line 21 assigns **circle1** (a reference to a derived-class object) to **point2** (a base-class reference). In C#, it is acceptable to assign a derived-class object to a base-class reference, because of the inheritance "is a" relationship. Class **Circle** inherits from class **Point**, because a **Circle** *is a* **Point** (in a structural sense, at least). However, assigning a base-class reference to a derived-class reference is potentially dangerous, as we will discuss.

Lines 23–24 invoke **point2.ToString** and append the result to **output**. When C# encounters a **virtual** method invocation (such as method **ToString**), C# determines which version of the method to call from the type of the object on which the method is called, not the type of the reference that refers to the object. In this case, **point2** refers to a **Circle** object, so C# calls **Circle** method **ToString**, rather than **Point** method **ToString** (as one might expect from the **point2** reference, which was declared as type **Point**). The decision about which method to call is an example of *polymorphism*, a concept that we discuss in detail throughout this chapter. Note that if **point2** referenced a **Point** object rather than a **Circle** object, C# would invoke **Point**'s **ToString** method.

Previous chapters used methods such as **Int32.Parse** and **Double.Parse** to convert between various built-in C# types. Now, we convert between object references of programmer-defined types. We use explicit casts to perform these conversions. If the cast is valid, our program can treat a base-class reference as a derived-class reference. If the cast is invalid, C# throws an **InvalidCastException**, which indicates that the cast operation is not allowed. Exceptions are discussed in detail in Chapter 8, Exception Handling.

Common Programming Error 7.1

Assigning a base-class object (or a base-class reference) to a derived-class reference (without an explicit cast) is a syntax error.

Software Engineering Observation 7.1

If a derived-class object has been assigned to a reference of one of its direct or indirect base classes, it is acceptable to cast that base-class reference back to a reference of the derived-class type. In fact, this must be done to send that object messages that do not appear in the base class. [Note: We sometimes use the term "messages" to represent the invocation of methods and the use of object properties.]

Line 28 casts **point2**, which currently refers to a **Circle** object (**circle1**), to a **Circle** and assigns the result to **circle2**. As we discuss momentarily, this cast would be dangerous if **point2** were referencing a **Point**. Lines 30–31 invoke method **ToString** of the **Circle** object to which **circle2** now refers (note that the fourth line of the output demonstrates that **Circle**'s **ToString** method is called). Lines 33–34 calculate and output **circle2**'s **Area**.

Line 39 explicitly casts reference **point1** to a **Circle**. This is a dangerous operation, because **point** refers to a **Point** object, and a **Point** is not a **Circle**. Objects can be cast only to their own type or to their base-class types. If this statement were to execute, C# would determine that **point1** references a **Point** object, recognize the cast to **Circle** as dangerous and indicate an improper cast with an **InvalidCastException** message. However, we prevent this statement from executing by including an **if/else** structure (lines 37–45). The condition at line 37 uses keyword *is* to determine whether the object to which **point1** refers "is a" **Circle**. Keyword *is* discovers the type of the object to which the left operand refers and compares this type to the right operand (in this case, **Circle**). In our example, **point1** does not refer to a **Circle**, so the condition fails, and line 44 appends to **output** a string that indicates the result. Note that the *is* comparison will be **true** if the left operand is a reference to an instance of the right operand or a derived class.

Common Programming Error 7.2

Attempting to cast a base-class reference to a derived-class type causes an **Invalid-CastException** *if the reference refers to a base-class object rather than an appropriate derived-class object.*

Software Engineering Observation 7.2

The **is** *keyword enables a program to determine whether a cast operation would be successful by ensuring that the reference type and target type are compatible.*

If we remove the **if** test and execute the program, C# displays a **MessageBox** that contains the message:

```
An unhandled exception of type 'System.InvalidCastException'
occurred in
```

followed by the name and path of the executing program. We discuss how to deal with such situations in Chapter 8.

Despite the fact that a derived-class object also "is a" base-class object, the derived-class and base-class objects are different. As we have discussed previously, derived-class objects can be treated as if they were base-class objects. This is a logical relationship, because the derived class contains members that correspond to all members in the base class, but the derived class can have additional members. For this reason, assigning a base-class object to a derived-class reference is not allowed without an explicit cast. Such an assignment would leave the additional derived-class members undefined.

There are four ways to mix base-class references and derived-class references with base-class objects and derived-class objects:

1. Referring to a base-class object with a base-class reference is straightforward.

2. Referring to a derived-class object with a derived-class reference is straightforward.

3. Referring to a derived-class object with a base-class reference is safe, because the derived-class object *is an* object of its base class. However, this reference can refer only to base-class members. If this code refers to derived-class-only members through the base-class reference, the compiler reports an error.

4. Referring to a base-class object with a derived-class reference generates a compiler error. To avoid this error, the derived-class reference first must be cast to a base-class reference explicitly. In this cast, the derived-class reference must reference a derived-class object, or C# generates an **InvalidCastException**.

Common Programming Error 7.3

After assigning a derived-class object to a base-class reference, attempting to reference derived-class-only members with the base-class reference is a compilation error.

Common Programming Error 7.4

Treating a base-class object as a derived-class object can cause errors.

Though it is convenient to treat derived-class objects as base-class objects by manipulating derived-class objects with base-class references, doing so can cause significant problems. For example, a payroll system, must be able to traverse an array of employees and calculate the weekly pay for each person. Intuition suggests that using base-class references would enable the program to call only the base-class payroll calculation routine (if there is such a routine in the base class). Using only base-class references, we can invoke the proper payroll calculation routine for each object, whether the object is a base-class object or a derived-class object. We learn how to create classes that exhibit this behavior as we introduce polymorphism throughout this chapter.

7.3 Type Fields and `switch` Statements

One way to determine the type of an object that is incorporated in a larger program is to use a **switch** structure. This allows us to distinguish among object types, then invoke an appropriate action for a particular object. For example, in a hierarchy of shapes in which each shape object has a **ShapeType** property, a **switch** structure could employ the object's **ShapeType** to determine which **Print** method to call.

However, using **switch** logic exposes programs to a variety of potential problems. For example, the programmer might forget to include a type test when one is warranted, or the programmer might forget to test all possible cases in a **switch** structure. When modifying a **switch**-based system by adding new types, the programmer might forget to insert the new cases in all relevant **switch** statements. Every addition or deletion of a class requires the modification of every **switch** statement in the system; tracking these statements down can be time consuming and error prone.

Software Engineering Observation 7.3

*Polymorphic programming can eliminate the need for unnecessary **switch** logic. By using C#'s polymorphism mechanism to perform the equivalent logic, programmers can avoid the kinds of errors typically associated with **switch** logic.*

Testing and Debugging Tip 7.1

An interesting consequence of using polymorphism is that programs take on a simplified appearance. They contain less branching logic and more simple, sequential code. This simplification facilitates testing, debugging and program maintenance.

7.4 Polymorphism Examples

In this section, we discuss several examples of polymorphism. If class **Rectangle** is derived from class **Quadrilateral**, then a **Rectangle** object is a more specific version of a **Quadrilateral** object. Any operation (such as calculating the perimeter or the area) that can be performed on an object of class **Quadrilateral** also can be performed on an object of class **Rectangle**. Such operations also can be performed on other kinds of **Quadrilateral**s, such as **Square**s, **Parallelogram**s and **Trapezoid**s. When a program invokes a derived-class method through a base-class (i.e., **Quadrilateral**) reference, C# polymorphically chooses the correct overriding method in the derived class from which the object was instantiated. We investigate this behavior in later examples.

Suppose that we design a video game that manipulates objects of many different types, including objects of classes **Martian**, **Venutian**, **Plutonian**, **SpaceShip** and **LaserBeam**. Also, imagine that each of these classes inherits from the common base class called **SpaceObject**, which contains method **DrawYourself**. Each derived class implements this method. A screen-manager program would maintain a container (such as a **SpaceObject** array) of references to objects of the various classes. To refresh the screen, the screen manager would periodically send each object the same message—namely, **DrawYourself**. However, each object responds in a unique way. For example, a **Martian** object would draw itself in red with the appropriate number of antennae. A **SpaceShip** object would draw itself as a bright, silver flying saucer. A **LaserBeam** object would draw itself as a bright red beam across the screen. Thus the same message sent to a variety of objects would have "many forms" of results—hence the term *polymorphism.*

A polymorphic screen manager facilitates adding new classes to a system with minimal modifications to the system's code. Suppose we want to add class **Mercurian**s to our video game. To do so, we must build a class **Mercurian** that inherits from **SpaceObject**, but provides its own definition of method **DrawYourself**. Then, when objects of class **Mercurian** appear in the container, the programmer does not need to modify the code for the screen manager. The screen manager invokes method **Draw-Yourself** on every object in the container, regardless of the object's type, so the new **Mercurian** objects simply "plug right in." Thus, without modifying the system (other than to build and include the classes themselves), programmers can use polymorphism to include additional types of classes that were not envisioned when the system was created.

With polymorphism, one method can cause different actions to occur, depending on the type of the object on which the method is invoked. This gives the programmer tremendous expressive capability. In the next several sections, we provide examples that demonstrate polymorphism.

Software Engineering Observation 7.4

With polymorphism, the programmer can deal in generalities and let the execution-time environment concern itself with the specifics. The programmer can command a wide variety of objects to behave in manners appropriate to those objects, even if the programmer does not know the objects' types.

Software Engineering Observation 7.5

Polymorphism promotes extensibility. Software used to invoke polymorphic behavior is written to be independent of the types of the objects to which messages (i.e., method calls) are sent. Thus, programmers can include into a system additional types of objects that respond to existing messages and can do this without modifying the base system.

7.5 Abstract Classes and Methods

When we think of a class as a type, we assume that programs will create objects of that type. However, there are cases in which it is useful to define classes for which the programmer never intends to instantiate any objects. Such classes are called *abstract classes*. Because such classes normally are used as base classes in inheritance hierarchies, we refer to such classes as *abstract base classes*. These classes cannot be used to instantiate objects, since abstract classes are incomplete. Derived classes must define the "missing pieces." Abstract classes normally contain one or more *abstract methods* or *abstract properties*, which are methods and properties that do not provide implementations. Derived classes must override inherited abstract methods and properties to enable objects of those derived classes to be instantiated. We discuss abstract classes extensively in Section 7.6 and Section 7.8.

The purpose of an abstract class is to provide an appropriate base class from which other classes may inherit. Classes from which objects can be instantiated are called *concrete classes*. Such classes provide implementations of every method and property they define. We could have an abstract base class **TwoDimensionalObject** and derive such concrete classes as **Square**, **Circle** and **Triangle**. We could also have an abstract base class **ThreeDimensionalObject** and derive such concrete classes as **Cube**, **Sphere** and **Cylinder**. Abstract base classes are too generic to define real objects; we need to be more specific before we can think of instantiating objects. For example, if someone tells you to "draw the shape," what shape would you draw? Concrete classes provide the specifics that make it reasonable to instantiate objects.

A class is made abstract by declaring it with keyword ***abstract***. An inheritance hierarchy does not need to contain any abstract classes, but, as we will see, many good object-oriented systems have class hierarchies headed by abstract base classes. In some cases, abstract classes constitute the top few levels of the hierarchy. A good example of this is the shape hierarchy in Fig. 6.3. The hierarchy begins with abstract base-class **Shape**. On the next level of the hierarchy, we have two more abstract base classes, namely **TwoDimensionalShape** and **ThreeDimensionalShape**. The next level of the hierarchy would define concrete classes for two-dimensional shapes, such as **Circle** and **Square**, and for three-dimensional shapes, such as **Sphere** and **Cube**.

Software Engineering Observation 7.6

*An abstract class defines a common set of **public** methods and properties for the various members of a class hierarchy. An abstract class typically contains one or more abstract methods and properties that derived classes will override. All classes in the hierarchy can use this common set of **public** methods and properties.*

Abstract classes must specify signatures for their abstract methods and properties. C# provides keyword ***abstract*** to declare a method or property as abstract. Methods and properties that are **abstract** do not provide implementations—attempting to do so is a syntax error. Every concrete derived class must override all base-class **abstract** methods and properties (using keyword **override**) and provide concrete implementations of those methods or properties. Any class with an **abstract** method in it must be declared **abstract**. The difference between an **abstract** method and a **virtual** method is that a **virtual** method has an implementation and provides the derived class with the option of overriding the method; by contrast, an **abstract** method does not provide an implementation and forces the derived class to override the method (for that derived class to be concrete).

Common Programming Error 7.5

*Defining an **abstract** method in a class that has not been declared as **abstract** results is a syntax error.*

Common Programming Error 7.6

*Attempting to instantiate an object of an **abstract** class results in a compilation error.*

Common Programming Error 7.7

*Failure to override an **abstract** method in a derived class is a syntax error, unless the derived class also is an **abstract** class.*

Software Engineering Observation 7.7

*An **abstract** class can have instance data and non-**abstract** methods (including constructors), which are subject to the normal rules of inheritance by derived classes.*

Although we cannot instantiate objects of abstract base classes, we *can* use abstract base classes to declare references; these references can refer to instances of any concrete classes derived from the abstract class. Programs can use such references to manipulate instances of the derived classes polymorphically.

Let us consider another application of polymorphism. A screen manager needs to display a variety of objects, including new types of objects that the programmer will add to the system after writing the screen manager. The system might need to display various shapes, such as **Circle**, **Triangle** or **Rectangle**, which are derived from abstract class **Shape**. The screen manager uses base-class references of type **Shape** to manage the objects that are displayed. To draw any object (regardless of the level at which that object's class appears in the inheritance hierarchy), the screen manager uses a base-class reference to the object to invoke the object's **Draw** method. Method **Draw** is an **abstract** method in base class **Shape**; therefore, each derived class must implement method **Draw**. Each **Shape** object in the inheritance hierarchy knows how to draw itself. The screen manager does not have to worry about the type of each object or whether the screen manager has ever encountered objects of that type.

Polymorphism is particularly effective for implementing layered software systems. In operating systems, for example, each type of physical device could operate quite differently from the others. Even so, commands to *read* or *write* data from and to devices may have a certain uniformity. The write message sent to a device-driver object needs to be interpreted specifically in the context of that device driver and how that device driver manipulates devices of a specific type. However, the write call itself really is no different from the write to any other device in the system—place some number of bytes from memory onto that device. An object-oriented operating system might use an abstract base class to provide an interface appropriate for all device drivers. Then, through inheritance from that abstract base class, derived classes are formed that all operate similarly. The capabilities (i.e., the **public** services) offered by the device drivers are provided as abstract methods in the abstract base class. The implementations of these abstract methods are provided in the derived classes that correspond to the specific types of device drivers.

It is common in object-oriented programming to define an *iterator class* that can traverse all the objects in a container (such as an array). For example, a program can print a list of objects in a linked list by creating an iterator object, then using the iterator to obtain the next element of the list each time the iterator is called. Iterators often are used in polymorphic programming to traverse an array or a linked list of objects from various levels of a hierarchy. The references in such a list are all base-class references. (See Chapter 20, Data Structures and Collections, to learn more about linked lists.) A list of objects of base class **TwoDimensionalShape** could contain objects from classes **Square**, **Circle**, **Triangle** and so on. Using polymorphism to send a **Draw** message to each object in the list would draw each object correctly on the screen.

7.6 Example: Inheriting Interface and Implementation

Our next example (Fig. 7.4–Fig. 7.8) reexamines the **Point**, **Circle**, **Cylinder** hierarchy that we explored in Chapter 6. In this example, the hierarchy begins with abstract base class **Shape** (Fig. 7.4). This hierarchy mechanically demonstrates the power of polymorphism.

```
1   // Fig. 7.4: Shape.cs
2   // Demonstrate a shape hierarchy using an abstract base class.
3   using System;
4
5   public abstract class Shape
6   {
7      // return Shape's area
8      public virtual double Area()
9      {
10        return 0;
11     }
12
13     // return Shape's volume
14     public virtual double Volume()
15     {
16        return 0;
17     }
18
19     // return Shape's name
20     public abstract string Name
21     {
22        get;
23     }
24  }
```

Fig. 7.4   Abstract **Shape** base class.

Class **Shape** defines two concrete methods and one **abstract** property. All shapes have an area and a volume, so we include virtual methods **Area** (lines 8–11) and **Volume** (lines 14–17), which return the shape's area and volume, respectively. The volume of two-dimensional shapes is always zero, whereas three-dimensional shapes have a positive, nonzero volume. In class **Shape**, methods **Area** and **Volume** return zero, by default. Programmers can override these methods in derived classes when those classes should have different area calculations [e.g., classes **Circle2** (Fig. 7.6) and **Cylinder2** (Fig. 7.7)] and/or different volume calculations (e.g., **Cylinder2**). Read-only property **Name** (lines 20–23) is declared **abstract**, so derived classes must implement this property to become concrete classes. Note that **abstract** methods and properties are implicitly **virtual**.

Class **Point2** (Fig. 7.5) inherits from abstract class **Shape** and overrides the **abstract** property **Name**, which makes **Point2** a concrete class. A point's area and volume are zero, so class **Point2** does not override base-class methods **Area** and **Volume**. Lines 59–65 implement property **Name**. If we did not provide this implementation, class **Point2** would be an **abstract** class that would require keyword **abstract** in the first line of the class definition.

```
1   // Fig. 7.5: Point2.cs
2   // Point2 inherits from abstract class Shape and represents
3   // an x-y coordinate pair.
4   using System;
5
6   // Point2 inherits from abstract class Shape
7   public class Point2 : Shape
8   {
9      private int x, y; // Point2 coordinates
10
11     // default constructor
12     public Point2()
13     {
14        // implicit call to Object constructor occurs here
15     }
16
17     // constructor
18     public Point2( int xValue, int yValue )
19     {
20        X = xValue;
21        Y = yValue;
22     }
23
24     // property X
25     public int X
26     {
27        get
28        {
29           return x;
30        }
31
```

Fig. 7.5   **Point2** class inherits from **abstract** class **Shape**. (Part 1 of 2.)

```
32            set
33            {
34                x = value; // no validation needed
35            }
36        }
37
38        // property Y
39        public int Y
40        {
41            get
42            {
43                return y;
44            }
45
46            set
47            {
48                y = value; // no validation needed
49            }
50        }
51
52        // return string representation of Point2 object
53        public override string ToString()
54        {
55            return "[" + X + ", " + Y + "]";
56        }
57
58        // implement abstract property Name of class Shape
59        public override string Name
60        {
61            get
62            {
63                return "Point2";
64            }
65        }
66
67    } // end class Point2
```

Fig. 7.5   **Point2** class inherits from **abstract** class **Shape**. (Part 2 of 2.)

Figure 7.6 defines class **Circle2**, which inherits from class **Point2**. Class **Circle2** contains property **Radius** (lines 24–37) for accessing the circle's radius. Note that we do not declare property **Radius** as **virtual**, so classes derived from this class cannot override this property. A circle has zero volume, so we do not override base-class method **Volume**. Rather, **Circle2** inherits this method from class **Point2**, which inherited the method from **Shape**. However, a circle does have an area, so **Circle2** overrides **Shape** method **Area** (lines 52–55). Property **Name** (lines 65–71) of class **Circle2** overrides property **Name** of class **Point2**. If this class did not override property **Name**, the class would inherit the **Point2** version of property **Name**. In that case, **Circle2**'s **Name** property would erroneously return "**Point2**."

```
1   // Fig. 7.6: Circle2.cs
2   // Circle2 inherits from class Point2 and overrides key members.
3   using System;
4
5   // Circle2 inherits from class Point2
6   public class Circle2 : Point2
7   {
8      private double radius; // Circle2 radius
9
10     // default constructor
11     public Circle2()
12     {
13        // implicit call to Point2 constructor occurs here
14     }
15
16     // constructor
17     public Circle2( int xValue, int yValue, double radiusValue )
18        : base( xValue, yValue )
19     {
20        Radius = radiusValue;
21     }
22
23     // property Radius
24     public double Radius
25     {
26        get
27        {
28           return radius;
29        }
30
31        set
32        {
33           // ensure non-negative radius value
34           if ( value >= 0 )
35              radius = value;
36        }
37     }
38
39     // calculate Circle2 diameter
40     public double Diameter()
41     {
42        return Radius * 2;
43     }
44
45     // calculate Circle2 circumference
46     public double Circumference()
47     {
48        return Math.PI * Diameter();
49     }
50
51     // calculate Circle2 area
52     public override double Area()
53     {
```

Fig. 7.6   **Circle2** class that inherits from class **Point2**. (Part 1 of 2.)

```
54          return Math.PI * Math.Pow( Radius, 2 );
55       }
56
57       // return string representation of Circle2 object
58       public override string ToString()
59       {
60          return "Center = " + base.ToString() +
61             "; Radius = " + Radius;
62       }
63
64       // override property Name from class Point2
65       public override string Name
66       {
67          get
68          {
69             return "Circle2";
70          }
71       }
72
73    } // end class Circle2
```

Fig. 7.6 **Circle2** class that inherits from class **Point2**. (Part 2 of 2.)

Figure 7.7 defines class **Cylinder2**, which inherits from class **Circle2**. Class **Cylinder2** contains property **Height** (lines 24–37) for accessing the cylinder's height. Note that we do not declare property **Height** as **virtual**, so classes derived from class **Cylinder2** cannot override this property. A cylinder has different area and volume calculations from those of a circle, so this class overrides method **Area** (lines 40–43) to calculate the cylinder's surface area (i.e., $2\pi r^2 + 2\pi rh$) and overrides method **Volume** (lines 46–49). Property **Name** (lines 58–64) overrides property **Name** of class **Circle2**. If this class did not override property **Name**, the class would inherit property **Name** of class **Circle2**, and this property would erroneously return "**Circle2**."

```
1    // Fig. 7.7: Cylinder2.cs
2    // Cylinder2 inherits from class Circle2 and overrides key
members.
3    using System;
4
5    // Cylinder2 inherits from class Circle2
6    public class Cylinder2 : Circle2
7    {
8       private double height; // Cylinder2 height
9
10      // default constructor
11      public Cylinder2()
12      {
13         // implicit call to Circle2 constructor occurs here
14      }
15
```

Fig. 7.7 **Cylinder2** class inherits from class **Circle2**. (Part 1 of 2.)

```
16       // constructor
17       public Cylinder2( int xValue, int yValue, double radiusValue,
18          double heightValue ) : base( xValue, yValue, radiusValue )
19       {
20          Height = heightValue;
21       }
22
23       // property Height
24       public double Height
25       {
26          get
27          {
28             return height;
29          }
30
31          set
32          {
33             // ensure non-negative height value
34             if ( value >= 0 )
35                height = value;
36          }
37       }
38
39       // calculate Cylinder2 area
40       public override double Area()
41       {
42          return 2 * base.Area() + base.Circumference() * Height;
43       }
44
45       // calculate Cylinder2 volume
46       public override double Volume()
47       {
48          return base.Area() * Height;
49       }
50
51       // return string representation of Cylinder2 object
52       public override string ToString()
53       {
54          return base.ToString() + "; Height = " + Height;
55       }
56
57       // override property Name from class Circle2
58       public override string Name
59       {
60          get
61          {
62             return "Cylinder2";
63          }
64       }
65
66    } // end class Cylinder2
```

Fig. 7.7   **Cylinder2** class inherits from class **Circle2**. (Part 2 of 2.)

Class **AbstractShapesTest** (Fig. 7.8), creates an object of each of the three concrete classes and manipulates those objects polymorphically using an array of **Shape** references. Lines 11–13 instantiate **Point2** object **point**, **Circle2** object **circle**, and **Cylinder2** object **cylinder**, respectively. Next, line 16 allocates array **arrayOfShapes**, which contains three **Shape** references. Line 19 assigns reference **point** to the array element **arrayOfShapes[0]**, line 22 assigns reference **circle** to the array element **arrayOfShapes[1]** and line 25 assigns reference **cylinder** to the array element **arrayOfShapes[2]**. These assignments are possible because a **Point2** is a **Shape**, a **Circle2** is a **Shape** and a **Cylinder2** is a **Shape**. Therefore, we can assign instances of derived classes **Point2**, **Circle2** and **Cylinder2** to base-class **Shape** references.

```
1   // Fig. 7.8: AbstractShapesTest.cs
2   // Demonstrates polymorphism in Point-Circle-Cylinder hierarchy.
3   using System;
4   using System.Windows.Forms;
5
6   public class AbstractShapesTest
7   {
8      public static void Main( string[] args )
9      {
10        // instantiate Point2, Circle2 and Cylinder2 objects
11        Point2 point = new Point2( 7, 11 );
12        Circle2 circle = new Circle2( 22, 8, 3.5 );
13        Cylinder2 cylinder = new Cylinder2( 10, 10, 3.3, 10 );
14
15        // create empty array of Shape base-class references
16        Shape[] arrayOfShapes = new Shape[ 3 ];
17
18        // arrayOfShapes[ 0 ] refers to Point2 object
19        arrayOfShapes[ 0 ] = point;
20
21        // arrayOfShapes[ 1 ] refers to Circle2 object
22        arrayOfShapes[ 1 ] = circle;
23
24        // arrayOfShapes[ 1 ] refers to Cylinder2 object
25        arrayOfShapes[ 2 ] = cylinder;
26
27        string output = point.Name + ": " + point + "\n" +
28           circle.Name + ": " + circle + "\n" +
29           cylinder.Name + ": " + cylinder;
30
31        // display Name, Area and Volume for each object
32        // in arrayOfShapes polymorphically
33        foreach ( Shape shape in arrayOfShapes )
34        {
35           output += "\n\n" + shape.Name + ": " + shape +
36              "\nArea = " + shape.Area().ToString( "F" ) +
37              "\nVolume = " + shape.Volume().ToString( "F" );
38        }
39
```

Fig. 7.8　**AbstractShapesTest** demonstrates polymorphism in Point-Circle-Cylinder hierarchy. (Part 1 of 2.)

```
40        MessageBox.Show( output, "Demonstrating Polymorphism" );
41    }
42  }
```

Fig. 7.8   **AbstractShapesTest** demonstrates polymorphism in Point-Circle-Cylinder hierarchy. (Part 2 of 2.)

Lines 27–29 access property **Name** and invoke method **ToString** (implicitly) for objects **point**, **circle** and **cylinder**. Property **Name** returns the object's class name and method **ToString** returns the object's **String** representation (i.e., *x-y* coordinate pair, radius and height, depending on each object's type). Note that lines 27–29 use derived-class references to invoke each derived-class object's methods and properties.

By contrast, the **foreach** structure (lines 33–38) uses base-class **Shape** references to invoke each derived-class object's methods and properties. The **foreach** structure calls property **Name** and methods **ToString**, **Area** and **Volume** for each **Shape** reference in **arrayOfShapes**. The property and methods are invoked on each object in **arrayOfShapes**. When the compiler looks at each method/property call, the compiler determines whether each **Shape** reference (in **arrayOfShapes**) can make these calls. This is the case for property **Name** and methods **Area** and **Volume**, because they are defined in class **Shape**. However, class **Shape** does not define method **ToString**. For this method, the compiler proceeds to **Shape**'s base class (class **Object**) and determines that **Shape** inherited a no-argument **ToString** method from class **Object**.

The screen capture of Fig. 7.8 illustrates that the "appropriate" property **Name** and methods **ToString**, **Area** and **Volume** were invoked for each type of object in **arrayOfShapes**. By "appropriate," we mean that C# maps each property and method call to the proper object. For example, in the **foreach** structure's first iteration, reference **arrayOfShapes[0]** (which is of type **Shape**) refers to the same object as **point** (which is of type **Point2**). Class **Point2** overrides property **Name**, and method **ToString** and inherits method **Area** and **Volume** from class **Shape**. At runtime, **arrayOfShapes[0]** accesses property **Name** and invokes methods **ToString**, **Area** and **Volume** of the **Point** object. C# determines the correct object type, then uses that type to determine the appropriate methods to invoke. Through polymorphism, the call to property **Name** returns the string **"Point2"**; the call to method **ToString** returns the **String** representation of **point**'s *x-y* coordinate pair; and methods **Area** and **Volume** each return **0** (as shown in the second group of outputs in Fig. 7.8).

Polymorphism occurs in the next two iterations of the **foreach** structure as well. Reference **arrayOfShapes[1]** refers to the same object as **circle** (which is of type **Circle2**). Class **Circle2** provides implementations for property **Name**, method **ToString** and method **Area**, and inherits method **Volume** from class **Point2** (which, in turn, inherited method **Volume** from class **Shape**). C# associates property **Name** and methods **ToString**, **Area** and **Volume** of the **Circle2** object to reference **arrayOfShapes[1]**. As a result, property **Name** returns the string **"Circle2"**; method **ToString** returns the **String** representation of **circle**'s *x-y* coordinate pair and radius; method **Area** returns the area (**38.48**); and method **Volume** returns **0**.

For the final iteration of the **foreach** structure, reference **arrayOfShapes[2]** refers to the same object as **cylinder** (which is of type **Cylinder2**). Class **Cylinder2** provides its own implementations for property **Name** and for methods **ToString**, **Area** and **Volume**. C# associates property **Name** and methods **ToString**, **Area** and **Volume** of the **Cylinder2** object to reference **arrayOfShapes[2]**. Property **Name** returns the string **"Cylinder2:"**; method **ToString** returns the **String** representation of **cylinder**'s *x-y* coordinate pair, radius and height; method **Area** returns the cylinder's surface area (**275.769…**); and method **Volume** returns the cylinder's volume (**342.119…**).

7.7 **sealed** Classes and Methods

In Chapter 5, Object-Based Programming, we saw that variables can be declared **const** and **readonly** to indicate that they cannot be modified after they are initialized. Variables declared with **const** must be initialized when they are declared; variables declared with **readonly** can be initialized in the constructor, but cannot be changed after they are initialized.

The keyword **sealed** is applied to methods and classes to prevent overriding and inheritance. A method that is declared **sealed** cannot be overridden in a derived class. Methods that are declared **static** and methods that are declared **private** are implicitly **sealed**.

Performance Tip 7.1

*The **sealed** keyword allows certain compiler optimizations. A **sealed** method's definition can never change, so the compiler can optimize the program by removing calls to **sealed** methods and replacing them with the expanded code of their definitions at each method call location—a technique known as inlining the code.*

Software Engineering Observation 7.8

*If a method is declared **sealed**, it cannot be overridden in derived classes. Method calls must not be sent polymorphically to objects of those derived classes. The method call still may be sent to derived classes, but they will respond identically, rather than polymorphically. Remember that a method cannot be overridden (using the keyword **override**) if it is not declared either **virtual** or **abstract**. Therefore, keyword **sealed** is not needed for these cases. Keyword **sealed** is used for methods that have been overridden, but that we do not want to be overridden in further derived classes.*

Performance Tip 7.2

*The compiler can decide to inline a **sealed** method call and will do so for small, simple **sealed** methods. Inlining does not violate encapsulation or information hiding (but does improve performance, because it eliminates the overhead of making a method call).*

Performance Tip 7.3

*Pipelined processors can improve performance by executing portions of the next several instructions simultaneously, but not if those instructions follow a method call. Inlining (which the compiler can perform on a **sealed** method) can improve performance in these processors as it eliminates the out-of-line transfer of control associated with a method call.*

Software Engineering Observation 7.9

*A class that is declared **sealed** cannot be a base class (i.e., a class cannot inherit from a **sealed** class). All methods in a **sealed** class are **sealed** implicitly.*

Using the **sealed** keyword with classes allows other runtime optimizations. For example, **virtual** method calls can be transformed into non-**virtual** method calls.

A **sealed** class is the opposite of an **abstract** class in certain ways. An **abstract** class cannot be instantiated—other classes derive from the abstract base class and implement the base class's **abstract** members. A **sealed** class, on the other hand, cannot have any derived classes. This relationship is similar with regard to methods. An **abstract** method must be overridden in a derived class. A **sealed** method cannot be overridden in a derived class.

7.8 Example: Payroll System Using Polymorphism

Let us use **abstract** classes, **abstract** methods and polymorphism to perform payroll calculations for various types of employees. We begin by creating abstract base class **Employee**. The derived classes of **Employee** are **Boss** (paid a fixed weekly salary, regardless of the number of hours worked), **CommissionWorker** (paid a flat base salary plus a percentage of the worker's sales), **PieceWorker** (paid a flat fee per item produced) and **HourlyWorker** (paid by the hour with "time-and-a-half" for overtime).

The application must determine the weekly earnings for all types of employees, so each class derived from **Employee** requires method **Earnings**. However, each derived class uses a different calculation to determine earnings for each specific type of employee. Therefore, we declare method **Earnings** as **abstract** in **Employee** and declare **Employee** to be an **abstract** class. Each derived class overrides this method to calculate earnings for that employee type.

To calculate any employee's earnings, the program can use a base-class reference to a derived-class object and invoke method **Earnings**. A real payroll system might reference the various **Employee** objects with individual elements in an array of **Employee** references. The program would traverse the array one element at a time, using the **Employee** references to invoke the appropriate **Earnings** method of each object.

Software Engineering Observation 7.10

The ability to declare an abstract method gives the class designer considerable control over how derived classes are defined in a class hierarchy. Any class that inherits directly from a base class containing an abstract method must override the abstract method. Otherwise, the new class also would be abstract, and attempts to instantiate objects of that class would fail.

Let us consider class **Employee** (Fig. 7.9). The **public** members include a constructor (lines 11–16) that takes as arguments the employee's first and last names; properties **FirstName** (lines 19–30) and **LastName** (lines 33–44); method **ToString** (lines

47–50), which returns the first name and last name separated by a space; and **abstract** method **Earnings** (line 54). The **abstract** keyword (line 5) indicates that class **Employee** is abstract; thus, it cannot be used to instantiate **Employee** objects. Method **Earnings** is declared **abstract**, so the class does not provide a method implementation. All classes derived directly from class **Employee**—except for abstract derived classes—must implement this method. Method **Earnings** is **abstract** in **Employee**, because we cannot calculate the earnings for a generic employee. To determine earnings, we first must know of what *kind* the employee is. By declaring this method **abstract**, we indicate that we will provide an implementation in each concrete derived class, but not in the base class itself.

```csharp
1   // Fig. 7.9: Employee.cs
2   // Abstract base class for company employees.
3   using System;
4
5   public abstract class Employee
6   {
7      private string firstName;
8      private string lastName;
9
10     // constructor
11     public Employee( string firstNameValue,
12        string lastNameValue )
13     {
14        FirstName = firstNameValue;
15        LastName = lastNameValue;
16     }
17
18     // property FirstName
19     public string FirstName
20     {
21        get
22        {
23           return firstName;
24        }
25
26        set
27        {
28           firstName = value;
29        }
30     }
31
32     // property LastName
33     public string LastName
34     {
35        get
36        {
37           return lastName;
38        }
39
```

Fig. 7.9   **abstract** class **Employee** definition. (Part 1 of 2.)

```
40          set
41          {
42              lastName = value;
43          }
44      }
45
46      // return string representation of Employee
47      public override string ToString()
48      {
49          return FirstName + " " + LastName;
50      }
51
52      // abstract method that must be implemented for each derived
53      // class of Employee to calculate specific earnings
54      public abstract decimal Earnings();
55
56  } // end class Employee
```

Fig. 7.9   **abstract** class **Employee** definition. (Part 2 of 2.)

Class **Boss** (Fig. 7.10) inherits from **Employee**. Class **Boss**'s constructor (lines 10–15) receives as arguments a first name, a last name and a salary. The constructor passes the first name and last name to the **Employee** constructor (line 12), which initializes the **FirstName** and **LastName** members of the base-class part of the derived-class object. Other **public** methods in class **Boss** include method **Earnings** (lines 34–37), which defines the calculation of a boss' earnings, and method **ToString** (lines 40–43), which returns a string that indicates the type of employee (i.e., **"Boss: "**) and the boss's name. Class **Boss** also includes property **WeeklySalary** (lines 18–31), which manipulates the value for member variable **salary**. Note that this property ensures only that **salary** cannot hold a negative value—in a real payroll system, this validation would be more extensive and carefully controlled.

```
1   // Fig. 7.10: Boss.cs
2   // Boss class derived from Employee.
3   using System;
4
5   public class Boss : Employee
6   {
7       private decimal salary; // Boss's salary
8
9       // constructor
10      public Boss( string firstNameValue, string lastNameValue,
11          decimal salaryValue)
12          : base( firstNameValue, lastNameValue )
13      {
14          WeeklySalary = salaryValue;
15      }
16
```

Fig. 7.10   **Boss** class inherits from class **Employee**. (Part 1 of 2.)

```
17      // property WeeklySalary
18      public decimal WeeklySalary
19      {
20         get
21         {
22            return salary;
23         }
24
25         set
26         {
27            // ensure positive salary value
28            if ( value > 0 )
29               salary = value;
30         }
31      }
32
33      // override base-class method to calculate Boss's earnings
34      public override decimal Earnings()
35      {
36         return WeeklySalary;
37      }
38
39      // return string representation of Boss
40      public override string ToString()
41      {
42         return "Boss: " + base.ToString();
43      }
44   }
```

Fig. 7.10 **Boss** class inherits from class **Employee**. (Part 2 of 2.)

Class **CommissionWorker** (Fig. 7.11) also inherits from class **Employee**. The constructor for this class (lines 12–20) receives as arguments a first name, a last name, a salary, a commission and a quantity of items sold. Line 15 passes the first name and last name to the base-class **Employee** constructor. Class **CommissionWorker** also provides properties **WeeklySalary** (lines 23–36), **Commission** (lines 39–52) and **Quantity** (lines 55–68); method **Earnings** (lines 72–75), which calculates the worker's wages; and method **ToString** (lines 78–81), which returns a string that indicates the employee type (i.e., **"CommissionWorker: "**) and the worker's name.

```
1    // Fig. 7.11: CommissionWorker.cs
2    // CommissionWorker class derived from Employee
3    using System;
4
5    public class CommissionWorker : Employee
6    {
7       private decimal salary;        // base weekly salary
8       private decimal commission;    // amount paid per item sold
9       private int quantity;          // total items sold
10
```

Fig. 7.11 **CommissionWorker** class inherits from class **Employee**. (Part 1 of 3.)

```
11        // constructor
12        public CommissionWorker( string firstNameValue,
13           string lastNameValue, decimal salaryValue,
14           decimal commissionValue, int quantityValue )
15           : base( firstNameValue, lastNameValue )
16        {
17           WeeklySalary = salaryValue;
18           Commission = commissionValue;
19           Quantity = quantityValue;
20        }
21
22        // property WeeklySalary
23        public decimal WeeklySalary
24        {
25           get
26           {
27              return salary;
28           }
29
30           set
31           {
32              // ensure non-negative salary value
33              if ( value > 0 )
34                 salary = value;
35           }
36        }
37
38        // property Commission
39        public decimal Commission
40        {
41           get
42           {
43              return commission;
44           }
45
46           set
47           {
48              // ensure non-negative commission value
49              if ( value > 0 )
50                 commission = value;
51           }
52        }
53
54        // property Quantity
55        public int Quantity
56        {
57           get
58           {
59              return quantity;
60           }
61
```

Fig. 7.11 CommissionWorker class inherits from class Employee. (Part 2 of 3.)

```
62          set
63          {
64              // ensure non-negative quantity value
65              if ( value > 0 )
66                  quantity = value;
67          }
68      }
69
70      // override base-class method to calculate
71      // CommissionWorker's earnings
72      public override decimal Earnings()
73      {
74          return WeeklySalary + Commission * Quantity;
75      }
76
77      // return string representation of CommissionWorker
78      public override string ToString()
79      {
80          return "CommissionWorker: " + base.ToString();
81      }
82
83  } // end class CommissionWorker
```

Fig. 7.11 **CommissionWorker** class inherits from class **Employee**. (Part 3 of 3.)

Class **PieceWorker** (Fig. 7.12) inherits from class **Employee**. The constructor for this class (lines 11–18) receives as arguments a first name, a last name, a wage per piece and a quantity of items produced. Line 14 then passes the first name and last name to the base-class **Employee** constructor. Class **PieceWorker** also provides properties **WagePerPiece** (lines 21–33) and **Quantity** (lines 36–48); method **Earnings** (lines 52–55), which calculates a piece worker's earnings; and method **ToString** (lines 58–61), which returns a string that indicates the type of the employee (i.e., **"PieceWorker: "**) and the piece worker's name.

```
1   // Fig. 7.12: PieceWorker.cs
2   // PieceWorker class derived from Employee.
3   using System;
4
5   public class PieceWorker : Employee
6   {
7       private decimal wagePerPiece; // wage per piece produced
8       private int quantity;          // quantity of pieces produced
9
10      // constructor
11      public PieceWorker( string firstNameValue,
12          string lastNameValue, decimal wagePerPieceValue,
13          int quantityValue )
14          : base( firstNameValue, lastNameValue )
15      {
16          WagePerPiece = wagePerPieceValue;
```

Fig. 7.12 **PieceWorker** class inherits from class **Employee**. (Part 1 of 2.)

```
17                Quantity = quantityValue;
18          }
19
20          // property WagePerPiece
21          public decimal WagePerPiece
22          {
23             get
24             {
25                return wagePerPiece;
26             }
27
28             set
29             {
30                if ( value > 0 )
31                   wagePerPiece = value;
32             }
33          }
34
35          // property Quantity
36          public int Quantity
37          {
38             get
39             {
40                return quantity;
41             }
42
43             set
44             {
45                if ( value > 0 )
46                   quantity = value;
47             }
48          }
49
50          // override base-class method to calculate
51          // PieceWorker's earnings
52          public override decimal Earnings()
53          {
54             return Quantity * WagePerPiece;
55          }
56
57          // return string representation of PieceWorker
58          public override string ToString()
59          {
60             return "PieceWorker: " + base.ToString();
61          }
62    }
```

Fig. 7.12   **PieceWorker** class inherits from class **Employee**. (Part 2 of 2.)

Class **HourlyWorker** (Fig. 7.13) inherits from class **Employee**. The constructor for this class (lines 11–17) receives as arguments a first name, a last name, a wage and the number of hours worked. Line 13 passes the first name and last name to the base-class

Employee constructor. Class **HourlyWorker** also provides properties **Wage** (lines 20–33) and **HoursWorked** (lines 36–49); method **Earnings** (lines 53–70), which calculates an hourly worker's earnings; and method **ToString** (lines 73–76), which returns a string that indicates the type of the employee (i.e., **"HourlyWorker:"**) and the hourly worker's name. Note that hourly workers are paid "time-and-a-half" for "overtime" (i.e., hours worked in excess of 40 hours).

```
1   // Fig. 7.13: HourlyWorker.cs
2   // HourlyWorker class derived from Employee.
3   using System;
4
5   public class HourlyWorker : Employee
6   {
7      private decimal wage;        // wage per hour of work
8      private double hoursWorked;  // hours worked during week
9
10     // constructor
11     public HourlyWorker( string firstNameValue, string
   LastNameValue,
12        decimal wageValue, double hoursWorkedValue )
13        : base( firstNameValue, LastNameValue )
14     {
15        Wage = wageValue;
16        HoursWorked = hoursWorkedValue;
17     }
18
19     // property Wage
20     public decimal Wage
21     {
22        get
23        {
24           return wage;
25        }
26
27        set
28        {
29           // ensure non-negative wage value
30           if ( value > 0 )
31              wage = value;
32        }
33     }
34
35     // property HoursWorked
36     public double HoursWorked
37     {
38        get
39        {
40           return hoursWorked;
41        }
42
```

Fig. 7.13 HourlyWorker class inherits from class **Employee**. (Part 1 of 2.)

```
43            set
44            {
45               // ensure non-negative hoursWorked value
46               if ( value > 0 )
47                  hoursWorked = value;
48            }
49         }
50
51         // override base-class method to calculate
52         // HourlyWorker earnings
53         public override decimal Earnings()
54         {
55            // compensate for overtime (paid "time-and-a-half")
56            if ( HoursWorked <= 40 )
57            {
58               return Wage * Convert.ToDecimal( HoursWorked );
59            }
60
61            else
62            {
63               // calculate base and overtime pay
64               decimal basePay = Wage * Convert.ToDecimal( 40 );
65               decimal overtimePay = Wage * 1.5M *
66                  Convert.ToDecimal( HoursWorked - 40 );
67
68               return basePay + overtimePay;
69            }
70         }
71
72         // return string representation of HourlyWorker
73         public override string ToString()
74         {
75            return "HourlyWorker: " + base.ToString();
76         }
77      }
```

Fig. 7.13 HourlyWorker class inherits from class **Employee**. (Part 2 of 2.)

Method **Main** (lines 9–48) of class **EmployeesTest** (Fig. 7.14) declares **Employee** reference **employee** (line 22). Each employee type is handled similarly in **Main**, so we discuss only the manipulations of the **Boss** object.

Line 11 assigns to **Boss** reference **boss** a **Boss** object and passes to its constructor the boss's first name ("**John**"), last name ("**Smith**") and fixed weekly salary (**800**). Line 22 assigns the derived-class reference **boss** to the base-class **Employee** reference **employee**, so we can demonstrate the polymorphic determination of **boss**'s earnings. Line 24 passes reference **employee** as an argument to method **GetString** (lines 51–55), which polymorphically invokes methods **ToString** and **Earnings** on the **Employee** object the method receives as an argument. At this point, C# determines that the object passed to **GetString** is of type **Boss**, so lines 53–54 invoke **Boss** methods **ToString** and **Earnings**. These are classic examples of polymorphic behavior.

```
1   // Fig. 7.14: EmployeesTest.cs
2   // Demonstrates polymorphism by displaying earnings
3   // for various Employee types.
4   using System;
5   using System.Windows.Forms;
6
7   public class EmployeesTest
8   {
9      public static void Main( string[] args )
10     {
11        Boss boss = new Boss( "John", "Smith", 800 );
12
13        CommissionWorker commissionWorker =
14           new CommissionWorker( "Sue", "Jones", 400, 3, 150 );
15
16        PieceWorker pieceWorker = new PieceWorker( "Bob", "Lewis",
17           Convert.ToDecimal( 2.5 ), 200 );
18
19        HourlyWorker hourlyWorker = new HourlyWorker( "Karen",
20           "Price", Convert.ToDecimal( 13.75 ), 50 );
21
22        Employee employee = boss;
23
24        string output = GetString( employee ) + boss + " earned " +
25              boss.Earnings().ToString( "C" ) + "\n\n";
26
27        employee = commissionWorker;
28
29        output += GetString( employee ) + commissionWorker +
30           " earned " +
31           commissionWorker.Earnings().ToString( "C" ) + "\n\n";
32
33        employee = pieceWorker;
34
35        output += GetString( employee ) + pieceWorker +
36           " earned " + pieceWorker.Earnings().ToString( "C" ) +
37           "\n\n";
38
39        employee = hourlyWorker;
40
41        output += GetString( employee ) + hourlyWorker +
42           " earned " + hourlyWorker.Earnings().ToString( "C" ) +
43           "\n\n";
44
45        MessageBox.Show( output, "Demonstrating Polymorphism",
46           MessageBoxButtons.OK, MessageBoxIcon.Information );
47
48     } // end method Main
49
50     // return string that contains Employee information
51     public static string GetString( Employee worker )
52     {
```

Fig. 7.14 **EmployeesTest** class tests the **Employee** class hierarchy. (Part 1 of 2.)

```
53                return worker.ToString() + " earned " +
54                    worker.Earnings().ToString( "C" ) + "\n";
55        }
56    }
```

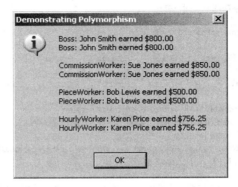

Fig. 7.14 **EmployeesTest** class tests the **Employee** class hierarchy. (Part 2 of 2.)

Method **Earnings** returns a **Decimal** object on which line 54 then calls method **ToString**. In this case, the string **"C"**, which is passed to an overloaded version of **Decimal** method **ToString**, stands for **Currency**, and **ToString** formats the string as a currency amount.

When method **GetString** returns to **Main**, lines 24–25 explicitly invoke methods **ToString** and **Earnings** through derived-class **Boss** reference **boss** to show the method invocations that do not use polymorphic processing. The output generated in lines 24–25 is identical to that generated by methods **ToString** and **Earnings** through base-class reference **employee** (i.e., the methods that use polymorphism), which verifies that the polymorphic methods invoke the appropriate methods in derived class **Boss**.

To prove that the base-class reference **employee** can invoke the proper derived-class versions of methods **ToString** and **Earnings** for the other types of employees, lines 27, 33 and 39 assign to base-class reference **employee** a different type of **Employee** object (**CommissionWorker**, **PieceWorker** and **HourlyWorker**, respectively). After each assignment, the application calls method **GetString** to return the results via the base-class reference. Then, the application calls methods **ToString** and **Earnings** of each derived-class reference to show that C# correctly associates each method call to its corresponding derived-class object.

7.9 Example: Creating and Using Interfaces

We now present two more examples of polymorphism using *interfaces* that specify sets of **public** services (i.e., methods and properties) that classes must implement. An interface is used when there is no default implementation to inherit (i.e., no instance variables and no default-method implementations). Whereas an abstract class is best used for providing data and services for objects in a hierarchical relationship, an interface can be used for providing services that "bring together" disparate objects that relate to one another only through that interface.

An interface definition begins with the keyword *interface* and contains a list of **public** methods and properties. To use an interface, a class must specify that it implements the interface and must provide implementations for every method and property specified in the interface definition. A class that implements an interface effectively signs a contract with the compiler that states, "this class will define all the methods and properties specified by the interface."

Common Programming Error 7.8

When a class implements an **interface**, *leaving even a single* **interface** *method or property undefined is an error. The class must define every method and property in the* **interface**.

Common Programming Error 7.9

In C#, an **interface** *can be declared only as* **public**; *the declaration of an* **interface** *as* **private** *or* **protected** *is an error.*

Interfaces provide uniform sets of methods and properties for objects of disparate classes. These methods and properties enable programs to process the objects of those disparate classes polymorphically. For example, consider disparate objects that represent a person, a tree, a car and a file. These objects have "nothing to do" with one another—a person has a first name and last name; a tree has a trunk, a set of branches and a bunch of leaves; a car has wheels, gears and several other mechanisms that enable the car to move; and a file contains data. Because of the lack of commonality among these classes, modeling them via an inheritance hierarchy with a common base class seems illogical. However, these objects certainly have at least one common characteristic—an age. A person's age is represented by the number of years since that person was born; a tree's age is represented by the number of rings in its trunk; a car's age is represented by its manufacture date; and file's age is represented by its creation date. We can use an interface that provides a method or property that objects of these disparate classes can implement to return each object's age.

In this example, we use interface **IAge** (Fig. 7.15) to return the age information for classes **Person** (Fig. 7.16) and **Tree** (Fig. 7.17). The definition of interface **IAge** begins at line 4 with **public interface** and ends at line 8 with a closing curly brace. Lines 6–7 specify read-only properties **Age** and **Name**, for which every class that implements interface **IAge** must provide implementations. Declaring these properties as read-only is not required—an interface can also provide methods, write-only properties and properties with both *get* and *set* accessors. By containing these property declarations, interface **IAge** provides an opportunity for an object that implements **IAge** to return its age and name, respectively. However, the classes that implement these methods are not "required" by either interface **IAge** or C# to return an age and a name. The compiler requires only that classes implementing interface **IAge** provide implementations for the interface's properties.

Line 5 of Fig. 7.16 use C#'s inheritance notation (i.e., *ClassName* **:** *InterfaceName*) to indicate that class **Person** implements interface **IAge**. In this example, class **Person** implements only one interface. A class can implement any number of interfaces in addition to inheriting from one class. To implement more than one interface, the class definition must provide a comma-separated list of interface names after the semicolon. Class **Person** has member variables **yearBorn**, **firstName** and **lastName** (lines 7–9), for which the constructor (lines 12–22) sets values. Because class **Person** implements interface **IAge**, class **Person** must implement properties **Age** and **Name**—defined on lines

25–31 and lines 34–40, respectively. Property **Age** allows the client to obtain the person's age, and property **Name** returns a **String** containing **firstName** and **lastName**. Note that property **Age** calculates the person's age by subtracting **yearBorn** from the current year (via property **Year** of property **DateTime.Now**, which returns the current date). These properties satisfy the implementation requirements defined in interface **IAge**, so class **Person** has fulfilled its "contract" with the compiler.

```
1   // Fig. 7.15: IAge.cs
2   // Interface IAge declares property for setting and getting age.
3
4   public interface IAge
5   {
6      int Age { get; }
7      string Name { get; }
8   }
```

Fig. 7.15   Interface for returning age of objects of disparate classes.

```
1   // Fig. 7.16: Person.cs
2   // Class Person has a birthday.
3   using System;
4
5   public class Person : IAge
6   {
7      private string firstName;
8      private string lastName;
9      private int yearBorn;
10
11     // constructor
12     public Person( string firstNameValue, string lastNameValue,
13        int yearBornValue )
14     {
15        firstName = firstNameValue;
16        lastName = lastNameValue;
17
18        if ( yearBornValue > 0 && yearBornValue <= DateTime.Now.Year )
19           yearBorn = yearBornValue;
20        else
21           yearBorn = DateTime.Now.Year;
22     }
23
24     // property Age implementation of interface IAge
25     public int Age
26     {
27        get
28        {
29           return DateTime.Now.Year - yearBorn;
30        }
31     }
32
```

Fig. 7.16   **Person** class implements **IAge** interface. (Part 1 of 2.)

```
33      // property Name implementation of interface IAge
34      public string Name
35      {
36         get
37         {
38            return firstName + " " + lastName;
39         }
40      }
41
42   } // end class Person
```

Fig. 7.16 **Person** class implements **IAge** interface. (Part 2 of 2.)

Class **Tree** (Fig. 7.17) also implements interface **IAge**. Class **Tree** has member variables **rings** (line 7), which represents the number of rings inside the tree's trunk—this variable corresponds directly to the tree's age. The **Tree** constructor (lines 10–14) receives as an argument an **int** that specifies in which year the tree was planted. Class **Tree** includes method **AddRing** (lines 17–20), which enables a program to increment the number of rings in the tree. Because class **Tree** implements interface **IAge**, class **Tree** must implement properties **Age** and **Name**—defined on lines 23–29 and lines 32–38, respectively. Property **Age** returns the value of **rings**, and property **Name** returns **string** "**Tree**."

```
1    // Fig. 7.17: Tree.cs
2    // Class Tree contains number of rings corresponding to its age.
3    using System;
4
5    public class Tree : IAge
6    {
7       private int rings; // number of rings in tree trunk
8
9       // constructor
10      public Tree( int yearPlanted )
11      {
12         // count number of rings in Tree
13         rings = DateTime.Now.Year - yearPlanted;
14      }
15
16      // increment rings
17      public void AddRing()
18      {
19         rings++;
20      }
21
22      // property Age implementation of interface IAge
23      public int Age
24      {
25         get
26         {
```

Fig. 7.17 **Tree** class implements **IAge** interface. (Part 1 of 2.)

```
27              return rings;
28          }
29      }
30
31      // property Name implementation of interface IAge
32      public string Name
33      {
34          get
35          {
36              return "Tree";
37          }
38      }
39
40  } // end class Tree
```

Fig. 7.17 **Tree** class implements **IAge** interface. (Part 2 of 2.)

Class **InterfacesTest** (Fig. 7.18) demonstrates polymorphism on the objects of disparate classes **Person** and **Tree**. Line 9 instantiates object **tree** of class **Tree**, and line 10 instantiates object **person** of class **Person**. Line 13 declares **iAgeArray**—an array of two references to **IAge** objects. Line 16 and 19 assign **tree** and **person** to the first and second reference in **iAgeArray**, respectively. Lines 22–23 invoke method **ToString** on **tree**, then invoke its properties **Age** and **Name** to return age and name information for object **tree**. Lines 26–27 invoke method **ToString** on **person**, then invoke its properties **Age** and **Name** to return age and name information for object **person**. Next, we manipulate these objects polymorphically through the **iAgeArray** of references to **IAge** objects. Lines 30–34 define a **foreach** structure that uses properties **Age** and **Name** to obtain age and name information for each **IAge** object in **iAgeArray**. Note that a program also can invoke class **Object**'s **public** methods (e.g., **ToString**) using any interface reference. This is possible because every object inherits directly or indirectly from class **Object**. Therefore, every object is guaranteed to have the class **Object**'s **public** methods.

Software Engineering Observation 7.11

*In C#, an interface reference may invoke methods and properties that the interface declares and the **public** methods of class **Object**.*

Software Engineering Observation 7.12

*In C#, an interface provides only those **public** services declared in the interface, whereas an abstract class provides the **public** services defined in the abstract class and those members inherited from the abstract class's base class.*

```
1   // Fig. 7.18: InterfacesTest.cs
2   // Demonstrating polymorphism with interfaces.
3   using System.Windows.Forms;
4
5   public class InterfacesTest
6   {
```

Fig. 7.18 Demonstrating polymorphism on objects of disparate classes. (Part 1 of 2.)

```
7     public static void Main( string[] args )
8     {
9        Tree tree = new Tree( 1978 );
10       Person person = new Person( "Bob", "Jones", 1971 );
11
12       // create array of IAge references
13       IAge[] iAgeArray = new IAge[ 2 ];
14
15       // iAgeArray[ 0 ] refers to Tree object polymorphically
16       iAgeArray[ 0 ] = tree;
17
18       // iAgeArray[ 1 ] refers to Person object polymorphically
19       iAgeArray[ 1 ] = person;
20
21       // display tree information
22       string output = tree + ": " + tree.Name + "\nAge is " +
23          tree.Age + "\n\n";
24
25       // display person information
26       output += person + ": " + person.Name + "\nAge is: "
27          + person.Age + "\n\n";
28
29       // display name and age for each IAge object in iAgeArray
30       foreach ( IAge ageReference in iAgeArray )
31       {
32          output += ageReference.Name + ": Age is " +
33             ageReference.Age + "\n";
34       }
35
36       MessageBox.Show( output, "Demonstrating Polymorphism" );
37
38    } // end method Main
39
40 } // end class InterfacesTest
```

Fig. 7.18 Demonstrating polymorphism on objects of disparate classes. (Part 2 of 2.)

Our next example reexamines the **Point–Circle–Cylinder** hierarchy using an interface, rather than using an abstract class, to describe the common methods and properties of the classes in the hierarchy. We now show how a class can implement an interface, then act as a base class for derived classes to inherit the implementation. We create interface **IShape** (Fig. 7.19), which specifies methods **Area** and **Volume** and property **Name** (lines 8–10). Every class that implements interface **IShape** must provide implementations for these two methods and this read-only property. Note that, even though the methods in this example interface do not receive arguments, interface methods can receive arguments (just as regular methods can).

Good Programming Practice 7.1

By convention, begin the name of each interface with "I."

Because class **Point3** (Fig. 7.20) implements interface **IShape**, class **Point3** must implement all three **IShape** members. Lines 59–62 implement method **Area**, which returns **0**, because points have an area of zero. Lines 65–68 implement method **Volume**, which also returns **0**, because points have a volume of zero. Lines 71–77 implement read-only property **Name**, which returns the class name as a **string** (**"Point3"**).

When a class implements an interface, the class enters the same kind of *is-a* relationship that inheritance establishes. In our example, class **Point3** implements interface **IShape**. Therefore, a **Point3** object *is an* **IShape**, and objects of any class that inherits from **Point3** are also **IShape**s. For example, class **Circle3** (Fig. 7.21) inherits from class **Point3**; thus, a **Circle3** *is an* **IShape**. Class **Circle3** implements interface **IShape** implicitly and inherits the **IShape** methods that class **Point** implemented. Because circles do not have volume, class **Circle3** does not override class **Point3**'s **Volume** method, which returns zero. However, we do not want to use the class **Point3** method **Area** or property **Name** for class **Circle3**. Class **Circle3** should provide its own implementation for these, because the area and name of a circle differ from those of a point. Lines 52–55 override method **Area** to return the circle's area, and lines 65–71 override property **Name** to return **String "Circle3"**.

Class **Cylinder3** (Fig. 7.22) inherits from class **Circle3**. **Cylinder3** implements interface **IShape** implicitly, because **Cylinder3** derives from **Point3**, which implements interface **IShape**. **Cylinder3** inherits method **Area** and property **Name** from **Circle3** and method **Volume** from **Point3**. However, **Cylinder3** overrides property **Name** and methods **Area** and **Volume** to perform **Cylinder3**-specific operations. Lines 40–43 override method **Area** to return the cylinder's surface area, lines 46–49 override method **Volume** to return the cylinder's volume and lines 59–65 override property **Name** to return **String "Cylinder3"**. Note that class **Point3** marks these methods/properties as **virtual**, enabling derived classes to override them.

```
1   // Fig. 7.19: IShape.cs
2   // Interface IShape for Point, Circle, Cylinder Hierarchy.
3
4   public interface IShape
5   {
6      // classes that implement IShape must implement these methods
7      // and this property
8      double Area();
9      double Volume();
10     string Name { get; }
11  }
```

Fig. 7.19 **IShape** interface provides methods **Area** and **Volume** and property **Name**.

```
1   // Fig. 7.20: Point3.cs
2   // Point3 implements interface IShape and represents
3   // an x-y coordinate pair.
4   using System;
5
6   // Point3 implements IShape
7   public class Point3 : IShape
8   {
9      private int x, y; // Point3 coordinates
10
11     // default constructor
12     public Point3()
13     {
14        // implicit call to Object constructor occurs here
15     }
16
17     // constructor
18     public Point3( int xValue, int yValue )
19     {
20        X = xValue;
21        Y = yValue;
22     }
23
24     // property X
25     public int X
26     {
27        get
28        {
29           return x;
30        }
31
32        set
33        {
34           x = value;
35        }
36     }
37
38     // property Y
39     public int Y
40     {
41        get
42        {
43           return y;
44        }
45
46        set
47        {
48           y = value;
49        }
50     }
51
```

Fig. 7.20 **Point3** class implements interface **IShape**. (Part 1 of 2.)

```
52       // return string representation of Point3 object
53       public override string ToString()
54       {
55          return "[" + X + ", " + Y + "]";
56       }
57
58       // implement interface IShape method Area
59       public virtual double Area()
60       {
61          return 0;
62       }
63
64       // implement interface IShape method Volume
65       public virtual double Volume()
66       {
67          return 0;
68       }
69
70       // implement property Name of IShape
71       public virtual string Name
72       {
73          get
74          {
75             return "Point3";
76          }
77       }
78
79    } // end class Point3
```

Fig. 7.20 **Point3** class implements interface **IShape**. (Part 2 of 2.)

```
1     // Fig. 7.21: Circle3.cs
2     // Circle3 inherits from class Point3 and overrides key members.
3     using System;
4
5     // Circle3 inherits from class Point3
6     public class Circle3 : Point3
7     {
8        private double radius; // Circle3 radius
9
10       // default constructor
11       public Circle3()
12       {
13          // implicit call to Point3 constructor occurs here
14       }
15
16       // constructor
17       public Circle3( int xValue, int yValue, double radiusValue )
18          : base( xValue, yValue )
19       {
20          Radius = radiusValue;
21       }
```

Fig. 7.21 **Circle3** class inherits from class **Point3**. (Part 1 of 2.)

```
22
23      // property Radius
24      public double Radius
25      {
26         get
27         {
28            return radius;
29         }
30
31         set
32         {
33            // ensure non-negative Radius value
34            if ( value >= 0 )
35               radius = value;
36         }
37      }
38
39      // calculate Circle3 diameter
40      public double Diameter()
41      {
42         return Radius * 2;
43      }
44
45      // calculate Circle3 circumference
46      public double Circumference()
47      {
48         return Math.PI * Diameter();
49      }
50
51      // calculate Circle3 area
52      public override double Area()
53      {
54         return Math.PI * Math.Pow( Radius, 2 );
55      }
56
57      // return string representation of Circle3 object
58      public override string ToString()
59      {
60         return "Center = " + base.ToString() +
61            "; Radius = " + Radius;
62      }
63
64      // override property Name from class Point3
65      public override string Name
66      {
67         get
68         {
69            return "Circle3";
70         }
71      }
72
73   } // end class Circle3
```

Fig. 7.21   **Circle3** class inherits from class **Point3**. (Part 2 of 2.)

```
1   // Fig. 7.22: Cylinder3.cs
2   // Cylinder3 inherits from class Circle2 and overrides key members.
3   using System;
4
5   // Cylinder3 inherits from class Circle3
6   public class Cylinder3 : Circle3
7   {
8      private double height; // Cylinder3 height
9
10     // default constructor
11     public Cylinder3()
12     {
13        // implicit call to Circle3 constructor occurs here
14     }
15
16     // constructor
17     public Cylinder3( int xValue, int yValue, double radiusValue,
18        double heightValue ) : base( xValue, yValue, radiusValue )
19     {
20        Height = heightValue;
21     }
22
23     // property Height
24     public double Height
25     {
26        get
27        {
28           return height;
29        }
30
31        set
32        {
33           // ensure non-negative Height value
34           if ( value >= 0 )
35              height = value;
36        }
37     }
38
39     // calculate Cylinder3 area
40     public override double Area()
41     {
42        return 2 * base.Area() + base.Circumference() * Height;
43     }
44
45     // calculate Cylinder3 volume
46     public override double Volume()
47     {
48        return base.Area() * Height;
49     }
50
51     // return string representation of Cylinder3 object
52     public override string ToString()
53     {
```

Fig. 7.22 **Cylinder3** class inherits from class **Circle3**. (Part 1 of 2.)

```
54        return "Center = " + base.ToString() +
55            "; Height = " + Height;
56     }
57
58     // override property Name from class Circle3
59     public override string Name
60     {
61        get
62        {
63           return "Cylinder3";
64        }
65     }
66
67  } // end class Cylinder3
```

Fig. 7.22 Cylinder3 class inherits from class **Circle3**. (Part 2 of 2.)

Class **Interfaces2Test** (Fig. 7.23) demonstrates our point-circle-cylinder hierarchy that uses interfaces. Class **Interfaces2Test** has only two differences from the example in Fig. 7.8, which tested the class hierarchy created from the **abstract** base class **Shape**. In Fig. 7.23, line 17 declares **arrayOfShapes** as an array of **IShape** interface references, rather than **Shape** base-class references.

```
1   // Fig. 7.23: Interfaces2Test.cs
2   // Demonstrating polymorphism with interfaces in
3   // Point-Circle-Cylinder hierarchy.
4
5   using System.Windows.Forms;
6
7   public class Interfaces2Test
8   {
9      public static void Main( string[] args )
10     {
11        // instantiate Point3, Circle3 and Cylinder3 objects
12        Point3 point = new Point3( 7, 11 );
13        Circle3 circle = new Circle3( 22, 8, 3.5 );
14        Cylinder3 cylinder = new Cylinder3( 10, 10, 3.3, 10 );
15
16        // create array of IShape references
17        IShape[] arrayOfShapes = new IShape[ 3 ];
18
19        // arrayOfShapes[ 0 ] references Point3 object
20        arrayOfShapes[ 0 ] = point;
21
22        // arrayOfShapes[ 1 ] references Circle3 object
23        arrayOfShapes[ 1 ] = circle;
24
25        // arrayOfShapes[ 2 ] references Cylinder3 object
26        arrayOfShapes[ 2 ] = cylinder;
27
```

Fig. 7.23 Interfaces2Test uses interfaces to demonstrate polymorphism in Point-Circle-Cylinder hierarchy. (Part 1 of 2.)

```
28        string output = point.Name + ": " + point + "\n" +
29           circle.Name + ": " + circle + "\n" +
30           cylinder.Name + ": " + cylinder;
31
32        foreach ( IShape shape in arrayOfShapes )
33        {
34           output += "\n\n" + shape.Name + ":\nArea = " +
35              shape.Area() + "\nVolume = " + shape.Volume();
36        }
37
38        MessageBox.Show( output, "Demonstrating Polymorphism" );
39     }
40  }
```

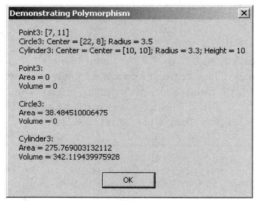

Fig. 7.23   Interfaces2Test uses interfaces to demonstrate polymorphism in
Point-Circle-Cylinder hierarchy. (Part 2 of 2.)

7.10 Delegates

In Chapter 4, Methods and Arrays, we discussed how objects can pass member variables as
arguments to methods. However, sometimes, it is beneficial for objects to pass methods as
arguments to other methods. For example, suppose that you wish to sort a series of values
in ascending and descending order. Rather than provide separate ascending and descending
sorting methods (one for each type of comparison), we could provide a single method that
receives as an argument a reference to the comparison method to use. To perform an ascending sort, we could pass to the sorting method the reference to the ascending-sort-com-
parison method; to perform a descending sort, we could pass to the sorting method the
reference to the descending-sort-comparison method. The sorting method then would use
this reference to sort the list—the sorting method would not need to know whether it is performing an ascending or descending sort.

C# does not allow the passing of method references directly as arguments to other
methods, but does provide *delegates*, which are classes that encapsulate sets of references to
methods. A delegate object that contains method references can be passed to another method.
Rather than send a method reference directly, an object can send the delegate instance, which
contains the reference of the method that we would like to send. The method that receives the
reference to the delegate then can invoke the methods the delegate contains.

A delegate that contains a single method is known as a *singlecast delegate* and is created or derived from class **Delegate**. Delegates that contain multiple methods are *multicast delegates* and are created or derived from class **MulticastDelegate**. Both delegate classes belong to namespace **System**.

To use a delegate, we first must declare one. The delegate's declaration specifies a method header (parameters and return value). Methods whose references will be contained within a delegate object must have the same method header as that defined in the delegate declaration. We then create methods that have this signature. The second step is to create a delegate instance that contains a reference to that method. After we create the delegate instance, we can invoke the method reference that it contains. We show this process in our next example.

Class **DelegateBubbleSort** (Fig. 7.24), which is a modified version of the bubble-sort algorithm, uses delegates to sort an integer array in ascending or descending order. Lines 6–7 provide the declaration for delegate **Comparator**. To declare a delegate (line 7), we declare a signature of a method—keyword **delegate** after the member-access modifier (in this case, **public**), followed by the return type, the delegate name and parameter list. Delegate **Comparator** defines a method signature for methods that receive two **int** arguments and return a **bool**. Note that delegate **Comparator** contains no body. As we soon demonstrate, our application (Fig. 7.25) implements methods that adhere to delegate **Comparator**'s signature, then passes these methods (as arguments of type **Comparator**) to method **SortArray**. The declaration of a delegate does not define its intended role or implementation; our application uses this particular delegate when comparing two **int**s, but other applications might use it for different purposes.

```cs
1   // Fig. 7.24: DelegateBubbleSort.cs
2   // Demonstrating delegates for sorting numbers.
3
4   public class DelegateBubbleSort
5   {
6      public delegate bool Comparator( int element1,
7         int element2 );
8
9      // sort array using Comparator delegate
10     public static void SortArray( int[] array,
11        Comparator Compare )
12     {
13        for ( int pass = 0; pass < array.Length; pass++ )
14
15           for ( int i = 0; i < array.Length - 1; i++ )
16
17              if ( Compare( array[ i ], array [ i + 1 ] ) )
18                 Swap( ref array[ i ], ref array[ i + 1 ] );
19     }
20
21     // swap two elements
22     private static void Swap( ref int firstElement,
23        ref int secondElement )
24     {
```

Fig. 7.24 Bubble sort using delegates. (Part 1 of 2.)

```
25              int hold = firstElement;
26              firstElement = secondElement;
27              secondElement = hold;
28          }
29      }
```

Fig. 7.24 Bubble sort using delegates. (Part 2 of 2.)

Lines 10–19 define method **SortArray**, which takes an array and a reference to a **Comparator** delegate object as arguments. Method **SortArray** modifies the array by sorting its contents. Line 17 uses the delegate method to determine how to sort the array. Line 17 invokes the method enclosed within the delegate object by treating the delegate reference as the method that the delegate object contains. C# invokes the enclosed method reference directly, passing it parameters **array[i]** and **array[i + 1]**. The **Comparator** determines the sorting order for its two arguments. If the **Comparator** returns **true**, the two elements are out of order, so line 18 invokes method **Swap** (lines 22–28) to swap the elements. If the **Comparator** returns **false**, the two elements are in the correct order. To sort in ascending order, the **Comparator** returns **true** when the first element being compared is greater than the second element being compared. Similarly, to sort in descending order, the **Comparator** returns **true** when the first element being compared is less than the second element being compared.

Class **BubbleSortForm** (Fig. 7.25) displays a **Form** with two text boxes and three buttons. The first text box displays a list of unsorted numbers, and the second box displays the same list of numbers after they are sorted. The **Create Data** button creates the list of unsorted values. The **Sort Ascending** and **Sort Descending** buttons sort the array in ascending and descending order, respectively. Methods **SortAscending** (lines 42–45) and **SortDescending** (lines 60–63) each have a signature that corresponds with the signature defined by the **Comparator** delegate declaration (i.e., each receives two **int**s and returns a **bool**). As we will see, the program passes to **DelegateBubbleSort** method **SortArray** delegates containing references to methods **SortAscending** and **Sort-Descending**, which will specify class **DelegateBubbleSort**'s sorting behavior.

```
1   // Fig. 7.25: BubbleSortForm.cs
2   // Demonstrates bubble sort using delegates to determine
3   // the sort order.
4   using System;
5   using System.Drawing;
6   using System.Collections;
7   using System.ComponentModel;
8   using System.Windows.Forms;
9
10  public class BubbleSortForm : System.Windows.Forms.Form
11  {
12      private System.Windows.Forms.TextBox originalTextBox;
13      private System.Windows.Forms.TextBox sortedTextBox;
14      private System.Windows.Forms.Button createButton;
15      private System.Windows.Forms.Button ascendingButton;
```

Fig. 7.25 Bubble-sort **Form** application. (Part 1 of 3.)

```
16      private System.Windows.Forms.Button descendingButton;
17      private System.Windows.Forms.Label originalLabel;
18      private System.Windows.Forms.Label sortedLabel;
19
20      private int[] elementArray = new int[ 10 ];
21
22      // create randomly generated set of numbers to sort
23      private void createButton_Click( object sender,
24         System.EventArgs e )
25      {
26         // clear TextBoxes
27         originalTextBox.Clear();
28         sortedTextBox.Clear();
29
30         // create random-number generator
31         Random randomNumber = new Random();
32
33         // populate elementArray with random integers
34         for ( int i = 0; i < elementArray.Length; i++ )
35         {
36            elementArray[ i ] = randomNumber.Next( 100 );
37            originalTextBox.Text += elementArray[ i ] + "\r\n";
38         }
39      }
40
41      // delegate implementation for ascending sort
42      private bool SortAscending( int element1, int element2 )
43      {
44         return element1 > element2;
45      }
46
47      // sort randomly generated numbers in ascending order
48      private void ascendingButton_Click( object sender,
49         System.EventArgs e )
50      {
51         // sort array, passing delegate for SortAscending
52         DelegateBubbleSort.SortArray( elementArray,
53            new DelegateBubbleSort.Comparator(
54               SortAscending ) );
55
56         DisplayResults();
57      }
58
59      // delegate implementation for descending sort
60      private bool SortDescending( int element1, int element2 )
61      {
62         return element1 < element2;
63      }
64
65      // sort randomly generating numbers in descending order
66      private void descendingButton_Click( object sender,
67         System.EventArgs e )
68      {
```

Fig. 7.25 Bubble-sort **Form** application. (Part 2 of 3.)

```
69              // sort array, passing delegate for SortDescending
70              DelegateBubbleSort.SortArray( elementArray,
71                  new DelegateBubbleSort.Comparator(
72                      SortDescending ) );
73
74          DisplayResults();
75      }
76
77      // display the sorted array in sortedTextBox
78      private void DisplayResults()
79      {
80          sortedTextBox.Clear();
81
82          foreach ( int element in elementArray )
83              sortedTextBox.Text += element + "\r\n";
84      }
85
86      // main entry point for application
87      public static void Main( string[] args )
88      {
89          Application.Run( new BubbleSortForm() );
90      }
91  }
```

Fig. 7.25   Bubble-sort **Form** application. (Part 3 of 3.)

Methods **ascendingButton_Click** (lines 48–57) and **descending-Button_Click** (lines 66–75) are invoked when the user clicks the **Sort Ascending** and **Sort Descending** buttons, respectively. Method **ascendingButton_Click**, passes to **DelegateBubbleSort** method **SortArray** the unsorted **elementArray** (line 52) and a reference to method **SortAscending**. The syntax on lines 53–54

> ***new* DelegateBubbleSort.Comparator(SortAscending)**

creates a **Comparator** delegate that contains a reference to method **SortAscending**. In method **descendingButton_Click**, lines 70–72 pass to method **SortArray** the unsorted array **elementArray** and a delegate reference to method **SortDescending**. We continue to use delegates in Chapters 9–11, when we discuss event handling and multithreading.

7.11 Operator Overloading

Manipulations on class objects are accomplished by sending messages (in the form of method calls) to the objects. This method-call notation is cumbersome for certain kinds of classes, especially mathematical classes. For these classes, it would be convenient to use C#'s rich set of built-in operators to specify object manipulations. In this section, we show how to enable C#'s operators to work with class objects—via a process called *operator overloading*.

Software Engineering Observation 7.13

Use operator overloading when it makes a program clearer than accomplishing the same operations with explicit method calls.

Software Engineering Observation 7.14

Avoid excessive or inconsistent use of operator overloading, as this can make a program cryptic and difficult to read.

C# enables the programmer to overload most operators to make them sensitive to the context in which they are used. Some operators are overloaded frequently, especially the assignment operator and various arithmetic operators, such as **+** and **−**. The job performed by overloaded operators also can be performed by explicit method calls, but operator notation often is more natural. Figure 7.27 provides an example of using operator overloading with a complex number class.

Class **ComplexNumber** (Fig. 7.26) overloads the plus (**+**), minus (**−**) and multiplication (*****) operators to enable programs to add, subtract and multiply instances of class **ComplexNumber** using common mathematical notation. Lines 7–8 declare data members for the real and imaginary parts of the complex number.

```
1   // Fig. 7.26: ComplexNumber.cs
2   // Class that overloads operators for adding, subtracting
3   // and multiplying complex numbers.
4
5   public class ComplexNumber
6   {
```

Fig. 7.26 Overloading operators for complex numbers. (Part 1 of 3.)

```
7        private int real;
8        private int imaginary;
9
10       // default constructor
11       public ComplexNumber() {}
12
13       // constructor
14       public ComplexNumber( int a, int b )
15       {
16          Real = a;
17          Imaginary = b;
18       }
19
20       // return string representation of ComplexNumber
21       public override string ToString()
22       {
23          return "( " + real +
24             ( imaginary < 0 ? " - " + ( imaginary * -1 ) :
25             " + "  + imaginary ) + "i )";
26       }
27
28       // property Real
29       public int Real
30       {
31          get
32          {
33             return real;
34          }
35
36          set
37          {
38             real = value;
39          }
40
41       } // end property Real
42
43       // property Imaginary
44       public int Imaginary
45       {
46          get
47          {
48             return imaginary;
49          }
50
51          set
52          {
53             imaginary = value;
54          }
55
56       } // end property Imaginary
57
```

Fig. 7.26   Overloading operators for complex numbers. (Part 2 of 3.)

```
58      // overload the addition operator
59      public static ComplexNumber operator + (
60         ComplexNumber x, ComplexNumber y )
61      {
62         return new ComplexNumber(
63            x.Real + y.Real, x.Imaginary + y.Imaginary );
64      }
65
66      // provide alternative to overloaded + operator
67      // for addition
68      public static ComplexNumber Add( ComplexNumber x,
69         ComplexNumber y )
70      {
71         return x + y;
72      }
73
74      // overload the subtraction operator
75      public static ComplexNumber operator - (
76         ComplexNumber x, ComplexNumber y )
77      {
78         return new ComplexNumber(
79            x.Real - y.Real, x.Imaginary - y.Imaginary );
80      }
81
82      // provide alternative to overloaded - operator
83      // for subtraction
84      public static ComplexNumber Subtract( ComplexNumber x,
85         ComplexNumber y )
86      {
87         return x - y;
88      }
89
90      // overload the multiplication operator
91      public static ComplexNumber operator * (
92         ComplexNumber x, ComplexNumber y )
93      {
94         return new ComplexNumber(
95            x.Real * y.Real - x.Imaginary * y.Imaginary,
96            x.Real * y.Imaginary + y.Real * x.Imaginary );
97      }
98
99      // provide alternative to overloaded * operator
100     // for multiplication
101     public static ComplexNumber Multiply( ComplexNumber x,
102        ComplexNumber y )
103     {
104        return x * y;
105     }
106
107  } // end class ComplexNumber
```

Fig. 7.26 Overloading operators for complex numbers. (Part 3 of 3.)

Lines 59–64 overload the plus operator (**+**) to perform addition of **ComplexNumber**s. Keyword *operator* followed by an operator indicates that a method overloads the specified operator. Methods that overload binary operators must take two arguments. The first argument is the left operand, and the second argument is the right operand. Class **ComplexNumber**'s overloaded plus operator takes two **ComplexNumber** references as arguments and returns a **ComplexNumber** that represents the sum of the arguments. Note that this method is marked **public** and **static**, which is required for overloaded operators. The body of the method (lines 62–63) performs the addition and returns the result as a new **ComplexNumber** reference.

Software Engineering Observation 7.15

Overload operators to perform the same function or similar functions on class objects as the operators perform on objects of built-in types. Avoid non-intuitive use of operators.

Software Engineering Observation 7.16

At least one argument of an operator overload method must be a reference to an object of the class in which the operator is overloaded. This prevents programmers from changing how operators work on built-in types.

Not all .NET languages support operator overloading. Therefore, to ensure that our **ComplexNumber** class can be used in other .NET languages, we must provide an alternative method for performing addition of **ComplexNumber**s. Method **Add** (lines 68–72) provides this alternative means to add **ComplexNumber**s. Lines 75–105 provide overloaded operators and alternative methods for subtracting and multiplying **ComplexNumber**s.

Class **ComplexTest** (Fig. 7.27) provides a user interface for adding, subtracting and multiplying **ComplexNumber**s. Method **firstButton_Click** and method **secondButton_Click** each read a **ComplexNumber** from textboxes **realTextBox** and **imaginaryTextBox**. Method **addButton_Click** (lines 56–59), method **subtractButton_Click** (lines 62–66) and method **multiplyButton_Click** (lines 69–73) use overloaded operators of class **ComplexNumber** to perform addition, subtraction and multiplication.

```
1   // Fig. 7.27: ComplexTest.cs
2   // An example that uses operator overloading
3
4   using System;
5   using System.Drawing;
6   using System.Collections;
7   using System.ComponentModel;
8   using System.Windows.Forms;
9   using System.Data;
10
11  public class ComplexTest : System.Windows.Forms.Form
12  {
13     private System.Windows.Forms.Label realLabel;
14     private System.Windows.Forms.Label imaginaryLabel;
15     private System.Windows.Forms.Label statusLabel;
16
17     private System.Windows.Forms.TextBox realTextBox;
18     private System.Windows.Forms.TextBox imaginaryTextBox;
19
```

Fig. 7.27   Using operator overloading. (Part 1 of 3.)

```
20       private System.Windows.Forms.Button firstButton;
21       private System.Windows.Forms.Button secondButton;
22       private System.Windows.Forms.Button addButton;
23       private System.Windows.Forms.Button subtractButton;
24       private System.Windows.Forms.Button multiplyButton;
25
26       private ComplexNumber x = new ComplexNumber();
27       private ComplexNumber y = new ComplexNumber();
28
29       [STAThread]
30       static void Main()
31       {
32          Application.Run( new ComplexTest() );
33       }
34
35       private void firstButton_Click(
36          object sender, System.EventArgs e )
37       {
38          x.Real = Int32.Parse( realTextBox.Text );
39          x.Imaginary = Int32.Parse( imaginaryTextBox.Text );
40          realTextBox.Clear();
41          imaginaryTextBox.Clear();
42          statusLabel.Text = "First Complex Number is: " + x;
43       }
44
45       private void secondButton_Click(
46          object sender, System.EventArgs e )
47       {
48          y.Real = Int32.Parse( realTextBox.Text );
49          y.Imaginary = Int32.Parse( imaginaryTextBox.Text );
50          realTextBox.Clear();
51          imaginaryTextBox.Clear();
52          statusLabel.Text = "Second Complex Number is: " + y;
53       }
54
55       // add complex numbers
56       private void addButton_Click( object sender, System.EventArgs e
)
57       {
58          statusLabel.Text = x + " + " + y + " = " + ( x + y );
59       }
60
61       // subtract complex numbers
62       private void subtractButton_Click(
63          object sender, System.EventArgs e )
64       {
65          statusLabel.Text = x + " - " + y + " = " + ( x - y );
66       }
67
68       // multiply complex numbers
69       private void multiplyButton_Click(
70          object sender, System.EventArgs e )
71       {
```

Fig. 7.27 Using operator overloading. (Part 2 of 3.)

```
72            statusLabel.Text = x + " * " + y + " = " + ( x * y );
73      }
74
75  } // end class ComplexTest
```

Fig. 7.27 Using operator overloading. (Part 3 of 3.)

7.12 Summary

Polymorphism enables programmers to write programs in a general fashion to handle a wide variety of existing and future related classes. One means of processing objects of many different types is to use a **switch** structure to perform an appropriate action on each object, based on that object's type. Polymorphic programming can eliminate the need for such **switch** logic.

Polymorphism allows one method call to perform different actions, depending on the type of the object receiving the call. The same message assumes many forms—hence, the term polymorphism. With polymorphism, the programmer can deal in generalities and let the executing program concern itself with the specifics.

Abstract classes define common behavior for an inheritance hierarchy. A program cannot instantiate objects of abstract classes, but can declare references to abstract classes. Such references can polymorphically manipulate instances of the derived classes.

A **sealed** class is a class that cannot be a base class and therefore represents the end of the inheritance hierarchy.

Delegates are classes that encapsulate a set of references to methods. Delegates facilitate polymorphism by enabling the programmer to specify calls to methods that will not be defined until later.

C# enables the programmer to overload most operators in order to make them sensitive to the context in which they are used. Operator overloading makes code more readable by providing intuitive operators that can be used in place of cumbersome method calls.

8

Exception Handling

Objectives

- To understand exceptions and error handling.
- To use **try** blocks to delimit code in which exceptions may occur.
- To **throw** exceptions.
- To use **catch** blocks to specify exception handlers.
- To use the **finally** block to release resources.
- To understand the C# exception-class hierarchy.
- To create programmer-defined exceptions.

It is common sense to take a method and try it. If it fails, admit it frankly and try another. But above all, try something.
Franklin Delano Roosevelt

O! throw away the worser part of it,
And live the purer with the other half.
William Shakespeare

If they're running and they don't look where they're going
I have to come out from somewhere and catch them.
Jerome David Salinger

And oftentimes excusing of a fault
Doth make the fault the worse by the excuse.
William Shakespeare

I never forget a face, but in your case I'll make an exception.
Groucho (Julius Henry) Marx

Outline

8.1	Introduction
8.2	Exception Handling Overview
8.3	Example: `DivideByZeroException`
8.4	.NET `Exception` Hierarchy
8.5	`finally` Block
8.6	`Exception` Properties
8.7	Programmer-Defined Exception Classes
8.8	Handling Overflows with Operators `checked` and `unchecked`
8.9	Summary

8.1 Introduction

In this chapter, we introduce *exception handling*. An *exception* is an indication of a problem that occurs during a program's execution. The name "exception" comes from the fact that although a problem can occur, the problem occurs infrequently—if the "rule" is that a statement normally executes correctly, then the "exception to the rule" is that a problem occurs. Exception handling enables programmers to create applications that can resolve (or handle) exceptions. In many cases, handling an exception allows a program to continue executing as if no problem was encountered. A more severe problem may prevent a program from continuing normal execution, instead requiring the program to notify the user of the problem, then terminate in a controlled manner. The features presented in this chapter enable programmers to write clear, robust and more *fault-tolerant programs*.

The style and details of exception handling in C# are based in part on the work of Andrew Koenig and Bjarne Stroustrup, as presented in their paper, "Exception Handling for C++ (revised)."[1] C#'s designers implemented an exception-handling mechanism similar to that used in C++, with Koenig's and Stroustrup's work as a model.

This chapter begins with an overview of exception-handling concepts, then demonstrates basic exception-handling techniques. The chapter continues with an overview of the exception-handling class hierarchy. Programs typically request and release resources (such as files on disk) during program execution. Often, these resources are in limited supply or can be used by only one program at a time. We demonstrate a part of the exception-handling mechanism that enables a program to use a resource, then guarantees that the program releases the resource for use by other programs. The chapter continues with an example that demonstrates several properties of class **System.Exception** (the base class of all exception classes), followed by an example that shows programmers how to create and use their own exception classes. The chapter concludes with a practical application of exception handling in which a program handles exceptions generated by arithmetic calculations that result in out-of-range values for a particular data type—a condition known as *arithmetic overflow*.

---

1. Koenig, A. and B. Stroustrup, "Exception Handling for C++ (revised)," *Proceedings of the Usenix C++ Conference*, 149-176, San Francisco, April 1990.

8.2 Exception Handling Overview

The logic of the program frequently tests conditions that determine how program execution proceeds. Consider the following pseudocode:

Perform a task

If the preceding task did not execute correctly
   Perform error processing

Perform next task

If the preceding task did not execute correctly
   Perform error processing

…

In this pseudocode, we begin by performing a task. We then test whether that task executed correctly. If not, we perform error processing. Otherwise we start the entire process again and continue with the next task. Although this form of error handling logic works, intermixing the logic of the program with the error-handling logic can make the program difficult to read, modify, maintain and debug—especially in large applications. In fact, if many of the potential problems occur infrequently, intermixing program logic and error handling can degrade the performance of the program, because the program must test extra conditions to determine whether the next task can be performed.

Exception handling enables the programmer to remove error-handling code from the "main line" of the program's execution. This improves program clarity and enhances modifiability. Programmers can decide to handle whatever exceptions they choose—all types of exceptions, all exceptions of a certain type or all exceptions of a group of related types. Such flexibility reduces the likelihood that errors will be overlooked and thereby increases a program's robustness.

Testing and Debugging Tip 8.1

Exception handling helps improve a program's fault tolerance. When it is easy to write error-processing code, programmers are more likely to use it.

Software Engineering Observation 8.1

Although it is possible to do so, do not use exceptions for conventional flow of control. It is difficult to keep track of a larger number of exception cases and programs with a large number of exception cases are hard to read and maintain.

Exception handling is designed to process *synchronous errors*—errors that occur during the normal program flow of control. Common examples of these errors are out-of-range array subscripts, arithmetic overflow (i.e., a value outside the representable range of values), division by zero, invalid method parameters and running out of available memory. Exception handling is not designed to process *asynchronous* events, such as disk I/O completions, network message arrivals, mouse clicks, keystrokes and the like.

Good Programming Practice 8.1

Avoid using exception handling for purposes other than error handling, because this can reduce program clarity.

With programming languages that do not support exception handling, programmers often delay the writing of error-processing code and sometimes simply forget to include it. This results in less robust software products. C# enables the programmer to deal with exception handling easily from the inception of a project. Still, the programmer must put considerable effort into incorporating an exception-handling strategy into software projects.

Software Engineering Observation 8.2

Try to incorporate the exception-handling strategy into a system from the inception of the design process. Adding effective exception handling after a system has been implemented can be difficult.

Software Engineering Observation 8.3

In the past, programmers used many techniques to implement error-processing code. Exception handling provides a single, uniform technique for processing errors. This helps programmers working on large projects to understand each other's error-processing code.

The exception-handling mechanism also is useful for processing problems that occur when a program interacts with software elements, such as methods, constructors, assemblies and classes. Rather than internally handling problems that occur, such software elements often use exceptions to notify programs when problems occur. This enables programmers to implement customized error handling for each application.

Common Programming Error 8.1

Aborting a program component could leave a resource—such as file stream or I/O device—in a state in which other programs are unable to acquire the resource. This is known as a "resource leak."

Performance Tip 8.1

When no exceptions occur, exception-handling code incurs little or no performance penalties. Thus, programs that implement exception handling operate more efficiently than programs that perform error handling throughout the program logic.

Performance Tip 8.2

Exception handling should be used only for problems that occur infrequently. As a "rule of thumb," if a problem occurs at least 30% of the time when a particular statement executes, the program should test for the error inline; otherwise, the overhead of exception handling will cause the program to execute more slowly.[2]

Software Engineering Observation 8.4

*Methods with common error conditions should return **null** (or another appropriate value) rather than throwing exceptions. A program calling such a method simply can check the return value to determine success or failure of the method call.[3]*

Complex applications normally consist of predefined software components (such as those defined in the .NET Framework) and components specific to the application that use the predefined components. When a predefined component encounters a problem, that component needs a mechanism to communicate the problem to the application-specific component—the predefined component cannot know in advance how each application will

---

2. "Best Practices for Handling Exceptions [C#]," *.NET Framework Developer's Guide*, Visual Studio .NET Online Help.
3. "Best Practices for Handling Exceptions [C#]."

process a problem that occurs. Exception handling simplifies combining software components and having them work together effectively by enabling predefined components to communicate problems that occur to application-specific components, which can then process the problems in an application-specific manner.

Exception handling is geared to situations in which the method that detects an error is unable to handle it. Such a method *throws an exception*. There is no guarantee that there will be an *exception handler*—code that executes when the program detects an exception—to process that kind of exception. If there is, the exception will be *caught* and *handled*. The result of an *uncaught exception* depends on whether the program executes in debug mode or standard execution mode. In debug mode, when the program detects an uncaught exception, a dialog box appears that enables the programmer to view the problem in the debugger or continue program execution by ignoring the problem that occurred. In standard execution mode, a Windows application presents a dialog that enables the user to continue or terminate program execution, and a console application presents a dialog that enables the user to open the program in the debugger or terminate program execution.

C# uses **try** *blocks* to enable exception handling. A **try** block consists of keyword **try** followed by braces (**{}**) that define a block of code in which exceptions may occur. The **try** block encloses statements that could cause exceptions. Immediately following the **try** block are zero or more **catch** *blocks* (also called **catch** *handlers*). Each **catch** handler specifies in parentheses an exception parameter that represents the type of exception the **catch** handler can handle. If an exception parameter includes an optional parameter name, the **catch** handler can use that parameter name to interact with a caught exception object. Optionally, programmers can include a *parameterless* **catch** *handler* that catches all exception types. After the last **catch** handler, an optional *finally block* contains code that always executes, regardless of whether an exception occurs.

Common Programming Error 8.2

The parameterless **catch** *handler must be the last* **catch** *handler following a particular* **try** *block; otherwise a syntax error occurs.*

When a method called in a program detects an exception or when the Common Language Runtime detects a problem, the method or CLR *throws an exception*. The point in the program at which an exception occurs is called the *throw point*—an important location for debugging purposes (as we demonstrate in Section 8.6). Exceptions are objects of classes that extend class **Exception** of namespace **System**. If an exception occurs in a **try** block, the **try** block *expires* (i.e., terminates immediately) and program control transfers to the first **catch** handler (if there is one) following the **try** block. C# is said to use the *termination model of exception handling*, because the **try** block enclosing a thrown exception expires immediately when that exception occurs.[4] As with any other block of code, when a **try** block terminates, local variables defined in the block go out of scope. Next, the CLR searches for the first **catch** handler that can process the type of exception that occurred. The CLR locates the matching **catch** by comparing the thrown exception's type to each **catch**'s exception-parameter type until the CLR finds a match. A match occurs if the types are identical or if the thrown exception's type is a derived class of the

---

4. Some languages use the *resumption model of exception handling*, in which, after the handling of the exception, control returns to the point at which the exception was thrown and execution resumes from that point.

exception-parameter type. When a **catch** handler finishes processing, local variables defined within the **catch** handler (including the **catch** parameter) go out of scope. If a match occurs, code contained within the matching **catch** handler is executed. All remaining **catch** handlers for that **try** block are ignored and execution resumes in the **finally** block (if included). The program then continues with the first statement after the **try**/**catch**/**finally** sequence.

If no exceptions occur in a **try** block, the CLR ignores the exception handlers for that block. Program execution resumes with the next statement after the **try**/**catch** sequence. If an exception that occurs in a **try** block has no matching **catch** handler, or if an exception occurs in a statement that is not in a **try** block, the method containing that statement terminates immediately and the CLR attempts to locate an enclosing **try** block in a calling method. This process is called *stack unwinding* (discussed in Section 8.6).

8.3 Example: **DivideByZeroException**

Let us consider a simple example of exception handling. The application in Fig. 8.1 uses **try** and **catch** to specify a block of code that may throw exceptions and to handle those exceptions if they occur. The application displays two **TextBox**es in which the user can type integers. When the user presses the **Click To Divide** button, the program invokes method **divideButton_Click** (lines 46–84), which obtains the user's input, converts the input values to type **int** and divides the first number (**numerator**) by the second number (**denominator**). Assuming that the user provides integers as input and does not specify 0 as the denominator for the division, **divideButton_Click** displays the division result in **outputLabel**. However, if the user inputs a non-integer value or supplies 0 as the denominator, an exception occurs. This program demonstrates how to catch these exceptions.

```
1   // Fig. 8.1: DivideByZeroTest.cs
2   // Basics of C# exception handling.
3
4   using System;
5   using System.Drawing;
6   using System.Collections;
7   using System.ComponentModel;
8   using System.Windows.Forms;
9   using System.Data;
10
11  // class demonstrates how to handle exceptions from
12  // division by zero in integer arithmetic and from
13  // improper numeric formatting
14  public class DivideByZeroTest : System.Windows.Forms.Form
15  {
16      private System.Windows.Forms.Label numeratorLabel;
17      private System.Windows.Forms.TextBox numeratorTextBox;
18
19      private System.Windows.Forms.Label denominatorLabel;
20      private System.Windows.Forms.TextBox denominatorTextBox;
21
22      private System.Windows.Forms.Button divideButton;
```

Fig. 8.1   Exception handlers for **FormatException** and **DivideByZeroException**. (Part 1 of 3.)

```
23         private System.Windows.Forms.Label outputLabel;
24
25         // required designer variable
26         private System.ComponentModel.Container components = null;
27
28         // default constructor
29         public DivideByZeroTest()
30         {
31             // required for Windows Form Designer support
32             InitializeComponent();
33         }
34
35         // main entry point for the application
36         [STAThread]
37         static void Main()
38         {
39             Application.Run( new DivideByZeroTest() );
40         }
41
42         // Visual Studio .NET generated code
43
44         // obtain integers input by user and divide numerator
45         // by denominator
46         private void divideButton_Click(
47             object sender, System.EventArgs e )
48         {
49             outputLabel.Text = "";
50
51             // retrieve user input and call Quotient
52             try
53             {
54                 // Convert.ToInt32 generates FormatException if
55                 // argument is not an integer
56                 int numerator = Convert.ToInt32( numeratorTextBox.Text );
57                 int denominator =
58                     Convert.ToInt32( denominatorTextBox.Text );
59
60                 // division generates DivideByZeroException if
61                 // denominator is 0
62                 int result = numerator / denominator;
63
64                 outputLabel.Text = result.ToString();
65
66             } // end try
67
68             // process invalid number format
69             catch ( FormatException )
70             {
71                 MessageBox.Show( "You must enter two integers",
72                     "Invalid Number Format",
73                     MessageBoxButtons.OK, MessageBoxIcon.Error );
74             }
```

Fig. 8.1   Exception handlers for **FormatException** and
              DivideByZeroException. (Part 2 of 3.)

```
75
76              // user attempted to divide by zero
77              catch ( DivideByZeroException divideByZeroException )
78              {
79                  MessageBox.Show( divideByZeroException.Message,
80                      "Attempted to Divide by Zero",
81                      MessageBoxButtons.OK, MessageBoxIcon.Error );
82              }
83
84          } // end method divideButton_Click
85
86      } // end class DivideByZeroTest
```

Fig. 8.1   Exception handlers for **FormatException** and
DivideByZeroException. (Part 3 of 3.)

Before we discuss the program details, consider the sample output windows in Fig. 8.1. The first window shows a successful calculation in which the user inputs the numerator **100** and the denominator **7**. Note that the result (**14**) is an integer, because integer division always yields integer results. The next two windows show the result of inputting a non-integer value—in this case, the user input **"hello"** in the second **TextBox**. When the user presses **Click To Divide**, the program attempts to convert the **string**s the user input into **int** values with method **Convert.ToInt32**. If the argument to **Convert.ToInt32** is not a valid representation of an integer (in this case a valid string representation of an integer), the method generates a **FormatException** (namespace **System**). The program detects the exception and displays an error message dialog, indicating that the user must enter two integers. The last two output windows demonstrate the result after an attempt to divide by zero. In integer arithmetic, the CLR automatically tests for division by zero and generates a **DivideByZeroException** (namespace **System**) if the denominator is zero. The program detects the exception and displays an error-message dialog, indicating an attempt to divide by zero.[5]

Let us consider the user interactions and flow of control that yield the results shown in the sample output windows. The user inputs values into the **TextBox**es that represent the numerator and denominator, then presses **ClicktoDivide**. At this point, the program invokes method **divideButton_Click** (lines 46–84). Line 49 assigns the empty **string** to **outputLabel** to clear any prior result, because the program is about to attempt a new calculation. Lines 52–66 define a **try** block that encloses the code that can throw exceptions, as well as the code that should not execute if an exception occurs. For example, the program should not display a new result in **outputLabel** (line 64) unless the calculation (line 62) completes successfully. Remember that the **try** block terminates immediately if an exception occurs, so the remaining code in the **try** block will not execute.

The two statements that read the integers from the **TextBox**es (lines 56–58) each call method **Convert.ToInt32** to convert **string**s to **int** values. This method throws a **FormatException** if it cannot convert its **string** argument to an integer. If lines 56–58 properly convert the values (i.e., no exceptions occur), then line 62 divides the **numerator** by the **denominator** and assigns the result to variable **result**. If the denominator is zero, line 62 causes the CLR to throw a **DivideByZeroException**. If line 62 does not cause an exception, then line 64 displays the result of the division. If no exceptions occur in the **try** block, the program successfully completes the **try** block by reaching line 66 by ignoring the **catch** handlers at lines 69–74 and 77–82—the program execution continues with the first statement following the **try/catch** sequence. In this example, the program reaches the end of event handler **divideButton_Click**, so the method terminates, and the program awaits the next user interaction.

Immediately following the **try** block are two **catch** handlers (also called *catch blocks*)—lines 69–74 define the exception handler for a **FormatException** and lines 77–82 define the exception handler for the **DivideByZeroException**. Each **catch** handler begins with keyword **catch** followed by an exception parameter in parentheses that specifies the type of exception handled by the **catch** handler. The exception-handling code appears in the **catch** handler. In general, when an exception occurs in a **try** block, a **catch** handler catches the exception and handles it. In Fig. 8.1, the first **catch** handler specifies that it catches the type **FormatException**s (thrown by method **Convert.ToInt32**) and the second **catch** handler specifies that it catches type **DivideByZeroException**s (thrown by the CLR). Only the matching **catch** handler executes if an exception occurs. Both the exception handlers in this example display an error-message dialog to the user. When program control reaches the end of a **catch** handler, the program considers the exception as having been handled, and program con-

---

5. The Common Language Runtime allows floating-point division by zero, which produces a positive or negative infinity result, depending on whether the numerator is positive or negative. Dividing zero by zero is a special case that results in a value called "not a number." Programs can test for these results using constants for positive infinity (**PositiveInfinity**), negative infinity (**NegativeInfinity**) and not a number (**NaN**) that are defined in structures **Double** (for **double** calculations) and **Single** (for **float** calculations).

trol continues with the first statement after the **try/catch** sequence (the end of the method in this example).

In the second sample output, the user input **hello** as the denominator. When lines 57–58 execute, **Convert.ToInt32** cannot convert this **string** to an **int**, so **Convert.ToInt32** creates a **FormatException** object and throws it to indicate that the method was unable to convert the **string** to an **int**. When an exception occurs, the **try** block expires (terminates). Any local variables defined in the **try** block go out of scope; therefore, those variables are not available to the exception handlers. Next, the CLR attempts to locate a matching **catch** handler, starting with the **catch** at line 69. The program compares the type of the thrown exception (**FormatException**) with the type in parentheses following keyword **catch** (also **FormatException**). A match occurs, so that exception handler executes and the program ignores all other exception handlers following the corresponding **try** block. Once the **catch** handler finishes processing, local variables defined within the **catch** handler go out of scope. If a match did not occur, the program compares the type of the thrown exception with the next **catch** handler in sequence and repeats the process until a match is found.

Software Engineering Observation 8.5

*Enclose in a **try** block a significant logical section of the program in which several statements can throw exceptions, rather than using a separate **try** block for every statement that throws an exception. However, for proper exception-handling granularity, each **try** block should enclose a section of code small enough, that when an exception occurs, the specific context is known and the **catch** handlers can process the exception properly.*

Common Programming Error 8.3

*Attempting to access a **try** block's local variables in one of that **try** block's associated **catch** handlers is a syntax error. Before a corresponding **catch** handler can execute, the **try** block expires, and its local variables go out of scope.*

Common Programming Error 8.4

*Specifying a comma-separated list of exception parameters in a **catch** handler is a syntax error. Each **catch** can have only one exception parameter.*

In the third sample output, the user input **0** as the denominator. When line 62 executes, the CLR throws a **DivideByZeroException** object to indicate an attempt to divide by zero. Once again, the **try** block terminates immediately upon encountering the exception, and the program attempts to locate a matching **catch** handler, starting from the **catch** handler at line 69. The program compares the type of the thrown exception (**DivideByZeroException**) with the type in parentheses following keyword **catch** (**FormatException**). In this case, there is no match, because they are not the same exception types and because **FormatException** is not a base class of **DivideByZeroException**. So, the program proceeds to line 77 and compares the type of the thrown exception (**DivideByZeroException**) with the type in parentheses following keyword **catch** (**DivideByZeroException**). A match occurs, so that exception handler executes. Line 79 in this handler uses property *Message* of class **Exception** to display the error message to the user. If there were additional **catch** handlers, the program would ignore them.

8.4 .NET **Exception** Hierarchy

The exception-handling mechanism allows only objects of class **Exception** and its derived classes to be thrown and caught.[6] This section overviews several of the .NET Framework's exception classes. In addition, we discuss how to determine whether a particular method throws exceptions.

Class **Exception** of namespace **System** is the base class of the .NET Framework exception hierarchy. Two of the most important derived classes of **Exception** are ***ApplicationException*** and ***SystemException***. **ApplicationException** is a base class programmers can extend to create exception data types that are specific to their applications. We discuss creating programmer-defined exception classes in Section 8.7. Programs can recover from most **ApplicationException**s and continue execution.

The CLR can generate **SystemException**s at any point during the execution of the program. Many of these exceptions can be avoided by coding properly. These are called *runtime exceptions* and they derive from class ***SystemException***. For example, if a program attempts to access an out-of-range array subscript, the CLR throws an exception of type **IndexOutOfRangeException** (a class derived from **SystemException**). Similarly, a runtime exception occurs when a program uses an object reference to manipulate an object that does not yet exist (i.e., the reference has a **null** value). Attempting to use such a **null** reference causes a ***NullReferenceException*** (another type of **SystemException**). According to Microsoft's "Best Practices for Handling Exceptions [C#],"[7] programs typically cannot recover from most exceptions the CLR throws. Therefore, programs generally should not throw or catch **SystemException**s. [*Note:* For a complete list of derived classes of **Exception**, look up "**Exception** class" in the **Index** of the Visual Studio .NET online documentation.]

A benefit of using the exception-class hierarchy is that a **catch** handler can catch exceptions of a particular type or can use a base-class type to catch exceptions in a hierarchy of related exception types. For example, a **catch** handler that specifies an exception parameter of type **Exception** also can catch exceptions of all classes that extend **Exception**, because **Exception** is the base class of all exception classes. This allows for polymorphic processing of related exceptions. The benefit of the latter approach is that the exception handler can use the exception parameter to manipulate the caught exception. If the exception handler does not need access to the caught exception, the exception parameter may be omitted. If no exception type is specified, the catch handler will catch all exceptions.

Using inheritance with exceptions enables an exception handler to catch related exceptions with a concise notation. An exception handler certainly could catch each derived-class exception type individually, but catching the base-class exception type is more concise. However, this makes sense only if the handling behavior is the same for a base class and derived classes. Otherwise, catch each derived-class exception individually.

---

6. Actually, it is possible to **catch** exceptions of types that are not derived from class **Exception** using the parameterless **catch** handler. This is useful for handling exceptions from code written in other languages that do not require all exception types to derive from class **Exception** in the .NET framework.
7. "Best Practices for Handling Exceptions [C#]," *.NET Framework Developer's Guide*, Visual Studio .NET Online Help.

At this point, we know that there are many different exception types. We also know that methods and the CLR can both throw exceptions. But, how do we determine that an exception could occur in a program? For methods in the .NET Framework classes, we can look at the detailed description of the methods in the online documentation. If a method throws an exception, its description contains a section called "Exceptions" that specifies the types of exceptions thrown by the method and briefly describes potential causes for the exceptions. For example, look up "**Convert.ToInt32** method" in the index of the Visual Studio .NET online documentation. In the document that describes the method, click the link "**public static int ToInt32(string);**." In the document that appears, the "Exceptions" section indicates that method **Convert.ToInt32** throws three exception types—**ArgumentException**, **FormatException** and **OverflowException**—and describes the reason that each exception type occurs.

Software Engineering Observation 8.6

*If a method is capable of throwing exceptions, statements that invoke that method should be placed in **try** blocks and those exceptions should be caught and handled.*

Determining when the CLR throws exceptions is more difficult. Typically, such information appears in the *C# Language Specification*, which is located in the online documentation. To access the language specification, select **Contents...** from the **Help** menu in Visual Studio. In the **Contents** window, expand **Visual Studio .NET**, **Visual Basic and Visual C#**, **Reference**, **Visual C# Language** and **C# Language Specification**.

The language specification defines the syntax of the language and specifies cases in which exceptions are thrown. For example, in Fig. 8.1, we demonstrated that the CLR throws a **DivideByZeroException** when a program attempts to divide by zero in integer arithmetic. The language specification, Section 7.7.2 discusses the division operator and its **Exception**s. In this section, you will find the details of when a **DivideByZeroException** occurs.

8.5 finally Block

Programs frequently request and release resources dynamically (i.e., at execution time). For example, a program that reads a file from disk first requests the opening of that file. If that request succeeds, the program reads the contents of the file. Operating systems typically prevent more than one program from manipulating a file at once. Therefore, when a program finishes processing a file, the program normally closes the file (i.e., releases the resource). This enables other programs to use the file. Closing the file helps prevent the *resource leak*, in which the file resource is unavailable to other programs because a program using the file never closed it. Programs that obtain certain types of resources (such as files) must return those resources explicitly to the system to avoid resource leaks.

In programming languages, like C and C++, in which the programmer is responsible for dynamic memory management, the most common type of resource leak is a *memory leak*. This happens when a program allocates memory (as we do with operator **new** in C#), but does not deallocate the memory when the memory is no longer needed in the program. In C#, this normally is not an issue, because the CLR performs "garbage collection" of memory no longer needed by an executing program. However, other kinds of resource leaks (such as the unclosed file mentioned previously) can occur in C#.

Testing and Debugging Tip 8.2

The CLR does not completely eliminate memory leaks. The CLR will not garbage-collect an object until the program has no more references to that object. Thus, memory leaks can occur if programmers erroneously keep references to unwanted objects.

Most resources that require explicit release have potential exceptions associated with the processing of the resource. For example, a program that processes a file might receive **IOException**s during the processing. For this reason, file-processing code normally appears in a **try** block. Regardless of whether a program successfully processes a file, the program should close the file when the file is no longer needed. Suppose a program places all resource-request and resource-release code in a **try** block. If no exceptions occur, the **try** block executes normally and releases the resources after using them. However, if an exception occurs, the **try** block may expire before the resource-release code can execute. We could duplicate all resource-release code in the **catch** handlers, but this makes the code more difficult to modify and maintain.

C#'s exception handling mechanism provides the *finally* block, which is guaranteed to execute if program control enters the corresponding **try** block. The **finally** block executes regardless of whether that **try** block executes successfully or an exception occurs. This guarantee makes the **finally** block an ideal location to place resource deallocation code for resources acquired and manipulated in the corresponding **try** block. If the **try** block executes successfully, the **finally** block executes immediately after the **try** block terminates. If an exception occurs in the **try** block, the **finally** block executes immediately after a **catch** handler completes exception handling. If the exception is not caught by a **catch** handler associated with that **try** block or if a **catch** handler associated with that **try** block throws an exception, the **finally** block executes, then the exception is processed by the next enclosing **try** block (if there is one).

Testing and Debugging Tip 8.3

A **finally** *block typically contains code to release resources acquired in the corresponding* **try** *block; this makes the* **finally** *block an effective way to eliminate resource leaks.*

Testing and Debugging Tip 8.4

The only reason a **finally** *block will not execute if program control entered the corresponding* **try** *block is that the application terminates before* **finally** *can execute.*

Performance Tip 8.3

As a rule, resources should be released as soon as it is apparent that they are no longer needed in a program, to make those resources immediately available for reuse, thus enhancing resource utilization in the program.

If one or more **catch** handlers follow a **try** block, the **finally** block is optional. If no **catch** handlers follow a **try** block, a **finally** block must appear immediately after the **try** block. If any **catch** handlers follow a **try** block, the **finally** block appears after the last **catch**. Only whitespace and comments can separate the blocks in a **try/catch/finally** sequence.

Common Programming Error 8.5

Placing the **finally** *block before a* **catch** *handler is a syntax error.*

The C# application in Fig. 8.2 demonstrates that the **finally** block always executes, even if no exception occurs in the corresponding **try** block. The program consists of method **Main** (lines 10–59) and four other **static** methods that **Main** invokes to demonstrate **finally**—**DoesNotThrowException** (lines 62–85), **ThrowExceptionWithCatch** (lines 88–114), **ThrowExceptionWithoutCatch** (lines 117–138) and **ThrowExceptionCatchRethrow** (lines 141–173). [*Note:* We use **static** methods in this example so that **Main** can invoke these methods directly without creating any objects of class **UsingExceptions**. This enables us to concentrate on the mechanics of **try/catch/finally**.]

Line 14 of **Main** invokes method **DoesNotThrowException** (lines 62–85). The **try** block (lines 65–68) begins by outputting a message (line 67). The **try** block does not throw any exceptions, so program control reaches the closing brace of the **try** block and the **catch** handler (lines 71–74) and executes the **finally** block (lines 77–81) which outputs a message. At this point, program control continues with the first statement after the **finally** block (line 83), which outputs a message indicating that the end of the method has been reached. Then, program control returns to **Main**.

Line 20 of **Main** invokes method **ThrowExceptionWithCatch** (lines 88–114), which begins in its **try** block (lines 91–97) by outputting a message. Next, the **try** block creates a new **Exception** object and uses a ***throw*** *statement* to throw the exception object (lines 95–96). The **string** passed to the constructor becomes the exception object's error message. When a **throw** statement in a **try** block executes, the **try** block expires immediately, and program control continues at the first **catch** (lines 100–103) following this **try** block. In this example, the type thrown (**Exception**) matches the type specified in the **catch**, so line 102 outputs a message indicating the exception that occurred. Then, the **finally** block (lines 106–110) executes and outputs a message. At this point, program control continues with the first statement after the **finally** block (line 112), which outputs a message indicating that the end of the method has been reached, then program control returns to **Main**. Note, that in line 102, we use the exception object's **Message** property to access the error message associated with the exception—(the message passed to the **Exception** constructor). Section 8.6 discusses several properties of class **Exception**.

Common Programming Error 8.6

*The expression of a **throw**—an exception object—must be of either class **Exception** or one of its derived classes.*

Lines 27–30 of **Main** define a **try** block in which **Main** invokes method **ThrowExceptionWithoutCatch** (lines 117–138). The **try** block enables **Main** to catch any exceptions thrown by **ThrowExceptionWithoutCatch**. The **try** block in lines 120–126 of **ThrowExceptionWithoutCatch** begins by outputting a message. Next, the **try** block throws an **Exception** (lines 124–125) and the **try** block expires immediately. Normally, program control would continue at the first **catch** following the **try** block. However, this **try** block does not have any corresponding **catch** handlers. Therefore, the exception is not caught in method **ThrowExceptionWithoutCatch**. Normal program control cannot continue until that exception is caught and processed. Thus, the CLR will terminate **ThrowExceptionWithoutCatch** and program control will return to **Main**. Before control returns to **Main**, the **finally** block (lines 129–133) executes and outputs a message. At this point, program control returns to **Main**—any statements appearing after the **finally** block would not execute. In this example, because the exception thrown at lines 127–128 is not caught. Method **ThrowExceptionWithoutCatch** always terminates after the **finally** block executes. In **Main**, the **catch** handler at lines 34–38 catches the exception and displays a message indicating that the exception was caught in **Main**.

```
1   // Fig. 8.2: UsingExceptions.cs
2   // Using finally blocks.
3
4   using System;
5
6   // demonstrating that finally always executes
7   class UsingExceptions
8   {
9      // entry point for application
10     static void Main( string[] args )
11     {
12        // Case 1: No exceptions occur in called method.
13        Console.WriteLine( "Calling DoesNotThrowException" );
14        DoesNotThrowException();
15
16        // Case 2: Exception occurs and is caught
17        // in called method.
18        Console.WriteLine( "\nCalling ThrowExceptionWithCatch" );
19        ThrowExceptionWithCatch();
20
21        // Case 3: Exception occurs, but not caught
22        // in called method, because no catch handlers.
23        Console.WriteLine(
24           "\nCalling ThrowExceptionWithoutCatch" );
25
26        // call ThrowExceptionWithoutCatch
27        try
28        {
29           ThrowExceptionWithoutCatch();
30        }
31
32        // process exception returned from
33        // ThrowExceptionWithoutCatch
34        catch
35        {
36           Console.WriteLine( "Caught exception from " +
37              "ThrowExceptionWithoutCatch in Main" );
38        }
39
40        // Case 4: Exception occurs and is caught
41        // in called method, then rethrown to caller.
42        Console.WriteLine(
43           "\nCalling ThrowExceptionCatchRethrow" );
44
```

Fig. 8.2   Demonstrating that **finally** blocks always execute regardless of whether an exception occurs. (Part 1 of 4.)

```
45          // call ThrowExceptionCatchRethrow
46          try
47          {
48              ThrowExceptionCatchRethrow();
49          }
50
51          // process exception returned from
52          // ThrowExceptionCatchRethrow
53          catch
54          {
55              Console.WriteLine( "Caught exception from " +
56                  "ThrowExceptionCatchRethrow in Main" );
57          }
58
59      } // end method Main
60
61      // no exceptions thrown
62      public static void DoesNotThrowException()
63      {
64          // try block does not throw any exceptions
65          try
66          {
67              Console.WriteLine( "In DoesNotThrowException" );
68          }
69
70          // this catch never executes
71          catch
72          {
73              Console.WriteLine( "This catch never executes" );
74          }
75
76          // finally executes because corresponding try executed
77          finally
78          {
79              Console.WriteLine(
80                  "Finally executed in DoesNotThrowException" );
81          }
82
83          Console.WriteLine( "End of DoesNotThrowException" );
84
85      } // end method DoesNotThrowException
86
87      // throws exception and catches it locally
88      public static void ThrowExceptionWithCatch()
89      {
90          // try block throws exception
91          try
92          {
93              Console.WriteLine( "In ThrowExceptionWithCatch" );
94
```

Fig. 8.2   Demonstrating that **finally** blocks always execute regardless of whether an exception occurs. (Part 2 of 4.)

```
95                throw new Exception(
96                   "Exception in ThrowExceptionWithCatch" );
97             }
98
99          // catch exception thrown in try block
100         catch ( Exception error )
101         {
102            Console.WriteLine( "Message: " + error.Message );
103         }
104
105         // finally executes because corresponding try executed
106         finally
107         {
108            Console.WriteLine(
109               "Finally executed in ThrowExceptionWithCatch" );
110         }
111
112         Console.WriteLine( "End of ThrowExceptionWithCatch" );
113
114      } // end method ThrowExceptionWithCatch
115
116      // throws exception and does not catch it locally
117      public static void ThrowExceptionWithoutCatch()
118      {
119         // throw exception, but do not catch it
120         try
121         {
122            Console.WriteLine( "In ThrowExceptionWithoutCatch" );
123
124            throw new Exception(
125               "Exception in ThrowExceptionWithoutCatch" );
126         }
127
128         // finally executes because corresponding try executed
129         finally
130         {
131            Console.WriteLine( "Finally executed in " +
132               "ThrowExceptionWithoutCatch" );
133         }
134
135         // unreachable code; would generate logic error
136         Console.WriteLine( "This will never be printed" );
137
138      } // end method ThrowExceptionWithoutCatch
139
140      // throws exception, catches it and rethrows it
141      public static void ThrowExceptionCatchRethrow()
142      {
143         // try block throws exception
144         try
145         {
146            Console.WriteLine( "In ThrowExceptionCatchRethrow" );
```

Fig. 8.2   Demonstrating that **finally** blocks always execute regardless of whether an exception occurs. (Part 3 of 4.)

```
147
148            throw new Exception(
149               "Exception in ThrowExceptionCatchRethrow" );
150         }
151
152         // catch any exception, place in object error
153         catch ( Exception error )
154         {
155            Console.WriteLine( "Message: " + error.Message );
156
157            // rethrow exception for further processing
158            throw error;
159
160            // unreachable code; would generate logic error
161         }
162
163         // finally executes because corresponding try executed
164         finally
165         {
166            Console.WriteLine( "Finally executed in " +
167               "ThrowExceptionCatchRethrow" );
168         }
169
170         // unreachable code; would generate logic error
171         Console.WriteLine( "This will never be printed" );
172
173      } // end method ThrowExceptionCatchRethrow
174
175 } // end class UsingExceptions
```

```
Calling DoesNotThrowException
In DoesNotThrowException
Finally executed in DoesNotThrowException
End of DoesNotThrowException

Calling ThrowExceptionWithCatch
In ThrowExceptionWithCatch
Message: Exception in ThrowExceptionWithCatch
Finally executed in ThrowExceptionWithCatch
End of ThrowExceptionWithCatch

Calling ThrowExceptionWithoutCatch
In ThrowExceptionWithoutCatch
Finally executed in ThrowExceptionWithoutCatch
Caught exception from ThrowExceptionWithoutCatch in Main

Calling ThrowExceptionCatchRethrow
In ThrowExceptionCatchRethrow
Message: Exception in ThrowExceptionCatchRethrow
Finally executed in ThrowExceptionCatchRethrow
Caught exception from ThrowExceptionCatchRethrow in Main
```

Fig. 8.2 Demonstrating that **finally** blocks always execute regardless of whether an exception occurs. (Part 4 of 4.)

Lines 46–49 of **Main** define a **try** block in which **Main** invokes method **Throw-ExceptionCatchRethrow** (lines 141–173). The **try** block enables **Main** to catch any exceptions thrown by **ThrowExceptionCatchRethrow**. The **try** block in lines 144–150 of **ThrowExceptionCatchRethrow** begins by outputting a message. Next, the **try** block throws an **Exception** (lines 148–149). The **try** block expires immediately, and program control continues at the first **catch** (lines 153–161) following the **try** block. In this example, the type thrown (**Exception**) matches the type specified in the **catch**, so line 155 outputs a message indicating the exception that occurred. Line 158 uses the **throw** statement to *rethrow* the exception. This indicates that the **catch** handler performed partial processing (or no processing) of the exception and is now passing the exception back to the calling method (in this case **Main**) for further processing. Note that the expression to the **throw** statement is the reference to the exception that was caught. When rethrowing the original exception, you can also use the statement

```
throw;
```

with no expression. Section 8.6 discusses the **throw** statement with an expression. Such a **throw** statement enables programmers to catch an exception, create an exception object, then throw a different type of exception from the **catch** handler. Class library designers often do this to customize the exception types thrown from methods in their class libraries or to provide additional debugging information.

Software Engineering Observation 8.7

Before throwing an exception to a calling method, the method that throws the exception should release any resources acquired within the method before the exception occurred.[8]

Software Engineering Observation 8.8

Whenever possible, a method should handle exceptions that are thrown in that method, rather than passing the exceptions to another region of the program.

The exception handling in method **ThrowExceptionCatchRethrow** did not complete, because the program cannot run code in the **catch** handler placed after the invocation of the **throw** statement (line 158). Therefore, method **ThrowExceptionCatchRethrow** will terminate and return control to **Main**. Once again, the **finally** block (lines 164–168) will execute and output a message before control returns to **Main**. When control returns to **Main**, the **catch** handler at lines 53–57 catches the exception and displays a message indicating that the exception was caught. Then the program terminates.

Note that the point at which program control continues after the **finally** block executes depends on the exception-handling state. If the **try** block successfully completes or if a **catch** handler catches and handles an exception, control continues with the next statement after the **finally** block. If an exception is not caught or if a **catch** handler rethrows an exception, program control continues in the next enclosing **try** block. The enclosing **try** may be in the calling method or one of its callers. Nesting a **try/catch** sequence in a **try** block is also possible, in which case the outer **try** block's catch handlers would process any exceptions that were not caught in the inner **try/catch** sequence. If a **try** block has a cor-

---

8. "Best Practices for Handling Exceptions [C#]," *.NET Framework Developer's Guide*, Visual Studio .NET Online Help.

responding **finally** block, the **finally** block executes even if the **try** block terminates due to a **return** statement; then the **return** occurs.

Common Programming Error 8.7

*Throwing an exception from a **finally** can be dangerous. If an uncaught exception is awaiting processing when the **finally** block executes and the **finally** block throws a new exception that is not caught in the **finally** block, the first exception is lost, and the new exception is the one passed to the next enclosing **try** block.*

Testing and Debugging Tip 8.5

*When placing code that can throw an exception in a **finally** block, always enclose that code in a **try/catch** sequence that catches the appropriate exception types. This prevents losing uncaught and rethrown exceptions that occur before the **finally** block executes.*

Software Engineering Observation 8.9

*C#'s exception-handling mechanism removes error-processing code from the main line of a program to improve program clarity. Do not place **try-catch-finally** around every statement that could throw an exception. Doing so makes programs difficult to read. Rather, place one **try** block around a significant portion of your code. Follow this **try** block with **catch** handlers that handle each of the possible exceptions and follow the **catch** handlers with a single **finally** block.*

8.6 **Exception** Properties

As we discussed in Section 8.4, exception data types derive from class **Exception**, which has several properties. These properties frequently are used to formulate error messages for a caught exception. Two important properties are *Message* and *StackTrace*. Property **Message** stores the error message associated with an **Exception** object. This message may be a default message associated with the exception type or a customized message passed to an exception object's constructor when the exception object is constructed. Property **StackTrace** contains a **string** that represents the *method call stack*. The runtime environment keeps a list of method calls that have been made up to a given moment. The **StackTrace string** represents this sequential list of methods that had not finished processing at the time the exception occurred. The exact location at which the exception occurs in the program is called the exception's *throw point*.

Testing and Debugging Tip 8.6

A stack trace shows the complete method call stack at the time an exception occurred. This lets the programmer view the series of method calls that led to the exception. Information in the stack trace includes names of the methods on the call stack at the time of the exception, names of the classes in which those methods are defined, names of the namespaces in which those classes are defined and line numbers. The first line number in the stack trace indicates the throw point. Subsequent line numbers indicate the locations from which each method in the stack trace was called.

Another property used frequently by class library programmers is *InnerException*. Typically, programmers use this property to "wrap" exception objects caught in their code, then throw new exception types that are specific to their libraries. For example, a programmer implementing an accounting system might have some account-number processing code in which account numbers are input as **string**s but represented with integers in the code. As you know, a program can convert **string**s to **int** values with **Convert.ToInt32**, which throws a **FormatException** when it encounters an invalid number format. When an invalid account-number format occurs, the accounting-system programmer might wish either to indicate an error message different from the default one supplied by **FormatException** or to indicate a new exception type, such as **InvalidAccountNumberFormatException**. In these cases, the programmer would provide code to catch the **FormatException**, then create an exception object in the **catch** handler, passing the original exception as one of the constructor arguments. The original exception object becomes the **InnerException** of the new exception object. When an **InvalidAccountNumberFormatException** occurs in code that uses the accounting-system library, the **catch** handler that catches the exception can view the original exception via the property **InnerException**. Thus, the exception indicates that an invalid account number was specified and that the particular problem was an invalid number format.

Our next example (Fig. 8.3) demonstrates properties **Message**, **StackTrace** and **InnerException** and method **ToString**. In addition, this example demonstrates *stack unwinding*—the process that attempts to locate an appropriate **catch** handler for an uncaught exception. As we discuss this example, we keep track of the methods on the call stack, so we can discuss property **StackTrace** and the stack-unwinding mechanism.

Program execution begins with the invocation of **Main**, which becomes the first method on the method call stack. Line 16 of the **try** block in **Main** invokes **Method1** (lines 43–46), which becomes the second method on the stack. If **Method1** throws an exception, the **catch** handler at lines 22–38 handle the exception and output information about the exception that occurred. Line 45 of **Method1** invokes **Method2** (lines 49–52), which becomes the third method on the stack. Then, line 51 of **Method2** invokes **Method3** (defined at lines 55–70) which becomes the fourth method on the stack.

Testing and Debugging Tip 8.7

When reading a stack trace, start from the top of the stack trace and read the error message first. Then, read the remainder of the stack trace, looking for the first line that indicates code that you wrote in your program. Normally, this is the location that caused the exception.

```
1   // Fig. 8.3: Properties.cs
2   // Stack unwinding and Exception class properties.
3
4   using System;
5
6   // demonstrates using the Message, StackTrace and
7   // InnerException properties
8   class Properties
9   {
10     static void Main( string[] args )
11     {
12        // call Method1, any Exception it generates will be
13        // caught in the catch handler that follows
14        try
15        {
16           Method1();
17        }
```

Fig. 8.3   **Exception** properties and stack unwinding. (Part 1 of 3.)

```
18
19          // Output string representation of Exception, then
20          // output values of InnerException, Message,
21          // and StackTrace properties
22          catch ( Exception exception )
23          {
24             Console.WriteLine(
25                "exception.ToString(): \n{0}\n",
26                exception.ToString() );
27
28             Console.WriteLine( "exception.Message: \n{0}\n",
29                exception.Message );
30
31             Console.WriteLine( "exception.StackTrace: \n{0}\n",
32                exception.StackTrace );
33
34             Console.WriteLine(
35                "exception.InnerException: \n{0}",
36                exception.InnerException );
37
38          } // end catch
39
40       } // end Main
41
42       // calls Method2
43       public static void Method1()
44       {
45          Method2();
46       }
47
48       // calls Method3
49       public static void Method2()
50       {
51          Method3();
52       }
53
54       // throws an Exception containing an InnerException
55       public static void Method3()
56       {
57          // attempt to convert non-integer string to int
58          try
59          {
60             Convert.ToInt32( "Not an integer" );
61          }
62
63          // catch FormatException and wrap it in new Exception
64          catch ( FormatException error )
65          {
66             throw new Exception(
67                "Exception occurred in Method3", error );
68          }
69
70       } // end method Method3
```

Fig. 8.3   **Exception** properties and stack unwinding. (Part 2 of 3.)

```
71
72  } // end class UsingExceptions
```

```
exception.ToString():
System.Exception: Exception occurred in Method3 --->
   System.FormatException: Input string was not in a correct format.
   at System.Number.ParseInt32(String s, NumberStyles style,
      NumberFormatInfo info)
   at System.Convert.ToInt32(String s)
   at Properties.Method3() in
      C:\books\2002\cspfep1\cspfep1_examples\ch08\Fig08_03\
         Properties\Properties.cs:line 60
   --- End of inner exception stack trace ---
   at Properties.Method3() in
      C:\books\2002\cspfep1\cspfep1_examples\ch08\Fig08_03\
         Properties\Properties.cs:line 66
   at Properties.Method2() in
      C:\books\2002\cspfep1\cspfep1_examples\ch08\Fig08_03\
         Properties\Properties.cs:line 51
   at Properties.Method1() in
      C:\books\2002\cspfep1\cspfep1_examples\ch08\Fig08_03\
         Properties\Properties.cs:line 45
   at Properties.Main(String[] args) in
      C:\books\2002\cspfep1\cspfep1_examples\ch08\Fig08_03\
         Properties\Properties.cs:line 16

exception.Message:
Exception occurred in Method3

exception.StackTrace:
   at Properties.Method3() in
      C:\books\2002\cspfep1\cspfep1_examples\ch08\Fig08_03\
         Properties\Properties.cs:line 66
   at Properties.Method2() in
      C:\books\2002\cspfep1\cspfep1_examples\ch08\Fig08_03\
         Properties\Properties.cs:line 51
   at Properties.Method1() in
      C:\books\2002\cspfep1\cspfep1_examples\ch08\Fig08_03\
         Properties\Properties.cs:line 45
   at Properties.Main(String[] args) in
      C:\books\2002\cspfep1\cspfep1_examples\ch08\Fig08_03\
         Properties\Properties.cs:line 16

exception.InnerException:
System.FormatException: Input string was not in a correct format.
   at System.Number.ParseInt32(String s, NumberStyles style,
      NumberFormatInfo info)
   at System.Convert.ToInt32(String s)
   at Properties.Method3() in
      C:\books\2002\cspfep1\cspfep1_examples\ch08\Fig08_03\
         Properties\Properties.cs:line 60
```

Fig. 8.3   **Exception** properties and stack unwinding. (Part 3 of 3.)

At this point, the method call stack for the program is

```
Method3
Method2
Method1
Main
```

with the last method called (**Method3**) at the top and the first method called (**Main**) at the bottom. The **try** block (lines 58–61) in **Method3** invokes method **Convert.ToInt32** (line 60) and attempts to convert a **string** to an **int**. At this point, **Convert.ToInt32** becomes the fifth and final method on the call stack.

The argument to **Convert.ToInt32** is not in integer format, so line 60 throws a **FormatException** that is caught at line 64 in **Method3**. The exception terminates the call to **Convert.ToInt32**, so the method is removed from the method call stack. The **catch** handler creates an **Exception** object, then throws it. The first argument to the **Exception** constructor is the custom error message for our example, "**Exception occurred in Method3**." The second argument is the **InnerException** object—the **FormatException** that was caught. Note that the **StackTrace** for this new exception object will reflect the point at which the exception was thrown (line 66). Now, **Method3** terminates, because the exception thrown in the **catch** handler is not caught in the method body. Thus, control will be returned to the statement that invoked **Method3** in the prior method in the call stack (**Method2**). This removes or *unwinds* **Method3** from the method-call stack.

Good Programming Practice 8.2

*When catching and rethrowing an exception, provide additional debugging information in the rethrown exception. To do so, create an **Exception** object with more specific debugging information and pass the original caught exception to the new exception object's constructor to initialize the **InnerException** property.[9]*

When control returns to line 51 in **Method2**, the CLR determines that line 51 is not in a **try** block. Therefore, the exception cannot be caught in **Method2**, and **Method2** terminates. This unwinds **Method2** from the method-call stack and returns control to line 45 in **Method1**. Here again, line 45 is not in a **try** block, so the exception cannot be caught in **Method1**. The method terminates and unwinds from the call stack, returning control to line 16 in **Main**, which is in a **try** block. The **try** block in **Main** expires, and the **catch** handler at lines (22–38) catches the exception. The **catch** handler uses method **ToString** and properties **Message**, **StackTrace** and **InnerException** to produce the output. Note that stack unwinding continues until either a **catch** handler catches the exception or the program terminates.

The first block of output (reformatted for readability) in Fig. 8.3 shows the exception's **string** representation returned from method **ToString**. This begins with the name of the exception class followed by the **Message** property value. The next eight lines show the **string** representation of the **InnerException** object. The remainder of that block of output shows the **StackTrace** for the exception thrown in **Method3**. Note that the **StackTrace** represents the state of the method-call stack at the throw

---

9. "Best Practices for Handling Exceptions [C#]," *.NET Framework Developer's Guide*, Visual Studio .NET Online Help.

point of the exception, not at the point where the exception eventually is caught. Each of the **StackTrace** lines that begins with "**at**" represents a method on the call stack. These lines indicate the method in which the exception occurred, the file in which that method resides and the line number in the file. Also, note that the stack trace includes the inner-exception stack trace.

Testing and Debugging Tip 8.8

*When catching and rethrowing an exception, provide additional debugging information in the rethrown exception. To do so, create an **Exception** object containing more specific debugging information and then pass the original caught exception to the new exception object's constructor to initialize the **InnerException** property.*

Method **ToString** of an exception returns a **string** containing the name of the exception, the optional character **string** supplied when the exception was constructed, the inner exception (if there is one) and a stack trace.

The next block of output (two lines) simply displays the **Message** property (**Exception occurred in Method3**) of the exception thrown in **Method3**.

The third block of output displays the **StackTrace** property of the exception thrown in **Method3**. Note that the **StackTrace** property includes the stack trace starting from line 66 in **Method3**, because that is the point at which the **Exception** object was created and thrown. The stack trace always begins from the exception's throw point.

Finally, the last block of output displays the **ToString** representation of the **InnerException** property, which includes the namespace and class names of that exception object, its **Message** property and its **StackTrace** property.

8.7 Programmer-Defined Exception Classes

In many cases, programmers can use existing exception classes from the .NET Framework to indicate exceptions that occur in their programs. However, in some cases, programmers may wish to create exception types that are more specific to the problems that occur in their programs. *Programmer-defined exception classes* should derive directly or indirectly from class **ApplicationException** of namespace **System**.

Good Programming Practice 8.3

Associating each type of malfunction with an appropriately named exception class improves program clarity.

Software Engineering Observation 8.10

Before creating programmer-defined exception classes, investigate the existing exception classes in the .NET Framework to determine whether an appropriate exception type already exists.

Software Engineering Observation 8.11

Programmers should create exception classes only if they need to catch and handle the new exceptions differently from other existing exception types.

Figure 8.4 and Fig. 8.5 demonstrate defining and using a programmer-defined exception class. Class **NegativeNumberException** (Fig. 8.4) is a programmer-defined exception class representing exceptions that occur when a program performs an illegal operation on a negative number, such as the square root of a negative number.

```
1   // Fig. 8.4: NegativeNumberException.cs
2   // NegativeNumberException represents exceptions caused by illegal
3   // operations performed on negative numbers
4
5   using System;
6
7   // NegativeNumberException represents exceptions caused by
8   // illegal operations performed on negative numbers
9   class NegativeNumberException : ApplicationException
10  {
11      // default constructor
12      public NegativeNumberException()
13          : base( "Illegal operation for a negative number" )
14      {
15      }
16
17      // constructor for customizing error message
18      public NegativeNumberException( string message )
19          : base( message )
20      {
21      }
22
23      // constructor for customizing error message and
24      // specifying inner exception object
25      public NegativeNumberException(
26          string message, Exception inner )
27              : base( message, inner )
28      {
29      }
30
31  } // end class NegativeNumberException
```

Fig. 8.4 **ApplicationException** subclass thrown when a program performs illegal operations on negative numbers.

According to Microsoft,[10] programmer-defined exceptions should extend class **ApplicationException**, should have a class name that ends with "Exception" and should define three constructors—a default constructor, a constructor that receives a **string** argument (the error message) and a constructor that receives a **string** argument and an **Exception** argument (the error message and the inner-exception object).

NegativeNumberExceptions most likely occur during arithmetic operations, so it seems logical to derive class **NegativeNumberException** from class **ArithmeticException**. However, class **ArithmeticException** derives from class **SystemException**—the category of exceptions thrown by the CLR. **ApplicationException** specifically is the base class for exceptions thrown by a user program, not by the CLR.

Class **SquareRootTest** (Fig. 8.5) demonstrates our programmer-defined exception class. The application enables the user to input a numeric value, then invokes method **SquareRoot** (lines 42–52) to calculate the square root of that value. For this purpose,

10. "Best Practices for Handling Exceptions [C#]," *.NET Framework Developer's Guide*, Visual Studio .NET Online Help.

SquareRoot invokes class **Math**'s *Sqrt* method, which receives a non-negative **double** value as its argument. If the argument is negative, method **Sqrt** normally returns constant **NaN** from class **Double**. In this program, we would like to prevent the user from calculating the square root of a negative number. If the numeric value received from the user is negative, **SquareRoot** throws a **NegativeNumberException** (lines 46–47). Otherwise, **SquareRoot** invokes class **Math**'s *Sqrt* method to compute the square root.

When the user inputs a value and clicks the **Square Root** button, the program invokes method **squareRootButton_Click** (lines 56–85). The **try** block (lines 62–68) attempts to invoke **SquareRoot** with the value input by the user. If the user input is not a valid number, a **FormatException** occurs, and the **catch** handler at lines 71–76 processes the exception. If the user inputs a negative number, method **SquareRoot** throws a **NegativeNumberException** (lines 46–47). The **catch** handler at lines 79–83 catches and handles that exception.

```
1   // Fig. 8.5: SquareRootTest.cs
2   // Demonstrating a programmer-defined exception class.
3
4   using System;
5   using System.Drawing;
6   using System.Collections;
7   using System.ComponentModel;
8   using System.Windows.Forms;
9   using System.Data;
10
11  // accepts input and computes the square root of that input
12  public class SquareRootTest : System.Windows.Forms.Form
13  {
14     private System.Windows.Forms.Label inputLabel;
15     private System.Windows.Forms.TextBox inputTextBox;
16
17     private System.Windows.Forms.Button squareRootButton;
18
19     private System.Windows.Forms.Label outputLabel;
20
21     // Required designer variable.
22     private System.ComponentModel.Container components = null;
23
24     // default constructor
25     public SquareRootTest()
26     {
27        // Required for Windows Form Designer support
28        InitializeComponent();
29     }
30
31     // Visual Studio .NET generated code
32
```

Fig. 8.5   **SquareRootTest** class throws an exception if error occurs when calculating the square root. (Part 1 of 3.)

```
33      // main entry point for the application
34      [STAThread]
35      static void Main()
36      {
37          Application.Run( new SquareRootTest() );
38      }
39
40      // computes the square root of its parameter; throws
41      // NegativeNumberException if parameter is negative
42      public double SquareRoot( double operand )
43      {
44          // if negative operand, throw NegativeNumberException
45          if ( operand < 0 )
46              throw new NegativeNumberException(
47                  "Square root of negative number not permitted" );
48
49          // compute the square root
50          return Math.Sqrt( operand );
51
52      } // end class SquareRoot
53
54      // obtain user input, convert to double and calculate
55      // square root
56      private void squareRootButton_Click(
57          object sender, System.EventArgs e )
58      {
59          outputLabel.Text = "";
60
61          // catch any NegativeNumberExceptions thrown
62          try
63          {
64              double result =
65                  SquareRoot( Double.Parse( inputTextBox.Text ) );
66
67              outputLabel.Text = result.ToString();
68          }
69
70          // process invalid number format
71          catch ( FormatException notInteger )
72          {
73              MessageBox.Show( notInteger.Message,
74                  "Invalid Operation", MessageBoxButtons.OK,
75                  MessageBoxIcon.Error );
76          }
77
78          // display MessageBox if negative number input
79          catch ( NegativeNumberException error )
80          {
81              MessageBox.Show( error.Message, "Invalid Operation",
82                  MessageBoxButtons.OK, MessageBoxIcon.Error );
83          }
84
```

Fig. 8.5   **SquareRootTest** class throws an exception if error occurs when calculating the square root. (Part 2 of 3.)

```
85        } // end method squareRootButton_Click
86
87    } // end class SquareRootTest
```

Fig. 8.5   SquareRootTest class throws an exception if error occurs when calculating the square root. (Part 3 of 3.)

8.8 Handling Overflows with Operators checked and unchecked

In .NET, the primitive data types are stored in fixed-size structures. For instance, the maximum value of an **int** is 2,147,483,647. In integer arithmetic, a value larger than 2,147,483,647 causes *overflow*—type **int** cannot represent such a number. Overflow also can occur with other C# primitive types. Overflows often cause programs to produce incorrect results.

C# provides operators **checked** and **unchecked** to specify whether integer arithmetic occurs in a *checked context* or *unchecked context*. In a checked context, the CLR throws an **OverflowException** (namespace **System**) if overflow occurs during evaluation of an arithmetic expression. In an unchecked context, the result is truncated if overflow occurs.

The operators **++**, **--**, *****, **/**, **+** and **-** (both unary and binary) may cause overflow when used with integral data types (such as **int** and **long**). Also, explicit conversions between integral data types can cause overflow. For example, converting the integer 1,000,000 from **int** to **short** results in overflow, because a **short** can store a maximum value of 32,767. Figure 8.6 demonstrates overflows occurring in both checked and unchecked contexts.

The program begins by defining **int** variables **number1** and **number2** (lines 11–12) and assigning each variable the maximum value for an **int**—2,147,483,647 (defined by **Int32.MaxValue**). Next, line 13 defines variable **sum** (initialized to 0) to store the **sum** of **number1** and **number2**. Then, lines 15–16 output the values of **number1** and **number2**.

Lines 19–25 define a **try** block in which line 24 adds **number1** and **number2** in a checked context. The expression to evaluate in a checked context appears in parentheses following keyword **checked**. Variables **number1** and **number2** already contain the maximum value for an **int**, so adding these values causes an **OverflowException**. The **catch** handler at lines 28–31 catches the exception and outputs its **string** representation.

Line 39 performs the same calculation in an unchecked context. The result of the calculation should be 4,294,967,294. However, this value requires more memory than an **int** can store, so operator **unchecked** truncates part of the value, resulting in **-2** in the output. As you can see, the result of the unchecked calculation is not the actual sum of the variables.

```
1    // Fig. 8.6: Overflow.cs
2    // Demonstrating operators checked and unchecked.
3
4    using System;
5
6    // demonstrates using the checked and unchecked operators
7    class Overflow
8    {
9       static void Main( string[] args )
10      {
11         int number1 = Int32.MaxValue;   // 2,147,483,647
12         int number2 = Int32.MaxValue;   // 2,147,483,647
13         int sum = 0;
14
15         Console.WriteLine(
16            "number1: {0}\nnumber2: {1}", number1, number2 );
17
18         // calculate sum of number1 and number2
19         try
20         {
21            Console.WriteLine(
22               "\nSum integers in checked context:" );
23
24            sum = checked( number1 + number2 );
25         }
26
27         // catch overflow exception
28         catch ( OverflowException overflowException )
29         {
30            Console.WriteLine( overflowException.ToString() );
31         }
32
33         Console.WriteLine(
34            "\nsum after checked operation: {0}", sum );
35
36         Console.WriteLine(
37            "\nSum integers in unchecked context:" );
38
39         sum = unchecked( number1 + number2 );
40
41         Console.WriteLine(
42            "sum after unchecked operation: {0}", sum );
43
44      } // end method Main
45
46   } // end class Overflow
```

Fig. 8.6   Operators **checked** and **unchecked** and the handling of arithmetic overflow. (Part 1 of 2.)

```
number1: 2147483647
number2: 2147483647

Sum integers in checked context:
System.OverflowException: Arithmetic operation resulted in an over-
flow.
   at Overflow.Overflow.Main(String[] args) in
      C:\books\2001\cspfep1\cspfep1_examples\ch08\Fig08_06\
         Overflow\Overflow.cs:line 24

sum after checked operation: 0

Sum integers in unchecked context:
sum after unchecked operation: -2
```

Fig. 8.6   Operators **checked** and **unchecked** and the handling of arithmetic overflow. (Part 2 of 2.)

By default, calculations occur in an unchecked context—a dangerous practice, unless the calculations are performed on constant expressions (such as literal integer values). Constant expressions are evaluated in a checked context at compile time. Overflows in such expressions results in compile-time errors. It is possible to specify in a project's properties that the default context for evaluating nonconstant expressions should be to check for arithmetic overflow. In the properties for your project, you can set the checked context as the default. To do so, first select your project in the **Solution Explorer**. Next, in the **View** menu, select **Property Pages**. In the **Property Pages** dialog, click the **Configuration Properties** folder. Under **Code Generation**, change the value of **Check for Arithmetic Overflow/Underflow** to `true`.

Good Programming Practice 8.4

Use a checked context when performing calculations that can result in overflows, and define exception handlers that can process any overflows that do occur.

Software Engineering Observation 8.12

Keywords **checked** *and* **unchecked** *can be used to evaluate blocks of statements in checked and unchecked contexts, respectively, by following the appropriate keyword with a block of code in braces (* **{}** *).*

In this chapter, we have demonstrated how the exception-handling mechanism works and discussed how to make applications more robust by writing exception handlers to process potential problems. As programmers develop new applications, it is important to investigate potential exceptions thrown by the methods your program invokes or by the CLR; then implement appropriate exception-handling code to make the applications more robust.

8.9 Summary

An exception is an indication of a problem that occurs during a program's execution. Exception handling enables programmers to create applications that can resolve exceptions, often allowing a program to continue execution as if no problems were encountered and thereby permitting programmers to write clear, robust and more fault-tolerant programs.

Exception handling also enables the programmer to remove error-handling code from the "main line" of the program's execution.

When a method detects an error and is unable to handle it, the method throws an exception. There is no guarantee that there will be an exception handler to process that kind of exception. If there is, the exception will be caught and handled. Exception-handling code uses **try/catch/finally** sequences.

A **try** block contains the code that could throw exceptions and the code that should not execute if an exception occurs. A **try** block consists of keyword **try** followed by braces (**{}**) that delimit a block of code in which exceptions could occur. If an exception occurs in a **try** block, the block expires, and program control transfers to the first **catch** handler following the **try** block. Each **catch** handler begins with keyword **catch** followed by an optional exception parameter that specifies the type of exception handled by the **catch** handler. The exception-handling code appears in the body of the **catch** handler. The CLR searches for the first **catch** handler that can process the type of exception that occurred. The appropriate handler is the first one in which the thrown exception's type matches, or is derived from, the exception type specified by the **catch** handler's exception parameter.

After the last **catch** handler, an optional **finally** block contains code that always executes, regardless of whether an exception occurs. The **finally** block is an ideal location to place resource-deallocation code for resources acquired and manipulated in the corresponding **try** block. If no exceptions occur or if an exception is caught and handled, the program resumes execution with the next statement after the **try/catch/finally** sequence.

Class **Exception** (of namespace **System**) is the base class of the .NET Framework exception hierarchy. **ApplicationException** is a base class that programmers can extend to create new exception data types that are specific to their applications. Programs can recover from most **ApplicationException**s and continue execution. The CLR generates **SystemException**s. Programs typically cannot recover from most exceptions thrown by the CLR. Therefore, programs generally should not throw **SystemException**s nor attempt to **catch** such exceptions.

A **throw** statement throws an exception object. A **throw** statement can be used in a **catch** handler to rethrow an exception. This event indicates that the **catch** handler performed partial processing of the exception and is now passing the exception back to a calling method for further processing.

Exception property **Message** stores the error message associated with an **Exception** object. This message may be a default message associated with the exception type or a customized message passed to an exception object's constructor at the time a program creates the exception. **Exception** property **StackTrace** contains a string that represents the method-call stack at the throw point of the exception. **Exception** property **InnerException** typically is used to "wrap" a caught exception object in a new exception object, and subsequently throw the object of that new exception type.

C# provides operators **checked** and **unchecked** to specify whether arithmetic occurs in a checked context or an unchecked context. In a checked context, operator **checked** throws an **OverflowException** if overflow occurs when evaluating an arithmetic expression. In an unchecked context, operator **unchecked** truncates the result if overflow occurs.

Graphical User Interface
Concepts: Part 1

Objectives

- To understand the design principles of graphical user interfaces.
- To understand, use and create events.
- To understand the namespaces containing graphical user interface components and event-handling classes and interfaces.
- To create graphical user interfaces.
- To create and manipulate buttons, labels, lists, textboxes and panels.
- To use mouse and keyboard events.

…the wisest prophets make sure of the event first.
Horace Walpole

…The user should feel in control of the computer; not the other way around. This is achieved in applications that embody three qualities: responsiveness, permissiveness, and consistency.
Inside Macintosh, Volume 1
Apple Computer, Inc. 1985

All the better to see you with my dear.
The Big Bad Wolf to Little Red Riding Hood

Outline

9.1	Introduction
9.2	Windows Forms
9.3	Event-Handling Model
	9.3.1 Basic Event Handling
9.4	Control Properties and Layout
9.5	Labels, TextBoxes and Buttons
9.6	GroupBoxes and Panels
9.7	CheckBoxes and RadioButtons
9.8	PictureBoxes
9.9	Mouse Event Handling
9.10	Keyboard Event Handling
9.11	Summary

9.1 Introduction

A *graphical user interface (GUI)* allows users to interact with a program visually. A GUI (pronounced "GOO-EE") gives a program a distinctive "look" and "feel." By providing different applications with a consistent set of intuitive user-interface components, GUIs allow users to spend less time trying to remember which keystroke sequences perform what functions and spend more time using the program in a productive manner.

 Look-and-Feel Observation 9.1

Consistent user interfaces enable users to learn new applications faster.

As an example of a GUI, Fig. 9.1 contains an Internet Explorer window with some of its *GUI components* labeled. In the window, there is a *menu bar* containing *menus*, including **File**, **Edit**, **View**, **Favorites**, **Tools** and **Help**. Below the menu bar is a set of *buttons*; each has a defined task in Internet Explorer. Below the buttons is a *textbox,* in which the user can type the location of a World Wide Web site to visit. To the left of the textbox is a *label* that indicates the textbox's purpose. On the far right and bottom there are *scrollbars*. Scrollbars are used when there is more information in a window than can be displayed at once. By moving the scrollbars back and forth, the user can view different portions of the Web page. The menus, buttons, textboxes, labels and scrollbars are part of Internet Explorer's GUI. They form a user-friendly interface through which the user interacts with the Internet Explorer Web browser.

GUIs are built from GUI components (sometimes called *controls* or *widgets*—short for *window gadgets*). A GUI component is an object with which the user interacts via the mouse or keyboard. Several common GUI components are listed in Fig. 9.2. In the sections that follow, we discuss each of these GUI components in detail. In the next chapter, we discuss more advanced GUI components.

Button   Label   Menu   Menu bar   Textbox   Scrollbar

Fig. 9.1   Sample Internet Explorer window with GUI components.

Control	Description
`Label`	An area in which icons or uneditable text can be displayed.
`TextBox`	An area in which the user inputs data from the keyboard. The area also can display information.
`Button`	An area that triggers an event when clicked.
`CheckBox`	A GUI control that is either selected or not selected.
`ComboBox`	A drop-down list of items from which the user can make a selection, by clicking an item in the list or by typing into the box, if permitted.
`ListBox`	An area in which a list of items is displayed from which the user can make a selection by clicking once on any element. Multiple elements can be selected.
`Panel`	A container in which components can be placed.
`ScrollBar`	Allows the user to access a range of values that cannot normally fit in its container.

Fig. 9.2   Some basic GUI components .

9.2 Windows Forms

Windows Forms (also called *WinForms*) create GUIs for programs. A form is a graphical element that appears on the desktop. A form can be a dialog, a window or an *MDI window*

(*multiple document interface window*, discussed in Chapter 10, GUI Graphical User Interface Concepts: Part 2). A *component* is a class that implements the **IComponent** *interface*, which defines the behaviors that components must implement. A *control*, such as a button or label, is a component with a graphical part. Controls are visible, whereas components, which lack graphical parts, are not.

Figure 9.3 displays the Windows Forms controls and components contained in the Visual Studio .NET **Toolbox**—the first two screens show the controls and the last screen shows the components. When the user selects a component or control, the user then can add that component or control to the form. Note that the **Pointer** (the icon at the top of the list) is not a component; rather it represents the default mouse action. Highlighting it allows the programmer to use the mouse cursor instead of adding an item. In this chapter and the next, we discuss many of these controls.

When interacting with windows, we say that the *active window* has the *focus*. The active window is the frontmost window and has a highlighted title bar. A window becomes the active window when the user clicks somewhere inside it. When a window has focus, the operating system directs user input from the keyboard and mouse to that application.

Fig. 9.3   Components and controls for Windows Forms.

The form acts as a *container* for components and controls. Controls must be added to the form using code. When we drag a control from the **Toolbox** onto the form, Visual Studio .NET generates this code for us, which instantiates the control and sets the control's basic properties. We could write the code ourselves, but it is much easier to create and modify controls using the **Toolbox** and **Properties** window, letting Visual Studio .NET handle the details. We introduced such *visual programming* earlier in the book. In the next several chapters, we build much richer GUIs through visual programming.

When the user interacts with a control by using the mouse or keyboard, events (discussed in Section 9.3) are generated, and event handlers process those events. Events typically cause something to happen in response. For example, clicking the **OK** button in a **MessageBox** generates an event. An event handler in class **MessageBox** closes the **MessageBox** in response to this event.

Each .NET Framework class (i.e., form, component and control) we present in this chapter is in the *System.Windows.Forms namespace*. Class **Form**, the basic window used by Windows applications, is fully qualified as **System.Windows.Forms.Form**. Likewise, class **Button** is actually **System.Windows.Forms.Button**.

The general design process for creating Windows applications requires creating a Windows Form, setting its properties, adding controls, setting their properties and implementing the event handlers. Figure 9.4 lists common **Form** properties and events.

Form Properties and Events	Description / Delegate and Event Arguments
Common Properties	
AcceptButton	Which button will be clicked when *Enter* is pressed.
AutoScroll	Whether scrollbars appear when needed (if data fill more than one screen).
CancelButton	Button that is clicked when the *Escape* key is pressed.
FormBorderStyle	Border of the form (e.g., **none**, **single**, **3D**, **sizable**).
Font	Font of text displayed on the form, as well as the default font of controls added to the form.
Text	Text in the form's title bar.
Common Methods	
Close	Closes form and releases all resources. A closed form cannot be reopened.
Hide	Hides form (does not release resources).
Show	Displays a hidden form.
Common Events	*(Delegate **EventHandler**, event arguments **EventArgs**)*
Load	Occurs before a form is shown. Visual Studio .NET generates a default event handler when the programmer double clicks on the form in the designer.

Fig. 9.4   Common **Form** properties and events.

Visual Studio .NET generates most GUI-related code when we create controls and event handlers. Programmers can use Visual Studio .NET to perform most of these tasks graphically, by dragging and dropping components onto the form and setting properties in the **Properties** window. In visual programming, the IDE generally maintains GUI-related code, and the programmer writes the event handlers.

9.3 Event-Handling Model

GUIs are *event driven* (i.e., they generate *events* when the program's user interacts with the GUI). Typical interactions include moving the mouse, clicking the mouse, clicking a button, typing in a textbox, selecting an item from a menu and closing a window. Event handlers are methods that process events and perform tasks. For example, consider a form that changes color when a button is clicked. When clicked, the button generates an event and passes it to the event handler, and the event-handler code changes the form's color.

Each control that can generate events has an associated delegate that defines the signature for that control's event handlers. Recall from Chapter 7 that delegates are objects that reference methods. Event delegates are *multicast* (class **MulticastDelegate**)— they contain lists of method references. Each method must have the same *signature* (i.e., the same list of parameters). In the event-handling model, delegates act as intermediaries between objects that generate events and methods that handle those events (Fig. 9.5).

Software Engineering Observation 9.1

Delegates enable classes to specify methods that will not be named or implemented until the class is instantiated. This is extremely helpful in creating event handlers. For instance, the creator of the **Form** *class does not need to name or define the method that will handle the* **Click** *event. Using delegates, the class can specify when such an event handler would be called. The programmers that create their own forms then can name and define this event handler. As long as it has been registered with the proper delegate, the method will be called at the proper time.*

Once an event is raised, every method that the delegate references is called. Every method in the delegate must have the same signature, because they are all passed the same information.

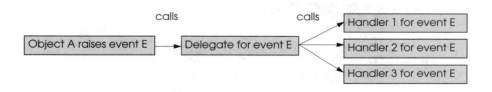

Fig. 9.5   Event-handling model using delegates.

9.3.1 Basic Event Handling

In most cases, we do not have to create our own events. Instead, we can handle the events generated by .NET controls such as buttons and text boxes. These controls already have delegates for every event they can raise. The programmer creates the event handler and registers it with the delegate—Visual Studio .NET helps with this task. In the following example, we create a form that displays a message box when clicked. Afterwards, we will analyze the event code that Visual Studio .NET generates.

First, create a new Windows application. To register and define an event handler, click the **Events** icon (the yellow lightning bolt) in the form's **Properties** window (Fig. 9.6). This window allows the programmer to access, modify and create event handlers for a control. The left panel lists the events that the object can generate. The right panel lists the registered event handlers for the corresponding event; this list is initially empty. The dropdown button indicates that multiple handlers can be registered for one event. A brief description of the event appears on the bottom of the window.

In this example, the form will take some action when clicked. Double-click the **Click** event in the **Properties** window to create an empty event handler in the program code.

```
private void FormName_Click( object sender, System.EventArgs e )
{

}
```

This is the method that will be called when the form is clicked. As a response, we will have the form display a message box. To do this, insert the statement

```
MessageBox.Show( "Form was pressed." );
```

Fig. 9.6   Events section of the **Properties** window.

into the event handler to get

```
private void FormName_Click( object sender, System.EventArgs e )
{
    MessageBox.Show( "Form was pressed" );
}
```

We can now compile and execute the program, which appears in Fig. 9.7. Whenever the form is clicked, a message box appears.

We now discuss the details of the program. First, we create an event handler (lines 26–29). Every event handler must have the signature that the corresponding event delegate specifies. Event handlers are passed two object references. The first is a reference to the object that raised the event (**sender**), and the second is a reference to an event arguments object (**e**). Argument **e** is of type **EventArgs**. Class **EventArgs** is the base class for objects that contain event information.

To create the event handler, we must find the delegate's signature. When we double-click an event name in the **Properties** window, Visual Studio .NET creates a method with the proper signature. The naming convention is *ControlName_EventName*; in our case the event handler is **MyForm_Click**. If we do not use the **Properties** window, we must look up the event arguments class. Consult the documentation index under *ControlName* **class** (i.e., **Form class**) and click the **events** section (Fig. 9.8). This displays a list of all the events the class can generate. Click the name of an event to bring up its delegate, event argument type and a description (Fig. 9.9).

```
1   // Fig. 9.7: SimpleEventExample.cs
2   // Using Visual Studio .NET to create event handlers.
3
4   using System;
5   using System.Drawing;
6   using System.Collections;
7   using System.ComponentModel;
8   using System.Windows.Forms;
9   using System.Data;
10
11  // program that shows a simple event handler
12  public class MyForm : System.Windows.Forms.Form
13  {
14      private System.ComponentModel.Container components = null;
15
16      // Visual Studio .NET generated code
17
18      [STAThread]
19      static void Main()
20      {
21          Application.Run( new MyForm() );
22      }
23
```

Fig. 9.7   Simple event-handling example using visual programming. (Part 1 of 2.)

```
24        // Visual Studio .NET creates an empty handler,
25        // we write definition: show message box when form clicked
26        private void MyForm_Click( object sender, System.EventArgs e )
27        {
28            MessageBox.Show( "Form was pressed" );
29        }
30
31    } // end class MyForm
```

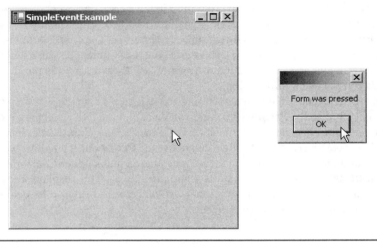

Fig. 9.7   Simple event-handling example using visual programming. (Part 2 of 2.)

Class name   List of events

Fig. 9.8   List of **Form** events.

Fig. 9.9   Details of **Click** event.

The format of the event-handling method is, in general,

```
void ControlName_EventName( object sender, EventArgs e )
{
    event-handling code
}
```

where the name of the event handler is by default the name of the control, followed by an underscore (_) and the name of the event. Event handlers have return type **void** and take two arguments—an **object** (usually **sender**) and an instance of an event argument class. The differences between the various **EventArgs** classes are discussed in the following sections.

Good Programming Practice 9.1

Use the event-handler naming convention ControlName_EventName *to keep methods organized. This tells a user which event a method handles, and for which control. Visual Studio .NET uses this naming convention when creating event handlers from the **Properties** window.*

After creating the event handler, we must *register* it with the delegate object, which contains a list of event handlers to call. Registering an event handler with a delegate object involves adding the event handler to the delegate's invocation list. Controls have a *delegate reference* for each of their events—the delegate reference has the same name as the event. For example, if we are handling event *EventName* for object **myControl**, then the delegate reference is **myControl.**EventName. Visual Studio .NET registers events for us with code such as the following from method **InitializeComponent**:

```
this.Click += new System.EventHandler( this.MyForm_Click );
```

The left-hand side is the delegate reference **MyForm.Click**. (**this** refers to an object of class **MyForm**.) The delegate reference is initially empty—we must assign to it an object reference (the right-hand side). We must create a new delegate object for each event handler. We create a new delegate object by writing

new System.EventHandler(*methodName* **)**

which returns a delegate object initialized with method *methodName*. The *methodName* is the name of the event handler, in our case it is **MyForm.MyForm_Click**. The **+=** operator adds an **EventHandler** delegate to the current delegate's invocation list. Since the delegate reference is initially empty, registering the first event handler creates a delegate object. In general, to register an event handler, write

objectName.*EventName* **+= new System.EventHandler(**
    MyEventHandler **);**

We can add more event handlers using similar statements. *Event multicasting* is the ability to have multiple handlers for one event. Each event handler is called when the event occurs, but the order in which the event handlers are called is indeterminate. Use the **-=** operator to remove the method from the delegate object.

Common Programming Error 9.1

Assuming that multiple event handlers registered for the same event are called in a particular order can lead to logic errors. If the order is important, register the first event handler and have it call the others in order, passing the sender and event arguments.

Software Engineering Observation 9.2

*Events for prepackaged .NET components usually have consistent naming schemes. If the event is named **EventName**, then its delegate is **EventNameEventHandler**, and the event arguments class is **EventNameEventArgs**. However, events that use class **EventArgs** use delegate **EventHandler**.*

To review: The information needed to register an event is the **EventArgs** class (a parameter for the event handler) and the **EventHandler** delegate (to register the event handler). Visual Studio .NET can create this code for us, or we can type it in ourselves. If Visual Studio .NET creates the code, the programmer does not have to deal with going through all the steps, but the programmer also does not have complete control of everything that is going on. For simple events and event handlers it is often easier to allow Visual Studio .NET to generate this code. For more complicated solutions, registering your own event handlers might be necessary. In the upcoming sections, we will indicate the **Event-Args** class and the **EventHandler** delegate for each event we cover. To find more information about a particular type of event, search the help documentation for *ClassName* **class** and refer to the **events** subcategory.

9.4 Control Properties and Layout

This section overviews properties that are common to many controls. Controls derive from class **Control** (namespace **System.Windows.Forms**). Figure 9.10 contains a list of common properties and events for class **Control**. The **Text** property specifies the text that appears on a control, which may vary depending on the context. For example, the text of a Windows Form is its title bar, and the text of a button appears on its face. The **Focus** method transfers the focus to a control. When the focus is on a control, it becomes the active control. When the *Tab* key is pressed, the **TabIndex** property determines the order in which controls are given focus. The **TabIndex** property is automatically set by Visual Studio .NET, but can be changed by the programmer. This is helpful for the user who enters information in many different locations—the user can enter information and quickly select the next control by pressing the *Tab* key. The **Enabled** property indicates whether the control can be used. Programs can set property **Enabled** to false when an option is unavailable to the user. In most cases, the control's text will appear gray (rather than black), when a control is disabled. Without having to disable a control, the control can be hidden from the user by setting the **Visible** property to **false** or by calling method **Hide**. When a control's **Visible** property is set to **false**, the control still exists, but it is not shown on the form.

Class **Control** Properties and Methods	Description
Common Properties	
BackColor	Background color of the control.
BackgroundImage	Background image of the control.
Enabled	Whether the control is enabled (i.e., if the user can interact with it). A disabled control will still be displayed, but "grayed-out"—portions of the control will become gray.
Focused	Whether a control has focus. (The control that is currently being used in some way.)
Font	**Font** used to display control's **Text**.
ForeColor	Foreground color of the control. This is usually the color used to display the control's **Text** property.
TabIndex	Tab order of the control. When the *Tab* key is pressed, the focus is moved to controls in increasing tab order. This order can be set by the programmer.
TabStop	If **true**, user can use the *Tab* key to select the control.
Text	Text associated with the control. The location and appearance varies with the type of control.
TextAlign	The alignment of the text on the control. One of three horizontal positions (left, center or right) and one of three vertical positions (top, middle or bottom).
Visible	Whether the control is visible.
Common Methods	
Focus	Transfers the focus to the control.
Hide	Hides the control (sets **Visible** to **false**).
Show	Shows the control (sets **Visible** to **true**).

Fig. 9.10 Class **Control** properties and methods.

Visual Studio .NET allows the programmer to *anchor* and *dock* controls, which help to specify the layout of controls inside a container (such as a form). Anchoring allows controls to stay a fixed distance from the sides of the container, even when the control is resized. Docking allows controls to extend themselves along the sides of their containers.

A user may want a control to appear in a certain position (top, bottom, left or right) in a form even when that form is resized. The user can specify this by *anchoring* the control to a side (top, bottom, left or right). The control then maintains a fixed distance from the side to its parent container. In most cases, the parent container is a form; however, other controls can act as a parent container.

When parent containers are resized, all controls move. Unanchored controls move relative to their original position on the form, while anchored controls move so that they will be the same distance from each side that they are anchored to. For example, in Fig. 9.11, the topmost button is anchored to the top and left sides of the parent form. When the form is resized, the anchored button moves so that it remains a constant distance from the top and left sides of the form (its parent). The unanchored button changes position as the form is resized.

Create a simple Windows application that contains two controls. Anchor one control to the right side by setting the **Anchor** property as shown in Fig. 9.12. Leave the other control unanchored. Now, resize the form by dragging the right side farther to the right. Notice that both controls move. The anchored control moves so that it is always the same distance to the right wall. The unanchored control moves so that it is in the same place on the form, relative to each side. This control will continue to be somewhat closer to whatever sides it was originally close to, but will still reposition itself when the user resizes the application window.

Sometimes a programmer wants a control to span the entire side of the form, even when the form is resized. This is useful when we want one control to remain prevalent on the form, such as the status bar that might appear at the bottom of a program. *Docking* allows a control to spread itself along an entire side (left, right, top or bottom) of its parent container. When the parent is resized, the docked control resizes as well. In Fig. 9.13, a button is docked to the top of the form. (It lays across the top portion.) When the form is resized, the button is resized as well—the button always fills the entire top portion of the form. The **Fill** dock option effectively docks the control to all sides of its parent, which causes it to fill its entire parent. Windows Forms contain property **DockPadding**, which sets the distance from docked controls to the edge of the form. The default value is zero, causing the controls to attach to the edge of the form. The control layout properties are summarized in Fig. 9.14.

Fig. 9.11 Anchoring demonstration.

Click down-arrow in **Anchor** property to display anchoring window

Darkened bar indicates side to which control is anchored

Fig. 9.12　Manipulating the **Anchor** property of a control.

Before resizing

After resizing

Control extends along top portion of form

Fig. 9.13　Docking demonstration.

Common Layout Properties	Description
Common Properties	
Anchor	Side of parent container at which to anchor control—values can be combined, such as **Top, Left**.
Dock	Side of parent container to dock control—values cannot be combined.
DockPadding (for containers)	Sets the dock spacing for controls inside the container. Default is zero, so controls appear flush against the side of the container.
Location	Location of the upper left corner of the control, relative to its container.

Fig. 9.14　Class **Control** layout properties. (Part 1 of 2.)

Common Layout Properties	Description
Size	Size of the control. Takes a **Size** structure, which has properties **Height** and **Width**.
MinimumSize, **MaximumSize** (for Windows Forms)	The minimum and maximum size of the form.

Fig. 9.14   Class **Control** layout properties. (Part 2 of 2.)

The docking and anchoring options refer to the parent container, which may or may not be the form. (We learn about other parent containers later this chapter.) The minimum and maximum form sizes can be set using properties **MinimumSize** and **MaximumSize**, respectively. Both properties use the **Size** structure, which has properties **Height** and **Width**, specifying the size of the form. These properties allow the programmer to design the GUI layout for a given size range. To set a form to a fixed size, set its minimum and maximum size to the same value.

Look-and-Feel Observation 9.2

Allow Windows forms to be resized—this enables users with limited screen space or multiple applications running at once to use the application more easily. Check that the GUI layout appears consistent for all permissible form sizes.

9.5 Labels, TextBoxes and Buttons

Labels provide text instructions or information about the program. Labels are defined with class **Label**, which derives from class **Control**. A **Label** displays *read-only text*, or text that the user cannot modify. Once labels are created, programs rarely change their contents. Figure 9.15 lists common **Label** properties.

A *textbox* (class **TextBox**) is an area in which text can be either input by the user from the keyboard or displayed. A *password textbox* is a **TextBox** that hides what the user entered. As the user types in characters, the password textbox displays only a certain character (usually *****). Altering the **PasswordChar** property of a textbox makes it a password textbox and sets the appropriate character to be displayed. Deleting the value of **PasswordChar** in the **Properties** window sets the textbox back to a regular textbox. Figure 9.16 lists the common properties and events of **TextBox**es.

A *button* is a control that the user clicks to trigger a specific action. A program can use several other types of buttons, such as *checkboxes* and *radio buttons*. All the button types are derived from **ButtonBase** (namespace **System.Windows.Forms**), which defines common button features. In this section, we concentrate on the class **Button**, which is often used to initiate a command. The other button types are covered in subsequent sections. The text on the face of a **Button** is called a *button label*. Figure 9.17 lists the common properties and events of **Button**s.

Label Properties	Description / Delegate and Event Arguments
Common Properties	
Font	The font used by the text on the **Label**.
Text	The text to appear on the **Label**.
TextAlign	The alignment of the **Label**'s text on the control. One of three horizontal positions (**left**, **center** or **right**) and one of three vertical positions (**top**, **middle** or **bottom**).

Fig. 9.15 **Label** properties.

TextBox Properties and Events	Description / Delegate and Event Arguments
Common Properties	
AcceptsReturn	If **true**, pressing *Enter* creates a new line if textbox spans multiple lines. If **false**, pressing *Enter* clicks the default button of the form.
Multiline	If **true**, textbox can span multiple lines. Default is **false**.
PasswordChar	Single character to display instead of typed text, making the **TextBox** a password box. If no character is specified, **Textbox** displays the typed text.
ReadOnly	If **true**, **TextBox** has a gray background and its text cannot be edited. Default is **false**.
ScrollBars	For multiline textboxes, indicates which scrollbars appear (**none**, **horizontal**, **vertical** or **both**).
Text	The text to be displayed in the text box.
Common Events	*(Delegate **EventHandler**, event arguments **EventArgs**)*
TextChanged	Raised when text changes in **TextBox** (the user added or deleted characters). Default event when this control is double clicked in the designer.

Fig. 9.16 **TextBox** properties and events.

Look-and-Feel Observation 9.3

*Although **Label**s, **TextBox**es and other controls can respond to mouse-button clicks, **Button**s naturally convey this meaning. Use **Button**s (e.g., **OK**), rather than other types of controls, to initiate user actions.*

The program in Fig. 9.18 uses a **TextBox**, a **Button** and a **Label**. The user enters text into a password box and clicks the **Button**. The text then appears in the **Label**. Normally, we would not display this text—the purpose of password textboxes is to hide the text being entered by the user from anyone who may be looking over a person's shoulder.

Button properties and events	Description / Delegate and Event Arguments
Common Properties	
Text	Text displayed on the **Button** face.
Common Events	*(Delegate **EventHandler**, event arguments **EventArgs**)*
Click	Raised when user clicks the control. Default event when this control is double clicked in the designer.

Fig. 9.17 Button properties and events.

```
1   // Fig. 9.18: LabelTextBoxButtonTest.cs
2   // Using a Textbox, Label and Button to display
3   // the hidden text in a password box.
4
5   using System;
6   using System.Drawing;
7   using System.Collections;
8   using System.ComponentModel;
9   using System.Windows.Forms;
10  using System.Data;
11
12  // namespace contains our form to display hidden text
13  namespace LabelTextBoxButtonTest
14  {
15     /// <summary>
16     /// form that creates a password textbox and
17     /// a label to display textbox contents
18     /// </summary>
19     public class LabelTextBoxButtonTest :
20        System.Windows.Forms.Form
21     {
22        private System.Windows.Forms.Button displayPasswordButton;
23        private System.Windows.Forms.Label displayPasswordLabel;
24        private System.Windows.Forms.TextBox inputPasswordTextBox;
25
26        /// <summary>
27        /// Required designer variable.
28        /// </summary>
29        private System.ComponentModel.Container components = null;
30
31        // default contructor
32        public LabelTextBoxButtonTest()
33        {
34           InitializeComponent();
35        }
36
```

Fig. 9.18 Program to display hidden text in a password box. (Part 1 of 4.)

```
37          /// <summary>
38          /// Clean up any resources being used.
39          /// </summary>
40          protected override void Dispose( bool disposing )
41          {
42             if ( disposing )
43             {
44                if ( components != null )
45                {
46                   components.Dispose();
47                }
48             }
49
50             base.Dispose( disposing );
51          }
52
53          #region Windows Form Designer generated code
54          /// <summary>
55          /// Required method for Designer support - do not modify
56          /// the contents of this method with the code editor.
57          /// </summary>
58          private void InitializeComponent()
59          {
60             this.displayPasswordButton =
61                new System.Windows.Forms.Button();
62             this.inputPasswordTextBox =
63                new System.Windows.Forms.TextBox();
64             this.displayPasswordLabel =
65                new System.Windows.Forms.Label();
66             this.SuspendLayout();
67
68             //
69             // displayPasswordButton
70             //
71             this.displayPasswordButton.Location =
72                new System.Drawing.Point( 96, 96 );
73             this.displayPasswordButton.Name =
74                "displayPasswordButton";
75             this.displayPasswordButton.TabIndex = 1;
76             this.displayPasswordButton.Text = "Show Me";
77             this.displayPasswordButton.Click +=
78                new System.EventHandler(
79                this.displayPasswordButton_Click );
80
81             //
82             // inputPasswordTextBox
83             //
84             this.inputPasswordTextBox.Location =
85                new System.Drawing.Point( 16, 16 );
86             this.inputPasswordTextBox.Name =
87                "inputPasswordTextBox";
88             this.inputPasswordTextBox.PasswordChar = '*';
```

Fig. 9.18   Program to display hidden text in a password box. (Part 2 of 4.)

```
89              this.inputPasswordTextBox.Size =
90                 new System.Drawing.Size( 264, 20 );
91              this.inputPasswordTextBox.TabIndex = 0;
92              this.inputPasswordTextBox.Text = "";
93
94              //
95              // displayPasswordLabel
96              //
97              this.displayPasswordLabel.BorderStyle =
98                 System.Windows.Forms.BorderStyle.Fixed3D;
99              this.displayPasswordLabel.Location =
100                new System.Drawing.Point( 16, 48 );
101             this.displayPasswordLabel.Name =
102                "displayPasswordLabel";
103             this.displayPasswordLabel.Size =
104                new System.Drawing.Size( 264, 23 );
105             this.displayPasswordLabel.TabIndex = 2;
106
107             //
108             // LabelTextBoxButtonTest
109             //
110             this.AutoScaleBaseSize =
111                new System.Drawing.Size( 5, 13 );
112             this.ClientSize =
113                new System.Drawing.Size( 292, 133 );
114             this.Controls.AddRange(
115                new System.Windows.Forms.Control[] {
116                   this.displayPasswordLabel,
117                   this.inputPasswordTextBox,
118                   this.displayPasswordButton});
119             this.Name = "LabelTextBoxButtonTest";
120             this.Text = "LabelTextBoxButtonTest";
121             this.ResumeLayout( false );
122
123          } // end method InitializeComponent
124
125          // end collapsible region started on line 53
126          #endregion
127
128          /// <summary>
129          /// The main entry point for the application.
130          /// </summary>
131          [STAThread]
132          static void Main()
133          {
134             Application.Run( new LabelTextBoxButtonTest() );
135          }
136
137          // display user input on label
138          protected void displayPasswordButton_Click(
139             object sender, System.EventArgs e )
140          {
```

Fig. 9.18   Program to display hidden text in a password box. (Part 3 of 4.)

```
141                    // text has not changed
142                    displayPasswordLabel.Text =
143                        inputPasswordTextBox.Text;
144                }
145
146        } // end class LabelTextBoxButtonTest
147
148 } // end namespace LabelTextBoxButtonTest
```

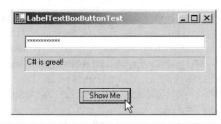

Fig. 9.18 Program to display hidden text in a password box. (Part 4 of 4.)

First, we create the GUI by dragging the components (a **Button**, a **Label** and a **TextBox**) onto the form. Once the components are positioned, we change their names in the **Properties** window (by setting the **(Name)** property) from the default values—**textBox1**, **label1**, **button1**—to the more descriptive **displayPasswordLabel**, **inputPasswordTextBox** and **displayPasswordButton**. Visual Studio .NET creates the code and places it inside method **InitializeComponent**. Now that the reader has an understanding of object-oriented programming, we can mention that the **(Name)** property is not really a property, but a means of changing the variable name of the object reference. For convenience, this value can be changed in the **Properties** window of Visual Studio .NET. This value, however, is not actually manipulated by a property.

We then set **displayPasswordLabel**'s **Text** property to "**Show Me**" and clear the **Text** of **displayPasswordLabel** and **inputPasswordTextBox** so that they are initially blank when the program runs. The **BorderStyle** property of **display-PasswordLabel** is set to **Fixed3D**, to give our **Label** a three-dimensional appearance. Notice that **TextBox**es have their **BorderStyle** property set to **Fixed3D** by default. The password character is set by assigning the asterisk character (*****) to the **PasswordChar** property. This property can take only one character.

Let us examine the code that Visual Studio .NET generates by right-clicking the design and selecting **View Code**. This is important because not every change can be made in the **Properties** window.

We have learned in previous chapters that Visual Studio .NET adds comments to our code. These comments appear throughout the code, such as on lines 15–18. In future examples we remove some of these generated comments to make programs more concise and readable (unless they illustrate a capability we have not yet covered).

Visual Studio .NET inserts declarations for the controls we add to the form (lines 22–24), namely, the **Label**, **TextBox** and **Button**. The IDE manages these declarations for us, making it easy to add and remove controls. Line 29 declares reference **components**—an array to hold the components that we add. We are not using any components in this program (only controls), and thus the reference is **null**.

The constructor for our form is created for us—it calls method **InitializeComponent**. Method **InitializeComponent** creates the components and controls in the form and sets their properties. The usual "to do" comments generated by Visual Studio .NET have been removed, because there is no more code that needs to be added to the constructor. When they existed, they would have appeared as a reminder in the **Task List** window. Method **Dispose** cleans up allocated resources, but is not called explicitly in our programs.

Lines 53–126 contain a collapsible region that encloses our **InitializeComponent** method. Recall that the **#region** and **#endregion** preprocessor directives allow the programmer to collapse code to a single line in Visual Studio .NET. This enables the programmer to focus on certain portions of a program.

Method **InitializeComponent** (lines 58–123) sets the properties of the controls added to the form (the **TextBox**, **Label** and **Button**). Lines 60–66 create new objects for the controls we add (a **Button**, a **TextBox** and a **Label**). Lines 86–88 and 92 set the **Name**, **PasswordChar** and **Text** properties for **inputPasswordTextBox**. The **TabIndex** property is initially set by Visual Studio .NET, but can be changed by the developer.

The comment on lines 54–57 advises us not to modify the contents of method **InitializeComponent**. We have altered it slightly for formatting purposes in this book, but this is not recommended. We have done this only so that the reader is able to see the important portions of the code. Visual Studio .NET examines this method to create the design view of the code. If we change this method, Visual Studio .NET may not recognize our modifications and show the design improperly. It is important to note that the design view is based on the code, and not vice versa.

Testing and Debugging Tip 9.1

To keep the design view accurate, do not modify the code in method **InitializeComponent**. *Make changes in the design window or property window.*

The **Click** event is triggered when a control is clicked. We create the handler using the procedure described in Section 9.3.1. We want to respond to the **Click** event **displayPasswordButton**, so we double click it in the **Events** window. (Alternately, we could simply have clicked on **displayPasswordButton**.) This creates an empty event handler named **displayPasswordButton_Click** (line 138). Visual Studio .NET also registers the event handler for us (line 77–79). It adds the event handler to the **Click** event, using the **EventHandler** delegate. We must then implement the event handler. Whenever **displayPasswordButton** is clicked, this method is called and displays **inputPasswordTextBox**'s text on **displayPasswordLabel**. Even though **inputPasswordTextBox** displays all asterisks, it still retains its input text in its **Text** property. To show the text, we set **displayPasswordLabel**'s **Text** to **inputPasswordTextBox**'s **Text** (line 142–143). The user must program this line manually. When **displayPasswordButton** is clicked, the **Click** event is triggered, and the event handler **displayPasswordButton_Click** runs (updating **displayPasswordLabel**).

Visual Studio .NET generated most of the code in this program. It simplifies tasks such as creating controls, setting their properties and registering event handlers. However, we should be aware of how this is done—in several programs we may set properties ourselves, using code.

9.6 GroupBoxes and Panels

GroupBoxes and *Panels* arrange components on a GUI. For example, buttons related to a particular task can be placed inside a **GroupBox** or **Panel** inside the Visual Studio .NET form designer. All these buttons move together when the **GroupBox** or **Panel** is moved.

The main difference between the two classes is that **GroupBox**es can display a caption, and **Panel**s can have scrollbars. The scrollbars allow the user to view additional controls inside the **Panel** by scrolling the visible area. **GroupBox**es have thin borders by default, but **Panel**s can be set to have borders by changing their **BorderStyle** property.

Look-and-Feel Observation 9.4

Panels and GroupBoxes can contain other Panels and GroupBoxes.

Look-and-Feel Observation 9.5

Organize the GUI by anchoring and docking controls (of similar function) inside a **Group-Box** *or* **Panel**. *The* **GroupBox** *or* **Panel** *then can be anchored or docked inside a form. This divides controls into functional "groups" that can be arranged easily.*

To create a **GroupBox**, drag it from the toolbar and place it on a form. Create new controls and place them inside the **GroupBox**, causing them to become part of this class. These controls are added to the **GroupBox**'s **Controls** property. The **GroupBox**'s **Text** property determines its caption. The following tables list the common properties of **GroupBox**es (Fig. 9.19) and **Panel**s (Fig. 9.20).

GroupBox Properties	Description
Common Properties	
Controls	The controls that the **GroupBox** contains.
Text	Text displayed on the top portion of the **GroupBox** (its caption).

Fig. 9.19   GroupBox properties.

Panel Properties	Description
Common Properties	
AutoScroll	Whether scrollbars appear when the **Panel** is too small to hold its controls. Default is **false**.
BorderStyle	Border of the **Panel** (default **None**; other options are **Fixed3D** and **FixedSingle**).
Controls	The controls that the **Panel** contains.

Fig. 9.20   Panel properties.

To create a **Panel**, drag it onto the form and add components to it. To enable the scrollbars, set the **Panel**'s **AutoScroll** property to **true**. If the **Panel** is resized and cannot hold its controls, scrollbars appear (Fig. 9.21). These scrollbars then can be used to view all the components in the **Panel** (both when running and designing the form). This allows the programmer to see the GUI exactly as it appears to the client.

Look-and-Feel Observation 9.6

*Use **Panel**s with scrollbars to avoid cluttering a GUI and to reduce the GUI's size.*

The program in Fig. 9.22 uses a **GroupBox** and a **Panel** to arrange buttons. These buttons change the text on a **Label**.

The **GroupBox** (named **mainGroupBox**) has two buttons, **hiButton** (labeled **Hi**) and **byeButton** (labeled **Bye**). The **Panel** (named **mainPanel**) has two buttons as well, **leftButton** (labeled **Far Left**) and **rightButton** (labeled **Far Right**). The **mainPanel** control also has its **AutoScroll** property set to **True**, allowing scrollbars to appear if needed (i.e., if the contents of the **Panel** take up more space than the **Panel** itself). The **Label** (named **messageLabel**) is initially blank.

The event handlers for the four buttons are located in lines 36–61. To create an empty **Click** event handler, double click the button in design mode (instead of using the **Events** window). We add a line in each handler to change the text of **messageLabel**.

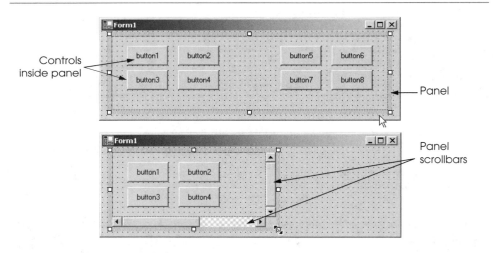

Fig. 9.21 Creating a **Panel** with scrollbars.

```
1    // Fig. 9.22: GroupBoxPanelExample.cs
2    // Using GroupBoxes and Panels to hold buttons.
3
4    using System;
5    using System.Drawing;
6    using System.Collections;
```

Fig. 9.22 Using **GroupBox**es and **Panel**s to arrange **Button**s. (Part 1 of 3.)

```
7    using System.ComponentModel;
8    using System.Windows.Forms;
9    using System.Data;
10
11   /// form to display a groupbox versus a panel
12   public class GroupBoxPanelExample : System.Windows.Forms.Form
13   {
14       private System.Windows.Forms.Button hiButton;
15       private System.Windows.Forms.Button byeButton;
16       private System.Windows.Forms.Button leftButton;
17       private System.Windows.Forms.Button rightButton;
18
19       private System.Windows.Forms.GroupBox mainGroupBox;
20       private System.Windows.Forms.Label messageLabel;
21       private System.Windows.Forms.Panel mainPanel;
22
23       private System.ComponentModel.Container components = null;
24
25       // Visual Studio .NET-generated Dispose method
26
27       [STAThread]
28       static void Main()
29       {
30           Application.Run( new GroupBoxPanelExample() );
31       }
32
33       // event handlers to change messageLabel
34
35       // event handler for hi button
36       private void hiButton_Click(
37           object sender, System.EventArgs e )
38       {
39           messageLabel.Text= "Hi pressed";
40       }
41
42       // event handler for bye button
43       private void byeButton_Click(
44           object sender, System.EventArgs e )
45       {
46           messageLabel.Text = "Bye pressed";
47       }
48
49       // event handler for far left button
50       private void leftButton_Click(
51           object sender, System.EventArgs e )
52       {
53           messageLabel.Text = "Far left pressed";
54       }
55
56       // event handler for far right button
57       private void rightButton_Click(
58           object sender, System.EventArgs e )
59       {
```

Fig. 9.22 Using **GroupBox**es and **Panel**s to arrange **Button**s. (Part 2 of 3.)

```
60              messageLabel.Text = "Far right pressed";
61      }
62
63  } // end class GroupBoxPanelExample
```

Fig. 9.22 Using **GroupBox**es and **Panel**s to arrange **Button**s. (Part 3 of 3.)

9.7 CheckBoxes and RadioButtons

C# has two types of *state buttons*—*CheckBox* and *RadioButton*—that can be in the
on/off or true/false state. Classes **CheckBox** and **RadioButton** are derived from class
ButtonBase. A **RadioButton** is different from a **CheckBox** in that there are normally several **RadioButton**s grouped together, and only one of the **RadioButton**s in the
group can be selected (true) at any time.

A checkbox is a small white square that can be blank or contain a checkmark. When a
checkbox is selected, a black checkmark appears in the box. There are no restrictions on
how checkboxes are used: Any number may be selected at a time. The text that appears
alongside a checkbox is referred to as the *checkbox label*. A list of common properties and
events of class **Checkbox** appears in Fig. 9.23.

CheckBox events and properties	Description / Delegate and Event Arguments
Common Properties	
Checked	Whether the **CheckBox** has been checked.
CheckState	Whether the **CheckBox** is checked (contains a black checkmark) or unchecked (blank). An *enumeration* (i.e., a series of related constants) with values **Checked**, **Unchecked** or **Indeterminate**.
Text	Text displayed to the right of the **CheckBox** (called the label).

Fig. 9.23 **CheckBox** properties and events. (Part 1 of 2.)

CheckBox events and properties	Description / Delegate and Event Arguments
Common Events	*(Delegate **EventHandler**, event arguments **EventArgs**)*
CheckedChanged	Raised every time the **CheckBox** is either checked or unchecked. Default event when this control is double clicked in the designer.
CheckState-Changed	Raised when the **CheckState** property changes.

Fig. 9.23 **CheckBox** properties and events. (Part 2 of 2.)

The program in Fig. 9.24 allows the user to select a **CheckBox** to change the font style of a **Label**. One **CheckBox** applies a bold style, the other an italic style. If both checkboxes are selected, the style of the font is bold and italic. When the program initially executes, neither **CheckBox** is checked.

The first **CheckBox**, named **boldCheckBox**, has its **Text** property set to **Bold**. The other **CheckBox** is named **italicCheckBox** and is labeled **Italic**. The **Label**, named **outputLabel**, is labeled **Watch the font style change**.

```
1   // Fig. 9.24: CheckBoxTest.cs
2   // Using CheckBoxes to toggle italic and bold styles.
3
4   using System;
5   using System.Drawing;
6   using System.Collections;
7   using System.ComponentModel;
8   using System.Windows.Forms;
9   using System.Data;
10
11  /// form contains checkboxes to allow
12  /// the user to modify sample text
13  public class CheckBoxTest : System.Windows.Forms.Form
14  {
15     private System.Windows.Forms.CheckBox boldCheckBox;
16     private System.Windows.Forms.CheckBox italicCheckBox;
17
18     private System.Windows.Forms.Label outputLabel;
19
20     private System.ComponentModel.Container components = null;
21
22     // Visual Studio .NET-generated Dispose method
23
24     /// The main entry point for the application.
25     [STAThread]
26     static void Main()
27     {
28        Application.Run( new CheckBoxTest() );
29     }
```

Fig. 9.24 Using **CheckBox**es to change font styles. (Part 1 of 2.)

```
30
31        // make text bold if not bold,
32        // if already bold make not bold
33        private void boldCheckBox_CheckedChanged(
34           object sender, System.EventArgs e )
35        {
36           outputLabel.Font =
37              new Font( outputLabel.Font.Name,
38              outputLabel.Font.Size,
39              outputLabel.Font.Style ^ FontStyle.Bold );
40        }
41
42        // make text italic if not italic,
43        // if already italic make not italic
44        private void italicCheckBox_CheckedChanged(
45           object sender, System.EventArgs e )
46        {
47           outputLabel.Font =
48              new Font( outputLabel.Font.Name,
49              outputLabel.Font.Size,
50              outputLabel.Font.Style ^ FontStyle.Italic );
51        }
52
53     } // end class CheckBoxTest
```

Fig. 9.24   Using **CheckBox**es to change font styles. (Part 2 of 2.)

After creating the components, we define their event handlers. Double clicking **bold-CheckBox** creates and registers an empty **CheckedChanged** event handler. To understand the code added to the event handler, we first discuss **outputLabel**'s **Font** property.

To change the font, the **Font** property must be set to a **Font** object. The **Font** constructor we use takes the font name, size and style. The first two arguments make use of **outputLabel**'s **Font** object, namely, **outputLabel.Font.Name** and **output-Label.Font.Size** (lines 37–38). The style is a member of the **FontStyle** enumeration, which contains the font styles **Regular**, **Bold**, **Italic**, **Strikeout** and **Underline**. (The **Strikeout** style displays text with a line through it, the **Underline** style displays text with a line below it.) A **Font** object's **Style** property is set when the **Font** object is created—the **Style** property itself is read-only.

Styles can be combined using *bitwise operators*, or operators that perform manipulation on bits. In this program, we need to set the font style so that the text will appear bold if it was not bold originally, and vice versa. Notice that on line 39 we use the bitwise XOR operator (**^**) to do this. Applying this operator to two bits does the following: If exactly 1 one of the corresponding bits is 1, set the result to 1. By using the **^** operator as we did on line 39, we are setting the bit values for bold in the same way. The operand on the right (**FontStyle.Bold**) always has bit values set to bold. The operand on the left, then (**outputLabel.Font.Style**) must not be bold for the resulting style to be bold. (Remember for XOR, if one value is set to 1, the other must be 0, or the result will not be 1.) If **outputLable.Font.Style** is bold, then the resulting style will not be bold. This operator also allows us to combine the styles. For instance, if the text were originally italicized, it would now be italicized and bold, rather than just bold.

We could have explicitly tested for the current style and changed it according to what we needed. For example, in the method **boldCheckBox_CheckChanged** we could have tested for the regular style, made it bold, tested for the bold style, made it regular, tested for the italic style, made it bold italic, or the italic bold style and made it italic. However, this method has a drawback—for every new style we add, we double the number of combinations. To add a checkbox for underline, we would have to test for eight possible styles. To add a checkbox for strikeout as well, we would have 16 tests in each event handler. By using the bitwise XOR operator, we save ourselves from this trouble. Each new style needs only a single statement in its event handler. In addition, styles can be removed easily, removing their handler. If we tested for every condition, we would have to remove the handler, and all the unnecessary test conditions in the other handlers.

Radio buttons (defined with class **RadioButton**) are similar to checkboxes, because they also have two states—*selected* and *not selected* (also called *deselected*). However, radio buttons normally appear as a *group* in which only one radio button can be selected at a time. Selecting a different radio button in the group forces all other radio buttons in the group to be deselected. Radio buttons represent a set of *mutually exclusive* options (i.e., a set in which multiple options cannot be selected at the same time).

Look-and-Feel Observation 9.7

Use ***RadioButton****s when the user should choose only one option in a group.*

Look-and-Feel Observation 9.8

Use ***CheckBox****es when the user should be able to choose many options in a group.*

All radio buttons added to a form become part of the same group. To create new groups, radio buttons must be added to **GroupBox**es or **Panel**s. The common properties and events of class **RadioButton** are listed in Fig. 9.25.

Software Engineering Observation 9.3

Forms, ***GroupBox****es, and* ***Panel****s can act as logical groups for radio buttons. The radio buttons within each group will be mutually exclusive to each other, but not to radio buttons in different groups.*

RadioButton properties and events	Description / Delegate and Event Arguments
Common Properties	
Checked	Whether the **RadioButton** is checked.
Text	Text displayed to the right of the **RadioButton** (called the label).
Common Events	*(Delegate **EventHandler**, event arguments **EventArgs**)*
Click	Raised when user clicks the control.
CheckedChanged	Raised every time the **RadioButton** is checked or unchecked. Default event when this control is double clicked in the designer.

Fig. 9.25   **RadioButton** properties and events.

The program in Fig. 9.26 uses radio buttons to select the options for a **MessageBox**. Users select the attributes they want then press the display button, which causes the **MessageBox** to appear. A **Label** in the lower-left corner shows the result of the **MessageBox** (**Yes**, **No**, **Cancel**, etc.). The different **MessageBox** icon and button types have been displayed in tables in Chapter 3, Control Structures.

```
1   // Fig. 9.26: RadioButtonsTest.cs
2   // Using RadioButtons to set message window options.
3
4   using System;
5   using System.Drawing;
6   using System.Collections;
7   using System.ComponentModel;
8   using System.Windows.Forms;
9   using System.Data;
10
11  /// form contains several radio buttons--user chooses one
12  /// from each group to create a custom MessageBox
13  public class RadioButtonsTest : System.Windows.Forms.Form
14  {
15     private System.Windows.Forms.Label promptLabel;
16     private System.Windows.Forms.Label displayLabel;
17     private System.Windows.Forms.Button displayButton;
18
19     private System.Windows.Forms.RadioButton questionButton;
20     private System.Windows.Forms.RadioButton informationButton;
21     private System.Windows.Forms.RadioButton exclamationButton;
22     private System.Windows.Forms.RadioButton errorButton;
23     private System.Windows.Forms.RadioButton retryCancelButton;
24     private System.Windows.Forms.RadioButton yesNoButton;
25     private System.Windows.Forms.RadioButton yesNoCancelButton;
26     private System.Windows.Forms.RadioButton okCancelButton;
27     private System.Windows.Forms.RadioButton okButton;
```

Fig. 9.26   Using **RadioButton**s to set message-window options. (Part 1 of 5.)

```
28      private System.Windows.Forms.RadioButton
29         abortRetryIgnoreButton;
30
31      private System.Windows.Forms.GroupBox groupBox2;
32      private System.Windows.Forms.GroupBox groupBox1;
33
34      private MessageBoxIcon iconType = MessageBoxIcon.Error;
35      private MessageBoxButtons buttonType =
36         MessageBoxButtons.OK;
37
38      /// The main entry point for the application.
39      [STAThread]
40      static void Main()
41      {
42         Application.Run( new RadioButtonsTest() );
43      }
44
45      // change button based on option chosen by sender
46      private void buttonType_CheckedChanged(
47         object sender, System.EventArgs e )
48      {
49         if ( sender == okButton ) // display OK button
50            buttonType = MessageBoxButtons.OK;
51
52         // display OK and Cancel buttons
53         else if ( sender == okCancelButton )
54            buttonType = MessageBoxButtons.OKCancel;
55
56         // display Abort, Retry and Ignore buttons
57         else if ( sender == abortRetryIgnoreButton )
58            buttonType = MessageBoxButtons.AbortRetryIgnore;
59
60         // display Yes, No and Cancel buttons
61         else if ( sender == yesNoCancelButton )
62            buttonType = MessageBoxButtons.YesNoCancel;
63
64         // display Yes and No buttons
65         else if ( sender == yesNoButton )
66            buttonType = MessageBoxButtons.YesNo;
67
68         // only one option left--display
69         // Retry and Cancel buttons
70         else
71            buttonType = MessageBoxButtons.RetryCancel;
72
73      } // end method buttonType_CheckedChanged
74
75      // change icon based on option chosen by sender
76      private void iconType_CheckedChanged(
77         object sender, System.EventArgs e )
78      {
79         if ( sender == errorButton ) // display error icon
80            iconType = MessageBoxIcon.Error;
```

Fig. 9.26 Using **RadioButton**s to set message-window options. (Part 2 of 5.)

```
81
82        // display exclamation point
83        else if ( sender == exclamationButton )
84            iconType = MessageBoxIcon.Exclamation;
85
86        // display information icon
87        else if ( sender == informationButton )
88            iconType = MessageBoxIcon.Information;
89
90        else // only one option left--display question mark
91            iconType = MessageBoxIcon.Question;
92
93     } // end method iconType_CheckedChanged
94
95     // display MessageBox and button user pressed
96     protected void displayButton_Click(
97        object sender, System.EventArgs e )
98     {
99        DialogResult result =
100           MessageBox.Show( "This is Your Custom MessageBox.",
101           "Custom MessageBox", buttonType, iconType, 0, 0 );
102
103        // check for dialog result and display it in label
104        switch ( result )
105        {
106           case DialogResult.OK:
107              displayLabel.Text = "OK was pressed.";
108              break;
109
110           case DialogResult.Cancel:
111              displayLabel.Text = "Cancel was pressed.";
112              break;
113
114           case DialogResult.Abort:
115              displayLabel.Text = "Abort was pressed.";
116              break;
117
118           case DialogResult.Retry:
119              displayLabel.Text = "Retry was pressed.";
120              break;
121
122           case DialogResult.Ignore:
123              displayLabel.Text = "Ignore was pressed.";
124              break;
125
126           case DialogResult.Yes:
127              displayLabel.Text = "Yes was pressed.";
128              break;
129
130           case DialogResult.No:
131              displayLabel.Text = "No was pressed.";
132              break;
133
```

Fig. 9.26   Using **RadioButton**s to set message-window options. (Part 3 of 5.)

```
134          } // end switch
135
136     } // end method displayButton_Click
137
138 } // end class RadioButtonsTest
```

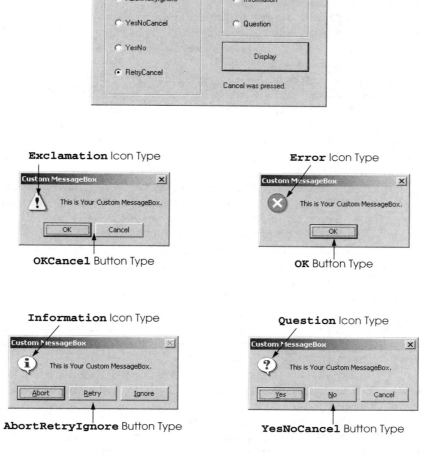

Exclamation Icon Type

OKCancel Button Type

Error Icon Type

OK Button Type

Information Icon Type

AbortRetryIgnore Button Type

Question Icon Type

YesNoCancel Button Type

Fig. 9.26 Using **RadioButton**s to set message-window options. (Part 4 of 5.)

YesNo Button Type

RetryCancel Button Type

Fig. 9.26   Using **RadioButton**s to set message-window options. (Part 5 of 5.)

To store the user's choice of options, the objects **iconType** and **buttonType** are created and initialized (lines 34–36). Object **iconType** is a **MessageBoxIcon** enumeration that can have values **Asterisk**, **Error**, **Exclamation**, **Hand**, **Information**, **Question**, **Stop** and **Warning**. In this example we use only **Error**, **Exclamation**, **Information** and **Question**.

Object **buttonType** is a **MessageBoxButton** enumeration with values **Abort-RetryIgnore**, **OK**, **OKCancel**, **RetryCancel**, **YesNo** and **YesNoCancel**. The name indicates which buttons will appear in the **MessageBox**. In this example we use all **MessageBoxButton** enumeration values.

Two **GroupBox**es are created, one for each enumeration. Their captions are **Button Type** and **Icon**. One label is used to prompt the user (**promptLabel**), while the other is used to display which button was pressed, once the custom **MessageBox** has been displayed (**displayLabel**). There is also a button (**displayButton**) that displays the text **Display**. **RadioButton**s are created for the enumeration options, with their labels set appropriately. The radio buttons are grouped, thus only one option can be selected from each **GroupBox**.

For event handling, one event handler exists for all the radio buttons in **groupBox1**, and another for all the radio buttons in **groupBox2**. Each radio button generates a **CheckedChanged** event when clicked.

Remember, to set the event handler for an event, use the events section of the **Properties** window. Create a new **CheckedChanged** event handler for one of the radio buttons in **buttonTypeGroupBox** and rename it **buttonType_CheckedChanged**. Then set the **CheckedChanged** event handlers for all the radio buttons in **buttonTypeGroupBox** to method **buttonType_CheckedChanged**. Create a second **CheckedChanged** event handler for a radio button in **iconTypeGroupBox** and rename it **iconType_CheckedChanged**. Finally, set the **CheckedChanged** event handlers for the radio buttons in **iconTypeGroupBox** to method **iconType_CheckedChanged**.

Both handlers compare the **sender** object with every radio button to determine which button was selected. Depending on the radio button selected, either **iconType** or **buttonType** changes (lines 46–93).

The **Click** handler for **displayButton** (lines 96–136) creates a **MessageBox** (lines 99–101). Some of the **MessageBox** options are set by **iconType** and **buttonType**. The result of the message box is a **DialogResult** enumeration, with values **Abort**, **Cancel**, **Ignore**, **No**, **None**, **OK**, **Retry** or **Yes**. The **switch** statement on lines 104–134 tests for the result and sets **displayLabel.Text** appropriately.

9.8 PictureBoxes

A picture box (class **PictureBox**) displays an image. The image, set by an object of class **Image**, can be in a bitmap (**.bmp**), **.gif**, **.jpg**, icon or metafile format. (Images and multimedia are discussed in Chapter 13, Graphics and Multimedia.) *GIF (Graphics Interchange Format)* and *JPEG (Joint Photographic Expert Group)* files are widely used file formats.

The **Image** property sets the **Image** object to use, and the **SizeMode** property sets how the image is displayed (**Normal**, **StretchImage**, **AutoSize** or **CenterImage**). Figure 9.27 describes the important properties and events of class **PictureBox**.

The program in Fig. 9.28 uses **PictureBox imagePictureBox** to display one of three bitmap images—**image0**, **image1** or **image2**. They are located in the directory **images** (as usual, located in the **bin/debug** directory of our project), where the executable file is located. Whenever the **imagePictureBox** is clicked, the image changes. The **Label** (named **promptLabel**) on the top of the form includes the instructions **Click On Picture Box to View Images**.

PictureBox properties and events	Description / Delegate and Event Arguments
Common Properties	
Image	Image to display in the **PictureBox**.
SizeMode	Enumeration that controls image sizing and positioning. Values **Normal** (default), **StretchImage**, **AutoSize** and **CenterImage**. **Normal** puts image in top-left corner of **PictureBox** and **CenterImage** puts image in middle. (Both cut off image if too large.) **StretchImage** resizes image to fit in **PictureBox**. **AutoSize** resizes **PictureBox** to hold image.
Common Events	*(Delegate **EventHandler**, event arguments **EventArgs**)*
Click	Raised when user clicks the control. Default event when this control is double clicked in the designer.

Fig. 9.27 **PictureBox** properties and events.

```
1   // Fig. 9.28: PictureBoxTest.cs
2   // Using a PictureBox to display images.
3
4   using System;
5   using System.Drawing;
6   using System.Collections;
7   using System.ComponentModel;
8   using System.Windows.Forms;
9   using System.Data;
10  using System.IO;
11
```

Fig. 9.28 Using a **PictureBox** to display images. (Part 1 of 2.)

```
12   /// form to display different images when clicked
13   public class PictureBoxTest : System.Windows.Forms.Form
14   {
15       private System.Windows.Forms.PictureBox imagePictureBox;
16       private System.Windows.Forms.Label promptLabel;
17
18       private int imageNum = -1;
19
20       /// The main entry point for the application.
21       [STAThread]
22       static void Main()
23       {
24           Application.Run( new PictureBoxTest() );
25       }
26
27       // change image whenever PictureBox clicked
28       private void imagePictureBox_Click(
29           object sender, System.EventArgs e )
30       {
31           imageNum = ( imageNum + 1 ) % 3; // imageNum from 0 to 2
32
33           // create Image object from file, display on PictureBox
34           imagePictureBox.Image = Image.FromFile(
35               Directory.GetCurrentDirectory() + "\\images\\image" +
36               imageNum + ".bmp" );
37       }
38
39   } // end class PictureBoxTest
```

Fig. 9.28   Using a `PictureBox` to display images. (Part 2 of 2.)

To respond to the user's clicks, we must handle the **Click** event (lines 28–37). Inside the event handler, we use an integer (**imageNum**) to store the image we want to display. We then set the **Image** property of **imagePictureBox** to an **Image**. Class **Image** is discussed in Chapter 13, Graphics and Multimedia, but here we overview method **From-File**, which takes a **string** (the path to the image file) and creates an **Image** object.

To find the images, we use class *Directory* (namespace **System.IO**, specified on line 10) method *GetCurrentDirectory* (line 35). This returns the current directory of the executable file (usually **bin\Debug**) as a **string**. To access the **images** subdirectory, we take the current directory and append "**\\images**" followed by "****" and the file name. We use a double slash because an escape sequence is needed to print a single slash.

Alternatively, we could have used **@** to avoid the escape character (i.e., **@"\"** will print a single slash—the slash does not need to be escaped by another slash). We use **imageNum** to append the proper number, so we can load either **image0**, **image1** or **image2**. Integer **imageNum** stays between **0** and **2**, due to the modulus calculation (line 31). Finally, we append **".bmp"** to the filename. Thus, if we want to load **image0**, the string becomes "*CurrentDir***images\image0.bmp**", where ***CurrentDir*** is the directory of the executable.

9.9 Mouse Event Handling

This section explains how to handle *mouse events,* such as *clicks, presses* and *moves.* Mouse events are generated when the mouse interacts with a control. They can be handled for any GUI control that derives from class **System.Windows.Forms.Control**. Mouse event information is passed using class ***MouseEventArgs***, and the delegate to create the mouse event handlers is ***MouseEventHandler***. Each mouse event-handling method must take an **object** and a **MouseEventArgs** object as arguments. The **Click** event, which we covered earlier, uses delegate **EventHandler** and event arguments **EventArgs**.

Class **MouseEventArgs** contains information about the mouse event, such as the *x*- and *y*-coordinates of the mouse pointer, the mouse button pressed, the number of clicks and the number of notches through which the mouse wheel turned. Note that the *x*- and *y*-coordinates of the **MouseEventArgs** object are relative to the control that raised the event. Point (0,0) is at the upper-left corner of the control. The various mouse events are described in Fig. 9.29.

Mouse Events, Delegates and Event Arguments	
*Mouse Events (Delegate **EventHandler**, event arguments **EventArgs**)*	
MouseEnter	Raised if the mouse cursor enters the area of the control.
MouseLeave	Raised if the mouse cursor leaves the area of the control.
*Mouse Events (Delegate **MouseEventHandler**, event arguments **MouseEventArgs**)*	
MouseDown	Raised if the mouse button is pressed while its cursor is over the area of the control.
MouseHover	Raised if the mouse cursor hovers over the area of the control.
MouseMove	Raised if the mouse cursor is moved while in the area of the control.
MouseUp	Raised if the mouse button is released when the cursor is over the area of the control.
*Class **MouseEventArgs** Properties*	
Button	Mouse button that was pressed (**left**, **right**, **middle** or **none**).
Clicks	The number of times the mouse button was clicked.
X	The *x*-coordinate of the event, relative to the control.
Y	The *y*-coordinate of the event, relative to the control.

Fig. 9.29 Mouse events, delegates and event arguments.

Figure 9.30 uses mouse events to draw on the form. Whenever the user drags the mouse (i.e., moves the mouse while holding down a button), a line is drawn on the form.

```
1   // Fig. 9.30: Painter.cs
2   // Using the mouse to draw on a form.
3
4   using System;
5   using System.Drawing;
6   using System.Collections;
7   using System.ComponentModel;
8   using System.Windows.Forms;
9   using System.Data;
10
11  /// creates a form as a drawing surface
12  public class Painter : System.Windows.Forms.Form
13  {
14     bool shouldPaint = false; // whether to paint
15
16     /// The main entry point for the application.
17     [STAThread]
18     static void Main()
19     {
20        Application.Run( new Painter() );
21     }
22
23     // should paint after mouse button has been pressed
24     private void Painter_MouseDown(
25        object sender, System.Windows.Forms.MouseEventArgs e )
26     {
27        shouldPaint = true;
28     }
29
30     // stop painting when mouse button released
31     private void Painter_MouseUp(
32        object sender, System.Windows.Forms.MouseEventArgs e )
33     {
34        shouldPaint = false;
35     }
36
37     // draw circle whenever mouse button
38     // moves (and mouse is down)
39     protected void Painter_MouseMove(
40        object sender, System.Windows.Forms.MouseEventArgs e )
41     {
42        if ( shouldPaint )
43        {
44           Graphics graphics = CreateGraphics();
45           graphics.FillEllipse(
46              new SolidBrush( Color.BlueViolet ),
47              e.X, e.Y, 4, 4 );
48        }
49
50     } // end Painter_MouseMove
```

Fig. 9.30 Using the mouse to draw on a form. (Part 1 of 2.)

```
51
52  } // end class Painter
```

Fig. 9.30   Using the mouse to draw on a form. (Part 2 of 2.)

On line 14 the program creates variable **shouldPaint**, which determines whether we should draw on the form. We want to draw only while the mouse button is pressed down. In the event handler for event **MouseDown**, **shouldPaint** is set to true (line 27). As soon as the mouse button is released the program stops drawing: **shouldPaint** is set to false in the **MouseUp** event handler (line 34).

Whenever the mouse moves while the button is pressed down, the **MouseMove** event is generated. The event will be generated repeatedly, at a rate set by the operating system. Inside the **Painter_MouseMove** event handler (lines 39–48), the program draws only if **shouldPaint** is **true** (indicating that the mouse button is down). Line 44 creates the **Graphics** object for the form, which provides methods for drawing various shapes. Method **FillEllipse** (lines 45–47) draws a circle at every point the mouse cursor moves over (while the mouse button is pressed). The first parameter to method **FillEllipse** is a **SolidBrush** object, which determines the color of the shape drawn. We create a new **SolidBrush** object by passing the constructor a **Color** value. Structure **Color** contains numerous predefined color constants—we selected **Color.BlueViolet** (line 46). The **SolidBrush** fills an elliptical region, which lies inside a bounding rectangle. The bounding rectangle is specified by the x- and y-coordinates of its upper-left corner, its height and its width. These four parameters are the final four arguments to method **FillEllipse**. The x- and y-coordinates are the location of the mouse event: They can be taken from the mouse event arguments (**e.X** and **e.Y**). To draw a circle, we set the height and width of the bounding rectangle equal—in this case, they are each 4 pixels.

9.10 Keyboard Event Handling

This section explains how to handle *key events*. Key events are generated when keys on the keyboard are pressed and released. These events can be handled by any control that inherits from **System.Windows.Forms.Control**. There are two types of key events. The first is event **KeyPress**, which fires when a key representing an ASCII character is pressed (determined by **KeyPressEventArgs** property **KeyChar**). ASCII is a 128-character set of alphanumeric symbols. (The full listing can be found in Appendix F, ASCII Character Set.)

Using the **KeyPress** event, we cannot determine if *modifier keys* (such as *Shift*, *Alt* and *Control*) were pressed. To determine such actions, handle the **KeyUp** or **KeyDown** events, which form the second type of key event. Class **KeyEventArgs** contains information about special modifier keys. The key's **Key** *enumeration* value can be returned, giving information about a wide range of non-ASCII keys. Modifier keys are often used in conjunction with the mouse to select or highlight information. The delegates for the two classes are **KeyPressEventHandler** (event argument class **KeyPressEventArgs**) and **KeyEventHandler** (event argument class **KeyEventArgs**). Figure 9.31 lists important information about key events.

Figure 9.32 demonstrates using the key event handlers to display the key that was pressed. The program's form contains two **Label**s. It displays the key pressed on one **Label** and modifier information on the other.

The two **Label**s (named **charLabel** and **keyInfoLabel**) are initially empty. The **KeyDown** and **KeyPress** events convey different information; thus, the form (**Key-Demo**) handles them both.

Keyboard Events, Delegates and Event Arguments	
*Key Events (Delegate **KeyEventHandler**, event arguments **KeyEventArgs**)*	
KeyDown	Raised when key is initially pushed down.
KeyUp	Raised when key is released.
*Key Events (Delegate **KeyPressEventHandler**, event arguments **KeyPressEventArgs**)*	
KeyPress	Raised when key is pressed. Occurs repeatedly while key is held down, at a rate specified by the operating system.
*Class **KeyPressEventArgs** Properties*	
KeyChar	Returns the ASCII character for the key pressed.
Handled	Whether the **KeyPress** event was handled.
*Class **KeyEventArgs** Properties*	
Alt	Indicates whether the *Alt* key was pressed.
Control	Indicates whether the *Control* key was pressed.
Shift	Indicates whether the *Shift* key was pressed.
Handled	Whether the event was handled.
KeyCode	Returns the key code for the key, as a **Keys** enumeration. This does not include modifier key information. Used to test for a specific key.
KeyData	Returns the key code as a **Keys** enumeration, combined with modifier information. Used to determine all information about the key pressed.
KeyValue	Returns the key code as an **int**, rather than as a **Keys** enumeration. Used to obtain a numeric representation of the key pressed.
Modifiers	Returns a **Keys** enumeration for any modifier keys pressed (*Alt*, *Control* and *Shift*). Used to determine modifier key information only.

Fig. 9.31 Keyboard events, delegates and event arguments.

```
1   // Fig. 9.32: KeyDemo.cs
2   // Displaying information about the key the user pressed.
3
4   using System;
5   using System.Drawing;
6   using System.Collections;
7   using System.ComponentModel;
8   using System.Windows.Forms;
9   using System.Data;
10
11  // form to display key press
12  // information--contains two labels
13  public class KeyDemo : System.Windows.Forms.Form
14  {
15      private System.Windows.Forms.Label charLabel;
16      private System.Windows.Forms.Label keyInfoLabel;
17
18      private System.ComponentModel.Container components = null;
19
20      /// The main entry point for the application.
21      [STAThread]
22      static void Main()
23      {
24          Application.Run( new KeyDemo() );
25      }
26
27      // display the character pressed using key char
28      protected void KeyDemo_KeyPress(
29          object sender, System.Windows.Forms.KeyPressEventArgs e )
30      {
31          charLabel.Text = "Key pressed: " + e.KeyChar;
32      }
33
34      // display modifier keys, key code, key data and key value
35      private void KeyDemo_KeyDown(
36          object sender, System.Windows.Forms.KeyEventArgs e )
37      {
38          keyInfoLabel.Text =
39              "Alt: " + ( e.Alt ? "Yes" : "No") + '\n' +
40              "Shift: " + ( e.Shift ? "Yes" : "No" ) + '\n' +
41              "Ctrl: " + ( e.Control ? "Yes" : "No" ) + '\n' +
42              "KeyCode: " + e.KeyCode + '\n' +
43              "KeyData: " + e.KeyData + '\n' +
44              "KeyValue: " + e.KeyValue;
45      }
46
47      // clear labels when key released
48      private void KeyDemo_KeyUp(
49          object sender, System.Windows.Forms.KeyEventArgs e )
50      {
51          keyInfoLabel.Text = "";
52          charLabel.Text = "";
53      }
```

Fig. 9.32   Demonstrating keyboard events (Part 1 of 2.).

```
54
55   } // end class KeyDemo
```

Fig. 9.32   Demonstrating keyboard events (Part 2 of 2.).

The **KeyPress** event handler (lines 28–32) accesses the **KeyChar** property of the **KeyPressEventArgs** object. This returns the key pressed as a **char** and displays in **charLabel** (line 31). If the key pressed was not an ASCII character, then the **KeyPress** event will not fire and **charLabel** remains empty. ASCII is a common encoding format for letters, numbers, punctuation marks and other characters. It does not support keys such as the *function keys* (like *F1*) or the modifier keys (*Alt*, *Control* and *Shift*).

The **KeyDown** event handler (lines 35–45) displays more information, all from its **KeyEventArgs** object. It tests for the *Alt*, *Shift* and *Control* keys (lines 39–41), using the **Alt**, **Shift** and **Control** properties, each of which returns **bool**. It then displays the **KeyCode**, **KeyData** and **KeyValue** properties.

The **KeyCode** property returns a **Keys** enumeration, which is converted to a **string** using method **ToString**. The **KeyCode** property returns the key that was pressed, but does not provide any information about modifier keys. Thus, both a capital and a lowercase "a" are represented as the *A* key.

The **KeyData** property returns a **Keys** enumeration as well, but also includes data about modifier keys. Thus, if "A" is input, the **KeyData** property shows that the *A* key and the *Shift* key were pressed. Finally, **KeyValue** returns the key code for the key that was pressed as an integer. This integer is the *Windows virtual key code*, which provides an integer value for a wide range of keys and for mouse buttons. The Windows virtual key code is useful when testing for non-ASCII keys (such as the *F12* key).

The **KeyUp** event handler clears both labels when the key is released (lines 48–53). As we can see from the output, non-ASCII keys are not displayed in the upper **charLabel**, because the **KeyPress** event was not generated. The **KeyDown** event is still raised, and **keyInfoLabel** displays information about the key. The **Keys** enumeration can be used to test for specific keys by comparing the key code for the key that was pressed with a specific **KeyCode**. The Visual Studio. NET documentation has a complete list of the **Keys** enumerations.

Software Engineering Observation 9.4

To cause a control to react when a certain key is pressed (such as the Enter *key), handle a key event and test for the particular key. To cause a button to be clicked when the* Enter *key is pressed on a form, set the form's* **AcceptButton** *property.*

9.11 Summary

A graphical user interface (GUI) presents a pictorial interface to a program. A GUI (pronounced "GOO-EE") gives a program a distinctive "look and feel." By providing different applications with a consistent set of intuitive user interface components, GUIs allow the user to concentrate on using programs productively.

GUIs are built from GUI components (sometimes called controls or widgets). A GUI control is a visual object with which the user interacts via the mouse or keyboard. When the user interacts with a control, an event is generated. The event can trigger methods that respond to the user's actions. Events are based on the notion of delegates. Delegates act as an intermediate step between the object creating (raising) the event and the method handling it.

The general design process for creating Windows applications involves creating a Windows Form, setting its properties, adding controls, setting their properties and configuring event handlers. All forms, components and controls are classes.

The information a programmer needs to register an event is the **EventArgs** class (to define the event handler) and the **EventHandler** delegate (to register the event handler). Visual Studio .NET usually can register the event handler on behalf of the programmer.

A **TextBox** is a single-line area in which text can be entered. A password text box masks each character input with a special character (e.g., *****). A **Button** is a control that the user clicks to trigger a specific action. **Button**s typically respond to the **Click** event.

GroupBoxes and **Panel**s help arrange components on a GUI. The main difference between these classes is that **GroupBox**es can display text, and **Panel**s can have scrollbars.

C# has two types of state buttons that have on/off (or true/false) values: **CheckBox**es and **RadioButton**s A check box is a small white square that is either empty or contains a check mark. Radio buttons appear as a group in which only one radio button can be selected at a time. In order to create a new group the radio buttons for the group must be added to a container (e.g., **GroupBox**es or **Panel**s). Radio buttons and check boxes raise the **CheckChanged** event.

Scrollbars are controls that allow the user to access a range of integer values. There are horizontal **HScrollBar**s and vertical **VScrollBar**s. Whenever a scrollbar is manipulated, it raises a **Scroll** event.

Mouse events (clicks, presses and moves) can be handled for any GUI control that derives from **System.Windows.Forms.Control**. Mouse events use class **MouseEventArgs** (whose corresponding delegate is **MouseEventHandler**) and **EventArgs** (whose corresponding delegate is **EventHandler**).

Class **MouseEventArgs** contains information about the cursor's x- and y-coordinates, the mouse button clicked, the number of clicks and the number of notches through which the mouse wheel was turned.

Key events are generated when the keyboard's keys are pressed and released. These events can be handled by any control that inherits from **System.Windows.Forms.Control**.

Event **KeyPress** can return a **char** for any ASCII character pressed. Events **KeyUp** and **KeyDown** test for special modifier keys (using **KeyEventArgs**). The delegates are **KeyPressEventHandler** (class **KeyPressEventArgs**) and **KeyEventHandler** (class **KeyEventArgs**).

Graphical User Interface Concepts: Part 2

Objectives

- To create menus, window tabs and multiple-document-interface (MDI) programs.
- To understand the use of the **ListView** and **TreeView** controls for displaying information.
- To use hyperlinks with the **LinkLabel** control.
- To display lists using **ListBox**es and **ComboBox**es.
- To create custom controls.

I claim not to have controlled events, but confess plainly that events have controlled me.
Abraham Lincoln

A good symbol is the best argument, and is a missionary to persuade thousands.
Ralph Waldo Emerson

Capture its reality in paint!
Paul Cézanne

But, soft! what light through yonder window breaks?
It is the east, and Juliet is the sun!
William Shakespeare

An actor entering through the door, you've got nothing. But if he enters through the window, you've got a situation.
Billy Wilder

Outline

10.1   Introduction

10.2   Menus

10.3   **LinkLabels**

10.4   **ListBoxes** and **CheckedListBoxes**

10.4.1   **ListBoxes**

10.4.2   **CheckedListBoxes**

10.5   **ComboBoxes**

10.6   **TreeViews**

10.7   **ListViews**

10.8   Tab Control

10.9   Multiple-Document-Interface (MDI) Windows

10.10   Visual Inheritance

10.11   User-Defined Controls

10.12   Summary

10.1 Introduction

This chapter continues our study of GUIs. We begin our discussion of more advanced topics with a commonly used GUI component, the *menu*, which presents a user with several logically organized options. The reader will learn how to develop menus with the tools provided by Visual Studio .NET. We introduce **LinkLabel**s, powerful GUI components that enable the user to click the mouse to be taken to one of several destinations.

We consider GUI components that encapsulate smaller GUI components. We demonstrate how to manipulate a list of values via a **ListBox** and how to combine several checkboxes in a **CheckedListBox**. We also create drop-down lists using **ComboBox**es and display data hierarchically with a **TreeView** control. We present two important GUI components—tab controls and multiple-document-interface windows. These components enable developers to create real-world programs with sophisticated graphical user interfaces.

Most of the GUI components used in this book are included with Visual Studio .NET. We show how to design custom controls and add those controls to the **ToolBox**. The techniques in this chapter form the groundwork for the creation of complex GUIs and custom controls.

10.2 Menus

Menus are used to provide groups of related commands for Windows applications. Although these commands depend on the program, some—such as **Open** and **Save**—are common to many applications. Menus are an integral part of GUIs, because they make user actions possible without unnecessary "cluttering" of GUIs.

In Fig. 10.1, an expanded menu lists various commands (called *menu items*), plus *submenus* (menus within a menu). Notice that the top-level menus appear in the left portion of the figure, whereas any submenus or menu items are displayed to the right. The menu that contains a menu item is called that menu item's *parent menu*. A menu item that contains a submenu is considered to be the parent of that submenu.

All menu items can have *Alt* key shortcuts (also called *access shortcuts* or *hot keys*), which are accessed by pressing *Alt* and the underlined letter (for example, *Alt + F* retrieves the **File** menu). Menus that are not top-level menus can have shortcut keys as well (combinations of *Ctrl, Shift, Alt, F1, F2*, letter keys etc.). Some menu items are preceded by checkmarks, which indicate that these features are enabled.

To create a menu, open the **Toolbox**, and drag a **MainMenu** control onto the form. This creates a menu bar on the top of the form and places a **MainMenu** icon underneath it. To select the **MainMenu**, click the icon. This setup is known as the Visual Studio .NET **Menu Designer**, which allows the user to create and edit menus. Menus are like other controls; they have properties, which can be accessed through the **Properties** window or the **Menu Designer** (Fig. 10.2), and events, which can be accessed through the **Class Name** and **Method Name** drop-down menus.

Look-and-Feel Observation 10.1

Buttons also can have access shortcuts. Place the & symbol just before the character [for which we wish to create a shortcut]. To click the button, the user then presses Alt *and the underlined character.*

Fig. 10.1 Expanded and checked menus.

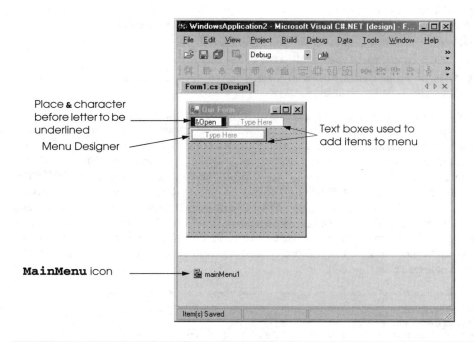

Place **&** character before letter to be underlined

Menu Designer

Text boxes used to add items to menu

MainMenu icon

Fig. 10.2   Visual Studio .NET **Menu Designer**.

To add entries to the menu, click the **Type Here** textbox and type the text that should appear in the menu. Each entry in the menu is of type *MenuItem* from the **System.Windows.Forms** namespace. The menu itself is of type *MainMenu*. After the programmer presses the *Enter* key, the menu item is added. Then, more **Type Here** text-boxes appear, allowing us to add items underneath or to the side of the original menu item (Fig. 10.2). To create an access shortcut, type an ampersand (**&**) in front of the character to be underlined. For example, to create the **File** menu item, type **&File**. The actual amper-sand character is displayed by typing **&&**. To add other shortcut keys (such as *Ctrl + F9*), set the **Shortcut** property of the **MenuItem**.

Programmers can remove a menu item by selecting it with the mouse and pressing the *Delete* key. Separator bars are inserted by right-clicking the menu and selecting **Insert Separator** or by typing "**-**" as the menu text.

Menu items generate a **Click** event when selected. To create an empty event handler, enter code-view mode, double click on the **MenuItem** in design view. Menus can also dis-play the names of open windows in multiple-document-interface (MDI) forms (see Section 10.9). Menu properties and events are summarized in Fig. 10.3.

Look-and-Feel Observation 10.2

It is conventional to place an ellipsis (...) after a menu item that brings up a dialog (such as **Save As...**). *Menu items that produce an immediate action without prompting the user (such as* **Save**) *should not have an ellipsis following their name.*

Class **MenuTest** (Fig. 10.4) creates a simple menu on a form. The form has a top-level **File** menu with menu items **About** (displays a message box) and **Exit** (terminates the program).The menu also includes a **Format** menu, which changes the text on a label. The **Format** menu has submenus **Color** and **Font**, which change the color and font of the text on a label.

Look-and-Feel Observation 10.3

Using common Windows shortcuts (such as Ctrl+F for Find operations and Ctrl+S for Save operations) decreases an application's learning curve.

We begin by dragging the **MainMenu** from the **ToolBox** onto the form. We then create our entire menu structure, using the **Menu Designer**. The **File** menu has items **About** (**aboutMenuItem**, line 21) and **Exit** (**exitMenuItem**, line 22); the **Format** menu (**formatMenu**, line 25) has two submenus. The first submenu, **Color** (**color-MenuItem**, line 28), contains menu items **Black** (**blackMenuItem**, line 29), **Blue** (**blueMenuItem**, line 30), **Red** (**redMenuItem**, line 31) and **Green** (**greenMenu-Item**, line 32). The second submenu, **Font** (**fontMenuItem**, line 40), contains menu items **Times New Roman** (**timesMenuItem**, line 35), **Courier** (**courierMenu-Item**, line 36), **Comic Sans** (**comicMenuItem**, line 37), a separator bar (**separa-torMenuItem**, line 42), **Bold** (**boldMenuItem**, line 38) and **Italic** (**italicMenuItem**, line 39).

MainMenu and **MenuItem** events and properties	Description / Delegate and Event Arguments
MainMenu *Properties*	
MenuItems	Lists the **MenuItem**s that are contained in the **MainMenu**.
RightToLeft	Causes text to display from right to left. Useful for languages (e.g., Arabic) that are read from right to left.
MenuItem *Properties*	
Checked	Indicates whether a menu item is checked (according to property **RadioCheck**). Default **False**, meaning that the menu item is not checked.
Index	Specifies an item's position in its parent menu.
MenuItems	Lists the submenu items for a particular menu item.
MergeOrder	Sets the position of a menu item when its parent menu is merged with another menu.
MergeType	Takes a value of the **MenuMerge** enumeration. Specifies how a parent menu merges with another menu. Possible values are **Add**, **MergeItems**, **Remove** and **Replace**.
RadioCheck	Indicates whether a selected menu item appears as a radio button (black circle) or displays a checkmark. **True** creates radio button, **False** displays checkmark; default **False**.
Shortcut	Specifies the shortcut key for the menu item (e.g., *Ctrl + F9* can be equivalent to clicking a specific item).

Fig. 10.3   MainMenu and **MenuItem** properties and events. (Part 1 of 2.)

MainMenu and MenuItem events and properties	Description / Delegate and Event Arguments
ShowShortcut	Indicates whether a shortcut key is shown beside menu item text. Default is **True**, which displays the shortcut key.
Text	Specifies the text to appear in the menu item. To create an *Alt* access shortcut, precede a character with **&** (e.g., **&File** for **File**).
Common Event	*(Delegate **EventHandler**, event arguments **EventArgs**)*
Click	Generated when item is clicked or shortcut key is used. Default when double-clicked in designer.

Fig. 10.3 **MainMenu** and **MenuItem** properties and events. (Part 2 of 2.)

```
1   // Fig. 10.4: MenuTest.cs
2   // Using menus to change font colors and styles.
3
4   using System;
5   using System.Drawing;
6   using System.Collections;
7   using System.ComponentModel;
8   using System.Windows.Forms;
9   using System.Data;
10
11  public class MenuTest : System.Windows.Forms.Form
12  {
13      // display label
14      private System.Windows.Forms.Label displayLabel;
15
16      // main menu (contains file and format menu)
17      private System.Windows.Forms.MainMenu mainMenu;
18
19      // file menu
20      private System.Windows.Forms.MenuItem fileMenuItem;
21      private System.Windows.Forms.MenuItem aboutMenuItem;
22      private System.Windows.Forms.MenuItem exitMenuItem;
23
24      // format menu
25      private System.Windows.Forms.MenuItem formatMenuItem;
26
27      // color submenu
28      private System.Windows.Forms.MenuItem colorMenuItem;
29      private System.Windows.Forms.MenuItem blackMenuItem;
30      private System.Windows.Forms.MenuItem blueMenuItem;
31      private System.Windows.Forms.MenuItem redMenuItem;
32      private System.Windows.Forms.MenuItem greenMenuItem;
33
34      // font submenu
35      private System.Windows.Forms.MenuItem timesMenuItem;
```

Fig. 10.4 Menus for changing text font and color. (Part 1 of 5.)

```
36    private System.Windows.Forms.MenuItem courierMenuItem;
37    private System.Windows.Forms.MenuItem comicMenuItem;
38    private System.Windows.Forms.MenuItem boldMenuItem;
39    private System.Windows.Forms.MenuItem italicMenuItem;
40    private System.Windows.Forms.MenuItem fontMenuItem;
41
42    private System.Windows.Forms.MenuItem separatorMenuItem;
43
44    [STAThread]
45    static void Main()
46    {
47        Application.Run( new MenuTest() );
48    }
49
50    // display MessageBox
51    private void aboutMenuItem_Click(
52        object sender, System.EventArgs e )
53    {
54        MessageBox.Show(
55            "This is an example\nof using menus.",
56            "About", MessageBoxButtons.OK,
57            MessageBoxIcon.Information );
58    }
59
60    // exit program
61    private void exitMenuItem_Click(
62        object sender, System.EventArgs e )
63    {
64        Application.Exit();
65    }
66
67    // reset color
68    private void ClearColor()
69    {
70        // clear all checkmarks
71        blackMenuItem.Checked = false;
72        blueMenuItem.Checked = false;
73        redMenuItem.Checked = false;
74        greenMenuItem.Checked = false;
75    }
76
77    // update menu state and color display black
78    private void blackMenuItem_Click(
79        object sender, System.EventArgs e )
80    {
81        // reset checkmarks for color menu items
82        ClearColor();
83
84        // set color to black
85        displayLabel.ForeColor = Color.Black;
86        blackMenuItem.Checked = true;
87    }
88
```

Fig. 10.4   Menus for changing text font and color. (Part 2 of 5.)

```
89          // update menu state and color display blue
90          private void blueMenuItem_Click(
91              object sender, System.EventArgs e )
92          {
93              // reset checkmarks for color menu items
94              ClearColor();
95
96              // set color to blue
97              displayLabel.ForeColor = Color.Blue;
98              blueMenuItem.Checked = true;
99          }
100
101         // update menu state and color display red
102         private void redMenuItem_Click(
103             object sender, System.EventArgs e )
104         {
105             // reset checkmarks for color menu items
106             ClearColor();
107
108             // set color to red
109             displayLabel.ForeColor = Color.Red;
110             redMenuItem.Checked = true;
111         }
112
113         // update menu state and color display green
114         private void greenMenuItem_Click(
115             object sender, System.EventArgs e )
116         {
117             // reset checkmarks for color menu items
118             ClearColor();
119
120             // set color to green
121             displayLabel.ForeColor = Color.Green;
122             greenMenuItem.Checked = true;
123         }
124
125         // reset font types
126         private void ClearFont()
127         {
128             // clear all checkmarks
129             timesMenuItem.Checked = false;
130             courierMenuItem.Checked = false;
131             comicMenuItem.Checked = false;
132         }
133
134         // update menu state and set font to Times
135         private void timesMenuItem_Click(
136             object sender, System.EventArgs e )
137         {
138             // reset checkmarks for font menu items
139             ClearFont();
140
```

Fig. 10.4   Menus for changing text font and color. (Part 3 of 5.)

```
141           // set Times New Roman font
142           timesMenuItem.Checked = true;
143           displayLabel.Font = new Font(
144              "Times New Roman", 14, displayLabel.Font.Style );
145        }
146
147        // update menu state and set font to Courier
148        private void courierMenuItem_Click(
149           object sender, System.EventArgs e )
150        {
151           // reset checkmarks for font menu items
152           ClearFont();
153
154           // set Courier font
155           courierMenuItem.Checked = true;
156           displayLabel.Font = new Font(
157              "Courier New", 14, displayLabel.Font.Style );
158        }
159
160        // update menu state and set font to Comic Sans MS
161        private void comicMenuItem_Click(
162           object sender, System.EventArgs e )
163        {
164           // reset checkmarks for font menu items
165           ClearFont();
166
167           // set Comic Sans font
168           comicMenuItem.Checked = true;
169           displayLabel.Font = new Font(
170              "Comic Sans MS", 14, displayLabel.Font.Style );
171        }
172
173        // toggle checkmark and toggle bold style
174        private void boldMenuItem_Click(
175           object sender, System.EventArgs e )
176        {
177           // toggle checkmark
178           boldMenuItem.Checked = !boldMenuItem.Checked;
179
180           // use Xor to toggle bold, keep all other styles
181           displayLabel.Font = new Font(
182              displayLabel.Font.FontFamily, 14,
183              displayLabel.Font.Style ^ FontStyle.Bold );
184        }
185
186        // toggle checkmark and toggle italic style
187        private void italicMenuItem_Click(
188           object sender, System.EventArgs e)
189        {
190           // toggle checkmark
191           italicMenuItem.Checked = !italicMenuItem.Checked;
192
```

Fig. 10.4   Menus for changing text font and color. (Part 4 of 5.)

```
193          // use Xor to toggle bold, keep all other styles
194          displayLabel.Font = new Font(
195             displayLabel.Font.FontFamily, 14,
196             displayLabel.Font.Style ^ FontStyle.Italic );
197      }
198
199  } // end class MenuTest
```

Fig. 10.4   Menus for changing text font and color. (Part 5 of 5.)

The **About** menu item in the **File** menu displays a **MessageBox** when clicked (lines 54–57). The **Exit** menu item closes the application through **static** method *Exit* of class *Application* (line 64). Class **Application** contains **static** methods used to control program execution. Method *Exit* causes our application to quit.

We made the items in the **Color** submenu (**Black**, **Blue**, **Red** and **Green**) mutually exclusive—the user can select only one at a time (we explain how we did this shortly). To indicate this behavior to the user, we set the menu item's *RadioCheck* properties to **True**. This causes a radio button to appear (instead of a checkmark) when a user selects a color-menu item.

Each **Color** menu item has its own event handler. The event handler for color **Black** is **blackMenuItem_Click** (lines 78–87). The event handlers for colors **Blue**, **Red** and **Green** are **blueMenuItem_Click** (lines 90–99), **redMenuItem_Click** (lines 102–111) and **greenMenuItem_Click** (lines 114–123), respectively. Each **Color** menu item must be mutually exclusive, so each event handler calls method **ClearColor** (lines 68–75) before setting its corresponding **Checked** property to **True**. Method **ClearColor** sets the **Checked** property of each color **MenuItem** to **False**, effectively preventing more than one menu item from being checked at a time.

Software Engineering Observation 10.1

The mutual exclusion of menu items is not enforced by the **MainMenu***, even when the* **RadioCheck** *property is* **True***. We must program this behavior.*

Look-and-Feel Observation 10.4

Set the **RadioCheck** *property to reflect the desired behavior of menu items. Use radio buttons (***RadioCheck** *property set to* **True***) to indicate mutually exclusive menu items. Use check marks (***RadioCheck** *property set to* **False***) for menu items that have no logical restriction.*

The **Font** menu contains three menu items for font types (**Courier, Times New Roman** and **Comic Sans**) and two menu items for font styles (**Bold** and *Italic*). We add a separator bar between the font-type and font-style menu items to indicate the distinction: Font types are mutually exclusive, but styles are not. This means that a **Font** object can specify only one font face at a time, but can set multiple styles at once (e.g., a font can be both bold and italic). We set the font-type menu items to display checks. As with the **Color** menu, we also must enforce mutual exclusion in our event handlers.

Event handlers for font-type menu items **TimesRoman, Courier** and **ComicSans** are **timesMenuItem_Click** (lines 135–145), **courierMenuItem_Click** (lines 148–158) and **comicMenuItem_Click** (lines 161–171), respectively. These event handlers behave in a manner similar to that of the event handlers for the **Color** menu items. Each event handler clears the **Checked** properties for all font-type menu items by calling method **ClearFont** (lines 126–132), then sets the **Checked** property of the menu item that generated the event to **True**. This enforces the mutual exclusion of the font-type menu items.

The event handlers for the **Bold** and *Italic* menu items (lines 174–197) use the bitwise **Xor** operator. For each font style, the exclusive or operator (**^**) changes the text to include the style or, if that style is already applied, to remove it. The toggling behavior provided by the **Xor** operator was explained in Chapter 9, Graphical User Interface Concepts: Part 1. As explained in Chapter 9, this program's event-handling structure allows us to add and remove menu entries while making minimal structural changes to the code.

10.3 **LinkLabels**

The ***LinkLabel*** control displays links to other objects, such as files or Web pages (Fig. 10.5). A **LinkLabel** appears as underlined text (colored blue by default). When the mouse moves over the link, the pointer changes to a hand; this is similar to the behavior of a hyperlink in a Web page. The link can change color to indicate whether the link is new, visited or active. When clicked, the **LinkLabel** generates a **LinkClicked** event (see Fig. 10.6). Class **LinkLabel** is derived from class **Label** and therefore inherits all of class **Label**'s functionality.

Class **LinkLabelTest** (Fig. 10.7) uses three **LinkLabel**s, to link to the **C:** drive, the Deitel Web page (**www.deitel.com**) and the Notepad application, respectively. The **Text** properties of the **LinkLabel**s **driveLinkLabel** (line 14), **deitelLinkLabel** (line 15) and **notepadLinkLabel** (line 16) are set to describe each link's purpose.

Look-and-Feel Observation 10.5

*Although other controls can perform actions similar to those of a **LinkLabel** (such as the opening of a Web page), **LinkLabel**s indicate that a link can be followed—a regular label or button does not necessarily convey that idea.*

The event handlers for the **LinkLabel** instances call static method **Start** of class **Process** (namespace **System.Diagnostics**). This method allows us to execute other programs from our application. Method **Start** can take as arguments either the file to open (a **String**) or the name of the application to run and its command-line arguments (two **String**s). Method **Start**'s arguments can be in the same form as if they were provided for input to the **Run** command in Windows. To open a file that has a file type that Windows recognizes, simply insert the file's full path name. The Windows operating system should be able to use the application associated with the given file's extension to open the file.

LinkLabel
on a form

Hand image displays when
mouse moves over **LinkLabel**

Fig. 10.5   LinkLabel control in running program.

LinkLabel properties and events	Description / Delegate and Event Arguments
Common Properties	
ActiveLinkColor	Specifies the color of the active link when clicked. Default is red.
LinkArea	Specifies which portion of text in the **LinkLabel** is treated as part of the link.
LinkBehavior	Specifies the link's behavior, such as how the link appears when the mouse is placed over it.
LinkColor	Specifies the original color of all links before they have been visited. Default is blue.
Links	Lists the **LinkLabel.Link** objects, which are the links contained in the **LinkLabel**.
LinkVisited	If **True**, link appears as if it were visited (its color is changed to that specified by property **VisitedLinkColor**). Default **False**.
Text	Specifies the text to appear on the control.
UseMnemonic	If **True**, **&** character in **Text** property acts as a shortcut (similar to the *Alt* shortcut in menus).
VisitedLinkColor	Specifies the color of visited links. Default is **Color.Purple**.

Fig. 10.6   LinkLabel properties and events. (Part 1 of 2.)

LinkLabel properties and events	Description / Delegate and Event Arguments
Common Event	*(Delegate* **LinkLabelLinkClickedEventHandler**, *event arguments* **LinkLabelLinkClickedEventArgs***)*
LinkClicked	Generated when link is clicked. Default when control is double-clicked in designer.

Fig. 10.6 **LinkLabel** properties and events. (Part 2 of 2.)

The event handler for **driveLinkLabel**'s **LinkClicked** events browses the **C:** drive (lines 25–30). Line 28 sets the **LinkVisited** property to **True**, which changes the link's color from blue to purple (we can configure the **LinkVisited** colors through the **Properties** window in the Visual Studio .NET IDE). The event handler then passes **"C:\"** to method **Start** (line 29), which opens a **Windows Explorer** window.

The event handler for **deitelLinkLabel**'s **LinkClicked** events (lines 33–39) opens the Web page **www.deitel.com** in Internet Explorer. We achieve this by passing the string **"IExplore"** and the Web-page address (lines 37–38), which opens Internet Explorer. Line 36 sets the **LinkVisited** property to **True**.

The event handler for **notepadLinkLabel**'s **LinkClicked** events opens the specified Notepad application (lines 42–51). Line 46 sets the link to appear as a visited link. Line 50 passes the argument **"notepad"** to method **Start**, which calls **notepad.exe**. Note that, in line 50, the **.exe** extension is not required—Windows can determine whether the argument given to method **Start** is an executable file.

```
1   // Fig. 10.7: LinkLabelTest.cs
2   // Using LinkLabels to create hyperlinks.
3
4   using System;
5   using System.Drawing;
6   using System.Collections;
7   using System.ComponentModel;
8   using System.Windows.Forms;
9   using System.Data;
10
11  public class LinkLabelTest : System.Windows.Forms.Form
12  {
13      // linklabels to C: drive, www.deitel.com and Notepad
14      private System.Windows.Forms.LinkLabel driveLinkLabel;
15      private System.Windows.Forms.LinkLabel deitelLinkLabel;
16      private System.Windows.Forms.LinkLabel notepadLinkLabel;
17
18      [STAThread]
19      static void Main()
20      {
21          Application.Run( new LinkLabelTest() );
22      }
```

Fig. 10.7 **LinkLabel**s used to link to a folder, a Web page and an application. (Part 1 of 3.)

```
23
24      // browse C:\ drive
25      private void driveLinkLabel_LinkClicked( object sender,
26         System.Windows.Forms.LinkLabelLinkClickedEventArgs e )
27      {
28         driveLinkLabel.LinkVisited = true;
29         System.Diagnostics.Process.Start( "C:\\" );
30      }
31
32      // load www.deitel.com in Web broswer
33      private void deitelLinkLabel_LinkClicked( object sender,
34         System.Windows.Forms.LinkLabelLinkClickedEventArgs e )
35      {
36         deitelLinkLabel.LinkVisited = true;
37         System.Diagnostics.Process.Start(
38            "IExplore", "http://www.deitel.com" );
39      }
40
41      // run application Notepad
42      private void notepadLinkLabel_LinkClicked(
43         object sender,
44         System.Windows.Forms.LinkLabelLinkClickedEventArgs e )
45      {
46         notepadLinkLabel.LinkVisited = true;
47
48         // program called as if in run
49         // menu and full path not needed
50         System.Diagnostics.Process.Start( "notepad" );
51      }
52
53   } // end class LinkLabelTest
```

Fig. 10.7   **LinkLabel**s used to link to a folder, a Web page and an application.
(Part 2 of 3.)

Fig. 10.7   **LinkLabel**s used to link to a folder, a Web page and an application. (Part 3 of 3.)

10.4 **ListBoxes** and **CheckedListBoxes**

The **ListBox** control allows the user to view and select from multiple items in a list. **ListBox**es are static GUI entities, which means that users cannot enter new items in the list. The **CheckedListBox** control extends a **ListBox** by including check boxes next to each item in the list. This allows users to place checks on multiple items at once, as is possible in a **CheckBox** control (users also can select multiple items simultaneously from a **ListBox**, but not by default). Figure 10.8 displays a sample **ListBox** and a sample **CheckedListBox**. In both controls, scroll bars appear if the number of items is too large to be displayed simultaneously in the component. Figure 10.9 lists common **ListBox** properties, methods and events.

The **SelectionMode** property determines the number of items that can be selected. This property has the possible values **None**, **One**, **MultiSimple** and **MultiExtended** (from the **SelectionMode** *enumeration*)—the differences among these settings are explained in Fig. 10.9. The **SelectedIndexChanged** event occurs when the user selects a new item.

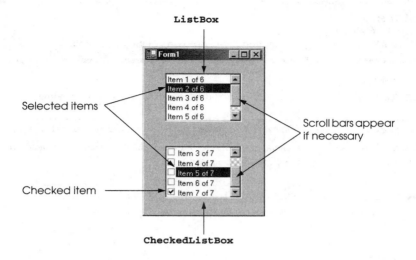

Fig. 10.8   ListBox and **CheckedListBox** on a form.

ListBox properties, methods and events	Description / Delegate and Event Arguments
Common Properties	
Items	Lists the collection of items within the **ListBox**.
MultiColumn	Indicates whether the **ListBox** can break a list into multiple columns. Multiple columns are used to make vertical scroll bars unnecessary.
SelectedIndex	Returns the index of the currently selected item. If the user selects multiple items, this method arbitrarily returns one of the selected indices; if no items have been selected, the method returns **-1**.
SelectedIndices	Returns a collection of the indices of all currently selected items.
SelectedItem	Returns a reference to the currently selected item (if multiple items are selected, it returns the item with the lowest index number).
SelectedItems	Returns a collection of the currently selected item(s).
SelectionMode	Determines the number of items that can be selected and the means through which multiple items can be selected. Values **None**, **One**, **MultiSimple** (multiple selection allowed) and **MultiExtended** (multiple selection allowed via a combination of arrow keys, mouse clicks and *Shift* and *Control* buttons).
Sorted	Indicates whether items appear in alphabetical order. **True** causes alphabetization; default is **False**.

Fig. 10.9   ListBox properties, methods and events. (Part 1 of 2.)

ListBox properties, methods and events	Description / Delegate and Event Arguments
Common Method	
GetSelected	Takes an index, and returns **True** if the corresponding item is selected.
Common Event	*(Delegate **EventHandler**, event arguments **EventArgs**)*
SelectedIndex-Changed	Generated when selected index changes. Default when control is double-clicked in designer.

Fig. 10.9 **ListBox** properties, methods and events. (Part 2 of 2.)

Both the **ListBox** and **CheckedListBox** have properties **Items**, **SelectedItem** and **SelectedIndex**. Property **Items** returns all the objects in the list as a collection. Collections are a common way of exposing lists of **Object**s in the .NET framework. Many .NET GUI components (e.g., **ListBox**es) use collections to expose lists of internal objects (e.g., items contained within a **ListBox**). We discuss collections further in Chapter 20, Data Structures and Collections. Property **SelectedItem** returns the currently selected item. If the user can select multiple items, use collection **SelectedItems** to return all the selected items as a collection. Property **SelectedIndex** returns the index of the selected item—if there could be more than one, use property **SelectedIndices**. If no items are selected, property **SelectedIndex** returns **-1**. Method **GetSelected** takes an index and returns **True** if the corresponding item is selected.

To add items to the **ListBox** or the **CheckedListBox** we must add objects to its **Items** collection. This can be accomplished by invoking method **Add** to add a **String** to the **ListBox**'s or **CheckedListBox**'s **Items** collection. For example, we could write

    myListBox.**Items.Add(** *"myListItem"* **)**

to add **String** *myListItem* to **ListBox** *myListBox*. To add multiple objects, programmers can either use method **Add** multiple times or use method **AddRange** to add an array of objects. Classes **ListBox** and **CheckedListBox** use each submitted object's **ToString** method to determine the label for the corresponding object's entry in the list. This allows developers to add different objects to a **ListBox** or a **CheckedListBox** that later can be returned through properties **SelectedItem** and **SelectedItems**.

Alternatively, we can add items to **ListBox**es and **CheckedListBox**es visually by examining the **Items** property in the **Properties** window. Clicking the ellipsis opens the **String Collection Editor**, a text area in which we can type the items to add; each item should appear on a separate line (Fig. 10.10). Visual Studio .NET then adds these **String**s to the **Items** collection inside method **InitializeComponent**.

Fig. 10.10 String Collection Editor.

10.4.1 ListBoxes

Class **ListBoxTest** (Fig. 10.11) enables the user to add, remove and clear items from **ListBox displayListBox** (line 14). Class **ListBoxTest** uses **TextBox input-TextBox** (line 17) to allow the user to type in a new item. When the user clicks button **addButton** (line 20), the new item appears in **displayListBox**. Similarly, if the user selects an item and clicks **removeButton** (line 21), the item is deleted. Control **clear-Button** (line 22) deletes all entries in **displayListBox**. The user terminates the application by clicking button **exitButton** (line 23).

The **addButton_Click** event handler (lines 33–38) calls method **Add** of the **Items** collection in the **ListBox**. This method takes a **String** as the item to add to **display-ListBox**. In this case, the **String** used is the user-input text, or **inputTextBox.Text** (line 36). After the item is added, **txtInput.Text** is cleared (line 37).

The **removeButton_Click** event handler (lines 41–48) calls method **Remove** of the **Items** collection. Event handler **removeButton_Click** first uses property **SelectedIndex** to check which index is selected. Unless **SelectedIndex** is **-1** (line 45), the handler removes the item that corresponds to the selected index.

```
1   // Fig. 10.11: ListBoxTest.cs
2   // Program to add, remove and clear list box items.
3
4   using System;
5   using System.Drawing;
6   using System.Collections;
7   using System.ComponentModel;
8   using System.Windows.Forms;
9   using System.Data;
10
11  public class ListBoxTest : System.Windows.Forms.Form
12  {
13      // contains user-input list of elements
14      private System.Windows.Forms.ListBox displayListBox;
15
```

Fig. 10.11 **ListBox** used in a program to add, remove and clear items. (Part 1 of 3.)

```
16        // user input textbox
17        private System.Windows.Forms.TextBox inputTextBox;
18
19        // add, remove, clear and exit command buttons
20        private System.Windows.Forms.Button addButton;
21        private System.Windows.Forms.Button removeButton;
22        private System.Windows.Forms.Button clearButton;
23        private System.Windows.Forms.Button exitButton;
24
25        [STAThread]
26        static void Main()
27        {
28           Application.Run( new ListBoxTest() );
29        }
30
31        // add new item (text from input box)
32        // and clear input box
33        private void addButton_Click(
34           object sender, System.EventArgs e )
35        {
36           displayListBox.Items.Add( inputTextBox.Text );
37           inputTextBox.Clear();
38        }
39
40        // remove item if one selected
41        private void removeButton_Click(
42           object sender, System.EventArgs e )
43        {
44           // remove only if item selected
45           if ( displayListBox.SelectedIndex != -1 )
46              displayListBox.Items.RemoveAt(
47                 displayListBox.SelectedIndex );
48        }
49
50        // clear all items
51        private void clearButton_Click(
52           object sender, System.EventArgs e )
53        {
54           displayListBox.Items.Clear();
55        }
56
57        // exit application
58        private void exitButton_Click(
59           object sender, System.EventArgs e )
60        {
61           Application.Exit();
62        }
63
64     } // end class ListBoxTest
```

Fig. 10.11 **ListBox** used in a program to add, remove and clear items. (Part 2 of 3.)

Fig. 10.11 ListBox used in a program to add, remove and clear items. (Part 3 of 3.)

The event handler for **clearButton_Click** (lines 51–55) calls method **Clear** of the **Items** collection (line 54). This removes all the entries in **displayListBox**. Finally, event handler **exitButton_Click** (lines 58–62) terminates the application, using method **Application.Exit** (line 61).

10.4.2 CheckedListBoxes

The **CheckedListBox** control derives from class **ListBox** and includes a checkbox next to each item in the list. As in **ListBox**es, items can be added via methods **Add** and **AddRange** or through the **String Collection Editor**. **CheckedListBox**es imply that multiple items can be selected, and the only possible values for the **SelectionMode** property are **SelectionMode.None** and **SelectionMode.One**. **Selection-Mode.One** allows multiple selection, because checkboxes imply that there are no logical restrictions on the items—the user can select as many items as required. Thus, the only choice is whether to give the user multiple selection or no selection at all. This keeps the **CheckedListBox**'s behavior consistent with that of **CheckBox**es. The programmer is unable to set the last two **SelectionMode** values, **MultiSimple** and **MultiEx-tended**, because the only logical selection modes are handled by **None** and **One**. Common properties and events of **CheckedListBox**es appear in Fig. 10.12.

Common Programming Error 10.1

*The IDE displays an error message if the programmer attempts to set the **Selection-Mode** property to **MultiSimple** or **MultiExtended** in the **Properties** window of a **CheckedListBox**; if this value is set by the programmer in the code, a runtime error occurs.*

Event **ItemCheck** is generated whenever a user checks or unchecks a **CheckedListBox** item. Event argument properties **CurrentValue** and **NewValue** return **CheckState** values for the current and the new state of the item, respectively. A comparison of these values allows us to determine whether the **CheckedListBox** item was checked or unchecked. The **CheckedListBox** control retains the **SelectedItems** and **SelectedIndices** properties (it inherits them from class **ListBox**). However, it also includes properties **CheckedItems** and **CheckedIndices**, which return information about the checked items and indices.

In Fig. 10.13, class **CheckedListBoxTest** uses a **CheckedListBox** and a **ListBox** to display a user's selection of books. The **CheckedListBox** named **inputCheckedListBox** (lines 14–15) allows the user to select multiple titles. In the **String Collection Editor**, items were added for some Deitel books: C++, Java, VB, Internet & WWW, Perl, Python, Wireless Internet and Advanced Java (the acronym HTP stands for "How to Program"). The **ListBox**, named **displayListBox** (line 18), displays the user's selection. In the screen shots accompanying this example, the **CheckedListBox** appears to the left, the **ListBox** to the right.

CheckedListBox properties, methods and events	Description / Delegate and Event Arguments
Common Properties	*(All the **ListBox** properties and events are inherited by **CheckedListBox**.)*
CheckedItems	Lists the collection of items that are checked. This is distinct from the selected items, which are highlighted (but not necessarily checked). *Note: There can be at most one selected item at any given time.*
CheckedIndices	Returns indices for the items that are checked. Not the same as the selected indices.
SelectionMode	Determines how many items can be checked. Only possible values are **One** (allows multiple checks to be placed) or **None** (does not allow any checks to be placed).
Common Method	
GetItemChecked	Takes an index, and returns **True** if corresponding item is checked.
Common Event	*(Delegate **ItemCheckEventHandler**, event arguments **ItemCheckEventArgs**)*
ItemCheck	Generated when an item is checked or unchecked.

Fig. 10.12 **CheckedListBox** properties, methods and events. (Part 1 of 2.)

CheckedListBox properties, methods and events	Description / Delegate and Event Arguments
ItemCheckEventArgs Properties	
CurrentValue	Indicates whether current item is checked or unchecked. Possible values are **Checked**, **Unchecked** and **Indeterminate**.
Index	Returns index of the item that changed.
NewValue	Specifies the new state of item.

Fig. 10.12 CheckedListBox properties, methods and events. (Part 2 of 2.)

```
1    // Fig. 10.13: CheckedListBoxTest.cs
2    // Using the checked list boxes to add items to a list box
3
4    using System;
5    using System.Drawing;
6    using System.Collections;
7    using System.ComponentModel;
8    using System.Windows.Forms;
9    using System.Data;
10
11   public class CheckedListBoxTest : System.Windows.Forms.Form
12   {
13       // list of available book titles
14       private System.Windows.Forms.CheckedListBox
15           inputCheckedListBox;
16
17       // user selection list
18       private System.Windows.Forms.ListBox displayListBox;
19
20       [STAThread]
21       static void Main()
22       {
23           Application.Run( new CheckedListBoxTest() );
24       }
25
26       // item about to change,
27       // add or remove from displayListBox
28       private void inputCheckedListBox_ItemCheck(
29           object sender,
30           System.Windows.Forms.ItemCheckEventArgs e )
31       {
32           // obtain reference of selected item
33           string item =
34               inputCheckedListBox.SelectedItem.ToString();
35
```

Fig. 10.13 CheckedListBox and ListBox used in a program to display a user selection. (Part 1 of 2.)

```
36              // if item checked add to listbox
37              // otherwise remove from listbox
38              if ( e.NewValue == CheckState.Checked )
39                  displayListBox.Items.Add( item );
40              else
41                  displayListBox.Items.Remove( item );
42
43          } // end method inputCheckedListBox_Click
44
45      } // end class CheckedListBox
```

Fig. 10.13 **CheckedListBox** and **ListBox** used in a program to display a user selection. (Part 2 of 2.)

When the user checks or unchecks an item in **CheckedListBox inputCheckedListBox**, the system generates an **ItemCheck** event. Event handler **inputCheckedListBox_ItemCheck** (lines 28–43) handles the event. An **if/else** control structure (lines 38–41) determines whether the user checked or unchecked an item in the **CheckedListBox**. Line 38 uses the **NewValue** property to test for whether the item is being checked (**CheckState.Checked**). If the user checks an item, line 39 adds the checked entry to the **ListBox displayListBox**. If the user unchecks an item, line 41 removes the corresponding item from **displayListBox**.

10.5 ComboBoxes

The **ComboBox** control combines **TextBox** features with a *drop-down list*. A drop-down list is a GUI component that contains a list from which values can be chosen. It usually appears as a text box with a down arrow to its right. By default, the user can enter text into the text box or click the down arrow to display a list of predefined items. If a user chooses an element from this list, that element is displayed in the text box. If the list contains more elements than can be displayed in the drop-down list, a scrollbar appears. The maximum number of items that a drop-down list can display at one time is set by property *MaxDropDownItems*. Figure 10.14 shows a sample **ComboBox** in three different states.

Fig. 10.14 ComboBox demonstration.

As with the **ListBox** control, the developer can add objects to collection **Items** programmatically, using methods **Add** and **AddRange**, or visually, with the **String Collection Editor**. Figure 10.15 lists common properties and events of class **ComboBox**.

ComboBox events and properties	Description / Delegate and Event Arguments
Common Properties	
DropDownStyle	Determines the type of combo box. Value **Simple** means that the text portion is editable and the list portion is always visible. Value **DropDown** (the default) means that the text portion is editable, but the user must click an arrow button to see the list portion. Value **DropDownList** means that the text portion is not editable and the user must click the arrow button to see the list portion.
Items	The collection of items in the **ComboBox** control.
MaxDropDownItems	Specifies the maximum number of items (between **1** and **100**) that can display in the drop-down list. If the number of items exceeds the maximum number of items to display, a scroll bar appears.
SelectedIndex	Returns index of currently selected item. If there is no currently selected item, **-1** is returned.
SelectedItem	Returns a reference to the currently selected item.
Sorted	Specifies whether items in a list are alphabetized. If **True**, items appear in alphabetical order. Default is **False**.
Common Event	*(Delegate **EventHandler**, event arguments **EventArgs**)*
SelectedIndex- Changed	Generated when the selected index changes (such as when a check box has been checked or unchecked). Default when control is double-clicked in designer.

Fig. 10.15 ComboBox properties and events.

Look-and-Feel Observation 10.6

*Use a **ComboBox** to save space on a GUI. The disadvantage is that, unlike with a **ListBox**, the user cannot see available items without scrolling.*

Property **DropDownStyle** determines the type of **ComboBox**. Style **Simple** does not display a drop-down arrow. Instead, a scrollbar appears next to the control, allowing the user to select a choice from the list. The user can also type in a selection. Style **DropDown** (the default) displays a drop-down list when the down arrow is clicked (or the down arrow key is pressed). The user can type a new item into the **ComboBox**.

The last style is **DropDownList**, which displays a drop-down list but does not allow the user to enter a new item. Drop-down lists save room, so a **ComboBox** should be used when GUI space is limited.

The **ComboBox** control has properties **Items** (a collection), **SelectedItem** and **SelectedIndex**, which are similar to the corresponding properties in **ListBox**. There can be at most one selected item in a **ComboBox** (if zero, then **SelectedIndex** is **-1**). When the selected item changes, event **SelectedIndexChanged** is generated.

Class **ComboBoxTest** (Fig. 10.16) allows users to select a shape to draw—an empty or filled circle, ellipse, square or pie—by using a **ComboBox**. The combo box in this example is uneditable, so the user cannot input a custom item.

Look-and-Feel Observation 10.7

*Make lists (such as **ComboBox**es) editable only if the program is designed to accept user-submitted elements. Otherwise, the user might enter a custom item and then be unable to use it.*

After creating **ComboBox imageComboBox** (line 14), we make it uneditable by setting its **DropDownStyle** to **DropDownList** in the **Properties** window. Next, we add items **Circle**, **Square**, **Ellipse**, **Pie**, **Filled Circle**, **Filled Square**, **Filled Ellipse** and **Filled Pie** to the **Items** collection. We added these items using the **String Collection Editor**. Whenever the user selects an item from **imageComboBox**, the system generates a **SelectedIndexChanged** event. Event handler **imageComboBox_SelectedIndexChanged** (lines 23–77) handles these events. Lines 27–34 create a **Graphics** object, a **Pen** and a **SolidBrush**, with which the program draws on the form. The **Graphics** object (line 22) allows a pen or brush to draw on a component, using one of several **Graphics** methods. The **Pen** object is used by methods **drawEllipse**, **drawRectangle** and **drawPie** (lines 43–56) to draw the outlines of their corresponding shapes. The **SolidBrush** object is used by methods **fillEllipse**, **fillRectangle** and **fillPie** (lines 59–72) to draw their corresponding solid shapes. Line 37 colors the entire form **White**, using **Graphics** method **Clear**. These methods are discussed in greater detail in Chapter 13, Graphics and Multimedia.

```
1   // Fig. 10.16: ComboBoxTest.cs
2   // Using ComboBox to select shape to draw
3
4   using System;
5   using System.Drawing;
6   using System.Collections;
```

Fig. 10.16 ComboBox used to draw a selected shape. (Part 1 of 3.)

```
7   using System.ComponentModel;
8   using System.Windows.Forms;
9   using System.Data;
10
11  public class ComboBoxTest : System.Windows.Forms.Form
12  {
13     // contains shape list (circle, square, ellipse, pie)
14     private System.Windows.Forms.ComboBox imageComboBox;
15
16     [STAThread]
17     static void Main()
18     {
19        Application.Run( new ComboBoxTest() );
20     }
21
22     // get selected index, draw shape
23     private void imageComboBox_SelectedIndexChanged(
24        object sender, System.EventArgs e )
25     {
26        // create graphics object, pen and brush
27        Graphics myGraphics = base.CreateGraphics();
28
29        // create Pen using color DarkRed
30        Pen myPen = new Pen( Color.DarkRed );
31
32        // create SolidBrush using color DarkRed
33        SolidBrush mySolidBrush =
34           new SolidBrush( Color.DarkRed );
35
36        // clear drawing area setting it to color White
37        myGraphics.Clear( Color.White );
38
39        // find index, draw proper shape
40        switch ( imageComboBox.SelectedIndex )
41        {
42           case 0: // case circle is selected
43              myGraphics.DrawEllipse(
44                 myPen, 50, 50, 150, 150 );
45              break;
46           case 1: // case rectangle is selected
47              myGraphics.DrawRectangle(
48                 myPen, 50, 50, 150, 150 );
49              break;
50           case 2: // case ellipse is selected
51              myGraphics.DrawEllipse(
52                 myPen, 50, 85, 150, 115 );
53              break;
54           case 3: // case pie is selected
55              myGraphics.DrawPie(
56                 myPen, 50, 50, 150, 150, 0, 45 );
57              break;
```

Fig. 10.16 ComboBox used to draw a selected shape. (Part 2 of 3.)

```
58                case 4: // case filled circle is selected
59                   myGraphics.FillEllipse(
60                      mySolidBrush, 50, 50, 150, 150 );
61                   break;
62                case 5: // case filled rectangle is selected
63                   myGraphics.FillRectangle(
64                      mySolidBrush, 50, 50, 150, 150 );
65                   break;
66                case 6: // case filled ellipse is selected
67                   myGraphics.FillEllipse(
68                      mySolidBrush, 50, 85, 150, 115 );
69                   break;
70                case 7: // case filled pie is selected
71                   myGraphics.FillPie(
72                      mySolidBrush, 50, 50, 150, 150, 0, 45 );
73                   break;
74
75         } // end switch
76
77      } // end method imageComboBox_SelectedIndexChanged
78
79   } // end class ComboBoxTest
```

Fig. 10.16 ComboBox used to draw a selected shape. (Part 3 of 3.)

The application draws a particular shape specified by the selected item's index. The **switch** structure (lines 40–75) uses **imageComboBox.SelectedIndex** to determine which item the user selected. Class **Graphics** method *DrawEllipse* (lines 43–44) takes a **Pen**, the *x*- and *y*-coordinates of the center and the width and height of the ellipse to draw. The origin of the coordinate system is in the upper left corner of the form; the *x*-coordinate increases to the right, the *y*-coordinate increases downward. A circle is a special case of an ellipse (the height and width are equal). Lines 43–44 draw a circle. Lines 51–52 draw an ellipse that has different values for height and width.

Class **Graphics** method *DrawRectangle* (lines 47–48) takes a **Pen**, the *x*- and *y*-coordinates of the upper-left corner and the width and height of the rectangle to draw. Method *DrawPie* (line 55–56) draws a pie as a portion of an ellipse. The ellipse is bounded by a rectangle. Method **DrawPie** takes a **Pen**, the *x*- and *y*-coordinates of the upper-left corner of the rectangle, its width and height, the start angle (in degrees) and the sweep angle (in degrees) of the pie. Angles increase clockwise. The *FillEllipse* (lines 59–60 and 67–68), *FillRectange* (lines 63–64) and *FillPie* (lines 71–72) methods are similar to their unfilled counterparts, except that they take a **SolidBrush** instead of a **Pen**. Some of the drawn shapes are illustrated in the screen shots at the bottom of Fig. 10.16.

10.6 TreeViews

The *TreeView* control displays *nodes* hierarchically on a *tree*. Traditionally, nodes are objects that contain values and can refer to other nodes. A *parent node* contains *child nodes*, and the child nodes can be parents to other nodes. Two child nodes that have the same parent node are considered *sibling nodes*. A tree is a collection of nodes, usually organized in a hierarchical manner. The first parent node of a tree is the *root* node (a **TreeView** can have multiple roots). For example, the file system of a computer can be represented as a tree. The top-level directory (perhaps **C:**) would be the root, each subfolder of **C:** would be a child node and each child folder could have its own children. **TreeView** controls are useful for displaying hierarchal information, such as the file structure that we just mentioned. We cover nodes and trees in greater detail in Chapter 20, Data Structures and Collections. Figure 10.17 displays a sample **TreeView** control on a form.

A parent node can be expanded or collapsed by clicking the plus or minus box to its left. Nodes without children do not have an expand or collapse box.

The nodes displayed in a **TreeView** are instances of class **TreeNode**. Each **TreeNode** has a **Nodes** collection (type **TreeNodeCollection**), which contains a list of other **TreeNode**s—its children. The **Parent** property returns a reference to the parent node (or **null** if the node is a root node). Figure 10.18 and Fig. 10.19 list the common properties of **TreeView**s and **TreeNode**s and an event of **TreeView**s.

To add nodes to the **TreeView** visually, click the ellipsis by the **Nodes** property in the **Properties** window. This opens the **TreeNode Editor**, which displays an empty tree representing the **TreeView** (Fig. 10.20). There are buttons to create a root, to add or delete a node.

To add nodes through code, we first must create a root node. Make a new **TreeNode** object and pass it a **String** to display. Then, use method **Add** to add this new **TreeNode** to the **TreeView**'s **Nodes** collection. Thus, to add a root node to **TreeView** *myTreeView*, write *myTreeView*.**Nodes.Add(** *new* **TreeNode(** *RootLabel* **))**

where *myTreeView* is the **TreeView** to which we are adding nodes, and *RootLabel* is the
text to display in *myTreeView*. To add children to a root node, add new **TreeNode**s to its
Nodes collection. We select the appropriate root node from the **TreeView** by writing

myTreeView.**Nodes[** *myIndex* **]**

where *myIndex* is the root node's index in *myTreeView*'s **Nodes** collection. We add nodes
to child nodes through the same process by which we added root nodes to *myTreeView*. To
add a child to the root node at index *myIndex*, write

myTreeView.**Nodes[** *myIndex* **].Nodes.Add(** *new* **TreeNode(** *ChildLabel* **))**

Fig. 10.17 TreeView displaying a sample tree.

TreeView properties and events	Description / Delegate and Event Arguments
Common Properties	
CheckBoxes	Indicates whether checkboxes appear next to nodes. **True** displays checkboxes. Default is **False**.
ImageList	Indicates the **ImageList** used to display icons by the nodes. An ***ImageList*** is a collection that contains a number of **Image** objects.
Nodes	Lists the collection of **TreeNode**s in the control. Contains methods **Add** (adds a **TreeNode** object), **Clear** (deletes the entire collection) and **Remove** (deletes a specific node). Removing a parent node deletes all its children.

Fig. 10.18 TreeView properties and events. (Part 1 of 2.)

TreeView properties and events	Description / Delegate and Event Arguments
`SelectedNode`	Currently selected node.
Common Event	*(Delegate **TreeViewEventHandler**, event arguments **TreeViewEventArgs**)*
`AfterSelect`	Generated after selected node changes. Default when double-clicked in designer.

Fig. 10.18 TreeView properties and events. (Part 2 of 2.)

TreeNode properties and methods	Description / Delegate and Event Arguments
Common Properties	
`Checked`	Indicates whether the **TreeNode** is checked. (**CheckBoxes** property must be set to **True** in parent **TreeView**.)
`FirstNode`	Specifies the first node in the **Nodes** collection (i.e., first child in tree).
`FullPath`	Indicates the path of the node, starting at the root of the tree.
`ImageIndex`	Specifies the index of the image to be shown when the node is deselected.
`LastNode`	Specifies the last node in the **Nodes** collection (i.e., last child in tree).
`NextNode`	Next sibling node.
`Nodes`	The collection of **TreeNode**s contained in the current node (i.e., all the children of the current node). Contains methods **Add** (adds a **TreeNode** object), **Clear** (deletes the entire collection) and **Remove** (deletes a specific node). Removing a parent node deletes all its children.
`PrevNode`	Indicates the previous sibling node.
`SelectedImageIndex`	Specifies the index of the image to use when the node is selected.
`Text`	Specifies the text to display in the **TreeView**.
Common Methods	
`Collapse`	Collapses a node.
`Expand`	Expands a node.
`ExpandAll`	Expands all the children of a node.
`GetNodeCount`	Returns the number of child nodes.

Fig. 10.19 TreeNode properties and methods.

Fig. 10.20 TreeNode Editor.

Class **TreeViewDirectoryStructureTest** (Fig. 10.21) uses a **TreeView** to display the directory file structure on a computer. The root node is the **C:** drive, and each subfolder of **C:** becomes a child. This layout is similar to that used in **Windows Explorer**. Folders can be expanded or collapsed by clicking the plus or minus boxes that appear to their left.

When **TreeViewDirectoryStructureTest** loads, the system generates a **Load** event, which is handled by event handler **TreeViewDirectoryStructureTest_Load** (lines 64–72). Line 69 adds a root node (**C:**) to our **TreeView**, named **directoryTreeView**. **C:** is the root folder for the entire directory structure. Lines 70–71 call method **PopulateTreeView** (lines 25–61), which takes a directory (a **String**) and a parent node. Method **PopulateTreeView** then creates child nodes corresponding to the subdirectories of the directory that was passed to it.

```
1   // Fig. 10.21: TreeViewDirectoryStructureTest.cs
2   // Using TreeView to display directory structure
3
4   using System;
5   using System.Drawing;
6   using System.Collections;
7   using System.ComponentModel;
8   using System.Windows.Forms;
9   using System.Data;
10  using System.IO;
11
```

Fig. 10.21 TreeView used to display directories. (Part 1 of 3.)

```
12  public class TreeViewDirectoryStructureTest
13     : System.Windows.Forms.Form
14  {
15     // contains view of c: drive directory structure
16     private System.Windows.Forms.TreeView directoryTreeView;
17
18     [STAThread]
19     static void Main()
20     {
21        Application.Run(
22           new TreeViewDirectoryStructureTest() );
23     }
24
25     public void PopulateTreeView(
26        string directoryValue, TreeNode parentNode )
27     {
28        // retrieve subdirectories
29        string[] directoryArray =
30           Directory.GetDirectories( directoryValue );
31
32        // populate current node with subdirectories
33        try
34        {
35           if ( directoryArray.Length != 0 )
36           {
37              // for every subdirectory, create new TreeNode,
38              // add as child of current node and recursively
39              // populate child nodes with subdirectories
40              foreach ( string directory in directoryArray )
41              {
42                 // create TreeNode for current directory
43                 TreeNode myNode = new TreeNode( directory );
44
45                 // add current directory node to parent node
46                 parentNode.Nodes.Add( myNode );
47
48                 // recursively populate every subdirectory
49                 PopulateTreeView( directory, myNode );
50              }
51
52           } // end if
53        }
54
55        // catch exception
56        catch ( UnauthorizedAccessException )
57        {
58           parentNode.Nodes.Add( "Access denied" );
59        }
60
61     } // end PopulateTreeView
62
```

Fig. 10.21 TreeView used to display directories. (Part 2 of 3.)

```
63        // called by system when form loads
64        private void TreeViewDirectoryStructureTest_Load(
65           object sender, System.EventArgs e)
66        {
67           // add c:\ drive to directoryTreeView and
68           // insert its subfolders
69           directoryTreeView.Nodes.Add( "C:\\" );
70           PopulateTreeView(
71              "C:\\", directoryTreeView.Nodes[ 0 ] );
72        }
73
74     } // end class TreeViewDirectoryStructure
```

Fig. 10.21 **TreeView** used to display directories. (Part 3 of 3.)

Method **PopulateTreeView** (lines 25–61) obtains a list of subdirectories, using method *GetDirectories* of class **Directory** (namespace **System.IO**) on lines 29–30. Method **GetDirectories** takes a **String** (the current directory) and returns an array of **String**s (the subdirectories). If a directory is not accessible for security reasons, an **UnauthorizedAccessException** is thrown. Lines 56–59 catch this exception and add a node containing "**Access Denied**" instead of displaying the subdirectories.

If there are accessible subdirectories, each **String** in the **directoryArray** is used to create a new child node (line 43). We use method **Add** (line 46) to add each child node to the parent. Then, method **PopulateTreeView** is called recursively on every subdirectory (line 49) and eventually populates the entire directory structure. Our recursive algorithm causes our program to have an initial delay when it loads—it must create a tree for the entire **C:** drive. However, once the drive folder names are added to the appropriate **Nodes** collection, they can be expanded and collapsed without delay. In the next section, we present an alternative algorithm to solve this problem.

10.7 ListViews

The *ListView* control is similar to a **ListBox**, in that both display lists from which the user can select one or more items (to see an example of a **ListView**, look ahead to the output of Fig. 10.24). The important difference between the two classes is that a **ListView** can display icons alongside the list items in a variety of ways (controlled by its **ImageList** property). Property *MultiSelect* (a boolean) determines whether multiple items can be selected. Checkboxes can be included by setting property **CheckBoxes** (a boolean) to **True**, making the **ListView**'s appearance similar to that of a **CheckedListBox**. The **View** property specifies the layout of the **ListBox**. Property *Activation* determines the method by which the user selects a list item. The details of these properties are explained in Fig. 10.22.

ListView allows us to define the images used as icons for **ListView** items. To display images, we must use an **ImageList** component. Create one by dragging it onto a form from the **ToolBox**. Then, click the **Images** collection in the **Properties** window to display the **Image Collection Editor** (Fig. 10.23). Here, developers can browse for images that they wish to add to the **ImageList**, which contains an array of **Image**s. Once the images have been defined, set property **SmallImageList** of the **ListView** to the new **ImageList** object. Property **SmallImageList** specifies the image list for the small icons. Property **LargeImageList** sets the **ImageList** for large icons. Icons for the **ListView** items are selected by setting the item's **ImageIndex** property to the appropriate array index.

ListView events and properties	Description / Delegate and Event Arguments
Common Properties	
Activation	Determines how the user activates an item. This property takes a value in the **ItemActivation** enumeration. Possible values are **OneClick** (single-click activation), **TwoClick** (double-click activation, item changes color when selected) and **Standard** (double-click activation).
CheckBoxes	Indicates whether items appear with checkboxes. **True** displays checkboxes. Default is **False**.
LargeImageList	Indicates the **ImageList** used when displaying large icons.

Fig. 10.22 ListView properties and events. (Part 1 of 2.)

ListView events and properties	Description / Delegate and Event Arguments
Items	Returns the collection of **ListViewItem**s in the control.
MultiSelect	Determines whether multiple selection is allowed. Default is **True**, which enables multiple selection.
SelectedItems	Lists the collection of currently selected items.
SmallImageList	Specifies the **ImageList** used when displaying small icons.
View	Determines appearance of **ListViewItems**. Values **LargeIcon** (large icon displayed, items can be in multiple columns), **Small-Icon** (small icon displayed), **List** (small icons displayed, items appear in a single column) and **Details** (like **List**, but multiple columns of information can be displayed per item).
Common Event	*(Delegate **EventHandler**, event arguments **EventArgs**)*
ItemActivate	Generated when an item in the **ListView** is activated. Does not specify which item is activated.

Fig. 10.22 **ListView** properties and events. (Part 2 of 2.)

Fig. 10.23 Image Collection Editor window for an **ImageList** component.

Class **ListViewTest** (Fig. 10.24) displays files and folders in a **ListView**, along with small icons representing each file or folder. If a file or folder is inaccessible because of permission settings, a message box appears. The program scans the contents of the directory as it browses, rather than indexing the entire drive at once.

```
1    // Fig. 10.24: ListViewTest.cs
2    // Displaying directories and their contents in ListView.
3
4    using System;
5    using System.Drawing;
6    using System.Collections;
7    using System.ComponentModel;
8    using System.Windows.Forms;
9    using System.Data;
10   using System.IO;
11
12   public class ListViewTest : System.Windows.Forms.Form
13   {
14      // display labels for current location
15      // in directory tree
16      private System.Windows.Forms.Label currentLabel;
17      private System.Windows.Forms.Label displayLabel;
18
19      // display contents of current directory
20      private System.Windows.Forms.ListView browserListView;
21
22      // specifies images for file icons and folder icons
23      private System.Windows.Forms.ImageList fileFolder;
24
25      // get current directory
26      string currentDirectory =
27         Directory.GetCurrentDirectory();
28
29      [STAThread]
30      static void Main()
31      {
32         Application.Run( new ListViewTest() );
33      }
34
35      // browse directory user clicked or go up one level
36      private void browserListView_Click(
37         object sender, System.EventArgs e )
38      {
39         // ensure item selected
40         if ( browserListView.SelectedItems.Count != 0 )
41         {
42            // if first item selected, go up one level
43            if ( browserListView.Items[ 0 ].Selected )
44            {
45               // create DirectoryInfo object for directory
46               DirectoryInfo directoryObject =
47                  new DirectoryInfo( currentDirectory );
48
49               // if directory has parent, load it
50               if ( directoryObject.Parent != null )
51                  LoadFilesInDirectory(
52                     directoryObject.Parent.FullName );
53            }
```

Fig. 10.24 ListView displaying files and folders. (Part 1 of 4.)

```
54
55          // selected directory or file
56          else
57          {
58             // directory or file chosen
59             string chosen =
60                browserListView.SelectedItems[ 0 ].Text;
61
62             // if item selected is directory
63             if ( Directory.Exists( currentDirectory +
64                "\\" + chosen ) )
65             {
66                // load subdirectory
67                // if in c:\, do not need '\',
68                // otherwise we do
69                if ( currentDirectory == "C:\\" )
70                   LoadFilesInDirectory(
71                      currentDirectory + chosen );
72                else
73                   LoadFilesInDirectory(
74                      currentDirectory + "\\" + chosen );
75             } //end if
76
77          } // end else
78
79          // update displayLabel
80          displayLabel.Text = currentDirectory;
81
82       } // end if
83
84    } // end method browserListView_Click
85
86    // display files/subdirectories of current directory
87    public void LoadFilesInDirectory(
88       string currentDirectoryValue )
89    {
90       // load directory information and display
91       try
92       {
93          // clear ListView and set first item
94          browserListView.Items.Clear();
95          browserListView.Items.Add( "Go Up One Level" );
96
97          // update current directory
98          currentDirectory = currentDirectoryValue;
99          DirectoryInfo newCurrentDirectory =
100             new DirectoryInfo( currentDirectory );
101
102          // put files and directories into arrays
103          DirectoryInfo[] directoryArray =
104             newCurrentDirectory.GetDirectories();
105
```

Fig. 10.24 ListView displaying files and folders. (Part 2 of 4.)

```
106                    FileInfo[] fileArray =
107                       newCurrentDirectory.GetFiles();
108
109                    // add directory names to ListView
110                    foreach ( DirectoryInfo dir in directoryArray )
111                    {
112                       // add directory to ListView
113                       ListViewItem newDirectoryItem =
114                          browserListView.Items.Add( dir.Name );
115
116                       // set directory image
117                       newDirectoryItem.ImageIndex = 0;
118                    }
119
120                    // add file names to ListView
121                    foreach ( FileInfo file in fileArray )
122                    {
123                       // add file to ListView
124                       ListViewItem newFileItem =
125                          browserListView.Items.Add( file.Name );
126
127                       newFileItem.ImageIndex = 1;   // set file image
128                    }
129              } // end try
130
131              // access denied
132              catch ( UnauthorizedAccessException exception )
133              {
134                 MessageBox.Show(
135                    "Warning: Some fields may not be " +
136                    "visible due to permission settings",
137                    "Attention", 0, MessageBoxIcon.Warning );
138              }
139
140        } // end method LoadFilesInDirectory
141
142        // handle load event when Form displayed for first time
143        private void ListViewTest_Load(
144           object sender, System.EventArgs e )
145        {
146           // set image list
147           Image folderImage = Image.FromFile(
148              currentDirectory + "\\images\\folder.bmp" );
149
150           Image fileImage = Image.FromFile( currentDirectory +
151              "\\images\\file.bmp" );
152
153           fileFolder.Images.Add( folderImage );
154           fileFolder.Images.Add( fileImage );
155
156           // load current directory into browserListView
157           LoadFilesInDirectory( currentDirectory );
158           displayLabel.Text = currentDirectory;
```

Fig. 10.24 ListView displaying files and folders. (Part 3 of 4.)

```
159
160    }   // end method ListViewTest_Load
161
162  }  // end class ListViewTest
```

Fig. 10.24 `ListView` displaying files and folders. (Part 4 of 4.)

To display icons beside list items, we must create an **ImageList** for the **ListView browserListView** (line 20). First, drag and drop an **ImageList** onto the form and open the **Image Collection Editor**. Create two simple bitmap images—one for a folder (array index 0) and another for a file (array index 1). Then, set the object **browserList-View** property **SmallImageList** to the new **ImageList** in the **Properties** window. Developers can create such icons with any image software, such as Adobe® Photoshop™, Jasc® Paint Shop Pro™, or Microsoft® Paint.

Method **LoadFilesInDirectory** (lines 87–140) is used to populate **browserListView** with the directory passed to it (**currentDirectoryValue**). It clears **browserListView** and adds the element **"Go Up One Level"**. When the user clicks this element, the program attempts to move up one level (we see how shortly). The method then creates a **DirectoryInfo** object initialized with the string **currentDirectory** (lines 99–100). If permission is not given to browse the directory, an exception is thrown (caught on lines 132–138). Method **LoadFilesInDirectory** works differently from method **PopulateTreeView** in the previous program (Fig. 10.21). Instead of loading all the folders in the entire hard drive, method **LoadFilesInDirectory** loads only the folders in the current directory.

Class *DirectoryInfo* (namespace **System.IO**) enables us to browse or manipulate the directory structure easily. Method **GetDirectories** (lines 103–104) returns an array of **DirectoryInfo** objects containing the subdirectories of the current directory. Similarly, method **GetFiles** (lines 106–107) returns an array of class **FileInfo** objects containing the files in the current directory. Property *Name* (of both class **DirectoryInfo** and class **FileInfo**) contains only the directory or file name, such as **temp** instead of **C:\myfolder\temp**. To access the full name, use property *FullName*.

Lines 110–118 and lines 121–128 iterate through the subdirectories and files of the current directory and add them to **browserListView**. Lines 117 and 127 set the **ImageIndex** properties of the newly created items. If an item is a directory, we set its icon to a directory icon (index 0); if an item is a file, we set its icon to a file icon (index 1).

Method **browserListView_Click** (lines 36–84) responds when the user clicks control **browserListView**. Line 40 checks on whether anything is selected. If a selection has been made, line 43 determines whether the user chose the first item in **browserListView**. The first item in **browserListView** is always **Go up one level**; if it is selected, the program attempts to go up a level. Lines 46–47 create a **DirectoryInfo** object for the current directory. Line 50 tests property **Parent** to ensure that the user is not at the root of the directory tree. Property **Parent** indicates the parent directory as a **DirectoryInfo** object; if it does not exist, **Parent** returns the value **null**. If a parent directory exists, then lines 51–52 pass the full name of the parent directory to method **LoadFilesInDirectory**.

If the user did not select the first item in **browserListView**, lines 56–77 allow the user to continue navigating through the directory structure. Lines 59–60 create **String chosen**, which receives the text of the selected item (the first item in collection **SelectedItems**). Lines 63–64 test whether the user has selected a valid directory (rather than a file). The program combines variables **currentDirectory** and **chosen** (the new directory), separated by a slash (****), and passes this value to class **Directory**'s method *Exists*. Method **Exists** returns **True** if its **String** parameter is a directory. If this occurs, the program passes the **String** to method **LoadFilesInDirectory**. The **C:** directory already includes a slash, so a slash is not needed when combining **currentDirectory** and **chosen** (line 71). However, other directories must include the slash (lines 73–74). Finally, **displayLabel** is updated with the new directory (line 80).

This program loads quickly, because it indexes only the files in the current directory. This means that, rather than having a large delay in the beginning, a small delay occurs whenever a new directory is loaded. In addition, changes in the directory structure can be shown by reloading a directory. The previous program (Fig. 10.21) needs to be restarted to reflect any changes in the directory structure. This type of trade-off is typical in the software world. When designing applications that run for long periods of time, developers might choose a large initial delay to improve performance throughout the rest of the program. However, when creating applications that run for only short periods of time, developers often prefer fast initial loading times and a small delay after each action.

10.8 Tab Control

The **TabControl** control creates tabbed windows, such as those we have seen in the Visual Studio .NET IDE (Fig. 10.25). This allows the programmer to design user interfaces that fit a large number of controls or a large amount of data without using up valuable screen "real estate."

TabControls contain **TabPage** objects, which are similar to **Panel**s and **Group-Box**es in that **TabPage**s also can contain controls. The programmer first adds controls to the **TabPage** objects, then adds the **TabPage**s to the **TabControl**. Only one **TabPage** is displayed at a time. Figure 10.26 depicts a sample **TabControl**.

Programmers can add **TabControl**s visually by dragging and dropping them onto a form in design mode. To add **TabPage**s in the Visual Studio .NET designer, right-click the **TabControl**, and select **Add Tab** (Fig. 10.27). Alternatively, click the **TabPages** collection in the **Properties** window, and add tabs in the dialog that appears. To change a tab label, set the **Text** property of the **TabPage**.

Tab Pages

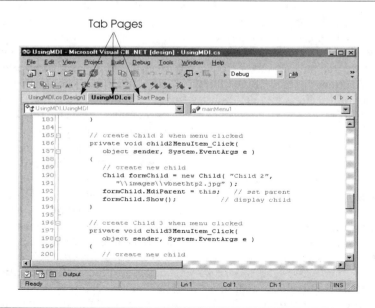

Fig. 10.25 Tabbed pages in Visual Studio .NET.

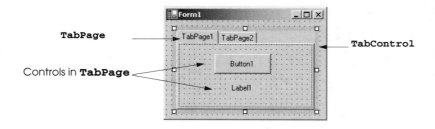

Fig. 10.26 TabControl with **TabPage**s example.

Note that clicking the tabs selects the **TabControl**—to select the **TabPage**, click the control area underneath the tabs. The developer can add controls to the **TabPage** by dragging and dropping items from the **ToolBox**. To view different **TabPage**s, click the appropriate tab (in either design or run mode). Common properties and events of **TabControl**s are described in Fig. 10.28.

Fig. 10.27 TabPages added to a **TabControl**.

TabControl properties and events	Description / Delegate and Event Arguments
Common Properties	
ImageList	Specifies images to be displayed on a tab.
ItemSize	Specifies tab size.
MultiLine	Indicates whether multiple rows of tabs can be displayed.

Fig. 10.28 TabControl properties and events. (Part 1 of 2.)

TabControl properties and events	Description / Delegate and Event Arguments
SelectedIndex	Indicates index of **TabPage** that is currently selected.
SelectedTab	Indicates the **TabPage** that is currently selected.
TabCount	Returns the number of tabs.
TabPages	Gets the collection of **TabPage**s within our **TabControl**.
Common Event	*(Delegate **EventHandler**, event arguments **EventArgs**)*
SelectedIndexChanged	Generated when **SelectedIndex** changes (i.e., another **TabPage** is selected).

Fig. 10.28 TabControl properties and events. (Part 2 of 2.)

Each **TabPage** generates its own **Click** event when its tab is clicked. Remember, events for controls can be handled by any event handler that is registered with the control's event delegate. This also applies to controls contained in a **TabPage**. For convenience, Visual Studio .NET generates the empty event handlers for these controls in the class in which we are currently working.

Class **UsingTabs** (Fig. 10.29) uses a **TabControl** to display various options relating to the text on a label (**Color**, **Size** and **Message**). The last **TabPage** displays an **About** message, which describes the use of **TabControl**s.

The **TabControl optionsTabControl** (lines 18–19) and **TabPage**s **colorTabPage** (line 22), **sizeTabPage** (line 30), **messageTabPage** (line 39) and **aboutTabPage** (line 46) are created in the designer (as described previously). **TabPage colorTabPage** contains three radio buttons—for colors black (**blackRadioButton**, lines 26–27), red (**redRadioButton**, line 25) and green (**greenRadioButton**, lines 23–24). The **CheckChanged** event handler for each button updates the color of the text in **displayLabel** (lines 59, 66 and 73). **TabPage sizeTabPage** has three radio buttons, corresponding to font sizes 12 (**size12RadioButton**, lines 35–36), 16 (**size16RadioButton**, lines 33–34) and 20 (**size20RadioButton**, lines 31–32), which change the font size of **displayLabel**—lines 80–81, 88–89 and 96–97, respectively. **TabPage messageTabPage** contains two radio buttons—for the messages **Hello!** (**helloRadioButton**, lines 42–43) and **Goodbye!** (**goodbyeRadioButton**, lines 40–41). The two radio buttons determine the text on **displayLabel** (lines 104 and 111, respectively).

```
1   // Fig. 10.29: UsingTabs.cs
2   // Using TabControl to display various font settings.
3
4   using System;
5   using System.Drawing;
6   using System.Collections;
7   using System.ComponentModel;
8   using System.Windows.Forms;
```

Fig. 10.29 TabControl used to display various font settings. (Part 1 of 4.)

```
 9   using System.Data;
10
11   public class UsingTabs : System.Windows.Forms.Form
12   {
13      // output label reflects text changes
14      private System.Windows.Forms.Label displayLabel;
15
16      // table control containing table pages colorTabPage,
17      // sizeTabPage, messageTabPage and aboutTabPage
18      private System.Windows.Forms.TabControl
19         optionsTabControl;
20
21      // table page containing color options
22      private System.Windows.Forms.TabPage colorTabPage;
23      private System.Windows.Forms.RadioButton
24         greenRadioButton;
25      private System.Windows.Forms.RadioButton redRadioButton;
26      private System.Windows.Forms.RadioButton
27         blackRadioButton;
28
29      // table page containing font size options
30      private System.Windows.Forms.TabPage sizeTabPage;
31      private System.Windows.Forms.RadioButton
32         size20RadioButton;
33      private System.Windows.Forms.RadioButton
34         size16RadioButton;
35      private System.Windows.Forms.RadioButton
36         size12RadioButton;
37
38      // table page containing text display options
39      private System.Windows.Forms.TabPage messageTabPage;
40      private System.Windows.Forms.RadioButton
41         goodByeRadioButton;
42      private System.Windows.Forms.RadioButton
43         helloRadioButton;
44
45      // table page containing about message
46      private System.Windows.Forms.TabPage aboutTabPage;
47      private System.Windows.Forms.Label messageLabel;
48
49      [STAThread]
50      static void Main()
51      {
52         Application.Run( new UsingTabs() );
53      }
54
55      // event handler for black color radio button
56      private void blackRadioButton_CheckedChanged(
57         object sender, System.EventArgs e )
58      {
59         displayLabel.ForeColor = Color.Black;
60      }
61
```

Fig. 10.29 TabControl used to display various font settings. (Part 2 of 4.)

```
62         // event handler for red color radio button
63         private void redRadioButton_CheckedChanged(
64            object sender, System.EventArgs e )
65         {
66            displayLabel.ForeColor = Color.Red;
67         }
68
69         // event handler for green color radio button
70         private void greenRadioButton_CheckedChanged(
71            object sender, System.EventArgs e )
72         {
73            displayLabel.ForeColor = Color.Green;
74         }
75
76         // event handler for size 12 radio button
77         private void size12RadioButton_CheckedChanged(
78            object sender, System.EventArgs e )
79         {
80            displayLabel.Font =
81               new Font( displayLabel.Font.Name, 12 );
82         }
83
84         // event handler for size 16 radio button
85         private void size16RadioButton_CheckedChanged(
86            object sender, System.EventArgs e )
87         {
88            displayLabel.Font =
89               new Font( displayLabel.Font.Name, 16 );
90         }
91
92         // event handler for size 20 radio button
93         private void size20RadioButton_CheckedChanged(
94            object sender, System.EventArgs e )
95         {
96            displayLabel.Font =
97               new Font( displayLabel.Font.Name, 20 );
98         }
99
100        // event handler for message "Hello!" radio button
101        private void helloRadioButton_CheckedChanged(
102           object sender, System.EventArgs e )
103        {
104           displayLabel.Text = "Hello!";
105        }
106
107        // event handler for message "Goodbye!" radio button
108        private void goodByeRadioButton_CheckedChanged(
109           object sender, System.EventArgs e )
110        {
111           displayLabel.Text = "Goodbye!";
112        }
113
114 } // end class UsingTabs
```

Fig. 10.29 TabControl used to display various font settings. (Part 3 of 4.)

Fig. 10.29 **TabControl** used to display various font settings. (Part 4 of 4.)

Software Engineering Observation 10.2

*A **TabPage** can act as a container for a single logical group of radio buttons and enforces their mutual exclusivity. To place multiple radio-button groups inside a single **TabPage**, programmers should group radio buttons within **Panel**s or **GroupBox**es contained within the **TabPage**.*

The last **TabPage** (**aboutTabPage**, line 46) contains a **Label** (**messageLabel**, line 47) that describes the purpose of **TabControl**s.

10.9 Multiple-Document-Interface (MDI) Windows

In previous chapters, we have built only *single-document-interface (SDI)* applications. Such programs (including Notepad or Paint) support only one open window or document at a time. SDI applications usually have contracted abilities—Paint and Notepad, for example, have limited image- and text-editing features. To edit multiple documents, the user must create additional instances of the SDI application.

Multiple document interface (MDI) programs (such as PaintShop Pro and Adobe Photoshop) enable users to edit multiple documents at once. MDI programs also tend to be more complex—PaintShop Pro and Photoshop have a greater number of image-editing features than does Paint. Until now, we had not mentioned that the applications we created were SDI applications. We define this here to emphasize the distinction between the two types of programs.

The application window of an MDI program is called the *parent window*, and each window inside the application is referred to as a *child window*. Although an MDI application can have many child windows, each has only one parent window. Furthermore, a maximum of one child window can be active at once. Child windows cannot be parents themselves and cannot be moved outside their parent. Otherwise, a child window behaves like any other window (with regard to closing, minimizing, resizing etc.). A child window's functionality can be different from the functionality of other child windows of the parent. For example, one child window might edit images, another might edit text and a third might display network traffic graphically, but all could belong to the same MDI parent. Figure 10.30 depicts a sample MDI application.

To create an MDI form, create a new **Form** and set its *IsMDIContainer* property to **True**. The form changes appearance, as in Fig. 10.31.

Fig. 10.30 MDI parent window and MDI child windows.

Fig. 10.31 SDI and MDI forms.

Next, create a child form class to be added to the form. To do this, right-click the project in the **Solution Explorer**, select **Add Windows Form...** and name the file. To add the child form to the parent, we must create a new child form object; set its **MdiParent** property to the parent form, and call method **Show**. The code to create a child usually lies inside an event handler, which creates a new window in response to a user action. Menu selections (such as **File** followed by a submenu option of **New** followed by a submenu option of **Window**) are common methods of creating new child windows.

Form property **MdiChildren** is an array of child **Form** references. This is useful if the parent window wants to check the status of all its children (such as to ensure that all are saved before the parent closes). Property **ActiveMdiChild** returns a reference to the active child window; it returns **null** if there are no active child windows. Other features of MDI windows are described in Fig. 10.32.

Child windows can be minimized, maximized and closed independently of each other and of the parent window. Figure 10.33 shows two images, one containing two minimized child windows and a second containing a maximized child window. When the parent is minimized or closed, the child windows are minimized or closed as well. Notice that the title bar in the second image of Fig. 10.33 is **Parent Window - [Child]**. When a child window is maximized, its title bar is inserted into the parent window's title bar. When a child window is minimized or maximized, its title bar displays a restore icon, which returns the child window to its previous size (its size before it was minimized or maximized).

MDI **Form** events and properties	Description / Delegate and Event Arguments
Common MDI Child Properties	
IsMdiChild	Indicates whether the **Form** is an MDI child. If **True**, **Form** is an MDI child (read-only property).
MdiParent	Specifies the MDI parent **Form** of the child.
Common MDI Parent Properties	
ActiveMdiChild	Returns the **Form** that is the currently active MDI child (returns **null** if no children are active).
IsMdiContainer	Indicates whether a **Form** can be an MDI. If **True**, the **Form** can be an MDI parent. Default is **False**.
MdiChildren	Returns the MDI children as an array of **Form**s.
Common Method	
LayoutMdi	Determines the display of child forms on an MDI parent. Takes as a parameter an **MdiLayout** enumeration with possible values **ArrangeIcons**, **Cascade**, **TileHorizontal** and **TileVertical**. Figure 10.35 depicts the effects of these values.
Common Event	*(Delegate **EventHandler**, event arguments **EventArgs**)*
MdiChildActivate	Generated when an MDI child is closed or activated.

Fig. 10.32 MDI parent and MDI child events and properties.

Parent window icons:
minimize, maximize and close

Maximized child window icons:
minimize, restore and close

Minimized child window icons:
restore, maximize and close

Parent title bar indicates
maximized child

Fig. 10.33 Minimized and maximized child windows.

The parent and child forms can have different menus, which are merged whenever a child window is selected. To specify how the menus merge, programmers can set the *MergeOrder* and the *MergeType* properties for each **MenuItem** (see Fig. 10.3). **MergeOrder** determines the order in which **MenuItem**s appear when two menus are merged. **MenuItem**s with a lower **MergeOrder** value will appear first. For example, if **Menu1** has items **File**, **Edit** and **Window** (and their orders are 0, 10 and 20) and **Menu2** has items **Format** and **View** (and their orders are 7 and 15), then the merged menu contains menu items **File**, **Format**, **Edit**, **View** and **Window**, in that order.

Each **MenuItem** instance has its own **MergeOrder** property. It is likely that, at some point in an application, two **MenuItem**s with the same **MergeOrder** value will merge. Property **MergeType** resolves this conflict by following the order in which the two menus are displayed.

The **MergeType** property takes a *MenuMerge* enumeration value and determines which menu items will be displayed when two menus are merged. A menu item with value *Add* is added to its parent's menu as a new menu on the menu bar (the parent's menu items come first). If a child form's menu item has value *Replace*, it attempts to take the place of its parent form's corresponding menu item during merging. A menu with value *Merge-Items* combines its items with that of its parent's corresponding menu (if parent and child menus originally occupy the same space, their submenus will be brought together as one large menu). A child's menu item with value *Remove* disappears when the menu is merged with that of its parent.

Value **MergeItems** acts passively—if the parent's menu has a **MergeType** that is different from the child menu's **MergeType**, the child's menu setting determines the outcome of the merge. When the child window is closed, the parent's original menu is restored.

 Good Programming Practice 10.1

*When creating MDI applications, include a menu item with its **MdiList** property set to **True**. This helps the user select a child window quickly, rather than having to search for it in the parent window.*

Software Engineering Observation 10.3

*Set the parent's menu items' **MergeType** property to value **MergeItems**. This allows the child window to add most menu items according to its own settings. Parent menu items that must remain should have value **Add**, and those that must be removed should have value **Remove**.*

C# provides a property that facilitates the tracking of which child windows are opened in an MDI container. Property **MdiList** (a boolean) of class **MenuItem** determines whether a **MenuItem** displays a list of open child windows. The list appears at the bottom of the menu following a separator bar (first screen in Figure 10.34). When a new child window is opened, an entry is added to the list. If nine or more child windows are open, the list includes the option **More Windows...**, which allows the user to select a window from a list, using a scrollbar. Multiple **MenuItem**s can have their **MdiList** property set; each displays a list of open child windows.

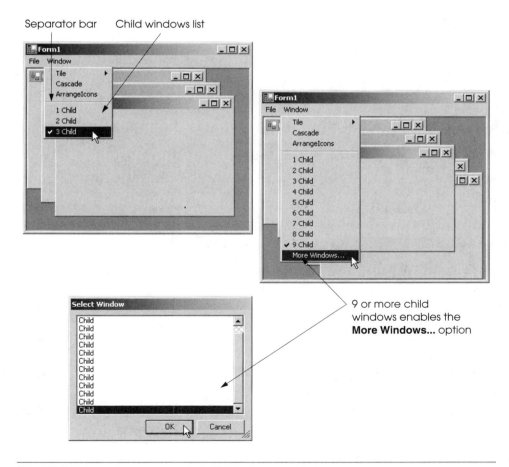

Fig. 10.34 **MenuItem** property **MdiList** example.

MDI containers allow developers to organize the placement of child windows. The child windows in an MDI application can be arranged by calling method **LayoutMdi** of the parent form. Method **LayoutMdi** takes a *MdiLayout* enumeration, which can have values **ArrangeIcons**, **Cascade**, **TileHorizontal** and **TileVertical**. *Tiled windows* completely fill the parent and do not overlap; such windows can be arranged horizontally (value **TileHorizontal**) or vertically (value **TileVertical**). *Cascaded windows* (value **Cascade**) overlap—each is the same size and displays a visible title bar, if possible. Value **ArrangeIcons** arranges the icons for any minimized child windows. If minimized windows are scattered around the parent window, value **ArrangeIcons** orders them neatly at the bottom-left corner of the parent window. Figure 10.35 illustrates the values of the **MdiLayout** enumeration.

Class **UsingMDI** (Fig. 10.36) demonstrates the use of MDI windows. Class **UsingMdi** uses three instances of class **Child** (Fig. 10.37), each of which contains a **PictureBox** and an image of a book cover. The parent MDI form contains a menu that enables users to create and arrange child forms.

ArrangeIcons   **Cascade**

TileHorizontal   **TileVertical**

Fig. 10.35 **MdiLayout** enumeration values.

The MDI parent form (Fig. 10.36) contains two top-level menus. The first of these menus, **File** (**fileMenuItem**, line 13), contains both an **Exit** item (**exitMenuItem**, line 18) and a **New** submenu (**newMenuItem**, line 14) consisting of items for each child window. The second menu, **Format** (**formatMenuItem**, line 19), provides options for laying out the MDI children, plus a list of the active MDI children.

In the **Properties** window, we set the **Form**'s **IsMdiContainer** property to **True**, making the **Form** an MDI parent. In addition, we set **formatMenuItem** property **MdiList** to **True**. This enables **formatMenuItem** to list the active child MDI windows.

```
1   // Fig. 10.36: UsingMDI.cs
2   // Demonstrating use of MDI parent and child windows.
3   using System;
4   using System.Drawing;
5   using System.Collections;
6   using System.ComponentModel;
7   using System.Windows.Forms;
8   using System.Data;
9
10  public class UsingMDI : System.Windows.Forms.Form
11  {
12     private System.Windows.Forms.MainMenu mainMenu1;
13     private System.Windows.Forms.MenuItem fileMenuItem;
14     private System.Windows.Forms.MenuItem newMenuItem;
15     private System.Windows.Forms.MenuItem child1MenuItem;
16     private System.Windows.Forms.MenuItem child2MenuItem;
17     private System.Windows.Forms.MenuItem child3MenuItem;
18     private System.Windows.Forms.MenuItem exitMenuItem;
19     private System.Windows.Forms.MenuItem formatMenuItem;
20     private System.Windows.Forms.MenuItem cascadeMenuItem;
21     private System.Windows.Forms.MenuItem
22        tileHorizontalMenuItem;
23     private System.Windows.Forms.MenuItem
24        tileVerticalMenuItem;
25
26     [STAThread]
27     static void Main()
28     {
29        Application.Run( new UsingMDI() );
30     }
31
32     // create Child 1 when menu clicked
33     private void child1MenuItem_Click(
34        object sender, System.EventArgs e )
35     {
36        // create new child
37        Child formChild = new Child( "Child 1",
38           "\\images\\csharphtp1.jpg" );
39        formChild.MdiParent = this;     // set parent
40        formChild.Show();               // display child
41     }
42
```

Fig. 10.36 MDI parent-window class. (Courtesy of Prentice Hall, Inc.) (Part 1 of 3.)

```
43        // create Child 2 when menu clicked
44        private void child2MenuItem_Click(
45           object sender, System.EventArgs e )
46        {
47           // create new child
48           Child formChild = new Child( "Child 2",
49              "\\images\\vbnethtp2.jpg" );
50           formChild.MdiParent = this;    // set parent
51           formChild.Show();              // display child
52        }
53
54        // create Child 3 when menu clicked
55        private void child3MenuItem_Click(
56           object sender, System.EventArgs e )
57        {
58           // create new child
59           Child formChild = new Child( "Child 3",
60              "\\images\\pythonhtp1.jpg" );
61           formChild.MdiParent = this;    // set parent
62           formChild.Show();              // display child
63        }
64
65        // exit application
66        private void exitMenuItem_Click(
67           object sender, System.EventArgs e )
68        {
69           Application.Exit();
70        }
71
72        // set cascade layout
73        private void cascadeMenuItem_Click(
74           object sender, System.EventArgs e )
75        {
76           this.LayoutMdi( MdiLayout.Cascade );
77        }
78
79        // set TileHorizontal layout
80        private void tileHorizontalMenuItem_Click(
81           object sender, System.EventArgs e )
82        {
83           this.LayoutMdi( MdiLayout.TileHorizontal );
84        }
85
86        // set TileVertical layout
87        private void tileVerticalMenuItem_Click(
88           object sender, System.EventArgs e )
89        {
90           this.LayoutMdi( MdiLayout.TileVertical );
91        }
92
93  } // end class UsingMDI
```

Fig. 10.36 MDI parent-window class. (Courtesy of Prentice Hall, Inc.) (Part 2 of 3.)

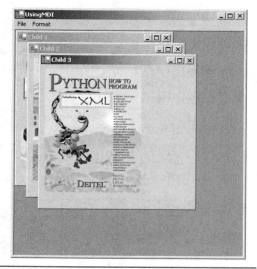

Fig. 10.36 MDI parent-window class. (Courtesy of Prentice Hall, Inc.) (Part 3 of 3.)

The **Cascade** menu item (**cascadeMenuItem**, line 20) has an event handler (**cascadeMenuItem_Click**, lines 73–77) that arranges the child windows in a cascading manner. The event handler calls method **LayoutMdi** with the argument **Cascade** from the **MdiLayout** enumeration (line 76).

The **Tile Horizontal** menu item (**tileHorizontalMenuItem**, lines 21–22) has an event handler (**mnuitmTileHorizontal_Click**, lines 80–84) that arranges the child windows in a horizontal manner. The event handler calls method **LayoutMdi** with the argument **TileHorizontal** from the **MdiLayout** enumeration (line 83).

Finally, the **Tile Vertical** menu item (**mnuitmTileVertical**, lines 23–24) has an event handler (**mnuitmTileVertical_Click**, lines 87–91) that arranges the child windows in a vertical manner. The event handler calls method **LayoutMdi** with the argument **TileVertical** from the **MdiLayout** enumeration (line 90).

To define the child class for the MDI application, right-click the project in the **Solution Explorer** and select first **Add** and then **Add Windows Form...**. Name the new class **Child** (Fig. 10.37).

Next, we add a **PictureBox** (**picDisplay**, line 11) to form **Child**. The constructor invokes method **InitializeComponent** (line 17) and initializes the form's title (line 19) and the image to display in the **PictureBox** (lines 22–23).

The parent MDI form (Fig. 10.36) creates new instances of class **Child** each time the user selects a new child window from the **File** menu. The event handlers in lines 33–63 create new child forms that contain images of Deitel and Associates, Inc. book covers. Each event handler creates a new instance of the child form, sets its **MdiParent** property to the parent form and calls method **Show** to display the child.

10.10 Visual Inheritance

In Chapter 6, Object-Oriented Programming: Inheritance, we discuss how to create classes by inheriting from other classes. In C#, we also can use inheritance to create **Form**s that display a GUI, because **Form**s are classes that derive from class **System.Windows.Forms.Form**. Visual inheritance allows us to create a new **Form** by inheriting from another **Form**. The derived **Form** class contains the functionality of its **Form** base class, including any base-class properties, methods, variables and controls. The derived class also inherits all visual aspects—such as sizing, component layout, spacing between GUI components, colors and fonts—from its base class.

Visual inheritance enables developers to achieve visual consistency across applications by reusing code. For example, a company could define a base form that contains a product's logo, a static background color, a predefined menu bar and other elements. Programmers then could use the base form throughout an application for purposes of uniformity and product branding.

```
1   // Fig. 10.37: Child.cs
2   // Child window of MDI parent.
3   using System;
4   using System.Drawing;
5   using System.Collections;
6   using System.ComponentModel;
7   using System.Windows.Forms;
8   using System.IO;
9
10  public class Child : System.Windows.Forms.Form
11  {
12     private System.Windows.Forms.PictureBox pictureBox;
13
14     public Child( string title, string fileName )
15     {
16        // Required for Windows Form Designer support
17        InitializeComponent();
```

Fig. 10.37 Child class for MDI demonstration. (Part 1 of 2.)

```
18
19              Text = title; // set title text
20
21              // set image to display in pictureBox
22              pictureBox.Image = Image.FromFile(
23                 Directory.GetCurrentDirectory() + fileName );
24           }
25      }
```

Fig. 10.37 Child class for MDI demonstration. (Part 2 of 2.)

Class **VisualInheritance** (Fig. 10.38) is a form that we use as a base class for demonstrating visual inheritance. The GUI contains two labels (one with text **Bugs, Bugs, Bugs** and one with **Copyright 2002, by Bug2Bug.com.**) and one button (displaying the text **Learn More**). When a user presses the **Learn More** button, method **learnMoreButton_Click** (lines 22–29) is invoked. This method displays a message box that provides some informative text.

```
1   // Fig. 10.38: VisualInheritance.cs
2   // Base Form for use with visual inheritance
3   using System;
4   using System.Drawing;
5   using System.Collections;
6   using System.ComponentModel;
7   using System.Windows.Forms;
8   using System.Data;
9
10  public class VisualInheritance : System.Windows.Forms.Form
11  {
12     private System.Windows.Forms.Label bugsLabel;
13     private System.Windows.Forms.Button learnMoreButton;
14     private System.Windows.Forms.Label label1;
15
16     [STAThread]
17     static void Main()
18     {
19        Application.Run( new VisualInheritance() );
20     }
21
22     private void learnMoreButton_Click( object sender,
23        System.EventArgs e )
24     {
25        MessageBox.Show(
26           "Bugs, Bugs, Bugs is a product of Bug2Bug.com",
27           "Learn More", MessageBoxButtons.OK,
28           MessageBoxIcon.Information );
29     }
30  }
```

Fig. 10.38 Class **VisualInheritance**, which inherits from class **Form**, contains a button (**Learn More**). (Part 1 of 2.)

Fig. 10.38 Class **VisualInheritance**, which inherits from class **Form**, contains a button (**Learn More**). (Part 2 of 2.)

Before deriving a form from class **VisualInheritance**, we must package class **VisualInheritance** in a **.dll**. Right click on the **VisualInheritance** project in the **Solution Explorer**, and select **Properties**. In **Common Properties > General**, change the **Output Type** to **Class Library**. Then, build the project to produce a **.dll** that contains the **VisualInheritance** class.

To create the derived form through visual inheritance, create an empty project. From the **Project** menu, select **Add Inherited Form....** This brings up the **Add New Item** window. Select **Inherited Form** from the templates window. Clicking **Open** displays the **Inheritance Picker**. The **Inheritance Picker** tool enables programmers to quickly create a form that inherits from a specified form. Click **Browse**, and select the **.dll** file for class **VisualInheritance**. The **.dll** file normally is located within the **bin\Debug** directory of the **VisualInheritance** project directory. Click **OK**. The Form Designer should now display the inherited form (Fig. 10.39).

Class **VisualInheritanceTest** (Fig. 10.40) derives from class **VisualInheritance**. The GUI contains those components derived from class **VisualInheritance**, plus a button with text **Learn The Program** that we added in class **VisualInheritanceTest**. When a user presses the **Learn The Program** button, method **learnProgramButton_Click** (lines 15–22) is invoked. This method displays a simple message box.

Figure 10.40 demonstrates that the components, their layouts and the functionality of the base class **VisualInheritance** (Fig. 10.38) are inherited by **VisualInheritanceTest**. If a user clicks button **Learn More**, the base-class event handler **learnMoreButton_Click** displays a **MessageBox**.

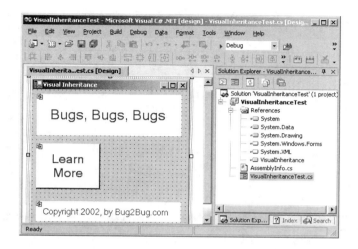

Fig. 10.39 Visual Inheritance through the Form Designer.

```
1   // Fig. 10.40: VisualInheritanceTest.cs
2   // Derived Form using visual inheritance.
3   using System;
4   using System.Collections;
5   using System.ComponentModel;
6   using System.Drawing;
7   using System.Windows.Forms;
8
9   public class VisualInheritanceTest :
10     VisualInheritance.VisualInheritance
11  {
12     private System.Windows.Forms.Button learnProgramButton;
13
14     // invoke when user clicks Learn the Program Button
15     private void learnProgramButton_Click( object sender,
16        System.EventArgs e )
17     {
18        MessageBox.Show(
19           "This program was created by Deitel & Associates",
20           "Learn the Program", MessageBoxButtons.OK,
21           MessageBoxIcon.Information );
22     }
23
24     public static void Main( string[] args )
25     {
26        Application.Run( new VisualInheritanceTest() );
27     }
28  }
```

Fig. 10.40 Class **VisualInheritanceTest**, which inherits from class
VisualInheritance.VisualInheritance, contains an
additional button. (Part 1 of 2.)

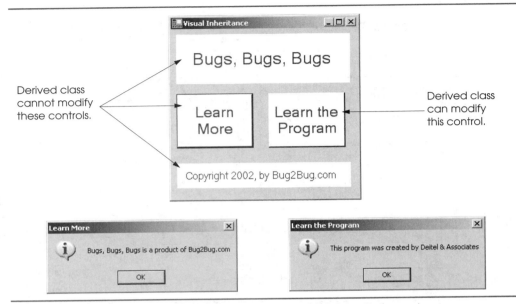

Fig. 10.40 Class **VisualInheritanceTest**, which inherits from class **VisualInheritance.VisualInheritance**, contains an additional button. (Part 2 of 2.)

10.11 User-Defined Controls

The .NET Framework allows programmers to create *custom controls* that inherit from a variety of classes. These custom controls appear in the user's **Toolbox** and can be added to **Form**s, **Panel**s or **GroupBox**es in the same way that we add **Button**s, **Label**s, and other predefined controls. The simplest way to create a custom control is to derive a class from an existing Windows Forms control, such as a **Label**. This is useful if the programmer wants to include functionality of an existing control, rather than having to reimplement the existing control in addition to including the desired new functionality. For example, we can create a new type of label that behaves like a normal **Label** but has a different appearance. We accomplish this by inheriting from class **Label** and overriding method **OnPaint**.

 Look-and-Feel Observation 10.8

*To change the appearance of any control, override method **OnPaint**.*

All controls contain method **OnPaint**, which the system calls when a component must be redrawn (such as when the component is resized). Method **OnPaint** is passed a *PaintEventArgs* object, which contains graphics information—property **Graphics** is the graphics object used to draw, and property *ClipRectangle* defines the rectangular boundary of the control. Whenever the system generates the **Paint** event, our control's base class catches the event. Through polymorphism, our control's **OnPaint** method is called. Our base class's **OnPaint** implementation is not called, so we must call it explicitly from our **OnPaint** implementation before we execute our custom-paint code. Alternatively, if we do not wish to let our base class paint itself, we should not call our base class's **OnPaint** method implementation.

To create a new control composed of existing controls, use class ***UserControl***. Controls added to a custom control are called *constituent controls*. For example, a programmer could create a **UserControl** composed of a button, a label and a text box, each associated with some functionality (such as that the button sets the label's text to that contained in the text box). The **UserControl** acts as a container for the controls added to it. The **UserControl** contains constituent controls, so it does not determine how these constituent controls are displayed. Method **OnPaint** cannot be overridden in these custom controls—their appearance can be modified only by handling each constituent control's **Paint** event. The **Paint** event handler is passed a **PaintEventArgs** object, which can be used to draw graphics (lines, rectangles etc.) on the constituent controls.

Using another technique, a programmer can create a brand-new control by inheriting from class **Control**. This class does not define any specific behavior; that task is left to the programmer. Instead, class **Control** handles the items associated with all controls, such as events and sizing handles. Method **OnPaint** should contain a call to the base class's **OnPaint** method, which calls the **Paint** event handlers. The programmer must then add code for custom graphics inside the overridden **OnPaint** method. This technique allows for the greatest flexibility, but also requires the most planning. All three approaches are summarized in Fig. 10.41.

Custom Control Techniques and **PaintEventArgs** Properties	Description
Inherit from Windows Forms control	Add functionality to a preexisting control. If overriding method **OnPaint**, call base class **OnPaint**. Can only add to the original control appearance, not redesign it.
*Create a **UserControl***	Create a **UserControl** composed of multiple preexisting controls (and combine their functionality). Cannot override **OnPaint** methods of custom controls. Instead, add drawing code to a **Paint** event handler. Can only add to the original control appearance, not redesign it.
*Inherit from class **Control***	Define a brand-new control. Override **OnPaint** method, call base class method **OnPaint** and include methods to draw the control. Can customize control appearance and functionality.
PaintEventArgs *Properties*	*Use this object inside method **OnPaint** or **Paint** to draw on the control.*
Graphics	Indicates the graphics object of control. Used to draw on control.
ClipRectangle	Specifies the rectangle indicating boundary of control.

Fig. 10.41 Custom control creation.

We create a "clock" control in Fig. 10.42. This is a **UserControl** composed of a label and a timer—whenever the timer generates an event, the label is updated to reflect the current time.

Timers (namespace **System.Windows.Forms**) are invisible components that reside on a form and generate *Tick* events at a set interval. This interval is set by the **Timer**'s *Interval* property, which defines the number of milliseconds (thousandths of a second) between events. By default, timers are disabled.

We create a **Form** that displays our custom control, **ClockUserControl** (Fig. 10.42). Create a **UserControl** class for the project by selecting **Project > Add User Control....** This displays a dialog from which we can select the type of control to add—user controls are already selected. We then name the file (and the class) **Clock-UserControl**. This brings up our empty **ClockUserControl** as a grey rectangle.

We can treat this control like a Windows **Form**, so we can add controls (using the **ToolBox**) and set properties (using the **Properties** window). However, instead of creating an application (notice there is no **Main** method in the **Control** class), we are simply creating a new control composed of other controls. We add a **Label** (**displayLabel**, line 15) and a **Timer** (**clockTimer**, line 14) to the **UserControl**. We set the **Timer** interval to 100 milliseconds and update **displayLabel**'s text with each event (lines 18–24). Note that **clockTimer** must be enabled by setting property **Enabled** to **True** in the **Properties** window.

Structure **DateTime** (namespace **System**) contains member **Now**, which is the current time. Method **ToLongTimeString** converts **Now** to a **String** that contains the current hour, minute, and second (along with AM or PM). We use this to set **display-Label**'s **Text** property on line 22.

Once created, our clock control appears as an item on the **ToolBox**. To use the control, we can simply drag it onto a Windows application in our project and run the Windows application. The **ClockUserControl** object has a white background to make it stand out in the form. Figure 10.42 shows the output of **ClockExample**, which is a simple form that contains our **ClockUserControl**.

```
1   // Fig. 10.42: ClockUserControl.cs
2   // User-defined control with a timer and a label.
3
4   using System;
5   using System.Collections;
6   using System.ComponentModel;
7   using System.Drawing;
8   using System.Data;
9   using System.Windows.Forms;
10
11  public class ClockUserControl
12      : System.Windows.Forms.UserControl
13  {
14      private System.Windows.Forms.Timer clockTimer;
15      private System.Windows.Forms.Label displayLabel;
16
```

Fig. 10.42 Programmer-defined control that displays the current time. (Part 1 of 2.)

```
17      // update label at every tick
18      private void clockTimer_Tick(
19         object sender, System.EventArgs e )
20      {
21         // get current time (Now), convert to string
22         displayLabel.Text = DateTime.Now.ToLongTimeString();
23
24      } // end method clockTimer_Tick
25
26  } // end class ClockUserControl
```

Fig. 10.42 Programmer-defined control that displays the current time. (Part 2 of 2.)

The above steps are useful when we need to define a custom control for the project on which we are working. Visual Studio .NET allows developers to share their custom controls with other developers. To create a **UserControl** that can be exported to other solutions, do the following:

1. Create a new **Windows Control Library** project.

2. Inside the project, add controls and functionality to the **UserControl** (Fig. 10.43).

3. Build the project. Visual Studio .NET creates a **.dll** file for the **UserControl** in the output directory. The file is not executable: **Control** classes do not have a **Main** method. Select **Project > Properties** to find the output directory and output file (Fig. 10.44).

4. Create a new Windows application.

5. Import the **UserControl**. In the new Windows application, right click the **ToolBox**, and select **Customize Toolbox...**. In the dialog that appears, select the **.NET Framework Components** tab. Browse for the **.dll** file, which is in the output directory for the Windows control library project. Click the checkbox next to the control, and click **OK** (Fig. 10.45).

6. The **UserControl** appears on the **ToolBox** and can be added to the form as if it were any other control (Fig. 10.46).

Testing and Debugging Tip 10.1

*Control classes do not have a **Main** method—they cannot be run by themselves. To test their functionality, add them to a sample Windows application and run them there.*

Fig. 10.43 Custom-control creation.

Fig. 10.44 Project properties dialog.

Fig. 10.45 Custom control added to the **ToolBox**.

New **ToolBox** icon   Newly inserted control

Fig. 10.46 Custom control added to a **Form**.

Many of today's most successful commercial programs provide GUIs that are easy to use and manipulate. Because of this demand for user-friendly GUIs, the ability to design sophisticated GUIs is an essential programming skill. Fortunately, Visual Studio .NET provides an IDE that makes GUI development quick and easy. In the last two chapters, we have presented the basic techniques required in order to add various GUI components to a program. The next chapter will explore a more behind-the-scenes topic, *multithreading*. In many programming languages, the programmer can create multiple *threads*, enabling several processes to occur at once. By learning to create and manage multithreading in C#, readers will begin their study of a more robust type of software.

10.12 Summary

Menus provide groups of related commands for Windows applications and enable user-application interaction without unnecessarily "cluttering" the GUI.

The **LinkLabel** control is used to display links to other objects, such as files or Web pages. When clicked, a **LinkLabel** generates a **LinkClicked** event.

The **ListBox** control allows the user to view and select multiple items from a list. The **CheckedListBox** control extends a **ListBox** by preceding each item in the list with a check box. This control allows multiple items to be selected with no logical restriction on them. The **SelectedIndexChanged** event occurs when the user selects a new item in a **CheckedListBox**. Property **SelectedItem** returns the currently selected item. **SelectedIndex** returns the index of the selected item.

The **ComboBox** control combines **TextBox** features with a drop-down list. The user can either select an option from the list or type one in (if allowed by the program). Property **DropDownStyle** determines the type of **ComboBox**. The **ComboBox** control has properties **Items** (a collection), **SelectedItem** and **SelectedIndex**, which are similar to the corresponding properties of **ListBox**.

The **TreeView** control can display nodes hierarchically in a tree. A node is one element in the tree. Nodes contain data as well as references to other nodes. A parent node contains child nodes, and the child nodes can be parents themselves. Each node has a **Nodes** collection, which contains a list of the node's children.

The **ListView** control is similar to a **ListBox** except that it can display icons alongside the list items in a variety of ways. To specify the images that will be used for the various icons, the programmer must use an **ImageList** component.

The **TabControl** control creates tabbed windows. This allows capability the programmer to organize information logically and save screen space. **TabControl**s contain **TabPage** objects, which can contain controls. Each **TabPage** generates its own **Click** event when its tab is clicked.

Multiple-document-interface (MDI) programs allow users to open multiple documents (i.e., windows) within the application's main window. Each window inside an MDI application is called a child window, and the application window is called the parent window. The parent and child windows of an application can have different menus, which are merged (combined) whenever a child window is selected.

The .NET Framework allows the programmer to create customized controls. To create a new control composed of existing controls, use class **UserControl**. To create a new control from the ground up, inherit from class **Control**. We create a **UserControl** class for the project by selecting **Project >Add User Control....** We can treat this control like a Windows Form.

Multithreading

Objectives

- To understand the notion of multithreading.
- To appreciate how multithreading can improve program performance.
- To understand how to create, manage and destroy threads.
- To understand the life cycle of a thread.
- To understand thread synchronization.
- To understand thread priorities and scheduling.
- To understand the role of a **ThreadPool** in efficient multithreading.

The spider's touch, how exquisitely fine!
Feels at each thread, and lives along the line.
Alexander Pope

A person with one watch knows what time it is; a person with two watches is never sure.
Proverb

Learn to labor and to wait.
Henry Wadsworth Longfellow

The most general definition of beauty...Multeity in Unity.
Samuel Taylor Coleridge

Outline

11.1   Introduction
11.2   Thread States: Life Cycle of a Thread
11.3   Thread Priorities and Thread Scheduling
11.4   Thread Synchronization and Class `Monitor`
11.5   Producer/Consumer Relationship without Thread Synchronization
11.6   Producer/Consumer Relationship with Thread Synchronization
11.7   Producer/Consumer Relationship: Circular Buffer
11.8   Summary

11.1 Introduction

It would be nice if we could perform one action at a time and perform it well, but that is usually difficult to do. The human body performs a great variety of operations *in parallel*— or, as we will say throughout this chapter, *concurrently*. Respiration, blood circulation and digestion, for example, can occur concurrently. All the senses—sight, touch, smell, taste and hearing—can occur at once. Computers, too, perform operations concurrently. It is common for desktop personal computers to be compiling a program, sending a file to a printer and receiving electronic mail messages over a network concurrently.

Ironically, most programming languages do not enable programmers to specify concurrent activities. Rather, programming languages generally provide only a simple set of control structures that enable programmers to perform one action at a time, proceeding to the next action after the previous one has finished. Historically, the type of concurrency that computers perform today generally has been implemented as operating system "primitives" available only to highly experienced "systems programmers."

The Ada programming language, developed by the United States Department of Defense, made concurrency primitives widely available to defense contractors building military command-and-control systems. However, Ada has not been widely used in universities and commercial industry.

The .NET Framework Class Library makes concurrency primitives available to the applications programmer. The programmer specifies that applications contain "threads of execution," each thread designating a portion of a program that may execute concurrently with other threads—this capability is called *multithreading*. Multithreading is available to all .NET programming languages, including C#, Visual Basic and Visual C++.

Software Engineering Observation 11.1

The .NET Framework Class Library includes multithreading capabilities in namespace `System.Threading`. This encourages the use of multithreading among a larger part of the applications-programming community.

We discuss many applications of concurrent programming. When programs download large files, such as audio clips or video clips from the World Wide Web, users do not want to wait until an entire clip downloads before starting the playback. To solve this problem, we can put multiple threads to work—one thread downloads a clip, and another plays the clip. These activities, or *tasks*, then may proceed concurrently. To avoid choppy playback, we *synchronize* the threads so that the player thread does not begin until there is a sufficient amount of the clip in memory to keep the player thread busy.

Another example of multithreading is C#'s automatic *garbage collection*. C and C++ place with the programmer the responsibility of reclaiming dynamically allocated memory. C# provides a *garbage-collector thread* that reclaims dynamically allocated memory that is no longer needed.

Performance Tip 11.1

One of the reasons for the popularity of C and C++ over the years was that their memory-management techniques were more efficient than those of languages that used garbage collectors. In fact, memory management in C# often is faster than in C or C++.[1]

Good Programming Practice 11.1

Set an object reference to **null** *when the program no longer needs that object. This enables the garbage collector to determine at the earliest possible moment that the object can be garbage collected. If such an object has other references to it, that object cannot be collected.*

Writing multithreaded programs can be tricky. Although the human mind can perform functions concurrently, people find it difficult to jump between parallel "trains of thought." To see why multithreading can be difficult to program and understand, try the following experiment: Open three books to page 1 and try reading the books concurrently. Read a few words from the first book, then read a few words from the second book, then read a few words from the third book, then loop back and read the next few words from the first book, etc. After this experiment, you will appreciate the challenges of multithreading—switching between books, reading briefly, remembering your place in each book, moving the book you are reading closer so you can see it, pushing books you are not reading aside—and amidst all this chaos, trying to comprehend the content of the books!

Performance Tip 11.2

A problem with single-threaded applications is that lengthy activities must complete before other activities can begin. In a multithreaded application, threads can share a processor (or set of processors), so that multiple tasks are performed in parallel.

11.2 Thread States: Life Cycle of a Thread

At any time, a thread is said to be in one of several *thread states* (illustrated in Fig. 11.1).[2] This section discusses these states and the transitions between states. Two classes critical for multithreaded applications are **Thread** and **Monitor** (**System.Threading** namespace). This section also discusses several methods of classes **Thread** and **Monitor** that cause state transitions.

---

1. E. Schanzer, "Performance Considerations for Run-Time Technologies in the .NET Framework," August 2001 **<http://msdn.microsoft.com/library/default.asp?url= /library/en-us/dndotnet/html/dotnetperftechs.asp>**.
2. As this book went to publication, Microsoft changed the names of the *Started* and *Blocked* thread states to *Running* and *WaitSleepJoin*, respectively.

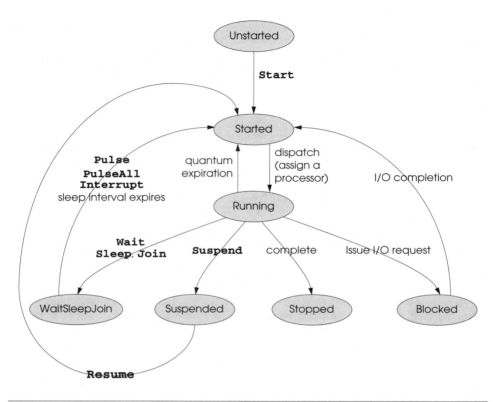

Fig. 11.1 Thread life cyle.

A new thread begins its lifecyle in the *Unstarted* state. The thread remains in the *Unstarted* state until the program calls **Thread** method **Start**, which places the thread in the *Started* state (sometimes called the *Ready* or *Runnable* state) and immediately returns control to the calling thread. Then the thread that invoked **Start**, the newly *Started* thread and any other threads in the program execute concurrently.

The highest priority *Started* thread enters the *Running* state (i.e., begins executing) when the operating system assigns a processor to the thread (Section 11.3 discusses thread priorities). When a *Started* thread receives a processor for the first time and becomes a *Running* thread, the thread executes its **ThreadStart** delegate, which specifies the actions the thread will perform during its lifecycle. When a program creates a new **Thread**, the program specifies the **Thread**'s **ThreadStart** delegate as the argument to the **Thread** constructor. The **ThreadStart** delegate must be a method that returns **void** and takes no arguments.

A *Running* thread enters the *Stopped* (or *Dead*) state when its **ThreadStart** delegate terminates. Note that a program can force a thread into the *Stopped* state by calling **Thread** method **Abort** on the appropriate **Thread** object. Method **Abort** throws a **ThreadAbortException** in the thread, normally causing the thread to terminate. When a thread is in the *Stopped* state and there are no references to the thread object, the garbage collector can remove the thread object from memory.

A thread enters the *Blocked* state when the thread issues an input/output request. The operating system blocks the thread from executing until the operating system can complete the I/O for which the thread is waiting. At that point, the thread returns to the *Started* state, so it can resume execution. A *Blocked* thread cannot use a processor even if one is available.

There are three ways in which a *Running* thread enters the *WaitSleepJoin* state. If a thread encounters code that it cannot execute yet (normally because a condition is not satisfied), the thread can call **Monitor** method **Wait** to enter the *WaitSleepJoin* state. Once in this state, a thread returns to the *Started* state when another thread invokes **Monitor** method **Pulse** or **PulseAll**. Method **Pulse** moves the next waiting thread back to the *Started* state. Method **PulseAll** moves all waiting threads back to the *Started* state.

A *Running* thread can call **Thread** method **Sleep** to enter the *WaitSleepJoin* state for a period of milliseconds specified as the argument to **Sleep**. A sleeping thread returns to the *Started* state when its designated sleep time expires. Sleeping threads cannot use a processor, even if one is available.

Any thread that enters the *WaitSleepJoin* state by calling **Monitor** method **Wait** or by calling **Thread** method **Sleep** also leaves the *WaitSleepJoin* state and returns to the *Started* state if the sleeping or waiting **Thread**'s **Interrupt** method is called by another thread in the program.

If a thread cannot continue executing (we will call this the dependent thread) unless another thread terminates, the dependent thread calls the other thread's **Join** method to "join" the two threads. When two threads are "joined," the dependent thread leaves the *WaitSleepJoin* state when the other thread finishes execution (enters the *Stopped* state).

If a *Running* **Thread**'s **Suspend** method is called, the *Running* thread enters the *Suspended* state. A *Suspended* thread returns to the *Started* state when another thread in the program invokes the Suspended thread's **Resume** method.

11.3 Thread Priorities and Thread Scheduling

Every thread has a priority in the range between **ThreadPriority.Lowest** to **ThreadPriority.Highest**. These two values come from the **ThreadPriority** enumeration (namespace **System.Threading**). The enumeration consists of the values **Lowest**, **BelowNormal**, **Normal**, **AboveNormal** and **Highest**. By default, each thread has priority **Normal**.

The Windows operating system supports a concept, called *timeslicing,* that enables threads of equal priority to share a processor. Without timeslicing, each thread in a set of equal-priority threads runs to completion (unless the thread leaves the *Running* state and enters the *WaitSleepJoin*, *Suspended* or *Blocked* state) before the thread's peers get a chance to execute. With timeslicing, each thread receives a brief burst of processor time, called a *quantum*, during which the thread can execute. At the completion of the quantum, even if the thread has not finished executing, the processor is taken away from that thread and given to the next thread of equal priority, if one is available.

The job of the thread scheduler is to keep the highest-priority thread running at all times and, if there is more than one highest-priority thread, to ensure that all such threads execute for a quantum in round-robin fashion (i.e., these threads can be timesliced). Figure 11.2 illustrates the multilevel priority queue for threads. In Fig. 11.2, assuming a single-processor computer, threads A and B each execute for a quantum in round-robin fashion until both threads complete execution. This means that A gets a quantum of time to run. Then B gets a quantum. Then A gets another quantum. Then B gets another quantum. This continues until one thread completes. The processor then devotes all its power to the thread that remains (unless another thread of that priority is *Started*). Next, thread C runs to completion. Threads D, E and F each execute for a quantum in round-robin fashion until they all complete execution. This process continues until all threads run to completion. Note that, depending on the operating system, new higher-priority threads could postpone—possibly indefinitely—the execution of lower-priority threads. Such *indefinite postponement* often is referred to more colorfully as *starvation*.

A thread's priority can be adjusted with the **Priority** property, which accepts values from the **ThreadPriority** enumeration. If the argument is not one of the valid thread-priority constants, an **ArgumentException** occurs.

A thread executes until it dies, becomes *Blocked* for input/output (or some other reason), calls **Sleep**, calls **Monitor** method **Wait** or **Join**, is preempted by a thread of higher priority or has its quantum expire. A thread with a higher priority than the *Running* thread can become *Started* (and hence preempt the *Running* thread) if a sleeping thread wakes up, if I/O completes for a thread that *Blocked* for that I/O, if either **Pulse** or **PulseAll** is called on an object on which **Wait** was called, or if a thread to which the high-priority thread was **Join**ed completes.

Figure 11.3 demonstrates basic threading techniques, including the construction of a **Thread** object and using the **Thread** class's **static** method **Sleep**. The program creates three threads of execution, each with the default priority **Normal**. Each thread displays a message indicating that it is going to sleep for a random interval of from 0 to 5000 milliseconds, then goes to sleep. When each thread awakens, the thread displays its name, indicates that it is done sleeping, terminates and enters the *Stopped* state. You will see that method **Main** (i.e., the *Main thread of execution*) terminates before the application terminates. The program consists of two classes—**ThreadTester** (lines 8–41), which creates the three threads, and **MessagePrinter** (lines 44–73), which defines a **Print** method containing the actions each thread will perform.

Objects of class **MessagePrinter** (lines 44–73) control the lifecycle of each of the three threads class **ThreadTester**'s **Main** method creates. Class **MessagePrinter** consists of instance variable **sleepTime** (line 46), **static** variable **random** (line 47), a constructor (lines 50–54) and a **Print** method (lines 57–71). Variable **sleepTime** stores a random integer value chosen when a new **MessagePrinter** object's constructor is called. Each thread controlled by a **MessagePrinter** object sleeps for the amount of time specified by the corresponding **MessagePrinter** object's **sleepTime**

The **MessagePrinter** constructor (lines 50–54) initializes **sleepTime** to a random integer from 0 up to, but not including, 5001 (i.e., from 0 to 5000).

Method **Print** begins by obtaining a reference to the currently executing thread (line 60) via class **Thread**'s **static** property *CurrentThread*. The currently executing thread is the one that invokes method **Print**. Next, lines 63–64 display a message indicating the name of the currently executing thread and stating that the thread is going to sleep for a certain number of milliseconds. Note that line 64 uses the currently executing thread's **Name** property to obtain the thread's name (set in method **Main** when each thread is created). Line 66 invokes **static Thread** method **Sleep** to place the thread into the *Wait-SleepJoin* state. At this point, the thread loses the processor and the system allows another thread to execute. When the thread awakens, it reenters the *Started* state again until the system assigns a processor to the thread. When the **MessagePrinter** object enters the *Running* state again, line 69 outputs the thread's name in a message that indicates the thread is done sleeping, and method **Print** terminates.

Class **ThreadTester**'s **Main** method (lines 10–39) creates three objects of class **MessagePrinter**, at lines 14, 19 and 24, respectively. Lines 15–16, 20–21 and 25–26 create and initialize three **Thread** objects. Lines 17, 22 and 27 set each **Thread**'s **Name** property, which we use for output purposes. Note that each **Thread**'s constructor receives a **ThreadStart** delegate as an argument. Remember that a **ThreadStart** delegate specifies the actions a thread performs during its lifecyle. Line 16 specifies that the delegate for **thread1** will be method **Print** of the object to which **printer1** refers. When **thread1** enters the *Running* state for the first time, **thread1** will invoke **printer1**'s **Print** method to perform the tasks specified in method **Print**'s body. Thus, **thread1** will print its name, display the amount of time for which it will go to sleep, sleep for that amount of time, wake up and display a message indicating that the thread is done sleeping. At that point method **Print** will terminate. A thread completes its task when the method specified by a **Thread**'s **ThreadStart** delegate terminates, placing the thread in the *Stopped* state. When **thread2** and **thread3** enter the *Running* state for the first time, they invoke the **Print** methods of **printer2** and **printer3**, respectively. Threads **thread2** and **thread3** perform the same tasks as **thread1** by executing the **Print** methods of the objects to which **printer2** and **printer3** refer (each of which has its own randomly chosen sleep time).

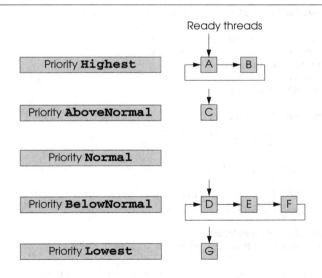

Fig. 11.2   Thread-priority scheduling.

```
1   // Fig. 11.3: ThreadTester.cs
2   // Multiple threads printing at different intervals.
3
```

Fig. 11.3   Threads sleeping and printing. (Part 1 of 3.)

```
 4   using System;
 5   using System.Threading;
 6
 7   // class ThreadTester demonstrates basic threading concepts
 8   class ThreadTester
 9   {
10      static void Main( string[] args )
11      {
12         // Create and name each thread. Use MessagePrinter's
13         // Print method as argument to ThreadStart delegate.
14         MessagePrinter printer1 = new MessagePrinter();
15         Thread thread1 =
16            new Thread ( new ThreadStart( printer1.Print ) );
17         thread1.Name = "thread1";
18
19         MessagePrinter printer2 = new MessagePrinter();
20         Thread thread2 =
21            new Thread ( new ThreadStart( printer2.Print ) );
22         thread2.Name = "thread2";
23
24         MessagePrinter printer3 = new MessagePrinter();
25         Thread thread3 =
26            new Thread ( new ThreadStart( printer3.Print  ) );
27         thread3.Name = "thread3";
28
29         Console.WriteLine( "Starting threads" );
30
31         // call each thread's Start method to place each
32         // thread in Started state
33         thread1.Start();
34         thread2.Start();
35         thread3.Start();
36
37         Console.WriteLine( "Threads started\n" );
38
39      } // end method Main
40
41   } // end class ThreadTester
42
43   // Print method of this class used to control threads
44   class MessagePrinter
45   {
46      private int sleepTime;
47      private static Random random = new Random();
48
49      // constructor to initialize a MessagePrinter object
50      public MessagePrinter()
51      {
52         // pick random sleep time between 0 and 5 seconds
53         sleepTime = random.Next( 5001 );
54      }
55
```

Fig. 11.3 Threads sleeping and printing. (Part 2 of 3.)

```
56      // method Print controls thread that prints messages
57      public void Print()
58      {
59          // obtain reference to currently executing thread
60          Thread current = Thread.CurrentThread;
61
62          // put thread to sleep for sleepTime amount of time
63          Console.WriteLine(
64              current.Name + " going to sleep for " + sleepTime );
65
66          Thread.Sleep ( sleepTime );
67
68          // print thread name
69          Console.WriteLine( current.Name + " done sleeping" );
70
71      } // end method Print
72
73  } // end class MessagePrinter
```

```
Starting threads
Threads started

thread1 going to sleep for 1977
thread2 going to sleep for 4513
thread3 going to sleep for 1261
thread3 done sleeping
thread1 done sleeping
thread2 done sleeping
```

```
Starting threads
Threads started

thread1 going to sleep for 1466
thread2 going to sleep for 4245
thread3 going to sleep for 1929
thread1 done sleeping
thread3 done sleeping
thread2 done sleeping
```

Fig. 11.3   Threads sleeping and printing. (Part 3 of 3.)

Testing and Debugging Tip 11.1

*Naming threads helps in the debugging of a multithreaded program. Visual Studio .NET's debugger provides a **Threads** window that displays the name of each thread and enables you to view the execution of any thread in the program.*

Lines 33–35 invoke each **Thread**'s **Start** method to place the threads in the *Started* state (sometimes called *launching a thread*). Method **Start** returns immediately from each invocation, then line 37 outputs a message indicating that the threads were started, and the **Main** thread of execution terminates. The program itself does not terminate, however, because there are still threads that are alive (i.e., the threads were *Started* and have not reached the *Stopped* state yet). The program will not terminate until its last thread dies. When the system assigns a processor to a thread, the thread enters the *Running* state and calls the method specified by the thread's **ThreadStart** delegate. In this program, each thread invokes method **Print** of the appropriate **MessagePrinter** object to perform the tasks discussed previously.

Note that the sample outputs for this program show each thread and the thread's sleep time as the thread goes to sleep. The thread with the shortest sleep time normally awakens first, then indicates that it is done sleeping and terminates. In Section 11.7, we discuss multithreading issues that could prevent the thread with the shortest sleep time from awakening first.

11.4 Thread Synchronization and Class Monitor

Often, multiple threads of execution manipulate shared data. If threads with access to shared data simply read that data, then there is no need to prevent the data from being accessed by more than one thread at a time. However, when multiple threads share data and that data is modified by one or more of those threads, then indeterminate results may occur. If one thread is in the process of updating the data and another thread tries to update it too, the data will reflect the update that occurs second. If the data is an array or other data structure in which the threads could update separate parts of the data concurrently, it is possible that part of the data will reflect the information from one thread while another part of the data will reflect information from a different thread. When this happens, the program has difficulty determining when the data has been updated properly.

The problem can be solved by giving one thread at a time exclusive access to code that manipulates the shared data. During that time, other threads desiring to manipulate the data should be kept waiting. When the thread with exclusive access to the data completes its manipulation of the data, one of the threads waiting to manipulate the data should be allowed to proceed. In this fashion, each thread accessing the shared data excludes all other threads from doing so simultaneously. This is called *mutual exclusion* or *thread synchronization*.

C# uses the .NET Framework's monitors[3] to perform synchronization. Class **Monitor** provides the methods for *locking objects* to implement synchronized access to shared data. Locking an object means that only one thread can access that object at a time. When a thread wishes to acquire exclusive control over an object, the thread invokes **Monitor** method *Enter* to acquire the lock on that data object. Each object has a *SyncBlock* that maintains the state of that object's lock. Methods of class **Monitor** use the data in an object's *SyncBlock* to determine the state of the lock for that object. After acquiring the lock for an object, a thread can manipulate that object's data. While the object is locked, all other threads attempting to acquire the lock on that object are blocked (i.e., they enter the *Blocked* state) from acquiring the lock. When the thread that locked the shared object no longer requires the lock, that thread invokes **Monitor** method *Exit* to release the lock. This updates the *SyncBlock* of the shared object to indicate that the lock for the object is avail-

---

3. Hoare, C. A. R., Monitors: An Operating System Structuring Concept, *Communications of the ACM*. Vol. 17, No. 10, October 1974: 549–557. *Corrigendum, Communications of the ACM*. Vol. 18, No. 2, February 1975: 95.

able again. At this point, if there is a thread that was previously blocked from acquiring the lock on the shared object, that thread acquires the lock to begin its processing of the object. If all threads with access to an object attempt to acquire the object's lock before manipulating the object, only one thread at a time will be allowed to manipulate the object. This helps ensure the integrity of the data.

Common Programming Error 11.1

Make sure that all code that updates a shared object locks the object before doing so. Otherwise a thread calling a method that does not lock the object can make the object unstable even when another thread has acquired the lock for the object.

Common Programming Error 11.2

Deadlock occurs when a waiting thread (let us call this thread1*) cannot proceed because it is waiting for another thread (let us call this* thread2*) to proceed. Similarly,* thread2 *cannot proceed because it is waiting for* thread1 *to proceed. The two threads are waiting for each other; therefore, the actions that would enable each thread to continue execution never occur.*

C# provides another means of manipulating an object's lock—keyword **lock**. Placing **lock** before a block of code (designated with braces) as in

```
lock ( objectReference )
{
    // code that requires synchronization goes here
}
```

obtains the lock on the object to which the *objectReference* in parentheses refers. The *objectReference* is the same reference that normally would be passed to **Monitor** methods **Enter**, **Exit**, **Pulse** and **PulseAll**. When a **lock** block terminates for any reason, C# releases the lock on the object to which the *objectReference* refers. We explain **lock** further in Section 11.7.

If a thread determines that it cannot perform its task on a locked object, the thread can call **Monitor** method **Wait** and pass as an argument the object on which the thread will wait until the thread can perform its task. Calling method **Monitor.Wait** from a thread releases the lock the thread has on the object **Wait** receives as an argument and places that thread into the *WaitSleepJoin* state for that object. A thread in the *WaitSleepJoin* state for an object leaves the *WaitSleepJoin* state when a separate thread invokes **Monitor** method **Pulse** or **PulseAll** with the object as an argument. Method **Pulse** transitions the object's first waiting thread from the *WaitSleepJoin* state to the *Started* state. Method **PulseAll** transitions all threads in the object's *WaitSleepJoin* state to the *Started* state. The transition to the *Started* state enables the thread (or threads) to get ready to continue executing.

There is a difference between threads waiting to acquire the lock for an object and threads waiting in an object's *WaitSleepJoin* state: The threads called **Monitor** method **Wait** with the object as an argument. Threads that are waiting to acquire the lock enter the *Blocked* state and wait there until the object's lock becomes available. Then, one of the blocked threads can acquire the object's lock.

Monitor methods **Enter**, **Exit**, **Wait**, **Pulse** and **PulseAll** all take a reference to an object—usually the keyword **this**—as their argument.

Common Programming Error 11.3

A thread in the WaitSleepJoin *state cannot reenter the* Started *state to continue execution until a separate thread invokes* **Monitor** *method* **Pulse** *or* **PulseAll** *with the appropriate object as an argument. If this does not occur, the waiting thread will wait forever and so can cause deadlock.*

Testing and Debugging Tip 11.2

When multiple threads manipulate a shared object, using monitors, ensure that, if one thread calls **Monitor** *method* **Wait** *to enter the* WaitSleepJoin *state for the shared object, a separate thread eventually will call* **Monitor** *method* **Pulse** *to transition the thread waiting on the shared object back to the* Started *state. If multiple threads may be waiting for the shared object, a separate thread can call* **Monitor** *method* **PulseAll** *as a safeguard to ensure that all waiting threads have another opportunity to perform their tasks.*

Performance Tip 11.3

Synchronization to achieve correctness in multithreaded programs can make programs run more slowly, as a result of monitor overhead and the frequent transitioning of threads among the Running, WaitSleepJoin *and* Started *states. There is not much to say, however, for highly efficient, incorrect multithreaded programs!*

11.5 Producer/Consumer Relationship without Thread Synchronization

In a *producer/consumer relationship*, the *producer* portion of an application generates data and the *consumer* portion of an application uses that data. In a multithreaded producer/consumer relationship, a *producer thread* calls a *produce method* to generate data and place it into a shared region of memory, called a *buffer*. A *consumer thread* calls a *consume method* to read that data. If the producer waiting to put the next data into the buffer determines that the consumer has not yet read the previous data from the buffer, the producer thread should call **Wait**; otherwise, the consumer never sees the previous data and that data is lost to that application. When the consumer thread reads the message, it should call **Pulse** to allow a waiting producer to proceed. If a consumer thread finds the buffer empty or finds that the previous data has already been read, the consumer should call **Wait**; otherwise, the consumer might read "garbage" from the buffer or the consumer might process a previous data item more than once—each of these possibilities results in a logic error in the application. When the producer places the next data into the buffer, the producer should call **Pulse** to allow the consumer thread to proceed.

Let us consider how logic errors can arise if we do not synchronize access among multiple threads manipulating shared data. Consider a producer/consumer relationship in which a producer thread writes a sequence of numbers (we use 1–4) into a *shared buffer*—a memory location shared between multiple threads. The consumer thread reads this data from the shared buffer then displays the data. We display in the program's output the values that the producer writes (produces) and that the consumer reads (consumes). Figure 11.4 demonstrates a producer and a consumer accessing a single shared cell (**int** variable **buffer**) of memory without any synchronization. Both the consumer and the producer threads access this single cell: The producer thread writes to the cell; the consumer thread reads from it. We would like each value the producer thread writes to the shared cell to be consumed exactly once by the consumer thread. However, the threads in this example are not synchronized. Therefore, data can be lost if the producer places new data into the slot before the consumer consumes the previous data. Also, data can be incorrectly repeated if the consumer consumes data again before the producer produces the next item. To show these possibilities, the consumer thread in the following example keeps a total of all the values it reads. The producer thread produces values from 1 to 4. If the consumer reads each value produced once and only once, the total would be 10. However, if you execute this program several times, you will see that the total is rarely, if ever, 10. Also, to emphasize our point, the producer and consumer threads in the example each sleep for random intervals of up to three seconds between performing their tasks. Thus, we do not know exactly when the producer thread will attempt to write a new value, nor do we know when the consumer thread will attempt to read a value.

The program consists of four classes—**HoldIntegerUnsynchronized** (lines 9–34), **Producer** (lines 37–70), **Consumer** (73–106) and **SharedCell** (109–144).

```
1   // Fig. 11.4: Unsynchronized.cs
2   // Showing multiple threads modifying a shared object without
3   // synchronization.
4
5   using System;
6   using System.Threading;
7
8   // this class represents a single shared int
9   public class HoldIntegerUnsynchronized
10  {
11      // buffer shared by producer and consumer threads
12      private int buffer = -1;
13
14      // property Buffer
15      public int Buffer
16      {
17          get
18          {
19              Console.WriteLine( Thread.CurrentThread.Name +
20                  " reads " + buffer );
21
22              return buffer;
23          }
24
25          set
26          {
27              Console.WriteLine( Thread.CurrentThread.Name +
28                  " writes " + value );
29
30              buffer = value;
31          }
32
33      } // end property Buffer
34
35  } // end class HoldIntegerUnsynchronized
```

Fig. 11.4   Producer and consumer threads accessing a shared object without synchronization. (Part 1 of 4.)

```
36
37   // class Producer's Produce method controls a thread that
38   // stores values from 1 to 4 in sharedLocation
39   class Producer
40   {
41      private HoldIntegerUnsynchronized sharedLocation;
42      private Random randomSleepTime;
43
44      // constructor
45      public Producer(
46         HoldIntegerUnsynchronized shared, Random random )
47      {
48         sharedLocation = shared;
49         randomSleepTime = random;
50      }
51
52      // store values 1-4 in object sharedLocation
53      public void Produce()
54      {
55         // sleep for random interval upto 3000 milliseconds
56         // then set sharedLocation's Buffer property
57         for ( int count = 1; count <= 4; count++ )
58         {
59            Thread.Sleep( randomSleepTime.Next( 1, 3000 ) );
60            sharedLocation.Buffer = count;
61         }
62
63         Console.WriteLine( Thread.CurrentThread.Name +
64            " done producing.\nTerminating " +
65            Thread.CurrentThread.Name + "." );
66
67      } // end method Produce
68
69   } // end class Producer
70
71   // class Consumer's Consume method controls a thread that
72   // loops four times and reads a value from sharedLocation
73   class Consumer
74   {
75      private HoldIntegerUnsynchronized sharedLocation;
76      private Random randomSleepTime;
77
78      // constructor
79      public Consumer(
80         HoldIntegerUnsynchronized shared, Random random )
81      {
82         sharedLocation = shared;
83         randomSleepTime = random;
84      }
85
```

Fig. 11.4   Producer and consumer threads accessing a shared object without synchronization. (Part 2 of 4.)

```
86      // read sharedLocation's value four times
87      public void Consume()
88      {
89         int sum = 0;
90
91         // sleep for random interval up to 3000 milliseconds
92         // then add sharedLocation's Buffer property value
93         // to sum
94         for ( int count = 1; count <= 4; count++ )
95         {
96            Thread.Sleep( randomSleepTime.Next( 1, 3000 ) );
97            sum += sharedLocation.Buffer;
98         }
99
100        Console.WriteLine( Thread.CurrentThread.Name +
101           " read values totaling: " + sum +
102           ".\nTerminating " + Thread.CurrentThread.Name + "." );
103
104     } // end method Consume
105
106  } // end class Consumer
107
108  // this class creates producer and consumer threads
109  class SharedCell
110  {
111     // create producer and consumer threads and start them
112     static void Main( string[] args )
113     {
114        // create shared object used by threads
115        HoldIntegerUnsynchronized holdInteger =
116           new HoldIntegerUnsynchronized();
117
118        // Random object used by each thread
119        Random random = new Random();
120
121        // create Producer and Consumer objects
122        Producer producer =
123           new Producer( holdInteger, random );
124
125        Consumer consumer =
126           new Consumer( holdInteger, random );
127
128        // create threads for producer and consumer and set
129        // delegates for each thread
130        Thread producerThread =
131           new Thread( new ThreadStart( producer.Produce ) );
132        producerThread.Name = "Producer";
133
134        Thread consumerThread =
135           new Thread( new ThreadStart( consumer.Consume ) );
136        consumerThread.Name = "Consumer";
137
```

Fig. 11.4 Producer and consumer threads accessing a shared object without synchronization. (Part 3 of 4.)

```
138        // start each thread
139        producerThread.Start();
140        consumerThread.Start();
141
142    } // end method Main
143
144 } // end class SharedCell
```

```
Consumer reads -1
Producer writes 1
Consumer reads 1
Consumer reads 1
Consumer reads 1
Consumer read values totaling: 2.
Terminating Consumer.
Producer writes 2
Producer writes 3
Producer writes 4
Producer done producing.
Terminating Producer.
```

```
Producer writes 1
Producer writes 2
Consumer reads 2
Producer writes 3
Consumer reads 3
Producer writes 4
Producer done producing.
Terminating Producer.
Consumer reads 4
Consumer reads 4
Consumer read values totaling: 13.
Terminating Consumer.
```

```
Producer writes 1
Consumer reads 1
Producer writes 2
Consumer reads 2
Producer writes 3
Consumer reads 3
Producer writes 4
Producer done producing.
Terminating Producer.
Consumer reads 4
Consumer read values totaling: 10.
Terminating Consumer.
```

Fig. 11.4 Producer and consumer threads accessing a shared object without synchronization. (Part 4 of 4.)

Class **HoldIntegerUnsynchronized** (lines 9–35) consists of instance variable **buffer** (line 12) and property **Buffer** (lines 15–33), which provides **get** and **set** accessors. Property **Buffer**'s accessors do not synchronize access to instance variable **buffer**. Note that each accessor uses class **Thread**'s **static** property **Current-Thread** to obtain a reference to the currently executing thread, then uses that thread's property **Name** to obtain the thread's name.

Class **Producer** (lines 39–69) consists of instance variable **sharedLocation** (line 41), instance variable **randomSleepTime** (line 42), a constructor (lines 45–50) to initialize the instance variables and a **Produce** method (lines 53–67). The constructor initializes instance variable **sharedLocation** to refer to the **HoldInteger-Unsynchronized** object received from method **Main** as the argument **shared**. The producer thread in this program executes the tasks specified in method **Produce** of class **Producer**. Method **Produce** contains a **for** structure (lines 57–61) that loops four times. Each iteration of the loop first invokes **Thread** method **Sleep** to place producer thread into the *WaitSleepJoin* state for a random time interval between 0 and 3 seconds. When the thread awakens, line 61 assigns the value of control variable **count** to the **HoldIntegerUnsynchronized** object's **Buffer** property, which causes the **set** accessor of **HoldIntegerUnsynchronized** to modify the **buffer** instance variable of the **HoldIntegerUnsynchronized** object. When the loop completes, lines 63–65 display a line of text in the console window indicating that the thread finished producing data and that the thread is terminating, then the **Produce** method terminates and so places the producer thread in the *Stopped* state.

Class **Consumer** (73–106) consists of instance variable **sharedLocation** (line 75), instance variable **randomSleepTime** (line 76), a constructor (lines 79–84) to initialize the instance variables and a **Consume** method (lines 87–104). The constructor initializes **sharedLocation** to refer to the **HoldIntegerUnsynchronized** received from **Main** as the argument **shared**. The consumer thread in this program performs the tasks specified in class **Consumer**'s **Consume** method. The method contains a **for** structure (lines 94–98) that loops four times. Each iteration of the loop invokes **Thread** method **Sleep** to put the consumer thread into the *WaitSleepJoin* state for a random time interval between 0 and 3 seconds. Next, line 97 gets the value of the **HoldIntegerUnsynchronized** object's **Buffer** property and adds the value to the variable **sum**. When the loop completes, lines 100–102 display a line in the console window indicating the sum of all values read, then the **Consume** method terminates, which places the consumer thread in the *Stopped* state.

Note: We use method **Sleep** in this example to emphasize the fact that, in multi-threaded applications, it is unclear when each thread will perform its task and for how long it will perform that task when it has the processor. Normally, these thread-scheduling issues are the job of the computer's operating system. In this program, our thread's tasks are quite simple—for the producer, loop four times and perform an assignment statement; for the consumer, loop four times and add a value to variable **sum**. Without the **Sleep** method call, and if the producer executes first, the producer would complete its task before the consumer ever gets a chance to execute. If the consumer executes first, it would consume -1 four times, then terminate before the producer can produce the first real value.

Class **SharedCell**'s **Main** method (lines 112–142) instantiates a shared **Hold-IntegerUnsynchronized** object (lines 115–116) and a **Random** object (line 119) for generating random sleep times and uses them as arguments to the constructors for the objects of classes **Producer** (lines 122–123) and **Consumer** (lines 125–126). The **HoldIntegerUnsynchronized** object contains the data that will be shared between the producer and consumer threads. Lines 130–132 create and name **producerThread**. The **ThreadStart** delegate for **producerThread** specifies that the thread will execute method **Produce** of object **producer**. Lines 134–136 create and name the **consumerThread**. The **ThreadStart** delegate for the **consumerThread** specifies that the thread will execute method **Consume** of object **consumer**. Finally, lines 139–140 place the two threads in the *Started* state by invoking each thread's **Start** method, then the **Main** thread terminates.

Ideally, we would like every value produced by the **Producer** object to be consumed exactly once by the **Consumer** object. However, when we study the first output of Fig. 11.4, we see that the consumer retrieved a value (-1) before the producer ever placed a value in the shared buffer and that the value 1 was consumed three times. The consumer finished executing before the producer had an opportunity to produce the values 2, 3 and 4. Therefore, those three values were lost. In the second output, we see that the value 1 was lost, because the values 1 and 2 were produced before the consumer thread could read the value 1. Also, the value 4 was consumed twice. The last sample output demonstrates that it is possible, with some luck, to get a proper output in which each value the producer produces is consumed once and only once by the consumer. This example clearly demonstrates that access to shared data by concurrent threads must be controlled carefully; otherwise, a program may produce incorrect results.

To solve the problems of lost data and data consumed more than once in the previous example, we will (in Fig. 11.5) synchronize access of the concurrent producer and consumer threads to the code that manipulates the shared data by using **Monitor** class methods **Enter**, **Wait**, **Pulse** and **Exit**. When a thread uses synchronization to access a shared object, the object is *locked*, so no other thread can acquire the lock for that shared object at the same time.

11.6 Producer/Consumer Relationship with Thread Synchronization

Figure 11.5 demonstrates a producer and a consumer accessing a shared cell of memory with synchronization, so that the consumer consumes only after the producer produces a value and the producer produces a new value only after the consumer consumes the previous value produced. Classes **Producer** (lines 90–123), **Consumer** (lines 126–162) and **SharedCell** (lines 165–200) are identical to Fig. 11.4, except that they use the new class **HoldIntegerSynchronized** in this example. [Note: In this example, we demonstrate synchronization with class **Monitor**'s **Enter** and **Exit** methods. In the next example, we demonstrate the same concepts via a **lock** block.]

```
1   // Fig. 11.5: Synchronized.cs
2   // Showing multiple threads modifying a shared object with
3   // synchronization.
```

Fig. 11.5 Producer and consumer threads accessing a shared object with synchronization. (Part 1 of 8.)

```
 4
 5   using System;
 6   using System.Threading;
 7
 8   // this class synchronizes access to an integer
 9   public class HoldIntegerSynchronized
10   {
11      // buffer shared by producer and consumer threads
12      private int buffer = -1;
13
14      // occupiedBufferCount maintains count of occupied buffers
15      private int occupiedBufferCount = 0;
16
17      // property Buffer
18      public int Buffer
19      {
20         get
21         {
22            // obtain lock on this object
23            Monitor.Enter( this );
24
25            // if there is no data to read, place invoking
26            // thread in WaitSleepJoin state
27            if ( occupiedBufferCount == 0 )
28            {
29               Console.WriteLine(
30                  Thread.CurrentThread.Name + " tries to read." );
31
32               DisplayState( "Buffer empty. " +
33                  Thread.CurrentThread.Name + " waits." );
34
35               Monitor.Wait( this );
36            }
37
38            // indicate that producer can store another value
39            // because a consumer just retrieved buffer value
40            --occupiedBufferCount;
41
42            DisplayState(
43               Thread.CurrentThread.Name + " reads " + buffer );
44
45            // tell waiting thread (if there is one) to
46            // become ready to execute (Started state)
47            Monitor.Pulse( this );
48
49            // Get copy of buffer before releasing lock.
50            // It is possible that the producer could be
51            // assigned the processor immediately after the
52            // monitor is released and before the return
53            // statement executes. In this case, the producer
54            // would assign a new value to buffer before the
55            // return statement returns the value to the
```

Fig. 11.5   Producer and consumer threads accessing a shared object with synchronization. (Part 2 of 8.)

```
56              // consumer. Thus, the consumer would receive the
57              // new value. Making a copy of buffer and
58              // returning the copy ensures that the
59              // consumer receives the proper value.
60              int bufferCopy = buffer;
61
62              // release lock on this object
63              Monitor.Exit( this );
64
65              return bufferCopy;
66
67          } // end get
68
69          set
70          {
71              // acquire lock for this object
72              Monitor.Enter( this );
73
74              // if there are no empty locations, place invoking
75              // thread in WaitSleepJoin state
76              if ( occupiedBufferCount == 1 )
77              {
78                  Console.WriteLine(
79                      Thread.CurrentThread.Name + " tries to write." );
80
81                  DisplayState( "Buffer full. " +
82                      Thread.CurrentThread.Name + " waits." );
83
84                  Monitor.Wait( this );
85              }
86
87              // set new buffer value
88              buffer = value;
89
90              // indicate producer cannot store another value
91              // until consumer retrieves current buffer value
92              ++occupiedBufferCount;
93
94              DisplayState(
95                  Thread.CurrentThread.Name + " writes " + buffer );
96
97              // tell waiting thread (if there is one) to
98              // become ready to execute (Started state)
99              Monitor.Pulse( this );
100
101             // release lock on this object
102             Monitor.Exit( this );
103
104         } // end set
105
106     }
107
```

Fig. 11.5 Producer and consumer threads accessing a shared object with synchronization. (Part 3 of 8.)

```
108        // display current operation and buffer state
109        public void DisplayState( string operation )
110        {
111           Console.WriteLine( "{0,-35}{1,-9}{2}\n",
112              operation, buffer, occupiedBufferCount );
113        }
114
115     } // end class HoldIntegerSynchronized
116
117     // class Producer's Produce method controls a thread that
118     // stores values from 1 to 4 in sharedLocation
119     class Producer
120     {
121        private HoldIntegerSynchronized sharedLocation;
122        private Random randomSleepTime;
123
124        // constructor
125        public Producer(
126           HoldIntegerSynchronized shared, Random random )
127        {
128           sharedLocation = shared;
129           randomSleepTime = random;
130        }
131
132        // store values 1-4 in object sharedLocation
133        public void Produce()
134        {
135           // sleep for random interval up to 3000 milliseconds
136           // then set sharedLocation's Buffer property
137           for ( int count = 1; count <= 4; count++ )
138           {
139              Thread.Sleep( randomSleepTime.Next( 1, 3000 ) );
140              sharedLocation.Buffer = count;
141           }
142
143           Console.WriteLine( Thread.CurrentThread.Name +
144              " done producing.\nTerminating " +
145              Thread.CurrentThread.Name + ".\n" );
146
147        } // end method Produce
148
149     } // end class Producer
150
151     // class Consumer's Consume method controls a thread that
152     // loops four times and reads a value from sharedLocation
153     class Consumer
154     {
155        private HoldIntegerSynchronized sharedLocation;
156        private Random randomSleepTime;
157
```

Fig. 11.5   Producer and consumer threads accessing a shared object with synchronization. (Part 4 of 8.)

```
158        // constructor
159        public Consumer(
160            HoldIntegerSynchronized shared, Random random )
161        {
162            sharedLocation = shared;
163            randomSleepTime = random;
164        }
165
166        // read sharedLocation's value four times
167        public void Consume()
168        {
169            int sum = 0;
170
171            // get current thread
172            Thread current = Thread.CurrentThread;
173
174            // sleep for random interval up to 3000 milliseconds
175            // then add sharedLocation's Buffer property value
176            // to sum
177            for ( int count = 1; count <= 4; count++ )
178            {
179                Thread.Sleep( randomSleepTime.Next( 1, 3000 ) );
180                sum += sharedLocation.Buffer;
181            }
182
183            Console.WriteLine( Thread.CurrentThread.Name +
184                " read values totaling: " + sum +
185                ".\nTerminating " + Thread.CurrentThread.Name + ".\n" );
186
187        } // end method Consume
188
189  } // end class Consumer
190
191  // this class creates producer and consumer threads
192  class SharedCell
193  {
194      // create producer and consumer threads and start them
195      static void Main( string[] args )
196      {
197          // create shared object used by threads
198          HoldIntegerSynchronized holdInteger =
199              new HoldIntegerSynchronized();
200
201          // Random object used by each thread
202          Random random = new Random();
203
204          // create Producer and Consumer objects
205          Producer producer =
206              new Producer( holdInteger, random );
207
208          Consumer consumer =
209              new Consumer( holdInteger, random );
```

Fig. 11.5 Producer and consumer threads accessing a shared object with synchronization. (Part 5 of 8.)

```
210
211            // output column heads and initial buffer state
212            Console.WriteLine( "{0,-35}{1,-9}{2}\n",
213               "Operation", "Buffer", "Occupied Count" );
214            holdInteger.DisplayState( "Initial state" );
215
216            // create threads for producer and consumer and set
217            // delegates for each thread
218            Thread producerThread =
219               new Thread( new ThreadStart( producer.Produce ) );
220            producerThread.Name = "Producer";
221
222            Thread consumerThread =
223               new Thread( new ThreadStart( consumer.Consume ) );
224            consumerThread.Name = "Consumer";
225
226            // start each thread
227            producerThread.Start();
228            consumerThread.Start();
229
230         } // end method Main
231
232      } // end class SharedCell
```

Operation	Buffer	Occupied Count
Initial state	-1	0
Producer writes 1	1	1
Consumer reads 1	1	0
Consumer tries to read. Buffer empty. Consumer waits.	1	0
Producer writes 2	2	1
Consumer reads 2	2	0
Producer writes 3	3	1
Producer tries to write. Buffer full. Producer waits.	3	1
Consumer reads 3	3	0
Producer writes 4	4	1
Producer done producing. Terminating Producer.		

continued on next page

Fig. 11.5 Producer and consumer threads accessing a shared object with synchronization. (Part 6 of 8.)

continued from previous page

Operation	Buffer	Occupied Count
Consumer reads 4	4	0
Consumer read values totaling: 10. Terminating Consumer.		

Operation	Buffer	Occupied Count
Initial state	-1	0
Consumer tries to read. Buffer empty. Consumer waits.	-1	0
Producer writes 1	1	1
Consumer reads 1	1	0
Producer writes 2	2	1
Consumer reads 2	2	0
Producer writes 3	3	1
Producer tries to write. Buffer full. Producer waits.	3	1
Consumer reads 3	3	0
Producer writes 4	4	1
Producer done producing. Terminating Producer.		
Consumer reads 4	4	0
Consumer read values totaling: 10. Terminating Consumer.		

Operation	Buffer	Occupied Count
Initial state	-1	0
Producer writes 1	1	1
Consumer reads 1	1	0
Producer writes 2	2	1

continued on next page

Fig. 11.5 Producer and consumer threads accessing a shared object with synchronization. (Part 7 of 8.)

```
                                                    continued from previous page

Consumer reads 2                    2        0

Producer writes 3                   3        1

Consumer reads 3                    3        0

Producer writes 4                   4        1

Producer done producing.
Terminating Producer.

Consumer reads 4                    4        0

Consumer read values totaling: 10.
Terminating Consumer.
```

Fig. 11.5   Producer and consumer threads accessing a shared object with synchronization. (Part 8 of 8.)

Class **HoldIntegerSynchronized** (lines 9–115) contains two instance variables—**buffer** (line 12) and **occupiedBufferCount** (line 15). Also, property **Buffer**'s **get** (lines 20–67) and **set** (lines 69–106) accessors now use methods of class **Monitor** to synchronize access to property **Buffer**. Thus, each object of class **HoldIntegerSynchronized** has a *SyncBlock* to maintain synchronization. Instance variable **occupiedBufferCount** is known as a *condition variable*—property **Buffer**'s accessors use this **int** in conditions to determine whether it is the producer's turn to perform a task or the consumer's turn to perform a task. If **occupiedBufferCount** is **0**, property **Buffer**'s **set** accessor can place a value into variable **buffer**, because the variable currently does not contain information. However, this means that property **Buffer**'s **get** accessor currently cannot read the value of **buffer**. If **occupiedBufferCount** is **1**, the **Buffer** property's **get** accessor can read a value from variable **buffer**, because the variable currently does contain information. In this case, property **Buffer**'s **set** accessor currently cannot place a value into **buffer**.

As in Fig. 11.4, the producer thread performs the tasks specified in the **producer** object's **Produce** method. When line 140 sets the value of **HoldIntegerSynchronized** property **Buffer**, the producer thread invokes the **set** accessor at lines 69–104. Line 72 invokes **Monitor** method **Enter** to acquire the lock on the **HoldIntegerSynchronized** object. The **if** structure at lines 76–85 determines whether **occupiedBufferCount** is **1**. If this condition is **true**, lines 78–79 output a message indicating that the producer thread tries to write a value, and lines 81–82 invoke method **DisplayState** (lines 109–113) to output another message indicating that the buffer is full and that the producer thread waits. Line 84 invokes **Monitor** method **Wait** to place the calling thread (i.e., the producer) in the *WaitSleepJoin* state for the **HoldIntegerSynchronized** object and releases the lock on the object. The *WaitSleepJoin* state for an object is maintained by that object's *SyncBlock*. Now another thread can invoke an accessor method of the **HoldIntegerSynchronized** object's **Buffer** property.

The producer thread remains in the *WaitSleepJoin* state until the thread is notified that it may proceed—at which point the thread returns to the *Started* state and waits for the system to assign a processor to the thread. When the thread returns to the *Running* state, the thread implicitly reacquires the lock on the **HoldIntegerSynchronized** object and the **set** accessor continues executing with the next statement after **Wait**. Line 88 assigns **value** to **buffer**. Line 92 increments the **occupiedBufferCount** to indicate that the shared buffer now contains a value (i.e., a consumer can read the value, and a producer cannot yet put another value there). Lines 94–95 invoke method **DisplayState** to output a line to the console window indicating that the producer is writing a new value into the **buffer**. Line 99 invokes **Monitor** method **Pulse** with the **HoldInteger-Synchronized** object as an argument. If there are any waiting threads in that object's *SyncBlock*, the first waiting thread enters the *Started* state, indicating that the thread can now attempt its task again (as soon as the thread is assigned a processor). The **Pulse** method returns immediately. Line 102 invokes **Monitor** method **Exit** to release the lock on the **HoldIntegerSynchronized** object, and the **set** accessor returns to its caller.

Common Programming Error 11.4

Forgetting to release the lock on an object when that lock is no longer needed is a logic error. This will prevent the threads in your program that require the lock from acquiring the lock to proceed with their tasks. These threads will be forced to wait (unnecessarily, because the lock is no longer needed). Such waiting can lead to deadlock and indefinite postponement.

The **get** and **set** accessors are implemented similarly. As in Fig. 11.4, the consumer thread performs the tasks specified in the **consumer** object's **Consume** method. The consumer thread gets the value of the **HoldIntegerSynchronized** object's **Buffer** property (line 180) by invoking the **get** accessor at lines 20–67. Line 23 invokes **Monitor** method **Enter** to acquire the lock on the **HoldIntegerSynchronized** object.

The **if** structure at lines 27–36 determines whether **occupiedBufferCount** is **0**. If this condition is **true**, lines 29–30 output a message indicating that the consumer thread tries to read a value, and lines 32–33 invoke method **DisplayState** to output another message indicating that the buffer is empty and that the consumer thread waits. Line 35 invokes **Monitor** method **Wait** to place the calling thread (i.e., the consumer) in the *WaitSleepJoin* state for the **HoldIntegerSynchronized** object and releases the lock on the object. Now another thread can invoke an accessor method of the **HoldInte-gerSynchronized** object's **Buffer** property.

The consumer thread object remains in the *WaitSleepJoin* state until the thread is notified that it may proceed—at which point the thread returns to the *Started* state and waits for the system to assign a processor to the thread. When the thread reenters the *Running* state, the thread implicitly reacquires the lock on the **HoldIntegerSynchronized** object, and the **get** accessor continues executing with the next statement after **Wait**. Line 40 decrements **occupiedBufferCount** to indicate that the shared buffer is now empty (i.e., a consumer cannot read the value, but a producer can place another value into the shared buffer), lines 42–43 output a line to the console window indicating the value the consumer is reading and line 47 invokes **Monitor** method **Pulse** with the **Hold-IntegerSynchronized** object as an argument. If there are any waiting threads in that object's *SyncBlock*, the first waiting thread enters the *Started* state, indicating that the thread can now attempt its task again (as soon as the thread is assigned a processor). The **Pulse** method returns immediately. Line 60 gets a copy of **buffer** before releasing lock.

It is possible that the producer could be assigned the processor immediately after the lock is released (line 63) and before the **return** statement executes (line 65). In this case, the producer would assign a new value to **buffer** before the **return** statement returns the value to the consumer. Thus, the consumer would receive the new value. Making a copy of **buffer** and returning the copy ensures that the consumer receives the proper value. Line 63 invokes **Monitor** method **Exit** to release the lock on the **HoldInteger-Synchronized** object and the **get** accessor returns **bufferCopy** to its caller.

Study the outputs in Fig. 11.5. Observe that every integer produced is consumed exactly once—no values are lost, and no values are consumed more than once. This occurs because the producer and consumer cannot perform tasks unless it is "their turn." The producer must go first; the consumer must wait if the producer has not produced, since the consumer last consumed; and the producer must wait if the consumer has not yet consumed the value the producer most recently produced. Execute this program several times to confirm that every integer produced is consumed once.

In the first and second sample outputs, notice the lines indicating when the producer and consumer must wait to perform their respective tasks. In the third sample output, notice that the producer and consumer were able to perform their tasks without waiting.

11.7 Producer/Consumer Relationship: Circular Buffer

Figure 11.5 uses thread synchronization to guarantee that two threads manipulate data in a shared buffer correctly. However, the application may not perform optimally. If the two threads operate at different speeds, one of the threads will spend more (or most) of its time waiting. For example, in Fig. 11.5 we shared a single integer between the two threads. If the producer thread produces values faster than the consumer can consume those values, then the producer thread waits for the consumer, because there are no other locations in memory to place the next value. Similarly, if the consumer consumes faster than the producer can produce values, the consumer waits until the producer places the next value into the shared location in memory. Even when we have threads that operate at the same relative speeds, over a period of time, those threads may become "out of sync," causing one of the threads to wait for the other. We cannot make assumptions about the relative speeds of asynchronous concurrent threads. There are too many interactions that occur with the operating system, the network, the user and other components, which can cause the threads to operate at different speeds. When this happens, threads wait. When threads wait, programs become less productive, user-interactive programs become less responsive and network applications suffer longer delays because the processor is not used efficiently.

To minimize the waiting for threads that share resources and operate at the same relative speeds, we can implement a *circular buffer* that provides extra buffers into which the producer can place values and from which the consumer can retrieve those values. Let us assume the buffer is implemented as an array. The producer and consumer work from the beginning of the array. When either thread reaches the end of the array, it simply returns to the first element of the array to perform its next task. If the producer temporarily produces values faster than the consumer can consume them, the producer can write additional values into the extra buffers (if cells are available). This enables the producer to perform its task even though the consumer is not ready to receive the current value being produced. Similarly, if the consumer consumes faster than the producer produces new values, the consumer can read additional values from the buffer (if there are any). This enables the consumer to perform its task even though the producer is not ready to produce additional values.

Note that the circular buffer would be inappropriate if the producer and consumer operate at different speeds. If the consumer always executes faster than the producer, then a buffer at one location is enough. Additional locations would waste memory. If the producer always executes faster, a buffer with an infinite number of locations would be required to absorb the extra production.

The key to using a circular buffer is to define it with enough extra cells to handle the anticipated "extra" production. If, over a period of time, we determine that the producer often produces as many as three more values than the consumer can consume, we can define a buffer of at least three cells to handle the extra production. We do not want the buffer to be too small, because that would cause threads to wait more. On the other hand, we do not want the buffer to be too large, because that would waste memory.

Performance Tip 11.4

Even when using a circular buffer, it is possible that a producer thread could fill the buffer, which would force the producer thread to wait until a consumer consumes a value to free an element in the buffer. Similarly, if the buffer is empty at any given time, the consumer thread must wait until the producer produces another value. The key to using a circular buffer is optimizing the buffer size to minimize the amount of thread-wait time.

Figure 11.6 demonstrates a producer and a consumer accessing a circular buffer (in this case, a shared array of two cells) with synchronization. In this version of the producer/consumer relationship, the consumer consumes a value only when the array is not empty and the producer produces a value only when the array is not full. This program is implemented as a Windows application that sends its output to a **TextBox**. Classes **Producer** (lines 174–210) and **Consumer** (lines 213–252) perform the same tasks as in Fig. 11.4 and Fig. 11.5, except that they output messages to the **TextBox** in the application window. The statements that created and started the thread objects in the **Main** methods of class **SharedCell** in Fig. 11.4 and Fig. 11.5 now appear in class **CircularBuffer** (lines 255–313), where the **Load** event handler (lines 278–311) performs the statements.

The most significant changes from Fig. 11.5 occur in class **HoldInteger-Synchronized**, which now contains six instance variables. Array **buffers** is a three-element integer array that represents the circular buffer. Variable **occupiedBuffer-Count** is the condition variable that can be used to determine whether a producer can write into the circular buffer (i.e., **occupiedBufferCount** is less than the number of elements in array **buffers**) and whether a consumer can read from the circular buffer (i.e., **occupiedBufferCount** is greater than **0**). Variable **readLocation** indicates the position from which the next value can be read by a consumer. Variable **writeLocation** indicates the next location in which a value can be placed by a producer. The program displays output in **outputTextBox** (a **TextBox** control).

```
1   // Fig. 11.6: CircularBuffer.cs
2   // Implementing the producer/consumer relationship with a
3   // circular buffer.
```

Fig. 11.6   Producer and consumer threads accessing a circular buffer. (Part 1 of 9.)

```
4
5    using System;
6    using System.Drawing;
7    using System.Collections;
8    using System.ComponentModel;
9    using System.Windows.Forms;
10   using System.Data;
11   using System.Threading;
12
13   // implement the shared integer with synchronization
14   public class HoldIntegerSynchronized
15   {
16      // each array element is a buffer
17      private int[] buffers = { -1, -1, -1 };
18
19      // occupiedBufferCount maintains count of occupied buffers
20      private int occupiedBufferCount = 0;
21
22      // variables that maintain read and write buffer locations
23      private int readLocation = 0, writeLocation = 0;
24
25      // GUI component to display output
26      private TextBox outputTextBox;
27
28      // constructor
29      public HoldIntegerSynchronized( TextBox output )
30      {
31         outputTextBox = output;
32      }
33
34      // property Buffer
35      public int Buffer
36      {
37         get
38         {
39            // lock this object while getting value
40            // from buffers array
41            lock ( this )
42            {
43               // if there is no data to read, place invoking
44               // thread in WaitSleepJoin state
45               if ( occupiedBufferCount == 0 )
46               {
47                  outputTextBox.Text += "\r\nAll buffers empty. " +
48                     Thread.CurrentThread.Name + " waits.";
49                  outputTextBox.ScrollToCaret();
50
51                  Monitor.Wait( this );
52               }
53
54               // obtain value at current readLocation, then
55               // add string indicating consumed value to output
56               int readValue = buffers[ readLocation ];
```

Fig. 11.6 Producer and consumer threads accessing a circular buffer. (Part 2 of 9.)

```
57
58              outputTextBox.Text += "\r\n" +
59                 Thread.CurrentThread.Name + " reads " +
60                 buffers[ readLocation ] + " ";
61
62              // just consumed a value, so decrement number of
63              // occupied buffers
64              --occupiedBufferCount;
65
66              // update readLocation for future read operation,
67              // then add current state to output
68              readLocation =
69                 ( readLocation + 1 ) % buffers.Length;
70              outputTextBox.Text += CreateStateOutput();
71              outputTextBox.ScrollToCaret();
72
73              // return waiting thread (if there is one)
74              // to Started state
75              Monitor.Pulse( this );
76
77              return readValue;
78
79          } // end lock
80
81       } // end accessor get
82
83       set
84       {
85          // lock this object while setting value
86          // in buffers array
87          lock ( this )
88          {
89             // if there are no empty locations, place invoking
90             // thread in WaitSleepJoin state
91             if ( occupiedBufferCount == buffers.Length )
92             {
93                outputTextBox.Text += "\r\nAll buffers full. " +
94                   Thread.CurrentThread.Name + " waits.";
95                outputTextBox.ScrollToCaret();
96
97                Monitor.Wait( this );
98             }
99
100            // place value in writeLocation of buffers, then
101            // add string indicating produced value to output
102            buffers[ writeLocation ] = value;
103
104            outputTextBox.Text += "\r\n" +
105               Thread.CurrentThread.Name + " writes " +
106               buffers[ writeLocation ] + " ";
107
```

Fig. 11.6   Producer and consumer threads accessing a circular buffer. (Part 3 of 9.)

```
108              // just produced a value, so increment number of
109              // occupied buffers
110              ++occupiedBufferCount;
111
112              // update writeLocation for future write operation,
113              // then add current state to output
114              writeLocation =
115                 ( writeLocation + 1 ) % buffers.Length;
116              outputTextBox.Text += CreateStateOutput();
117              outputTextBox.ScrollToCaret();
118
119              // return waiting thread (if there is one)
120              // to Started state
121              Monitor.Pulse( this );
122
123           } // end lock
124
125        } // end accessor set
126
127     } // end property Buffer
128
129     // create state output
130     public string CreateStateOutput()
131     {
132        // display first line of state information
133        string output = "(buffers occupied: " +
134           occupiedBufferCount + ")\r\nbuffers: ";
135
136        for ( int i = 0; i < buffers.Length; i++ )
137           output += "  " + buffers[ i ] + "   ";
138
139        output += "\r\n";
140
141        // display second line of state information
142        output += "             ";
143
144        for ( int i = 0; i < buffers.Length; i++ )
145           output += "---- ";
146
147        output += "\r\n";
148
149        // display third line of state information
150        output += "             ";
151
152        // display readLocation (R) and writeLocation (W)
153        // indicators below appropriate buffer locations
154        for ( int i = 0; i < buffers.Length; i++ )
155
156           if ( i == writeLocation &&
157                writeLocation == readLocation )
158              output += " WR  ";
159           else if ( i == writeLocation )
160              output += " W   ";
```

Fig. 11.6 Producer and consumer threads accessing a circular buffer. (Part 4 of 9.)

```
161              else if  ( i == readLocation )
162                 output += "   R   ";
163              else
164                 output += "       ";
165
166          output += "\r\n";
167
168          return output;
169       }
170
171    } // end class HoldIntegerSynchronized
172
173    // produce the integers from 11 to 20 and place them in buffer
174    public class Producer
175    {
176       private HoldIntegerSynchronized sharedLocation;
177       private TextBox outputTextBox;
178       private Random randomSleepTime;
179
180       // constructor
181       public Producer( HoldIntegerSynchronized shared,
182          Random random, TextBox output )
183       {
184          sharedLocation = shared;
185          outputTextBox = output;
186          randomSleepTime = random;
187       }
188
189       // produce values from 11-20 and place them in
190       // sharedLocation's buffer
191       public void Produce()
192       {
193          // sleep for random interval up to 3000 milliseconds
194          // then set sharedLocation's Buffer property
195          for ( int count = 11; count <= 20; count++ )
196          {
197             Thread.Sleep( randomSleepTime.Next( 1, 3000 ) );
198             sharedLocation.Buffer = count;
199          }
200
201          string name = Thread.CurrentThread.Name;
202
203          outputTextBox.Text += "\r\n" + name +
204             " done producing.\r\n" + name + " terminated.\r\n";
205
206          outputTextBox.ScrollToCaret();
207
208       } // end method Produce
209
210    } // end class Producer
211
```

Fig. 11.6   Producer and consumer threads accessing a circular buffer. (Part 5 of 9.)

```
212   // consume the integers 12 to 20 from circular buffer
213   public class Consumer
214   {
215      private HoldIntegerSynchronized sharedLocation;
216      private TextBox outputTextBox;
217      private Random randomSleepTime;
218
219      // constructor
220      public Consumer( HoldIntegerSynchronized shared,
221         Random random, TextBox output )
222      {
223         sharedLocation = shared;
224         outputTextBox = output;
225         randomSleepTime = random;
226      }
227
228      // consume 10 integers from buffer
229      public void Consume()
230      {
231         int sum = 0;
232
233         // loop 10 times and sleep for random interval up to
234         // 3000 milliseconds then add sharedLocation's
235         // Buffer property value to sum
236         for ( int count = 1; count <= 10; count++ )
237         {
238            Thread.Sleep( randomSleepTime.Next( 1, 3000 ) );
239            sum += sharedLocation.Buffer;
240         }
241
242         string name = Thread.CurrentThread.Name;
243
244         outputTextBox.Text += "\r\nTotal " + name +
245            " consumed: " + sum + ".\r\n" + name +
246            " terminated.\r\n";
247
248         outputTextBox.ScrollToCaret();
249
250      } // end method Consume
251
252   } // end class Consumer
253
254   // set up the producer and consumer and start them
255   public class CircularBuffer : System.Windows.Forms.Form
256   {
257      private System.Windows.Forms.TextBox outputTextBox;
258
259      // required designer variable
260      private System.ComponentModel.Container components = null;
261
```

Fig. 11.6 Producer and consumer threads accessing a circular buffer. (Part 6 of 9.)

```
262     // no-argument constructor
263     public CircularBuffer()
264     {
265        InitializeComponent();
266     }
267
268     // Visual Studio .NET GUI code appears here in source file
269
270     // main entry point for the application
271     [STAThread]
272     static void Main()
273     {
274        Application.Run( new CircularBuffer() );
275     }
276
277     // Load event handler creates and starts threads
278     private void CircularBuffer_Load(
279        object sender, System.EventArgs e )
280     {
281        // create shared object
282        HoldIntegerSynchronized sharedLocation =
283           new HoldIntegerSynchronized( outputTextBox );
284
285        // display sharedLocation state before producer
286        // and consumer threads begin execution
287        outputTextBox.Text = sharedLocation.CreateStateOutput();
288
289        // Random object used by each thread
290        Random random = new Random();
291
292        // create Producer and Consumer objects
293        Producer producer =
294           new Producer( sharedLocation, random, outputTextBox );
295        Consumer consumer =
296           new Consumer( sharedLocation, random, outputTextBox );
297
298        // create and name threads
299        Thread producerThread =
300           new Thread( new ThreadStart( producer.Produce ) );
301        producerThread.Name = "Producer";
302
303        Thread consumerThread =
304           new Thread( new ThreadStart( consumer.Consume ) );
305        consumerThread.Name = "Consumer";
306
307        // start threads
308        producerThread.Start();
309        consumerThread.Start();
310
311     } // end CircularBuffer_Load method
312
313  } // end class CircularBuffer
```

Fig. 11.6 Producer and consumer threads accessing a circular buffer. (Part 7 of 9.)

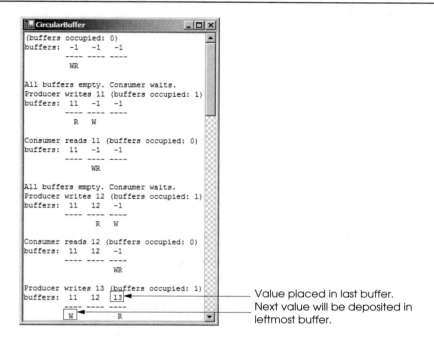

Value placed in last buffer.
Next value will be deposited in
leftmost buffer.

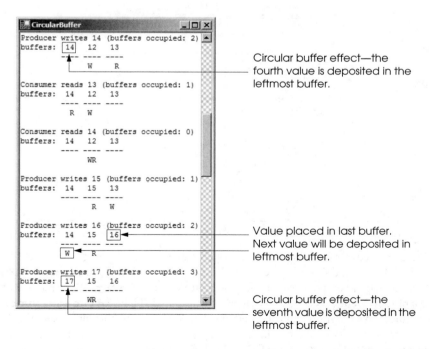

Circular buffer effect—the
fourth value is deposited in the
leftmost buffer.

Value placed in last buffer.
Next value will be deposited in
leftmost buffer.

Circular buffer effect—the
seventh value is deposited in the
leftmost buffer.

Fig. 11.6 Producer and consumer threads accessing a circular buffer. (Part 8 of 9.)

Fig. 11.6 Producer and consumer threads accessing a circular buffer. (Part 9 of 9.)

The **set** accessor (lines 83–125) of property **Buffer** performs the same tasks that it did in Fig. 11.5, with a few modifications. Rather than using **Monitor** methods **Enter** and **Exit** to acquire and release the lock on the **HoldIntegerSynchronized** object, we use a block of code preceded by keyword **lock** to lock the **HoldIntegerSynchronized** object. As program control enters the **lock** block, the currently executing thread acquires the lock (assuming the lock is currently available) on the **HoldInteger-Synchronized** object (i.e., **this**). When the **lock** block terminates, the thread releases the lock automatically.

Common Programming Error 11.5

*When using class **Monitor**'s **Enter** and **Exit** methods to manage an object's lock, **Exit** must be called explicitly to release the lock. If an exception occurs in a method before **Exit** can be called and that exception is not caught, the method could terminate without calling **Exit**. If so, the lock is not released. To avoid this error, place code that could throw exceptions in a **try** block, and place the call to **Exit** in the corresponding **finally** block to ensure that the lock is released.*

Software Engineering Observation 11.2

*Using a **lock** block to manage the lock on a synchronized object eliminates the possibility of forgetting to relinquish the lock with a call to **Monitor** method **Exit**. C# implicitly calls **Monitor** method **Exit** when a **lock** block terminates for any reason. Thus, even if an exception occurs in the block, the lock will be released.*

The **if** structure at lines 91–98 in the **set** accessor determines whether the producer must wait (i.e., all buffers are full). If the producer thread must wait, lines 93–94 append text to the **outputTextBox** indicating that the producer is waiting to perform its task and line 97 invokes **Monitor** method **Wait** to place the producer thread in the *WaitSleepJoin* state of the **HoldIntegerSynchronized** object. When execution continues at line 102 after the **if** structure, the value written by the producer is placed in the circular buffer at location **writeLocation**. Next, lines 104–106 append a message containing the value produced to the **TextBox**. Line 110 increments **occupiedBufferCount**, because there is now at least one value in the buffer that the consumer can read. Then, lines 114–115 update **writeLocation** for the next call to the **set** accessor of property **Buffer**. The output continues at line 116 by invoking method **CreateStateOutput** (lines 130–169), which outputs the number of occupied buffers, the contents of the buffers and the current **writeLocation** and **readLocation**. Finally, line 121 invokes **Monitor** method **Pulse** to indicate that a thread waiting on the **HoldIntegerSynchronized** object (if there is a waiting thread) should transition to the *Started* state. Note that reaching the closing right brace of the **lock** block at line 123 causes the thread to release the lock on the **HoldIntegerSynchronized** object.

The **get** accessor (lines 37–81) of property **Buffer** also performs the same tasks in this example that it did in Fig. 11.5, with a few minor modifications. The **if** structure at lines 45–52 in the **get** accessor determines whether the consumer must wait (i.e., all buffers are empty). If the consumer thread must wait, lines 47–48 append text to the **outputTextBox** indicating that the consumer is waiting to perform its task, and line 51 invokes **Monitor** method **Wait** to place the consumer thread in the *WaitSleepJoin* state of the **HoldIntegerSynchronized** object. Once again, we use a **lock** block to acquire and release the lock on the **HoldIntegerSynchronized** object, rather than using **Monitor** methods **Enter** and **Exit**. When execution continues at line 56 after the **if** structure, **readValue** is assigned the value at location **readLocation** in the circular buffer. Lines 58–60 appends the value consumed to the **TextBox**. Line 64 decrements the **occupiedBufferCount**, because there is at least one open position in the buffer in which the producer thread can place a value. Then, lines 68–69 update **readLocation** for the next call to the **get** accessor of **Buffer**. Line 70 invokes method **CreateStateOutput** to output the number of occupied buffers, the contents of the buffers and the current **writeLocation** and **readLocation**. Finally, line 80 invokes method **Pulse** to transition the next thread waiting for the **HoldIntegerSynchron-**

ized object into the *Started* state, and line 82 returns the consumed value to the calling method.

In Fig. 11.6, the outputs include the current **occupiedBufferCount**, the contents of the buffers, and the current **writeLocation** and **readLocation**. In the output, the letters **W** and **R** represent the current **writeLocation** and **readLocation**, respectively. Notice that, after the third value is placed in the third element of the buffer, the fourth value is inserted at the beginning of the array. This procedure provides the circular buffer effect.

11.8 Summary

Computers perform operations concurrently. Programming languages generally provide only a simple set of control structures that enable programmers to perform one action at a time and proceed to the next action after the previous one finishes. The FCL provides the C# programmer with the ability to specify that applications contain threads of execution, where each thread designates a portion of a program that may execute concurrently with other threads; this capability is called multithreading.

A thread is initialized using the **Thread** class's constructor, which receives a **ThreadStart** delegate. The delegate specifies the method that contains the tasks which a thread will perform. A thread remains in the *Unstarted* state until the thread's **Start** method is called; when the method is called, the thread enters the *Started* state. A thread in the *Started* state enters the *Running* state when the system assigns a processor to the thread. The system assigns the processor to the highest-priority *Started* thread. A thread enters the *Stopped* state when its **ThreadStart** delegate completes or terminates. A thread is forced into the *Stopped* state when its **Abort** method is called (by itself or by another thread). A *Running* thread enters the *Blocked* state when the thread issues an input/output request. A *Blocked* thread becomes *Started* when the I/O it is waiting for completes. A *Blocked* thread cannot use a processor, even if one is available.

If a thread needs to sleep, it calls method **Sleep**. A thread wakes up when the designated sleep interval expires. If a thread cannot continue executing unless another thread terminates, the first thread, called the dependent thread, calls the other thread's **Join** method to "join" the two threads. When two threads are joined, the dependent thread leaves the *WaitSleepJoin* state when the other thread finishes execution.

When a thread encounters code that it cannot yet run, the thread can call **Monitor** method **Wait** until certain actions occur that enable the thread to continue executing. This method call puts the thread into the *WaitSleepJoin* state. Any thread in the *WaitSleepJoin* state can leave that state if another thread invokes **Thread** method **Interrupt** on the thread in the *WaitSleepJoin* state. If a thread calls **Monitor** method **Wait**, a corresponding call to the **Monitor** method **Pulse** or **PulseAll** by another thread in the program will transition the original thread from the *WaitSleepJoin* state to the *Started* state.

If **Thread** method **Suspend** is called on a thread, the thread enters the *Suspended* state. A thread leaves the *Suspended* state when a separate thread invokes **Thread** method **Resume** on the suspended thread.

Every C# thread has a priority. The job of the thread scheduler is to keep the highest-priority thread running at all times and, if there is more than one highest-priority thread, to ensure that all equally high-priority threads execute for a quantum at a time in round-robin fashion. A thread's priority can be adjusted with the **Priority** property, which is assigned an argument from the **ThreadPriority** enumeration.

A thread that updates shared data calls **Monitor** method **Enter** to acquire the lock on those data. It updates the data and calls **Monitor** method **Exit** upon completion of the update. While the data are locked, all other threads attempting to acquire the lock on the data must wait. If you place the **lock** keyword before a block of code, the lock is acquired on the specified object as program control enters the block; the lock is released when the block terminates.

Strings, Characters and Regular Expressions

Objectives

- To create and manipulate immutable character string objects of class **String**.
- To create and manipulate mutable character string objects of class **StringBuilder**.
- To use regular expressions in conjunction with classes **Regex** and **Match**.

*The chief defect of Henry King
Was chewing little bits of string.*
Hilaire Belloc

Vigorous writing is concise. A sentence should contain no unnecessary words, a paragraph no unnecessary sentences.
William Strunk, Jr.

I have made this letter longer than usual, because I lack the time to make it short.
Blaise Pascal

The difference between the almost-right word & the right word is really a large matter—it's the difference between the lightning bug and the lightning.
Mark Twain

Mum's the word.
Miguel de Cervantes

Outline

12.1	Introduction
12.2	Fundamentals of Characters and Strings
12.3	**String** Constructors
12.4	**String** Indexer, **Length** Property and **CopyTo** Method
12.5	Comparing **Strings**
12.6	**String** Method **GetHashCode**
12.7	Locating Characters and Substrings in **Strings**
12.8	Extracting Substrings from **Strings**
12.9	Concatenating **Strings**
12.10	Miscellaneous **String** Methods
12.11	Class **StringBuilder**
12.12	**StringBuilder** Indexer, **Length** and **Capacity** Properties, and **EnsureCapacity** Method
12.13	**StringBuilder** **Append** and **AppendFormat** Methods
12.14	**StringBuilder** **Insert**, **Remove** and **Replace** Methods
12.15	**Char** Methods
12.16	Card Shuffling and Dealing Simulation
12.17	Regular Expressions and Class **Regex**
12.18	Summary

12.1 Introduction

In this chapter, we introduce the Framework Class Library's string and character processing capabilities and demonstrate the use of regular expressions to search for patterns in text. The techniques presented in this chapter can be employed to develop text editors, word processors, page-layout software, computerized typesetting systems and other kinds of text-processing software. Previous chapters have already presented several string-processing capabilities. In this chapter, we expand on this information by detailing the capabilities of class *String* and type *char* from the *System* namespace, class *StringBuilder* from the *System.Text* namespace and classes *Regex* and *Match* from the *System.Text.RegularExpressions* namespace.

12.2 Fundamentals of Characters and Strings

Characters are the fundamental building blocks of C# source code. Every program is composed of characters that, when grouped together meaningfully, create a sequence that the compiler interprets as a series of instructions that describe how to accomplish a task. In addition to normal characters, a program also can contain *character constants*. A character constant is a character that is represented as an integer value, called a *character code*. For example, the integer value **122** corresponds to the character constant **'z'**. The integer value **10** corresponds to the new line character **'\n'**. Character constants are established according to the *Unicode character set*, an international character set that contains many more symbols and letters than does the ASCII character set (see Appendix F, ASCII Character Set). To learn more about Unicode®, see Appendix G, Unicode®.

A string is a series of characters treated as a single unit. These characters can be uppercase letters, lowercase letters, digits and various *special characters,* such as **+**, **-**, *****, **/**, **$** and others. A string is an object of class **String** in the **System** namespace.[1] We write *string literals*, or *string constants* (often called *literal **string**s*), as sequences of characters in double quotation marks, as follows:

```
"John Q. Doe"
"9999 Main Street"
"Waltham, Massachusetts"
"(201) 555-1212"
```

A declaration can assign a **string** literal to a **string** reference. The declaration

```
string color = "blue";
```

initializes **string** reference **color** to refer to the **string** literal object **"blue"**.

Performance Tip 12.1

*If there are multiple occurrences of the same **string** literal object in an application, a single copy of the **string** literal object will be referenced from each location in the program that uses that **string** literal. It is possible to share the object in this manner, because **string** literal objects are implicitly constant. Such sharing conserves memory.*

On occasion, a **string** will contain multiple backslash characters (this often occurs in the name of a file). It is possible to exclude escape sequences and interpret all the characters in a **string** literally, using the **@** character. Backslashes within the double quotation marks are not considered escape sequences, but rather regular backslash characters. Often this simplifies programming and makes the code easier to read. For example, consider the string "**C:\MyFolder\MySubFolder\MyFile.txt**" with the following assignment:

```
string file = "C:\\MyFolder\\MySubFolder\\MyFile.txt";
```

Using the verbatim string syntax, the assignment can be altered to

```
string file = @"C:\MyFolder\MySubFolder\MyFile.txt";
```

This approach also has the advantage of allowing strings to span multiple lines by preserving all newlines, spaces and tabs.

---

1. C# provides the **string** keyword as an alias for class **String**. In this book, we use **String** to refer to the class **String** and **string** to refer to an object of class **String**.

12.3 `String` Constructors

Class **String** provides eight constructors for initializing **string**s in various ways. Figure 12.1 demonstrates the use of three of the constructors.

Lines 14–16 declare **string**s **output**, **originalString**, **string1**, **string2**, **string3** and **string4**. Lines 18–19 allocate the **char** array **characterArray**, which contains nine characters. Line 22 assigns literal **string "Welcome to C# programming!"** to **string** reference **originalString**. Line 23 sets **string1** to reference the same **string** literal.

Line 24 assigns to **string2** a new **string**, using the **String** constructor that takes a character array as an argument. The new **string** contains a copy of the characters in array **characterArray**.

```
1   // Fig. 12.1: StringConstructor.cs
2   // Demonstrating String class constructors.
3
4   using System;
5   using System.Windows.Forms;
6
7   // test several String class constructors
8   class StringConstructor
9   {
10      // The main entry point for the application.
11      [STAThread]
12      static void Main( string[] args )
13      {
14         string output;
15         string originalString, string1, string2,
16            string3, string4;
17
18         char[] characterArray =
19            { 'b', 'i', 'r', 't', 'h', ' ', 'd', 'a', 'y' };
20
21         // string initialization
22         originalString = "Welcome to C# programming!";
23         string1 = originalString;
24         string2 = new string( characterArray );
25         string3 = new string( characterArray, 6, 3 );
26         string4 = new string( 'C', 5 );
27
28         output = "string1 = " + "\"" + string1 + "\"\n" +
29            "string2 = " + "\"" + string2 + "\"\n" +
30            "string3 = " + "\"" + string3 + "\"\n" +
31            "string4 = " + "\"" + string4 + "\"\n";
32
33         MessageBox.Show( output, "String Class Constructors",
34            MessageBoxButtons.OK, MessageBoxIcon.Information );
35
36      } // end method Main
37
38   } // end class StringConstructor
```

Fig. 12.1 String constructors. (Part 1 of 2.)

Fig. 12.1   **String** constructors. (Part 2 of 2.)

Software Engineering Observation 12.1

*In most cases, it is not necessary to make a copy of an existing **string**. All **string**s are immutable—their character contents cannot be changed after they are created. Also, if there are one or more references to a **string** (or any object for that matter), the object cannot be reclaimed by the garbage collector.*

Line 25 assigns to **string3** a new **string**, using the **String** constructor that takes a **char** array and two **int** arguments. The second argument specifies the starting index position (the *offset*) from which characters in the array are copied. The third argument specifies the number of characters (the *count*) to be copied from the specified starting position in the array. The new **string** contains a copy of the specified characters in the array. If the specified offset or count indicates that the program should access an element outside the bounds of the character array, an ***ArgumentOutOfRangeException*** is thrown.

Line 26 assigns to **string4** a new **string**, using the **String** constructor that takes as arguments a character and an **int** specifying the number of times to repeat that character in the **string**.

12.4 String Indexer, Length Property and CopyTo Method

The application in Fig. 12.2 presents the **String** indexer, which facilitates the retrieval of any character in the **string**, and the **String** property *Length*, which returns the length of the **string**. The **String** method *CopyTo* copies a specified number of characters from a **string** into a **char** array.

In this example, we create an application that determines the length of a **string**, reverses the order of the characters in the **string** and copies a series of characters from the **string** into a character array.

```
1   // Fig. 12.2: StringMethods.cs
2   // Using the indexer, property Length and method CopyTo
3   // of class String.
4
5   using System;
6   using System.Windows.Forms;
7
```

Fig. 12.2   **String** indexer, **Length** property and **CopyTo** method. (Part 1 of 2.)

```
 8      // creates string objects and displays results of using
 9      // indexer and methods Length and CopyTo
10      class StringMethods
11      {
12          // The main entry point for the application.
13          [STAThread]
14          static void Main( string[] args )
15          {
16              string string1, output;
17              char[] characterArray;
18
19              string1 = "hello there";
20              characterArray = new char[ 5 ];
21
22              // output string
23              output =
24                  "string1: \"" + string1 + "\"";
25
26              // test Length property
27              output += "\nLength of string1: " + string1.Length;
28
29              // loop through character in string1 and display
30              // reversed
31              output += "\nThe string reversed is: ";
32
33              for ( int i = string1.Length - 1; i >= 0; i-- )
34                  output += string1[ i ];
35
36              // copy characters from string1 into characterArray
37              string1.CopyTo( 0, characterArray, 0, 5 );
38              output += "\nThe character array is: ";
39
40              for ( int i = 0 ; i < characterArray.Length; i++ )
41                  output += characterArray[ i ];
42
43              MessageBox.Show( output, "Demonstrating the string " +
44                  "Indexer, Length Property and CopyTo method",
45                  MessageBoxButtons.OK, MessageBoxIcon.Information );
46
47          } // end method Main
48
49      } // end class StringMethods
```

Fig. 12.2   **String** indexer, **Length** property and **CopyTo** method. (Part 2 of 2.)

Line 27 uses **String** property **Length** to determine the number of characters in **string string1**. Like arrays, **string**s always know their own size.

Lines 33–34 append to **output** the characters of the **string string1** in reverse order. The **string** indexer returns the character at a specific position in the **string**. The **string** indexer treats a **string** as an array of **char**s. The indexer receives an integer argument as the *position number* and returns the character at that position. As with arrays, the first element of a **string** is considered to be at position 0.

Common Programming Error 12.1

*Attempting to access a character that is outside the bounds of a **string** (i.e., an index less than 0 or an index greater than or equal to the **string**'s length) results in an **IndexOutOfRangeException**.*

Line 37 uses **String** method **CopyTo** to copy the characters of a **string** (**string1**) into a character array (**characterArray**). The first argument given to method **CopyTo** is the index from which the method begins copying characters in the **string**. The second argument is the character array into which the characters are copied. The third argument is the index specifying the location at which the method places the copied characters in the character array. The last argument is the number of characters that the method will copy from the **string**. Lines 40–41 append the **char** array contents to **string output** one character at a time.

12.5 Comparing **Strings**

The next two examples demonstrate the various methods that C# provides for comparing **string**s. To understand how one **string** can be "greater than" or "less than" another **string**, consider the process of alphabetizing a series of last names. The reader would, no doubt, place **"Jones"** before **"Smith"**, because the first letter of **"Jones"** comes before the first letter of **"Smith"** in the alphabet. The alphabet is more than just a set of 26 letters—it is an ordered list of characters in which each letter occurs in a specific position. For example, **z** is more than just a letter of the alphabet; **z** is specifically the twenty-sixth letter of the alphabet.

Computers can order characters alphabetically because the characters are represented internally as Unicode numeric codes. When comparing two **string**s, C# simply compares the numeric codes of the characters in the **string**s.

Class **String** provides several ways to compare **string**s. The application in Fig. 12.3 demonstrates the use of method *Equals*, method *CompareTo* and the equality operator (**==**).

The condition in the **if** structure (line 27) uses instance method **Equals** to compare **string1** and literal **string "hello"** to determine whether they are equal. Method **Equals** (inherited by **String** from class **Object**) tests any two objects for equality (i.e., checks whether the objects contain identical contents). The method returns **true** if the objects are equal and **false** otherwise. In this instance, the preceding condition returns **true**, because **string1** references **string** literal object **"hello"**. Method **Equals** uses a *lexicographical comparison*—the integer Unicode values that represent each character in each **string** are compared. Method **Equals** compares the numeric Unicode values that represent the characters in each **string**. A comparison of the **string "hello"** with the **string "HELLO"** would return **false**, because the numeric representations of lowercase letters are different from the numeric representations of corresponding uppercase letters.

The condition in the second **if** structure (line 33) uses the equality operator (**==**) to compare **string string1** with the literal **string "hello"** for equality. In C#, the equality operator also uses a lexicographical comparison to compare two **string**s. Thus, the condition in the **if** structure evaluates to **true**, because the values of **string1** and **"hello"** are equal. To compare the references of two **string**s, we must explicitly cast the **string**s to type **object** and use the equality operator (**==**).

```
1    // Fig. 12.3: StringCompare.cs
2    // Comparing strings.
3
4    using System;
5    using System.Windows.Forms;
6
7    // compare a number of strings
8    class StringCompare
9    {
10       // The main entry point for the application.
11       [STAThread]
12       static void Main( string[] args )
13       {
14          string string1 = "hello";
15          string string2 = "good bye";
16          string string3 = "Happy Birthday";
17          string string4 = "happy birthday";
18          string output;
19
20          // output values of four strings
21          output = "string1 = \"" + string1 + "\"" +
22             "\nstring2 = \"" + string2 + "\"" +
23             "\nstring3 = \"" + string3 + "\"" +
24             "\nstring4 = \"" + string4 + "\"\n\n";
25
26          // test for equality using Equals method
27          if ( string1.Equals( "hello" ) )
28             output += "string1 equals \"hello\"\n";
29          else
30             output += "string1 does not equal \"hello\"\n";
31
32          // test for equality with ==
33          if ( string1 == "hello" )
34             output += "string1 equals \"hello\"\n";
35          else
36             output += "string1 does not equal \"hello\"\n";
37
38          // test for equality comparing case
39          if ( String.Equals( string3, string4 ) )
40             output += "string3 equals string4\n";
41          else
42             output += "string3 does not equal string4\n";
43
```

Fig. 12.3 **String** test to determine equality. (Part 1 of 2.)

```
44          // test CompareTo
45          output += "\nstring1.CompareTo( string2 ) is " +
46             string1.CompareTo( string2 ) + "\n" +
47             "string2.CompareTo( string1 ) is " +
48             string2.CompareTo( string1 ) + "\n" +
49             "string1.CompareTo( string1 ) is " +
50             string1.CompareTo( string1 ) + "\n" +
51             "string3.CompareTo( string4 ) is " +
52             string3.CompareTo( string4 ) + "\n" +
53             "string4.CompareTo( string3 ) is " +
54             string4.CompareTo( string3 ) + "\n\n";
55
56          MessageBox.Show( output, "Demonstrating string " +
57             "comparisons", MessageBoxButtons.OK,
58             MessageBoxIcon.Information );
59
60       } // end method Main
61
62    } // end class StringCompare
```

Fig. 12.3 **String** test to determine equality. (Part 2 of 2.)

We present the test for **string** equality between **string3** and **string4** (line 39) to illustrate that comparisons are indeed case sensitive. Here, **static** method **Equals** (as opposed to the instance method in line 27) is used to compare the values of two **string**s. **"Happy Birthday"** does not equal **"happy birthday"**, so the condition of the **if** structure fails, and the message **"string3 does not equal string4"** is added to the output message (line 42).

Lines 46–54 use the **String** method **CompareTo** to compare **string**s. Method **CompareTo** returns **0** if the **string**s are equal, a **-1** if the **string** that invokes **CompareTo** is less than the **string** that is passed as an argument and a **1** if the **string** that invokes **CompareTo** is greater than the **string** that is passed as an argument. Method **CompareTo** uses a lexicographical comparison.

Notice that **CompareTo** considers **string3** to be larger than **string4**. The only difference between these two **string**s is that **string3** contains two uppercase letters. This example illustrates that an uppercase letter has a higher value in the Unicode character set than its corresponding lowercase letter.

The application in Fig. 12.4 shows how to test whether a **string** instance begins or ends with a given **string**. Method *StartsWith* determines whether a **string** instance starts with the **string** text passed to it as an argument. Method *EndsWith* determines whether a **string** instance ends with the **string** text passed to it as an argument. Application **StringStartEnd**'s **Main** method defines an array of **string**s (called **strings**), which contains **"started"**, **"starting"**, **"ended"** and **"ending"**. The remainder of method **Main** tests the elements of the array to determine whether they start or end with a particular set of characters.

Line 21 uses method **StartsWith**, which takes a **string** argument. The condition in the **if** structure determines whether the **string** at index **i** of the array starts with the characters **"st"**. If so, the method returns **true** and appends **strings[i]** to **string output** for display purposes.

Line 30 uses method **EndsWith**, which also takes a **string** argument. The condition in the **if** structure determines whether the **string** at index **i** of the array ends with the characters **"ed"**. If so, the method returns **true**, and **strings[i]** is appended to **string output** for display purposes.

```
1    // Fig. 12.4: StringStartEnd.cs
2    // Demonstrating StartsWith and EndsWith methods.
3
4    using System;
5    using System.Windows.Forms;
6
7    // testing StartsWith and EndsWith
8    class StringStartEnd
9    {
10       // The main entry point for the application.
11       [STAThread]
12       static void Main( string[] args )
13       {
14          string[] strings =
15               { "started", "starting", "ended", "ending" };
16          string output = "";
17
18          //test every string to see if it starts with "st"
19          for ( int i = 0; i < strings.Length; i++ )
20
21             if ( strings[ i ].StartsWith( "st" ) )
22                output += "\"" + strings[ i ] + "\"" +
23                   " starts with \"st\"\n";
24
25          output += "\n";
26
27          // test every string to see if it ends with "ed"
28          for ( int i = 0; i < strings.Length; i ++ )
29
30             if ( strings[ i ].EndsWith( "ed" ) )
31                output += "\"" + strings[ i ] + "\"" +
32                   " ends with \"ed\"\n";
33
```

Fig. 12.4　**StartsWith** and **EndsWith** methods. (Part 1 of 2.)

```
34              MessageBox.Show( output, "Demonstrating StartsWith and " +
35                 "EndsWith methods", MessageBoxButtons.OK,
36                 MessageBoxIcon.Information );
37
38        } // end method Main
39
40    } // end class StringStartEnd
```

Fig. 12.4 **StartsWith** and **EndsWith** methods. (Part 2 of 2.)

12.6 String Method GetHashCode

Often, it is necessary to store **string**s and other data types in a manner that enables the information to be found quickly. One of the best ways to make information easily accessible is to store it in a hash table. A *hash table* stores an object by performing a special calculation on that object, which produces a *hash code*. The object then is stored at a location in the hash table determined by the calculated hash code. When a program needs to retrieve the information, the same calculation is performed, generating the same hash code. Any object can be stored in a hash table. Class **Object** defines method *Get-HashCode* to perform the hash-code calculation. Although all classes inherit this method from class **Object**, it is recommended that they override **Object**'s default implementation. Class **String override**s method **GetHashCode** to provide a good hash-code distribution based on the contents of the **string**. We will discuss hashing in detail in Chapter 20, Data Structures and Collections.

The example in Fig. 12.5 demonstrates the application of the **GetHashCode** method to two **string**s (**"hello"** and **"Hello"**). Here, the hash-code value for each **string** is different. However, **string**s that are not identical can have the same hash-code value.

```
1    // Fig. 12.5: StringHashCode.cs
2    // Demonstrating method GetHashCode of class String.
3
4    using System;
5    using System.Windows.Forms;
6
```

Fig. 12.5 **GetHashCode** method demonstration. (Part 1 of 2.)

```
7    // testing the GetHashCode method
8    class StringHashCode
9    {
10      // The main entry point for the application.
11      [STAThread]
12      static void Main( string[] args )
13      {
14
15         string string1 = "hello";
16         string string2 = "Hello";
17         string output;
18
19         output = "The hash code for \"" + string1 +
20            "\" is " + string1.GetHashCode() + "\n";
21
22         output += "The hash code for \"" + string2 +
23            "\" is " + string2.GetHashCode() + "\n";
24
25         MessageBox.Show( output, "Demonstrating String " +
26            "method GetHashCode", MessageBoxButtons.OK,
27            MessageBoxIcon.Information );
28
29      } // end method Main
30
31   } // end class StringHashCode
```

Fig. 12.5 **GetHashCode** method demonstration. (Part 2 of 2.)

12.7 Locating Characters and Substrings in Strings

In many applications, it is necessary to search for a character or set of characters in a **string**. For example, a programmer creating a word processor would want to provide capabilities for searching through documents. The application in Fig. 12.6 demonstrates some of the many versions of **String** methods *IndexOf*, *IndexOfAny*, *LastIndexOf* and *LastIndexOfAny*, which search for a specified character or substring in a **string**. We perform all searches in this example on the **string letters** (initialized with "ab-cdefghijklmabcdefghijklm") located in method **Main** of class **StringIndexMethods**.

```
1    // Fig. 12.6: StringIndexMethods.cs
2    // Using String searching methods.
3
```

Fig. 12.6 Searching for characters and substrings in **string**s. (Part 1 of 3.)

```
 4   using System;
 5   using System.Windows.Forms;
 6
 7   // testing indexing capabilities of strings
 8   class StringIndexMethods
 9   {
10      // The main entry point for the application.
11      [STAThread]
12      static void Main( string[] args )
13      {
14         string letters = "abcdefghijklmabcdefghijklm";
15         string output = "";
16         char[] searchLetters = { 'c', 'a', '$' };
17
18         // test IndexOf to locate a character in a string
19         output += "'c' is located at index " +
20            letters.IndexOf( 'c' );
21
22         output += "\n'a' is located at index " +
23            letters.IndexOf( 'a', 1 );
24
25         output += "\n'$' is located at index " +
26            letters.IndexOf( '$', 3, 5 );
27
28         // test LastIndexOf to find a character in a string
29         output += "\n\nLast 'c' is located at " +
30            "index " + letters.LastIndexOf( 'c' );
31
32         output += "\nLast 'a' is located at index " +
33            letters.LastIndexOf( 'a', 25 );
34
35         output += "\nLast '$' is located at index " +
36            letters.LastIndexOf( '$', 15, 5 );
37
38         // test IndexOf to locate a substring in a string
39         output += "\n\n\"def\" is located at" +
40            " index " + letters.IndexOf( "def" );
41
42         output += "\n\"def\" is located at index " +
43            letters.IndexOf( "def", 7 );
44
45         output += "\n\"hello\" is located at index " +
46            letters.IndexOf( "hello", 5, 15 );
47
48         // test LastIndexOf to find a substring in a string
49         output += "\n\nLast \"def\" is located at index " +
50            letters.LastIndexOf( "def" );
51
52         output += "\nLast \"def\" is located at " +
53            letters.LastIndexOf( "def", 25 );
54
55         output += "\nLast \"hello\" is located at index " +
56            letters.LastIndexOf( "hello", 20, 15 );
```

Fig. 12.6 Searching for characters and substrings in **string**s. (Part 2 of 3.)

```
57
58        // test IndexOfAny to find first occurrence of character
59        // in array
60        output += "\n\nFirst occurrence of 'c', 'a', '$' is " +
61           "located at " + letters.IndexOfAny( searchLetters );
62
63        output += "\nFirst occurrence of 'c, 'a' or '$' is " +
64           "located at " + letters.IndexOfAny( searchLetters, 7 );
65
66        output += "\nFirst occurrence of 'c', 'a' or '$' is " +
67           "located at " + letters.IndexOfAny( searchLetters, 20, 5 );
68
69        // test LastIndexOfAny to find last occurrence of character
70        // in array
71        output += "\n\nLast occurrence of 'c', 'a' or '$' is " +
72           "located at " + letters.LastIndexOfAny( searchLetters );
73
74        output += "\nLast occurrence of 'c', 'a' or '$' is " +
75           "located at " + letters.LastIndexOfAny( searchLetters, 1 );
76
77        output += "\nLast occurrence of 'c', 'a' or '$' is " +
78           "located at " + letters.LastIndexOfAny(
79           searchLetters, 25, 5 );
80
81        MessageBox.Show( output,
82           "Demonstrating class index methods",
83           MessageBoxButtons.OK, MessageBoxIcon.Information );
84
85     } // end method Main
86
87  } // end class StringIndexMethods
```

Fig. 12.6 Searching for characters and substrings in **string**s. (Part 3 of 3.)

Lines 20, 23 and 26 use method **IndexOf** to locate the first occurrence of a character or substring in a **string**. If **IndexOf** finds a character, **IndexOf** returns the index of the specified character in the **string**; otherwise, **IndexOf** returns **-1**. The expression on line 23 uses a version of method **IndexOf** that takes two arguments—the character to search for and the starting index at which the search of the **string** should begin. The method does not examine any characters that occur prior to the starting index (in this case **1**). The expression in line 26 uses another version of method **IndexOf** that takes three arguments—the character to search for, the index at which to start searching and the number of characters to search.

Lines 30, 33 and 36 use method **LastIndexOf** to locate the last occurrence of a character in a **string**. Method **LastIndexOf** performs the search from the end of the **string** toward the beginning of the **string**. If method **LastIndexOf** finds the character, **LastIndexOf** returns the index of the specified character in the **string**; otherwise, **LastIndexOf** returns **-1**. There are three versions of **LastIndexOf** that search for characters in a **string**. The expression in line 30 uses the version of method **LastIndexOf** that takes as an argument the character for which to search. The expression in line 33 uses the version of method **LastIndexOf** that takes two arguments—the character for which to search and the highest index from which to begin searching backward for the character. The expression in line 36 uses a third version of method **LastIndexOf** that takes three arguments—the character for which to search, the starting index from which to start searching backward and the number of characters (the portion of the **string**) to search.

Lines 40–56 use versions of **IndexOf** and **LastIndexOf** that take a **string** instead of a character as the first argument. These versions of the methods perform identically to those described above except that they search for sequences of characters (or substrings) that are specified by their **string** arguments.

Lines 61–79 use methods **IndexOfAny** and **LastIndexOfAny**, which take an array of characters as the first argument. These versions of the methods also perform identically to those described above except that they return the index of the first occurrence of any of the characters in the character array argument.

Common Programming Error 12.2

In the overloaded methods **LastIndexOf** *and* **LastIndexOfAny** *that take three parameters, the second argument must always be bigger than or equal to the third argument. This might seem counterintuitive, but remember that the search moves from the end of the string toward the start of the string.*

12.8 Extracting Substrings from **Strings**

Class **String** provides two *Substring* methods, which are used to create a new **string** by copying part of an existing **string**. Each method returns a new **string**. The application in Fig. 12.7 demonstrates the use of both methods.

```
1   // Fig. 12.7: SubString.cs
2   // Demonstrating the String Substring method.
3
```

Fig. 12.7   Substrings generated from **string**s. (Part 1 of 2.)

```
4    using System;
5    using System.Windows.Forms;
6
7    // creating substrings
8    class SubString
9    {
10      // The main entry point for the application.
11      [STAThread]
12      static void Main( string[] args )
13      {
14         string letters = "abcdefghijklmabcdefghijklm";
15         string output = "";
16
17         // invoke Substring method and pass it one parameter
18         output += "Substring from index 20 to end is \"" +
19            letters.Substring( 20 ) + "\"\n";
20
21         // invoke Substring method and pass it two parameters
22         output += "Substring from index 0 to 6 is \"" +
23            letters.Substring( 0, 6 ) + "\"";
24
25         MessageBox.Show( output,
26            "Demonstrating String method Substring",
27            MessageBoxButtons.OK, MessageBoxIcon.Information );
28
29      } // end method Main
30
31   } // end class SubString
```

Fig. 12.7 Substrings generated from **string**s. (Part 2 of 2.)

The statement in line 19 uses the **Substring** method that takes one **int** argument. The argument specifies the starting index from which the method copies characters in the original **string**. The substring returned contains a copy of the characters from the starting index to the end of the **string**. If the index specified in the argument is outside the bounds of the **string**, the program throws an **ArgumentOutOfRangeException**.

The second version of method **Substring** (line 23) takes two **int** arguments. The first argument specifies the starting index from which the method copies characters from the original **string**. The second argument specifies the length of the substring to be copied. The substring returned contains a copy of the specified characters from the original **string**.

12.9 Concatenating Strings

The + operator (discussed in Chapter 2, Introduction to the Visual Studio .NET IDE and C# Programming) is not the only way to perform **string** concatenation. The **static** method **Concat** of class **String** (Fig. 12.8) concatenates two **string**s and returns a new **string** containing the combined characters from both original **string**s. Line 23 appends the characters from **string2** to the end of **string1**, using method **Concat**. The statement on line 23 does not modify the original **string**s.

12.10 Miscellaneous String Methods

Class **String** provides several methods that return modified copies of **string**s. The application in Fig. 12.9 demonstrates the use of these methods, which include **String** methods *Replace*, *ToLower*, *ToUpper*, *Trim* and *ToString*.

```
1    // Fig. 12.8: SubConcatenation.cs
2    // Demonstrating String class Concat method.
3
4    using System;
5    using System.Windows.Forms;
6
7    // concatenates strings using String method Concat
8    class StringConcatenation
9    {
10       // The main entry point for the application.
11       [STAThread]
12       static void Main( string[] args )
13       {
14          string string1 = "Happy ";
15          string string2 = "Birthday";
16          string output;
17
18          output = "string1 = \"" + string1 + "\"\n" +
19             "string2 = \"" + string2 + "\"";
20
21          output +=
22             "\n\nResult of String.Concat( string1, string2 ) = " +
23             String.Concat( string1, string2 );
24
25          output += "\nstring1 after concatenation = " + string1;
26
27          MessageBox.Show( output,
28             "Demonstrating String method Concat",
29             MessageBoxButtons.OK, MessageBoxIcon.Information );
30
31       } // end method Main
32
33    } // end class StringConcatenation
```

Fig. 12.8   Concat **static** method.

Line 27 uses **String** method **Replace** to return a new **string**, replacing every occurrence in **string1** of character **'e'** with character **'E'**. Method **Replace** takes two arguments—a **string** for which to search and another **string** with which to replace all matching occurrences of the first argument. The original **string** remains unchanged. If there are no occurrences of the first argument in the **string**, the method returns the original **string**.

String method **ToUpper** generates a new **string** (line 31) that replaces any lowercase letters in **string1** with their uppercase equivalent. The method returns a new **string** containing the converted **string**; the original **string** remains unchanged. If there are no characters to convert to uppercase, the method returns the original **string**. Line 32 uses **String** method **ToLower** to return a new **string** in which any uppercase letters in **string2** are replaced by their lowercase equivalents. The original **string** is unchanged. As with **ToUpper**, if there are no characters to convert to lowercase, method **ToLower** returns the original **string**.

```
1   // Fig. 12.9: StringMiscellaneous2.cs
2   // Demonstrating String methods Replace, ToLower, ToUpper, Trim
3   // and ToString.
4
5   using System;
6   using System.Windows.Forms;
7
8   // creates strings using methods Replace, ToLower, ToUpper, Trim
9   class StringMethods2
10  {
11     // The main entry point for the application.
12     [STAThread]
13     static void Main( string[] args )
14     {
15        string string1 = "cheers!";
16        string string2 = "GOOD BYE ";
17        string string3 = "   spaces   ";
18        string output;
19
20        output = "string1 = \"" + string1 + "\"\n" +
21           "string2 = \"" + string2 + "\"\n" +
22           "string3 = \"" + string3 + "\"";
23
24        // call method Replace
25        output +=
26           "\n\nReplacing \"e\" with \"E\" in string1: \"" +
27           string1.Replace( 'e', 'E' ) + "\"";
28
29        // call ToLower and ToUpper
30        output += "\n\nstring1.ToUpper() = \"" +
31           string1.ToUpper() + "\"\nstring2.ToLower() = \"" +
32           string2.ToLower() + "\"";
33
```

Fig. 12.9 **String** methods **Replace**, **ToLower**, **ToUpper**, **Trim** and **ToString**. (Part 1 of 2.)

```
34            // call Trim method
35            output += "\n\nstring3 after trim = \"" +
36               string3.Trim() + "\"";
37
38            // call ToString method
39            output += "\n\nstring1 = \"" + string1.ToString() + "\"";
40
41            MessageBox.Show( output,
42               "Demonstrating various string methods",
43               MessageBoxButtons.OK, MessageBoxIcon.Information );
44
45         } // end method Main
46
47      } // end class StringMethods2
```

Fig. 12.9 **String** methods **Replace**, **ToLower**, **ToUpper**, **Trim** and **ToString**. (Part 2 of 2.)

Line 36 uses **String** method **Trim** to remove all whitespace characters that appear at the beginning and end of a **string**. Without otherwise altering the original **string**, the method returns a new **string** that contains the **string**, but omits leading or trailing whitespace characters. Another version of method **Trim** takes a character array and returns a **string** that does not contain the characters in the array argument.

Line 39 uses class **String**'s method **ToString** to show that the various other methods employed in this application have not modified **string1**. Why is the **ToString** method provided for class **String**? In C#, all objects are derived from class **Object**, which defines **virtual** method **ToString**. Thus, method **ToString** can be called to obtain a **string** representation of any object. If a class that inherits from **Object** (such as **String**) does not override method **ToString**, the class uses the default version from class **Object**, which returns a **string** consisting of the object's class name. Classes usually override method **ToString** to express the contents of an object as text. Class **String** overrides method **ToString** so that, instead of returning the class name, it simply returns the **string**.

12.11 Class **StringBuilder**

The **String** class provides many capabilities for processing **string**s. However a **string**'s contents can never change. Operations that seem to concatenate **string**s are in fact assigning **string** references to newly created **string**s (e.g., the **+=** operator creates a new **string** and assigns the initial **string** reference to the newly created **string**).

The next several sections discuss the features of class **StringBuilder** (namespace **System.Text**), used to create and manipulate dynamic string information—i.e., mutable strings. Every **StringBuilder** can store a certain number of characters that is specified by its capacity. Exceeding the capacity of a **StringBuilder** causes the capacity to expand to accommodate the additional characters. As we will see, members of class **StringBuilder**, such as methods **Append** and **AppendFormat**, can be used for concatenation like the operators **+** and **+=** for class **String**.

Software Engineering Observation 12.2

*Objects of class **String** are constant strings, whereas object of class **StringBuilder** are mutable strings. C# can perform certain optimizations involving **string**s (such as the sharing of one **string** among multiple references), because it knows these objects will not change.*

Performance Tip 12.2

*When given the choice between using a **string** to represent a string and using a **StringBuilder** object to represent that string, always use a **string** if the contents of the object will not change. When appropriate, using **string**s instead of **StringBuilder** objects improves performance.*

Class **StringBuilder** provides six overloaded constructors. Class **StringBuilderConstructor** (Fig. 12.10) demonstrates the use of three of these overloaded constructors.

```
1   // Fig. 12.10: StringBuilderConstructor.cs
2   // Demonstrating StringBuilder class constructors.
3
4   using System;
5   using System.Windows.Forms;
6   using System.Text;
7
8   // creates three StringBuilder with three constructors
9   class StringBuilderConstructor
10  {
11     // The main entry point for the application.
12     [STAThread]
13     static void Main( string[] args )
14     {
15        StringBuilder buffer1, buffer2, buffer3;
16        string output;
17
18        buffer1 = new StringBuilder();
19        buffer2 = new StringBuilder( 10 );
20        buffer3 = new StringBuilder( "hello" );
21
22        output = "buffer1 = \"" + buffer1.ToString() + "\"\n";
23
24        output += "buffer2 = \"" + buffer2.ToString() + "\"\n";
25
```

Fig. 12.10 StringBuilder class constructors. (Part 1 of 2.)

```
26              output += "buffer3 = \"" + buffer3.ToString() + "\"\n";
27
28          MessageBox.Show( output,
29              "Demonstrating StringBuilder class constructors",
30              MessageBoxButtons.OK, MessageBoxIcon.Information );
31
32      } // end method Main
33
34  } // end class StringBuilderConstructor
```

Fig. 12.10 `StringBuilder` class constructors. (Part 2 of 2.)

Line 18 employs the no-argument **StringBuilder** constructor to create a **StringBuilder** that contains no characters and has a default initial capacity of 16 characters. Line 19 uses the **StringBuilder** constructor that takes an **int** argument to create a **StringBuilder** that contains no characters and has the initial capacity specified in the **int** argument (i.e., **10**). Line 20 uses the **StringBuilder** constructor that takes a **string** argument to create a **StringBuilder** containing the characters of the **string** argument. The initial capacity is the smallest power of two greater than the number of characters in the **string** passed as an argument.

Lines 22–26 use **StringBuilder** method **ToString** to obtain a **string** representation of the **StringBuilder**s' contents. This method returns the **StringBuilder**s' underlying string.

12.12 StringBuilder Indexer, Length and Capacity Properties, and EnsureCapacity Method

Class **StringBuilder** provides the *Length* and *Capacity* properties to return the number of characters currently in a **StringBuilder** and the number of characters that a **StringBuilder** can store without allocating more memory, respectively. These properties also can increase or decrease the length or the capacity of the **StringBuilder**.

Method *EnsureCapacity* allows programmers to guarantee that a **StringBuilder** has a capacity that reduces the number of times the capacity must be increased. Method **EnsureCapacity** doubles the **StringBuilder** instance's current capacity. If this doubled value is greater than the value that the programmer wishes to ensure, it becomes the new capacity. Otherwise, **EnsureCapacity** alters the capacity to make it one more than the requested number. For example, if the current capacity is 17 and we wish to make it 40, 17 multiplied by 2 is not greater than 40, so the call will result in a new capacity of 41. If the current capacity is 23 and we wish to make it 40, 23 will be multiplied by 2 to result in a new capacity of 46. Both 41 and 46 are greater than 40, and so a capacity of 40 is indeed ensured by method **EnsureCapacity**. The program in Fig. 12.11 demonstrates the use of these methods and properties.

The program contains one **StringBuilder**, called **buffer**. Lines 15–16 of the program use the **StringBuilder** constructor that takes a **string** argument to instantiate the **StringBuilder** and initialize its value to **"Hello, how are you?"**. Lines 19–21 append to **output** the content, length and capacity of the **StringBuilder**. In the output window, notice that the capacity of the **StringBuilder** is initially 32. Remember, the **StringBuilder** constructor that takes a **string** argument creates a **StringBuilder** object with an initial capacity that is the smallest power of two greater than the number of characters in the **string** passed as an argument.

Line 24 expands the capacity of the **StringBuilder** to a minimum of 75 characters. The current capacity (**32**) multiplied by two is less than 75, so method **EnsureCapacity** increases the capacity to one greater than 75 (i.e., 76). If new characters are added to a **StringBuilder** so that its length exceeds its capacity, the capacity grows to accommodate the additional characters in the same manner as if method **EnsureCapacity** had been called.

```
1   // Fig. 12.11: StringBuilderFeatures.cs
2   // Demonstrating some features of class StringBuilder.
3
4   using System;
5   using System.Windows.Forms;
6   using System.Text;
7
8   // uses some of class StringBuilder's methods
9   class StringBuilderFeatures
10  {
11      // The main entry point for the application.
12      [STAThread]
13      static void Main( string[] args )
14      {
15          StringBuilder buffer =
16              new StringBuilder( "Hello, how are you?" );
17
18          // use Length and Capacity properties
19          string output = "buffer = " + buffer.ToString() +
20              "\nLength = " + buffer.Length +
21              "\nCapacity = " + buffer.Capacity;
22
23          // use EnsureCapacity method
24          buffer.EnsureCapacity( 75 );
25
26          output += "\n\nNew capacity = " +
27              buffer.Capacity;
28
29          // truncate StringBuilder by setting Length property
30          buffer.Length = 10;
31
32          output += "\n\nNew length = " +
33              buffer.Length + "\nbuffer = ";
34
```

Fig. 12.11 StringBuilder size manipulation. (Part 1 of 2.)

```
35            // use StringBuilder indexer
36            for ( int i = 0; i < buffer.Length; i++ )
37               output += buffer[ i ];
38
39            MessageBox.Show( output, "StringBuilder features",
40               MessageBoxButtons.OK, MessageBoxIcon.Information );
41
42      } // end method Main
43
44 } // end class StringBuilderFeatures
```

Fig. 12.11 StringBuilder size manipulation. (Part 2 of 2.)

Line 30 uses **Length**'s **Set** accessor to set the length of the **StringBuilder** to **10**. If the specified length is less than the current number of characters in the **String-Builder**, the contents of **StringBuilder** are truncated to the specified length (i.e., the program discards all characters in the **StringBuilder** that occur after the specified length). If the specified length is greater than the number of characters currently in the **StringBuilder**, null characters (characters with the numeric representation **0** that signal the end of a **string**) are appended to the **StringBuilder** until the total number of characters in the **StringBuilder** is equal to the specified length.

Common Programming Error 12.3

*Assigning **null** to a **string** reference can lead to logic errors. The keyword **null** is a null reference, not a **string**. Do not confuse **null** with the empty string, **""** (the **string** that is of length 0 and contains no characters).*

12.13 StringBuilder Append and AppendFormat Methods

Class **StringBuilder** provides 19 overloaded **Append** methods that allow various data-type values to be added to the end of a **StringBuilder**. C# provides versions for each of the primitive data types and for character arrays, **String**s and **Object**s. (Remember that method **ToString** produces a **string** representation of any **Object**.) Each of the methods takes an argument, converts it to a **string** and appends it to the **StringBuilder**. Figure 12.12 demonstrates the use of several **Append** methods.

Lines 29–47 use 10 different overloaded **Append** methods to attach the objects created in lines 15–26 to the end of the **StringBuilder**. **Append** behaves similarly to the **+** operator which is used with **string**s. Just as **+** seems to append objects to a **string**, method **Append** can append data types to a **StringBuilder**'s underlying string.

Class **StringBuilder** also provides method ***AppendFormat***, which converts a **string** to a specified format and then appends it to the **StringBuilder**. The example in Fig. 12.13 demonstrates the use of this method.

```
1   // Fig. 12.12: StringBuilderAppend.cs
2   // Demonstrating StringBuilder Append methods.
3
4   using System;
5   using System.Windows.Forms;
6   using System.Text;
7
8   // testing the Append method
9   class StringBuilderAppend
10  {
11      // The main entry point for the application.
12      [STAThread]
13      static void Main( string[] args )
14      {
15          object objectValue = "hello";
16          string stringValue = "good bye";
17          char[] characterArray = { 'a', 'b', 'c', 'd',
18                                     'e', 'f' };
19
20          bool booleanValue = true;
21          char characterValue = 'Z';
22          int integerValue = 7;
23          long longValue = 1000000;
24          float floatValue = 2.5F;
25          double doubleValue = 33.333;
26          StringBuilder buffer = new StringBuilder();
27
28          // use method Append to append values to buffer
29          buffer.Append( objectValue );
30          buffer.Append( "  " );
31          buffer.Append( stringValue );
32          buffer.Append( "  " );
33          buffer.Append( characterArray );
34          buffer.Append( "  " );
35          buffer.Append( characterArray, 0, 3 );
36          buffer.Append( "  " );
37          buffer.Append( booleanValue );
38          buffer.Append( "  " );
39          buffer.Append( characterValue );
40          buffer.Append( "  " );
41          buffer.Append( integerValue );
42          buffer.Append( "  " );
43          buffer.Append( longValue );
44          buffer.Append( "  " );
45          buffer.Append( floatValue );
46          buffer.Append( "  " );
47          buffer.Append( doubleValue );
48
```

Fig. 12.12 Append methods of **StringBuilder**. (Part 1 of 2.)

```
49              MessageBox.Show( "buffer = " + buffer.ToString(),
50                  "Demonstrating StringBuilder append method",
51                  MessageBoxButtons.OK, MessageBoxIcon.Information );
52
53      } // end method Main
54
55  } // end class StringBuilderAppend
```

Fig. 12.12 Append methods of **StringBuilder**. (Part 2 of 2.)

```
1   // Fig. 12.13: StringBuilderAppendFormat.cs
2   // Demonstrating method AppendFormat.
3
4   using System;
5   using System.Windows.Forms;
6   using System.Text;
7
8   // use the AppendFormat method
9   class StringBuilderAppendFormat
10  {
11      // The main entry point for the application.
12      [STAThread]
13      static void Main( string[] args )
14      {
15          StringBuilder buffer = new StringBuilder();
16          string string1, string2;
17
18          // formatted string
19          string1 = "This {0} costs: {1:C}.\n";
20
21          // string1 argument array
22          object[] objectArray = new object[ 2 ];
23
24          objectArray[ 0 ] = "car";
25          objectArray[ 1 ] = 1234.56;
26
27          // append to buffer formatted string with argument
28          buffer.AppendFormat( string1, objectArray );
29
30          // formatted string
31          string2 = "Number:{0:d3}.\n" +
32              "Number right aligned with spaces:{0, 4}.\n" +
33              "Number left aligned with spaces:{0, -4}.";
34
```

Fig. 12.13 StringBuilder's AppendFormat method. (Part 1 of 2.)

```
35        // append to buffer formatted string with argument
36        buffer.AppendFormat( string2, 5 );
37
38        // display formatted strings
39        MessageBox.Show( buffer.ToString(), "Using AppendFormat",
40           MessageBoxButtons.OK, MessageBoxIcon.Information );
41
42     } // end method Main
43
44  } // end class StringBuilderAppendFormat
```

Fig. 12.13 **StringBuilder**'s **AppendFormat** method. (Part 2 of 2.)

Line 19 creates a **string** that contains formatting information. The information enclosed within the braces determines how to format a specific piece of information. Formats have the form **{X[,Y][:FormatString]}**, where **X** is the number of the argument to be formatted, counting from zero. **Y** is an optional argument, which can be positive or negative, indicating how many characters should be in the result of formatting. If the resulting **string** is less than the number **Y**, the **string** will be padded with spaces to make up for the difference. A positive integer aligns the **string** to the right; a negative integer aligns it to the left. The optional **FormatString** applies a particular format to the argument: Currency, decimal or scientific, among others. In this case, "**{0}**" means the first argument will be printed out. "**{1:C}**" specifies that the second argument will be formatted as a currency value.

Line 28 shows a version of **AppendFormat**, which takes two parameters—a **string** specifying the format and an array of objects to serve as the arguments to the format **string**. The argument referred to by "**{0}**" is in the object array at index **0**, and so on.

Lines 31–33 define another **string** used for formatting. The first format "**{0:D3}**" specifies that the first argument will be formatted as a three-digit decimal, meaning any number that has fewer than three digits will have leading zeros placed in front to make up the difference. The next format, "**{0, 4}**" specifies that the formatted **string** should have four characters and should be right aligned. The third format, "**{0, -4}**" specifies that the **string**s should be aligned to the left. For more formatting options, please refer to the documentation.

Line 36 uses a version of **AppendFormat** that takes two parameters: A **string** containing a format and an object to which the format is applied. In this case, the object is the number **5**. The output of Fig. 12.13 displays the result of applying these two version of **AppendFormat** with their respective arguments.

12.14 StringBuilder Insert, Remove and Replace Methods

Class **StringBuilder** provides 18 overloaded *Insert* methods to allow various data-type values to be inserted at any position in a **StringBuilder**. The class provides versions for each of the primitive data types and for character arrays, **String**s and **Object**s. (Remember that method **ToString** produces a **string** representation of any **Object**.) Each method takes its second argument, converts it to a **string** and inserts the **string** into the **StringBuilder** in front of the index specified by the first argument. The index specified by the first argument must be greater than or equal to **0** and less than the length of the **StringBuilder**; otherwise, the program throws an **ArgumentOutOfRange-Exception**.

Class **StringBuilder** also provides method *Remove* for deleting any portion of a **StringBuilder**. Method **Remove** takes two arguments—the index at which to begin deletion and the number of characters to delete. The sum of the starting subscript and the number of characters to be deleted must always be less than the length of the **String-Builder**; otherwise, the program throws an **ArgumentOutOfRangeException**. The **Insert** and **Remove** methods are demonstrated in Fig. 12.14.

```
1   // Fig. 12.14: StringBuilderInsertRemove.cs
2   // Demonstrating methods Insert and Remove of the
3   // StringBuilder class.
4
5   using System;
6   using System.Windows.Forms;
7   using System.Text;
8
9   // test the Insert and Remove methods
10  class StringBuilderInsertRemove
11  {
12     // The main entry point for the application.
13     [STAThread]
14     static void Main( string[] args )
15     {
16        object objectValue = "hello";
17        string stringValue = "good bye";
18        char[] characterArray = { 'a', 'b', 'c',
19                                  'd', 'e', 'f' };
20
21        bool booleanValue = true;
22        char characterValue = 'K';
23        int integerValue = 7;
24        long longValue = 10000000;
25        float floatValue = 2.5F;
26        double doubleValue = 33.333;
27        StringBuilder buffer = new StringBuilder();
28        string output;
29
30        // insert values into buffer
31        buffer.Insert( 0, objectValue );
```

Fig. 12.14 StringBuilder text insertion and removal. (Part 1 of 2.)

```
32          buffer.Insert(0, "   ");
33          buffer.Insert(0, stringValue);
34          buffer.Insert(0, "   ");
35          buffer.Insert(0, characterArray);
36          buffer.Insert(0, "   ");
37          buffer.Insert(0, booleanValue);
38          buffer.Insert(0, "   ");
39          buffer.Insert(0, characterValue);
40          buffer.Insert(0, "   ");
41          buffer.Insert(0, integerValue);
42          buffer.Insert(0, "   ");
43          buffer.Insert(0, longValue);
44          buffer.Insert(0, "   ");
45          buffer.Insert(0, floatValue);
46          buffer.Insert(0, "   ");
47          buffer.Insert(0, doubleValue);
48          buffer.Insert(0, "   ");
49
50          output = "buffer after inserts: \n" +
51             buffer.ToString() + "\n\n";
52
53          buffer.Remove( 10, 1 ); // delete 2 in 2.5
54          buffer.Remove( 2, 4 );  // delete 33.3 in 33.333
55
56          output += "buffer after Removes:\n" +
57             buffer.ToString();
58
59          MessageBox.Show( output, "Demonstrating StringBuilder " +
60             "Insert and Remove methods", MessageBoxButtons.OK,
61             MessageBoxIcon.Information );
62
63       } // end method Main
64
65    } // end class StringBuilderInsertRemove
```

Fig. 12.14 StringBuilder text insertion and removal. (Part 2 of 2.)

Another useful method included with **StringBuilder** is **Replace**. **Replace** searches for a specified **string** or character and substitutes another **string** or character in its place. Figure 12.15 demonstrates this method.

```
1    // Fig. 12.15: StringBuilderReplace.cs
2    // Demonstrating method Replace.
3
```

Fig. 12.15 StringBuilder text replacement. (Part 1 of 2.)

```
 4   using System;
 5   using System.Windows.Forms;
 6   using System.Text;
 7
 8   // testing the Replace method
 9   class StringBuilderReplace
10   {
11      // The main entry point for the application.
12      [STAThread]
13      static void Main( string[] args )
14      {
15         StringBuilder builder1 =
16            new StringBuilder( "Happy Birthday Jane" );
17
18         StringBuilder builder2 =
19            new StringBuilder( "good bye greg" );
20
21         string output = "Before replacements:\n" +
22            builder1.ToString() + "\n" + builder2.ToString();
23
24         builder1.Replace( "Jane", "Greg" );
25         builder2.Replace( 'g', 'G', 0, 5 );
26
27         output += "\n\nAfter replacements:\n" +
28            builder1.ToString() + "\n" + builder2.ToString();
29
30         MessageBox.Show( output,
31            "Using StringBuilder method Replace",
32            MessageBoxButtons.OK, MessageBoxIcon.Information );
33
34      } // end method Main
35
36   } // end class StringBuilderReplace
```

Fig. 12.15 StringBuilder text replacement. (Part 2 of 2.)

Line 24 uses method **Replace** to replace all instances of the **string "Jane"** with the **string "Greg"** in **builder1**. Another overload of this method takes two characters as parameters and replaces each occurrence of the first with one of the second. Line 25 uses an overload of **Replace** that takes four parameters, the first two of which are characters and the second two of which are **int**s. The method replaces all instances of the first character with the second, beginning at the index specified by the first **int** and continuing for a count specified by the second. Thus, in this case, **Replace** looks through only five characters starting with the character at index **0**. As the outputs illustrates, this version of

Replace replaces **g** with **G** in the word **"good"**, but not in **"greg"**. This is because the **g**s in **"greg"** do not fall in the range indicated by the **int** arguments (i.e., between indexes **0** and **4**).

12.15 Char Methods

C# provides a data type, called a *structure*, that is similar to a class. Although structures and classes are comparable in many ways, structures are a value type. Like classes, structures include methods and properties. Both use the same modifiers (such as **public**, **private** and **protected**) and access members via the member access operator (**.**). However, classes are created by using the keyword **class**, but structures are created using the keyword *struct*.

Many of the primitive data types that we have used in this book are actually aliases for different structures. For instance, an **int** is defined by structure **System.Int32**, a **Long** by **System.Int64**, and so on. These structures are derived from class *ValueType*, which in turn is derived from class **Object**. In this section, we present structure *Char*, which is the structure for characters.

Most **Char** methods are **static**, take at least one character argument and perform either a test or a manipulation on the character. We present several of these methods in the next example. Figure 12.16 demonstrates **static** methods that test characters to determine whether they are of a specific character type and **static** methods that perform case conversions on characters.

This Windows application contains a prompt, a **TextBox** into which the user can input a character, a button that the user can press after entering a character and a second **TextBox** that displays the output of our analysis. When the user clicks the **Analyze Character** button, event handler **analyzeButton_Click** (lines 32–37) is invoked. This method converts the entered data from a **string** to a **Char**, using method **Convert.ToChar** (line 35). On line 36, we call method **BuildOutput**, which is defined in lines 40–72.

Line 45 uses **Char** method *IsDigit* to determine whether character **input-Character** is defined as a digit. If so, the method returns **true**; otherwise, it returns **false**.

Line 48 uses **Char** method *IsLetter* to determine whether character **inputCh-aracter** is a letter. If so, the method returns **true**; otherwise, it returns **false**. Line 51 uses **Char** method *IsLetterOrDigit* to determine whether character **inputChar-acter** is a letter or a digit. If so, the method returns **true**; otherwise, it returns **false**.

```
1   // Fig. 12.16: CharMethods.cs
2   // Demonstrates static character testing methods
3   // from Char structure
4
5   using System;
6   using System.Drawing;
7   using System.Collections;
8   using System.ComponentModel;
9   using System.Windows.Forms;
10  using System.Data;
```

Fig. 12.16 Char's static character-testing methods and case-conversion methods. (Part 1 of 3.)

```
11
12      // Form displays information about specific characters.
13      public class StaticCharMethods : System.Windows.Forms.Form
14      {
15         private System.Windows.Forms.Label enterLabel;
16         private System.Windows.Forms.TextBox inputTextBox;
17         private System.Windows.Forms.Button analyzeButton;
18         private System.Windows.Forms.TextBox outputTextBox;
19
20         private System.ComponentModel.Container components = null;
21
22         // The main entry point for the application.
23         [STAThread]
24         static void Main()
25         {
26            Application.Run( new StaticCharMethods() );
27         }
28
29         // Visual Studio .NET generated code
30
31         // handle analyzeButton_Click
32         private void analyzeButton_Click(
33            object sender, System.EventArgs e )
34         {
35            char character = Convert.ToChar( inputTextBox.Text );
36            BuildOutput( character );
37         }
38
39         // display character information in outputTextBox
40         private void BuildOutput( char inputCharacter )
41         {
42            string output;
43
44            output = "is digit: " +
45               Char.IsDigit( inputCharacter ) + "\r\n";
46
47            output += "is letter: " +
48               Char.IsLetter( inputCharacter ) + "\r\n";
49
50            output += "is letter or digit: " +
51               Char.IsLetterOrDigit( inputCharacter ) + "\r\n";
52
53            output += "is lower case: " +
54               Char.IsLower( inputCharacter ) + "\r\n";
55
56            output += "is upper case: " +
57               Char.IsUpper( inputCharacter ) + "\r\n";
58
59            output += "to upper case: " +
60               Char.ToUpper( inputCharacter ) + "\r\n";
61
```

Fig. 12.16 Char's **static** character-testing methods and case-conversion methods. (Part 2 of 3.)

```
62              output += "to lower case: " +
63                  Char.ToLower( inputCharacter ) + "\r\n";
64
65              output += "is punctuation: " +
66                  Char.IsPunctuation( inputCharacter ) + "\r\n";
67
68              output += "is symbol: " + Char.IsSymbol( inputCharacter );
69
70              outputTextBox.Text = output;
71
72          } // end method BuildOutput
73
74      } // end class StaticCharMethods
```

Fig. 12.16 **Char**'s **static** character-testing methods and case-conversion methods. (Part 3 of 3.)

Line 54 uses **Char** method *IsLower* to determine whether character **inputCharacter** is a lowercase letter. If so, the method returns **true**; otherwise, it returns **false**. Line 57 uses **Char** method *IsUpper* to determine whether character **inputCharacter** is an uppercase letter. If so, the method returns **true**; otherwise, it returns **false**. Line 60 uses **Char** method *ToUpper* to convert the character **inputCharacter** to its uppercase equivalent. The method returns the converted character if the character has an uppercase equivalent; otherwise, the method returns its original argument. Line 63 uses **Char** method *ToLower* to convert the character **inputCharacter** to its lowercase equivalent. The method returns the converted character if the character has a lowercase equivalent; otherwise, the method returns its original argument.

Line 66 uses **Char** method *IsPunctuation* to determine whether character **inputCharacter** is a punctuation mark. If so, the method returns **true**; otherwise, it returns **false**. Line 68 uses **Char** method *IsSymbol* to determine whether character **inputCharacter** is a symbol. If so, the method returns **true**; otherwise it returns **false**.

Structure type **Char** also contains other methods not shown in this example. Many of the **static** methods are similar; for instance, *IsWhiteSpace* is used to determine whether a certain character is a whitespace character (e.g., newline, tab or space). The structure also contains several **public** instance methods; many of these, such as methods

ToString and **Equals**, are methods that we have seen before in other classes. This group includes method *CompareTo*, which is used to compare two character values with one another.

12.16 Card Shuffling and Dealing Simulation

In this section, we use random-number generation to develop a program that simulates the shuffling and dealing of cards. Once created, this program can be implemented in programs that imitate specific card games.

Class **Card** (Fig. 12.17) contains two **string** instance variables—**face** and **suit**—that store references to the face name and suit name of a specific card. The constructor for the class receives two **string**s that it uses to initialize **face** and **suit**. Method **ToString** (lines 20–24) creates a **string** consisting of the **face** of the card and the **suit** of the card.

We develop application **DeckForm** (Fig. 12.18), which creates a deck of 52 playing cards, using **Card** objects. Users can deal each card by clicking the **Deal Card** button. Each dealt card is displayed in a **Label**. Users can also shuffle the deck at any time by clicking the **Shuffle Cards** button.

Method **DeckForm_Load** (lines 35–53 of Fig. 12.18) uses the **for** structure (lines 50–51) to fill the **deck** array with **Card**s. Note that each **Card** is instantiated and initialized with two **string**s—one from the **faces** array (**string**s **"Ace"** through **"King"**) and one from the **suits** array (**"Hearts"**, **"Diamonds"**, **"Clubs"** or **"Spades"**). The calculation **i % 13** always results in a value from **0** to **12** (the thirteen subscripts of the **faces** array), and the calculation **i % 4** always results in a value from **0** to **3** (the four subscripts in the **suits** array). The initialized **deck** array contains the cards with faces ace through king for each suit.

```
1   // Fig. 12.17: Card.cs
2   // Stores suit and face information on each card.
3
4   using System;
5
6   // the representation of a card
7   public class Card
8   {
9      private string face;
10     private string suit;
11
12     public Card( string faceValue,
13        string suitValue )
14     {
15        face = faceValue;
16        suit = suitValue;
17
18     } // end constructor
19
```

Fig. 12.17 Card class. (Part 1 of 2.)

```
20          public override string ToString()
21          {
22              return face + " of " + suit;
23
24          } // end method ToString
25
26      } // end class Card
```

Fig. 12.17 Card class. (Part 2 of 2.)

```
1   // Fig. 12.18: DeckOfCards.cs
2   // Simulating card drawing and shuffling.
3
4   using System;
5   using System.Drawing;
6   using System.Collections;
7   using System.ComponentModel;
8   using System.Windows.Forms;
9   using System.Data;
10
11  // provides the functionality for the form
12  public class DeckForm : System.Windows.Forms.Form
13  {
14      private System.Windows.Forms.Button dealButton;
15      private System.Windows.Forms.Button shuffleButton;
16
17      private System.Windows.Forms.Label displayLabel;
18      private System.Windows.Forms.Label statusLabel;
19
20      private System.ComponentModel.Container components = null;
21
22      private Card[] deck = new Card[ 52 ];
23      private int currentCard;
24
25      // main entry point for application
26      [STAThread]
27      static void Main()
28      {
29          Application.Run( new deckForm() );
30      }
31
32      // Visual Studio .NET generated code
33
34      // handles form at load time
35      private void DeckForm_Load(
36          object sender, System.EventArgs e )
37      {
38          string[] faces = { "Ace", "Deuce", "Three", "Four",
39                             "Five", "Six", "Seven", "Eight",
40                             "Nine", "Ten", "Jack", "Queen",
41                             "King" };
```

Fig. 12.18 Card dealing and shuffling simulation. (Part 1 of 4.)

```
42
43          string[] suits = { "Hearts", "Diamonds", "Clubs",
44                             "Spades" };
45
46          // no cards have been drawn
47          currentCard = -1;
48
49          // initialize deck
50          for ( int i = 0; i < deck.Length; i++ )
51             deck[ i ] = new Card( faces[ i % 13 ], suits[ i % 4 ] );
52
53       } // end method deckForm_Load
54
55       // handles dealButton Click
56       private void dealButton_Click(
57          object sender, System.EventArgs e )
58       {
59          Card dealt = DealCard();
60
61          // if dealt card is null, then no cards left
62          // player must shuffle cards
63          if ( dealt != null )
64          {
65             displayLabel.Text = dealt.ToString();
66             statusLabel.Text = "Card #: " + currentCard;
67          }
68          else
69          {
70             displayLabel.Text = "NO MORE CARDS TO DEAL";
71             statusLabel.Text = "Shuffle cards to continue";
72          }
73       }
74
75       // shuffle cards
76       private void Shuffle()
77       {
78          Random randomNumber = new Random();
79          Card temporaryValue;
80
81          currentCard = -1;
82
83          // swap each card with random card
84          for ( int i = 0; i < deck.Length; i++ )
85          {
86             int j = randomNumber.Next( 52 );
87
88             // swap cards
89             temporaryValue = deck[ i ];
90             deck[ i ] = deck[ j ];
91             deck[ j ] = temporaryValue;
92          }
93
```

Fig. 12.18 Card dealing and shuffling simulation. (Part 2 of 4.)

```
94            dealButton.Enabled = true;
95
96      } // end method Shuffle
97
98      private Card DealCard()
99      {
100         // if there is a card to deal then deal it
101         // otherwise signal that cards need to be shuffled by
102         // disabling dealButton and returning null
103         if ( currentCard + 1 < deck.Length )
104         {
105            currentCard++;
106            return deck[ currentCard ];
107         }
108         else
109         {
110            dealButton.Enabled = false;
111            return null;
112         }
113
114      } // end method DealCard
115
116      // handles shuffleButton Click
117      private void shuffleButton_Click(
118         object sender, System.EventArgs e )
119      {
120         displayLabel.Text = "SHUFFLING...";
121         Shuffle();
122         displayLabel.Text = "DECK IS SHUFFLED";
123         statusLabel.Text = "";
124      } // end method shuffleButton_Click
125
126   } // end class deckForm
```

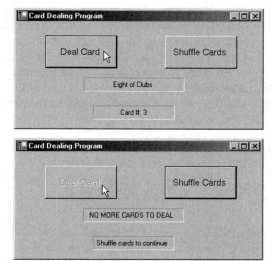

Fig. 12.18 Card dealing and shuffling simulation. (Part 3 of 4.)

Fig. 12.18 Card dealing and shuffling simulation. (Part 4 of 4.)

When users click the **Deal Card** button, event handler **dealButton_Click** (lines 56–73) invokes method **DealCard** (defined in lines 98–114) to get the next card in the **deck** array. If the **deck** is not empty, the method returns a **Card** object reference; otherwise, it returns **null**. If the reference is not **null**, lines 65–66 display the **Card** in **displayLabel** and display the card number in the **statusLabel**.

If **DealCard** returns a **null** reference, the **string "NO MORE CARDS TO DEAL"** is displayed in **displayLabel**, and the **string "Shuffle cards to continue"** is displayed in **statusLabel**.

When users click the **Shuffle Cards** button, its event-handling method **shuffleButton_Click** (lines 117–124) invokes method **Shuffle** (defined on lines 76–96) to shuffle the cards. The method loops through all 52 cards (array subscripts **0–51**). For each card, the method randomly picks a number between **0** and **51**. Then the current **Card** object and the randomly selected **Card** object are swapped in the array. To shuffle the cards, method **Shuffle** makes a total of only 52 swaps during a single pass of the entire array. When the shuffling is complete, **displayLabel** displays the **string "DECK IS SHUFFLED"** and **statusLabel** is cleared.

12.17 Regular Expressions and Class Regex

Regular expressions are specially formatted **string**s used to find patterns in text and can be useful during information validation, to ensure that data is in a particular format. For example, a ZIP code must consist of five digits, and a last name must start with a capital letter. One application of regular expressions is to facilitate the construction of a compiler. Often, a large and complex regular expression is used to validate the syntax of a program. If the program code does not match the regular expression, the compiler knows that there is a syntax error within the code.

The .NET Framework provides several classes to help developers recognize and manipulate regular expressions. Class **Regex** (**System.Text.RegularExpressions** namespace) represents an immutable regular expression. It contains static methods that allow use of the **Regex** class without explicitly instantiating objects of that class. Class **Match** represents the results of a regular expression matching operation.

Class **Regex** provides method **Match**, which returns an object of class **Match** that represents a single regular expression match. **Regex** also provides method **Matches**, which finds all matches of a regular expression in an arbitrary **string** and returns a **MatchCollection** object—i.e., a set of **Match**es.

Common Programming Error 12.4

*When using regular expressions, do not confuse class **Match** with the method **Match**, which belongs to class **Regex**.*

Common Programming Error 12.5

*Visual Studio does not add **System.Text.RegularExpressions** to the list of namespaces imported in the project properties, so a programmer must import it manually with the statement **using System.Text.RegularExpressions**.*

The table in Fig. 12.19 specifies some *character classes* that can be used with regular expressions. A character class is an escape sequence that represents a group of characters.

A *word character* is any alphanumeric character or underscore. A *whitespace* character is a space, a tab, a carriage return, a newline or a form feed. A *digit* is any numeric character. Regular expressions are not limited to these character classes, however. The expressions employ various operators and other forms of notation to search for complex patterns. We discuss several of these techniques in the context of the next example.

Figure 12.20 presents a simple example that employs regular expressions. This program takes birthdays and tries to match them to a regular expression. The expression matches only birthdays that do not occur in April and that belong to people whose names begin with **"J"**.

Character	Matches	Character	Matches
\d	any digit	\D	any non-digit
\w	any word character	\W	any non-word character
\s	any whitespace	\S	any non-whitespace

Fig. 12.19 Character classes.

```
1   // Fig. 12.20: RegexMatches.cs
2   // Demonstrating Class Regex.
3
4   using System;
5   using System.Windows.Forms;
6   using System.Text.RegularExpressions;
7
```

Fig. 12.20 Regular expressions checking birthdays. (Part 1 of 2.)

```
 8    // test out regular expressions
 9    class RegexMatches
10    {
11        // The main entry point for the application.
12        [STAThread]
13        static void Main( string[] args )
14        {
15            string output = "";
16
17            // create regular expression
18            Regex expression =
19                new Regex( @"J.*\d[0-35-9]-\d\d-\d\d" );
20
21            string string1 = "Jane's Birthday is 05-12-75\n" +
22                "Dave's Birthday is 11-04-68\n" +
23                "John's Birthday is 04-28-73\n" +
24                "Joe's Birthday is 12-17-77";
25
26            // match regular expression to string and
27            // print out all matches
28            foreach ( Match myMatch in expression.Matches( string1 ) )
29                output += myMatch.ToString() + "\n";
30
31            MessageBox.Show( output, "Using class Regex",
32                MessageBoxButtons.OK, MessageBoxIcon.Information );
33
34        } // end method Main
35
36    } // end class RegexMatches
```

Fig. 12.20 Regular expressions checking birthdays. (Part 2 of 2.)

Line 19 creates an instance of class **Regex** and defines the regular expression pattern for which **Regex** will search. The first character in the regular expression, **"J"**, is treated as a literal character. This means that any **string** matching this regular expression is required to start with **"J"**.

In a regular expression, the dot character **"."** matches any single character except a newline character. However, when the dot character is followed by an asterisk, as in the expression **".*"**, it matches any number of unspecified characters. In general, when the operator **"*"** is applied to any expression, the expression will match zero or more occurrences of the expression. By contrast, the application of the operator **"+"** to an expression causes the expression to match one or more occurrences of that expression. For example, both **"A*"** and **"A+"** will match **"A"**, but only **"A*"** will match an empty **string**.

As indicated in Fig. 12.19, **"\d"** matches any numeric digit. To specify sets of characters other than those that have a character class, characters can be listed in square brackets, **[]**. For example, the pattern **"[aeiou]"** can be used to match any vowel. Ranges of characters can be represented by placing a dash (-) between two characters. In the example, **"[0-35-9]"** matches only digits in the ranges specified by the pattern. In this case, the pattern matches any digit between **0** and **3** or between **5** and **9**; therefore, it matches any digit except **4**. If the first character in the brackets is the **"^"**, the expression accepts any character other than those indicated. However, it is important to note that **"[^4]"** is not the same as **"[0-35-9]"**; the former matches any nondigit, in addition to the digits other than **4**.

Although the **"-"** character indicates a range when it is enclosed in square brackets, instances of the **"-"** character outside grouping expressions are treated as literal characters. Thus, the regular expression in line 19 searches for a **string** that starts with the letter **"J"**, followed by any number of characters, followed by a two-digit number (of which the second digit cannot be **4**), followed by a dash, another two-digit number, a dash and another two-digit number.

Lines 28–29 use a **foreach** loop to iterate through each **Match** obtained from **expression.Matches**, which used **string1** as an argument. The output in Fig. 12.20 indicates the two matches that were found in **string1**. Notice that both matches conform to the pattern specified by the regular expression.

The asterisk (*****) and plus (**+**) in the previous example are called *quantifiers*. Figure 12.21 lists various quantifiers and their uses.

We have already discussed how the asterisk (*****) and plus (**+**) work. The question mark (**?**) matches zero or one occurrences of the expression that it quantifies. A set of braces containing one number (**{n}**) matches exactly **n** occurrences of the expression it quantifies. We demonstrate this quantifier in the next example. Including a comma after the number enclosed in braces matches at least **n** occurrences of the quantified expression. The set of braces containing two numbers (**{n,m}**), matches between **n** and **m** occurrences of the expression that it qualifies. All of the quantifiers are *greedy*. This means that they will match as many occurrences as they can as long as the match is successful. However, if any of these quantifiers is followed by a question mark (**?**), the quantifier becomes *lazy*. It then will match as few occurrences as possible as long as the match is successful.

The Windows application in Fig. 12.22 presents a more involved example that validates user input via regular expressions.

When a user clicks the **OK** button, the program checks to make sure that none of the fields is empty (lines 49–52). If one or more fields are empty, the program signals the user that all fields must be filled before the program can validate the input information (lines 55–56). Line 59 calls instance method **Focus** of class **TextBox**. Method **Focus** places the cursor within the **TextBox** that made the call. The program then exits the event handler (line 61). If there are no empty fields, the user input is validated. The **Last Name** is validated first (lines 65–74). If it passes the test (i.e., if the *Success* property of the **Match** instance is **true**), control moves on to validate the **First Name** (lines 77–86). This process continues until all **TextBox**es are validated or until a test fails (**Success** is **false**) and the program sends an appropriate error message. If all fields contain valid information, success is signaled, and the program quits.

In the previous example, we searched for substrings that matched a regular expression. In this example, we want to check whether an entire **string** conforms to a regular expression. For example, we want to accept **"Smith"** as a last name, but not **"9@Smith#"**. We achieve this effect by beginning each regular expression with a **"^"** character and ending it with a **"$"** character. The **"^"** and **"$"** characters match the positions at the beginning and end of a **string**, respectively. This forces the regular expression to evaluate the entire **string** and not return a match if a substring matches successfully.

In this program, we use the **static** version of **Regex** method *Match*, which takes an additional parameter specifying the regular expression that we are trying to match. The expression in line 66 uses the square bracket and range notation to match an uppercase first letter, followed by letters of any case—**a-z** matches any lowercase letter, and **A-Z** matches any uppercase letter. The ***** quantifier signifies that the second range of characters may occur zero or more times in the **string**. Thus, this expression matches any **string** consisting of one uppercase letter, followed by zero or more additional letters.

The notation **\s** matches a single whitespace character (lines 90, 102 and 114). The expression **\d{5}**, used in the **Zip** (zip code) field, matches any five digits (line 125). In general, an expression with a positive integer **x** in the curly braces will match any **x** digits. (Notice the importance of the **"^"** and **"$"** characters to prevent zip codes with extra digits from being validated.)

Quantifier	Matches
*	Matches zero or more occurrences of the pattern.
+	Matches one or more occurrences of the pattern.
?	Matches zero or one occurrences of the pattern.
{n}	Matches exactly **n** occurrences.
{n,}	Matches at least **n** occurrences.
{n,m}	Matches between **n** and **m** (inclusive) occurrences.

Fig. 12.21 Quantifiers used in regular expressions.

```
1    // Fig. 12.22: Validate.cs
2    // Validate user information using regular expressions.
3
4    using System;
5    using System.Drawing;
6    using System.Collections;
7    using System.ComponentModel;
8    using System.Windows.Forms;
9    using System.Data;
10   using System.Text.RegularExpressions;
11
12   // use regular expressions to validate strings
13   public class ValidateForm : System.Windows.Forms.Form
14   {
15       private System.Windows.Forms.Label phoneLabel;
16       private System.Windows.Forms.Label zipLabel;
17       private System.Windows.Forms.Label stateLabel;
18       private System.Windows.Forms.Label cityLabel;
19       private System.Windows.Forms.Label addressLabel;
```

Fig. 12.22 Validating user information using regular expressions. (Part 1 of 5.)

```
20      private System.Windows.Forms.Label firstLabel;
21      private System.Windows.Forms.Label lastLabel;
22
23      private System.Windows.Forms.Button okButton;
24
25      private System.Windows.Forms.TextBox phoneTextBox;
26      private System.Windows.Forms.TextBox zipTextBox;
27      private System.Windows.Forms.TextBox stateTextBox;
28      private System.Windows.Forms.TextBox cityTextBox;
29      private System.Windows.Forms.TextBox addressTextBox;
30      private System.Windows.Forms.TextBox firstTextBox;
31      private System.Windows.Forms.TextBox lastTextBox;
32
33      private System.ComponentModel.Container components = null;
34
35      // The main entry point for the application.
36      [STAThread]
37      static void Main()
38      {
39          Application.Run( new validateForm() );
40      }
41
42      // Visual Studio .NET generated code
43
44      // handles okButton Click event
45      private void okButton_Click(
46          object sender, System.EventArgs e )
47      {
48          // ensures no textboxes are empty
49          if ( lastTextBox.Text == "" || firstTextBox.Text == "" ||
50              addressTextBox.Text == "" || cityTextBox.Text == "" ||
51              stateTextBox.Text == "" || zipTextBox.Text == "" ||
52              phoneTextBox.Text == "" )
53          {
54              // display popup box
55              MessageBox.Show( "Please fill in all fields", "Error",
56                  MessageBoxButtons.OK, MessageBoxIcon.Error );
57
58              // set focus to lastTextBox
59              lastTextBox.Focus();
60
61              return;
62          }
63
64          // if last name format invalid show message
65          if ( !Regex.Match( lastTextBox.Text,
66              @"^[A-Z][a-zA-Z]*$" ).Success )
67          {
68              // last name was incorrect
69              MessageBox.Show( "Invalid Last Name", "Message",
70                  MessageBoxButtons.OK, MessageBoxIcon.Error );
71              lastTextBox.Focus();
72
```

Fig. 12.22 Validating user information using regular expressions. (Part 2 of 5.)

```
73          return;
74       }
75
76       // if first name format invalid show message
77       if ( !Regex.Match( firstTextBox.Text,
78          @"^[A-Z][a-zA-Z]*$" ).Success )
79       {
80          // first name was incorrect
81          MessageBox.Show( "Invalid First Name", "Message",
82             MessageBoxButtons.OK, MessageBoxIcon.Error );
83          firstTextBox.Focus();
84
85          return;
86       }
87
88       // if address format invalid show message
89       if ( !Regex.Match( addressTextBox.Text,
90          @"^[0-9]+\s+([a-zA-Z]+|[a-zA-Z]+\s[a-zA-Z]+)$" ).Success )
91       {
92          // address was incorrect
93          MessageBox.Show( "Invalid Address", "Message",
94             MessageBoxButtons.OK, MessageBoxIcon.Error );
95          addressTextBox.Focus();
96
97          return;
98       }
99
100      // if city format invalid show message
101      if ( !Regex.Match( cityTextBox.Text,
102         @"^([a-zA-Z]+|[a-zA-Z]+\s[a-zA-Z]+)$" ).Success )
103      {
104         // city was incorrect
105         MessageBox.Show( "Invalid City", "Message",
106            MessageBoxButtons.OK, MessageBoxIcon.Error );
107         cityTextBox.Focus();
108
109         return;
110      }
111
112      // if state format invalid show message
113      if ( !Regex.Match( stateTextBox.Text,
114         @"^([a-zA-Z]+|[a-zA-Z]+\s[a-zA-Z]+)$" ).Success )
115      {
116         // state was incorrect
117         MessageBox.Show( "Invalid State", "Message",
118            MessageBoxButtons.OK, MessageBoxIcon.Error );
119         stateTextBox.Focus();
120
121         return;
122      }
123
```

Fig. 12.22 Validating user information using regular expressions. (Part 3 of 5.)

```
124           // if zip code format invalid show message
125           if ( !Regex.Match( zipTextBox.Text, @"^\d{5}$" ).Success )
126           {
127              // zip was incorrect
128              MessageBox.Show( "Invalid Zip Code", "Message",
129                 MessageBoxButtons.OK, MessageBoxIcon.Error );
130              zipTextBox.Focus();
131
132              return;
133           }
134
135           // if phone number format invalid show message
136           if ( !Regex.Match( phoneTextBox.Text,
137              @"^[1-9]\d{2}-[1-9]\d{2}-\d{4}$" ).Success )
138           {
139              // phone number was incorrect
140              MessageBox.Show( "Invalid Phone Number", "Message",
141                 MessageBoxButtons.OK, MessageBoxIcon.Error );
142              phoneTextBox.Focus();
143
144              return;
145           }
146
147           // information is valid, signal user and exit application
148           this.Hide();
149           MessageBox.Show( "Thank You!", "Information Correct",
150              MessageBoxButtons.OK, MessageBoxIcon.Information );
151
152           Application.Exit();
153
154        } // end method okButton_Click
155
156   } // end class ValidateForm
```

Fig. 12.22 Validating user information using regular expressions. (Part 4 of 5.)

Fig. 12.22 Validating user information using regular expressions. (Part 5 of 5.)

The character "|" matches the expression to its left or to its right. For example, **Hi (John|Jane)** matches both **Hi John** and **Hi Jane**. Note the use of parentheses to group parts of the regular expression. Quantifiers may be applied to patterns enclosed in parentheses to create more complex regular expressions.

The **Last Name** and **First Name** fields both accept **string**s of any length, that begin with an uppercase letter. The **Address** field matches a number of at least one digit, followed by a space and then either one or more letters or else one or more letters followed by a space and another series of one or more letters (line 90). Therefore, **"10 Broadway"** and **"10 Main Street"** are both valid addresses. The **City** (line 102) and **State** (line 114) fields match any word of at least one character or, alternatively, any two words of at least one character if the words are separated by a single space. This means both **Waltham** and **West Newton** would match. As previously stated, the **Zip** code must be a five-digit number (line 125). The **Phone** number must be of the form **xxx-yyy-yyyy**, where the **x**s represent the area code and **y**s the number (line 137). The first **x** and the first **y** cannot be zero.

Sometimes it is useful to replace parts of a **string** with another, or split a **string** according to a regular expression. For this purpose, the **Regex** class provides **static** and instance versions of methods *Replace* and *Split*, which are demonstrated in Fig. 12.23.

```csharp
1   // Fig. 12.23: RegexSubstitution.cs
2   // Using Regex method Replace.
3
4   using System;
5   using System.Text.RegularExpressions;
6   using System.Windows.Forms;
7
8   // Summary description for RegexSubstitution.
9   public class RegexSubstitution1
10  {
11
12      // The main entry point for the application.
13      static void Main( string[] args )
14      {
15          string testString1 =
16              "This sentence ends in 5 stars *****";
17
18          string testString2 = "1, 2, 3, 4, 5, 6, 7, 8";
19          Regex testRegex1 = new Regex( "stars" );
20          Regex testRegex2 = new Regex( @"\d" );
21          string[] results;
22          string output = "Original String 1\t\t\t" + testString1;
23
24          testString1 = Regex.Replace( testString1, @"\*", "^" );
25
26          output += "\n^ substituted for *\t\t\t" + testString1;
27
28          testString1 = testRegex1.Replace( testString1, "carets" );
29
30          output += "\n\"carets\" substituted for \"stars\"\t\t" +
31              testString1;
32
33          output += "\nEvery word replaced by \"word\"\t" +
34              Regex.Replace( testString1, @"\w+", "word" );
35
36          output += "\n\nOriginal String 2\t\t\t" + testString2;
37
38          output += "\nFirst 3 digits replaced by \"digit\"\t\t" +
39              testRegex2.Replace( testString2, "digit", 3 );
40
41          output += "\nString split at commas\t\t[";
42
43          results = Regex.Split( testString2, @",\s*" );
44
```

Fig. 12.23 Regex methods **Replace** and **Split**. (Part 1 of 2.)

```
45          foreach ( string resultString in results )
46          {
47              output += "\"" + resultString + "\", ";
48          }
49
50          output = output.Substring( 0, output.Length - 2 ) + "]";
51
52          MessageBox.Show( output,
53              "Substitution using regular expressions" );
54
55      } // end method Main
56
57  } // end class RegexSubstitution
```

Fig. 12.23 Regex methods **Replace** and **Split**. (Part 2 of 2.)

Method **Replace** replaces text in a **string** with new text wherever the original **string** matches a regular expression. We present two versions of this method in Fig. 12.23. The first version (line 24) is **static** and takes three parameters—the **string** to modify, the **string** containing the regular expression to match and the replacement **string**. Here, **Replace** replaces every instance of **"*"** in **testString1** with **"^"**. Notice that the regular expression (**@"*"**) precedes character ***** with a backslash, ****. Normally, ***** is a quantifier indicating that a regular expression should match any number of occurrences of a preceding pattern. However, in line 24, we want to find all occurrences of the literal character *****; to do this, we must escape character ***** with character ****. By escaping a special regular expression character with a ****, we inform the regular-expression matching engine to find the actual character, as opposed to what it represents in a regular expression. The second version of method **Replace** (line 28) is an instance method that uses the regular expression passed to the constructor for **testRegex1** (line 19) to perform the replacement operation. In this case, every match for the regular expression **"stars"** in **testString1** is replaced with **"carets"**.

Line 20 instantiates **testRegex2** with argument **@"\d"**. The call to instance method **Replace** in line 39 takes three arguments—a **string** to modify, a **string** containing the replacement text and an **int** specifying the number of replacements to make. In other words, this version of **Replace** replaces the first three instances of a digit (**"\d"**) in **testString2** with the text **"digit"** (line 39).

Method **Split** divides a **string** into several substrings. The original **string** is broken in any location that matches a specified regular expression. Method **Split** returns an array containing the substrings between matches for the regular expression. In line 43, we use the **static** version of method **Split** to separate a **string** of comma-separated integers. The first argument is the **string** to split; the second argument is the regular expression. In this case, we use the regular expression **@",\s*"** to separate the substrings wherever a comma occurs. By matching any whitespace characters, we eliminate extra spaces from the resulting substrings.

12.18 Summary

Characters are the fundamental building blocks of C# program code. Every program is composed of a sequence of characters that is interpreted by the compiler as a series of instructions used to accomplish a task.

A **string** is a series of characters that is treated as a single unit. A **string** may include letters, digits and various special characters, such as **+**, **-**, *****, **/** and **$**. All characters correspond to numeric codes. When the computer compares two **string**s, it actually compares the numeric codes of the characters in the **string**s. Once a **string** is created, its contents can never change. Class **StringBuilder** provides a modifiable **string** like entity that can grow and shrink in size.

A hash table stores information, using a special calculation on the object to be stored that produces a hash code. The hash code is used to choose the location in the table at which to store the object. Class **Object** defines method **GetHashCode** to perform the hash-code calculation.

The braces in a format **string** specify how to format a particular piece of information. Formats have the form **{X[,Y][:FormatString]}**, where **X** is the number of the argument to be formatted, counting from zero. **Y** is an optional argument that can be positive or negative. **Y** indicates how many characters should be in the formatted result; if the resulting **string** is less than this number, it will be padded with spaces to make up for the difference. If **Y** is a positive integer, the **string** will be right aligned; if **Y** is a negative integer, it will be left aligned. The optional **FormatString** indicates what kind of formatting should be applied to the argument—i.e., currency, decimal, or scientific.

Structures are similar to classes; in many ways the primary difference between them is that structures encapsulate value types, whereas classes encapsulate reference types. Many of the primitive data types that we have been using are actually aliases for different structures. These structures are derived from class **ValueType**, which, in turn, is derived from class **Object**. **Char** is a structure that represents characters.

Regular expressions match patterns in text. The .NET Framework provides class **Regex** to aid developers in recognizing and manipulating regular expressions. **Regex** provides method **Match**, which returns an object of class **Match**. This object represents a single match in a regular expression. **Regex** also provides method **Matches**, which finds all matches of a regular expression in an arbitrary **string** and returns a **MatchCollection**—a set of **Match**es.

Graphics and Multimedia

Objectives

- To understand graphics contexts and graphics objects.
- To manipulate colors and fonts.
- To understand and be able to use GDI+ **Graphics** methods to draw lines, rectangles, **string**s and images.
- To use class **Image** to manipulate and display images.
- To draw complex shapes from simple shapes with class **GraphicsPath**.
- To use Windows Media Player and Microsoft Agent in C# applications.

One picture is worth ten thousand words.
Chinese proverb

Treat nature in terms of the cylinder, the sphere, the cone, all in perspective.
Paul Cezanne

Nothing ever becomes real till it is experienced—even a proverb is no proverb to you till your life has illustrated it.
John Keats

A picture shows me at a glance what it takes dozens of pages of a book to expound.
Ivan Sergeyevich

Outline

13.1   Introduction
13.2   Graphics Contexts and Graphics Objects
13.3   Color Control
13.4   Font Control
13.5   Drawing Lines, Rectangles and Ovals
13.6   Drawing Arcs
13.7   Drawing Polygons and Polylines
13.8   Advanced Graphics Capabilities
13.9   Introduction to Multimedia
13.10   Loading, Displaying and Scaling Images
13.11   Animating a Series of Images
13.12   Windows Media Player
13.13   Microsoft Agent
13.14   Summary

13.1 Introduction

In this chapter, we overview C#'s tools for drawing two-dimensional shapes and for controlling colors and fonts. C# supports graphics that enable programmers to enhance their Windows applications visually. The FCL contains many sophisticated drawing capabilities as part of namespace **System.Drawing** and the other namespaces that make up the .NET resource *GDI+*. GDI+, an extension of the Graphical Device Interface, is an application programming interface (API) that provides classes for creating two-dimensional vector graphics (a way of describing graphics so that they may be easily manipulated with high-performance techniques), manipulating fonts and inserting images. GDI+ expands GDI by simplifying the programming model and introducing several new features, such as graphics paths, extended image file format support and "alpha blending." Using the GDI+ API, programmers can create images without worrying about the platform-specific details of their graphics hardware.

We begin with an introduction to the .NET framework's drawing capabilities. We then present more powerful drawing capabilities, such as changing the styles of lines used to draw shapes and controlling the colors and patterns of filled shapes.

Figure 13.1 depicts a portion of the **System.Drawing** class hierarchy, which includes several of the basic graphics classes and structures covered in this chapter. The most commonly used components of GDI+ reside in the **System.Drawing** and **System.Drawing.Drawing2D** namespaces.

Class *Graphics* contains methods used for drawing **string**s, lines, rectangles and other shapes on a **Control**. The drawing methods of class **Graphics** usually require a **Pen** or **Brush** object to render a specified shape. The **Pen** draws shape outlines; the **Brush** draws solid objects.

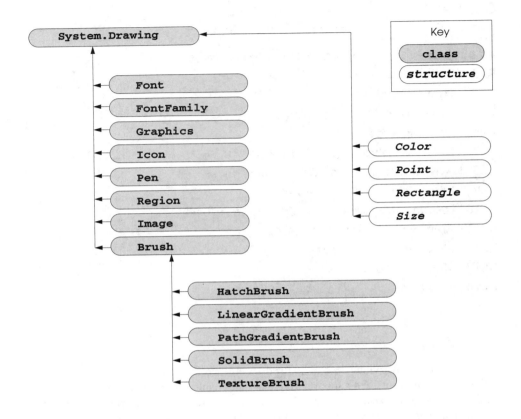

Fig. 13.1   **System.Drawing** namespace's classes and structures.

Structure **Color** contains numerous **static** properties, which set the colors of various graphical components, plus methods that allow users to create new colors. Class ***Font*** contains properties that define unique fonts. Class ***FontFamily*** contains methods for obtaining font information.

To begin drawing in C#, we first must understand GDI+'s *coordinate system* (Fig. 13.2), a scheme for identifying every point on the screen. By default, the upper-left corner of a GUI component (such as a **Panel** or a **Form**) has the coordinates (0, 0). A coordinate pair has both an *x-coordinate* (the *horizontal coordinate*) and a *y-coordinate* (the *vertical coordinate*). The *x*-coordinate is the horizontal distance (to the right) from the upper-left corner. The *y*-coordinate is the vertical distance (downward) from the upper-left corner. The *x-axis* defines every horizontal coordinate, and the *y-axis* defines every vertical coordinate. Programmers position text and shapes on the screen by specifying their (*x,y*) coordinates. Coordinate units are measured in *pixels* ("picture elements"), which are the smallest units of resolution on a display monitor.

The **System.Drawing** namespace provides structures **Rectangle** and **Point**. The ***Rectangle*** *structure* defines rectangular shapes and dimensions. The ***Point*** *structure* represents the *x-y* coordinates of a point on a two-dimensional plane.

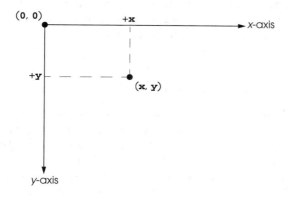

Fig. 13.2   GDI+ coordinate system. Units are measured in pixels.

Portability Tip 13.1

Different display monitors have different resolutions, so the density of pixels on such monitors will vary. This might cause the sizes of graphics to appear different on different monitors.

In the remainder of this chapter, we explore techniques for manipulating images and creating smooth animations. We also discuss class ***Image***, which can store and manipulate images from various file formats. Later, we explain how to combine the graphical rendering capabilities covered in the early sections of the chapter with those for image manipulation.

13.2 Graphics Contexts and Graphics Objects

A C# *graphics context* represents a drawing surface that enables drawing on the screen. A **Graphics** object manages a graphics context by controlling how information is drawn. **Graphics** objects contain methods for drawing, font manipulation, color manipulation and other graphics-related actions. Every Windows application that derives from class **System.Windows.Forms.Form** inherits a **virtual** *OnPaint* event handler where most graphics operations are performed. The arguments to the **OnPaint** method include a **PaintEventArgs** object from which we can obtain a **Graphics** object for the control. We must obtain the **Graphics** object on each call to the method, because the properties of the graphics context that the graphics object represents could change. The **OnPaint** method triggers the **Control**'s *Paint* event.

When displaying graphical information on a **Form**'s client area, programmers can override the **OnPaint** method to retrieve a **Graphics** object from argument **PaintEventArgs** or to create a new **Graphics** object associated with the appropriate surface. We demonstrate these techniques of drawing in C# later in the chapter.

To override the inherited **OnPaint** method, use the following method definition:

```
protected override void OnPaint( PaintEventArgs e )
```

Next, extract the incoming **Graphics** object from the **PaintEventArgs** argument:

```
Graphics graphicsObject = e.Graphics;
```

Variable **graphicsObject** now is available to draw shapes and **string**s on the form.

Calling the **OnPaint** method raises the **Paint** event. Instead of overriding the **OnPaint** method, programmers can add an event handler for the **Paint** event. Visual Studio .NET generates the **Paint** event handler in this form:

```
protected void MyEventHandler_Paint(
    object sender, PaintEventArgs e )
```

Programmers seldom call the **OnPaint** method directly, because the drawing of graphics is an *event-driven process*. An event—such as the covering, uncovering or resizing of a window—calls the **OnPaint** method of that form. Similarly, when any control (such as a **TextBox** or **Label**) is displayed, the program calls that control's **Paint** method.

If programmers need to cause method **OnPaint** to run explicitly, they should not call method **OnPaint**. Rather, they can call the *Invalidate* method (inherited from **Control**). This method refreshes a control's client area and implicitly repaints all graphical components. C# contains several overloaded **Invalidate** methods that allow programmers to update portions of the client area.

Performance Tip 13.1

*Calling the **Invalidate** method to refresh the **Control** often is inefficient. Instead, call **Invalidate** with a **Rectangle** parameter to refresh only the area designated by the rectangle. This improves program performance.*

Controls, such as **Label**s and **Button**s, do not have their own graphics contexts, but one can be created. To draw on a control, first create its graphics object by invoking the **CreateGraphics** method:

```
Graphics graphicsObject = controlName.CreateGraphics();
```

where *graphicsObject* represents an instance of class **Graphics** and *controlName* is any control. Now, a programmer can use the methods provided in class **Graphics** to draw on the control.

13.3 Color Control

Colors can enhance a program's appearance and help convey meaning. For example, a red traffic light indicates stop, yellow indicates caution and green indicates go.

Structure **Color** defines methods and constants used to manipulate colors. Because it is a lightweight object that performs only a handful of operations and stores **static** fields, **Color** is implemented as a structure, rather than as a class.

Every color can be created from a combination of alpha, red, green and blue components. Together, these components are called *ARGB values*. All four ARGB components are **byte**s that represent integer values in the range from 0 to 255. The alpha value determines the opacity of the color. For example, the alpha value 0 results in a transparent color, the value 255 in an opaque color. Alpha values between 0 and 255 result in a weighted blending effect of the color's RGB value with that of any background color, causing a semi-transparent effect. The first number in the RGB value defines the amount of red in the color, the second defines the amount of green and the third defines the amount of blue. The larger the value, the greater the amount of that particular color. C# enables programmers to choose from almost 17 million colors. If a particular computer cannot display all these colors, it will display the color closest to the one specified. Figure 13.3 summarizes some predefined **Color** constants, and Fig. 13.4 describes several **Color** methods and properties.

The table in Fig. 13.4 describes two *FromArgb* method calls. One takes three **int** arguments, and one takes four **int** arguments (all argument values must be between 0 and 255). Both take **int** arguments specifying the amount of red, green and blue. The overloaded version takes four arguments and allows the user to specify alpha; the three-argument version defaults the alpha to 255. Both methods return a **Color** object representing the specified values. **Color** properties *A*, *R*, *G* and *B* return **byte**s that represent **int** values from 0 to 255, corresponding to the amounts of alpha, red, green and blue, respectively.

Programmers draw shapes and **string**s with **Brush**es and **Pen**s. A **Pen**, which functions similarly to an ordinary pen, is used to draw lines. Most drawing methods require a **Pen** object. The overloaded **Pen** constructors allow programmers to specify the colors and widths of the lines that they wish to draw. The **System.Drawing** namespace also provides a **Pens** collection containing predefined **Pen**s.

Constants in structure Color (all are public static)	RGB value	Constants in structure Color (all are public static)	RGB value
Orange	255, 200, 0	White	255, 255, 255
Pink	255, 175, 175	Gray	128, 128, 128
Cyan	0, 255, 255	DarkGray	64, 64, 64
Magenta	255, 0, 255	Red	255, 0, 0
Yellow	255, 255, 0	Green	0, 255, 0
Black	0, 0, 0	Blue	0, 0, 255

Fig. 13.3 **Color** structure **static** constants and their RGB values.

Structure Color methods and properties	Description
Common Methods	
static FromArgb	Creates a color based on red, green and blue values expressed as **int**s from 0 to 255. Overloaded version allows specification of alpha, red, green and blue values.
static FromName	Creates a color from a name, passed as a **string**.
Common Properties	
A	**byte** between 0 and 255, representing the alpha component.
R	**byte** between 0 and 255, representing the red component.

Fig. 13.4 **Color** structure members. (Part 1 of 2.)

Structure Color methods and properties	Description
G	**byte** between 0 and 255, representing the green component.
B	**byte** between 0 and 255, representing the blue component.

Fig. 13.4 **Color** structure members. (Part 2 of 2.)

All classes derived from abstract class **Brush** define objects that color the interiors of graphical shapes (for example, the **SolidBrush** constructor takes a **Color** object—the color to draw). In most **Fill** methods, **Brush**es fill a space with a color, pattern or image. Figure 13.5 summarizes various **Brush**es and their functions.

The application in Fig. 13.6 demonstrates several of the methods and properties described in Fig. 13.4. It displays two overlapping rectangles, allowing the user to experiment with color values and color names.

Class	Description
HatchBrush	Uses a rectangular brush to fill a region with a pattern. The pattern is defined by a member of the **HatchStyle** enumeration, a foreground color (with which the pattern is drawn) and a background color.
LinearGradient-Brush	Fills a region with a gradual blend of one color into another. Linear gradients are defined along a line. They can be specified by the two colors, the angle of the gradient and either the width of a rectangle or two points.
SolidBrush	Fills a region with one color. Defined by a **Color** object.
TextureBrush	Fills a region by repeating a specified **Image** across the surface.

Fig. 13.5 Classes that derive from class **Brush**.

```
1   // Fig. 13.6: ShowColors.cs
2   // Using different colors in C#.
3
4   using System;
5   using System.Drawing;
6   using System.Collections;
7   using System.ComponentModel;
8   using System.Windows.Forms;
9   using System.Data;
10
```

Fig. 13.6 Color value and alpha demonstration. (Part 1 of 3.)

```
11    // allows users to change colors using the name of
12    // the color or argb values
13    class ShowColors : System.Windows.Forms.Form
14    {
15       private System.ComponentModel.Container components = null;
16
17       // color for back rectangle
18       private Color behindColor = Color.Wheat;
19       private System.Windows.Forms.GroupBox nameGroup;
20       private System.Windows.Forms.GroupBox colorValueGroup;
21       private System.Windows.Forms.TextBox colorNameTextBox;
22       private System.Windows.Forms.TextBox alphaTextBox;
23       private System.Windows.Forms.TextBox redTextBox;
24       private System.Windows.Forms.TextBox greenTextBox;
25       private System.Windows.Forms.TextBox blueTextBox;
26       private System.Windows.Forms.Button colorValueButton;
27       private System.Windows.Forms.Button colorNameButton;
28
29       // color for front rectangle
30       private Color frontColor =
31          Color.FromArgb( 100, 0 , 0, 255 );
32
33       [STAThread]
34       static void Main()
35       {
36          Application.Run( new ShowColors() );
37       }
38
39       // Visual Studio .NET generated code
40
41       // override Form OnPaint method
42       protected override void OnPaint( PaintEventArgs e )
43       {
44          Graphics graphicsObject = e.Graphics; // get graphics
45
46          // create text brush
47          SolidBrush textBrush = new SolidBrush( Color.Black );
48
49          // create solid brush
50          SolidBrush brush = new SolidBrush( Color.White );
51
52          // draw white background
53          graphicsObject.FillRectangle( brush, 4, 4, 275, 180 );
54
55          // display name of behindColor
56          graphicsObject.DrawString( behindColor.Name, this.Font,
57             textBrush, 40, 5 );
58
59          // set brush color and display back rectangle
60          brush.Color = behindColor;
61
62          graphicsObject.FillRectangle( brush, 45, 20, 150, 120 );
63
```

Fig. 13.6   Color value and alpha demonstration. (Part 2 of 3.)

```
64          // display Argb values of front color
65          graphicsObject.DrawString( "Alpha: " + frontColor.A +
66             " Red: " + frontColor.R + " Green: " + frontColor.G
67             + " Blue: " + frontColor.B, this.Font, textBrush,
68             55, 165 );
69
70          // set brush color and display front rectangle
71          brush.Color = frontColor;
72
73          graphicsObject.FillRectangle( brush, 65, 35, 170, 130 );
74
75       } // end method OnPaint
76
77       // handle colorValueButton click event
78       private void colorValueButton_Click(
79          object sender, System.EventArgs e )
80       {
81          // obtain new front color from text boxes
82          frontColor = Color.FromArgb( Convert.ToInt32(
83             alphaTextBox.Text ),
84             Convert.ToInt32( redTextBox.Text ),
85             Convert.ToInt32( greenTextBox.Text ),
86             Convert.ToInt32( blueTextBox.Text ) );
87
88          Invalidate(); // refresh Form
89       }
90
91       // handle colorNameButton click event
92       private void colorNameButton_Click(
93          object sender, System.EventArgs e )
94       {
95          // set behindColor to color specified in text box
96          behindColor = Color.FromName( colorNameTextBox.Text );
97
98          Invalidate(); // refresh Form
99       }
100
101   } // end class ShowColors
```

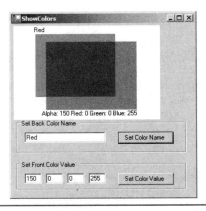

Fig. 13.6   Color value and alpha demonstration. (Part 3 of 3.)

When the application begins its execution, it calls class **ShowColors**'s **OnPaint** method to paint the window. Line 44 gets a reference to **PaintEventArgs e**'s **Graphics** object and assigns it to **Graphics** object **graphicsObject**. Lines 47–50 create a black and a white **SolidBrush** for drawing on the form. Class **SolidBrush** derives from abstract base class **Brush**; programmers can draw solid shapes with the **SolidBrush**.

Graphics method *FillRectangle* draws a solid white rectangle with the **Brush** supplied as a parameter (line 53). It takes as parameters a brush, the *x*- and *y*-coordinates of a point and the width and height of the rectangle to draw. The point represents the upper-left corner of the rectangle. Lines 56–57 display the **string Name** property of the **Brush**'s **Color** property with the **Graphics DrawString** method. The programmer has access to several overloaded **DrawString** methods; the version demonstrated in lines 56–57 takes a **string** to display, the display **Font**, a **Brush** and the x- and y-coordinates of the location for the **string**'s first character.

Lines 60–62 assign the **Color behindColor** value to the **Brush**'s **Color** property and display a rectangle. Lines 65–68 extract and display the ARGB values of **Color frontColor** and then display a filled rectangle that overlaps the first.

Button event handler **colorValueButton_Click** (lines 78–89) uses **Color** method **FromArgb** to construct a new **Color** object from the ARGB values that a user specifies via text boxes. It then assigns the newly created **Color** to **frontColor**. **Button** event handler **colorNameButton_Click** (lines 92–99) uses the **Color** method **FromName** to create a new **Color** object from the **colorName** that a user enters in a text box. This **Color** is assigned to **behindColor**.

If the user assigns an alpha value between 0 and 255 for the **frontColor**, the effects of alpha blending are apparent. In the screenshot output, the red back rectangle blends with the blue front rectangle to create purple where the two overlap.

 Software Engineering Observation 13.1

*No methods in class **Color** enable programmers to change the characteristics of the current color. To use a different color, create a new **Color** object.*

The predefined GUI component *ColorDialog* is a dialog box that allows users to select from a palette of available colors. It also offers the option of creating custom colors. The program in Fig. 13.7 demonstrates the use of such a dialog. When a user selects a color and presses **OK**, the application retrieves the user's selection via the **ColorDialog**'s **Color** property.

The GUI for this application contains two **Button**s. The top one, **background-ColorButton**, allows the user to change the form and button background colors. The bottom one, **textColorButton**, allows the user to change the button text colors.

```
1   // Fig. 13.7: ShowColorsComplex.cs
2   // Change the background and text colors of a form.
3
4   using System;
5   using System.Drawing;
6   using System.Collections;
```

Fig. 13.7 **ColorDialog** used to change background and text color. (Part 1 of 3.)

```
 7  using System.ComponentModel;
 8  using System.Windows.Forms;
 9  using System.Data;
10
11  // allows users to change colors using a ColorDialog
12  public class ShowColorsComplex : System.Windows.Forms.Form
13  {
14     private System.Windows.Forms.Button backgroundColorButton;
15     private System.Windows.Forms.Button textColorButton;
16
17     private System.ComponentModel.Container components = null;
18
19     [STAThread]
20     static void Main()
21     {
22        Application.Run( new ShowColorsComplex() );
23     }
24
25     // Visual Studio .NET generated code
26
27     // change text color
28     private void textColorButton_Click(
29        object sender, System.EventArgs e )
30     {
31        // create ColorDialog object
32        ColorDialog colorChooser = new ColorDialog();
33        DialogResult result;
34
35        // get chosen color
36        result = colorChooser.ShowDialog();
37
38        if ( result == DialogResult.Cancel )
39           return;
40
41        // assign forecolor to result of dialog
42        backgroundColorButton.ForeColor = colorChooser.Color;
43        textColorButton.ForeColor = colorChooser.Color;
44
45     } // end method textColorButton_Click
46
47     // change background color
48     private void backgroundColorButton_Click(
49        object sender, System.EventArgs e )
50     {
51        // create ColorDialog object
52        ColorDialog colorChooser = new ColorDialog();
53        DialogResult result;
54
55        // show ColorDialog and get result
56        colorChooser.FullOpen = true;
57        result = colorChooser.ShowDialog();
58
```

Fig. 13.7 ColorDialog used to change background and text color. (Part 2 of 3.)

```
59          if ( result == DialogResult.Cancel )
60             return;
61
62          // set background color
63          this.BackColor = colorChooser.Color;
64
65      } // end method backgroundColorButton_Click
66
67  } // end class ShowColorsComplex
```

Fig. 13.7 **ColorDialog** used to change background and text color. (Part 3 of 3.)

Lines 28–45 define the event handler that is called when the user clicks **Button tex-tColorButton**. The event handler creates a new **ColorDialog** named **color-Chooser** and invokes its **ShowDialog** method, which displays the window. Property **Color** of **colorChooser** stores users' selections. Lines 42–43 set the text color of both buttons to the selected color.

Lines 48–65 define the event handler for button **backgroundColorButton**. The method modifies the background color of the form by setting **BackColor** equal to the dialog's **Color** property. The method creates a new **ColorDialog** and sets the dialog's **FullOpen** property to **true**. The dialog now displays all available colors, as shown in the screen capture in Fig. 13.7. The regular color display does not show the right-hand portion of the screen.

Users are not restricted to the **ColorDialog**'s 48 colors. To create a custom color, users can click anywhere in the **ColorDialog**'s large rectangle—this displays the various color shades. Adjust the slider, hue and other features to refine the color. When finished, click the **Add to Custom Colors** button, which adds the custom color to a square in the custom colors section of the dialog. Clicking **OK** sets the **Color** property of the

ColorDialog to that color. Selecting a color and pressing the dialog's **OK** button causes the application's background color to change.

13.4 Font Control

This section introduces methods and constants that are related to font control. Once a **Font** has been created, its properties cannot be modified. If programmers require a different **Font**, they must create a new **Font** object—there are many overloaded versions of the **Font** constructor for creating custom **Font**s. Some properties of class **Font** are summarized in Fig. 13.8.

Note that the **Size** property returns the font size as measured in design units, whereas **SizeInPoints** returns the font size as measured in points (the more common measurement). When we say that the **Size** property measures the size of the font in *design units*, we mean that the font size can be specified in a variety of ways, such as inches or millimeters. Some versions of the **Font** constructor accept a **GraphicsUnit** argument—an enumeration that allows users to specify the unit of measurement employed to describe the font size. Members of the **GraphicsUnit** enumeration include **Point** (1/72 inch), **Display** (1/75 inch), **Document** (1/300 inch), **Millimeter**, **Inch** and **Pixel**. If this argument is provided, the **Size** property contains the size of the font as measured in the specified design unit, and the **SizeInPoints** property converts the size of the font into points. For example, if we create a **Font** having size **1** and specify that **GraphicsUnit.Inch** be used to measure the font, the **Size** property will be **1**, and the **SizeInPoints** property will be **72**. If we employ a constructor that does not accept a member of the **GraphicsUnit**, the default measurement for the font size is **GraphicsUnit.Point** (thus, the **Size** and **SizeInPoints** properties will be equal).

Property	Description
Bold	Tests a font for a bold font style. Returns **true** if the font is bold.
FontFamily	Represents the **FontFamily** of the **Font** (a grouping structure to organize fonts and define their similar properties).
Height	Represents the height of the font.
Italic	Tests a font for an italic font style. Returns **true** if the font is italic.
Name	Represents the font's name as a **string**.
Size	Returns a **float** value indicating the current font size measured in design units (design units are any specified units of measurement for the font).
SizeInPoints	Returns a **float** value indicating the current font size measured in points.
Strikeout	Tests a font for a strikeout font style. Returns **true** if the font is in strikeout format.
Underline	Tests a font for a underline font style. Returns **true** if the font is underlined.

Fig. 13.8   Font class read-only properties.

Class **Font** has a number of constructors. Most require a *font name*, which is a **string** representing a font currently supported by the system. Common fonts include Microsoft *SansSerif* and *Serif*. Constructors also usually require the *font size* as an argument. Lastly, **Font** constructors usually require a *font style*, specified by the **FontStyle** enumeration: **Bold**, **Italic**, **Regular**, **Strikeout**, **Underline**. Font styles can be combined via the '|' operator (for example, **FontStyle.Italic | FontStyle.Bold**, makes a font both italic and bold).

Graphics method **DrawString** sets the current drawing font—the font in which the text displays—to its **Font** argument.

Common Programming Error 13.1

Specifying a font that is not available on a system is a logic error. If this occurs, C# will substitute that system's default font.

The program in Fig. 13.9 displays text in four different fonts, each of a different size. The program uses the **Font** constructor to initialize **Font** objects (lines 32–47). Each call to the **Font** constructor passes a font name (e.g., Arial, Times New Roman, Courier New or Tahoma) as a **string**, a font size (a **float**) and a **FontStyle** object (**style**). **Graphics** method **DrawString** sets the font and draws the text at the specified location. Note that line 29 creates a **DarkBlue SolidBrush** object (**brush**), causing all **string**s drawn with that brush to appear in **DarkBlue**.

Software Engineering Observation 13.2

There is no way to change the properties of a **Font** *object—to use a different font, programmers must create a new* **Font** *object.*

```
1   // Fig. 13.9: UsingFonts.cs
2   // Demonstrating various font settings.
3
4   using System;
5   using System.Drawing;
6   using System.Collections;
7   using System.ComponentModel;
8   using System.Windows.Forms;
9   using System.Data;
10
11  // demonstrate font constructors and properties
12  public class UsingFonts : System.Windows.Forms.Form
13  {
14     private System.ComponentModel.Container components = null;
15
16     [STAThread]
17     static void Main()
18     {
19        Application.Run( new UsingFonts() );
20     }
21
22     // Visual Studio .NET generated code
23
```

Fig. 13.9 **Font**s and **FontStyle**s. (Part 1 of 2.)

```
24      // demonstrate various font and style settings
25      protected override void OnPaint(
26         PaintEventArgs paintEvent )
27      {
28         Graphics graphicsObject = paintEvent.Graphics;
29         SolidBrush brush = new SolidBrush( Color.DarkBlue );
30
31         // arial, 12 pt bold
32         FontStyle style = FontStyle.Bold;
33         Font arial =
34            new Font( new FontFamily( "Arial" ), 12, style );
35
36         // times new roman, 12 pt regular
37         style = FontStyle.Regular;
38         Font timesNewRoman =
39            new Font( "Times New Roman", 12, style );
40
41         // courier new, 16 pt bold and italic
42         style = FontStyle.Bold | FontStyle.Italic;
43         Font courierNew = new Font( "Courier New", 16, style );
44
45         // tahoma, 18 pt strikeout
46         style = FontStyle.Strikeout;
47         Font tahoma = new Font( "Tahoma", 18, style );
48
49         graphicsObject.DrawString( arial.Name +
50            " 12 point bold.", arial, brush, 10, 10 );
51
52         graphicsObject.DrawString( timesNewRoman.Name +
53            " 12 point plain.", timesNewRoman, brush, 10, 30 );
54
55         graphicsObject.DrawString( courierNew.Name +
56            " 16 point bold and italic.", courierNew,
57            brush, 10, 54 );
58
59         graphicsObject.DrawString( tahoma.Name +
60            " 18 point strikeout.", tahoma, brush, 10, 75 );
61
62      } // end method OnPaint
63
64   } // end class UsingFonts
```

Fig. 13.9 Fonts and FontStyles. (Part 2 of 2.)

Programmers can define precise information about a font's *metrics* (or properties), such as *height*, *descent* (the amount that characters dip below the baseline), *ascent* (the amount that characters rise above the baseline) and *leading* (the difference between the ascent of one line and the decent of the previous line). Figure 13.10 illustrates these properties.

Class **FontFamily** defines characteristics common to a group of related fonts. Class **FontFamily** provides several methods used to determine the font metrics that are shared by members of a particular family. These methods are summarized in Fig. 13.11.

The program shown in Fig. 13.12 calls method **ToString** to display the metrics of two fonts. Line 32 creates **Font arial** and sets it to 12-point Arial font. Line 33 uses class **Font** property **FontFamily** to obtain object **arial**'s **FontFamily** object. Lines 38–39 call **ToString** to output the **string** representation of the font. Lines 41–55 then use methods of class **FontFamily** to return integers specifying the ascent, descent, height and leading of the font. Lines 58–77 repeat this process for font **sansSerif**, a **Font** object derived from the MS Sans Serif **FontFamily**.

Fig. 13.10 An illustration of font metrics.

Method	Description
GetCellAscent	Returns an **int** representing the ascent of a font as measured in design units.
GetCellDescent	Returns an **int** representing the descent of a font as measured in design units.
GetEmHeight	Returns an **int** representing the height of a font as measured in design points.
GetLineSpacing	Returns an **int** representing the distance between two consecutive lines of text as measured in design units.

Fig. 13.11 **FontFamily** methods that return font-metric information.

```
1   // Fig. 13.12: UsingFontMetrics.cs
2   // Displaying font metric information.
3
4   using System;
5   using System.Drawing;
6   using System.Collections;
7   using System.ComponentModel;
```

Fig. 13.12 **FontFamily** class used to obtain font-metric information. (Part 1 of 3.)

```
8   using System.Windows.Forms;
9   using System.Data;
10
11  // displays font information
12  public class UsingFontMetrics : System.Windows.Forms.Form
13  {
14     private System.ComponentModel.Container components = null;
15
16     [STAThread]
17     static void Main()
18     {
19        Application.Run( new UsingFontMetrics() );
20     }
21
22     // Visual Studio .NET generated code
23
24     // displays font information
25     protected override void OnPaint(
26        PaintEventArgs paintEvent )
27     {
28        Graphics graphicsObject = paintEvent.Graphics;
29        SolidBrush brush = new SolidBrush( Color.DarkBlue );
30
31        // Arial font metrics
32        Font arial = new Font( "Arial", 12 );
33        FontFamily family = arial.FontFamily;
34        Font sanSerif = new Font( "Microsoft Sans Serif",
35           14, FontStyle.Italic );
36
37        // display Arial font metrics
38        graphicsObject.DrawString( "Current Font: " +
39           arial.ToString(), arial, brush, 10, 10 );
40
41        graphicsObject.DrawString( "Ascent: " +
42           family.GetCellAscent( FontStyle.Regular ), arial,
43           brush, 10, 30 );
44
45        graphicsObject.DrawString( "Descent: " +
46           family.GetCellDescent( FontStyle.Regular ), arial,
47           brush, 10, 50 );
48
49        graphicsObject.DrawString( "Height: " +
50           family.GetEmHeight( FontStyle.Regular ), arial,
51           brush, 10, 70 );
52
53        graphicsObject.DrawString( "Leading: " +
54           family.GetLineSpacing( FontStyle.Regular ), arial,
55           brush, 10, 90 );
56
57        // display Sans Serif font metrics
58        family = sanSerif.FontFamily;
59
```

Fig. 13.12 FontFamily class used to obtain font-metric information. (Part 2 of 3.)

```
60        graphicsObject.DrawString( "Current Font: " +
61            sanSerif.ToString(), sanSerif, brush, 10, 130 );
62
63        graphicsObject.DrawString( "Ascent: " +
64            family.GetCellAscent( FontStyle.Regular ), sanSerif,
65            brush, 10, 150 );
66
67        graphicsObject.DrawString( "Descent: " +
68            family.GetCellDescent( FontStyle.Regular ), sanSerif,
69            brush, 10, 170 );
70
71        graphicsObject.DrawString( "Height: " +
72            family.GetEmHeight( FontStyle.Regular ), sanSerif,
73            brush, 10, 190 );
74
75        graphicsObject.DrawString( "Leading: " +
76            family.GetLineSpacing( FontStyle.Regular ), sanSerif,
77            brush, 10, 210 );
78
79    } // end method OnPaint
80
81 } // end class UsingFontMetrics
```

Fig. 13.12 FontFamily class used to obtain font-metric information. (Part 3 of 3.)

13.5 Drawing Lines, Rectangles and Ovals

This section presents a variety of **Graphics** methods for drawing lines, rectangles and ovals. Each of the drawing methods has several overloaded versions. When employing methods that draw shape outlines, we use versions that take a **Pen** and four **int**s; when employing methods that draw solid shapes, we use versions that take a **Brush** and four **int**s. In both instances, the first two **int** arguments represent the coordinates of the upper-left corner of the shape or its enclosing area, and the last two **int**s indicate the shape's width and height. Figure 13.13 summarizes the **Graphics** methods and their parameters.

The application in Fig. 13.14 draws lines, rectangles and ellipses. In this application, we also demonstrate methods that draw filled and unfilled shapes.

Methods *FillRectangle* and *DrawRectangle* (lines 33 and 42) draw rectangles on the screen. For each method, the first argument specifies the drawing object to use. The **DrawRectangle** method uses a **Pen** object, whereas the **FillRectangle** method uses a **Brush** object (in this case, an instance of **SolidBrush**—a class that derives from **Brush**). The next two arguments specify the coordinates of the upper-left corner of the *bounding rectangle*, which represents the area in which the rectangle will be drawn. The fourth and fifth arguments specify the rectangle's width and height. Method *DrawLine* (lines 36–39) takes a **Pen** and two pairs of **int**s, specifying the start and endpoint of the line. The method then draws a line, using the **Pen** object passed to it.

Methods *DrawEllipse* and *FillEllipse* each provide overloaded versions that take five arguments. In both methods, the first argument specifies the drawing object to use. The next two arguments specify the upper-left coordinates of the bounding rectangle representing the area in which the ellipse will be drawn. The last two arguments specify the bounding rectangle's width and height, respectively. Figure 13.15 depicts an ellipse bounded by a rectangle. The ellipse touches the midpoint of each of the four sides of the bounding rectangle. The bounding rectangle is not displayed on the screen.

Graphics Drawing Methods and Descriptions.

Note: Many of these methods are overloaded—consult the documentation for a full listing.

DrawLine(Pen p, int x1, int y1, int x2, int y2)
Draws a line from ($x1$, $y1$) to ($x2$, $y2$). The **Pen** determines the color, style and width of the line.

DrawRectangle(Pen p, int x, int y, int width, int height)
Draws a rectangle of the specified width and height. The top-left corner of the rectangle is at point (x, y). The **Pen** determines the color, style, and border width of the rectangle.

FillRectangle(Brush b, int x, int y, int width, int height)
Draws a solid rectangle of the specified width and height. The top-left corner of the rectangle is at point (x, y). The **Brush** determines the fill pattern inside the rectangle.

DrawEllipse(Pen p, int x, int y, int width, int height)
Draws an ellipse inside a rectangle. The width and height of the rectangle are as specified, and its top-left corner is at point (x, y). The **Pen** determines the color, style and border width of the ellipse.

FillEllipse(Brush b, int x, int y, int width, int height)
Draws a filled ellipse inside a rectangle. The width and height of the rectangle are as specified, and its top-left corner is at point (x, y). The **Brush** determines the pattern inside the ellipse.

Fig. 13.13 Graphics methods that draw lines, rectangles and ovals.

```
1   // Fig. 13.14: LinesRectanglesOvals.cs
2   // Demonstrating lines, rectangles and ovals.
3
4   using System;
5   using System.Drawing;
6   using System.Collections;
7   using System.ComponentModel;
```

Fig. 13.14 Demonstration of methods that draw lines, rectangles and ellipses. (Part 1 of 3.)

```
 8   using System.Windows.Forms;
 9   using System.Data;
10
11   // draws shapes on the Form
12   public class LinesRectanglesOvals : System.Windows.Forms.Form
13   {
14       private System.ComponentModel.Container components = null;
15
16       [STAThread]
17       static void Main()
18       {
19           Application.Run( new LinesRectanglesOvals() );
20       }
21
22       // Visual Studio .NET generated code
23
24       protected override void OnPaint(
25           PaintEventArgs paintEvent )
26       {
27           // get graphics object
28           Graphics g = paintEvent.Graphics;
29           SolidBrush brush = new SolidBrush( Color.Blue );
30           Pen pen = new Pen( Color.AliceBlue );
31
32           // create filled rectangle
33           g.FillRectangle( brush, 90, 30, 150, 90 );
34
35           // draw lines to connect rectangles
36           g.DrawLine( pen, 90, 30, 110, 40 );
37           g.DrawLine( pen, 90, 120, 110, 130 );
38           g.DrawLine( pen, 240, 30, 260, 40 );
39           g.DrawLine( pen, 240, 120, 260, 130 );
40
41           // draw top rectangle
42           g.DrawRectangle( pen, 110, 40, 150, 90 );
43
44           // set brush to red
45           brush.Color = Color.Red;
46
47           // draw base Ellipse
48           g.FillEllipse( brush, 280, 75, 100, 50 );
49
50           // draw connecting lines
51           g.DrawLine( pen, 380, 55, 380, 100 );
52           g.DrawLine( pen, 280, 55, 280, 100 );
53
54           // draw Ellipse outline
55           g.DrawEllipse( pen, 280, 30, 100, 50 );
56
57       } // end method OnPaint
58
59   } // end class LinesRectanglesOvals
```

Fig. 13.14 Demonstration of methods that draw lines, rectangles and ellipses. (Part 2 of 3.)

Fig. 13.14 Demonstration of methods that draw lines, rectangles and ellipses. (Part 3 of 3.)

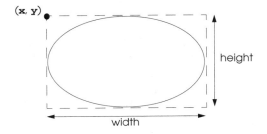

Fig. 13.15 Ellipse bounded by a rectangle.

13.6 Drawing Arcs

*Arc*s are portions of ellipses and are measured in degrees, beginning at a *starting angle* and continuing for a specified number of degrees called the *arc angle*. An arc is said to *sweep* (traverse) its arc angle, beginning from its starting angle. Arcs that sweep in a clockwise direction are measured in positive degrees, whereas arcs that sweep in a counterclockwise direction are measured in negative degrees. Figure 13.16 depicts two arcs. Note that the left portion of the figure sweeps downward from zero degrees to approximately 110 degrees. Similarly, the arc in the right portion of the figure sweeps upward from zero degrees to approximately –110 degrees.

Notice the dashed boxes around the arcs in Fig. 13.16. We draw each arc as part of an oval (the rest of which is not visible). When drawing an oval, we specify the oval's dimensions in the form of a bounding rectangle that encloses the oval. The boxes in Fig. 13.16 correspond to these bounding rectangles. The **Graphics** methods used to draw arcs—**DrawArc**, **DrawPie** and **FillPie**—are summarized in Fig. 13.17.

The program in Fig. 13.18 draws six images (three arcs and three filled pie slices) to demonstrate the arc methods listed in Fig. 13.17. To illustrate the bounding rectangles that determine the sizes and locations of the arcs, the arcs are displayed inside red rectangles that have the same *x*-coordinates, *y*-coordinates and width and height arguments as those that define the bounding rectangles for the arcs.

Lines 28–35 create the objects that we need to draw various arcs: **Graphics** objects, **Rectangle**s, **SolidBrush**es and **Pen**s. Lines 38–39 then draw a rectangle and an arc inside the rectangle. The arc sweeps 360 degrees, forming a circle. Line 42 changes the location of the **Rectangle** by setting its **Location** property to a new **Point**. The **Point** constructor takes the *x*- and *y*-coordinates of the new point. The **Location** property determines the upper-left corner of the **Rectangle**. After drawing the rectangle, the program draws an arc that starts at 0 degrees and sweeps 110 degrees. Because angles in C# increase in a clockwise direction, the arc sweeps downward.

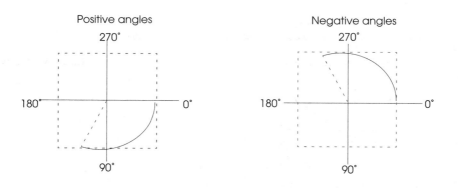

Fig. 13.16 Positive and negative arc angles.

Graphics Methods And Descriptions

Note: Many of these methods are overloaded—consult the documentation for a complete listing.

DrawArc(Pen p, *int* x, *int* y, *int* width, *int* height,
   int startAngle, int sweepAngle)
Draws an arc of an ellipse, beginning from angle **startAngle** (in degrees) and sweeping **sweepAngle** degrees. The ellipse is defined by a bounding rectangle of width **w**, height **h** and upper-left corner (**x,y**). The **Pen** determines the color, border width and style of the arc.

DrawPie(Pen p, *int* x, *int* y, *int* width, *int* height,
   int startAngle, int sweepAngle)
Draws a pie section of an ellipse, beginning from angle **startAngle** (in degrees) and sweeping **sweepAngle** degrees. The ellipse is defined by a bounding rectangle of width **w**, height **h** and upper-left corner (**x,y**). The **Pen** determines the color, border width and style of the arc.

FillPie(Brush b, *int* x, *int* y, *int* width, *int* height,
   int startAngle, int sweepAngle)
Functions similarly to **DrawPie**, except draws a solid arc (i.e., a sector). The **Brush** determines the fill pattern for the solid arc.

Fig. 13.17 Graphics methods for drawing arcs.

```
1   // Fig. 13.18: DrawArcs.cs
2   // Drawing various arcs on a form.
```

Fig. 13.18 Arc-method demonstration. (Part 1 of 3.)

```
3
4    using System;
5    using System.Drawing;
6    using System.Collections;
7    using System.ComponentModel;
8    using System.Windows.Forms;
9    using System.Data;
10
11   // draws various arcs
12   public class DrawArcs : System.Windows.Forms.Form
13   {
14      private System.ComponentModel.Container components = null;
15
16      [STAThread]
17      static void Main()
18      {
19         Application.Run( new DrawArcs() );
20      }
21
22      // Visual Studio .NET generated code
23
24      private void DrawArcs_Paint(
25         object sender, System.Windows.Forms.PaintEventArgs e )
26      {
27         // get graphics object
28         Graphics graphicsObject = e.Graphics;
29         Rectangle rectangle1 =
30            new Rectangle( 15, 35, 80, 80 );
31         SolidBrush brush1 =
32            new SolidBrush( Color.Firebrick );
33         Pen pen1 = new Pen( brush1, 1 );
34         SolidBrush brush2 = new SolidBrush( Color.DarkBlue );
35         Pen pen2 = new Pen( brush2, 1 );
36
37         // start at 0 and sweep 360 degrees
38         graphicsObject.DrawRectangle( pen1, rectangle1 );
39         graphicsObject.DrawArc( pen2, rectangle1, 0, 360 );
40
41         // start at 0 and sweep 110 degrees
42         rectangle1.Location = new Point( 100, 35 );
43         graphicsObject.DrawRectangle( pen1, rectangle1 );
44         graphicsObject.DrawArc( pen2, rectangle1, 0, 110 );
45
46         // start at 0 and sweep -270 degrees
47         rectangle1.Location = new Point( 185, 35 );
48         graphicsObject.DrawRectangle( pen1, rectangle1 );
49         graphicsObject.DrawArc( pen2, rectangle1, 0, -270 );
50
51         // start at 0 and sweep 360 degrees
52         rectangle1.Location = new Point( 15, 120 );
53         rectangle1.Size = new Size( 80, 40 );
54         graphicsObject.DrawRectangle( pen1, rectangle1 );
55         graphicsObject.FillPie( brush2, rectangle1, 0, 360 );
```

Fig. 13.18 Arc-method demonstration. (Part 2 of 3.)

```
56
57        // start at 270 and sweep -90 degrees
58        rectangle1.Location = new Point( 100, 120 );
59        graphicsObject.DrawRectangle( pen1, rectangle1 );
60        graphicsObject.FillPie(
61           brush2, rectangle1, 270, -90 );
62
63        // start at 0 and sweep -270 degrees
64        rectangle1.Location = new Point( 185, 120 );
65        graphicsObject.DrawRectangle( pen1, rectangle1 );
66        graphicsObject.FillPie(
67           brush2, rectangle1, 0, -270 );
68
69     } // end method DrawArcs_Paint
70
71 } // end class DrawArcs
```

Fig. 13.18 Arc-method demonstration. (Part 3 of 3.)

Lines 47–49 perform similar functions, except that the specified arc sweeps -270 degrees. The **Size** property of a **Rectangle** determines the arc's height and width. Line 53 sets the **Size** property to a new **Size** object, which changes the size of the rectangle.

The remainder of the program is similar to the portions described above, except that a **SolidBrush** is used with method **FillPie**. The resulting arcs, which are filled, can be seen in the bottom half of the screenshot Fig. 13.18.

13.7 Drawing Polygons and Polylines

Polygons are multisided shapes. There are several **Graphics** methods used to draw polygons: **DrawLines** draws a series of connected points, **DrawPolygon** draws a closed polygon and **FillPolygon** draws a solid polygon. These methods are described in Fig. 13.19. The program in Fig. 13.20 allows users to draw polygons and connected lines via the methods listed in Fig. 13.19.

To allow the user to specify a variable number of points, line 26 declares **ArrayList points** as a container for our **Point** objects. Lines 29–31 declare the **Pen** and **Brush** used to color our shapes. The **MouseDown** event handler (lines 42–49) for **Panel drawPanel** stores mouse-click locations in the **points ArrayList**. It then calls method **Invalidate** of **drawPanel** to ensure that the panel refreshes to accommodate the new point. Method **drawPanel_Paint** (lines 51–82) handles the **Panel**'s **Paint** event. It obtains the panel's **Graphics** object (line 55) and, if the **ArrayList points** contains two or more **Points**, displays the polygon with the method that the user selected via the GUI radio buttons (lines 58–80). In lines 61–63, we extract an **Array** from the **Array-List** via method **ToArray**. Method **ToArray** can take a single argument to determine the type of the returned array; we obtain the type from the first element in the **ArrayList**.

Method	Description
DrawLines	Draws a series of connected lines. The coordinates of each point are specified in an array of **Point**s. If the last point is different from the first point, the figure is not closed.
DrawPolygon	Draws a polygon. The coordinates of each point are specified in an array of **Point** objects. This method draws a closed polygon, even if the last point is different from the first point.
FillPolygon	Draws a solid polygon. The coordinates of each point are specified in an array of **Points**. This method draws a closed polygon, even if the last point is different from the first point.

Fig. 13.19 Graphics methods for drawing polygons.

```
1   // Fig. 13.20: DrawPolygons.cs
2   // Demonstrating polygons.
3
4   using System;
5   using System.Drawing;
6   using System.Collections;
7   using System.ComponentModel;
8   using System.Windows.Forms;
9   using System.Data;
10
11  public class PolygonForm : System.Windows.Forms.Form
12  {
13     private System.Windows.Forms.Button colorButton;
14     private System.Windows.Forms.Button clearButton;
15     private System.Windows.Forms.GroupBox typeGroup;
16     private System.Windows.Forms.RadioButton
17        filledPolygonOption;
18     private System.Windows.Forms.RadioButton lineOption;
19     private System.Windows.Forms.RadioButton polygonOption;
20     private System.Windows.Forms.Panel drawPanel;
21
22     private
23        System.ComponentModel.Container components = null;
24
25     // contains list of polygon vertices
26     private ArrayList points = new ArrayList();
27
```

Fig. 13.20 Polygon-drawing demonstration. (Part 1 of 4.)

```
28      // initialize default pen and brush
29      Pen pen = new Pen( Color.DarkBlue );
30
31      SolidBrush brush = new SolidBrush( Color.DarkBlue );
32
33      [STAThread]
34      static void Main()
35      {
36         Application.Run( new PolygonForm() );
37      }
38
39      // Visual Studio .NET generated code
40
41      // draw panel mouse down event handler
42      private void drawPanel_MouseDown(
43         object sender, System.Windows.Forms.MouseEventArgs e )
44      {
45         // add mouse position to vertex list
46         points.Add( new Point( e.X, e.Y ) );
47         drawPanel.Invalidate(); // refresh panel
48
49      } // end method drawPanel_MouseDown
50
51      private void drawPanel_Paint(
52         object sender, System.Windows.Forms.PaintEventArgs e )
53      {
54         // get graphics object for panel
55         Graphics graphicsObject = e.Graphics;
56
57         // if arraylist has 2 or more points, display shape
58         if ( points.Count > 1 )
59         {
60            // get array for use in drawing functions
61            Point[] pointArray =
62               ( Point[] )points.ToArray(
63               points[ 0 ].GetType() );
64
65            if ( polygonOption.Checked )
66
67               // draw polygon
68               graphicsObject.DrawPolygon( pen, pointArray );
69
70            else if ( lineOption.Checked )
71
72               // draw lines
73               graphicsObject.DrawLines( pen, pointArray );
74
75            else if ( filledPolygonOption.Checked )
76
77               // draw filled
78               graphicsObject.FillPolygon(
79                  brush, pointArray );
80         }
```

Fig. 13.20 Polygon-drawing demonstration. (Part 2 of 4.)

```
81
82       } // end method drawPanel_Paint
83
84       // handle clearButton click event
85       private void clearButton_Click(
86          object sender, System.EventArgs e )
87       {
88          points = new ArrayList(); // remove points
89
90          drawPanel.Invalidate(); // refresh panel
91
92       } // end method clearButton_Click
93
94       // handle polygon radio button CheckedChanged event
95       private void polygonOption_CheckedChanged(
96          object sender, System.EventArgs e)
97       {
98          drawPanel.Invalidate(); // refresh panel
99
100      } // end method polygonOption_CheckedChanged
101
102      // handle line radio button CheckedChanged event
103      private void lineOption_CheckedChanged(
104         object sender, System.EventArgs e)
105      {
106         drawPanel.Invalidate(); // refresh panel
107
108      } // end method lineOption_CheckedChanged
109
110      // handle filled polygon radio button
111      // CheckedChanged event
112      private void filledPolygonOption_CheckedChanged(
113         object sender, System.EventArgs e)
114      {
115         drawPanel.Invalidate(); // refresh panel
116
117      } // end method filledPolygonOption_CheckedChanged
118
119      // handle colorButton click event
120      private void colorButton_Click(
121         object sender, System.EventArgs e)
122      {
123         // create new color dialog
124         ColorDialog dialogColor = new ColorDialog();
125
126         // show dialog and obtain result
127         DialogResult result = dialogColor.ShowDialog();
128
129         // return if user cancels
130         if ( result == DialogResult.Cancel )
131            return;
132
133         pen.Color = dialogColor.Color;   // set pen to color
```

Fig. 13.20 Polygon-drawing demonstration. (Part 3 of 4.)

```
134          brush.Color = dialogColor.Color; // set brush
135          drawPanel.Invalidate();          // refresh panel
136
137     } // end method colorButton_Click
138
139 } // end class PolygonForm
```

Fig. 13.20 Polygon-drawing demonstration. (Part 4 of 4.)

Method **clearButton_Click** (lines 85–92) handles the **Clear** button's click event, creates an empty **ArrayList** (causing the old list to be erased) and refreshes the display. Lines 95–117 define the event handlers for the radio buttons' **CheckedChanged** event. Each method refreshes **Panel drawPanel** to ensure that the panel display reflects the selected drawing type. Event method **colorButton_Click** (120–137) allows the user to select a new drawing color with a **ColorDialog**, using the same technique demonstrated in Fig. 13.7.

13.8 Advanced Graphics Capabilities

C# offers many additional graphics capabilities. The **Brush** hierarchy, for example, also includes *HatchBrush*, *LinearGradientBrush*, *PathGradientBrush* and *TextureBrush*.

The program in Fig. 13.21 demonstrates several graphics features, such as dashed lines, thick lines and the ability to fill shapes with patterns. These represent just a few of the additional capabilities of the **System.Drawing** namespace.

```
1    // Fig. 13.21: DrawShapes.cs
2    // Drawing various shapes on a form.
3
4    using System;
5    using System.Drawing;
6    using System.Collections;
7    using System.ComponentModel;
8    using System.Windows.Forms;
9    using System.Data;
10   using System.Drawing.Drawing2D;
11
12   // draws shapes with different brushes
13   public class DrawShapesForm : System.Windows.Forms.Form
14   {
15      private System.ComponentModel.Container components = null;
16
17      [STAThread]
18      static void Main()
19      {
20         Application.Run( new DrawShapesForm() );
21      }
22
23      // Visual Studio .NET generated code
24
25      // draw various shapes on form
26      private void DrawShapesForm_Paint(
27         object sender, System.Windows.Forms.PaintEventArgs e )
28      {
29         // references to object we will use
30         Graphics graphicsObject = e.Graphics;
31
32         // ellipse rectangle and gradient brush
33         Rectangle drawArea1 =
34            new Rectangle( 5, 35, 30, 100 );
35         LinearGradientBrush linearBrush =
36            new LinearGradientBrush( drawArea1, Color.Blue,
37            Color.Yellow, LinearGradientMode.ForwardDiagonal );
38
39         // pen and location for red outline rectangle
40         Pen thickRedPen = new Pen( Color.Red, 10 );
41         Rectangle drawArea2 = new Rectangle( 80, 30, 65, 100 );
42
43         // bitmap texture
44         Bitmap textureBitmap = new Bitmap( 10, 10 );
45
46         // get bitmap graphics
47         Graphics graphicsObject2 =
48            Graphics.FromImage( textureBitmap );
```

Fig. 13.21 Shapes drawn on a form. (Part 1 of 3.)

```
49
50      // brush and pen used throughout program
51      SolidBrush solidColorBrush =
52          new SolidBrush( Color.Red );
53      Pen coloredPen = new Pen( solidColorBrush );
54
55      // draw ellipse filled with a blue-yellow gradient
56      graphicsObject.FillEllipse(
57          linearBrush, 5, 30, 65, 100 );
58
59      // draw thick rectangle outline in red
60      graphicsObject.DrawRectangle( thickRedPen, drawArea2 );
61
62      // fill textureBitmap with yellow
63      solidColorBrush.Color = Color.Yellow;
64      graphicsObject2.FillRectangle(
65          solidColorBrush, 0, 0, 10, 10 );
66
67      // draw small black rectangle in textureBitmap
68      coloredPen.Color = Color.Black;
69      graphicsObject2.DrawRectangle(
70          coloredPen, 1, 1, 6, 6 );
71
72      // draw small blue rectangle in textureBitmpa
73      solidColorBrush.Color = Color.Blue;
74      graphicsObject2.FillRectangle(
75          solidColorBrush, 1, 1, 3, 3 );
76
77      // draw small red square in textureBitmap
78      solidColorBrush.Color = Color.Red;
79      graphicsObject2.FillRectangle(
80          solidColorBrush, 4, 4, 3, 3 );
81
82      // create textured brush and
83      // display textured rectangle
84      TextureBrush texturedBrush =
85          new TextureBrush( textureBitmap );
86      graphicsObject.FillRectangle(
87          texturedBrush, 155, 30, 75, 100 );
88
89      // draw pie-shaped arc in white
90      coloredPen.Color = Color.White;
91      coloredPen.Width = 6;
92      graphicsObject.DrawPie(
93          coloredPen, 240, 30, 75, 100, 0, 270 );
94
95      // draw lines in green and yellow
96      coloredPen.Color = Color.Green;
97      coloredPen.Width = 5;
98      graphicsObject.DrawLine(
99          coloredPen, 395, 30, 320, 150 );
100
```

Fig. 13.21 Shapes drawn on a form. (Part 2 of 3.)

```
101         // draw a rounded, dashed yellow line
102         coloredPen.Color = Color.Yellow;
103         coloredPen.DashCap = DashCap.Round;
104         coloredPen.DashStyle = DashStyle.Dash;
105         graphicsObject.DrawLine(
106            coloredPen, 320, 30, 395, 150 );
107
108    } // end method DrawShapesForm_Paint
109
110 } // end class DrawShapesForm
```

Fig. 13.21 Shapes drawn on a form. (Part 3 of 3.)

Lines 26–108 define the **Paint** event handler for our form. Lines 35–37 create **LinearGradientBrush** object **linearBrush**, which resides in namespace **System.Drawing.Drawing2D**. A **LinearGradientBrush** enables users to draw with a color gradient. The **LinearGradientBrush** used in this example takes four arguments: A **Rectangle**, two **Color**s and a member of enumeration **LinearGradientMode**. In C#, all linear gradients are defined along a line that determines the gradient endpoint. This line can be specified either by starting and ending points or by the diagonal of a rectangle. The first argument, **Rectangle drawArea1**, specifies the defining line for **LinearGradientBrush linearBrush**. This **Rectangle** argument represents the endpoints of the linear gradient—the upper-left corner is the starting point, and the bottom-right corner is the ending point. The second and third arguments specify the colors that the gradient will use. In this case, the color of the ellipse will gradually change from **Color.Blue** to **Color.Yellow**. The last argument, a type from the enumeration *LinearGradientMode*, specifies the linear gradient's direction. In our case, we use *LinearGradientMode.ForwardDiagonal*, which creates a gradient from the upper-left to the lower-right corner. We then use **Graphics** method **FillEllipse** in lines 56–57 to draw an ellipse with **linearBrush**; the color gradually changes from blue to yellow, as described above.

In line 40, we create a **Pen** object **thickRedPen**. We pass to **thickRedPen**'s constructor **Color.Red** and **int** argument **10**, indicating that we want **thickRedPen** to draw red lines that are 10 pixels wide.

Line 44 creates a new *Bitmap* image, which initially is empty. Class **Bitmap** can produce images in color and gray scale; this particular **Bitmap** is 10 pixels wide and 10 pixels tall. Method *FromImage* (line 47–48) is a **static** member of class **Graphics** and retrieves the **Graphics** object associated with an **Image**, which may be used to draw on an image. Lines 63–80 draw on the **Bitmap** a pattern consisting of black, blue, red and yellow rectangles and lines. A **TextureBrush** is a brush that fills the interior of a shape with an image, rather than a solid color. In line 86–87, **TextureBrush** object **textureBrush** fills a rectangle with our **Bitmap**. The **TextureBrush** constructor version that we use takes as an argument an image that defines its texture.

Next, we draw a pie-shaped arc with a thick white line. Lines 90–91 set **coloredPen**'s color to **White** and modify its width to be six pixels. We then draw the pie on the form by specifying the **Pen** the *x*-coordinate, *y*-coordinate, length and width of the bounding rectangle and the start angle and sweep angle.

Finally, lines 103–104 make use of **System.Drawing.Drawing2D** enumerations *DashCap* and *DashStyle* to draw a diagonal dashed line. Line 103 sets the *DashCap* property of **coloredPen** (not to be confused with the **DashCap** enumeration) to a member of the **DashCap** enumeration. The **DashCap** enumeration specifies the styles for the start and end of a dashed line. In this case, we want both ends of the dashed line to be rounded, so we use *DashCap.Round*. Line 104 sets the *DashStyle* property of **coloredPen** (not to be confused with the **DashStyle** enumeration) to *DashStyle.Dash*, indicating that we want our line to consist entirely of dashes.

Our next example demonstrates the use of a *general path*. A general path is a shape constructed from straight lines and complex curves. An object of class *GraphicsPath* (**System.Drawing.Drawing2D** namespace) represents a general path. The **GraphicsPath** class provides functionality that enables the creation of complex shapes from vector-based primitive graphics objects. A **GraphicsPath** object consists of figures defined by simple shapes. The start point of each vector-graphics object (such as a line or arc) that is added to the path is connected by a straight line to the end point of the previous object. When called, the **CloseFigure** method attaches the final vector-graphic object endpoint to the initial starting point for the current figure by a straight line, then starts a new figure. Method **StartFigure** begins a new figure within the path without closing the previous figure.

The program of Fig. 13.22 draws general paths in the shape of five-pointed stars. Line 45 sets the origin of the **Graphics** object. The arguments to method **TranslateTransform** indicate that the origin should be translated to the coordinates (150, 150). Lines 36–39 define two **int** arrays, representing the *x*- and *y*-coordinates of the points in the star, and line 42 defines **GraphicsPath** object **star**. A **for** loop then creates lines to connect the points of the star and adds these lines to **star**. We use **GraphicsPath** method *AddLine* to append a line to the shape. The arguments of **AddLine** specify the coordinates for the line's endpoints; each new call to **AddLine** adds a line from the previous point to the current point. Line 38 uses **GraphicsPath** method *CloseFigure* to complete the shape.

```
1   // Fig. 13.22: DrawStarsForm.cs
2   // Using paths to draw stars on the form.
3
4   using System;
5   using System.Drawing;
6   using System.Collections;
7   using System.ComponentModel;
```

Fig. 13.22 Paths used to draw stars on a form. (Part 1 of 3.)

```
8   using System.Windows.Forms;
9   using System.Data;
10  using System.Drawing.Drawing2D;
11
12  // draws randomly colored stars
13  public class DrawStarsForm : System.Windows.Forms.Form
14  {
15     private
16        System.ComponentModel.Container components = null;
17
18     [STAThread]
19     static void Main()
20     {
21        Application.Run( new DrawStarsForm() );
22     }
23
24     // Visual Studio .NET generated code
25
26     // create path and draw stars along it
27     private void DrawStarsForm_Paint(
28        object sender, System.Windows.Forms.PaintEventArgs e )
29     {
30        Graphics graphicsObject = e.Graphics;
31        Random random = new Random();
32        SolidBrush brush =
33           new SolidBrush( Color.DarkMagenta );
34
35        // x and y points of the path
36        int[] xPoints =
37           { 55, 67, 109, 73, 83, 55, 27, 37, 1, 43 };
38        int[] yPoints =
39           { 0, 36, 36, 54, 96, 72, 96, 54, 36, 36 };
40
41        // create graphics path for star;
42        GraphicsPath star = new GraphicsPath();
43
44        // translate the origin to (150, 150)
45        graphicsObject.TranslateTransform( 150, 150 );
46
47        // create star from series of points
48        for ( int i = 0; i <= 8; i += 2 )
49           star.AddLine( xPoints[ i ], yPoints[ i ],
50              xPoints[ i + 1 ], yPoints[ i + 1 ] );
51
52        // close the shape
53        star.CloseFigure();
54
55        // rotate the origin and draw stars in random colors
56        for ( int i = 1; i <= 18; i++ )
57        {
58           graphicsObject.RotateTransform( 20 );
59
```

Fig. 13.22 Paths used to draw stars on a form. (Part 2 of 3.)

```
60              brush.Color = Color.FromArgb(
61                 random.Next( 200, 255 ), random.Next( 255 ),
62                 random.Next( 255 ), random.Next( 255 ) );
63
64              graphicsObject.FillPath( brush, star );
65           }
66
67        } // end method DrawStarsForm_Paint
68
69     } // end class DrawStarsForm
```

Fig. 13.22 Paths used to draw stars on a form. (Part 3 of 3.)

The **for** structure in lines 56–65 draws the **star** 18 times, rotating it around the origin. Line 58 uses **Graphics** method *RotateTransform* to move to the next position on the form; the argument specifies the rotation angle in degrees. **Graphics** method **FillPath** (line 64) then draws a filled version of the **star** with the **Brush** created on lines 60–62. The application determines the **SolidBrush**'s color randomly, using **Random** method **Next**.

13.9 Introduction to Multimedia

C# offers many convenient ways to include images and animations in programs. People who entered the computing field decades ago used computers primarily to perform arithmetic calculations. As the discipline evolves, we are beginning to realize the importance of computers' data-manipulation capabilities. We are seeing a wide variety of exciting new three-dimensional applications. Multimedia programming is an entertaining and innovative field, but one that presents many challenges.

Multimedia applications demand extraordinary computing power. Until recently, affordable computers with this amount of power were not available. However, today's ultrafast processors are making multimedia-based applications commonplace. As the market for multimedia explodes, users are purchasing the faster processors, larger memories and wider communications bandwidths needed to support multimedia applications. This benefits the computer and communications industries, which provide the hardware, software and services fueling the multimedia revolution.

In the remaining sections of this chapter, we introduce the use and manipulation of images and other multimedia features and capabilities. Section 13.10 discusses how to load, display and scale images; Section 13.11 demonstrates image animation; Section 13.12 presents the video capabilities of the Windows Media Player control; and Section 13.13 explores Microsoft Agent technology.

13.10 Loading, Displaying and Scaling Images

C#'s multimedia capabilities include graphics, images, animations and video. Previous sections demonstrated C#'s vector-graphics capabilities; this section concentrates on image manipulation. The Windows form that we create in Fig. 13.23 demonstrates the loading of an **Image** (**System.Drawing** namespace). The application allows users to enter a desired height and width for the **Image**, which then is displayed in the specified size.

Lines 23–24 declare **Image** reference **image**. The **static Image** method *From-File* then retrieves an image stored on disk and assigns it to **image** (line 24). Line 31 uses **Form** method *CreateGraphics* to create a **Graphics** object associated with the **Form**; we use this object to draw on the **Form**. Method **CreateGraphics** is inherited from class **Control**; all Windows controls, such as **Button**s and **Panel**s, also provide this method. When users click **Set**, the width and height parameters are validated to ensure that they are not too large. If the parameters are valid, line 59 calls **Graphics** method *Clear* to paint the entire **Form** in the current background color. Lines 62–63 call **Graphics** method *DrawImage* with the following parameters: the image to draw, the *x*-coordinate of the upper-left corner, the *y*-coordinate of the upper-left corner, the width of the image and the height of the image. If the width and height do not correspond to the image's original dimensions, the image is scaled to fit the new specifications.

```
1   // Fig. 13.23: DisplayLogoForm.cs
2   // Displaying and resizing an image.
3
4   using System;
5   using System.Drawing;
6   using System.Collections;
7   using System.ComponentModel;
8   using System.Windows.Forms;
9   using System.Data;
10
11  // displays an image and allows the user to resize it
12  public class DisplayLogoForm : System.Windows.Forms.Form
13  {
14      private System.Windows.Forms.Button setButton;
15      private System.Windows.Forms.TextBox heightTextBox;
16      private System.Windows.Forms.Label heightLabel;
```

Fig. 13.23 Image resizing. (Part 1 of 3.)

```
17      private System.Windows.Forms.TextBox widthTextBox;
18      private System.Windows.Forms.Label widthLabel;
19
20      private
21         System.ComponentModel.Container components = null;
22
23      private
24         Image image = Image.FromFile( "images/Logo.gif" );
25      private Graphics graphicsObject;
26
27      public DisplayLogoForm()
28      {
29         InitializeComponent();
30
31         graphicsObject = this.CreateGraphics();
32      }
33
34      [STAThread]
35      static void Main()
36      {
37         Application.Run( new DisplayLogoForm() );
38      }
39
40      // Visual Studio .NET generated code
41
42      private void setButton_Click(
43         object sender, System.EventArgs e )
44      {
45         // get user input
46         int width = Convert.ToInt32( widthTextBox.Text );
47         int height = Convert.ToInt32( heightTextBox.Text );
48
49         // if dimensions specified are too large
50         // display problem
51         if ( width > 375 || height > 225 )
52         {
53            MessageBox.Show( "Height or Width too large" );
54
55            return;
56         }
57
58         // clear Windows Form
59         graphicsObject.Clear( this.BackColor );
60
61         // draw image
62         graphicsObject.DrawImage(
63            image, 5, 5, width, height );
64
65      } // end method setButton_Click
66
67   } // end class DisplayLogoForm
```

Fig. 13.23 Image resizing. (Part 2 of 3.)

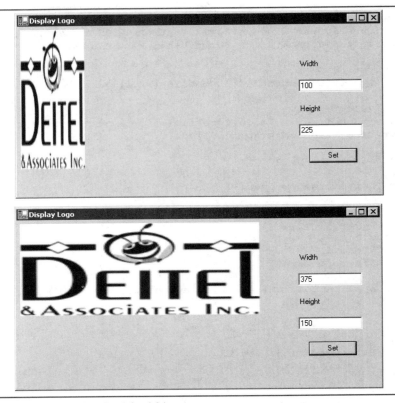

Fig. 13.23 Image resizing. (Part 3 of 3.)

13.11 Animating a Series of Images

The next example animates a series of images stored in an array. The application uses the same techniques to load and display **Image**s as those illustrated in Fig. 13.23. The images were created with Adobe® Photoshop™.

The animation in Fig. 13.24 uses a **PictureBox**, which contains the images that we animate. We use a **Timer** to cycle through the images, causing a new image to display every 50 milliseconds. Variable **count** keeps track of the current image number and increases by one every time we display a new image. The array includes 30 images (numbered 0–29); when the application reaches image 29, it returns to image 0. The 30 images were prepared in advance and placed in the **images** folder inside the **bin/Debug** directory of the project.

```
1   // Fig. 13.24: LogoAnimator.cs
2   // Program that animates a series of images.
3
```

Fig. 13.24 Animation of a series of images. (Part 1 of 3.)

```
4    using System;
5    using System.Drawing;
6    using System.Collections;
7    using System.ComponentModel;
8    using System.Windows.Forms;
9    using System.Data;
10
11   // animates a series of 30 images
12   public class LogoAnimator : System.Windows.Forms.Form
13   {
14      private System.Windows.Forms.PictureBox logoPictureBox;
15      private System.Windows.Forms.Timer Timer;
16      private System.ComponentModel.IContainer components;
17
18      private ArrayList images = new ArrayList();
19      private int count = -1;
20
21      public LogoAnimator()
22      {
23         InitializeComponent();
24
25         for ( int i = 0; i < 30; i++ )
26            images.Add( Image.FromFile( "images/deitel" + i +
27               ".gif" ) );
28
29         // load first image
30         logoPictureBox.Image = ( Image ) images[ 0 ];
31
32         // set PictureBox to be the same size as Image
33         logoPictureBox.Size = logoPictureBox.Image.Size;
34
35      } // end constructor
36
37      [STAThread]
38      static void Main()
39      {
40         Application.Run( new LogoAnimator() );
41      }
42
43      // Visual Studio .NET generated code
44
45      private void Timer_Tick(
46         object sender, System.EventArgs e )
47      {
48         // increment counter
49         count = ( count + 1 ) % 30;
50
51         // load next image
52         logoPictureBox.Image = ( Image )images[ count ];
53
54      } // end method Timer_Tick
55
56   } // end class LogoAnimator
```

Fig. 13.24 Animation of a series of images. (Part 2 of 3.)

Fig. 13.24 Animation of a series of images. (Part 3 of 3.)

Lines 25–27 load each of 30 images and place them in an **ArrayList**. **ArrayList** method **Add** allows us to add objects to the **ArrayList**; we use this method in lines 26–27 to add each **Image**. Line 30 places the first image in the **PictureBox**, using the **ArrayList** indexer. Line 33 modifies the size of the **PictureBox** so that it is equal to the size of the **Image** it is displaying. The event handler for **timer**'s **Tick** event (line 45–54) then displays the next image from the **ArrayList**.

Performance Tip 13.2

It is more efficient to load an animation's frames as one image than to load each image separately. (A painting program, such as Adobe® Photoshop™, or Jasc® Paint Shop Pro™, can be used to combine the animation's frames into one image.) If the images are being loaded separately from the Web, each loaded image requires a separate connection to the site on which the images are stored; this process can result in poor performance.

Performance Tip 13.3

Loading animation frames can cause program delays, because the program waits for all frames to load before displaying them.

The following chess example demonstrates the capabilities of GDI+ as they pertain to a chess-game application. These include techniques for two-dimensional *collision detection*, the selection of single frames from a multi-frame image and *regional invalidation* (refreshing only the required parts of the screen) to increase performance. Two-dimensional collision detection is the detection of an overlap between two shapes. In the next example, we demonstrate the simplest form of collision detection, which determines whether a point (the mouse-click location) is contained within a rectangle (a chess-piece image).

Class **ChessPiece** (Fig. 13.25) is a container class for the individual chess pieces. Lines 11–19 define a public enumeration of constants that identify each chess-piece type. The constants also serve to identify the location of each piece in the chess-piece image file. **Rectangle** object **targetRectangle** (lines 25–26) identifies the image location on the chess board. The **x** and **y** properties of the rectangle are assigned in the **ChessPiece** constructor, and all chess-piece images have height and width **75**.

The **ChessPiece** constructor (lines 29–40) requires that the calling class define a chess-piece type, its **x** and **y** location and the **Bitmap** containing all chess-piece images. Rather than loading the chess-piece image within the class, we allow the calling class to pass the image. This avoids the image-loading overhead for each piece. It also increases the flexibility of the class by allowing the user to change images; for example, in this case, we use the class for both black and white chess-piece images. Lines 37–39 extract a subimage that contains only the current piece's bitmap data. Our chess-piece images are defined in a specific manner: One image contains six chess-piece images, each defined within a 75-pixel block, resulting in a total image size of 450-by-75. We obtain a single image via **Bitmap**'s **Clone** method, which allows us to specify a rectangle image location and the desired pixel format. The location is a 75-by-75 pixel block with its upper-left corner **x** equal to **75 * type** and the corresponding **y** equal to **0**. For the pixel format, we specify constant **DontCare**, causing the format to remain unchanged.

Method **Draw** (lines 43–46) causes the **ChessPiece** to draw **pieceImage** in **targetRectangle** on the passed **Graphics** object. **Method GetBounds** returns the object **targetRectangle** for use in collision detection, and **SetLocation** allows the calling class to specify a new piece location.

```
1   // Fig. 13.25: ChessPiece.cs
2   // Storage class for chess piece attributes.
3
4   using System;
5   using System.Drawing;
6
7   // represents a chess piece
8   public class ChessPiece
9   {
10     // define chess-piece type constants
11     public enum Types
12     {
13        KING,
14        QUEEN,
15        BISHOP,
16        KNIGHT,
17        ROOK,
18        PAWN
19     }
20
21     private int currentType; // this object's type
22     private Bitmap pieceImage; // this object's image
23
24     // default display location
25     private Rectangle targetRectangle =
26        new Rectangle( 0, 0, 75, 75 );
27
28     // construct piece
29     public ChessPiece( int type, int xLocation,
30        int yLocation, Bitmap sourceImage )
31     {
32        currentType = type; // set current type
33        targetRectangle.X = xLocation; // set current x location
34        targetRectangle.Y = yLocation; // set current y location
35
36        // obtain pieceImage from section of sourceImage
37        pieceImage = sourceImage.Clone(
38           new Rectangle( type * 75, 0, 75, 75 ),
39           System.Drawing.Imaging.PixelFormat.DontCare );
40     }
```

Fig. 13.25 Container class for chess pieces. (Part 1 of 2.)

```
41
42      // draw chess piece
43      public void Draw( Graphics graphicsObject )
44      {
45         graphicsObject.DrawImage( pieceImage, targetRectangle );
46      }
47
48      // obtain this piece's location rectangle
49      public Rectangle GetBounds()
50      {
51         return targetRectangle;
52      } // end method GetBounds
53
54      // set this piece's location
55      public void SetLocation( int xLocation, int yLocation )
56      {
57         targetRectangle.X = xLocation;
58         targetRectangle.Y = yLocation;
59
60      } // end method SetLocation
61
62   } // end class ChessPiece
```

Fig. 13.25 Container class for chess pieces. (Part 2 of 2.)

Class **ChessGame** (Fig. 13.26) defines the game and graphics code for our chess game. Lines 23–33 define class-scope variables the program requires. **ArrayList chessTile** (line 23) stores the board tile images. It contains four images: Two light tiles and two dark tiles (to increase board variety). **ArrayList chessPieces** (line 26) stores all active **ChessPiece** objects and **int selectedIndex** (line 29) identifies the index in **chess-Pieces** of the currently selected piece. The **board** (line 30) is an 8-by-8, two-dimensional **int** array corresponding to the squares of a chess board. Each board element is an integer from 0 to 3 that corresponds to an index in **chessTile** and is used to specify the chessboard-square image. **const int TILESIZE** (line 33) defines the size of each tile in pixels.

The chess game GUI consists of **Form ChessGame**, the area in which we draw the tiles; **PictureBox pieceBox**, the window in which we draw the pieces (note that **pieceBox** background color is set to **"transparent"**); and a **Menu** that allows the user to begin a new game. Although the pieces and tiles could have been drawn on the same form, doing so would decrease performance. We would be forced to refresh the board as well as the pieces every time we refreshed the control.

The **ChessGame Load** event (lines 44–56) loads each tile image into **chessTile**. It then calls method **ResetBoard** to refresh the **Form** and begin the game. Method **Reset-Board** (lines 59–169) assigns **chessPieces** to a new **ArrayList**, loading images for both the black and the white chess-piece sets, and creates **Bitmap selected** to define the currently selected **Bitmap** set. Lines 82–167 loop through 64 positions on the chess board, setting the tile color and piece for each tile. Lines 86–87 cause the currently selected image to switch to the **blackPieces** after the fifth row. If the row counter is on the first or last row, lines 94–134 add a new piece to **chessPieces**. The type of the piece is based on the current column we are initializing. Pieces in chess are positioned in the following order, from left to right: Rook, knight, bishop, queen, king, bishop, knight and rook. Lines 137–146 add a new pawn at the current location if the current **row** is second or seventh.

A chess board is defined by alternating light and dark tiles across a row in a pattern where the color that starts each row is equal to the color of the last tile of the previous row. Lines 151–162 assign the current board-tile color as an index in the **board** array. Based on the alternating value of **bool** variable **light** and the results of the random operation on line 149, **0** and **1** are light tiles, whereas **2** and **3** are dark tiles. Line 166 inverts the value of **light** at the end of each row to maintain the staggered effect of a chess board.

```
1    // Fig. 13.26: ChessGame.cs
2    // Chess Game graphics code.
3
4    using System;
5    using System.Drawing;
6    using System.Collections;
7    using System.ComponentModel;
8    using System.Windows.Forms;
9    using System.Data;
10
11   // allows 2 players to play chess
12   public class ChessGame : System.Windows.Forms.Form
13   {
14       private System.Windows.Forms.PictureBox pieceBox;
15       private System.Windows.Forms.MainMenu GameMenu;
16       private System.Windows.Forms.MenuItem gameItem;
17       private System.Windows.Forms.MenuItem newGameItem;
18
19       private
20          System.ComponentModel.Container components = null;
21
22       // ArrayList for board tile images
23       ArrayList chessTile = new ArrayList();
24
25       // ArrayList for chess pieces
26       ArrayList chessPieces = new ArrayList();
27
28       // define index for selected piece
29       int selectedIndex = -1;
30       int[,] board = new int[ 8, 8 ]; // board array
31
32       // define chess tile size in pixels
33       private const int TILESIZE = 75;
34
35       [STAThread]
36       static void Main()
37       {
38          Application.Run( new ChessGame() );
39       }
40
41       // Visual Studio .NET generated code
42
```

Fig. 13.26 Chess-game code. (Part 1 of 8.)

```
43          // load tile bitmaps and reset game
44          private void ChessGame_Load(
45             object sender, System.EventArgs e)
46          {
47             // load chess board tiles
48             chessTile.Add( Bitmap.FromFile( "lightTile1.png" ) );
49             chessTile.Add( Bitmap.FromFile( "lightTile2.png" ) );
50             chessTile.Add( Bitmap.FromFile( "darkTile1.png" ) );
51             chessTile.Add( Bitmap.FromFile( "darkTile2.png" ) );
52
53             ResetBoard(); // initialize board
54             Invalidate(); // refresh form
55
56          } // end method ChessGame_Load
57
58          // initialize pieces to start and rebuild board
59          private void ResetBoard()
60          {
61             int current = -1;
62             ChessPiece piece;
63             Random random = new Random();
64             bool light = true;
65             int type;
66
67             // ensure empty arraylist
68             chessPieces = new ArrayList();
69
70             // load whitepieces image
71             Bitmap whitePieces =
72                ( Bitmap )Image.FromFile( "whitePieces.png" );
73
74             // load blackpieces image
75             Bitmap blackPieces =
76                ( Bitmap )Image.FromFile( "blackPieces.png" );
77
78             // set whitepieces drawn first
79             Bitmap selected = whitePieces;
80
81             // traverse board rows in outer loop
82             for ( int row = 0;
83                row <= board.GetUpperBound( 0 ); row++ )
84             {
85                // if at bottom rows, set to black pieces images
86                if ( row > 5 )
87                   selected = blackPieces;
88
89                // traverse board columns in inner loop
90                for ( int column = 0;
91                   column <= board.GetUpperBound( 1 ); column++ )
92                {
93                   // if first or last row, organize pieces
94                   if ( row == 0 || row == 7 )
95                   {
```

Fig. 13.26 Chess-game code. (Part 2 of 8.)

```
96                 switch( column )
97                 {
98                     case 0:
99                     case 7: // set current piece to rook
100                        current =
101                           ( int )ChessPiece.Types.ROOK;
102                        break;
103
104                     case 1:
105                     case 6: // set current piece to knight
106                        current =
107                           ( int )ChessPiece.Types.KNIGHT;
108                        break;
109
110                     case 2:
111                     case 5: // set current piece to bishop
112                        current =
113                           ( int )ChessPiece.Types.BISHOP;
114                        break;
115
116                     case 3: // set current piece to king
117                        current =
118                           ( int )ChessPiece.Types.KING;
119                        break;
120
121                     case 4: // set current piece to queen
122                        current =
123                           ( int )ChessPiece.Types.QUEEN;
124                        break;
125                 }
126
127                 // create current piece at start position
128                 piece = new ChessPiece( current,
129                    column * TILESIZE, row * TILESIZE,
130                    selected );
131
132                 // add piece to arraylist
133                 chessPieces.Add( piece );
134             }
135
136             // if second or seventh row, organize pawns
137             if ( row == 1 || row == 6 )
138             {
139                 piece = new ChessPiece(
140                    ( int )ChessPiece.Types.PAWN,
141                    column * TILESIZE, row * TILESIZE,
142                    selected );
143
144                 // add piece to arraylist
145                 chessPieces.Add( piece );
146             }
147
```

Fig. 13.26 Chess-game code. (Part 3 of 8.)

```
148                // determine board piece type
149                type = random.Next( 0, 2 );
150
151                if ( light )
152                {
153                   // set light tile
154                   board[ row, column ] = type;
155                   light = false;
156                }
157                else
158                {
159                   // set dark tile
160                   board[ row, column ] = type + 2;
161                   light = true;
162                }
163             }
164
165             // account for new row tile color switch
166             light = !light;
167          }
168
169       } // end method ResetBoard
170
171       // display board in form OnPaint event
172       private void ChessGame_Paint(
173          object sender, System.Windows.Forms.PaintEventArgs e)
174       {
175          // obtain graphics object
176          Graphics graphicsObject = e.Graphics;
177
178          for ( int row = 0;
179             row <= board.GetUpperBound( 0 ); row++ )
180          {
181             for ( int column = 0;
182                column <= board.GetUpperBound( 1 ); column++ )
183             {
184                // draw image specified in board array
185                graphicsObject.DrawImage(
186                   (Image)chessTile[ board[ row, column ] ],
187                   new Point( TILESIZE * column,
188                   TILESIZE * row ) );
189             }
190          }
191
192       } // end method ChessGame_Paint
193
194       // return index of piece that intersects point
195       // optionally exclude a value
196       private int CheckBounds( Point point, int exclude )
197       {
198          Rectangle rectangle; // current bounding rectangle
199
```

Fig. 13.26 Chess-game code. (Part 4 of 8.)

```
200          for ( int i = 0; i < chessPieces.Count; i++ )
201          {
202             // get piece rectangle
203             rectangle = GetPiece( i ).GetBounds();
204
205             // check if rectangle contains point
206             if ( rectangle.Contains( point ) && i != exclude )
207                return i;
208          }
209
210          return -1;
211
212       } // end method CheckBounds
213
214       // handle pieceBox paint event
215       private void pieceBox_Paint(
216          object sender, System.Windows.Forms.PaintEventArgs e)
217       {
218          // draw all pieces
219          for ( int i = 0; i < chessPieces.Count; i++ )
220             GetPiece( i ).Draw( e.Graphics );
221
222       } // end method pieceBox_Paint
223
224       private void pieceBox_MouseDown(
225          object sender, System.Windows.Forms.MouseEventArgs e)
226       {
227          // determine selected piece
228          selectedIndex =
229             CheckBounds( new Point( e.X, e.Y ), -1 );
230
231       } // end method pieceBox_MouseDown
232
233       // if piece is selected, move it
234       private void pieceBox_MouseMove(
235          object sender, System.Windows.Forms.MouseEventArgs e)
236       {
237          if ( selectedIndex > -1 )
238          {
239             Rectangle region = new Rectangle(
240                e.X - TILESIZE * 2, e.Y - TILESIZE * 2,
241                TILESIZE * 4, TILESIZE * 4 );
242
243             // set piece center to mouse
244             GetPiece( selectedIndex ).SetLocation(
245                e.X - TILESIZE / 2, e.Y - TILESIZE / 2 );
246
247             // refresh immediate area
248             pieceBox.Invalidate( region );
249          }
250
251       } // end method pieceBox_MouseMove
```

Fig. 13.26 Chess-game code. (Part 5 of 8.)

```
252
253    // on mouse up deselect piece and remove taken piece
254    private void pieceBox_MouseUp(
255       object sender, System.Windows.Forms.MouseEventArgs e)
256    {
257       int remove = -1;
258
259       //if chess piece was selected
260       if ( selectedIndex > -1 )
261       {
262          Point current = new Point( e.X, e.Y );
263          Point newPoint = new Point(
264             current.X - ( current.X % TILESIZE ),
265             current.Y - ( current.Y % TILESIZE ) );
266
267          // check bounds with point, exclude selected piece
268          remove = CheckBounds( current, selectedIndex );
269
270          // snap piece into center of closest square
271          GetPiece( selectedIndex ).SetLocation( newPoint.X,
272             newPoint.Y );
273
274          // deselect piece
275          selectedIndex = -1;
276
277          // remove taken piece
278          if ( remove > -1 )
279             chessPieces.RemoveAt( remove );
280       }
281
282       // refresh pieceBox to ensure artifact removal
283       pieceBox.Invalidate();
284
285    } // end method pieceBox_MouseUp
286
287    // helper function to convert
288    // ArrayList object to ChessPiece
289    private ChessPiece GetPiece( int i )
290    {
291       return (ChessPiece)chessPieces[ i ];
292    } // end method GetPiece
293
294    // handle NewGame menu option click
295    private void newGameItem_Click(
296       object sender, System.EventArgs e)
297    {
298       ResetBoard(); // reinitialize board
299       Invalidate(); // refresh form
300
301    } // end method newGameItem_Click
302
303 } // end class ChessGame
```

Fig. 13.26 Chess-game code. (Part 6 of 8.)

Fig. 13.26 Chess-game code. (Part 7 of 8.)

Fig. 13.26 Chess-game code. (Part 8 of 8.)

Method **ChessGame_Paint** (lines 172–192) handles this class **Form**'s **Paint** event and draws the tiles according to their values in the board array. Method **pieceBox_Paint**, which handles the **pieceBox PictureBox paint** event, iterates through each element of the **chessPiece ArrayList** and calls its **Draw** method.

The **MouseDown** event handler (lines 224–231) calls method **CheckBounds** with the location of the user's click to determine whether the user selected a piece. **Check-Bounds** returns an integer locating a collision from a given point.

The **MouseMove** event handler (lines 234–251) moves the currently selected piece with the mouse. Lines 244–245 set the selected piece location to the mouse-cursor position, adjusting the location by up to half a tile to center the image on the mouse. Lines 239–241 define and refresh a region of the **PictureBox** that spans two tiles in every direction from the mouse. As mentioned earlier in the chapter, the **Invalidate** method is slow. This means that the **MouseMove** event handler might be called again several times before the **Invalidate** method completes. If a user working on a slow computer moves the mouse quickly, the application could leave behind *artifacts*. An artifact is any unintended visual abnormality in a graphical program. By causing the program to refresh a two-square rectangle, which should suffice in most cases, we achieve a significant performance enhancement over an entire component refresh during each **MouseMove** event.

Lines 254–285 define the **MouseUp** event handler. If a piece has been selected, lines 260–280 determine the index in **chessPieces** of any piece collision, remove the collided piece, snap (align) the current piece into a valid location and deselect the piece. We check for piece collisions to allow the chess piece to "take" other chess pieces. Line 268 checks whether any piece (excluding the currently selected piece) is beneath the current mouse location. If a collision is detected, the returned piece index is assigned to **int remove**. Lines 271–272 determine the closest valid chess tile and "snap" the selected piece to that location. If **remove** contains a positive value, line 279 removes the object at that index from the **chessPieces ArrayList**. Finally, the entire **PictureBox** is **Invalidate**d in line 283 to display the new piece location and remove any artifacts created during the move.

Method **CheckBounds** (lines 196–212) is a collision-detection helper method; it iterates through the **chessPieces ArrayList** and returns the index of any piece rectangle containing the point value passed to the method (the mouse location, in this example). Method **CheckBounds** optionally can exclude a single piece index (to ignore the selected index in the **MouseUp** event handler, in this example).

Lines 289–292 define helper function **GetPiece**, which simplifies the conversion from **object**s in the **ArrayList chessPieces** to **ChessPiece** types. Method **newGameItem_Click** handles the **NewGame** menu item click event, calls **Refresh-Board** to reset the game and **Invalidate**s the entire form.

13.12 Windows Media Player

The Windows Media Player control enables an application to play video and sound in many multimedia formats. These include MPEG (Motion Pictures Experts Group) audio and video, AVI (audio-video interleave) video, WAV (Windows wave-file format) audio and MIDI (Musical Instrument Digital Interface) audio. Users can find preexisting audio and video on the Internet, or they can create their own files, using available sound and graphics packages.

The application in Fig. 13.27 demonstrates the Windows Media Player control, which enables users to play multimedia files. To use the Windows Media Player control, programmers must add the control to the **Toolbox**. This is accomplished by first selecting **Customize Toolbox** from the **Tool** menu to display the **Customize Toolbox** dialog box. In the dialog box, scroll down and select the option **Windows Media Player**. Then, click the **OK** button to dismiss the dialog box. The icon for the Windows Media Player control now should appear at the bottom of the **Toolbox**.

```
1   // Fig. 13.27: MediaPlayerTest.cs
2   // Demonstrates the Windows Media Player control
3
4   using System;
5   using System.Drawing;
6   using System.Collections;
7   using System.ComponentModel;
8   using System.Windows.Forms;
9   using System.Data;
10
11  // allows users to play media files using a
12  // Windows Media Player control
13  public class MediaPlayer : System.Windows.Forms.Form
14  {
15      private System.Windows.Forms.MainMenu applicationMenu;
```

Fig. 13.27 Windows Media Player demonstration. (Part 1 of 3.)

```
16        private System.Windows.Forms.MenuItem fileItem;
17        private System.Windows.Forms.MenuItem openItem;
18        private System.Windows.Forms.MenuItem exitItem;
19        private System.Windows.Forms.MenuItem aboutItem;
20        private System.Windows.Forms.MenuItem aboutMessageItem;
21        private System.Windows.Forms.OpenFileDialog
22           openMediaFileDialog;
23        private AxMediaPlayer.AxMediaPlayer player;
24
25        private
26           System.ComponentModel.Container components = null;
27
28        [STAThread]
29        static void Main()
30        {
31           Application.Run( new MediaPlayer() );
32        }
33
34        // Visual Studio .NET generated code
35
36        // open new media file in Windows Media Player
37        private void openItem_Click(
38           object sender, System.EventArgs e)
39        {
40           openMediaFileDialog.ShowDialog();
41
42           player.FileName = openMediaFileDialog.FileName;
43
44           // adjust the size of the Media Player control and
45           // the Form according to the size of the image
46           player.Size = new Size( player.ImageSourceWidth,
47              player.ImageSourceHeight );
48
49           this.Size = new Size( player.Size.Width + 20,
50              player.Size.Height + 60 );
51
52        } // end method openItem_Click
53
54        private void exitItem_Click(
55           object sender, System.EventArgs e)
56        {
57           Application.Exit();
58
59        } // end method exitItem_Click
60
61        private void aboutMessageItem_Click(
62           object sender, System.EventArgs e)
63        {
64           player.AboutBox();
65
66        } // end method aboutMessageItem_Click
67
68     } // end class MediaPlayer
```

Fig. 13.27 Windows Media Player demonstration. (Part 2 of 3.)

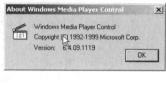

Fig. 13.27 Windows Media Player demonstration. (Part 3 of 3.)

The Windows Media Player control provides several buttons that allow the user to play the current file, pause, stop, play the previous file, rewind, forward and play the next file. The control also includes a volume control and trackbars to select a specific position in the media file.

The application provides a **MainMenu**, which includes **File** and **About** menus. The **File** menu contains the **Open** and **Exit** menu items; the **About** menu contains the **About Windows Media Player** menu item.

When a user chooses **Open** from the **File** menu, event handler **openItem_Click** (lines 37–52) executes. An **OpenFileDialog** box displays (line 40), allowing the user to select a file. The program then sets the **FileName** property of the player (the Windows Media Player control object of type **AxMediaPlayer**) to the name of the file chosen by the user. The **FileName** property specifies the file that Windows Media Player currently is using. Lines 46–50 adjust the size of **player** and the application to reflect the size of the media contained in the file.

The event handler that executes when the user selects **Exit** from the **File** menu (lines 54–59) simply calls **Application.Exit** to terminate the application. The event handler that executes when the user chooses **About Windows Media Player** from the **About** menu (lines 61–66) calls the **AboutBox** method of the player. **AboutBox** simply displays a preset message box containing information about Windows Media Player.

13.13 Microsoft Agent

Microsoft Agent is a technology used to add *interactive animated characters* to Windows applications or Web pages. Interactivity is the key function of Microsoft Agent technology: Microsoft Agent characters can speak and respond to user input via speech recognition and synthesis. Microsoft employs its Agent technology in applications such as Word, Excel and PowerPoint. Agents in these programs aid users in finding answers to questions and in understanding how the applications function.

The Microsoft Agent control provides programmers with access to four predefined characters—*Genie* (a genie), *Merlin* (a wizard), *Peedy* (a parrot) and *Robby* (a robot). Each character has a unique set of animations that programmers can use in their applications to illustrate different points and functions. For instance, the Peedy character-animation set includes different flying animations, which the programmer might use to move Peedy on the screen. Microsoft provides basic information on Agent technology at its Web site,

> **www.microsoft.com/msagent**

Microsoft Agent technology enables users to interact with applications and Web pages through speech, the most natural form of human communication. When the user speaks into a microphone, the control uses a *speech recognition engine,* an application that translates vocal sound input from a microphone into language that the computer understands. The Microsoft Agent control also uses a *text-to-speech engine*, which generates characters' spoken responses. A text-to-speech engine is an application that translates typed words into audio sound that users hear through headphones or speakers connected to a computer. Microsoft provides speech recognition and text-to-speech engines for several languages at its Web site,

> **www.microsoft.com/products/msagent/downloads.htm**

Programmers can even create their own animated characters with the help of the *Microsoft Agent Character Editor* and the *Microsoft Linguistic Sound Editing Tool*. These products are available free for download from

> **www.microsoft.com/products/msagent/devdownloads.htm**

This section introduces the basic capabilities of the Microsoft Agent control. For complete details on downloading this control, visit

> **www.microsoft.com/products/msagent/downloads.htm**

The following example, Peedy's Pizza Palace, was developed by Microsoft to illustrate the capabilities of the Microsoft Agent control. Peedy's Pizza Palace is an online pizza shop where users can place their orders via voice input. The Peedy character interacts with users by helping them choose toppings and then calculating the totals for their orders.

Readers can view this example at

agent.microsoft.com/agent2/sdk/samples/html/peedypza.htm

To run this example, readers must download the Peedy character file, a text-to-speech engine and a speech-recognition engine. When the page loads, the browser prompts for these downloads. Follow the directions provided by Microsoft to complete installation.

When the window opens, Peedy introduces himself (Fig. 13.28), and the words he speaks appear in a cartoon bubble above his head. Notice that Peedy's animations correspond to the words he speaks.

Programmers can synchronize character animations with speech output to illustrate a point or to convey a character's mood. For instance, Fig. 13.29 depicts Peedy's *Pleased* animation. The Peedy character-animation set includes eighty-five different animations, each of which is unique to the Peedy character.

Look-and-Feel Observation 13.1

Agent characters remain on top of all active windows while a Microsoft Agent application is running. Their motions are not limited to within the boundaries of the browser or application window.

Peedy also responds to input from the keyboard and mouse. Figure 13.30 shows what happens when a user clicks Peedy with the mouse pointer. Peedy jumps up, ruffles his feathers and exclaims, "Hey that tickles!" or, "Be careful with that pointer!" Users can relocate Peedy on the screen by clicking and dragging him with the mouse. However, even when the user moves Peedy to a different part of the screen, he continues to perform his preset animations and location changes.

Bubble contains text equivalent to words Peedy speaks —

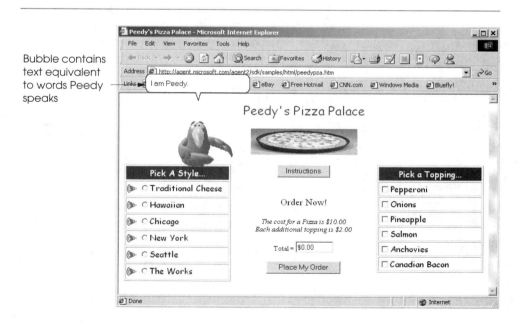

Fig. 13.28 Peedy introducing himself when the window opens.

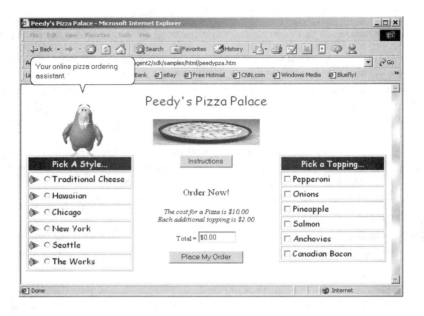

Fig. 13.29 Peedy's *Pleased* animation.

Fig. 13.30 Peedy's reaction when he is clicked.

Many location changes involve animations. For instance, Peedy can hop from one screen location to another, or he can fly (Fig. 13.31).

Fig. 13.31 Peedy flying animation.

Once Peedy completes the ordering instructions, a text box appears beneath him indicating that he is listening for a voice command (Fig. 13.32). A user can enter the type of pizza to order either by speaking the style name into a microphone or by clicking the radio button corresponding to their choice.

If a user chooses speech input, a box appears below Peedy displaying the words that Peedy "heard" (i.e., the words translated to the program by the speech-recognition engine). Once he recognizes the user input, Peedy gives the user a description of the selected pizza. Figure 13.33 shows what happens when the user chooses **Seattle** as the pizza style.

Peedy then asks the user to choose additional toppings. Again, the user can either speak or use the mouse to make a selection. Check boxes corresponding to toppings that come with the selected pizza style are checked for the user. Figure 13.34 shows what happens when a user chooses anchovies as an additional topping. Peedy makes a wisecrack about the user's choice.

The user can submit the order either by pressing the **Place My Order** button or by speaking "Place order" into the microphone. Peedy recounts the order while writing down the order items on his notepad (Fig. 13.35). He then calculates the figures on his calculator and reports the total to the user (Fig. 13.36).

The following example (Fig. 13.37) demonstrates how to build a simple application with the Microsoft Agent control. This application contains two drop-down lists from which the user can choose an Agent character and a character animation. When the user chooses from these lists, the chosen character appears and performs the chosen animation. The application uses speech recognition and synthesis to control the character animations and speech: Users can tell the character which animation to perform by pressing the *Scroll Lock* key and then speaking the animation name into a microphone.

Fig. 13.32 Peedy waiting for speech input.

Text box
indicates that
Peedy is waiting
for user input

Radio buttons
corresponding
to different
pizza styles

Text box
indicates
recognized
speech

Fig. 13.33 Peedy repeating the user's request for Seattle-style pizza.

Fig. 13.34 Peedy repeating the user's request for anchovies as an additional topping.

Fig. 13.35 Peedy recounting the order.

Fig. 13.36 Peedy calculating the total.

The example also allows the user to switch to a new character by speaking its name and also creates a custom command, **MoveToMouse**. In addition, the characters also speak any text that a user enters into the text box. Before running this example, readers first must download and install the control, speech-recognition engine, text-to-speech engine and character definitions from the Microsoft Agent Web site listed previously.

To use the Microsoft Agent control, the programmer first must add it to the **Toolbox**. Begin by selecting **Customize Toolbox** from the **Tools** menu to display the **Customize Toolbox** dialog. In the dialog, scroll down and select the option **Microsoft Agent Control 2.0**. When this option is selected properly, a small check mark appears in the box to the left of the option. Then, click **OK** to dismiss the dialog. The icon for the Microsoft Agent control now should appear at the bottom of the **Toolbox**.

In addition to the Microsoft Agent object **mainAgent** (of type **AxAgent**) that manages all the characters, we also need an object (of type **IAgentCtlCharacter**) to represent the current character. We create this object, named **speaker**, in line 30.

```
1   // Fig. 13.37: Agent.cs
2   // Demonstrates microsoft agent
3
4   using System;
5   using System.Drawing;
6   using System.Collections;
7   using System.ComponentModel;
8   using System.Windows.Forms;
9   using System.Data;
```

Fig. 13.37 Microsoft Agent demonstration. (Part 1 of 7.)

```
10   using System.IO;
11
12   public class Agent : System.Windows.Forms.Form
13   {
14      // options
15      private System.Windows.Forms.ComboBox actionsCombo;
16      private System.Windows.Forms.ComboBox characterCombo;
17
18      private System.Windows.Forms.Button speakButton;
19      private System.Windows.Forms.GroupBox characterGroup;
20      private AxAgentObjects.AxAgent mainAgent;
21
22      // input
23      private System.Windows.Forms.TextBox speechTextBox;
24      private System.Windows.Forms.TextBox locationTextBox;
25
26      private
27         System.ComponentModel.Container components = null;
28
29      // current agent object
30      private AgentObjects.IAgentCtlCharacter speaker;
31
32      [STAThread]
33      static void Main()
34      {
35         Application.Run( new Agent() );
36      }
37
38      // Visual Studio .NET generated code
39
40      // KeyDown event handler for locationTextBox
41      private void locationTextBox_KeyDown(
42         object sender, System.Windows.Forms.KeyEventArgs e )
43      {
44         if ( e.KeyCode == Keys.Enter )
45         {
46            // set character location to text box value
47            string location = locationTextBox.Text;
48
49            // initialize the characters
50            try
51            {
52               // load characters into agent object
53               mainAgent.Characters.Load( "Genie",
54                  location + "Genie.acs" );
55
56               mainAgent.Characters.Load( "Merlin",
57                  location + "Merlin.acs" );
58
59               mainAgent.Characters.Load( "Peedy",
60                  location + "Peedy.acs" );
61
```

Fig. 13.37 Microsoft Agent demonstration. (Part 2 of 7.)

```
62                    mainAgent.Characters.Load( "Robby",
63                       location + "Robby.acs" );
64
65                    // disable TextBox for entering the location
66                    // and enable other controls
67                    locationTextBox.Enabled = false;
68                    speechTextBox.Enabled = true;
69                    speakButton.Enabled = true;
70                    characterCombo.Enabled = true;
71                    actionsCombo.Enabled = true;
72
73                    // set current character to Genie and show him
74                    speaker = mainAgent.Characters[ "Genie" ];
75
76                    // obtain an animation name list
77                    GetAnimationNames();
78                    speaker.Show( 0 );
79                 }
80                 catch( FileNotFoundException )
81                 {
82                    MessageBox.Show( "Invalid character location",
83                       "Error", MessageBoxButtons.OK,
84                       MessageBoxIcon.Error );
85                 }
86              }
87
88        } // end method locationTextBox_KeyDown
89
90        private void speakButton_Click(
91           object sender, System.EventArgs e )
92        {
93           // if textbox is empty, have the character ask
94           // user to type the words into textbox, otherwise
95           // have character say the words in textbox
96           if ( speechTextBox.Text == "" )
97              speaker.Speak(
98                 "Please, type the words you want me to speak",
99                 "" );
100          else
101             speaker.Speak( speechTextBox.Text, "" );
102
103       } // end method speakButton_Click
104
105       // click event for agent
106       private void mainAgent_ClickEvent( object sender,
107          AxAgentObjects._AgentEvents_ClickEvent e )
108       {
109          speaker.Play( "Confused" );
110          speaker.Speak( "Why are you poking me?", "" );
111          speaker.Play( "RestPose" );
112
113       } // end method mainAgent_ClickEvent
114
```

Fig. 13.37 Microsoft Agent demonstration. (Part 3 of 7.)

```
115    // combobox changed event, switch active agent
116    private void characterCombo_SelectedIndexChanged(
117       object sender, System.EventArgs e )
118    {
119       ChangeCharacter( characterCombo.Text );
120
121    } // end method characterCombo_SelectedIndexChanged
122
123    private void ChangeCharacter( string name )
124    {
125       speaker.Hide( 0 );
126       speaker = mainAgent.Characters[ name ];
127
128       // regenerate animation name list
129       GetAnimationNames();
130       speaker.Show( 0 );
131
132    } // end method ChangeCharacter
133
134    // get animation names and store in arraylist
135    private void GetAnimationNames()
136    {
137       // ensure thread safety
138       lock( this )
139       {
140
141          // get animation names
142          IEnumerator enumerator =
143             mainAgent.Characters[
144             speaker.Name ].AnimationNames.GetEnumerator();
145
146          string voiceString;
147
148          // clear actionsCombo
149          actionsCombo.Items.Clear();
150          speaker.Commands.RemoveAll();
151
152          // copy enumeration to ArrayList
153          while ( enumerator.MoveNext() )
154          {
155             //remove underscores in speech string
156             voiceString = ( string )enumerator.Current;
157             voiceString =
158                voiceString.Replace( "_", "underscore" );
159
160             actionsCombo.Items.Add( enumerator.Current );
161
162             // add all animations as voice enabled commands
163             speaker.Commands.Add(
164                ( string )enumerator.Current,
165                enumerator.Current,
166                voiceString, true, false );
167          }
```

Fig. 13.37 Microsoft Agent demonstration. (Part 4 of 7.)

```
168
169             // add custom command
170             speaker.Commands.Add(
171                "MoveToMouse", "MoveToMouse",
172                "MoveToMouse", true, true );
173          }
174
175       } // end method GetAnimationNames
176
177       // user selects new action
178       private void actionsCombo_SelectedIndexChanged(
179          object sender, System.EventArgs e )
180       {
181          speaker.StopAll( "Play" );
182          speaker.Play( actionsCombo.Text );
183          speaker.Play( "RestPose" );
184
185       } // end method actionsCombo_SelectedIndexChanged
186
187       // handles agent commands
188       private void mainAgent_Command( object sender,
189          AxAgentObjects._AgentEvents_CommandEvent e )
190       {
191          // get userInput property
192          AgentObjects.IAgentCtlUserInput command =
193             ( AgentObjects.IAgentCtlUserInput )e.userInput;
194
195          // change character if user speaks character name
196          if ( command.Voice == "Peedy" ||
197             command.Voice == "Robby" ||
198             command.Voice == "Merlin" ||
199             command.Voice == "Genie" )
200          {
201             ChangeCharacter( command.Voice );
202
203             return;
204          }
205
206          // send agent to mouse
207          if ( command.Voice == "MoveToMouse" )
208          {
209             speaker.MoveTo(
210                Convert.ToInt16( Cursor.Position.X - 60 ),
211                Convert.ToInt16( Cursor.Position.Y - 60 ), 5 );
212             return;
213          }
214
215          // play new animation
216          speaker.StopAll( "Play" );
217          speaker.Play( command.Name );
218
219       } // end method mainAgent_Command
220    } // end class Agent
```

Fig. 13.37 Microsoft Agent demonstration. (Part 5 of 7.)

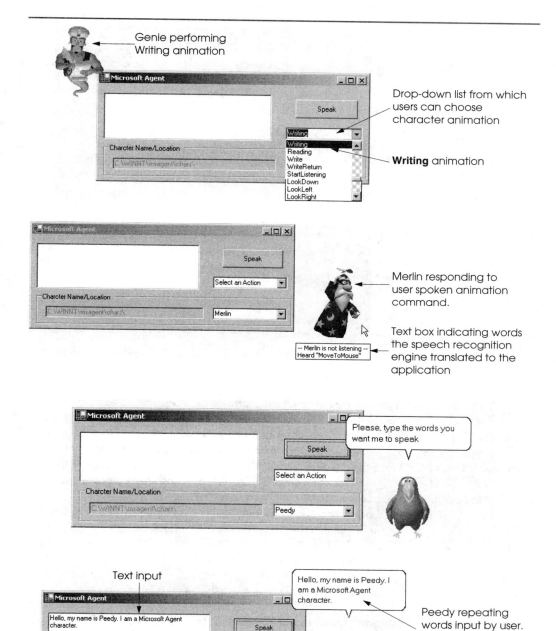

Genie performing Writing animation

Drop-down list from which users can choose character animation

Writing animation

Merlin responding to user spoken animation command.

Text box indicating words the speech recognition engine translated to the application

Please, type the words you want me to speak

Text input

Hello, my name is Peedy. I am a Microsoft Agent character.

Peedy repeating words input by user. Peedy's speech can be heard through computer audio output.

Fig. 13.37 Microsoft Agent demonstration. (Part 6 of 7.)

Fig. 13.37 Microsoft Agent demonstration. (Part 7 of 7.)

When the program begins, the only enabled control is the **locationTextBox**. This text box contains the default location for the character files, but the user can change this location if the files are located elsewhere on the user's computer. Once the user presses *Enter* in the **TextBox**, event handler **locationTextBox_KeyDown** (lines 41–88) executes. Lines 53–63 load the character descriptions for the predefined animated characters. If the specified location of the characters is incorrect, or if any character is missing, a **FileNotFoundException** is thrown.

Lines 67–71 disable **locationTextBox** and enable the rest of the controls. Lines 74–78 set Genie as the default character, obtain all animation names via method **GetAnimationNames** and then call **IAgentCtlCharacter** method *Show* to display the character. We access characters through property *Characters* of **mainAgent**, which contains all characters that have been loaded. We use the indexer of the **Characters** property to specify the name of the character that we wish to load (Genie).

When a user clicks the character (i.e., pokes it with the mouse), event handler **mainAgent_ClickEvent** (lines 106–113) executes. First, **speaker** method **Play** plays an animation. This method accepts as an argument a **string** representing one of the predefined animations for the character (a list of animations for each character is available at the Microsoft Agent Web site; each character provides over 70 animations). In our example, the argument to **Play** is **"Confused"**—this animation is defined for all four characters, each of which expresses this emotion in a unique way. The character then speaks, **"Why are you poking me?"** via a call to method *Speak*. Finally, the *RestPose* animation is played, which returns the character to its neutral, resting pose.

The list of valid commands for a character is contained in property **Commands** of the **IAgentCtlCharacter** object (**speaker**, in this example). The commands for an Agent character can be viewed in the **Commands** pop-up window, which displays when the user right-clicks an Agent character (the last screenshot in Fig. 13.37). Method **Add** of property **Commands** adds a new command to the command list. Method **Add** takes three **string** arguments and two **bool** arguments. The first **string** argument identifies the name of the command, which we use to identify the command programmatically. The second **string** defines the command name as it appears in the **Commands** pop-up window. The third **string** defines the voice input that triggers the command. The first **bool** specifies whether the command is active, and the second **bool** indicates whether the command is visible in the **Commands** pop-up window. A command is triggered when the user selects the command from the **Commands** pop-up window or speaks the voice input into a microphone. Command logic is handled in the **Command** event of the **AxAgent** control (**mainAgent**, in this example). In addition, Agent defines several global commands that have predefined functions (for example, speaking a character name causes that character to appear).

Method **GetAnimationNames** (lines 135–175) fills the **actionsCombo** ComboBox with the current character's animation listing and defines the valid commands that can be used with the character. The method contains a **lock** block to prevent errors resulting from rapid character changes. The method obtains the current character's animations as an enumerator (142–144), then clears the existing items in the **ComboBox** and character's **Commands** property. Lines 153–167 iterate through all items in the animation-name enumerator. For each animation, in line 156, we assign the animation name to **string voiceString**. Lines 157–158 remove any underscore characters (_) and replaces them with the **string "underscore"**; this changes the **string** so that a user can pronounce and employ it as a command activator. The **Add** method (lines 163–166) of the **Commands** property adds a new command to the current character. The **Add** method adds all animations as commands by providing the following arguments: The animation name as the new command's **name** and caption, and **voiceString** for the voice activation **string**. The method's **bool** arguments enable the command, but make it unavailable in the **Commands** pop-up window. Thus, the command can be activated only by voice input. Lines 170–172 create a new command, named **MoveToMouse**, which is visible in the **Commands** pop-up window.

After the **GetAnimationNames** method has been called, the user can select a value from the **actionsCombo** ComboBox. Event handler **actionsCombo.SelectedIndexChanged** stops any current animation and then displays the animation that the user selected from the **ComboBox**.

The user also can type text into the **TextBox** and click **Speak**. This causes event handler **speakButton_Click** (line 90–103) to call **speaker**'s method **Speak**, supplying as an argument the text in **speechTextBox**. If the user clicks **Speak** without providing text, the character speaks, **"Please, type the words you want me to speak"**.

At any point in the program, the user can choose to display a different character from the **ComboBox**. When this happens, the **SelectedIndexChanged** event handler for **characterCombo** (lines 116–121) executes. The event handler calls method **ChangeCharacter** (lines 123–132) with the text in the **characterCombo ComboBox** as an argument. Method **ChangeCharacter** calls the **Hide** method of **speaker** (line 125) to remove the current character from view. Line 126 assigns the newly selected character to **speaker**, line 129 generates the character's animation names and commands, and line 130 displays the character via a call to method **Show**.

Each time a user presses the *Scroll Lock* key and speaks into a microphone or selects a command from the **Commands** pop-up window, event handler **main-Agent_Command** is called. This method is passed an argument of type **AxAgentObjects._AgentEvents_CommandEvent**, which contains a single property, **userInput**. The **userInput** property returns an **Object** that can be converted to type **AgentObjects.IAgentCtlUserInput**. The **userInput** object is assigned to a **IAgentCtlUserInput** object **command**, which is used to identify the command and take appropriate action. Lines 196–204 use method **ChangeCharacter** to change the current Agent character if the user speaks a character name. Microsoft Agent always will show a character when a user speaks its name; however, by controlling the character change, we can ensure that only one Agent character is displayed at a time. Lines 207–213 move the character to the current mouse location if the user invokes the **MoveToMouse** command. The Agent method *MoveTo* takes *x*- and *y*-coordinate arguments and moves the character to the specified screen position, applying appropriate movement animations. For all other commands, we **Play** the command name as an animation on line 217.

In this chapter, we have explored various graphics capabilities of GDI+, including pens, brushes, images and some multimedia capabilities of the .NET Framework Class Library. In the next chapter, we cover the reading, writing and accessing of sequential- and random-access files. We also explore several types of streams included in Visual Studio .NET.

13.14 Summary

A coordinate system identifies every possible point on the screen. The upper left corner of a GUI component has coordinates (0, 0). A coordinate pair is composed of an *x*-coordinate (the horizontal coordinate) and a *y*-coordinate (the vertical coordinate). Coordinate units are measured in pixels. A pixel is the smallest unit of resolution on a display monitor.

A graphics context represents a drawing surface on the screen. A **Graphics** object provides access to the graphics context of a control. **Graphics** objects contain methods for drawing, font manipulation, color manipulation and other graphics-related actions.

Class **Graphics** provides methods **DrawLine**, **DrawRectangle**, **DrawEllipse**, **DrawArc**, **DrawLines**, **DrawPolygon** and **DrawPie**, which draw lines and outlines of shapes. Methods **FillRectangle**, **FillEllipse**, **FillPolygon** and **FillPie** draw solid shapes. Classes **HatchBrush**, **LinearGradientBrush**, **PathGradientBrush** and **TextureBrush** all derive from class **Brush** and represent shape-filling styles.

Method **OnPaint** normally is called in response to an event, such as the uncovering of a window. This method, in turn, triggers a **Paint** event.

Structure **Color** defines constants for manipulating colors in a C# program. **Color** properties **R**, **G** and **B** return **int** values from 0 to 255, representing the amounts of red, green and blue, respectively, that exist in a **Color**. The larger the value for a particular color, the greater is the amount of that color.

Class **Font**'s constructors all take at least three arguments—the font name, the font size and the font style. The font name can be that of any font currently supported by the system. The font style is a member of the **FontStyle** enumeration. Class **FontMetrics** defines several methods for obtaining font metrics (e.g., ascent and descent). The

FontFamily class provides information about such font metrics as the family's spacing and height.

Using Visual Studio .NET and C#, programmers can create applications that use components such as Windows Media Player and Microsoft Agent. Windows Media Player allows programmers to create applications that can play multimedia files. Microsoft Agent is a technology that allows programmers to include interactive animated characters in their applications.

Files and Streams

Objectives

- To create, read, write and update files.
- To understand the C# streams class hierarchy.
- To use classes **File** and **Directory**.
- To use the **FileStream** and **BinaryFormatter** classes to read objects from, and write objects to, files.
- To become familiar with sequential-access and random-access file processing.

I can only assume that a "Do Not File" document is filed in a "Do Not File" file.
Senator Frank Church
Senate Intelligence Subcommittee Hearing, 1975

Consciousness … does not appear to itself chopped up in bits. … A "river" or a "stream" are the metaphors by which it is most naturally described.
William James

I read part of it all the way through.
Samuel Goldwyn

Outline

14.1   Introduction
14.2   Data Hierarchy
14.3   Files and Streams
17.4   Classes `File` and `Directory`
14.5   Creating a Sequential-Access File
14.6   Reading Data from a Sequential-Access File
14.7   Random-Access Files
14.8   Creating a Random-Access File
14.9   Writing Data Randomly to a Random-Access File
14.10 Reading Data Sequentially from a Random-Access File
14.11 Case Study: A Transaction-Processing Program
14.12 Summary

14.1 Introduction

Variables and arrays offer only temporary storage of data—the data are lost when an object is garbage collected or when the program terminates. By contrast, *files* are used for long-term storage of large amounts of data and can retain data even after the program that created the data terminates. Data maintained in files often are called *persistent data*. Computers can store files on *secondary storage devices*, such as magnetic disks, optical disks and magnetic tapes. In this chapter, we explain how to create, update and process data files in C# programs. We consider both "sequential-access" files and "random-access" files, indicating the kinds of applications for which each is best suited. We have two goals in this chapter: To introduce the sequential-access and random-access file-processing paradigms and to provide the reader with sufficient stream-processing capabilities to support the networking features that we introduce in Chapter 19, Networking: Streams-Based Sockets and Datagrams.

File processing is one of the most important capabilities of a programming language, because it enables a language to support commercial applications that typically process massive amounts of persistent data. This chapter discusses C#'s powerful and abundant file-processing and stream-input/output features.

14.2 Data Hierarchy

Ultimately, all data items processed by a computer are reduced to combinations of zeros and ones. This is because it is simple and economical to build electronic devices that can assume two stable states—**0** represents one state, and **1** represents the other. It is remarkable that the impressive functions performed by computers involve only the most fundamental manipulations of **0**s and **1**s.

The smallest data items that computers support are called *bits* (short for "binary digit"—a digit that can assume one of two values). Each data item, or bit, can assume either the value **0** or the value **1**. Computer circuitry performs various simple bit manipulations, such as examining the value of a bit, setting the value of a bit and reversing a bit (from **1** to **0** or from **0** to **1**).

Programming with data in the low-level form of bits is cumbersome. It is preferable to program with data in forms such as *decimal digits* (i.e., 0, 1, 2, 3, 4, 5, 6, 7, 8 and 9), *letters* (i.e., A through Z and a through z) and *special symbols* (i.e., $, @, %, &, *, (,), -, +, ", :, ?, / and many others). Digits, letters and special symbols are referred to as *characters.* The set of all characters used to write programs and represent data items on a particular computer is called that computer's *character set.* Because computers can process only **1**s and **0**s, every character in a computer's character set is represented as a pattern of **1**s and **0**s. *Bytes* are composed of eight bits (characters in C# are *Unicode* characters, which are composed of 2 bytes). Programmers create programs and data items with characters; computers manipulate and process these characters as patterns of bits.

In the same way that characters are composed of bits, *fields* are composed of characters. A field is a group of characters that conveys some meaning. For example, a field consisting of uppercase and lowercase letters can represent a person's name.

The various kinds of data items processed by computers form a *data hierarchy* (Fig. 14.1) in which data items become larger and more complex in structure as we progress from bits, to characters, to fields and up to larger data structures.

Typically, a *record* is composed of several fields. In a payroll system, for example, a record for a particular employee might include the following fields:

1. Employee identification number

2. Name

3. Address

4. Hourly pay rate

5. Number of exemptions claimed

6. Year-to-date earnings

7. Amount of taxes withheld

Thus, a record is a group of related fields. In the preceding example, each field is associated with the same employee. A *file* is a group of related records.[1] A company's payroll file normally contains one record for each employee. Thus, a payroll file for a small company might contain only 22 records, whereas a payroll file for a large company might contain 100,000 records. It is not unusual for a company to have many files, some containing millions, billions or even trillions of bits of information.

To facilitate the retrieval of specific records from a file, at least one field in each record is chosen as a unique *record key.* A record key identifies a record as belonging to a particular person or entity and distinguishes that record from all other records. In the payroll record described previously, the employee identification number normally would be chosen as the record key.

---

1. More generally, a file can contain arbitrary data in arbitrary formats. In some operating systems, a file is viewed as nothing more than a collection of bytes. In such an operating system, any organization of the bytes in a file (such as organizing the data into records) is a view created by the applications programmer.

Fig. 14.1   Data hierarchy.

There are many ways of organizing records in a file. The most common type of organization is called a *sequential file*, in which records typically are stored in order by the record-key field. In a payroll file, records usually are placed in order by employee-identification numbers. The first employee record in the file contains the lowest employee-identification number, and subsequent records contain increasingly higher employee-identification numbers.

Most businesses use many different files to store data. For example, a company might have payroll files, accounts receivable files (listing money due from clients), accounts payable files (listing money due to suppliers), inventory files (listing facts about all the items handled by the business) and many other types of files. Sometimes, a group of related files is called a *database*. A collection of programs designed to create and manage databases is called a *database management system* (DBMS). We discuss databases in detail in Chapter 16, Database, SQL and ADO .NET.

14.3 Files and Streams

C# views each file as a sequential *stream* of bytes (Fig. 14.2). Each file ends either with an *end-of-file marker* or at a specific byte number that is recorded in a system-maintained administrative data structure. When a file is *opened*, C# creates an object, then associates a stream with that object. The runtime environment creates three stream objects upon program execution, which are accessible via properties **Console.Out**, **Console.In** and **Console.Error**, respectively. These objects facilitate communication between a program and a particular file or device. Property **Console.In** returns the *standard input* *stream object*, which enables a program to input data from the keyboard. Property **Console.Out** returns the *standard output stream object*, which enables a program to output data to the screen. Property **Console.Error** returns the *standard error stream object*, which enables a program to output error messages to the screen. We have been using **Console.Out** and **Console.In** in our console applications—**Console** methods **Write** and **WriteLine** use **Console.Out** to perform output, and methods **Read** and **ReadLine** use **Console.In** to perform input.

To perform file processing in C#, namespace **System.IO** must be referenced. This namespace includes definitions for stream classes such as *StreamReader* (for text input from a file), *StreamWriter* (for text output to a file) and *FileStream* (for both input from and output to a file). Files are opened by creating objects of these stream classes, which inherit from **abstract** classes *TextReader*, *TextWriter* and *Stream*, respectively. Actually, **Console.In** and **Console.Out** are properties of class **TextReader** and **TextWriter**, respectively.

C# provides class *BinaryFormatter*, which is used in conjunction with a **Stream** object to perform input and output of objects. *Serialization* involves converting an object into a format that can be written to a file without losing any of that object's data. *Deserialization* consists of reading this format from a file and reconstructing the original object from it. A **BinaryFormatter** can serialize objects to, and deserialize objects from, a specified **Stream**.

Class *System.IO.Stream* provides functionality for representing streams as bytes. This class is **abstract**, so objects of this class cannot be instantiated. Classes *FileStream*, *MemoryStream* and *BufferedStream* (all from namespace **System.IO**) inherit from class **Stream**. Later in the chapter, we use **FileStream** to read data from, and write data to, sequential-access and random-access files. Class **MemoryStream** enables the transferal of data directly to and from memory—this type of transfer is much faster than are other types of data transfer (e.g., to and from disk). Class **BufferedStream** uses *buffering* to transfer data to or from a stream. Buffering is an I/O-performance-enhancement technique in which each output operation is directed to a region in memory called a *buffer* that is large enough to hold the data from many output operations. Then, actual transfer to the output device is performed in one large *physical output operation* each time the buffer fills. The output operations directed to the output buffer in memory often are called *logical output operations*.

C# offers many classes for performing input and output. In this chapter, we use several key stream classes to implement a variety of file-processing programs that create, manipulate and destroy sequential-access files and random-access files. In Chapter 19, Networking: Streams-Based Sockets and Datagrams, we use stream classes extensively to implement networking applications.

Fig. 14.2   *C#'s view of an n-byte file.*

14.4 Classes `File` and `Directory`

Information on computers is stored in files, which are organized in directories. Class *File* is provided for manipulating files, and class *Directory* is provided for manipulating directories. Class **File** cannot write to or read from files directly; we discuss methods for reading and writing files in subsequent sections.

Note that the **** *separator character* separates directories and files in a path. On UNIX systems, the separator character is **/**. C# actually processes both characters as identical in a path name. This means that, if we specified the path **c:\C_Sharp/README**, which uses one of each separator character, C# still would process the file properly.

Figure 14.3 lists some methods contained in class **File** for manipulating and determining information about particular files. Class **File** contains only **static** methods—you cannot instantiate objects of type **File**. We use several of these methods in the example of Fig. 14.5.

Class **Directory** provides capabilities for manipulating directories. Figure 14.4 lists some methods that can be used for directory manipulation. We employ several of these methods in the example of Fig. 14.5

The *DirectoryInfo* object returned by method **CreateDirectory** contains information about a directory. Much of the information contained in this class also can be accessed via the methods of class **Directory**.

`static` Method	Description
AppendText	Returns a **StreamWriter** that appends to an existing file or creates a file if one does not exist.
Copy	Copies a file to a new file.
Create	Creates a file and returns its associated **FileStream**.
CreateText	Creates a text file and returns its associated **StreamWriter**.
Delete	Deletes the specified file.
GetCreationTime	Returns a **DateTime** object representing the time that the file was created.
GetLastAccessTime	Returns a **DateTime** object representing the time that the file was last accessed.
GetLastWriteTime	Returns a **DateTime** object representing the time that the file was last modified.
Move	Moves the specified file to a specified location.
Open	Returns a **FileStream** associated with the specified file and equipped with the specified read/write permissions.
OpenRead	Returns a read-only **FileStream** associated with the specified file.
OpenText	Returns a **StreamReader** associated with the specified file.
OpenWrite	Returns a read/write **FileStream** associated with the specified file.

Fig. 14.3 `File` class methods (partial list).

`static` Method	Description
`CreateDirectory`	Creates a directory and returns its associated `Directory-Info`.
`Delete`	Deletes the specified directory.
`Exists`	Returns `true` if the specified directory exists; otherwise, it returns `false`.
`GetLastWriteTime`	Returns a `DateTime` object representing the time that the directory was last modified.
`GetDirectories`	Returns a `string` array representing the names of the subdirectories in the specified directory.
`GetFiles`	Returns a `string` array representing the names of the files in the specified directory.
`GetCreationTime`	Returns a `DateTime` object representing the time that the directory was created.
`GetLastAccessTime`	Returns a `DateTime` object representing the time that the directory was last accessed.
`GetLastWriteTime`	Returns a `DateTime` object representing the time that items were last written to the directory.
`Move`	Moves the specified directory to a specified location.

Fig. 14.4   `Directory` class methods (partial list).

Class **`FileTestForm`** (Fig. 14.5) uses methods described in Fig. 14.3 and Fig. 14.4 to access file and directory information. This class contains **`TextBox inputTextBox`** (line 18), which enables the user to input a file or directory name. For each key that the user presses in the text box, the program calls method **`inputTextBox_KeyDown`** (lines 31–93). If the user presses the *Enter* key (line 35), this method displays either file or directory contents, depending on the text the user input in the **`TextBox`**. (Note that, if the user does not press the *Enter* key, this method returns without displaying any content.) Line 43 uses method **`Exists`** of class **`File`** to determine whether the user-specified text is a name of an existing file. If the user specifies an existing file, line 47 invokes **`private`** method **`GetInformation`** (lines 96–115), which calls methods **`GetCreationTime`** (line 103), **`GetLastWriteTime`** (line 107) and **`GetLastAccessTime`** (line 111) of class **`File`** to access file information. When method **`GetInformation`** returns, line 53 instantiates a **`StreamReader`** for reading text from the file. The **`StreamReader`** constructor takes as an argument a **`string`** containing the name of the file to open. Line 54 calls method **`ReadToEnd`** of the **`StreamReader`** to read the file content from the file, then displays the content.

```
1   // Fig. 14.5: FileTest.cs
2   // Using classes File and Directory.
3
```

Fig. 14.5   Testing classes **`File`** and **`Directory`**. (Part 1 of 4.)

```
4   using System;
5   using System.Drawing;
6   using System.Collections;
7   using System.ComponentModel;
8   using System.Windows.Forms;
9   using System.Data;
10  using System.IO;
11
12  // displays contents of files and directories
13  public class FileTestForm : System.Windows.Forms.Form
14  {
15     private System.Windows.Forms.Label directionsLabel;
16
17     private System.Windows.Forms.TextBox outputTextBox;
18     private System.Windows.Forms.TextBox inputTextBox;
19
20     private System.ComponentModel.Container components = null;
21
22     [STAThread]
23     static void Main()
24     {
25        Application.Run( new FileTestForm() );
26     }
27
28     // Visual Studio .NET generated code
29
30     // invoked when user presses key
31     private void inputTextBox_KeyDown(
32        object sender, System.Windows.Forms.KeyEventArgs e )
33     {
34        // determine whether user pressed Enter key
35        if ( e.KeyCode == Keys.Enter )
36        {
37           string fileName; // name of file or directory
38
39           // get user-specified file or directory
40           fileName = inputTextBox.Text;
41
42           // determine whether fileName is a file
43           if ( File.Exists( fileName ) )
44           {
45              // get file's creation date,
46              // modification date, etc.
47              outputTextBox.Text = GetInformation( fileName );
48
49              // display file contents through StreamReader
50              try
51              {
52                 // obtain reader and file contents
53                 StreamReader stream = new StreamReader( fileName );
54                 outputTextBox.Text += stream.ReadToEnd();
55              }
```

Fig. 14.5   Testing classes **File** and **Directory**. (Part 2 of 4.)

```
56                      // handle exception if StreamReader is unavailable
57                      catch( IOException )
58                      {
59                         MessageBox.Show( "File Error", "File Error",
60                            MessageBoxButtons.OK, MessageBoxIcon.Error );
61                      }
62                   }
63
64                   // determine whether fileName is a directory
65                   else if ( Directory.Exists( fileName ) )
66                   {
67                      // array for directories
68                      string[] directoryList;
69
70                      // get directory's creation date,
71                      // modification date, etc.
72                      outputTextBox.Text = GetInformation( fileName );
73
74                      // obtain file/directory list of specified directory
75                      directoryList = Directory.GetDirectories( fileName );
76
77                      outputTextBox.Text +=
78                         "\r\n\r\nDirectory contents:\r\n";
79
80                      // output directoryList contents
81                      for ( int i = 0; i < directoryList.Length; i++ )
82                         outputTextBox.Text += directoryList[ i ] + "\r\n";
83                   }
84                   else
85                   {
86                      // notify user that neither file nor directory exists
87                      MessageBox.Show( inputTextBox.Text +
88                         " does not exist", "File Error",
89                         MessageBoxButtons.OK, MessageBoxIcon.Error );
90                   }
91                } // end if
92
93             } // end method inputTextBox_KeyDown
94
95             // get information on file or directory
96             private string GetInformation( string fileName )
97             {
98                // output that file or directory exists
99                string information = fileName + " exists\r\n\r\n";
100
101                // output when file or directory was created
102                information += "Created: " +
103                   File.GetCreationTime( fileName ) + "\r\n";
104
105                // output when file or directory was last modified
106                information += "Last modified: " +
107                   File.GetLastWriteTime( fileName ) + "\r\n";
108
```

Fig. 14.5   Testing classes **File** and **Directory**. (Part 3 of 4.)

```
109        // output when file or directory was last accessed
110        information += "Last accessed: " +
111           File.GetLastAccessTime( fileName ) + "\r\n" + "\r\n";
112
113        return information;
114
115     } // end method GetInformation
116
117  } // end class FileTestForm
```

Fig. 14.5   Testing classes **File** and **Directory**. (Part 4 of 4.)

If line 43 determines that the user-specified text is not a file, line 65 determines whether it is a directory using method **Exists** of class **Directory**. If the user specified an existing directory, line 72 invokes method **GetInformation** to access the directory information. Line 75 calls method **GetDirectories** of class **Directory** to obtain a **string** array containing the names of subdirectories in the specified directory. Lines 81–82 display each element in the **string** array. Note that, if line 65 determines that the user-specified text is neither a file nor a directory, lines 87–89 notify the user (via a **MessageBox**) that the file or directory does not exist.

We now consider another example that uses C#'s file- and directory-manipulation capabilities. Class **FileSearchForm** (Fig. 14.6) uses classes **File** and **Directory** in conjunction with classes for performing regular expressions to report the number of files of each file type that exist in the specified directory path. The program also serves as a "clean-up" utility—when the program encounters a file that has the **.bak** extension (i.e., a backup file), the program displays a **MessageBox** asking whether that file should be removed, then responds appropriately to the user's input.

When the user presses the *Enter* key or clicks the **Search Directory** button, the program invokes method **searchButton_Click** (lines 52–92), which searches recursively through the directory path that the user provides. If the user inputs text in the **TextBox**, line 59 calls method **Exists** of class **Directory** to determine whether that text indicates a valid directory. If the user specifies an invalid directory, lines 70–71 notify the user of the error.

If the user specifies a valid directory, line 80 passes the directory name as an argument to **private** method **SearchDirectory** (lines 95–185). This method locates files that match the regular expression defined in lines 103–104, which matches any sequence of numbers or letters followed by a period and one or more letters. Notice the substring of format **(?<extension>***regular-expression***)** in the argument to the **Regex** constructor (line 104). All **string**s with the substring *regular-expression* are tagged with the name **extension**. In this program, we assign to the variable **extension** any **string** matching one or more characters.

Lines 115–116 call method **GetDirectories** of class **Directory** to retrieve the names of all subdirectories that belong to the current directory. Line 119 calls method **GetFiles** of class **Directory** to store in **string** array **fileArray** the names of files in the current directory. The **foreach** loop in lines 122–170 searches for all files with extension **bak**; it then calls **SearchDirectory** recursively for each subdirectory in the current directory. Lines 125–126 eliminate the directory path, so the program can test only the file name when using the regular expression. Line 129 uses method **Match** of the **Regex** object to match the regular expression with the file name, then returns the result to object **matchResult** of type **Match**. If the match is successful, lines 133–134 use method **Result** of object **matchResult** to store the extension **string** from object **matchResult** in **fileExtension** (the **string** that will contain the current file's extension). If the match is unsuccessful, line 136 sets **fileExtension** to hold a value of **"[no extension]"**.

```
1   // Fig. 14.6: FileSearch.cs
2   // Using regular expressions to determine file types.
3
4   using System;
5   using System.Drawing;
6   using System.Collections;
7   using System.ComponentModel;
8   using System.Windows.Forms;
9   using System.Data;
10  using System.IO;
11  using System.Text.RegularExpressions;
12  using System.Collections.Specialized;
13
```

Fig. 14.6   Regular expression used to determine file types. (Part 1 of 5.)

```
14   public class FileSearchForm : System.Windows.Forms.Form
15   {
16      private System.Windows.Forms.Label directionsLabel;
17      private System.Windows.Forms.Label directoryLabel;
18
19      private System.Windows.Forms.Button searchButton;
20
21      private System.Windows.Forms.TextBox outputTextBox;
22      private System.Windows.Forms.TextBox inputTextBox;
23
24      private System.ComponentModel.Container components = null;
25
26      string currentDirectory = Directory.GetCurrentDirectory();
27      string[] directoryList; // subdirectories
28      string[] fileArray;
29
30      // store extensions found and number found
31      NameValueCollection found = new NameValueCollection();
32
33      [STAThread]
34      static void Main()
35      {
36         Application.Run( new FileSearchForm() );
37      }
38
39      // Visual Studio .NET generated code
40
41      // invoked when user types in text box
42      private void inputTextBox_KeyDown(
43         object sender, System.Windows.Forms.KeyEventArgs e )
44      {
45         // determine whether user pressed Enter
46         if ( e.KeyCode == Keys.Enter )
47            searchButton_Click( sender, e );
48
49      } // end method inputTextBox_KeyDown
50
51      // invoked when user clicks "Search Directory" button
52      private void searchButton_Click(
53         object sender, System.EventArgs e )
54      {
55         // check for user input; default is current directory
56         if ( inputTextBox.Text != "" )
57         {
58            // verify that user input is valid directory name
59            if ( Directory.Exists( inputTextBox.Text ) )
60            {
61               currentDirectory = inputTextBox.Text;
62
63               // reset input text box and update display
64               directoryLabel.Text = "Current Directory:" +
65                  "\r\n" + currentDirectory;
66            }
```

Fig. 14.6   Regular expression used to determine file types. (Part 2 of 5.)

```
67                 else
68                 {
69                     // show error if user does not specify valid directory
70                     MessageBox.Show( "Invalid Directory", "Error",
71                         MessageBoxButtons.OK, MessageBoxIcon.Error );
72                 }
73             }
74
75             // clear text boxes
76             inputTextBox.Clear();
77             outputTextBox.Clear();
78
79             // search directory
80             SearchDirectory( currentDirectory );
81
82             // summarize and print results
83             foreach ( string current in found )
84             {
85                 outputTextBox.Text += "* Found " +
86                     found[ current ] + " " + current + " files.\r\n";
87             }
88
89             // clear output for new search
90             found.Clear();
91
92         } // end method searchButton_Click
93
94         // search directory using regular expression
95         private void SearchDirectory( string currentDirectory )
96         {
97             // search directory
98             try
99             {
100                string fileName = "";
101
102                // regular expression for extensions matching pattern
103                Regex regularExpression = new Regex(
104                    "[a-zA-Z0-9]+\\.(?<extension>\\w+)" );
105
106                // stores regular-expression-match result
107                Match matchResult;
108
109                string fileExtension; // holds file extensions
110
111                // number of files with given extension in directory
112                int extensionCount;
113
114                // get directories
115                directoryList =
116                    Directory.GetDirectories( currentDirectory );
117
118                // get list of files in current directory
119                fileArray = Directory.GetFiles( currentDirectory );
```

Fig. 14.6   Regular expression used to determine file types. (Part 3 of 5.)

```
120
121            // iterate through list of files
122            foreach ( string myFile in fileArray )
123            {
124               // remove directory path from file name
125               fileName = myFile.Substring(
126                  myFile.LastIndexOf( "\\" ) + 1 );
127
128               // obtain result for regular-expression search
129               matchResult = regularExpression.Match( fileName );
130
131               // check for match
132                  ( matchResult.Success )
133                  fileExtension =
134                     matchResult.Result( "${extension}" );
135               else
136                  fileExtension = "[no extension]";
137
138               // store value from container
139               if ( found[ fileExtension ] == null )
140                  found.Add( fileExtension, "1" );
141               else
142               {
143                  extensionCount = Int32.Parse(
144                     found[ fileExtension ] ) + 1;
145
146                  found[ fileExtension ] = extensionCount.ToString();
147               }
148
149               // search for backup(.bak) files
150               if ( fileExtension == "bak" )
151               {
152                  // prompt user to delete (.bak) file
153                  DialogResult result =
154                     MessageBox.Show( "Found backup file " +
155                     fileName + ". Delete?", "Delete Backup",
156                     MessageBoxButtons.YesNo,
157                     MessageBoxIcon.Question );
158
159                  // delete file if user clicked 'yes'
160                  if ( result == DialogResult.Yes )
161                  {
162                     File.Delete( myFile );
163
164                     extensionCount =
165                        Int32.Parse( found[ "bak" ] ) - 1;
166
167                     found[ "bak" ] = extensionCount.ToString();
168                  }
169               }
170            }
171
```

Fig. 14.6   Regular expression used to determine file types. (Part 4 of 5.)

```
172              // recursive call to search files in subdirectory
173              foreach ( string myDirectory in directoryList )
174                  SearchDirectory( myDirectory );
175          }
176
177          // handle exception if files have unauthorized access
178          catch( UnauthorizedAccessException )
179          {
180              MessageBox.Show( "Some files may not be visible" +
181                  " due to permission settings", "Warning",
182                  MessageBoxButtons.OK, MessageBoxIcon.Information );
183          }
184
185      } // end method SearchDirectory
186
187 } // end class FileSearchForm
```

Fig. 14.6   Regular expression used to determine file types. (Part 5 of 5.)

Class **FileSearchForm** uses an instance of class ***NameValueCollection*** (declared in line 31) to store each file-extension type and the number of files for each type. A **NameValueCollection** contains a collection of key/value pairs, each of which is a **string**, and provides method **Add** to add a key/value pair. The indexer for this pair can index according to the order that the items were added or according to the entry key. Line

139 uses **NameValueCollection found** to determine whether this is the first occurrence of the file extension. If so, line 140 adds that extension to **found** as a key with the value **1**. If the extension is in **found** already, lines 143–144 increment the value associated with the extension in **found** to indicate another occurrence of that file extension.

Line 150 determines whether **fileExtension** equals "**bak**"—i.e., whether the file is a backup file. If so, lines 153–157 prompt the user to indicate whether the file should be removed; if the user clicks **Yes** (line 160), lines 162–167 delete the file and decrement the value for the "**bak**" file type in **found**.

Lines 173–174 call method **SearchDirectory** for each subdirectory. Using recursion, we ensure that the program performs the same logic for finding **bak** files on each subdirectory. After each subdirectory has been checked for **bak** files, method **SearchDirectory** completes, and lines 83–87 display the results.

14.5 Creating a Sequential-Access File

C# imposes no structure on files. Thus, concepts like that of a "record" do not exist in C# files. This means that the programmer must structure files to meet the requirements of applications. In this example, we use text and special characters to organize our own concept of a "record."

The following examples demonstrate file processing in a bank-account maintenance application. These programs have similar user interfaces, so we created class **BankUIForm** (Fig. 14.7) to encapsulate a base-class GUI (see the screen capture in Fig. 14.7). Class **BankUIForm** contains four **Label**s (lines 15, 18, 21 and 24) and four **TextBox**es (lines 16, 19, 22 and 25). Methods **ClearTextBoxes** (lines 49–64), **SetTextBoxValues** (lines 67–91) and **GetTextBoxValues** (lines 94–110) clear, set the values of, and get the values of the text in the **TextBox**es, respectively.

To reuse class **BankUIForm**, we compile the GUI into a DLL library by creating a project of type **Windows Control Library** (the DLL we create is called **BankLibrary**). This library, as well as all the code in this book, can be found at our Web site, **www.deitel.com**, under the **Downloads/Resources** link. However, readers might need to change the reference to this library, as it most likely resides in a different location on their systems.

Figure 14.8 contains class **Record** that Fig. 14.9, Fig. 14.11 and Fig. 14.12 use for reading records from, and writing records to, a file sequentially. This class also belongs to the **BankLibrary** DLL, so it is located in the same project as is class **BankUIForm**.

The **Serializable** attribute (line 6) indicates to the compiler that objects of class **Record** can be *serialized*, or represented as sets of bytes—we can read and write these bytes to our streams. Objects that we wish to write to or read from a stream must include this attribute in their class definitions.

Class **Record** contains **private** data members **account**, **firstName**, **lastName** and **balance** (lines 9–12), which collectively represent all information necessary to store record data. The default constructor (lines 15–17) sets these members to their default (i.e., empty) values, and the overloaded constructor (lines 20–28) sets these members to specified parameter values. Class **Record** also provides properties **Account** (lines 31–43), **FirstName** (lines 46–58), **LastName** (lines 61–73) and **Balance** (lines 76–88) for accessing the account number, first name, last name and balance of each customer, respectively.

```csharp
1    // Fig. 14.7: BankUI.cs
2    // A reusable windows form for the examples in this chapter.
3
4    using System;
5    using System.Drawing;
6    using System.Collections;
7    using System.ComponentModel;
8    using System.Windows.Forms;
9    using System.Data;
10
11   public class BankUIForm : System.Windows.Forms.Form
12   {
13      private System.ComponentModel.Container components = null;
14
15      public System.Windows.Forms.Label accountLabel;
16      public System.Windows.Forms.TextBox accountTextBox;
17
18      public System.Windows.Forms.Label firstNameLabel;
19      public System.Windows.Forms.TextBox firstNameTextBox;
20
21      public System.Windows.Forms.Label lastNameLabel;
22      public System.Windows.Forms.TextBox lastNameTextBox;
23
24      public System.Windows.Forms.Label balanceLabel;
25      public System.Windows.Forms.TextBox balanceTextBox;
26
27      // number of TextBoxes on Form'
28      protected int TextBoxCount = 4;
29
30      // enumeration constants specify TextBox indices
31      public enum TextBoxIndices
32      {
33         ACCOUNT,
34         FIRST,
35         LAST,
36         BALANCE
37
38      } // end enum
39
40      [STAThread]
41      static void Main()
42      {
43         Application.Run( new BankUIForm() );
44      }
45
46      // Visual Studio .NET generated code
47
48      // clear all TextBoxes
49      public void ClearTextBoxes()
50      {
51         // iterate through every Control on form
52         for ( int i = 0; i < Controls.Count; i++ )
53         {
```

Fig. 14.7   Base class for GUIs in our file-processing applications. (Part 1 of 3.)

```
54                Control myControl = Controls[ i ]; // get control
55
56                // determine whether Control is TextBox
57                if ( myControl is TextBox )
58                {
59                   // clear Text property (set to empty strng)
60                   myControl.Text = "";
61                }
62          }
63
64    } // end method ClearTextBoxes
65
66    // set text box values to string array values
67    public void SetTextBoxValues( string[] values )
68    {
69       // determine whether string array has correct length
70       if ( values.Length != TextBoxCount )
71       {
72          // throw exception if not correct length
73          throw( new ArgumentException( "There must be " +
74             (TextBoxCount + 1) + " strings in the array" ) );
75       }
76
77       // set array values if array has correct length
78       else
79       {
80          // set array values to text box values
81          accountTextBox.Text =
82             values[ ( int )TextBoxIndices.ACCOUNT ];
83          firstNameTextBox.Text =
84             values[ ( int )TextBoxIndices.FIRST ];
85          lastNameTextBox.Text =
86             values[ ( int )TextBoxIndices.LAST ];
87          balanceTextBox.Text =
88             values[ ( int )TextBoxIndices.BALANCE ];
89       }
90
91    } // end method SetTextBoxValues
92
93    // return text box values as string array
94    public string[] GetTextBoxValues()
95    {
96       string[] values = new string[ TextBoxCount ];
97
98       // copy text box fields to string array
99       values[ ( int )TextBoxIndices.ACCOUNT ] =
100         accountTextBox.Text;
101      values[ ( int )TextBoxIndices.FIRST ] =
102         firstNameTextBox.Text;
103      values[ ( int )TextBoxIndices.LAST ] =
104         lastNameTextBox.Text;
105      values[ ( int )TextBoxIndices.BALANCE ] =
106         balanceTextBox.Text;
```

Fig. 14.7   Base class for GUIs in our file-processing applications. (Part 2 of 3.)

```
107
108         return values;
109
110     } // end method GetTextBoxValues
111
112 } // end class BankUIForm
```

Fig. 14.7   Base class for GUIs in our file-processing applications. (Part 3 of 3.)

```
1   // Fig. 14.8: Record.cs
2   // Serializable class that represents a data record.
3
4   using System;
5
6   [Serializable]
7   public class Record
8   {
9      private int account;
10     private string firstName;
11     private string lastName;
12     private double balance;
13
14     // default constructor sets members to default values
15     public Record() : this( 0, "", "", 0.0 )
16     {
17     }
18
19     // overloaded constructor sets members to parameter values
20     public Record( int accountValue, string firstNameValue,
21        string lastNameValue, double balanceValue )
22     {
23        Account = accountValue;
24        FirstName = firstNameValue;
25        LastName = lastNameValue;
26        Balance = balanceValue;
27
28     } // end constructor
29
```

Fig. 14.8   Record for sequential-access file-processing applications. (Part 1 of 3.)

```
30          // property Account
31          public int Account
32          {
33             get
34             {
35                return account;
36             }
37
38             set
39             {
40                account = value;
41             }
42
43          } // end property Account
44
45          // property FirstName
46          public string FirstName
47          {
48             get
49             {
50                return firstName;
51             }
52
53             set
54             {
55                firstName = value;
56             }
57
58          } // end property FirstName
59
60          // property LastName
61          public string LastName
62          {
63             get
64             {
65                return lastName;
66             }
67
68             set
69             {
70                lastName = value;
71             }
72
73          } // end property LastName
74
75          // property Balance
76          public double Balance
77          {
78             get
79             {
80                return balance;
81             }
82
```

Fig. 14.8   Record for sequential-access file-processing applications. (Part 2 of 3.)

```
83          set
84          {
85             balance = value;
86          }
87
88       } // end property Balance
89
90    } // end class Record
```

Fig. 14.8   Record for sequential-access file-processing applications. (Part 3 of 3.)

Class **CreateFileForm** (Fig. 14.9) uses instances of class **Record** to create a sequential-access file that might be used in an accounts receivable system—i.e., a program that organizes data regarding money owed by a company's credit clients. For each client, the program obtains an account number and the client's first name, last name and balance (i.e., the amount of money that the client owes to the company for previously received goods or services). The data obtained for each client constitutes a record for that client. In this application, the account number represents the record key—files are created and maintained in account-number order. This program assumes that the user enters records in account-number order. However, a comprehensive accounts receivable system would provide a sorting capability. The user could enter the records in any order, and the records then could be sorted and written to the file in order. (Note that all outputs in this chapter should be read row by row, from left to right in each row.)

Figure 14.9 contains the code for class **CreateFileForm**, which either creates or opens a file (depending on whether one exists), then allows the user to write bank information to that file. Line 16 imports the **BankLibrary** namespace; this namespace contains class **BankUIForm**, from which class **CreateFileForm** inherits (line 18). Because of this inheritance relationship, the **CreateFileForm** GUI is similar to that of class **BankUIForm** (shown in the Fig. 14.9 output), except that the inherited class contains buttons **Save As**, **Enter** and **Exit**.

When the user clicks the **Save As** button, the program invokes method **saveButton_Click** (lines 41–85). Line 45 instantiates an object of class **SaveFileDialog**, which belongs to the **System.Windows.Forms** namespace. Objects of this class are used for selecting files (see the second screen in Fig. 14.9). Line 46 calls method **ShowDialog** of the **SaveFileDialog** object to display the **SaveFileDialog**. When displayed, a **SaveFileDialog** prevents the user from interacting with any other window in the program until the user closes the **SaveFileDialog** by clicking either **Save** or **Cancel**. Dialogs that behave in this fashion are called *modal dialogs*. The user selects the appropriate drive, directory and file name, then clicks **Save**. Method **ShowDialog** returns an integer specifying which button (**Save** or **Cancel**) the user clicked to close the dialog. In this example, the **Form** property **DialogResult** receives this integer. Line 53 tests whether the user clicked **Cancel** by comparing the value returned by property **DialogResult** to constant *DialogResult.Cancel*. If the values are equal, method **saveButton_Click** returns (line 54). If the values are unequal (i.e., the user clicked **Save**, instead of clicking **Cancel**), line 57 uses property *FileName* of class **SaveFileDialog** to obtain the user-selected file.

```
1   // Fig. 14.9: CreateSequentialAccessFile.cs
2   // Creating a sequential-access file.
3
4   // C# namespaces
5   using System;
6   using System.Drawing;
7   using System.Collections;
8   using System.ComponentModel;
9   using System.Windows.Forms;
10  using System.Data;
11  using System.IO;
12  using System.Runtime.Serialization.Formatters.Binary;
13  using System.Runtime.Serialization;
14
15  // Deitel namespace
16  using BankLibrary;
17
18  public class CreateFileForm : BankUIForm
19  {
20     private System.Windows.Forms.Button saveButton;
21     private System.Windows.Forms.Button enterButton;
22     private System.Windows.Forms.Button exitButton;
23
24     private System.ComponentModel.Container components = null;
25
26     // serializes Record in binary format
27     private BinaryFormatter formatter = new BinaryFormatter();
28
29     // stream through which serializable data is written to file
30     private FileStream output;
31
32     [STAThread]
33     static void Main()
34     {
35        Application.Run( new CreateFileForm() );
36     }
37
38     // Visual Studio .NET generated code
39
40     // invoked when user clicks Save button
41     private void saveButton_Click(
42        object sender, System.EventArgs e )
43     {
44        // create dialog box enabling user to save file
45        SaveFileDialog fileChooser = new SaveFileDialog();
46        DialogResult result = fileChooser.ShowDialog();
47        string fileName; // name of file to save data
48
49        // allow user to create file
50        fileChooser.CheckFileExists = false;
51
```

Fig. 14.9   Create and write to a sequential-access file. (Part 1 of 5.)

```
52          // exit event handler if user clicked "Cancel"
53          if ( result == DialogResult.Cancel )
54             return;
55
56          // get specified file name
57          fileName = fileChooser.FileName;
58
59          // show error if user specified invalid file
60          if ( fileName == "" || fileName == null )
61             MessageBox.Show( "Invalid File Name", "Error",
62                MessageBoxButtons.OK, MessageBoxIcon.Error );
63          else
64          {
65             // save file via FileStream if user specified valid file
66             try
67             {
68                // open file with write access
69                output = new FileStream( fileName,
70                   FileMode.OpenOrCreate, FileAccess.Write );
71
72                // disable Save button and enable Enter button
73                saveButton.Enabled = false;
74                enterButton.Enabled = true;
75             }
76
77             // handle exception if file does not exist
78             catch ( FileNotFoundException )
79             {
80                // notify user if file does not exist
81                MessageBox.Show( "File Does Not Exist", "Error",
82                   MessageBoxButtons.OK, MessageBoxIcon.Error );
83             }
84          }
85       } // end method saveButton_Click
86
87       // invoke when user clicks Enter button
88       private void enterButton_Click(
89          object sender, System.EventArgs e )
90       {
91          // store TextBox values string array
92          string[] values = GetTextBoxValues();
93
94          // Record containing TextBox values to serialize
95          Record record = new Record();
96
97          // determine whether TextBox account field is empty
98          if ( values[ ( int )TextBoxIndices.ACCOUNT ] != "" )
99          {
100             // store TextBox values in Record and serialize Record
101             try
102             {
```

Fig. 14.9   Create and write to a sequential-access file. (Part 2 of 5.)

```
103                    // get account number value from TextBox
104                    int accountNumber = Int32.Parse(
105                       values[ ( int )TextBoxIndices.ACCOUNT ] );
106
107                    // determine whether accountNumber is valid
108                    if ( accountNumber > 0 )
109                    {
110                       // store TextBox fields in Record
111                       record.Account = accountNumber;
112                       record.FirstName =
113                          values[ ( int )TextBoxIndices.FIRST ];
114                       record.LastName =
115                          values[ ( int )TextBoxIndices.LAST ];
116                       record.Balance = Double.Parse( values[
117                          ( int )TextBoxIndices.BALANCE ] );
118
119                       // write Record to FileStream (serialize object)
120                       formatter.Serialize( output, record );
121                    }
122                    else
123                    {
124                       // notify user if invalid account number
125                       MessageBox.Show( "Invalid Account Number", "Error",
126                          MessageBoxButtons.OK, MessageBoxIcon.Error );
127                    }
128                 }
129
130                 // notify user if error occurs in serialization
131                 catch( SerializationException )
132                 {
133                    MessageBox.Show( "Error Writing to File", "Error",
134                       MessageBoxButtons.OK, MessageBoxIcon.Error );
135                 }
136
137                 // notify user if error occurs regarding parameter format
138                 catch( FormatException )
139                 {
140                    MessageBox.Show( "Invalid Format", "Error",
141                       MessageBoxButtons.OK, MessageBoxIcon.Error );
142                 }
143              }
144
145           ClearTextBoxes(); // clear TextBox values
146
147       } // end method enterButton_Click
148
149       // invoked when user clicks Exit button
150       private void exitButton_Click(
151          object sender, System.EventArgs e )
152       {
153          // determine whether file exists
154          if ( output != null )
155          {
```

Fig. 14.9   Create and write to a sequential-access file. (Part 3 of 5.)

```
156              // close file
157              try
158              {
159                  output.Close();
160              }
161
162              // notify user of error closing file
163              catch( IOException )
164              {
165                  MessageBox.Show( "Cannot close file", "Error",
166                      MessageBoxButtons.OK, MessageBoxIcon.Error );
167              }
168          }
169
170          Application.Exit();
171
172      } // end method exitButton_Click
173
174  } // end class CreateFileForm
```

BankUI graphical
user interface

SaveFileDialog

Files and directories

Fig. 14.9   Create and write to a sequential-access file. (Part 4 of 5.)

Fig. 14.9   Create and write to a sequential-access file. (Part 5 of 5.)

As we stated previously in this chapter, we can open files to perform text manipulation by creating objects of classes **FileStream**. In this example, we want the file to be opened for output, so lines 69–70 instantiate a **FileStream** object. The **FileStream** constructor that we use receives three arguments—a **string** containing the name of the file to be opened, a constant describing how to open the file and a constant describing the file permissions. Line 70 passes constant **FileMode.OpenOrCreate** to the **FileStream** constructor as the constructor's second argument. This constant indicates that the **FileStream** object should open the file if the file exists or create the file if the file does not exist. C# offers other **FileMode** constants describing how to open files; we introduce these constants as we use them in examples. Line 70 passes constant **FileAccess.Write** to the **FileStream** constructor as the constructor's third argument. This constant ensures that the program can perform write-only operations on the **FileStream** object. C# provides two other constants for this parameter—**FileAccess.Read** for read-only access and **FileAccess.ReadWrite** for both read and write access.

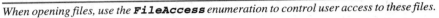

Good Programming Practice 14.1

*When opening files, use the **FileAccess** enumeration to control user access to these files.*

After the user types information in each **TextBox**, the user clicks the **Enter** button, which calls method **enterButton_Click** (lines 88–147) to save data from the **TextBox** in the user-specified file. If the user entered a valid account number (i.e., an integer greater than zero), lines 112–118 store the **TextBox** values in an object of type **Record**. If the user entered invalid data in one of the **TextBox**es (such as entering non-numeric characters in the **Balance** field), the program throws a **FormatException**. The **catch** block in lines 138–142 handles such an exception by notifying the user (via a **MessageBox**) of the improper format. If the user entered valid data, line 120 writes the record to the file by invoking method **Serialize** of the **BinaryFormatter** object (instantiated in line 27). Class **BinaryFormatter** uses methods **Serialize** and **Deserialize** to write and read objects into streams, respectively. Method **Serialize** writes the object's representation to a file. Method **Deserialize** reads this representation from a file and reconstructs the original object. Both methods throw a **SerializationException** if an error occurs during serialization or deserialization (errors result when the methods attempt to access streams or records that do not exist). Both methods **Serialize** and **Deserialize** require a **Stream** object (e.g., the **FileStream**) as a parameter so that the **BinaryFormatter** can access the correct file; the **BinaryFormatter** must receive an instance of a class that derives from class **Stream**, because **Stream** is **abstract**. Class **BinaryFormatter** belongs to the *System.Runtime.Serialization.Formatters.Binary* namespace.

Common Programming Error 14.1

Failure to open a file before attempting to reference it in a program is a logic error.

When the user clicks the **Exit** button, the program invokes method **exitButton_Click** (lines 150–172) to exit the application. Line 159 closes the **FileStream** if one has been opened, and line 170 exits the program.

Performance Tip 14.1

Close each file explicitly when the program no longer needs to reference the file. This can reduce resource usage in programs that continue executing long after they finish using a specific file. The practice of explicitly closing files also improves program clarity.

Performance Tip 14.2

Releasing resources explicitly when they are no longer needed makes them immediately available for reuse by the program, thus improving resource utilization.

In the sample execution for the program in Fig. 14.9, we entered information for five accounts (Fig. 14.10). The program does not depict how the data records are rendered in

Account Number	First Name	Last Name	Balance
100	Nancy	Brown	-25.54
200	Stacey	Dunn	314.33
300	Doug	Barker	0.00
400	Dave	Smith	258.34
500	Sam	Stone	34.98

Fig. 14.10 Sample data for the program of Fig. 14.9.

the file. To verify that the file has been created successfully, in the next section, we create a program to read and display the file.

14.6 Reading Data from a Sequential-Access File

Data are stored in files so that they can be retrieved for processing when they are needed. The previous section demonstrated how to create a file for use in sequential-access applications. In this section, we discuss how to read (or retrieve) data sequentially from a file.

Class **ReadSequentialAccessFileForm** (Fig. 14.11) reads records from the file created by the program in Fig. 14.9, then displays the contents of each record. Much of the code in this example is similar to that of Fig. 14.9, so we discuss only the unique aspects of the application.

When the user clicks the **Open File** button, the program calls method **open-Button_Click** (lines 40–70). Line 44 instantiates an object of class *OpenFile-Dialog*, and line 45 calls the object's *ShowDialog* method to display the **Open** dialog (see the second screenshot in Fig. 14.11). The behavior and GUI for the two dialog types are the same (except that **Save** is replaced by **Open**). If the user inputs a valid file name, lines 63–64 create a **FileStream** object and assign it to reference **input**. We pass constant **FileMode.Open** as the second argument to the **FileStream** constructor. This constant indicates that the **FileStream** should open the file if the file exists or should throw a **FileNotFoundException** if the file does not exist. (In this example, the **FileStream** constructor will not throw a **FileNotFoundException**, because the **OpenFileDialog** requires the user to enter a name of a file that exists.) In the last example (Fig. 14.9), we wrote text to the file using a **FileStream** object with write-only access. In this example, (Fig. 14.11), we specify read-only access to the file by passing constant **FileAccess.Read** as the third argument to the **FileStream** constructor.

Testing and Debugging Tip 14.1

*Open a file with the **FileAccess.Read** file-open mode if the contents of the file should not be modified. This prevents unintentional modification of the file's contents.*

When the user clicks the **Next Record** button, the program calls method **nextButton_Click** (lines 73–113), which reads the next record from the user-specified file. (The user must click **Next Record** after opening the file to view the first record.) Lines 80–81 call method **Deserialize** of the **BinaryFormatter** object to read the next record. Method **Deserialize** reads the data and casts the result to a **Record**—this cast is necessary, because **Deserialize** returns a reference of type **Object**. Lines 84–91 then display the **Record** values in the **TextBox**es. When method **Deserialize** attempts to deserialize a record that does not exist in the file (i.e., the program has displayed all file records), the method throws a **SerializationException**. The **catch** block (lines 95–111) that handles this exception closes the **FileStream** object (line 98) and notifies the user that there are no more records (lines 109–110).

```
1   // Fig. 14.11: ReadSequentialAccessFile.cs
2   // Reading a sequential-access file.
3
4   // C# namespaces
5   using System;
6   using System.Drawing;
7   using System.Collections;
8   using System.ComponentModel;
9   using System.Windows.Forms;
10  using System.Data;
11  using System.IO;
12  using System.Runtime.Serialization.Formatters.Binary;
13  using System.Runtime.Serialization;
14
15  // Deitel namespaces
16  using BankLibrary;
17
18  public class ReadSequentialAccessFileForm : BankUIForm
19  {
20     System.Windows.Forms.Button openButton;
21     System.Windows.Forms.Button nextButton;
22
23     private System.ComponentModel.Container components = null;
24
25     // stream through which serializable data are read from file
26     private FileStream input;
27
28     // object for deserializing Record in binary format
29     private BinaryFormatter reader = new BinaryFormatter();
30
31     [STAThread]
32     static void Main()
33     {
34        Application.Run( new ReadSequentialAccessFileForm() );
35     }
36
37     // Visual Studio .NET generated code
38
39     // invoked when user clicks Open button
40     private void openButton_Click(
41        object sender, System.EventArgs e )
42     {
43        // create dialog box enabling user to open file
44        OpenFileDialog fileChooser = new OpenFileDialog();
45        DialogResult result = fileChooser.ShowDialog();
```

Fig. 14.11 Reading sequential-access files. (Part 1 of 4.)

```
46          string fileName; // name of file containing data
47
48          // exit event handler if user clicked Cancel
49          if ( result == DialogResult.Cancel )
50             return;
51
52          // get specified file name
53          fileName = fileChooser.FileName;
54          ClearTextBoxes();
55
56          // show error if user specified invalid file
57          if ( fileName == "" || fileName == null )
58             MessageBox.Show( "Invalid File Name", "Error",
59                MessageBoxButtons.OK, MessageBoxIcon.Error );
60          else
61          {
62             // create FileStream to obtain read access to file
63             input = new FileStream( fileName, FileMode.Open,
64                FileAccess.Read );
65
66             // enable next record button
67             nextButton.Enabled = true;
68          }
69
70       } // end method openButton_Click
71
72       // invoked when user clicks Next button
73       private void nextButton_Click(
74          object sender, System.EventArgs e )
75       {
76          // deserialize Record and store data in TextBoxes
77          try
78          {
79             // get next Record available in file
80             Record record =
81                ( Record )reader.Deserialize( input );
82
83             // store Record values in temporary string array
84             string[] values = new string[] {
85                record.Account.ToString(),
86                record.FirstName.ToString(),
87                record.LastName.ToString(),
88                record.Balance.ToString() };
89
90             // copy string array values to TextBox values
91             SetTextBoxValues( values );
92          }
93
94          // handle exception when no Records in file
95          catch( SerializationException )
96          {
97             // close FileStream if no Records in file
98             input.Close();
```

Fig. 14.11 Reading sequential-access files. (Part 2 of 4.)

```
99
100          // enable Open Record button
101          openButton.Enabled = true;
102
103          // disable Next Record button
104          nextButton.Enabled = false;
105
106          ClearTextBoxes();
107
108          // notify user if no Records in file
109          MessageBox.Show( "No more records in file", "",
110             MessageBoxButtons.OK, MessageBoxIcon.Information );
111       }
112
113    } // end method nextButton_Click
114
115 } // end class ReadSequentialAccessFileForm
```

Fig. 14.11 Reading sequential-access files. (Part 3 of 4.)

Fig. 14.11 Reading sequential-access files. (Part 4 of 4.)

To retrieve data sequentially from a file, programs normally start from the beginning of the file, reading data consecutively until the desired data are found. It sometimes is necessary to process a file sequentially several times (from the beginning of the file) during the execution of a program. A **FileStream** object can reposition its *file-position pointer* (which contains the byte number of the next byte to be read from or written to the file) to any position in the file—we show this feature when we introduce random-access file-processing applications. When a **FileStream** object is opened, its file-position pointer is set to zero (i.e., the beginning of the file)

Performance Tip 14.3

It is time-consuming to close and reopen a file for the purpose of moving the file-position pointer to the file's beginning. Doing so frequently could slow program performance.

We now present a more substantial program that builds on the concepts employed in Fig. 14.11. Class **creditInquiryForm** (Fig. 14.12) is a credit-inquiry program that enables a credit manager to display account information for those customers with credit balances (i.e., customers to whom the company owes money), zero balances (i.e., customers who do not owe the company money) and debit balances (i.e., customers who owe the company money for previously received goods and services). Note that line 21 declares a **RichTextBox** that will display the account information. **RichTextBox**es provide more functionality than do regular **TextBox**es—for example, **RichTextBox**es offer method **Find** for searching individual strings and method **LoadFile** for displaying file contents. Class **RichTextBox** does not inherit from class **TextBox**; rather, both classes inherit directly from abstract class **System.Windows.Forms.TextBoxBase**. We use a **RichTextBox** in this example, because a **RichTextBox** displays multiple lines of text by default, whereas a regular **TextBox** displays only one. Alternatively, we could have specified that a **TextBox** object display multiple lines of text by setting its **Multiline** property to **true**

The program in Fig. 14.12 displays buttons that enable a credit manager to obtain credit information. The **Open File** button opens a file for gathering data. The **Credit Balances** button displays a list of accounts that have credit balances, the **Debit Balances** button displays a list of accounts that have debit balances, and the **Zero Balances** button displays a list of accounts that have zero balances. The **Done** button exits the application.

When the user clicks the **Open File** button, the program calls method **openButton_Click** (lines 49–76). Line 53 instantiates an object of class **OpenFileDialog**, and line 54 calls the object's **ShowDialog** method to display the **Open** dialog, in which the user inputs the name of the file to open.

When the user clicks **Credit Balances**, **Debit Balances** or **Zero Balances**, the program invokes method **get_Click** (lines 80–142). Line 83 casts the **sender** parameter, which is a reference to the object that sent the event, to a **Button** object. Line 86 extracts the **Button** object's text, which the program uses to determine which GUI **Button** the user clicked. Lines 96–97 create a **FileStream** object with read-only file access and assign it to reference **input**. Lines 102–125 define a **while** loop that uses **private** method **ShouldDisplay** (lines 145–170) to determine whether to display each record in the file. The **while** loop obtains each record by calling method **Deserialize** of the **FileStream** object repeatedly (line 105). When the file-position pointer reaches the end of file, method **Deserialize** throws a **SerializationException**, which the **catch** block in lines 136–140 handles: Line 139 calls the **Close** method of **FileStream** to close the file, and method **get_Click** returns.

```
1   // Fig. 14.12: CreditInquiry.cs
2   // Read a file sequentially and display contents based on
3   // account type specified by user (credit, debit or zero balances).
4
```

Fig. 14.12 Credit-inquiry program. (Part 1 of 7.)

```csharp
5     // C# namespaces
6     using System;
7     using System.Drawing;
8     using System.Collections;
9     using System.ComponentModel;
10    using System.Windows.Forms;
11    using System.Data;
12    using System.IO;
13    using System.Runtime.Serialization.Formatters.Binary;
14    using System.Runtime.Serialization;
15
16    // Deitel namespaces
17    using BankLibrary;
18
19    public class CreditInquiryForm : System.Windows.Forms.Form
20    {
21       private System.Windows.Forms.RichTextBox displayTextBox;
22
23       private System.Windows.Forms.Button doneButton;
24       private System.Windows.Forms.Button zeroButton;
25       private System.Windows.Forms.Button debitButton;
26       private System.Windows.Forms.Button creditButton;
27       private System.Windows.Forms.Button openButton;
28
29       private System.ComponentModel.Container components = null;
30
31       // stream through which serializable data are read from file
32       private FileStream input;
33
34       // object for deserializing Record in binary format
35       BinaryFormatter reader = new BinaryFormatter();
36
37       // name of file that stores credit, debit and zero balances
38       private string fileName;
39
40       [STAThread]
41       static void Main()
42       {
43          Application.Run( new CreditInquiryForm() );
44       }
45
46       // Visual Studio .NET generated code
47
48       // invoked when user clicks Open File button
49       private void openButton_Click(
50          object sender, System.EventArgs e )
51       {
52          // create dialog box enabling user to open file
53          OpenFileDialog fileChooser = new OpenFileDialog();
54          DialogResult result = fileChooser.ShowDialog();
55
```

Fig. 14.12   Credit-inquiry program. (Part 2 of 7.)

```
56            // exit event handler if user clicked Cancel
57            if ( result == DialogResult.Cancel )
58               return;
59
60            // get name from user
61            fileName = fileChooser.FileName;
62
63            // show error if user specified invalid file
64            if ( fileName == "" || fileName == null )
65               MessageBox.Show( "Invalid File Name", "Error",
66                  MessageBoxButtons.OK, MessageBoxIcon.Error );
67            else
68            {
69               // enable all GUI buttons, except for Open file button
70               openButton.Enabled = false;
71               creditButton.Enabled = true;
72               debitButton.Enabled = true;
73               zeroButton.Enabled = true;
74            }
75
76      } // end method openButton_Click
77
78      // invoked when user clicks credit balances,
79      // debit balances or zero balances button
80      private void get_Click( object sender, System.EventArgs e )
81      {
82         // convert sender explicitly to object of type button
83         Button senderButton = ( Button )sender;
84
85         // get text from clicked Button, which stores account type
86         string accountType = senderButton.Text;
87
88         // read and display file information
89         try
90         {
91            // close file from previous operation
92            if ( input != null )
93               input.Close();
94
95            // create FileStream to obtain read access to file
96            input = new FileStream( fileName, FileMode.Open,
97               FileAccess.Read );
98
99            displayTextBox.Text = "The accounts are:\r\n";
100
101            // traverse file until end of file
102            while ( true )
103            {
104               // get next Record available in file
105               Record record = ( Record )reader.Deserialize( input );
106
107               // store record's last field in balance
108               Double balance = record.Balance;
```

Fig. 14.12   Credit-inquiry program. (Part 3 of 7.)

```
109
110                        // determine whether to display balance
111                        if ( ShouldDisplay( balance, accountType ) )
112                        {
113                           // display record
114                           string output = record.Account + "\t" +
115                              record.FirstName + "\t" + record.LastName +
116                              new string( ' ', 6 ) + "\t";
117
118                           // display balance with correct monetary format
119                           output += String.Format(
120                              "{0:F}", balance ) + "\r\n";
121
122                           // copy output to screen
123                           displayTextBox.Text += output;
124                        }
125                     }
126                  }
127
128                  // handle exception when file cannot be closed
129                  catch( IOException )
130                  {
131                     MessageBox.Show( "Cannot Close File", "Error",
132                        MessageBoxButtons.OK, MessageBoxIcon.Error );
133                  }
134
135                  // handle exception when no more records
136                  catch( SerializationException )
137                  {
138                     // close FileStream if no Records in file
139                     input.Close();
140                  }
141
142          } // end method get_Click
143
144          // determine whether to display given record
145          private bool ShouldDisplay( double balance, string accountType )
146          {
147             if ( balance > 0 )
148             {
149                // display credit balances
150                if ( accountType == "Credit Balances" )
151                   return true;
152             }
153
154             else if ( balance < 0 )
155             {
156                // display debit balances
157                if ( accountType == "Debit Balances" )
158                   return true;
159             }
160
```

Fig. 14.12 Credit-inquiry program. (Part 4 of 7.)

```
161            else // balance == 0
162            {
163               // display zero balances
164               if ( accountType == "Zero Balances" )
165                  return true;
166            }
167
168            return false;
169
170         } // end method ShouldDisplay
171
172         // invoked when user clicks Done button
173         private void doneButton_Click(
174            object sender, System.EventArgs e )
175         {
176            // determine whether file exists
177            if ( input != null )
178            {
179               // close file
180               try
181               {
182                  input.Close();
183               }
184
185               // handle exception if FileStream does not exist
186               catch( IOException )
187               {
188                  // notify user of error closing file
189                  MessageBox.Show( "Cannot close file", "Error",
190                     MessageBoxButtons.OK, MessageBoxIcon.Error);
191               }
192            }
193
194            Application.Exit();
195
196         } // end method doneButton_Click
197
198   } // end class CreditInquiryForm
```

Fig. 14.12 Credit-inquiry program. (Part 5 of 7.)

Fig. 14.12   Credit-inquiry program. (Part 6 of 7.)

Fig. 14.12   Credit-inquiry program. (Part 7 of 7.)

14.7 Random-Access Files

So far, we have explained how to create sequential-access files and how to search through such files to locate particular information. However, sequential-access files are inappropriate for so-called *"instant-access" applications*, in which a particular record of information must be located immediately. Popular instant-access applications include airline-reservation systems, banking systems, point-of-sale systems, database systems, automated-teller machines and other kinds of *transaction-processing systems* requiring rapid access to specific data. The bank at which an individual has an account might have hundreds of thousands or even millions of other customers; however, when that individual uses an automated teller machine, the appropriate account is checked for sufficient funds in seconds. This type of instant access is made possible by *random-access files*. Individual records of a random-access file can be accessed directly (and quickly), without searching through potentially large numbers of other records, as is necessary with sequential-access files. Random-access files sometimes are called *direct-access files*.

As we discussed earlier in this chapter, C# does not impose structure on files, so applications that use random-access files must implement the random-access capability. There are a variety of techniques for creating random-access files. Perhaps the simplest involves requiring that all records in a file be of a uniform, fixed length. The use of fixed-length records enables a program to calculate (as a function of the record size and the record key) the exact location of any record in relation to the beginning of the file. We soon demonstrate how this facilitates immediate access to specific records, even in large files.

Figure 14.13 illustrates the organization of a random-access file composed of fixed-length records (each record in this figure is 100 bytes long). Readers can consider a random-access file as analogous to a railroad train with many cars, some of which are empty and some of which contain contents.

Data can be inserted into a random-access file without destroying other data in the file. In addition, previously stored data can be updated or deleted without rewriting the entire file. In the following sections, we explain how to create a random-access file, write data to that file, read data both sequentially and randomly, update data and delete data that is no longer needed.

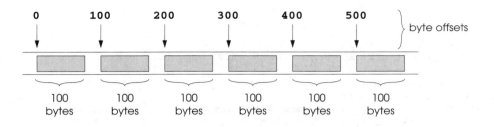

Fig. 14.13 Random-access file with fixed-length records.

Figure 14.14 contains class **RandomAccessRecord**, which is used in the random-access file-processing applications in this chapter. This class also belongs to the **Bank-Library** DLL—i.e., it is part of the project that contains classes **BankUIForm** and **Record**. (When adding class **RandomAccessRecord** to the project containing **BankUIForm** and **Record**, remember to rebuild the project.)

Like class **Record** (Fig. 14.8), class **RandomAccessRecord** contains **private** data members (lines 20–23) for storing record information, two constructors for setting these members to default and parameter-specified values, respectively, and properties for accessing these members. However, class **RandomAccessRecord** does not contain attribute **[Serializable]** before its class definition. We do not serialize this class, because C# does not provide a means to obtain an object's size at runtime. This means that, if we serialize the class, we cannot guarantee a fixed-length record size.

Instead of serializing the class, we fix the length of the **private** data members, then write those data as a byte stream to the file. To fix this length, the **set** accessors of properties **FirstName** (lines 58–91) and **LastName** (lines 94–127) ensure that members **firstName** and **lastName** are **char** arrays of exactly 15 elements. Each **set** accessor receives as an argument a **string** representing the first name and last name, respectively. If the **string** parameter contains fewer than 15 characters, the property's **set** accessor copies the **string**'s values to the **char** array, then populates the remainder with spaces. If the **string** parameter contains more than 15 characters, the **set** accessor stores only the first 15 characters of the **string** parameter into the **char** array.

```
1   // Fig. 14.14: RandomAccessRecord.cs
2   // Data-record class for random-access applications.
3
4   using System;
5
6   public class RandomAccessRecord
7   {
8      // length of firstName and lastName
9      private const int CHAR_ARRAY_LENGTH = 15;
10
11     private const int SIZE_OF_CHAR = 2;
12     private const int SIZE_OF_INT32 = 4;
13     private const int SIZE_OF_DOUBLE = 8;
```

Fig. 14.14 Record for random-access file-processing applications. (Part 1 of 4.)

```
14
15        // length of record
16        public const int SIZE = SIZE_OF_INT32 +
17           2 * ( SIZE_OF_CHAR * CHAR_ARRAY_LENGTH ) + SIZE_OF_DOUBLE;
18
19        // record data
20        private int account;
21        private char[] firstName = new char[ CHAR_ARRAY_LENGTH ];
22        private char[] lastName = new char[ CHAR_ARRAY_LENGTH ];
23        private double balance;
24
25        // default constructor sets members to default values
26        public RandomAccessRecord() : this( 0, "", "", 0.0 )
27        {
28        }
29
30        // overloaded counstructor sets members to parameter values
31        public RandomAccessRecord( int accountValue,
32           string firstNameValue, string lastNameValue,
33           double balanceValue )
34        {
35           Account = accountValue;
36           FirstName = firstNameValue;
37           LastName = lastNameValue;
38           Balance = balanceValue;
39
40        } // end constructor
41
42        // property Account
43        public int Account
44        {
45           get
46           {
47              return account;
48           }
49
50           set
51           {
52              account = value;
53           }
54
55        } // end property Account
56
57        // property FirstName
58        public string FirstName
59        {
60           get
61           {
62              return new string( firstName );
63           }
64
```

Fig. 14.14 Record for random-access file-processing applications. (Part 2 of 4.)

```
65            set
66            {
67               // determine length of string parameter
68               int stringSize = value.Length;
69
70               // firstName string representation
71               string firstNameString = value;
72
73               // append spaces to string parameter if too short
74               if ( CHAR_ARRAY_LENGTH >= stringSize )
75               {
76                  firstNameString = value +
77                     new string( ' ', CHAR_ARRAY_LENGTH - stringSize );
78               }
79               else
80               {
81                  // remove characters from string parameter if too long
82                  firstNameString =
83                     value.Substring( 0, CHAR_ARRAY_LENGTH );
84               }
85
86               // convert string parameter to char array
87               firstName = firstNameString.ToCharArray();
88
89            } // end set
90
91         } // end property FirstName
92
93         // property LastName
94         public string LastName
95         {
96            get
97            {
98               return new string( lastName );
99            }
100
101           set
102           {
103              // determine length of string parameter
104              int stringSize = value.Length;
105
106              // lastName string representation
107              string lastNameString = value;
108
109              // append spaces to string parameter if too short
110              if ( CHAR_ARRAY_LENGTH >= stringSize )
111              {
112                 lastNameString = value +
113                    new string( ' ', CHAR_ARRAY_LENGTH - stringSize );
114              }
```

Fig. 14.14 Record for random-access file-processing applications. (Part 3 of 4.)

```
115              else
116              {
117                  // remove characters from string parameter if too long
118                  lastNameString =
119                      value.Substring( 0, CHAR_ARRAY_LENGTH );
120              }
121
122              // convert string parameter to char array
123              lastName = lastNameString.ToCharArray();
124
125          } // end set
126
127      } // end property LastName
128
129      // property Balance
130      public double Balance
131      {
132          get
133          {
134              return balance;
135          }
136
137          set
138          {
139              balance = value;
140          }
141
142      } // end property Balance
143
144  } // end class RandomAccessRecord
```

Fig. 14.14 Record for random-access file-processing applications. (Part 4 of 4.)

Lines 16–17 declare **const SIZE**, which specifies the record's length. Each record contains **account** (4-byte **int**), **firstName** and **lastName** (two 15-element **char** arrays, where each **char** occupies two bytes, resulting in a total of 60 bytes) and **balance** (8-byte **double**). In this example, each record (i.e., the four **private** data members that our programs will read to and write from files) occupies 72 bytes (4 bytes + 60 bytes + 8 bytes).

14.8 Creating a Random-Access File

Consider the following problem statement for a credit-processing application:

> *Create a transaction-processing program capable of storing a maximum of 100 fixed-length records for a company that can have a maximum of 100 customers. Each record consists of an account number (which acts as the record key), a last name, a first name and a balance. The program can update an account, create an account and delete an account.*

The next several sections introduce the techniques necessary to create this credit-processing program. We now discuss the program used to create the random-access file that the programs of Fig. 14.16 and Fig. 14.17 and the transaction-processing application use to manipulate data. Class **CreateRandomAccessFile** (Fig. 14.15) creates a random-access file.

```
1    // Fig. 14.15: CreateRandomAccessFile.cs
2    // Creating a random file.
3
4    // C# namespaces
5    using System;
6    using System.IO;
7    using System.Windows.Forms;
8
9    // Deitel namespaces
10   using BankLibrary;
11
12   class CreateRandomAccessFile
13   {
14      // number of records to write to disk
15      private const int NUMBER_OF_RECORDS = 100;
16
17      [STAThread]
18      static void Main(string[] args)
19      {
20         // create random file, then save to disk
21         CreateRandomAccessFile file = new CreateRandomAccessFile();
22         file.SaveFile();
23
24      } // end method Main
25
26      // write records to disk
27      private void SaveFile()
28      {
29         // record for writing to disk
30         RandomAccessRecord blankRecord = new RandomAccessRecord();
31
32         // stream through which serializable data are written to file
33         FileStream fileOutput = null;
34
35         // stream for writing bytes to file
36         BinaryWriter binaryOutput = null;
37
38         // create dialog box enabling user to save file
39         SaveFileDialog fileChooser = new SaveFileDialog();
40         DialogResult result = fileChooser.ShowDialog();
41
42         // get file name from user
43         string fileName = fileChooser.FileName;
44
45         // exit event handler if user clicked Cancel
46         if ( result == DialogResult.Cancel )
47            return;
48
49         // show error if user specified invalid file
50         if ( fileName == "" || fileName == null )
51            MessageBox.Show("Invalid File Name", "Error",
52               MessageBoxButtons.OK, MessageBoxIcon.Error);
```

Fig. 14.15 Creating files for random-access file-processing applications. (Part 1 of 3.)

```
53          else
54          {
55              // write records to file
56              try
57              {
58                  // create FileStream to hold records
59                  fileOutput = new FileStream( fileName,
60                      FileMode.Create, FileAccess.Write );
61
62                  // set length of file
63                  fileOutput.SetLength( RandomAccessRecord.SIZE *
64                      NUMBER_OF_RECORDS );
65
66                  // create object for writing bytes to file
67                  binaryOutput = new BinaryWriter( fileOutput );
68
69                  // write empty records to file
70                  for ( int i = 0; i < NUMBER_OF_RECORDS; i++ )
71                  {
72                      // set file position pointer in file
73                      fileOutput.Position = i * RandomAccessRecord.SIZE;
74
75                      // write blank record to file
76                      binaryOutput.Write( blankRecord.Account );
77                      binaryOutput.Write( blankRecord.FirstName );
78                      binaryOutput.Write( blankRecord.LastName );
79                      binaryOutput.Write( blankRecord.Balance );
80                  }
81
82                  // notify user of success
83                  MessageBox.Show("File Created", "Success",
84                      MessageBoxButtons.OK, MessageBoxIcon.Information);
85              }
86
87              // handle exception if error occurs during writing
88              catch( IOException )
89              {
90                  // notify user of error
91                  MessageBox.Show( "Cannot write to file", "Error",
92                      MessageBoxButtons.OK, MessageBoxIcon.Error );
93              }
94          }
95
96          // close FileStream
97          if ( fileOutput == null )
98              fileOutput.Close();
99
100         // close BinaryWriter
101         if ( binaryOutput == null )
102             binaryOutput.Close();
103
104     } // end method SaveFile
105 } // end class CreateRandomAccessFile
```

Fig. 14.15 Creating files for random-access file-processing applications. (Part 2 of 3.)

Fig. 14.15 Creating files for random-access file-processing applications. (Part 3 of 3.)

Method **Main** (lines 18–24) starts the application, which creates a random-access file by calling user-defined method **SaveFile** (lines 27–104). Method **SaveFile** populates a file with 100 copies of the default (i.e., empty) values for **private** data members **account**, **firstName**, **lastName** and **balance** of class **RandomAccessRecord**. Lines 39–40 create and display the **SaveFileDialog**, which enables a user to specify the file to which the program writes data. Using this file, lines 59–60 instantiate the **FileStream**. Note that line 60 passes constant **FileMode.Create**, which either creates the specified file, if the file does not exist, or overwrites the specified file if it does exist. Lines 63–64 sets the **FileStream**'s length, which is equal to the size of an individual **RandomAccessRecord** (obtained through constant **RandomAccess-Record.SIZE**) multiplied by the number of records we want to copy (obtained through constant **NUMBER_OF_RECORDS** in line 15, which we set to value **100**).

We now require a means to write bytes to a file. Class ***BinaryWriter*** of namespace **System.IO** provides methods for writing bytes to streams. The **BinaryWriter** constructor takes as an argument a reference to an instance of class **System.IO.Stream**, through which the **BinaryWriter** can write bytes. Class **FileStream** provides methods for writing streams to files and inherits from class **Stream**, so we can pass the **FileStream** object as an argument to the **BinaryWriter** constructor (line 67). Now, we can use the **BinaryWriter** to write bytes directly to the file.

Lines 70–80 populate the file with 100 copies of the empty record values (i.e., default values for **private** data members of class **RandomAccessRecord**). Line 73 changes the file-position pointer to specify the location in the file at which to write the next empty record. Now that we are working with a random-access file, we must set the file-pointer explicitly, using the **FileStream** object's **Position** property. This property receives as an argument a **long** value describing where to position the pointer relative to the beginning of the file—in this example, we set the pointer so that it advances a number of bytes that is equal to the record size (obtained by **RandomAccessRecord.SIZE**). Lines 76–79 call method **Write** of the **BinaryWriter** object to write the data. Method **Write** is an overloaded method that receives as an argument any primitive data type, then writes that type to a stream of bytes. After the **for** loop exits, lines 97–102 close the **FileStream** and **BinaryWriter** objects.

14.9 Writing Data Randomly to a Random-Access File

Now that we have created a random-access file, we use class **WriteRandomAccess-FileForm** (Fig. 14.16) to write data to that file. When a user clicks the **Open File** button, the program invokes method **openButton_Click** (lines 41–84), which displays the **OpenFileDialog** for specifying the file in which to serialize data (lines 45–46); the program then uses the specified file to create a **FileStream** object with write-only access (lines 65–66). Line 69 uses the **FileStream** reference to instantiate an object of class **BinaryWriter**, enabling the program to write bytes to files. We used the same approach when working with class **CreateRandomAccessFile** (Fig. 14.15).

The user enters values in the **TextBox**es for the account number, first name, last name and balance. When the user clicks the **Enter** button, the program invokes method **enterButton_Click** (lines 87–139), which writes the data in the **TextBox**es to the file. Line 91 calls method **GetTextBoxValues** (provided by base class **BankUIForm**) to retrieve the data. Lines 104–105 determine whether the **Account Number TextBox** holds valid information (i.e., the account number is in the **1–100** range).

```
1   // Fig. 14.16: WriteRandomAccessFile.cs
2   // Write data to a random-access file.
3
4   // C# namespaces
5   using System;
6   using System.Drawing;
7   using System.Collections;
8   using System.ComponentModel;
9   using System.Windows.Forms;
10  using System.Data;
11  using System.IO;
12
13  // Deitel namespaces
14  using BankLibrary;
15
16  public class WriteRandomAccessFileForm : BankUIForm
17  {
18      private System.Windows.Forms.Button openButton;
19      private System.Windows.Forms.Button enterButton;
20
21      private System.ComponentModel.Container components = null;
22
```

Fig. 14.16 Writing records to random-access files. (Part 1 of 5.)

```
23      // number of RandomAccessRecords to write to disk
24      private const int NUMBER_OF_RECORDS = 100;
25
26      // stream through which data are written to file
27      private FileStream fileOutput;
28
29      // stream for writing bytes to file
30      private BinaryWriter binaryOutput;
31
32      [STAThread]
33      static void Main()
34      {
35         Application.Run( new WriteRandomAccessFileForm() );
36      }
37
38      // Visual Studio .NET generated code
39
40      // invoked when user clicks Open button
41      private void openButton_Click(
42         object sender, System.EventArgs e )
43      {
44         // create dialog box enabling user to open file
45         OpenFileDialog fileChooser = new OpenFileDialog();
46         DialogResult result = fileChooser.ShowDialog();
47
48         // get file name from user
49         string fileName = fileChooser.FileName;
50
51         // exit event handler if user clicked Cancel
52         if ( result == DialogResult.Cancel )
53            return;
54
55         // show error if user specified invalid file
56         if ( fileName == "" || fileName == null )
57            MessageBox.Show("Invalid File Name", "Error",
58               MessageBoxButtons.OK, MessageBoxIcon.Error);
59         else
60         {
61            // open file if file already exists
62            try
63            {
64               // create FileStream to hold records
65               fileOutput = new FileStream( fileName,
66                  FileMode.Open, FileAccess.Write );
67
68               // create object for writing bytes to file
69               binaryOutput = new BinaryWriter( fileOutput );
70
71               // disable Open button and enable Enter button
72               openButton.Enabled = false;
73               enterButton.Enabled = true;
74            }
75
```

Fig. 14.16 Writing records to random-access files. (Part 2 of 5.)

```
76                  // notify user if file does not exist
77                  catch( IOException )
78                  {
79                     MessageBox.Show("File Does Not Exits", "Error",
80                        MessageBoxButtons.OK, MessageBoxIcon.Error);
81                  }
82              }
83
84          } // end method openButton_Click
85
86          // invoked when user clicks Enter button
87          private void enterButton_Click(
88             object sender, System.EventArgs e )
89          {
90             // TextBox values string array
91             string[] values = GetTextBoxValues();
92
93             // determine whether TextBox account field is empty
94             if ( values[ ( int )TextBoxIndices.ACCOUNT ] != "" )
95             {
96                // write record to file at appropriate position
97                try
98                {
99                   // get account number value from TextBox
100                  int accountNumber = Int32.Parse(
101                     values[ ( int )TextBoxIndices.ACCOUNT ] );
102
103                  // determine whether accountNumber is valid
104                  if ( accountNumber > 0 &&
105                     accountNumber <= NUMBER_OF_RECORDS )
106                  {
107                     // move file position pointer
108                     fileOutput.Seek( ( accountNumber - 1 ) *
109                        RandomAccessRecord.SIZE, SeekOrigin.Begin );
110
111                     // write data to file
112                     binaryOutput.Write( accountNumber );
113                     binaryOutput.Write(
114                        values[ ( int )TextBoxIndices.FIRST ] );
115                     binaryOutput.Write(
116                        values[ ( int )TextBoxIndices.LAST ] );
117                     binaryOutput.Write( Double.Parse( values[
118                        ( int )TextBoxIndices.BALANCE ] ) );
119                  }
120                  else
121                  {
122                     // notify user if invalid account number
123                     MessageBox.Show("Invalid Account Number", "Error",
124                        MessageBoxButtons.OK, MessageBoxIcon.Error);
125                  }
126               }
127
```

Fig. 14.16 Writing records to random-access files. (Part 3 of 5.)

```
128           // handle number-format exception
129           catch( FormatException )
130           {
131              // notify user if error occurs when formatting numbers
132              MessageBox.Show("Invalid Balance", "Error",
133                 MessageBoxButtons.OK, MessageBoxIcon.Error );
134           }
135        }
136
137        ClearTextBoxes(); // clear text box values
138
139     } // end method enterButton_Click
140
141  } // end class WriteRandomAccessFileForm
```

Fig. 14.16 Writing records to random-access files. (Part 4 of 5.)

Fig. 14.16 Writing records to random-access files. (Part 5 of 5.)

Class **WriteRandomAccessFileForm** must determine the location in the **FileStream** at which to insert the data from the **TextBox**es. Lines 108–109 use method **Seek** of the **FileStream** object to locate an exact point in the file. In this case, method **Seek** sets the position of the file-position pointer for the **FileStream** object to the byte location calculated by **(accountNumber - 1) * RandomAccessRecord.SIZE**. Because the account numbers range from **1** to **100**, we subtract **1** from the account number when calculating the byte location of the record. For example, our use of method **Seek** sets the first record's file-position pointer to byte 0 of the file (the file's beginning). The second argument to method **Seek** is a member of the enumeration *SeekOrigin* and specifies the location at which the method should begin seeking. We use **const *SeekOrigin.Begin***, because we want the method to seek in relation to the beginning of the file. After the program determines the file location at which to place the record, lines 112–118 write the record to the file using the **BinaryWriter** (discussed in the previous section).

14.10 Reading Data Sequentially from a Random-Access File

In the previous sections, we created a random-access file and wrote data to that file. Here, we develop a program (Fig. 14.17) that opens the file, reads records from it and displays only the records that contain data (i.e., those records in which the account number is not zero). This program also provides an additional benefit. Readers should attempt to determine what it is—we will reveal it at the end of this section.

When the user clicks the **Open File** button, class **ReadRandomAccessFileForm** invokes method **openButton_Click** (lines 41–75), which displays the **OpenFile-Dialog** for specifying the file from which to read data. Lines 62–63 instantiate a **FileStream** object that opens a file with read-only access. Line 66 creates an instance of class **BinaryReader**, which reads bytes from a stream. We pass the **FileStream** object as an argument to the **BinaryReader** constructor, thus enabling the **BinaryReader** to read bytes from the file.

```
1   // Fig. 14.17: ReadRandomAccessFile.cs
2   // Reads and displays random-access file contents.
3
4   // C# namespaces
5   using System;
6   using System.Drawing;
7   using System.Collections;
8   using System.ComponentModel;
9   using System.Windows.Forms;
10  using System.Data;
11  using System.IO;
12
13  // Deitel namespaces
14  using BankLibrary;
15
16  public class ReadRandomAccessFileForm : BankUIForm
17  {
18      private System.Windows.Forms.Button openButton;
19      private System.Windows.Forms.Button nextButton;
20
21      private System.ComponentModel.Container components = null;
22
23      // stream through which data are read from file
24      private FileStream fileInput;
25
26      // stream for reading bytes from file
27      private BinaryReader binaryInput;
28
29      // index of current record to be displayed
30      private int currentRecordIndex;
31
```

Fig. 14.17 Reading records from random-access files sequentially. (Part 1 of 5.)

```
32      [STAThread]
33      static void Main()
34      {
35          Application.Run( new ReadRandomAccessFileForm() );
36      }
37
38      // Visual Studio .NET generated code
39
40      // invoked when user clicks Open button
41      private void openButton_Click(
42          object sender, System.EventArgs e )
43      {
44          // create dialog box enabling user to open file
45          OpenFileDialog fileChooser = new OpenFileDialog();
46          DialogResult result = fileChooser.ShowDialog();
47
48          // get file name from user
49          string fileName = fileChooser.FileName;
50
51          // exit eventhandler if user clicked Cancel
52          if ( result == DialogResult.Cancel )
53              return;
54
55          // show error if user specified invalid file
56          if ( fileName == "" || fileName == null )
57              MessageBox.Show( "Invalid File Name", "Error",
58                  MessageBoxButtons.OK, MessageBoxIcon.Error );
59          else
60          {
61              // create FileStream to obtain read access to file
62              fileInput = new FileStream( fileName,
63                  FileMode.Open, FileAccess.Read );
64
65              // use FileStream for BinaryWriter to read bytes from file
66              binaryInput = new BinaryReader( fileInput );
67
68              openButton.Enabled = false; // disable Open button
69              nextButton.Enabled = true; // enable Next button
70
71              currentRecordIndex = 0;
72              ClearTextBoxes();
73          }
74
75      } // end method openButton_Click
76
77      // invoked when user clicks Next button
78      private void nextButton_Click(
79          object sender, System.EventArgs e )
80      {
81          // record to store file data
82          RandomAccessRecord record = new RandomAccessRecord();
83
```

Fig. 14.17 Reading records from random-access files sequentially. (Part 2 of 5.)

```
84          // read record and store data in TextBoxes
85          try
86          {
87             string[] values; // for storing TextBox values
88
89             // get next record available in file
90             while( record.Account == 0 )
91             {
92                // set file position pointer to next record in file
93                fileInput.Seek(
94                   currentRecordIndex * RandomAccessRecord.SIZE, 0 );
95
96                currentRecordIndex += 1;
97
98                // read data from record
99                record.Account = binaryInput.ReadInt32();
100               record.FirstName = binaryInput.ReadString();
101               record.LastName = binaryInput.ReadString();
102               record.Balance = binaryInput.ReadDouble();
103            }
104
105            // store record values in temporary string array
106            values = new string[] {
107               record.Account.ToString(),
108               record.FirstName,
109               record.LastName,
110               record.Balance.ToString() };
111
112            // copy string array values to TextBox values
113            SetTextBoxValues( values );
114         }
115
116         // handle exception when no records in file
117         catch( IOException )
118         {
119            // close streams if no records in file
120            fileInput.Close();
121            binaryInput.Close();
122
123            openButton.Enabled = true; // enable Open button
124            nextButton.Enabled = false; // disable Next button
125            ClearTextBoxes();
126
127            // notify user if no records in file
128            MessageBox.Show("No more records in file", "",
129               MessageBoxButtons.OK, MessageBoxIcon.Information);
130         }
131
132      } // end method nextButton_Click
133
134 } // end class ReadRandomAccessFileForm
```

Fig. 14.17 Reading records from random-access files sequentially. (Part 3 of 5.)

Fig. 14.17 Reading records from random-access files sequentially. (Part 4 of 5.)

Fig. 14.17 Reading records from random-access files sequentially. (Part 5 of 5.)

When the user clicks the **Next** button, the program calls method **nextButton_Click** (lines 78–132), which reads the next record from the file. Line 82 instantiates a **RandomAccessRecord** for storing the record data from the file. Lines 90–114 define a **while** loop that reads from the file until it reaches a record that has a non-zero account number (**0** is the initial value for the account number). Lines 93–94 call method **Seek** of the **FileStream** object, which moves the file-position pointer to the appropriate place in the file where the record must be read. To accomplish this, method **Seek** uses **int currentRecordIndex**, which stores the number of records that have been read. Lines 99–102 use the **BinaryReader** object to store the file data in the **RandomAccessRecord** object. Recall that class **BinaryWriter** provides overloaded **Write** methods for writing data. However, class **BinaryReader** does not provide overloaded **Read** methods to read data. This means that we must use method **ReadInt32** to read an **int**, method **ReadString** to read a **string** and method **ReadDouble** to read a **double**. Note that the order of these method invocations must correspond to the order in which the **BinaryWriter** object wrote each data type. When the **BinaryReader** reads a valid account number (i.e., a non-zero value), the loop terminates, and lines 106–113 display the record values in the **TextBox**es. When the program has displayed all records, method **Seek** throws an **IOException** (because method **Seek** tries to position the file-position pointer to a location that is beyond the end-of-file marker). The **catch** block (lines 117–130) handles this exception by closing the **FileStream** and **BinaryReader** objects (lines 120–121) and notifying the user that no more records exist (lines 128–129).

What about that additional benefit we promised? If readers examine the GUI as the program executes, they will notice that the program displays the records in ascending order by account number! This is a simple consequence of using our direct-access techniques to store these records in the file. We achieve this improved speed by making the file large enough to hold every possible record that a user might create. Of course, this means that the file could be sparsely occupied most of the time, resulting in a waste of storage. Here is yet another example of the space/time trade-off: By using large amounts of space, we are able to develop a faster sorting algorithm.

14.11 Case Study: A Transaction-Processing Program

We now develop a substantial transaction-processing program (Fig. 14.18–Fig. 14.23) using a random-access file to achieve "instant-access" processing. The program maintains a bank's account information. Users of this program can add new accounts, update existing accounts and delete accounts that are no longer needed. First, we discuss the transaction-processing behavior (i.e., the class that enables the addition, updating and removal of accounts). We then discuss the GUI, which contains windows that display the account information and enable the user to invoke the application's transaction-processing behavior.

Transaction-Processing Behavior

In this case study, we create class **Transaction** (Fig. 14.18), which acts as a *proxy* to handle all transaction processing. Rather than providing the transaction-processing behavior themselves, the objects in this application use an instance of **Transaction** to provide the necessary functionality. By using a proxy, we can encapsulate transaction-processing behavior in only one class, enabling various other classes in our application to reuse this behavior. Furthermore, if we decide to modify this behavior, we modify only the proxy (i.e., class **Transaction**), instead of having to modify the behavior of each class that uses the proxy.

Class **Transaction** contains methods **OpenFile**, **GetRecord** and **AddRecord**. Method **OpenFile** (lines 27–74) uses constant **FileMode.OpenOrCreate** (line 33) to create a **FileStream** object from either an existing file or one not yet created. Lines 36–39 use this **FileStream** to create **BinaryReader** and **BinaryWriter** objects for reading and writing bytes to the file, respectively. If the file is new, lines 42–64 populate the **FileStream** object with empty records. Readers might recall that we used these techniques in Section 14.8.

```
1   // Fig. 14.18: Transaction.cs
2   // Handles record transactions.
3
4   // C# namespaces
5   using System;
6   using System.IO;
7   using System.Windows.Forms;
8
```

Fig. 14.18 Record-transaction class for the transaction-processor case study. (Part 1 of 4.)

```
 9      // Deitel namespaces
10      using BankLibrary;
11
12      public class Transaction
13      {
14         // number of records to write to disk
15         private const int NUMBER_OF_RECORDS = 100;
16
17         // stream through which data move to and from file
18         private FileStream file;
19
20         // stream for reading bytes from file
21         private BinaryReader binaryInput;
22
23         // stream for writing bytes to file
24         private BinaryWriter binaryOutput;
25
26         // create/open file containing empty records
27         public void OpenFile( string fileName )
28         {
29            // write empty records to file
30            try
31            {
32               // create FileStream from new file or existing file
33               file = new FileStream( fileName, FileMode.OpenOrCreate );
34
35               // use FileStream for BinaryWriter to read bytes from file
36               binaryInput = new BinaryReader( file );
37
38               // use FileStream for BinaryWriter to write bytes to file
39               binaryOutput = new BinaryWriter( file );
40
41               // determine whether file has just been created
42               if ( file.Length == 0 )
43               {
44                  // record to be written to file
45                  RandomAccessRecord blankRecord =
46                     new RandomAccessRecord();
47
48                  // new record can hold NUMBER_OF_RECORDS records
49                  file.SetLength( RandomAccessRecord.SIZE *
50                     NUMBER_OF_RECORDS );
51
52                  // write blank records to file
53                  for ( int i = 0; i < NUMBER_OF_RECORDS; i++ )
54                  {
55                     // move file-position pointer to next position
56                     file.Position = i * RandomAccessRecord.SIZE;
57
58                     // write blank record to file
59                     binaryOutput.Write( blankRecord.Account );
60                     binaryOutput.Write( blankRecord.FirstName );
```

Fig. 14.18 Record-transaction class for the transaction-processor case study. (Part 2 of 4.)

```
61                       binaryOutput.Write( blankRecord.LastName );
62                       binaryOutput.Write( blankRecord.Balance );
63                    }
64                 }
65              }
66
67              // notify user of error during writing of blank records
68              catch( IOException )
69              {
70                 MessageBox.Show("Cannot create file", "Error",
71                    MessageBoxButtons.OK, MessageBoxIcon.Error);
72              }
73
74           } // end method OpenFile
75
76           // retrieve record depending on whether account is valid
77           public RandomAccessRecord GetRecord( string accountValue )
78           {
79              // store file data associated with account in record
80              try
81              {
82                 // record to store file data
83                 RandomAccessRecord record = new RandomAccessRecord();
84
85                 // get value from TextBox's account field
86                 int accountNumber = Int32.Parse( accountValue );
87
88                 // if account is invalid, do not read data
89                 if ( accountNumber < 1 ||
90                    accountNumber > NUMBER_OF_RECORDS )
91                 {
92                    // set record's account field with account number
93                    record.Account = accountNumber;
94                 }
95
96                 // get data from file if account is valid
97                 else
98                 {
99                    // locate position in file where record exists
100                   file.Seek( ( accountNumber - 1 ) *
101                      RandomAccessRecord.SIZE, 0 );
102
103                   // read data from record
104                   record.Account = binaryInput.ReadInt32();
105                   record.FirstName = binaryInput.ReadString();
106                   record.LastName = binaryInput.ReadString();
107                   record.Balance = binaryInput.ReadDouble();
108                }
109
110                return record;
111             }
112
```

Fig. 14.18 Record-transaction class for the transaction-processor case study. (Part 3 of 4.)

```
113          // notify user of error during reading
114          catch( IOException )
115          {
116             MessageBox.Show( "Cannot read file", "Error",
117                MessageBoxButtons.OK, MessageBoxIcon.Error );
118          }
119
120          return null;
121
122       } // end method GetRecord;
123
124       // add record to file at position determined by accountNumber
125       public bool AddRecord(
126          RandomAccessRecord record, int accountNumber )
127       {
128          // write record to file
129          try
130          {
131             // move file position pointer to appropriate position
132             file.Seek( ( accountNumber - 1 ) *
133                RandomAccessRecord.SIZE, 0 );
134
135             // write data to file
136             binaryOutput.Write(record.Account);
137             binaryOutput.Write(record.FirstName);
138             binaryOutput.Write(record.LastName);
139             binaryOutput.Write(record.Balance);
140          }
141
142          // notify user if error occurs during writing
143          catch( IOException )
144          {
145             MessageBox.Show( "Error Writing To File", "Error",
146                MessageBoxButtons.OK, MessageBoxIcon.Error );
147
148             return false; // failure
149          }
150
151          return true; // success
152
153       } // end method AddRecord
154
155    } // end class Transaction
```

Fig. 14.18 Record-transaction class for the transaction-processor case study.
(Part 4 of 4.)

Method **GetRecord** (lines 77–122) returns the record associated with the account-number parameter. Line 83 instantiates a **RandomAccessRecord** object that will store the file data. If the account parameter is valid, lines 100–101 call method **Seek** of the **FileStream** object, which uses the parameter to determine the position of the specified record in the file. Lines 104–107 then call methods **ReadInt32**, **ReadString** and **ReadDouble** of the **BinaryReader** object to store the file data in the **Random-**

AccessRecord object. Line 110 returns the **RandomAccessRecord** object. We used these techniques in Section 14.10.

Method **AddRecord** (lines 125–153) inserts a record into the file. Lines 132–133 call method **Seek** of the **FileStream** object, which uses the account-number parameter to locate the position at which to insert the record in the file. Lines 136–139 call the overloaded **Write** methods of the **BinaryWriter** object to write the **RandomAccessRecord** object's data to the file. We used these techniques in Section 14.9. Note that, if an error occurs when adding the record (i.e., either the **FileStream** or the **BinaryWriter** throws an **IOException**), lines 145–146 notify the user of the error and return **false** (failure).

Transaction-Processor GUI

The GUI for this program uses a multiple-document interface. Class **Transaction-ProcessorForm** (Fig. 14.19) is the parent window, and contains corresponding child windows **StartDialogForm** (Fig. 14.20), **NewDialogForm** (Fig. 14.22), **Update-DialogForm** (Fig. 14.21) and **DeleteDialogForm** (Fig. 14.23). **StartDialog-Form** allows the user to open a file containing account information and provides access to the **NewDialogForm**, **UpdateDialogForm** and **DeleteDialogForm** internal frames. These frames allow users to update, create and delete records, respectively.

Initially, **TransactionProcessorForm** displays the **StartDialogForm** object; this window provides the user with various options. It contains four buttons, which enable the user to create or open a file, create a record, update an existing record or delete an existing record.

```
1   // Fig. 14.19: TransactionProcessor.cs
2   // MDI parent for transaction-processor application.
3
4   using System;
5   using System.Drawing;
6   using System.Collections;
7   using System.ComponentModel;
8   using System.Windows.Forms;
9   using System.Data;
10
11  public class TransactionProcessorForm
12     : System.Windows.Forms.Form
13  {
14     private System.ComponentModel.Container components = null;
15     private System.Windows.Forms.MdiClient MdiClient1;
16
17     // reference to StartDialog
18     private StartDialogForm startDialog;
19
20     // constructor
21     public TransactionProcessorForm()
22     {
23        // required for Windows Form Designer support
24        InitializeComponent();
25
```

Fig. 14.19 **TransactionProcessorForm** class runs the transaction-processor application. (Part 1 of 2.)

```
26          startDialog = new StartDialogForm();
27          startDialog.MdiParent = this;
28          startDialog.Show();
29       }
30
31       [STAThread]
32       static void Main()
33       {
34          Application.Run( new TransactionProcessorForm() );
35       }
36
37       // Visual Studio .NET generated code
38
39  } // end class TransactionProcessorForm
```

Fig. 14.19 `TransactionProcessorForm` class runs the transaction-processor application. (Part 2 of 2.)

Before the user can modify records, the user must either create or open a file. When the user clicks the **New/Open File** button, the program calls method **open-Button_Click** (lines 42–100), which opens a file that the application uses for modifying records. Lines 46–62 display the **OpenFileDialog** for specifying the file from which to read data, then use this file to create the **FileStream** object. Note that line 52 sets property **CheckFileExists** of the **OpenFileDialog** object to **false**—this enables the user to create a file if the specified file does not exist. If this property were **true** (its default value), the dialog would notify the user that the specified file does not exist, thus preventing the user from creating a file.

```
1   // Fig. 14.20: StartDialog.cs
2   // Initial dialog box displayed to user. Provides buttons for
3   // creating/opening file and for adding, updating and removing
4   // records from file.
5
6   // C# namespaces
7   using System;
8   using System.Drawing;
9   using System.Collections;
10  using System.ComponentModel;
11  using System.Windows.Forms;
12
13  // Deitel namespaces
14  using BankLibrary;
15
16  public delegate void MyDelegate();
17
18  public class StartDialogForm : System.Windows.Forms.Form
19  {
20     private System.Windows.Forms.Button updateButton;
21     private System.Windows.Forms.Button newButton;
```

Fig. 14.20 `StartDialogForm` class enables users to access dialog boxes associated with various transactions. (Part 1 of 4.)

```
22      private System.Windows.Forms.Button deleteButton;
23      private System.Windows.Forms.Button openButton;
24
25      private System.ComponentModel.Container components = null;
26
27      // reference to dialog box for adding record
28      private NewDialogForm newDialog;
29
30      // reference to dialog box for updating record
31      private UpdateDialogForm updateDialog;
32
33      // reference to dialog box for removing record
34      private DeleteDialogForm deleteDialog;
35
36      // reference to object that handles transactions
37      private Transaction transactionProxy;
38
39      // Visual Studio .NET generated code
40
41      // invoked when user clicks New/Open File button
42      private void openButton_Click(
43         object sender, System.EventArgs e )
44      {
45         // create dialog box enabling user to create or open file
46         OpenFileDialog fileChooser = new OpenFileDialog();
47         DialogResult result;
48         string fileName;
49
50         // enable user to create file if file does not exist
51         fileChooser.Title = "Create File / Open File";
52         fileChooser.CheckFileExists = false;
53
54         // show dialog box to user
55         result = fileChooser.ShowDialog();
56
57         // exit event handler if user clicked Cancel
58         if ( result == DialogResult.Cancel )
59            return;
60
61         // get file name from user
62         fileName = fileChooser.FileName;
63
64         // show error if user specified invalid file
65         if ( fileName == "" || fileName == null )
66            MessageBox.Show( "Invalid File Name", "Error",
67               MessageBoxButtons.OK, MessageBoxIcon.Error );
68
69         // open or create file if user specified valid file
70         else
71         {
72            // create Transaction with specified file
73            transactionProxy = new Transaction();
```

Fig. 14.20 StartDialogForm class enables users to access dialog boxes associated with various transactions. (Part 2 of 4.)

```
74              transactionProxy.OpenFile( fileName );
75
76              // enable GUI buttons except for New/Open File button
77              newButton.Enabled = true;
78              updateButton.Enabled = true;
79              deleteButton.Enabled = true;
80              openButton.Enabled = false;
81
82              // instantiate dialog box for creating records
83              newDialog = new NewDialogForm( transactionProxy,
84                 new MyDelegate( ShowStartDialog ) );
85
86              // instantiate dialog box for updating records
87              updateDialog = new UpdateDialogForm( transactionProxy,
88                 new MyDelegate( ShowStartDialog ) );
89
90              // instantiate dialog box for removing records
91              deleteDialog = new DeleteDialogForm( transactionProxy,
92                 new MyDelegate( ShowStartDialog ) );
93
94              // set StartDialog as MdiParent for dialog boxes
95              newDialog.MdiParent = this.MdiParent;
96              updateDialog.MdiParent = this.MdiParent;
97              deleteDialog.MdiParent = this.MdiParent;
98           }
99
100     } // end method openButton_Click
101
102     // invoked when user clicks New Record button
103     private void newButton_Click(
104        object sender, System.EventArgs e )
105     {
106        Hide(); // hide StartDialog
107        newDialog.Show(); // show NewDialog
108
109     } // end method newButton_Click
110
111     private void updateButton_Click(
112        object sender, System.EventArgs e )
113     {
114        Hide(); // hide StartDialog
115        updateDialog.Show(); // show UpdateDialog
116
117     } // end method updateButton_Click
118
119     private void deleteButton_Click(
120        object sender, System.EventArgs e )
121     {
122        Hide(); // hide StartDialog
123        deleteDialog.Show(); // show DeleteDialog
124
125     } // end method deleteButton_Click
```

Fig. 14.20 **StartDialogForm** class enables users to access dialog boxes associated with various transactions. (Part 3 of 4.)

```
126
127     protected void ShowStartDialog()
128     {
129         Show();
130     }
131
132  } // end class StartDialogForm
```

Fig. 14.20 StartDialogForm class enables users to access dialog boxes
associated with various transactions. (Part 4 of 4.)

If the user specifies a file name, line 73 instantiates an object of class **Transaction** (Fig. 14.18), which acts as the proxy for creating, reading records from and writing records to random-access files. Line 74 calls **Transaction**'s method **OpenFile**, which either creates or opens the specified file, depending on whether the file exists.

Class **StartDialogForm** also creates internal windows that enable the user to create, update and delete records. We do not use the default constructor created by Visual Studio .NET for these classes; instead, we use an overloaded constructor that takes as arguments the **Transaction** object and a delegate object that references method **ShowStartDialog** (lines 127–130). Each child window uses the second delegate parameter to display the **StartDialogForm** GUI when the user closes a child window. Lines 83–92 instantiate objects of classes **UpdateDialogForm**, **NewDialogForm** and **DeleteDialogForm**, which serve as the child windows.

When the user clicks the **New Record** button in the **Start Dialog**, the program invokes method **newButton_Click** of class **StartDialogForm** (Fig. 14.20, lines 103–109), which displays the **NewDialogForm** internal frame (Fig. 14.22). Class **NewDialogForm** enables the user to create records in the file that **StartDialogForm** opened (or created). Line 25 of Fig. 14.22 defines **MyDelegate** as a delegate to a method that does not return a value and has no parameters; method **ShowStartDialog** of class **StartDialogForm** (Fig. 14.20, lines 127–130) conforms to these requirements. Class **NewDialogForm** receives a **MyDelegate** object, which references this method as a parameter—therefore, **NewDialogForm** can invoke this method to display the start window when the user exits the **NewDialogForm**. Classes **UpdateDialogForm** and **DeleteDialogForm** also receive **MyDelegate** references as arguments, enabling them to display **StartDialogForm** after completing their tasks.

After the user enters data in the **TextBox**es and clicks the **Save Record** button, the program invokes method **saveButton_Click** (lines 51–66) to write the record to disk. Lines 54–56 call method **GetRecord** of the **Transaction** object, which should return an empty **RandomAccessRecord**. If method **GetRecord** returns a **RandomAccessRecord** that contains data, the user is attempting to overwrite that **RandomAccessRecord** with a new one. Line 60 calls **private** method **InsertRecord** (lines 69–116). If the **RandomAccessRecord** is empty, method **InsertRecord** calls method **AddRecord** of the **Transaction** object (lines 100–101), which adds the newly created **RandomAccessRecord** to the file. If the user is attempting to overwrite an existing record, lines 81–83 notify the user that the record already exists and return from the method.

When the user clicks the **Update Record** button in the **Start Dialog**, the program invokes method **updateButton_Click** of class **StartDialogForm** (Fig. 14.20, lines 111–117), which displays the **UpdateDialogForm** internal frame (Fig. 14.21). Class **UpdateDialogForm** enables the user to update existing records in the file.

To update a record, the user must enter the account number associated with that record. When the user presses *Enter*, **UpdateDialogForm** calls method **accountTextBox_KeyDown** (lines 45–84) to display the record contents. This method calls method **GetRecord** of the **Transaction** object (lines 52–54) to retrieve the specified **RandomAccessRecord**. If the record is not empty, lines 64–72 populate the **TextBox**es with the **RandomAccessRecord** values.

The **Transaction** **TextBox** initially contains the string **Charge or Payment**. The user should select this text, type the transaction amount (a positive value for a charge or a

negative value for a payment), then press *Enter*. The program calls method
transactionTextBox_KeyDown (lines 87–132) to add the user-specified transaction
amount to the current balance.

```
1    // Fig. 14.21: UpdateDialog.cs
2    // Enables user to update records in file.
3
4    // C# namespaces
5    using System;
6    using System.Drawing;
7    using System.Collections;
8    using System.ComponentModel;
9    using System.Windows.Forms;
10
11   // Deitel namespaces
12   using BankLibrary;
13
14   public class UpdateDialogForm : BankUIForm
15   {
16      private System.Windows.Forms.Label transactionLabel;
17      private System.Windows.Forms.TextBox transactionTextBox;
18
19      private System.Windows.Forms.Button saveButton;
20      private System.Windows.Forms.Button cancelButton;
21
22      private System.ComponentModel.Container components = null;
23
24      // reference to object that handles transactions
25      private Transaction transactionProxy;
26
27      // delegate for method that displays previous window
28      private MyDelegate showPreviousWindow;
29
30      // initialize components and set members to parameter values
31      public UpdateDialogForm(
32         Transaction transactionProxyValue,
33         MyDelegate delegateValue )
34      {
35         InitializeComponent();
36         showPreviousWindow = delegateValue;
37
38         // instantiate object that handles transactions
39         transactionProxy = transactionProxyValue;
40      }
41
42      // Visual Studio .NET generated code
43
44      // invoked when user enters text in account TextBox
45      private void accountTextBox_KeyDown(
46         object sender, System.Windows.Forms.KeyEventArgs e )
47      {
```

Fig. 14.21 UpdateDialogForm class enables users to update records in transaction-processor case study. (Part 1 of 5.)

```
48          // determine whether user pressed Enter key
49          if ( e.KeyCode == Keys.Enter )
50          {
51             // retrieve record associated with account from file
52             RandomAccessRecord record =
53                transactionProxy.GetRecord( GetTextBoxValues()
54                [ ( int )TextBoxIndices.ACCOUNT ] );
55
56             // return if record does not exist
57             if ( record == null )
58                return;
59
60             // determine whether record is empty
61             if ( record.Account != 0 )
62             {
63                // store record values in string array
64                string[] values = {
65                   record.Account.ToString(),
66                   record.FirstName.ToString(),
67                   record.LastName.ToString(),
68                   record.Balance.ToString() };
69
70                // copy string array value to TextBox values
71                SetTextBoxValues( values );
72                transactionTextBox.Text = "[Charge or Payment]";
73
74             }
75             else
76             {
77                // notify user if record does not exist
78                MessageBox.Show(
79                   "Record Does Not Exist", "Error",
80                   MessageBoxButtons.OK, MessageBoxIcon.Error );
81             }
82          }
83
84       } // end method accountTextBox_KeyDown
85
86       // invoked when user enters text in transaction TextBox
87       private void transactionTextBox_KeyDown(
88          object sender, System.Windows.Forms.KeyEventArgs e )
89       {
90          // determine whether user pressed Enter key
91          if ( e.KeyCode == Keys.Enter )
92          {
93             // calculate balance using transaction TextBox value
94             try
95             {
96                // retrieve record associated with account from file
97                RandomAccessRecord record =
98                   transactionProxy.GetRecord( GetTextBoxValues()
99                   [ ( int )TextBoxIndices.ACCOUNT ] );
```

Fig. 14.21 UpdateDialogForm class enables users to update records in transaction-processor case study. (Part 2 of 5.)

```
100
101                // get transaction TextBox value
102                double transactionValue =
103                   Double.Parse( transactionTextBox.Text );
104
105                // calculate new balance (old balance + transaction)
106                double newBalance =
107                   record.Balance + transactionValue;
108
109                // store record values in string array
110                string[] values = {
111                   record.Account.ToString(),
112                   record.FirstName.ToString(),
113                   record.LastName.ToString(),
114                   newBalance.ToString() };
115
116                // copy string array value to TextBox values
117                SetTextBoxValues( values );
118
119                // clear transaction TextBox
120                transactionTextBox.Text = "";
121             }
122
123             // notify user if error occurs in parameter mismatch
124             catch( FormatException )
125             {
126                MessageBox.Show(
127                   "Invalid Transaction", "Error",
128                   MessageBoxButtons.OK, MessageBoxIcon.Error );
129             }
130          }
131
132       } // end method transactionTextBox_KeyDown
133
134       // invoked when user clicks Save button
135       private void saveButton_Click(
136          object sender, System.EventArgs e )
137       {
138          RandomAccessRecord record =
139             transactionProxy.GetRecord( GetTextBoxValues()
140             [ ( int )TextBoxIndices.ACCOUNT ] );
141
142          // if record exists, update in file
143          if ( record != null )
144             UpdateRecord( record );
145
146          Hide();
147          ClearTextBoxes();
148          showPreviousWindow();
149
150       } // end method saveButton_Click
151
```

Fig. 14.21 UpdateDialogForm class enables users to update records in transaction-processor case study. (Part 3 of 5.)

```
152     // invoked when user clicks Cancel button
153     private void cancelButton_Click(
154        object sender, System.EventArgs e )
155     {
156        Hide();
157        ClearTextBoxes();
158        showPreviousWindow();
159
160     } // end method cancelButton_Click
161
162     // update record in file at position specified by accountNumber
163     public void UpdateRecord( RandomAccessRecord record )
164     {
165        // store TextBox values in record and write record to file
166        try
167        {
168           int accountNumber = record.Account;
169           string[] values = GetTextBoxValues();
170
171           // store values in record
172           record.Account = accountNumber;
173           record.FirstName =
174              values[ ( int )TextBoxIndices.FIRST ];
175           record.LastName =
176              values[ ( int )TextBoxIndices.LAST ];
177           record.Balance =
178              Double.Parse(
179              values[ ( int )TextBoxIndices.BALANCE ] );
180
181           // add record to file
182           if ( transactionProxy.AddRecord(
183              record, accountNumber ) == false )
184
185              return; // if error
186        }
187
188        // notify user if error occurs in parameter mismatch
189        catch( FormatException )
190        {
191           MessageBox.Show( "Invalid Balance", "Error",
192              MessageBoxButtons.OK, MessageBoxIcon.Error );
193
194           return;
195        }
196
197        MessageBox.Show( "Record Updated", "Success",
198           MessageBoxButtons.OK,
199           MessageBoxIcon.Information );
200
201     } // end method UpdateRecord
202
203  } // end class UpdateDialogForm
```

Fig. 14.21 UpdateDialogForm class enables users to update records in transaction-processor case study. (Part 4 of 5.)

Fig. 14.21 UpdateDialogForm class enables users to update records in transaction-processor case study. (Part 5 of 5.)

The user clicks the **Save Changes** button to write the altered contents of the **Text-Box**es to the file. (Note that pressing **Save Changes** does not update the **Balance** field—the user must press *Enter* to update this field before pressing **Save Changes**.) When the user clicks **Save Changes**, the program invokes method **saveButton_Click** (lines 135–150), which calls **private** method **UpdateRecord** (lines 163–201). This method calls method **AddRecord** of the **Transaction** object (lines 182–183) to store the **TextBox** values in a **RandomAccessRecord** and over-write the existing file record with the **RandomAccessRecord** containing the new data.

When the user clicks the **Delete Record** button of the **Start Dialog**, the program invokes method **deleteButton_Click** of class **StartDialogForm** (Fig. 14.20, lines 119–125), which displays the **DeleteDialogForm** internal frame (Fig. 14.23). Class **DeleteDialogForm** enables the user to remove existing records from the file. To remove a record, the user must enter the account number associated with that record. When the user clicks the **Delete Record** button (now, from the **DeleteDialogForm** internal frame), **DeleteDialogForm** calls method **deleteButton_Click** (lines 44–57). This method calls method **DeleteRecord** (lines 69–102), which ensures that the record to be deleted exists, then calls method **AddRecord** of the **Transaction** object (lines 87–88) to overwrite the file record with an empty one.

In this chapter, we demonstrated how to read data from files and write data to files via both sequential-access and random-access file-processing techniques. Using class **BinaryFormatter**, we serialized and deserialized objects to and from streams; we then employed **FileStream**, **BinaryWriter** and **BinaryReader** to transfer the objects' byte representation to and from files. In Chapter 15, we discuss the Extensible Markup Language (XML), a widely supported technology for describing data. Using XML, we can describe any type of data, such as mathematical formulas, music and financial reports.

```
1   // Fig. 14.22: NewDialog.cs
2   // Enables user to insert new record into file.
3
4   // C# namespaces
5   using System;
6   using System.Drawing;
7   using System.Collections;
8   using System.ComponentModel;
9   using System.Windows.Forms;
10
11  // Deitel namespaces
12  using BankLibrary;
13
14  public class NewDialogForm : BankUIForm
15  {
16      private System.Windows.Forms.Button saveButton;
17      private System.Windows.Forms.Button cancelButton;
```

Fig. 14.22 **NewDialogForm** class enables users to create records in transaction-processor case study. (Part 1 of 4.)

```
18
19        private System.ComponentModel.Container components = null;
20
21        // reference to object that handles transactions
22        private Transaction transactionProxy;
23
24        // delegate for method that displays previous window
25        public MyDelegate showPreviousWindow;
26
27        // constructor
28        public NewDialogForm( Transaction transactionProxyValue,
29           MyDelegate delegateValue )
30        {
31           InitializeComponent();
32           showPreviousWindow = delegateValue;
33
34           // instantiate object that handles transactions
35           transactionProxy = transactionProxyValue;
36        }
37
38        // Visual Studio .NET generated code
39
40        // invoked when user clicks Cancel button
41        private void cancelButton_Click(
42           object sender, System.EventArgs e )
43        {
44           Hide();
45           ClearTextBoxes();
46           showPreviousWindow();
47
48        } // end method cancelButton_Click
49
50        // invoked when user clicks Save As button
51        private void saveButton_Click(
52           object sender, System.EventArgs e )
53        {
54           RandomAccessRecord record =
55              transactionProxy.GetRecord( GetTextBoxValues()
56              [ ( int )TextBoxIndices.ACCOUNT ] );
57
58           // if record exists, add it to file
59           if ( record != null )
60              InsertRecord( record );
61
62           Hide();
63           ClearTextBoxes();
64           showPreviousWindow();
65
66        } // end method saveButton_Click
67
```

Fig. 14.22 **NewDialogForm** class enables users to create records in transaction-processor case study. (Part 2 of 4.)

```
68        // insert record in file at position specified by accountNumber
69        private void InsertRecord( RandomAccessRecord record )
70        {
71           //store TextBox values in string array
72           string[] textBoxValues = GetTextBoxValues();
73
74           // store TextBox account field
75           int accountNumber = Int32.Parse(
76              textBoxValues[ ( int )TextBoxIndices.ACCOUNT ] );
77
78           // notify user and return if record account is not empty
79           if ( record.Account != 0 )
80           {
81              MessageBox.Show(
82                 "Record Already Exists or Invalid Number", "Error",
83                 MessageBoxButtons.OK, MessageBoxIcon.Error);
84
85              return;
86           }
87
88           // store values in record
89           record.Account = accountNumber;
90           record.FirstName =
91              textBoxValues[ ( int )TextBoxIndices.FIRST];
92           record.LastName =
93              textBoxValues[ ( int )TextBoxIndices.LAST];
94           record.Balance = Double.Parse(
95              textBoxValues[ ( int )TextBoxIndices.BALANCE ] );
96
97           // add record to file
98           try
99           {
100             if ( transactionProxy.AddRecord(
101                record, accountNumber ) == false )
102
103                return; // if error
104          }
105
106          // notify user if error occurs in parameter mismatch
107          catch( FormatException )
108          {
109             MessageBox.Show( "Invalid Balance", "Error",
110                MessageBoxButtons.OK, MessageBoxIcon.Error );
111          }
112
113          MessageBox.Show( "Record Created", "Success",
114             MessageBoxButtons.OK, MessageBoxIcon.Information );
115
116       } // end method InsertRecord
117
118    } // end class NewDialogForm
```

Fig. 14.22 NewDialogForm class enables users to create records in transaction-processor case study. (Part 3 of 4.)

Fig. 14.22 **NewDialogForm** class enables users to create records in transaction-processor case study. (Part 4 of 4.)

```
1   // Fig. 14.23: DeleteDialog.cs
2   // Enables user to delete records in file.
3
4   // C# namespaces
5   using System;
6   using System.Drawing;
7   using System.Collections;
8   using System.ComponentModel;
9   using System.Windows.Forms;
10
11  // Deitel namespaces
12  using BankLibrary;
13
14  public class DeleteDialogForm : System.Windows.Forms.Form
15  {
16     private System.Windows.Forms.Label accountLabel;
17     private System.Windows.Forms.TextBox accountTextBox;
18
19     private System.Windows.Forms.Button deleteButton;
20     private System.Windows.Forms.Button cancelButton;
21
22     private System.ComponentModel.Container components = null;
23
24     // reference to object that handles transactions
25     private Transaction transactionProxy;
```

Fig. 14.23 **DeleteDialogForm** class enables users to remove records from files in transaction-processor case study. (Part 1 of 3.)

```
26
27      // delegate for method that displays previous window
28      private MyDelegate showPreviousWindow;
29
30      // initialize components and set members to parameter values
31      public DeleteDialogForm( Transaction transactionProxyValue,
32         MyDelegate delegateValue)
33      {
34         InitializeComponent();
35         showPreviousWindow = delegateValue;
36
37         // instantiate object that handles transactions
38         transactionProxy = transactionProxyValue;
39      }
40
41      // Visual Studio .NET generated code
42
43      // invoked when user clicks Delete Record button
44      private void deleteButton_Click(
45         object sender, System.EventArgs e)
46      {
47         RandomAccessRecord record =
48            transactionProxy.GetRecord( accountTextBox.Text );
49
50         // if record exists, delete it in file
51         if ( record != null )
52            DeleteRecord( record );
53
54         this.Hide();
55         showPreviousWindow();
56
57      } // end method deleteButton_Click
58
59      // invoked when user clicks Cancel button
60      private void cancelButton_Click(
61         object sender, System.EventArgs e)
62      {
63         this.Hide();
64         showPreviousWindow();
65
66      } // end method cancelButton_Click
67
68      // delete record in file at position specified by accountNumber
69      public void DeleteRecord( RandomAccessRecord record )
70      {
71         int accountNumber = record.Account;
72
73         // display error message if record does not exist
74         if ( record.Account == 0 )
75         {
76            MessageBox.Show( "Record Does Not Exist", "Error",
77               MessageBoxButtons.OK, MessageBoxIcon.Error );
```

Fig. 14.23 DeleteDialogForm class enables users to remove records from files in transaction-processor case study. (Part 2 of 3.)

```
78              accountTextBox.Clear();
79
80              return;
81           }
82
83           // create blank record
84           record = new RandomAccessRecord();
85
86           // write over file record with empty record
87           if ( transactionProxy.AddRecord(
88              record, accountNumber ) == true )
89
90              // notify user of successful deletion
91              MessageBox.Show( "Record Deleted", "Success",
92                 MessageBoxButtons.OK, MessageBoxIcon.Information );
93           else
94
95              // notify user of failure
96              MessageBox.Show(
97                 "Record could not be deleted", "Error",
98                 MessageBoxButtons.OK, MessageBoxIcon.Error );
99
100          accountTextBox.Clear();
101
102       } // end method DeleteRecord
103
104    } // end class DeleteDialogForm
```

Fig. 14.23 DeleteDialogForm class enables users to remove records from files in transaction-processor case study. (Part 3 of 3.)

14.12 Summary

All data items processed by a computer ultimately are reduced to combinations of zeros and ones. The smallest data items that computers support are called bits and can assume either the value **0** or the value **1**. Digits, letters and special symbols are referred to as characters. The set of all characters used to write programs and represent data items on a particular computer is called that computer's character set. Every character in a computer's character set is represented as a pattern of **1**s and **0**s.

A field is a group of characters that conveys some meaning. A record is a group of related fields. At least one field in a record is chosen as a record key, which identifies that record as belonging to a particular person or entity and distinguishes that record from all other records in the file. A file is a group of related records. Files are used for long-term retention of large amounts of data and can store those data even after the program that created the data terminates. Data maintained in files often are called persistent data.

C# imposes no structure on files. This means that concepts like that of a record do not exist in C#. The programmer must structure each file appropriately to meet the requirements of an application. C# views each file as a sequential stream of bytes. Each file ends in some machine-dependent form of end-of-file marker.

To perform file processing in C#, the namespace **System.IO** must be referenced. This namespace includes definitions for stream classes such as **StreamReader**, **StreamWriter** and **FileStream**. Files are opened by instantiating objects of these classes. When a file is opened, an object is created, and a stream is associated with the object. Streams provide communication channels between files and programs.

The most common type of file organization is the sequential file, in which records typically are stored in order by the record-key field. To retrieve data sequentially from a file, programs normally start from the beginning of the file, reading all data consecutively until the desired data are found. With a sequential-access file, each successive input/output request reads or writes the next consecutive set of data in the file.

BinaryFormatter provides methods **Serialize** and **Deserialize** for writing and reading objects, respectively. Only classes with the **Serializable** attribute can be serialized to and deserialized from files. Method **Serialize** writes the object's representation to a stream. Method **Deserialize** reads the representation from a stream and reconstructs the original object. Methods **Serialize** and **Deserialize** each require a **Stream** object as a parameter, enabling the **BinaryFormatter** to access the correct file.

Instant data access is possible with random-access files. A program can access individual records of a random-access file directly (and quickly) without searching through other records. Random-access files sometimes are called direct-access files. With a random-access file, each successive input/output request can be directed to any part of the file, which can be at any distance from the part of the file referenced in the previous request.

There is a variety of techniques for creating random-access files. Perhaps the simplest involves requiring that all records in a file be of the same fixed length. The use of fixed-length records makes it easy for a program to calculate (as a function of the record size and the record key) the exact location of any record in relation to the beginning of the file.

Classes **BinaryReader** and **BinaryWriter** provide methods for reading and writing bytes to streams, respectively. The **BinaryReader** and **BinaryWriter** constructors receive references to instances of class **System.IO.Stream** as arguments. Class **FileStream** inherits from class **Stream**, so we can pass the **FileStream** object as an argument to either the **BinaryReader** or the **BinaryWriter** constructor in order to create an object that can transfer bytes directly to or from a file.

Extensible Markup Language (XML)

Objectives

- To mark up data, using XML.
- To understand the concept of an XML namespace.
- To understand the relationship between DTDs, Schemas and XML.
- To create Schemas.
- To create and use simple XSLT documents.
- To transform XML documents into XHTML, using class **XslTransform**.
- To become familiar with BizTalk™.

Knowing trees, I understand the meaning of patience.
Knowing grass, I can appreciate persistence.
Hal Borland

Like everything metaphysical, the harmony between thought and reality is to be found in the grammar of the language.
Ludwig Wittgenstein

I played with an idea and grew willful, tossed it into the air; transformed it; let it escape and recaptured it; made it iridescent with fancy, and winged it with paradox.
Oscar Wilde

Outline

15.1   **Introduction**

15.2   **XML Documents**

15.3   **XML Namespaces**

15.4   **Document Object Model (DOM)**

15.5   **Document Type Definitions (DTDs), Schemas and Validation**

      15.5.1   **Document Type Definitions**

      15.5.2   **Microsoft XML Schemas**

      15.5.3   **W3C XML Schema**

      15.5.4   **Schema Validation in C#**

15.6   **Extensible Stylesheet Language and XslTransform**

15.7   **Microsoft BizTalk™**

15.8   **Summary**

15.9   **Internet and World Wide Web Resources**

15.1 Introduction

The *Extensible Markup Language* (XML) was developed in 1996 by the *World Wide Web Consortium's (W3C's) XML Working Group*. XML is a portable, widely supported, *open technology* (i.e., non-proprietary technology) for describing data. XML is becoming the standard for storing data that is exchanged between applications. Using XML, document authors can describe any type of data, including mathematical formulas, software-configuration instructions, music, recipes and financial reports. XML documents are readable by both humans and machines.

The .NET Framework uses XML extensively. The Framework Class Library (FCL) provides an extensive set of XML-related classes. Much of Visual Studio's internal implementation also employs XML. In this chapter, we introduce XML, XML-related technologies and key classes for creating and manipulating XML documents.

15.2 XML Documents

In this section, we present our first XML document, which describes an article (Fig. 15.1). [*Note:* The line numbers shown are not part of the XML document.]

```xml
1   <?xml version = "1.0"?>
2
3   <!-- Fig. 15.1: article.xml      -->
4   <!-- Article structured with XML -->
5
6   <article>
7
8       <title>Simple XML</title>
```

Fig. 15.1   XML used to mark up an article. (Part 1 of 2.)

```
 9
10      <date>December 6, 2001</date>
11
12      <author>
13         <firstName>John</firstName>
14         <lastName>Doe</lastName>
15      </author>
16
17      <summary>XML is pretty easy.</summary>
18
19      <content>In this chapter, we present a wide variety of examples
20         that use XML.
21      </content>
22
23   </article>
```

Fig. 15.1   XML used to mark up an article. (Part 2 of 2.)

This document begins with an optional *XML declaration* (line 1), which identifies the document as an XML document. The **version** *information parameter* specifies the version of XML that is used in the document. XML comments (lines 3–4), which begin with **<!--** and end with **-->**, can be placed almost anywhere in an XML document. As in a C# program, comments are used in XML for documentation purposes.

Common Programming Error 15.1

The placement of any characters, including whitespace, before the XML declaration is an error.

Portability Tip 15.1

Although the XML declaration is optional, documents should include the declaration to identify the version of XML used. Otherwise, in the future, a document that lacks an XML declaration might be assumed to conform to the latest version of XML, and errors could result.

In XML, data are marked up using *tags*, which are names enclosed in *angle brackets* (**<>**). Tags are used in pairs to delimit character data (e.g., **Simple XML** in line 8). A tag that begins *markup* (i.e., XML data) is called a *start tag*, whereas a tag that terminates markup is called an *end tag*. Examples of start tags are **<article>** and **<title>** (lines 6 and 8, respectively). End tags differ from start tags in that they contain a *forward slash* (**/**) character immediately after the **<** character. Examples of end tags are **</title>** and **</article>** (lines 8 and 23, respectively). XML documents can contain any number of tags.

Common Programming Error 15.2

Failure to provide a corresponding end tag for a start tag is an error.

Individual units of markup (i.e., everything included between a start tag and its corresponding end tag) are called *elements*. An XML document includes one element (called a *root element*) that contains every other element. The root element must be the first element after the XML declaration. In Fig. 15.1, **article** (line 6) is the root element. Elements are *nested* within each other to form hierarchies—with the root element at the top of the hierarchy. This allows document authors to create explicit relationships between data. For example, elements **title**, **date**, **author**, **summary** and **content** are nested within **article**. Elements **firstName** and **lastName** are nested within **author**.

Common Programming Error 15.3

Attempting to create more than one root element in an XML document is a syntax error.

Element **title** (line 8) contains the title of the article, **Simple XML**, as character data. Similarly, **date** (line 10), **summary** (line 17) and **content** (lines 19–21) contain as character data the date, summary and content, respectively. XML element names can be of any length and may contain letters, digits, underscores, hyphens and periods—they must begin with a letter or an underscore.

Common Programming Error 15.4

XML is case sensitive. The use of the wrong case for an XML element name is a syntax error.

By itself, this document is simply a text file named **article.xml**. Although it is not required, most XML documents end in the file extension **.xml**. The processing of XML documents requires a program called an *XML parser* also called *XML processors*. Parsers are responsible for checking an XML document's syntax and making the XML document's data available to applications. Often, XML parsers are built into applications such as Visual Studio or available for download over the Internet. Popular parsers include Microsoft's *msxml*, the Apache Software Foundation's *Xerces* and IBM's *XML4J*. In this chapter, we use msxml.

When the user loads **article.xml** into Internet Explorer (IE),[1] msxml parses the document and passes the parsed data to IE. IE then uses a built-in *style sheet* to format the data. Notice that the resulting format of the data (Fig. 15.2) is similar to the format of the XML document shown in Fig. 15.1. As we soon demonstrate, style sheets play an important and powerful role in the transformation of XML data into formats suitable for display.

Notice the minus (−) and plus (+) signs in Fig. 15.2. Although these are not part of the XML document, IE places them next to all *container elements* (i.e., elements that contain other elements). Container elements also are called *parent elements*. A minus sign indicates that the parent element's *child elements* (i.e., nested elements) are being displayed. When clicked, a minus sign becomes a plus sign (which collapses the container element and hides all children). Conversely, clicking a plus sign expands the container element and changes the plus sign to a minus sign. This behavior is similar to the viewing of the directory structure on a Windows system using Windows Explorer. In fact, a directory structure often is modeled as a series of tree structures, in which each drive letter (e.g., **C:**, etc.) represents the *root* of a tree. Each folder is a *node* in the tree. Parsers often place XML data into trees to facilitate efficient manipulation, as discussed in Section 15.4.

Common Programming Error 15.5

*Nesting XML tags improperly is a syntax error. For example, **<x><y>hello</x></y>** is a error, because the **</y>** tag must precede the **</x>** tag.*

---

1. IE 5 and higher.

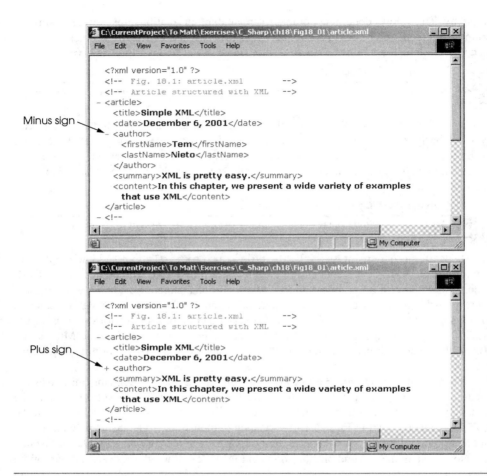

Fig. 15.2 `article.xml` displayed by Internet Explorer.

We now present a second XML document (Fig. 15.3), which marks up a business letter. This document contains significantly more data than did the previous XML document.

```
1    <?xml version = "1.0"?>
2
3    <!-- Fig. 15.3: letter.xml              -->
4    <!-- Business letter formatted with XML -->
5
6    <letter>
7       <contact type = "from">
8          <name>Jane Doe</name>
9          <address1>Box 12345</address1>
10         <address2>15 Any Ave.</address2>
11         <city>Othertown</city>
12         <state>Otherstate</state>
```

Fig. 15.3 XML to mark up a business letter. (Part 1 of 2.)

```
13              <zip>67890</zip>
14              <phone>555-4321</phone>
15              <flag gender = "F" />
16          </contact>
17
18          <contact type = "to">
19              <name>John Doe</name>
20              <address1>123 Main St.</address1>
21              <address2></address2>
22              <city>Anytown</city>
23              <state>Anystate</state>
24              <zip>12345</zip>
25              <phone>555-1234</phone>
26              <flag gender = "M" />
27          </contact>
28
29          <salutation>Dear Sir:</salutation>
30
31              <paragraph>It is our privilege to inform you about our new
32              database managed with <technology>XML</technology>. This
33              new system allows you to reduce the load on
34              your inventory list server by having the client machine
35              perform the work of sorting and filtering the data.
36              </paragraph>
37
38              <paragraph>Please visit our Web site for availability
39              and pricing.
40              </paragraph>
41
42          <closing>Sincerely</closing>
43
44          <signature>Ms. Doe</signature>
45      </letter>
```

Fig. 15.3 XML to mark up a business letter. (Part 2 of 2.)

Root element **letter** (lines 6–45) contains the child elements **contact** (lines 7–16 and 18–27), **salutation**, **paragraph** (lines 31–36 and 38–40), **closing** and **signature**. In addition to being placed between tags, data also can be placed in *attributes*, which are name-value pairs in start tags. Elements can have any number of attributes in their start tags. The first **contact** element (lines 7–16) has attribute **type** with attribute *value* **"from"**, which indicates that this **contact** element marks up information about the letter's sender. The second **contact** element (lines 18–27) has attribute **type** with value **"to"**, which indicates that this **contact** element marks up information about the letter's recipient. Like element names, attribute names are case sensitive, can be any length; may contain letters, digits, underscores, hyphens and periods; and must begin with either a letter or underscore character. A **contact** element stores a contact's name, address and phone number. Element **salutation** (line 29) marks up the letter's salutation. Lines 31–40 mark up the letter's body with **paragraph** elements. Elements **closing** (line 42) and **signature** (line 44) mark up the closing sentence and the signature of the letter's author, respectively.

Common Programming Error 15.6

Failure to enclose attribute values in either double (" ") or single (' ') quotes is a syntax error.

Common Programming Error 15.7

Attempting to provide two attributes with the same name for an element is a syntax error.

In line 15, we introduce *empty element* **flag**, which indicates the gender of the contact. Empty elements do not contain character data (i.e., they do not contain text between the start and end tags). Such elements are closed either by placing a slash at the end of the element (as shown in line 15) or by explicitly writing a closing tag, as in

```
<flag gender = "F"></flag>
```

15.3 XML Namespaces

Object-oriented programming languages, such as C# and Visual Basic .NET, provide massive class libraries that group their features into namespaces. These namespaces prevent *naming collisions* between programmer-defined identifiers and identifiers in class libraries. For example, we might use class **Book** to represent information on one of our publications; however, a stamp collector might use class **Book** to represent a book of stamps. A naming collision would occur if we use these two classes in the same assembly, without using namespaces to differentiate them.

Like C#, XML also provides *namespaces*, which provide a means of uniquely identifying XML elements. In addition, XML-based languages—called *vocabularies*, such as XML Schema (Section 15.5), Extensible Stylesheet Language (Section 15.6) and BizTalk (Section 15.7)—often use namespaces to identify their elements.

Elements are differentiated via *namespace prefixes*, which identify the namespace to which an element belongs. For example,

```
<deitel:book>C# For Experienced Programmers</deitel:book>
```

qualifies element **book** with namespace prefix **deitel**. This indicates that element **book** is part of namespace **deitel**. Document authors can use any name for a namespace prefix except the reserved namespace prefix **xml**.

Common Programming Error 15.8

*Attempting to create a namespace prefix named **xml** in any mixture of case is a syntax error.*

The mark up in Fig. 15.4 demonstrates the use of namespaces. This XML document contains two **file** elements that are differentiated using namespaces.

```
1   <?xml version = "1.0"?>
2
3   <!-- Fig. 15.4: namespace.xml -->
4   <!-- Demonstrating namespaces -->
```

Fig. 15.4 XML namespaces demonstration. (Part 1 of 2.)

```
5
6    <text:directory xmlns:text = "urn:deitel:textInfo"
7       xmlns:image = "urn:deitel:imageInfo">
8
9       <text:file filename = "book.xml">
10         <text:description>A book list</text:description>
11      </text:file>
12
13      <image:file filename = "funny.jpg">
14         <image:description>A funny picture</image:description>
15         <image:size width = "200" height = "100" />
16      </image:file>
17
18   </text:directory>
```

Fig. 15.4 XML namespaces demonstration. (Part 2 of 2.)

Software Engineering Observation 15.1

A programmer has the option of qualifying an attribute with a namespace prefix. However, it is not required, because attributes always are associated with elements.

Lines 6–7 use attribute **xmlns** to create two namespace prefixes: **text** and **image**. Each namespace prefix is bound to a series of characters called a *uniform resource identifier (URI)* that uniquely identifies the namespace. Document authors create their own namespace prefixes and URIs.

To ensure that namespaces are unique, document authors must provide unique URIs. Here, we use the text **urn:deitel:textInfo** and **urn:deitel:imageInfo** as URIs. A common practice is to use *Universal Resource Locators (URLs)* for URIs, because the domain names (such as, **www.deitel.com**) used in URLs are guaranteed to be unique. For example, lines 6–7 could have been written as

```
<text:directory xmlns:text =
    "http://www.deitel.com/xmlns-text"
    xmlns:image = "http://www.deitel.com/xmlns-image">
```

In this example, we use URLs related to the Deitel & Associates, Inc, domain name to iden-tify namespaces. The parser never visits these URLs—they simply represent a series of characters used to differentiate names. The URLs need not refer to actual Web pages or be formed properly.

Lines 9–11 use the namespace prefix **text** to qualify elements **file** and **description** as belonging to the namespace **"urn:deitel:textInfo"**. Notice that the namespace prefix **text** is applied to the end tags as well. Lines 13–16 apply namespace prefix **image** to elements **file**, **description** and **size**.

To eliminate the need to precede each element with a namespace prefix, document authors can specify a *default namespace*. Figure 15.5 demonstrates the creation and use of default namespaces.

```xml
1   <?xml version = "1.0"?>
2
3   <!-- Fig. 15.5: defaultnamespace.xml -->
4   <!-- Using default namespaces        -->
5
6   <directory xmlns = "urn:deitel:textInfo"
7      xmlns:image = "urn:deitel:imageInfo">
8
9      <file filename = "book.xml">
10         <description>A book list</description>
11     </file>
12
13     <image:file filename = "funny.jpg">
14         <image:description>A funny picture</image:description>
15         <image:size width = "200" height = "100" />
16     </image:file>
17
18  </directory>
```

Fig. 15.5   Default namespace demonstration.

Line 6 declares a default namespace using attribute **xmlns** with a URI as its value. Once we define this default namespace, child elements belonging to the namespace need not be qualified by a namespace prefix. Element **file** (line 9–11) is in the namespace **urn:deitel:textInfo**. Compare this to Fig. 15.4, where we prefixed **file** and **description** with **text** (lines 9–11).

The default namespace applies to the **directory** element and all elements that are not qualified with a namespace prefix. However, we can use a namespace prefix to specify a different namespace for particular elements. For example, the **file** element in line 13 is prefixed with **image** to indicate that it is in the namespace **urn:deitel:imageInfo**, rather than the default namespace.

15.4 Document Object Model (DOM)

Although XML documents are text files, retrieving data from them via sequential-file access techniques is neither practical nor efficient, especially in situations where data must be added or deleted dynamically.

Upon successful parsing, some XML parsers store document data as tree structures in memory. Figure 15.6 illustrates the tree structure for the document **article.xml** discussed in Fig. 15.1. This hierarchical tree structure is called a *Document Object Model (DOM)* tree, and an XML parser that creates this type of structure is known as a *DOM parser*. The DOM tree represents each component of the XML document (e.g., **article**, **date**, **firstName**, etc.) as a node in the tree. Nodes (such as, **author**) that contain other nodes (called *child nodes*) are called *parent nodes*. Nodes that have the same parent (such as, **firstName** and **lastName**) are called *sibling nodes*. A node's *descendant nodes* include that node's children, its children's children and so on. Similarly, a node's *ancestor nodes* include that node's parent, its parent's parent and so on. Every DOM tree has a single *root node* that contains all other nodes in the document, such as comments, elements, etc.

Classes for creating, reading and manipulating XML documents are located in the C# namespace **System.Xml**. This namespace also contains additional namespaces that contain other XML-related operations.

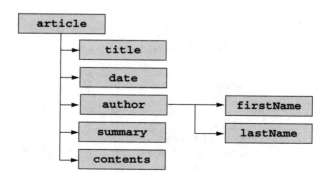

Fig. 15.6   Tree structure for Fig. 15.1.

In this section, we present several examples that use DOM trees. Our first example, the program in Fig. 15.7, loads the XML document presented in Fig. 15.1 and displays its data in a text box. This example uses class *XmlNodeReader* which is derived from *Xml-Reader*, which iterates through each node in the XML document. Class **XmlReader** is an **abstract** class that defines the interface for reading XML documents.

```csharp
1   // Fig. 15.7: XmlReaderTest.cs
2   // Reading an XML document.
3
4   using System;
5   using System.Windows.Forms;
6   using System.Xml;
7
8   public class XmlReaderTest : System.Windows.Forms.Form
9   {
10      private System.Windows.Forms.TextBox outputTextBox;
11      private System.ComponentModel.Container components = null;
12
13      public XmlReaderTest()
14      {
15         InitializeComponent();
16
17         // reference to "XML document"
18         XmlDocument document = new XmlDocument();
19         document.Load( "..\\..\\article.xml" );
20
21         // create XmlNodeReader for document
22         XmlNodeReader reader = new XmlNodeReader( document );
23
24         // show form before outputTextBox is populated
25         this.Show();
26
27         // tree depth is -1, no indentation
28         int depth = -1;
29
30         // display each node's content
31         while ( reader.Read() )
32         {
33            switch ( reader.NodeType )
34            {
35               // if Element, display its name
36               case XmlNodeType.Element:
37
38                  // increase tab depth
39                  depth++;
40                  TabOutput( depth );
41                  outputTextBox.Text += "<" + reader.Name + ">" +
42                     "\r\n";
43
```

Fig. 15.7 **XmlNodeReader** used to iterate through an XML document. (Part 1 of 3.)

```
44              // if empty element, decrease depth
45              if ( reader.IsEmptyElement )
46                 depth--;
47
48              break;
49
50          // if Comment, display it
51          case XmlNodeType.Comment:
52             TabOutput( depth );
53             outputTextBox.Text +=
54                "<!--" + reader.Value + "-->\r\n";
55             break;
56
57          // if Text, display it
58          case XmlNodeType.Text:
59             TabOutput( depth );
60             outputTextBox.Text += "\t" + reader.Value +
61                "\r\n";
62             break;
63
64          // if XML declaration, display it
65          case XmlNodeType.XmlDeclaration:
66             TabOutput( depth );
67             outputTextBox.Text += "<?" + reader.Name + " "
68                + reader.Value + " ?>\r\n";
69             break;
70
71          // if EndElement, display it and decrement depth
72          case XmlNodeType.EndElement:
73             TabOutput( depth );
74             outputTextBox.Text += "</" + reader.Name
75                + ">\r\n";
76             depth--;
77             break;
78          } // end switch statement
79       } // end while loop
80    } // End XmlReaderTest constructor
81
82    // insert tabs
83    private void TabOutput( int number )
84    {
85       for ( int i = 0; i < number; i++ )
86          outputTextBox.Text += "\t";
87    } // end TabOutput
88
89    // Windows Form Designer generated code
90
91    [STAThread]
92    static void Main()
93    {
94       Application.Run( new XmlReaderTest() );
95    } // end Main
96 } // end XmlReaderTest
```

Fig. 15.7 XmlNodeReader used to iterate through an XML document. (Part 2 of 3.)

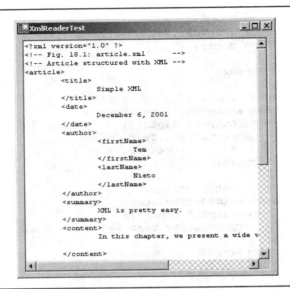

Fig. 15.7   XmlNodeReader used to iterate through an XML document. (Part 3 of 3.)

Line 6 includes the **System.Xml** namespace, which contains the XML classes used in this example. Line 18 creates a reference to an *XmlDocument* object that conceptually represents an empty XML document. The XML document **article.xml** is parsed and loaded into this **XmlDocument** object when method *Load* is invoked in line 19. Once an XML document is loaded into an **XmlDocument**, its data can be read and manipulated programmatically. In this example, we read each node in the **XmlDocument**, which is the DOM tree. In successive examples, we demonstrate how to manipulate node values.

In line 22, we create an **XmlNodeReader** and assign it to reference **reader**, which enables us to read one node at a time from the **XmlDocument**. Method *Read* of **XmlReader** reads one node from the DOM tree. Placing this statement in the **while** loop (lines 31–78) makes **reader Read** all the document nodes. The **switch** statement (lines 33–77) processes each node. Either the *Name* property (line 41), which contains the node's name, or the *Value* property (line 53), which contains the node's data, is formatted and concatenated to the **string** assigned to the text box **Text** property. The **NodeType** property contains the node type (specifying whether the node is an element, comment, text, etc.). Notice that each **case** specifies a node type, using *XmlNodeType* enumeration constants.

Notice that the displayed output emphasizes the structure of the XML document. Variable **depth** (line 28) sets the number of tab characters used to indent each element. The depth is incremented each time an **Element** type is encountered and is decremented each time an **EndElement** or empty element is encountered. We use a similar technique in the next example to emphasize the tree structure of the XML document in the display.

Notice that our line breaks use the character sequence **"\r\n"**, which denotes a carriage return followed by a line feed. This is the standard line break for Windows-based applications and controls.

The C# program in Fig. 15.8 demonstrates how to manipulate DOM trees programmatically. This program loads **letter.xml** (Fig. 15.3) into the DOM tree and then creates a second DOM tree that duplicates the DOM tree containing **letter.xml**'s contents. The GUI for this application contains a text box, a **TreeView** control and three buttons— **Build**, **Print** and **Reset**. When clicked, **Build** copies **letter.xml** and displays the document's tree structure in the **TreeView** control, **Print** displays the XML element values and names in a text box and **Reset** clears the **TreeView** control and text box content.

Lines 20 and 23 create references to **XmlDocument**s **source** and **copy**. Line 32 assigns a new **XmlDocument** object to reference **source**. Line 33 then invokes method **Load** to parse and load **letter.xml**. We discuss reference **copy** shortly.

Unfortunately, **XmlDocument**s do not provide any features for displaying their content graphically. In this example, we display the document's contents via a **TreeView** control. We use objects of class *TreeNode* to represent each node in the tree. Class **TreeView** and class **TreeNode** are part of the **System.Windows.Forms** namespace. **TreeNode**s are added to the **TreeView** to emphasize the structure of the XML document.

```
1   // Fig. 15.8: XmlDom.cs
2   // Demonstrates DOM tree manipulation.
3
4   using System;
5   using System.Windows.Forms;
6   using System.Xml;
7   using System.IO;
8   using System.CodeDom.Compiler;   // contains TempFileCollection
9
10  // Class XmlDom demonstrates the DOM
11  public class XmlDom : System.Windows.Forms.Form
12  {
13     private System.Windows.Forms.Button buildButton;
14     private System.Windows.Forms.Button printButton;
15     private System.Windows.Forms.TreeView xmlTreeView;
16     private System.Windows.Forms.TextBox consoleTextBox;
17     private System.Windows.Forms.Button resetButton;
18     private System.ComponentModel.Container components = null;
19
20     private XmlDocument source; // reference to "XML document"
21
22     // reference copy of source's "XML document"
23     private XmlDocument copy;
24
25     private TreeNode tree; // TreeNode reference
26
27     public XmlDom()
28     {
29        InitializeComponent();
30
31        // create XmlDocument and load letter.xml
32        source = new XmlDocument();
33        source.Load( "..\\..\\letter.xml" );
34
35        // initialize references to null
36        copy = null;
```

Fig. 15.8 DOM structure of an XML document illustrated by a class. (Part 1 of 6.)

```
37          tree = null;
38      } // end XmlDom
39
40      [STAThread]
41      static void Main()
42      {
43          Application.Run( new XmlDom() );
44      }
45
46      // event handler for buildButton click event
47      private void buildButton_Click( object sender,
48          System.EventArgs e )
49      {
50          // determine if copy has been built already
51          if ( copy != null )
52              return;  // document already exists
53
54          // instantiate XmlDocument and TreeNode
55          copy = new XmlDocument();
56          tree = new TreeNode();
57
58          // add root node name to TreeNode and add
59          // TreeNode to TreeView control
60          tree.Text = source.Name;      // assigns #root
61          xmlTreeView.Nodes.Add( tree );
62
63          // build node and tree hierarchy
64          BuildTree( source, copy, tree );
65
66          printButton.Enabled = true;
67          resetButton.Enabled = true;
68      } // end buildButton_Click
69
70      // event handler for printButton click event
71      private void printButton_Click( object sender,
72          System.EventArgs e )
73      {
74          // exit if copy does not reference an XmlDocument
75          if ( copy == null )
76              return;
77
78          // create temporary XML file
79          TempFileCollection file = new TempFileCollection();
80
81          // create file that is deleted at program termination
82          file.AddExtension( "xml", false );
83          string[] filename = new string[ 1 ];
84          file.CopyTo( filename, 0 );
85
86          // write XML data to disk
87          XmlTextWriter writer = new XmlTextWriter( filename[ 0 ],
88              System.Text.Encoding.UTF8 );
89          copy.WriteTo( writer );
```

Fig. 15.8   DOM structure of an XML document illustrated by a class. (Part 2 of 6.)

```
90              writer.Close();
91
92              // parse and load temporary XML document
93              XmlTextReader reader = new XmlTextReader( filename[ 0 ] );
94
95              // read, format and display data
96              while( reader.Read() )
97              {
98                 if ( reader.NodeType == XmlNodeType.EndElement )
99                    consoleTextBox.Text += "/";
100
101                if ( reader.Name != String.Empty )
102                   consoleTextBox.Text += reader.Name + "\r\n";
103
104                if ( reader.Value != String.Empty )
105                   consoleTextBox.Text += "\t" + reader.Value +
106                      "\r\n";
107             } // end while
108
109             reader.Close();
110          } // end printButton_Click
111
112          // handle resetButton click event
113          private void resetButton_Click( object sender,
114             System.EventArgs e )
115          {
116             // remove TreeView nodes
117             if ( tree != null )
118                xmlTreeView.Nodes.Remove( tree );
119
120             xmlTreeView.Refresh(); // force TreeView update
121
122             // delete XmlDocument and tree
123             copy = null;
124             tree = null;
125
126             consoleTextBox.Text = "";   // clear text box
127
128             printButton.Enabled = false;
129             resetButton.Enabled = false;
130
131          } // end resetButton_Click
132
133          // construct DOM tree
134          private void BuildTree( XmlNode xmlSourceNode,
135             XmlNode document, TreeNode treeNode )
136          {
137             // create XmlNodeReader to access XML document
138             XmlNodeReader nodeReader = new XmlNodeReader(
139                xmlSourceNode );
140
141             // represents current node in DOM tree
142             XmlNode currentNode = null;
```

Fig. 15.8 DOM structure of an XML document illustrated by a class. (Part 3 of 6.)

```
143
144          // treeNode to add to existing tree
145          TreeNode newNode = new TreeNode();
146
147          // references modified node type for CreateNode
148          XmlNodeType modifiedNodeType;
149
150          while ( nodeReader.Read() )
151          {
152             // get current node type
153             modifiedNodeType = nodeReader.NodeType;
154
155             // check for EndElement, store as Element
156             if ( modifiedNodeType == XmlNodeType.EndElement )
157                modifiedNodeType = XmlNodeType.Element;
158
159             // create node copy
160             currentNode = copy.CreateNode( modifiedNodeType,
161                nodeReader.Name, nodeReader.NamespaceURI );
162
163             // build tree based on node type
164             switch ( nodeReader.NodeType )
165             {
166                // if Text node, add its value to tree
167                case XmlNodeType.Text:
168                   newNode.Text = nodeReader.Value;
169                   treeNode.Nodes.Add( newNode );
170
171                   // append Text node value to currentNode data
172                   ( ( XmlText ) currentNode ).AppendData(
173                      nodeReader.Value );
174                   document.AppendChild( currentNode );
175                   break;
176
177                // if EndElement, move up tree
178                case XmlNodeType.EndElement:
179                   document = document.ParentNode;
180                   treeNode = treeNode.Parent;
181                   break;
182
183                // if new element, add name and traverse tree
184                case XmlNodeType.Element:
185
186                   // determine if element contains content
187                   if ( !nodeReader.IsEmptyElement )
188                   {
189                      // assign node text, add newNode as child
190                      newNode.Text = nodeReader.Name;
191                      treeNode.Nodes.Add( newNode );
192
193                      // set treeNode to last child
194                      treeNode = newNode;
195
```

Fig. 15.8   DOM structure of an XML document illustrated by a class. (Part 4 of 6.)

```
196                    document.AppendChild( currentNode );
197                    document = document.LastChild;
198                }
199                else // do not traverse empty elements
200                {
201                    // assign NodeType string to newNode
202                    newNode.Text =
203                       nodeReader.NodeType.ToString();
204
205                    treeNode.Nodes.Add( newNode );
206                    document.AppendChild( currentNode );
207                }
208
209                break;
210
211             // all other types, display node type
212             default:
213                newNode.Text = nodeReader.NodeType.ToString();
214                treeNode.Nodes.Add( newNode );
215                document.AppendChild( currentNode );
216                break;
217         }  // end switch
218
219         newNode = new TreeNode();
220      } // end while
221
222      // update the TreeView control
223      xmlTreeView.ExpandAll();
224      xmlTreeView.Refresh();
225
226   } // end BuildTree
227 } // end XmlDom
```

Fig. 15.8   DOM structure of an XML document illustrated by a class. (Part 5 of 6.)

Fig. 15.8 DOM structure of an XML document illustrated by a class. (Part 6 of 6.)

When clicked, button **Build** triggers event handler **buildButton_Click** (lines 47–68), which copies **letter.xml** dynamically. The new **XmlDocument** and **TreeNode**s (i.e., the nodes used for graphical representation in the **TreeView**) are created in lines 55–56. Line 60 retrieves the **Name** of the node referenced by **source** (i.e., **#root**, which represents the document root) and assigns it to **tree**'s **Text** property. This **TreeNode** then is inserted into the **TreeView** control's node list. Method **Add** is called to add each new **TreeNode** to the **TreeView**'s **Nodes** collection. Line 64 calls method **BuildTree** to copy the **XMLDocument** referenced by **source** and to update the **TreeView**.

Method **BuildTree** (line 134–226) receives an **XmlNode** representing the source node, an empty **XmlNode** and a **treeNode** to place in the DOM tree. Parameter **treeNode** references the current location in the tree (i.e., the **TreeNode** most recently added to the **TreeView** control). Lines 138–139 instantiate a new **XmlNodeReader** for iterating through the DOM tree. Lines 142–145 declare **XmlNode** and **TreeNode** references that indicate the next nodes added to **document** (i.e., the DOM tree referenced by **copy**) and **treeNode**. Lines 150–220 iterate through each node in the tree.

Lines 153–161 create a node containing a copy of the current **nodeReader** node. Method *CreateNode* of **XmlDocument** takes a **NodeType**, a **Name** and a *NamespaceURI* as arguments. The **NodeType** cannot be an **EndElement**. If the **NodeType** is of an **EndElement** type, lines 156–157 assign **modifiedNodeType** type **Element**.

The **switch** statement in lines 164–217 determines the node type, creates and adds nodes to the **TreeView** and updates the DOM tree. When a text node is encountered, the new **TreeNode**'s **newNode**'s **Text** property is assigned the current node's value. This **TreeNode** is added to the **TreeView** control. In lines 172–174, we downcast **currentNode** to **XmlText** and append the node's value. The **currentNode** then is appended to the **document**. Lines 178–181 match an **EndElement** node type. This **case** moves up the tree, because the end of an element has been encountered. The *ParentNode* and *Parent* properties retrieve the **document**'s and **treeNode**'s parents, respectively.

Line 184 matches **Element** node types. Each nonempty **Element NodeType** (line 187) increases the depth of the tree; thus, we assign the current **nodeReader Name** to the **newNode**'s **Text** property and add the **newNode** to the **treeNode** node list. Lines 194–197 reorder the nodes in the node list to ensure that **newNode** is the last **TreeNode** in the node list. **XmlNode currentNode** is appended to **document** as the last child, and **document** is set to its *LastChild*, which is the child we just added. If it is an empty element (line 199), we assign to the **newNode**'s **Text** property the **string** representation of the **NodeType**. Next, the **newNode** is added to the **treeNode** node list. Line 206 appends the **currentNode** to the **document**. The **default** case assigns the string representation of the node type to the **NewNode Text** property, adds the **newNode** to the **TreeNode** node list and appends the **currentNode** to the **document**.

After building the DOM trees, the **TreeNode** node list displays in the **TreeView** control. Clicking the nodes (i.e., the **+** or **–** boxes) in the **TreeView** either expands or collapses them. Clicking **Print** invokes event handler **printButton_Click** (line 71). Lines 79–84 create a temporary file for storing the XML. Line 87 creates an **XmlTextWriter** for streaming the XML data to disk. Method *WriteTo* is called to write the XML representation to the *XmlTextWriter* stream (line 89). Line 93 creates an *XmlTextReader* to read from the file. The **while** loop (line 96–107) reads each node in the DOM tree and writes tag names and character data to the text box. If it is an end element, a slash is concatenated. If the node has a **Name** or **Value**, that name or value is concatenated to the textbox text.

The **Reset** button's event handler, **resetButton_Click**, deletes both dynamically generated trees and updates the **TreeView** control's display. Reference **copy** is assigned **null** (to allow its tree to be garbage collected in line 123), and the **TreeNode** node list reference **tree** is assigned **null**.

Although **XmlReader** includes methods for reading and modifying node values, it is not the most efficient means of locating data in a DOM tree. The .NET framework provides class *XPathNavigator* in the *System.Xml.XPath* namespace for iterating through node lists that match search criteria, which are written as an *XPath expression*. XPath (XML Path Language) provides a syntax for locating specific nodes in XML documents effectively and efficiently. XPath is a string-based language of expressions used by XML and many of its related technologies (such as, XSLT, discussed in Section 15.6).

Figure 15.9 demonstrates how to navigate through an XML document with an **XPathNavigator**. Like Fig. 15.8, this program uses a **TreeView** control and **TreeNode** objects to display the XML document's structure. However, instead of displaying the entire DOM tree, the **TreeNode** node list is updated each time the **XPath-Navigator** is positioned to a new node. Nodes are added to and deleted from the **TreeView** to reflect the **XPathNavigator**'s location in the DOM tree. The XML document **sports.xml** that we use in this example is presented in Figure 15.10.

This program loads XML document **sports.xml** into an *XPathDocument* object by passing the document's file name to the **XPathDocument** constructor (line 36). Method *CreateNavigator* (line 39) creates and returns an **XPathNavigator** reference to the **XPathDocument**'s tree structure.

The navigation methods of **XPathNavigator** used in Fig. 15.9 are *MoveTo-FirstChild* (line 66), *MoveToParent* (line 94), *MoveToNext* (line 122) and *MoveToPrevious* (line 151). Each method performs the action that its name implies. Method **MoveToFirstChild** moves to the first child of the node referenced by the

XPathNavigator, **MoveToParent** moves to the parent node of the node referenced by the **XPathNavigator**, **MoveToNext** moves to the next sibling of the node referenced by the **XPathNavigator** and **MoveToPrevious** moves to the previous sibling of the node referenced by the **XPathNavigator**. Each method returns a **bool** indicating whether the move was successful. In this example, we display a warning in a **MessageBox** whenever a move operation fails. Furthermore, each of these methods is called in the event handler of the button that matches its name (e.g., button **First Child** triggers **firstChildButton_Click**, which calls **MoveToFirstChild**).

Whenever we move forward via the **XPathNavigator**, as with **MoveToFirstChild** and **MoveToNext**, nodes are added to the **TreeNode** node list. Method **DetermineType** is a **private** method (defined in lines 208–229) that determines whether to assign the **Node**'s *Name* property or *Value* property to the **TreeNode** (lines 218 and 225). Whenever **MoveToParent** is called, all children of the parent node are removed from the display. Similarly, a call to **MoveToPrevious** removes the current sibling node. Note that the nodes are removed only from the **TreeView**, not from the tree representation of the document.

The other event handler corresponds to button **Select** (line 173–174). Method **Select** (line 182) takes search criteria in the form of either an *XPathExpression* or a **string** that represents an XPath expression and returns as an **XPathNodeIterator** object any nodes that match the search criteria. The XPath expressions provided by this program's combo box are summarized in Fig. 15.11.

Method **DisplayIterator** (defined in lines 195–204) appends the node values from the given **XPathNodeIterator** to the **selectTreeViewer** text box. Note that we call the **string** method **Trim** to remove unnecessary whitespace. Method *MoveNext* (line 200) advances to the next node, which can be accessed via property *Current* (line 202).

```
1   // Fig. 15.9: PathNavigator.cs
2   // Demonstrates Class XPathNavigator.
3
4   using System;
5   using System.Windows.Forms;
6   using System.Xml.XPath; // contains XPathNavigator
7
8   public class PathNavigator : System.Windows.Forms.Form
9   {
10      private System.Windows.Forms.Button firstChildButton;
11      private System.Windows.Forms.Button parentButton;
12      private System.Windows.Forms.Button nextButton;
13      private System.Windows.Forms.Button previousButton;
14      private System.Windows.Forms.Button selectButton;
15      private System.Windows.Forms.TreeView pathTreeViewer;
16      private System.Windows.Forms.ComboBox selectComboBox;
17      private System.ComponentModel.Container components = null;
18      private System.Windows.Forms.TextBox selectTreeViewer;
19      private System.Windows.Forms.GroupBox navigateBox;
20      private System.Windows.Forms.GroupBox locateBox;
21
```

Fig. 15.9   XPathNavigator class used to navigate selected nodes. (Part 1 of 7.)

```
22        // navigator to traverse document
23        private XPathNavigator xpath;
24
25        // references document for use by XPathNavigator
26        private XPathDocument document;
27
28        // references TreeNode list used by TreeView control
29        private TreeNode tree;
30
31        public PathNavigator()
32        {
33           InitializeComponent();
34
35           // load XML document
36           document = new XPathDocument( "..\\..\\sports.xml" );
37
38           // create navigator
39           xpath = document.CreateNavigator();
40
41           // create root node for TreeNodes
42           tree = new TreeNode();
43
44           tree.Text = xpath.NodeType.ToString(); // #root
45           pathTreeViewer.Nodes.Add( tree );        // add tree
46
47           // update TreeView control
48           pathTreeViewer.ExpandAll();
49           pathTreeViewer.Refresh();
50           pathTreeViewer.SelectedNode = tree;      // highlight root
51        } // end constructor
52
53        [STAThread]
54        static void Main()
55        {
56           Application.Run( new PathNavigator() );
57        }
58
59        // traverse to first child
60        private void firstChildButton_Click( object sender,
61           System.EventArgs e )
62        {
63           TreeNode newTreeNode;
64
65           // move to first child
66           if ( xpath.MoveToFirstChild() )
67           {
68              newTreeNode = new TreeNode(); // create new node
69
70              // set node's Text property to either
71              // navigator's name or value
72              DetermineType( newTreeNode, xpath );
73
```

Fig. 15.9 XPathNavigator class used to navigate selected nodes. (Part 2 of 7.)

```
74                  // add node to TreeNode node list
75                  tree.Nodes.Add( newTreeNode );
76                  tree = newTreeNode; // assign tree newTreeNode
77
78                  // update TreeView control
79                  pathTreeViewer.ExpandAll();
80                  pathTreeViewer.Refresh();
81                  pathTreeViewer.SelectedNode = tree;
82               }
83            else // node has no children
84               MessageBox.Show( "Current Node has no children.",
85                  "", MessageBoxButtons.OK,
86                  MessageBoxIcon.Information );
87         }
88
89         // traverse to node's parent on parentButton click event
90         private void parentButton_Click( object sender,
91            System.EventArgs e )
92         {
93            // move to parent
94            if ( xpath.MoveToParent() )
95            {
96               tree = tree.Parent;
97
98               // get number of child nodes, not including subtrees
99               int count = tree.GetNodeCount( false );
100
101              // remove all children
102              tree.Nodes.Clear();
103
104              // update TreeView control
105              pathTreeViewer.ExpandAll();
106              pathTreeViewer.Refresh();
107              pathTreeViewer.SelectedNode = tree;
108           }
109           else // if node has no parent (root node)
110              MessageBox.Show( "Current node has no parent.", "",
111                 MessageBoxButtons.OK,
112                 MessageBoxIcon.Information );
113        }
114
115        // find next sibling on nextButton click event
116        private void nextButton_Click( object sender,
117           System.EventArgs e )
118        {
119           TreeNode newTreeNode = null, newNode = null;
120
121           // move to next sibling
122           if ( xpath.MoveToNext() )
123           {
124              newTreeNode = tree.Parent; // get parent node
125
126              newNode = new TreeNode(); // create new node
```

Fig. 15.9 **XPathNavigator** class used to navigate selected nodes. (Part 3 of 7.)

```
127              DetermineType( newNode, xpath );
128              newTreeNode.Nodes.Add( newNode );
129
130              // set current position for display
131              tree = newNode;
132
133              // update TreeView control
134              pathTreeViewer.ExpandAll();
135              pathTreeViewer.Refresh();
136              pathTreeViewer.SelectedNode = tree;
137           }
138        else // node has no additional siblings
139           MessageBox.Show( "Current node is last sibling.",
140              "", MessageBoxButtons.OK,
141              MessageBoxIcon.Information );
142     } // end nextButton_Click
143
144     // get previous sibling on previousButton click
145     private void previousButton_Click( object sender,
146        System.EventArgs e )
147     {
148        TreeNode parentTreeNode = null;
149
150        // move to previous sibling
151        if ( xpath.MoveToPrevious() )
152        {
153           parentTreeNode = tree.Parent; // get parent node
154
155           // delete current node
156           parentTreeNode.Nodes.Remove( tree );
157
158           // move to previous node
159           tree = parentTreeNode.LastNode;
160
161           // update TreeView control
162           pathTreeViewer.ExpandAll();
163           pathTreeViewer.Refresh();
164           pathTreeViewer.SelectedNode = tree;
165        }
166        else // if current node has no previous siblings
167           MessageBox.Show( "Current node is first sibling.",
168              "", MessageBoxButtons.OK,
169              MessageBoxIcon.Information );
170     } // end previousButton_Click
171
172     // process selectButton click event
173     private void selectButton_Click( object sender,
174        System.EventArgs e )
175     {
176        XPathNodeIterator iterator; // enables node iteration
177
```

Fig. 15.9   **XPathNavigator** class used to navigate selected nodes. (Part 4 of 7.)

```
178            // get specified node from ComboBox
179            try
180            {
181               iterator = xpath.Select( selectComboBox.Text );
182               DisplayIterator( iterator ); // print selection
183            }
184
185            // catch invalid expressions
186            catch ( System.ArgumentException argumentException )
187            {
188               MessageBox.Show( argumentException.Message,
189                  "Error", MessageBoxButtons.OK,
190                  MessageBoxIcon.Error );
191            }
192         } // end selectButton_Click
193
194         // print values for XPathNodeIterator
195         private void DisplayIterator( XPathNodeIterator iterator )
196         {
197            selectTreeViewer.Text = "";
198
199            // prints selected node's values
200            while ( iterator.MoveNext() )
201               selectTreeViewer.Text +=
202                  iterator.Current.Value.Trim()
203                  + "\r\n";
204         } // end DisplayIterator
205
206         // determine if TreeNode should display current node
207         // name or value
208         private void DetermineType( TreeNode node,
209            XPathNavigator xPath )
210         {
211            // determine NodeType
212            switch ( xPath.NodeType )
213            {
214               // if Element, get its name
215               case XPathNodeType.Element:
216
217                  // get current node name, and remove whitespace
218                  node.Text = xPath.Name.Trim();
219                  break;
220
221               // obtain node values
222               default:
223
224                  // get current node value and remove whitespace
225                  node.Text = xPath.Value.Trim();
226                  break;
227
228            } // end switch
229         } // end DetermineType
230      } // end PathNavigator
```

Fig. 15.9 XPathNavigator class used to navigate selected nodes. (Part 5 of 7.)

Fig. 15.9   **XPathNavigator** class used to navigate selected nodes. (Part 6 of 7.)

Fig. 15.9   XPathNavigator class used to navigate selected nodes. (Part 7 of 7.)

```
1    <?xml version = "1.0"?>
2
3    <!-- Fig. 15.10: sports.xml -->
4    <!-- Sports Database       -->
5
6    <sports>
7
8       <game id = "783">
9          <name>Cricket</name>
10
11         <paragraph>
12            More popular among commonwealth nations.
13         </paragraph>
14      </game>
15
16      <game id = "239">
17         <name>Baseball</name>
18
19         <paragraph>
20            More popular in America.
21         </paragraph>
22      </game>
23
24      <game id = "418">
25         <name>Soccer(Futbol)</name>
26         <paragraph>Most popular sport in the world</paragraph>
27      </game>
28   </sports>
```

Fig. 15.10 XML document that describes various sports.

15.5 Document Type Definitions (DTDs), Schemas and Validation

XML documents can reference optional documents that specify how the XML documents should be structured. These optional documents are called *Document Type Definitions* (*DTDs*) and *Schemas*. When a DTD or Schema document is provided, some parsers (called *validating parsers*) can read the DTD or Schema and check the XML document's structure against it. If the XML document conforms to the DTD or Schema, then the XML document is *valid*. Parsers that cannot check for document conformity against the DTD or Schema are called *non-validating parsers*. If an XML parser (validating or non-validating) is able to process an XML document (that does not reference a DTD or Schema), the XML document is considered to be *well formed* (i.e., it is syntactically correct). By definition, a valid XML document is also a well-formed XML document. If a document is not well formed, parsing halts, and the parser issues an error.

Software Engineering Observation 15.2

DTD and Schema documents are essential components for XML documents used in business-to-business (B2B) transactions and mission-critical systems. These documents help ensure that XML documents are valid.

Software Engineering Observation 15.3

Because XML document content can be structured in many different ways, an application cannot determine whether the document data it receives is complete, missing data or ordered properly. DTDs and Schemas solve this problem by providing an extensible means of describing a document's contents. An application can use a DTD or Schema document to perform a validity check on the document's contents.

Expression	Description
`/sports`	Matches the **sports** node that is child node of the document root node. This node contains the root element.
`/sports/game/name`	Matches all **name** nodes that are child nodes of **game**. The **game** node must be a child of **sports** and **sports** must be a root element node.
`/sports/game/paragraph`	Matches all **paragraph** nodes that are child nodes of **game**. The **game** node must be a child of **sports**, and **sports** must be a root element node.
`/sports/ game[name='Cricket']`	Matches all **game** nodes that contain a child element **name** whose value is **Cricket**. The **game** node must be a child of **sports**, and **sports** must be a root element node.

Fig. 15.11 XPath expressions and descriptions.

15.5.1 Document Type Definitions

Document type definitions (DTDs) provide a means for type checking XML documents and thus verifying their *validity* (confirming that elements contain the proper attributes, elements are in the proper sequence, etc.). DTDs use *EBNF* (*Extended Backus-Naur Form*) *grammar* to describe an XML document's content. XML parsers need additional functionality to read EBNF grammar, because it is not XML syntax. Although DTDs are optional, they are recommended to ensure document conformity. The DTD in Fig. 15.12 defines the set of rules (i.e., the grammar) for structuring the business letter document contained in Fig. 15.13.

 Portability Tip 15.2

DTDs can ensure consistency among XML documents generated by different programs.

Line 4 uses the ***ELEMENT*** *element type declaration* to define rules for element **letter**. In this case, **letter** contains one or more **contact** elements, one **salutation** element, one or more **paragraph** elements, one **closing** element and one **signature** element, in that sequence. The *plus sign* (**+**) *occurrence indicator* specifies that an element must occur one or more times. Other indicators include the *asterisk* (*****), which indicates an optional element that can occur any number of times, and the *question mark* (**?**), which indicates an optional element that can occur at most once. If an occurrence indicator is omitted, exactly one occurrence is expected.

The **contact** element definition (line 7) specifies that it contains the **name**, **address1**, **address2**, **city**, **state**, **zip**, **phone** and **flag** elements—in that order. Exactly one occurrence of each is expected.

```
1   <!-- Fig. 15.12: letter.dtd       -->
2   <!-- DTD document for letter.xml -->
3
4   <!ELEMENT letter ( contact+, salutation, paragraph+,
5      closing, signature )>
6
7   <!ELEMENT contact ( name, address1, address2, city, state,
8      zip, phone, flag )>
9   <!ATTLIST contact type CDATA #IMPLIED>
10
11  <!ELEMENT name ( #PCDATA )>
12  <!ELEMENT address1 ( #PCDATA )>
13  <!ELEMENT address2 ( #PCDATA )>
14  <!ELEMENT city ( #PCDATA )>
15  <!ELEMENT state ( #PCDATA )>
16  <!ELEMENT zip ( #PCDATA )>
17  <!ELEMENT phone ( #PCDATA )>
18  <!ELEMENT flag EMPTY>
19  <!ATTLIST flag gender (M | F) "M">
20
21  <!ELEMENT salutation ( #PCDATA )>
22  <!ELEMENT closing ( #PCDATA )>
23  <!ELEMENT paragraph ( #PCDATA )>
24  <!ELEMENT signature ( #PCDATA )>
```

Fig. 15.12 Document Type Definition (DTD) for a business letter.

Line 9 uses the ***ATTLIST*** *element type declaration* to define an attribute (i.e., **type**) for the **contact** element. Keyword ***#IMPLIED*** specifies that, if the parser finds a **contact** element without a **type** attribute, the application can provide a value or ignore the missing attribute. The absence of a **type** attribute cannot invalidate the document. Other types of default values include ***#REQUIRED*** and ***#FIXED***. Keyword ***#REQUIRED*** specifies that the attribute must be present in the document and the keyword ***#FIXED*** specifies that the attribute (if present) must always be assigned a specific value. For example,

```
<!ATTLIST address zip #FIXED "01757">
```

indicates that the value **01757** must be used for attribute **zip**; otherwise, the document is invalid. If the attribute is not present, then the parser, by default, uses the fixed value that is specified in the **ATTLIST** declaration. Flag ***CDATA*** specifies that attribute **type** contains a **String** that is not processed by the parser, but instead is passed to the application as is.

Software Engineering Observation 15.4

DTD syntax does not provide any mechanism for describing an element's (or attribute's) data type.

Flag ***#PCDATA*** (line 11) specifies that the element can store *parsed character data* (i.e., text). Parsed character data cannot contain markup. The characters less than (**<**) and ampersand (**&**) must be replaced by their *entities* (i.e., **<** and **&**). However, the ampersand character can be inserted when used with entities. See Appendix M, HTML/XHTML Special Characters, for a list of pre-defined entities.

Line 18 defines an empty element named **flag**. Keyword ***EMPTY*** specifies that the element cannot contain character data. Empty elements commonly are used for their attributes.

Common Programming Error 15.9

Any element, attribute or relationship not explicitly defined by a DTD results in an invalid document.

Many XML documents explicitly reference a DTD. Figure 15.13 is an XML document that conforms to **letter.dtd** (Fig. 15.12).

```
1   <?xml version = "1.0"?>
2
3   <!-- Fig. 15.13: letter2.xml          -->
4   <!-- Business letter formatted with XML -->
5
6   <!DOCTYPE letter SYSTEM "letter.dtd">
7
8   <letter>
9      <contact type = "from">
10        <name>Jane Doe</name>
11        <address1>Box 12345</address1>
12        <address2>15 Any Ave.</address2>
13        <city>Othertown</city>
14        <state>Otherstate</state>
15        <zip>67890</zip>
16        <phone>555-4321</phone>
```

Fig. 15.13 XML document referencing its associated DTD. (Part 1 of 2.)

```
17            <flag gender = "F" />
18      </contact>
19
20      <contact type = "to">
21            <name>John Doe</name>
22            <address1>123 Main St.</address1>
23            <address2></address2>
24            <city>Anytown</city>
25            <state>Anystate</state>
26            <zip>12345</zip>
27            <phone>555-1234</phone>
28            <flag gender = "M" />
29      </contact>
30
31      <salutation>Dear Sir:</salutation>
32
33      <paragraph>It is our privilege to inform you about our new
34            database managed with XML. This new system
35            allows you to reduce the load on your inventory list
36            server by having the client machine perform the work of
37            sorting and filtering the data.
38      </paragraph>
39
40      <paragraph>Please visit our Web site for availability
41            and pricing.
42      </paragraph>
43      <closing>Sincerely</closing>
44      <signature>Ms. Doe</signature>
45   </letter>
```

Fig. 15.13 XML document referencing its associated DTD. (Part 2 of 2.)

This XML document is similar to that in Fig. 15.3. Line 6 references a DTD file. This markup contains three pieces: The name of the root element (**letter** in line 8) to which the DTD is applied, the keyword **SYSTEM** (which in this case denotes an *external DTD*—a DTD defined in a separate file) and the DTD's name and location (i.e., **letter.dtd** in the current directory). Though almost any file extension can be used, DTD documents typically end with the **.dtd** extension.

Various tools (many of which are free) check document conformity against DTDs and Schemas (discussed momentarily). The output in Fig. 15.14 shows the results of the validation of **letter2.xml** using Microsoft's *XML Validator*. Visit **www.w3.org/XML/ Schema.html** for a list of validating tools. Microsoft XML Validator is available free for download from

```
msdn.microsoft.com/downloads/samples/Internet/xml/
xml_validator/sample.asp
```

Microsoft XML Validator can validate XML documents against DTDs locally or by uploading the documents to the XML Validator Web site. Here, **letter2.xml** and **letter.dtd** are placed in folder **C:\XML**. This XML document (**letter2.xml**) is well formed and conforms to **letter.dtd**.

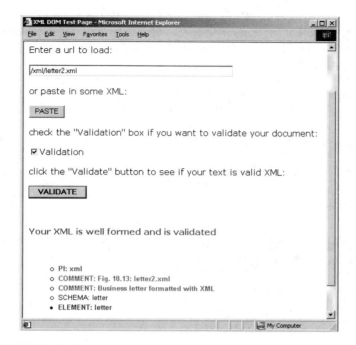

Fig. 15.14 XML Validator validates an XML document against a DTD.

XML documents that fail validation are still well-formed documents. When a document fails to conform to a DTD or Schema, Microsoft XML Validator displays an error message. For example, the DTD in Fig. 15.12 indicates that the **contacts** element must contain child element **name**. If the document omits this child element, the document is well formed, but not valid. In such a scenario, Microsoft XML Validator displays the error message shown in Fig. 15.15.

C# programs can use msxml to validate XML documents against DTDs. For information on how to accomplish this, visit:

> **msdn.microsoft.com/library/default.asp?url=/library/en-us/**
> **cpguidnf/html/cpconvalidationagainstdtdwithxmlvalidatin-**
> **greader.asp**

Schemas are the preferred means of defining structures for XML documents in .NET. Although, several types of Schemas exist, the two most popular are Microsoft Schema and W3C Schema. We begin our discussion of Schemas in the next section.

15.5.2 Microsoft XML Schemas[2]

In this section, we introduce an alternative to DTDs—called Schemas—for defining an XML document's structure. Many developers in the XML community feel that DTDs are

---

2. W3C Schema, which we discuss in Section 15.5.3, is emerging as the industry standard for describing an XML document's structure. Within the next two years, we expect most developers will be using W3C Schema.

not flexible enough to meet today's programming needs. For example, DTDs cannot be manipulated (e.g., searched, programmatically modified, etc.) in the same manner that XML documents can, because DTDs are not XML documents. Furthermore, DTDs do not provide features for describing an element's (or attribute's) data type.

Unlike DTDs, Schemas do not use Extended Backus-Naur Form (EBNF) grammar. Instead, Schemas are XML documents that can be manipulated (e.g., elements can be added or removed, etc.) like any other XML document. As with DTDs, Schemas require validating parsers.

In this section, we focus on Microsoft's *XML Schema* vocabulary. Figure 15.16 presents an XML document that conforms to the Microsoft Schema document shown in Fig. 15.17. By convention, Microsoft XML Schema documents use the file extension **.xdr**, which is short for *XML-Data Reduced*. Line 6 (Fig. 15.16) references the Schema document **book.xdr**.

Fig. 15.15 XML Validator displaying an error message.

```
1   <?xml version = "1.0"?>
2
3   <!-- Fig. 15.16: bookxdr.xml          -->
4   <!-- XML file that marks up book data -->
5
6   <books xmlns = "x-schema:book.xdr">
7      <book>
8         <title>C# How to Program</title>
9      </book>
10
11     <book>
12        <title>Java How to Program, 4/e</title>
13     </book>
14
15     <book>
16        <title>Visual Basic .NET How to Program</title>
17     </book>
18
19     <book>
20        <title>Advanced Java 2 Platform How to Program</title>
21     </book>
```

Fig. 15.16 XML document that conforms to a Microsoft Schema document. (Part 1 of 2.)

```
22
23      <book>
24         <title>Python How to Program</title>
25      </book>
26   </books>
```

Fig. 15.16 XML document that conforms to a Microsoft Schema document. (Part 2 of 2.)

```
1    <?xml version = "1.0"?>
2
3    <!-- Fig. 15.17: book.xdr                        -->
4    <!-- Schema document to which book.xml conforms -->
5
6    <Schema xmlns = "urn:schemas-microsoft-com:xml-data">
7       <ElementType name = "title" content = "textOnly"
8          model = "closed" />
9
10      <ElementType name = "book" content = "eltOnly" model = "closed">
11         <element type = "title" minOccurs = "1" maxOccurs = "1" />
12      </ElementType>
13
14      <ElementType name = "books" content = "eltOnly" model = "closed">
15         <element type = "book" minOccurs = "0" maxOccurs = "*" />
16      </ElementType>
17   </Schema>
```

Fig. 15.17 Microsoft Schema file that contains structure to which **bookxdr.xml** conforms.

Software Engineering Observation 15.5

Schemas are XML documents that conform to DTDs, which define the structure of a Schema. These DTDs, which are bundled with the parser, are used to validate the Schemas that authors create.

Software Engineering Observation 15.6

Many organizations and individuals are creating DTDs and Schemas for a broad range of categories (e.g., financial transactions, medical prescriptions, etc.). Often, these collections—called repositories—*are available free for download from the Web.[3]*

In line 6, root element **Schema** begins the Schema markup. Microsoft Schemas use the namespace URI **"urn:schemas-microsoft-com:xml-data"**. Line 7 uses element **ElementType** to define element **title**. Attribute **content** specifies that this element contains parsed character data (i.e., text only). Element **title** is not permitted to contain child elements. Setting the **model** *attribute* to **"closed"** specifies that a conforming XML document can contain only elements defined in this Schema. Line 10 defines element **book**; this element's **content** is "elements only" (i.e., **eltOnly**). This means that the element cannot contain mixed content (i.e., text and other elements). Within the **ElementType** element named **book**, the **element** element indicates that **title** is a **child** element of **book**. Attributes **minOccurs** and **maxOccurs** are set to **"1"**, indicating that a **book** ele-

---

3. See, for example, **opengis.net/schema.htm**.

ment must contain exactly one **title** element. The asterisk (*****) in line 15 indicates that the Schema permits any number of **book** elements in element **books**. We discuss how to validate **bookxdr.xml** against **book.xdr** in Section 15.5.4.

15.5.3 W3C XML Schema[4]

In this section, we focus on *W3C XML Schema*[5]—the schema that the W3C created. XML Schema is a *Recommendation* (i.e., a stable release suitable for use in industry). Figure 15.18 shows a Schema-valid XML document named **bookxsd.xml** and Fig. 15.19 shows the W3C XML Schema document (**book.xsd**) that defines the structure for **bookxsd.xml**. Although Schema authors can use virtually any filename extension, W3C XML Schemas typically use the *.xsd* extension. We discuss how to validate **bookxsd.xml** against **book.xsd** in the next section.

```
1   <?xml version = "1.0"?>
2
3   <!-- Fig. 15.18: bookxsd.xml                  -->
4   <!-- Document that conforms to W3C XML Schema -->
5
6   <deitel:books xmlns:deitel = "http://www.deitel.com/booklist">
7      <book>
8         <title>e-Business and e-Commerce How to Program</title>
9      </book>
10     <book>
11        <title>Python How to Program</title>
12     </book>
13  </deitel:books>
```

Fig. 15.18 XML document that conforms to W3C XML Schema.

```
1   <?xml version = "1.0"?>
2
3   <!-- Fig. 15.19: book.xsd       -->
4   <!-- Simple W3C XML Schema document -->
5
6   <xsd:schema xmlns:xsd = "http://www.w3.org/2001/XMLSchema"
7      xmlns:deitel = "http://www.deitel.com/booklist"
8      targetNamespace = "http://www.deitel.com/booklist">
9
10     <xsd:element name = "books" type = "deitel:BooksType"/>
11
12     <xsd:complexType name = "BooksType">
13        <xsd:sequence>
14           <xsd:element name = "book" type = "deitel:BookType"
15           minOccurs = "1" maxOccurs = "unbounded"/>
16        </xsd:sequence>
17     </xsd:complexType>
```

Fig. 15.19 XSD Schema document to which **bookxsd.xml** conforms. (Part 1 of 2.)

---

4. We provide a detailed treatment of W3C Schema in *XML for Experienced Programmers* (2003).
5. For the latest on W3C XML Schema, visit **www.w3.org/XML/Schema**.

```
18
19     <xsd:complexType name = "BookType">
20        <xsd:sequence>
21           <xsd:element name = "title" type = "xsd:string"/>
22        </xsd:sequence>
23     </xsd:complexType>
24
25  </xsd:schema>
```

Fig. 15.19 XSD Schema document to which **bookxsd.xml** conforms. (Part 2 of 2.)

W3C XML Schema use the namespace URI *http://www.w3.org/2001/*
XMLSchema and often use *namespace prefix xsd* (line 6 in Fig. 15.19). Root element
schema contains elements that define the XML document's structure. Line 7 binds the
URI **http://www.deitel.com/booklist** to namespace prefix **deitel**. Line 8
specifies the *targetNamespace*, which is the namespace for elements and attributes
that this schema defines.

In W3C XML Schema, element *element* (line 10) defines an element. Attributes
name and *type* specify the **element**'s name and data type, respectively. In this case, the
name of the element is **books** and the data type is **deitel:BooksType**. Any element
(e.g., **books**) that contains attributes or child elements must define a *complex type*, which
defines each attribute and child element. Type **deitel:BooksType** (lines 12–17) is an
example of a complex type. We prefix **BooksType** with **deitel**, because this is a complex type that we have created, not an existing W3C XML Schema complex type.

Lines 12–17 use element *complexType* to define an element type that has a child
element named **book**. Because **book** contains a child element, its type must be a complex
type (e.g., **BookType**). Attribute *minOccurs* specifies that **books** must contain a minimum of one **book** element. Attribute *maxOccurs*, with value *unbounded* (line 14)
specifies that **books** may have any number of **book** child elements. Element *sequence*
specifies the order of elements in the complex type.

Lines 19–23 define the **complexType BookType**. Line 21 defines element **title**
with **type xsd:string**. When an element has a *simple type* such as **xsd:string**, it
is prohibited from containing attributes and child elements. W3C XML Schema provides a
large number of data types such as *xsd:date* for dates, *xsd:int* for integers,
xsd:double for floating-point numbers and *xsd:time* for time.

Good Programming Practice 15.1

*By convention, W3C XML Schema authors use namespace prefix **xsd** when referring to the
URI **http://www.w3.org/2001/XMLSchema**.*

15.5.4 Schema Validation in C#

In this section, we present a C# application (Fig. 15.20) that uses classes from the .NET
Framework Class Library to validate the XML documents presented in the last two sections
against their respective Schemas. We use an instance of *XmlValidatingReader* to
perform the validation.

Line 17 creates an *XmlSchemaCollection* reference named **schemas**. Line 28
calls method *Add* to add an *XmlSchema* object to the Schema collection. Method **Add** is
passed a name that identifies the Schema (i.e., **"book"**) and the name of the Schema file

(i.e., **`book.xdr`**). Line 29 calls method **Add** to add a W3C XML Schema. The first argument specifies the namespace URI (i.e., line 18 in Fig. 15.19) and the second argument identifies the schema file (i.e., **`book.xsd`**). This is the Schema that is used to validate **`bookxsd.xml`**.

```
1    // Fig. 15.20: ValidationTest.cs
2    // Validating XML documents against Schemas.
3
4    using System;
5    using System.Windows.Forms;
6    using System.Xml;
7    using System.Xml.Schema;            // contains Schema classes
8
9    // determines XML document Schema validity
10   public class ValidationTest : System.Windows.Forms.Form
11   {
12       private System.Windows.Forms.ComboBox filesComboBox;
13       private System.Windows.Forms.Button validateButton;
14       private System.Windows.Forms.Label consoleLabel;
15       private System.ComponentModel.Container components = null;
16
17       private XmlSchemaCollection schemas;    // Schemas
18       private bool valid;                     // validation result
19
20       public ValidationTest()
21       {
22           InitializeComponent();
23
24           valid = true;   // assume document is valid
25
26           // get Schema(s) for validation
27           schemas = new XmlSchemaCollection();
28           schemas.Add( "book", "book.xdr" );
29           schemas.Add( "http://www.deitel.com/booklist", "book.xsd" );
30       } // end constructor
31
32       // Visual Studio .NET generated code
33
34       [STAThread]
35       static void Main()
36       {
37           Application.Run( new ValidationTest() );
38       } // end Main
39
40       // handle validateButton click event
41       private void validateButton_Click( object sender,
42           System.EventArgs e )
43       {
44           // get XML document
45           XmlTextReader reader =
46               new XmlTextReader( filesComboBox.Text );
47
```

Fig. 15.20 Schema-validation example. (Part 1 of 2.)

```
48           // get validator
49           XmlValidatingReader validator =
50              new XmlValidatingReader( reader );
51
52           // assign Schema(s)
53           validator.Schemas.Add( schemas );
54
55           // set validation type
56           validator.ValidationType = ValidationType.Auto;
57
58           // register event handler for validation error(s)
59           validator.ValidationEventHandler +=
60              new ValidationEventHandler( ValidationError );
61
62           // validate document node-by-node
63           while ( validator.Read() ) ; // empty body
64
65           // check validation result
66           if ( valid )
67              consoleLabel.Text = "Document is valid";
68
69           valid = true; // reset variable
70
71           // close reader stream
72           validator.Close();
73        }  // end validateButton_Click
74
75        // event handler for validation error
76        private void ValidationError( object sender,
77           ValidationEventArgs arguments )
78        {
79           consoleLabel.Text = arguments.Message;
80           valid = false; // validation failed
81        } // end ValidationError
82     } // end ValidationTest
```

Fig. 15.20 Schema-validation example. (Part 2 of 2.)

Lines 45–46 create an **XmlReader** for the file that the user selected from **file-sComboBox**. The XML document to be validated against a Schema contained in the **XmlSchemaCollection** must be passed to the **XmlValidatingReader** constructor (lines 49–50).

Line 53 **Add**s the Schema collection referenced by **Schemas** to the *Schemas* property. This property sets the Schema used to validate the document. The *ValidationType* property (line 56) is set to the *ValidationType enumeration* constant for **Auto**matically identifying the Schema's type (i.e., XDR or XSD). Lines 59–60 register method **ValidationError** with *ValidationEventHandler*. Method **ValidationError** (lines 76–81) is called if the document is invalid or an error occurs, such as if the document cannot be found. Failure to register a method with **ValidationEventHandler** causes an exception to be thrown when the document is missing or invalid.

Validation is performed node-by-node by calling the method *Read* (line 63). Each call to **Read** validates the next node in the document. The loop terminates either when all nodes have been validated successfully or a node fails validation. When validated against their respective Schemas, the XML documents in Fig. 15.16 and Fig. 15.18 validate successfully.

Figure 15.21 and Fig. 15.22 list two XML documents that fail to conform to **book.xdr** and **book.xsd**, respectively. In Fig. 15.21, the extra **title** element in **book** (lines 19–22) invalidate the document. In Fig. 15.22, the extra **title** element in **book** (lines 7–10) invalidates the document. Although both documents are invalid, they are well formed.

```
1   <?xml version = "1.0"?>
2
3   <!-- Fig. 15.21: bookxsdfail.xml               -->
4   <!-- Document that does not conforms to W3C Schema -->
5
6   <deitel:books xmlns:deitel = "http://www.deitel.com/booklist">
7      <book>
8         <title>e-Business and e-Commerce How to Program</title>
9         <title>C# How to Program</title>
10     </book>
11     <book>
12        <title>Python How to Program</title>
13     </book>
14  </deitel:books>
```

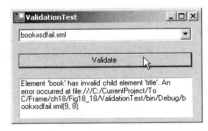

Fig. 15.21 XML document that does not conform to the XSD schema of Fig. 15.19.

```
1   <?xml version = "1.0"?>
2
3   <!-- Fig. 15.22: bookxdrfail.xml                -->
4   <!-- XML file that does not conform to Schema book.xdr -->
5
```

Fig. 15.22 XML file that does not conform to the Schema in Fig. 15.17. (Part 1 of 2.)

```
 6    <books xmlns = "x-schema:book.xdr">
 7       <book>
 8          <title>XML How to Program</title>
 9       </book>
10
11       <book>
12          <title>Java How to Program, 4/e</title>
13       </book>
14
15       <book>
16          <title>Visual Basic .NET How to Program</title>
17       </book>
18
19       <book>
20          <title>C++ How to Program, 3/e</title>
21          <title>Python How to Program</title>
22       </book>
23
24       <book>
25          <title>C# How to Program</title>
26       </book>
27    </books>
```

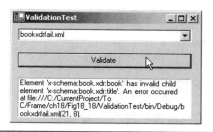

Fig. 15.22 XML file that does not conform to the Schema in Fig. 15.17. (Part 2 of 2.)

15.6 Extensible Stylesheet Language and `XslTransform`

Extensible Stylesheet Language (XSL) is an XML vocabulary for formatting XML data. In this section, we discuss the portion of XSL—called *XSL Transformations (XSLT)*—that creates formatted text-based documents from XML documents. This process is called a *transformation* and involves two tree structures: The *source tree*, which is the XML document being transformed, and the *result tree*, which is the result (i.e., any text-based format such as XHTML) of the transformation.[6] The source tree is not modified when a transformation occurs.

To perform transformations, an XSLT processor is required. Popular XSLT processors include Microsoft's msxml and the Apache Software Foundation's *Xalan*. The XML document, shown in Fig. 15.23, is transformed by msxml into an XHTML document (Fig. 15.24).

---

6. Extensible Hypertext Markup Language (XHTML) is the W3C technical recommendation that replaces HTML for marking up content for the Web. For more information on XHTML, see the XHTML Appendices K and L and visit **www.w3.org**.

```
1    <?xml version = "1.0"?>
2
3    <!-- Fig. 15.23: sorting.xml                      -->
4    <!-- XML document containing book information -->
5
6    <?xml:stylesheet type = "text/xsl" href = "sorting.xsl"?>
7
8    <book isbn = "999-99999-9-X">
9       <title>Deitel&apos;s XML Primer</title>
10
11      <author>
12         <firstName>Paul</firstName>
13         <lastName>Deitel</lastName>
14      </author>
15
16      <chapters>
17         <frontMatter>
18            <preface pages = "2" />
19            <contents pages = "5" />
20            <illustrations pages = "4" />
21         </frontMatter>
22
23         <chapter number = "3" pages = "44">
24            Advanced XML</chapter>
25
26         <chapter number = "2" pages = "35">
27            Intermediate XML</chapter>
28
29         <appendix number = "B" pages = "26">
30            Parsers and Tools</appendix>
31
32         <appendix number = "A" pages = "7">
33            Entities</appendix>
34
35         <chapter number = "1" pages = "28">
36            XML Fundamentals</chapter>
37      </chapters>
38
39      <media type = "CD" />
40   </book>
```

Fig. 15.23 XML document containing book information.

Line 6 is a *processing instruction* (*PI*), which contains application-specific informa-tion that is embedded into the XML document. In this particular case, the processing instruction is specific to IE and specifies the location of an XSLT document with which to transform the XML document. The characters **<?** and **?>** delimit a processing instruction, which consists of a *PI target* (e.g., **xml:stylesheet**) and *PI value* (e.g., **type = "text/xsl" href = "sorting.xsl"**). The portion of this particular PI value that follows **href** specifies the name and location of the style sheet to apply—in this case, **sorting.xsl**, which is located in the same directory as this XML document.

Fig. 15.24 presents the XSLT document (**sorting.xsl**) that transforms **sorting.xml** (Fig. 15.23) to XHTML.

Performance Tip 15.1

Using Internet Explorer on the client to process XSLT documents conserves server resources by using the client's processing power (instead of having the server process XSLT documents for multiple clients).

Line 1 of Fig. 15.23 contains the XML declaration. Recall that an XSL document is an XML document. Line 6 is the **xsl:stylesheet** root element. Attribute **version** specifies the version of XSLT to which this document conforms. Namespace prefix **xsl** is defined and is bound to the XSLT URI defined by the W3C. When processed, lines 11–13 write the document type declaration to the result tree. Attribute **method** is assigned **"xml"**, which indicates that XML is being output to the result tree. Attribute **omit-xml-declaration** is assigned **"no"**, which outputs an XML declaration to the result tree. Attribute **doctype-system** and **doctype-public** write the **Doctype** DTD information to the result tree.

XSLT documents contain one or more **xsl:template** elements that specify which information is output to the result tree. The template on line 16 **match**es the source tree's document root. When the document root is encountered, this template is applied, and any text marked up by this element that is not in the namespace referenced by **xsl** is output to the result tree. Line 18 calls for all the **template**s that match children of the document root to be applied. Line 23 specifies a **template** that **match**es element **book**.

```
1   <?xml version = "1.0"?>
2
3   <!-- Fig. 15.24: sorting.xsl                    -->
4   <!-- Transformation of book information into XHTML -->
5
6   <xsl:stylesheet version = "1.0"
7      xmlns:xsl = "http://www.w3.org/1999/XSL/Transform">
8
9      <!-- write XML declaration and DOCTYPE DTD information -->
10     <xsl:output method = "xml" omit-xml-declaration = "no"
11        doctype-system =
12           "http://www.w3.org/TR/xhtml1/DTD/xhtml1-strict.dtd"
13        doctype-public = "-//W3C//DTD XHTML 1.0 Strict//EN"/>
14
15     <!-- match document root -->
16     <xsl:template match = "/">
17        <html xmlns = "http://www.w3.org/1999/xhtml">
18           <xsl:apply-templates/>
19        </html>
20     </xsl:template>
21
22     <!-- match book -->
23     <xsl:template match = "book">
24        <head>
25           <title>ISBN <xsl:value-of select = "@isbn" /> -
26              <xsl:value-of select = "title" /></title>
27        </head>
```

Fig. 15.24 XSL document that transforms **sorting.xml** (Fig. 15.23) into XHTML. (Part 1 of 3.)

```
28
29        <body>
30          <h1 style = "color: blue">
31            <xsl:value-of select = "title"/></h1>
32
33          <h2 style = "color: blue">by <xsl:value-of
34            select = "author/lastName" />,
35            <xsl:value-of select = "author/firstName" /></h2>
36
37          <table style =
38            "border-style: groove; background-color: wheat">
39
40            <xsl:for-each select = "chapters/frontMatter/*">
41              <tr>
42                <td style = "text-align: right">
43                  <xsl:value-of select = "name()" />
44                </td>
45
46                <td>
47                  ( <xsl:value-of select = "@pages" /> pages )
48                </td>
49              </tr>
50            </xsl:for-each>
51
52            <xsl:for-each select = "chapters/chapter">
53              <xsl:sort select = "@number" data-type = "number"
54                order = "ascending" />
55              <tr>
56                <td style = "text-align: right">
57                  Chapter <xsl:value-of select = "@number" />
58                </td>
59
60                <td>
61                  ( <xsl:value-of select = "@pages" /> pages )
62                </td>
63              </tr>
64            </xsl:for-each>
65
66            <xsl:for-each select = "chapters/appendix">
67              <xsl:sort select = "@number" data-type = "text"
68                order = "ascending" />
69              <tr>
70                <td style = "text-align: right">
71                  Appendix <xsl:value-of select = "@number" />
72                </td>
73
74                <td>
75                  ( <xsl:value-of select = "@pages" /> pages )
76                </td>
77              </tr>
78            </xsl:for-each>
79          </table>
```

Fig. 15.24 XSL document that transforms **sorting.xml** (Fig. 15.23) into XHTML. (Part 2 of 3.)

```
80
81              <br /><p style = "color: blue">Pages:
82                 <xsl:variable name = "pagecount"
83                    select = "sum(chapters//*/@pages)" />
84                 <xsl:value-of select = "$pagecount" />
85              <br />Media Type:
86                 <xsl:value-of select = "media/@type" /></p>
87           </body>
88        </xsl:template>
89
90     </xsl:stylesheet>
```

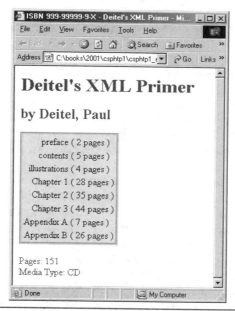

Fig. 15.24 XSL document that transforms **sorting.xml** (Fig. 15.23) into XHTML. (Part 3 of 3.)

Lines 25–26 create the title for the XHTML document. We use the ISBN of the book from attribute **isbn** and the contents of element **title** to create the title string **ISBN 999-99999-9-X - Deitel's XML Primer**. Element **xsl:value-of** selects the **book** element's **isbn** attribute.

Lines 33–35 create a header element that contains the book's author. Because the *context node* (i.e., the current node being processed) is **book**, the XPath expression **author/lastName** selects the author's last name, and the expression **author/firstName** selects the author's first name.

Line 40 selects each element (indicated by an asterisk) that is a child of element **frontMatter**. Line 43 calls *node-set function* **name** to retrieve the current node's element name (e.g., **preface**). The current node is the context node specified in the **xsl:for-each** (line 40).

Lines 53–54 sort **chapter**s by number in ascending order. Attribute **select** selects the value of context node **chapter**'s attribute **number**. Attribute *data-type* with value **"number"**, specifies a numeric sort and attribute *order* specifies **"ascending"** order. Attribute **data-type** also can, be assigned the value *"text"* (line 67) and attribute **order** also may be assigned the value *"descending"*.

Lines 82–83 use an *XSL variable* to store the value of the book's page count and output it to the result tree. Attribute **name** specifies the variable's name, and attribute **select** assigns it a value. Function *sum* totals the values for all **page** attribute values. The two slashes between **chapters** and * indicate that all descendent nodes of **chapters** are searched for elements that contain an attribute named **pages**.

The *System.Xml.Xsl* namespace provides classes for applying XSLT style sheets to XML documents. Specifically, an object of class *XslTransform* performs the transformation.

Figure 15.25 applies a style sheet (**sports.xsl**) to **sports.xml** (Fig. 15.10). The transformation result is written to a text box and to a file. We also show the transformation results rendered in IE.

Line 20 declares **XslTransform** reference **transformer**. An object of this type is necessary to transform the XML data to another format. In line 29, the XML document is parsed and loaded into memory with a call to method **Load**. Method **CreateNavigator** is called in line 32 to create an **XPathNavigator** object, which is used to navigate the XML document during the transformation. A call to method *Load* of class **XslTransform** (line 36) parses and loads the style sheet that this application uses. The argument that is passed contains the name and location of the style sheet.

Event handler **transformButton_Click** calls method *Transform* of class **XslTransform** to apply the style sheet (**sports.xsl**) to **sports.xml** (line 53). This method takes three arguments: An **XPathNavigator** (created from **sports.xml**'s **XmlDocument**), an instance of class *XsltArgumentList*, which is a list of **string** parameters that can be applied to a style sheet—**null**, in this case and an instance of a derived class of **TextWriter** (in this example, an instance of class **StringWriter**). The results of the transformation are stored in the **StringWriter** object referenced by **output**. Lines 59–62 write the transformation results to disk. The third screen shot depicts the created XHTML document when it is rendered in IE.

```
1   // Fig. 15.25: TransformTest.cs
2   // Applying a style sheet to an XML document.
3
4   using System;
5   using System.Windows.Forms;
6   using System.Xml;
7   using System.Xml.XPath;      // contains XPath classes
8   using System.Xml.Xsl;        // contains style sheet classes
9   using System.IO;             // contains stream classes
10
11  // transforms XML document to XHTML
12  public class TransformTest : System.Windows.Forms.Form
13  {
14      private System.Windows.Forms.TextBox consoleTextBox;
15      private System.Windows.Forms.Button transformButton;
16      private System.ComponentModel.Container components = null;
```

Fig. 15.25 XSL style sheet applied to an XML document. (Part 1 of 3.)

```
17
18      private XmlDocument document;        // Xml document root
19      private XPathNavigator navigator;    // navigate document
20      private XslTransform transformer;    // transform document
21      private StringWriter output;         // display document
22
23      public TransformTest()
24      {
25          InitializeComponent();
26
27          // load XML data
28          document = new XmlDocument();
29          document.Load( "..\\..\\sports.xml" );
30
31          // create navigator
32          navigator = document.CreateNavigator();
33
34          // load style sheet
35          transformer = new XslTransform();
36          transformer.Load( "..\\..\\sports.xsl" );
37      } // end constructor
38
39      // Windows Form Designer generated code
40
41      [STAThread]
42      static void Main()
43      {
44          Application.Run( new TransformTest() );
45      } // end Main
46
47      // transformButton click event
48      private void transformButton_Click( object sender,
49          System.EventArgs e )
50      {
51          // transform XML data
52          output = new StringWriter();
53          transformer.Transform( navigator, null, output );
54
55          // display transformation in text box
56          consoleTextBox.Text = output.ToString();
57
58          // write transformation result to disk
59          FileStream stream = new FileStream( "..\\..\\sports.html",
60              FileMode.Create );
61          StreamWriter writer = new StreamWriter( stream );
62          writer.Write( output.ToString() );
63
64          // close streams
65          writer.Close();
66          output.Close();
67      } // end transformButton_Click
68  }       // end TransformTest
```

Fig. 15.25 XSL style sheet applied to an XML document. (Part 2 of 3.)

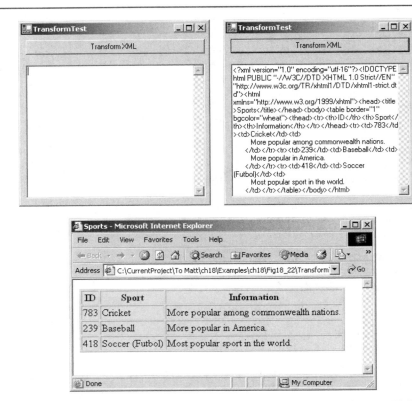

Fig. 15.25 XSL style sheet applied to an XML document. (Part 3 of 3.)

15.7 Microsoft BizTalk™

Increasingly, organizations are using the Internet to exchange critical data between business partners and their own business divisions. However, transferring data between organizations can become difficult, because companies often use different platforms, applications and data specifications that complicate data transfer. For example, consider a business that supplies raw materials to a variety of industries. If the supplier cannot receive all orders electronically because their customers use different computing platforms, an employee must input order data manually. If the supplier receives hundreds of orders a day, typing mistakes are likely, resulting in incorrect inventories or wrong order fulfillments, thereby jeopardizing the business by losing customers.

The supplier has several options—either continue to have data entered manually, purchase the same software packages as the ones their customers use or encourage customers to adopt the applications used by the supply company. In a growing economy, a business would have to purchase and maintain disparate software packages, spend money for more employees to process data or force their business partners to standardize their own organizational software programs. To facilitate the flow of information between businesses, Microsoft developed *BizTalk* ("business talk"), an XML-based technology that helps to manage and facilitate business transactions.

BizTalk creates an environment in which data marked up as XML is used to exchange business-specific information, regardless of platform or programming applications. This section overviews BizTalk and presents a code example to illustrate the business-specific information included in the markup.

BizTalk consists of three parts: The BizTalk Server, the BizTalk Framework and the BizTalk Schema Library. The *BizTalk Server* (*BTS*) parses and translates all inbound and outbound messages (or documents) that are sent to and from a business, using Internet standards such as HTTP. The *BizTalk Framework* is a Schema for structuring those messages. The Framework offers a specific set of core tags. Businesses can download the Framework to use in their organizations and can submit new schemas to the BizTalk organization, at **www.biztalk.org**. Once the BizTalk organization verifies and validates the submissions, the Schemas become BizTalk Framework Schemas. The *BizTalk Schema Library* is a collection of Framework Schemas. Figure 15.26 summarizes BizTalk terminology.

Fig. 15.27 is an example BizTalk message for a product offer from a clothing company. The message Schema for this example was developed by Microsoft to facilitate online purchases by a retailer from a wholesaler. We use this Schema for a fictitious company, named ExComp.

BizTalk	Description
Framework	A specification that defines a format for messages.
Schema library	A repository of Framework XML Schemas.
Server	An application that assists vendors in converting their messages to BizTalk format. For more information, visit **www.microsoft.com/biztalkserver**
JumpStart Kit	A set of tools for developing BizTalk applications.

Fig. 15.26 BizTalk terminology.

```
1   <?xml version = "1.0"?>
2   <BizTalk xmlns =
3      "urn:schemas-biztalk-org:BizTalk/biztalk-0.81.xml">
4
5   <!-- Fig. 15.27: biztalkmarkup.xml      -->
6   <!-- Example of standard BizTalk markup -->
7
8      <Route>
9         <From locationID = "8888888" locationType = "DUNS"
10           handle = "23" />
11
12        <To locationID = "454545445" locationType = "DUNS"
13           handle = "45" />
14     </Route>
15
```

Fig. 15.27 BizTalk markup using an offer Schema. (Part 1 of 3.)

```
16        <Body>
17          <Offers xmlns =
18            "x-schema:http://schemas.biztalk.org/eshop_msn_com/
t7ntoqnq.xml">
19            <Offer>
20              <Model>12-a-3411d</Model>
21              <Manufacturer>ExComp, Inc.</Manufacturer>
22              <ManufacturerModel>DCS-48403</ManufacturerModel>
23
24              <MerchantCategory>
25                Clothes | Sports wear
26              </MerchantCategory>
27
28              <MSNClassId></MSNClassId>
29
30              <StartDate>2001-06-05 T13:12:00</StartDate>
31              <EndDate>2001-12-05T13:12:00</EndDate>
32
33              <RegularPrice>89.99</RegularPrice>
34              <CurrentPrice>25.99</CurrentPrice>
35              <DisplayPrice value = "3" />
36              <InStock value = "15" />
37
38              <ReferenceImageURL>
39                http://www.Example.com/clothes/index.jpg
40              </ReferenceImageURL>
41
42              <OfferName>Clearance sale</OfferName>
43
44              <OfferDescription>
45                This is a clearance sale
46              </OfferDescription>
47
48              <PromotionalText>Free Shipping</PromotionalText>
49
50              <Comments>
51                Clothes that you would love to wear.
52              </Comments>
53
54              <IconType value = "BuyNow" />
55
56              <ActionURL>
57                http://www.example.com/action.htm
58              </ActionURL>
59
60              <AgeGroup1 value = "Infant" />
61              <AgeGroup2 value = "Adult" />
62
63              <Occasion1 value = "Birthday" />
64              <Occasion2 value = "Anniversary" />
65              <Occasion3 value = "Christmas" />
66
67            </Offer>
```

Fig. 15.27 BizTalk markup using an offer Schema. (Part 2 of 3.)

```
68              </Offers>
69          </Body>
70      </BizTalk>
```

Fig. 15.27 BizTalk markup using an offer Schema. (Part 3 of 3.)

All Biztalk documents have the root element **BizTalk** (line 2). Line 3 defines a default namespace for the **BizTalk** framework elements. Element **Route** (lines 8–14) contains the routing information, which is mandatory for all BizTalk documents. Element **Route** also contains elements **To** and **From** (lines 9–12), which indicate the document's destination and source, respectively. This makes it easier for the receiving application to communicate with the sender. Attribute **locationType** specifies the type of business that sends or receives the information, and attribute **locationID** specifies a business identity (the unique identifier for a business). These attributes facilitate source and destination organization. Attribute **handle** provides information to routing applications that handle the document.

Element **Body** (lines 16–69) contains the actual message, whose Schema is defined by the businesses themselves. Lines 17–18 specify the default namespace for element **Offers** (lines 17–68), which is contained in element **Body** (note that line 18 wraps—if we split this line, Internet Explorer cannot locate the namespace). Each offer is marked up using an **Offer** element (lines 19–67) that contains elements describing the offer. Note that the tags all are business-related elements, and easily understood. For additional information on BizTalk, visit **www.biztalk.com**.

In this chapter, we studied the Extensible Markup Language and several of its related technologies. In Chapter 16, we begin our discussion of databases, which are crucial to the development of multi-tier Web-based applications.

15.8 Summary

XML is a widely supported, open (i.e., nonproprietary) technology for data exchange. XML is quickly becoming the standard by which applications maintain data. XML is highly portable. Any text editor that supports ASCII or Unicode characters can render or display XML documents. Because XML elements describe the data they contain, they are readable by both humans and machines.

XML permits document authors to create custom markup for virtually any type of information. This extensibility enables document authors to create entirely new markup languages that describe specific types of data—i.e., mathematical formulas, chemical molecular structures, music and recipes.

The processing of XML documents—which programs typically store in files whose names end with the **.xml** extension—requires a program called an XML parser. An XML parser is responsible for identifying components of XML documents and for storing those components in a data structure for manipulation.

An XML document can reference an optional document that defines the XML document's structure. Two types of optional structure-defining documents are Document Type Definitions (DTDs) and Schemas.

Data are marked up with tags whose names are enclosed in angle brackets (<>). Tags are used in pairs to delimit markup. A tag that begins markup is called a start tag, and a tag that terminates markup is called an end tag. End tags differ from start tags in that end tags contain a forward-slash (**/**) character.

Individual units of markup are called elements, which are the most fundamental XML building blocks. XML documents contain one element, called a root element, that contains every other element in the document. Elements are embedded or nested within each other to form hierarchies, with the root element at the top of the hierarchy.

In addition to being placed between tags, data also can be placed in attributes, which are name–value pairs in start tags. Elements can have any number of attributes.

Because XML allows document authors to create their own tags, naming collisions (i.e., two different elements that have the same name) can occur. As in C#, XML namespaces provide a means for document authors to prevent collisions. Elements are qualified with namespace prefixes that specify the namespace to which they belong.

Each namespace prefix is bound to a uniform resource identifier (URI) that uniquely identifies the namespace. A URI is a series of characters that differentiates names. Document authors create their own namespace prefixes. Virtually any name can be used as a namespace prefix, except the reserved namespace prefix **xml**. To eliminate the need to place a namespace prefix in each element, document authors can specify a default namespace for an element and its children.

When an XML parser successfully parses a document, the parser stores a tree structure containing the document's data in memory. This hierarchical tree structure is called a Document Object Model (DOM) tree. The DOM tree represents each component of the XML document as a node in the tree. Nodes that contain other nodes (called child nodes) are called parent nodes. Nodes that have the same parent are called sibling nodes. A node's descendant nodes include that node's children, its children's children and so on. A node's ancestor nodes include that node's parent, its parent's parent and so on. The DOM tree has a single root node that contains all other nodes in the document.

Namespace **System.Xml** contains classes for creating, reading and manipulating XML documents. **XmlReader**-derived class **XmlNodeReader** iterates through each node in the XML document. An **XmlDocument** object conceptually represents an empty XML document. XML documents are parsed and loaded into an **XmlDocument** object when method **Load** is invoked. Once an XML document is loaded into an **XmlDocument**, its data can be read and manipulated programmatically. An **XmlNodeReader** allows programmers to read one node at a time from an **XmlDocument**. An **XmlText-Writer** streams XML data to disk. An **XmlTextReader** reads XML data from a file.

XPath (XML Path Language) provides syntax for locating specific nodes in XML documents effectively and efficiently. XPath is a string-based language of expressions used by XML and many of its related technologies. Class **XPathNavigator** in the **System.Xml.XPath** namespace can iterate through node lists that match search criteria, written as an XPath expression.

XML documents contain only data; however, XSLT is capable of transforming XML documents into any text-based format. XSLT documents typically have the extension **.xsl**. When transforming an XML document via XSLT, two tree structures are involved—the source tree, which is the XML document being transformed, and the result tree, which is the result (e.g., XHTML) of the transformation. XML documents can be transformed programmatically through C#. The **System.Xml.Xsl** namespace facilities the application of XSLT style sheets to XML documents.

15.9 Internet and World Wide Web Resources

www.w3.org/xml

The W3C (World Wide Web Consortium) facilitates the development of common protocols to ensure interoperability on the Web. Their XML page includes information about upcoming events, publications, software and discussion groups. Visit this site to read about the latest developments in XML.

www.xml.org

xml.org is a reference for XML, DTDs, schemas and namespaces.

www.w3.org/style/XSL

This W3C page provides information on XSL, including topics such as XSL development, learning XSL, XSL-enabled tools, XSL specification, FAQs and XSL history.

www.w3.org/TR

This is the W3C technical reports and publications page. It contains links to working drafts, proposed recommendations and other resources.

www.xmlbooks.com

This site provides a list of XML books recommended by Charles Goldfarb, one of the original designers of GML (General Markup Language), from which SGML was derived.

www.xml-zone.com

The Development Exchange XML Zone is a complete resource for XML information. This site includes a FAQ, news, articles and links to other XML sites and newsgroups.

wdvl.internet.com/Authoring/Languages/XML

Web Developer's Virtual Library XML site includes tutorials, FAQs, the latest news, and numerous links to XML sites and software downloads.

www.xml.com

XML.com provides the latest news and information about XML, conference listings, links to XML Web resources organized by topic, tools and other resources.

msdn.microsoft.com/xml/default.asp

The MSDN Online XML Development Center features articles on XML, "Ask the Experts" chat sessions, samples and demos, newsgroups and other helpful information.

msdn.microsoft.com/downloads/samples/Internet/xml/xml_validator/ sample.asp

The microsoft XML validator, which can be downloaded from this site, can validate both online and off-line documents.

www.oasis-open.org/cover/xml.html

The SGML/XML Web Page is an extensive resource that includes links to several FAQs, online resources, industry initiatives, demos, conferences and tutorials.

www.gca.org/whats_xml/default.htm

The GCA site offers an XML glossary, list of books on XML, brief descriptions of the draft standards for XML and links to online drafts.

www-106.ibm.com/developerworks/xml

The IBM XML Zone site is a great resource for developers. It provides news, tools, a library, case studies, and information about events and standards.

developer.netscape.com/tech/xml/index.html

The XML and Metadata Developer Central site has demos, technical notes and news articles related to XML.

www.projectcool.com/developer/xmlz
The Project Cool Developer Zone site includes several tutorials covering introductory through advanced XML topics.

www.ucc.ie/xml
This site is a detailed set of FAQs on XML. Developers can check out responses to some popular questions or submit their own questions through the site.

16

Database, SQL and ADO .NET

Objectives

- To understand the relational database model.
- To understand basic database queries using Structured Query Language (SQL).
- To use the classes and interfaces of namespace **System.Data** to manipulate databases.
- To understand and use ADO .NET's disconnected model.
- To use the classes and interfaces of namespace **System.Data.OleDb**.

It is a capital mistake to theorize before one has data.
Arthur Conan Doyle

Now go, write it before them in a table, and note it in a book, that it may be for the time to come for ever and ever.
The Holy Bible: The Old Testament

Let's look at the record.
Alfred Emanuel Smith

Get your facts first, and then you can distort them as much as you please.
Mark Twain

I like two kinds of men: domestic and foreign.
Mae West

Outline

16.1   Introduction
16.2   Relational Database Model
16.3   Relational Database Overview: Books Database
16.4   Structured Query Language (SQL)
        16.4.1   Basic SELECT Query
        16.4.2   WHERE Clause
        16.4.3   ORDER BY Clause
        16.4.4   Merging Data from Multiple Tables: INNER JOIN
        16.4.5   Joining Data from Tables Authors, AuthorISBN,
                  Titles and Publishers
        16.4.6   INSERT Statement
        16.4.7   UPDATE Statement
        16.4.8   DELETE Statement
16.5   ADO .NET Object Model
16.6   Programming with ADO .NET: Extracting Information from a
        Database
        16.6.1   Connecting to and Querying an Access Data Source
        16.6.2   Querying the Books Database
16.7   Programming with ADO.NET: Modifying a Database
16.8   Reading and Writing XML Files
16.9   Summary

16.1 Introduction

A *database* is an integrated collection of data. Many different strategies exist for organizing data in databases to facilitate easy access to and manipulation of the data. A *database management system* (*DBMS*) provides mechanisms for storing and organizing data in a manner that is consistent with the database's format. Database management systems enable programmers to access and store data without worrying about the internal representation of databases.

Today's most popular database systems are *relational databases* (*RDBMS*). Almost universally, relational databases use a language called *Structured Query Language* (*SQL*— pronounced as its individual letters or as "sequel") to perform *queries* (i.e., to request information that satisfies given criteria) and to manipulate data. [*Note*: The writing in this chapter assumes that SQL is pronounced as its individual letters. For this reason, we often precede SQL with the article "an," as in "an SQL database" or "an SQL statement."]

Some popular, enterprise-level relational database systems include Microsoft SQL Server, Oracle™, Sybase™, DB2™, Informix™ and MySQL™. This chapter presents examples using Microsoft Access—a relational database system that is packaged with Microsoft Office.

A programming language connects to, and interacts with, a relational database via an *interface*—software that facilitates communication between a database management system and a program. C# programmers communicate with databases and manipulate their data through *Microsoft ActiveX Data Objects™* (ADO), *ADO .NET*.

16.2 Relational Database Model

The *relational database model* is a logical representation of data that allows relationships among data to be considered without concern for the physical structure of the data. A relational database is composed of *tables*. Figure 16.1 illustrates an example table that might be used in a personnel system. The table name is **Employee**, and its primary purpose is to illustrate the specific attributes of various employees. A particular row of the table is called a *record* (or *row*). This table consists of six records. The **number** *field* (or *column*) of each record in the table is the *primary key* for referencing data in the table. A primary key is a field (or fields) in a table that contain(s) unique data—i.e, data that is not duplicated in other records of that table. This guarantees that each record can be identified by at least one distinct value. Examples of primary-key fields are columns that contain social security numbers, employee IDs and part numbers in an inventory system. The records of Fig. 16.1 are *ordered* by primary key. In this case, the records are listed in increasing order (they also could be listed in decreasing order).

Each column of the table represents a different field. Records normally are unique (by primary key) within a table, but particular field values might be duplicated in multiple records. For example, three different records in the **Employee** table's **Department** field contain the number 413.

number	name	department	salary	location
23603	Jones	413	1100	New Jersey
24568	Kerwin	413	2000	New Jersey
34589	Larson	642	1800	Los Angeles
35761	Myers	611	1400	Orlando
47132	Neumann	413	9000	New Jersey
78321	Stephens	611	8500	Orlando

Record/Row

Primary key   Field/Column

Fig. 16.1 Relational-database structure of an **Employee** table.

Often, different users of a database are interested in different data and different relationships among those data. Some users require only subsets of the table columns. To obtain table subsets, we use SQL statements to specify certain data we wish to *select* from a table. SQL provides a complete set of commands (including **SELECT**) that enable programmers to define complex *queries* to select data from a table. The results of a query commonly are called *result sets* (or *record sets*). For example, we might select data from the table in Fig. 16.1 to create a new result set containing only the location of each department. This result set appears in Fig. 16.2. SQL queries are discussed in detail in Section 16.4.

16.3 Relational Database Overview: Books Database

The next section provides an overview of SQL in the context of a sample **Books** database that we created for this chapter. However, before we discuss SQL, we must explain the various tables of the **Books** database. We use this database to introduce various database concepts, including the use of SQL to manipulate and obtain useful information from the database.

The database consists of four tables: **Authors**, **Publishers**, **AuthorISBN** and **Titles**. The **Authors** table (described in Fig. 16.3) consists of three fields (or columns) that maintain each author's unique ID number, first name and last name. Figure 16.4 contains the data from the **Authors** table of the **Books** database.

department	location
413	New Jersey
611	Orlando
642	Los Angeles

Fig. 16.2 Result set formed by selecting **Department** and **Location** data from the **Employee** table.

Field	Description
authorID	Author's ID number in the database. In the **Books** database, this **int** field is defined as an *auto-incremented field*. For each new record inserted in this table, the database increments the **authorID** value, ensuring that each record has a unique **authorID**. This field represents the table's primary key.
firstName	Author's first name (a **string**).
lastName	Author's last name (a **string**).

Fig. 16.3 **Authors** table from **Books**.

The **Publishers** table (described in Fig. 16.5) consists of two fields, representing each publisher's unique ID and name. Figure 16.6 contains the data from the **Publishers** table of the **Books** database.

The **AuthorISBN** table (described in Fig. 16.7) consists of two fields that maintain the authors' ID numbers and the corresponding ISBN numbers of their books. This table helps associate the names of the authors with the titles of their books. Figure 16.8 contains the data from the **AuthorISBN** table of the **Books** database. ISBN is an abbreviation for "International Standard Book Number"—a numbering scheme by which publishers worldwide assign every book a unique identification number. [*Note*: To save space, we have split the contents of this figure into two columns, each containing the **authorID** and **isbn** fields.

authorID	firstName	lastName
1	Harvey	Deitel
2	Paul	Deitel
3	Tem	Nieto
4	Kate	Steinbuhler
5	Sean	Santry
6	Ted	Lin
7	Praveen	Sadhu
8	David	McPhie
9	Cheryl	Yaeger
10	Marina	Zlatkina
11	Ben	Wiedermann
12	Jonathan	Liperi
13	Jeffrey	Listfield

Fig. 16.4 Data from the **Authors** table of **Books**.

Field	Description
publisherID	The publisher's ID number in the database. This auto-incremented **int** field is the table's primary-key field.
publisherName	The name of the publisher (a **string**).

Fig. 16.5 **Publishers** table from **Books**.

publisherID	publisherName
1	Prentice Hall
2	Prentice Hall PTG

Fig. 16.6 Data from the **Publishers** table of **Books**.

Field	Description
authorID	The author's ID number, which allows the database to associate each book with a specific author. The integer ID number in this field must also appear in the **Authors** table.
isbn	The ISBN number for a book (a **string**).

Fig. 16.7 **AuthorISBN** table from **Books**.

authorID	isbn	authorID	isbn
1	0130895725	2	0139163050
1	0132261197	2	013028419x
1	0130895717	2	0130161438
1	0135289106	2	0130856118
1	0139163050	2	0130125075
1	013028419x	2	0138993947
1	0130161438	2	0130852473
1	0130856118	2	0130829277
1	0130125075	2	0134569555
1	0138993947	2	0130829293
1	0130852473	2	0130284173
1	0130829277	2	0130284181
1	0134569555	2	0130895601
1	0130829293	3	013028419x
1	0130284173	3	0130161438
1	0130284181	3	0130856118
1	0130895601	3	0134569555
2	0130895725	3	0130829293
2	0132261197	3	0130284173
2	0130895717	3	0130284181
2	0135289106	4	0130895601

Fig. 16.8 Data from **AuthorISBN** table in **Books**.

The **Titles** table (described in Fig. 16.9) consists of seven fields that maintain general information about the books in the database. This information includes each book's ISBN number, title, edition number, copyright year and publisher's ID number, as well as the name of a file containing an image of the book cover and, finally, each book's price. Figure 16.10 contains the data from the **Titles** table.

Field	Description
isbn	ISBN number of the book (a **string**).
title	Title of the book (a **string**).
editionNumber	Edition number of the book (a **string**).
copyright	Copyright year of the book (an **int**).
publisherID	Publisher's ID number (an **int**). This value must correspond to an ID number in the **Publishers** table.
imageFile	Name of the file containing the book's cover image (a **string**).
price	Suggested retail price of the book (a real number). [*Note*: The prices shown in this database are for example purposes only.]

Fig. 16.9 **Titles** table from **Books**.

isbn	title	edition-Number	publish-erID	copy-right	imageFile	price
0130923613	Python How to Program	1	1	2002	**python.jpg**	$69.95
0130622214	C# How to Program	1	1	2002	**cshtp.jpg**	$69.95
0130341517	Java How to Program	4	1	2002	**jhtp4.jpg**	$69.95
0130649341	The Complete Java Training Course	4	2	2002	**javactc4.jpg**	$109.95
0130895601	Advanced Java 2 Platform How to Program	1	1	2002	**advjhtp1.jpg**	$69.95
0130308978	Internet and World Wide Web How to Program	2	1	2002	**iw3htp2.jpg**	$69.95
0130293636	Visual Basic .NET How to Program	2	1	2002	**vbnet.jpg**	$69.95
0130895636	The Complete C++ Training Course	3	2	2001	**cppctc3.jpg**	$109.95

Fig. 16.10 Data from the **Titles** table of **Books**. (Part 1 of 3.)

isbn	title	edition-Number	publish-erID	copy-right	imageFile	price
0130895512	The Complete e-Business & e-Commerce Programming Training Course	1	2	2001	`ebecctc.jpg`	$109.95
013089561X	The Complete Internet & World Wide Web Programming Training Course	2	2	2001	`iw3ctc2.jpg`	$109.95
0130895547	The Complete Perl Training Course	1	2	2001	`perl.jpg`	$109.95
0130895563	The Complete XML Programming Training Course	1	2	2001	`xmlctc.jpg`	$109.95
0130895725	C How to Program	3	1	2001	`chtp3.jpg`	$69.95
0130895717	C++ How to Program	3	1	2001	`cpphtp3.jpg`	$69.95
013028419X	e-Business and e-Commerce How to Program	1	1	2001	`ebechtp1.jpg`	$69.95
0130622265	Wireless Internet and Mobile Business How to Program	1	1	2001	`wireless.jpg`	$69.95
0130284181	Perl How to Program	1	1	2001	`perlhtp1.jpg`	$69.95
0130284173	XML How to Program	1	1	2001	`xmlhtp1.jpg`	$69.95
0130856118	The Complete Internet and World Wide Web Programming Training Course	1	2	2000	`iw3ctc1.jpg`	$109.95
0130125075	Java How to Program (Java 2)	3	1	2000	`jhtp3.jpg`	$69.95
0130852481	The Complete Java 2 Training Course	3	2	2000	`javactc3.jpg`	$109.95
0130323640	e-Business and e-Commerce for Managers	1	1	2000	`ebecm.jpg`	$69.95
0130161438	Internet and World Wide Web How to Program	1	1	2000	`iw3htp1.jpg`	$69.95

Fig. 16.10 Data from the **Titles** table of **Books**. (Part 2 of 3.)

isbn	title	edition-Number	publish-erID	copy-right	imageFile	price
0130132497	Getting Started with Visual C++ 6 with an Introduction to MFC	1	1	1999	gsvc.jpg	$49.95
0130829293	The Complete Visual Basic 6 Training Course	1	2	1999	vbctc1.jpg	$109.95
0134569555	Visual Basic 6 How to Program	1	1	1999	vbhtp1.jpg	$69.95
0132719746	Java Multimedia Cyber Classroom	1	2	1998	javactc.jpg	$109.95
0136325890	Java How to Program	1	1	1998	jhtp1.jpg	$69.95
0139163050	The Complete C++ Training Course	2	2	1998	cppctc2.jpg	$109.95
0135289106	C++ How to Program	2	1	1998	cpphtp2.jpg	$49.95
0137905696	The Complete Java Training Course	2	2	1998	javactc2.jpg	$109.95
0130829277	The Complete Java Training Course (Java 1.1)	2	2	1998	javactc2.jpg	$99.95
0138993947	Java How to Program (Java 1.1)	2	1	1998	jhtp2.jpg	$49.95
0131173340	C++ How to Program	1	1	1994	cpphtp1.jpg	$69.95
0132261197	C How to Program	2	1	1994	chtp2.jpg	$49.95
0131180436	C How to Program	1	1	1992	chtp.jpg	$69.95

Fig. 16.10 Data from the **Titles** table of **Books**. (Part 3 of 3.)

Figure 16.11 illustrates the relationships among the tables in the **Books** database. The first line in each table is the table's name. The field whose name appears in italics contains that table's primary key. A table's primary key uniquely identifies each record in the table. Every record must have a value in the primary-key field, and the value must be unique. This is known as the *Rule of Entity Integrity*. Note that the **AuthorISBN** table contains two fields whose names are italicized. This indicates that these two fields form a *compound primary key*—each record in the table must have a unique **authorID–isbn** combination. For example, several records might have an **authorID** of **2**, and several records might have an **isbn** of **0130895601**, but only one record can have both an **authorID** of **2** and an **isbn** of **0130895601**.

Fig. 16.11 Table relationships in **Books**.

Common Programming Error 16.1

Failure to provide a value for a primary-key field in every record breaks the Rule of Entity Integrity and causes the DBMS to report an error.

Common Programming Error 16.2

Providing duplicate values for the primary-key field of multiple records causes the DBMS to report an error.

The lines connecting the tables in Fig. 16.11 represent the *relationships* among the tables. Consider the line between the **Publishers** and **Titles** tables. On the **Publishers** end of the line, there is a **1**, and, on the **Titles** end, there is an infinity (∞) symbol. This line indicates a *one-to-many relationship*, in which every publisher in the **Publishers** table can have an arbitrarily large number of books in the **Titles** table. Note that the relationship line links the **publisherID** field in the **Publishers** table to the **publisherID** field in **Titles** table. In the **Titles** table, the **publisherID** field is a *foreign key*—a field for which every entry has a unique value in another table and where the field in the other table is the primary key for that table (e.g., **publisherID** in the **Publishers** table). Programmers specify foreign keys when creating a table. The foreign key helps maintain the *Rule of Referential Integrity*: Every foreign-key field value must appear in another table's primary-key field. Foreign keys enable information from multiple tables to be *joined* together for analysis purposes. There is a one-to-many relationship between a primary key and its corresponding foreign key. This means that a foreign-key field value can appear many times in its own table, but must appear exactly once as the primary key of another table. The line between the tables represents the link between the foreign key in one table and the primary key in another table.

Common Programming Error 16.3

Providing a foreign-key value that does not appear as a primary-key value in another table breaks the Rule of Referential Integrity and causes the DBMS to report an error.

The line between the **AuthorISBN** and **Authors** tables indicates that, for each author in the **Authors** table, the **AuthorISBN** table can contain an arbitrary number of ISBNs for books written by that author. The **authorID** field in the **AuthorISBN** table is a foreign key of the **authorID** field (the primary key) of the **Authors** table. Note, again, that the line between the tables links the foreign key in table **AuthorISBN** to the corresponding primary key in table **Authors**. The **AuthorISBN** table links information in the **Titles** and **Authors** tables.

The line between the **Titles** and **AuthorISBN** tables illustrates another one-to-many relationship; a title can be written by any number of authors. In fact, the sole purpose of the **AuthorISBN** table is to represent a many-to-many relationship between the **Authors** and **Titles** tables; an author can write any number of books, and a book can have any number of authors.

16.4 Structured Query Language (SQL)

In this section, we provide an overview of Structured Query Language (SQL) in the context of our **Books** sample database. The SQL queries discussed here form the foundation for the SQL used in the chapter examples.

Figure 16.12 lists SQL keywords and provides a description of each. In the next several subsections, we discuss these SQL keywords in the context of complete SQL queries. Other SQL keywords exist, but are beyond the scope of this text. [*Note*: To locate additional information on SQL, please refer to the bibliography at the end of this chapter.]

16.4.1 Basic **SELECT** Query

Let us consider several SQL queries that extract information from database **Books**. A typical SQL query "selects" information from one or more tables in a database. Such selections are performed by *SELECT queries*. The basic format for a **SELECT** query is:

> *SELECT * FROM* tableName

In this query, the asterisk (*****) indicates that all columns from the *tableName* table of the database should be selected. For example, to select the entire contents of the **Authors** table (i.e., all data depicted in Fig. 16.4), use the query:

> *SELECT * FROM* Authors

SQL keyword	Description
SELECT	Selects (retrieves) fields from one or more tables.
FROM	Specifies tables from which to get fields or delete records. Required in every *SELECT* and *DELETE* statement.
WHERE	Specifies criteria that determine the rows to be retrieved.
INNER JOIN	Joins records from multiple tables to produce a single set of records.
GROUP BY	Specifies criteria for grouping records.
ORDER BY	Specifies criteria for ordering records.
INSERT	Inserts data into a specified table.
UPDATE	Updates data in a specified table.
DELETE	Deletes data from a specified table.

Fig. 16.12 SQL query keywords.

To select specific fields from a table, replace the asterisk (*****) with a comma-separated list of the field names to select. For example, to select only the fields **authorID** and **lastName** for all rows in the **Authors** table, use the query:

> *SELECT* authorID, lastName *FROM* Authors

This query returns only the data presented in Fig. 16.13. [*Note*: If a field name contains spaces, the entire field name must be enclosed in square brackets (**[]**) in the query. For example, if the field name is **first name**, it must appear in the query as **[first name]**.]

![icon] **Common Programming Error 16.4**

If a program assumes that an SQL statement using the asterisk (***) to select fields always returns those fields in the same order, the program could process the result set incorrectly. If the field order in the database table(s) changes, the order of the fields in the result set would change accordingly.

![icon] **Performance Tip 16.1**

If a program does not know the order of fields in a result set, the program must process the fields by name. This could require a linear search of the field names in the result set. If users specify the field names that they wish to select from a table (or several tables), the application receiving the result set knows the order of the fields in advance. When this occurs, the program can process the data more efficiently, because fields can be accessed directly by column number.

16.4.2 WHERE Clause

In most cases, users search a database for records that satisfy certain *selection criteria*. Only records that match the selection criteria are selected. SQL uses the optional **WHERE** *clause* in a **SELECT** query to specify the selection criteria for the query. The simplest format for a **SELECT** query that includes selection criteria is:

> *SELECT* fieldName1, fieldName2, ... *FROM* tableName *WHERE* criteria

For example, to select the **title**, **editionNumber** and **copyright** fields from those rows of table **Titles** in which the **copyright** date is greater than **1999**, use the query:

authorID	lastName	authorID	lastName
1	Deitel	8	McPhie
2	Deitel	9	Yaeger
3	Nieto	10	Zlatkina
4	Steinbuhler	12	Wiedermann
5	Santry	12	Liperi
6	Lin	13	Listfield
7	Sadhu		

Fig. 16.13 **authorID** and **lastName** from the **Authors** table.

```
SELECT title, editionNumber, copyright
FROM Titles
WHERE copyright > 1999
```

Figure 16.14 shows the result set of the preceding query. [*Note*: When we construct a query for use in C#, we simply create a **string** containing the entire query. However, when we display queries in the text, we often use multiple lines and indentation to enhance readability.]

Performance Tip 16.2

Using selection criteria improves performance, because queries that involve such criteria normally select a portion of the database that is smaller than the entire database. Working with a smaller portion of the data is more efficient than working with the entire set of data stored in the database.

title	editionNumber	copyright
Internet and World Wide Web How to Program	2	2002
Java How to Program	4	2002
The Complete Java Training Course	4	2002
The Complete e-Business & e-Commerce Programming Training Course	1	2001
The Complete Internet & World Wide Web Programming Training Course	2	2001
The Complete Perl Training Course	1	2001
The Complete XML Programming Training Course	1	2001
C How to Program	3	2001
C++ How to Program	3	2001
The Complete C++ Training Course	3	2001
e-Business and e-Commerce How to Program	1	2001
Internet and World Wide Web How to Program	1	2000
The Complete Internet and World Wide Web Programming Training Course	1	2000
Java How to Program (Java 2)	3	2000
The Complete Java 2 Training Course	3	2000
XML How to Program	1	2001
Perl How to Program	1	2001
Advanced Java 2 Platform How to Program	1	2002
e-Business and e-Commerce for Managers	1	2000
Wireless Internet and Mobile Business How to Program	1	2001
C# How To Program	1	2002
Python How to Program	1	2002
Visual Basic .NET How to Program	2	2002

Fig. 16.14 Titles with copyrights after 1999 from table **Titles**.

The **WHERE** clause condition can contain operators **<, >, <=, >=, =, <>** and **LIKE**. Operator **LIKE** is used for *pattern matching* with wildcard characters *asterisk* (*****) and *question mark* (**?**). Pattern matching allows SQL to search for strings that "match a pattern."

A pattern that contains an asterisk (*****) searches for strings in which zero or more characters take the asterisk character's place in the pattern. For example, the following query locates the records of all authors whose last names start with the letter **D**:

```
SELECT authorID, firstName, lastName
FROM Authors
WHERE lastName LIKE 'D*'
```

The preceding query selects the two records shown in Fig. 16.15, because two of the authors in our database have last names that begin with the letter **D** (followed by zero or more characters). The ***** in the **WHERE** clause's **LIKE** pattern indicates that any number of characters can appear after the letter **D** in the **lastName** field. Notice that the pattern string is surrounded by single-quote characters.

Portability Tip 16.1

Not all database systems support the ***LIKE*** *operator, so be sure to read the database system's documentation carefully before employing this operator.*

Portability Tip 16.2

Most databases use the **%** *character in place of the* ***** *character in* ***LIKE*** *expressions.*

Portability Tip 16.3

In some databases, string data is case sensitive.

Portability Tip 16.4

In some databases, table names and field names are case sensitive.

Good Programming Practice 16.1

By convention, SQL keywords should be written entirely in uppercase letters on systems that are not case sensitive. This emphasizes the SQL keywords in an SQL statement.

A pattern string including a question mark (**?**) character searches for strings in which exactly one character takes the question mark's place in the pattern. For example, the following query locates the records of all authors whose last names start with any character (specified with **?**), followed by the letter **i**, followed by any number of additional characters (specified with *****):

authorID	firstName	lastName
1	Harvey	Deitel
2	Paul	Deitel

Fig. 16.15 Authors from the **Authors** table whose last names start with **D**.

```
SELECT authorID, firstName, lastName
FROM Authors
WHERE lastName LIKE '?i*'
```

The preceding query produces the records listed in Fig. 16.16; five authors in our database have last names in which the letter **i** is the second letter.

Portability Tip 16.5

*Most databases use the _ character in place of the ? character in **LIKE** expressions.*

16.4.3 ORDER BY Clause

The results of a query can be arranged in ascending or descending order using the optional ***ORDER BY*** *clause*. The simplest forms for an **ORDER BY** clause are:

```
SELECT fieldName1, fieldName2, ... FROM tableName ORDER BY field ASC
SELECT fieldName1, fieldName2, ... FROM tableName ORDER BY field DESC
```

where **ASC** specifies ascending order (lowest to highest), **DESC** specifies descending order (highest to lowest) and *field* specifies the field whose values determine the sorting order.

For example, to obtain a list of authors arranged in ascending order by last name (Fig. 16.17), use the query:

```
SELECT authorID, firstName, lastName
FROM Authors
ORDER BY lastName ASC
```

Note that the default sorting order is ascending; therefore, **ASC** is optional.

authorID	firstName	lastName
3	Tem	Nieto
6	Ted	Lin
11	Ben	Wiedermann
12	Jonathan	Liperi
13	Jeffrey	Listfield

Fig. 16.16 Authors from table **Authors** whose last names contain **i** as the second letter.

authorID	firstName	lastName
2	Paul	Deitel
1	Harvey	Deitel

Fig. 16.17 Authors from table **Authors** in ascending order by **lastName**. (Part 1 of 2.)

authorID	firstName	lastName
6	Ted	Lin
12	Jonathan	Liperi
13	Jeffrey	Listfield
8	David	McPhie
3	Tem	Nieto
7	Praveen	Sadhu
5	Sean	Santry
4	Kate	Steinbuhler
11	Ben	Wiedermann
9	Cheryl	Yaeger
10	Marina	Zlatkina

Fig. 16.17 Authors from table **Authors** in ascending order by **lastName**. (Part 2 of 2.)

To obtain the same list of authors arranged in descending order by last name (Fig. 16.18), use the query:

```
SELECT authorID, firstName, lastName
FROM Authors
ORDER BY lastName DESC
```

authorID	firstName	lastName
10	Marina	Zlatkina
9	Cheryl	Yaeger
11	Ben	Wiedermann
4	Kate	Steinbuhler
5	Sean	Santry
7	Praveen	Sadhu
3	Tem	Nieto
8	David	McPhie
13	Jeffrey	Listfield
12	Jonathan	Liperi
6	Ted	Lin
2	Paul	Deitel
1	Harvey	Deitel

Fig. 16.18 Authors from table **Authors** in descending order by **lastName**.

The **ORDER BY** clause also can be used to order records by multiple fields. Such queries are written in the form:

> **ORDER BY** *field1 sortingOrder*, *field2 sortingOrder*, ...

where *sortingOrder* is either **ASC** or **DESC**. Note that the *sortingOrder* does not have to be identical for each field.

For example, the query:

```
SELECT authorID, firstName, lastName
FROM Authors
ORDER BY lastName, firstName
```

sorts all authors in ascending order by last name, then by first name. This means that, if any authors have the same last name, their records are returned sorted by first name (Fig. 16.19).

The **WHERE** and **ORDER BY** clauses can be combined in one query. For example, the query:

```
SELECT isbn, title, editionNumber, copyright, price
FROM Titles
WHERE title
LIKE '*How to Program' ORDER BY title ASC
```

returns the ISBN, title, edition number, copyright and price of each book in the **Titles** table that has a **title** ending with "**How to Program**"; it lists these records in ascending order by **title**. The results of the query are depicted in Fig. 16.20.

authorID	firstName	lastName
1	Harvey	Deitel
2	Paul	Deitel
6	Ted	Lin
12	Jonathan	Liperi
13	Jeffrey	Listfield
8	David	McPhie
3	Tem	Nieto
7	Praveen	Sadhu
5	Sean	Santry
4	Kate	Steinbuhler
11	Ben	Wiedermann
9	Cheryl	Yaeger
10	Marina	Zlatkina

Fig. 16.19 Authors from table **Authors** in ascending order by **lastName** and by **firstName**.

isbn	title	edition-Number	copy-right	price
0130895601	Advanced Java 2 Platform How to Program	1	2002	$69.95
0131180436	C How to Program	1	1992	$69.95
0130895725	C How to Program	3	2001	$69.95
0132261197	C How to Program	2	1994	$49.95
0130622214	C# How To Program	1	2002	$69.95
0135289106	C++ How to Program	2	1998	$49.95
0131173340	C++ How to Program	1	1994	$69.95
0130895717	C++ How to Program	3	2001	$69.95
013028419X	e-Business and e-Commerce How to Program	1	2001	$69.95
0130308978	Internet and World Wide Web How to Program	2	2002	$69.95
0130161438	Internet and World Wide Web How to Program	1	2000	$69.95
0130341517	Java How to Program	4	2002	$69.95
0136325890	Java How to Program	1	1998	$49.95
0130284181	Perl How to Program	1	2001	$69.95
0130923613	Python How to Program	1	2002	$69.95
0130293636	Visual Basic .NET How to Program	2	2002	$69.95
0134569555	Visual Basic 6 How to Program	1	1999	$69.95
0130622265	Wireless Internet and Mobile Business How to Program	1	2001	$69.95
0130284173	XML How to Program	1	2001	$69.95

Fig. 16.20 Books from table **Titles** whose titles end with **How to Program** in ascending order by **title**.

16.4.4 Merging Data from Multiple Tables: INNER JOIN

Database designers often split related data into separate tables to ensure that a database does not store data redundantly. For example, the **Books** database has tables **Authors** and **Titles**. We use an **AuthorISBN** table to provide "links" between authors and their corresponding titles. If we did not separate this information into individual tables, we would need to include author information with each entry in the **Titles** table. This would result in the database storing duplicate author information for authors who wrote multiple books.

Often, it is necessary for analysis purposes to merge data from multiple tables into a single set of data. Referred to as *joining* the tables, this is accomplished via an **INNER JOIN** operation in the **SELECT** query. An **INNER JOIN** merges records from two or more tables by testing for matching values in a field that is common to the tables. The simplest format for an **INNER JOIN** clause is:

```
SELECT fieldName1, fieldName2, ...
FROM table1
INNER JOIN table2
    ON table1.fieldName = table2.fieldName
```

The **ON** part of the **INNER JOIN** clause specifies the fields from each table that are compared to determine which records are joined. For example, the following query produces a list of authors accompanied by the ISBN numbers for books written by each author:

```
SELECT firstName, lastName, isbn
FROM Authors
INNER JOIN AuthorISBN
    ON Authors.authorID = AuthorISBN.authorID
ORDER BY lastName, firstName
```

The query merges the **firstName** and **lastName** fields from table **Authors** with the **isbn** field from table **AuthorISBN**, sorting the results in ascending order by **lastName** and **firstName**. Notice the use of the syntax *tableName.fieldName* in the **ON** part of the **INNER JOIN**. This syntax (called a *fully qualified name*) specifies the fields from each table that should be compared to join the tables. The "*tableName.*" syntax is required if the fields have the same name in both tables. The same syntax can be used in any query to distinguish among fields in different tables that have the same name. Fully qualified names that start with the database name can be used to perform cross-database queries.

Software Engineering Observation 16.1

*If an SQL statement includes fields from multiple tables that have the same name, the statement must precede those field names with their table names and the dot operator (e.g., **Authors.authorID**).*

Common Programming Error 16.5

In a query, failure to provide fully qualified names for fields that have the same name in two or more tables is an error.

As always, the query can contain an **ORDER BY** clause. Figure 16.21 depicts the results of the preceding query, ordered by **lastName** and **firstName**. [*Note:* To save space, we split the results of the query into two columns, each containing the **firstName**, **lastName** and **isbn** fields.]

firstName	lastName	isbn	firstName	lastName	isbn
Harvey	Deitel	0130895601	Harvey	Deitel	0130829293
Harvey	Deitel	0130284181	Harvey	Deitel	0134569555
Harvey	Deitel	0130284173	Harvey	Deitel	0130829277

Fig. 16.21 Authors from table **Authors** and ISBN numbers of the authors' books, sorted in ascending order by **lastName** and **firstName**. (Part 1 of 2.)

firstName	lastName	isbn	firstName	lastName	isbn
Harvey	Deitel	0130852473	Paul	Deitel	0130125075
Harvey	Deitel	0138993947	Paul	Deitel	0130856118
Harvey	Deitel	0130856118	Paul	Deitel	0130161438
Harvey	Deitel	0130161438	Paul	Deitel	013028419x
Harvey	Deitel	013028419x	Paul	Deitel	0139163050
Harvey	Deitel	0139163050	Paul	Deitel	0130895601
Harvey	Deitel	0135289106	Paul	Deitel	0135289106
Harvey	Deitel	0130895717	Paul	Deitel	0130895717
Harvey	Deitel	0132261197	Paul	Deitel	0132261197
Harvey	Deitel	0130895725	Paul	Deitel	0130895725
Harvey	Deitel	0130125075	Tem	Nieto	0130284181
Paul	Deitel	0130284181	Tem	Nieto	0130284173
Paul	Deitel	0130284173	Tem	Nieto	0130829293
Paul	Deitel	0130829293	Tem	Nieto	0134569555
Paul	Deitel	0134569555	Tem	Nieto	0130856118
Paul	Deitel	0130829277	Tem	Nieto	0130161438
Paul	Deitel	0130852473	Tem	Nieto	013028419x
Paul	Deitel	0138993947			

Fig. 16.21 Authors from table **Authors** and ISBN numbers of the authors' books, sorted in ascending order by **lastName** and **firstName**. (Part 2 of 2.)

16.4.5 Joining Data from Tables Authors, AuthorISBN, Titles and Publishers

The **Books** database contains one predefined query (**TitleAuthor**), which selects as its results the title, ISBN number, author's first name, author's last name, copyright year and publisher's name for each book in the database. For books that have multiple authors, the query produces a separate composite record for each author. The **TitleAuthor** query is depicted in Fig. 16.22. Figure 16.23 contains a portion of the query results.

```
1   SELECT Titles.title, Titles.isbn, Authors.firstName,
2       Authors.lastName, Titles.copyright,
3         Publishers.publisherName
4   FROM
5   ( Publishers INNER JOIN Titles
6       ON Publishers.publisherID = Titles.publisherID )
7       INNER JOIN
```

Fig. 16.22 TitleAuthor query of **Books** database. (Part 1 of 2.)

```
 8        ( Authors INNER JOIN AuthorISBN
 9        ON Authors.authorID = AuthorISBN.authorID )
10     ON Titles.isbn = AuthorISBN.isbn
11     ORDER BY Titles.title
```

Fig. 16.22 `TitleAuthor` query of **Books** database. (Part 2 of 2.)

Title	isbn	first-Name	last-Name	copy-right	publisher-Name
Advanced Java 2 Platform How to Program	0130895601	Paul	Deitel	2002	Prentice Hall
Advanced Java 2 Platform How to Program	0130895601	Harvey	Deitel	2002	Prentice Hall
Advanced Java 2 Platform How to Program	0130895601	Sean	Santry	2002	Prentice Hall
C How to Program	0131180436	Harvey	Deitel	1992	Prentice Hall
C How to Program	0131180436	Paul	Deitel	1992	Prentice Hall
C How to Program	0132261197	Harvey	Deitel	1994	Prentice Hall
C How to Program	0132261197	Paul	Deitel	1994	Prentice Hall
C How to Program	0130895725	Harvey	Deitel	2001	Prentice Hall
C How to Program	0130895725	Paul	Deitel	2001	Prentice Hall
C# How To Program	0130622214	Tem	Nieto	2002	Prentice Hall
C# How To Program	0130622214	Paul	Deitel	2002	Prentice Hall
C# How To Program	0130622214	Jeffrey	Listfield	2002	Prentice Hall
C# How To Program	0130622214	Cheryl	Yaeger	2002	Prentice Hall
C# How To Program	0130622214	Marina	Zlatkina	2002	Prentice Hall
C# How To Program	0130622214	Harvey	Deitel	2002	Prentice Hall
C++ How to Program	0130895717	Paul	Deitel	2001	Prentice Hall
C++ How to Program	0130895717	Harvey	Deitel	2001	Prentice Hall
C++ How to Program	0131173340	Paul	Deitel	1994	Prentice Hall
C++ How to Program	0131173340	Harvey	Deitel	1994	Prentice Hall
C++ How to Program	0135289106	Harvey	Deitel	1998	Prentice Hall
C++ How to Program	0135289106	Paul	Deitel	1998	Prentice Hall
e-Business and e-Commerce for Managers	0130323640	Harvey	Deitel	2000	Prentice Hall
e-Business and e-Commerce for Managers	0130323640	Kate	Stein-buhler	2000	Prentice Hall

Fig. 16.23 Portion of the result set produced by the query in Fig. 16.22. (Part 1 of 2.)

Title	isbn	first-Name	last-Name	copy-right	publisher-Name
e-Business and e-Commerce for Managers	0130323640	Paul	Deitel	2000	Prentice Hall
e-Business and e-Commerce How to Program	013028419X	Harvey	Deitel	2001	Prentice Hall
e-Business and e-Commerce How to Program	013028419X	Paul	Deitel	2001	Prentice Hall
e-Business and e-Commerce How to Program	013028419X	Tem	Nieto	2001	Prentice Hall

Fig. 16.23 Portion of the result set produced by the query in Fig. 16.22. (Part 2 of 2.)

We added indentation to the query in Fig. 16.22 to make the query more readable. Let us now break down the query into its various parts. Lines 1–3 contain a comma-separated list of the fields that the query returns; the order of the fields from left to right specifies the fields' order in the returned table. This query selects fields **title** and **isbn** from table **Titles**, fields **firstName** and **lastName** from table **Authors**, field **copyright** from table **Titles** and field **publisherName** from table **Publishers**. For purposes of clarity, we fully qualified each field name with its table name (e.g., **Titles.isbn**).

Lines 5–10 specify the **INNER JOIN** operations used to combine information from the various tables. There are three **INNER JOIN** operations. It is important to note that, although an **INNER JOIN** is performed on two tables, either of those two tables can be the result of another query or another **INNER JOIN**. We use parentheses to nest the **INNER JOIN** operations; SQL evaluates the innermost set of parentheses first and then moves outward. We begin with the **INNER JOIN**:

```
( Publishers INNER JOIN Titles
    ON Publishers.publisherID = Titles.publisherID )
```

which joins the **Publishers** table and the **Titles** table **ON** the condition that the **publisherID** numbers in each table match. The resulting temporary table contains information about each book and its publisher.

The other nested set of parentheses contains the **INNER JOIN**:

```
( Authors INNER JOIN AuthorISBN ON
    Authors.AuthorID = AuthorISBN.AuthorID )
```

which joins the **Authors** table and the **AuthorISBN** table **ON** the condition that the **authorID** fields in each table match. Remember that the **AuthorISBN** table has multiple entries for **ISBN** numbers of books that have more than one author. The third **INNER JOIN**:

```
( Publishers INNER JOIN Titles
    ON Publishers.publisherID = Titles.publisherID )
INNER JOIN
( Authors INNER JOIN AuthorISBN
    ON Authors.authorID = AuthorISBN.authorID )
ON Titles.isbn = AuthorISBN.isbn
```

joins the two temporary tables produced by the two prior inner joins **ON** the condition that the **Titles.isbn** field for each record in the first temporary table matches the corresponding **AuthorISBN.isbn** field for each record in the second temporary table. The result of all these **INNER JOIN** operations is a temporary table from which the appropriate fields are selected to produce the results of the query.

Finally, line 11 of the query:

```
ORDER BY Titles.title
```

indicates that all the records should be sorted in ascending order (the default) by title.

16.4.6 INSERT Statement

The *INSERT* statement inserts a new record in a table. The simplest form for this statement is:

```
INSERT INTO tableName ( fieldName1, fieldName2, ..., fieldNameN )
       VALUES ( value1, value2, ..., valueN )
```

where *tableName* is the table in which to insert the record. The *tableName* is followed by a comma-separated list of field names in parentheses. The list of field names is followed by the SQL keyword **VALUES** and a comma-separated list of values in parentheses. The specified values in this list must match the field names listed after the table name in both order and type (for example, if *fieldName1* is specified as the **firstName** field, then *value1* should be a string in single quotes representing the first name). The **INSERT** statement:

```
INSERT INTO Authors ( firstName, lastName )
       VALUES ( 'Sue', 'Smith' )
```

inserts a record into the **Authors** table. The first comma-separated list indicates that the statement provides data for the **firstName** and **lastName** fields. The corresponding values to insert, which are contained in the second comma-separated list, are **'Sue'** and **'Smith'**. We do not specify an **authorID** in this example, because **authorID** is an auto-increment field in the database. Every new record that we add to this table is assigned a unique **authorID** value that is the next value in the auto-increment sequence (i.e., 1, 2, 3, etc.). In this case, **Sue Smith** would be assigned **authorID** number 14. Figure 16.24 shows the **Authors** table after we perform the **INSERT** operation.

authorID	firstName	lastName
1	Harvey	Deitel
2	Paul	Deitel
3	Tem	Nieto
4	Kate	Steinbuhler
5	Sean	Santry
6	Ted	Lin
7	Praveen	Sadhu

Fig. 16.24 Authors after an **INSERT** operation to add a record. (Part 1 of 2.)

authorID	firstName	lastName
8	David	McPhie
9	Cheryl	Yaeger
10	Marina	Zlatkina
11	Ben	Wiedermann
12	Jonathan	Liperi
13	Jeffrey	Listfield
14	Sue	Smith

Fig. 16.24 Authors after an **INSERT** operation to add a record. (Part 2 of 2.)

Common Programming Error 16.6

SQL statements use the single-quote (') character as a delimiter for strings. To specify a string containing a single quote (such as O'Malley) in an SQL statement, the string must include two single quotes in the position where the single-quote character should appear in the string (e.g., **'O''Malley'***). The first of the two single-quote characters acts as an escape character for the second. Failure to escape single-quote characters in a string that is part of an SQL statement is an SQL syntax error.*

16.4.7 UPDATE Statement

An **UPDATE** statement modifies data in a table. The simplest form for an **UPDATE** statement is:

```
UPDATE tableName
    SET fieldName1 = value1, fieldName2 = value2, ..., fieldNameN = valueN
    WHERE criteria
```

where *tableName* is the table in which to update a record (or records). The *tableName* is followed by keyword **SET** and a comma-separated list of field name/value pairs written in the format, *fieldName = value*. The **WHERE** clause specifies the criteria used to determine which record(s) to update. For example, the **UPDATE** statement:

```
UPDATE Authors
    SET lastName = 'Jones'
    WHERE lastName = 'Smith' AND firstName = 'Sue'
```

updates a record in the **Authors** table. The statement indicates that **lastName** will be assigned the new value **Jones** for the record in which **lastName** currently is equal to **Smith** and **firstName** is equal to **Sue**. If we know the **authorID** in advance of the **UPDATE** operation (possibly because we searched for the record previously), the **WHERE** clause could be simplified as follows:

```
WHERE AuthorID = 14
```

Figure 16.25 depicts the **Authors** table after we perform the **UPDATE** operation.

authorID	firstName	lastName
1	Harvey	Deitel
2	Paul	Deitel
3	Tem	Nieto
4	Kate	Steinbuhler
5	Sean	Santry
6	Ted	Lin
7	Praveen	Sadhu
8	David	McPhie
9	Cheryl	Yaeger
10	Marina	Zlatkina
11	Ben	Wiedermann
12	Jonathan	Liperi
13	Jeffrey	Listfield
14	Sue	Jones

Fig. 16.25 Table **Authors** after an **UPDATE** operation to change a record.

Common Programming Error 16.7

*Failure to use a **WHERE** clause with an **UPDATE** statement could lead to logic errors.*

16.4.8 DELETE Statement

An SQL **DELETE** statement removes data from a table. The simplest form for a **DELETE** statement is:

> *DELETE FROM* tableName *WHERE* criteria

where *tableName* is the table from which to delete a record (or records). The **WHERE** clause specifies the criteria used to determine which record(s) to delete. For example, the **DELETE** statement:

> *DELETE FROM* Authors
>   *WHERE* lastName = 'Jones' *AND* firstName = 'Sue'

deletes the record for **Sue Jones** from the **Authors** table.

Common Programming Error 16.8

***WHERE** clauses can match multiple records. When deleting records from a database, be sure to define a **WHERE** clause that matches only the records to be deleted.*

Figure 16.26 depicts the **Authors** table after we perform the **DELETE** operation.

authorID	firstName	lastName
1	Harvey	Deitel
2	Paul	Deitel
3	Tem	Nieto
4	Kate	Steinbuhler
5	Sean	Santry
6	Ted	Lin
7	Praveen	Sadhu
8	David	McPhie
9	Cheryl	Yaeger
10	Marina	Zlatkina
11	Ben	Wiedermann
12	Jonathan	Liperi
13	Jeffrey	Listfield

Fig. 16.26 Table **Authors** after a **DELETE** operation to remove a record.

16.5 ADO .NET Object Model

The ADO .NET object model provides an API for accessing database systems programmatically. ADO .NET was created for the .NET Framework and is the next generation of *ActiveX Data Objects*™ (ADO).

Namespace *System.Data* is the root namespace for the ADO .NET API. The primary namespaces for ADO .NET, *System.Data.OleDb* and *System.Data.SqlClient*, contain classes that enable programs to connect with and modify datasources. Namespace **System.Data.OleDb** contains classes that are designed to work with any datasource, whereas the **System.Data.SqlClient** namespace contains classes that are optimized to work with Microsoft SQL Server 2000 databases.

Instances of class *System.Data.DataSet*, which consist of a set of **DataTable**s and relationships among those **DataTable**s, represent *caches* of data—data that a program stores temporarily in local memory. The structure of a **DataSet** mimics the structure of a relational database. An advantage of using class **DataSet** is that it is *disconnected*—the program does not need a persistent connection to the datasource to work with data in a **DataSet**. The program connects to the datasource only during the initial population of the **DataSet** and then to store any changes made in the **DataSet**. Hence, the program does not require any active, permanent connection to the datasource.

Instances of class *OleDbConnection* (namespace **System.Data.OleDb**) represent connections to a datasource. An instance of class *OleDbDataAdapter* connects to a datasource through an instance of class **OleDbConnection** and can populate a **DataSet** with data from that datasource. We discuss the details of creating and populating **DataSet**s later in this chapter. An instance of class *OleDbCommand* (namespace **System.Data.OleDb**) represents an arbitrary SQL command to be executed on a datasource. A program can use instances of class **OleDbCommand** to manipulate a datasource through an **OleDbConnection**. The programmer must close the active connection to the datasource explicitly once no further changes are to be made. Unlike **DataSet**s, **OleDbCommand** objects do not cache data in local memory.

Instances of classes *SqlDataReader* (namespace **System.Data.SqlClient**) and *OleDbDataReader* (namespace **System.Data.OleDb**) represent read-only connections to a datasource. Data readers provide a performance-optimized way to retrieve large amounts of data. Chapter 17, ASP .NET, Web Forms and Web Controls, contains an application using an **OleDbDataReader**.

16.6 Programming with ADO .NET: Extracting Information from a Database

In this section, we present two examples that introduce how to connect to a database, query the database and display the results of the query. The database used in these examples is the Microsoft Access **Books** database that we have discussed throughout this chapter. It can be found in the project directory for the application of Fig. 16.27. Each program must specify the location of this database on the computer's hard drive. When executing these examples, readers must update this location for each program. For example, before readers can run the application in Fig. 16.27 on their computers, they must change lines 234–247 so that the code specifies the correct location of the database file.

16.6.1 Connecting to and Querying an Access Data Source

The first example (Fig. 16.27) performs a simple query on the **Books** database that retrieves the entire **Authors** table and displays the data in a *DataGrid* (a **System.Windows.Forms** component class that can display a datasource in a GUI). The program illustrates the process of connecting to the database, querying the database and displaying the results in a **DataGrid**. The discussion following the example presents the key aspects of the program. [*Note*: We present all of Visual Studio's auto-generated code in Fig. 16.27 so that readers are aware of the code that Visual Studio generates for the example.]

This example uses an Access database. To register the **Books** database as a datasource, select **View > Server Explorer**. Right click the **Data Connections** node in the **Server Explorer** and then double click **<Add Connection>**. In the **Provider** tab of the window that appears, choose **Microsoft Jet 4.0 OLE DB Provider**, which is the driver for Access databases. In the **Connection** tab, click the ellipses button (**...**) to the right of the textbox for the database name, which opens the **Select Access Database** window. Go to the appropriate folder, select the **Books** database and click **OK**. Now, this database is listed as a connection in the **Server Explorer**. Drag the database node onto the Windows Form. This creates an **OleDbConnection** to the source, which the Windows Form designer displays as **oleDbConnection1**.

```
1   // Fig. 16.27: TableDisplay.cs
2   // Displays data from a database table.
3
```

Fig. 16.27 Accessing and displaying a database's data. (Part 1 of 7.)

```
 4   using System;
 5   using System.Drawing;
 6   using System.Collections;
 7   using System.ComponentModel;
 8   using System.Windows.Forms;
 9   using System.Data;
10
11   // Summary description for TableDisplay.cs.
12   public class TableDisplay : System.Windows.Forms.Form
13   {
14      private System.Data.DataSet dataSet1;
15      private System.Data.OleDb.OleDbDataAdapter oleDbDataAdapter1;
16      private System.Windows.Forms.DataGrid dataGrid1;
17      private System.Data.OleDb.OleDbCommand oleDbSelectCommand1;
18      private System.Data.OleDb.OleDbCommand oleDbInsertCommand1;
19      private System.Data.OleDb.OleDbCommand oleDbUpdateCommand1;
20      private System.Data.OleDb.OleDbCommand oleDbDeleteCommand1;
21      private System.Data.OleDb.OleDbConnection oleDbConnection1;
22
23      private System.ComponentModel.Container components = null;
24
25      public TableDisplay()
26      {
27         InitializeComponent();
28
29         // Fill dataSet1 with data
30         oleDbDataAdapter1.Fill( dataSet1, "Authors" );
31
32         // bind data in Authors table in dataSet1 to dataGrid1
33         dataGrid1.SetDataBinding( dataSet1, "Authors" );
34      }
35
36      private void InitializeComponent()
37      {
38         this.dataSet1 = new System.Data.DataSet();
39         this.oleDbDataAdapter1 =
40            new System.Data.OleDb.OleDbDataAdapter();
41         this.dataGrid1 = new System.Windows.Forms.DataGrid();
42         this.oleDbSelectCommand1 =
43            new System.Data.OleDb.OleDbCommand();
44         this.oleDbInsertCommand1 =
45            new System.Data.OleDb.OleDbCommand();
46         this.oleDbUpdateCommand1 =
47            new System.Data.OleDb.OleDbCommand();
48         this.oleDbDeleteCommand1 =
49            new System.Data.OleDb.OleDbCommand();
50         this.oleDbConnection1 =
51            new System.Data.OleDb.OleDbConnection();
52         ((System.ComponentModel.ISupportInitialize)
53            (this.dataSet1)).BeginInit();
54         ((System.ComponentModel.ISupportInitialize)
55            (this.dataGrid1)).BeginInit();
56         this.SuspendLayout();
```

Fig. 16.27 Accessing and displaying a database's data. (Part 2 of 7.)

```
57            //
58            // dataSet1
59            //
60            this.dataSet1.DataSetName = "NewDataSet";
61            this.dataSet1.Locale =
62               new System.Globalization.CultureInfo("en-US");
63            //
64            // oleDbDataAdapter1
65            //
66            this.oleDbDataAdapter1.DeleteCommand =
67               this.oleDbDeleteCommand1;
68            this.oleDbDataAdapter1.InsertCommand =
69               this.oleDbInsertCommand1;
70            this.oleDbDataAdapter1.SelectCommand =
71               this.oleDbSelectCommand1;
72            this.oleDbDataAdapter1.TableMappings.AddRange(
73               new System.Data.Common.DataTableMapping[] {
74                  new System.Data.Common.DataTableMapping(
75                     "Table", "Authors",
76                     new System.Data.Common.DataColumnMapping[] {
77                        new System.Data.Common.DataColumnMapping(
78                           "authorID", "authorID"),
79                        new System.Data.Common.DataColumnMapping(
80                           "firstName", "firstName"),
81                        new System.Data.Common.DataColumnMapping(
82                           "lastName", "lastName")})});
83            this.oleDbDataAdapter1.UpdateCommand =
84               this.oleDbUpdateCommand1;
85            //
86            // dataGrid1
87            //
88            this.dataGrid1.DataMember = "";
89            this.dataGrid1.HeaderForeColor =
90               System.Drawing.SystemColors.ControlText;
91            this.dataGrid1.Location =
92               new System.Drawing.Point(16, 16);
93            this.dataGrid1.Name = "dataGrid1";
94            this.dataGrid1.Size = new System.Drawing.Size(264, 248);
95            this.dataGrid1.TabIndex = 0;
96            //
97            // oleDbSelectCommand1
98            //
99            this.oleDbSelectCommand1.CommandText =
100              "SELECT authorID, firstName, lastName FROM Authors";
101           this.oleDbSelectCommand1.Connection =
102              this.oleDbConnection1;
103           //
104           // oleDbInsertCommand1
105           //
106           this.oleDbInsertCommand1.CommandText =
107              "INSERT INTO Authors(firstName, lastName) VALUES " +
108              "(?, ?)";
```

Fig. 16.27 Accessing and displaying a database's data. (Part 3 of 7.)

```
109          this.oleDbInsertCommand1.Connection =
110             this.oleDbConnection1;
111          this.oleDbInsertCommand1.Parameters.Add(
112             new System.Data.OleDb.OleDbParameter("firstName",
113                System.Data.OleDb.OleDbType.VarWChar, 50,
114                "firstName"));
115          this.oleDbInsertCommand1.Parameters.Add(
116             new System.Data.OleDb.OleDbParameter("lastName",
117                System.Data.OleDb.OleDbType.VarWChar, 50,
118                "lastName"));
119          //
120          // oleDbUpdateCommand1
121          //
122          this.oleDbUpdateCommand1.CommandText =
123             "UPDATE Authors SET firstName = ?, lastName = ? WHERE" +
124             " (authorID = ?) AND (firstNam" +
125             "e = ? OR ? IS NULL AND firstName IS NULL) AND " +
126             "(lastName = ? OR ? IS NULL AND las" +
127             "tName IS NULL)";
128          this.oleDbUpdateCommand1.Connection =
129             this.oleDbConnection1;
130          this.oleDbUpdateCommand1.Parameters.Add(
131             new System.Data.OleDb.OleDbParameter(
132                "firstName",
133                System.Data.OleDb.OleDbType.VarWChar,
134                50, "firstName"));
135          this.oleDbUpdateCommand1.Parameters.Add(
136             new System.Data.OleDb.OleDbParameter(
137                "lastName",
138                System.Data.OleDb.OleDbType.VarWChar, 50,
139                "lastName"));
140          this.oleDbUpdateCommand1.Parameters.Add(
141             new System.Data.OleDb.OleDbParameter(
142                "Original_authorID",
143                System.Data.OleDb.OleDbType.Integer, 0,
144                System.Data.ParameterDirection.Input, false,
145                ((System.Byte)(10)), ((System.Byte)(0)),
146                "authorID", System.Data.DataRowVersion.Original,
147                null));
148          this.oleDbUpdateCommand1.Parameters.Add(
149             new System.Data.OleDb.OleDbParameter(
150                "Original_firstName",
151                System.Data.OleDb.OleDbType.VarWChar, 50,
152                System.Data.ParameterDirection.Input, false,
153                ((System.Byte)(0)), ((System.Byte)(0)),
154                "firstName", System.Data.DataRowVersion.Original,
155                null));
156          this.oleDbUpdateCommand1.Parameters.Add(
157             new System.Data.OleDb.OleDbParameter(
158                "Original_firstName1",
159                System.Data.OleDb.OleDbType.VarWChar, 50,
160                System.Data.ParameterDirection.Input, false,
161                ((System.Byte)(0)), ((System.Byte)(0)),
```

Fig. 16.27 Accessing and displaying a database's data. (Part 4 of 7.)

```
162                      "firstName", System.Data.DataRowVersion.Original,
163                      null));
164         this.oleDbUpdateCommand1.Parameters.Add(
165            new System.Data.OleDb.OleDbParameter(
166                "Original_lastName",
167                System.Data.OleDb.OleDbType.VarWChar, 50,
168                System.Data.ParameterDirection.Input, false,
169                ((System.Byte)(0)), ((System.Byte)(0)),
170                "lastName", System.Data.DataRowVersion.Original,
171                null));
172         this.oleDbUpdateCommand1.Parameters.Add(
173            new System.Data.OleDb.OleDbParameter(
174                "Original_lastName1",
175                System.Data.OleDb.OleDbType.VarWChar, 50,
176                System.Data.ParameterDirection.Input, false,
177                ((System.Byte)(0)), ((System.Byte)(0)),
178                "lastName", System.Data.DataRowVersion.Original,
179                null));
180         //
181         // oleDbDeleteCommand1
182         //
183         this.oleDbDeleteCommand1.CommandText =
184            "DELETE FROM Authors WHERE (authorID = ?) AND " +
185            "(firstName = ? OR ? IS NULL AND firs" +
186            "tName IS NULL) AND (lastName = ? OR ? IS NULL AND " +
187            "lastName IS NULL)";
188         this.oleDbDeleteCommand1.Connection =
189            this.oleDbConnection1;
190         this.oleDbDeleteCommand1.Parameters.Add(
191            new System.Data.OleDb.OleDbParameter(
192                "Original_authorID",
193                System.Data.OleDb.OleDbType.Integer, 0,
194                System.Data.ParameterDirection.Input, false,
195                ((System.Byte)(10)), ((System.Byte)(0)),
196                "authorID", System.Data.DataRowVersion.Original,
197                null));
198         this.oleDbDeleteCommand1.Parameters.Add(
199            new System.Data.OleDb.OleDbParameter(
200                "Original_firstName",
201                System.Data.OleDb.OleDbType.VarWChar, 50,
202                System.Data.ParameterDirection.Input, false,
203                ((System.Byte)(0)), ((System.Byte)(0)),
204                "firstName", System.Data.DataRowVersion.Original,
205                null));
206         this.oleDbDeleteCommand1.Parameters.Add(
207            new System.Data.OleDb.OleDbParameter(
208                "Original_firstName1",
209                System.Data.OleDb.OleDbType.VarWChar, 50,
210                System.Data.ParameterDirection.Input, false,
211                ((System.Byte)(0)), ((System.Byte)(0)),
212                "firstName", System.Data.DataRowVersion.Original,
213                null));
```

Fig. 16.27 Accessing and displaying a database's data. (Part 5 of 7.)

```
214          this.oleDbDeleteCommand1.Parameters.Add(
215             new System.Data.OleDb.OleDbParameter(
216                "Original_lastName",
217                System.Data.OleDb.OleDbType.VarWChar, 50,
218                System.Data.ParameterDirection.Input, false,
219                ((System.Byte)(0)), ((System.Byte)(0)),
220                "lastName", System.Data.DataRowVersion.Original,
221                null));
222          this.oleDbDeleteCommand1.Parameters.Add(
223             new System.Data.OleDb.OleDbParameter(
224                "Original_lastName1",
225                System.Data.OleDb.OleDbType.VarWChar, 50,
226                System.Data.ParameterDirection.Input, false,
227                ((System.Byte)(0)), ((System.Byte)(0)),
228                "lastName", System.Data.DataRowVersion.Original,
229                null));
230          //
231          // oleDbConnection1
232          //
233          this.oleDbConnection1.ConnectionString =
234             @"Provider=Microsoft.Jet.OLEDB.4.0;Password="""";" +
235             @"User ID=Admin;Data Source=C:\Books\2001\csphtp1\" +
236             @"csphtp1_examples\ch19\Books.mdb;Mode=Share " +
237             @"Deny None;Extended Properties="""";Jet OLEDB:" +
238             @"System database="""";Jet OLEDB:Registry " +
239             @"Path="""";Jet OLEDB:Database Password="""";" +
240             @"Jet OLEDB:Engine Type=5;Jet OLEDB:Database " +
241             @"Locking Mode=1;Jet OLEDB:Global Partial Bulk " +
242             @"Ops=2;Jet OLEDB:Global Bulk Transactions=1;Jet " +
243             @"OLEDB:New Database Password="""";Jet OLEDB:" +
244             @"Create System Database=False;Jet OLEDB:Encrypt " +
245             @"Database=False;Jet OLEDB:Don't Copy Locale on " +
246             @"Compact=False;Jet OLEDB:Compact Without Replica " +
247             @"Repair=False;Jet OLEDB:SFP=False";
248          //
249          // TableDisplay
250          //
251          this.AutoScaleBaseSize = new System.Drawing.Size(5, 13);
252          this.ClientSize = new System.Drawing.Size(292, 273);
253          this.Controls.AddRange(
254             new System.Windows.Forms.Control[] {
255                this.dataGrid1});
256          this.Name = "TableDisplay";
257          this.Text = "TableDisplay";
258          ((System.ComponentModel.ISupportInitialize)
259             (this.dataSet1)).EndInit();
260          ((System.ComponentModel.ISupportInitialize)
261             (this.dataGrid1)).EndInit();
262          this.ResumeLayout(false);
263
264       }    // end of InitializeComponent
265
```

Fig. 16.27 Accessing and displaying a database's data. (Part 6 of 7.)

```
266    [STAThread]
267    static void Main()
268    {
269        Application.Run( new TableDisplay() );
270    }
271 }
```

Fig. 16.27 Accessing and displaying a database's data. (Part 7 of 7.)

Next, drag an *OleDbDataAdapter* from the **Toolbox**'s *Data* group onto the Windows Form designer. This displays the **Data Adapter Configuration Wizard** for configuring the **OleDbDataAdapter** instance with a custom query for populating a **DataSet**. Click **Next** to select a connection to use. Select the connection created in the previous step from the drop-down list and click **Next**. The resulting screen allows us to choose how the **OleDbDataAdapter** should access the database. Keep the default **Use SQL Statement** option and then click **Next**. Click the **Query Builder** button, select the **Authors** table from the **Add** menu and **Close** that menu. Place a check mark in the ***All Columns** box from the **Authors** window. Notice how that particular window lists all columns of the **Authors** table.

Next, we must create a **DataSet** to store the query results. To do so, drag **DataSet** from the **Data** group in the **Toolbox**. This displays the **Add DataSet** window. Choose the **Untyped DataSet (no schema)**, because the query with which we populate the **DataSet** dictates the **DataSet**'s *schema*, or structure.

Figure 16.27 shows all of the code generated by Visual Studio. Normally, we omit this code, because it usually only contains GUI related code. In this case, however, the code contains database functionality that we must discuss. Furthermore, we have left the default naming conventions of Visual Studio in this example to demonstrate the exact format of the auto-generated code that Visual Studio creates. Normally, we would change these names to conform to our programming conventions and style. The code generated by Visual Studio has also been formatted for presentation purposes.

 Good Programming Practice 16.2

Use clear, descriptive variable names in code. This makes programs easier to understand.

Lines 233–247 initialize the **oleDbConnection** for this program. Property **ConnectionString** specifies the path to the database file on the computer's hard drive.

An instance of class **OleDbDataAdapter** populates the **DataSet** in this example with data from the **Books** database. The instance properties *DeleteCommand* (lines 66–67), *InsertCommand* (lines 68–69), *SelectCommand* (lines 70–71) and *Update-Command* (lines 83–84) are **OleDbCommand** objects that specify how the **OleDbData-Adapter** deletes, inserts, selects and updates data in the database, respectively.

Each **OleDbCommand** object must have an **OleDbConnection** through which the **OleDbCommand** can communicate with the database. Property **Connection** is set to the **OleDbConnection** to the **Books** database. For **oleDbUpdateCommand1**, lines 128–129 set the **Connection** property, and lines 122–127 set the **CommandText**.

Although Visual Studio generates most of this program's code, we enter code in the **TableDisplay** constructor (lines 25–34) for populating **dataSet1** using an **OleDb-DataAdapter**. Line 30 calls **OleDbDataAdapter** method *Fill* to retrieve information from the database associated with the **OleDbConnection**, placing the information in the **DataSet** provided as an argument. The second argument to this method is a **string** that specifies the name of the table in the database from which to **Fill** the **DataSet**.

Line 33 invokes **DataGrid** method *SetDataBinding* to bind the **DataGrid** to a datasource. The first argument is the **DataSet**—in this case, **dataSet1**—whose data the **DataGrid** should display. The second argument is a **string** representing the name of the table within the datasource we want to bind to the **DataGrid**. Once this line executes, the **DataGrid** is filled with the information in the **DataSet**—the number of rows and number of columns are set from the information in **dataSet1**.

16.6.2 Querying the Books Database

The example in Fig. 16.28 demonstrates how to execute SQL **SELECT** statements on database **Books.mdb** and display the results. Although Fig. 16.28 uses only **SELECT** statements to query the data, the same program could be used to execute many different SQL statements if we made a few minor modifications.

Method **submitButton_Click** is the key part of this program. When the program invokes this event handler, lines 47–48 assign the **SELECT** query **string** to **OleDb-DataAdapter**'s **SelectCommand** property. This **string** is parsed into an SQL query and executed on the database via the **OleDbDataAdapter**'s **Fill** method (line 55). As we discussed in the previous section, method **Fill** places data from the database into **dataSet1**.

```
1   // Fig. 16.28: DisplayQueryResults.cs
2   // Displays the contents of the authors database.
3
4   using System;
5   using System.Drawing;
6   using System.Collections;
7   using System.ComponentModel;
8   using System.Windows.Forms;
9   using System.Data;
```

Fig. 16.28 Execute SQL statements on a database. (Part 1 of 3.)

```
10
11   public class DisplayQueryResults : System.Windows.Forms.Form
12   {
13      private System.Data.OleDb.OleDbConnection oleDbConnection1;
14      private System.Data.DataSet dataSet1;
15      private System.Data.OleDb.OleDbDataAdapter oleDbDataAdapter1;
16      private System.Data.OleDb.OleDbCommand oleDbSelectCommand1;
17      private System.Data.OleDb.OleDbCommand oleDbInsertCommand1;
18      private System.Data.OleDb.OleDbCommand oleDbUpdateCommand1;
19      private System.Data.OleDb.OleDbCommand oleDbDeleteCommand1;
20      private System.Windows.Forms.TextBox queryTextBox;
21      private System.Windows.Forms.Button submitButton;
22      private System.Windows.Forms.DataGrid dataGrid1;
23      private System.ComponentModel.Container components = null;
24
25      public DisplayQueryResults()
26      {
27
28         InitializeComponent();
29      }
30
31      // Visual Studio.NET generated code
32
33      [STAThread]
34      static void Main()
35      {
36         Application.Run( new DisplayQueryResults() );
37      }
38
39      // perform SQL query on data
40      private void submitButton_Click( object sender,
41         System.EventArgs e )
42      {
43         try
44         {
45            // set SQL query to what user
46            // input into queryTextBox
47            oleDbDataAdapter1.SelectCommand.CommandText =
48               queryTextBox.Text;
49
50            // clear DataSet from previous operation
51            dataSet1.Clear();
52
53            // Fill data set with information that results
54            // from SQL query
55            oleDbDataAdapter1.Fill( dataSet1, "Authors" );
56
57            // bind DataGrid to contents of DataSet
58            dataGrid1.SetDataBinding( dataSet1, "Authors" );
59         }
60
```

Fig. 16.28 Execute SQL statements on a database. (Part 2 of 3.)

```
61              catch ( System.Data.OleDb.OleDbException oleException )
62              {
63                  MessageBox.Show( "Invalid query" );
64              }
65
66          }  // end of submitButton_Click
67      }
```

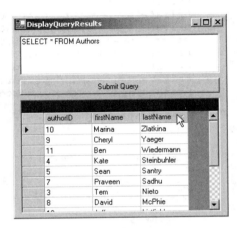

Fig. 16.28 Execute SQL statements on a database. (Part 3 of 3.)

Common Programming Error 16.9

*If a **DataSet** has been **Fill**ed at least once, forgetting to call a **DataSet**'s **Clear** method before calling the **Fill** method again will lead to logic errors.*

To display, or redisplay, contents in the **DataGrid**, use method **SetDataBinding**. The first argument is the datasource to be displayed in the table—a **DataSet**, in this case. The second argument is the **string** name of the datasource member to be displayed (line 58). Readers can try entering their own queries in the text box and then pressing the **Submit Query** button to execute the query.

16.7 Programming with ADO.NET: Modifying a Database

Our next example implements a simple address-book application that enables the user to insert, locate and update records in the Microsoft Access database **Addressbook**.

The **Addressbook** application (Fig. 16.29) provides a GUI enabling users to execute SQL statements on the database. Earlier in the chapter, we presented examples demonstrating the use of **SELECT** statements to query a database. Here, that same functionality is provided.

```
1    // Fig. 16.29: AddressBook.cs
2    // Using SQL statements to manipulate a database.
```

Fig. 16.29 Modifying a database. (Part 1 of 8.)

```
3
4    using System;
5    using System.Drawing;
6    using System.Collections;
7    using System.ComponentModel;
8    using System.Windows.Forms;
9    using System.Data;
10
11   public class AddressBook : System.Windows.Forms.Form
12   {
13       private System.Windows.Forms.TextBox faxTextBox;
14       private System.Windows.Forms.TextBox homeTextBox;
15       private System.Windows.Forms.TextBox firstTextBox;
16       private System.Windows.Forms.TextBox stateTextBox;
17       private System.Windows.Forms.TextBox idTextBox;
18       private System.Windows.Forms.TextBox lastTextBox;
19       private System.Windows.Forms.TextBox postalTextBox;
20       private System.Windows.Forms.TextBox addressTextBox;
21       private System.Windows.Forms.TextBox cityTextBox;
22       private System.Windows.Forms.TextBox countryTextBox;
23       private System.Windows.Forms.TextBox emailTextBox;
24       private System.Data.DataSet dataSet1;
25       private System.Data.OleDb.OleDbDataAdapter oleDbDataAdapter1;
26       private System.Data.OleDb.OleDbCommand oleDbSelectCommand1;
27       private System.Data.OleDb.OleDbCommand oleDbInsertCommand1;
28       private System.Data.OleDb.OleDbCommand oleDbUpdateCommand1;
29       private System.Data.OleDb.OleDbCommand oleDbDeleteCommand1;
30       private System.Data.OleDb.OleDbConnection oleDbConnection1;
31       private System.Windows.Forms.TextBox statusTextBox;
32       private System.Windows.Forms.Label addressLabel;
33       private System.Windows.Forms.Label cityLabel;
34       private System.Windows.Forms.Label stateLabel;
35       private System.Windows.Forms.Label idLabel;
36       private System.Windows.Forms.Label firstLabel;
37       private System.Windows.Forms.Label lastLabel;
38       private System.Windows.Forms.Label postalLabel;
39       private System.Windows.Forms.Label countryLabel;
40       private System.Windows.Forms.Label emailLabel;
41       private System.Windows.Forms.Button clearButton;
42       private System.Windows.Forms.Button helpButton;
43       private System.Windows.Forms.Button findButton;
44       private System.Windows.Forms.Button addButton;
45       private System.Windows.Forms.Button updateButton;
46       private System.Windows.Forms.Label faxLabel;
47       private System.Windows.Forms.Label homeLabel;
48       private System.ComponentModel.Container components = null;
49
50       public AddressBook()
51       {
52           InitializeComponent();
53           oleDbConnection1.Open();
54       }
55
```

Fig. 16.29 Modifying a database. (Part 2 of 8.)

```
56          // Visual Studio.NET generated code
57
58          [STAThread]
59          static void Main()
60          {
61             Application.Run( new AddressBook() );
62          }
63
64          private void findButton_Click( object sender,
65                System.EventArgs e )
66          {
67             try
68             {
69                if ( lastTextBox.Text != "" )
70                {
71                   // clear DataSet from last operation
72                   dataSet1.Clear();
73
74                   // create SQL query to find contact with
75                   // specified last name
76                   oleDbDataAdapter1.SelectCommand.CommandText =
77                      "SELECT * FROM addresses WHERE lastname = '" +
78                      lastTextBox.Text + "'";
79
80                   // fill dataSet1 with rows resulting from
81                   // query
82                   oleDbDataAdapter1.Fill( dataSet1 );
83
84                   // display information
85                   Display( dataSet1 );
86                   statusTextBox.Text += "\r\nQuery successful\r\n";
87                }
88                else
89                   lastTextBox.Text =
90                      "Enter last name here then press Find";
91             }
92
93             catch ( System.Data.OleDb.OleDbException oleException )
94             {
95                Console.WriteLine( oleException.StackTrace );
96                statusTextBox.Text += oleException.ToString();
97             }
98
99             catch ( InvalidOperationException invalidException )
100            {
101               MessageBox.Show( invalidException.Message );
102            }
103
104         }  // end of findButton_Click
105
106         private void addButton_Click( object sender, System.EventArgs e )
107         {
```

Fig. 16.29 Modifying a database. (Part 3 of 8.)

```
108          try
109          {
110              if ( lastTextBox.Text != "" && firstTextBox.Text != "" )
111              {
112                  // create SQL query to insert row
113                  oleDbDataAdapter1.InsertCommand.CommandText =
114                      "INSERT INTO addresses (" +
115                      "firstname, lastname, address, city, " +
116                      "stateorprovince, postalcode, country, " +
117                      "emailaddress, homephone, faxnumber" +
118                      ") VALUES ('" +
119                      firstTextBox.Text + "', '" +
120                      lastTextBox.Text + "', '" +
121                      addressTextBox.Text + "', '" +
122                      cityTextBox.Text + "', '" +
123                      stateTextBox.Text + "', '" +
124                      postalTextBox.Text + "', '" +
125                      countryTextBox.Text + "', '" +
126                      emailTextBox.Text + "', '" +
127                      homeTextBox.Text + "', '" +
128                      faxTextBox.Text + "')";
129
130                  // notify user that query is being sent
131                  statusTextBox.Text += "\r\nSending query: " +
132                      oleDbDataAdapter1.InsertCommand.CommandText +
133                      "\r\n" ;
134
135                  // send query
136                  oleDbDataAdapter1.InsertCommand.ExecuteNonQuery();
137
138                  statusTextBox.Text += "\r\nQuery successful\r\n";
139              }
140              else
141                  statusTextBox.Text += "\r\nEnter at least first " +
142                      "and last name then press Add\r\n";
143          }
144
145          catch ( System.Data.OleDb.OleDbException oleException )
146          {
147              Console.WriteLine( oleException.StackTrace );
148              statusTextBox.Text += oleException.ToString();
149          }
150
151      } // end of addButton_Click
152
153      private void updateButton_Click( object sender,
154          System.EventArgs e )
155      {
156          try
157          {
```

Fig. 16.29 Modifying a database. (Part 4 of 8.)

```
158                   // make sure users have found record
159                   // they wish to update
160                   if ( idTextBox.Text != "" )
161                   {
162                      // set SQL query to update all fields in
163                      // table where id number matches id
164                      // in idTextBox
165                      oleDbDataAdapter1.UpdateCommand.CommandText =
166                         "UPDATE addresses SET " +
167                         "firstname ='" + firstTextBox.Text +
168                         "', lastname='" + lastTextBox.Text +
169                         "', address='" + addressTextBox.Text +
170                         "', city='" + cityTextBox.Text +
171                         "', stateorprovince='" + stateTextBox.Text +
172                         "', postalcode='" + postalTextBox.Text +
173                         "', country='" + countryTextBox.Text +
174                         "', emailaddress='" + emailTextBox.Text +
175                         "', homephone='" + homeTextBox.Text +
176                         "', faxnumber='" + faxTextBox.Text +
177                         "' WHERE id=" + idTextBox.Text;
178
179                      // notify user that query is being set
180                      statusTextBox.Text += "\r\nSending query: " +
181                         oleDbDataAdapter1.UpdateCommand.CommandText +
182                         "\r\n";
183
184                      // execute query
185                      oleDbDataAdapter1.UpdateCommand.ExecuteNonQuery();
186
187                      statusTextBox.Text += "\r\nQuery successful\r\n";
188                   }
189                   else
190                      statusTextBox.Text += "\r\nYou may only update " +
191                         "an existing record. Use Find to locate the" +
192                         "record, then modify the information and " +
193                         "press Update.\r\n";
194                }
195
196             catch ( System.Data.OleDb.OleDbException oleException )
197             {
198                Console.WriteLine( oleException.StackTrace );
199                statusTextBox.Text += oleException.ToString();
200             }
201
202          } // end of updateButton_Click
203
204          private void clearButton_Click( object sender,
205                System.EventArgs e )
206          {
207             idTextBox.Clear();
208             ClearTextBoxes();
209          }
210
```

Fig. 16.29 Modifying a database. (Part 5 of 8.)

```
211      private void helpButton_Click( object sender,
212          System.EventArgs e )
213      {
214         statusTextBox.AppendText(
215            "\r\nClick Find to locate a record\r\n" +
216            "Click Add to insert a new record.\r\n" +
217            "Click Update to update the information in a record "
218            + "\r\nClick Clear to empty the textboxes" );
219      }
220
221      private void Display( DataSet dataSet )
222      {
223         try
224         {
225            // get first DataTable--there always will be one
226            DataTable dataTable = dataSet.Tables[ 0 ];
227
228            if ( dataTable.Rows.Count != 0 )
229            {
230               int recordNumber = ( int ) dataTable.Rows[ 0 ][ 0 ];
231
232               idTextBox.Text = recordNumber.ToString();
233               firstTextBox.Text =
234                  ( string ) dataTable.Rows[ 0 ][ 1 ];
235               lastTextBox.Text =
236                  ( string ) dataTable.Rows[ 0 ][ 2 ];
237               addressTextBox.Text =
238                  ( string ) dataTable.Rows[ 0 ][ 3 ];
239               cityTextBox.Text =
240                  ( string ) dataTable.Rows[ 0 ][ 4 ];
241               stateTextBox.Text =
242                  ( string ) dataTable.Rows[ 0 ][ 5 ];
243               postalTextBox.Text =
244                  ( string ) dataTable.Rows[ 0 ][ 6 ];
245               countryTextBox.Text =
246                  ( string ) dataTable.Rows[ 0 ][ 7 ];
247               emailTextBox.Text =
248                  ( string ) dataTable.Rows[ 0 ][ 8 ];
249               homeTextBox.Text =
250                  ( string ) dataTable.Rows[ 0 ][ 9 ];
251               faxTextBox.Text =
252                  ( string ) dataTable.Rows[ 0 ][ 10 ];
253            }
254
255            else
256               statusTextBox.Text += "\r\nNo record found\r\n";
257         }
258
259         catch( System.Data.OleDb.OleDbException oleException )
260         {
261            Console.WriteLine( oleException.StackTrace );
262            statusTextBox.Text += oleException.ToString();
263         }
```

Fig. 16.29 Modifying a database. (Part 6 of 8.)

```
264
265     } // end Display
266
267     private void ClearTextBoxes()
268     {
269        firstTextBox.Clear();
270        lastTextBox.Clear();
271        addressTextBox.Clear();
272        cityTextBox.Clear();
273        stateTextBox.Clear();
274        postalTextBox.Clear();
275        countryTextBox.Clear();
276        emailTextBox.Clear();
277        homeTextBox.Clear();
278        faxTextBox.Clear();
279     }
280  }
```

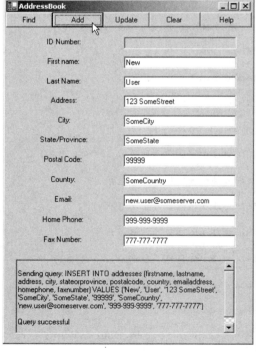

Fig. 16.29 Modifying a database. (Part 7 of 8.)

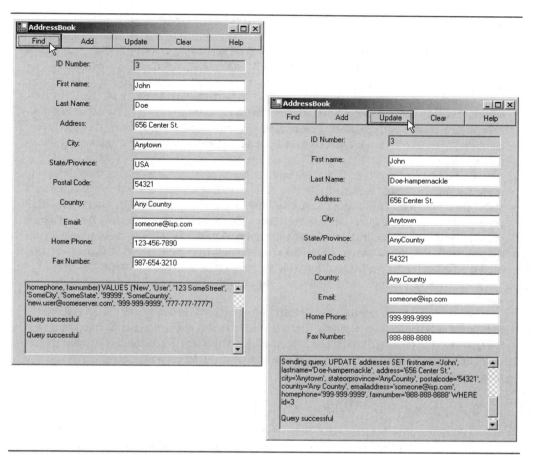

Fig. 16.29 Modifying a database. (Part 8 of 8.)

Event handler **findButton_Click** performs the **SELECT** query on the database for the record associated with the **string** in **lastTextBox**. This represents the last name of the person whose record the user wishes to retrieve. Line 72 invokes method **Clear** of class **DataSet** to empty the **DataSet** of any prior data. Lines 76–78 then modify the text of the SQL query to perform the appropriate **SELECT** operation. This statement is executed by the **OleDbDataAdapter** method **Fill** (line 82), which is passed the **DataSet** as an argument. Finally, the **TextBox**es are updated with a call to method **Display** (line 85).

Methods **addButton_Click** and **updateButton_Click** perform **INSERT** and **UPDATE** operations, respectively. Each method uses members of class **OleDbCommand** to perform operations on a database. The instance properties **InsertCommand** and **Update-Command** of class **OleDbDataAdapter** are instances of class **OleDbCommand**.

Property **CommandText** of class **OleDbCommand** is a **string** representing the SQL statement that the **OleDbCommand** object executes. Method **addButton_Click** sets this property of **InsertCommand** to execute the appropriate **INSERT** statement on the database (lines 113–128). Method **updateButton_Click** sets this property of

UpdateCommand to execute the appropriate **UPDATE** statement on the database (lines 165–177).

Method *ExecuteNonQuery* of class **OleDbCommand** performs the action specified by **CommandText**. Hence, the **INSERT** statement defined by **oleDbData-Adapter1.InsertCommand.CommandText** in event handler **addButton_Click** is executed when line 136 invokes method **oleDbDataAdapter1.InsertCom-mand.ExecuteNonQuery**. Similarly, the **UPDATE** statement defined by **oleDbData-Adapter1.DeleteCommand.CommandText** in **updateButton_Click** event handler is executed by **oleDbDataAdapter1.UpdateCommand.ExecuteNon-Query** (line 185).

Method **Display** (lines 221–265) updates the user interface with data from the newly retrieved address-book record. Line 226 obtains a **DataTable** from the **DataSet**'s **Tables** collection. This **DataTable** contains the results of our SQL query. Line 228 determines whether the query returned any rows. The **Rows** property in class **DataTable** provides access to all records retrieved by the query. The **Rows** property is similar to a two-dimensional rectangular array. Line 230 retrieves the field with index *0, 0* (i.e., the first record's first column of data) and stores the value in variable **recordNumber**. Lines 232–252 then retrieve the remaining fields of data from the **DataTable** to populate the user interface.

When clicked, the application's **Help** button prints instructions in the console at the bottom of the application window (lines 214–218). The event handler for this button is **helpButton_Click**. The **Clear** button clears the text from the **TextBox**es. This event handler is defined in the method **clearButton_Click** and uses the utility method **ClearTextBoxes** (line 208).

16.8 Reading and Writing XML Files

A powerful feature of ADO .NET is its ability to convert data stored in a datasource to XML. Class **DataSet** of namespace **System.Data** provides methods *WriteXml*, *ReadXml* and *GetXml*, which enable developers to create XML documents from datasources and to convert data from XML into datasources. The application in Fig. 16.30 populates a **DataSet** with statistics about baseball players and then writes the data to a file as XML. The application also displays the XML in a **TextBox**.

The **DatabaseXMLWriter** constructor (lines 25–41) establishes a connection to the **Baseball** database in line 33. Line 36 then calls method **Fill** of class **OleDbData-Adapter** to populate **playersDataSet** with data from the **Players** table in the **Baseball** database. Line 39 binds **playersDataGrid** to **playersDataSet** to display the information to the user.

```
1   // Fig. 16.30 XMLWriter.cs
2   // Demonstrates generating XML from an ADO .NET DataSet.
3
4   using System;
5   using System.Drawing;
6   using System.Collections;
7   using System.ComponentModel;
```

Fig. 16.30 Application that writes **DataSet** XML representation to a file. (Part 1 of 3.)

```
8    using System.Windows.Forms;
9    using System.Data;
10
11   public class DatabaseXMLWriter : System.Windows.Forms.Form
12   {
13      private System.Data.OleDb.OleDbConnection baseballConnection;
14      private System.Data.OleDb.OleDbDataAdapter playersDataAdapter;
15      private System.Data.OleDb.OleDbCommand oleDbSelectCommand1;
16      private System.Data.OleDb.OleDbCommand oleDbInsertCommand1;
17      private System.Data.OleDb.OleDbCommand oleDbUpdateCommand1;
18      private System.Data.OleDb.OleDbCommand oleDbDeleteCommand1;
19      private System.Data.DataSet playersDataSet;
20      private System.Windows.Forms.DataGrid playersDataGrid;
21      private System.Windows.Forms.Button writeButton;
22      private System.Windows.Forms.TextBox outputTextBox;
23      private System.ComponentModel.Container components = null;
24
25      public DatabaseXMLWriter()
26      {
27         //
28         // Required for Windows Form Designer support
29         //
30         InitializeComponent();
31
32         // open database connection
33         baseballConnection.Open();
34
35         // fill DataSet with data from OleDbDataAdapter
36         playersDataAdapter.Fill( playersDataSet, "Players" );
37
38         // bind DataGrid to DataSet
39         playersDataGrid.SetDataBinding( playersDataSet, "Players" );
40
41      }
42
43      // Visual Studio .NET generated code
44
45      // main entry point for application.
46      [STAThread]
47      static void Main()
48      {
49         Application.Run( new DatabaseXMLWriter() );
50      }
51
52      // write XML representation of DataSet when button is clicked
53      private void writeButton_Click(
54         object sender, System.EventArgs e)
55      {
56         // write XML representation of DataSet to file
57         playersDataSet.WriteXml( "Players.xml" );
58
```

Fig. 16.30 Application that writes **DataSet** XML representation to a file. (Part 2 of 3.)

```
59              // display XML in TextBox
60              outputTextBox.Text += "Writing the following XML:\n\n" +
61                 playersDataSet.GetXml() + "\n\n";
62
63          }
64      }
```

Fig. 16.30 Application that writes **DataSet** XML representation to a file. (Part 3 of 3.)

Method **writeButton_Click** defines the event handler for the **Write to XML** button. When the user clicks this button, line 57 invokes **DataSet** method **WriteXml**, which generates an XML representation of the data contained in the **DataSet** and writes the XML to the specified file. Figure 16.31 depicts this XML representation. Each **Players** element represents a record in the **Players** table. The **firstName, lastName, battingAverage** and **playerID** elements correspond to the fields of the same names in the **Players** table. Method **GetXml** returns a **string** representing the **DataSet**'s data in XML form. Lines 60–61 append the XML **string** to **outputTextBox**.

```
1    <?xml version="1.0" standalone="yes"?>
2    <NewDataSet>
3        <Players>
4            <firstName>John</firstName>
5            <lastName>Doe</lastName>
6            <battingAverage>0.375</battingAverage>
7            <playerID>1</playerID>
8        </Players>
9
10       <Players>
11           <firstName>Jack</firstName>
12           <lastName>Smith</lastName>
```

Fig. 16.31 XML document generated from **DataSet** in **DatabaseXMLWriter**. (Part 1 of 2.)

```
13              <battingAverage>0.223</battingAverage>
14              <playerID>2</playerID>
15          </Players>
16
17          <Players>
18              <firstName>George</firstName>
19              <lastName>O'Malley</lastName>
20              <battingAverage>0.444</battingAverage>
21              <playerID>3</playerID>
22          </Players>
23      </NewDataSet>
```

Fig. 16.31 XML document generated from **DataSet** in **DatabaseXMLWriter**. (Part 2 of 2.)

In this chapter, we have discussed the fundamentals of Structured Query Language (SQL) and C#'s database capabilities. We learned that C# programmers communicate with databases and manipulate their data through *Microsoft ActiveX Data Objects*™ (ADO) .NET, or *ADO .NET*. In the next chapter, we discuss ASP .NET Web Forms. Web Forms allow programmers to develop dynamic Web content using databases and ASP .NET features.

16.9 Summary

A database is an integrated collection of data. A database management system (DBMS) provides mechanisms for storing and organizing data. Today's most popular database systems are relational databases.

A relational database is composed of tables. A row of a table is called a record. A primary key is a field in a record that contains unique data, or data that are not duplicated in other records of that table. Each column in a table represents a different field. A primary key can be composed of more than one column (or field) in the database. A one-to-many relationship between tables indicates that a record in one table can have many corresponding records in a separate table. A foreign key is a field for which every entry in one table has a unique value in another table and where the field in the latter table is the primary key for that table.

A language called Structured Query Language (SQL) is used almost universally with relational-database systems to perform queries and manipulate data. SQL provides a complete set of commands, enabling programmers to define complex queries to select data from a table. The results of a query commonly are called result sets (or record sets).

The **SELECT** query is used to extract data from a database. The optional **WHERE** clause specifies the selection criteria for the query. The **WHERE** clause's condition can contain operators <, >, <=, >=, =, <> and **LIKE**. Operator **LIKE** is used for pattern matching with wildcard characters asterisk (*) and question mark (?). The results of a query can be arranged in ascending or descending order via the optional **ORDER BY** clause. A join merges records from two or more tables by testing for matching values in a field that is common to both tables. An **INSERT** statement inserts a new record in a table. An **UPDATE** statement modifies data in a table. A **DELETE** statement removes data from a table.

A programming language connects to, and interacts with, relational databases via an interface. C# programmers communicate with databases and manipulate their data via

ADO .NET. **System.Data**, **System.Data.OleDb** and **System.Data.Sql-Client** are the three main namespaces in ADO .NET. Class **DataSet** is from the **System.Data** namespace. Instances of this class represent in-memory caches of data. The advantage of using class **DataSet** is that it allows the contents of a datasource to be modified without having to maintain an active connection. Class **OleDbCommand** of the **System.Data.OleDb** namespace enables the programmer to execute SQL statements directly on the datasource.

Use the **Add Connection** option to create a database connection. Use the **Data Adapter Configuration Wizard** to set up an **OleDbDataAdapter** and generate queries. **OleDbCommand** commands are what the **OleDbDataAdapter** executes on the database in the form of SQL queries. **OleDbCommand** instance property **Connection** is set to the **OleDbConnection** on which the command will be executed, and the instance property **CommandText** is set to the SQL query that will be executed on the database.

OleDbDataAdapter method **Fill** retrieves information from the database associated with the **OleDbConnection** and places this information in the **DataSet** provided as an argument. **DataGrid** method **SetDataBinding** binds a **DataGrid** to a datasource. Method **ExecuteNonQuery** of class **OleDbCommand** performs the action specified by **CommandText** on the database.

A powerful feature of ADO .NET is its ability to convert data stored in a datasource to XML, and vice versa. Method **WriteXml** of class **DataSet** writes the XML representation of the **DataSet** instance to the first argument passed to it. Method **ReadXml** of class **DataSet** reads the XML representation of the first argument passed to it into its own **DataSet**.

ASP .NET, Web Forms and Web Controls

Objectives

- To become familiar with Web Forms in ASP .NET.
- To create Web Forms.
- To create an ASP .NET application that consists of multiple Web Forms.
- To control user access to Web applications through forms authentication.
- To use files and databases in ASP .NET applications.
- To learn how to use tracing with Web Forms.

If any man will draw up his case, and put his name at the foot of the first page, I will give him an immediate reply. Where he compels me to turn over the sheet, he must wait my leisure.
Lord Sandwich

Rule One: Our client is always right
Rule Two: If you think our client is wrong, see Rule One.
Anonymous

A fair question should be followed by a deed in silence.
Dante Alighieri

You will come here and get books that will open your eyes, and your ears, and your curiosity, and turn you inside out or outside in.
Ralph Waldo Emerson

Outline

17.1   Introduction
17.2   Simple HTTP Transaction
17.3   System Architecture
17.4   Creating and Running a Simple Web Form Example
17.5   Web Controls
    17.5.1   Text and Graphics Controls
    17.5.2   `AdRotator` Control
    17.5.3   Validation Controls
17.6   Session Tracking
    17.6.1   Cookies
    17.6.2   Session Tracking with `HttpSessionState`
17.7   Case Study: Online Guest Book
17.8   Case Study: Connecting to a Database in ASP .NET
17.9   Tracing
17.10   Summary
17.11   Internet and Web Resources

17.1 Introduction

In previous chapters, we used Windows Forms and Windows controls to develop Windows applications. In this chapter, we introduce *Web-based application development* with Microsoft's ASP .NET technology. Web-based applications create content for Web browser clients. This Web content can include HyperText Markup Language (HTML),[1] client-side scripting, images and binary data.

We present several examples that demonstrate Web-based applications development using *Web Forms* (also known as *Web Form pages*), *Web controls* (also known as *ASP .NET server controls*) and C# programming. Web Form files have the file extension `.aspx` and contain the Web page's GUI. Programmers customize Web Forms by adding Web controls, which include labels, text boxes, images, buttons and other GUI components. The Web Form file represents what the Web page that is sent to the client browser will look like. [*Note*: From this point onward, we refer to Web Form files as *ASPX files.*]

Every ASPX file created in Visual Studio has a corresponding class written in a .NET-compliant language, such as C#. This class includes event handlers, initialization code, utility methods and other supporting code for the user interface in the ASPX file. The C# file that contains this class is called the *code-behind file* and provides the ASPX file's programmatic implementation.

---

1. Readers not familiar with HTML should read Appendices I–J before studying this chapter.

17.2 Simple HTTP Transaction

Before exploring Web-based applications development further, a basic understanding of networking and the World Wide Web is necessary. In this section, we examine the inner workings of the *HyperText Transfer Protocol (HTTP)* and discuss what occurs behind the scenes when a browser displays a Web page. HTTP is a protocol that specifies a set of *methods* and *headers* that allow clients and servers to interact and exchange information in a uniform and predictable way.

In their simplest form, Web pages are HTML documents, these are plain-text files that contains markings (*markup* or *tags*) describing the structures of the documents. For example, the HTML markup:

```
<title>My Web Page</title>
```

indicates that the text contained between the **`<title>`** *start tag* and the **`</title>`** *end tag* is the Web page's title. HTML documents also can contain *hyperlinks*, which enable users to navigate their Web browsers to other Web pages. When the user activates a hyperlink (usually by clicking it with the mouse), the requested Web page (or different part of the same Web page) is loaded into the user's browser window.

Any HTML document available on the Web has a *Uniform Resource Locator (URL)*, which indicates the location of a resource. The URL contains information that directs Web browsers to the document. Computers that run *Web server* software provide such resources. Microsoft *Internet Information Services (IIS)* is the Web server that programmers use when developing ASP .NET Web applications in Visual Studio.

Let us examine the components of the URL:

```
http://www.deitel.com/books/downloads.htm
```

The **`http://`** indicates that the resource is to be obtained using HTTP. The middle portion—**`www.deitel.com`**—is the fully qualified *hostname* of the server. The hostname is the name of the computer on which the resource resides. This computer usually is referred to as the *host*, because it houses and maintains resources. The hostname **`www.deitel.com`** is translated into an *IP address* (**`63.110.43.82`**) that identifies the server in a manner similar to that by which a telephone number uniquely defines a particular phone line. The translation of the hostname into an IP address normally is performed by a *domain name server (DNS)*—a computer that maintains a database of hostnames and their corresponding IP addresses. This translation operation is called a *DNS lookup*.

The remainder of the URL provides the name and location of the requested resource, **`/books/downloads.htm`** (an HTML document). This portion of the URL specifies both the name of the resource (**`downloads.htm`**) and its path, or location (**`/books`**), on the Web server. The path could specify the location of an actual directory on the Web server's file system. However, for security reasons, paths often specify the locations of a *virtual directory*. In such systems, the server translates the virtual directory into a real location on the server (or on another computer on the server's network), thus hiding the true location of the resource. Furthermore, some resources are created dynamically and do not reside anywhere on the server computer. The hostname in the URL for such a resource specifies the correct server, and the path and resource information identifies the location of the resource with which to respond to the client's request.

When given a URL, a browser performs a simple HTTP transaction to retrieve and display a Web page. Figure 17.1 illustrates this transaction in detail. The transaction consists of interaction between the Web browser (the client side) and the Web-server application (the server side).

In Fig. 17.1, the Web browser sends an HTTP request to the server. The request (in its simplest form) is

GET /books/downloads.htm HTTP/1.1

The word ***GET*** is an HTTP method indicating that the client wishes to obtain a resource from the server. The remainder of the request provides the path name of the resource and the protocol's name and version number (**HTTP/1.1**).

Any server that understands HTTP (version 1.1) can translate this request and respond appropriately. Figure 17.2 depicts a Web server's response for a successful request. The server first responds by sending a line of text that indicates the HTTP version, followed by a numeric code and phrase, both of which describe the status of the transaction. For example,

HTTP/1.1 200 OK

indicates success, whereas

HTTP/1.1 404 Not found

informs the client that the Web server could not locate the requested resource.

Fig. 17.1   Web server/client interaction. Step 1: The **GET** request, **GET /books/downloads.htm HTTP/1.1**.

Fig. 17.2   Client interacting with Web server. Step 2: The HTTP response, **HTTP/1.1 200 OK**.

The server then sends one or more *HTTP headers,* which provide information about the data that will be sent. In this case, the server is sending an HTML text document, so the HTTP header for this example reads:

```
Content-type: text/html
```

This header specifies the *Multipurpose Internet Mail Extensions* (*MIME*) type of the content that the server is transmitting to the browser. MIME is an Internet standard used to identify various types of data so that programs can interpret those data correctly. For example, the MIME type **text/plain** indicates that the information is plain-text, which a Web browser can display directly without any special formatting. Similarly, the MIME type **image/gif** indicates that the transmitted content is a GIF image, enabling the Web browser to display the image appropriately.

The set of headers is followed by a blank line, which indicates to the client that the server is finished sending HTTP headers. The server then sends the contents of the requested HTML document (**downloads.htm**). The server terminates the connection when the transfer of the resource is complete. At this point, the client-side browser parses the HTML it has received and *renders* (or displays) the results.

17.3 System Architecture

Most Web-based applications are *multi-tier applications* (sometimes referred to as *n-tier* applications). Multi-tier applications divide functionality into separate *tiers* (i.e., logical groupings of functionality). Although tiers can be located on the same computer, the tiers of Web-based applications typically reside on separate computers. Figure 17.3 presents the basic structure of a three-tier Web-based application.

The *information tier* (also called the *data tier* or the *bottom tier*) maintains data that pertains to the application. This tier typically stores data in a *relational database management system (RDBMS).* We discussed RDBMSs in Chapter 16, Database, SQL and ADO .NET. For example, a retail store might maintain a database for storing product information, such as descriptions, prices and quantities in stock. The same database also might contain customer information, such as user names, billing addresses and credit-card numbers. This tier can be comprised of multiple databases, which together contain the data needed for our application.

Fig. 17.3   Three-tier architecture.

The *middle tier* implements *business logic*, *controller logic* and *presentation logic* to control interactions between application clients and application data. The middle tier acts as an intermediary between data in the information tier and the application's clients. The middle-tier controller logic processes client requests (such as requests to view a product catalog) and retrieves data from the database. The middle-tier presentation logic then processes data from the information tier and presents the content to the client. Web applications typically present data to clients in the form of HTML documents.

Business logic in the middle tier enforces *business rule*s and ensures that data are reliable before the server application updates the database or presents data to users. Business rules dictate how clients can and cannot access application data and how applications process data.

The *client tier*, or *top tier*, is the application's user interface, which typically is a Web browser. Users interact directly with the application through the user interface. The client tier interacts with the middle tier to make requests and to retrieve data from the information tier. The client tier then displays to the user the data retrieved by the middle tier.

17.4 Creating and Running a Simple Web Form Example

In this section, we present our first example of an ASP .NET application. When run, this program displays the text **A Simple Web Form Example**, followed by the Web server's time. As mentioned previously, the program consists of two related files—an ASPX file (Fig. 17.4) and a C# code-behind file (Fig. 17.5). We present the markup in the ASPX file, the code in the code-behind file and the output of the application first; then, we carefully guide the reader through the step-by-step process of creating this program. [*Note*: The markup in Fig. 17.4 and other ASPX file listings in this chapter has been reformatted for presentation purposes.]

```
1   <%-- Fig. 17.4: WebTime.aspx          --%>
2   <%-- A page that contains two labels. --%>
3
4   <%@ Page language="c#" Codebehind="WebTime.aspx.cs"
5       AutoEventWireup="false" Inherits="WebTime.WebTimeTest"
6       EnableSessionState="False" enableViewState="False"%>
7
8   <!DOCTYPE HTML PUBLIC "-//W3C//DTD HTML 4.0 Transitional//EN" >
9
10  <HTML>
11     <HEAD>
12        <title>WebTime</title>
13           <meta name="GENERATOR"
14              Content="Microsoft Visual Studio 7.0">
15           <meta name="CODE_LANGUAGE" Content="C#">
16           <meta name="vs_defaultClientScript"
17              content="JavaScript">
18           <meta name="vs_targetSchema"
19              content="http://schemas.microsoft.com/intellisense/ie5">
20     </HEAD>
```

Fig. 17.4   ASPX page that displays the Web server's time. (Part 1 of 2.)

```
21
22    <body MS_POSITIONING="GridLayout">
23        <form id="WebForm1" method="post" runat="server">
24            <asp:Label id="promptLabel" style="Z-INDEX: 101;
25                LEFT: 25px; POSITION: absolute; TOP: 23px"
26                runat="server" Font-Size="Medium">
27                A Simple Web Form Example
28            </asp:Label>
29
30            <asp:Label id="timeLabel" style="Z-INDEX: 102;
31                LEFT: 25px; POSITION: absolute; TOP: 55px"
32                runat="server" Font-Size="XX-Large"
33                BackColor="Black" ForeColor="LimeGreen">
34            </asp:Label>
35        </form>
36    </body>
37 </HTML>
```

Fig. 17.4   ASPX page that displays the Web server's time. (Part 2 of 2.)

Visual Studio generates the markup shown in Fig. 17.4 when the programmer drags two **Label**s onto a Web Form and sets their properties. Notice that the ASPX file contains other information, in addition to HTML.

Lines 1–2 of Fig. 17.4 are *ASP .NET comments* that indicate the figure number, the file name and the purpose of the file. ASP.NET comments begin with **<%--** and terminate with **--%>**. Lines 4–6 use a **<%@ Page...%>** *directive* to specify information needed to process this file. The **language** of the code-behind file is specified as **C#**, and the code-behind file is named **WebTime.aspx.cs**.

The **AutoEventWireup** attribute determines how event handlers are linked to a control's events. When **AutoEventWireup** is set to **true**, ASP .NET determines which methods in the class to call in response to an event generated by a user's interaction with the Web page. ASP .NET will call the proper event handlers for a Web control (based on a specific naming convention for event handlers) without using a delegate, thus eliminating the need for the programmer to add a delegate for the event handler. This elimination is particularly convenient when developers are not using Visual Studio and therefore must add all code themselves. When Visual Studio .NET generates an ASPX file, it sets **AutoEventWireup** to **false**, because Visual Studio generates the necessary event delegates for us. If we were to set **AutoEventWireup** to **true** in Visual Studio (where all the delegates are added automatically) an event handler could be called twice—once through the delegate, and once as a result of **AutoEventWireup**.

The **Inherits** attribute specifies the class in the code-behind file from which this ASP .NET document inherits—in this case, **WebTimeTest**. We say more about **Inherits** momentarily. [*Note*: We explicitly set the **EnableViewState** attribute and the **EnableSessionState** attribute to **false**. We explain the significance of these attributes later in the chapter.]

Line 8 is called the *document type declaration*, which specifies the document element name (**HTML**) and the uniform resource identifier (URI) for the DTD. Lines 10–11 contain the **<HTML>** and **<HEAD>** start tags, respectively. **HTML** documents have root element

HTML and mark up information about the document in the **HEAD** element. Line 12 sets the title for this Web page. Lines 13–19 display a series of *meta elements* that contain information about the document. Two important **meta**-element attributes are *name*, which identifies the **meta** element, and *content*, which stores the **meta** element's data. Visual Studio generates these **meta** elements when an ASPX file is created.

Line 22 contains the **<body>** start tag, which marks the beginning of the Web page's viewable content; the body contains the content that the browser displays. The **Form** that contains our controls is defined in lines 23–35. Notice the *runat* attribute in line 23, which is set to *"server"*. This attribute indicates that the server processes the **form** and generates HTML to send to the client.

Lines 24–28 and 30–34 display the markup for two **Label** Web controls. The properties that we set in the **Properties** window, such as **Font-Size** and **Text**, are attributes here. The *asp: tag prefix* in the declaration of the *Label* tag indicates that the label is an ASP .NET Web control. Each Web control maps to a corresponding HTML element.

Portability Tip 17.1

A single type of Web control can map to different HTML elements, depending on the client browser and the Web control's property settings.

In this example, the **asp:Label** control maps to the HTML *span* element. A **span** element simply contains text. This particular element is used because **span** elements facilitate the application of styles to text. Several of the property values that were applied to our labels are represented as part of the **style** attribute of the **span** element. We will see the **span** elements that are created by this control shortly.

Each Web control in our example contains the **runat="server"** attribute-value pair, because these controls must be processed on the server. If this attribute pair is not present, the **asp:Label** element is written to the client. (i.e., the control will not be converted into a **span** element, and the Web browser will not render the element properly.)

Figure 17.5 presents the code-behind file for our example. Recall that the ASPX file in Fig. 17.4 references this file in line 4. We present the complete code listing here. In the remaining examples, we omit portions of the generated code that are not relevant to our discussion. In such examples, we insert a comment to indicate where the generated code would appear.

```
1   // Fig. 17.5: WebTime.aspx.cs
2   // The code-behind file for a page
3   // that displays the Web server's time.
4
5   using System;
6   using System.Collections;
7   using System.ComponentModel;
8   using System.Data;
9   using System.Drawing;
10  using System.Web;
11  using System.Web.SessionState;
12
```

Fig. 17.5   Code-behind file for a page that displays the Web server's time. (Part 1 of 3.)

```
13    // definitions for graphical controls used in Web Forms
14    using System.Web.UI;
15    using System.Web.UI.WebControls;
16    using System.Web.UI.HtmlControls;
17
18    namespace WebTime
19    {
20       /// <summary>
21       /// display current time
22       /// </summary>
23       public class WebTimeTest : System.Web.UI.Page
24       {
25          protected System.Web.UI.WebControls.Label promptLabel;
26          protected System.Web.UI.WebControls.Label timeLabel;
27
28          // event handler for Load event
29          private void Page_Load(
30             object sender, System.EventArgs e )
31          {
32             // display current time
33             timeLabel.Text =
34                String.Format( "{0:D2}:{1:D2}:{2:D2}",
35                DateTime.Now.Hour, DateTime.Now.Minute,
36                DateTime.Now.Second );
37          }
38
39          // event handler for Init event; sets
40          // timeLabel to Web server's time
41          #region Web Form Designer generated code
42          override protected void OnInit( EventArgs e )
43          {
44             //
45             // CODEGEN: This call is required by the
46             // ASP.NET Web Form Designer.
47             //
48             InitializeComponent();
49             base.OnInit( e );
50          }
51
52          /// <summary>
53          /// Required method for Designer support - do not modify
54          /// the contents of this method with the code editor.
55          /// </summary>
56          private void InitializeComponent()
57          {
58             this.Load += new System.EventHandler(
59                this.Page_Load );
60          }
61          #endregion
62
63       } // end class WebTimeTest
64
65    } // end namespace WebTime
```

Fig. 17.5 Code-behind file for a page that displays the Web server's time. (Part 2 of 3.)

Fig. 17.5 Code-behind file for a page that displays the Web server's time. (Part 3 of 3.)

Notice the **using** statements on lines 10–16. These statements specify namespaces that contain classes for developing Web-based applications. The key namespace on which we initially focus is *System.Web*, which contains classes that manage client requests and server responses. Some of the other namespaces define the available controls and various manipulations of these controls; we discuss the other namespaces throughout the chapter as they become more relevant.

Line 23 begins the class definition for **WebTimeTest**, which inherits from class *Page*. This class defines the requested Web page and is located in the *System.Web.UI* namespace (line 14), which contains classes for the creation of Web-based applications and controls. Class **Page** also provides event handlers and objects necessary for creating Web-based applications. In addition to the **Page** class (from which all Web Forms directly or indirectly inherit), **System.Web.UI** also includes the *Control* class. This class is the base class that provides common functionality for all Web controls.

Lines 25–26 declare references to two **Label**s. These **Label**s are Web controls, defined in namespace *System.Web.UI.WebControls* (line 15). This namespace contains Web controls employed in the design of the page's user interface. Web controls in this namespace derive from class *WebControl*.

Lines 42–50 define method *OnInit*, which is called when the *Init* event is raised. This event, which is the first event raised when a client requests the Web form, indicates that the page is ready to be initialized. Method **OnInit** calls method **InitializeComponent** (defined in lines 56–60). As in Windows Forms, this method is used to set some initial properties of the application's components. The method also can be used to register events. Method **InitializeComponent** creates and attaches an event handler for the *Load* event, which is raised when the page loads (this event occurs after all the Web controls on the page have been initialized and loaded). After **InitializeComponent** executes, method **OnInit** calls the base class's (**Page**'s) **OnInit** method to perform any additional initialization that might be required (line 49).

How are the ASPX file and the code-behind file used to create the Web page that is sent to the client? First, recall that class **WebTimeTest** is the base class specified in line 5 of the ASPX file (Fig. 17.4). Class **WebTimeTest** inherits from **Page**, which defines the general functionality of a Web page. In addition to inheriting this functionality, **WebTimeTest** defines some of its own (i.e., displaying the current time). The code-behind file is the file that defines this functionality, whereas the ASPX file defines the GUI. When a client requests an ASPX file, a class is created behind the scenes that contains both the visual aspect of our page (defined in the ASPX file) and the logic of our page (defined in the code-behind file). The new class inherits from **Page**. The first time that our Web page is requested, this class is compiled, and an instance is created. This instance represents our page—it creates the HTML that is sent to the client. The assembly created from our compiled class is placed in the project's **bin** directory.

Performance Tip 17.1

Once an instance of the Web page has been created, multiple clients can use that instance to access the page—no recompilation is necessary. The project will be recompiled only when a programmer modifies the application; such changes are detected by the runtime environment, and the project is recompiled to reflect the altered content.

Let us look briefly at how the code in our Web page executes. When the Web server creates an instance of our page to serve a client request, the **Init** event occurs first, invoking method **OnInit**. This method calls **InitializeComponent**. In addition, method **OnInit** might contain code for initializing objects. After this occurs, the **Load** event is generated, which calls method **Page_Load**. This event handler executes any processing that is necessary to restore data that was used in previous requests to the page. Lines 33–36 of the **Load** event handler set **timeLabel**'s **Text** property to the Web server's time. We include this code in the **Load** event handler so that the time will be updated with every page request. After this event handler finishes executing, the page processes any events raised by the page's controls. This includes the handling of any events generated by the user, such as button clicks. When the Web Form object is ready for garbage collection, an **Unload** event is generated. Although not present in our example, event handler **Page_Unload** is inherited from class **Page**. This event handler contains code that releases resources, especially any *unmanaged resources* (i.e., resources not managed by the CLR).

Figure 17.6 depicts the HTML generated by the ASP .NET application. To view this HTML, select **View > Source** in Internet Explorer.

```
1   <!-- Fig. 17.6: WebTime.html                    -->
2   <!-- The HTML generated when WebTime is loaded. -->
3
4   <!DOCTYPE HTML PUBLIC "-//W3C//DTD HTML 4.0 Transitional//EN" >
5
6   <HTML>
7      <HEAD>
8         <title>WebTime</title>
9         <meta name="GENERATOR"
10           Content="Microsoft Visual Studio 7.0">
11        <meta name="CODE_LANGUAGE" Content="C#">
12        <meta name="vs_defaultClientScript" content="JavaScript">
13        <meta name="vs_targetSchema"
14           content="http://schemas.microsoft.com/intellisense/ie5">
15     </HEAD>
16
```

Fig. 17.6 HTML response when the browser requests **WebTime.aspx**. (Part 1 of 2.)

```
17    <body MS_POSITIONING="GridLayout">
18       <form name="WebForm1" method="post"
19          action="WebTime.aspx" id="WebForm1">
20          <input type="hidden" name="__VIEWSTATE"
21             value="dDwtNjA2MTkwMTQ5Ozs+" />
22
23          <span id="promptLabel"
24             style="font-size:Medium;Z-INDEX: 101; LEFT: 25px;
25             POSITION: absolute; TOP: 23px">
26             A Simple Web Form Example
27          </span>
28
29          <span id="timeLabel" style="color:LimeGreen;
30             background-color:Black;font-size:XX-Large;
31             Z-INDEX: 102; LEFT: 25px; POSITION: absolute;
32             TOP: 55px">10:39:35
33          </span>
34       </form>
35    </body>
36 </HTML>
```

Fig. 17.6   HTML response when the browser requests **WebTime.aspx**. (Part 2 of 2.)

The contents of this page are similar to those of the ASPX file. Lines 7–15 define a document header similar to the one in Fig. 17.4. Lines 17–35 define the body of the document. Line 18 begins the form, which is a mechanism for collecting user information and sending it to the Web server. In this particular program, the user does not submit data to the Web server for processing.

HTML forms can contain visual and nonvisual components. Visual components include buttons and other GUI components with which users interact. Nonvisual components, called *hidden inputs*, store any data that the document author specifies, such as e-mail addresses entered by users of the Web page. One of these hidden inputs is defined in lines 20–21. We discuss the precise meaning of this hidden input later in the chapter. Attribute **method** of element **form** (line 18) specifies the method by which the Web browser submits the form to the server (in this example **post**). The **action** attribute in the **form** element identifies the name and location of the resource that will be requested when this form is submitted; in this case, **WebTime.aspx**. Recall that the ASPX file's **form** element contained the **runat="server"** attribute-value pair. When the **form** is processed on the server, the **name="WebForm1"** and **action="WebTime.aspx"** attribute-value pairs are added to the HTML **form** sent to the client browser.

In the ASPX file, the form's labels were Web controls. Here, we are viewing the HTML created by our application, so the **form** contains **span** elements to represent the text in our labels. In this particular case, ASP .NET maps the **Label** Web controls to HTML **span** elements. Each **span** element contains formatting information, such as size and placement of the text being displayed. Most of the information specified as properties of **timeLabel** and **promptLabel** are specified in the **style** attribute of each **span**.

Now that we have presented the ASPX file and the code-behind file, we outline the process by which we created this application:[2]

1. *Create the project.* Select **File > New > Project...** to display the **New Project** dialog (Fig. 17.7). In this dialog, select **Visual C# Projects** in the left pane and then ***ASP.NET Web Application*** in the right pane. Notice that the field for the project is grayed out. Rather than using this field, we specify the name and location of the project in the **Location** field. We want the project to be located at the Web address **http://localhost**, which is the URL for IIS's root directory (typically **C:\InetPub\wwwroot**). The name *localhost* indicates that the client and server reside on the same machine. If the Web server were located on a different machine, **localhost** would be replaced with the appropriate IP address or hostname. By default, Visual Studio assigns the project name **WebApplication1**, which we changed to **WebTime**. IIS must be running to create the project successfully. IIS can be started by executing **inetmgr.exe**, right clicking **Default Web Site** in the dialog that appears and selecting **Start**. [*Note:* Readers might need to expand the node representing their computer to display the **Default Web Site**.] Below the **Location** text box, the text "**Project will be created at http://localhost/WebTime**" appears. This indicates that the project's folder is located in the Web server's root directory. When the developer clicks **OK**, the project is created; this action also produces a virtual directory, which is linked to the project folder. The ***Create New Web*** dialog is displayed next, while Visual Studio creates the Web site on the server (Fig. 17.8).

Fig. 17.7   Creating an **ASP.NET Web Application** in Visual Studio.

2. The steps provided in this chapter enable readers to create Web applications of their own. If the readers would like to run the examples for this chapter (located on our Web site), they must first create a virtual directory in Microsoft Internet Information Services. For instructions, visit the **Downloads/Resources** link at **www.deitel.com**. Once the virtual directory has been created and the application has been opened, readers will need to set the start page for the Web application. To do this, right-click the ASPX file and select **Set as Start Page**.

Fig. 17.8 Visual Studio creating and linking a virtual directory for the **WebTime** project folder.

2. *Examine the newly created project.* The next several figures describe the new project's content; we begin with the **Solution Explorer**, shown in Fig. 17.9. As with Windows applications, Visual Studio creates several files when a new **ASP .NET Web Application** is created. **WebForm1.aspx** is the Web Form. (**WebForm1** is the default name for this file.) A code-behind file also is included as part of the project. To view the ASPX file's code-behind file, right click the ASPX file and select **View Code**. Alternatively, the programmer can click an icon to display all files, then expand the node for our ASPX page (see Fig. 17.9.). [*Note*: To see the code-behind file listed in the **Solution Explorer**, the reader might need to select the icon that displays all files.]

The next figure, Fig. 17.10, shows the **Web Forms** listed in the **Toolbox**. The left figure displays the beginning of the Web controls list, and the right figure displays the remaining Web controls. Notice that some controls are similar to the Windows controls presented earlier in the book.

Figure 17.11 shows the Web Form designer for **WebForm1.aspx**. It consists of a grid on which users drag and drop components, such as buttons and labels, from the **Toolbox**.

The Web Form designer's *HTML* mode (Fig. 17.12) allows the programmer to view the markup that represents the user interface. Clicking the **HTML** button in the lower-left corner of the Web Form designer switches the Web Form designer to HTML mode. Similarly, clicking the *Design* button (to the left of the **HTML** button) returns the Web Form designer to design mode.

Fig. 17.9 **Solution Explorer** window for project **WebTime**.

Fig. 17.10 Web Forms menu in the Toolbox.

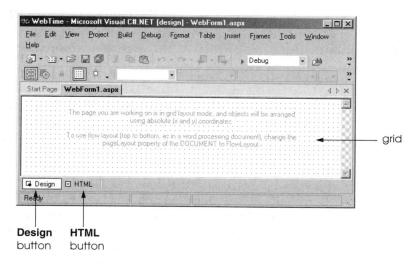

Fig. 17.11 Design mode of Web Form designer.

The next figure (Fig. 17.13) displays **WebForm1.aspx.cs**—the code-behind file for **WebForm1.aspx**. Recall that Visual Studio .NET generates this code-behind file when the project is created. This file can be viewed by right-clicking the ASPX file in the **Solution Explorer** and selecting **View Code**.

3. *Rename the ASPX file.* We have displayed the contents of the default ASPX and code-behind files. We now rename these files. Right click the ASPX file in the **Solution Explorer** and select **Rename**. Enter the new file name and hit *Enter*. This updates the name of both the ASPX file and the code-behind file. In this example, we use the name **WebTime.aspx**.

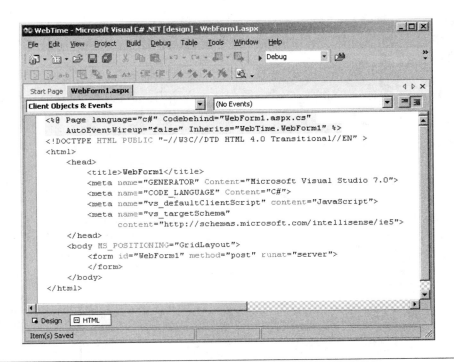

Fig. 17.12 HTML mode of Web Form designer.

4. *Design the page.* Designing a Web Form is as simple as designing a Windows Form. To add controls to the page, drag and drop them from the **Toolbox** onto the Web Form. Like the Web Form itself, each control is an object that has properties, methods and events. Developers can set these properties and events using the **Properties** window.

The *PageLayout* property determines how controls are arranged on the form (Fig. 17.14). By default, property **PageLayout** is set to *GridLayout*, which specifies that all controls are located exactly where they are dropped on the Web Form. This is called *absolute positioning*. Alternatively, the developer can set the Web Form's **PageLayout** property to *FlowLayout*, which causes controls to be placed sequentially on the Web Form. This is called *relative positioning*, because the controls' positions are relative to the Web Form's upper left corner. We use **GridLayout** for many of our examples. To view the Web Form's properties, select *Document* from the drop-down list in the **Properties** window; **Document** is the name used to represent the Web Form in the **Properties** window.

In this example, we use two **Label**s, which developers can place on the Web Form either by drag-and-drop or by double-clicking the **Toolbox**'s **Label** control. Name the first **Label promptLabel** and the second **timeLabel**. We delete **timeLabel**'s text, because this text is set in the code-behind file. When a **Label** does not contain text, the **Label** displays its name in square brackets in the Web Form designer (Fig. 17.15), but this name is not displayed at runtime. We set the text for **promptLabel** to **A Simple Web Form Example**.

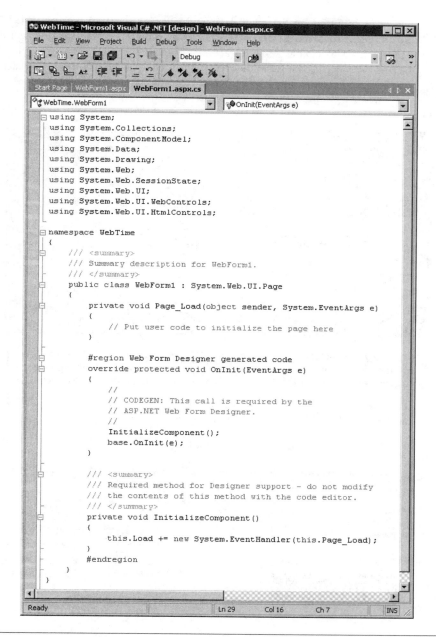

Fig. 17.13 Code-behind file for **WebForm1.aspx** generated by Visual Studio .NET.

We set **timeLabel**'s **BackColor**, **ForeColor** and **Font-Size** properties to **Black**, **LimeGreen** and **XX-Large**, respectively. To change font properties, the programmer must expand the **Font** node in the **Properties** window, then change each relevant property individually. We also set the labels' locations and sizes by dragging the controls. Finally, we set the Web Form's **Enable-SessionState** and **EnableViewState** properties to **false** (these properties are used to enable session-tracking, discussed in Section 17.6.). Once the **Label**s' properties are set in the **Properties** window, Visual Studio updates the ASPX file's contents. Figure 17.15 shows the IDE after these properties are set.

GridLayout—Controls are placed where they are dropped on the page

FlowLayout—Controls are placed one after the other

Cursor indicates where next control will be located

Fig. 17.14 GridLayout and **FlowLayout** illustration.

Labels   Web Form

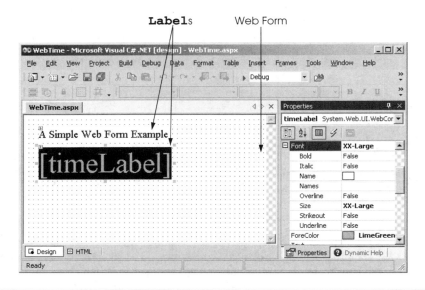

Fig. 17.15 WebForm.aspx after adding two **Label**s and setting their properties.

5. *Add page logic*. Once the user interface has been designed, C# code must be added to the code-behind file. In this example, lines 33–36 of Fig. 17.5 are added to the code-behind file. The statement retrieves the current time and formats it so that the time is in the format *HH*:*MM*:*SS*. For example, 9 a.m. is formatted as **09:00:00**.

6. *Run the program*. Select **Debug > Start**. An Internet Explorer window opens and loads the Web page (the ASPX file). Notice that the URL is **http://local-host/WebTime/WebTime.aspx** (Fig. 17.4), indicating that our ASPX file is located within the directory **WebTime**, which is located in the Web server's root directory.

   After the Web Form is created, the programmer can view it three different ways. First, the programmer can select **Debug >Start** (as described previously), which runs the application by opening a browser window. The IDE exits **Run** or **Debug** mode when the browser is closed.

   The programmer also can right-click either the Web Form designer or the ASPX file name (in the **Solution Explorer**) and select *View In Browser*. This opens a browser window within Visual Studio and displays a preview of the page. This technique allows developers to view what the page will look like when it is requested by a client, but does not compile the code-behind file. The third way to run an ASP .NET application is to open a browser window and type in the Web page's URL. When testing an ASP .NET application on the local computer, type **http://localhost/***ProjectFolder***/***PageName***.aspx**, where *ProjectFold-er* is the folder in which the page resides (usually the name of the project), and *PageName* is the name of the ASP .NET page. Note that, if this technique is used, the page must already be compiled.

17.5 Web Controls

This section introduces some of the Web controls located on the **Web Form** tab in the **Toolbox** (Fig. 17.10). Figure 17.16 summarizes some of the Web controls used in the chapter examples.[3]

Web Control	Description
Label	Displays text that the user cannot edit.
Button	Displays a button control.
TextBox	Gathers user input and displays text.
Image	Displays images (e.g., GIF and JPG).
RadioButtonList	Groups radio buttons.
DropDownList	Displays a drop-down list of choices from which the user can select one item.

Fig. 17.16 Web controls commonly used in ASP.NET applications.

3. ASP .NET also provides controls known as *HTML controls*, which represent standard HTML components. Because of the sophisticated functionality provided by the Web controls in ASP .NET, we use these types of controls in the chapter.

17.5.1 Text and Graphics Controls

The form in Fig. 17.17 gathers user input using the controls listed in Fig. 17.16. [*Note*: This example does not contain any functionality (i.e., no action occurs when the user clicks **Register**). We ask the reader to provide the functionality as an exercise. In successive examples, we demonstrate how to add functionality to many of these Web controls.]

Lines 34–37 define an *Image* control, which places an image into a Web page. The *ImageUrl* property (line 36) specifies the file location of the image to display. To specify an image, click the ellipsis button next to the **ImageUrl** property in the **Properties** window; the resulting dialog enables the programmer to browse for the desired image. The top of this dialog displays the contents of this application. If the image is not explicitly part of the project, the programmer will need to use the **Browse** button or add the image to the project. If the image is within the project directory (or any subdirectories thereof), that image can be added explicitly to the project by displaying all files in the **Solution Explorer**, right-clicking the image and selecting **Include in Project**. Once this has been done, the image will be displayed in the list of project files in the dialog that appears when the programmer selects the **ImageUrl** property. Within the dialog, the user is given the option to choose **URL TYPE**, which defines how the location of the image will be specified in the program. Developers have various options for the **URL Type**: They can specify whether they want the image to be referenced as being located on the server, on the local machine or relative to the current path. We have chosen for the location to be specified as a relative path.

Lines 49–52 define a *TextBox* control, which allows the programmer to read and display text. Lines 69–86 define a *RadioButtonList* control, which provides a series of radio buttons from which the user can select only one. Each radio button is defined using a *ListItem* element (lines 73–84). The *HyperLink* control (lines 88–92) adds a hyperlink to a Web page. The *NavigateUrl* property (line 90) of this control specifies the resource that is requested (such as **http://www.deitel.com**) when a user clicks the hyperlink. Lines 94–114 define a *DropDownList*. This control is similar to a **RadioButtonList** in that it allows the user to select exactly one option. When a user clicks the drop-down list, it expands and displays a list from which the user can make a selection. Lines 98–112 define the **ListItem**s that display when the drop-down list is expanded. Like the **Button** Windows control, the *Button* Web control (lines 137–140) represents a button; a button Web control typically maps to an **input** HTML element that has attribute **type** and value **"button"**.

```
1   <%-- Fig. 17.17: WebControls.aspx      --%>
2   <%-- Demonstrating some Web controls. --%>
3
4   <%@ Page language="c#" Codebehind="WebControls.aspx.cs"
5       AutoEventWireup="false" Inherits="WebControls.WebForm1"
6       EnableSessionState="False" enableViewState="False"%>
7
8   <!DOCTYPE HTML PUBLIC "-//W3C//DTD HTML 4.0 Transitional//EN" >
9
10  <HTML>
11     <HEAD>
12
```

Fig. 17.17 Web controls demonstration. (Part 1 of 5.)

```
13          <title>WebForm1</title>
14          <meta name="GENERATOR"
15            Content="Microsoft Visual Studio 7.0">
16          <meta name="CODE_LANGUAGE" Content="C#">
17          <meta name="vs_defaultClientScript"
18            content="JavaScript">
19          <meta name="vs_targetSchema"
20          content="http://schemas.microsoft.com/intellisense/ie5">
21
22      </HEAD>
23
24      <body MS_POSITIONING="GridLayout">
25
26          <form id="Form1" method="post" runat="server">
27
28              <asp:Label id="welcomeLabel" style="Z-INDEX: 101;
29                  LEFT: 21px; POSITION: absolute; TOP: 17px"
30                  runat="server" Font-Bold="True" Font-Size="Medium">
31                  This is a sample registration form.
32              </asp:Label>
33
34              <asp:Image id="operatingImage" style="Z-INDEX: 121;
35                  LEFT: 21px; POSITION: absolute; TOP: 371px"
36                  runat="server" ImageUrl="images\os.png">
37              </asp:Image>
38
39              <asp:Image id="publicationImage" style="Z-INDEX: 120;
40                  LEFT: 21px; POSITION: absolute; TOP: 245px"
41                  runat="server" ImageUrl="images\downloads.png">
42              </asp:Image>
43
44              <asp:Image id="userImage" style="Z-INDEX: 119;
45                  LEFT: 21px; POSITION: absolute; TOP: 91px"
46                  runat="server" ImageUrl="images\user.png">
47              </asp:Image>
48
49              <asp:TextBox id="emailTextBox" style="Z-INDEX: 118;
50                  LEFT: 95px; POSITION: absolute;
51                  TOP: 161px" runat="server">
52              </asp:TextBox>
53
54              <asp:TextBox id="firstTextBox" style="Z-INDEX: 117;
55                  LEFT: 95px; POSITION: absolute; TOP: 127px"
56                  runat="server">
57              </asp:TextBox>
58
59              <asp:TextBox id="lastTextBox" style="Z-INDEX: 116;
60                  LEFT: 341px; POSITION: absolute;
61                  TOP: 127px" runat="server">
62              </asp:TextBox>
63
64              <asp:TextBox id="phoneTextBox" style="Z-INDEX: 115;
65                  LEFT: 341px; POSITION: absolute;
```

Fig. 17.17 Web controls demonstration. (Part 2 of 5.)

```
66                 TOP: 161px" runat="server">
67           </asp:TextBox>
68
69           <asp:RadioButtonList id="operatingRadioButtonList"
70              style="Z-INDEX: 114; LEFT: 21px;
71              POSITION: absolute; TOP: 409px" runat="server">
72
73              <asp:ListItem Value="Windows NT">Windows NT
74              </asp:ListItem>
75
76              <asp:ListItem Value="Windows 2000">Windows 2000
77              </asp:ListItem>
78
79              <asp:ListItem Value="Windows XP">Windows XP
80              </asp:ListItem>
81
82              <asp:ListItem Value="Linux">Linux</asp:ListItem>
83
84              <asp:ListItem Value="Other">Other</asp:ListItem>
85
86           </asp:RadioButtonList>
87
88           <asp:HyperLink id="booksHyperLink" style="Z-INDEX: 113;
89              LEFT: 21px; POSITION: absolute; TOP: 316px"
90              runat="server" NavigateUrl="http://www.deitel.com">
91              Click here to view more information about our books.
92           </asp:HyperLink>
93
94           <asp:DropDownList id="booksDropDownList"
95              style="Z-INDEX: 112; LEFT: 21px;
96              POSITION: absolute; TOP: 282px" runat="server">
97
98              <asp:ListItem Value="XML How to Program 1e">
99                 XML How to Program 1e
100             </asp:ListItem>
101
102             <asp:ListItem Value="C# How to Program 1e">
103                C# How to Program 1e
104             </asp:ListItem>
105
106             <asp:ListItem Value="Visual Basic .NET How to Program 2e">
107                Visual Basic .NET How to Program 2e
108             </asp:ListItem>
109
110             <asp:ListItem Value="C++ How to Program 3e">
111                C++ How to Program 3e
112             </asp:ListItem>
113
114          </asp:DropDownList>
115
116          <asp:Image id="phoneImage" style="Z-INDEX: 111;
117             LEFT: 266px; POSITION: absolute; TOP: 161px"
118             runat="server" ImageUrl="images\phone.png">
```

Fig. 17.17 Web controls demonstration. (Part 3 of 5.)

```
119                   </asp:Image>
120
121            <asp:Image id="emailImage" style="Z-INDEX: 110;
122               LEFT: 21px; POSITION: absolute; TOP: 161px"
123               runat="server" ImageUrl="images\email.png">
124            </asp:Image>
125
126            <asp:Image id="lastImage" style="Z-INDEX: 109;
127               LEFT: 266px; POSITION: absolute; TOP: 127px"
128               runat="server" ImageUrl="images\lname.png">
129            </asp:Image>
130
131            <asp:Image id="firstImage" style="Z-INDEX: 108;
132               LEFT: 21px; POSITION: absolute;
133               TOP: 127px" runat="server"
134               ImageUrl="images\fname.png">
135            </asp:Image>
136
137            <asp:Button id="registerButton" style="Z-INDEX: 107;
138               LEFT: 21px; POSITION: absolute; TOP: 547px"
139               runat="server" Text="Register">
140            </asp:Button>
141
142            <asp:Label id="bookLabel" style="Z-INDEX: 106;
143               LEFT: 216px; POSITION: absolute; TOP: 245px"
144               runat="server" ForeColor="DarkCyan">
145               Which book would you like information about?
146            </asp:Label>
147
148            <asp:Label id="fillLabel" style="Z-INDEX: 105;
149               LEFT: 218px; POSITION: absolute; TOP: 91px"
150               runat="server" ForeColor="DarkCyan">
151               Please fill out the fields below.
152            </asp:Label>
153
154            <asp:Label id="phoneLabel" style="Z-INDEX: 104;
155               LEFT: 266px; POSITION: absolute;
156               TOP: 198px" runat="server">
157               Must be in the form (555)555-5555.
158            </asp:Label>
159
160            <asp:Label id="operatingLabel" style="Z-INDEX: 103;
161               LEFT: 220px; POSITION: absolute; TOP: 371px"
162               runat="server" Height="9px" ForeColor="DarkCyan">
163               Which operating system are you using?
164            </asp:Label>
165
166            <asp:Label id="registerLabel" style="Z-INDEX: 102;
167               LEFT: 21px; POSITION: absolute; TOP: 46px"
168               runat="server" Font-Italic="True">
169               Please fill in all fields and click Register.
170            </asp:Label>
171
```

Fig. 17.17 Web controls demonstration. (Part 4 of 5.)

```
172          </form>
173      </body>
174  </HTML>
```

Image control

TextBox control

DropDownList control

HyperLink control

RadioButtonList control

Button control

Fig. 17.17 Web controls demonstration. (Part 5 of 5.)

17.5.2 **AdRotator** Control

Web pages often contain product and service advertisements; these advertisements usually consist of images. Although Web site authors want to sell advertisements to as many sponsors as possible, Web pages can display only a limited number of advertisements at once. To address this problem, ASP .NET provides the **AdRotator** Web control for displaying advertisements. Using advertisement data located in an XML file, the **AdRotator** control randomly selects an image to display and generates a hyperlink to the Web page associated with that image. Browsers that do not support images display a text alternative, which is specified in the XML document.

Figure 17.18 demonstrates the **AdRotator** Web control. The images that we rotate in this example include the flags of eleven countries. When a user clicks the displayed flag

```
1   <%-- Fig. 17.18: AdRotator.aspx                    --%>
2   <%-- A Web Form that demonstrates class AdRotator. --%>
3
4   <%@ Page language="c#" Codebehind="AdRotator.aspx.cs"
5       AutoEventWireup="false" Inherits="AdRotatorTest.AdRotator"
6       EnableSessionState="False" enableViewState="False"%>
7
8   <!DOCTYPE HTML PUBLIC "-//W3C//DTD HTML 4.0 Transitional//EN" >
9   <HTML>
10     <HEAD>
11        <title>WebForm1</title>
12        <meta name="GENERATOR"
13           Content="Microsoft Visual Studio 7.0">
14        <meta name="CODE_LANGUAGE" Content="C#">
15        <meta name="vs_defaultClientScript"
16           content="JavaScript">
17        <meta name="vs_targetSchema"
18           content="http://schemas.microsoft.com/intellisense/ie5">
19     </HEAD>
20
21     <body MS_POSITIONING="GridLayout">
22        background="images/background.png">
23        <form id="Form1" method="post" runat="server">
24
25           <asp:AdRotator id="adRotator" style="Z-INDEX: 101;
26              LEFT: 17px; POSITION: absolute; TOP: 69px"
27              runat="server" Width="86px" Height="60px"
28              AdvertisementFile="AdRotatorInformation.xml">
29           </asp:AdRotator>
30
31           <asp:Label id="adRotatorLabel" style="Z-INDEX: 102;
32              LEFT: 17px; POSITION: absolute; TOP: 26px"
33              runat="server" Font-Size="Large">
34              AdRotator Example
35           </asp:Label> 
36
37        </form>
38     </body>
39   </HTML>
```

Fig. 17.18 AdRotator class demonstrated on a Web form.

image, the browser is redirected to a Web page containing information about the country that the flag represents. If a user clicks refresh or re-requests the page, one of the eleven flags is chosen again at random and displayed.

The ASPX file in Fig. 17.18 is similar to that of Fig. 17.4. However, instead of two **Label**s, this page contains one **Label** and one **AdRotator** control, named **adRotator**. The **background** property for our page is set to display the image **background.png**. To specify this file, click the ellipsis button provided next to the **Background** property and use the resulting dialog to browse for **background.png**.

In the **Properties** window, we set the **AdRotator** control's **Advertisement-File** property to **AdRotatorInformation.xml** (line 28). The Web control determines which advertisement from this file to display. We present the contents of this XML file momentarily. As illustrated in Fig. 17.19, the programmer does not need to add any code to the code-behind file, because the **AdRotator** control does "all the work."

The output depicts two different requests—the first time the page is requested, the American flag is shown, and, in the second request, the Latvian flag is displayed. The last image depicts the Web page that loads when a user clicks the Latvian flag.

```
1    // Fig. 17.19: AdRotator.aspx.cs
2    // The code-behind file for a page that
3    // demonstrates the AdRotator class.
4
5    using System;
6    using System.Collections;
7    using System.ComponentModel;
8    using System.Data;
9    using System.Drawing;
10   using System.Web;
11   using System.Web.SessionState;
12   using System.Web.UI;
13   using System.Web.UI.WebControls;
14   using System.Web.UI.HtmlControls;
15
16   namespace AdRotatorTest
17   {
18      /// page that demonstrates AdRotator
19      public class AdRotator : System.Web.UI.Page
20      {
21         protected System.Web.UI.WebControls.AdRotator adRotator;
22         protected System.Web.UI.WebControls.Label adRotatorLabel;
23
24         // Visual Studio .NET generated code
25
26      } // end class AdRotator
27
28   } // end namespace AdRotatorTest
```

Fig. 17.19 Code-behind file for page demonstrating the **AdRotator** class. (Part 1 of 2.)

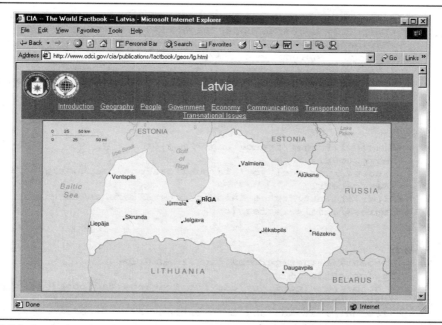

Fig. 17.19 Code-behind file for page demonstrating the **AdRotator** class. (Part 2 of 2.)

XML document **AdRotatorInformation.xml** (Fig. 17.20) contains several *Ad* elements, each of which provides information about an advertisement for the **AdRotator**. Element *ImageUrl* specifies the relative path (location) of the advertisement's image, and element *NavigateUrl* specifies the URL for the Web page that loads when a user clicks the advertisement. The **AlternateText** element contains text that displays in place of the image when the browser cannot locate or render the image (i.e., because the file is missing, or because the browser is not capable of displaying it). The **AlternateText** element's text also is a *tooltip* that the Web browser displays when a user places the mouse pointer over the image (Fig. 17.19). A tooltip is a caption that appears when the mouse hovers over a control and provides the user with information about that control. The *Impressions* element specifies how often a particular image appears, relative to the other images. An advertisement that has a higher **Impressions** value displays more frequently than an advertisement with a lower value. In our example, the advertisements display with equal probability, because each **Impressions**' value is set to **1**. Advertisers often purchase advertisements on Web sites based on the number of impressions the advertisement will receive.

```
1   <?xml version="1.0" encoding="utf-8"?>
2
3   <!-- Fig. 17.20: AdRotatorInformation.xml       -->
4   <!-- XML file containing advertisement information. -->
5
6   <Advertisements>
```

Fig. 17.20 **AdvertisementFile** used in **AdRotator** example. (Part 1 of 3.)

```
 7      <Ad>
 8          <ImageUrl>images/us.png</ImageUrl>
 9          <NavigateUrl>
10             http://www.odci.gov/cia/publications/factbook/geos/us.html
11          </NavigateUrl>
12          <AlternateText>United States Information</AlternateText>
13          <Impressions>1</Impressions>
14      </Ad>
15
16      <Ad>
17          <ImageUrl>images/france.png</ImageUrl>
18          <NavigateUrl>
19             http://www.odci.gov/cia/publications/factbook/geos/fr.html
20          </NavigateUrl>
21          <AlternateText>France Information</AlternateText>
22          <Impressions>1</Impressions>
23      </Ad>
24
25      <Ad>
26          <ImageUrl>images/germany.png</ImageUrl>
27          <NavigateUrl>
28             http://www.odci.gov/cia/publications/factbook/geos/gm.html
29          </NavigateUrl>
30          <AlternateText>Germany Information</AlternateText>
31          <Impressions>1</Impressions>
32      </Ad>
33
34      <Ad>
35          <ImageUrl>images/italy.png</ImageUrl>
36          <NavigateUrl>
37             http://www.odci.gov/cia/publications/factbook/geos/it.html
38          </NavigateUrl>
39          <AlternateText>Italy Information</AlternateText>
40          <Impressions>1</Impressions>
41      </Ad>
42
43      <Ad>
44          <ImageUrl>images/spain.png</ImageUrl>
45          <NavigateUrl>
46             http://www.odci.gov/cia/publications/factbook/geos/sp.html
47          </NavigateUrl>
48          <AlternateText>Spain Information</AlternateText>
49          <Impressions>1</Impressions>
50      </Ad>
51
52      <Ad>
53          <ImageUrl>images/latvia.png</ImageUrl>
54          <NavigateUrl>
55             http://www.odci.gov/cia/publications/factbook/geos/lg.html
56          </NavigateUrl>
57          <AlternateText>Latvia Information</AlternateText>
58          <Impressions>1</Impressions>
59      </Ad>
```

Fig. 17.20 AdvertisementFile used in AdRotator example. (Part 2 of 3.)

```
60
61      <Ad>
62          <ImageUrl>images/peru.png</ImageUrl>
63          <NavigateUrl>
64              http://www.odci.gov/cia/publications/factbook/geos/pe.html
65          </NavigateUrl>
66          <AlternateText>Peru Information</AlternateText>
67          <Impressions>1</Impressions>
68      </Ad>
69
70      <Ad>
71          <ImageUrl>images/senegal.png</ImageUrl>
72          <NavigateUrl>
73              http://www.odci.gov/cia/publications/factbook/geos/sg.html
74          </NavigateUrl>
75          <AlternateText>Senegal Information</AlternateText>
76          <Impressions>1</Impressions>
77      </Ad>
78
79      <Ad>
80          <ImageUrl>images/sweden.png</ImageUrl>
81          <NavigateUrl>
82              http://www.odci.gov/cia/publications/factbook/geos/sw.html
83          </NavigateUrl>
84          <AlternateText>Sweden Information</AlternateText>
85          <Impressions>1</Impressions>
86      </Ad>
87
88      <Ad>
89          <ImageUrl>images/thailand.png</ImageUrl>
90          <NavigateUrl>
91              http://www.odci.gov/cia/publications/factbook/geos/th.html
92          </NavigateUrl>
93          <AlternateText>Thailand Information</AlternateText>
94          <Impressions>1</Impressions>
95      </Ad>
96
97      <Ad>
98          <ImageUrl>images/unitedstates.png</ImageUrl>
99          <NavigateUrl>
100             http://www.odci.gov/cia/publications/factbook/geos/us.html
101         </NavigateUrl>
102         <AlternateText>United States Information</AlternateText>
103         <Impressions>1</Impressions>
104     </Ad>
105 </Advertisements>
```

Fig. 17.20 **AdvertisementFile** used in **AdRotator** example. (Part 3 of 3.)

17.5.3 Validation Controls

This section introduces ASP .NET *validation controls* (or *validators*), which determine whether the data in other Web controls are in the proper format. For example, validators could determine whether a user has provided information in a required field, or whether a

ZIP-code field contains exactly five digits. Validators provide a mechanism for validating user input on the client-side. When the HTML for our page is created, the validator is converted to *ECMAScript*[4] that performs the validation. ECMAScript is a scripting language that enhances the functionality and appearance of Web pages. ECMAScript typically is executed on the client-side. However, if the client does not support scripting or scripting is disabled, validation is performed on the server.

The example in this section prompts the user to input a phone number in the form 555–4567 (i.e., three digits, followed by a hyphen and four more digits.) After the user enters a number, validators ensure that the phone-number field is filled and that the number is in the correct format before the program sends the number to the Web server for further processing. Once the phone number is submitted, the Web server responds with an HTML page containing all possible letter combinations that represent the phone number. The letters used for each digit are the letters found on a phone's key pad. For instance, the 5 button displays the letters j, k and l. For the position in the phone number where a 5 appears, we can substitute one of these three letters. Businesses often use this technique to make their phone numbers easy to remember. Figure 17.21 presents the ASPX file.

```
1   <%-- Fig. 17.21: Generator.aspx                          --%>
2   <%-- A Web Form demonstrating the use of validators. --%>
3
4   <%@ Page language="c#" Codebehind="Generator.aspx.cs"
5   AutoEventWireup="false" Inherits="WordGenerator.Generator" %>
6
7   <!DOCTYPE HTML PUBLIC "-//W3C//DTD HTML 4.0 Transitional//EN" >
8
9   <HTML>
10     <HEAD>
11        <title>WebForm1</title>
12        <meta name="GENERATOR"
13           Content="Microsoft Visual Studio 7.0">
14        <meta name="CODE_LANGUAGE" Content="C#">
15        <meta name="vs_defaultClientScript" content="JavaScript">
16        <meta name="vs_targetSchema" content=
17           "http://schemas.microsoft.com/intellisense/ie5">
18     </HEAD>
19
20     <body MS_POSITIONING="GridLayout">
21        <form id="Form1" method="post" runat="server">
22           <asp:Label id="promptLabel" style="Z-INDEX: 101;
23              LEFT: 16px; POSITION: absolute; TOP: 23px"
24              runat="server">
25              Please enter a phone number in the form 555-4567:
26           </asp:Label>
```

Fig. 17.21 Validators used in a Web Form that generates possible letter combinations from a phone number. (Part 1 of 2.)

4. ECMAScript (commonly known as JavaScript) is a scripting standard created by the ECMA (European Computer Manufacturer's Association). Both Netscape's JavaScript and Microsoft's JScript comply with the ECMAScript standard, but each provides additional features beyond the specification. For information on the current ECMAScript standard, visit **www.ecma.ch/ ecma1/stand/ecma-262.htm**.

```
27
28          <asp:RegularExpressionValidator
29              id="phoneNumberValidator" style="Z-INDEX: 106;
30          LEFT: 217px; POSITION: absolute; TOP: 73px"
31              runat="server" ErrorMessage=
32          "The phone number must be in the form 555-4567."
33              ControlToValidate="inputTextBox"
34              ValidationExpression="^\d{3}-\d{4}$">
35          </asp:RegularExpressionValidator>
36
37          <asp:RequiredFieldValidator
38              id="phoneInputValidator" style="Z-INDEX: 105;
39          LEFT: 217px; POSITION: absolute; TOP: 47px"
40              runat="server" ErrorMessage=
41          "Please enter a phone number."
42              ControlToValidate="inputTextBox">
43          </asp:RequiredFieldValidator>
44
45          <asp:TextBox id="outputTextBox" style="Z-INDEX: 104;
46          LEFT: 16px; POSITION: absolute; TOP: 146px"
47              runat="server" Visible="False" TextMode="MultiLine"
48              Height="198px" Width="227px" Font-Bold="True"
49              Font-Names="Courier New">
50          </asp:TextBox>
51
52          <asp:Button id="submitButton" style="Z-INDEX: 103;
53          LEFT: 16px; POSITION: absolute; TOP: 86px"
54              runat="server" Text="Submit">
55          </asp:Button>
56
57          <asp:TextBox id="inputTextBox" style="Z-INDEX: 102;
58          LEFT: 16px; POSITION: absolute; TOP: 52px"
59              runat="server">
60          </asp:TextBox>
61      </form>
62   </body>
63 </HTML>
```

Fig. 17.21 Validators used in a Web Form that generates possible letter combinations from a phone number. (Part 2 of 2.)

The HTML page sent to the client browser accepts a phone number in the form *555–4567* and then lists all the possible letter combinations that can be generated from both the first three digits and the last four digits. This example uses a **RegularExpression-Validator** to match another Web control's content against a regular expression. (The use of regular expressions is introduced in Chapter 12, Strings, Characters and Regular Expressions.) Lines 28–35 create a **RegularExpressionValidator** named **phoneNumberValidator**. Property **ErrorMessage**'s text (lines 31–32) is displayed on the Web Form when the validation fails. Property **ValidationExpression** specifies the regular expression with which to validate the user input (line 34). The input is valid if it matches the regular expression, **^\d{3}-\d{4}$** (i.e., the beginning of the string, followed by 3 digits, a hyphen, four additional digits and the end of the string).

Clicking property **ValidationExpression** in the **Properties** window displays a dialog containing a list of regular expressions for phone numbers, ZIP codes and other common data. However, we write our own regular expression in this example, because the phone number input should not contain an area code. Line 33 associates **inputTextBox** with **phoneNumberValidator** by setting property *ControlToValidate* to **inputTextBox**. This indicates that **phoneNumberValidator** verifies the **inputTextBox**'s contents. If the user inputs text that does not have the correct format and attempts to submit the form, the **ErrorMessage** text is displayed in red.

This example also uses a *RequiredFieldValidator*, which ensures that data has been entered in a specific control. Lines 37–43 define **RequiredFieldValidator phoneInputValidator**, which confirms that **inputTextBox**'s content is not empty. If the user does not input any data in **inputTextBox** and attempts to submit the form, validation fails, and the **ErrorMessage** for this validator is displayed in red. If validation is successful, **outputTextBox** (lines 45–50) displays the words generated from the phone number.

Figure 17.22 is the code-behind file for the ASPX file in Fig. 17.21. Note that this code-behind file does not contain any implementation related to the validators. We say more about this momentarily.

```
1    // Fig. 17.22: Generator.aspx.cs
2    // The code-behind file for a page that
3    // generates words from a phone number.
4
5    using System;
6    using System.Collections;
7    using System.ComponentModel;
8    using System.Data;
9    using System.Drawing;
10   using System.Web;
11   using System.Web.SessionState;
12   using System.Web.UI;
13   using System.Web.UI.WebControls;
14   using System.Web.UI.HtmlControls;
15
16   namespace WordGenerator
17   {
18      // page that computes all combinations of letters for first
19      // three digits and last four digits in phone number
20      public class Generator : System.Web.UI.Page
21      {
22         protected System.Web.UI.WebControls.TextBox
23            outputTextBox;
24         protected System.Web.UI.WebControls.TextBox
25            inputTextBox;
26
27         protected
28            System.Web.UI.WebControls.RegularExpressionValidator
29            phoneNumberValidator;
```

Fig. 17.22 Code-behind file for the word-generator page. (Part 1 of 5.)

```
30      protected
31         System.Web.UI.WebControls.RequiredFieldValidator
32         phoneInputValidator;
33
34      protected System.Web.UI.WebControls.Button submitButton;
35      protected System.Web.UI.WebControls.Label promptLabel;
36
37      private void Page_Load(
38         object sender, System.EventArgs e )
39      {
40         // if page loaded due to a postback
41         if ( IsPostBack )
42         {
43            outputTextBox.Text = "";
44
45            // retrieve number and remove "-"
46            string number = Request.Form[ "inputTextBox" ];
47            number = number.Remove( 3, 1 );
48
49            // generate words for first 3 digits
50            outputTextBox.Text += "Here are the words for\n";
51            outputTextBox.Text +=
52               "the first three digits:\n\n";
53            ComputeWords( number.Substring( 0, 3 ), "" );
54            outputTextBox.Text += "\n";
55
56            // generate words for last 4 digits
57            outputTextBox.Text += "Here are the words for\n";
58            outputTextBox.Text +=
59               "the last four digits:\n\n";
60            ComputeWords( number.Substring( 3 ), "" );
61
62            outputTextBox.Visible = true;
63
64         } // end if
65
66      } // end method Page_Load
67
68      // Visual Studio .NET generated code
69
70      private void ComputeWords(
71         string number, string temporaryWord )
72      {
73         if ( number == "" )
74         {
75            outputTextBox.Text += temporaryWord + "\n";
76            return;
77         }
78
79         int current =
80            Int32.Parse( number.Substring( 0, 1 ) );
81
82         number = number.Remove( 0, 1 );
```

Fig. 17.22 Code-behind file for the word-generator page. (Part 2 of 5.)

```
83
84          switch ( current )
85          {
86              // 0 can be q or z
87              case 0:
88                  ComputeWords( number, temporaryWord + "q" );
89                  ComputeWords( number, temporaryWord + "z" );
90                  break;
91
92              // 1 has no letters associated with it
93              case 1:
94                  ComputeWords( number, temporaryWord + " " );
95                  break;
96
97              // 2 can be a, b or c
98              case 2:
99                  ComputeWords( number, temporaryWord + "a" );
100                 ComputeWords( number, temporaryWord + "b" );
101                 ComputeWords( number, temporaryWord + "c" );
102                 break;
103
104             // 3 can be d, e or f
105             case 3:
106                 ComputeWords( number, temporaryWord + "d" );
107                 ComputeWords( number, temporaryWord + "e" );
108                 ComputeWords( number, temporaryWord + "f" );
109                 break;
110
111             // 4 can be g, h or i
112             case 4:
113                 ComputeWords( number, temporaryWord + "g" );
114                 ComputeWords( number, temporaryWord + "h" );
115                 ComputeWords( number, temporaryWord + "i" );
116                 break;
117
118             // 5 can be j, k or l
119             case 5:
120                 ComputeWords( number, temporaryWord + "j" );
121                 ComputeWords( number, temporaryWord + "k" );
122                 ComputeWords( number, temporaryWord + "l" );
123                 break;
124
125             // 6 can be m, n or o
126             case 6:
127                 ComputeWords( number, temporaryWord + "m" );
128                 ComputeWords( number, temporaryWord + "n" );
129                 ComputeWords( number, temporaryWord + "o" );
130                 break;
131
132             // 7 can be p, r or s
133             case 7:
134                 ComputeWords( number, temporaryWord + "p" );
135                 ComputeWords( number, temporaryWord + "r" );
```

Fig. 17.22 Code-behind file for the word-generator page. (Part 3 of 5.)

```
136                    ComputeWords( number, temporaryWord + "s" );
137                    break;
138
139              // 8 can be t, u or v
140              case 8:
141                    ComputeWords( number, temporaryWord + "t" );
142                    ComputeWords( number, temporaryWord + "u" );
143                    ComputeWords( number, temporaryWord + "v" );
144                    break;
145
146              // 9 can be w, x or y
147              case 9:
148                    ComputeWords( number, temporaryWord + "w" );
149                    ComputeWords( number, temporaryWord + "x" );
150                    ComputeWords( number, temporaryWord + "y" );
151                    break;
152
153           } // end switch
154
155        } // end method ComputeWords
156
157     } // end class Generator
158
159 } // end namespace WordGenerator
```

Fig. 17.22 Code-behind file for the word-generator page. (Part 4 of 5.)

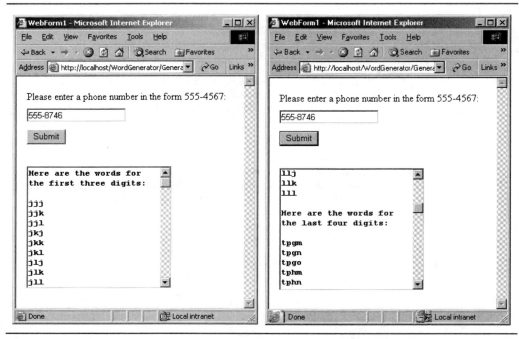

Fig. 17.22 Code-behind file for the word-generator page. (Part 5 of 5.)

ASP .NET developers often design their Web pages such that the current page reloads when the user submits the form to process the input. This practice—known as a *postback*—groups input and processing logic, which makes the ASPX file easier to maintain. In our example, the page provides a text box where users can enter their phone numbers. Once this information has been submitted, the same page reloads, displaying the results below the original text box. One advantage of this is that the user can continue entering phone numbers without having to navigate back to an earlier page. Line 41 uses the **IsPostBack** property of class **Page** to determine whether the page is being loaded due to a postback. The first time that the Web page is requested, **IsPostBack** is **false**. When the postback occurs (due to the user clicking **Submit**), **IsPostBack** is **true**. To prepare the **outputTextBox** for display, its **Text** property is set to an empty string (**""**) in line 43. Line 46 then uses the **Request** object to retrieve **phoneTextBox**'s value from the **Form** array. When data are posted to the Web server, the HTML **form**'s data are accessible to the Web application through the **Request** object's **Form** array. Line 47 removes the hyphen from the phone number string. Method **ComputeWords** is passed a substring containing the first three numbers and an empty **string** (line 53). Line 62 sets the **outputTextBox**'s **Visible** property to **true**.

Method **ComputeWords**, defined in lines 70–155, is a recursive method that generates a list of words from the **string** containing the digits of the phone number, minus the hyphen. The first argument—**number**—contains the digits that are being converted to letters. The first call to method **ComputeWords** (line 53) passes in the first three digits, and the second call (line 60) passes in the last four digits. The second argument, **temporaryWord**, builds up the list that the program displays. Each time this method is called, **number** contains one less character than the previous call, whereas **temporaryWord** contains one more character. Lines 73–77 define the recursion's base case, which occurs when **number** equals the empty string. When this occurs, the **temporaryWord** that has been built up from the previous calls is added to **outputTextBox**, and the method returns.

Let us discuss how **ComputeWords** works when the base case does not evaluate to **true**. On line 79, we declare variable **current** and initialize its value to the first character in **number**. We then remove this character from **number**. The remainder of the method uses a **switch** structure (lines 84–153) to make the correct recursive calls based on the number in **current**. For each digit, we wish to add the appropriate letter to **temporaryWord**. For most of the digits, there are two or three letters that the number in **current** can represent. The keypad button for the number 3, for instance, also represents the letters d, e and f. In this example, we want to exhaust all possible letter combinations, so we make a recursive call to **ComputeWords** for each option (lines 105–109). Each call passes **number** as the first argument (which contains one less digit as a result of the call to method **Remove** on line 82). The second argument contains **temporaryWord**, concatenated with the new letter. Each call adds a letter for the current number until all the numbers have been processed. At this point, we have reached the base case, and **temporaryWord** is appended to **outputTextBox**.

Figure 17.23 shows the HTML sent to the client browser. Notice that lines 25–28 and lines 72–113 contain ECMAScript, which provides the implementation for the validation controls. ASP .NET generates this ECMAScript. The programmer does not need to be able to create or even understand ECMAScript—the functionality defined for the controls in our application is converted to working ECMAScript for us.

```
1   <!-- Fig. 17.23: Generator.html                        -->
2   <!-- The HTML page that is sent to the client browser. -->
3
4   <!DOCTYPE HTML PUBLIC "-//W3C//DTD HTML 4.0 Transitional//EN" >
5   <HTML>
6      <HEAD>
7         <title>WebForm1</title>
8         <meta name="GENERATOR"
9            content="Microsoft Visual Studio 7.0">
10        <meta name="CODE_LANGUAGE" content="C#" >
11        <meta name="vs_defaultClientScript"
12           content="JavaScript">
13        <meta name="vs_targetSchema"
14           content="http://schemas.microsoft.com/intellisense/ie5">
15     </HEAD>
16
17     <body MS_POSITIONING="GridLayout">
18
19        <form name="Form1" method="post"
20           action="Generator.aspx" language="javascript"
21           onsubmit="ValidatorOnSubmit();" id="FORM1">
22           <input type="hidden" name="__VIEWSTATE"
23              value="dDwxMjgyMzM3ozs+" />
24
```

Fig. 17.23 HTML and ECMAScript sent to the client browser. (Part 1 of 3.)

```
25              <script language="javascript"
26                src=
27              "/aspnet_client/system_web/1_0_3215_11/WebUIValidation.js">
28              </script>
29
30              <span id="phoneNumberValidator"
31                controltovalidate="inputTextBox"
32                errormessage=
33                  "The phone number must be in the form 555-4567."
34                evaluationfunction=
35                  "RegularExpressionValidatorEvaluateIsValid"
36                validationexpression="^\d{3}-\d{4}$"
37                style="color:Red;Z-INDEX:106;LEFT:217px;
38                  POSITION:absolute;TOP:73px;visibility:hidden;">
39                  The phone number must be in the form 555-4567.
40              </span>
41
42              <input name="inputTextBox" type="text"
43                id="inputTextBox"
44                style="Z-INDEX: 102; LEFT: 16px;
45                POSITION: absolute; TOP: 52px" />
46
47              <input type="submit" name="submitButton"
48                value="Submit"
49                onclick= "if ( " +
50                  "typeof(Page_ClientValidate) == 'function') " +
51                  "Page_ClientValidate(); " language="javascript"
52                  id="submitButton" style="Z-INDEX: 103;
53                LEFT: 16px;
54                POSITION: absolute;
55                TOP: 86px" />
56
57              <span id="phoneInputValidator"
58                controltovalidate="inputTextBox"
59                errormessage="Please enter a phone number."
60                evaluationfunction=
61                  "RequiredFieldValidatorEvaluateIsValid"
62                initialvalue="" style="color:Red;Z-INDEX:105;
63                  LEFT:217px;POSITION:absolute;TOP:47px;
64                  visibility:hidden;">Please enter a phone number.
65              </span>
66
67              <span id="promptLabel" style="Z-INDEX: 101;
68                LEFT: 16px; POSITION: absolute; TOP: 23px">
69                Please enter a phone number in the form 555-4567:
70              </span>
71
72              <script language="javascript">
73              <!--
74                var Page_Validators = new Array(
75                  document.all["phoneNumberValidator"],
76                  document.all["phoneInputValidator"] );
77              // -->
```

Fig. 17.23 HTML and ECMAScript sent to the client browser. (Part 2 of 3.)

```
78         </script>
79
80         <script language="javascript">
81         <!--
82             var Page_ValidationActive = false;
83
84             if (
85                 typeof(clientInformation) != "undefined" &&
86                 clientInformation.appName.indexOf("Explorer")
87                 != -1 ) {
88
89                 if ( typeof(Page_ValidationVer) == "undefined" )
90                     alert(
91                         "Unable to find script library " +
92                         "'/aspnet_client/system_web/'"+
93                         "'1_0_3215_11/WebUIValidation.js'. " +
94                         "Try placing this file manually, or " +
95                         "reinstall by running 'aspnet_regiis -c'.");
96                 else if ( Page_ValidationVer != "125" )
97                     alert(
98                         "This page uses an incorrect version " +
99                         "of WebUIValidation.js. The page " +
100                        "expects version 125. " +
101                        "The script library is " +
102                        Page_ValidationVer + ".");
103                else
104                    ValidatorOnLoad();
105            }
106
107            function ValidatorOnSubmit() {
108                if (Page_ValidationActive) {
109                    ValidatorCommonOnSubmit();
110                }
111            }
112        // -->
113        </script>
114    </form>
115    </body>
116 </HTML>
```

Fig. 17.23 HTML and ECMAScript sent to the client browser. (Part 3 of 3.)

In earlier ASPX files, we explicitly set attribute **EnableViewState** to **false**. This attribute determines whether a Web control's properties persist (i.e., is retained) when a postback occurs. By default, this attribute is **true**, which indicates that control values persist. A **hidden** input in the HTML document (line 22–23) stores the properties of the controls on this page between client requests. This element always is named **__VIEWSTATE** and stores the controls' properties as encoded data.

Performance Tip 17.2

*The setting of **EnabledViewState** to **false** reduces the amount of data passed to the Web server.*

17.6 Session Tracking

Originally, critics accused the Internet and e-businesses of failing to provide the customized services typically experienced in brick-and-mortar stores. To address this problem, e-businesses began to establish mechanisms by which they could personalize users' browsing experiences, tailoring content to individual users while enabling them to bypass irrelevant information. Businesses achieve this level of service by tracking each customer's movement through the Internet and combining the collected data with information that the consumer provides, including billing information, personal preferences, interests and hobbies.

Personalization makes it possible for e-businesses to communicate effectively with their customers and improves users' ability to locate desired products and services. Companies that provide content of particular interest to users can establish relationships with customers and build on those relationships over time. Furthermore, by targeting consumers with personal offers, advertisements, promotions and services, e-businesses create customer loyalty. At Web sites such as **MSN.com** and **CNN.com**, sophisticated technology allows visitors to customize home pages to suit their individual needs and preferences. Similarly, online shopping sites often store personal information for customers and target them with notifications and special offers tailored to their interests. Such services can create customer bases that visit sites more frequently and make purchases from those sites more regularly.

A trade-off exists, however, between personalized e-business service and *privacy protection*. Whereas some consumers embrace the idea of tailored content, others fear the release of information that they provide to e-businesses or that is collected about them by tracking technologies will have adverse consequences on their lives. Consumers and privacy advocates ask: What if the e-businesses to which we give personal data sell or give that information to other organizations without our knowledge? What if we do not want our actions on the Internet—a supposedly anonymous medium—to be tracked and recorded by unknown parties? What if unauthorized parties gain access to sensitive private data, such as credit-card numbers or medical history? All of these are questions that must be debated and addressed by consumers, e-businesses and lawmakers alike.

To provide personalized services to consumers, e-businesses must be able to recognize specific clients when they request information from a site. As we have discussed, HTTP enables the request/response system on which the Web operates. Unfortunately, HTTP is a stateless protocol—it does not support persistent connections that would enable Web servers to maintain state information for particular clients. This means that Web servers have no capacity to determine whether a request comes from a particular client or whether the same or different clients generate a series of requests. To circumvent this problem, sites such as **MSN.com** and **CNN.com** provide mechanisms by which they identify individual clients. A *session ID* represents a unique client on the Internet. If the client leaves a site and then returns later, the client will be recognized as the same user. To help the server distinguish among clients, each client must identify itself to the server. The tracking of individual clients, known as *session tracking*, can be achieved in one of a number of ways. One popular technique uses cookies (Section 17.6.1), whereas another employs .NET's **HttpSessionState** object (Section 17.6.2). Additional session-tracking techniques include the use of hidden input form elements and URL rewriting. Using hidden form elements, the Web Form writes its session-tracking data into a **form** in the Web page that it returns to the client in response to a prior request. When the user submits the form in the new Web page, all the form data, including the hidden fields, are sent to the form handler on the Web server. When a Web site employs URL rewriting, the Web Form embeds session-tracking information directly in the URLs of hyperlinks that the user clicks to send subsequent requests to the Web server.

The reader should note that, in previous examples, we set the Web Form's **EnableSessionState** property to **false**. However, because we wish to use session tracking in the following examples, we leave this property in its default mode, which is **true**.

17.6.1 Cookies

A popular way to customize Web pages for particular users is via *cookies*. A cookie is a text file that a Web site stores on an individual's computer to enable the site to track that individual's actions and preferences. The first time a user visits the Web site, the user's computer might receive a cookie that contains a unique identifier for that user. This cookie is reactivated each subsequent time the user visits that site. The Web site uses this cookie to identify the user and to store information, such as the user's zip code or other data that might facilitate the distribution of user-specific content. The collected information is intended to be an anonymous record for personalizing the user's future visits to the site. Cookies in a shopping application might store unique identifiers for users. When a user adds items to an online shopping cart or performs another task resulting in a request to the Web server, the server receives a cookie containing the user's unique identifier. The server then uses the unique identifier to locate the user's shopping cart and perform any necessary processing.

In addition to identifying users, cookies also can indicate a client's preferences. When a Web Form receives a communication from a client, the Web Form could examine the cookie(s) it sent to the client during previous communications, identify the client's preferences and immediately display products that are of interest to the client.

Every HTTP-based interaction between a client and a server includes a header that contains information either about the request (when the communication is from the client to the server) or about the response (when the communication is from the server to the client). When a Web Form receives a request, the header includes information such as the request type (e.g., **GET**) and any cookies that the server has stored on the client machine. When the server formulates its response, the header information includes any cookies the server wants to store on the client computer, as well as information such as the MIME type of the response.

If the Web server does not set an *expiration date* for a cookie, the Web browser maintains the cookie for the duration of the browsing session (which usually ends when the user closes the Web browser). Otherwise, the Web browser maintains the cookie until the expiration date. The expiration date of a cookie can be set using the cookie's **Expires** property. When the browser requests a resource from a Web server, cookies previously sent to the client by that Web server are returned to the Web server as part of the request. Cookies are deleted when they expire.

The next Web application demonstrates the use of cookies. The example contains two pages. In the first page (Fig. 17.24 and Fig. 17.25), users select their favorite programming language from a group of radio buttons, then submit the HTML **form** to the Web server for processing. The Web server responds by creating a cookie that stores a record of the chosen language, as well as the ISBN number for a book on that topic. The server then returns an HTML document to the browser, allowing the user either to select another programming language or to view the second page in the application (Fig. 17.26 and Fig. 17.27), which lists recommended books pertaining to the programming language that

the user selected previously. When the user clicks the hyperlink, the cookies previously
stored on the client are read and used to form the list of book recommendations.

```
1    <%-- Fig. 17.24: OptionsPage.aspx                        --%>
2    <%-- This ASPX page allows the user to choose a language. --%>
3
4    <%@ Page language="c#" Codebehind="OptionsPage.aspx.cs"
5       AutoEventWireup="false"
6       Inherits="Cookies.OptionsPage" %>
7
8    <!DOCTYPE HTML PUBLIC "-//W3C//DTD HTML 4.0 Transitional//EN" >
9
10   <HTML>
11      <HEAD>
12         <title>RecommendationsPage</title>
13            <meta name="GENERATOR" Content=
14               "Microsoft Visual Studio 7.0">
15            <meta name="CODE_LANGUAGE" Content="C#">
16            <meta name="vs_defaultClientScript" content=
17               "JavaScript">
18            <meta name="vs_targetSchema" content=
19               "http://schemas.microsoft.com/intellisense/ie5">
20      </HEAD>
21
22      <body>
23         <form id="RecommendationsPage" method="post"
24            runat="server">
25         <P>
26            <asp:Label id="promptLabel" runat="server"
27               Font-Bold="True">Select a programming language:
28            </asp:Label>
29
30            <asp:Label id="welcomeLabel" runat="server"
31               Font-Bold="True" Visible="False">
32               Welcome to Cookies! You selected
33            </asp:Label>
34         </P>
35
36         <P>
37            <asp:RadioButtonList id="languageList" runat=
38               "server">
39            <asp:ListItem Value="C#">C#</asp:ListItem>
40
41            <asp:ListItem Value="C++">C++</asp:ListItem>
42
43            <asp:ListItem Value="C">C</asp:ListItem>
44
45            <asp:ListItem Value="Python">Python
46            </asp:ListItem>
47
48            <asp:ListItem Value="Visual Basic .NET">
49               Visual Basic .NET
50            </asp:ListItem>
```

Fig. 17.24 ASPX file that presents a list of programming languages. (Part 1 of 2.)

```
51                    </asp:RadioButtonList>
52                </P>
53
54                <P>
55                    <asp:Button id="submitButton" runat="server" Text=
56                        "Submit">
57                    </asp:Button>
58                </P>
59
60                <P>
61                    <asp:HyperLink id="languageLink" runat="server"
62                        NavigateUrl="OptionsPage.aspx" Visible="False">
63                        Click here to choose another language.
64                    </asp:HyperLink>
65                </P>
66
67                <P>
68                    <asp:HyperLink id="recommendationsLink" runat=
69                        "server" NavigateUrl="RecommendationsPage.aspx"
70                        Visible="False">Click here to get book recommendations.
71                    </asp:HyperLink>
72                </P>
73            </form>
74        </body>
75    </HTML>
```

Fig. 17.24 ASPX file that presents a list of programming languages. (Part 2 of 2.)

The ASPX file in Fig. 17.24 contains five radio buttons (lines 39–50) with values **C#**, **C++**, **C**, **Python** and **Visual Basic .NET**. A programmer sets these values by clicking the **Items** property in the **Properties** window, then adding items via the **List Item Collection Editor**. This process is similar to that of customizing a **ListBox** in a Windows application. The user selects a programming language by clicking one of the radio buttons. The page also contains a **Submit** button, which, when clicked, creates a cookie that contains a record of the selected language. Once created, this cookie is added to the HTTP response header, and a postback occurs. Each time the user chooses a language and clicks **Submit**, a cookie is written to the client.

When the postback occurs, certain components are hidden, whereas others are displayed. Toward the bottom of the page, two hyperlinks are displayed: One that requests the current page (lines 61–64) and one that requests **Recommendations.aspx** (lines 68–71). Notice that clicking the first hyperlink (the one that requests the current page) does not cause a postback to occur. The file **OptionsPage.aspx** is specified in the **NavigateUrl** property of the hyperlink. When the hyperlink is clicked, this page is requested as a completely new request to allow the user to select a new programming language.

Figure 17.25 presents the code-behind file. Line 35 defines **books** as a **Hashtable** (namespace **System.Collections**), which is a data structure that stores *key-value pairs* (we covered **Hashtable** briefly in Chapter 12, Strings, Characters and Regular Expressions). The program uses the key to store and retrieve the associated value in the **Hashtable**. In this example, the keys are **string**s that contain the programming language names, and the values are **string**s that contain the ISBN numbers for the recommended books. Class **Hashtable** provides method **Add**, which takes as arguments a key and a value. The value for a specific **Hashtable** entry can be obtained by indexing the hash table with that value's key. For instance,

HashtableName[*keyName*];

returns the value from the key-value pair in which *keyName* is the key. An example of this is shown in line 92—**books[language]** returns the value that corresponds to the key contained in **language**. Class **Hashtable** is discussed in detail in Chapter 20, Data Structures and Collections.

```
1   // Fig. 17.25: OptionPage.aspx.cs
2   // A listing of program languages that the user can choose from.
3
4   using System;
5   using System.Collections;
6   using System.ComponentModel;
7   using System.Data;
8   using System.Drawing;
9   using System.Web;
10  using System.Web.SessionState;
11  using System.Web.UI;
12  using System.Web.UI.WebControls;
13  using System.Web.UI.HtmlControls;
14
15  namespace Cookies
16  {
17     // page contains language options in a RadioButtonList,
18     // will add a cookie to store their choice
19     public class OptionsPage : System.Web.UI.Page
20     {
21        protected System.Web.UI.WebControls.Label promptLabel;
22        protected System.Web.UI.WebControls.Label welcomeLabel;
23
24        protected System.Web.UI.WebControls.RadioButtonList
25           languageList;
26
27        protected System.Web.UI.WebControls.HyperLink
28           languageLink;
29        protected System.Web.UI.WebControls.HyperLink
30           recommendationsLink;
31
32        protected System.Web.UI.WebControls.Button
33           submitButton;
34
35        protected Hashtable books = new Hashtable();
36
37        // event handler for Load event
38        private void Page_Load(
39           object sender, System.EventArgs e )
40        {
```

Fig. 17.25 Code-behind file that writes cookies to the client. (Part 1 of 3.)

```
41              if ( IsPostBack )
42              {
43                  // if postback has occurred, user has submitted
44                  // information, so display welcome message
45                  // and appropriate hyperlinks
46                  welcomeLabel.Visible = true;
47                  languageLink.Visible = true;
48                  recommendationsLink.Visible = true;
49
50                  // hide option information
51                  submitButton.Visible = false;
52                  promptLabel.Visible = false;
53                  languageList.Visible = false;
54
55                  // notify user of what they have chosen
56                  if ( languageList.SelectedItem != null )
57                      welcomeLabel.Text +=
58                          languageList.SelectedItem.ToString() + ".";
59                  else
60                      welcomeLabel.Text += "no language.";
61
62              } // end if
63
64          } // end method Page_Load
65
66          override protected void OnInit( EventArgs e )
67          {
68              // add values to Hashtable
69              books.Add( "C#", "0-13-062221-4" );
70              books.Add( "C++", "0-13-089571-7" );
71              books.Add( "C", "0-13-089572-5" );
72              books.Add( "Python", "0-13-092361-3" );
73              books.Add( "Visual Basic .NET", "0-13-456955-5" );
74
75              InitializeComponent();
76              base.OnInit( e );
77          }
78
79          // Visual Studio .NET generated code
80
81          // when user clicks Submit button
82          // create cookie to store user's choice
83          private void submitButton_Click(
84              object sender, System.EventArgs e )
85          {
86              // if choice was made by user
87              if ( languageList.SelectedItem != null )
88              {
89                  string language =
90                      languageList.SelectedItem.ToString();
91
92                  string ISBN = books[ language ].ToString();
93
```

Fig. 17.25 Code-behind file that writes cookies to the client. (Part 2 of 3.)

```
94              // create cookie, name-value pair is
95              // language chosen and ISBN number from Hashtable
96              HttpCookie cookie = new HttpCookie(
97                 language, ISBN );
98
99              // add cookie to response,
100             // thus placing it on user's machine
101             Response.Cookies.Add( cookie );
102
103          } // end if
104
105       } // end method submitButton_Click
106
107    } // end class OptionsPage
108
109 } // end namespace Cookies
```

Fig. 17.25 Code-behind file that writes cookies to the client. (Part 3 of 3.)

As mentioned earlier, clicking the **Submit** button causes a postback to occur. As a result, the condition in the **if** structure of **Page_Load** (line 41) evaluates to **true**, and lines 46–60 execute. Line 56 determines whether the user selected a language. If so, that language is displayed in **welcomeLabel** (lines 57–58). Otherwise, text indicating that a language was not selected is displayed in **welcomeLabel** (line 60). The two hyperlinks are made visible in lines 47–48.

A new cookie object (of type *HttpCookie*) is created to store the **language** and its corresponding **ISBN** number (lines 96–97). This cookie then is **Add**ed to the *Cookies* collection sent as part of the HTTP response header (line 101).

```
1   <%-- Fig. 17.26: RecommendationsPage.aspx --%>
2   <%-- This page shows recommendations     --%>
3   <%-- retrieved from the Hashtable.        --%>
4
5   <%@ Page language="c#" Codebehind="RecommendationsPage.aspx.cs"
6       AutoEventWireup="false"
7       Inherits="Cookies.RecommendationsPage" %>
8
9   <!DOCTYPE HTML PUBLIC "-//W3C//DTD HTML 4.0 Transitional//EN" >
10
11  <HTML>
12     <HEAD>
13        <title>WebForm1</title>
14        <meta name="GENERATOR" Content=
15           "Microsoft Visual Studio 7.0">
16        <meta name="CODE_LANGUAGE" Content="C#">
17        <meta name="vs_defaultClientScript" content="JavaScript">
18        <meta name="vs_targetSchema" content=
19           "http://schemas.microsoft.com/intellisense/ie5">
20     </HEAD>
21
22     <body MS_POSITIONING="GridLayout">
23
24        <form id="Form1" method="post" runat="server">
25
26           <asp:Label id="recommendationsLabel"
27              style="Z-INDEX: 101; LEFT: 21px; POSITION: absolute;
28              TOP: 25px" runat="server" Font-Bold="True"
29              Font-Size="X-Large">Recommendations
30           </asp:Label>
31
32           <asp:ListBox id="booksListBox" style="Z-INDEX: 102;
33              LEFT: 21px; POSITION: absolute; TOP: 82px" runat=
34              "server" Width="383px" Height="91px">
35           </asp:ListBox>
36        </form>
37     </body>
38  </HTML>
```

Fig. 17.26 ASPX page that displays book information.

RecommendationsPage.aspx contains a label (lines 26–30) and a list box (lines 32–35). The label displays the text **Recommendations** if the user has selected one or more languages; otherwise, it displays **No Recommendations**. The list box displays the recommendations created by the code-behind file, which is shown in Fig. 17.27.

```
1    // Fig. 17.27: RecommendationsPage.aspx.cs
2    // Reading cookie data from the client.
3
4    using System;
5    using System.Collections;
6    using System.ComponentModel;
7    using System.Data;
8    using System.Drawing;
9    using System.Web;
10   using System.Web.SessionState;
11   using System.Web.UI;
12   using System.Web.UI.WebControls;
13   using System.Web.UI.HtmlControls;
14
15   namespace Cookies
16   {
17      // page displays cookie information and recommendations
18      public class RecommendationsPage : System.Web.UI.Page
19      {
20         protected System.Web.UI.WebControls.ListBox booksListBox;
21         protected System.Web.UI.WebControls.Label
22            recommendationsLabel;
23
24         // Visual Studio .NET generated code
25
26         override protected void OnInit( EventArgs e )
27         {
28            InitializeComponent();
29            base.OnInit( e );
30
31            // retrieve client's cookies
32            HttpCookieCollection cookies = Request.Cookies;
33
34            // if there are cookies other than the ID cookie,
35            // list appropriate books and ISBN numbers
36            if ( cookies != null && cookies.Count != 1 )
37               for ( int i = 1; i < cookies.Count; i++ )
38                  booksListBox.Items.Add(
39                     cookies[ i ].Name +
40                     " How to Program. ISBN#: " +
41                     cookies[ i ].Value );
42
43            // if no cookies besides ID, no options were
44            // chosen, so no recommendations made
45            else
46            {
47               recommendationsLabel.Text = "No Recommendations.";
```

Fig. 17.27 Cookies being read from a client in an ASP .NET application. (Part 1 of 2.)

```
48                        booksListBox.Items.Clear();
49                        booksListBox.Visible = false;
50                  }
51
52            } // end method OnInit
53
54        } // end class RecommendationsPage
55
56  } // end namespace Cookies
```

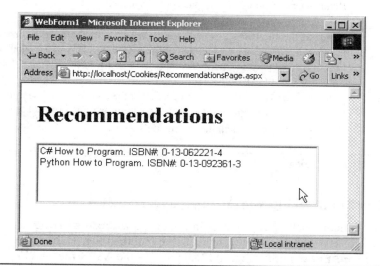

Fig. 17.27 Cookies being read from a client in an ASP .NET application. (Part 2 of 2.)

Method **OnInit** (lines 26–52) retrieves the cookies from the client using the **Request** object's **Cookies** property (line 32). This returns a collection of type **Http-CookieCollection** that contains cookies that have been written to the client previously. Cookies can be read by an application only if they were created in the domain in which that application is running—a Web server can never access cookies created outside the domain associated with that server. For example, a cookie created by a Web server in the **deitel.com** domain cannot be downloaded by a Web server in the **bug2bug.com** domain.

Line 36 determines whether at least two cookies exist. ASP .NET always adds a cookie named **ASP.NET_SessionId** to the response, so line 36 ensures that there is at least one cookie besides the **ASP.NET_SessionId** cookie. Lines 38–41 add the information in the other cookie(s) to our list box. The **for** structure iterates through all the cookies except for the first one (the **ASP.NET_SessionID** cookie). The application retrieves the name and value of each cookie by using **i**, the control variable in our **for** structure, to determine the current value in our cookie collection. The **Name** and **Value** properties of class **Http-Cookie** which contain the language and corresponding ISBN, respectively, are concatenated with **" How to Program. ISBN# "** and added to the **ListBox**. The list box displays a maximum of five books. Lines 47–49 execute if no language was selected. We summarize some commonly used **HttpCookie** properties in Fig. 17.28.

Properties	Description
Domain	Returns a **string** that contains the cookie's domain (i.e., the domain of the Web server from which the cookie was downloaded). This determines which Web servers can receive the cookie. By default, cookies are sent to the Web server that originally sent the cookie to the client.
Expires	Returns a **DateTime** object indicating when the browser can delete the cookie.
Name	Returns a **string** containing the cookie's name.
Path	Returns a **string** containing the URL prefix for the cookie. Cookies can be "targeted" to specific URLs that include directories on the Web server, enabling the programmer to specify the location of the cookie. By default, a cookie is returned to services that operates in the same directory as the service that sent the cookie or a subdirectory of that directory.
Secure	Returns a **bool**ean value indicating whether the cookie should be transmitted using a secure protocol. A value of **true** causes a secure protocol to be used.
Value	Returns a **string** containing the cookie's value.

Fig. 17.28 **HttpCookie** properties.

17.6.2 Session Tracking with **HttpSessionState**

C# provides session-tracking capabilities in the FCL's **HttpSessionState** class. To demonstrate basic session-tracking techniques, we modified Fig. 17.27 so that it employs **HttpSessionState** objects. Figure 17.29 presents the ASPX file, and Fig. 17.30 presents the code-behind file. The ASPX file is similar to that presented in Fig. 17.24.

```
1   <%-- Fig. 17.29: OptionsPage.aspx                    --%>
2   <%-- Page that presents a list of language options. --%>
3
4   <%@ Page language="c#" Codebehind="OptionsPage.aspx.cs"
5      AutoEventWireup="false" Inherits=
6      "Sessions.OptionsPage" %>
7
8   <!DOCTYPE HTML PUBLIC "-//W3C//DTD HTML 4.0 Transitional//EN" >
9   <HTML>
10     <HEAD>
11        <title>RecommendationsPage</title>
12        <meta name="GENERATOR" Content=
13           "Microsoft Visual Studio 7.0">
14        <meta name="CODE_LANGUAGE" Content="C#">
15        <meta name="vs_defaultClientScript" content="JavaScript">
16        <meta name="vs_targetSchema" content=
17           "http://schemas.microsoft.com/intellisense/ie5">
18     </HEAD>
19
```

Fig. 17.29 Options supplied on an ASPX page. (Part 1 of 3.)

```
20     <body>
21        <form id="RecommendationsPage" method="post"
22          runat="server">
23          <P>
24              <asp:Label id="promptLabel" runat="server"
25                Font-Bold="True">Select a programming language:
26              </asp:Label>
27
28              <asp:Label id="welcomeLabel" runat="server"
29                Font-Bold="True" Visible="False">
30                Welcome to Cookies! You selected
31              </asp:Label>
32          </P>
33
34          <P>
35              <asp:RadioButtonList id="languageList" runat=
36                "server">
37
38                  <asp:ListItem Value="C#">C#</asp:ListItem>
39
40                  <asp:ListItem Value="C++">C++</asp:ListItem>
41
42                  <asp:ListItem Value="C">C</asp:ListItem>
43
44                  <asp:ListItem Value="Python">Python
45                  </asp:ListItem>
46
47                  <asp:ListItem Value="Visual Basic .NET">
48                     Visual Basic .NET
49                  </asp:ListItem>
50              </asp:RadioButtonList>
51          </P>
52
53          <P>
54              <asp:Button id="submitButton" runat="server"
55                Text="Submit">
56              </asp:Button>
57          </P>
58
59          <P>
60              <asp:Label id="idLabel" runat="server">
61              </asp:Label>
62          </P>
63
64          <P>
65              <asp:Label id="timeoutLabel" runat="server">
66              </asp:Label>
67          </P>
68
69          <P>
70              <asp:Label id="newSessionLabel" runat="server">
71              </asp:Label>
72          </P>
```

Fig. 17.29 Options supplied on an ASPX page. (Part 2 of 3.)

```
73
74                <P>
75                    <asp:HyperLink id="languageLink" runat="server"
76                        NavigateUrl="OptionsPage.aspx" Visible="False">
77                        Click here to choose another language.
78                    </asp:HyperLink>
79                </P>
80
81                <P>
82                    <asp:HyperLink id="recommendationsLink" runat=
83                        "server" NavigateUrl="RecommendationsPage.aspx"
84                        Visible="False">
85                        Click here to get book recommendations.
86                    </asp:HyperLink>
87                </P>
88            </form>
89        </body>
90    </HTML>
```

Fig. 17.29 Options supplied on an ASPX page. (Part 3 of 3.)

Every Web Form includes an **HttpSessionState** object, which is accessible through property **Session** of class **Page**. Throughout this section, we use property **Session** to manipulate our page's **HttpSessionState** object. When the Web page is requested, an **HttpSessionState** object is created and assigned to the **Page**'s **Session** property. We often refer to property **Session** as the **Session** object. When the user presses **Submit**, **submitButton_Click** is invoked in the code-behind file (Fig. 17.30). Method **submitButton_Click** adds a key-value pair to our **Session** object specifying the language chosen and the ISBN number for a book on that language. Next, a postback occurs. Each time the user clicks **Submit**, **submitButton_Click** adds a new language/ISBN pair to the **HttpSessionState** object. Because much of this example is similar to the last example, we concentrate on the new features.

Software Engineering Observation 17.1

*A Web Form must not use instance variables to maintain client state information, because clients accessing that Web Form in parallel might overwrite the shared instance variables. Web Forms should maintain client state information in **HttpSessionState** objects, because such objects are specific to each client.*

```
1    // Fig. 17.30: OptionsPage.aspx.cs
2    // A listing of programming languages,
3    // choice is stored in page's Session object.
4
5    using System;
6    using System.Collections;
7    using System.ComponentModel;
8    using System.Data;
9    using System.Drawing;
```

Fig. 17.30 Sessions are created for each user in an ASP .NET Web application. (Part 1 of 4.)

```
10   using System.Web;
11   using System.Web.SessionState;
12   using System.Web.UI;
13   using System.Web.UI.WebControls;
14   using System.Web.UI.HtmlControls;
15
16   namespace Sessions
17   {
18      // page contains language options in a RadioButtonList
19      // will add cookie to store user's choice
20      public class OptionsPage : System.Web.UI.Page
21      {
22         protected System.Web.UI.WebControls.Label promptLabel;
23         protected System.Web.UI.WebControls.Label welcomeLabel;
24         protected System.Web.UI.WebControls.Label idLabel;
25         protected System.Web.UI.WebControls.Label timeoutLabel;
26
27         protected System.Web.UI.WebControls.HyperLink
28            languageLink;
29         protected System.Web.UI.WebControls.HyperLink
30            recommendationsLink;
31
32         protected System.Web.UI.WebControls.RadioButtonList
33            languageList;
34         protected System.Web.UI.WebControls.Button submitButton;
35
36         private Hashtable books = new Hashtable();
37
38         // event handler for Load event
39         private void Page_Load(
40            object sender, System.EventArgs e )
41         {
42            // if page is loaded due to postback, load session
43            // information, hide language options from user
44            if ( IsPostBack )
45            {
46               // display components that contain session information
47               welcomeLabel.Visible = true;
48               languageLink.Visible = true;
49               recommendationsLink.Visible = true;
50
51               // hide components
52               submitButton.Visible = false;
53               promptLabel.Visible = false;
54               languageList.Visible = false;
55
56               // set labels to display Session information
57               if ( languageList.SelectedItem != null )
58                  welcomeLabel.Text +=
59                     languageList.SelectedItem.ToString() + ".";
60               else
61                  welcomeLabel.Text += "no language.";
```

Fig. 17.30 Sessions are created for each user in an ASP .NET Web application. (Part 2 of 4.)

```
62
63                    idLabel.Text += "Your unique session ID is: " +
64                        Session.SessionID;
65
66                    timeoutLabel.Text += "Timeout: " + Session.Timeout +
67                        " minutes";
68
69               } // end if
70
71          } // end method Page_Load
72
73          override protected void OnInit( EventArgs e )
74          {
75             // add values to Hashtable
76             books.Add( "C#", "0-13-062221-4" );
77             books.Add( "C++", "0-13-089571-7" );
78             books.Add( "C", "0-13-089572-5" );
79             books.Add( "Python", "0-13-092361-3" );
80             books.Add( "Visual Basic .NET", "0-13-456955-5" );
81
82             InitializeComponent();
83             base.OnInit( e );
84          }
85
86          // Visual Studio .NET generated code
87
88          // when user clicks Submit button,
89          // store user's choice in session object
90          private void submitButton_Click(
91             object sender, System.EventArgs e )
92          {
93             if ( languageList.SelectedItem != null )
94             {
95                string language =
96                    languageList.SelectedItem.ToString();
97                string ISBN = books[ language ].ToString();
98
99                // store in session object as name-value pair
100               // name is language chosen, value is
101               // ISBN number for corresponding book
102               Session.Add( language, ISBN );
103
104            } // end if
105
106         } // end method submitButton_Click
107
108      } // end class OptionsPage
109
110  } // end namespace Sessions
```

Fig. 17.30 Sessions are created for each user in an ASP .NET Web application. (Part 3 of 4.)

Fig. 17.30 Sessions are created for each user in an ASP .NET Web application. (Part 4 of 4.)

Like a cookie, an **HttpSessionState** object can store name—value pairs. In session terminology, these are called *session items*, and they are placed into an **HttpSession-State** object by calling method **Add**. Line 102 calls **Add** to place the language and its corresponding recommended book's ISBN number into the **HttpSessionState** object. One of the primary benefits of using **HttpSessionState** objects (rather than cookies) is that **HttpSessionState** objects can store any type of object (not just **string**s) as an attribute value. This provides C# programmers with increased flexibility in determining the type of state information they wish to maintain for their clients. If the application calls method **Add** to add an attribute that has the same name as an attribute previously stored in a session, the object associated with that attribute is replaced.

After the values are added to the **HttpSessionState** object, the application handles the postback event (lines 44–70) in method **Page_Load**. Here, we retrieve information about the current client's session from the **Session** object's properties and display this information in the Web page. The ASP .NET application contains information about the **HttpSessionState** object for the current client. Property *SessionID* (lines 63–64) contains the *session's unique ID*. The first time a client connects to the Web server, a unique session ID is created for that client. When the client makes additional requests, the client's session ID is compared with the session IDs stored in the Web server's memory. Property *Timeout* (line 66) specifies the maximum amount of time that an **HttpSessionState** object can be inactive before it is discarded. Figure 17.31 list some common **HttpSessionState** properties.

As in the cookies example, this application provides a link to **RecommendationsPage.aspx** (Fig. 17.32), which displays a list of book recommendations on the basis of the user's language selections. Lines 30–33 define a **ListBox** Web control that is used to present the recommendations to the user. Figure 17.33 presents the code-behind file for this ASPX file.

Properties	Description
Count	Specifies the number of key-value pairs in the **Session** object.
IsNewSession	Indicates whether this is a new session (i.e., whether the session was created when this page was loaded).
IsReadOnly	Indicates whether the **Session** object is read-only.
Keys	Returns a collection containing the **Session** object's keys.
SessionID	Returns the session's unique ID.
Timeout	Specifies the maximum number of minutes during which a session can be inactive (i.e., no requests are made) before the session expires. By default, this property is set to 20 minutes.

Fig. 17.31 **HttpSessionState** properties.

```
1   <%-- Fig. 17.32: RecommendationsPage.aspx --%>
2   <%-- Read the user's session data.        --%>
3
4   <%@ Page language="c#" Codebehind="RecommendationsPage.aspx.cs"
5       AutoEventWireup="false"
6       Inherits="Sessions.RecommendationsPage" %>
7
8   <!DOCTYPE HTML PUBLIC "-//W3C//DTD HTML 4.0 Transitional//EN" >
9
10  <HTML>
11      <HEAD>
12          <title>WebForm1</title>
13              <meta name="GENERATOR" Content=
14                  "Microsoft Visual Studio 7.0">
```

Fig. 17.32 Session information displayed in a **ListBox**. (Part 1 of 2.)

```
15          <meta name="CODE_LANGUAGE" Content="C#">
16          <meta name="vs_defaultClientScript" content=
17             "JavaScript">
18          <meta name="vs_targetSchema" content=
19             "http://schemas.microsoft.com/intellisense/ie5">
20       </HEAD>
21
22       <body MS_POSITIONING="GridLayout">
23          <form id="Form1" method="post" runat="server">
24             <asp:Label id="recommendationsLabel"
25                style="Z-INDEX: 101; LEFT: 21px; POSITION: absolute;
26                TOP: 25px" runat="server" Font-Bold="True"
27                Font-Size="X-Large">Recommendations
28             </asp:Label>
29
30             <asp:ListBox id="booksListBox" style="Z-INDEX: 102;
31                LEFT: 21px; POSITION: absolute; TOP: 84px" runat=
32                "server" Width="383px" Height="91px">
33             </asp:ListBox>
34          </form>
35       </body>
36    </HTML>
```

Fig. 17.32 Session information displayed in a **ListBox**. (Part 2 of 2.)

```
1    // Fig. 17.33: RecommendationsPage.aspx.cs
2    // Reading session data from the user.
3
4    using System;
5    using System.Collections;
6    using System.ComponentModel;
7    using System.Data;
8    using System.Drawing;
9    using System.Web;
10   using System.Web.SessionState;
11   using System.Web.UI;
12   using System.Web.UI.WebControls;
13   using System.Web.UI.HtmlControls;
14
15   namespace Sessions
16   {
17      // page displaying session information and recommendations
18      public class RecommendationsPage : System.Web.UI.Page
19      {
20         protected System.Web.UI.WebControls.ListBox booksListBox;
21
22         protected System.Web.UI.WebControls.Label
23            recommendationsLabel;
24
25         // Visual Studio .NET generated code
26
```

Fig. 17.33 Session data read by an ASP .NET Web application to provide recommendations for the user. (Part 1 of 2.)

```
27           // event handler for Init event
28           override protected void OnInit( EventArgs e )
29           {
30              InitializeComponent();
31              base.OnInit( e );
32
33              // determine if Session contains information
34              if ( Session.Count != 0 )
35              {
36                 // iterate through Session values,
37                 // display in ListBox
38                 for ( int i = 0; i < Session.Count; i++ )
39                 {
40                    // store current key in sessionName
41                    string keyName = Session.Keys[ i ];
42
43                    // use current key to display
44                    // Session's name/value pairs
45                    booksListBox.Items.Add( keyName +
46                       " How to Program. ISBN#: " +
47                       Session[ keyName ] );
48
49                 } // end for
50
51              }
52              else
53              {
54                 recommendationsLabel.Text = "No Recommendations";
55                 booksListBox.Visible = false;
56              }
57
58           } // end method OnInit
59
60        } // end class RecommendationsPage
61
62     } // end namespace Sessions
```

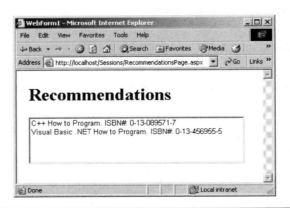

Fig. 17.33 Session data read by an ASP .NET Web application to provide recommendations for the user. (Part 2 of 2.)

Event handler **OnInit** (lines 28–58) retrieves the session information. If a user has never selected languages during any visit to this site, our **Session** object's **Count** property will be zero. This property provides the number of session items contained in a **Session** object. If **Session** object's **Count** property is zero (i.e., no language was ever selected), then we display the text **No Recommendations**.

If the user has chosen a language, the **for** structure (lines 38–49) iterates through the **Session** object. Property *Count* contains the number of key-value pairs stored in this session. The value in a key-value pair is retrieved from the **Session** object by indexing the **Session** object with the key name, using the same process by which we retrieved a value from our hash table in the last section.

We then access the *Keys* property of class **HttpSessionState** (line 41), which returns a collection that contains all the keys in the session. This line indexes our collection to retrieve the current key. Lines 45–47 concatenate **keyName**'s value to the **string " How to Program. ISBN#: "** and to the value from the session object for which **keyName** is the key. The resulting **string** is the recommendation that appears in the **ListBox**.

17.7 Case Study: Online Guest Book

Many Web sites allow users to provide feedback about the Web site in a *guest book*. Typically, users click a link on the Web site's home page to request the guest-book page. This page usually consists of an HTML **form** that contains fields for the user's name, e-mail address, and a message. Data submitted to the guest book often are stored in a database located on the Web server's machine. In this section, we create a guest-book Web Form application. The GUI is slightly more complex than the one we just described; it contains a **DataGrid**, as shown in Fig. 17.34.

The HTML **form** presented to the user consists of a user-name field, an e-mail address field and a message field. Figure 17.35 presents the ASPX file, and Fig. 17.36 presents the code-behind file for the guest book application. For the sake of simplicity, we write the guest-book information to a text file.

The ASPX file generated by the GUI is shown in Fig. 17.35. After dragging the two buttons onto the form, double-click each button to create its corresponding event handler. Visual Studio adds the event handlers to the code-behind file (Fig. 17.36). A **DataGrid** named **dataGrid** displays all guest-book entries. This control can be added from the **Toolbox**. The colors for the **DataGrid** are specified using the **Auto Format...** link located near the bottom of the **Properties** window. This link will appear only when the developer is looking at the properties of a **DataGrid**. A dialog will open with several choices. In this example, we chose the **Colorful 4** option in this dialog. We discuss adding information to the **DataGrid** shortly.

The event handler for **clearButton** (lines 114–121) clears all the **TextBox**es by setting their **Text** properties to empty strings. Lines 90–111 contain the event-handling code for **submitButton**, which adds the user's information to **guestbook.txt**, a text file stored in our project. The various entries in this file, including the newest entry, will be displayed in the **DataGrid**. Let us look at how this is done in the code.

Lines 94–96 create a **StreamWriter** that references the file containing the guest-book entries. We use the **Request** object's *PhysicalApplicationPath* property to retrieve the path of the application's root directory (this will be the path of the project folder for the current application) and then concatenate to it the file name (i.e., **guestbook.txt**). The second argument (**true**) specifies that new information will be appended to the file (i.e., added to the end of the file). Lines 99–102 append the appropriate message to the guest-book file. Before the event handler exits, it calls method **FillMessageTable** (line 110).

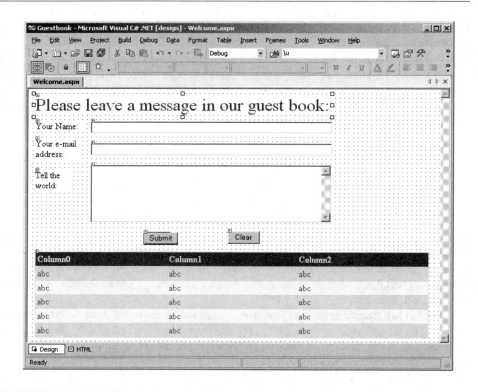

Fig. 17.34 Guest-book application GUI.

```
1   <%-- Fig. 17.35: Welcome.aspx                    --%>
2   <%-- A Web Form demonstrating a guest book. --%>
3
4   <%@ Page language="c#" Codebehind="Welcome.aspx.cs"
5      AutoEventWireup="false"
6      Inherits="Guestbook.GuestBookTest" %>
7
8   <!DOCTYPE HTML PUBLIC "-//W3C//DTD HTML 4.0 Transitional//EN" >
9
10  <HTML>
11     <HEAD>
12        <title>WebForm1</title>
```

Fig. 17.35 ASPX file for the guest book application. (Part 1 of 3.)

```
13        <meta name="GENERATOR" Content=
14          "Microsoft Visual Studio 7.0">
15        <meta name="CODE_LANGUAGE" Content="C#">
16        <meta name="vs_defaultClientScript" content="JavaScript">
17        <meta name="vs_targetSchema" content=
18          "http://schemas.microsoft.com/intellisense/ie5">
19      </HEAD>
20
21      <body MS_POSITIONING="GridLayout">
22        <form id="Form1" method="post" runat="server">
23          <asp:DataGrid id="dataGrid" style="Z-INDEX: 101;
24            LEFT: 13px; POSITION: absolute; TOP: 301px" runat=
25            "server" Width="698px" HorizontalAlign="Left"
26            BorderColor="#E7E7FF" BorderWidth="1px"
27            GridLines="Horizontal" BackColor="White"
28            DataSource="<%# dataView %>" BorderStyle="None"
29            CellPadding="3">
30
31            <SelectedItemStyle Font-Bold="True" ForeColor=
32              "#F7F7F7" BackColor="#738A9C">
33            </SelectedItemStyle>
34
35            <AlternatingItemStyle BackColor="#F7F7F7">
36            </AlternatingItemStyle>
37
38            <ItemStyle HorizontalAlign="Left" ForeColor=
39              "#4A3C8C" BackColor="#E7E7FF">
40            </ItemStyle>
41
42            <HeaderStyle Font-Bold="True" ForeColor="#F7F7F7"
43              BackColor="#4A3C8C">
44            </HeaderStyle>
45
46            <FooterStyle ForeColor="#4A3C8C" BackColor=
47              "#B5C7DE">
48            </FooterStyle>
49
50            <PagerStyle HorizontalAlign="Right" ForeColor=
51              "#4A3C8C" BackColor="#E7E7FF" Mode=
52              "NumericPages">
53            </PagerStyle>
54          </asp:DataGrid>
55
56          <asp:Button id="clearButton" style="Z-INDEX: 111;
57            LEFT: 354px; POSITION: absolute; TOP: 262px"
58            runat="server" Width="57px" Text="Clear">
59          </asp:Button>
60
61          <asp:Button id="submitButton" style="Z-INDEX: 110;
62            LEFT: 205px; POSITION: absolute; TOP: 264px"
63            runat="server" Text="Submit">
64          </asp:Button>
65
```

Fig. 17.35 ASPX file for the guest book application. (Part 2 of 3.)

```
66              <asp:TextBox id="messageTextBox" style="Z-INDEX: 109;
67                 LEFT: 111px; POSITION: absolute; TOP: 139px"
68                 runat="server" Width="427px" Height="107px"
69                 TextMode="MultiLine">
70              </asp:TextBox>
71
72              <asp:Label id="messageLabel" style="Z-INDEX: 108;
73                 LEFT: 13px; POSITION: absolute; TOP: 149px"
74                 runat="server" Width="59px" Height="9px">
75                 Tell the world:
76              </asp:Label>
77
78              <asp:Label id="emailLabel" style="Z-INDEX: 107;
79                 LEFT: 13px; POSITION: absolute; TOP: 91px"
80                 runat="server" Width="76px">E-mail address:
81              </asp:Label>
82
83              <asp:TextBox id="emailTextBox" style="Z-INDEX: 106;
84                 LEFT: 111px; POSITION: absolute; TOP: 99px"
85                 runat="server" Width="428px">
86              </asp:TextBox>
87
88              <asp:Label id="nameLabel" style="Z-INDEX: 104;
89                 LEFT: 13px; POSITION: absolute; TOP: 59px"
90                 runat="server" Width="84px">First Name:
91              </asp:Label>
92
93              <asp:TextBox id="nameTextBox" style="Z-INDEX: 105;
94                 LEFT: 111px; POSITION: absolute; TOP: 59px"
95                 runat="server" Width="428px">
96              </asp:TextBox>
97
98              <asp:Label id="promptLabel" style="Z-INDEX: 102;
99                 LEFT: 13px; POSITION: absolute; TOP: 12px"
100                runat="server" ForeColor="Blue" Font-Size="X-Large">
101                Please leave a message in our guest book:
102             </asp:Label>
103         </form>
104      </body>
105  </HTML>
```

Fig. 17.35 ASPX file for the guest book application. (Part 3 of 3.)

```
1    // Fig. 17.36: Welcome.aspx.cs
2    // The code-behind file for the guest book page.
3
4    using System;
5    using System.Collections;
6    using System.ComponentModel;
7    using System.Data;
8    using System.Drawing;
9    using System.Web;
```

Fig. 17.36 Code-behind file for the guest book application. (Part 1 of 4.)

```
10   using System.Web.SessionState;
11   using System.Web.UI;
12   using System.Web.UI.WebControls;
13   using System.Web.UI.HtmlControls;
14   using System.IO;
15
16   namespace Guestbook
17   {
18      // allows user to leave messages
19      public class GuestBookForm : System.Web.UI.Page
20      {
21         protected System.Web.UI.WebControls.Label promptLabel;
22         protected System.Web.UI.WebControls.Label nameLabel;
23         protected System.Web.UI.WebControls.Label emailLabel;
24         protected System.Web.UI.WebControls.Label messageLabel;
25
26         protected System.Web.UI.WebControls.DataGrid dataGrid;
27
28         protected System.Web.UI.WebControls.Button submitButton;
29         protected System.Web.UI.WebControls.Button clearButton;
30
31         protected System.Web.UI.WebControls.TextBox nameTextBox;
32         protected System.Web.UI.WebControls.TextBox
33            emailTextBox;
34         protected System.Web.UI.WebControls.TextBox
35            messageTextBox;
36
37         protected System.Data.DataView dataView;
38
39         // handle Page's Load event
40         private void Page_Load(
41            object sender, System.EventArgs e )
42         {
43            dataView = new DataView( new DataTable() );
44
45         } // end method Page_Load
46
47         // Visual Studio .NET generated code
48
49         // places all the messages in the guest book into a
50         // table; messages are separated by horizontal rules
51         public void FillMessageTable()
52         {
53            DataTable table = dataView.Table;
54            table.Columns.Add( "Date" );
55            table.Columns.Add( "First Name" );
56            table.Columns.Add( "e-mail" );
57            table.Columns.Add( "Message" );
58
59            // open guest book file for reading
60            StreamReader reader = new StreamReader(
61               Request.PhysicalApplicationPath +
62               "guestbook.txt" );
```

Fig. 17.36 Code-behind file for the guest book application. (Part 2 of 4.)

```
63
64          char[] separator = { '\t' };
65
66          // read in line from file
67          string message = reader.ReadLine();
68
69          while ( message != null )
70          {
71             // split the string into its four parts
72             string[] parts = message.Split( separator );
73
74             // load data into table
75             table.LoadDataRow( parts, true );
76
77             // read in one line from file
78             message = reader.ReadLine();
79          }
80
81          // update grid
82          dataGrid.DataSource = table;
83          dataGrid.DataBind();
84
85          reader.Close();
86
87       } // end method FillMessageTable
88
89       // add user's entry to guest book
90       private void submitButton_Click(
91          object sender, System.EventArgs e )
92       {
93          // open stream for appending to file
94          StreamWriter guestbook =
95             new StreamWriter( Request.PhysicalApplicationPath +
96             "guestbook.txt", true );
97
98          // write new message to file
99          guestbook.WriteLine(
100            DateTime.Now.Date.ToString().Substring( 0, 10 ) +
101            "\t" + nameTextBox.Text + "\t" + emailTextBox.Text
102            + "\t" + messageTextBox.Text );
103
104         // clear textboxes and close stream
105         nameTextBox.Text = "";
106         emailTextBox.Text = "";
107         messageTextBox.Text = "";
108         guestbook.Close();
109
110         FillMessageTable();
111      } // end method submitButton_Click
112
```

Fig. 17.36 Code-behind file for the guest book application. (Part 3 of 4.)

```
113        // clear all text boxes
114        private void clearButton_Click(
115           object sender, System.EventArgs e )
116        {
117           nameTextBox.Text = "";
118           emailTextBox.Text = "";
119           messageTextBox.Text = "";
120
121        } // end method clearButton_Click
122
123     } // end class GuestBookForm
124
125  } // end namespace Guestbook
```

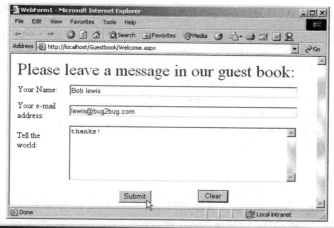

Fig. 17.36 Code-behind file for the guest book application. (Part 4 of 4.)

Method **FillMessageTable** (lines 51–87) places the guest-book entries in **DataTable table**. Lines 53–57 create a **DataTable** object from our **DataView**'s **Table** property and then form the necessary columns using the **Columns** collection's **Add** method. Lines 67–79 read each line in the text file. Method **Split** breaks each line read from the file into four tokens, which are added to the **table** by calling method **LoadDataRow** (line 75). The second argument to method **LoadDataRow** is **true**, indicating that any changes resulting from the addition will be accepted. The **DataTable** places one piece of data in each column. After the **DataTable** is populated, the data are bound to the **DataGrid**. Method **DataBind** is called to refresh the **DataView**. [*Note*: **DataView dataView** was assigned to the **DataSource** property of the **DataGrid** in the **Properties** window after it was declared in the code.]

17.8 Case Study: Connecting to a Database in ASP .NET

This case study presents a Web-based application in which a user can view a list of publications by a specified author. This program consists of two Web Forms. The first page that a user requests is **Login.aspx** (Fig. 17.37). After accessing this page, users select their names from the drop-down list and then enter their passwords. If their passwords are valid, they are redirected to **Authors.aspx** (Fig. 17.40), which provides a list of authors. When the user chooses an author and clicks the **Select** button, a postback occurs, and the updated page displays a table that contains the titles, ISBNs and publishers of books written by the selected author.

```
1   <%-- Fig. 17.37: Login.aspx                    --%>
2   <%-- A page that allows the user to log in. --%>
3
4   <%@ Page language="c#" Codebehind="login.aspx.cs"
5      AutoEventWireup="false" Inherits="Database.Login" %>
6   <%@ Register TagPrefix="Header" TagName="ImageHeader"
7      Src="ImageHeader.ascx" %>
8
9   <!DOCTYPE HTML PUBLIC "-//W3C//DTD HTML 4.0 Transitional//EN" >
10  <HTML>
11     <HEAD>
12        <title>WebForm1</title>
13        <meta name="GENERATOR" Content="Microsoft Visual Studio 7.0">
14        <meta name="CODE_LANGUAGE" Content="C#">
15        <meta name="vs_defaultClientScript" content="JavaScript">
16        <meta name="vs_targetSchema"
17           content="http://schemas.microsoft.com/intellisense/ie5">
18     </HEAD>
19     <body MS_POSITIONING="GridLayout" bgColor="#ffebff">
20        <form id="Form1" method="post" runat="server">
21           <asp:label id="nameLabel" style="Z-INDEX: 101;
22              LEFT: 15px; POSITION: absolute; TOP: 188px"
23              runat="server">Name
24           </asp:label>
25
```

Fig. 17.37 Log-in Web Form. (Part 1 of 2.)

```
26        <asp:label id="promptLabel" style="Z-INDEX: 108;
27           LEFT: 15px; POSITION: absolute; TOP: 145px"
28           runat="server">Please select your name and
29           enter your password to log in:
30        </asp:label>
31
32        <asp:customvalidator id="invalidPasswordValidator"
33           style="Z-INDEX: 107; LEFT: 262px; POSITION: absolute;
34           TOP: 221px" runat="server"
35           ControlToValidate="passwordTextBox" Font-Bold="True"
36           ForeColor="DarkCyan" ErrorMessage="Invalid password!">
37        </asp:customvalidator>
38
39        <asp:requiredfieldvalidator id="requiredPasswordValidator"
40           style="Z-INDEX: 106; LEFT: 262px; POSITION: absolute;
41           TOP: 221px" runat="server"
42           ControlToValidate="passwordTextBox" Font-Bold="True"
43           ForeColor="DarkCyan"
44           ErrorMessage="Please enter a password!">
45        </asp:requiredfieldvalidator>
46
47        <asp:dropdownlist id="nameList" style="Z-INDEX: 105;
48           LEFT: 92px; POSITION: absolute; TOP: 185px"
49           runat="server" Width="154px">
50        </asp:dropdownlist>
51
52        <asp:button id="submitButton" style="Z-INDEX: 104;
53           LEFT: 92px; POSITION: absolute; TOP: 263px"
54           runat="server" Text="Submit">
55        </asp:button>
56
57        <asp:textbox id="passwordTextBox" style="Z-INDEX: 103;
58           LEFT: 92px; POSITION: absolute; TOP: 221px"
59           runat="server" TextMode="Password">
60        </asp:textbox>
61
62        <asp:label id="passwordLabel" style="Z-INDEX: 102;
63           LEFT: 15px; POSITION: absolute; TOP: 220px"
64           runat="server">Password
65        </asp:label>
66
67        <Header:ImageHeader id="ImageHeader1" runat="server">
68        </Header:ImageHeader>
69     </form>
70   </body>
71 </HTML>
```

Fig. 17.37 Log-in Web Form. (Part 2 of 2.)

Much of the information provided by this Web page is accessed through databases stored in our project. **Login.aspx** retrieves valid user names for this site through **Login.mdb**, whereas all author information is retrieved from the **Books.mdb** database (also used in Chapter 16, Database, SQL and ADO .NET). The reader can view these databases by opening the **Database** directory for this chapter.

Lines 6–7 add a *Web user control* to the ASPX file. Readers might recall that we covered the definition of user controls for Windows applications in Chapter 10, Graphical User Interface Concepts: Part 2; we can define user controls for Web Forms using a similar technique. Because the ASPX files that users request do not define user controls for Web Forms, such controls do not have **HTML** or **BODY** elements. Rather, programmers specify these controls using the **<%@Register...%>** directive. For example, a programmer might want to include a *navigation bar* (i.e., a series of buttons for navigating a Web site) on every page of a site. If the site consists of a large number of pages, adding markup to create the navigation bar for each page could be time-consuming. Moreover, if the programmer subsequently modifies the navigation bar, every page on the site that uses the navigation bar must be updated. By creating a user control, the programmer can specify where on each page the navigation bar is placed using only a few lines of markup. If the navigation bar changes, the pages that use it are updated when those pages are requested in the future.

Like Web Forms, most Web user controls consist of two pages: An *ASCX file* and a code-behind file. Lines 6–7 define the user control's *tag name* (the name of this instance of the control) and tag prefix, which are **ImageHeader** and **Header**, respectively. The **ImageHeader** element is added to the file in lines 67–68. The tag definition is located in the *Src* file **HeaderImage.ascx** (Fig. 17.38). The programmer can create this file by right clicking the project name in the **Solution Explorer** and selecting **Add > Add New Item...**. From the dialog that opens, select **Web User Control**, and a new ASCX file will be added to the solution. At this point, the programmer can add controls and define any functionality in the Web user control's code-behind file. After creating the user control, the programmer can drag it from the **Solution Explorer** directly onto an open ASPX file. An instance of the control then will be created and added to the Web Form.

The form (Fig. 17.39) includes several **Label**s, a **TextBox (passwordTextbox)** and a **DropDownList (nameList)**, which is populated in the code-behind file (**Login.aspx.cs**) with user names retrieved from a database. We also include two validators: A **RequiredFieldValidator** and a *CustomValidator*. A **CustomValidator** allows us to specify the conditions under which a field is valid. We define these conditions in the event handler for the *ServerValidate* event of the **CustomValidator**. The event-handling code, which is placed in the code-behind file for **Login.aspx.cs**, is discussed shortly. Both validators' **ControlToValidate** properties are set to **passwordTextbox**.

```
1   <%-- Fig. 17.38: ImageHeader.ascx          --%>
2   <%-- Listing for the header user control. --%>
3
4   <%@ Control Language="c#" AutoEventWireup="false"
5       Codebehind="ImageHeader.ascx.cs"
6       Inherits="Database.ImageHeader"
7       TargetSchema="http://schemas.microsoft.com/intellisense/ie5" %>
8
9   <asp:Image id="Image1" runat="server" ImageUrl="bug2bug.png">
10  </asp:Image>
```

Fig. 17.38 ASCX code for the header. (Part 1 of 2.)

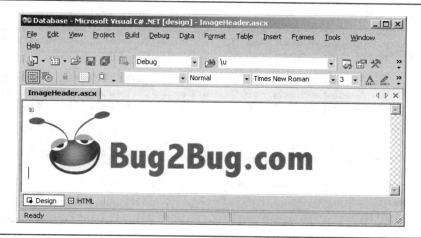

Fig. 17.38 ASCX code for the header. (Part 2 of 2.)

```
1   // Fig. 17.39: Login.aspx.cs
2   // The code-behind file for the page that logs the user in.
3
4   using System;
5   using System.Collections;
6   using System.ComponentModel;
7   using System.Data;
8   using System.Drawing;
9   using System.Web;
10  using System.Web.SessionState;
11  using System.Web.UI;
12  using System.Web.UI.WebControls;
13  using System.Web.UI.HtmlControls;
14  using System.Web.Security;
15
16  namespace Database
17  {
18     // allows users to log in
19     public class Login : System.Web.UI.Page
20     {
21        protected System.Data.OleDb.OleDbDataAdapter
22           oleDbDataAdapter1;
23        protected System.Data.OleDb.OleDbCommand
24           oleDbSelectCommand1;
25        protected System.Data.OleDb.OleDbCommand
26           oleDbInsertCommand1;
27        protected System.Data.OleDb.OleDbCommand
28           oleDbUpdateCommand1;
29        protected System.Data.OleDb.OleDbCommand
30           oleDbDeleteCommand1;
31        protected System.Data.OleDb.OleDbConnection
32           oleDbConnection1;
```

Fig. 17.39 Code-behind file for the log-in page of authors application. (Part 1 of 4.)

```
33
34        protected System.Web.UI.WebControls.Label passwordLabel;
35        protected System.Web.UI.WebControls.Label nameLabel;
36        protected System.Web.UI.WebControls.Label promptLabel;
37
38        protected System.Web.UI.WebControls.DropDownList nameList;
39        protected System.Web.UI.WebControls.Button submitButton;
40        protected System.Web.UI.WebControls.RequiredFieldValidator
41           requiredPasswordValidator;
42        protected System.Web.UI.WebControls.CustomValidator
43           invalidPasswordValidator;
44        protected System.Web.UI.WebControls.TextBox passwordTextBox;
45
46        protected System.Data.OleDb.OleDbDataReader dataReader;
47
48        // handle Page's Load event
49        private void Page_Load( object sender, System.EventArgs e )
50        {
51           // if page loads due to postback, process information
52           // otherwise, page is loading for first time, so
53           // do nothing
54           if ( !IsPostBack )
55           {
56              // open database connection
57              oleDbConnection1.Open();
58
59              // execute query
60              dataReader =
61                 oleDbDataAdapter1.SelectCommand.ExecuteReader();
62
63              // while we can read a row from query result,
64              // add first item to drop-down list
65              while ( dataReader.Read() )
66                 nameList.Items.Add( dataReader.GetString( 0 ) );
67
68              // close database connection
69              oleDbConnection1.Close();
70           }
71        } // end Page_Load
72
73        // Visual Studio .NET generated code
74
75        // validate user name and password
76        private void invalidPasswordValidator_ServerValidate(
77           object source,
78           System.Web.UI.WebControls.ServerValidateEventArgs args )
79        {
80           // open database connection
81           oleDbConnection1.Open();
82
83           // set select command to find password of username
84           // from drop-down list
85           oleDbDataAdapter1.SelectCommand.CommandText =
```

Fig. 17.39 Code-behind file for the log-in page of authors application. (Part 2 of 4.)

```
86              "SELECT * FROM Users WHERE loginID = '" +
87              Request.Form[ "nameList" ].ToString() + "'";
88
89        dataReader =
90           oleDbDataAdapter1.SelectCommand.ExecuteReader();
91
92        dataReader.Read();
93
94        // if password is correct, create
95        // authentication ticket for this user and redirect
96        // user to Authors.aspx; otherwise set IsValid to false
97        if ( args.Value == dataReader.GetString( 1 ) )
98        {
99           FormsAuthentication.SetAuthCookie(
100             Request.Form[ "namelist" ], false );
101          Session.Add(
102             "name", Request.Form[ "nameList" ].ToString() );
103          Response.Redirect( "Authors.aspx" );
104       }
105       else
106          args.IsValid = false;
107
108       // close database connection
109       oleDbConnection1.Close();
110
111    } // end method invalidPasswordValidator_ServerValidate
112
113 } // end class Login
114
115 } // end namespace Database
```

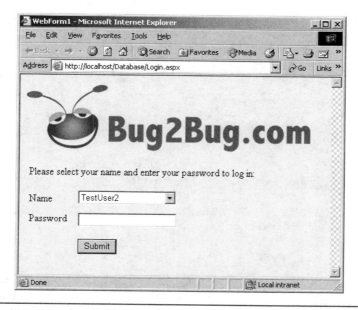

Fig. 17.39 Code-behind file for the log-in page of authors application. (Part 3 of 4.)

Fig. 17.39 Code-behind file for the log-in page of authors application. (Part 4 of 4.)

In Fig. 17.39, the **Page_Load** event handler is defined in lines 49–71. If the page is being loaded for the first time, lines 55–70 execute. Lines 60–61 execute the SQL query that Visual Studio generates at design time—this query simply retrieves all the rows from the **Authors** table of the **Books** database. Lines 65–66 iterate through the rows, placing the item in the first column of each row (the author name) into **nameList**.

The reader might notice that we use an *OleDbDataReader*, an object that reads data from a database. We did not use an object of this type before, because the **OleDbDataReader** is not as flexible as other readers we discussed in Chapter 16. The object can read, but not update, data. We use **OleDbDataReader** in this example, because we need only to read the authors' names, and this object provides a fast and simple way to do so.

In this example, we use a **CustomValidator** to validate the user's password. We define a handler (lines 76–111) for the *ServerValidate* event of the **CustomValidator**, which executes every time the user clicks **Submit**. This event handler receives a *ServerValidateEventArgs* parameter called **args**. The object referenced by **args** has two important properties: *Value*, which contains the value of the control that the **CustomValidator** is validating, and *IsValid*, which contains a **bool**ean representing the validation result. Once the event handler completes, if **IsValid** is **true**, the HTML form is submitted to the Web server; if **IsValid** is **false**, the **CustomValidator**'s **ErrorMessage** is displayed, and the HTML **form** is not submitted to the Web server.

To create and attach an event handler for the **ServerValidate** event, double-click **CustomValidator**. The definition for this event handler (lines 76–111) tests the selected user name and the password provided by the user. If they match a valid user name and password in the database, the user is *authenticated* (i.e., the user's identity is confirmed), and the browser is redirected to **Authors.aspx** (Fig. 17.40). Lines 99–103 authenticate the user and provide access to **Authors.aspx** by calling **static** method *SetAuthCookie* of class *FormsAuthentication*. This class is in the **System.Web.Security** namespace (line 14). Method **SetAuthCookie** writes an *encrypted* cookie to the client containing information necessary to authenticate the user. Encrypted data are translated into code that only the sender and receiver can understand, thereby keeping those data private. Method **SetAuthCookie** takes two arguments: A **string** that contains the user name and a **bool**ean value that specifies whether this cookie should persist (i.e., remain on the client's computer) beyond the current session. Because we want the application to authenticate the user only for the current session, we set the **bool** value to **false**. After the user is authenticated, the user's Web browser is redirected to **Authors.aspx**. If the database query did not verify the user's identity, property *IsValid* of the **CustomValidator** is set to **false**; in this case, the application displays the *ErrorMessage*, and the user can attempt to log in again.

This example uses a technique known as *forms authentication*, which protects a page so that only authenticated users can access that page. Authentication is a crucial tool for sites that allow only members to enter the site or a portion of the site. Authentication and denial of access to unauthorized users requires several lines in *Web.config* (a file used for application configuration). This XML file is a part of every ASP .NET application created in Visual Studio. The default authentication element:

```
<authentication mode="None" />
```

disables authentication. To deny access to unauthorized users, replace this line with:

```
<authentication mode="Forms">
   <forms name="DatabaseCookie"
      loginUrl="Login.aspx" protection="Encryption" />
</authentication>
```

```
<authorization>
    <deny users="?" />
</authorization>
```

This replacement alters the value of the *mode* attribute in the **authentication** element from **"None"** to **"Forms"**, which specifies that we want to use forms authentication. The *forms* element defines the way in which users are validated. Inside the forms element, attribute **name** sets the name of the cookie that is created on the user's machine—in this case, we name it **DatabaseCookie**. Attribute *loginUrl* specifies the log-in page for our application; users that attempt to access any page in our application without logging in are redirected to this page. Attribute *protection* specifies whether the value of the cookie is encrypted. In this case, we set the value of **protection** to **"Encryption"** to encrypt the cookie's data.

Element *authorization* indicates the type of access that specific users can have. In this application, we want to allow authenticated users access to all pages on the site. We place the *deny* element inside the **authorization** element to specify users to which we wish to deny access. When we set this attribute's value to **"?"**, all anonymous (i.e., unauthenticated) users are denied access to the site.

After the user has been authenticated, they will be redirected to **Authors.aspx** (Fig. 17.40). This page provides a list of authors from which the user can choose one. After a choice has been made, a table is displayed containing information about books that author has written.

```
1   <%-- Fig. 17.40: Authors.aspx                        --%>
2   <%-- This page allows a user to chose an author and display --%>
3   <%-- that author's books.                            --%>
4
5   <%@ Page language="c#" Codebehind="Authors.aspx.cs"
6      AutoEventWireup="false" Inherits="Database.Authors" %>
7   <%@ Register TagPrefix="Header" TagName="ImageHeader"
8      Src="ImageHeader.ascx" %>
9   <!DOCTYPE HTML PUBLIC "-//W3C//DTD HTML 4.0 Transitional//EN" >
10  <HTML>
11     <HEAD>
12        <title>Authors</title>
13        <meta name="GENERATOR" Content="Microsoft Visual Studio 7.0">
14        <meta name="CODE_LANGUAGE" Content="C#">
15        <meta name="vs_defaultClientScript" content="JavaScript">
16        <meta name="vs_targetSchema"
17           content="http://schemas.microsoft.com/intellisense/ie5">
18     </HEAD>
19     <body MS_POSITIONING="GridLayout" bgColor="#ffebff">
20        <form id="Authors" method="post" runat="server">
21           <asp:DropDownList id="nameList" style="Z-INDEX: 103;
22              LEFT: 90px; POSITION: absolute; TOP: 157px"
23              runat="server" Width="158px" Height="22px">
24           </asp:DropDownList>
25
```

Fig. 17.40 ASPX file that allows a user to select an author from a drop-down list. (Part 1 of 2.)

```
26        <Header:ImageHeader id="Head1" runat="server">
27        </Header:ImageHeader>
28
29        <asp:Label id="Label2" style="Z-INDEX: 102; LEFT: 28px;
30           POSITION: absolute; TOP: 157px" runat="server"
31           Width="48px" Height="22px">Authors:
32        </asp:Label>
33
34        <asp:Button id="Button1" style="Z-INDEX: 104; LEFT: 29px;
35           POSITION: absolute; TOP: 188px" runat="server"
36           Width="78px" Text="Select">
37        </asp:Button>
38
39        <asp:Label id="Label3" style="Z-INDEX: 105; LEFT: 19px;
40           POSITION: absolute; TOP: 127px" runat="server"
41           Width="210px" Visible="False">You chose
42        </asp:Label>
43
44        <asp:DataGrid id="dataGrid" style="Z-INDEX: 106;
45           LEFT: 12px; POSITION: absolute; TOP: 151px"
46           runat="server" Height="23px" Width="700px"
47           ForeColor="Black" AllowPaging="True"
48           DataSource="<%# dataView1 %>" Visible="False"
49           AllowSorting="True">
50
51           <EditItemStyle BackColor="White"></EditItemStyle>
52
53           <AlternatingItemStyle ForeColor="Black"
54              BackColor="LightGoldenrodYellow">
55           </AlternatingItemStyle>
56
57           <ItemStyle BackColor="White"></ItemStyle>
58
59           <HeaderStyle BackColor="LightGreen"></HeaderStyle>
60
61           <PagerStyle NextPageText="Next &amp;gt;"
62              PrevPageText="&amp;lt; Previous">
63           </PagerStyle>
64        </asp:DataGrid>
65     </form>
66  </body>
67 </HTML>
```

Fig. 17.40 ASPX file that allows a user to select an author from a drop-down list. (Part 2 of 2.)

The ASPX file (Fig. 17.40) for this page creates a number of controls: A **DropDown-List**, three **Label**s, a **Button** and a **DataGrid**. Notice that some of the controls—one of the **Label**s and the **DataGrid**—have their **Visible** properties set to **false** (line 41 and line 48). This means that the controls are not visible when the page first loads; because the user has not yet chosen an author, there is no information to display. Users select an author from the **DropDownList** and click **Submit**, causing a postback to occur.

When the postback is handled, the **DataGrid** is filled and displayed. Figure 17.41 presents the code-behind file for this ASPX file.

```
1   // Fig. 17.41: Authors.aspx.cs
2   // The code-behind file for a page that allows a user to choose an
3   // author and then view a list of that author's books.
4
5   using System;
6   using System.Collections;
7   using System.ComponentModel;
8   using System.Data;
9   using System.Drawing;
10  using System.Web;
11  using System.Web.SessionState;
12  using System.Web.UI;
13  using System.Web.UI.WebControls;
14  using System.Web.UI.HtmlControls;
15
16  namespace Database
17  {
18     // let user pick an author, then display that author's books
19     public class Authors : System.Web.UI.Page
20     {
21        protected System.Web.UI.WebControls.DropDownList nameList;
22        protected System.Web.UI.WebControls.Label choseLabel;
23        protected System.Web.UI.WebControls.Button selectButton;
24        protected System.Web.UI.WebControls.Label authorsLabel;
25        protected System.Web.UI.WebControls.DataGrid dataGrid;
26
27        protected System.Data.OleDb.OleDbDataAdapter
28           oleDbDataAdapter1;
29        protected System.Data.OleDb.OleDbConnection
30           oleDbConnection1;
31        protected System.Data.OleDb.OleDbDataReader dataReader;
32
33        protected System.Data.OleDb.OleDbCommand
34           oleDbSelectCommand1;
35        protected System.Data.OleDb.OleDbCommand
36           oleDbInsertCommand1;
37        protected System.Data.OleDb.OleDbCommand
38           oleDbUpdateCommand1;
39        protected System.Data.OleDb.OleDbCommand
40           oleDbDeleteCommand1;
41
42        protected System.Data.DataTable dataTable1 =
43           new DataTable();
44        protected System.Data.DataView dataView1;
45
46        protected static string sortString = "Title";
47
48        // on page load
49        private void Page_Load( object sender, System.EventArgs e )
50        {
```

Fig. 17.41 Database information input into a **DataGrid**. (Part 1 of 4.)

```
51      // test whether page was loaded due to postback
52      if ( !IsPostBack )
53      {
54         // open database connection
55         try
56         {
57            oleDbConnection1.Open();
58
59            // execute query
60            dataReader =
61               oleDbDataAdapter1.SelectCommand.ExecuteReader();
62
63            // while we can read a row from result of
64            // query, add first item to dropdown list
65            while ( dataReader.Read() )
66               nameList.Items.Add( dataReader.GetString( 0 ) +
67                  " " + dataReader.GetString( 1 ) );
68         }
69
70         // if database cannot be found
71         catch( System.Data.OleDb.OleDbException )
72         {
73            authorsLabel.Text =
74               "Server Error: Unable to load database!";
75         }
76
77         // close database connection
78         finally
79         {
80            oleDbConnection1.Close();
81         }
82      }
83      else
84      {
85         // set some controls to be invisible
86         nameList.Visible = false;
87         selectButton.Visible = false;
88         choseLabel.Visible = false;
89
90         // set other controls to be visible
91         authorsLabel.Visible = true;
92         dataGrid.Visible = true;
93
94         // add author name to label
95         authorsLabel.Text =
96            "You Chose " + nameList.SelectedItem + ".";
97         int authorID = nameList.SelectedIndex + 1;
98
99         try
100        {
101           // open database connection
102           oleDbConnection1.Open();
103
```

Fig. 17.41 Database information input into a **DataGrid**. (Part 2 of 4.)

```
104                    // grab title, ISBN and publisher name for each book
105                    oleDbDataAdapter1.SelectCommand.CommandText =
106                        "SELECT Titles.Title, Titles.ISBN, " +
107                        "Publishers.PublisherName FROM AuthorISBN " +
108                        "INNER JOIN Titles ON AuthorISBN.ISBN = " +
109                        "Titles.ISBN, Publishers WHERE " +
110                        "(AuthorISBN.AuthorID = " + authorID + ")";
111
112                    // fill dataview with results
113                    oleDbDataAdapter1.Fill( dataTable1 );
114                    dataView1 = new DataView( dataTable1 );
115                    dataView1.Sort = sortString;
116                    dataGrid.DataBind(); // bind grid to data source
117                }
118
119                // if database cannot be found
120                catch( System.Data.OleDb.OleDbException )
121                {
122                    authorsLabel.Text =
123                        "Server Error: Unable to load database!";
124                }
125
126                // close database connection
127                finally
128                {
129                    oleDbConnection1.Close();
130                }
131            }
132
133        } // end method Page_Load
134
135        // on new page
136        private void OnNewPage( object sender,
137            DataGridPageChangedEventArgs e )
138        {
139            // set current page to next page
140            dataGrid.CurrentPageIndex = e.NewPageIndex;
141
142            dataView1.Sort = sortString;
143            dataGrid.DataBind(); // rebind data
144
145        } // end method OnNewPage
146
147        // Visual Studio .NET generated code
148
149        // handles Sort event
150        private void dataGrid_SortCommand( object source,
151            System.Web.UI.WebControls.DataGridSortCommandEventArgs e )
152        {
153            // get table to sort
154            sortString = e.SortExpression.ToString();
155            dataView1.Sort = sortString; // sort
156            dataGrid.DataBind(); // rebind data
```

Fig. 17.41 Database information input into a **DataGrid**. (Part 3 of 4.)

```
157
158         } // end method dataGrid_SortCommand
159
160      } // end class Authors
161
162  } // end namespace Database
```

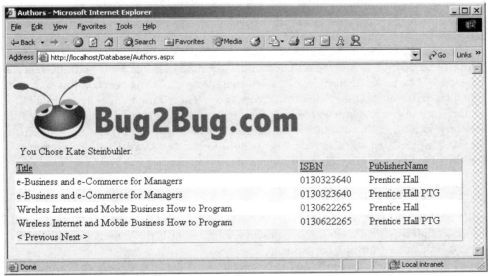

Fig. 17.41 Database information input into a **DataGrid**. (Part 4 of 4.)

Method **Page_Load** (lines 49–133) contains most of the code for this example. The condition (line 52) determines whether the page was loaded as a result of a postback event. Line 57 then opens the database connection, and lines 60–61 execute the database command, which retrieves all the authors' first and last names from the database. Lines 65–67 iterate through the result set and add the authors' first and last names to **nameList**.

Once the user has selected an author and submitted the form, the condition (line 52) becomes **false**, which causes lines 86–131 to execute. The initial set of controls displayed to the user (i.e., the label, drop-down list and button) are hidden in the postback. However, the label and the data grid that previously were invisible are made visible. Lines 95–96 add the selected author's name to the label control.

Lines 105–110 create a database query to retrieve the title, ISBN and publisher name for each of the author's books and assign them to the command's **CommandText** property. Method **fill** (line 113) populates its **DataTable** argument with the rows returned by our query on lines 106–110. The **DataView** class's *Sort* property sorts its data by the **string sortString** assigned it (line 115). Line 46 initially sets this **string** to **"Title"**, indicating that the rows in our table are to be sorted in ascending order by title. Ascending order is the default. If **sortString** where **"TitleDESC"**, the rows in our table would be sorted in descending order by title.

Method **OnNewPage** (lines 136–145) handles the **DataGrid**'s **PageIndex-Changed** event, which is fired when the user clicks the **Next** link at the bottom of the **DataGrid** control to display the next page of data. To enable paging, the **AllowPaging** property of the **DataGrid** is set to **true** in the Web Form designer. **DataGrid**'s **PageSize** property determines the number of entries per page, and its **PagerStyle** property customizes the display of our **DataGrid** during paging. This **DataGrid** control displays ten books per page. After the **DataGrid**'s **CurrentPageIndex** property is assigned the event argument **NewPageIndex** (line 140), we sort the data and rebind it so that the next page of data can be displayed (lines 142–143). This technique for displaying data makes the site more readable and enables pages to load more quickly (due to the fact that less data are displayed at one time).

Method **dataGrid_SortCommand** (lines 150–158) handles the **Sort** event of the **DataGrid** control. When the **AllowSorting** property in the Web Form designer is enabled, the **DataGrid** displays all table headings as *LinkButton* controls (i.e., buttons that act as hyperlinks). The **SortCommand** event is raised when the user clicks a column header name. On line 154, we use the *SortExpression* property of **e**. This property indicates the column by which the data is sorted. This value is assigned to **string sortString**, which then is assigned to our **DataView**'s **Sort** property on line 155. On line 156, we rebind the sorted data to our **DataGrid**.

17.9 Tracing

ASP .NET provides a *tracing* feature for debugging Web-based applications. Tracing is the process of placing statements throughout the code-behind file that output information during execution about the program's status.

In Windows applications, message boxes can aid in debugging; in Web Forms, a programmer might use **Response.Write** for this purpose. However, using **Response.Write** for tracing in ASP .NET has several drawbacks.

One of these drawbacks is that, once an application is executing correctly, the programmer must remove all tracing statements from the program. This is time-consuming and can introduce errors, because the programmer must differentiate between statements that are part of the program's logic and statements that are used for testing purposes. ASP .NET provides the programmer with two forms of built-in tracing: *Page tracing* and *application tracing*.

Page tracing involves the tracing of the actions of an individual page. Setting the **Trace** property of the page to **True** in the **Properties** window enables tracing for that page. Instead of calling the **Response** object's **Write** method, we call the **Trace** object's **Write** method. Object **Trace** is an instance of the **TraceContext** class and provides tracing capabilities. In addition to method **Write**, the **Trace** object includes method **Warn**, which prints warning statements in red. When tracing is disabled by setting the **Trace** property to **false**, **Trace** statements are not executed.

Figure 17.42 depicts a simple page that displays a sentence (we do not show the code for this page, as it is quite simple). The **Page_Load** event for this page includes the statement **Trace.Warn("Using warnings")**. The **Trace** property is set to **false** so **"Using warnings"** is not displayed on the page; we will see shortly when and where trace statements are displayed.

Figure 17.43 displays the same page when the **Trace** property is set to **True**. The top of the figure depicts the original page, and the tracing information generated by ASP .NET appears below. The **Request Details** section provides information about the request. The **Trace Information** section contains the information output by calling the **Write** and **Warn** methods. The second row contains the message, which displays in red.

The **Control Tree** section lists all the controls contained on the page. Several additional tables also appear in this page. The **Cookies Collection** section contains information about the program's cookies, the **Headers Collection** section catalogs the HTTP headers for the page and the **Server Variables** section provides a list of server variables (i.e., information sent by the browser with each request) and their values.

Tracing for entire projects also is available. To turn on application-level tracing, open the **Web.config** file for the project and set the **enabled** property to **true** in the **trace** element. To view the project's tracing information, navigate the browser to the **trace.axd** file in the project folder. This file does not actually exist on the hard drive; it is generated when the user requests **trace.axd**. Figure 17.44 shows the Web page that is generated when the programmer views the **trace.axd** file.

This page lists all the requests made to this application and the times when the pages were accessed. Clicking one of the **View Details** links directs the browser to a page similar to the one portrayed in Fig. 17.43.

In this chapter, we discussed ASP .NET with C# and its role in a three tier architecture. Readers now should be able to create dynamic Web forms that respond to user input, track and maintain a user's session information and interact with a back-end database from a Web form. In the next chapter, we introduce ASP .NET Web services, which allow remote software to interact with methods and objects on a Web server.

Fig. 17.42 ASPX page with tracing turned off.

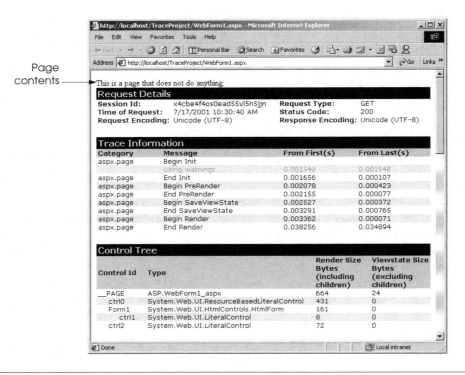

Fig. 17.43 Tracing enabled on a page.

Fig. 17.44 Tracing information for a project.

17.10 Summary

Microsoft's ASP .NET technology is used for Web-based application development. Web-based applications create Web content for Web browser clients, using Web-Form files. The Web-Form file represents the Web page that is sent to the client browser. Web-Form files have the file extension **.aspx** and contain the GUI of the Web page being developed. Programmers customize Web Forms by adding Web controls, which include text boxes, images and buttons. Every ASPX file created in Visual Studio.NET has a corresponding class located in the code-behind file that provides the ASPX file's programmatic implementation.

Visual Studio.NET generates the markup in the ASPX page when controls are dragged onto the Web Form. When a control's **runat** attribute is set to **"server"**, the control is executed on a server, generating HTML equivalent markup for the control. The **asp:** tag prefix in the declaration of a control indicates that the control is an ASP .NET Web control. Each Web control maps to a corresponding HTML element.

Class **Page** defines a standard Web page, providing event handlers and objects necessary for creating Web-based applications. All code-behind classes for ASPX forms inherit from class **Page**. When a client requests an ASPX file, a class is created behind the scenes that contains both the visual aspect of the page (defined in the ASPX file) and the page's logic (defined in the code-behind file). This new class inherits from **Page**. The first time that a Web page is requested, this class is compiled, and an instance is created. The instance represents the page—it will create the HTML that is sent to the client.

Method **OnInit** is called when the **Init** event is raised. This event indicates that the page is ready to be initialized. The **Load** event is raised every time a page is requested or reloaded. The **Page_Load** event handler typically is used to execute any processing that is necessary to restore data from previous requests. After **Page_Load** has finished executing, the page processes any events raised by the page's controls.

The **PageLayout** property determines how controls are arranged on the form. By default, property **PageLayout** is set to **GridLayout**, which specifies that all controls remain exactly where they are dropped on the Web Form.

Image controls insert an image onto a Web page. A **TextBox** control allows the programmer to read and display text. A **RadioButtonList** control provides a series of radio buttons from which the user can select. A **DropDownList** control provides a list of options to the user. The **HyperLink** control adds a hyperlink to a Web page. The **AdRotator** Web control is used for displaying advertisements.

A validation control (or validator) checks whether the data in another Web control are in the proper format. A **RegularExpressionValidator** matches a Web control's content against a regular expression. The regular expression that validates the input is assigned to property **ValidationExpressison**. A validator's **ControlToValidate** property indicates which control will be validated. A **RequiredFieldValidator** is used to ensure that a control receives input from the user when the form is submitted. A **CustomValidator** allows programmers to specify the circumstances under which a field is valid. We define these circumstances in the event handler for the **ServerValidate** event of the **CustomValidator**.

Web programmers using ASP .NET often design their Web pages so that, when submitted, the current page is requested again. This event is known as a postback. The **Page**'s **IsPostBack** property can be used to determine whether the page is being loaded as a result of a postback. The **EnableViewState** attribute determines whether a Web control's state persists (i.e., is retained) when a postback occurs.

A session represents a unique client. If a client leaves a site and then returns later, the client should still be recognized as the same user. To help the server distinguish among clients, each client must identify itself to the server. The tracking of individual clients is known as session tracking.

A cookie is a text file stored by a Web site on an individual's computer that allows the site to track the actions of the visitor. When a Web Form receives a request, the header includes such information as the request type and any cookies that have been sent previously from the server to be stored on the client machine. When the server formulates its response, the header information includes any cookies the server wants to store on the client computer and other information, such as the MIME type of the response.

A cookie object is of type **HttpCookie**. Cookies are sent and received in the form of a collection of cookies, of type **HttpCookieCollection**. The **Name** and **Value** properties of class **HttpCookie** can be used to retrieve the key and value, respectively, of the key-value pair in a cookie.

C# provides session-tracking capabilities in the FCL's **HttpSessionState** class. Every Web Form includes an **HttpSessionState** object, which is accessible through property **Session** of class **Page**. When the Web page is requested, an **HttpSessionState** object is created and is assigned to the **Page**'s **Session** property.

Web Forms should maintain client state information in **HttpSessionState** objects, because such objects are specific to each client. Like a cookie, an **HttpSessionState** object can store name-value pairs. **HttpSessionState** objects can store any type of object (not just **string**s) as attribute values. The value in a key-value pair is retrieved from the **Session** object by indexing the **Session** object with the name of the key, using the same process by which a value can be retrieved from a hash table. The **Keys** property of class **HttpSessionState** returns a collection containing all the keys in the session.

When a user's identity is confirmed, the user has been authenticated. Method **SetAuthCookie** writes to the client an encrypted cookie containing information necessary to authenticate the user. Encrypted data are data that have been translated into a code that only the sender and receiver can understand, thereby keeping it private.

A technique known as forms authentication protects a page so that only authenticated users can access it. Specifying that a page perform authentication and denial of access to unauthorized users involves the placement of several lines in **Web.config** (a file used for application configuration).

ASP .NET provides a tracing feature for the debugging of Web-based applications. Tracing is the process of placing statements throughout the code-behind file that output information during execution about the program's status. ASP .NET provides the programmer with two forms of built-in tracing—page tracing and application tracing. Page tracing involves tracing the actions of an individual page. Application-level tracing enables the programmer to trace the entire project, rather than simply one ASPX page. When tracing is disabled by setting the **Trace** property to **false**, **Trace** statements are not executed.

17.11 Internet and Web Resources

www.asp.net
The Microsoft site overviews ASP .NET and provides a link for downloading ASP .NET. This site includes the IBuy Spy e-commerce storefront example that uses ASP .NET. Links to the Amazon and Barnes & Noble Web sites, at which the user can purchase books on ASP .NET, also are included.

www.asp101.com/aspdotnet/aspplus/index.asp

This site overviews ASP .NET and includes articles, code examples and links to ASP .NET resources. The code samples demonstrate the use of cookies in an ASP .NET application and show how to establish a connection to a database—two key capabilities of multi-tier applications.

www.411asp.net

This resource site provides programmers with ASP .NET tutorials and code samples. The community pages allows programmers to ask questions, answer questions and post messages.

www.aspfree.com

This site provides free ASP .NET demos and source code. The site also provides a list of articles for various topics and a frequently asked questions (FAQs) page.

www.aspng.com/aspng/index.asp

This site offers tutorials, links and recommendations for books on ASP. NET. Links to different mailing lists also are provided. These links are organized by topic. This site also contains articles related to many ASP. NET topics, such as "Performance Tips and Tricks."

www.aspnetfaq.com

This site provides answers to frequently asked questions (FAQs) about ASP. NET.

www.123aspx.com

This site offers a directory of links to ASP .NET resources. The site also includes daily and weekly newsletters.

18

ASP .NET and Web Services

Objectives

- To understand what a Web service is.
- To create Web services.
- To understand the elements that comprise a Web service, such as service descriptions and discovery files.
- To create a client that uses a Web service.
- To be able to use Web services with Windows and Web applications.
- To understand session tracking in Web services.
- To pass user-defined data types between Web services and Web clients.

A client is to me a mere unit, a factor in a problem.
Sir Arthur Conan Doyle

...if the simplest things of nature have a message that you understand, rejoice, for your soul is alive.
Eleonora Duse

Protocol is everything.
Francoise Giuliani

They also serve who only stand and wait.
John Milton

Outline

18.1   Introduction
18.2   Web Services
18.3   Simple Object Access Protocol (SOAP) and Web Services
18.4   Publishing and Consuming Web Services
18.5   Session Tracking in Web Services
18.6   Using Web Forms and Web Services
18.7   Case Study: Temperature Information Application
18.8   User-Defined Types in Web Services
18.9   Summary

18.1 Introduction[1]

Throughout this book, we have created dynamic link libraries (DLLs) to facilitate software reusability and modularity—the cornerstones of good object-oriented programming. However, the use of DLLs is limited by the fact that DLLs must reside on the same machine as the programs that use them. This chapter introduces the use of Web services (sometimes called *XML Web services*) to promote software reusability in distributed systems. Distributed-systems technologies allow applications to execute across multiple computers on a network. A Web service is an application that enables distributed computing by allowing one machine to call methods on other machines via common data formats and protocols, such as XML and HTTP. In .NET, these method calls are implemented using the Simple Object Access Protocol (SOAP), an XML-based protocol describing how to mark up requests and responses so that they can be transferred via protocols such as HTTP. Using SOAP, applications represent and transmit data in a standardized format—XML. The underlying implementation of the Web service is irrelevant to clients using the Web service.

Microsoft is encouraging software vendors and e-businesses to deploy Web services. As more and more people worldwide connect to the Internet via networks, applications that call methods across a network become more practical. Earlier in this text, we discussed the merits of object-oriented programming. Web services represents the next step in object-oriented programming: Instead of developing software from a small number of class libraries provided at one location, programmers can access countless libraries in multiple locations.

This technology also makes it easier for businesses to collaborate and grow together. By subscribing Web services that are relevant to their businesses, companies that create applications can spend less time coding and more time developing new products from existing components. In addition, e-businesses can employ Web services to provide their customers with an enhanced shopping experience. As a simple example, consider an online music store that enables users to purchase music CDs or to obtain information about artists. Now, suppose another company that sells concert tickets provides a Web service that determines the dates of upcoming concerts by various artists and allows users to buy concert tickets. By licensing the concert-ticket Web service for use on its site, the online music

---

1. Internet Information Services (IIS) must be running to create a Web service in Visual Studio.

store can sell concert tickets to its customers, which likely will result in increased traffic to its site. The company that sells concert tickets also benefits from the business relationship. In addition to selling more tickets, the company receives revenue from the online music store in exchange for the use of its Web service.

Visual Studio and the .NET Framework provide a simple way to create Web services like the one discussed in this example. In this chapter, we explore the steps involved in both the creation and accessing of Web services. For each example, we provide the code for the Web service, then give an example of an application that might use the Web service. Our initial examples are designed to offer a brief introduction to Web services and how they work in Visual Studio. In later sections, we move on to demonstrate more sophisticated Web services.

18.2 Web Services

A Web service is an application stored on one machine that can be accessed on another machine over a network. Due to the nature of this relationship, the machine on which the Web service resides commonly is referred to as a *remote machine*. The application that accesses the Web service sends a method call to the remote machine, which processes the call and sends a response to the application. This kind of distributed computing benefits various systems, including those without access to certain data and those lacking the processing power necessary to perform specific computations.

A Web service is, in its simplest form, a class. In previous chapters, when we wanted to include a class in a project, we would either define the class in our project or add a reference to the compiled DLL. This compiled DLL is placed in the **bin** directory of an application by default. As a result, all pieces of our application reside on one machine. When using Web services, the class (and its compiled DLL) we wish to include in our project are stored on a remote machine—a compiled version of this class is not placed in the current application.

Methods in a Web service are remotely invoked using a *Remote Procedure Call* (*RPC*). These methods, which are marked with the **WebMethod** attribute, often are referred to as *Web-service methods*. Declaring a method with this attribute makes the method accessible to other classes via an RPC. The declaration of a Web-service method with attribute **WebMethod** is known as *exposing* the method, or enabling it to be called remotely.

Common Programming Error 18.1

Attempting to call a remote method from a Web service if the method is not declared with the **WebMethod** *attribute is a compilation error.*

Most requests to and responses from Web services are transmitted via SOAP. This means that any client capable of generating and processing SOAP messages can use a Web service, regardless of the language in which the Web service is written.

Web services have important implications for *business-to-business (B2B) transactions*, (i.e., transactions that occur between two or more businesses). Now, instead of using proprietary applications, businesses can conduct transactions via Web services—a much simpler and more efficient means of conducting business. Because Web services and SOAP are platform-independent, companies can collaborate and use Web services without worrying about the compatibility of various technologies or programming languages. In this way, Web services are an inexpensive, readily-available solution to facilitate B2B transactions.

A Web service created in Visual Studio .NET has two parts: An *ASMX* file and a code-behind file. The ASMX file by default can be viewed in any Web browser and contains valuable information about the Web service, such as descriptions of Web-service methods and ways to test these methods. The code-behind file provides the implementation for the methods that the Web service encompasses. Figure 18.1 depicts Internet Explorer rendering an ASMX file.

The top of the page provides a link to the Web service's ***Service Description***. A service description is an XML document that conforms to the *Web Service Description Language* (*WSDL*), an XML vocabulary that defines the methods that the Web service makes available and the ways in which clients can interact with those methods. The WSDL document also specifies lower-level information that clients might need, such as the required formats for requests and responses. Visual Studio .NET generates the WSDL service description. Client programs can use the service description to confirm the correctness of method calls when the client programs are compiled.

The programmer should not alter the service description, as it defines how a Web service works. When a user clicks the **Service Description** link at the top of the ASMX page, WSDL is displayed that defines the service description for this Web service (Fig. 18.2).

Fig. 18.1   ASMX file rendered in Internet Explorer.

Fig. 18.2   Service description for a Web service.

Below the **Service Description** link, the Web page shown in Fig. 18.1 lists the methods that the Web service provides (i.e., all methods in the application that are declared with **WebMethod** attributes). Clicking any method name requests a test page that describes the method (Fig. 18.3). After explaining the method's arguments, the test page allows users to test the method by entering the proper parameters and clicking **Invoke**. (We discuss the process of testing a Web-service method shortly.) Below the **Invoke** button, the page displays sample request and response messages using SOAP, HTTP GET and HTTP POST. These protocols are the three options for sending and receiving messages in Web services. The protocol used to transmit request and response messages is sometimes known as the Web service's *wire protocol* or *wire format*, because the protocol specifies how information is sent "along the wire." Notice that Fig. 18.3 uses the HTTP GET protocol to test a method. Later in this chapter, when we use Web services in our C# programs, we use SOAP as the wire protocol. The advantages of using SOAP over HTTP GET and HTTP POST are discussed in the next section.

On the page depicted in Fig. 18.3, users can test a method by entering **Value**s in the **first:** and **second:** fields and then clicking **Invoke** (in this example, we tested method **Bigger**). The method executes, and a new Web browser window opens to display an XML document containing the result (Fig. 18.4). Now that we have introduced a simple example using a Web service, the next several sections explore the role of XML in Web services, as well as other aspects of Web service functionality.

Fig. 18.3   Invoking a method of a Web service from a Web browser.

Fig. 18.4   Results of invoking a Web-service method from a Web browser.

 Testing and Debugging Tip 18.1

Using the ASMX page of a Web service to test and debug methods makes that Web service more reliable and robust; it also reduces the likelihood that clients using the Web service will encounter errors.

18.3 Simple Object Access Protocol (SOAP) and Web Services

The Simple Object Access Protocol (SOAP) is a platform-independent protocol that uses XML to make remote-procedure calls over HTTP. Each request and response is packaged in a *SOAP message*—an XML message that contains all the information necessary to process its contents. SOAP messages are quite popular, because they are written in the easy-to-understand and platform-independent XML. Similarly, HTTP was chosen to transmit SOAP messages, because HTTP is a standard protocol for sending information across the Internet. The use of XML and HTTP enables different operating systems to send and receive SOAP messages. Another benefit of HTTP is that it can be used with networks that contain *firewalls*—security barriers that restrict communication among networks.

SOAP supports an extensive set of data types. Readers should note that the wire format used to transmit requests and responses must support all data types passed between the applications. Web services that use SOAP support a wider variety of data types than do Web services that employ other wire formats. The data types supported by SOAP include most basic data types, as well as **DataSet**, **DateTime**, **XmlNode** and several others. SOAP also permits the transmission of arrays of all these types. In addition, user-defined types can be used—we demonstrate how to do this in Section 18.8.

Applications send requests and responses to and from Web services via SOAP. When a program invokes a Web-service method, the request and all relevant information are packaged in a SOAP message and sent to the appropriate destination. When the Web service receives the SOAP message, it begins to process the contents (called the *SOAP envelope*), which specifies the method that the client wishes to execute and the arguments the client is passing to that method. After the Web service receives this request and parses it, the proper method is called with the specified arguments (if there are any), and the response is sent back to the client in another SOAP message. The client parses the response to retrieve the result of the method call.

The SOAP request portrayed in Fig. 18.5 was taken directly from the **Bigger** method of the **HugeInteger** Web service (Fig. 18.3). This Web service provides programmers with several methods that manipulate integers larger than those that can be stored in a **long** variable. Most programmers do not manipulate SOAP messages, allowing the Web service to handle the details of transmission.

Figure 18.5 displays a standard SOAP request that is created when a client wishes to execute the **HugeInteger** Web service's method **Bigger**. When a request to a Web service causes such a SOAP request to be created, the elements **first** and **second**'s character data (**string**s) would contain the actual values that the user entered (lines 16–17). If this envelope contained the request from Fig. 18.3, element **first** and element **second** would contain the values entered in Fig. 18.3. Placeholder **length** would contain the length of this SOAP message.

```
1   POST /HugeIntegerWebService/HugeInteger.asmx HTTP/1.1
2   Host: localhost
3   Content-Type: text/xml; charset=utf-8
4   Content-Length: length
5   SOAPAction: "http://www.deitel.com/cspfep1/ch18/Bigger"
6
7   <?xml version="1.0" encoding="utf-8"?>
8
9   <soap:Envelope
10     xmlns:xsi="http://www.w3.org/2001/XMLSchema-instance"
```

Fig. 18.5 SOAP request for the **HugeInteger** Web service. (Part 1 of 2.)

```
11     xmlns:xsd="http://www.w3.org/2001/XMLSchema"
12     xmlns:soap="http://schemas.xmlsoap.org/soap/envelope/">
13
14     <soap:Body>
15         <Bigger xmlns="http://www.deitel.com/cspfep1/ch18/">
16             <first>string</first>
17             <second>string</second>
18         </Bigger>
19     </soap:Body>
20
21 </soap:Envelope>
```

Fig. 18.5 SOAP request for the **HugeInteger** Web service. (Part 2 of 2.)

18.4 Publishing and Consuming Web Services

This section presents several examples of creating (also known as *publishing*) and using (also known as *consuming*) a Web service. An application that consumes a Web service actually consists of two parts: A *proxy* class that represents the Web service and a client application that accesses the Web service via an instance of the proxy class. The proxy class handles the transferal of the arguments for the Web-service method from the client application to the Web service, as well as the transferal of the result from the Web-service method back to the client application. Visual Studio can generate proxy classes—we demonstrate how to do this momentarily.

Figure 18.6 presents the code-behind file for the **HugeInteger** Web service (Fig. 18.1). The name of the Web service is based on the name of the class that defines it (in this case, **HugeInteger**). This Web service is designed to perform calculations with integers that contain a maximum of 100 digits. As we mentioned earlier, **long** variables cannot handle integers of this size (i.e., an overflow would occur). The Web service provides a client with methods that take two "huge integers" and determine which one is larger or smaller, whether the two numbers are equal, their sum or their difference. The reader can think of these methods as services that one application provides for the programmers of other applications (hence the term, "Web services"). Any programmer can access this Web service, use its methods and thus avoid the writing, testing and debugging of over 200 lines of code. In the remaining examples, we hide portions of the Visual Studio generated code in the code-behind files. We do this both for brevity and for presentation purposes.

```
1  // Fig. 18.6: HugeInteger.asmx.cs
2  // HugeInteger Web Service.
3
4  using System;
5  using System.Text;
6  using System.Collections;
7  using System.ComponentModel;
8  using System.Data;
9  using System.Diagnostics;
10 using System.Web;
11 using System.Web.Services; // contains Web service related classes
```

Fig. 18.6 **HugeInteger** Web service. (Part 1 of 6.)

```
12
13   namespace HugeIntegerWebService
14   {
15       /// <summary>
16       /// performs operations on large integers
17       /// </summary>
18       [ WebService(
19          Namespace = "http://www.deitel.com/cspfep1/ch18/",
20          Description = "A Web service which provides methods that" +
21          " can manipulate large integer values." ) ]
22       public class HugeInteger : System.Web.Services.WebService
23       {
24          // default constructor
25          public HugeInteger()
26          {
27             // CODEGEN: This call is required by the ASP .NET Web
28             // Services Designer
29             InitializeComponent();
30
31             number = new int[ MAXIMUM ];
32          }
33
34          #region Component Designer generated code
35          /// <summary>
36          /// Required method for Designer support - do not modify
37          /// the contents of this method with the code editor.
38          /// </summary>
39          private void InitializeComponent()
40          {
41          }
42          #endregion
43
44          /// <summary>
45          /// Clean up any resources being used.
46          /// </summary>
47          protected override void Dispose( bool disposing )
48          {
49          }
50
51          // WEB SERVICE EXAMPLE
52          // The HelloWorld() example service returns
53          // the string Hello World
54          // To build, uncomment the following lines
55          // then save and build the project
56          // To test this web service, press F5
57
58          //    [WebMethod]
59          //    public string HelloWorld()
60          //    {
61          //       return "Hello World";
62          //    }
63
64          private const int MAXIMUM = 100;
```

Fig. 18.6 HugeInteger Web service. (Part 2 of 6.)

```
65
66      public int[] number;
67
68      // indexer that accepts an integer parameter
69      public int this[ int index ]
70      {
71         get
72         {
73            return number[ index ];
74         }
75
76         set
77         {
78            number[ index ] = ( value >= 0 ? value : 0 );
79         }
80
81      } // end indexer
82
83      // returns string representation of HugeInteger
84      public override string ToString()
85      {
86         StringBuilder returnString = new StringBuilder();
87
88         foreach ( int digit in number )
89            returnString.Insert( 0, digit );
90
91         return returnString.ToString();
92      }
93
94      // creates HugeInteger based on argument
95      public static HugeInteger FromString( string integer )
96      {
97         HugeInteger parsedInteger = new HugeInteger();
98
99         for ( int i = 0; i < integer.Length; i++ )
100           parsedInteger[ i ] = Int32.Parse(
101              integer[ integer.Length - i - 1 ].ToString() );
102
103        return parsedInteger;
104     }
105
106     // WebMethod that performs integer addition
107     // represented by string arguments
108     [ WebMethod ( Description = "Adds two huge integers." ) ]
109     public string Add( string first, string second )
110     {
111        int carry = 0;
112
113        HugeInteger operand1 = HugeInteger.FromString( first );
114        HugeInteger operand2 =
115           HugeInteger.FromString( second );
116
```

Fig. 18.6 HugeInteger Web service. (Part 3 of 6.)

```
117            // store result of addition
118            HugeInteger result = new HugeInteger();
119
120            // perform addition algorithm for each digit
121            for ( int i = 0; i < MAXIMUM; i++ )
122            {
123                // add two digits in same column
124                // result is their sum, plus carry from
125                // previous operation modulus 10
126                result[ i ] =
127                    ( operand1[ i ] + operand2[ i ] ) % 10 + carry;
128
129                // store remainder of dividing
130                // sums of two digits by 10
131                carry = ( operand1[ i ] + operand2[ i ] ) / 10;
132            }
133
134            return result.ToString();
135
136        } // end method Add
137
138        // WebMethod that performs the subtraction of integers
139        // represented by string arguments
140        [ WebMethod (
141            Description = "Subtracts two huge integers." ) ]
142        public string Subtract( string first, string second )
143        {
144            HugeInteger operand1 = HugeInteger.FromString( first );
145            HugeInteger operand2 =
146                HugeInteger.FromString( second );
147            HugeInteger result = new HugeInteger();
148
149            // subtract top digit from bottom digit
150            for ( int i = 0; i < MAXIMUM; i++ )
151            {
152                // if top digit is smaller than bottom
153                // digit we need to borrow
154                if ( operand1[ i ] < operand2[ i ] )
155                    Borrow( operand1, i );
156
157                // subtract bottom from top
158                result[ i ] = operand1[ i ] - operand2[ i ];
159            }
160
161            return result.ToString();
162
163        } // end method Subtract
164
165        // borrows 1 from next digit
166        private void Borrow( HugeInteger integer, int place )
167        {
```

Fig. 18.6 HugeInteger Web service. (Part 4 of 6.)

```
168            // if no place to borrow from, signal problem
169            if ( place >= MAXIMUM - 1 )
170               throw new ArgumentException();
171
172            // otherwise if next digit is zero,
173            // borrow from digit to left
174            else if ( integer[ place + 1 ] == 0 )
175               Borrow( integer, place + 1 );
176
177            // add ten to current place because we borrowed
178            // and subtract one from previous digit -
179            // this is digit borrowed from
180            integer[ place ] += 10;
181            integer[ place + 1 ] -= 1;
182
183         } // end method Borrow
184
185         // WebMethod that returns true if first integer is
186         // bigger than second
187         [ WebMethod ( Description = "Determines whether first " +
188            "integer is larger than the second integer." ) ]
189         public bool Bigger( string first, string second )
190         {
191            char[] zeroes = { '0' };
192
193            try
194            {
195               // if elimination of all zeroes from result
196               // of subtraction is an empty string,
197               // numbers are equal, so return false,
198               // otherwise return true
199               if ( Subtract( first, second ).Trim( zeroes ) == "" )
200                  return false;
201               else
202                  return true;
203            }
204
205            // if ArgumentException occurs, first number
206            // was smaller, so return false
207            catch ( ArgumentException )
208            {
209               return false;
210            }
211
212         } // end method Bigger
213
214         // WebMethod returns true if first integer is
215         // smaller than second
216         [ WebMethod ( Description = "Determines whether the " +
217            "first integer is smaller than the second integer." ) ]
218         public bool Smaller( string first, string second )
219         {
```

Fig. 18.6   HugeInteger Web service. (Part 5 of 6.)

```
220                // if second is bigger than first, then first is
221                // smaller than second
222                return Bigger( second, first );
223            }
224
225            // WebMethod that returns true if two integers are equal
226            [ WebMethod ( Description = "Determines whether the " +
227                "first integer is equal to the second integer." ) ]
228            public bool EqualTo( string first, string second )
229            {
230                // if either first is bigger than second, or first is
231                // smaller than second, they are not equal
232                if ( Bigger( first, second ) ||
233                    Smaller( first, second ) )
234                    return false;
235                else
236                    return true;
237            }
238
239        } // end class HugeInteger
240
241    } // end namespace HugeIntegerWebService
```

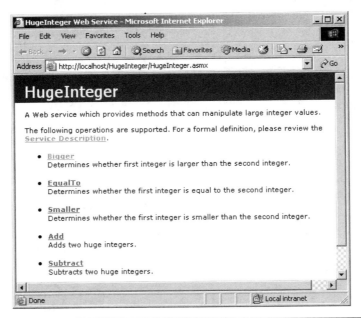

Fig. 18.6 HugeInteger Web service. (Part 6 of 6.)

Line 13 places class **HugeInteger** in namespace **HugeIntegerWebService**. Line 19 assigns the Web service namespace to **www.deitel.com/cspfep1/ch18/** to uniquely identify this Web service. The namespace is specified using the ***Namespace*** property of the ***WebService*** attribute. In lines 20–21, we use property ***Description*** to provide information about our Web service that appears in the ASMX file. Line 22 specifies that our class derives from **System.Web.Services.WebService**. By default, Visual Studio defines our Web service so that it inherits from the **WebService** class. Although a Web service class is not required to subclass **WebService**, class **WebService** provides members that are useful in determining information about the client and the Web service itself. Several methods in class **HugeInteger** are tagged with the **WebMethod** attribute, which *exposes* the method such that it can be called remotely. When this attribute is absent, the method is not accessible through the Web service. Notice that the **WebMethod** attribute, like the **WebService** attribute, contains a **Description** property, which provides information about the method to the ASMX page. Readers can see these descriptions in the output of Fig. 18.6.

Good Programming Practice 18.1

Specify a namespace for each Web service so that it can be uniquely identified.

Good Programming Practice 18.2

Specify descriptions for all Web services and Web-service methods so that clients can obtain additional information about the Web service and its contents.

Common Programming Error 18.2

*Web-service methods cannot be declared **static**, or a runtime error will occur when attempting to view the ASMX page. For a client to access a Web-service method, an instance of that Web service must exist.*

Lines 69–81 define an indexer for our class. This enables us to access any digit in **HugeInteger** as if we were accessing it through array **number**. Lines 108–136 and 142–163 define **WebMethod**s **Add** and **Subtract**, which perform addition and subtraction, respectively. Method **Borrow** (lines 166–183) handles the case in which the digit in the left operand is smaller than the corresponding digit in the right operand. For instance, when we subtract 19 from 32, we usually go digit by digit, starting from the right. The number 2 is smaller than 9, so we add 10 to 2 (resulting in 12), which subtracts 9, resulting in 3 for the rightmost digit in the solution. We then subtract 1 from the next digit over (3), making it 2. The corresponding digit in the right operand is now the "1" in 19. The subtraction of 1 from 2 is 1, making the corresponding digit in the result 1. The final result, when both resulting digits are combined, is 13. Method **Borrow** adds 10 to the appropriate digits and subtracts 1 from the digit to the left. Because this is a utility method that is not intended to be called remotely, it is not qualified with attribute **WebMethod**.

The screen capture in Fig. 18.6 is identical to the one in Fig. 18.1. A client application can invoke only the five methods listed in the screen shot (i.e., the methods qualified with the **WebMethod** attribute).

Now, let us demonstrate how to create this Web service. To begin, we must create a project of type **ASP.NET Web Service**. Like Web Forms, Web services are by default placed in the Web server's **wwwroot** directory on the server (**localhost**). By default, Visual Studio places the solution file (**.sln**) in the **Visual Studio Projects** folder, in a directory for the solution. (The **Visual Studio Projects** folder is usually located in the **My Documents** folder.)

Notice that, when the project is created, the code-behind file is displayed in design view by default (Fig. 18.7). If this file is not open, it can be opened by clicking

Service1.asmx. The file that will be opened, however, is **Service1.asmx.cs** (the code-behind file for our Web service). This is because, when creating Web services in Visual Studio, programmers work almost exclusively in the code-behind file. In fact, if a programmer were to open the ASMX file, it would contain only the lines:

```
<%@ WebService Language="c#" Codebehind="Service1.asmx.cs"
      Class="WebService1.Service1" %>
```

indicating the name of the code-behind file, the programming language in which the code-behind file is written and the class that defines our Web service. This is the extent of the information that this file must contain. [*Note*: By default, the code-behind file is not listed in the **Solution Explorer**. The code-behind file is displayed when the ASMX file is double clicked in the **Solution Explorer**. This file can be listed in the **Solution Explorer** by clicking the icon to show all files.]

It might seem strange that there is a design view for Web services, given that Web services do not have graphical user interfaces. A design view is provided because more sophisticated Web services contain methods that manipulate more than just strings or numbers. For example, a Web-service method could manipulate a database. Instead of typing all the code necessary to create a database connection, developers can simply drop the proper ADO .NET components into the design view and manipulate them as we would in a Windows or Web application. We show an example of this in Section 18.6.

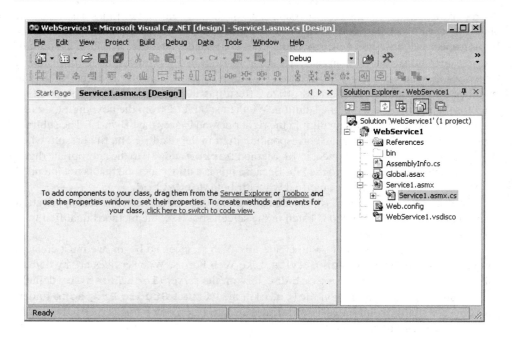

Fig. 18.7   Design view of a Web service.

Now that we have defined our Web service, we demonstrate how to use it. First, a client application must be created. In this first example, we create a Windows application as our client. Once this application has been created, the client must add a proxy class for accessing the Web service. A proxy class (or proxy) is a class created from the Web service's WSDL file that enables the client to call Web-service methods over the Internet. The proxy class handles all the "plumbing" required for Web-service method calls. Whenever a call is made in the client application to a Web-service method, the application actually calls a corresponding method in the proxy class. This method takes the name of the method and its arguments, then formats them so that they can be sent as a request in a SOAP message. The Web service receives this request and executes the method call, sending back the result as another SOAP message. When the client application receives the SOAP message containing the response, the proxy class decodes it and formats the results so that they are understandable to the client. This information then is returned to the client. It is important to note that the proxy class essentially is hidden from the programmer. We cannot, in fact, view it in the **Solution Explorer** unless we choose to show all the files. The purpose of the proxy class is to make it seem to clients as though they are calling the Web-service methods directly. It is rarely necessary for the client to view or manipulate the proxy class.

The next example demonstrates how to create a Web service client and its corresponding proxy class. We must begin by creating a project and adding a *Web reference* to that project. When we add a Web reference to a client application, the proxy class is created. The client then creates an instance of the proxy class, which is used to call methods included in the Web service.

To create a proxy in Visual Studio, right click the **References** folder in **Solution Explorer** and select ***Add Web Reference*** (Fig. 18.8). In the **Add Web Reference** dialog that appears (Fig. 18.9), enter the Web address of the Web service and press *Enter*. Once a Web service is chosen the description of that Web service appears, and the developer can click **Add Reference** (Fig. 18.9). This adds to the **Solution Explorer** (Fig. 18.10) a **Web References** folder with a node named for the domain where the Web service is located. In this case, the name is `localhost`, because we are using the local Web server. This means that, when we reference class `HugeInteger`, we will be doing so through class `HugeInteger` in namespace `localhost`, instead of class `HugeInteger` in namespace `HugeIntegerWebService` [*Note*: The Web service class and the proxy class have the same name. Visual Studio generates a proxy for the Web service and adds it as a reference (Fig. 18.10).]

Fig. 18.8   Adding a Web service reference to a project.

Fig. 18.9   Web reference selection and description.

    Good Programming Practice 18.3

When creating a program that will use Web services, add the Web reference first. This will enable Visual Studio .NET to recognize an instance of the Web service class, allowing Intellisense to help the developer use the Web service.

The steps that we described previously work well if the programmer knows the appropriate Web services reference. However, what if we are trying to locate a new Web service? There are two technologies that facilitate this process: *Universal Description, Discovery and Integration (UDDI)* and *Discovery files (DISCO)*. UDDI is a project for developing a set of specifications that define how Web services should be published so that programmers searching for Web services can find them. Microsoft began this ongoing project to facilitate the locating of Web services that conform to certain specifications, allowing programmers to find different Web services using search engines. UDDI organizes and describes Web services and then places this information in a central location. Although UDDI is beyond the scope of what we are teaching, the reader can learn more about this project and view a demonstration by visiting **www.uddi.org** and **uddi.microsoft.com**. These sites contain search tools that make finding Web services fast and easy.

Fig. 18.10 Solution Explorer after adding a Web reference to a project.

A DISCO file catalogs Web services in a particular directory. There are two types of discovery files: *Dynamic discovery* files (with a **.vsdisco** extension) and *static discovery* files (with a **.disco** extension). These files indicate both the location of the ASMX file and the service description (a WSDL file) for each Web service in the current directory, as well as any Web services in the current directory's subdirectories. When a programmer creates a Web service, Visual Studio generates a dynamic discovery file for that Web service. When a Web reference is added, the client uses the dynamic discovery file to select the desired Web service. Once the Web reference is created, a static discovery file is placed in the client's project. The static discovery file hard codes the location for the ASMX and WSDL files. (By "hard code", we mean that the location is entered directly into the file.) Dynamic discovery files, on the other hand, are created such that a list of Web services is created dynamically on the server when a client is searching for a Web service. The use of dynamic discovery enables certain extra options, such as hiding of certain Web services in subdirectories. Discovery files are a Microsoft-specific technology, whereas UDDI is not. However, the two can work together to enable a client to find a Web service. Using both technologies, the client can use a search engine to find a location with various Web services on a topic, and then use discovery files to view all the Web services in that location.

Once the Web reference is added, the client can access the Web service through our proxy. Because our proxy class is named **HugeInteger** and is located in namespace **localhost**, we must use **localhost.HugeInteger** to reference this class. The Windows Form in Fig. 18.11 uses the **HugeInteger** Web service to perform computations with positive integers up to **100** digits long. [*Note:* If using the examples for this book located on our Web site, the reader might need to regenerate the proxy.]

```
1   // Fig. 18.11: UsingHugeIntegerService.cs
2   // Using the HugeInteger Web Service.
3
```

Fig. 18.11 Using the **HugeInteger** Web service. (Part 1 of 6.)

```csharp
 4   using System;
 5   using System.Drawing;
 6   using System.Collections;
 7   using System.ComponentModel;
 8   using System.Windows.Forms;
 9   using System.Web.Services.Protocols;
10
11   // allows user to perform operations on large integers
12   public class UsingHugeIntService : System.Windows.Forms.Form
13   {
14      private System.Windows.Forms.Label promptLabel;
15      private System.Windows.Forms.Label resultLabel;
16
17      private System.Windows.Forms.TextBox firstTextBox;
18      private System.Windows.Forms.TextBox secondTextBox;
19
20      private System.Windows.Forms.Button addButton;
21      private System.Windows.Forms.Button subtractButton;
22      private System.Windows.Forms.Button biggerButton;
23      private System.Windows.Forms.Button smallerButton;
24      private System.Windows.Forms.Button equalButton;
25
26      private System.ComponentModel.Container components = null;
27
28      // declare a reference Web service
29      private localhost.HugeInteger remoteInteger;
30
31      private char[] zeroes = { '0' };
32
33      // default constructor
34      public UsingHugeIntService()
35      {
36         InitializeComponent();
37
38         // instantiate remoteInteger
39         remoteInteger = new localhost.HugeInteger();
40      }
41
42      // Visual Studio .NET generated code
43
44      [STAThread]
45      static void Main()
46      {
47         Application.Run( new UsingHugeIntService() );
48
49      } // end Main
50
51      // checks whether two numbers user input are equal
52      protected void equalButton_Click(
53         object sender, System.EventArgs e )
54      {
```

Fig. 18.11 Using the **HugeInteger** Web service. (Part 2 of 6.)

```
55          // make sure HugeIntegers do not exceed 100 digits
56          if ( CheckSize( firstTextBox, secondTextBox ) )
57             return;
58
59          // call Web-service method to determine
60          // whether integers are equal
61          if ( remoteInteger.EqualTo(
62             firstTextBox.Text, secondTextBox.Text ) )
63
64             resultLabel.Text =
65                firstTextBox.Text.TrimStart( zeroes ) +
66                " is equal to " +
67                secondTextBox.Text.TrimStart( zeroes );
68          else
69             resultLabel.Text =
70                firstTextBox.Text.TrimStart( zeroes ) +
71                " is NOT equal to " +
72                secondTextBox.Text.TrimStart( zeroes );
73
74       } // end method equalButton_Click
75
76       // checks whether first integer input
77       // by user is smaller than second
78       protected void smallerButton_Click(
79          object sender, System.EventArgs e )
80       {
81          // make sure HugeIntegers do not exceed 100 digits
82          if ( CheckSize( firstTextBox, secondTextBox ) )
83             return;
84
85          // call Web-service method to determine whether first
86          // integer is smaller than second
87          if ( remoteInteger.Smaller(
88             firstTextBox.Text, secondTextBox.Text ) )
89
90             resultLabel.Text =
91                firstTextBox.Text.TrimStart( zeroes ) +
92                " is smaller than " +
93                secondTextBox.Text.TrimStart( zeroes );
94          else
95             resultLabel.Text =
96                firstTextBox.Text.TrimStart( zeroes ) +
97                " is NOT smaller than " +
98                secondTextBox.Text.TrimStart( zeroes );
99
100      } // end method smallerButton_Click
101
102      // checks whether first integer input
103      // by user is bigger than second
104      protected void biggerButton_Click(
105         object sender, System.EventArgs e )
106      {
```

Fig. 18.11 Using the **HugeInteger** Web service. (Part 3 of 6.)

```
107        // make sure HugeIntegers do not exceed 100 digits
108        if ( CheckSize( firstTextBox, secondTextBox ) )
109           return;
110
111        // call Web-service method to determine whether first
112        // integer is larger than the second
113        if ( remoteInteger.Bigger( firstTextBox.Text,
114           secondTextBox.Text ) )
115
116           resultLabel.Text =
117              firstTextBox.Text.TrimStart( zeroes ) +
118              " is larger than " +
119              secondTextBox.Text.TrimStart( zeroes );
120        else
121           resultLabel.Text =
122              firstTextBox.Text.TrimStart( zeroes ) +
123              " is NOT larger than " +
124              secondTextBox.Text.TrimStart( zeroes );
125
126     } // end method biggerButton_Click
127
128     // subtract second integer from first
129     protected void subtractButton_Click(
130        object sender, System.EventArgs e )
131     {
132        // make sure HugeIntegers do not exceed 100 digits
133        if ( CheckSize( firstTextBox, secondTextBox ) )
134           return;
135
136        // perform subtraction
137        try
138        {
139           string result = remoteInteger.Subtract(
140              firstTextBox.Text,
141              secondTextBox.Text ).TrimStart( zeroes );
142
143           resultLabel.Text = ( ( result == "" ) ? "0" : result );
144        }
145
146        // if WebMethod throws an exception, then first
147        // argument was smaller than second
148        catch ( SoapException )
149        {
150           MessageBox.Show(
151              "First argument was smaller than the second" );
152        }
153
154     } // end method subtractButton_Click
155
156     // adds two integers input by user
157     protected void addButton_Click(
158        object sender, System.EventArgs e )
159     {
```

Fig. 18.11 Using the **HugeInteger** Web service. (Part 4 of 6.)

```
160          // make sure HugeInteger does not exceed 100 digits
161          // and is not situation where both integers are 100
162          // digits long--result in overflow
163          if ( firstTextBox.Text.Length > 100 ||
164             secondTextBox.Text.Length > 100   ||
165             ( firstTextBox.Text.Length == 100 &&
166             secondTextBox.Text.Length == 100 ) )
167          {
168             MessageBox.Show( "HugeIntegers must not be more "
169                + "than 100 digits\nBoth integers cannot be of"
170                + " length 100: this causes an overflow",
171                "Error", MessageBoxButtons.OK,
172                MessageBoxIcon.Information );
173
174             return;
175          }
176
177          // perform addition
178          resultLabel.Text = remoteInteger.Add( firstTextBox.Text,
179             secondTextBox.Text ).TrimStart( zeroes ).ToString();
180
181       } // end method addButton_Click
182
183       // determines whether size of integers is too big
184       private bool CheckSize( TextBox first, TextBox second )
185       {
186          if ( first.Text.Length > 100 || second.Text.Length > 100 )
187          {
188             MessageBox.Show( "HugeIntegers must be less than 100"
189                + " digits", "Error", MessageBoxButtons.OK,
190                MessageBoxIcon.Information );
191
192             return true;
193          }
194
195          return false;
196
197       } // end method CheckSize
198
199 } // end class UsingHugeIntegerService
```

Fig. 18.11 Using the **HugeInteger** Web service. (Part 5 of 6.)

Fig. 18.11 Using the **HugeInteger** Web service. (Part 6 of 6.)

The user inputs two integers, each up to 100 digits long. The clicking of any button invokes a remote method to perform the appropriate calculation and return the result. The return value of each operation is displayed, and all leading zeroes are eliminated using **string** method **TrimStart**. Note that **UsingHugeInteger** does not have the capability to perform operations with 100-digit numbers. Instead, it creates **string** representations of these numbers and passes them as arguments to Web-service methods that handle such tasks for us.

18.5 Session Tracking in Web Services

In Chapter 17, ASP .NET, Web Forms and Web Controls, we described the importance of maintaining information about users to personalize their experiences. In the context of this discussion, we explored session tracking using cookies and sessions. In this section, we incorporate session tracking into a Web service. Sometimes, it makes sense for client applications to call several methods from the same Web service, and to call some methods several times. It would be beneficial for the Web service to maintain state information for the client. Using session tracking can be beneficial, because information that is stored as part of the session will not need to be passed back and forth between the Web service and the client. This will not only cause the client application to run faster, but it will require less effort on the part of the programmer (who likely will have to pass less information to a Web-service method).

Storing session information also can provide for a more intuitive Web service. In the following example, we create a Web service designed to assist with the computations involved in playing a game of Blackjack (Fig. 18.12). We then use this Web service to create a dealer for a game of Blackjack. This dealer handles the details for our deck of cards. The information is stored as part of the session, so that one set of cards does not get mixed up with another deck of cards being used by another client application. Our example uses casino Blackjack rules as follows:

> *Two cards each are dealt to each the dealer and the player. The player's cards are dealt face up. Only one of the dealer's cards is dealt face up. Then, the player can begin taking additional cards, one at a time. These cards are dealt face up, and the player decides when to stop taking cards. If the sum of the player's cards exceeds 21, the game is over, and the player loses. When the player is satisfied with the current set of cards, the player "stays" (i.e., stops taking cards), and the dealer's hidden card is revealed. If the dealer's total is less than 17, the dealer must take another card; otherwise, the dealer must stay. The dealer must continue to take cards until the sum of the dealer's cards is greater than or equal to 17. If the dealer exceeds 21, the player wins. Otherwise, the hand with the higher point total wins. If both sets of cards have the same point total, the game is a "push" (i.e., a tie), and no one wins. Finally, if a player's first two cards total 21, the player immediately wins. This type of win is known as a "Blackjack."*

The Web service that we create provides methods to deal a card and to count cards in a hand, determining a value for a specific hand. Each card is represented by a string in the form "**face suit**," where **face** is a digit that represents the face of the card, and **suit** is a digit that represents the suit of the card. After the Web service is created, we create a Windows application that uses these methods to implement a game of Blackjack.

```
1    // Fig. 18.12: BlackjackService.asmx.cs
2    // Blackjack Web Service which manipulates a deck of cards.
3
4    using System;
5    using System.Collections;
6    using System.ComponentModel;
7    using System.Data;
8    using System.Diagnostics;
9    using System.Web;
10   using System.Web.Services;
11
12   namespace BlackjackWebService
13   {
14      [ WebService(
15         Namespace = "http://www.deitel.com/cspfep1/ch18/",
16         Description = "A Web service that provides methods " +
17         "to manipulate a deck of cards." ) ]
18      public class BlackjackService : System.Web.Services.WebService
19      {
20
21         // Visual Studio .NET generated code
22
```

Fig. 18.12 Blackjack Web service. (Part 1 of 3.)

```
23          // deal new card
24          [ WebMethod( EnableSession = true,
25             Description = "Deal a new card from the deck." ) ]
26          public string DealCard()
27          {
28             string card = "2 2";
29
30             // get client's deck
31             ArrayList deck = ( ArrayList ) Session[ "deck" ];
32             card = ( string ) deck[ 0 ];
33             deck.RemoveAt( 0 );
34             return card;
35
36          } // end method DealCard
37
38          [ WebMethod( EnableSession = true,
39             Description = "Create and shuffle a deck of cards." ) ]
40          public void Shuffle() .
41          {
42             Random randomObject = new Random();
43
44             ArrayList deck = new ArrayList();
45
46             // generate all possible cards
47             for ( int i = 1; i < 14; i++ ) {
48                for ( int j = 0; j < 4; j++ ) {
49                   deck.Add( i + " " + j );
50                }
51             }
52
53             // swap each card with another card randomly
54             for ( int i = 0; i < deck.Count; i++ )
55             {
56                int newIndex = randomObject.Next( deck.Count );
57                object temporary = deck[ i ];
58                deck[ i ] = deck[ newIndex ];
59                deck[ newIndex ] = temporary;
60             }
61
62             // add this deck to user's session state
63             Session[ "deck" ] = deck;
64          }
65
66          // computes value of hand
67          [ WebMethod ( Description = "Compute a " +
68             "numerical value for the current hand." ) ]
69          public int CountCards( string dealt )
70          {
71             // split string containing cards
72             char[] tab = { '\t' };
73             string[] cards = dealt.Split( tab );
74             int total = 0, face, aceCount = 0;
75
```

Fig. 18.12 Blackjack Web service. (Part 2 of 3.)

```
76              foreach ( string drawn in cards )
77              {
78                  // get face of card
79                  face =
80                      Int32.Parse( drawn.Substring(
81                          0, drawn.IndexOf( " " ) ) );
82
83                  switch ( face )
84                  {
85                      // if ace, increment number of aces in hand
86                      case 1:
87                          aceCount++;
88                          break;
89
90                      // if Jack, Queen or King, add 10 to total
91                      case 11:  case 12:  case 13:
92                          total += 10;
93                          break;
94
95                      // otherwise, add value of face
96                      default:
97                          total += face;
98                          break;
99
100                 } // end switch
101
102             } // end foreach
103
104             // if any aces, calculate optimum total
105             if ( aceCount > 0 )
106             {
107                 // if it is possible to count one ace as 11, and rest
108                 // 1 each, do so; otherwise, count all aces as 1 each
109                 if ( total + 11 + aceCount - 1 <= 21 )
110                     total += 11 + aceCount - 1;
111                 else
112                     total += aceCount;
113             }
114
115             return total;
116
117         }  // end method CountCards
118
119     } // end class BlackjackService
120
121 } // end namespace BlackjackWebService
```

Fig. 18.12 Blackjack Web service. (Part 3 of 3.)

Lines 24–36 define method **DealCard** as a **WebMethod**, with property **EnableSession** set to **true**. This property needs to be set to **true** to maintain session information. This simple step provides an important advantage to our Web service. The Web service now can use an **HttpSessionState** object (called **Session**) to maintain the deck of cards for each client application that wishes to use this Web service (line 31).

We can use **Session** to store objects for a specific client between method calls. We discussed session state in detail in Chapter 17, ASP .NET, Web Forms and Web Controls.

As we discuss shortly, method **DealCard** removes a card from the deck and returns it to the client. If we were not using a session variable, the deck of cards would need to be passed back and forth with each method call. Not only does the use of session state make the method easier to call (it now requires no arguments), but we avoid the overhead that would occur from sending this information back and forth, making our Web service faster.

In our current implementation, we simply have methods that use session variables. The Web service, however, still cannot determine which session variables belong to which user. This is an important point—if the Web service cannot uniquely identify a user, it has failed to perform session-tracking properly. If the same client called method **DealCard** twice, two different decks would be manipulated (as if two different users had called **Deal-Card**). To identify various users, the Web service creates a cookie for each user. Unfortunately, the Web service has no way of determining whether or not cookies are enabled on the client's machine. If the client application wishes to use this Web service, the client must accept this cookie in a *CookieContainer* object. We discuss this in more detail shortly, when we look into the client application that uses the **Blackjack** Web service.

Method **DealCard** (lines 24–36) obtains the current user's deck as an *ArrayList* from the Web service's **Session** object (line 31). You can think of an **ArrayList** as a dynamic array (i.e., its size can change at runtime). Class **ArrayList** is discussed in greater detail in Chapter 20, Data Structures and Collections. The class's method **Add** places an **object** in the **ArrayList**. Method **DealCard** then removes the top card from the deck (line 33) and returns the card's value as a **string** (line 34).

Method **Shuffle** (lines 38–64) generates an **ArrayList** representing a card deck, shuffles it and stores the shuffled cards in the client's **Session** object. Lines 47–51 include **for** loops to generate **string**s in the form "**face suit**" to represent each possible card in a deck. Lines 54–60 shuffle the re-created deck by swapping each card with another card in the deck. Line 63 adds the **ArrayList** to the **Session** object to maintain the deck between method calls.

Method **CountCards** (lines 67–117) counts the values of the cards in a hand by trying to attain the highest score possible without going over 21. Precautions need to be taken when calculating the value of the cards, because an ace can be counted as either 1 or 11, and all face cards count as 10.

The string **dealt** is tokenized into its individual cards by calling **string** method **Split** and passing it an array that contains the tab character. The **foreach** loop (line 76–102) counts the value of each card. Lines 79–81 retrieve the first integer—the face—and use that value as input to the **switch** statement in line 83. If the card is 1 (an ace), the program increments variable **aceCount**. Because an ace can have two values, additional logic is required to process aces. If the card is a 13, 12 or 11 (King, Queen or Jack), the program adds 10 to the total. If the card is anything else, the program increases the total by that value.

In lines 105–113, the aces are counted after all the other cards. If several aces are included in a hand, only one can be counted as 11 (e.g., if two were counted as 11 we would already have a hand value of 22, which is a losing hand). We then determine if we can count an ace as 11 without exceeding 21. If this is possible, line 110 adjusts the total accordingly. Otherwise, line 112 adjusts the total by counting each ace as 1 point.

CountCards attempts to maximize the value of the current cards without exceeding 21. Imagine, for example, that the dealer has a 7 and then receives an ace. The new total could be either 8 or 18. However, **CountCards** always tries the maximize the value of the cards without going over 21, so the new total is 18.

Now, we use the **Blackjack** Web service in a Windows application called **Game** (Fig. 18.13). This program uses an instance of **BlackjackWebService** to represent the dealer, calling its **DealCard** and **CountCards** methods. The Web service keeps track of both the player's and the dealer's cards (i.e., all the cards that have been dealt).

Each player has 11 **PictureBox**es—the maximum number of cards that can be dealt without exceeding 21. These **PictureBox**es are placed in an **ArrayList**, allowing us to index the **ArrayList** to determine which **PictureBox** displays the card image.

Previously we mentioned that the client must provide a way to accept any cookies created by the Web service to identify users. Line 64 in the constructor creates a new **CookieContainer** object for the **CookieContainer** property of **dealer**. Class **CookieContainer** (defined in namespace **System.Net**) acts as a storage space for an object of the **HttpCookie** class. Creating the **CookieContainer** allows the Web service to maintain session state for the current client. This **CookieContainer** stores a **Cookie** with a unique identifier that the server can use to recognize the client when the client makes future requests. By default, the **CookieContainer** is **null**, and a new **Session** object is created by the Web Service for each client.

```
1   // Fig. 18.13: Blackjack.cs
2   // Blackjack game that uses the Blackjack Web service.
3
4   using System;
5   using System.Drawing;
6   using System.Collections;
7   using System.ComponentModel;
8   using System.Windows.Forms;
9   using System.Data;
10  using System.Net;
11
12  // game that uses Blackjack Web Service
13  public class Blackjack : System.Windows.Forms.Form
14  {
15     private System.Windows.Forms.PictureBox pictureBox1;
16     private System.Windows.Forms.PictureBox pictureBox2;
17     private System.Windows.Forms.PictureBox pictureBox3;
18     private System.Windows.Forms.PictureBox pictureBox4;
19     private System.Windows.Forms.PictureBox pictureBox5;
20     private System.Windows.Forms.PictureBox pictureBox6;
21     private System.Windows.Forms.PictureBox pictureBox7;
22     private System.Windows.Forms.PictureBox pictureBox8;
23     private System.Windows.Forms.PictureBox pictureBox9;
24     private System.Windows.Forms.PictureBox pictureBox10;
25     private System.Windows.Forms.PictureBox pictureBox11;
26     private System.Windows.Forms.PictureBox pictureBox12;
27     private System.Windows.Forms.PictureBox pictureBox13;
28     private System.Windows.Forms.PictureBox pictureBox14;
```

Fig. 18.13 Blackjack game that uses **Blackjack** Web service. (Part 1 of 8.)

```
29        private System.Windows.Forms.PictureBox pictureBox15;
30        private System.Windows.Forms.PictureBox pictureBox16;
31        private System.Windows.Forms.PictureBox pictureBox17;
32        private System.Windows.Forms.PictureBox pictureBox18;
33        private System.Windows.Forms.PictureBox pictureBox19;
34        private System.Windows.Forms.PictureBox pictureBox20;
35        private System.Windows.Forms.PictureBox pictureBox21;
36        private System.Windows.Forms.PictureBox pictureBox22;
37
38        private System.Windows.Forms.Button dealButton;
39        private System.Windows.Forms.Button hitButton;
40        private System.Windows.Forms.Button stayButton;
41
42        private System.ComponentModel.Container components = null;
43
44        private localhost.BlackjackService dealer;
45        private string dealersCards, playersCards;
46        private ArrayList cardBoxes;
47        private int playerCard, dealerCard;
48
49        // labels displaying game status, dealer and player
50        private System.Windows.Forms.Label dealerLabel;
51        private System.Windows.Forms.Label playerLabel;
52        private System.Windows.Forms.Label statusLabel;
53
54        public enum GameStatus :
55           int { PUSH, LOSE, WIN, BLACKJACK };
56
57        public Blackjack()
58        {
59           InitializeComponent();
60
61           dealer = new localhost.BlackjackService();
62
63           // allow session state
64           dealer.CookieContainer = new CookieContainer();
65
66           cardBoxes = new ArrayList();
67
68           // put PictureBoxes into cardBoxes
69           cardBoxes.Add( pictureBox1 );
70           cardBoxes.Add( pictureBox2 );
71           cardBoxes.Add( pictureBox3 );
72           cardBoxes.Add( pictureBox4 );
73           cardBoxes.Add( pictureBox5 );
74           cardBoxes.Add( pictureBox6 );
75           cardBoxes.Add( pictureBox7 );
76           cardBoxes.Add( pictureBox8 );
77           cardBoxes.Add( pictureBox9 );
78           cardBoxes.Add( pictureBox10 );
79           cardBoxes.Add( pictureBox11 );
80           cardBoxes.Add( pictureBox12 );
81           cardBoxes.Add( pictureBox13 );
```

Fig. 18.13 Blackjack game that uses **Blackjack** Web service. (Part 2 of 8.)

```
82          cardBoxes.Add( pictureBox14 );
83          cardBoxes.Add( pictureBox15 );
84          cardBoxes.Add( pictureBox16 );
85          cardBoxes.Add( pictureBox17 );
86          cardBoxes.Add( pictureBox18 );
87          cardBoxes.Add( pictureBox19 );
88          cardBoxes.Add( pictureBox20 );
89          cardBoxes.Add( pictureBox21 );
90          cardBoxes.Add( pictureBox22 );
91
92      } // end method Blackjack
93
94      // Visual Studio .NET generated code
95
96      [STAThread]
97      static void Main()
98      {
99          Application.Run( new Blackjack() );
100
101     } // end Main
102
103     // deals cards to dealer while dealer's total is
104     // less than 17, then computes value of each hand
105     // and determines winner
106     protected void stayButton_Click(
107        object sender, System.EventArgs e )
108     {
109        stayButton.Enabled = false;
110        hitButton.Enabled = false;
111        dealButton.Enabled = true;
112        DealerPlay();
113     }
114
115     // process dealers turn
116     private void DealerPlay()
117     {
118        // while value of dealer's hand is below 17,
119        // dealer must take cards
120        while ( dealer.CountCards( dealersCards ) < 17 )
121        {
122           dealersCards += "\t" + dealer.DealCard();
123           DisplayCard( dealerCard, "" );
124           dealerCard++;
125           MessageBox.Show( "Dealer takes a card" );
126        }
127
128        int dealersTotal = dealer.CountCards( dealersCards );
129        int playersTotal = dealer.CountCards( playersCards );
130
131        // if dealer busted, player wins
132        if ( dealersTotal > 21 )
133        {
134           GameOver( GameStatus.WIN );
```

Fig. 18.13 Blackjack game that uses **Blackjack** Web service. (Part 3 of 8.)

```
135          return;
136      }
137
138      // if dealer and player have not exceeded 21,
139      // higher score wins; equal scores is a push.
140      if ( dealersTotal > playersTotal )
141         GameOver( GameStatus.LOSE );
142      else if ( playersTotal > dealersTotal )
143         GameOver( GameStatus.WIN );
144      else
145         GameOver( GameStatus.PUSH );
146
147   } // end method DealerPlay
148
149   // deal another card to player
150   protected void hitButton_Click(
151      object sender, System.EventArgs e )
152   {
153      // get player another card
154      string card = dealer.DealCard();
155      playersCards += "\t" + card;
156      DisplayCard( playerCard, card );
157      playerCard++;
158
159      int total = dealer.CountCards( playersCards );
160
161      // if player exceeds 21, house wins
162      if ( total > 21 )
163         GameOver( GameStatus.LOSE );
164
165      // if player has 21, they cannot take more cards
166      // the dealer plays
167      if ( total == 21 )
168      {
169         hitButton.Enabled = false;
170         DealerPlay();
171      }
172
173   } // end method hitButton_Click
174
175   // deal two cards each to dealer and player
176   protected void dealButton_Click(
177      object sender, System.EventArgs e )
178   {
179      string card;
180
181      // clear card images
182      foreach ( PictureBox cardImage in cardBoxes )
183         cardImage.Image = null;
184
185      // clear status from previous game
186      statusLabel.Text = "";
187
```

Fig. 18.13 Blackjack game that uses **Blackjack** Web service. (Part 4 of 8.)

```
188            // shuffle cards
189            dealer.Shuffle();
190
191            // deal two cards to player
192            playersCards = dealer.DealCard();
193            DisplayCard( 11, playersCards );
194            card = dealer.DealCard();
195            DisplayCard( 12, card );
196            playersCards += "\t" + card;
197
198            // deal two cards to dealer, only display face
199            // of first card
200            dealersCards = dealer.DealCard() ;
201            DisplayCard( 0, dealersCards );
202            card = dealer.DealCard();
203            DisplayCard( 1, "" );
204            dealersCards += "\t" + card;
205
206            stayButton.Enabled = true;
207            hitButton.Enabled = true;
208            dealButton.Enabled = false;
209
210            int dealersTotal = dealer.CountCards( dealersCards );
211            int playersTotal = dealer.CountCards( playersCards );
212
213            // if hands equal 21, it is a push
214            if ( dealersTotal == playersTotal &&
215               dealersTotal == 21 )
216               GameOver( GameStatus.PUSH );
217
218            // if player has 21 player wins with blackjack
219            else if ( playersTotal == 21 )
220               GameOver( GameStatus.BLACKJACK );
221
222            // if dealer has 21, dealer wins
223            else if ( dealersTotal == 21 )
224               GameOver( GameStatus.LOSE );
225
226            dealerCard = 2;
227            playerCard = 13;
228
229         } // end method dealButton_Click
230
231         // displays card represented by cardValue in
232         // PictureBox with number card
233         public void DisplayCard( int card, string cardValue )
234         {
235            // retrieve appropriate PictureBox from ArrayList
236            PictureBox displayBox = ( PictureBox ) cardBoxes[ card ];
237
```

Fig. 18.13 Blackjack game that uses **Blackjack** Web service. (Part 5 of 8.)

```
238          // if string representing card is empty,
239          // set displayBox to display back of card
240          if ( cardValue == "" )
241          {
242             displayBox.Image =
243                Image.FromFile( "blackjack_images\\cardback.png" );
244             return;
245          }
246
247          // retrieve face value of card from cardValue
248          int faceNumber = Int32.Parse( cardValue.Substring( 0,
249             cardValue.IndexOf( " " ) ) );
250
251          string face = faceNumber.ToString();
252
253          // retrieve the suit of the card from cardValue
254          string suit = cardValue.Substring(
255             cardValue.IndexOf( " " ) + 1 );
256
257          char suitLetter;
258
259          // determine if suit is other than clubs
260          switch ( Convert.ToInt32( suit ) )
261          {
262             // suit is clubs
263             case 0:
264                suitLetter = 'c';
265                break;
266
267             // suit is diamonds
268             case 1:
269                suitLetter = 'd';
270                break;
271
272             // suit is hearts
273             case 2:
274                suitLetter = 'h';
275                break;
276
277             // else suit is spades
278             default:
279                suitLetter = 's';
280                break;
281          }
282
283          // set displayBox to display appropriate image
284          displayBox.Image = Image.FromFile(
285             "blackjack_images\\" + face + suitLetter + ".png"  );
286
287       } // end method DisplayCard
288
289    // displays all player cards and shows
290    // appropriate game status message
```

Fig. 18.13 Blackjack game that uses **Blackjack** Web service. (Part 6 of 8.)

```
291      public void GameOver( GameStatus winner )
292      {
293         char[] tab = { '\t' };
294         string[] cards = dealersCards.Split( tab );
295
296         for ( int i = 0; i < cards.Length; i++ )
297            DisplayCard(  i, cards[ i ] );
298
299         // push
300         if ( winner == GameStatus.PUSH )
301            statusLabel.Text = "It's a tie!";
302
303         // player loses
304         else if ( winner == GameStatus.LOSE )
305            statusLabel.Text = "You Lose Try Again!";
306
307         // player wins
308         else if ( winner == GameStatus.WIN )
309            statusLabel.Text = "You Win!";
310
311         // player has won with blackjack
312         else
313            statusLabel.Text = "BlackJack!";
314
315         stayButton.Enabled = false;
316         hitButton.Enabled = false;
317         dealButton.Enabled = true;
318
319      } // end method GameOver
320
321   } // end class Blackjack
```

Fig. 18.13 Blackjack game that uses **Blackjack** Web service. (Part 7 of 8.)

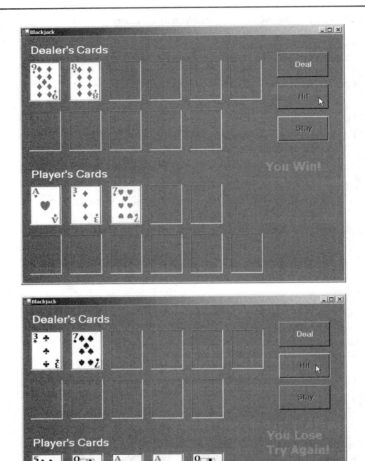

Fig. 18.13 Blackjack game that uses **Blackjack** Web service. (Part 8 of 8.)

Method **GameOver** (lines 291–319) displays all the dealer's cards (many of which are turned face down during the game) and shows the appropriate message in the status **PictureBox**. Method **GameOver** receives as an argument a member of the **GameStatus** enumeration (defined in lines 54–55). The enumeration represents whether the player tied, lost or won the game; its four members are: **PUSH**, **LOSE**, **WIN** and **BLACKJACK**.

When the player clicks the **Deal** button (in the event handler on lines 176–229), all the **PictureBox**es are cleared, the deck is shuffled and the player and dealer receive two cards each. If both obtain scores of 21, method **GameOver** is called and is passed **GameStatus.PUSH**. If the player has 21, **GameOver** is called and is passed **GameStatus.BLACKJACK**. Finally, if only the dealer has 21, method **GameOver** is called and is passed **GameStatus.LOSE**.

If **GameOver** is not called, the player can take additional cards by clicking the **Hit** button (in the event handler on lines 150–173). Each time a player clicks **Hit**, the player is dealt one card, which is displayed in the GUI. If the player exceeds 21, the game is over, and the player loses. If the player has exactly 21, the player is not allowed to take any more cards.

Players can click the **Stay** button to indicate that they do not want to risk being dealt another card. In the event handler for this event (lines 106–113), all three buttons are disabled, and method **DealerPlay** is called. This method (lines 116–147) causes the dealer to keep taking cards until the dealer's hand is worth 17 or more. If the dealer's hand exceeds 21, the player wins; otherwise, the values of the hands are compared, and **GameOver** is called with the appropriate argument.

Method **DisplayCard** (lines 233–287) retrieves the appropriate card image. It takes as arguments an integer representing the index of the **PictureBox** in the **ArrayList** that must have its image set and a **string** representing the card. An empty **string** indicates that we wish to display the back of a card; otherwise, the program extracts the face and suit from the **string** and uses this information to find the correct image. The **switch** statement (lines 260–281) converts the number representing the suit into an integer and assigns the appropriate character to **suitLetter** (**c** for Clubs, **d** for Diamonds, **h** for Hearts and **s** for Spades). The character **suitLetter** completes the image's file name.

18.6 Using Web Forms and Web Services

In the previous examples, we have accessed Web services from Windows applications. However, we can just as easily use them in Web applications. Because Web-based business is becoming more and more prevalent, it often is more practical for programmers to design Web services as part of Web applications. Figure 18.14 presents an airline-reservation Web service that receives information regarding the type of seat the customer wishes to reserve and then makes a reservation if such a seat is available.

The airline-reservation Web service has a single **WebMethod**—**Reserve** (lines 36–85)—which searches its seat database to locate a seat matching a user's request. If it finds an appropriate seat, **Reserve** updates the database, makes the reservation and returns **true**; otherwise, no reservation is made, and the method returns **false**.

Reserve takes two arguments: A **string** representing the desired type of seat (the choices are window, middle or aisle) and a **string** representing the desired class type (the choices are economy or first class). Our database contains four columns: The seat number, the seat type, the class type and a column containing either 0 or 1 to indicate whether the seat is taken. Lines 48–51 define an SQL command that retrieves the number of available seats matching the requested seat and class types. The statement in lines 52–53 executes the query. If the result of the query is not empty, the application reserves the first seat number that the query returns. The database is updated with an **UPDATE** command, and **Reserve** returns **true**, indicating that the reservation was successful. If the result of the **SELECT** query is not successful, **Reserve** returns **false**, indicating that no available seats matched the request.

```
1    // Fig. 18.14: Reservation.asmx.cs
2    // Airline reservation Web Service.
3
4    using System;
5    using System.Data;
6    using System.Diagnostics;
7    using System.Web;
8    using System.Web.Services;
9    using System.Data.OleDb;
10
11   namespace AirlineReservation
12   {
13      // performs reservation of a seat
14      [ WebService( Namespace = "http://www.deitel.com/cspfep1/ch18/",
15         Description = "Service that enables a user to " +
16         "reserve a seat on a plane." ) ]
17      public class Reservation : System.Web.Services.WebService
18      {
19         private System.Data.OleDb.OleDbCommand
20            oleDbSelectCommand1;
21         private System.Data.OleDb.OleDbCommand
22            oleDbInsertCommand1;
23         private System.Data.OleDb.OleDbCommand
24            oleDbUpdateCommand1;
25         private System.Data.OleDb.OleDbCommand
26            oleDbDeleteCommand1;
27         private System.Data.OleDb.OleDbConnection
28            oleDbConnection1;
29         private System.Data.OleDb.OleDbDataAdapter
30            oleDbDataAdapter1;
31
32         // Visual Studio .NET generated code
33
34         // checks database to determine whether
35         // matching seat is available
36         [ WebMethod ( Description = "Method to reserve seat." ) ]
37         public bool Reserve( string seatType, string classType )
38         {
39            OleDbDataReader dataReader;
40
41            // try database connection
42            try
43            {
44               // open database connection
45               oleDbConnection1.Open();
46
47               // set and execute SQL query
48               oleDbDataAdapter1.SelectCommand.CommandText =
49                  "SELECT Number FROM Seats WHERE Type = '" +
50                  seatType + "' AND Class = '" + classType +
51                  "' AND Taken = '0'" ;
52               dataReader =
53                  oleDbDataAdapter1.SelectCommand.ExecuteReader();
```

Fig. 18.14 Airline reservation Web service. (Part 1 of 2.)

```
54
55              // if there were results, seat is available
56              if ( dataReader.Read() )
57              {
58                 string seatNumber = dataReader.GetString( 0 );
59
60                 dataReader.Close();
61
62                 // update first available seat to be taken
63                 oleDbDataAdapter1.UpdateCommand.CommandText =
64                    "Update Seats Set Taken = '1' WHERE Number = '"
65                    + seatNumber + "'";
66                 oleDbDataAdapter1.UpdateCommand.ExecuteNonQuery();
67
68                 return true;
69
70              } // end if
71              dataReader.Close();
72           }
73           catch ( OleDbException ) // if connection problem
74           {
75              return false;
76           }
77           finally
78           {
79              oleDbConnection1.Close();
80           }
81
82           // no seat was reserved
83           return false;
84
85        } // end method Reserve
86
87     } // end class Reservation
88
89  } // end namespace AirlineReservation
```

Fig. 18.14 Airline reservation Web service. (Part 2 of 2.)

Earlier in the chapter, we displayed a Web service in design view (Fig. 18.7), and we explained that this design view allows the programmer to add components to a Web service. In our airline-reservation Web service (Fig. 18.14), we used various data components. Figure 18.16 shows these components in design view. Notice that it is easier to drop these components into our Web service using the **Toolbox** than to type the equivalent code.

Figure 18.16 presents the ASPX listing for the Web Form through which users can select seat types. This page allows a user to reserve a seat on the basis of its class and location in a row of seats. The page then uses the airline-reservation Web service to carry out the user's request. If the database request is not successful, the user is instructed to modify the request and try again.

Fig. 18.15 Airline Web Service in design view.

```
1   <%-- Fig. 18.16: TicketReservation.aspx            --%>
2   <%-- A Web Form to allow users to select the kind of seat --%>
3   <%-- they wish to reserve.                          --%>
4
5   <%@ Page language="c#" Codebehind="TicketReservation.aspx.cs"
6       AutoEventWireup="false"
7       Inherits="MakeReservation.TicketReservation" %>
8
9   <!DOCTYPE HTML PUBLIC "-//W3C//DTD HTML 4.0 Transitional//EN" >
10  <HTML>
11     <HEAD>
12        <meta name="GENERATOR" Content="Microsoft Visual Studio 7.0">
13        <meta name="CODE_LANGUAGE" Content="C#">
14        <meta name="vs_defaultClientScript"
15              content="JavaScript (ECMAScript)">
16        <meta name="vs_targetSchema"
17              content="http://schemas.microsoft.com/intellisense/ie5">
18     </HEAD>
19     <body MS_POSITIONING="GridLayout">
20
21        <form id="MakeReservation" method="post" runat="server">
22
23           <asp:DropDownList id="seatList" style="Z-INDEX: 101;
24              LEFT: 16px; POSITION: absolute; TOP: 43px"
25              runat="server" Width="105px" Height="22px">
26
27              <asp:ListItem Value="Aisle">Aisle</asp:ListItem>
28              <asp:ListItem Value="Middle">Middle</asp:ListItem>
29              <asp:ListItem Value="Window">Window</asp:ListItem>
30
31           </asp:DropDownList>
32
33           <asp:DropDownList id="classList" style="Z-INDEX: 102;
34              LEFT: 145px; POSITION: absolute; TOP: 43px"
35              runat="server" Width="98px" Height="22px">
36
```

Fig. 18.16 ASPX file that takes reservation information. (Part 1 of 2.)

```
37              <asp:ListItem Value="Economy">Economy</asp:ListItem>
38              <asp:ListItem Value="First">First</asp:ListItem>
39
40          </asp:DropDownList>
41
42          <asp:Button id="reserveButton" style="Z-INDEX: 103;
43            LEFT: 21px; POSITION: absolute; TOP: 83px" runat="server"
44            Text="Reserve">
45          </asp:Button>
46
47          <asp:Label id="Label1" style="Z-INDEX: 104;
48            LEFT: 17px; POSITION: absolute; TOP: 13px"
49            runat="server">Please select the type of seat and
50            class you wish to reserve:
51          </asp:Label>
52
53        </form>
54      </body>
55  </HTML>
```

Fig. 18.16 ASPX file that takes reservation information. (Part 2 of 2.)

The page in Fig. 18.16 defines two **DropDownList** objects and a **Button**. One **DropDownList** displays all the seat types from which users can select. The second lists choices for the class type. Users click the **Button**, named **reserveButton**, to submit requests after making selections from the **DropDownList**s. The code-behind file (Fig. 18.17) attaches an event handler for this button.

Lines 30–31 create a **Reservation** object. When the user clicks **Reserve**, the **reserveButton_Click** event handler executes, and the page reloads. The event handler (lines 48–63) calls the Web service's **Reserve** method and passes it the selected seat and class types as arguments. If **Reserve** returns **true**, the application displays a message thanking the user for making a reservation; otherwise, the user is notified that the type of seat requested is not available, and the user is instructed to try again.

```
1   // Fig. 18.17: TicketReservation.aspx.cs
2   // Making a Reservation using a Web Service.
3
4   using System;
5   using System.Collections;
6   using System.ComponentModel;
7   using System.Data;
8   using System.Drawing;
9   using System.Web;
10  using System.Web.SessionState;
11  using System.Web.UI;
12  using System.Web.UI.WebControls;
13  using System.Web.UI.HtmlControls;
14
```

Fig. 18.17 Code-behind file for the reservation page. (Part 1 of 3.)

```
15   namespace MakeReservation
16   {
17      // allows visitors to select seat type to reserve, and
18      // then make reservation
19      public class TicketReservation : System.Web.UI.Page
20      {
21         protected System.Web.UI.WebControls.DropDownList
22            seatList;
23         protected System.Web.UI.WebControls.DropDownList
24            classList;
25
26         protected System.Web.UI.WebControls.Button
27            reserveButton;
28         protected System.Web.UI.WebControls.Label Label1;
29
30         private localhost.Reservation agent =
31            new localhost.Reservation();
32
33         private void Page_Load(
34            object sender, System.EventArgs e )
35         {
36            if ( IsPostBack )
37            {
38               seatList.Visible =        ;
39               classList.Visible =         ;
40               reserveButton.Visible =         ;
41               Label1.Visible =        ;
42            }
43         }
44
45         // Visual Studio .NET generated code
46
47         // calls Web Service to try to reserve specified seat
48         public void reserveButton_Click (
49            object sender, System.EventArgs e )
50         {
51            // if Web-service method returned true, signal success
52            if ( agent.Reserve( seatList.SelectedItem.Text,
53               classList.SelectedItem.Text ) )
54               Response.Write( "Your reservation has been made."
55                  + "  Thank you." );
56
57            // Web-service method returned false, so signal failure
58            else
59               Response.Write( "This seat is not available, " +
60                  "please hit the back button on your browser " +
61                  "and try again." );
62
63         } // end method reserveButton_Click
64
65      } // end class TicketReservation
66
67   } // end namespace MakeReservation
```

Fig. 18.17 Code-behind file for the reservation page. (Part 2 of 3.)

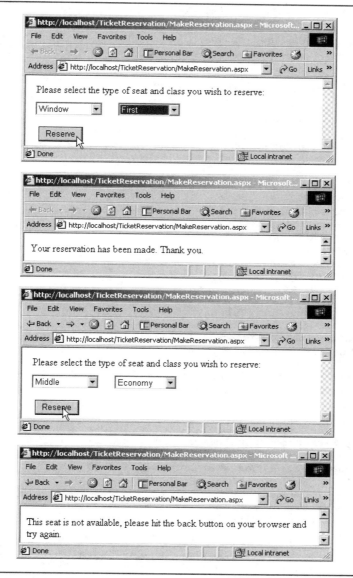

Fig. 18.17 Code-behind file for the reservation page. (Part 3 of 3.)

18.7 Case Study: Temperature Information Application

This case study discusses both a Web service that presents weather forecasts for various cities around the United States and a windows application that employs the Web service. The Web service uses networking capabilities to display the forecasts; it parses a Web page containing the required information and then extracts weather forecast data.

First, we present Web service **TemperatureServer** in Fig. 18.18. This Web service reads a Web page and collects information about the temperature and weather conditions in an assortment of American cities. [*Note*: At the time of publication, this program runs in the manner that we describe. However, if changes are made to the Web page from which the program retrieves data, the program might work differently or not at all. Please check our Web site at **www.deitel.com** for updates.]

```
1   // Fig. 18.18: TemperatureServer.asmx.cs
2   // TemperatureServer Web Service that extracts weather
3   // information from a Web page.
4
5   using System;
6   using System.Collections;
7   using System.ComponentModel;
8   using System.Data;
9   using System.Diagnostics;
10  using System.Web;
11  using System.Web.Services;
12  using System.IO;
13  using System.Net;
14
15  namespace TemperatureWebService
16  {
17     [ WebService( Namespace = "http://www.deitel.com/cspfep1/ch18/",
18        Description = "A Web service that provides information " +
19        "from the National Weather Service." ) ]
20     public class TemperatureServer :
21        System.Web.Services.WebService
22     {
23        // Visual Studio .NET generated code
24
25        [ WebMethod( EnableSession = true, Description =
26           "Method to read information from the weather service." ) ]
27        public void UpdateWeatherConditions()
28        {
29           // create WebClient to get access to Web page
30           WebClient myClient = new WebClient();
31           ArrayList cityList = new ArrayList();
32
33           // get StreamReader for response so we can read page
34           StreamReader input = new StreamReader(
35              myClient.OpenRead(
36              "http://iwin.nws.noaa.gov/iwin/us/" +
37              "traveler.html" ) );
38
39           string separator = "TAV12";
40
41           // locate first horizontal line on Web page
42           while ( !input.ReadLine().StartsWith(
43              separator ) ) ; // do nothing
44
```

Fig. 18.18 TemperatureServer Web service. (Part 1 of 3.)

```
45            // day format and night format
46            string dayFormat =
47               "CITY            WEA      HI/LO    WEA      " +
48               "HI/LO";
49            string nightFormat =
50               "CITY            WEA      LO/HI    WEA      " +
51               "LO/HI";
52            string inputLine = "";
53
54            // locate header that begins weather information
55            do
56            {
57               inputLine = input.ReadLine();
58            } while ( !inputLine.Equals( dayFormat ) &&
59               !inputLine.Equals( nightFormat ) );
60
61            // get first city's data
62            inputLine = input.ReadLine();
63
64            while ( inputLine.Length > 28 )
65            {
66               // create CityWeather object for city
67               CityWeather weather = new CityWeather(
68                  inputLine.Substring( 0, 16 ),
69                  inputLine.Substring( 16, 7 ),
70                  inputLine.Substring( 23, 7 ) );
71
72               // add to List
73               cityList.Add( weather );
74
75               // get next city's data
76               inputLine = input.ReadLine();
77            }
78
79            // close connection to NWS server
80            input.Close();
81
82            // add city list to user session
83            Session.Add( "cityList", cityList );
84
85         } // end UpdateWeatherConditions
86
87         // gets all city names
88         [ WebMethod( EnableSession = true, Description =
89            "Method to retrieve a list of cities." ) ]
90         public string[] Cities()
91         {
92            ArrayList cityList = ( ArrayList ) Session[ "cityList" ];
93            string[] cities= new string[ cityList.Count ];
94
95            // retrieve names for cities
96            for ( int i = 0; i < cityList.Count; i++ )
97            {
```

Fig. 18.18 TemperatureServer Web service. (Part 2 of 3.)

```
98                  CityWeather weather = ( CityWeather ) cityList[ i ];
99
100                 cities[ i ] = weather.CityName;
101              }
102
103              return cities;
104
105           } // end method Cities
106
107           // gets all city descriptions
108           [ WebMethod( EnableSession = true, Description = "Method" +
109              " to retrieve weather descriptions for a " +
110              "list of cities." )]
111           public string[] Descriptions()
112           {
113              ArrayList cityList = ( ArrayList ) Session[ "cityList" ];
114              string[] descriptions= new string[ cityList.Count ];
115
116              // retrieve weather descriptions for all cities
117              for ( int i = 0; i < cityList.Count; i++ )
118              {
119                 CityWeather weather = ( CityWeather )cityList[ i ];
120
121                 descriptions[ i ] = weather.Description;
122              }
123
124              return descriptions;
125
126           } // end method Descriptions
127
128           // obtains each city temperature
129           [ WebMethod( EnableSession = true, Description = "Method " +
130              "to retrieve the temperature for a list of cities." ) ]
131           public string[] Temperatures()
132           {
133              ArrayList cityList = ( ArrayList ) Session[ "cityList" ];
134              string[] temperatures= new string[ cityList.Count ];
135
136              // retrieve temperatures for all cities
137              for ( int i = 0; i < cityList.Count; i++ )
138              {
139                 CityWeather weather = ( CityWeather )cityList[ i ];
140                 temperatures[ i ] = weather.Temperature;
141              }
142
143              return temperatures;
144
145           } // end method Temperatures
146
147        } // end class TemperatureServer
148
149     } // end namespace TemperatureWebService
```

Fig. 18.18 TemperatureServer Web service. (Part 3 of 3.)

Method **UpdateWeatherConditions**, which gathers weather data from a Web page, is the first **WebMethod** that a client must call from the Web service. The service also provides **WebMethod**s **Cities**, **Descriptions** and **Temperatures**, which return different kinds of forecast-related information.

When **UpdateWeatherConditions** (lines 25–85) is invoked, the method connects to a Web site containing the traveler's forecasts from the National Weather Service (NWS). Line 30 creates a *WebClient* object, which we use because the **WebClient** class is designed for interaction with a source specified by a URL. In this case, the URL for the NWS page is **http://iwin.nws.noaa.gov/iwin/us/traveler.html**. Lines 34–37 call **WebClient** method *OpenRead*; the method retrieves a **Stream** from the URL containing the weather information and then uses this **Stream** to create a **StreamReader** object. Using a **StreamReader** object, the program can read the Web page's HTML markup line by line.

The section of the Web page in which we are interested starts with the **string** "**TAV12**." Therefore, lines 42–43 read the HTML markup one line at a time until this **string** is encountered. Once the string "**TAV12**" is reached, the **do/while** structure (lines 55–59) continues to read the page one line at a time until it finds the header line (i.e., the line at the beginning of the forecast table). This line starts with either **dayFormat**, indicating day format, or **nightFormat**, indicating night format. Because the line could be in either format, the structure checks for both. Line 62 reads the next line from the page, which is the first line containing temperature information.

The **while** structure (lines 64–77) creates a new **CityWeather** object to represent the current city. It parses the **string** containing the current weather data, separating the city name, the weather condition and the temperature. The **CityWeather** object is added to **cityList** (an **ArrayList** that contains a list of the cities, their descriptions and their current temperatures); then, the next line from the page is read and stored in **inputLine** for the next iteration. This process continues until the length of the **string** read from the Web page is less than or equal to **28**. This signals the end of the temperature section. Line 83 adds the **ArrayList cityList** to the **Session** object so that the values are maintained between method calls.

Method **Cities** (lines 88–105) creates an array of **string**s that can contain as many **string** elements as there are elements in **cityList**. Line 92 obtains the list of cities from the **Session** object. Lines 96–101 iterate through each **CityWeather** object in **cityList** and insert the city name into the array, which is returned in line 103. Methods **Descriptions** (lines 108–126) and **Temperatures** (lines 129–145) behave similarly, except that they return weather descriptions and temperatures, respectively.

Figure 18.19 contains the code listing for the **CityWeather** class. The constructor takes three arguments: The city's name, the weather description and the current temperature. The class provides the read-only properties **CityName**, **Temperature** and **Description** so that these values can be retrieved by the Web service.

```
1   // Fig. 18.19: CityWeather.cs
2   // Class representing the weather information for one city.
3
4   using System;
```

Fig. 18.19 Class that stores weather information about a city. (Part 1 of 2.)

```
 5
 6   namespace TemperatureWebService
 7   {
 8      public class CityWeather
 9      {
10         private string cityName;
11         private string temperature;
12         private string description;
13
14         public CityWeather(
15            string city, string information, string degrees )
16         {
17            cityName = city;
18            description = information;
19            temperature = degrees;
20         }
21
22         // city name
23         public string CityName
24         {
25            get
26            {
27               return cityName;
28            }
29         }
30
31         // city temperature
32         public string Temperature
33         {
34            get
35            {
36               return temperature;
37            }
38         }
39
40         // forecast description
41         public string Description
42         {
43            get
44            {
45               return description;
46            }
47         }
48
49      } // end class CityWeather
50   } // end namespace TemperatureWebService
```

Fig. 18.19 Class that stores weather information about a city. (Part 2 of 2.)

The Windows application in Fig. 18.20 uses the **TemperatureServer** Web service to display weather information in a user-friendly format.

TemperatureClient (Fig. 18.20) is a Windows application that uses the **TemperatureServer** Web service to display weather information in a graphical and easy-to-read manner. The application consists of 36 **Label**s, which are placed in two columns. Each **Label** displays the weather information for a different city.

```csharp
1   // Fig. 18.20: Client.cs
2   // Class that displays weather information that it receives
3   // from a Web service.
4
5   using System;
6   using System.Drawing;
7   using System.Collections;
8   using System.ComponentModel;
9   using System.Windows.Forms;
10  using System.Net;
11
12  namespace TemperatureClient
13  {
14     public class Client : System.Windows.Forms.Form
15     {
16        private System.Windows.Forms.Label label1;
17        private System.Windows.Forms.Label label2;
18        private System.Windows.Forms.Label label3;
19        private System.Windows.Forms.Label label4;
20        private System.Windows.Forms.Label label5;
21        private System.Windows.Forms.Label label6;
22        private System.Windows.Forms.Label label7;
23        private System.Windows.Forms.Label label8;
24        private System.Windows.Forms.Label label9;
25        private System.Windows.Forms.Label label10;
26        private System.Windows.Forms.Label label11;
27        private System.Windows.Forms.Label label12;
28        private System.Windows.Forms.Label label13;
29        private System.Windows.Forms.Label label14;
30        private System.Windows.Forms.Label label15;
31        private System.Windows.Forms.Label label16;
32        private System.Windows.Forms.Label label17;
33        private System.Windows.Forms.Label label18;
34        private System.Windows.Forms.Label label19;
35        private System.Windows.Forms.Label label20;
36        private System.Windows.Forms.Label label21;
37        private System.Windows.Forms.Label label22;
38        private System.Windows.Forms.Label label23;
39        private System.Windows.Forms.Label label24;
40        private System.Windows.Forms.Label label25;
41        private System.Windows.Forms.Label label26;
42        private System.Windows.Forms.Label label27;
43        private System.Windows.Forms.Label label28;
44        private System.Windows.Forms.Label label29;
45        private System.Windows.Forms.Label label30;
46        private System.Windows.Forms.Label label31;
47        private System.Windows.Forms.Label label32;
48        private System.Windows.Forms.Label label33;
49        private System.Windows.Forms.Label label34;
```

Fig. 18.20 Receiving temperature and weather data from a Web service. (Part 1 of 4.)

```
50          private System.Windows.Forms.Label label36;
51          private System.Windows.Forms.Label label35;
52
53          private System.ComponentModel.Container components =
54             null;
55
56          public Client()
57          {
58             InitializeComponent();
59
60             localhost.TemperatureServer client =
61                new localhost.TemperatureServer();
62             client.CookieContainer = new CookieContainer();
63             client.UpdateWeatherConditions();
64
65             string[] cities = client.Cities();
66             string[] descriptions = client.Descriptions();
67             string[] temperatures = client.Temperatures();
68
69             label35.BackgroundImage = new Bitmap(
70                "images/header.png" );
71             label36.BackgroundImage = new Bitmap(
72                "images/header.png" );
73
74             // create Hashtable and populate it with every label
75             Hashtable cityLabels = new Hashtable();
76             cityLabels.Add( 1, label1 );
77             cityLabels.Add( 2, label2 );
78             cityLabels.Add( 3, label3 );
79             cityLabels.Add( 4, label4 );
80             cityLabels.Add( 5, label5 );
81             cityLabels.Add( 6, label6 );
82             cityLabels.Add( 7, label7 );
83             cityLabels.Add( 8, label8 );
84             cityLabels.Add( 9, label9 );
85             cityLabels.Add( 10, label10 );
86             cityLabels.Add( 11, label11 );
87             cityLabels.Add( 12, label12 );
88             cityLabels.Add( 13, label13 );
89             cityLabels.Add( 14, label14 );
90             cityLabels.Add( 15, label15 );
91             cityLabels.Add( 16, label16 );
92             cityLabels.Add( 17, label17 );
93             cityLabels.Add( 18, label18 );
94             cityLabels.Add( 19, label19 );
95             cityLabels.Add( 20, label20 );
96             cityLabels.Add( 21, label21 );
97             cityLabels.Add( 22, label22 );
98             cityLabels.Add( 23, label23 );
99             cityLabels.Add( 24, label24 );
100            cityLabels.Add( 25, label25 );
101            cityLabels.Add( 26, label26 );
102            cityLabels.Add( 27, label27 );
```

Fig. 18.20 Receiving temperature and weather data from a Web service. (Part 2 of 4.)

```
103        cityLabels.Add( 28, label28 );
104        cityLabels.Add( 29, label29 );
105        cityLabels.Add( 30, label30 );
106        cityLabels.Add( 31, label31 );
107        cityLabels.Add( 32, label32 );
108        cityLabels.Add( 33, label33 );
109        cityLabels.Add( 34, label34 );
110
111        // create Hashtable and populate with
112        // all weather conditions
113        Hashtable weather = new Hashtable();
114        weather.Add( "SUNNY", "sunny" );
115        weather.Add( "PTCLDY", "pcloudy" );
116        weather.Add( "CLOUDY", "mcloudy" );
117        weather.Add( "MOCLDY", "mcloudy" );
118        weather.Add( "TSTRMS", "rain" );
119        weather.Add( "RAIN", "rain" );
120        weather.Add( "SNOW", "snow" );
121        weather.Add( "VRYHOT", "vryhot" );
122        weather.Add( "FAIR", "fair" );
123        weather.Add( "RNSNOW", "rnsnow" );
124        weather.Add( "SHWRS", "showers" );
125        weather.Add( "WINDY", "windy" );
126        weather.Add( "NOINFO", "noinfo" );
127        weather.Add( "MISG", "noinfo" );
128        weather.Add( "DRZL", "rain" );
129        weather.Add( "HAZE", "noinfo" );
130        weather.Add( "SMOKE", "mcloudy" );
131
132        Bitmap background = new Bitmap( "images/back.png" );
133        Font font = new Font( "Courier New", 8,
134           FontStyle.Bold );
135
136        // for every city
137        for ( int i = 0; i < cities.Length; i++ )
138        {
139           // use Hashtable cityLabels to find the next Label
140           Label currentCity = ( Label )cityLabels[ i + 1 ];
141
142           // set current Label's image to image
143           // corresponding to the city's weather condition -
144           // find correct image name in Hashtable weather
145           currentCity.Image = new Bitmap( "images/" +
146              weather[ descriptions[ i ].Trim() ] + ".png" );
147
148           // set background image, font and forecolor
149           // of Label
150           currentCity.BackgroundImage = background;
151           currentCity.Font = font;
152           currentCity.ForeColor = Color.White;
153
```

Fig. 18.20 Receiving temperature and weather data from a Web service. (Part 3 of 4.)

```
154                    // set label's text to city name
155                    currentCity.Text = "\r\n" + cities[ i ] + " " +
156                        temperatures[ i ];
157                }
158
159        } // end of constructor
160
161        // Visual Studio .NET generated code
162
163        [STAThread]
164        static void Main()
165        {
166            Application.Run( new Client() );
167        }
168
169    } // end class Client
170
171 } // end namespace TemperatureClient
```

Fig. 18.20 Receiving temperature and weather data from a Web service. (Part 4 of 4.)

Lines 60–63 of the constructor instantiate a **TemperatureServer** object, create a new **CookieContainer** object and update the weather data by calling method **UpdateWeatherConditions**. Lines 65–67 call **TemperatureServer** methods **Cities**, **Descriptions** and **Temperatures** to retrieve the city's weather and description information. Because the application presents weather data for so many cities, we must establish a way to organize the information in the **Label**s and to ensure that each weather description is accompanied by an appropriate image. To address these concerns, the program uses class **Hashtable** (discussed further in Chapter 20, Data Structures and Collections) to store all the **Label**s and weather descriptions and the names of their corresponding images. A **Hashtable** stores key-value pairs, in which both the key and the value can be any type of object. Method **Add** adds key-value pairs to a **Hashtable**. The class also provides an indexer to return the key value on which the **Hashtable** is indexed. Line 75 creates a **Hashtable** object, and lines 76–109 add the **Label**s to the **Hashtable**, using the numbers **1** through **36** as keys. Then, line 113 creates a second **Hashtable** object (**weather**) to contain pairs of weather conditions and the images associated with those conditions. Note that a given weather description does not necessarily correspond to the name of the PNG file containing the correct image. For example, both "**TSTRMS**" and "**RAIN**" weather conditions use the **rain.png** file.

Lines 137–157 set each **Label** so that it contains a city name, the current temperature in the city and an image corresponding to the weather condition for that city. Line 140 uses the **Hashtable** indexer to retrieve the next **Label** by passing as an argument the current value of **i** plus **1**. We add **1** because the **Hashtable** indexer begins at 0, despite the fact that both the labels and the **Hashtable** keys are numbered from 1–36.

Lines 145–146 set the **Label**'s image to the PNG image that corresponds to the city's weather condition. The application does this by retrieving the name of the PNG image from the **weather Hashtable**. The program eliminates any spaces in the description **string** by calling **string** method **Trim**. Lines 150–156 set several **Label**s' properties to achieve the visual effect seen in the output. For each label, we specify a blue-and-black background image (line 150). Lines 155–156 set each label's text so that it displays the correct information for each city (i.e., the city's name and temperature).

18.8 User-Defined Types in Web Services

The Web service discussed in the previous section returns arrays of **string**s. It would be much more convenient if **TemperatureServer** could return an array of **CityWeather** objects, instead of an array of **string**s. Fortunately, it is possible to define and employ user-defined types (also known as custom types) in a Web service. These types can be passed into or returned from Web-service methods. Web-service clients also can use these user-defined types, because the proxy class created for the client contains these type definitions. There are, however, some subtleties to keep in mind when using user-defined types in Web services; we point these out as we encounter them in the next example.

The case study in this section presents a math-tutoring program. The Web service generates random equations of type **Equation**. The client inputs information about the kind of mathematical example that the user wants (addition, subtraction or multiplication) and the skill level of the user (1 creates equations using one-digit numbers, 2 specifies more difficult equations involving two-digit numbers and 3 specifies the most difficult equations, containing three-digit numbers). It then generates an equation consisting of random numbers that have the proper number of digits. The client receives the **Equation** and uses a Windows Form to display the sample questions to the user.

We mentioned earlier that all data types passed to and from Web services must be supported by SOAP. How, then, can SOAP support a type that is not even created yet? In Chapter 14, Files and Streams, we discussed the serializing of data types, which enables them to be written to files. Similarly, custom types that are sent to or from a Web service are serialized, enabling them to be passed in XML format. This process is referred to as *XML serialization*.

When defining objects to be returned from Web-service methods, there are several subtleties to understand. For example, any object returned by a Web-service method must have a default constructor. Although all objects can be instantiated using a default **public** constructor (even if this constructor is not defined explicitly), a class returned from a Web service must have an explicitly defined constructor, even if its body is empty.

Common Programming Error 18.3

*Failure to define explicitly a **public** constructor for a type being used in a Web service results in a run-time error.*

A few additional requirements apply to custom types in Web services. Any variables of our user-defined type that we wish to access on the client-side must be declared **public**. We also must define both the **get** and **set** accessors of any properties that we wish to access at runtime. The Web service needs to have a way both to retrieve and manipulate such properties, because objects of the user-defined type will be converted into XML (when the objects are serialized) then converted back to objects (when they are de-serialized). During serialization, the property value must be read (through the **get** accessor); during de-serialization, the property value of the new object must be set (through the **set** accessor). If only one accessor is present, the client application will not have access to the property.

Common Programming Error 18.4

*Defining only the **get** or **set** accessor of a property for a user-defined type being used in a Web service results in a property that is inaccessible to the client.*

Common Programming Error 18.5

*Clients of a Web service can access only that service's **public** members. To allow access to **private** data, the programmer should provide **public** properties.*

Figure 18.21 displays class **Equation**. The constructor that is called (lines 18–37) takes three arguments—two integers representing the left and right operands and a **string** representing the algebraic operation to carry out. We define a default constructor (line 13–15) that calls another constructor (lines 18–37) and passes some default values. The constructor sets the **left**, **right** and **operation** fields, then calculates the appropriate result. We do not use this default constructor, but it must be defined in the program.

Class **Equation** defines properties **LeftHandSide**, **RightHandSide**, **Left**, **Right**, **Operation** and **Result**. The program does not need to modify the values of some of these properties, but implementation for the **set** accessor must be provided. **LeftHandSide** returns a **string** representing everything to the left of the "**=**" sign, and **RightHandSide** returns a **string** representing everything to the right of the "**=**" sign. **Left** returns the **int** to the left of the operator (known as the left operand), and **Right** returns the **int** to the right of the operator (known as the right operand). **Result** returns

```csharp
1   // Fig. 18.21: Equation.cs
2   // Class Equation that contains
3   // information about an equation.
4
5   using System;
6
7   public class Equation
8   {
9      private int left, right, result;
10     private string operation;
11
12     // required default constructor
13     public Equation() : this( 0, 0, "+" )
14     {
15     }
16
17     // constructor for class Equation
18     public Equation( int leftValue, int rightValue,
19        string operationType )
20     {
21        Left = leftValue;
22        Right = rightValue;
23        Operation = operationType;
24
25        switch ( operationType )
26        {
27           case "+":
28              Result = Left + Right;
29              break;
30           case "-":
31              Result = Left - Right;
32              break;
33           case "*":
34              Result = Left * Right;
35              break;
36        }
37     }
38
39     public override string ToString()
40     {
41        return Left.ToString() + " " + Operation + " " +
42           Right.ToString() + " = " + Result.ToString();
43     }
44
45     // property returning string representing
46     // left-hand side
47     public string LeftHandSide
48     {
49        get
50        {
51           return Left.ToString() + " " + Operation + " " +
52              Right.ToString();
53        }
```

Fig. 18.21 Class that stores equation information. (Part 1 of 3.)

```
54
55        set
56        {
57        }
58     }
59
60     // property returning string representing
61     // right-hand side
62     public string RightHandSide
63     {
64        get
65        {
66           return Result.ToString();
67        }
68
69        set
70        {
71        }
72     }
73
74     // left operand get and set property
75     public int Left
76     {
77        get
78        {
79           return left;
80        }
81
82        set
83        {
84           left = value;
85        }
86     }
87
88     // right operand get and set property
89     public int Right
90     {
91        get
92        {
93           return right;
94        }
95
96        set
97        {
98           right = value;
99        }
100    }
101
102    // get and set property of result of applying
103    // operation to left and right operands
104    public int Result
105    {
```

Fig. 18.21 Class that stores equation information. (Part 2 of 3.)

```
106            get
107            {
108                return result;
109            }
110
111            set
112            {
113                result = value;
114            }
115        }
116
117        // get and set property for operation
118        public string Operation
119        {
120            get
121            {
122                return operation;
123            }
124
125            set
126            {
127                operation = value;
128            }
129        }
130
131    } // end class Equation
```

Fig. 18.21 Class that stores equation information. (Part 3 of 3.)

the answer to the equation, and **Operation** returns the operator. The program does not actually need the **RightHandSide** property, but we have chosen to include it in case other clients choose to use it. Figure 18.22 presents the **Generator** Web service that creates random, customized **Equation**s.

```
1   // Fig. 18.22: Generator.asmx.cs
2   // Web Service to generate random equations based on a
3   // specified operation and difficulty level.
4
5   using System;
6   using System.Collections;
7   using System.ComponentModel;
8   using System.Data;
9   using System.Diagnostics;
10  using System.Web;
11  using System.Web.Services;
12
13  namespace EquationGenerator
14  {
15      [ WebService( Namespace = "http://www.deitel.com/cspfep1/ch18",
16          Description = "A Web service that generates questions " +
17          "based on the specified mathematical operation and " +
18          "level of difficulty chosen." ) ]
```

Fig. 18.22 Web service that generates random equations. (Part 1 of 2.)

```
19        public class Generator : System.Web.Services.WebService
20        {
21
22            // Visual Studio .NET generated code
23
24            [ WebMethod ( Description =
25                "Method that generates a random equation." ) ]
26            public Equation GenerateEquation( string operation,
27                int level )
28            {
29                // find maximum and minimum number to be used
30                int maximum = ( int ) Math.Pow( 10, level ),
31                    minimum = ( int ) Math.Pow( 10, level - 1 );
32
33                Random random = new Random();
34
35                // create equation consisting of two random numbers
36                // between minimum and maximum parameters
37                Equation equation = new Equation(
38                    random.Next( minimum, maximum ),
39                    random.Next( minimum, maximum ), operation );
40
41                return equation;
42
43            } // end method GenerateEquation
44
45        } // end class Generator
46
47    } // end namespace EquationGenerator
```

Fig. 18.22 Web service that generates random equations. (Part 2 of 2.)

Web service **Generator** contains only one method, **GenerateEquation**. This method takes as arguments a **string** representing the operation we wish to perform and an **integer** representing the desired difficulty level of the equation. Figure 18.23 demonstrates the result of executing a test call of this Web service. Notice that the return value from our Web-service method is marked up as XML. However, this example differs from previous ones in that the XML specifies the values for all **public** properties and fields of the object that is being returned. The return object has been serialized into XML. Our proxy class takes this return value and deserializes it into an object (containing the **public** data from the original object) that then is passed back to the client.

Lines 30–31 define the lower and upper bounds for the random numbers that the method generates. To set these limits, the program first calls **static** method **Pow** of class **Math**—this method raises its first argument to the power of its second argument. Integer **maximum** represents the upper bound for a randomly generated number. The program raises **10** to the power of the specified **level** argument and then passes this value as the upper bound. For instance, if **level** is **1**, **maximum** is **10**; if **level** is **2**; **maximum** is **100** and so on. Variable **minimum**'s value is determined by raising **10** to a power one less then **level**. This calculates the smallest number with **level** digits. If **level** is **2**, **minimum** is **10**; if **level** is **3**, **minimum** is **100** and so on.

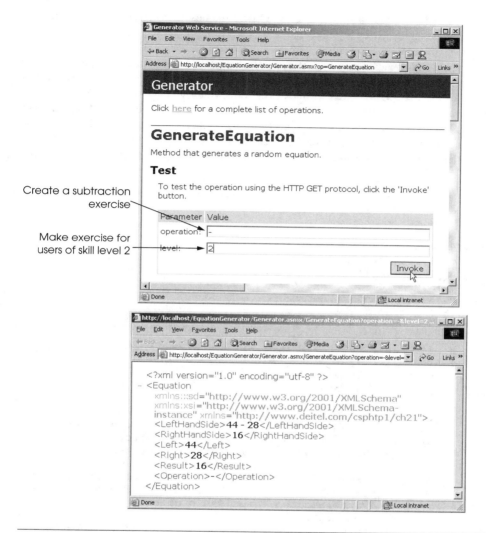

Create a subtraction exercise

Make exercise for users of skill level 2

Fig. 18.23 Returning an object from a Web-service method.

Lines 37–39 create a new **Equation** object. The program calls **Random** method **Next**, which returns an integer that is greater than or equal to a specified lower bound, but less than a specified upper bound. In this example, **Random** generates a left operand value that is greater than or equal to **minimum**, but less than **maximum** (i.e., a number with **level** digits). The right operand is another random number with the same characteristics. The operation passed to the **Equation** constructor is the **string operation** that was received by **GenerateEquation**. The new **Equation** object is returned.

Figure 18.24 lists the math-tutoring application that uses the **Generator** Web service. The application calls **Generator**'s **GenerateEquation** method to create an **Equation** object. The application then displays the left-hand side of the **Equation** and waits for user input. In this example, the program accesses both class **Generator** and class **Equation** from within the **localhost** namespace—both are placed in this namespace when the proxy is generated.

The math-tutoring application displays a question and waits for input. The default setting for the difficulty level is **1**, but the user can change this at any time by choosing a level from among the top row of **RadioButton**s. Clicking any of the level options invokes **levelRadioButtons_Click** (lines 110–120), which sets integer **level** to the level selected by the user. Although the default setting for the question type is **Addition**, the user also can change this at any time by selecting one of the bottom-row **RadioButton**s. Doing so invokes the **operationRadioButtons_Click** (lines 91–107) event handler, which sets **string operation** so that it contains the symbol corresponding to the user's selection.

```
1   // Fig. 18.24: Tutor.cs
2   // Math tutor program.
3
4   using System;
5   using System.Drawing;
6   using System.Collections;
7   using System.ComponentModel;
8   using System.Windows.Forms;
9
10  namespace EquationGeneratorClient
11  {
12     public class Tutor : System.Windows.Forms.Form
13     {
14        private System.Windows.Forms.Panel panel1;
15        private System.Windows.Forms.Panel panel2;
16
17        private System.Windows.Forms.Label questionLabel;
18        private System.Windows.Forms.TextBox answerTextBox;
19        private System.Windows.Forms.Button okButton;
20        private System.Windows.Forms.Button generateButton;
21
22        private System.Windows.Forms.RadioButton oneRadioButton;
23        private System.Windows.Forms.RadioButton twoRadioButton;
24        private System.Windows.Forms.RadioButton
25           threeRadioButton;
26        private System.Windows.Forms.RadioButton addRadioButton;
27        private System.Windows.Forms.RadioButton
28           subtractRadioButton;
29        private System.Windows.Forms.RadioButton
30           multiplyRadioButton;
31
32        private System.ComponentModel.Container components =
33           null;
34        private int level = 1;
35
36        private localhost.Equation equation;
37        private localhost.Generator generator =
38           new localhost.Generator();
39        private string operation = "+";
```

Fig. 18.24 Math tutor application. (Part 1 of 4.)

```
40
41        // Visual Studio .NET generated code
42
43        [STAThread]
44        static void Main()
45        {
46            Application.Run( new Tutor() );
47        }
48
49        // generates new equation on click event
50        protected void generateButton_Click( object sender,
51           System.EventArgs e )
52        {
53            // generate equation using current operation
54            // and level
55            equation = generator.GenerateEquation( operation,
56               level );
57
58            // display left-hand side of equation
59            questionLabel.Text = equation.LeftHandSide;
60
61            okButton.Enabled = true;
62            answerTextBox.Enabled = true;
63
64        } // end method generateButton_Click
65
66        // check users answer
67        protected void okButton_Click( object sender,
68           System.EventArgs e )
69        {
70            // determine correct result from Equation
71            // object
72            int answer = equation.Result;
73
74            // get user's answer
75            int myAnswer = Int32.Parse( answerTextBox.Text );
76
77            // test if user's answer is correct
78            if ( answer == myAnswer )
79            {
80               questionLabel.Text = "";
81               answerTextBox.Text = "";
82               okButton.Enabled = false;
83               MessageBox.Show( "Correct! Good job!" );
84            }
85            else
86               MessageBox.Show( "Incorrect. Try again." );
87
88        } // end method okButton_Click
89
```

Fig. 18.24 Math tutor application. (Part 2 of 4.)

```
90              // set the selected operation
91              protected void operationRadioButtons_Click( object sender,
92                 EventArgs e )
93              {
94                 RadioButton item = ( RadioButton ) sender;
95
96                 // set the operation to be the appropriate symbol
97                 if ( item == addRadioButton )
98                    operation = "+";
99                 else if ( item == subtractRadioButton )
100                   operation = "-";
101                else
102                   operation = "*";
103
104                generateButton.Text = "Generate " + item.Text +
105                   " Example";
106
107             } // end method operationRadioButtons_Click
108
109             // set the current level
110             protected void levelRadioButtons_Click( object sender,
111                EventArgs e )
112             {
113                if ( sender == oneRadioButton )
114                   level = 1;
115                else if ( sender == twoRadioButton )
116                   level = 2;
117                else
118                   level = 3;
119
120             } // end method levelRadioButtons_Click
121
122          } // end class Tutor
123
124       } // end namespace EquationGeneratorClient
```

Fig. 18.24 Math tutor application. (Part 3 of 4.)

Fig. 18.24 Math tutor application. (Part 4 of 4.)

Event handler **generateButton_Click** (lines 50–64) invokes **Generator** method **GenerateEquation**. The left-hand side of the equation is displayed in **questionLabel** (line 59), and **okButton** is enabled so that the user can enter an answer. When the user clicks **OK**, **okButton_Click** (lines 67–88) checks whether the user provided the correct answer.

This chapter and the previous one have familiarized readers with the creation of Web applications and Web services, both of which enable users to request and receive data via the Internet. In the next chapter, we discuss the low-level details of how data are sent from one location to another (this process is called *networking*). Topics discussed in the next chapter include the implementation of servers and clients and the sending of data via sockets.

18.9 Summary

A Web service is an application stored on a remote machine and accessed through a remote procedure call. Web-service method calls are implemented using Simple Object Access Protocol (SOAP), an XML-based protocol describing how requests and responses are marked up so that they can be transferred via protocols such as HTTP. These methods are marked with the **WebMethod** attribute and are often referred to as Web-service methods. By default, requests to and responses from Web services are sent as SOAP messages. As long as a client can create and understand SOAP messages, the client can use Web services, regardless of the programming languages in which the Web services are written.

A Web service in .NET has two parts—an ASMX file and a code-behind file. The ASMX file can be viewed in any Web browser and displays information about the Web service. The code-behind file contains the definition for the methods in the Web service.

A service description is an XML document that conforms to the Web Service Description Language (WSDL). WSDL is an XML vocabulary that describes how Web services behave. The service description can be used by a client program to confirm the correctness of method calls at compile time.

The Simple Object Access Protocol (SOAP) is a platform-independent protocol that uses XML to describe remote-procedure calls over HTTP. Requests to and responses from a Web-service method are packaged in a SOAP message—an XML message containing all the information necessary to process its contents. SOAP allows Web services to employ a variety of data types, including user-defined data types. When a program invokes a Web-service method, the request and all relevant information are packaged in a SOAP message and sent to the appropriate destination. When the Web service receives the SOAP message, it processes the message's contents, which specify the method that the client wishes to execute and the arguments the client is passing to that method. The method is then executed, and the response is sent back to the client as another SOAP message.

An application that uses a Web service consists of two parts—a proxy class for the Web service and a client application that accesses the Web service via the proxy. The proxy class handles the task of transferring the arguments passed from the client into a SOAP message that is sent to the Web service. The proxy likewise handles the transfer of information in the SOAP response to the client. The proxy class is created from the Web service's WSDL file that enables the client to call Web-service methods over the Internet. Whenever a call is made in a client application to a Web-service method, a method in the proxy class is called. This method takes the method name and arguments passed by the client and formats them so that they can be sent as a request in a SOAP message.

Class **WebService** provides members that determine information about the user, the application and other topics relevant to the Web service. A Web service is not required to inherit from class **WebService**. A programmer specifies a class as a Web service by tagging it with the **WebService** attribute.

UDDI (Universal Description, Discovery and Integration) is a project for developing a set of specifications that define how Web services should be discovered so that clients searching for Web services can find them. A DISCO (discovery) file specifies any Web services that are available in the current directory. There are two types of discovery files—dynamic discovery files (**.vsdisco** extension) and static discovery files (**.disco** extension). Once a Web reference is created, a static discovery file is placed in the client's project. The static discovery file contains the locations of the ASMX and WSDL files. Dynamic discovery files consist of a list of Web services that is created when a client is searching for Web services.

To store session information, the **EnableSession** property of the **WebMethod** attribute must be set to **true**. When storing session information, a Web service must have a way of identifying users between method calls. The approach is implemented using cookies, which are stored in a **CookieContainer**.

Types can be defined by a programmer and used in a Web service. The types can be passed into or returned from Web-service methods. User-defined types can be sent to or returned from Web-service methods, because the types are defined in the proxy class created for the client. Custom types that are sent to or from a Web service are serialized as XML. When an object is returned from a Web service, all its **public** properties and fields are marked up in XML. This information can then be transferred back into an object on the client side.

Networking: Streams-Based Sockets and Datagrams

Objectives

- To implement C# networking applications that use sockets and datagrams.
- To understand how to implement C# clients and servers that communicate with one another.
- To understand how to implement network-based collaborative applications.
- To construct a multithreaded server.

If the presence of electricity can be made visible in any part of a circuit, I see no reason why intelligence may not be transmitted instantaneously by electricity.
Samuel F. B. Morse

Mr. Watson, come here, I want you.
Alexander Graham Bell

What networks of railroads, highways and canals were in another age, the networks of telecommunications, information and computerization … are today.
Bruno Kreisky

Science may never come up with a better office-communication system than the coffee break.
Earl Wilson

Outline

19.1   Introduction

19.2   Establishing a Simple Server (Using Stream Sockets)

19.3   Establishing a Simple Client (Using Stream Sockets)

19.4   Client/Server Interaction with Stream-Socket Connections

19.5   Connectionless Client/Server Interaction with Datagrams

19.6   Client/Server Tic-Tac-Toe Using a Multithreaded Server

19.7   Summary

19.1 Introduction

The Internet and the World Wide Web have generated a great deal of excitement in the business and computing communities. The Internet ties the "information world" together; the Web makes the Internet easy to use while providing the flair of multimedia. Organizations see both the Internet and the Web as crucial to their information-systems strategies. C# and the .NET Framework offer a number of built-in networking capabilities that facilitate Internet-based and Web-based applications development. C# not only can specify parallelism through multithreading, but also can enable programs to search the Web for information and collaborate with programs running on other computers internationally.

In Chapters 17 and 18, we began our presentation of C#'s networking and distributed-computing capabilities. We discussed Web Forms and Web Services, two high-level networking technologies that enable programmers to develop distributed applications in C#. In this chapter, we focus on the networking technologies that support C#'s ASP.NET capabilities and can be used to build distributed applications.

Our discussion of networking focuses on both sides of a *client–server relationship*. The *client* requests that some action be performed; the *server* performs the action and responds to the client. A common implementation of this request–response model is between Web browsers and Web servers. When users select Web sites that they wish to view through a browser (the client application), the browser makes a request to the appropriate Web server (the server application). The server normally responds to the client by sending the appropriate HTML Web pages.

C#'s networking capabilities are grouped into several namespaces. The fundamental networking capabilities are defined by classes and interfaces of namespace **System.Net.Sockets**. Through this namespace, C# offers *socket-based communications*, which enable developers to view networking as if it were file I/O. This means that a program can read from a *socket* (network connection) or write to a socket as easily as it can read from or write to a file. Sockets are the fundamental way to perform network communications in the .NET Framework. The term "socket" refers to the Berkeley Sockets Interface, which was developed in 1978 for network programming with UNIX and was popularized by C and C++ programmers.

The classes and interfaces of namespace **System.Net.Sockets** also offer *packet-based communications*, through which individual *packets* of information are transmitted—

this is a common method of transmitting audio and video over the Internet. In this chapter, we show how to create and manipulate sockets and how to communicate via packets of data.

Socket-based communications in C# employ *stream sockets*. With stream sockets, a *process* (running program) establishes a *connection* to another process. While the connection is in place, data flows between the processes in continuous *streams*. For this reason, stream sockets are said to provide a *connection-oriented service*. The popular *TCP (Transmission Control Protocol)* facilitates stream-socket transmission.

By contrast, packet-based communications in C# employ *datagram sockets*, through which individual *packets* of information are transmitted. Unlike TCP, the protocol used to enable datagram sockets—*UDP, the User Datagram Protocol*—is a *connectionless service* and does not guarantee that packets will arrive in any particular order. In fact, packets can be lost or duplicated and can arrive out of sequence. Applications that use UDP often require significant extra programming to deal with these problems. UDP is most appropriate for network applications that do not require the error checking and reliability of TCP. For example, several online multi-player games use UDP, because speed is more important than perfect accuracy in these types of applications. Stream sockets and the TCP protocol will be the most desirable method of communication for the vast majority of C# programmers.

Performance Tip 19.1

Connectionless services generally offer better performance but less reliability than do connection-oriented services.

Portability Tip 19.1

The TCP protocol and its related set of protocols enable intercommunication among a wide variety of heterogeneous computer systems (i.e., computer systems with different processors and different operating systems).

19.2 Establishing a Simple Server (Using Stream Sockets)

Typically, with TCP and stream sockets, a server "waits" for a connection request from a client. Often, the server program contains a control structure or block of code that executes continuously until the server receives a request. On receiving a request, the server establishes a connection with the client. The server then uses this connection to handle future requests from that client and to send data to the client.

The establishment of a simple server with TCP and stream sockets in C# requires five steps. The first step is to create an object of class **TcpListener**, which belongs to namespace **System.Net.Sockets**. This class represents a TCP stream socket through which a server can listen for requests. A call to the **TcpListener** constructor, such as

```
TcpListener server = new TcpListener( port );
```

binds (assigns) the server to the specified *port number*. A port number is a numeric identifier that a process uses to identify itself at a given *network address*, also known as an *Internet Protocol Address (IP Address)*. IP addresses identify computers on the Internet. In fact, Web-site names, such as **www.deitel.com**, are aliases for IP addresses. Any process that performs networking identifies itself via an *IP address/port number pair*. Hence, no two processes can have the same port number at a given IP address. The explicit binding of a socket to a port (using method **Bind** of class **Socket**) is usually unnecessary, because class **TcpListener** and other classes discussed in this chapter hide this binding (i.e., bind sockets to ports implicitly), plus they perform other socket-initialization operations.

Software Engineering Observation 19.1

Port numbers can have values between 0 and 65535. Many operating systems reserve port numbers below 1024 for system services (such as e-mail and Web servers). Applications must be granted special privileges to use these reserved port numbers. Usually, a server-side application should not specify port numbers below 1024 as connection ports, because some operating systems might reserve these numbers.

Common Programming Error 19.1

Attempting to bind an already assigned port at a given IP address is a logic error.

To receive requests, the **TcpListener** first must listen for them. The second step in our connection process is to call **TcpListener**'s **Start** method, which causes the **TcpListener** object to begin listening for connection requests. The third step establishes the connection between the server and client. The server listens indefinitely for a request—i.e., the execution of the server-side application waits until some client attempts to connect with it. The server creates a connection to the client upon receipt of a connection request. An object of class **System.Net.Sockets.Socket** manages each connection to the client. Method **AcceptSocket** of class **TcpListener** waits for a connection request, then creates a connection when a request is received. This method returns a **Socket** object upon connection, as in the statement

```
Socket connection = server.AcceptSocket();
```

When the server receives a request, method **AcceptSocket** calls method **Accept** of the **TcpListener**'s underlying **Socket** to make the connection. This is an example of C#'s hiding of networking complexity from the programmer. The programmer can write the preceding statement into a server-side program, then allow the classes of namespace **System.Net.Sockets** to handle the details of accepting requests and establishing connections.

Step four is the processing phase, in which the server and the client communicate via methods **Receive** and **Send** of class **Socket**. Note that these methods, as well as TCP and stream sockets, can be used only when the server and client are connected. By contrast, through **Socket** methods **SendTo** and **ReceiveFrom**, UDP and datagram sockets can be used when no connection exists.

The fifth step is the connection-termination phase. When the client and server have finished communicating, the server uses method **Close** of the **Socket** object to close the connection. Most servers then return to step two (i.e., wait for another client's connection request).

One problem associated with the server scheme described in this section is that step four *blocks* other requests while processing a client's request, so that no other client can connect with the server while the code that defines the processing phase is executing. The most common technique for addressing this problem is to use multithreaded servers, which place the processing-phase code in a separate thread. When the server receives a connection request, the server *spawns*, or creates, a **Thread** to process the connection, leaving its **TcpListener** (or **Socket**) free to receive other connections.

Software Engineering Observation 19.2

Using C#'s multithreading capabilities, we can create servers that can manage simultaneous connections with multiple clients. This multithreaded-server architecture is precisely what popular UNIX and Windows network servers use.

Software Engineering Observation 19.3

*A multithreaded server can be implemented to create a thread that manages network I/O across a reference to a **Socket** object returned by method **AcceptSocket**. A multithreaded server also can be implemented to maintain a pool of threads that manage network I/O across newly created **Socket**s.*

Performance Tip 19.2

*In high-performance systems with abundant memory, a multithreaded server can be implemented to create a pool of threads. These threads can be assigned quickly to handle network I/O across each multiple **Socket**. Thus, when a connection is received, the server does not incur the overhead of thread creation.*

19.3 Establishing a Simple Client (Using Stream Sockets)

We create TCP-stream-socket clients via a process that requires four steps. In the first step, we create an object of class **TcpClient** (which belongs to namespace **System.Net.Sockets**) to connect to the server. This connection is established through method **Connect** of class **TcpClient**. One overloaded version of this method receives two arguments—the server's IP address and the port number—as in the following:

```
TcpClient client = new TcpClient();
client.Connect( serverAddress, serverPort );
```

Here, **serverPort** is an **int** that represents the server's port number; **serverAddress** can be either an **IPAddress** instance (that encapsulates the server's IP address) or a **string** that specifies the server's hostname. Alternatively, the programmer could pass an object reference of class **IPEndPoint**, which represents an IP address/port number pair, to a different overload of method **Connect**. Method **Connect** of class **TcpClient** calls method **Connect** of class **Socket** to establish the connection. If the connection is successful, method **TcpClient.Connect** returns a positive integer; otherwise, it returns **0**.

In step two, the **TcpClient** uses its method **GetStream** to get a **NetworkStream** so that it can write to and read from the server. **NetworkStream** methods **WriteByte** and **Write** can be used to output individual bytes or sets of bytes to the server, respectively; similarly, **NetworkStream** methods **ReadByte** and **Read** can be used to input individual bytes or sets of bytes from the server, respectively.

The third step is the processing phase, in which the client and the server communicate. In this phase, the client uses methods **Read**, **ReadByte**, **Write** and **WriteByte** of class **NetworkStream** to perform the appropriate communications. Using a process similar to that used by servers, a client can employ threads to prevent blocking of communications with other servers while processing data from one connection.

After the transmission is complete, step four requires the client to close the connection by calling method **Close** of the **NetworkStream** object. This closes the underlying

Socket (if the **NetworkStream** has a reference to that **Socket**). Then, the client calls method *Close* of class **TcpClient** to terminate the TCP connection. At this point, a new connection can be established through method **Connect**, as we have described.

19.4 Client/Server Interaction with Stream-Socket Connections

The applications in Fig. 19.1 and Fig. 19.2 use the classes and techniques discussed in the previous two sections to construct a simple *client/server chat application.* The server waits for a client's request to make a connection. When a client application connects to the server, the server application sends an array of bytes to the client, indicating that the connection was successful. The client then displays a message notifying the user that a connection has been established.

Both the client and the server applications contain **TextBox**es that enable users to type messages and send them to the other application. When either the client or the server sends message "**TERMINATE**," the connection between the client and the server terminates. The server then waits for another client to request a connection. Figure 19.1 and Fig. 19.2 provide the code for classes **Server** and **Client**, respectively. Figure 19.2 also contains screen captures displaying the execution between the client and the server.

```
1   // Fig. 19.1: Server.cs
2   // Set up a Server that will receive a connection from a client,
3   // send a string to the client, and close the connection.
4
5   using System;
6   using System.Drawing;
7   using System.Collections;
8   using System.ComponentModel;
9   using System.Windows.Forms;
10  using System.Threading;
11  using System.Net.Sockets;
12  using System.IO;
13
14  // server that awaits client connections (one at a time) and
15  // allows a conversation between client and server
16  public class Server : System.Windows.Forms.Form
17  {
18      private System.Windows.Forms.TextBox inputTextBox;
19      private System.Windows.Forms.TextBox displayTextBox;
20      private Socket connection;
21      private Thread readThread;
22
23      private System.ComponentModel.Container components = null;
24      private NetworkStream socketStream;
25      private BinaryWriter writer;
26      private BinaryReader reader;
27
```

Fig. 19.1 Server portion of a client/server stream-socket connection. (Part 1 of 4.)

```
28        // default constructor
29        public Server()
30        {
31           InitializeComponent();
32
33           // create a new thread from the server
34           readThread = new Thread( new ThreadStart( RunServer ) );
35           readThread.Start();
36        }
37
38        // Visual Studio .NET generated code
39
40        [STAThread]
41        static void Main()
42        {
43           Application.Run( new Server() );
44        }
45
46        protected void Server_Closing(
47           object sender, CancelEventArgs e )
48        {
49           System.Environment.Exit( System.Environment.ExitCode );
50        }
51
52        // sends the text typed at the server to the client
53        protected void inputTextBox_KeyDown(
54           object sender, KeyEventArgs e )
55        {
56           // sends the text to the client
57           try
58           {
59              if ( e.KeyCode == Keys.Enter && connection != null )
60              {
61                 writer.Write( "SERVER>>> " + inputTextBox.Text );
62
63                 displayTextBox.Text +=
64                    "\r\nSERVER>>> " + inputTextBox.Text;
65
66                 // if the user at the server signaled termination
67                 // sever the connection to the client
68                 if ( inputTextBox.Text == "TERMINATE" )
69                    connection.Close();
70
71                 inputTextBox.Clear();
72              }
73           }
74           catch ( SocketException )
75           {
76              displayTextBox.Text += "\nError writing object";
77           }
78        } // inputTextBox_KeyDown
79
```

Fig. 19.1   Server portion of a client/server stream-socket connection. (Part 2 of 4.)

```
80      // allows a client to connect and displays the text it sends
81      public void RunServer()
82      {
83         TcpListener listener;
84         int counter = 1;
85
86         // wait for a client connection and display the text
87         // that the client sends
88         try
89         {
90            // Step 1: create TcpListener
91            listener = new TcpListener( 5000 );
92
93            // Step 2: TcpListener waits for connection request
94            listener.Start();
95
96            // Step 3: establish connection upon client request
97            while ( true )
98            {
99               displayTextBox.Text = "Waiting for connection\r\n";
100
101              // accept an incoming connection
102              connection = listener.AcceptSocket();
103
104              // create NetworkStream object associated with socket
105              socketStream = new NetworkStream( connection );
106
107              // create objects for transferring data across stream
108              writer = new BinaryWriter( socketStream );
109              reader = new BinaryReader( socketStream );
110
111              displayTextBox.Text += "Connection " + counter +
112                 " received.\r\n";
113
114              // inform client that connection was successfull
115              writer.Write( "SERVER>>> Connection successful" );
116
117              inputTextBox.ReadOnly = false;
118              string theReply = "";
119
120              // Step 4: read String data sent from client
121              do
122              {
123                 try
124                 {
125                    // read the string sent to the server
126                    theReply = reader.ReadString();
127
128                    // display the message
129                    displayTextBox.Text += "\r\n" + theReply;
130                 }
131
```

Fig. 19.1 Server portion of a client/server stream-socket connection. (Part 3 of 4.)

```
132                    // handle exception if error reading data
133                    catch ( Exception )
134                    {
135                        break;
136                    }
137
138                } while ( theReply != "CLIENT>>> TERMINATE"  &&
139                    connection.Connected );
140
141                displayTextBox.Text +=
142                    "\r\nUser terminated connection";
143
144                // Step 5: close connection
145                inputTextBox.ReadOnly = true;
146                writer.Close();
147                reader.Close();
148                socketStream.Close();
149                connection.Close();
150
151                ++counter;
152            }
153        } // end try
154
155        catch ( Exception error )
156        {
157            MessageBox.Show( error.ToString() );
158        }
159
160    } // end method RunServer
161
162 } // end class Server
```

Fig. 19.1 Server portion of a client/server stream-socket connection. (Part 4 of 4.)

```
1   // Fig. 19.2: Client.cs
2   // Set up a Client that will read information sent from a Server
3   // and display the information.
4
5   using System;
6   using System.Drawing;
7   using System.Collections;
8   using System.ComponentModel;
9   using System.Windows.Forms;
10  using System.Threading;
11  using System.Net.Sockets;
12  using System.IO;
13
14  // connects to a chat server
15  public class Client : System.Windows.Forms.Form
16  {
17      private System.Windows.Forms.TextBox inputTextBox;
```

Fig. 19.2 Client portion of a client/server stream-socket connection. (Part 1 of 5.)

```
18        private System.Windows.Forms.TextBox displayTextBox;
19
20        private NetworkStream output;
21        private BinaryWriter writer;
22        private BinaryReader reader;
23
24        private string message = "";
25
26        private Thread readThread;
27
28        private System.ComponentModel.Container components = null;
29
30        // default constructor
31        public Client()
32        {
33           InitializeComponent();
34
35           readThread = new Thread( new ThreadStart( RunClient ) );
36           readThread.Start();
37        }
38
39        // Visual Studio .NET-generated code
40
41        [STAThread]
42        static void Main()
43        {
44           Application.Run( new Client() );
45        }
46
47        protected void Client_Closing(
48           object sender, CancelEventArgs e )
49        {
50           System.Environment.Exit( System.Environment.ExitCode );
51        }
52
53        // sends text the user typed to server
54        protected void inputTextBox_KeyDown (
55           object sender, KeyEventArgs e )
56        {
57           try
58           {
59              if ( e.KeyCode == Keys.Enter )
60              {
61                 writer.Write( "CLIENT>>> " + inputTextBox.Text );
62
63                 displayTextBox.Text +=
64                    "\r\nCLIENT>>> " + inputTextBox.Text;
65
66                 inputTextBox.Clear();
67              }
68           }
```

Fig. 19.2 Client portion of a client/server stream-socket connection. (Part 2 of 5.)

```
69          catch ( SocketException ioe )
70          {
71             displayTextBox.Text += "\nError writing object";
72          }
73
74    } // end method inputTextBox_KeyDown
75
76    // connect to server and display server-generated text
77    public void RunClient()
78    {
79       TcpClient client;
80
81       // instantiate TcpClient for sending data to server
82       try
83       {
84          displayTextBox.Text += "Attempting connection\r\n";
85
86          // Step 1: create TcpClient and connect to server
87          client = new TcpClient();
88          client.Connect( "localhost", 5000 );
89
90          // Step 2: get NetworkStream associated with TcpClient
91          output = client.GetStream();
92
93          // create objects for writing and reading across stream
94          writer = new BinaryWriter( output );
95          reader = new BinaryReader( output );
96
97          displayTextBox.Text += "\r\nGot I/O streams\r\n";
98
99          inputTextBox.ReadOnly = false;
100
101          // loop until server signals termination
102          do
103          {
104
105             // Step 3: processing phase
106             try
107             {
108                // read message from server
109                message = reader.ReadString();
110                displayTextBox.Text += "\r\n" + message;
111             }
112
113             // handle exception if error in reading server data
114             catch ( Exception )
115             {
116                System.Environment.Exit(
117                   System.Environment.ExitCode );
118             }
119          } while( message != "SERVER>>> TERMINATE" );
120
```

Fig. 19.2   Client portion of a client/server stream-socket connection. (Part 3 of 5.)

```
121                displayTextBox.Text += "\r\nClosing connection.\r\n";
122
123            // Step 4: close connection
124            writer.Close();
125            reader.Close();
126            output.Close();
127            client.Close();
128            Application.Exit();
129        }
130
131        // handle exception if error in establishing connection
132        catch ( Exception error )
133        {
134            MessageBox.Show( error.ToString() );
135        }
136
137    } // end method RunClient
138
139 } // end class Client
```

Fig. 19.2   Client portion of a client/server stream-socket connection. (Part 4 of 5.)

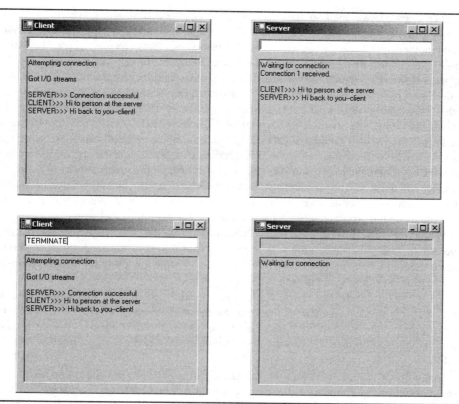

Fig. 19.2   Client portion of a client/server stream-socket connection. (Part 5 of 5.)

As we analyze this example, we begin by discussing class **Server** (Fig. 19.1). In the constructor, line 34 creates a **Thread** that will accept connections from clients. Line 35 starts the **Thread**, which invokes method **RunServer** (lines 81–160). Method **Run-Server** initializes the server to receive connection requests and process connections. Line 91 instantiates the **TcpListener** to listen for a connection request from a client at port **5000** (Step 1). Line 94 then calls method **Start** of the **TcpListener** object, which causes the **TcpListener** to begin waiting for requests (Step 2).

Lines 97–152 declare an infinite **while** loop that establishes connections requested by clients (Step 3). Line 102 calls method **AcceptSocket** of the **TcpListener** object, which returns a **Socket** upon successful connection. The thread in which method **AcceptSocket** is called stops executing until a connection is established. The **Socket** object will manage the connection. Line 105 passes this **Socket** object as an argument to the constructor of a **NetworkStream** object. Class **NetworkStream** provides access to streams across a network—in this example, the **NetworkStream** object provides access to the **Socket** connection. Lines 108–109 create instances of the *BinaryWriter* and *BinaryReader* classes for writing and reading data. We pass the **Network-Stream** object as an argument to each constructor; **BinaryWriter** can write bytes to the **NetworkStream**, and **BinaryReader** can read bytes from **NetworkStream**. Lines 111–112 append text to the **TextBox**, indicating that a connection was received.

BinaryWriter method *Write* has many overloaded versions, which enable the method to write various types to a stream. (You might remember that we used these overloaded methods in Chapter 14 to write record data to files.) Line 115 uses method **Write** to send to the client a **string** notifying the user of a successful connection. Lines 121–139 declare a **do/while** structure that executes until the server receives a message indicating connection termination (i.e., **CLIENT>>> TERMINATE**). Line 126 uses **BinaryReader** method *ReadString* to read a **string** from the stream (Step 4). (You might remember that we also used this method in Chapter 14 to read records' first-name and last-name **string**s from files.) Method **ReadString** blocks until a **string** is read. To prevent the whole server from blocking, we use a separate **Thread** to handle the transfer of information. The **while** statement loops until there is more information to read—this results in I/O blocking, which causes the program always to appear frozen. However, if we run this portion of the program in a separate **Thread**, the user can interact with the Windows **Form** and send messages while the program waits in the background for incoming messages.

When the chat is complete, lines 146–149 close the **BinaryWriter**, **BinaryReader**, **NetworkStream** and **Socket** (Step 5) by invoking their respective **Close** methods. The server then waits for another client connection request by returning to the beginning of the **while** loop (line 97).

When the user of the server application enters a **string** in the **TextBox** and presses the *Enter* key, event handler **inputTextBox_KeyDown** (lines 53–78) reads the **string** and sends it via method **Write** of class **BinaryWriter**. If a user terminates the server application, line 69 calls method **Close** of the **Socket** object to close the connection.

Lines 46–50 define the **Server_Closing** event handler for the **Closing** event. The event closes the application and uses **System.Environment.Exit** method with parameter **System.Environment.ExitCode** to terminate all threads. Method **Exit** of class **Environment** closes all threads associated with the application.

Figure 19.2 lists the code for the **Client** object. Like the **Server** object, the **Client** object creates a **Thread** (lines 35–36) in its constructor to handle all incoming messages. **Client** method **RunClient** (lines 77–137) connects to the **Server**, receives data from the **Server** and sends data to the **Server** (when the user presses *Enter*). Lines 87–88 instantiate a **TcpClient** object, then call its method **Connect** to establish a connection (Step 1). The first argument to method **Connect** is the name of the server—in our case, the server's name is *"localhost"*, meaning that the server is located on the same machine as the client. The **localhost** is also known as the *loopback IP address* and is equivalent to the IP address *127.0.0.1*. This value sends the data transmission back to the sender's IP address. [*Note:* We chose to demonstrate the client/server relationship by connecting between programs that are executing on the same computer (**localhost**). Normally, this argument would contain the Internet address of another computer.] The second argument to method **Connect** is the server port number. This number must match the port number at which the server waits for connections.

The **Client** uses a **NetworkStream** to send data to and receive data from the server. The client obtains the **NetworkStream** on line 91 through a call to **TcpClient** method **GetStream** (Step 2). The **do/while** structure in lines 102–119 loops until the client receives the connection-termination message (**SERVER>>> TERMINATE**). Line 109 uses **BinaryReader** method **ReadString** to obtain the next message from the server (Step

3). Line 110 displays the message, and lines 124–127 close the **BinaryWriter, BinaryReader, NetworkStream** and **TcpClient** objects (Step 4).

When the user of the client application enters a **string** in the **TextBox** and presses the *Enter* key, the event handler **inputTextBox_KeyDown** (lines 54–74) reads the **string** from the **TextBox** and sends it via **BinaryWriter** method **Write**. Notice that, here, the **Server** receives a connection, processes it, closes it and waits for the next one. In a real-world application, a server would likely receive a connection, set up the connection to be processed as a separate thread of execution and wait for new connections. The separate threads that process existing connections can continue to execute while the **Server** concentrates on new connection requests.

19.5 Connectionless Client/Server Interaction with Datagrams

Up to this point, we have discussed connection-oriented, streams-based transmission. Now, we consider connectionless transmission using datagrams.

Connection-oriented transmission is similar to interaction over a telephone system, in which a user dials a number and is *connected* to the telephone of the party they wish to connect. The system maintains the connection for the duration of the phone call, regardless of whether the users are speaking.

By contrast, connectionless transmission via *datagrams* more closely resembles the method by which the postal service carries and delivers mail. Connectionless transmission bundles and sends information in *packets* called datagrams, which can be thought of as similar to posted letters. If a large message will not fit in one envelope, that message is broken into separate message pieces and placed in separate, sequentially numbered envelopes. All the letters are mailed at once. The letters might arrive in order, out of order or not at all. The person at the receiving end reassembles the message pieces into sequential order before attempting to interpret the message. If the message is small enough to fit in one envelope, the sequencing problem is eliminated, but it is still possible that the message will never arrive. (Unlike with posted mail, duplicate of datagrams could reach receiving computers.) C# provides the **UdpClient** class for connectionless transmission. Like **TcpListener** and **TcpClient**, **UdpClient** uses methods from class **Socket**. The **UdpClient** methods **Send** and **Receive** are used to transmit data with **Socket**'s **SendTo** method and to read data with **Socket**'s **ReceiveFrom** method, respectively.

The programs in Fig. 19.3 and Fig. 19.4 use datagrams to send *packets* of information between a client and server applications. In the **Client** application, the user types a message into a **TextBox** and presses *Enter*. The client converts the message to a **byte** array and sends it to the server. The server receives the packet and displays the packet's information, then *echoes*, or returns, the packet back to the client. When the client receives the packet, the client displays the packet's information. In this example, the implementations of the **Client** and **Server** classes are similar.

```
1   // Fig. 19.3: Server.cs
2   // Set up a Server that will receive packets from a
3   // client and send packets to a client.
4
```

Fig. 19.3   Server-side portion of connectionless client/server computing. (Part 1 of 3.)

```
5   using System;
6   using System.Drawing;
7   using System.Collections;
8   using System.ComponentModel;
9   using System.Windows.Forms;
10  using System.Data;
11  using System.Net;
12  using System.Net.Sockets;
13  using System.Threading;
14
15  // create the UDP server
16  public class Server : System.Windows.Forms.Form
17  {
18     private System.Windows.Forms.TextBox displayTextBox;
19     private UdpClient client;
20     private IPEndPoint receivePoint;
21     private System.ComponentModel.Container components = null;
22
23     // no-argument constructor
24     public Server()
25     {
26        InitializeComponent();
27
28        client = new UdpClient( 5000 );
29        receivePoint = new IPEndPoint( new IPAddress( 0 ), 0 );
30        Thread readThread = new Thread(
31           new ThreadStart( WaitForPackets ) );
32
33        readThread.Start();
34     }
35
36     // Visual Studio .NET generated code
37
38     [STAThread]
39     static void Main()
40     {
41        Application.Run( new Server() );
42     }
43
44     // shut down the server
45     protected void Server_Closing(
46        object sender, CancelEventArgs e )
47     {
48        System.Environment.Exit( System.Environment.ExitCode );
49     }
50
51     // wait for a packet to arrive
52     public void WaitForPackets()
53     {
54        while ( true )
55        {
56           // receive byte array from client
57           byte[] data = client.Receive( ref receivePoint );
```

Fig. 19.3 Server-side portion of connectionless client/server computing. (Part 2 of 3.)

```
58
59            // output packet data to TextBox
60            displayTextBox.Text += "\r\nPacket received:" +
61               "\r\nLength: " + data.Length + "\r\nContaining: " +
62               System.Text.Encoding.ASCII.GetString( data );
63
64            displayTextBox.Text +=
65               "\r\n\r\nEcho data back to client...";
66
67            // echo information from packet back to client
68            client.Send( data, data.Length, receivePoint );
69            displayTextBox.Text += "\r\nPacket sent\r\n";
70         }
71
72      } // end method WaitForPackets
73
74   } // end class Server
```

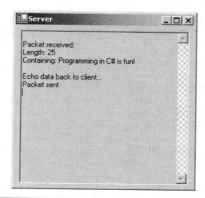

Fig. 19.3   Server-side portion of connectionless client/server computing. (Part 3 of 3.)

```
1    // Fig. 19.4: Client.cs
2    // Set up a Client that sends packets to a server and receives
3    // packets from a server.
4
5    using System;
6    using System.Drawing;
7    using System.Collections;
8    using System.ComponentModel;
9    using System.Windows.Forms;
10   using System.Data;
11   using System.Net;
12   using System.Net.Sockets;
13   using System.Threading;
14
```

Fig. 19.4   Client portion of connectionless client/server computing. (Part 1 of 3.)

```
15     // run the UDP client
16     public class Client : System.Windows.Forms.Form
17     {
18        private System.Windows.Forms.TextBox inputTextBox;
19        private System.Windows.Forms.TextBox displayTextBox;
20
21        private UdpClient client;
22        private IPEndPoint receivePoint;
23
24        private System.ComponentModel.Container components = null;
25
26        // no-argument constructor
27        public Client()
28        {
29           InitializeComponent();
30
31           receivePoint = new IPEndPoint( new IPAddress( 0 ), 0 );
32           client = new UdpClient( 5001 );
33           Thread thread =
34              new Thread( new ThreadStart( WaitForPackets ) );
35           thread.Start();
36        }
37
38        // Visual Studio.NET generated code
39
40        [STAThread]
41        static void Main()
42        {
43           Application.Run( new Client() );
44        }
45
46        // shut down the client
47        protected void Client_Closing(
48           object sender, CancelEventArgs e )
49        {
50           System.Environment.Exit( System.Environment.ExitCode );
51        }
52
53        // send a packet
54        protected void inputTextBox_KeyDown(
55           object sender, KeyEventArgs e )
56        {
57           if ( e.KeyCode == Keys.Enter )
58           {
59              // create packet (datagram) as string
60              string packet = inputTextBox.Text;
61              displayTextBox.Text +=
62                 "\r\nSending packet containing: " + packet;
63
64              // convert packet to byte array
65              byte[] data =
66                 System.Text.Encoding.ASCII.GetBytes( packet );
67
```

Fig. 19.4   Client portion of connectionless client/server computing. (Part 2 of 3.)

```
68              // send packet to server on port 5000
69              client.Send( data, data.Length, "localhost", 5000 );
70              displayTextBox.Text += "\r\nPacket sent\r\n";
71              inputTextBox.Clear();
72          }
73       } // end method inputTextBox_KeyDown
74
75       // wait for packets to arrive
76       public void WaitForPackets()
77       {
78           while ( true )
79           {
80               // receive byte array from server
81               byte[] data = client.Receive( ref receivePoint );
82
83               // output packet data to TextBox
84               displayTextBox.Text += "\r\nPacket received:" +
85                   "\r\nLength: " + data.Length + "\r\nContaining: " +
86                   System.Text.Encoding.ASCII.GetString( data ) +
87                   "\r\n";
88           }
89
90       } // end method WaitForPackets
91
92    } // end class Client
```

Client window before
sending a packet to the server

Client window after sending a packet
to the server and receiving it back

Fig. 19.4   Client portion of connectionless client/server computing. (Part 3 of 3.)

The code in Fig. 19.3 defines the **Server** for this application. Line 28 in the constructor for class **Server** creates an instance of the **UdpClient** class that receives data at port **5000**. This initializes the underlying **Socket** for communications. Line 29 creates an instance of class **IPEndPoint** to hold the IP address and port number of the client(s) that transmit to **Server**. The first argument to the constructor of **IPEndPoint** is an **IPAddress** object; the second argument to the constructor for **IPEndPoint** is the port number of the endpoint. These values are both **0**, because we need only instantiate an empty **IPEndPoint** object. The IP addresses and port numbers of clients are copied into the **IPEndPoint** when datagrams are received from clients.

Server method **WaitForPackets** (lines 52–72) executes an infinite loop while waiting for data to arrive at the **Server**. When information arrives, the **UdpClient** method **Receive** (line 57) receives a **byte** array from the client. We include **Receive** in the **IPEndPoint** object created in the constructor; this provides the method with a reference to an **IPEndPoint** into which the program copies the client's IP address and port number. This program will compile and run without an exception even if the reference to the **IPEndPoint** object is **null**, because method **Receive** initializes the **IPEndPoint** if it is **null**.

Good Programming Practice 19.1

*Initialize all references to objects (to a value other than **null**). This protects code from methods that do not check their parameters for **null** references.*

Lines 60–65 update the **Server**'s display to include the packet's information and content. Line 68 echoes the data back to the client, using **UdpClient** method **Send**. This version of **Send** takes three arguments: The byte array to send, an **int** representing the array's length and the **IPEndPoint** to which to send the data. We use array **data** returned by method **Receive** as the data, the length of array **data** as the length and the **IPEndPoint** passed to method **Receive** as the data's destination. The IP address and port number of the client that sent the data to **Server** are stored in **receivePoint**, so merely passing **receivePoint** to **Send** allows **Server** to respond to the client.

Class **Client** (Fig. 19.4) works similarly to class **Server**, except that the **Client** object sends packets only when the user types a message in a **TextBox** and presses the *Enter* key. When this occurs, event handler **inputTextBox_KeyDown** (lines 54–73) is called. Lines 65–66 convert the **string** that the user entered in the **TextBox** to a **byte** array. Line 69 calls **UdpClient** method **Send** to send the **byte** array to the **Server** that is located on **localhost** (i.e., the same machine). We specify the port as **5000**, which we know to be **Server**'s port.

Line 32 instantiates a **UdpClient** object to receive packets at port **5001**—we choose port **5001**, because the **Server** already occupies port **5000**. Method **WaitForPackets** of class **Client** (lines 76–90) uses an infinite loop to wait for these packets. The **UdpClient** method **Receive** blocks until a packet of data is received (line 81). The blocking performed by method **Receive** does not prevent class **Client** from performing other services (e.g., handling user input), because a separate thread runs method **WaitForPackets**.

When a packet arrives, lines 84–87 display its contents in the **TextBox**. The user can type information into the **Client** window's **TextBox** and press the *Enter* key at any time, even while a packet is being received. The event handler for the **TextBox** processes the event and sends the data to the server.

19.6 Client/Server Tic-Tac-Toe Using a Multithreaded Server

In this section, we present our capstone networking example—the popular game Tic-Tac-Toe, implemented with stream sockets and client/server techniques. The program consists of a **Server** application (Fig. 19.5) and two **Client** applications (Fig. 19.6); **Server** allows the **Client**s to connect to the server and play Tic-Tac-Toe. We depict the output in Fig. 19.6. When the server receives a client connection, lines 72–83 of Fig. 19.5 create an instance of class **Player** to process the client in a separate thread of execution. This enables the server to handle requests from both clients. The server assigns value **"X"** to the first client that connects (player **X** makes the first move), then assigns value **"O"** to the second client. Throughout the game, the server maintains information regarding the status of the board so that the server can validate players' requested moves. However, neither the server nor the client can establish whether a player has won the game—in this application, method **GameOver** (lines 143–147) always returns **false**. Each **Client** maintains its own GUI version of the Tic-Tac-Toe board to display the game. The clients can place marks only in empty squares on the board. Class **Square** (Fig. 19.7) is used to define squares on the Tic-Tac-Toe board.

```
1   // Fig. 19.5: Server.cs
2   // This class maintains a game of Tic-Tac-Toe for two
3   // client applications.
4
5   using System;
6   using System.Drawing;
7   using System.Collections;
8   using System.ComponentModel;
9   using System.Windows.Forms;
10  using System.Data;
11  using System.Net.Sockets;
12  using System.Threading;
13  using System.IO;
14
15  // awaits connections from two clients and allows them to
16  // play tic-tac-toe against each other
17  public class Server : System.Windows.Forms.Form
18  {
19      private System.Windows.Forms.TextBox displayTextBox;
20
21      private byte[] board;
22
23      private Player[] players;
24      private Thread[] playerThreads;
25
26      private TcpListener listener;
27      private int currentPlayer;
28      private Thread getPlayers;
29
30      private System.ComponentModel.Container components = null;
31
32      internal bool disconnected = false;
33
34      // default constructor
35      public Server()
36      {
37          InitializeComponent();
38
39          board = new byte[ 9 ];
```

Fig. 19.5   Server side of client/server Tic-Tac-Toe program. (Part 1 of 6.)

```
40
41          players = new Player[ 2 ];
42          playerThreads = new Thread[ 2 ];
43          currentPlayer = 0;
44
45          // accept connections on a different thread
46          getPlayers = new Thread( new ThreadStart( SetUp ) );
47          getPlayers.Start();
48       }
49
50       // Visual Studio .NET-generated code
51
52       [STAThread]
53       static void Main()
54       {
55          Application.Run( new Server() );
56       }
57
58       protected void Server_Closing(
59          object sender, CancelEventArgs e )
60       {
61          disconnected = true;
62       }
63
64       // accepts connections from 2 players
65       public void SetUp()
66       {
67          // set up Socket
68          listener = new TcpListener( 5000 );
69          listener.Start();
70
71          // accept first player and start a thread for him or her
72          players[ 0 ] =
73             new Player( listener.AcceptSocket(), this, 0 );
74          playerThreads[ 0 ] = new Thread(
75             new ThreadStart( players[ 0 ].Run ) );
76          playerThreads[ 0 ].Start();
77
78          // accept second player and start a thread for him or her
79          players[ 1 ] =
80             new Player( listener.AcceptSocket(), this, 1 );
81          playerThreads[ 1 ] =
82             new Thread( new ThreadStart( players[ 1 ].Run ) );
83          playerThreads[ 1 ].Start();
84
85          // let the first player know that the other player has
86          // connected
87          lock ( players[ 0 ] )
88          {
89             players[ 0 ].threadSuspended = false;
90             Monitor.Pulse( players[ 0 ] );
91          }
92       } // end method SetUp
```

Fig. 19.5   Server side of client/server Tic-Tac-Toe program. (Part 2 of 6.)

```
93
94      // appends the argument to text in displayTextBox
95      public void Display( string message )
96      {
97          displayTextBox.Text += message + "\r\n";
98      }
99
100     // determine if a move is valid
101     public bool ValidMove( int location, int player )
102     {
103         // prevent another thread from making a move
104         lock ( this )
105         {
106             // while it is not the current player's turn, wait
107             while ( player != currentPlayer )
108                 Monitor.Wait( this );
109
110             // if the desired square is not occupied
111             if ( !IsOccupied( location ) )
112             {
113                 // set the board to contain the current player's mark
114                 board[ location ] = ( byte ) ( currentPlayer == 0 ?
115                     'X' : 'O' );
116
117                 // set the currentPlayer to be the other player
118                 currentPlayer = ( currentPlayer + 1 ) % 2;
119
120                 // notify the other player of the move
121                 players[ currentPlayer ].OtherPlayerMoved( location );
122
123                 // alert the other player it's time to move
124                 Monitor.Pulse( this );
125
126                 return true;
127             }
128             else
129                 return false;
130         }
131     } // end method ValidMove
132
133     // determines whether the specified square is occupied
134     public bool IsOccupied( int location )
135     {
136         if ( board[ location ] == 'X' || board[ location ] == 'O' )
137             return true;
138         else
139             return false;
140     }
141
142     // determines if the game is over
143     public bool GameOver()
144     {
```

Fig. 19.5 Server side of client/server Tic-Tac-Toe program. (Part 3 of 6.)

```
145         // place code here to test for a winner of the game
146         return false;
147      }
148
149 } // end class Server
150
151 public class Player
152 {
153    internal Socket connection;
154    private NetworkStream socketStream;
155    private Server server;
156    private BinaryWriter writer;
157    private BinaryReader reader;
158
159    private int number;
160    private char mark;
161    internal bool threadSuspended = true;
162
163    // constructor requiring Socket, Server and int objects
164    // as arguments
165    public Player( Socket socket, Server serverValue, int newNumber )
166    {
167       mark = ( newNumber == 0 ? 'X' : 'O' );
168
169       connection = socket;
170
171       server = serverValue;
172       number = newNumber;
173
174       // create NetworkStream object for Socket
175       socketStream = new NetworkStream( connection );
176
177       // create Streams for reading/writing bytes
178       writer = new BinaryWriter( socketStream );
179       reader = new BinaryReader( socketStream );
180
181    } // end constructor
182
183    // signal other player of move
184    public void OtherPlayerMoved( int location )
185    {
186       // signal that opponent moved
187       writer.Write( "Opponent moved" );
188       writer.Write( location ); // send location of move
189    }
190
191    // allows the players to make moves and receives moves
192    // from other player
193    public void Run()
194    {
195       bool done = false;
196
```

Fig. 19.5 Server side of client/server Tic-Tac-Toe program. (Part 4 of 6.)

```
197         // display on the server that a connection was made
198         server.Display( "Player " + ( number == 0 ? 'X' : 'O' )
199            + " connected" );
200
201         // send the current player's mark to the server
202         writer.Write( mark );
203
204         // if number equals 0 then this player is X, so send
205         writer.Write( "Player " + ( number == 0 ?
206            "X connected\r\n" : "O connected, please wait\r\n" ) );
207
208         // wait for another player to arrive
209         if ( mark == 'X' )
210         {
211            writer.Write( "Waiting for another player" );
212
213            // wait for notification from server that another
214            // player has connected
215            lock ( this )
216            {
217               while ( threadSuspended )
218                  Monitor.Wait( this );
219            }
220
221            writer.Write( "Other player connected. Your move" );
222
223         } // end if
224
225         // play game
226         while ( !done )
227         {
228            // wait for data to become available
229            while ( connection.Available == 0 )
230            {
231               Thread.Sleep( 1000 );
232
233               if ( server.disconnected )
234                  return;
235            }
236
237            // receive data
238            int location = reader.ReadInt32();
239
240            // if the move is valid, display the move on the
241            // server and signal the move is valid
242            if ( server.ValidMove( location, number ) )
243            {
244               server.Display( "loc: " + location );
245               writer.Write( "Valid move." );
246            }
247
```

Fig. 19.5　Server side of client/server Tic-Tac-Toe program. (Part 5 of 6.)

```
248              // signal the move is invalid
249              else
250                 writer.Write( "Invalid move, try again" );
251
252              // if game is over, set done to true to exit while loop
253              if ( server.GameOver() )
254                 done = true;
255
256           } // end while loop
257
258           // close the socket connection
259           writer.Close();
260           reader.Close();
261           socketStream.Close();
262           connection.Close();
263
264        } // end method Run
265
266  } // end class Player
```

Fig. 19.5 Server side of client/server Tic-Tac-Toe program. (Part 6 of 6.)

Server (Fig. 19.5) uses its constructor (lines 35–48) to create a **byte** array to store the moves the players have made (line 39). The program creates an array of two references to **Player** objects (line 41) and an array of two references to **Thread** objects (line 42). Each element in both arrays corresponds to a Tic-Tac-Toe player. Variable **current-Player** is set to **0**, which corresponds to player **"X"**. In our program, player **"X"** makes the first move (line 43). Lines 46–47 create and start **Thread getPlayers**, which the **Server** uses to accept connections so that the current **Thread** does not block while awaiting players.

Thread **getPlayers** executes method **SetUp** (lines 65–92), which creates a **TcpListener** object to listen for requests on port **5000** (lines 68–69). This object then listens for connection requests from the first and second players. Lines 72–73 and 79–80 instantiate **Player** objects representing the players, and lines 74–75 and 81–82 create two **Thread**s that execute the **Run** methods of each **Player** object.

The **Player** constructor (Fig. 19.5, lines 165–181) receives as arguments a reference to the **Socket** object (i.e., the connection to the client), a reference to the **Server** object and an **int** indicating the mark (**"X"** or **"O"**) used by that player. In this case study, **Server** calls method **Run** (lines 193–264) after instantiating a **Player** object. Lines 198–206 notify the server of a successful connection and send to the client the **char** that the client will place on the board when making a move. If **Run** is executing for **Player "X"**, lines 211–221 execute, causing **Player "X"** to wait for a second player to connect. Lines 217–218 define a **while** loop that suspends the **Player "X" Thread** until the server signals that **Player "O"** has connected. The server notifies the **Player** of the connection by setting the **Player**'s **threadSuspended** variable to **false** (line 89). When **threadSuspended** becomes **false**, **Player** exits the **while** loop of lines 217–218.

Method **Run** executes the **while** structure (lines 226–256), enabling the user to play the game. Each iteration of this structure waits for the client to send an **int** specifying where on the board to place the **"X"** or **"O"**—the **Player** then places the mark on the board, if the specified mark location is valid (e.g., that location does not already contain a mark). Note that the **while** structure continues execution only if **bool** variable **done** is **false**. This variable is set to **true** by event handler **Server_Closing** of class **Server**, which is invoked when the server closes the connection.

```csharp
1   // Fig. 19.6: Client.cs
2   // Client for the TicTacToe program.
3
4   using System;
5   using System.Drawing;
6   using System.Collections;
7   using System.ComponentModel;
8   using System.Windows.Forms;
9   using System.Data;
10  using System.Net.Sockets;
11  using System.Threading;
12  using System.IO;
13
14  // represents a tic-tac-toe player
15  public class Client : System.Windows.Forms.Form
16  {
17      private System.Windows.Forms.Label idLabel;
18
19      private System.Windows.Forms.TextBox displayTextBox;
20
21      private System.Windows.Forms.Panel panel1;
22      private System.Windows.Forms.Panel panel2;
23      private System.Windows.Forms.Panel panel3;
24      private System.Windows.Forms.Panel panel5;
25      private System.Windows.Forms.Panel panel6;
26      private System.Windows.Forms.Panel panel4;
27      private System.Windows.Forms.Panel panel7;
28      private System.Windows.Forms.Panel panel8;
29      private System.Windows.Forms.Panel panel9;
30
31      private Square[ , ] board;
32      private Square currentSquare;
33
34      private Thread outputThread;
35
36      private TcpClient connection;
37      private NetworkStream stream;
38      private BinaryWriter writer;
39      private BinaryReader reader;
40
41      private char myMark;
42      private bool myTurn;
43
44      private SolidBrush brush;
45      private System.ComponentModel.Container components = null;
46
47      bool done = false;
```

Fig. 19.6   Client side of client/server Tic-Tac-Toe program. (Part 1 of 7.)

```
48
49      // default constructor
50      public Client()
51      {
52          InitializeComponent();
53
54          board = new Square[ 3, 3 ];
55
56          // create 9 Square objects and place them on the board
57          board[ 0, 0 ] = new Square( panel1, ' ', 0 );
58          board[ 0, 1 ] = new Square( panel2, ' ', 1 );
59          board[ 0, 2 ] = new Square( panel3, ' ', 2 );
60          board[ 1, 0 ] = new Square( panel4, ' ', 3 );
61          board[ 1, 1 ] = new Square( panel5, ' ', 4 );
62          board[ 1, 2 ] = new Square( panel6, ' ', 5 );
63          board[ 2, 0 ] = new Square( panel7, ' ', 6 );
64          board[ 2, 1 ] = new Square( panel8, ' ', 7 );
65          board[ 2, 2 ] = new Square( panel9, ' ', 8 );
66
67          // create a SolidBrush for writing on the Squares
68          brush = new SolidBrush( Color.Black );
69
70          // Make connection to sever and get the associated
71          // network stream. Start separate thread to allow this
72          // program to continually update its output in textbox.
73          connection = new TcpClient( "localhost", 5000 );
74          stream = connection.GetStream();
75
76          writer = new BinaryWriter( stream );
77          reader = new BinaryReader( stream );
78
79          // start a new thread for sending and receiving messages
80          outputThread = new Thread( new ThreadStart( Run ) );
81          outputThread.Start();
82      }   // end Client constructor
83
84      // Visual Studio .NET-generated code
85
86      [STAThread]
87      static void Main()
88      {
89          Application.Run( new Client() );
90      }
91
92      protected void Client_Paint (
93          object sender, System.Windows.Forms.PaintEventArgs e )
94      {
95          PaintSquares();
96      }
97
```

Fig. 19.6   Client side of client/server Tic-Tac-Toe program. (Part 2 of 7.)

```
98      protected void Client_Closing(
99         object sender, CancelEventArgs e )
100     {
101         done = true;
102     }
103
104     // draws the mark of each square
105     public void PaintSquares()
106     {
107         Graphics g;
108
109         // draw the appropriate mark on each panel
110         for ( int row = 0; row < 3; row++ )
111            for ( int column = 0; column < 3; column++ )
112            {
113               // get the Graphics for each Panel
114               g = board[ row, column ].SquarePanel.CreateGraphics();
115
116               // draw the appropriate letter on the panel
117               g.DrawString( board[ row, column ].Mark.ToString(),
118                  this.Font, brush, 8, 8 );
119            }
120     } // end method PaintSquares
121
122     // send location of the clicked square to server
123     protected void square_MouseUp(
124        object sender, System.Windows.Forms.MouseEventArgs e )
125     {
126        // for each square check if that square was clicked
127        for ( int row = 0; row < 3; row++ )
128           for ( int column = 0; column < 3; column++ )
129              if ( board[ row, column ].SquarePanel == sender )
130              {
131                 CurrentSquare = board[ row, column ];
132
133                 // send the move to the server
134                 SendClickedSquare( board[ row, column ].Location );
135              }
136     } // end method square_MouseUp
137
138     // control thread that allows continuous update of the
139     // textbox display
140     public void Run()
141     {
142        // first get players's mark (X or O)
143        myMark = reader.ReadChar();
144        idLabel.Text = "You are player \"" + myMark + "\"";
145        myTurn = ( myMark == 'X' ? true : false );
146
147        // process incoming messages
148        try
149        {
```

Fig. 19.6 Client side of client/server Tic-Tac-Toe program. (Part 3 of 7.)

```
150              // receive messages sent to client
151              while ( true )
152                 ProcessMessage( reader.ReadString() );
153           }
154           catch ( EndOfStreamException )
155           {
156              MessageBox.Show( "Server is down, game over", "Error",
157                 MessageBoxButtons.OK, MessageBoxIcon.Error );
158           }
159
160        } // end method Run
161
162        // process messages sent to client
163        public void ProcessMessage( string message )
164        {
165           // if the move player sent to the server is valid
166           // update the display, set that square's mark to be
167           // the mark of the current player and repaint the board
168           if ( message == "Valid move." )
169           {
170              displayTextBox.Text +=
171                 "Valid move, please wait.\r\n";
172              currentSquare.Mark = myMark;
173              PaintSquares();
174           }
175
176           // if the move is invalid, display that and it is now
177           // this player's turn again
178           else if ( message == "Invalid move, try again" )
179           {
180              displayTextBox.Text += message + "\r\n";
181              myTurn = true;
182           }
183
184           // if opponent moved
185           else if ( message == "Opponent moved" )
186           {
187              // find location of their move
188              int location = reader.ReadInt32();
189
190              // set that square to have the opponents mark and
191              // repaint the board
192              board[ location / 3, location % 3 ].Mark =
193                 ( myMark == 'X' ? 'O' : 'X' );
194              PaintSquares();
195
196              displayTextBox.Text +=
197                 "Opponent moved.  Your turn.\r\n";
198
199              // it is now this player's turn
200              myTurn = true;
201           }
202
```

Fig. 19.6 Client side of client/server Tic-Tac-Toe program. (Part 4 of 7.)

```
203              // display the message
204              else
205                  displayTextBox.Text += message + "\r\n";
206
207          } // end method ProcessMessage
208
209          // sends the server the number of the clicked square
210          public void SendClickedSquare( int location )
211          {
212              // if it is the current player's move right now
213              if ( myTurn )
214              {
215                  // send the location of the move to the server
216                  writer.Write( location );
217
218                  // it is now the other player's turn
219                  myTurn = false;
220              }
221          }
222
223          // write-only property for the current square
224          public Square CurrentSquare
225          {
226              set
227              {
228                  currentSquare = value;
229              }
230          }
231
232      } // end class Client
```

1.

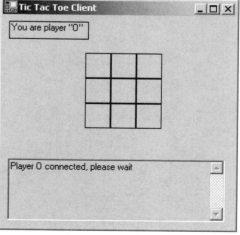

Fig. 19.6 Client side of client/server Tic-Tac-Toe program. (Part 5 of 7.)

2.

3.

4.

Fig. 19.6   Client side of client/server Tic-Tac-Toe program. (Part 6 of 7.)

server output after (1.)

server output after (2.)

server output after (3.)

server output after (4.)

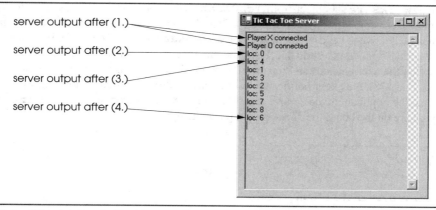

Fig. 19.6   Client side of client/server Tic-Tac-Toe program. (Part 7 of 7.)

Line 229 of Fig. 19.5 begins a **while** that loops until **Socket** property **Available** indicates that there is information to receive from the **Socket** (or until the server disconnects from the client). If there is no information, the thread goes to sleep for one second. Upon awakening, the thread uses property **Disconnected** to check for whether server variable **disconnect** is **true**. If the value is **true**, the **Thread** exits the method (thus terminating the **Thread**); otherwise, the **Thread** loops again. However, if property **Available** indicates that there is data to receive, the **while** loop of lines 229–235 terminates, enabling the information to be processed.

This information contains an **int** representing the location in which the client wants to place a mark. Line 238 calls method **ReadInt32** of the **BinaryReader** object (which reads from the **NetworkStream** created with the **Socket**) to read this **int**. Line 242 then passes the **int** to **Server** method **ValidMove**. If this method validates the move, the **Player** places the mark in the desired location.

Method **ValidMove** (lines 101–131) sends to the client a message indicating whether the move was valid. Locations on the board correspond to numbers from **0–8** (**0–2** for the first row, **3–5** for the second and **6–8** for the third). All statements in method **ValidMove** are enclosed in a **lock** statement that allows only one move to be attempted at a time. This prevents two players from modifying the game's state information simultaneously. If the **Player** attempting to validate a move is not the current player (i.e., the one allowed to make a move), that **Player** is placed in a *wait* state until it is that **Player**'s turn to move. If the user attempts to place a mark on a location that already contains a mark, method **ValidMove** returns **false**. However, if the user has selected an unoccupied location (line 111), lines 114–115 place the mark on the local representation of the board. Line 121 notifies the other **Player** that a move has been made, and line 124 invokes the **Pulse** method so that the waiting **Player** can validate a move. The method then returns **true** to indicate that the move is valid.

When a **Client** application (Fig. 19.6) executes, it creates a **TextBox** to display messages from the server and the Tic-Tac-Toe board representation. The board is created out of nine **Square** objects (Fig. 19.7) that contain **Panel**s on which the user can click, indicating the position on the board in which to place a mark. The **Client**'s constructor (line 50–82) opens a connection to the server (line 73) and obtains a reference to the connection's associated **NetworkStream** object from **TcpClient** (line 74). Lines 80–81 start a thread to read messages sent from the server to the client. The server passes messages (for example, whether each move is valid) to method **ProcessMessage** (lines 163–207). If the message indicates that a move is valid (line 168), the client sets its mark to the current square (the square that the user clicked) and repaints the board. If the message indicates that a move is invalid (line 178), the client notifies the user to click a different square. If the message indicates that the opponent made a move (line 185), line 188 reads from the server an **int** specifying where on the board the client should place the opponent's mark.

```
1    // Fig. 19.7: Square.cs
2    // A Square on the TicTacToe board.
3
4    using System.Windows.Forms;
5
6    // the representation of a square in a tic-tac-toe grid
7    public class Square
8    {
9       private Panel panel;
10      private char mark;
11      private int location;
12
13      // constructor
14      public Square( Panel newPanel, char newMark, int newLocation )
15      {
16         panel = newPanel;
17         mark = newMark;
18         location = newLocation;
19      }
20
21      // property SquarePanel; the panel which the square represents
22      public Panel SquarePanel
23      {
24         get
25         {
26            return panel;
27         }
28      } // end property SquarePanel
29
30      // property Mark; the mark of the square
31      public char Mark
32      {
33         get
34         {
35            return mark;
36         }
37
38         set
39         {
40            mark = value;
41         }
42      } // end property Mark
```

Fig. 19.7 Class **Square**. (Part 1 of 2.)

```
43
44      // property Location; the square's location on the board
45      public int Location
46      {
47         get
48         {
49            return location;
50         }
51      } // property Location
52
53   } // end class Square
```

Fig. 19.7 Class **Square**. (Part 2 of 2.)

In this chapter, we have discussed how to use C#'s networking technologies by providing both connection-oriented (i.e., streams-based) transmission and connectionless (i.e., packet-based) transmission. We have shown how to create a simple server and client via stream sockets and how to create a multithreaded server. In Chapter 20, Data Structures and Collections, we discuss how to store data dynamically and discuss several of the key classes that belong to the C# **System.Collections** namespace.

19.7 Summary

The two most popular types of sockets are stream sockets and datagram sockets. Stream sockets provide a connection-oriented service, meaning that one process establishes a connection to another process, and data can flow between the processes in continuous streams. Datagram sockets provide a connectionless service that uses messages to transmit data. Connectionless services generally offer greater performance, but less reliability, than connection-oriented services.

Transmission Control Protocol (TCP) is the preferred protocol for stream sockets. It is a reliable and relatively fast way to send data through a network. The User Datagram Protocol (UDP) is the preferred protocol for datagram sockets. UDP is unreliable. There is no guarantee that packets sent with UDP will arrive in the order in which they were sent or that they will arrive at all.

The establishment of a simple server with TCP and stream sockets in C# requires five steps. Step 1 is to create a **TcpListener** object. This class represents a TCP stream socket that a server can use to receive connections. To receive connections, the **TcpListener** must be listening for them. For the **TcpListener** to listen for client connections, its **Start** method must be called (Step 2). **TcpListener** method **AcceptSocket** blocks indefinitely until a connection is established, at which point it returns a **Socket** (Step 3). Step 4 is the processing phase, in which the server and the client communicate using methods **Read** and **Write** via a **NetworkStream** object. When the client and server have finished communicating, the server closes the connection by using the **Close** method on the **Socket** (Step 5). Most servers will then, by means of a control loop, return to the **AcceptSocket** call step to wait for another client's connection.

A port number, also known as an Internet Protocol Address (IP Address), is a numeric ID number that a process uses to identify itself at a given network address. An individual process running on a computer is identified by an IP-address/port-number pair. Hence, no two processes can have the same port number at a given IP address. Class **IPAddress** represents an Internet Protocol address. Class **IPEndPoint** represents an end point on a network, including an IP-address/port-number pair.

The establishment of a simple client requires four steps. Step 1, is to create a **Tcp-Client** to connect to the server. This connection is established through a call to the **Tcp-Client** method **Connect**, containing two arguments—the server's IP address and the port number. In Step 2, the **TcpClient** uses method **GetStream** to get a **Stream** to write to and read from the server. Step 3 is the processing phase, in which the client and the server communicate. Step 4 has the client close the connection by calling the **Close** method on the **NetworkStream**. **NetworkStream** methods **WriteByte** and **Write** can be used to output individual bytes or sets of bytes to a stream, respectively. **Network-Stream** methods **ReadByte** and **Read** can be used to read individual bytes or sets of bytes from a stream, respectively.

Class **UdpClient** is provided for connectionless transmission of data. Class **Udp-Client** methods **Send** and **Receive** are used to transmit data.

Multithreaded servers can manage many simultaneous connections with multiple clients. Using multithreaded servers, the programmer can place processing-phase code into a separate thread. This arrangement leaves the **TCPListener** free to listen for other connections.

Data Structures and Collections

Objectives

- To form linked data structures using references, self-referential classes and recursion.
- To create and manipulate dynamic data structures such as linked lists, queues, stacks and binary trees.
- To understand various important applications of linked data structures.
- To understand how to create reusable data structures with classes, inheritance and composition.

Much that I bound, I could not free;
Much that I freed returned to me.
Lee Wilson Dodd

'Will you walk a little faster?' said a whiting to a snail,
'There's a porpoise close behind us, and he's treading on my
tail.'
Lewis Carroll

There is always room at the top.
Daniel Webster

Push on—keep moving.
Thomas Morton

I think that I shall never see
A poem lovely as a tree.
Joyce Kilmer

Outline

20.1   **Introduction**
20.2   **Self-Referential Classes**
20.3   **Linked Lists**
20.4   **Stacks**
20.5   **Queues**
20.6   **Trees**
    20.6.1   **Binary Search Tree of Integer Values**
    20.6.2   **Binary Search Tree of `IComparable` Objects**
20.7   **Collection Classes**
    20.7.1   **Class `Array`**
    20.7.2   **Class `ArrayList`**
    20.7.3   **Class `Stack`**
    20.7.4   **Class `Hashtable`**
20.8   **Summary**

20.1 Introduction

The *data structures* that we have studied thus far have had fixed size, such as single- and double-subscripted arrays. This chapter introduces *dynamic data structures* that grow and shrink at execution time. *Linked lists* are collections of data items "lined up in a row"—users can make insertions and deletions anywhere in a linked list. *Stacks* are important in compilers and operating systems because insertions and deletions are made at only one end—its *top*. *Queues* represent waiting lines; insertions are made at the back (also referred to as the *tail*) of a queue, and deletions are made from the front (also referred to as the *head*) of a queue. *Binary trees* facilitate high-speed searching and sorting of data, efficient elimination of duplicate data items, representation of file system directories and compilation of expressions into machine language. These data structures have many other interesting applications as well.

We will discuss each of the major types of data structures and implement programs that create and manipulate them. We use classes, inheritance and composition to create and package these data structures for reusability and maintainability.

The chapter examples are practical programs that will be useful in more advanced courses and in industrial applications. The programs devote special attention to and focus on reference manipulation. The exercises offer a rich collection of useful applications.

20.2 Self-Referential Classes

A *self-referential class* contains a reference member that refers to an object of the same class type. For example, the class definition in Fig. 20.1 defines a type, **Node**. This type has two **private** instance variables—integer **data** and **Node** reference **next**. Member **next** references an object of type **Node**, an object of the same type as the one being declared here—hence, the term "self-referential class." Member **next** is referred to as a *link* (i.e., **next** can be used to "tie" an object of type **Node** to another object of the same type). Class **Node** also has two properties: One for variable **data** (named **Data**), and another for variable **next** (named **Next**).

Self-referential objects can be linked together to form useful data structures, such as lists, queues, stacks and trees. Figure 20.2 illustrates two self-referential objects linked together to form a list. A backslash (representing a **null** reference) is placed in the link member of the second self-referential object to indicate that the link does not refer to another object. The slash is for illustration purposes; it does not correspond to the backslash character in C#. A **null** reference normally indicates the end of a data structure.

Common Programming Error 20.1

*Not setting the link in the last node of a list (or other linear data structure) to **null** is a common logic error.*

```
1   class Node
2   {
3       private int data;
4       private Node next;
5
6       public Node( int d )
7       {
8           // constructor body
9       }
10
11      public int Data
12      {
13          get
14          {
15              // get body
16          }
17
18          set
19          {
20              // set body
21          }
22      }
23
24      public Node Next
25      {
26          get
27          {
28              // get body
29          }
30
31          set
32          {
33              // set body
34          }
35      }
36  }
```

Fig. 20.1   Sample self-referential **Node** class definition.

Fig. 20.2   Two self-referential class objects linked together.

Creating and maintaining dynamic data structures requires *dynamic memory alloca-tion*—a program's ability to obtain more memory space at execution time to hold new nodes and to release space no longer needed. As we have already learned, C# programs do not explicitly release dynamically allocated memory. Rather, C# performs automatic gar-bage collection.

The limit for dynamic memory allocation can be as large as the amount of available disk space in a virtual-memory system. Often, the limits are much smaller, because the computer's available memory must be shared among many users.

Operator **new** is essential to dynamic memory allocation. Operator **new** takes as an operand the type of the object being dynamically allocated and returns a reference to a newly created object of that type. For example, the statement

```
Node nodeToAdd = new Node( 10 );
```

allocates the appropriate amount of memory to store a **Node** and stores a reference to this object in **nodeToAdd**. If no memory is available, **new** throws an **OutOfMemoryEx-ception**. The 10 is the **Node** object's data.

The following sections discuss lists, stacks, queues and trees. These data structures are created and maintained with dynamic memory allocation and self-referential classes.

 Good Programming Practice 20.1

When creating a very large number of objects, test for an **OutOfMemoryException** *Per-form appropriate error processing if the requested memory is not allocated.*

20.3 Linked Lists

A *linked list* is a linear collection (i.e., a sequence) of self-referential class objects, called *nodes,* connected by reference links—hence, the term "linked" list. A program accesses a linked list via a reference to the first node of the list. Each subsequent node is accessed via the link-reference member stored in the previous node. By convention, the link ref-erence in the last node of a list is set to **null** to mark the end of the list. Data are stored in a linked list dynamically—that is, each node is created as necessary. A node can con-tain data of any type, including objects of other classes. Stacks and queues are also linear data structures, and they are constrained versions of linked lists. Trees are nonlinear data structures.

Lists of data can be stored in arrays, but linked lists provide several advantages. A linked list is appropriate when the number of data elements to be represented in the data structure is unpredictable. Unlike a linked list, the size of a conventional C# array cannot be altered, because the array size is fixed at creation time. Conventional arrays can become full, but linked lists become full only when the system has insufficient memory to satisfy dynamic storage allocation requests.

Performance Tip 20.1

An array can be declared to contain more elements than the number of items expected, at the expense of wasting memory. Linked lists provide better memory utilization in these situations and they allow the program to adapt at run time.

Performance Tip 20.2

After locating the insertion point for a new item in a sorted linked list, inserting an element in the list is fast—only two references have to be modified. All existing nodes remain at their current locations in memory.

Programmers can maintain linked lists in sorted order simply by inserting each new element at the proper point in the list (locating the proper insertion point does take time). They do not need to move existing list elements.

Performance Tip 20.3

The elements of an array are stored contiguously in memory to allow immediate access to any array element—the address of any element can be calculated directly from its offset from the beginning of the array. Linked lists do not afford such immediate access to their elements—an element can be accessed only by traversing the list from the front.

Memory does not normally store linked list nodes contiguously. Rather, the nodes are logically contiguous. Figure 20.3 illustrates a linked list with several nodes.

Performance Tip 20.4

Using dynamic memory allocation (instead of arrays) for data structures that grow and shrink at execution time can save memory. Keep in mind, however, that references occupy space, and that dynamic memory allocation incurs the overhead of method calls.

The program of Fig. 20.4–Fig. 20.5 uses an object of class **List** to manipulate a list of miscellaneous object types. The **Main** method of class **ListTest** (Fig. 20.5) creates a list of objects, inserts objects at the beginning of the list using **List** method **InsertAtFront**, inserts objects at the end of the list using **List** method **InsertAtBack**, deletes objects from the front of the list using **List** method **RemoveFromFront** and deletes objects from the end of the list using **List** method **RemoveFromBack**. Each insertion and deletion operation invokes **List** method **Print** to display the current list contents. A detailed discussion of the program follows. If an attempt is made to remove an item from an empty list, an **EmptyListException** occurs.

Fig. 20.3 A graphical representation of a linked list.

Performance Tip 20.5

Insertion and deletion in a sorted array can be time consuming—all the elements following the inserted or deleted element must be shifted appropriately.

The program consists of four classes—**ListNode** (Fig. 20.4, lines 9–52), **List** (Fig. 20.4, lines 55–193), **EmptyListException** (Fig. 20.4, lines 196–203) and class **ListTest** (Fig. 20.5). The classes in Fig. 20.4 create a linked-list library (defined in namespace **LinkedListLibrary**) that can be reused throughout this chapter.

Encapsulated in each **List** object is a linked list of **ListNode** objects. Class **ListNode** (Fig. 20.4, lines 9–52) consists of two member variables—**data** and **next**. Member **data** can refer to any object. Member **next** stores a reference to the next **ListNode** object in the linked list. A **List** accesses the **ListNode** member variables via the properties **Data** (lines 44–50) and **Next** (lines 30–41), respectively.

Class **List** contains **private** members **firstNode** (a reference to the first **ListNode** in a **List**) and **lastNode** (a reference to the last **ListNode** in a **List**). The constructors (lines 62–66 and 69–71) initialize both references to **null**. **InsertAtFront** (lines 76–87), **InsertAtBack** (lines 92–104), **RemoveFromFront** (lines 107–125) and **RemoveFromBack** (lines 128–156) are the primary methods of class **List**. Each method uses a **lock** block to ensure that **List** objects are *multithread safe* when used in a multithreaded program. If one thread is modifying the contents of a **List** object, no other thread can modify the same **List** object at the same time. Method **IsEmpty** (lines 159–165) is a *predicate method* that determines whether the list is empty (i.e., the reference to the first node of the list is **null**). Predicate methods typically test a condition and do not modify the object on which they are called. If the list is empty, method **IsEmpty** returns **true**; otherwise, it returns **false**. Method **Print** (lines 168–191) displays the list's contents. Both **IsEmpty** and **Print** also use **lock** blocks so that the state of the list does not change while those methods are performing their tasks.

Class **EmptyListException** (lines 196–203) defines an exception class to handle illegal operations on an empty **List**.

Class **ListTest** (Fig. 20.5) uses the linked-list library to create and manipulate a linked list. Line 14 creates a new instance of type **List** named **list**. Lines 17–20 create data to add to the list. Lines 23–30 use **List** insertion methods to insert these objects and use **List** method **Print** to output the contents of **list** after each insertion. The code inside the **try** block (lines 36–53) removes objects via **List** deletion methods, outputs the object removed and outputs **list** after every deletion. If there is an attempt to remove an object from an empty list, this **try** block catches the **EmptyListException**. Note that class **ListTest** uses namespace **LinkedListLibrary** (Fig. 20.4); thus, the solution for class **ListTest** must have a reference to the **LinkedListLibrary** class library.

Over the next several pages, we discuss each of the methods of class **List** in detail. Method **InsertAtFront** (Fig. 20.4, lines 76–87) places a new node at the front of the list. The method consists of three steps (illustrated in Fig. 20.6):

1. Call **IsEmpty** to determine whether the list is empty (line 80).

2. If the list is empty, set both **firstNode** and **lastNode** to refer to a new **ListNode** initialized with **insertItem** (lines 81–82). The **ListNode** constructor at lines 16–19 (Fig. 20.4) calls the **ListNode** constructor at lines 23–27

(Fig. 20.4) to set instance variable **data** to refer to the **object** passed as the first argument and sets the **next** reference to **null**.

3. If the list is not empty, the new node is "threaded" (not to be confused with *multithreading*) into the list by setting **firstNode** to refer to a new **ListNode** object initialized with **insertItem** and **firstNode** (lines 84–85). When the **List-Node** constructor (lines 23–27 of Fig. 20.4) executes, it sets instance variable **data** to refer to the **object** passed as the first argument and performs the insertion by setting the **next** reference to the **ListNode** passed as the second argument.

```
1   // Fig. 20.4: LinkedListLibrary.cs
2   // Class ListNode and class List definitions.
3
4   using System;
5
6   namespace LinkedListLibrary
7   {
8      // class to represent one node in a list
9      class ListNode
10     {
11        private object data;
12        private ListNode next;
13
14        // constructor to create ListNode that refers to dataValue
15        // and is last node in list
16        public ListNode( object dataValue )
17           : this( dataValue, null )
18        {
19        }
20
21        // constructor to create ListNode that refers to dataValue
22        // and refers to next ListNode in List
23        public ListNode( object dataValue, ListNode nextNode )
24        {
25           data = dataValue;
26           next = nextNode;
27        }
28
29        // property Next
30        public ListNode Next
31        {
32           get
33           {
34              return next;
35           }
36
37           set
38           {
39              next = value;
40           }
41        }
```

Fig. 20.4 Definitions of classes **ListNode**, **List** and **EmptyListException**. (Part 1 of 5.)

```
42
43          // property Data
44          public object Data
45          {
46              get
47              {
48                  return data;
49              }
50          }
51
52      } // end class ListNode
53
54      // class List definition
55      public class List
56      {
57          private ListNode firstNode;
58          private ListNode lastNode;
59          private string name;      // string like "list" to display
60
61          // construct empty List with specified name
62          public List( string listName )
63          {
64              name = listName;
65              firstNode = lastNode = null;
66          }
67
68          // construct empty List with "list" as its name
69          public List() : this( "list" )
70          {
71          }
72
73          // Insert object at front of List. If List is empty,
74          // firstNode and lastNode will refer to same object.
75          // Otherwise, firstNode refers to new node.
76          public void InsertAtFront( object insertItem )
77          {
78              lock ( this )
79              {
80                  if ( IsEmpty() )
81                      firstNode = lastNode =
82                          new ListNode( insertItem );
83                  else
84                      firstNode =
85                          new ListNode( insertItem, firstNode );
86              }
87          }
88
89          // Insert object at end of List. If List is empty,
90          // firstNode and lastNode will refer to same object.
91          // Otherwise, lastNode's Next property refers to new node.
92          public void InsertAtBack( object insertItem )
93          {
```

Fig. 20.4 Definitions of classes **ListNode**, **List** and **EmptyListException**.
(Part 2 of 5.)

```
 94                    lock ( this )
 95                    {
 96                       if ( IsEmpty() )
 97                          firstNode = lastNode =
 98                             new ListNode( insertItem );
 99
100                       else
101                          lastNode = lastNode.Next =
102                             new ListNode( insertItem );
103                    }
104                 }
105
106                 // remove first node from List
107                 public object RemoveFromFront()
108                 {
109                    lock ( this )
110                    {
111                       if ( IsEmpty() )
112                          throw new EmptyListException( name );
113
114                       object removeItem = firstNode.Data;   // retrieve data
115
116                       // reset firstNode and lastNode references
117                       if ( firstNode == lastNode )
118                          firstNode = lastNode = null;
119
120                       else
121                          firstNode = firstNode.Next;
122
123                       return removeItem;   // return removed data
124                    }
125                 }
126
127                 // remove last node from List
128                 public object RemoveFromBack()
129                 {
130                    lock ( this )
131                    {
132                       if ( IsEmpty() )
133                          throw new EmptyListException( name );
134
135                       object removeItem = lastNode.Data;    // retrieve data
136
137                       // reset firstNode and lastNode references
138                       if ( firstNode == lastNode )
139                          firstNode = lastNode = null;
140
141                       else
142                       {
143                          ListNode current = firstNode;
144
```

Fig. 20.4 Definitions of classes **ListNode**, **List** and **EmptyListException**.
(Part 3 of 5.)

```
145                    // loop while current node is not lastNode
146                    while ( current.Next != lastNode )
147                       current = current.Next;     // move to next node
148
149                    // current is new lastNode
150                    lastNode = current;
151                    current.Next = null;
152                 }
153
154              return removeItem;   // return removed data
155           }
156        }
157
158        // return true if List is empty
159        public bool IsEmpty()
160        {
161           lock ( this )
162           {
163              return firstNode == null;
164           }
165        }
166
167        // output List contents
168        virtual public void Print()
169        {
170           lock ( this )
171           {
172              if ( IsEmpty() )
173              {
174                 Console.WriteLine( "Empty " + name );
175                 return;
176              }
177
178              Console.Write( "The " + name + " is: " );
179
180              ListNode current = firstNode;
181
182              // output current node data while not at end of list
183              while ( current != null )
184              {
185                 Console.Write( current.Data + " " );
186                 current = current.Next;
187              }
188
189              Console.WriteLine( "\n" );
190           }
191        }
192
193     } // end class List
194
```

Fig. 20.4 Definitions of classes **ListNode**, **List** and **EmptyListException**. (Part 4 of 5.)

```
195      // class EmptyListException definition
196      public class EmptyListException : ApplicationException
197      {
198         public EmptyListException( string name )
199            : base( "The " + name + " is empty" )
200         {
201         }
202
203      } // end class EmptyListException
204
205  } // end namespace LinkedListLibrary
```

Fig. 20.4   Definitions of classes **ListNode**, **List** and **EmptyListException**.
(Part 5 of 5.)

```
1    // Fig. 20.5: ListTest.cs
2    // Testing class List.
3
4    using System;
5    using LinkedListLibrary;
6
7    namespace ListTest
8    {
9       // class to test List class functionality
10      class ListTest
11      {
12         static void Main( string[] args )
13         {
14            List list = new List();  // create List container
15
16            // create data to store in List
17            bool aBoolean = true;
18            char aCharacter = '$';
19            int anInteger =  34567;
20            string aString = "hello";
21
22            // use List insert methods
23            list.InsertAtFront( aBoolean );
24            list.Print();
25            list.InsertAtFront( aCharacter );
26            list.Print();
27            list.InsertAtBack( anInteger );
28            list.Print();
29            list.InsertAtBack( aString );
30            list.Print();
31
32            // use List remove methods
33            object removedObject;
34
```

Fig. 20.5   Demonstrating the linked list. (Part 1 of 2.)

```
35                // remove data from list and print after each removal
36                try
37                {
38                    removedObject = list.RemoveFromFront();
39                    Console.WriteLine( removedObject + " removed" );
40                    list.Print();
41
42                    removedObject = list.RemoveFromFront();
43                    Console.WriteLine( removedObject + " removed" );
44                    list.Print();
45
46                    removedObject = list.RemoveFromBack();
47                    Console.WriteLine( removedObject + " removed" );
48                    list.Print();
49
50                    removedObject = list.RemoveFromBack();
51                    Console.WriteLine( removedObject + " removed" );
52                    list.Print();
53                }
54
55                // process exception if list empty when attempt is
56                // made to remove item
57                catch ( EmptyListException emptyListException )
58                {
59                    Console.Error.WriteLine( "\n" + emptyListException );
60                }
61
62        } // end method Main
63
64    } // end class ListTest
65 }
```

```
The list is: True

The list is: $ True

The list is: $ True 34567

The list is: $ True 34567 hello

$ removed
The list is: True 34567 hello

True removed
The list is: 34567 hello

hello removed
The list is: 34567

34567 removed
Empty list
```

Fig. 20.5   Demonstrating the linked list. (Part 2 of 2.)

Figure 20.6 illustrates method **InsertAtFront**. Part (a) of the figure shows the list and the new node during the **InsertAtFront** operation and before the threading of the new node into the list. The dotted arrows in part (b) illustrate step 3 of the **InsertAtFront** operation, which enables the node containing **12** to become the new list front.

Method **InsertAtBack** (Fig. 20.4, lines 92–104) places a new node at the back of the list. The method consists of three steps (illustrated in Fig. 20.7):

1. Call **IsEmpty** to determine whether the list is empty (line 96).

2. If the list is empty, set both **firstNode** and **lastNode** to refer to a new **ListNode** initialized with **insertItem** (lines 97–98). The **ListNode** constructor at lines 16–19 (Fig. 20.4) calls the **ListNode** constructor at lines 23–27 (Fig. 20.4) to set instance variable **data** to refer to the **object** passed as the first argument and sets the **next** reference to **null**.

3. If the list is not empty, thread the new node into the list by setting **lastNode** and **lastNode.next** to refer to a new **ListNode** object initialized with **insertItem** (lines 101–102). When the **ListNode** constructor (lines 16–19 of Fig. 20.4) executes, it sets instance variable **data** to refer to the **object** passed as an argument and sets the **next** reference to **null**.

Fig. 20.7 illustrates an **InsertAtBack** operation. Part a) of the figure shows the list and the new node during the **InsertAtBack** operation and before the new node has been threaded into the list. The dotted arrows in part b) illustrate the steps of method **InsertAtBack** that enable a new node to be added to the end of a list that is not empty.

Method **RemoveFromFront** (Fig. 20.4, lines 107–127) removes the front node of the list and returns a reference to the removed data. The method throws an **EmptyListException** (line 114) if the programmer tries to remove a node from an empty list. Otherwise, the method returns a reference to the removed data. The method consists of four steps (illustrated in Fig. 20.8):

1. Assign **firstNode.Data** (the data being removed from the list) to reference **removeItem** (line 116).

2. If the objects to which **firstNode** and **lastNode** refer are the same object, the list has only one element prior to the removal attempt. In this case, the method sets **firstNode** and **lastNode** to **null** (line 120) to "dethread" (remove) the node from the list (leaving the list empty).

3. If the list has more than one node prior to removal, then the method leaves reference **lastNode** as is and simply assigns **firstNode.Next** to reference **firstNode** (line 123). Thus, **firstNode** references the node that was the second node prior to the **RemoveFromFront** call.

4. Return the **removeItem** reference.

Fig. 20.8 illustrates method **RemoveFromFront**. Part a) illustrates the list before the removal operation. Part b) shows actual reference manipulations.

Method **RemoveFromBack** (Fig. 20.4, lines 130–160) removes the last node of a list and returns a reference to the removed data. The method throws an **EmptyListException** (line 137) if the program attempts to remove a node from an empty list. The method consists of several steps (illustrated in Fig. 20.9):

1. Assign **lastNode.Data** (the data being removed from the list) to reference **removeItem** (line 139).

2. If the objects to which **firstNode** and **lastNode** refer are the same object (line 142), the list has only one element prior to the removal attempt. In this case, the method sets **firstNode** and **lastNode** to **null** (line 143) to dethread (remove) that node from the list (leaving the list empty).

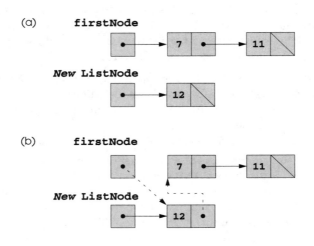

Fig. 20.6 A graphical representation of the **InsertAtFront** operation.

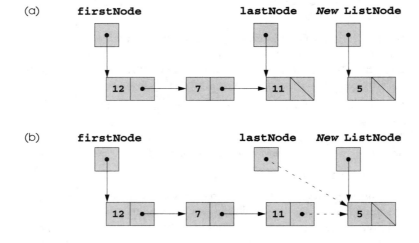

Fig. 20.7 A graphical representation of the **InsertAtBack** operation.

3. If the list has more than one node prior to removal, create the **ListNode** reference **current** and assign it **firstNode** (line 147).

4. Now "walk the list" with **current** until it references the node before the last node. The **while** loop (lines 150–151) assigns **current.Next** to reference **current** as long as **current.Next** is not equal to **lastNode**.

5. After locating the second-to-last node, assign **current** to **lastNode** (line 154) to dethread the last node from the list.

6. Set **current.Next** to **null** (line 155) in the new last node of the list to ensure proper list termination.

7. Return the **removeItem** reference (line 140).

Fig. 20.9 illustrates method **RemoveFromBack**. Part a) illustrates the list before the removal operation. Part b) shows the actual reference manipulations.

Method **Print** (Fig. 20.4, lines 172–195) first determines whether the list is empty (line 176). If so, **Print** displays a **string** consisting of the string **"Empty "** and the list's **name**, then returns control to the calling method. Otherwise, **Print** outputs the data in the list. The method prints a string consisting of the string **"The "**, the **name** and the string **" is: "**. Then, line 184 creates **ListNode** reference **current** and initializes it with **firstNode**. While **current** is not **null**, there are more items in the list. Therefore, the method prints **current.Data** (line 189), then assigns **current.Next** to **current** (line 190) to move to the next node in the list. Note that, if the link in the last node of the list is not **null**, the printing algorithm will erroneously attempt to print past the end of the list. The printing algorithm is identical for linked lists, stacks and queues.

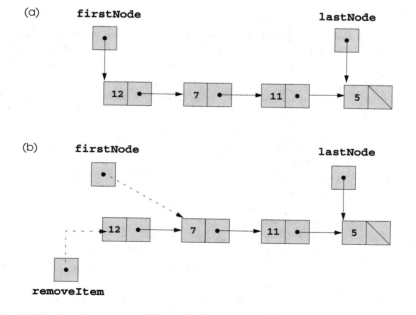

Fig. 20.8   A graphical representation of the **RemoveFromFront** operation.

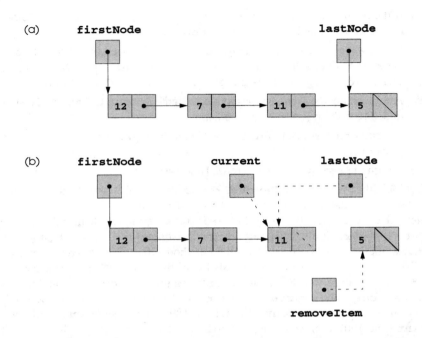

Fig. 20.9 A graphical representation of the **RemoveFromBack** operation.

20.4 Stacks

A *stack* is a constrained version of a linked list—a stack takes new nodes and releases nodes only at the top. For this reason, a stack is referred to as a *last-in, first-out (LIFO)* data structure. The link member in the bottom (i.e., last) node of the stack is set to **null** to indicate the bottom of the stack.

The primary operations to manipulate a stack are *push* and *pop*. Operation push adds a new node to the top of the stack. Operation pop removes a node from the top of the stack and returns the item from the popped node.

Stacks have many interesting applications. For example, when a program calls a method, the called method must know how to return to its caller, so the return address is pushed onto the *program execution stack*. If a series of method calls occurs, the successive return values are pushed onto the stack in last-in, first-out order so that each method can return to its caller. Stacks support recursive method calls in the same manner that they do conventional nonrecursive method calls.

The program-execution stack contains the space created for local variables on each invocation of a method during a program's execution. When the method returns to its caller, the space for that method's local variables is popped off the stack, and those variables are no longer known to the program.

The *System.Collections* namespace contains class **Stack** for implementing and manipulating stacks that can grow and shrink during program execution. Section 20.7 discusses class **Stack**.

We take advantage of the close relationship between lists and stacks to implement a stack class by reusing a list class. We demonstrate two different forms of reusability. First, we implement the stack class by inheriting from class **List** of Fig. 20.4. Then, we implement an identically performing stack class through composition by including a **List** object as a **private** member of a stack class. This chapter implements list, stack and queue data structures to store **object** references to encourage further reusability. Thus, any object type can be stored in a list, stack or queue.

The program of Fig. 20.10 and Fig. 20.11 creates a stack class by inheriting from class **List** of Fig. 20.4. We want the stack to have methods **Push**, **Pop**, **IsEmpty** and **Print**. Essentially, these are the methods **InsertAtFront**, **RemoveFromFront**, **IsEmpty** and **Print** of class **List**. Of course, class **List** contains other methods (such as **InsertAtBack** and **RemoveFromBack**) that we would rather not make accessible through the **public** interface of the stack. It is important to remember that all methods in the **public** interface of class **List** are also **public** methods of the derived class **StackInheritance** (Fig. 20.10).

When we implement the stack's methods, we have each **StackInheritance** method call the appropriate **List** method—method **Push** calls **InsertAtFront**, method **Pop** calls **RemoveFromFront**. Class **StackInheritance** does not define methods **IsEmpty** and **Print**, because **StackInheritance** inherits these methods from class **List** into **StackInheritance**'s **public** interface. The methods in class **StackInheritance** do not use **lock** statements. Each of the methods in this class calls a method from class **List** that uses **lock**. If two threads call **Push** on the same stack object, only one of the threads at a time will be able to call **List** method **InsertAtFront**. Note that class **StackInheritance** uses namespace **LinkedListLibrary** (Fig. 20.4); thus, the solution for the class library that defines **StackInheritance** must have a reference to the **LinkedListLibrary** class library.

StackInheritanceTest's **Main** method (Fig. 20.11) uses class **StackInheritance** to instantiate a stack of **object**s called **stack**. Lines 18–21 define four objects that will be pushed onto the stack and popped off the stack. The program pushes onto the stack (lines 24, 26, 28 and 30) a **bool** containing **true**, a **char** containing **$**, an **int** containing **34567** and a **string** containing **hello**. An infinite **while** loop (lines 36–41) pops the elements from the stack. When there are no objects left to pop, method **Pop** throws an **EmptyListException** and the program displays the exception's stack trace, which shows the program execution stack at the time the exception occurred. The program uses method **Print** (inherited from class **List**) to output the contents of the stack after each operation. Note that class **StackInheritanceTest** uses namespace **LinkedListLibrary** (Fig. 20.4) and namespace **StackInheritanceLibrary** (Fig. 20.10); thus, the solution for class **StackInheritanceTest** must have references to both class libraries.

```
1   // Fig. 20.10: StackInheritanceLibrary.cs
2   // Implementing a stack by inheriting from class List.
3
4   using System;
5   using LinkedListLibrary;
```

Fig. 20.10 StackInheritance extends class **List**. (Part 1 of 2.)

```
6
7   namespace StackInheritanceLibrary
8   {
9      // class StackInheritance inherits class List's capabilities
10     public class StackInheritance : List
11     {
12        // pass name "stack" to List constructor
13        public StackInheritance() : base( "stack" )
14        {
15        }
16
17        // place dataValue at top of stack by inserting
18        // dataValue at front of linked list
19        public void Push( object dataValue )
20        {
21           InsertAtFront( dataValue );
22        }
23
24        // remove item from top of stack by removing
25        // item at front of linked list
26        public object Pop()
27        {
28           return RemoveFromFront();
29        }
30
31     } // end class StackInheritance
32  }
```

Fig. 20.10 `StackInheritance` extends class `List`. (Part 2 of 2.)

Another way to implement a stack class is by reusing a list class through composition. The class in Fig. 20.12 uses a **private** object of class **List** (line 12) in the definition of class **StackComposition**. Composition enables us to hide the methods of class **List** that should not be in our stack's **public** interface by providing **public** interface methods only to the required **List** methods. This class implements each stack method by delegating its work to an appropriate **List** method. In particular, **StackComposition** calls **List** methods **InsertAtFront**, **RemoveFromFront**, **IsEmpty** and **Print**. In this example, we do not show class **StackCompositionTest**, because the only difference in this example is that we change the type of the stack from **StackInheritance** to **StackComposition**. If you execute the application from the code located on our Web site, you will see that the output is identical.

```
1   // Fig. 20.11: StackInheritanceTest.cs
2   // Testing class StackInheritance.
3
4   using System;
5   using StackInheritanceLibrary;
6   using LinkedListLibrary;
7
```

Fig. 20.11 Using class `StackInheritance`. (Part 1 of 3.)

```
8   namespace StackInheritanceTest
9   {
10      // demonstrate functionality of class StackInheritance
11      class StackInheritanceTest
12      {
13          static void Main( string[] args )
14          {
15              StackInheritance stack = new StackInheritance();
16
17              // create objects to store in the stack
18              bool aBoolean = true;
19              char aCharacter = '$';
20              int anInteger = 34567;
21              string aString = "hello";
22
23              // use method Push to add items to stack
24              stack.Push( aBoolean );
25              stack.Print();
26              stack.Push( aCharacter );
27              stack.Print();
28              stack.Push( anInteger );
29              stack.Print();
30              stack.Push( aString );
31              stack.Print();
32
33              // use method Pop to remove items from stack
34              try
35              {
36                  while ( true )
37                  {
38                      object removedObject = stack.Pop();
39                      Console.WriteLine( removedObject + " popped" );
40                      stack.Print();
41                  }
42              }
43
44              // if exception occurs, print stack trace
45              catch ( EmptyListException emptyListException )
46              {
47                  Console.Error.WriteLine(
48                      emptyListException.StackTrace );
49              }
50
51          } // end method Main
52
53      } // end class StackInheritanceTest
54  }
```

```
The stack is: True

The stack is: $ True
```
(continued on next page)

Fig. 20.11 Using class **StackInheritance**. (Part 2 of 3.)

```
                                                 (continued from previous page)
The stack is: 34567 $ True

The stack is: hello 34567 $ True

hello popped
The stack is: 34567 $ True

34567 popped
The stack is: $ True

$ popped
The stack is: True

True popped
Empty stack
   at LinkedListLibrary.List.RemoveFromFront()
      in z:\ch20\Linkedlistlibrary\Linkedlistlibrary.cs:line 114
   at StackInheritanceLibrary.StackInheritance.Pop()
      in z:\ch20\Stackinheritancelibrary\
      Stackinheritancelibrary.cs:line 28
   at StackInheritanceTest.StackInheritanceTest.Main(String[] args
      in z:\ch20\Fig20_11\Stackinheritancetest.cs:line 41
```

Fig. 20.11 Using class **StackInheritance**. (Part 3 of 3.)

```
 1   // Fig. 20.12: StackCompositionLibrary.cs
 2   // StackComposition definition with composed List object.
 3
 4   using System;
 5   using LinkedListLibrary;
 6
 7   namespace StackCompositionLibrary
 8   {
 9      // class StackComposition encapsulates List's capabilities
10      public class StackComposition
11      {
12         private List stack;
13
14         // construct empty stack
15         public StackComposition()
16         {
17            stack = new List( "stack" );
18         }
19
20         // add object to stack
21         public void Push( object dataValue )
22         {
23            stack.InsertAtFront( dataValue );
24         }
25
```

Fig. 20.12 StackComposition class encapsulates functionality of class **List**.
(Part 1 of 2.)

```
26        // remove object from stack
27        public object Pop()
28        {
29            return stack.RemoveFromFront();
30        }
31
32        // determine whether stack is empty
33        public bool IsEmpty()
34        {
35            return stack.IsEmpty();
36        }
37
38        // output stack contents
39        public void Print()
40        {
41            stack.Print();
42        }
43
44    } // end class StackComposition
45 }
```

Fig. 20.12 `StackComposition` class encapsulates functionality of class `List`. (Part 2 of 2.)

20.5 Queues

Another common data structure is the *queue*. A queue is similar to a checkout line in a super-market—the first person in line is served first; customers enter the line only at the end, and they wait to be served. Queue nodes are removed only from the *head* of the queue and are inserted only at the *tail* of the queue. For this reason, a queue is a *first-in, first-out* (*FIFO*) data structure. The insert and remove operations are known as *enqueue* and *dequeue*.

Queues have many applications in computer systems. Most computers have only a single processor, so they can only serve one user at a time. Entries for the other users are placed in a queue. The entry at the front of the queue receives the first available service. Each entry gradually advances to the front of the queue as users receive service.

Queues also support print spooling. A multiuser environment may have only one printer. Several users may send output to the printer. If the printer is busy, users may still generate other outputs, which are "spooled" to disk (much as thread is wound onto a spool), where they wait in a queue until the printer becomes available.

Information packets also wait in queues in computer networks. Each time a packet arrives at a network node, the routing node must route it to the next node on the network along the path to the packet's final destination. The routing node routes one packet at a time, so additional packets are enqueued until the router can route them.

A file server in a computer network handles file access requests from many clients throughout the network. Servers have a limited capacity to service requests from clients. When client requests exceed that capacity, the requests wait in queues.

The program of Fig. 20.13 and Fig. 20.14 creates a queue class through inheritance from a list class. We want the **QueueInheritance** class (Fig. 20.13) to have methods **Enqueue**, **Dequeue**, **IsEmpty** and **Print**. Note that these methods are essentially the **InsertAtBack**, **RemoveFromFront**, **IsEmpty** and **Print** methods of class **List**.

Of course, the list class contains other methods (such as **InsertAtFront** and **Remove-FromBack**) that we would rather not make accessible through the **public** interface to the queue class. Remember that all methods in the **public** interface of the **List** class are also **public** methods of the derived class **QueueInheritance**.

When we implement the queue's methods, we have each **QueueInheritance** method call the appropriate **List** method—method **Enqueue** calls **InsertAtBack**, method **Dequeue** calls **RemoveFromFront**, and **IsEmpty** and **Print** calls invoke their base-class versions. Class **QueueInheritance** does not define methods **IsEmpty** and **Print**, because **QueueInheritance** inherits these methods from class **List** into **QueueInheritance**'s **public** interface. Also, the methods in class **QueueInheritance** do not use **lock** statements. Each of the methods in this class calls a method from class **List** that uses **lock**. Note that class **QueueInheritance** uses namespace **LinkedListLibrary** (Fig. 20.4); thus, the solution for the class library that defines **QueueInheritance** must have a reference to the **LinkedListLibrary** class library.

Class **QueueInheritanceTest**'s **Main** method (Fig. 20.14) uses class **QueueInheritance** to instantiate a queue of **object**s called **queue**. Lines 18–21 define four objects that will be enqueued and dequeued. The program enqueues (lines 24, 26, 28 and 30) a **bool** containing **true**, a **char** containing **$**, an **int** containing **34567** and a **string** containing **hello**.

```
1    // Fig. 20.13: QueueInheritanceLibrary.cs
2    // Implementing a queue by inheriting from class List.
3
4    using System;
5    using LinkedListLibrary;
6
7    namespace QueueInheritanceLibrary
8    {
9       // class QueueInheritance inherits List's capabilities
10      public class QueueInheritance : List
11      {
12         // pass name "queue" to List constructor
13         public QueueInheritance() : base( "queue" )
14         {
15         }
16
17         // place dataValue at end of queue by inserting
18         // dataValue at end of linked list
19         public void Enqueue( object dataValue )
20         {
21            InsertAtBack( dataValue );
22         }
23
24         // remove item from front of queue by removing
25         // item at front of linked list
26         public object Dequeue( )
27         {
28            return RemoveFromFront();
29         }
```

Fig. 20.13 QueueInheritance extends class **List**. (Part 1 of 2.)

```
30
31      } // end of QueueInheritance
32   }
```

Fig. 20.13 `QueueInheritance` extends class **List**. (Part 2 of 2.)

An infinite **while** loop (lines 39–44) dequeues the elements from the queue in FIFO order. When there are no objects left to dequeue, method **Dequeue** throws an **Empty-ListException** and the program displays the exception's stack trace, which shows the program execution stack at the time the exception occurred. The program uses method **Print** (inherited from class **List**) to output the contents of the queue after each operation. Note that class **QueueInheritanceTest** uses namespace **LinkedListLibrary** (Fig. 20.4) and namespace **QueueInheritanceLibrary** (Fig. 20.13); thus, the solution for class **QueueInheritanceTest** must have references to both class libraries.

```
1    // Fig. 20.14: QueueTest.cs
2    // Testing class QueueInheritance.
3
4    using System;
5    using QueueInheritanceLibrary;
6    using LinkedListLibrary;
7
8    namespace QueueTest
9    {
10      // demonstrate functionality of class QueueInheritance
11      class QueueTest
12      {
13         static void Main( string[] args )
14         {
15            QueueInheritance queue = new QueueInheritance();
16
17            // create objects to store in the stack
18            bool aBoolean = true;
19            char aCharacter = '$';
20            int anInteger = 34567;
21            string aString = "hello";
22
23            // use method Enqueue to add items to queue
24            queue.Enqueue( aBoolean );
25            queue.Print();
26            queue.Enqueue( aCharacter );
27            queue.Print();
28            queue.Enqueue( anInteger );
29            queue.Print();
30            queue.Enqueue( aString );
31            queue.Print();
32
33            // use method Dequeue to remove items from queue
34            object removedObject = null;
35
```

Fig. 20.14 Using inheritance to create a queue. (Part 1 of 2.)

```
36              // remove items from queue
37              try
38              {
39                  while ( true )
40                  {
41                      removedObject = queue.Dequeue();
42                      Console.WriteLine( removedObject + " dequeue" );
43                      queue.Print();
44                  }
45              }
46
47              // if exception occurs, print stack trace
48              catch ( EmptyListException emptyListException )
49              {
50                  Console.Error.WriteLine(
51                      emptyListException.StackTrace );
52              }
53
54          } // end method Main
55
56      } // end class QueueTest
57  }
```

```
The queue is: True

The queue is: True $

The queue is: True $ 34567

The queue is: True $ 34567 hello

True dequeue
The queue is: $ 34567 hello

$ dequeue
The queue is: 34567 hello

34567 dequeue
The queue is: hello

hello dequeue
Empty queue
   at LinkedListLibrary.List.RemoveFromFront()
      in z:\ch20\Linkedlistlibrary\Linkedlistlibrary.cs:line 114
   at QueueInheritanceLibrary.QueueInheritance.Dequeue()
      in z:\ch20\Queueinheritancelibrary\
      Queueinheritancelibrary.cs:line 28
   at QueueTest.QueueTest.Main(String[] args)
      in z:\ch20\Fig20_14\Queuetest.cs:line 41
```

Fig. 20.14 Using inheritance to create a queue. (Part 2 of 2.)

20.6 Trees

Linked lists, stacks and queues are *linear data structures* (i.e., *sequences*). A *tree* is a non-linear, two-dimensional data structure with special properties. Tree nodes contain two or more links. This section discusses *binary trees* (Fig. 20.15)—trees whose nodes all contain two links (none, one or both of which may be **null**). The *root node* is the first node in a tree. Each link in the root node refers to a *child*. The *left child* is the first node in the *left subtree,* and the *right child* is the first node in the *right subtree.* The children of a specific node are called *siblings.* A node with no children is called a *leaf node.* Computer scientists normally draw trees from the root node down—exactly the opposite of the way most trees grow in nature.

Common Programming Error 20.2

*Not setting to **null** the links in leaf nodes of a tree is a common logic error.*

In our binary tree example, we create a special binary tree called a *binary search tree.* A binary search tree (with no duplicate node values) has the characteristic that the values in any left subtree are less than the value in the subtree's parent node, and the values in any right subtree are greater than the value in the subtree's parent node. Figure 20.16 illustrates a binary search tree with 12 integer values. Note that the shape of the binary search tree that corresponds to a set of data can depend on the order in which the values are inserted into the tree.

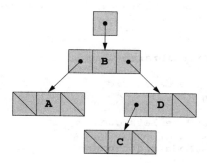

Fig. 20.15 A graphical representation of a binary tree.

Fig. 20.16 A binary search tree containing 12 values.

20.6.1 Binary Search Tree of Integer Values

The application of Fig. 20.17 and Fig. 20.18 creates a binary search tree of integers and traverses it (i.e., walks through all its nodes) in three ways—using recursive *inorder, preorder* and *postorder traversals*. The program generates 10 random numbers and inserts each into the tree. Figure 20.17 defines class **Tree** in namespace **BinaryTreeLibrary** for reuse purposes. Figure 20.18 defines class **TreeTest** to demonstrate class **Tree**'s functionality. Method **Main** of class **TreeTest** instantiates an empty **Tree** object, then randomly generates 10 integers and inserts each value in the binary tree by calling **Tree** method **InsertNode**. The program then performs preorder, inorder and postorder traversals of the tree. We will discuss these traversals shortly.

Class **TreeNode** (lines 9–95 of Fig. 20.17) is a self-referential class containing three **private** data members—**leftNode** and **rightNode**, of type **TreeNode**, and **data**, of type **int**. Initially, every **TreeNode** is a leaf node, so the constructor (lines 16–20) initializes references **leftNode** and **rightNode** to **null**. Properties **LeftNode** (lines 23–34), **Data** (lines 37–48) and **RightNode** (lines 51–62) provide access to a **ListNode**'s **private** data members. We discuss **TreeNode** method **Insert** (lines 67–93) shortly.

```
1   // Fig. 20.17: BinaryTreeLibrary.cs
2   // Definition of class TreeNode and class Tree.
3
4   using System;
5
6   namespace BinaryTreeLibrary
7   {
8      // class TreeNode definition
9      class TreeNode
10     {
11        private TreeNode leftNode;
12        private int data;
13        private TreeNode rightNode;
14
15        // initialize data and make this a leaf node
16        public TreeNode( int nodeData )
17        {
18           data = nodeData;
19           leftNode = rightNode = null;  // node has no children
20        }
21
22        // LeftNode property
23        public TreeNode LeftNode
24        {
25           get
26           {
27              return leftNode;
28           }
29
```

Fig. 20.17 Definitions of **TreeNode** and **Tree** for a binary search tree. (Part 1 of 5.)

```
30              set
31              {
32                 leftNode = value;
33              }
34           }
35
36           // Data property
37           public int Data
38           {
39              get
40              {
41                 return data;
42              }
43
44              set
45              {
46                 data = value;
47              }
48           }
49
50           // RightNode property
51           public TreeNode RightNode
52           {
53              get
54              {
55                 return rightNode;
56              }
57
58              set
59              {
60                 rightNode = value;
61              }
62           }
63
64
65           // insert TreeNode into Tree that contains nodes;
66           // ignore duplicate values
67           public void Insert( int insertValue )
68           {
69              // insert in left subtree
70              if ( insertValue < data )
71              {
72                 // insert new TreeNode
73                 if ( leftNode == null )
74                    leftNode = new TreeNode( insertValue );
75
76                 // continue traversing left subtree
77                 else
78                    leftNode.Insert( insertValue );
79              }
80
```

Fig. 20.17 Definitions of **TreeNode** and **Tree** for a binary search tree. (Part 2 of 5.)

```
81              // insert in right subtree
82              else if ( insertValue > data )
83              {
84                  // insert new TreeNode
85                  if ( rightNode == null )
86                      rightNode = new TreeNode( insertValue );
87
88                  // continue traversing right subtree
89                  else
90                      rightNode.Insert( insertValue );
91              }
92
93          }  // end method Insert
94
95      }  // end class TreeNode
96
97      // class Tree definition
98      public class Tree
99      {
100         private TreeNode root;
101
102         // construct an empty Tree of integers
103         public Tree()
104         {
105             root = null;
106         }
107
108         // Insert a new node in the binary search tree.
109         // If the root node is null, create the root node here.
110         // Otherwise, call the insert method of class TreeNode.
111         public void InsertNode( int insertValue )
112         {
113             lock ( this )
114             {
115                 if ( root == null )
116                     root = new TreeNode( insertValue );
117
118                 else
119                     root.Insert( insertValue );
120             }
121         }
122
123         // begin preorder traversal
124         public void PreorderTraversal()
125         {
126             lock ( this )
127             {
128                 PreorderHelper( root );
129             }
130         }
131
```

Fig. 20.17 Definitions of **TreeNode** and **Tree** for a binary search tree. (Part 3 of 5.)

```
132          // recursive method to perform preorder traversal
133          private void PreorderHelper( TreeNode node )
134          {
135             if ( node == null )
136                return;
137
138             // output node data
139             Console.Write( node.Data + " " );
140
141             // traverse left subtree
142             PreorderHelper( node.LeftNode );
143
144             // traverse right subtree
145             PreorderHelper( node.RightNode );
146          }
147
148          // begin inorder traversal
149          public void InorderTraversal()
150          {
151             lock ( this )
152             {
153                InorderHelper( root );
154             }
155          }
156
157          // recursive method to perform inorder traversal
158          private void InorderHelper( TreeNode node )
159          {
160             if ( node == null )
161                return;
162
163             // traverse left subtree
164             InorderHelper( node.LeftNode );
165
166             // output node data
167             Console.Write( node.Data + " " );
168
169             // traverse right subtree
170             InorderHelper( node.RightNode );
171          }
172
173          // begin postorder traversal
174          public void PostorderTraversal()
175          {
176             lock ( this )
177             {
178                PostorderHelper( root );
179             }
180          }
181
```

Fig. 20.17 Definitions of **TreeNode** and **Tree** for a binary search tree. (Part 4 of 5.)

```
182          // recursive method to perform postorder traversal
183          private void PostorderHelper( TreeNode node )
184          {
185             if ( node == null )
186                return;
187
188             // traverse left subtree
189             PostorderHelper( node.LeftNode );
190
191             // traverse right subtree
192             PostorderHelper( node.RightNode );
193
194             // output node data
195             Console.Write( node.Data + " " );
196          }
197
198       }  // end class Tree
199  }
```

Fig. 20.17 Definitions of **TreeNode** and **Tree** for a binary search tree. (Part 5 of 5.)

```
1   // Fig. 20.18: TreeTest.cs
2   // This program tests class Tree.
3
4   using System;
5   using BinaryTreeLibrary;
6
7   namespace TreeTest
8   {
9      // class TreeTest definition
10     public class TreeTest
11     {
12        // test class Tree
13        static void Main( string[] args )
14        {
15           Tree tree = new Tree();
16           int insertValue;
17
18           Console.WriteLine( "Inserting values: " );
19           Random random = new Random();
20
21           // insert 10 random integers from 0-99 in tree
22           for ( int i = 1; i <= 10; i++ )
23           {
24              insertValue = random.Next( 100 );
25              Console.Write( insertValue + " " );
26
27              tree.InsertNode( insertValue );
28           }
29
30           // perform preorder traversal of tree
31           Console.WriteLine( "\n\nPreorder traversal" );
```

Fig. 20.18 Creating and traversing a binary tree. (Part 1 of 2.)

```
32              tree.PreorderTraversal();
33
34              // perform inorder traversal of tree
35              Console.WriteLine( "\n\nInorder traversal" );
36              tree.InorderTraversal();
37
38              // perform postorder traversal of tree
39              Console.WriteLine( "\n\nPostorder traversal" );
40              tree.PostorderTraversal();
41              Console.WriteLine();
42           }
43
44        }  // end class TreeTest
45  }
```

```
Inserting values:
39 69 94 47 50 72 55 41 97 73

Preorder traversal
39 69 47 41 50 55 94 72 73 97

Inorder traversal
39 41 47 50 55 69 72 73 94 97

Postorder traversal
41 55 50 47 73 72 97 94 69 39
```

Fig. 20.18 Creating and traversing a binary tree. (Part 2 of 2.)

Class **Tree** (lines 98–198 of Fig. 20.17) manipulates objects of class **TreeNode**. Class **Tree** has as **private** data **root** (line 100)—a reference to the root node of the tree. The class contains **public** method **InsertNode** (lines 111–121) to insert a new node in the tree and **public** methods **PreorderTraversal** (lines 124–130), **InorderTraversal** (lines 149–155) and **PostorderTraversal** (lines 174–180) to begin traversals of the tree. Each of these methods calls a separate recursive utility method to perform the traversal operations on the internal representation of the tree. The **Tree** constructor (lines 103–106) initializes **root** to **null** to indicate that the tree initially is empty.

The **Tree** class's method **InsertNode** (lines 111–121) first locks the **Tree** object for thread safety, then determines whether the tree is empty. If so, line 116 allocates a new **TreeNode**, initializes the node with the integer being inserted in the tree and assigns the new node to **root**. If the tree is not empty, **InsertNode** calls **TreeNode** method **Insert** (lines 67–93), which recursively determines the location for the new node in the tree and inserts the node at that location. *A node can be inserted only as a leaf node in a binary search tree.*

The **TreeNode** method **Insert** compares the value to insert with the **data** value in the root node. If the insert value is less than the root-node data, the program determines whether the left subtree is empty (line 73). If so, line 74 allocates a new **TreeNode**, initializes it with the integer being inserted and assigns the new node to reference **leftNode**. Otherwise, line 78 recursively calls **Insert** for the left subtree to insert the value into the left subtree. If the insert value is greater than the root-node data, the program determines whether the right subtree is empty (line 85). If so, line 86 allocates a new **TreeNode**, initializes it with the integer being inserted and assigns the new node to reference **right-Node**. Otherwise, line 90 recursively calls **Insert** for the right subtree to insert the value in the right subtree.

Methods **InorderTraversal**, **PreorderTraversal** and **PostorderTraversal** call helper methods **InorderHelper** (lines 158–171), **PreorderHelper** (lines 133–146) and **PostorderHelper** (lines 183–196), respectively, to traverse the tree and print the node values. The purpose of the helper methods in class **Tree** is to allow the programmer to start a traversal without the need to obtain a reference to the **root** node first, then call the recursive method with that reference. Methods **InorderTraversal**, **PreorderTraversal** and **PostorderTraversal** simply take the **private** reference **root** and pass it to the appropriate helper method to initiate a traversal of the tree. For the following discussion, we use the binary search tree shown in Fig. 20.19.

Method **InorderHelper** (lines 158–171) defines the steps for an inorder traversal. Those steps are as follows:

1. If the argument is **null**, return immediately.
2. Traverse the left subtree with a call to **InorderHelper** (line 164).
3. Process the value in the node (line 167).
4. Traverse the right subtree with a call to **InorderHelper** (line 170).

The inorder traversal does not process the value in a node until the values in that node's left subtree are processed. The inorder traversal of the tree in Fig. 20.19 is

```
6  13  17  27  33  42  48
```

Note that the inorder traversal of a binary search tree prints the node values in ascending order. The process of creating a binary search tree actually sorts the data—thus, this process is called the *binary tree sort*.

Method **PreorderHelper** (lines 133–146) defines the steps for a preorder traversal. Those steps are as follows:

1. If the argument is **null**, return immediately.
2. Process the value in the node (line 139).
3. Traverse the left subtree with a call to **PreorderHelper** (line 142).
4. Traverse the right subtree with a call to **PreorderHelper** (line 145).

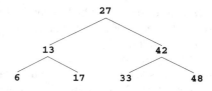

Fig. 20.19 A binary search tree.

The preorder traversal processes the value in each node as the node is visited. After processing the value in a given node, the preorder traversal processes the values in the left subtree, then the values in the right subtree. The preorder traversal of the tree in Fig. 20.19 is

       27 13 6 17 42 33 48

Method **PostorderHelper** (lines 183–198) defines the steps for a postorder traversal. Those steps are as follows:

1. If the argument is **null**, return immediately.

2. Traverse the left subtree with a call to **PostorderHelper** (line 189).

3. Traverse the right subtree with a call to **PostorderHelper** (line 192).

4. Process the value in the node (line 195).

The postorder traversal processes the value in each node after the values of all that node's children are processed. The postorder traversal of the tree in Fig. 20.19 is

       6 17 13 33 48 42 27

The binary search tree facilitates *duplicate elimination*. While building a tree, the insertion operation recognizes attempts to insert a duplicate value, because a duplicate follows the same "go left" or "go right" decisions on each comparison as the original value did. Thus, the insertion operation eventually compares the duplicate with a node containing the same value. At this point, the insertion operation might simply discard the duplicate value.

Searching a binary tree for a value that matches a key value is fast, especially for *tightly packed* trees. In a tightly packed tree, each level contains about twice as many elements as the previous level. Figure 20.19 is a tightly packed binary tree. A binary search tree with n elements has a minimum of $\log_2 n$ levels. Thus, at most $\log_2 n$ comparisons are required either to find a match or to determine that no match exists. Searching a (tightly packed) 1000-element binary search tree requires at most 10 comparisons, because $2^{10} > 1000$. Searching a (tightly packed) 1,000,000-element binary search tree requires at most 20 comparisons, because $2^{20} > 1,000,000$.

20.6.2 Binary Search Tree of **IComparable** Objects

The binary tree example in Section 20.6.1 works nicely when all the data is of type **int**. Suppose that you want to manipulate a binary tree of double values. You could rewrite the **TreeNode** and **Tree** classes with different names and customize the classes to manipulate double values. Similarly, for each data type you could create customized versions of classes **TreeNode** and **Tree**. This results in a proliferation of code, which can become difficult to manage and maintain. The C++ programming language provides a technology called templates that enables us to write a class definition once, then have the compiler generate new versions of the class for any data type we choose.

Ideally, we would like to define the functionality of a binary tree once and reuse that functionality for many data types. Languages like Java™ and C# provide polymorphic capabilities that enable all objects to be manipulated in a uniform manner. Using such capabilities enables us to design a more flexible data structure.

In our next example, we take advantage of C#'s polymorphic capabilities by implementing **TreeNode** and **Tree** classes that manipulate objects of any type that implements interface **IComparable** (namespace **System**). It is imperative that we be able to compare objects stored in a binary search, so we can determine the path to the insertion point of a new node. Classes that implement **IComparable** define method **CompareTo**, which compares the object that invokes the method with the object that the method receives as an argument. The method returns an **int** value less than zero if the calling object is less than the argument object, zero if the objects are equal, a positive value if the calling object is greater than the argument object. Also, both the calling and argument objects must be of the same data type; otherwise, the method throws an **ArgumentException**.

The program of Fig. 20.20 and Fig. 20.21 enhances the program from Section 20.6.1 to manipulate **IComparable** objects. One restriction on the new versions of classes **TreeNode** and **Tree** in Fig. 20.20 is that each **Tree** object can contain objects of only one data type (e.g., all **string**s or all **double**s). If a program attempts to insert multiple data types in the same **Tree** object, **ArgumentException**s will occur. We modified only six lines of code in class **TreeNode** (lines 13, 17, 38, 67, 70 and 82) and one line of code in class **Tree** (line 111) to enable processing of **IComparable** objects. With the exception of lines 70 and 82, all other changes simply replaced the type **int** with the type **IComparable**. Lines 70 and 82 previously used the **<** and **>** operators to compare the value being inserted with the value in a given node. These lines now compare **IComparable** objects via the interface's method **CompareTo**, then test the method's return value to determine whether it is less than zero (the calling object is less than the argument object) or greater than zero (the calling object is greater than the argument object), respectively.

Class **TreeTest** (Fig. 20.21) creates three **Tree** objects to store **int**, **double** and **string** values, all of which the .NET Framework defines as **IComparable** types. The program populates the trees with the values in arrays **intArray** (line 15), **doubleArray** (lines 16–17) and **stringArray** (lines 18–19), respectively.

Method **PopulateTree** (lines 38–48) receives an **Array** containing the initializer values for the **Tree**, a **Tree** into which the array elements will be placed and a **string** representing the **Tree** name as arguments, then inserts each **Array** element in the **Tree**. Method **TraverseTree** (lines 51–68) receives a **Tree** and a **string** representing the **Tree** name as arguments, then outputs the preorder, inorder and postorder traversals of the **Tree**. Note that the inorder traversal of each **Tree** outputs the data in sorted order regardless of the data type stored in the **Tree**. Our polymorphic implementation of class Tree invokes the appropriate data type's **CompareTo** method to determine the path to each value's insertion point by using the standard binary search tree insertion rules. Also, notice that the **Tree** of **string**s appears in alphabetical order.

```
1   // Fig. 20.20: BinaryTreeLibrary2.cs
2   // Definition of class TreeNode and class Tree for IComparable
3   // objects.
4
```

Fig. 20.20 Definitions of class **TreeNode** and **Tree** for manipulating **IComparable** objects. (Part 1 of 5.)

```
 5   using System;
 6
 7   namespace BinaryTreeLibrary2
 8   {
 9      // class TreeNode definition
10      class TreeNode
11      {
12         private TreeNode leftNode;
13         private IComparable data;
14         private TreeNode rightNode;
15
16         // initialize data and make this a leaf node
17         public TreeNode( IComparable nodeData )
18         {
19            data = nodeData;
20            leftNode = rightNode = null;   // node has no children
21         }
22
23         // LeftNode property
24         public TreeNode LeftNode
25         {
26            get
27            {
28               return leftNode;
29            }
30
31            set
32            {
33               leftNode = value;
34            }
35         }
36
37         // Data property
38         public IComparable Data
39         {
40            get
41            {
42               return data;
43            }
44
45            set
46            {
47               data = value;
48            }
49         }
50
51         // RightNode property
52         public TreeNode RightNode
53         {
54            get
55            {
```

Fig. 20.20 Definitions of class **TreeNode** and **Tree** for manipulating **IComparable** objects. (Part 2 of 5.)

```
56                  return rightNode;
57              }
58
59              set
60              {
61                  rightNode = value;
62              }
63          }
64
65          // insert TreeNode into Tree that contains nodes;
66          // ignore duplicate values
67          public void Insert( IComparable insertValue )
68          {
69              // insert in left subtree
70              if ( insertValue.CompareTo( data ) < 0 )
71              {
72                  // insert new TreeNode
73                  if ( leftNode == null )
74                      leftNode = new TreeNode( insertValue );
75
76                  // continue traversing left subtree
77                  else
78                      leftNode.Insert( insertValue );
79              }
80
81              // insert in right subtree
82              else if ( insertValue.CompareTo( data ) > 0 )
83              {
84                  // insert new TreeNode
85                  if ( rightNode == null )
86                      rightNode = new TreeNode( insertValue );
87
88                  // continue traversing right subtree
89                  else
90                      rightNode.Insert( insertValue );
91              }
92
93          }  // end method Insert
94
95      }  // end class TreeNode
96
97      // class Tree definition
98      public class Tree
99      {
100         private TreeNode root;
101
102         // construct an empty Tree of integers
103         public Tree()
104         {
105             root = null;
106         }
107
```

Fig. 20.20 Definitions of class **TreeNode** and **Tree** for manipulating **IComparable** objects. (Part 3 of 5.)

```
108          // Insert a new node in the binary search tree.
109          // If the root node is null, create the root node here.
110          // Otherwise, call the insert method of class TreeNode.
111          public void InsertNode( IComparable insertValue )
112          {
113             lock ( this )
114             {
115                if ( root == null )
116                   root = new TreeNode( insertValue );
117
118                else
119                   root.Insert( insertValue );
120             }
121          }
122
123          // begin preorder traversal
124          public void PreorderTraversal()
125          {
126             lock ( this )
127             {
128                PreorderHelper( root );
129             }
130          }
131
132          // recursive method to perform preorder traversal
133          private void PreorderHelper( TreeNode node )
134          {
135             if ( node == null )
136                return;
137
138             // output node data
139             Console.Write( node.Data + " " );
140
141             // traverse left subtree
142             PreorderHelper( node.LeftNode );
143
144             // traverse right subtree
145             PreorderHelper( node.RightNode );
146          }
147
148          // begin inorder traversal
149          public void InorderTraversal()
150          {
151             lock ( this )
152             {
153                InorderHelper( root );
154             }
155          }
156
157          // recursive method to perform inorder traversal
158          private void InorderHelper( TreeNode node )
159          {
```

Fig. 20.20 Definitions of class **TreeNode** and **Tree** for manipulating **IComparable** objects. (Part 4 of 5.)

```
160                 if ( node == null )
161                     return;
162
163                 // traverse left subtree
164                 InorderHelper( node.LeftNode );
165
166                 // output node data
167                 Console.Write( node.Data + " " );
168
169                 // traverse right subtree
170                 InorderHelper( node.RightNode );
171             }
172
173             // begin postorder traversal
174             public void PostorderTraversal()
175             {
176                 lock ( this )
177                 {
178                     PostorderHelper( root );
179                 }
180             }
181
182             // recursive method to perform postorder traversal
183             private void PostorderHelper( TreeNode node )
184             {
185                 if ( node == null )
186                     return;
187
188                 // traverse left subtree
189                 PostorderHelper( node.LeftNode );
190
191                 // traverse right subtree
192                 PostorderHelper( node.RightNode );
193
194                 // output node data
195                 Console.Write( node.Data + " " );
196             }
197
198         }   // end class Tree
199     }
```

Fig. 20.20 Definitions of class **TreeNode** and **Tree** for manipulating **IComparable** objects. (Part 5 of 5.)

```
1    // Fig. 20.21: TreeTest.cs
2    // This program tests class Tree.
3
4    using System;
5    using BinaryTreeLibrary2;
```

Fig. 20.21 Demonstrating class **Tree** with **IComparable** objects. (Part 1 of 3.)

```
6
7   namespace TreeTest
8   {
9      // class TreeTest definition
10     public class TreeTest
11     {
12        // test class Tree
13        static void Main( string[] args )
14        {
15           int[] intArray = { 8, 2, 4, 3, 1, 7, 5, 6 };
16           double[] doubleArray =
17              { 8.8, 2.2, 4.4, 3.3, 1.1, 7.7, 5.5, 6.6 };
18           string[] stringArray = { "eight", "two", "four",
19              "three", "one", "seven", "five", "six" };
20
21           // create int Tree
22           Tree intTree = new Tree();
23           PopulateTree( intArray, intTree, "intTree" );
24           TraverseTree( intTree, "intTree" );
25
26           // create double Tree
27           Tree doubleTree = new Tree();
28           PopulateTree( doubleArray, doubleTree, "doubleTree" );
29           TraverseTree( doubleTree, "doubleTree" );
30
31           // create string Tree
32           Tree stringTree = new Tree();
33           PopulateTree( stringArray, stringTree, "stringTree" );
34           TraverseTree( stringTree, "stringTree" );
35        }
36
37        // populate Tree with array elements
38        static void populateTree(
39           Array array, Tree tree, string name )
40        {
41           Console.WriteLine( "\nInserting into " + name + ":" );
42
43           foreach ( IComparable data in array )
44           {
45              Console.Write( data + " " );
46              tree.InsertNode( data );
47           }
48        }
49
50        // insert perform traversals
51        static void traverseTree( Tree tree, string treeType )
52        {
53           // perform preorder traversal of tree
54           Console.WriteLine(
55              "\n\nPreorder traversal of " + treeType );
56           tree.PreorderTraversal();
57
```

Fig. 20.21 Demonstrating class **Tree** with **IComparable** objects. (Part 2 of 3.)

```
58              // perform inorder traversal of tree
59              Console.WriteLine(
60                 "\n\nInorder traversal of " + treeType );
61              tree.InorderTraversal();
62
63              // perform postorder traversal of tree
64              Console.WriteLine(
65                 "\n\nPostorder traversal of " + treeType );
66              tree.PostorderTraversal();
67              Console.WriteLine( "\n" );
68           }
69
70        }  // end class TreeTest
71     }
```

```
Inserting into intTree:
8 2 4 3 1 7 5 6

Preorder traversal of intTree
8 2 1 4 3 7 5 6

Inorder traversal of intTree
1 2 3 4 5 6 7 8

Postorder traversal of intTree
1 3 6 5 7 4 2 8


Inserting into doubleTree:
8.8 2.2 4.4 3.3 1.1 7.7 5.5 6.6

Preorder traversal of doubleTree
8.8 2.2 1.1 4.4 3.3 7.7 5.5 6.6

Inorder traversal of doubleTree
1.1 2.2 3.3 4.4 5.5 6.6 7.7 8.8

Postorder traversal of doubleTree
1.1 3.3 6.6 5.5 7.7 4.4 2.2 8.8


Inserting into stringTree:
eight two four three one seven five six

Preorder traversal of stringTree
eight two four five three one seven six

Inorder traversal of stringTree
eight five four one seven six three two

Postorder traversal of stringTree
five six seven one three four two eight
```

Fig. 20.21 Demonstrating class **Tree** with **IComparable** objects. (Part 3 of 3.)

20.7 Collection Classes

The previous sections of this chapter discussed how to create and manipulate data structures. The discussion was "low level," in the sense that we painstakingly created each element of each data structure dynamically with **new** and modified the data structures by directly manipulating their elements and references to their elements. In this section, we consider the prepackaged data-structure classes provided by the .NET Framework. These classes are known as *collection classes*—they store collections of data. Each instance of one of these classes is known as a *collection*, which is a set of items.

With collection classes, instead of creating data structures, the programmer simply uses existing data structures, without concern for how the data structures are implemented. This methodology is a marvelous example of code reuse. Programmers can code faster and can expect excellent performance, maximizing execution speed and minimizing memory consumption.

Some examples of collections are the cards you hold in a card game, your favorite songs stored in your computer and the real-estate records in your local registry of deeds (which map book numbers and page numbers to property owners). The .NET Framework provides several collections. We demonstrate four collection classes—**Array**, **ArrayList**, **Stack** and **Hashtable**—all from namespace **System.Collections**, plus built-in array capabilities. In addition, namespace **System.Collections** provides several other data structures, including **BitArray** (a collection of true/false values), **Queue** and **SortedList** (a collection of key/value pairs that are sorted by key and can be accessed either by key or by index).

The .NET Framework provides ready-to-go, reusable components; you do not need to write your own collection classes. The collections are standardized so applications can share them easily, without having to be concerned with the details of their implementation. These collections are written for broad reuse. They are tuned for rapid execution and for efficient use of memory. As new data structures and algorithms are developed that fit this framework, a large base of programmers already will be familiar with the interfaces and algorithms implemented by those data structures.

20.7.1 Class **Array**

Chapter 4 presented basic array-processing capabilities, and many subsequent chapters used the techniques shown there. We discussed briefly that all arrays inherit from class **Array** (namespace **System**) which defines a **Length** property that specifies the number of elements in an array. In addition, class **Array** provides **static** methods that provide algorithms for processing arrays. Typically, class **Array** overloads these methods to provide multiple options for performing algorithms. For example, **Array** method **Reverse** can reverse the order of the elements in an entire array or can reverse the elements in a specified range of elements in an array. For a complete list of class **Array**'s **static** methods and their overloaded versions, see the online documentation for the class. Figure 20.22 demonstrates several **static** methods of class **Array**.

Line 28 uses **static Array** method *Sort* to sort an array of **double** values. When this method returns, the array contains its original elements sorted in ascending order.

Lines 31–32 uses **static Array** method *Copy* to copy elements from array **intArray** into array **intArrayCopy**. The first argument is the array to copy

(**intValues**), the second argument is the destination array (**intValuesCopy**) and the
third argument is an integer representing the number of elements to copy (in this case,
intValues.Length specifies all elements).

```
1   // Fig. 20.22: UsingArray.cs
2   // Using Array class to perform common array manipulations.
3
4   using System;
5   using System.Windows.Forms;
6   using System.Collections;
7
8   namespace UsingArray
9   {
10     // demonstrate algorithms of class Array
11     class UsingArray
12     {
13        private int[] intValues = { 1, 2, 3, 4, 5, 6 };
14        private double[] doubleValues =
15           { 8.4, 9.3, 0.2, 7.9, 3.4 };
16        private int[] intValuesCopy;
17        private string output;
18
19        // method to build and display program output
20        public void Start()
21        {
22           intValuesCopy = new int[ intValues.Length ];
23
24           output = "Initial array values:\n";
25           PrintArray();  // output initial array contents
26
27           // sort doubleValues
28           Array.Sort( doubleValues );
29
30           // copy intValues into intValuesCopy
31           Array.Copy( intValues, intValuesCopy,
32              intValues.Length );
33
34           output += "\nArray values after Sort and Copy:\n";
35           PrintArray();  // output array contents
36           output += "\n";
37
38           // search for 5 in intValues
39           int result = Array.BinarySearch( intValues, 5 );
40           output +=
41              ( result >= 0 ? "5 found at element " + result :
42                  "5 not found" ) + " in intValues\n";
43
44           // search for 8763 in intValues
45           result = Array.BinarySearch( intValues, 8763 );
46           output +=
47              ( result >= 0 ? "8763 found at element " + result :
48                  "8763 not found" ) + " in intValues";
```

Fig. 20.22 Program that demonstrates class **Array**. (Part 1 of 2.)

```
49
50              MessageBox.Show( output, "Using Class Array",
51                  MessageBoxButtons.OK, MessageBoxIcon.Information );
52          }
53
54          // append array content to output string
55          private void PrintArray()
56          {
57              output += "doubleValues: ";
58
59              foreach ( double element in doubleValues )
60                  output += element + " ";
61
62              output += "\nintValues: ";
63
64              foreach ( int element in intValues )
65                  output += element + " ";
66
67              output += "\nintValuesCopy: ";
68
69              foreach ( int element in intValuesCopy )
70                  output += element + " ";
71
72              output += "\n";
73          }
74
75          // main entry point for application
76          static void Main( string[] args )
77          {
78              UsingArray application = new UsingArray();
79
80              application.Start();
81          }
82
83      } // end class UsingArray
84  }
```

Fig. 20.22 Program that demonstrates class **Array**. (Part 2 of 2.)

Lines 39 and 45 invoke **static Array** method *BinarySearch* to perform binary searches on array **intValues**. Method **BinarySearch** receives the *sorted* array in which to search and the key for which to search. The method returns the index in the array at which it finds the key (but a negative number if the key was not found).

Other **static Array** methods include **Clear** (to set a range of elements to 0 or null), **CreateInstance** (to create a new array of a specified data type), **IndexOf** (to locate the first occurrence of an object in an array or portion of an array), **LastIndexOf** (to locate the last occurrence of an object in an array or portion of an array) and **Reverse** (to reverse the contents of an array or portion of an array).

20.7.2 Class **ArrayList**

In most programming languages, conventional arrays have a fixed size—they cannot be changed dynamically to conform to an application's execution-time memory requirements. In some applications, this fixed-size limitation presents a problem for programmers. They must choose between using fixed-size arrays that are large enough to store the maximum number of elements the program may require and using dynamic data structures that can grow and shrink the amount of memory required to store data in response to the changing requirements of a program at execution time.

The .NET Framework's class **ArrayList** collection mimics the functionality of conventional arrays and provides dynamic resizing of the collection through the class's methods. At any time an **ArrayList** contains a certain number of elements less than or equal to its *capacity*—the number of elements currently reserved for an **ArrayList**. A program can manipulate the capacity with **ArrayList** property **Capacity**. If an **ArrayList** needs to grow, it by default doubles its current **Capacity**.

Performance Tip 20.6

*As with linked lists, inserting additional elements into an **ArrayList** whose current size is less than its capacity is a fast operation.*

Performance Tip 20.7

*It is a slow operation to insert an element into an **ArrayList** that needs to grow larger to accommodate a new element.*

Performance Tip 20.8

*If storage is at a premium, use method **TrimToSize** of class **ArrayList** to trim an **ArrayList** to its exact size. This will optimize an **ArrayList**'s memory use. Be careful—if the program needs to insert additional elements, the process will be slower because the **ArrayList** must grow dynamically (trimming leaves no room for growth).*

Performance Tip 20.9

*The default capacity increment, doubling the size of the **ArrayList**, may seem to waste storage, but doubling is an efficient way for an **ArrayList** to grow quickly to "about the right size." This is a much more efficient use of time than growing the **ArrayList** by one element at a time in response to insert operations.*

ArrayLists store references to **object**s. All classes derive from class **Object**, so an **ArrayList** can contain objects of any type. Figure 20.23 lists some useful methods of class **ArrayList**.

Figure 20.24 demonstrates class **ArrayList** and several of its methods. Users can type a **string** into the user interface's **TextBox**, then press a button representing an **ArrayList** method to see that method's functionality. A **TextBox** displays messages indicating each operation's results.

Method	Description
Add	Adds an **object** to the **ArrayList**. Returns an **int** specifying the index at which the **object** was added.
Clear	Removes all the elements from the **ArrayList**.
Contains	Returns **true** if the specified **object** is in the **ArrayList**; otherwise, returns **false**.
IndexOf	Returns the index of the first occurrence of the specified **object** in the **ArrayList**.
Insert	Inserts an **object** at the specified index.
Remove	Removes the first occurrence of the specified **object**.
RemoveAt	Removes an object at the specified index.
RemoveRange	Removes a specified number of elements starting at a specified index in the **ArrayList**.
Sort	Sorts the **ArrayList**.
TrimToSize	Sets the **Capacity** of the **ArrayList** to be the number of elements the **ArrayList** currently contains.

Fig. 20.23 Some methods of class **ArrayList**.

```
1   // Fig. 20.24: ArrayListTest.cs
2   // Using class ArrayList.
3
4   using System;
5   using System.Drawing;
6   using System.Collections;
7   using System.ComponentModel;
8   using System.Windows.Forms;
9   using System.Data;
10  using System.Text;
11
12  namespace ArrayListTest
13  {
14      // demonstrating ArrayList functionality
15      public class ArrayListTest : System.Windows.Forms.Form
16      {
17          private System.Windows.Forms.Button addButton;
18          private System.Windows.Forms.TextBox inputTextBox;
19          private System.Windows.Forms.Label inputLabel;
20          private System.Windows.Forms.Button removeButton;
21          private System.Windows.Forms.Button firstButton;
22          private System.Windows.Forms.Button lastButton;
23          private System.Windows.Forms.Button isEmptyButton;
24          private System.Windows.Forms.Button containsButton;
25          private System.Windows.Forms.Button locationButton;
```

Fig. 20.24 Demonstrating the **ArrayList** class. (Part 1 of 5.)

```
26          private System.Windows.Forms.Button trimButton;
27          private System.Windows.Forms.Button statisticsButton;
28          private System.Windows.Forms.Button displayButton;
29
30          // Required designer variable.
31          private System.ComponentModel.Container components = null;
32          private System.Windows.Forms.TextBox consoleTextBox;
33
34          // ArrayList for manipulating strings
35          private ArrayList arrayList = new ArrayList( 1 );
36
37          public ArrayListTest()
38          {
39              // Required for Windows Form Designer support
40              InitializeComponent();
41          }
42
43          // Visual Studio.NET generated code
44
45          // main entry point for the application
46          [STAThread]
47          static void Main()
48          {
49              Application.Run( new ArrayListTest() );
50          }
51
52          // add item to end of arrayList
53          private void addButton_Click(
54              object sender, System.EventArgs e )
55          {
56              arrayList.Add( inputTextBox.Text );
57              consoleTextBox.Text =
58                  "Added to end: " + inputTextBox.Text;
59              inputTextBox.Clear();
60          }
61
62          // remove specified item from arrayList
63          private void removeButton_Click(
64              object sender, System.EventArgs e )
65          {
66              arrayList.Remove( inputTextBox.Text );
67              consoleTextBox.Text = "Removed: " + inputTextBox.Text;
68              inputTextBox.Clear();
69          }
70
71          // display first element
72          private void firstButton_Click(
73              object sender, System.EventArgs e )
74          {
75              // get first element
76              try
77              {
```

Fig. 20.24 Demonstrating the **ArrayList** class. (Part 2 of 5.)

```
 78              consoleTextBox.Text =
 79                 "First element: " + arrayList[ 0 ];
 80           }
 81
 82           // show exception if no elements in arrayList
 83           catch ( ArgumentOutOfRangeException outOfRange )
 84           {
 85              consoleTextBox.Text = outOfRange.ToString();
 86           }
 87        }
 88
 89        // display last element
 90        private void lastButton_Click(
 91           object sender, System.EventArgs e )
 92        {
 93           // get last element
 94           try
 95           {
 96              consoleTextBox.Text = "Last element: " +
 97                 arrayList[ arrayList.Count - 1 ];
 98           }
 99
100           // show exception if no elements in arrrayList
101           catch ( ArgumentOutOfRangeException outOfRange )
102           {
103              consoleTextBox.Text = outOfRange.ToString();
104           }
105        }
106
107        // determine whether arrayList is empty
108        private void isEmptyButton_Click(
109           object sender, System.EventArgs e )
110        {
111           consoleTextBox.Text = ( arrayList.Count == 0 ?
112              "arrayList is empty" : "arrayList is not empty" );
113        }
114
115        // determine whether arrayList contains specified object
116        private void containsButton_Click(
117           object sender, System.EventArgs e )
118        {
119           if ( arrayList.Contains( inputTextBox.Text ) )
120              consoleTextBox.Text = "arrayList contains " +
121                 inputTextBox.Text;
122           else
123              consoleTextBox.Text = inputTextBox.Text +
124                 " not found";
125        }
126
127        // determine location of specified object
128        private void locationButton_Click(
129           object sender, System.EventArgs e )
130        {
```

Fig. 20.24 Demonstrating the **ArrayList** class. (Part 3 of 5.)

```
131             consoleTextBox.Text = "Element is at location " +
132                arrayList.IndexOf( inputTextBox.Text );
133          }
134
135          // trim arrayList to current size
136          private void trimButton_Click(
137             object sender, System.EventArgs e )
138          {
139             arrayList.TrimToSize();
140             consoleTextBox.Text = "Vector trimmed to size";
141          }
142
143          // show arrayList current size and capacity
144          private void statisticsButton_Click(
145             object sender, System.EventArgs e )
146          {
147             consoleTextBox.Text = "Size = " + arrayList.Count +
148                "; capacity = " + arrayList.Capacity;
149          }
150
151          // display contents of arrayList
152          private void displayButton_Click(
153             object sender, System.EventArgs e )
154          {
155             IEnumerator enumerator = arrayList.GetEnumerator();
156             StringBuilder buffer = new StringBuilder();
157
158             while ( enumerator.MoveNext() )
159                buffer.Append( enumerator.Current + "   " );
160
161             consoleTextBox.Text = buffer.ToString();
162          }
163       }
164    }
```

Fig. 20.24 Demonstrating the **ArrayList** class. (Part 4 of 5.)

Fig. 20.24 Demonstrating the **ArrayList** class. (Part 5 of 5.)

The **ArrayList** in this example stores **string**s that users input in the **TextBox**. Line 35 creates an **ArrayList** with an initial capacity of one element. This **ArrayList** will double in size each time the user fills the array and attempts to add another element.

ArrayList method *Add* appends a new element at the end of an **ArrayList**. When the user clicks **Add**, event handler **addButton_Click** (lines 53–60) invokes method **Add** (line 56) to append the **string** in the **inputTextBox** to the **ArrayList**.

ArrayList method *Remove* deletes a specified item from an **ArrayList**. When the user clicks **Remove**, event handler **removeButton_Click** (line 63–69) invokes **Remove** (line 66) to remove the **string** specified in the **inputTextBox** from the **ArrayList**. If the object passed to **Remove** is in the **ArrayList**, the first occurrence of that object is removed, and all subsequent elements shift toward the beginning of the **ArrayList** to fill the empty position.

A program can access **ArrayList** elements like conventional array elements by following the **ArrayList** reference name with the array subscript operator (**[]**) and the desired index of the element. Event handlers **firstButton_Click** (lines 72–87) and **lastButton_Click** (lines 90–105) use the **ArrayList** subscript operator to retrieve the first element (line 79) and last element (line 97), respectively. An **ArgumentOutOf-RangeException** occurs if the specified index is not both greater than 0 and less than the number of elements currently stored in the **ArrayList**.

Event handler **isEmptyButton_Click** (lines 108–113) uses **ArrayList** property *Count* (line 111) to determine whether the **ArrayList** is empty. Event handler **containsButton_Click** (lines 116–125) uses **ArrayList** method **Contains** (line 119) to determine whether the given object is currently in the **ArrayList**. If so, the method returns **true**; otherwise, it returns **false**.

Performance Tip 20.10

*ArrayList method **Contains** performs a linear search, which is a costly operation for large **ArrayLists**. If the **ArrayList** is sorted, use **ArrayList** method **Binary-Search** to perform a more efficient search.*

When the user clicks **Location**, event handler **locationButton_Click** (lines 128–133) invokes **ArrayList** method *IndexOf* (line 132) to determine the index of a particular object in the **ArrayList**. **IndexOf** returns **-1** if the element is not found.

When the user clicks **Trim**, event handler **trimButton_Click** (lines 136–141) invokes method *TrimToSize* (line 139) to set the *Capacity* property to equal the **Count** property. This reduces the storage capacity of the **ArrayList** to the exact number of elements currently in the **ArrayList**.

When the user clicks **Statistics**, **statisticsButton_Click** (lines 144–149) uses the **Count** and **Capacity** properties to display the current number of elements in the **ArrayList** and the maximum number of elements that can be stored without allocating more memory to the **ArrayList**.

When users click **Display**, **displayButton_Click** (lines 152–162) outputs the contents of the **ArrayList**. This event handler uses an *IEnumerator* (sometimes called an *enumerator* or an *iterator*) to traverse the elements of an **ArrayList** one element at a time. Interface **IEnumerator** defines methods *MoveNext* and *Reset* and property *Current*. **MoveNext** moves the enumerator to the next element in the **Array-List**. The first call to **MoveNext** positions the enumerator at the first element of the **ArrayList**. **MoveNext** returns **true** if there is at least one more element in the **ArrayList**; otherwise, the method returns **false**. Method **Reset** positions the enumerator before the first element of the **ArrayList**. Methods **MoveNext** and **Reset** throw an **InvalidOperationException** if the contents of the collection are modified in any way after the enumerator's creation. Property **Current** returns the object at the current location in the **ArrayList**.

Line 155 creates an **IEnumerator** called **enumerator** and assigns it the result of calling **ArrayList** method *GetEnumerator*. Lines 158–159 iterate while **MoveNext** returns **true**, retrieve the current item via property **Count** and append it to **buffer**. When the loop terminates, line 161 displays the contents of **buffer**.

20.7.3 Class **Stack**

The **Stack** class, as its name implies, implements a stack data structure. This class provides much of the functionality that we defined in our implementation in Section 20.4. Refer back to that section for a discussion of stack data structure concepts. The application in Fig. 20.25 provides a GUI that enables the user to test many **Stack** methods. Line 38 of the **Stack-Test** constructor creates a **Stack** with the default initial capacity (10 elements).

As one might expect, class **Stack** has methods **Push** and **Pop** to perform the basic stack operations. Method **Push** takes an **object** as an argument and adds it to the top of the **Stack**. If the number of items on the **Stack** (the **Count** property) is equal to the capacity at the time of the **Push** operation, the **Stack** grows to accommodate more **object**s. Event handler **pushButton_Click** (lines 51–56) uses method **Push** to add a user-specified string to the stack (line 54).

Method **Pop** takes no arguments. This method removes and returns the object currently on top of the **Stack**. Event handler **popButton_Click** (lines 59–73) calls method **Pop** (line 57) to remove an object from the **Stack**. An **InvalidOperationException** occurs if the **Stack** is empty when the program calls **Pop**.

```csharp
1   // Fig. 20.25: StackTest.cs
2   // Demonstrates class Stack of namespace System.Collections.
3
4   using System;
5   using System.Drawing;
6   using System.Collections;
7   using System.ComponentModel;
8   using System.Windows.Forms;
9   using System.Data;
10  using System.Text;
11
12  namespace StackTest
13  {
14     // demonstrate Stack collection
15     public class StackTest : System.Windows.Forms.Form
16     {
17        private System.Windows.Forms.Label inputLabel;
18        private System.Windows.Forms.TextBox inputTextBox;
19        private System.Windows.Forms.Button pushButton;
20        private System.Windows.Forms.Button popButton;
21        private System.Windows.Forms.Button peekButton;
22        private System.Windows.Forms.Button isEmptyButton;
23        private System.Windows.Forms.Button searchButton;
24        private System.Windows.Forms.Button displayButton;
25        private System.Windows.Forms.Label statusLabel;
26
27        // Required designer variable.
28        private System.ComponentModel.Container components = null;
29
30        private Stack stack;
31
32        public StackTest()
33        {
34           // Required for Windows Form Designer support
35           InitializeComponent();
36
37           // create Stack
38           stack = new Stack();
39        }
40
41        // Visual Studio.NET generated code
42
```

Fig. 20.25 Using the **Stack** class. (Part 1 of 4.)

```
43          // main entry point for the application
44          [STAThread]
45          static void Main()
46          {
47              Application.Run( new StackTest() );
48          }
49
50          // push element onto stack
51          private void pushButton_Click(
52              object sender, System.EventArgs e )
53          {
54              stack.Push( inputTextBox.Text );
55              statusLabel.Text = "Pushed: " + inputTextBox.Text;
56          }
57
58          // pop element from stack
59          private void popButton_Click(
60              object sender, System.EventArgs e )
61          {
62              // pop element
63              try
64              {
65                  statusLabel.Text = "Popped: " + stack.Pop();
66              }
67
68              // print message if stack is empty
69              catch ( InvalidOperationException invalidOperation )
70              {
71                  statusLabel.Text = invalidOperation.ToString();
72              }
73          }
74
75          // peek at top element of stack
76          private void peekButton_Click(
77              object sender, System.EventArgs e )
78          {
79              // view top element
80              try
81              {
82                  statusLabel.Text = "Top: " + stack.Peek();
83              }
84
85              // print message if stack is empty
86              catch ( InvalidOperationException invalidOperation )
87              {
88                  statusLabel.Text = invalidOperation.ToString();
89              }
90          }
91
92          // determine whether stack is empty
93          private void isEmptyButton_Click(
94              object sender, System.EventArgs e )
95          {
```

Fig. 20.25 Using the **Stack** class. (Part 2 of 4.)

```
96              statusLabel.Text = ( stack.Count == 0 ?
97                 "Stack is empty" : "Stack is not empty" );
98           }
99
100          // determine whether specified element is on stack
101          private void searchButton_Click(
102             object sender, System.EventArgs e )
103          {
104             string result = stack.Contains( inputTextBox.Text ) ?
105                " found" : " not found";
106
107             statusLabel.Text = inputTextBox.Text + result;
108          }
109
110          // display stack contents
111          private void displayButton_Click(
112             object sender, System.EventArgs e )
113          {
114             IEnumerator enumerator = stack.GetEnumerator();
115             StringBuilder buffer = new StringBuilder();
116
117             // while the enumerator can move on to the next element
118             // print that element out.
119             while ( enumerator.MoveNext() )
120                buffer.Append( enumerator.Current + " " );
121
122             statusLabel.Text = buffer.ToString();
123          }
124       }
125    }
```

Fig. 20.25 Using the **Stack** class. (Part 3 of 4.)

Fig. 20.25 Using the **Stack** class. (Part 4 of 4.)

Method **Peek** returns the value of the top stack element, but does not remove the element from the **Stack**. We demonstrate **Peek** at line 82 in event handler **peekButton_Click** (lines 76–90) to view the object on top of the **Stack**. As with **Pop**, an **InvalidOperationException** occurs if the **Stack** is empty when the program calls **Peek**.

Common Programming Error 20.3

*Attempting to **Peek** or **Pop** an empty **Stack** (a **Stack** whose **Count** property equals 0) causes an **InvalidOperationException**.*

Event handler **isEmptyButton_Click** (lines 93–98) determines whether the **Stack** is empty by comparing the **Stack**'s **Count** property to 0. If it is 0, the **Stack** is empty; otherwise, it is not. Event handler **searchButton_Click** (lines 101–108) uses **Stack** method **Contains** (lines 104–105) to determine whether the **Stack** contains the object specified as its argument. **Contains** returns **true** if the **Stack** contains the specified object, **false** otherwise.

Event handler **isEmptyButton_Click** (lines 111–123) uses an IEnumerator to traverse the **Stack** and display its contents.

20.7.4 Class **Hashtable**

Object-oriented programming languages facilitate creating new types. When a program creates objects of new or existing types, it then needs to manage those objects efficiently. This includes sorting and retrieving objects. Sorting and retrieving information with arrays is efficient if some aspect of your data directly matches the key value and if those keys are unique and tightly packed. If you have 100 employees with nine-digit Social Security numbers and you want to store and retrieve employee data by using the Social Security number as a key, it would nominally require an array with 999,999,999 elements, because there are 999,999,999 unique nine-digit numbers. This is impractical for virtually all applications that key on Social Security numbers. If you could have an array that large, you could get very high performance storing and retrieving employee records by simply using the Social Security number as the array index.

A large variety of applications have this problem—namely, that either the keys are of the wrong type (i.e., not nonnegative integers), or they are of the right type, but they are sparsely spread over a large range.

What is needed is a high-speed scheme for converting keys such as Social Security numbers and inventory part numbers into unique array subscripts. Then, when an application needs to store something, the scheme could convert the application key rapidly into a subscript and the record of information could be stored at that location in the array. Retrieval occurs the same way—once the application has a key for which it wants to retrieve the data record, the application simply applies the conversion to the key, which produces the array subscript where the data resides in the array and retrieves the data.

The scheme we describe here is the basis of a technique called *hashing*. Why the name? Because, when we convert a key into an array subscript, we literally scramble the bits, forming a kind of "mishmash" number. The number actually has no real significance beyond its usefulness in storing and retrieving this particular data record.

A glitch in the scheme occurs when *collisions* occur [i.e., two different keys "hash into" the same cell (or element) in the array]. Since we cannot sort two different data records into the same space, we need to find an alternative home for all records beyond the first that hash to a particular array subscript. Many schemes exist for doing this. One is to "hash again" (i.e., to reapply the hashing transformation to the key to provide a next candidate cell in the array). The hashing process is designed to be quite random, so the assumption is that with just a few hashes, an available cell will be found.

Another scheme uses one hash to locate the first candidate cell. If the cell is occupied, successive cells are searched linearly until an available cell is found. Retrieval works the same way—the key is hashed once, the resulting cell is checked to determine whether it contains the desired data. If it does, the search is complete. If it does not, successive cells are searched linearly until the desired data is found.

The most popular solution to hash-table collisions is to have each cell of the table be a hash "bucket," typically a linked list of all the key/value pairs that hash to that cell. This is the solution that the .NET Framework's **Hashtable** class implements.

The *load factor* is one factor that affects the performance of hashing schemes. The load factor is the ratio of the number of occupied cells in the hash table to the size of the hash table. The closer the ratio gets to 1.0, the greater the chance of collisions.

Performance Tip 20.11

The load factor in a hash table is a classic example of a space/time trade-off: By increasing the load factor, we get better memory utilization, but the program runs slower due to increased hashing collisions. By decreasing the load factor, we get better program speed because of reduced hashing collisions, but we get poorer memory utilization because a larger portion of the hash table remains empty.

Programming hash tables properly is too complex for most casual programmers. Computer science students study hashing schemes thoroughly in courses called "Data Structures" and "Algorithms." Recognizing the value of hashing, C# provides class **Hashtable** and some related features to enable programmers to take advantage of hashing without the complex details.

The preceding sentence is profoundly important in our study of object-oriented programming. Classes encapsulate and hide complexity (i.e., implementation details) and offer user-friendly interfaces. Crafting classes to do this properly is one of the most valued skills in the field of object-oriented programming.

A *hash function* performs a calculation that determines where to place data in the hashtable. The hash function is applied to the key in a key/value pair of objects. Class **Hash-**

table can accept any object as a key. For this reason, class **Object** defines method **GetHashCode**, which all objects in C# inherit. Most classes that are candidates to be used as keys in a hash table override this method to provide one that performs efficient hashcode calculations for a specific data type. For example, a **string** has a hashcode calculation that is based on the contents of the **string**. Figure 20.26 demonstrates several methods of class **Hashtable**.

```
1   // Fig. 20.26: HashtableTest.cs
2   // Demonstrate class Hashtable of namespace System.Collections.
3
4   using System;
5   using System.Drawing;
6   using System.Collections;
7   using System.ComponentModel;
8   using System.Windows.Forms;
9   using System.Data;
10  using System.Text;
11
12  namespace HashTableTest
13  {
14     // demonstrate Hashtable functionality
15     public class HashTableTest : System.Windows.Forms.Form
16     {
17        private System.Windows.Forms.Label firstNameLabel;
18        private System.Windows.Forms.Label lastNameLabel;
19        private System.Windows.Forms.Button addButton;
20        private System.Windows.Forms.TextBox lastNameTextBox;
21        private System.Windows.Forms.TextBox consoleTextBox;
22        private System.Windows.Forms.TextBox firstNameTextBox;
23        private System.Windows.Forms.Button getButton;
24        private System.Windows.Forms.Button removeButton;
25        private System.Windows.Forms.Button emptyButton;
26        private System.Windows.Forms.Button containsKeyButton;
27        private System.Windows.Forms.Button clearTableButton;
28        private System.Windows.Forms.Button listObjectsButton;
29        private System.Windows.Forms.Button listKeysButton;
30        private System.Windows.Forms.Label statusLabel;
31
32        // Required designer variable.
33        private System.ComponentModel.Container components = null;
34
35        // Hashtable to demonstrate functionality
36        private Hashtable table;
37
38        public HashTableTest()
39        {
40           // Required for Windows Form Designer support
41           InitializeComponent();
42
43           // create Hashtable object
44           table = new Hashtable();
45        }
```

Fig. 20.26 Using the **Hashtable** class. (Part 1 of 5.)

```
46
47        // Visual Studio.NET generated code
48
49        // main entry point for the application
50        [STAThread]
51        static void Main()
52        {
53           Application.Run( new HashTableTest() );
54        }
55
56        // add last name and Employee object to table
57        private void addButton_Click(
58           object sender, System.EventArgs e )
59        {
60           Employee employee = new Employee( firstNameTextBox.Text,
61              lastNameTextBox.Text );
62
63           // add new key/value pair
64           try
65           {
66              table.Add( lastNameTextBox.Text, employee );
67              statusLabel.Text = "Put: " + employee.ToString();
68           }
69
70           // if key is null or already in table, output message
71           catch ( ArgumentException argumentException )
72           {
73              statusLabel.Text = argumentException.ToString();
74           }
75        }
76
77        // get object for given key
78        private void getButton_Click(
79           object sender, System.EventArgs e )
80        {
81           object result = table[ lastNameTextBox.Text ];
82
83           if ( result != null )
84              statusLabel.Text = "Get: " + result.ToString();
85           else
86              statusLabel.Text = "Get: " + lastNameTextBox.Text +
87                 " not in table";
88        }
89
90        // remove key/value pair from table
91        private void removeButton_Click(
92           object sender, System.EventArgs e )
93        {
94           table.Remove( lastNameTextBox.Text );
95           statusLabel.Text = "Object Removed";
96        }
97
```

Fig. 20.26 Using the **Hashtable** class. (Part 2 of 5.)

```
98          // determine whether table is empty
99          private void emptyButton_Click(
100            object sender, System.EventArgs e )
101         {
102            statusLabel.Text = "Table is " + (
103               table.Count == 0 ? "empty" : "not empty" );
104         }
105
106         // determine whether table contains specified key
107         private void containsKeyButton_Click(
108            object sender, System.EventArgs e )
109         {
110            statusLabel.Text = "Contains key: " +
111               table.ContainsKey( lastNameTextBox.Text );
112         }
113
114         // discard all table contents
115         private void clearTableButton_Click(
116            object sender, System.EventArgs e )
117         {
118            table.Clear();
119            statusLabel.Text = "Clear: Table is now empty";
120         }
121
122         // display list of objects in table
123         private void listObjectsButton_Click(
124            object sender, System.EventArgs e )
125         {
126            IDictionaryEnumerator enumerator =
127               table.GetEnumerator();
128            StringBuilder buffer = new StringBuilder();
129
130            while ( enumerator.MoveNext() )
131               buffer.Append( enumerator.Value + "\r\n" );
132
133            consoleTextBox.Text = buffer.ToString();
134         }
135
136         // display list of keys in table
137         private void listKeysButton_Click(
138            object sender, System.EventArgs e )
139         {
140            IDictionaryEnumerator enumerator =
141               table.GetEnumerator();
142            StringBuilder buffer = new StringBuilder();
143
144            while ( enumerator.MoveNext() )
145               buffer.Append( enumerator.Key + "\r\n" );
146
147            consoleTextBox.Text = buffer.ToString();
148         }
149
150      } // end class HashtableTest
```

Fig. 20.26 Using the **Hashtable** class. (Part 3 of 5.)

```
151
152     // class Employee for use with HashtableTest
153     class Employee
154     {
155        private string first, last;
156
157        // constructor
158        public Employee( string fName, string lName )
159        {
160           first = fName;
161           last = lName;
162        }
163
164        // return Employee first and last names as string
165        public override string ToString()
166        {
167           return first + " " + last;
168        }
169
170     } // end class Employee
171 }
```

Fig. 20.26 Using the **Hashtable** class. (Part 4 of 5.)

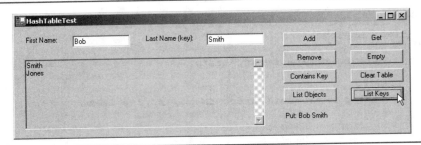

Fig. 20.26 Using the **Hashtable** class. (Part 5 of 5.)

Event handler **addButton_Click** (lines 57–75) reads the first name and last name of an employee from the user interface, creates an object of class Employee (defined at lines 153–170) and adds that **Employee** to the **Hashtable**, using method *Add* (line 66). This method receives two arguments—a key object and a value object. In this example, the key is the last name of the **Employee** (a **string**), and the value is the corresponding **Employee** object. An **ArgumentException** occurs if the **Hashtable** already contains the key or if the key is **null**.

Event handler **getButton_Click** (lines 78–88) retrieves the object associated with a specific key, using the **Hashtable**'s subscript operator as shown on line 81. The expression in square brackets is the key for which the **Hashtable** should return the corresponding object. If the key is not found, the result is **null**.

Event handler **removeButton_Click** (lines 91–96) invokes **Hashtable** method *Remove* to delete a key and its associated object from the **Hashtable**. If the key does not exist in the table, nothing happens.

Event handler **emptyButton_Click** (lines 99–104) uses **Hashtable** property *Count* to determine whether the **Hashtable** is empty (i.e., whether **Count** is **0**).

Event handler **containsKeyButton_Click** (lines 107–112) invokes **Hashtable** method *ContainsKey* to determine whether the **Hashtable** contains the specified key. If so, the method returns **true**; otherwise, it returns **false**.

Event handler **clearTableButton_Click** (lines 115–120) invokes **Hashtable** method *Clear* to delete all **Hashtable** entries.

Class **Hashtable** provides method **GetEnumerator**, which returns an enumerator of type *IDictionaryEnumerator*, which derives from **IEnumerator**. Such enumerators provide properties *Key* and *Value* to access the information for a key/value pair. The event handler at lines 123–134 (**listObjectsButton_click**) uses the **Value** property of the enumerator to output the objects in the **Hashtable**. The event handler at lines 123–134 (**listKeysButton_click**) uses the **Key** property of the enumerator to output the keys in the **Hashtable**.

20.8 Summary

Dynamic data structures can grow and shrink at run time. Creating and maintaining dynamic data structures requires dynamic memory allocation—the ability for a program to obtain more memory at execution time (to hold new nodes) and to release memory that is no longer needed. The limit for dynamic memory allocation can be as large as the available physical memory in the computer or the amount of available disk space in a virtual-memory system.

A self-referential class contains a data member that refers to an object of the same class type. Self-referential objects can be linked to form useful data structures such as lists, queues, stacks and trees.

A linked list is a linear collection (i.e., a sequence) of self-referential class objects called nodes, connected by reference links. A node can contain data of any type, including objects of other classes. A linked list is accessed via a reference to the first node of the list. Each subsequent node is accessed via the link-reference member stored in the previous node. By convention, the link reference in the last node of a list is set to **null** to mark the end of the list.

Stacks are important in compilers and operating systems. A stack is a constrained version of a linked list; new nodes can be added to a stack and removed from a stack only at the top. A stack is referred to as a last-in, first-out (LIFO) data structure. The primary stack operations are push and pop. Operation push adds a new node to the top of the stack. Operation pop removes a node from the top of the stack and returns the data object from the popped node.

Queues represent waiting lines. Insertions occur at the back (also referred to as the tail) of a queue and deletions occur from the front (also referred to as the head) of a queue. A queue is similar to a checkout line in a supermarket: The first person in line is served first; other customers enter the line only at the end and wait to be served. Likewise, queue nodes are removed only from the head of the queue and are inserted only at the tail of the queue. For this reason, a queue is referred to as a first-in, first-out (FIFO) data structure. The insert and remove operations for a queue are known as enqueue and dequeue, respectively.

Binary trees facilitate high-speed searching and sorting of data. Tree nodes generally contain two or more links. A binary tree is a tree whose nodes all contain exactly two links. The root node is the first node in a tree. Each link in the root node refers to a child. The left child is the first node in the left subtree, and the right child is the first node in the right subtree. The children of a node are called siblings. A node with no children is called a leaf node.

A binary search tree (with no duplicate node values) has the characteristic that the values in any left subtree are less than the values that subtree's parent node, and the values in any right subtree are greater than the values in that subtree's parent node. A node can be inserted only as a leaf node in a binary search tree.

An inorder traversal of a binary search tree processes the node values in ascending order. The process of creating a binary search tree actually sorts the data—hence the term "binary-tree sort." In a preorder traversal, the value in each node is processed as the node is visited. After the value in a given node is processed, the values in the node's left subtree are processed; then the values in the node's right subtree are processed. In a postorder traversal, the value in each node is processed after the node's left and right subtrees are processed.

The binary search tree facilitates elimination of duplicate values. As the tree is created, attempts to insert a duplicate value are recognized, because a duplicate follows the same "go left" or "go right" decisions on each comparison as the original value did. Thus, the duplicate eventually is compared with a node containing the same value. The duplicate value may simply be discarded at this point.

The prepackaged data-structure classes provided by the .NET Framework are known as collection classes; they store collections of data. Each instance of one of these classes is known as a collection, which is a set of items.

21

Accessibility

Objectives

- To introduce the World Wide Web Consortium's Web Content Accessibility Guidelines 1.0 (WCAG 1.0).
- To understand how to use the **alt** attribute of the HTML **<img>** tag to describe images to people with visual impairments, mobile-Web-device users and others unable to view images.
- To understand how to make tables more accessible to page readers.
- To understand how to verify that XHTML tags are used properly and to ensure that Web pages can be viewed on any type of display or reader.
- To understand how VoiceXML™ and CallXML™ are changing the way in which people with disabilities access information on the Web.
- To introduce the various accessibility aids offered in Windows 2000.

'Tis the good reader that makes the good book...
Ralph Waldo Emerson

I once was lost, but now am found,
Was blind, but now I see.
John Newton

Outline

21.1   Introduction
21.2   Regulations and Resources
21.3   Web Accessibility Initiative
21.4   Providing Alternatives for Images
21.5   Maximizing Readability by Focusing on Structure
21.6   Accessibility in Visual Studio .NET
        21.6.1   Enlarging Toolbar Icons
        21.6.2   Enlarging the Text
        21.6.3   Modifying the Toolbox
        21.6.4   Modifying the Keyboard
        21.6.5   Rearranging Windows
21.7   Accessibility in C#
21.8   Accessibility in XHTML Tables
21.9   Accessibility in XHTML Frames
21.10   Accessibility in XML
21.11   Using Voice Synthesis and Recognition with VoiceXML™
21.12   CallXML™
21.13   JAWS® for Windows
21.14   Other Accessibility Tools
21.15   Accessibility in Microsoft® Windows® 2000
        21.15.1   Tools for People with Visual Impairments
        21.15.2   Tools for People with Hearing Impairments
        21.15.3   Tools for Users Who Have Difficulty Using the Keyboard
        21.15.4   Microsoft Narrator
        21.15.5   Microsoft On-Screen Keyboard
        21.15.6   Accessibility Features in Microsoft Internet Explorer 6.0
21.16   Summary
21.17   Internet and Web Resources

21.1 Introduction

Throughout this book, we discuss the creation of C# applications. Later chapters also introduced the development of Web-based content using Web Forms, ASP .NET, XHTML and XML. In this chapter, we explore the topic of *accessibility*, which refers to the level of usability that an application or Web site provides to people with various disabilities. Disabilities that might affect an individual's computer or Internet usage are common; they include visual impairments, hearing impairments, other physical injuries (such as the inability to use a keyboard or a mouse) and learning disabilities. In today's computing environment, such impediments prevent many users from taking full advantage of applications and Web content.

The design of applications and sites to meet the needs of individuals with disabilities should be a priority for all software companies and e-businesses. People affected by disabilities represent a significant portion of the population, and legal ramifications could exist for companies that discriminate by failing to provide adequate and universal access to their resources. In this chapter, we explore the World Wide Web Consortium's *Web Accessibility Initiative* and its guidelines and review various laws regarding the availability of computing and Internet resources to people with disabilities. We also highlight companies that have developed systems, products and services that meet the needs of this demographic. As readers use C# and its related technologies to design applications and Web sites, they should keep in mind the accessibility requirements and recommendations that we discuss in this chapter.

21.2 Regulations and Resources

Over the past several years, the United States has taken legislative steps to ensure that people with disabilities are given the tools they need to use computers and access the Web. A wide variety of legislation, including the *Americans With Disabilities Act* (ADA) of 1990, governs the provision of computer and Web accessibility (Fig. 21.1). These laws have inspired significant legal action. For example, according to the ADA, companies are required to offer equal access to individuals with visual problems. The National Federation for the Blind (NFB) cited this law in a 1999 suit against AOL, responding to the company's failure to make its services available to individuals with disabilities.

There are 54 million Americans with disabilities, and these individuals represent an estimated \$1 trillion in annual purchasing power. In addition to legislation, many organizations and resources focus on assisting individuals with disabilities to access computers and the Internet. **WeMedia.com**™ (Fig. 21.2) is a Web site that provides news, information, products and services to the millions of people with disabilities and to their families, friends and caregivers.

Act	Purpose
Americans with Disabilities Act	The ADA prohibits discrimination on the basis of disability in employment, state and local government, public accommodations, commercial facilities, transportation and telecommunications.
Telecommunications Act of 1996	The Telecommunications Act of 1996 contains two amendments to Section 255 and Section 251(a)(2) of the Communications Act of 1934. These amendments require that communication devices, such as cell phones, telephones and pagers, be accessible to individuals with disabilities.

Fig. 21.1   Acts designed to improve Internet and computer accessibility for people with disabilities. (Part 1 of 2.)

Act	Purpose
Individuals with Disabilities Education Act of 1997	The Individuals with Disabilities Education Act stipulates that education materials in schools must be made accessible to children with disabilities.
Rehabilitation Act	Section 504 of the Rehabilitation Act states that college sponsored activities receiving federal funding cannot discriminate against individuals with disabilities. Section 508 mandates that all government institutions receiving federal funding must design their Web sites so that they are accessible to individuals with disabilities. Businesses that sell services to the government also must abide by this act.

Fig. 21.1   Acts designed to improve Internet and computer accessibility for people with disabilities. (Part 2 of 2.)

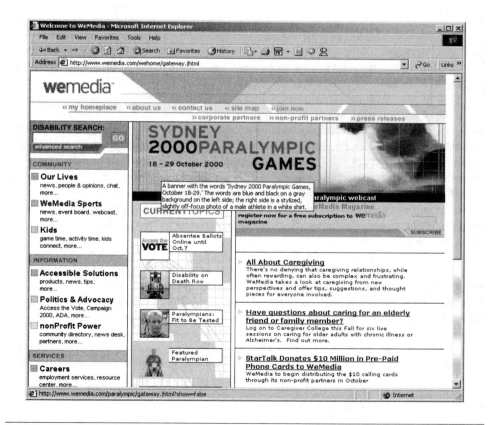

Fig. 21.2   WeMedia's home page. (**Wemedia.com** home page courtesy of WeMedia, Inc.)

As these laws and resources exemplify, computer and Internet accessibility for individuals with disabilities is quickly becoming a reality. Such accessibility enables individuals with disabilities to work in a vast array of new fields. This is partly because the Internet provides a medium through which disabled people can telecommute to jobs and interact easily with others without traveling. Such technologies as voice activation, visual enhancers and auditory aids create additional employment opportunities. For example, people with visual impairments can use computer monitors with enlarged text, and people with physical impairments can use head pointers with on-screen keyboards. In the remaining sections of this chapter, we explore various organizations, techniques, products and services that help provide computer and Internet access to people with disabilities.

21.3 Web Accessibility Initiative

Currently, most Web sites are considered to be either partially or totally inaccessible to people with visual, learning or mobility impairments. Total accessibility is difficult to achieve, because of the variety of disabilities that must be accommodated and because of problems resulting from language barriers and hardware and software inconsistencies. However, a high level of accessibility is attainable. As more people with disabilities begin to use the Internet, it is imperative that Web-site designers increase the accessibility of their sites. Although computer and Web accessibility is the focus of some recent legislation, standards organizations also see the need for industry recommendations. In an attempt to address issues of accessibility, the World Wide Web Consortium (W3C) launched the *Web Accessibility Initiative* (WAI™) in April 1997. To learn more about the WAI or to read its mission statement, visit **www.w3.org/WAI**.

This chapter explains various techniques used to develop accessible Web sites. In 1999, the WAI published the *Web Content Accessibility Guidelines (WCAG) 1.0* to help businesses determine whether their Web sites are universally accessible. The WCAG 1.0 (available at **www.w3.org/TR/WCAG10**) uses checkpoints to list specific accessibility requirements. Each checkpoint is accompanied by a corresponding priority rating that indicates the requirement's level of importance. *Priority-one checkpoints* are goals that must be met to ensure accessibility; we focus on these points in this chapter. *Priority-two checkpoints*, though not essential, are highly recommended. If these checkpoints are not satisfied, people with certain disabilities will experience difficulty accessing Web sites. *Priority-three checkpoints* slightly improve accessibility.

At the time of publication, the WAI was working on *WCAG 2.0*; a working draft of this publication can be found at **www.w3.org/TR/WCAG20**. A single checkpoint in the WCAG 2.0 Working Draft might encompass several checkpoints from WCAG 1.0. Once WCAG 2.0 has been reviewed and published by the W3C, its checkpoints will supersede those of WCAG 1.0. Furthermore, the new version can be applied to a wider range of markup languages (i.e., XML, WML, etc.) and content types than can its predecessor.

The WAI also presents a supplemental checklist of *quick tips*, which reinforce ten important points relating to accessible Web–site design. More information on the WAI Quick Tips can be found at **www.w3.org/WAI/References/Quicktips**.

21.4 Providing Alternatives for Images

One important WAI requirement specifies that every image on a Web page should be accompanied by a textual description that clearly defines the purpose of the image. To accomplish this task, Web developers can use the **alt** attribute of the **img** and **input** tags to include a textual equivalent for every image or graphic included on a site.

Web developers who do not use the **alt** attribute to provide text equivalents increase the difficulties that people with visual impairments experience in navigating the Web. Specialized *user agent*s (or *accessibility aids*), such as *screen readers* (programs that allow users to hear all text that is displayed on their screens) and *braille displays* (devices that receive data from screen-reading software and then output the data as braille), enable people with visual impairments to access text-based information that normally is displayed on the screen. A user agent visually interprets Web-page source code and translates it into a format that is accessible to people with various disabilities. Web browsers, such as Microsoft Internet Explorer and Netscape Communicator, and the screen readers mentioned throughout this chapter are examples of user agents.

Similarly, Web pages that do not provide text equivalents for video and audio clips are difficult for people with visual and hearing impairments to access. Screen readers cannot interpret images, movies and most other non-XHTML content from these Web pages. However, by providing multimedia-based information in a variety of ways (e.g., using the **alt** attribute or providing in-line descriptions of images), Web designers can help maximize the accessibility of their sites' content.

Web designers should provide useful and appropriate text equivalents in the **alt** attribute for use by nonvisual user agents. For example, if the **alt** attribute describes a sales-growth chart, it should provide a brief summary of the data, but should not describe the data in the chart. Instead, a complete description of the chart's data should be included in the **_longdesc_** (long description) *attribute*, which is intended to augment the **alt** attribute's description. The **longdesc** attribute contains a link to a Web page describing the image or multimedia content. Currently, most Web browsers do not support the **longdesc** attribute. An alternative to the **longdesc** attribute is *D-link*, which provides descriptive text about graphs and charts. More information on D-links can be obtained at the *CORDA Technologies* Web site (**www.corda.com**).

The use of a screen reader to facilitate Web-site navigation can be time-consuming and frustrating, because screen readers cannot interpret pictures and other graphical content. The inclusion of a link at the top of each Web page providing direct access to the page's content could allow disabled users to bypass long lists of navigation links and other irrelevant or inaccessible content. This jump can save time and eliminate frustration for individuals with visual impairments.

Emacspeak (**www.cs.cornell.edu/home/raman/emacspeak/emacspeak.html**) is a screen interface that improves the quality of Internet access for individuals with visual disabilities by translating text to voice data. The open-source product also implements auditory icons that play various sounds. Emacspeak can be customized with Linux operating systems and provides support for the IBM *ViaVoice* speech engine.

In March 2001, We Media introduced another user agent, the *WeMedia Browser*, which allows people with vision impairments and cognitive disabilities (such as dyslexia) to use the Internet more conveniently. The WeMedia Browser enhances traditional browser capabilities by providing oversized buttons and keystroke commands that assist in navigation. The browser "reads" text that the user selects, allowing the user to control the speed and volume at which the browser reads the contents of the Web page. The WeMedia Browser free download is available at **www.wemedia.com**

IBM Home Page Reader (HPR) is another browser that "reads" text selected by the user. The HPR uses IBM ViaVoice technology to synthesize an audible voice. A trial version of HPR is available at **www-3.ibm.com/able/hpr.html**.

21.5 Maximizing Readability by Focusing on Structure

Many Web sites use XHTML tags for aesthetic purposes, ignoring the tags' intended functions. For example, the **<h1>** heading tag often is used erroneously to make text large and bold, rather than to indicate a major section head for content. This practice might create a desired visual effect, but it causes problems for screen readers. When the screen-reader software encounters the **<h1>** tag, it might verbally inform the user that a new section has been reached. If this is not in fact the case, the **<h1>** tag might confuse users. Therefore, developers should use the **h1** only in accordance with its XHTML specifications (e.g., to mark up a heading that introduces an important section of a document). Instead of using **h1** to make text large and bold, developers can use CSS (Cascading Style Sheets) or XSL (Extensible Stylesheet Language) to format and style the text. For further examples of this nature, refer to the WCAG 1.0 Web site at **www.w3.org/TR/WCAG10**. [*Note:* The **<strong>** tag also can be used to make text bold; however, screen readers emphasize bold text, which affects the inflection of what is spoken.]

Another accessibility issue is *readability*. When creating a Web page intended for the general public, it is important to consider the reading level (i.e., level of difficulty to read and understand) at which content is written. Web-site designers can make their sites easier to read by using shorter words. Furthermore, slang terms and other nontraditional language could be problematic for users from other countries, so developers should limit the use of such words.

WCAG 1.0 suggests using a paragraph's first sentence to convey its subject. When a Web site states the point of a paragraph in this paragraph's first sentence, it is easier for individuals with disabilities both to find crucial information and to bypass unwanted material.

The *Gunning Fog Index*, a formula that produces a readability grade when applied to a text sample, can evaluate a Web site's readability. To obtain more information about the Gunning Fog Index, visit **www.trainingpost.org/3-2-inst.htm**.

21.6 Accessibility in Visual Studio .NET

In the previous sections, we have outlined various accessibility guidelines presented in the W3C's Web Accessibility initiative. However, Visual Studio .NET provides its own guidelines for designing accessible software within its programming environment. For instance, one guideline recommends reserving the use of color for the enhancement or emphasis of information, instead of for aesthetic purposes. A second guideline recommends providing information about objects (e.g., desktop icons and open windows) to the accessibility aids (specialized software that renders applications to individuals with disabilities). Such information might include the name, location and size of a window. A third guideline recommends designing user interfaces so that they can accommodate user preferences. For example, people with visual disabilities should be able to modify the font size of a user interface. A fourth guideline recommends allowing users to adjust the time setting for applications that have time constraints. For example, users with mobility or speech disabilities

might experience difficulty when using applications that require users to enter input within
a predetermined period of time (such as 10 seconds). However, if such applications provide
adjustable time settings, users can modify the settings to suit their needs.

In addition to suggesting guidelines the help developers create accessible applications,
Visual Studio .NET also offers features that enable disabled individuals to use the development environment itself. For example, users can enlarge icons and text, customize the toolbox
and keyboard and rearrange windows. The next subsections illustrate these capabilities.

21.6.1 Enlarging Toolbar Icons

To enlarge icons in Visual Studio, select **Customize** from the **Tools** menu. In the **Customize** window's **Options** tab, select the **Large Icons** check box (Fig. 21.3), and select
Close. Figure 21.4 depicts the enlarged icons on the Visual Studio development window.

Fig. 21.3   Enlarging icons using the **Customize** feature.

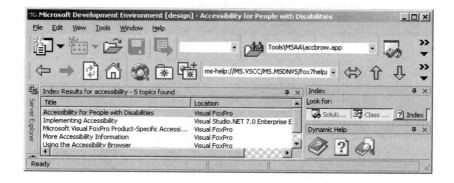

Fig. 21.4   Enlarged icons in the development window.

21.6.2 Enlarging the Text

Visual Studio uses the default operating-system font settings when displaying text. However, some individuals cannot read these default font settings, causing the applications to be inaccessible to them. To remedy this, Visual Studio allows users to modify the font size. Select **Options** from the **Tools** menu. In the **Options** window, open the **Environment** directory and choose **Fonts and Colors**. In the **Show settings for** drop-down box, select **Text Editor**. In the **Font** drop-down box, select a different style of font and, in the **Size** drop-down box, select a different font size. Figure 21.5 depicts the **Text Editor** before we modified the font size, Fig. 21.6 shows the **Options** window with new font settings and Fig. 21.7 displays the **Text Editor** after the changes have been applied.

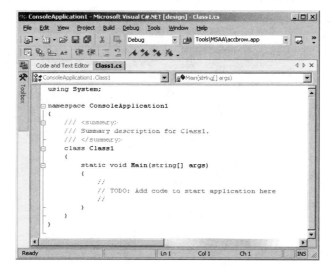

Fig. 21.5   Text Editor before modifying the font size.

Fig. 21.6   Enlarging text in the **Options** window.

Fig. 21.7 Text Editor after the font size is modified.

21.6.3 Modifying the Toolbox

The **Toolbox** feature of Visual Studio contains numerous design elements that facilitate the creation of Web applications; however, some developers might use only a few of these design elements. To accommodate the needs of individual developers, Visual Studio allows programmers to customize the toolbox by creating new tabs and then inserting design elements into the tabs. This eliminates the need for users with disabilities to navigate among multiple tabs or scroll through long lists in search of design elements. To create a new tab, right-click any existing tab and select **Add Tab** from the context menu. In the text box, type an identifier for the tab (such as "Frequently Used") and click *Enter*. By default, the **Pointer** element is placed in all tabs (Fig. 21.8). The **Pointer** element simply allows the cursor to function normally.

To insert elements into the newly created tab, select **Customize Toolbox** from the **Tools** menu. In the **.NET Framework Components** tab, select the elements to include in the new tab and click **OK**. The selected elements now will appear in the tab.

21.6.4 Modifying the Keyboard

Another accessibility feature in Visual Studio .NET allows individuals with disabilities to customize their keyboards by creating *shortcut keys* (i.e., combinations of keyboard keys that, when pressed together, perform frequent tasks; for example, *Ctrl + V* causes text to be pasted from the clipboard). To create a shortcut key, begin by selecting **Options** from the **Tools** menu. In the **Options** window, select the **Keyboard** item from the **Environment** directory. From the **Keyboard mapping scheme** drop-down list, select a scheme and click the **Save As** button. Then, assign a name to the scheme in the **Save Scheme** dialog box and click **OK**. Enter the task of the shortcut key in the **Show commands containing** text box. For example, if we were creating a shortcut key for the paste function, we would enter **Paste** in the text box, or we would select the proper task from the selection list directly below the text box. Then, in the **Use new shortcut** drop-down list, select the applications that will use the shortcut key. If the shortcut key will be used in all applications, select **Global**. Finally, in the **Press shortcut key(s)** text box, assign a shortcut key to the task in the form *non-text key + text key*. Valid non-text keys include *Ctrl*, *Shift* and *Alt*; valid text keys include A–Z, inclusive. [*Note*: To enter a non-text key, select the key itself—do not type the word *Ctrl*, *Shift* or *Alt*. It is possible to include more than one non-text key as part of a shortcut key. Do not enter the + symbol.] Thus, a valid shortcut key might be *Ctrl+Alt+D*. After assigning a shortcut key, select **Assign** and then **OK**. Figure 21.9 illustrates the process of creating a shortcut key for the `NewBreakpoint` function. The shortcut key (*Ctrl+Alt+D*) is valid only in the **Text Editor**.

21.6.5 Rearranging Windows

Some screen readers have difficulty interpreting user interfaces that include multiple tabs; this is because most screen readers can read information on only one screen. To accommodate such screen readers, Visual Studio allows developers to customize their user interfaces so that only the console window appears. To remove tabs, select **Options** from the **Tools** menu. Then, in the **Options** window, select the **General** item from the **Environment** directory. In the **Settings** section, select the **MDI environment** radio button and click **OK**. Figure 21.10 depicts the **Options** window, and Fig. 21.11 illustrates a console window with and without tabs.

Fig. 21.8   Adding tabs to the **Toolbox**.

operation selection   application to
apply shortcuts   mapping scheme   key designation

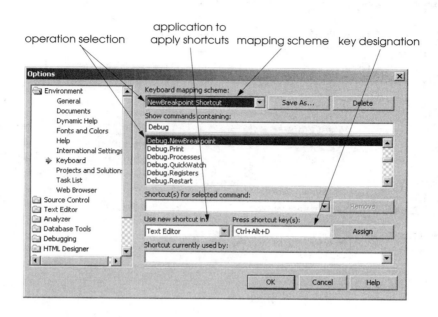

Fig. 21.9 Shortcut key creation.

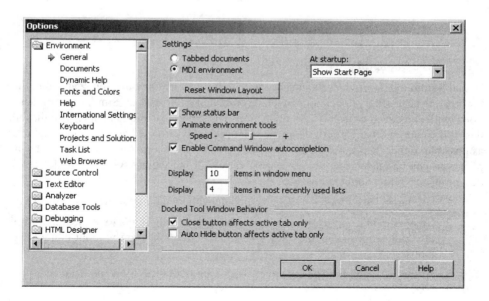

Fig. 21.10 Removing tabs from Visual Studio environment.

Fig. 21.11 Console windows with tabs and without tabs.

21.7 Accessibility in C#

Visual Studio .NET provides extensive accessibility features and also presents guidelines for creating accessible applications in its development environment. Similar recommendations guide the development of C# applications that are accessible to people with disabilities. It is important that C# programmers gear applications toward as many potential users as possible, rather then toward only the average user. With some modifications, most applications can be made accessible to a wide variety of individuals. General guidelines for designing accessible applications are:

1. Use larger-sized fonts—this helps people with visual impairments see the text.

2. Create flexible applications that provide keyboard shortcuts for all features within the application—this allows people to use the application without employing a mouse.

3. Allow information to be conveyed to the user both in a visual and in an audio context.

4. Use graphics and images whenever helpful—visual cues can increase accessibility for people who have trouble reading text on the screen.

5. Never signal information with sound only—someone accessing the information might not have speakers or might have hearing impairments.[1]

6. Test the application without using either a mouse or a keyboard. Access to an application's functionality should not be limited to one input device.

For more information on these and other design guidelines for accessible applications, please refer to the Visual Studio .NET documentation under the **overview** subsection of the index topic **accessibility**. This section provides links to discussions of how to design more accessible Windows and ASP.NET applications.

One specific way that programmers can make their applications more accessible is to use a *text-to-speech* control in their programs. A text-to-speech control can convert text into speech—a computerized voice speaks the words provided as text to the control. Text-to-speech controls facilitate access for people who cannot see the screen.

Another way to make applications more accessible is to use *tab stops*. A tab stop occurs when the user presses the *Tab* key, causing the focus to transfer to another control. The order in which the controls gain focus is called the *tab order*, which is determined by the **TabIndex** value of the controls (controls gain focus in ascending order). Each control also has a **TabStop** property—if this property is **true**, the control is included in the tab order; otherwise, it is not. Using the **TabIndex** and **TabStop** properties makes it simple to create more easily navigable applications. If these properties are set incorrectly, the logical ordering of the application might not be maintained. Consider an application that has **TextBox**es in which a user inputs a first name, a last name and an address. The logical tab order would take the user from the **TextBox** for the first name to the one for the last name and then to the one for the address.

A third and important way in which programmers can increase the accessibility of their applications is to use specific classes provided by .NET. Class **Control**, for example, has many properties designed for conveying information to users. These applications can then, in turn, find the required information stored as properties. Figure 21.12 lists some properties of class **Control** that are designed to provide information to users.

Property	Purpose
AccessibleDescription	Describes the control to an accessibility client application. For example, a **CheckBox** that says **"New User"** would not require more description, but a **CheckBox** with an image of a cat would have its **AccessibleDescription** property set to something like, **"A CheckBox with an image of a cat on it"**.
AccessibleName	Contains a short name or identifier for the control.

Fig. 21.12 Properties of class **Control** related to accessibility. (Part 1 of 2.)

---

1. "Basic Principles of Accessible Design," *.NET Framework Developer's Guide*, Visual Studio .NET Online Help

Property	Purpose
AccessibleRole	Member of the **AccessibleRole** enumeration. Represents the role of this control in the application—this information might help the accessibility client application determine what actions it should take.
IsAccessible	Contains a **bool** value specifying whether the control is visible to accessibility client applications.

Fig. 21.12 Properties of class **Control** related to accessibility. (Part 2 of 2.)

The application in Fig. 21.13 uses a text-to-speech control, tab stops and class **Control**'s accessibility-related properties. It consists of a form with three **Label**s, three **TextBox**es and a **Button**, enabling a user to submit the information. Submitting the information simply terminates the application—the application is intended only to demonstrate the use of the text-to-speech control.

The accessibility features in this program work as follows: When the mouse is over a **Label**, the text-to-speech control prompts the user to enter the appropriate information in the **TextBox** located to the right of the **Label**. If the mouse is over a **TextBox**, the contents of the **TextBox** are spoken. Lastly, if the mouse is over **Button Submit**, the user is told that the button should be clicked to submit the information. The tab order is the following: The **TextBox**es where the user inputs the name, phone number and password, then the **Button**. The **Label**s and text-to-speech control are not included in the tab order, because the user cannot interact with them, and their inclusion would serve no purpose. The accessibility properties are set so that accessibility client applications will obtain appropriate information about the controls. Please note that only the relevant code generated by Visual Studio .NET is included in Fig. 21.13. To use the text-to-speech control, first add it to the **Toolbox**. This is accomplished by selecting **Customize Toolbox** from the **Tools** menu. The **Customize Toolbox** dialog pops up—check the box next to the **TextToSpeech Class** option. Click **OK** to dismiss the dialog box. The **VText** control now is in the **ToolBox** and can be dragged onto a form int he same way that any other control.

The application has three **Label**s that prompts for the user's name, phone number and password. Three corresponding **TextBox**es accept the user's input and, a **Button** allows the user to submit the form. Line 25 declares a text-to-speech control named **speaker**. We want the user to hear audio descriptions of controls when the mouse is located over those controls. Lines 112–139 define the **controls_MouseHover** event handler—we attach this method to the three **TextBox**es and the **Button** as the event handler for the **MouseHover** event.

```
1   // Fig. 21.13: TextToSpeech.cs
2   // Providing audio for people with visual impairments.
3
4   using System;
5   using System.Drawing;
```

Fig. 21.13 Application with accessibility features. (Part 1 of 4.)

```
 6    using System.Collections;
 7    using System.ComponentModel;
 8    using System.Windows.Forms;
 9    using System.Data;
10
11    // helps users navigate form with aid of audio cues
12    public class TextToSpeech : System.Windows.Forms.Form
13    {
14       private System.Windows.Forms.Label nameLabel;
15       private System.Windows.Forms.Label phoneLabel;
16
17       private System.Windows.Forms.TextBox nameTextBox;
18       private System.Windows.Forms.TextBox phoneTextBox;
19       private System.Windows.Forms.TextBox passwordTextBox;
20
21       private System.Windows.Forms.Button submitButton;
22
23       private System.Windows.Forms.Label passwordLabel;
24
25       private AxHTTSLib.AxTextToSpeech speaker;
26
27       private System.ComponentModel.Container components = null;
28
29       // default constructor
30       public TextToSpeech()
31       {
32          InitializeComponent();
33
34          // set Form to be visible to accessibility applications
35          this.IsAccessible = true;
36
37          // let all controls be visible to accessibility applications
38          foreach ( Control current in this.Controls )
39             current.IsAccessible = true;
40       }
41
42       private void InitializeComponent()
43       {
44          this.nameLabel.AccessibleDescription = "User Name";
45          this.nameLabel.AccessibleName = "User Name";
46          this.nameLabel.TabIndex = 5;
47          this.nameLabel.MouseHover +=
48             new System.EventHandler( this.controls_MouseHover );
49
50          this.phoneLabel.AccessibleDescription =
51             "Phone Number Label";
52          this.phoneLabel.AccessibleName = "Phone Number Label";
53          this.phoneLabel.TabIndex = 6;
54          this.phoneLabel.MouseHover +=
55             new System.EventHandler( this.controls_MouseHover );
56
57          this.nameTextBox.AccessibleDescription =
58             "Enter User Name";
```

Fig. 21.13 Application with accessibility features. (Part 2 of 4.)

```
59          this.nameTextBox.AccessibleName = "User Name TextBox";
60          this.nameTextBox.TabIndex = 1;
61          this.nameTextBox.MouseHover +=
62             new System.EventHandler( this.controls_MouseHover );
63
64          this.phoneTextBox.AccessibleDescription =
65             "Enter Phone Number";
66          this.phoneTextBox.AccessibleName = "Phone Number TextBox";
67          this.phoneTextBox.TabIndex = 2;
68          this.phoneTextBox.MouseHover +=
69             new System.EventHandler( this.controls_MouseHover );
70
71          this.passwordTextBox.AccessibleDescription =
72             "Enter Password";
73          this.passwordTextBox.AccessibleName = "Password TextBox";
74          this.passwordTextBox.TabIndex = 3;
75          this.passwordTextBox.MouseHover +=
76             new System.EventHandler( this.controls_MouseHover );
77
78          this.submitButton.AccessibleDescription =
79             "Submit the Information";
80          this.submitButton.AccessibleName = "Submit Information";
81          this.submitButton.TabIndex = 4;
82          this.submitButton.Text = "&Submit";
83          this.submitButton.Click +=
84             new System.EventHandler( this.submitButton_Click );
85          this.submitButton.MouseHover +=
86             new System.EventHandler( this.controls_MouseHover );
87
88          this.passwordLabel.AccessibleDescription =
89             "Password Label";
90          this.passwordLabel.AccessibleName = "Password Label";
91          this.passwordLabel.TabIndex = 7;
92          this.passwordLabel.MouseHover +=
93             new System.EventHandler( this.controls_MouseHover );
94
95          this.speaker.AccessibleDescription =
96             "Give Information about Form";
97          this.speaker.AccessibleName = "Speaker";
98          this.speaker.TabIndex = 8;
99          this.speaker.TabStop = false;
100
101          this.AccessibleDescription = "Registration Form";
102          this.AccessibleName = "Registration Form";
103       }
104
105       [STAThread]
106       static void Main()
107       {
108          Application.Run( new TextToSpeech() );
109       }
110
```

Fig. 21.13 Application with accessibility features. (Part 3 of 4.)

```
111    // tell user over which control mouse is
112    private void controls_MouseHover(
113       object sender, System.EventArgs e )
114    {
115       // if mouse is over Label, tell user to enter information
116       if ( sender.GetType() == nameLabel.GetType() )
117       {
118          Label temporary = ( Label) sender;
119          speaker.Speak( "Please enter your " + temporary.Text +
120             " in the textbox to the right" );
121       }
122
123       // if mouse is over TextBox, tell user what
124       // information was entered
125       else if ( sender.GetType() == nameTextBox.GetType() )
126       {
127          TextBox temporary = ( TextBox ) sender;
128          speaker.Speak( "You have entered " +
129             ( temporary.Text == "" ? "nothing" :
130             temporary.Text ) + " in the " + temporary.Name );
131       }
132
133       // otherwise, user is over Button, so tell user to click
134       // it to submit information
135       else
136          speaker.Speak(
137             "Click on this button to submit your information" );
138
139    } // end method controls_MouseHover
140
141    // thank user for information submission
142    private void submitButton_Click(
143       object sender, System.EventArgs e )
144    {
145       speaker.Speak(
146          "Thank you, your information has been submitted." );
147
148       Application.Exit();
149    }
150
151 } // end class TextToSpeech
```

Fig. 21.13 Application with accessibility features. (Part 4 of 4.)

Method **controls_MouseHover** determines which type of control the mouse is hovering over and generates the appropriate audio. Line 116 determines whether the type of the control calling the method is the same as that of **nameLabel**. Here, we use method **GetType** of class **Type**, which returns an instance of class **Type**; this class represents information about a particular class. We call method **GetType** on object **sender**. Event-handler argument **sender** is a reference to the control that triggered the event. When the condition at line 116 evaluates to **true** (i.e., the control that triggered the event is **nameLabel**), lines 118–120 execute. Line 118 casts **sender** to a **Label** (now that we know it is one) and assigns it to **Label temporary**. Lines 119–120 call **speaker**'s method **Speak**, which provides the **string** that should be converted to speech.

A similar process is performed to determine whether the mouse is over a **TextBox** (line 125) and to generate the appropriate audio (lines 127–130). Lastly, if the control over which the mouse is hovering is neither a **Label** nor a **TextBox**, it must be the **Button**; lines 136–137 tell the user to click the button to submit information. Method **submitButton_Click** (lines 142–149) executes when the user clicks the **Button**. This event handler calls **speaker**'s method **Speak**, providing as an argument a thank-you message, and then exits the application.

Line 82 sets the **Text** property of **submitButton** to **"&Submit"**. This is an example of providing keyboard access to the functionality of the application. Recall that, in Chapter 10, we assigned shortcut keys by placing **"&"** in front of the letter that would become the shortcut key. Here, we do the same for **submitButton**—pressing **Alt+S** on the keyboard is equivalent to clicking the **submitButton**.

We establish the tab order in this application by setting the **TabIndex** and **TabStop** properties. The **TabIndex** properties of the controls are assigned in lines 46, 60, 67, 74, 81, 91 and 98. The **TextBox**es are assigned the tab indices 1–3, in order of their appearance (vertically) on the form. The **Button** is assigned tab index 4, and the rest of the controls are given tab indices 5–8. We want the tab order to include only the **TextBox**es and the **Button**. The default setting for the **TabStop** property of **Label**s is **false**—thus, we do not need to change it; the labels will not be included in the tab order. The **TabStop** property of **TextBox**es and **Button**s is **true**, which means that we do not need to change the values for those controls either. The **TabStop** property of **speaker**, however, is **true** by default. We set it to **false**, indicating that we do not want **speaker** included in the tab order. In general, those controls with which the user cannot directly interact should have their **TabStop** properties set to **false**.

The last accessibility feature in this application involves setting the accessibility properties of the controls so that client accessibility applications can access and process the controls properly. Lines 44, 50–51, 57–58, 64–65, 71–72, 78–79, 88–89 and 95–96 set the **AccessibleDescription** properties of all the controls (including the Form). Lines 45, 52, 59, 66, 73, 80, 90 and 97 set the **AccessibleName** properties of all the controls (again including the Form). The **IsAccessible** property is not visible in the **Properties** window during design time, so we must write code to set it to **true**. Line 35 sets the **IsAccessible** property of **TextToSpeech** to **true**. Lines 38–39 loop through each control on the form and set each **IsAccessible** property to **true**. The Form and all its controls now will be visible to client accessibility applications.

21.8 Accessibility in XHTML Tables

Complex Web pages often contain tables that format content and present data. However, many screen readers are incapable of translating tables correctly unless developers design the tables with screen-reader requirements in mind. For example, the *CAST eReader*, a screen reader developed by the Center for Applied Special Technology (**www.cast.org**), starts at the top-left-hand cell and reads columns from left to right, top to bottom. This technique of reading data from a table is referred to as *linearized*. Figure 21.14 creates a simple table listing the costs of various fruits; later, we provide this table to the CAST eReader to demonstrate its linear reading of the table. The CAST eReader reads the table in Fig. 21.14 as follows:

> *Price of Fruit Fruit Price Apple $0.25 Orange $0.50 Banana $1.00 Pineapple $2.00*

This reading does not present the content of the table adequately: The reading neither specifies caption and header information nor links data contained in cells to the column headers that describe them. WCAG 1.0 recommends using Cascading Style Sheets (CSS) instead of tables, unless a table's content linearizes in an understandable manner.

```
1   <?xml version = "1.0"?>
2   <!DOCTYPE html PUBLIC "-//W3C//DTD XHTML 1.0 Strict//EN"
3      "http://www.w3.org/TR/xhtml1/DTD/xhtml1-strict.dtd">
4
5   <!-- Fig. 21.14: withoutheaders.html -->
6   <!-- Table without headers            -->
7
8   <html xmlns = "http://www.w3.org/1999/xhtml">
9      <head>
10        <title>XHTML Table Without Headers</title>
11
12        <style type = "text/css">
13           body { background-color: #ccffaa;
14                  text-align: center }
15        </style>
16     </head>
17
18     <body>
19
20        <p>Price of Fruit</p>
21
22        <table border = "1" width = "50%">
23
24           <tr>
25              <td>Fruit</td>
26              <td>Price</td>
27           </tr>
28
29           <tr>
30              <td>Apple</td>
31              <td>$0.25</td>
32           </tr>
33
```

Fig. 21.14 XHTML table without accessibility modifications. (Part 1 of 2.)

```
34              <tr>
35                  <td>Orange</td>
36                  <td>$0.50</td>
37              </tr>
38
39              <tr>
40                  <td>Banana</td>
41                  <td>$1.00</td>
42              </tr>
43
44              <tr>
45                  <td>Pineapple</td>
46                  <td>$2.00</td>
47              </tr>
48
49          </table>
50
51      </body>
52  </html>
```

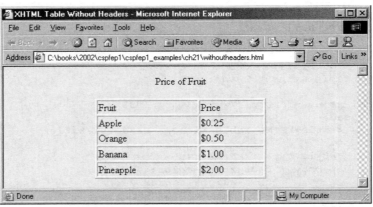

Fig. 21.14 XHTML table without accessibility modifications. (Part 2 of 2.)

If the table in Fig. 21.14 were large, the screen reader's linearized reading would be even more confusing to users. However, modifying the **<td>** tag with the **headers** attribute and modifying *header cells* (cells specified by the **<th>** tag) with the **id** attribute causes the table to be read as intended. Figure 21.15 demonstrates how these modifications change the way in which a screen reader interprets the table.

```
1   <?xml version = "1.0"?>
2   <!DOCTYPE html PUBLIC "-//W3C//DTD XHTML 1.0 Strict//EN"
3       "http://www.w3.org/TR/xhtml1/DTD/xhtml1-strict.dtd">
4
5   <!-- Fig. 21.15: withheaders.html -->
6   <!-- Table with headers              -->
7
```

Fig. 21.15 Table optimized for screen reading, using attribute **headers**. (Part 1 of 3.)

```
 8    <html xmlns = "http://www.w3.org/1999/xhtml">
 9       <head>
10          <title>XHTML Table With Headers</title>
11
12          <style type = "text/css">
13             body { background-color: #ccffaa;
14                    text-align: center }
15          </style>
16       </head>
17
18       <body>
19
20       <!-- This table uses the id and headers attributes to    -->
21       <!-- ensure readability by text-based browsers. It also   -->
22       <!-- uses a summary attribute, used by screen readers to  -->
23       <!-- describe the table.                                  -->
24
25          <table width = "50%" border = "1"
26             summary = "This table uses th elements and id and
27             headers attributes to make the table readable
28             by screen readers">
29
30             <caption><strong>Price of Fruit</strong></caption>
31
32             <tr>
33                <th id = "fruit">Fruit</th>
34                <th id = "price">Price</th>
35             </tr>
36
37             <tr>
38                <td headers = "fruit">Apple</td>
39                <td headers = "price">$0.25</td>
40             </tr>
41
42             <tr>
43                <td headers = "fruit">Orange</td>
44                <td headers = "price">$0.50</td>
45             </tr>
46
47             <tr>
48                <td headers = "fruit">Banana</td>
49                <td headers = "price">$1.00</td>
50             </tr>
51
52             <tr>
53                <td headers = "fruit">Pineapple</td>
54                <td headers = "price">$2.00</td>
55             </tr>
56
57          </table>
58
59       </body>
60    </html>
```

Fig. 21.15 Table optimized for screen reading, using attribute **headers**. (Part 2 of 3.)

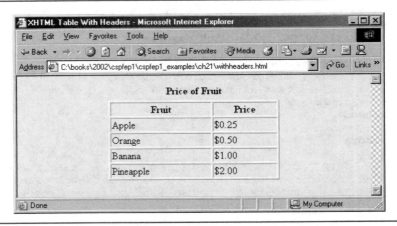

Fig. 21.15 Table optimized for screen reading, using attribute **headers**. (Part 3 of 3.)

This table does not appear to be different from the standard XHTML table shown in Fig. 21.14. However, the formatting of this table allows a screen reader to read the contained data more intelligently. A screen reader vocalizes the data from the table in Fig. 21.15 as follows:

```
Caption: Price of Fruit
Summary: This table uses th elements and id and headers
attributes to make the table readable by screen readers
Fruit: Apple, Price: $0.25
Fruit: Orange, Price: $0.50
Fruit: Banana, Price: $1.00
Fruit: Pineapple, Price: $2.00
```

Every cell in the table is preceded by its corresponding header when read by the screen reader. This format helps the listener understand the table. The **headers** *attribute* is intended specifically for use in tables that hold large amounts of data. Most small tables linearize fairly well, as long as the **<th>** tag is used properly. We also suggest using the **summary** attribute and **caption** element to enhance clarity. To view additional examples that demonstrate how to make tables accessible, visit **www.w3.org/TR/WCAG**.

21.9 Accessibility in XHTML Frames

Web designers often use frames to display more than one XHTML file in a single browser window. Frames are a convenient way to ensure that certain content always displays on the screen. Unfortunately, frames often lack proper descriptions, and this prevents users with text-based browsers and users listening via speech synthesizers from navigating the Web site.

A site that uses frames must provide a meaningful description of each frame in the frame's **<title>** tag. Examples of good titles include *"Navigation Frame"* and *"Main Content Frame."* Users navigating via text-based browsers, such as Lynx, must choose which frame they want to open; descriptive titles make this choice simpler. However, the assignment of titles to frames does not solve all the navigation problems associated with frames. Web designers also should use the **<noframes>** tag, which provides alternative content for browsers that do not support frames.

Look-and-Feel Observation 21.1

Always provide titles for frames to ensure that user agents that do not support frames have alternatives.

Look-and-Feel Observation 21.2

Include a title for each frame's contents with the **frame** *element; if possible, provide links to the individual pages within the frameset, so that users still can navigate through the Web pages. To provide alternative content to browsers that do not support frames, use the* **<noframes>** *tag. This also improves access for browsers that offer limited support for frames.*

WCAG 1.0 suggests using Cascading Style Sheets (CSS) as an alternative to frames, because CSS can provide similar functionality and is highly customizible. Unfortunately, the ability to display multiple XHTML documents in a single browser window requires the complete support of HTML 4, which is not widespread. However, the second generation of Cascading Style Sheets (CSS2) can display a single document as if it were several documents. CSS2 is not yet fully supported by many user agents.

21.10 Accessibility in XML

XML gives developers the freedom to create new markup languages. Although this feature provides many advantages, the new languages might not incorporate accessibility features. To prevent the proliferation of inaccessible languages, the WAI is developing guidelines—the *XML Guidelines (XML GL)*—to facilitate the creation of accessible XML documents. The XML Guidelines recommend including a text description, similar to XHTML's **<alt>** tag, for each non-text object on a page. To enhance accessibility further, element types should allow grouping and classification and should identify important content. Without an accessible user interface, other efforts to implement accessibility are less effective. Therefore, it is essential to create stylesheets that can produce multiple outputs, including document outlines.

Many XML languages, including Synchronized Multimedia Integration Language (SMIL) and Scalable Vector Graphics (SVG), have implemented several of the WAI guidelines. The WAI XML Accessibility Guidelines can be found at **www.w3.org/WAI/PF/xmlgl.htm**.

21.11 Using Voice Synthesis and Recognition with VoiceXML™

A joint effort by AT&T®, IBM®, Lucent™ and Motorola® has created an XML vocabulary that marks up information for use by *speech synthesizers*, or tools that enable computers to speak to users. This technology, called *VoiceXML*, can provide tremendous benefits to people with visual impairments and to people who are illiterate. VoiceXML-enabled applications read Web pages to the user and then employ *speech recognition* technology to understand words spoken into a microphone. An example of a speech-recognition tool is IBM's *ViaVoice* (**www-4.ibm.com/software/speech**). To learn more about speech recognition and synthesis, consult Chapter 13, Graphics and Multimedia.

The VoiceXML interpreter and the VoiceXML browser process VoiceXML. In the future, Web browsers might incorporate these interpreters. VoiceXML is derived from XML, so VoiceXML is platform–independent. When a VoiceXML document is loaded, a *voice server* sends a message to the VoiceXML browser and begins a verbal conversation between the user and the computer.

The IBM *WebSphere Voice Server SDK 1.5* is a VoiceXML interpreter that can be used to test VoiceXML documents on the desktop. To download the VoiceServer SDK, visit **www.alphaworks.ibm.com/tech/voiceserversdk**. [*Note*: To run the VoiceXML program in Fig. 21.16, download *Java 2 Platform Standard Edition* (Java SDK) 1.4 from **www.java.sun.com/j2se/1.4**. Installation instructions for both the VoiceServerSDK and the Java SDK are located on the Deitel & Associates, Inc., Web site at **www.deitel.com**.]

Figure 21.16 and Fig. 21.17 depict examples of VoiceXML that could be included on a Web site. The computer speaks a document's text to the user, and the text embedded in the VoiceXML tags enables verbal interaction between the user and the browser. The output included in Fig. 21.17 demonstrates a conversation that might take place between a user and a computer after this document is loaded.

```
1    <?xml version = "1.0"?>
2    <vxml version = "1.0">
3
4    <!-- Fig. 21.16: main.vxml -->
5    <!-- Voice page            -->
6
7    <link next = "#home">
8        <grammar>home</grammar>
9    </link>
10
11   <link next = "#end">
12       <grammar>exit</grammar>
13   </link>
14
15   <var name = "currentOption" expr = "'home'"/>
16
17   <form>
18       <block>
19           <emp>Welcome</emp> to the voice page of Deitel and
20           Associates. To exit any time say exit.
21           To go to the home page any time say home.
22       </block>
23
24       <subdialog src = "#home"/>
25   </form>
26
27   <menu id = "home">
28       <prompt count = "1" timeout = "10s">
29           You have just entered the Deitel home page.
30           Please make a selection by speaking one of the
31           following options:
32           <break msecs = "1000" />
33           <enumerate/>
34       </prompt>
35
36       <prompt count = "2">
37           Please say one of the following.
38           <break msecs = "1000" />
```

Fig. 21.16 Home page written in VoiceXML. (Part 1 of 3.)

```
39              <enumerate/>
40         </prompt>
41
42         <choice next = "#about">About us</choice>
43         <choice next = "#directions">Driving directions</choice>
44         <choice next = "publications.vxml">Publications</choice>
45    </menu>
46
47    <form id = "about">
48       <block>
49          About Deitel and Associates, Inc.
50          Deitel and Associates, Inc. is an internationally
51          recognized corporate training and publishing
52          organization, specializing in programming languages,
53          Internet and World Wide Web technology and object
54          technology education. Deitel and Associates, Inc. is a
55          member of the World Wide Web Consortium. The company
56          provides courses on Java, C++, Visual Basic, C, Internet
57          and World Wide Web programming and Object Technology.
58          <assign name = "currentOption" expr = "'about'"/>
59          <goto next = "#repeat"/>
60       </block>
61    </form>
62
63    <form id = "directions">
64       <block>
65          Directions to Deitel and Associates, Inc.
66          We are located on Route 20 in Sudbury,
67          Massachusetts, equidistant from route
68          <sayas class = "digits">128</sayas> and route
69          <sayas class = "digits">495</sayas>.
70          <assign name = "currentOption" expr = "'directions'"/>
71          <goto next = "#repeat"/>
72       </block>
73    </form>
74
75    <form id = "repeat">
76       <field name = "confirm" type = "boolean">
77          <prompt>
78             To repeat say yes. To go back to home, say no.
79          </prompt>
80
81          <filled>
82             <if cond = "confirm == true">
83                <goto expr = "'#' + currentOption"/>
84             <else/>
85                <goto next = "#home"/>
86             </if>
87          </filled>
88
89       </field>
90    </form>
91
```

Fig. 21.16 Home page written in VoiceXML. (Part 2 of 3.)

```
92   <form id = "end">
93      <block>
94         Thank you for visiting Deitel and Associates voice page.
95         Have a nice day.
96         <exit/>
97      </block>
98   </form>
99
100  </vxml>
```

Fig. 21.16 Home page written in VoiceXML. (Part 3 of 3.)

```
101  <?xml version = "1.0"?>
102  <vxml version = "1.0">
103
104  <!-- Fig. 21.17: publications.vxml       -->
105  <!-- Voice page for various publications -->
106
107  <link next = "main.vxml#home">
108     <grammar>home</grammar>
109  </link>
110
111  <link next = "main.vxml#end">
112     <grammar>exit</grammar>
113  </link>
114
115  <link next = "#publication">
116     <grammar>menu</grammar>
117  </link>
118
119  <var name = "currentOption" expr = "'home'"/>
120
121  <menu id = "publication">
122
123     <prompt count = "1" timeout = "12s">
124        Following are some of our publications. For more
125        information visit our web page at www.deitel.com.
126        To repeat the following menu, say menu at any time.
127        Please select by saying one of the following books:
128        <break msecs = "1000" />
129        <enumerate/>
130     </prompt>
131
132     <prompt count = "2">
133        Please select from the following books.
134        <break msecs = "1000" />
135        <enumerate/>
136     </prompt>
137
138     <choice next = "#java">Java.</choice>
139     <choice next = "#c">C.</choice>
```

Fig. 21.17 Publication page of Deitel and Associates' VoiceXML page. (Part 1 of 4.)

```
140        <choice next = "#cplus">C plus plus.</choice>
141    </menu>
142
143    <form id = "java">
144        <block>
145            Java How to program, third edition.
146            The complete, authoritative introduction to Java.
147            Java is revolutionizing software development with
148            multimedia-intensive, platform-independent,
149            object-oriented code for conventional, Internet,
150            Intranet and Extranet-based applets and applications.
151            This Third Edition of the world's most widely used
152            university-level Java textbook carefully explains
153            Java's extraordinary capabilities.
154            <assign name = "currentOption" expr = "'java'"/>
155            <goto next = "#repeat"/>
156        </block>
157    </form>
158
159    <form id = "c">
160        <block>
161            C How to Program, third edition.
162            This is the long-awaited, thorough revision to the
163            world's best-selling introductory C book! The book's
164            powerful "teach by example" approach is based on
165            more than 10,000 lines of live code, thoroughly
166            explained and illustrated with screen captures showing
167            detailed output.World-renowned corporate trainers and
168            best-selling authors Harvey and Paul Deitel offer the
169            most comprehensive, practical introduction to C ever
170            published with hundreds of hands-on exercises, more
171            than 250 complete programs written and documented for
172            easy learning, and exceptional insight into good
173            programming practices, maximizing performance, avoiding
174            errors, debugging, and testing. New features include
175            thorough introductions to C++, Java, and object-oriented
176            programming that build directly on the C skills taught
177            in this book; coverage of graphical user interface
178            development and C library functions; and many new,
179            substantial hands-on projects.For anyone who wants to
180            learn C, improve their existing C skills, and understand
181            how C serves as the foundation for C++, Java, and
182            object-oriented development.
183            <assign name = "currentOption" expr = "'c'"/>
184            <goto next = "#repeat"/>
185        </block>
186    </form>
187
188    <form id = "cplus">
189        <block>
190            The C++ how to program, second edition.
191            With nearly 250,000 sold, Harvey and Paul Deitel's C++
192            How to Program is the world's best-selling introduction
```

Fig. 21.17 Publication page of Deitel and Associates' VoiceXML page. (Part 2 of 4.)

```
193            to C++ programming. Now, this classic has been thoroughly
194            updated! The new, full-color Third Edition has been
195            completely revised to reflect the ANSI C++ standard, add
196            powerful new coverage of object analysis and design with
197            UML, and give beginning C++ developers even better live
198            code examples and real-world projects. The Deitels' C++
199            How to Program is the most comprehensive, practical
200            introduction to C++ ever published with hundreds of
201            hands-on exercises, roughly 250 complete programs written
202            and documented for easy learning, and exceptional insight
203            into good programming practices, maximizing performance,
204            avoiding errors, debugging, and testing. This new Third
205            Edition covers every key concept and technique ANSI C++
206            developers need to master: control structures, functions,
207            arrays, pointers and strings, classes and data
208            abstraction, operator overloading, inheritance, virtual
209            functions, polymorphism, I/O, templates, exception
210            handling, file processing, data structures, and more. It
211            also includes a detailed introduction to Standard
212            Template Library containers, container adapters,
213            algorithms, and iterators.
214            <assign name = "currentOption" expr = "'cplus'"/>
215            <goto next = "#repeat"/>
216         </block>
217    </form>
218
219    <form id = "repeat">
220       <field name = "confirm" type = "boolean">
221
222          <prompt>
223             To repeat say yes. Say no, to go back to home.
224          </prompt>
225
226          <filled>
227             <if cond = "confirm == true">
228                <goto expr = "'#' + currentOption"/>
229             <else/>
230                <goto next = "#publication"/>
231             </if>
232          </filled>
233       </field>
234    </form>
235    </vxml>
```

> *Computer speaks:*
> **Welcome to the voice page of Deitel and Associates. To exit any time**
> **say exit. To go to the home page any time say home.**
>
> *User speaks:*
> **Home**
>
> *(continued on next page)*

Fig. 21.17 Publication page of Deitel and Associates' VoiceXML page. (Part 3 of 4.)

(continued from previous page)

Computer speaks:
`You have just entered the Deitel home page. Please make a selection`
`by speaking one of the following options: About us, Driving direc-`
`tions, Publications.`

User speaks:
`Driving directions`

Computer speaks:
`Directions to Deitel and Associates, Inc.`
`We are located on Route 20 in Sudbury,`
`Massachusetts, equidistant from route 128`
`and route 495.`
`To repeat say yes. To go back to home, say no.`

Fig. 21.17 Publication page of Deitel and Associates' VoiceXML page. (Part 4 of 4.)

A VoiceXML document contains a series of dialogs and subdialogs, resulting in spoken interaction between the user and the computer. The **<form>** and **<menu>** tags implement the dialogs. A **form** element both presents information to the user and gathers data from the user. A **menu** element provides the user with list options and then transfers control to another dialog in response to the user's selection.

Lines 7–9 (of Fig. 21.16) use element **link** to create an active link to the home page. Attribute **next** specifies the URL to which the browser is directed when a user selects the link. Element **grammar** marks up the text that the user must speak to select the link. In the **link** element, we navigate to the element containing **id home** when a user speaks the word **home**. Lines 11–13 use element **link** to create a link to **id end** when a user speaks the word **exit**.

Lines 17–25 create a form dialog using element **form**, which collects information from the user. Lines 18–22 present introductory text. Element **block**, which can exist only within a **form** element, groups together elements that perform an action or an event. Element **emp** indicates that a section of text should be spoken with emphasis. If the level of emphasis is not specified, then the default level—*moderate*—is used. Our example uses the default level. [*Note*: To specify an emphasis level, use the **level** attribute. This attribute accepts the following values: *strong*, *moderate*, *none* and *reduced*.]

The **menu** element in line 27 enables users to select the page to which they would like to link. The **choice** element, which always is part of either a **menu** or a **form**, presents the options. The **next** attribute indicates the page that is loaded when a user makes a selection. The user selects a **choice** element by speaking the text marked up between the tags into a microphone. In this example, the first and second **choice** elements in lines 42–43 transfer control to a *local dialog* (i.e., a location within the same document) when they are selected. The third **choice** element transfers the user to the document **publications.vxml**. Lines 28–34 use element **prompt** to instruct the user to make a selection. Attribute **count** maintains a record of the number of times that a prompt is spoken (i.e., each time the computer reads a prompt, **count** increments by one). The **count** attribute transfers control to another prompt once a certain limit has been reached. Attribute

timeout specifies how long the program should wait after outputting the prompt for users to respond. In the event that the user does not respond before the timeout period expires, lines 36–40 provide a second, shorter prompt that reminds the user to make a selection.

When the user chooses the **publications** option, **publications.vxml** (Fig. 21.17) loads into the browser. Lines 107–113 define **link** elements that provide links to **main.vxml**. Lines 115–117 provide links to the **menu** element (lines 121–141), which asks users to select one of the following publications: Java, C or C++. The **form** elements in lines 143–217 describe books that correspond to these topics. Once the browser speaks the description, control transfers to the **form** element with an **id** attribute whose value equals **repeat** (lines 219–234).

Figure 21.18 provides a brief description of each VoiceXML tag that we used in the previous example (Fig. 21.17).

VoiceXML Tag	Description
<assign>	Assigns a value to a variable.
<block>	Presents information to users without any interaction between the user and the computer (i.e., the computer does not expect any input from the user).
<break>	Instructs the computer to pause its speech output for a specified period of time.
<choice>	Specifies an option in a *menu* element.
<enumerate>	Lists all the available options to the user.
<exit>	Exits the program.
<filled>	Contains elements that execute when the computer receives input for a *form* element from the user.
<form>	Gathers information from the user for a set of variables.
<goto>	Transfers control from one dialog to another.
<grammar>	Specifies grammar for the expected input from the user.
<if>, <else>, <elseif>	Indicates a control statement used for making logic decisions.
<link>	Performs a transfer of control similar to the *goto* statement, but a *link* can be executed at any time during the program's execution.
<menu>	Provides user options and then transfers control to other dialogs on the basis of the selected option.
<prompt>	Specifies text to be read to users when they must make a selection.
<subdialog>	Calls another dialog. After executing the subdialog, the calling dialog resumes control.
<var>	Declares a variable.
<vxml>	Top-level tag that specifies that the document should be processed by a VoiceXML interpreter.

Fig. 21.18 VoiceXML tags.

21.12 CallXML™

Another advancement benefiting people with visual impairments is *CallXML*, a voice technology created and supported by *Voxeo* (**www.voxeo.com**). CallXML creates phone-to-Web applications that control incoming and outgoing telephone calls. Examples of CallXML applications include voice mail, interactive voice-response systems and Internet call waiting. VoiceXML allows computers to read Web pages to users with visual impairments; CallXML reads Web content to users via a telephone. CallXML has important implications for individuals who do not have a computer, but do have a telephone.

When users access CallXML applications, a *text-to-speech (TTS)* engine converts text to an automated voice. The TTS engine then reads information contained within CallXML elements to the users. CallXML applications are tailored to respond to input from callers. [*Note*: Users must have a touch-tone phone to access CallXML applications.]

Typically, CallXML applications play prerecorded audio clips or text as output, requesting responses as input. An audio clip might contain a greeting that introduces callers to the application, or it might recite a menu of options, requesting that callers make a touch-tone entry. Certain applications, such as voice mail, might require both verbal and touch-tone input. Once the application receives the necessary input, it responds by invoking CallXML elements (such as **text**) that contain the information a TTS engine reads to users. If the application does not receive input within a designated time frame, it prompts the user to enter valid input.

When a user accesses a CallXML application, the incoming telephone call is referred to as a *session*. A CallXML application can support multiple sessions, which means that the application can process multiple telephone calls at once. Each session is independent of the others and is assigned a unique *sessionID* for identification. A session terminates either when the user hangs up the telephone or when the CallXML application invokes the **hangup** element.

Our first CallXML application demonstrates the classic "Hello World" example (Fig. 21.19). Line 1 contains the optional *XML declaration*. Value **version** indicates the XML version to which the document conforms. The current XML recommendation is version **1.0**. Value **encoding** indicates the type of *Unicode* encoding that the application uses. For this example, we empty UTF-8, which requires eight bits to transfer and receive data. More information on Unicode® can be found in Appendix G, Unicode®.

The **<callxml>** tag in line 6 declares that the content is a CallXML document. Line 7 contains the **Hello World text**. All text that is to be spoken by a text-to-speech (TTS) engine must be placed within **<text>** tags.

```
1    <?xml version = "1.0" encoding = "UTF-8"?>
2
3    <!-- Fig. 21.19: hello.xml          -->
4    <!-- The classic Hello World example -->
5
6    <callxml>
7       <text>Hello World.</text>
8    </callxml>
```

Fig. 21.19 Hello World CallXML example. (Part 1 of 2.) (Courtesy of Voxeo, © Voxeo Corporation 2000–2002.)

Fig. 21.19 **Hello World** CallXML example. (Part 2 of 2.) (Courtesy of Voxeo, © Voxeo Corporation 2000–2002.)

To deploy a CallXML application, register with the *Voxeo* Community (**community.voxeo.com**), a Web resource that facilitates the creation, debugging and deployment of phone applications. For the most part, Voxeo resources are free, but the company does charge fees when CallXML applications are deployed commercially. The Voxeo Community assigns a unique telephone number to each CallXML application so that external users can access and interact with the application. [*Note*: Voxeo assigns telephone numbers only to applications that reside on the Internet. If you have access to a Web server (such as IIS, PWS or Apache), use it to post your CallXML application. Otherwise, open an Internet account through one of the many Internet-service companies (such as **www.geocities.com**, **angelfire.lycos.com**, **www.stormpages.com**, **www.freewebsites.com**, or **www.brinkster.com**). These companies allow individuals to post documents on the Internet using their Web servers.]

Figure 21.19 also demonstrates the *logging* feature of the **Voxeo Account Manager**, which is accessible to registered members. The logging feature records and displays the "conversation" between the user and the application. The first row of the logging feature lists the URL of the CallXML application and the *global variables* associated with that session. When a session begins, the application creates and assigns values to global variables that the entire application can access and modify. The subsequent row(s) display the "conversation." This example demonstrates a one-way conversation (i.e., the application does not accept any input from the user) in which the TTS engine says **Hello World**. The last row displays the **end of session** message, which states that the phone call has terminated. The logging feature assists developers in the debugging of their applications. By observing a CallXML "conversation," a developer can determine the point at which the application terminates. If the application terminates abruptly ("crashes"), the logging feature displays information regarding the type and location of the error, pointing the developer toward the section of the application that is causing the problem.

The next example (Fig. 21.20) depicts a CallXML application that reads the ISBN numbers of three Deitel textbooks—*Internet and World Wide Web How to Program: Second Edition*, *XML How to Program* and *Java How to Program: Fourth Edition*—on the basis of a user's touch-tone input. [*Note*: The code has been formatted for presentation purposes.]

```
1   <?xml version = "1.0" encoding = "UTF-8"?>
2
3   <!-- Fig. 21.20: isbn.xml                        -->
4   <!-- Reads the ISBN value of three Deitel books -->
5
6   <callxml>
7      <block>
8         <text>
9            Welcome. To obtain the ISBN of the Internet and World
10           Wide Web How to Program: Second Edition, please enter 1.
11           To obtain the ISBN of the XML How to Program,
12           please enter 2. To obtain the ISBN of the Java How
13           to Program: Fourth Edition, please enter 3. To exit the
14           application, please enter 4.
15        </text>
16
17        <!-- Obtains the numeric value entered by the user and -->
18        <!-- stores it in the variable ISBN. The user has 60   -->
19        <!-- seconds to enter one numeric value               -->
20        <getDigits var = "ISBN"
21           maxDigits = "1"
22           termDigits = "1234"
23           maxTime = "60s" />
24
25        <!-- Requests that the user enter a valid numeric -->
26        <!-- value after the elapsed time of 60 seconds   -->
27        <onMaxSilence>
28           <text>
29              Please enter either 1, 2, 3 or 4.
30           </text>
31
32           <getDigits var = "ISBN"
33              termDigits = "1234"
34              maxDigits = "1"
35              maxTime = "60s" />
36
37        </onMaxSilence>
38
39        <onTermDigit value = "1">
40           <text>
41              The ISBN for the Internet book is 0130308978.
42              Thank you for calling our CallXML application.
43              Good-bye.
44           </text>
45        </onTermDigit>
46
```

Fig. 21.20 CallXML example that reads three ISBN values. (Part 1 of 2.) (Courtesy of Voxeo, © Voxeo Corporation 2000–2002.)

```
47              <onTermDigit value = "2">
48                  <text>
49                      The ISBN for the XML book is 0130284173.
50                      Thank you for calling our CallXML application.
51                      Good-bye.
52                  </text>
53              </onTermDigit>
54
55              <onTermDigit value = "3">
56                  <text>
57                      The ISBN for the Java book is 0130341517.
58                      Thank you for calling our CallXML application.
59                      Good-bye.
60                  </text>
61              </onTermDigit>
62
63              <onTermDigit value = "4">
64                  <text>
65                      Thank you for calling our CallXML application.
66                      Good-bye.
67                  </text>
68              </onTermDigit>
69          </block>
70
71          <!-- Event handler that terminates the call -->
72          <onHangup />
73      </callxml>
```

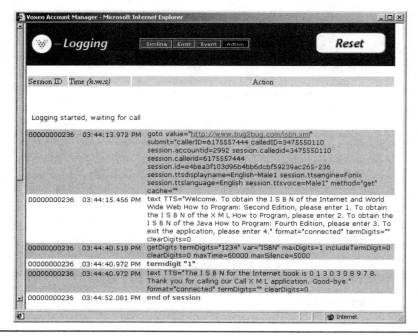

Fig. 21.20 CallXML example that reads three ISBN values. (Part 2 of 2.) (Courtesy of Voxeo, © Voxeo Corporation 2000–2002.)

The **<block>** tag (line 7) encapsulates other CallXML tags. Usually, sets of CallXML tags that perform similar tasks are enclosed within **<block>...</block>**. The **block** element in this example encapsulates the **<text>**, **<getDigits>**, **<onMaxSilence>** and **<onTermDigit>** tags. A **block** element also can be nested in other **block** elements.

Lines 20–23 contain some attributes of the **<getDigits>** tag. The **getDigits** element obtains the user's touch-tone response and stores it in the variable declared by the **var** attribute (i.e., **ISBN**). The **maxDigits** attribute (line 21) indicates the maximum number of digits that the application can accept. This application accepts only one character. If no maximum is stated, then the application uses the default value, *nolimit*.

The **termDigits** attribute (line 22) contains the list of characters that terminate user input. When a user inputs a character from this list, the application is notified that it has received the last acceptable input; any character entered after this point is invalid. These characters do not terminate the call; they simply notify the application to proceed to the next instruction, because the necessary input has been received. In our example, the values for **termDigits** are **1**, **2**, **3** and **4**. The default value for **termDigits** is the null value (**""**).

The **maxTime** attribute (line 23) indicates the maximum amount of time that the application will wait for a user response. If the user fails to enter input within the given time frame, then the CallXML application invokes the event handler **onMaxSilence**. The default value for this attribute is 30 seconds.

The **onMaxSilence** element (lines 27–37) is an event handler that is invoked when attribute **maxTime** (or **maxSilence**) expires. The event handler notifies the application of the appropriate action to perform when a user fails to respond. In this case, the application asks the user to enter a value, because the **maxTime** has expired. After receiving input, **getDigits** (line 32) stores the entered value in the **ISBN** variable.

The **onTermDigit** element (lines 39–68) is an event handler that notifies the application of the appropriate action to perform when a user selects one of the **termDigits** characters. At least one **<onTermDigit>** tag must be associated with (i.e., must appear after) the **getDigits** element, even if the default value (**""**) is used. We provide four actions that the application can perform in response to the specific **termDigits** value entered by the user. For example, if the user enters **1**, the application reads the ISBN value for the *Internet and World Wide Web How to Program: Second Edition* textbook.

Line 72 contains the **<onHangup/>** event handler, which terminates the telephone call when the user hangs up the telephone. Our **<onHangup>** event handler is an empty tag (i.e., no action is performed when this tag is invoked).

The logging feature (Fig. 21.20) displays the "conversation" between the application and the user. As in the previous example, the first row specifies the URL of the application and the global variables of the session. The subsequent rows display the "conversation": The application asks the caller which ISBN value to read; the caller enters **1** (*Internet and World Wide Web How to Program: Second Edition*), and the application reads the corresponding ISBN. The **end of session** message states that the application has terminated.

We provide brief descriptions of various logic and action CallXML elements in Fig. 21.21. *Logic elements* assign values to, and clear values from, the session variables; *action elements* perform specified tasks, such as answering and terminating a telephone call during the current session. A complete list of CallXML elements is available at:

www.oasis-open.org/cover/callxmlv2.html

21.13 JAWS® for Windows

JAWS (Job Access with Sound) is one of the leading screen readers currently on the market. Henter-Joyce, a division of Freedom Scientific™, created this application to help people with visual impairments interact with technology.

To download a demonstration version of JAWS, visit **www.freedomscientific.com**. The JAWS demo is fully functional and includes an extensive, highly customized help system. Users can select the voice that "reads" Web content and the rate at which text is spoken. Users also can create keyboard shortcuts. Although the demo is in English, the full version of JAWS allows the user to choose one of several supported languages.

JAWS also includes special key commands for popular programs, such as Microsoft Internet Explorer and Microsoft Word. For example, when browsing in Internet Explorer, JAWS' capabilities extend beyond the reading of content on the screen. If JAWS is enabled, pressing *Insert + F7* in Internet Explorer opens a **Links List** dialog, which displays all the links available on a Web page. For more information about JAWS and the other products offered by Henter-Joyce, visit **www.freedomscientific.com**.

Elements	Description
assign	Assigns a **value** to a variable, **var**.
clear	Clears the contents of the **var** attribute.
clearDigits	Clears all digits that the user has entered.
goto	Navigates to another section of the current CallXML application or to a different CallXML application. The **value** attribute specifies the URL of the invoked application. The **submit** attribute lists the variables that are passed to the invoked application. The **method** attribute states whether to use the HTTP *get* or *post* request type when sending and retrieving information. A *get* request retrieves data from a Web server without modifying the contents, whereas the *post* request receives modified data.
run	Starts a new CallXML session for each call. The **value** attribute specifies the CallXML application to retrieve. The **submit** attribute lists the variables that are passed to the invoked application. The **method** attribute states whether to use the HTTP *get* or *post* request type. The **var** attribute stores the identification number of the session.
sendEvent	Allows multiple sessions to exchange messages. The **value** attribute stores the message, and the **session** attribute specifies the identification number of the session that receives the message.
answer	Answers an incoming telephone call.
call	Calls the URL specified by the **value** attribute. The **callerID** attribute contains the phone number that is displayed on a CallerID device. The **maxTime** attribute specifies the length of time to wait for the call to be answered before disconnecting.

Fig. 21.21 CallXML elements. (Part 1 of 2.)

Elements	Description
`conference`	Connects multiple sessions so that individuals can participate in a conference call. The `targetSessions` attribute specifies the identification numbers of the sessions, and the `termDigits` attribute indicates the touch-tone keys that terminate the call.
`wait`	Waits for user input. The `value` attribute specifies how long to wait. The `termDigits` attribute indicates the touch-tone keys that terminate the `wait` element.
`play`	Plays an audio file or pronounces a value that is stored as a number, date or amount of money and is indicated by the `format` attribute. The `value` attribute contains the information (location of the audio file, number, date or amount of money) that corresponds to the `format` attribute. The `clearDigits` attribute specifies whether or not to delete the previously entered input. The `termDigits` attribute indicates the touch-tone keys that terminate the audio file, etc.
`recordAudio`	Records an audio file and stores it at the URL specified by `value`. The `format` attribute indicates the file extension of the audio clip. Other attributes include `termDigits`, `clearDigits`, `maxTime` and `maxSilence`.

Fig. 21.21 CallXML elements. (Part 2 of 2.)

21.14 Other Accessibility Tools

Many accessibility products are available to assist people with disabilities. One such technology, Microsoft's *Active Accessibility*®, establishes a protocol by which an accessibility aid can retrieve information about an application's user interface in a consistent manner. Accessibility aids require information such as the name, location and layout of particular GUI elements within an application, so that the accessibility aid can render the information properly to the intended audience. Active Accessibility also enables software developers and accessibility-aid developers to design programs and products that are compatible with each other. Moreover, Active Accessibility is packaged in two components, enabling both programmers and individuals who use accessibility aids to employ the software. The *Software Development Kit (SDK)* component is intended for programmers: It includes testing tools, programmatic libraries and header files. The *Redistribution Kit (RDK)* component is intended for those who use accessibility aids: It installs a runtime component into the Microsoft operating system. Accessibility aids use the Active Accessibility runtime component to interact with and obtain information from any application software. For more information on Active Accessibility, visit:

> `www.msdn.microsoft.com/library/default.asp?url=/nhp/`
> `Default.asp?contentid=28000544`

Another important accessibility tool for individuals with visual impairments is the *braille keyboard*. In addition to providing keys labeled with the letters they represent, a braille keyboard also has the equivalent braille symbol printed on each key. Most often, braille keyboards are combined with a speech synthesizer or a braille display, enabling users to interact with the computer to verify that their typing is correct.

Speech synthesis also provides benefits to people with disabilities. *Speech synthesizers* have been used for many years to aid people who are unable to communicate verbally. However, the growing popularity of the Web has prompted a surge of interest in the fields of speech synthesis and speech recognition. Now, these technologies are allowing individuals with disabilities to use computers more than ever before. The development of speech synthesizers also is enabling the improvement of other technologies, such as VoiceXML and *AuralCSS* (**www.w3.org/TR/REC-CSS2/aural.html**). These tools allow people with visual impairments and illiterate people to access Web sites.

Despite the existence of adaptive software and hardware for people with visual impairments, the accessibility of computers and the Internet is still hampered by the high costs, rapid obsolescence and unnecessary complexity of current technology. Moreover, almost all software currently available requires installation by a person who can see. *Ocularis* is a project launched in the open-source community that aims to address these problems. (Open-source software for people with visual impairments already exists; although it is often superior to its proprietary, closed-source counterparts, it has not yet reached its full potential.) Ocularis ensures that the blind can access and use all aspects of the Linux operating system. Products that integrate with Ocularis include word processors, calculators, basic finance applications, Internet browsers and e-mail clients. In addition, a screen reader is included for use with programs that have a command-line interface. The official Ocularis Web site is located at

ocularis.sourceforge.net.

People with visual impairments are not the only beneficiaries of efforts to improve markup languages. People with hearing impairments also have a number of tools to help them interpret auditory information delivered over the Web. One of these tools, *Synchronized Multimedia Integration Language* (SMIL™), is designed to add extra *tracks (*layers of content found within a single audio or video file) to multimedia content. The additional tracks can contain closed captioning.

Technologies are being designed to help people with severe disabilities, such as quadriplegia, a form of paralysis that affects the body from the neck down. One such technology, *EagleEyes*, developed by researchers at Boston College (**www.bc.edu/eagleeyes**), is a system that translates eye movements into mouse movements. A user moves the mouse cursor by moving his or her eyes or head and is thereby able to control the computer.

GW Micro, Henter-Joyce and Adobe Systems, Inc., also are working on software that assists people with disabilities. Adobe Acrobat 5.0 complies with Microsoft's application programming interface (API) to allow businesses to provide information to a wider audience. JetForm Corp is also accommodating the needs of people with disabilities by developing server-based XML software. The new software allows users to download information in a format that best meets their needs.

There are many services on the Web that assist e-businesses in designing Web sites so that they are accessible to individuals with disabilities. For additional information, the U.S. Department of Justice (**www.usdoj.gov**) provides extensive resources detailing legal and technical issues related to people with disabilities.

21.15 Accessibility in Microsoft® Windows® 2000

Because of the prominence of the Windows operating system, it is crucial that this operating system provide proper accessibility to individuals with disabilities. Beginning with Microsoft *Windows 95*, Microsoft has included accessibility features in its operating systems and many of its applications, including *Office 97*, *Office 2000* and *Netmeeting*. In Microsoft *Windows 2000*, Microsoft significantly enhanced the operating system's accessibility features. All the accessibility options provided by Windows 2000 are available through the **Accessibility Wizard**, which guides users through Windows 2000 accessibility features and then configures users' computers in accordance with the chosen specifications. This section uses the **Accessibility Wizard** to guide users through the configuration of their Windows 2000 accessibility options.

To access the **Accessibility Wizard**, users' computers must be equipped with Microsoft Windows 2000. Click the **Start** button and select **Programs,** followed by **Accessories, Accessibility** and **Accessibility Wizard**. When the wizard starts, the **Welcome** screen displays. Click **Next**. The next dialog (Fig. 21.22) asks the user to select a font size. Modify the font size if necessary and then click **Next**.

Figure 21.22 depicts the **Display Settings** dialog. This dialog allows the user to activate the font-size settings chosen in the previous window, change the screen resolution, enable the *Microsoft Magnifier* (a program that displays an enlarged section of the screen in a separate window) and disable personalized menus. Personalized menus hide rarely used programs from the start menu and can be a hindrance to users with disabilities. Make appropriate selections and click **Next**.

The **Set Wizard Options** dialog (Fig. 21.23) asks questions about the user's disabilities; the answers to these questions allow the **Accessibility Wizard** to customize Windows to better suit the user's needs. For demonstration purposes, we selected every type of disability included in the dialogue. Click **Next** to continue.

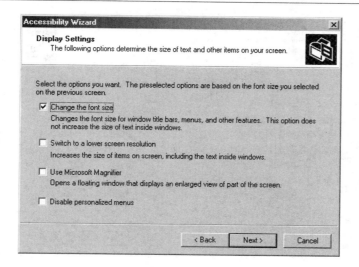

Fig. 21.22 Display Settings dialog.

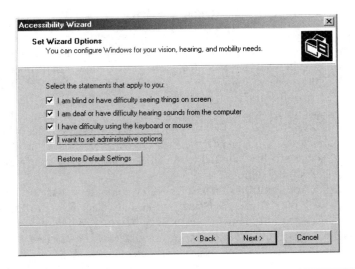

Fig. 21.23 Accessibility Wizard initialization options.

21.15.1 Tools for People with Visual Impairments

When we check all the options in Fig. 21.23, the wizard begins to configure Windows so that it is accessible to people with visual impairments. The dialog box shown in Fig. 21.24 allows the user to resize the scroll bars and window borders to increase their visibility. Click **Next** to proceed to the next dialog.

Figure 21.25 contains a dialog that allows the user to resize icons. Users with poor vision and users who are illiterate or have trouble reading benefit from large icons.

Fig. 21.24 Scroll Bar and Window Border Size dialog.

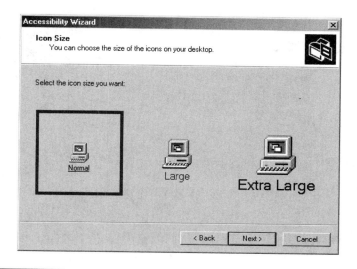

Fig. 21.25 Adjusting window-element sizes.

Clicking **Next** displays the **Display Color Settings** dialog (Fig. 21.26). These settings enable the user to change the Windows color scheme and resize various screen elements.

Click **Next** to view the dialog (Fig. 21.27) that enables customization of the mouse cursor. Anyone who has ever used a laptop computer knows how difficult it can be to see the mouse cursor. This is even more problematic for people with visual impairments. To address this problem, the wizard offers users the options of larger cursors, black cursors and cursors that invert the colors of objects underneath them. Click **Next**.

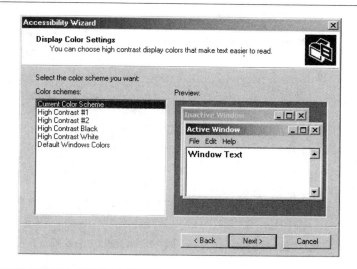

Fig. 21.26 Display Color Settings options.

Fig. 21.27 **Accessibility Wizard** mouse cursor adjustment tool.

21.15.2 Tools for People with Hearing Impairments

This section, which focuses on accessibility for people with hearing impairments, begins with the **SoundSentry** window (Fig. 21.28). **SoundSentry** is a tool that creates visual signals to notify users of system events. For example, people with hearing impairments are unable to hear the beeps that normally indicate warnings, so **SoundSentry** flashes the screen when a beep occurs. To continue on to the next dialog, click **Next**.

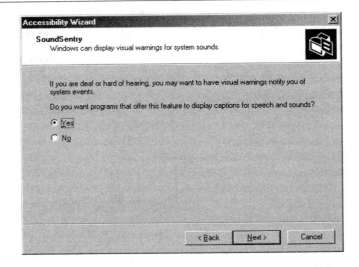

Fig. 21.28 **SoundSentry** dialog.

The next window is the **ShowSounds** window (Fig. 21.29). **ShowSounds** adds captions to spoken text and other sounds produced by today's multimedia-rich software. Note that, for **ShowSounds** to work in a specific application, developers must provide the captions and spoken text specifically within their software. Make selections and click **Next**.

21.15.3 Tools for Users Who Have Difficulty Using the Keyboard

The next dialog describes **StickyKeys** (Fig. 21.30). **StickyKeys** is a program that helps users who have difficulty pressing multiple keys at the same time. Many important computer commands can be invoked only by pressing specific key combinations. For example, the reboot command requires the user to press *Ctrl+Alt+Delete* simultaneously. **StickyKeys** enables the user to press key combinations in sequence, rather than at the same time. Click **Next** to continue to the **BounceKeys** dialog (Fig. 21.31).

Fig. 21.29 ShowSounds dialog.

Fig. 21.30 StickyKeys window.

Fig. 21.31 BounceKeys dialog.

Another common problem that affects certain users with disabilities is the accidental pressing of the same key multiple times. This problem typically is caused by holding a key down too long. **BounceKeys** forces the computer to ignore repeated keystrokes. Click **Next**.

ToggleKeys (Fig. 21.32) alerts users that they have pressed one of the lock keys (i.e., *Caps Lock*, *Num Lock* or *Scroll Lock*) by sounding an audible beep. Make selections and click **Next**.

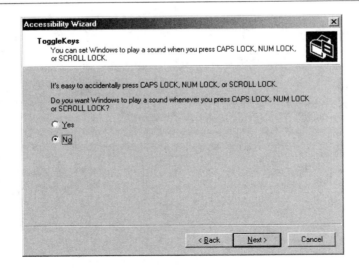

Fig. 21.32 ToggleKeys window.

Next, the **Extra Keyboard Help** dialog (Fig. 21.33) is displayed. This dialog can activate a tool that displays information such as keyboard shortcuts and tool tips when such information is available. Like **ShowSounds**, this tool requires that software developers provide the content to be displayed.

Clicking **Next** will load the **MouseKeys** (Fig. 21.34) customization window. **MouseKeys** is a tool that uses the keyboard to imitate mouse movements. The arrow keys direct the mouse, and the 5 key indicates a single click. To double click, the user must press the + key; to simulate the holding down of the mouse button, the user must press the *Ins* (Insert) key. To release the mouse button, the user must press the *Del* (*Delete*) key. Choose whether to enable **MouseKeys** and then click **Next.**

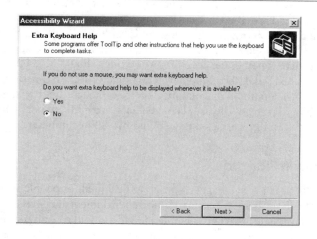

Fig. 21.33 Extra Keyboard Help dialog.

Fig. 21.34 MouseKeys window.

Today's computer tools, including most mice, are designed almost exclusively for right-handed users. Microsoft recognized this problem and added the **Mouse Button Settings** window (Fig. 21.35) to the **Accessibility Wizard**. This tool allows the user to create a virtual left-handed mouse by swapping the button functions. Click **Next**.

Users can adjust mouse speed through the **MouseSpeed** (Fig. 21.36) section of the **Accessibility Wizard**. Dragging the scroll bar changes the speed. Clicking the **Next** button sets the speed and displays the wizard's **Set Automatic Timeouts** window (Fig. 21.37). Although accessibility tools are important to users with disabilities, they can be a hindrance to users who do not need them. In situations where varying accessibility needs exist, it is important that the user be able to turn the accessibility tools on and off as necessary. The **Set Automatic Timeouts** window specifies a *timeout* period for enabling or disabling accessibility tools. A timeout either enables or disables a certain action after the computer has idled for a specified amount of time. A screen saver is a common example of a program with a timeout period. Here, a timeout is set to toggle the accessibility tools.

After the user clicks **Next**, the **Save Settings to File** dialog appears (Fig. 21.38). This dialog determines whether the accessibility settings should be used as the *default settings*, which are loaded when the computer is rebooted or after a timeout. Set the accessibility settings as the default if the majority of users needs them. Users also can save multiple accessibility settings. The user can create an **.acw** file, which, when chosen, activates the saved accessibility settings on any Windows 2000 computer.

21.15.4 Microsoft Narrator

Microsoft Narrator is a text-to-speech program designed for people with visual impairments. It reads text, describes the current desktop environment and alerts the user when certain Windows events occur. **Narrator** is intended to aid in the configuration of Microsoft Windows. It is a screen reader that works with Internet Explorer, Wordpad, Notepad and most programs in the **Control Panel**. Although its capabilities are limited outside these applications, **Narrator** is excellent at navigating the Windows environment.

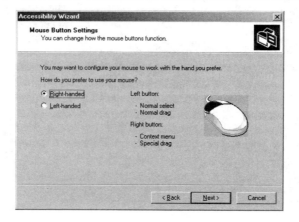

Fig. 21.35 Mouse Button Settings window.

To explore **Narrator**'s functionality, we explain how to use the program in conjunction with several Windows applications. Click the **Start** button and select **Programs**, followed by **Accessories**, **Accessibility** and **Narrator**. Once **Narrator** is open, it describes the current foreground window. It then reads the text inside the window aloud to the user. When the user clicks **OK**, the dialog in Fig. 21.39 displays.

Fig. 21.36 Mouse Speed dialog.

Fig. 21.37 Set Automatic Timeouts dialog.

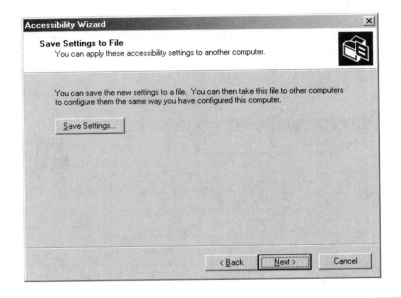

Fig. 21.38 Saving new accessibility settings.

Fig. 21.39 Narrator window.

Checking the first option instructs **Narrator** to describe menus and new windows when they are opened. The second option instructs **Narrator** to speak the characters that users type as they type them. The third option moves the mouse cursor to the region currently being read by **Narrator**. Clicking the **Voice...** button enables the user to change the pitch, volume and speed of the narrator voice (Fig. 21.40).

Now, we demonstrate **Narrator** in various applications. When **Narrator** is running, open **Notepad** and click the **File** menu. **Narrator** announces the opening of the program and begins to describe the items in the **File** menu. As a user scrolls down the list, **Narrator** reads the item to which the mouse currently is pointing. Type some text and press *Ctrl-Shift-Enter* to hear **Narrator** read it (Fig. 21.41). If the **Read typed characters** option is checked, **Narrator** reads each character as it is typed. Users also can employ the keyboard's direction arrows to make **Narrator** read. The up and down arrows cause **Narrator** to speak the lines adjacent to the current mouse position, and the left and right arrows cause **Narrator** to speak the characters adjacent to the current mouse position.

Fig. 21.40 Voice-settings window.

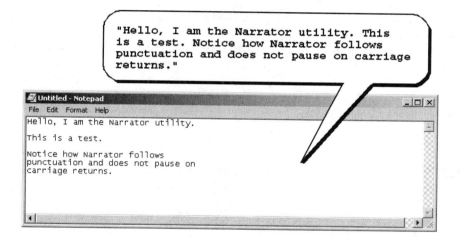

Fig. 21.41 Narrator reading **Notepad** text.

21.15.5 Microsoft On-Screen Keyboard

Some computer users lack the ability to use a keyboard, but are able to use a pointing device, such as a mouse. For these users, the *On-Screen Keyboard* is helpful. To access
the On-Screen Keyboard, click the **Start** button and select **Programs,** followed by **Accessories, Accessibility** and **On-Screen Keyboard.** Figure 21.42 depicts the layout
of the Microsoft On-Screen Keyboard.

Users who have difficulty using the On-Screen Keyboard can purchase more sophisticated products, such as *Clicker 4*™ by *Inclusive Technology.* Clicker 4 is an aid designed
for people who cannot use a keyboard effectively. Its best feature is that it can be customized. Keys can have letters, numbers, entire words or even pictures on them. For more
information regarding Clicker 4, visit **www.inclusive.co.uk/catalog/
clicker.shtml**.

Fig. 21.42 Microsoft **On-Screen Keyboard**.

21.15.6 Accessibility Features in Microsoft Internet Explorer 6.0

Internet Explorer 6.0 offers a variety of options that can improve usability. To access IE6.0's accessibility features, launch the program, click the **Tools** menu and select **Internet Options....** Then, from the **Internet Options** menu, press the button labeled **Accessibility...** to open the accessibility options (Fig. 21.43).

The accessibility options in IE6.0 are designed to improve the Web browsing experiences of users with disabilities. Users are able to ignore Web colors, Web fonts and font-size tags. This eliminates accessibility problems arising from poor Web-page design and allows users to customize their Web browsing. Users can even specify a *style sheet,* which formats every Web site that users visit according to their personal preferences.

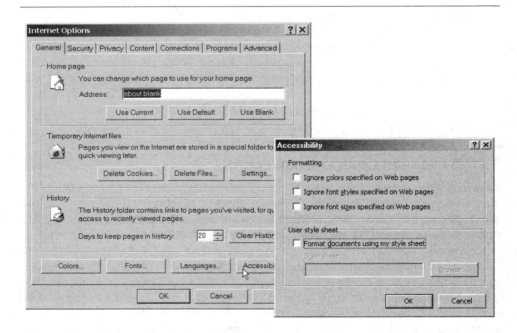

Fig. 21.43 Microsoft Internet Explorer 6.0's accessibility options.

In the **Internet Options** dialog, click the **Advanced** tab. This opens the dialog depicted in Fig. 21.44. The first available option is labeled **Always expand ALT text for images**. By default, IE6.0 hides some of the `<alt>` text if the size of the text exceeds that of the image it describes. This option forces IE6.0 to show all the text. The second option reads: **Move system caret with focus/selection changes**. This option is intended to make screen reading more effective. Some screen readers use the *system caret* (the blinking vertical bar associated with editing text) to determine what to read. If this option is not activated, screen readers might not read Web pages correctly.

Web designers often forget to take accessibility into account when creating Web sites, and, in attempts to provide large amounts of content, they use fonts that are too small. Many user agents have addressed this problem by allowing the user to adjust the text size. Click the **View** menu and select **Text Size** to change the font size in pages rendered by IE6.0. By default, the text size is set to **Medium**.

In this chapter, we presented a wide variety of technologies that help people with various disabilities use computers and the Internet. We hope that all our readers will join us in emphasizing the importance of these capabilities in their schools and workplaces.

21.16 Summary

In 1997, the World Wide Web Consortium (W3C) launched the Web Accessibility Initiative (WAI). The WAI is an attempt to make the Web more accessible; its mission is described at **www.w3.org/WAI**. One important WAI requirement is to ensure that every image, movie and sound on a Web site is accompanied by a description that clearly defines the item's purpose; the description is called an `<alt>` tag.

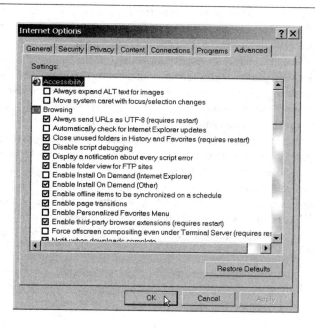

Fig. 21.44 Advanced accessibility settings in Microsoft Internet Explorer 6.0.

Accessibility refers to the level of usability of an application or Web site for people with disabilities. Total accessibility is difficult to achieve, because there are many different disabilities, languages used, and hardware and software inconsistencies.

Specialized user agents, such as screen readers (programs that allow users to hear what is being displayed on their screen) and braille displays (devices that receive data from screen-reading software and output the data as braille), allow people with visual impairments to access text-based information that normally is displayed on the screen.

Web pages with large amounts of multimedia content are difficult for user agents to interpret unless they are designed properly. Images, movies and most non-XHTML objects cannot be read by screen readers.

When creating a Web page for the general public, it is important to consider the reading level at which it is written. Web site designers can make their sites more readable through the use of shorter words; some users may have difficulty understanding slang and other nontraditional language.

Web designers often use frames to display more than one XHTML file at a time. Unfortunately, frames often lack proper descriptions, which prevents users with text-based browsers and users with visual impairments from navigating the Web site.

VoiceXML, a speech recognition and synthesis technology, has tremendous implications for people with visual impairments and for illiterate people. It reads Web pages to users and "understands" words spoken into a microphone.

CallXML, a language created and supported by Voxeo, creates phone-to-Web applications. These applications tailor themselves to the user's input.

Braille keyboards are similar to standard keyboards, except that, in addition to having each key labeled with the letter it represents, braille keyboards have the equivalent braille symbol printed on the key. Most often, braille keyboards are combined with a speech synthesizer or a braille display, so that users are able to interact with the computer to verify that their typing is correct.

People with visual impairments are not the only beneficiaries of the effort being made to improve markup languages. Individuals with hearing impairments also have a great number of tools to help them interpret auditory information delivered over the Web.

Open-source software for people with visual impairments already exists and is often superior to most of its proprietary, closed-source counterparts.

People with hearing impairments will soon benefit from Synchronized Multimedia Integration Language (SMIL). This markup language is designed to add extra tracks—layers of content found within a single audio or video file. The additional tracks can contain such data as closed captioning.

All of the accessibility options provided by Windows 2000 are available through the **Accessibility Wizard**. The **Accessibility Wizard** guides users step by step through all of the Windows accessibility features and configures their computer according to the chosen specifications.

21.17 Internet and Web Resources

There are many accessibility resources available on the Internet and World Wide Web; this section lists a variety of these resources.

General Information, Guidelines and Definitions

www.w3.org/WAI

The World Wide Web Consortium's *Web Accessibility Initiative (WAI)* site promotes the design of universally accessible Web sites. This site contains the current guidelines and forthcoming standards for Web accessibility.

www.w3.org/TR/xhtml1

The *XHTML 1.0 Recommendation* contains XHTML 1.0 general information, compatibility issues, document type definition information, definitions, terminology and much more.

www.abledata.com/text2/icg_hear.htm

This page contains a consumer guide that discusses technologies designed for people with hearing impairments.

www.washington.edu/doit

The University of Washington's DO-IT (Disabilities, Opportunities, Internetworking and Technology) site provides information and Web-development resources for the creation of universally accessible Web sites.

www.webable.com

The *WebABLE* site contains links to many disability-related Internet resources; the site is geared towards those developing technologies for people with disabilities.

www.webaim.org

The *WebAIM* site provides a number of tutorials, articles, simulations and other useful resources that demonstrate how to design accessible Web sites. The site provides a screen-reader simulation.

deafness.about.com/health/deafness/msubvib.htm

This site provides information on vibrotactile devices, which allow individuals with hearing impairments to experience audio in the form of vibrations.

Developing Accessible Applications with Existing Technologies

wdvl.com/Authoring/Languages/XML/XHTML

The Web Developers Virtual Library provides an introduction to XHTML. This site also contains articles, examples and links to other technologies.

www.w3.org/TR/1999/xhtml-modularization-19990406/DTD/doc

The XHTML 1.0 DTD documentation site provides links to DTD documentation for the strict, transitional and frameset document type definitions.

www.webreference.com/xml/reference/xhtml.html

This Web page contains a list of the frequently used XHTML tags, such as header tags, table tags, frame tags and form tags. It also provides a description of each tag.

www.w3.org/TR/REC-CSS2/aural.html

This site discusses Aural Style Sheets, outlining the purpose and uses of this new technology.

www.trill-home.com/lynx/public_lynx.html

This site allows users to browse the Web with a Lynx browser. Users can view how Web pages appear to users who are not using the most current technologies.

java.sun.com/products/java-media/speech/forDevelopers/JSML

This site outlines the specifications for JSML, Sun Microsystem's Java Speech Markup Language. This language, like VoiceXML, helps improve accessibility for people with visual impairments.

ocfo.ed.gov/coninfo/clibrary/software.htm
This is the U.S. Department of Education's Web site that outlines software accessibility requirements. The site helps developers produce accessible products.

www.speech.cs.cmu.edu/comp.speech/SpeechLinks.html
The *Speech Technology Hyperlinks* page has over 500 links to sites related to computer-based speech and speech-recognition tools.

www.islandnet.com/accessibility.html
This page provides a list of tips for creating accessible Web pages.

www.chantinc.com/technology
This page is the *Chant* Web site, which discusses speech technology and how it works. Chant also provides speech–synthesis and speech-recognition software.

www.searchWebServices.com
This site provides definitions and information about several topics, including CallXML. Its thorough definition of CallXML differentiates CallXML from VoiceXML, another technology developed by Voxeo. The site also contains links to other published articles that discuss CallXML.

www.oasis-open.org/cover/callxmlv2.html
This site provides a comprehensive list of the CallXML tags, complete with a description of each tag. The site also provides short examples on how to apply the tags in various applications.

www.freedomscientific.com
Henter-Joyce is a division of Freedom Scientific that provides software for people with visual impairments. It is the homepage of JAWS (Job Access with Sound).

www-3.ibm.com/able/
This is the homepage of IBM's accessibility site. It provides information on IBM products and their accessibility and discusses hardware, software and Web accessibility.

www.w3.org/TR/voice-tts-reqs
This page explains the speech-synthesis markup requirements for voice markup languages.

www.cast.org
CAST (Center for Applied Special Technology) offers software, including a valuable accessibility checker, that can help individuals with disabilities use computers. The accessibility checker is a Web-based program that validates the accessibility of Web sites.

www.cs.cornell.edu/home/raman/emacspeak/emacspeak.html
The site for Emacspeak, a screen interface that improves the quality of Internet access for individuals with visual disabilities.

Information on Disabilities

deafness.about.com/health/deafness/msubmenu6.htm
This is the home page of **deafness.about.com**. It provides a wealth of information on the history of hearing loss, the current state of medical developments and other resources related to these topics.

www.trainingpost.org/3-2-inst.htm
This site presents a tutorial on the Gunning Fog Index. The Gunning Fog Index is a method of grading text according to its readability.

laurence.canlearn.ca/English/learn/accessibility2001/neads/index.shtml
INDIE stands for "Integrated Network of Disability Information and Education." This site is home to a search engine that helps users find information on disabilities.

22

Mobile Internet Toolkit

Objectives

- To become familiar with the Mobile Internet Toolkit (MIT).
- To use ASP .NET and C# to create mobile Web content.
- To use Mobile Web controls.
- To create code-behind files.
- To create scripts for mobile Web Forms.
- To use style sheets and templates with a Web Form.
- To access Web services from mobile applications.

It was ordained at the beginning of the world that certain signs should prefigure certain events.
Marcus Tullius Cicero

Oh, never mind the fashion. When one has a style of one's own, it is always twenty times better.
Margaret Oliphant

Outline

22.1   Introduction
22.2   Mobile Internet Toolkit Client Devices
22.3   Introduction to the Mobile Internet Toolkit and Mobile Web Forms
22.4   Advanced Mobile Web Forms Controls
22.5   Example: Deitel Wireless Portal
22.6   Device-Independent Web Design Using Style Sheets and
        Templates
22.7   Consuming a Web Service from a Mobile Application
22.8   Summary
22.9   Internet and World Wide Web Resources

22.1 Introduction

Wireless technologies bring the power of communications and the Internet to users worldwide. Wireless communications affect many aspects of society, including business management and operations, employee productivity, consumer purchasing behavior, marketing strategies and personal communications. In addition to Web applications and Windows applications, programmers must develop applications for wireless platforms.

In this chapter, we introduce the Microsoft® *Mobile Internet Toolkit (MIT)*,[1] which allows programmers to create mobile Web applications. The MIT extends Visual Studio .NET's functionality and uses the .NET Framework to create Web content for mobile devices using languages such as C# and Visual Basic .NET. In this chapter, we explore the MIT in depth as we create wireless applications using ASP .NET, XML and C#. We discuss handling user input, displaying images, accessing Web services, mobile Web design and how to make Web pages accessible to multiple devices with the MIT.

22.2 Mobile Internet Toolkit Client Devices

In 1997, the *Wireless Application Protocol (WAP)* was developed by dominant cell-phone manufacturers Nokia, Ericsson, Motorola and others to facilitate the introduction and standardization of wireless Internet access.[2] WAP is a set of communications protocols that are designed to enable wireless devices to access the Internet.

The *Wireless Markup Language (WML)*, which is an XML vocabulary, is the markup language used to describe content for WAP devices. *Microbrowsers*, browsers designed with limited bandwidth and memory requirements, can access the Web via the wireless Internet. WAP supports WML to deliver the content to microbrowsers.

---

1. Setup instructions for the Mobile Internet Toolkit 1.0, Microsoft Mobile Explorer (MME) 3.0 and Pocket PC 2002 can be downloaded from the **Downloads/Resources** page at **www.deitel.com**.
2. T. Hughes, "The Web Unwired," *Global Technology Business* December 1999: 33.

Although WAP and WML have many proponents, they also have many opponents. WAP technology is viewed as a short-term solution for the delivery of wireless Internet access. WAP opponents cite various disadvantages that are associated with the protocol, including possible security breaches, limited bandwidth and unreliability.[3] Another disadvantage cited is that the WAP standard has been implemented only loosely for the various WAP microbrowsers on the market. This means that some microbrowsers only support a subset of WML tags and thus have limited functionality.

 Portability Tip 22.1

Different WAP microbrowsers can have inconsistent WML implementations. This makes it difficult to use WML uniformly across a wide variety of WAP microbrowsers.

The fast pace at which the wireless community is growing has led to the development of other standards, some of which will be discussed shortly. Multiple standards have created a significant challenge for wireless developers. In a world of clients attempting to communicate over disparate technologies, it is a difficult task to build one application that will run correctly on a variety of wireless devices. This chapter introduces the MIT, which helps developers handle disparate mobile devices uniformly. Before we begin our discussion of the MIT's features, let us briefly overview the types of devices that can be targeted by the MIT.

The MIT supports three main clients—*HTML devices*, *WAP devices* and *iMode devices*. HTML devices are those that display HTML markup, such as Internet Explorer (IE), Pocket PC and Palm-based browsers. WAP devices are those that support WAP microbrowsers, which render WML markup. WAP devices can include mobile phones equipped with Nokia or Openwave WAP microbrowsers.

The relationship between WAP browsers and WML is similar to that of IE and HTML. WML's design fits the needs of small devices with low memory capabilities and limited display screens.

Finally, iMode devices are those that support *cHTML (compact HyperText Markup Language) content*. cHTML conforms to a subset of the HTML 2.0 specification. Unlike HTML, cHTML does not support image maps, tables, frames or JPEG images. cHTML pages cannot have a background color or image. Style sheets (e.g., CSS) and scripts (e.g., JavaScript) cannot be used with cHTML.

When learning about mobile communications, it is vital to understand that the process by which mobile devices connect to and interact with the Internet is different for each application type. For example, WAP applications communicate with a WAP gateway using WAP, and the WAP gateway communicates with a Web server via HTTP; whereas iMode applications communicate with a Web server directly via HTTP. The MIT eliminates the burden of understanding the various protocols and languages. Rather than creating WML markup for WAP devices, cHTML markup for iMode devices and HTML markup for HTML devices, the developer can now create one application that produces the proper markup needed for a number of different devices. For a list of mobile devices supported by the MIT, visit **msdn.microsoft.com/vstudio/device/ mitdevices.asp**.

---

3. Further information about WAP can be found at the WAP Forum Web site, **www.wapforum.org**.

22.3 Introduction to the Mobile Internet Toolkit and Mobile Web Forms

The MIT extends ASP .NET (Chapter 17) functionality to include mobile clients. When an ASPX page is requested by the *incoming device* (i.e., the mobile device), the MIT generates HTML for IE 6.0 and Pocket IE, cHTML for iMode clients, and WML for WAP clients.

Creating a mobile Web application in Visual Studio .NET generates an ASPX page (with the `.aspx` file extension), which contains the markup for the page's user interface. The business logic (e.g., event handlers for buttons) for the application can be embedded in the ASPX file as a script or in a code-behind file. The business logic is executed on the Web server. In this chapter, we use both methods of code containment.

 Software Engineering Observation 22.1

Most developers use a code-behind file, especially when an application contains significant amounts of code. Using a code-behind file makes programs easier to maintain, debug and modify because the interface is separated from the implementation.

In this section, we present two mobile Web applications and guide the reader through the steps necessary to create the applications. Figure 22.1 displays the **Welcome.aspx** Web page. The markup in this example is generated by Visual Studio .NET when the user interface is created in design view. Later, we manipulate this markup to include C# code and device-specific functionality. Lines 6–7 use the **Page** directive to set the language (via the **Language** attribute) in which the code-behind file is written to C# and set the code-behind file (**CodeBehind** attribute) to **Welcome.aspx.cs**. We discuss this code-behind file (Fig. 22.2) momentarily. Attribute **Inherits** indicates the class from which this page inherits. In this example, we are inheriting from the class **Welcome.Welcome-Page**, defined in the code-behind file.

```
1   <%-- Fig. 22.1: Welcome.aspx --%>
2   <%-- A simple Web Form.        --%>
3
4   <%-- directive specifies file where code is stored and --%>
5   <%-- programming language in which the code is written --%>
6   <%@ Page language="c#" Codebehind="Welcome.aspx.cs"
7       Inherits="Welcome.WelcomePage" AutoEventWireup="false" %>
8
9   <%@ Register TagPrefix="mobile"
10      Namespace="System.Web.UI.MobileControls"
11      Assembly="System.Web.Mobile, Version=1.0.3300.0,
Culture=neutral, PublicKeyToken=b03f5f7f11d50a3a" %>
12
13  <meta name="GENERATOR" content="Microsoft Visual Studio 7.0">
14  <meta name="CODE_LANGUAGE" content="C#">
15  <meta name="vs_targetSchema"
16      content="http://schemas.microsoft.com/Mobile/Page">
17
18  <body Xmlns:mobile="http://schemas.microsoft.com/Mobile/WebForm">
19
20      <mobile:Form id="startForm" runat="server">
21
```

Fig. 22.1   Multiple forms in a mobile Web Form page. (Part 1 of 2.)

```
22          <mobile:Label id="startLabel" runat="server">
23             Click Start!
24          </mobile:Label>
25
26          <%-- Command control --%>
27          <%-- invokes method startCommand_Click when clicked --%>
28          <mobile:Command id="startCommand" runat="server">
29             Start
30          </mobile:Command>
31       </mobile:Form>
32
33       <%-- Form resultForm --%>
34       <%-- when activated, method resultForm_Activate is called --%>
35       <mobile:Form id="resultForm" runat="server">
36          <mobile:Label id="resultLabel" runat="server"></mobile:Label>
37       </mobile:Form>
38
39    </body>
```

Fig. 22.1   Multiple forms in a mobile Web Form page. (Part 2 of 2.)

The **Register** directive (lines 9–11) specifies the namespace and assembly to which this mobile Web Form's controls belong and the *tag prefix*, which qualifies the Mobile control tag names. The tag prefix is assigned to **Register's** **TagPrefix** attribute. The default value for this attribute is **mobile**. The **Namespace** attribute's value (**System.Web.UI.MobileControls**) indicates that any control with the prefix **mobile** is defined in the namespace **System.Web.UI.MobileControls**. The **Assembly** attribute's value (**System.Web.Mobile**) specifies the library file where the mobile FCL classes are located.

Mobile Web Form controls (or *mobile controls*) are the objects used to create mobile applications. Some basic mobile controls include labels and buttons. Every mobile control's start tag has its **runat** attribute set to **"server"** to indicate that the control must be executed on the server. Lines 20–31 define the first mobile control, a **Form**. The **id** attribute's value (line 20) provides a programmatic identifier for the control. In this case, we chose the identifier **startForm**, because this is the initial form that is displayed to mobile clients. Programmers can assign almost any value to the **id** attribute via the **(ID)** property, provided that it is a valid C# identifier. Programmers can access and manipulate this control in their code-behind files using the identifier **startForm**.

This form contains a **Label** control and a **Command** control. Like Web Form **Label** controls, mobile **Label** controls display textual information. Setting the **Label**'s **Text** property to **Click Start!** and its **(ID)** property to **startLabel** in design view creates a **Label** control in the markup, such as

```
<mobile:Label id="startLabel" runat="server">
   Click Start!
</mobile:Label>
```

Look-and-Feel Observation 22.1

*In design view, **Command** controls look like buttons. However, some microbrowsers, such as the Openwave™ 5.0 browser, render **Command** controls as hyperlinks.*

When users click the **Command** control, method **startCommand_Click** is called to handle the **Click** event. This method is defined in the code-behind file (discussed in Fig. 22.2). Notice that, in the output of Fig. 22.2, the **Command** control is rendered below the **Label** control. By default, controls are placed one below the other on the form in design view. We discuss how to change the layout of the form's controls later in the chapter. Screen size is limited on most mobile devices; therefore, content usually is divided into multiple forms, which reduces the user's need to scroll through the page. On lines 35–37 of Fig. 22.1, the second form is provided, which is the equivalent of another Web page. When this form becomes *active* (i.e., is being displayed), its code-behind file's **resultForm_Activate** method is called to handle the ***Activate*** event. [*Note*: The form being displayed is called the *active form*. Only one form can be active at a time.]

Common Programming Error 22.1

Web Form pages must contain a minimum of one form. A page with no forms results in a compilation error.

In Fig. 22.2, we present the code-behind file **Welcome.aspx.cs** for the ASPX file presented in Fig. 22.1. On line 18, we add a reference to namespace ***System.Web.UI.MobileControls*** that includes base class ***MobilePage***. This class is required for mobile Web Forms. Class **WelcomePage** begins on line 24 and is the base class specified on line 7 in Fig. 22.1. On lines 46–52, we define method **startCommand_Click**, which handles the **Click** event raised when the user presses the **Start** button. Line 50 sets **resultForm** as the active form by assigning it to property **ActiveForm**. Forms must be activated in this manner because ASPX files can contain multiple forms, but only one form can be active at a time. Method **resultForm_Activate** (lines 55–62) sets **resultLabel**'s **Text** property to a welcome message (lines 59–60). In this example, the text displayed by **resultLabel** is **"Welcome to the Microsoft Mobile Internet Toolkit!"**.

The *Microsoft Mobile Explorer* (MME) is a phone emulator that includes two *soft keys* (labeled in Fig. 22.2). These keys allow users to interact with the application. For example, the left MME output window in Fig. 22.2 shows the **Start** button highlighted and the left soft key displaying **OK**. Pressing the left soft key selects (i.e., presses) the **Start** button. The *scroll keys* allow users to scroll through Web pages.

```
1   // Fig. 22.2: Welcome.aspx.cs
2   // Code-behind file for Welcome.aspx.
3
4   using System;
5   using System.Collections;
6   using System.ComponentModel;
7   using System.Data;
8   using System.Drawing;
9
10  // contains classes that manage client requests and
11  // server responses
12  using System.Web;
13  using System.Web.Mobile;
14  using System.Web.SessionState;
```

Fig. 22.2   Code-behind file for the mobile application. (Part 1 of 3.)

```
15
16   // definitions for graphical controls used in Web Forms
17   using System.Web.UI;
18   using System.Web.UI.MobileControls;
19   using System.Web.UI.WebControls;
20   using System.Web.UI.HtmlControls;
21
22   namespace Welcome
23   {
24      public class WelcomePage :
25         System.Web.UI.MobileControls.MobilePage
26      {
27         // forms
28         protected System.Web.UI.MobileControls.Form startForm;
29         protected System.Web.UI.MobileControls.Form resultForm;
30
31         // labels
32         protected System.Web.UI.MobileControls.Label startLabel;
33         protected System.Web.UI.MobileControls.Label resultLabel;
34
35         // button
36         protected System.Web.UI.MobileControls.Command startCommand;
37
38         private void Page_Load( object sender, System.EventArgs e )
39         {
40            // Put user code to initialize the page here
41         }
42
43         // Visual Studio .NET generated code
44
45         // sets resultForm as active form when Start is clicked
46         private void startCommand_Click(
47            object sender, System.EventArgs e )
48         {
49            // change current form to resultForm
50            ActiveForm = resultForm;
51
52         } // end startCommand_Click
53
54         // displays text when resultForm becomes active
55         private void resultForm_Activate(
56            object sender, System.EventArgs e )
57         {
58            // set value to be displayed
59            resultLabel.Text =
60               "Welcome to the Microsoft Mobile Internet Toolkit!";
61
62         } // end resultForm_Activate
63
64      } // end class WelcomePage
65
66   } // end namespace Welcome
```

Fig. 22.2 Code-behind file for the mobile application. (Part 2 of 3.)

Fig. 22.2   Code-behind file for the mobile application. (Part 3 of 3.)

Now that we have presented the ASPX file and the code-behind file,[4] we outline the process by which we created this application. To create the application, perform the following steps:[5]

1. *Create the project.* Open Visual Studio .NET, and select **File > New > Project...** to display the **New Project** dialog (Fig. 22.3). In this dialog, select **Visual C#**

---

4. To run the chapter examples provided at **www.deitel.com**, you must create a virtual directory in IIS. For instructions on how to create a virtual directory, visit the **Downloads/Resources** link at **www.deitel.com**.

5. IIS must be running for this project to be created successfully. IIS can be started by executing **inetmgr.exe**, right-clicking **Default Web Site** and selecting **Start**. You might need to expand the node representing your computer to display the **Default Web Site**.

Projects in the left pane and then **Mobile Web Application** in the right pane.[6] Notice that the field for the project name is disabled (i.e., grayed out). Rather than using this field, we specify the name and location of the project in the **Location** field. We want our project to be located in `http://localhost`, which is the URL for IIS' root directory (typically `C:\InetPub\wwwroot`). The name *localhost* indicates that the client and server reside on the same machine. If the Web server were located on a different machine, `localhost` would be replaced with the appropriate IP address or hostname. By default, Visual Studio .NET assigns the project name **MobileWebApplication1**, which we changed to `Welcome`. Below the **Location** textbox, the text **Project will be created at http://localhost/Welcome.** appears. This indicates that the project's folder is located in the root directory on the Web server. Clicking **OK** creates the project and creates a virtual directory, which is linked to the project folder. The **Create New Web** dialog is displayed next, while Visual Studio .NET is creating the Web site on the server (Fig. 22.4).

Fig. 22.3   Creating a **Mobile Web Application** in Visual Studio .NET.

Fig. 22.4   Visual Studio .NET creating and linking a virtual directory for the **Welcome** project folder.

6. The **Mobile Web Application** project will not appear in the **New Project** dialog until after the MIT has been installed.

3. *Examine the newly created project.* The next several figures describe the new project's content; we begin with the **Solution Explorer** shown in Fig. 22.5. Visual Studio .NET generates several files when a new **Mobile Web Application** project is created. **MobileWebForm1.aspx** is the mobile Web Form, which includes a code-behind file. To view the ASPX file's code-behind file, right click the ASPX file, and select **View Code**. Alternatively, the programmer can click the icon to display all files, then expand the node for the ASPX page as shown in Fig. 22.5.

Figure 22.6 shows the *Mobile Web Form Designer* for ASPX page **MobileWebForm1.aspx** in *design mode.* It consists of a form on which programmers drag and drop controls, such as buttons and labels, from the **Toolbox**.

Fig. 22.5 **Solution Explorer** window for project **Welcome**.

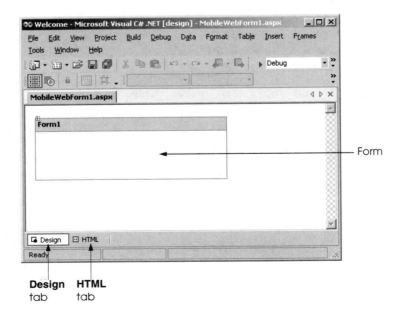

Fig. 22.6 Design mode of the Mobile Web Form Designer.

Figure 22.7 shows the Mobile Web Form Designer in *HTML mode*, which allows the programmer to view the markup that represents the user interface shown in design mode. A developer can switch to HTML mode by clicking the **HTML** *tab* in the lower-left corner of the Mobile Web Form Designer. Similarly, clicking the **Design** tab (to the left of the **HTML** tab) returns the Mobile Web Form Designer to design mode.

The next figure (Fig. 22.8) displays **MobileWebForm1.aspx.cs**—the code-behind file for **MobileWebForm1.aspx**. Recall that Visual Studio .NET generates this code-behind file when the project is created; we have reformatted the file's contents for presentation purposes.

4. *Rename the ASPX file.* We have displayed the contents of the default ASPX and code-behind files. We now rename these files. Right click the ASPX file in the **Solution Explorer**, and select **Rename**. Enter the new file name, and press *Enter*. This updates the name of both the ASPX file and the code-behind file. In this example, we use the name **Welcome.aspx**.

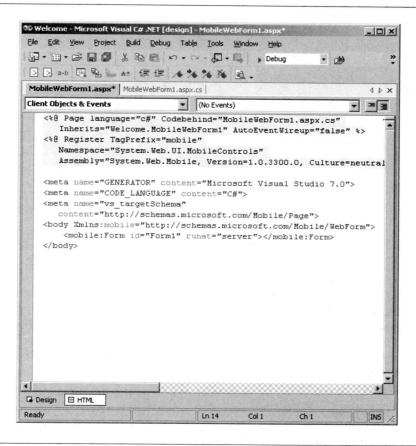

Fig. 22.7   HTML mode of Mobile Web Form Designer.

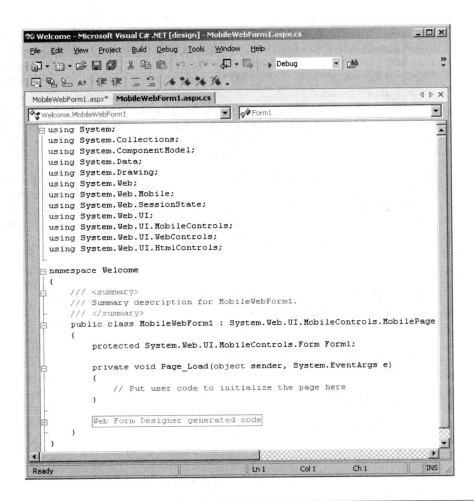

Fig. 22.8   Code-behind file for `MobileWebForm1.aspx` generated by Visual Studio .NET.

5. *Design the page.* The process of designing a mobile Web Form is the same as designing a Web Form. To add mobile controls to the page, drag and drop them from the **Toolbox** onto the mobile Web Form. Like the mobile Web Form itself, each control is an object that has properties, methods and events. Programmers can set these properties and events using the **Properties** window. To view the properties of the mobile Web Form, select **Document** from the drop-down list in the **Properties** window.

Figure 22.9 shows the **Mobile Web Forms** controls listed in the **Toolbox**. The left figure displays the beginning of the Mobile Web controls list, and the right figure displays the remaining Mobile Web controls. Many of these controls are similar to the Windows controls and Web controls presented earlier in the book.

Fig. 22.9   Mobile Web Forms group in the **Toolbox**.

We set the form's **(ID)** property to **startForm**. We then add a **Label** control and a **Command** control to the form. We set the **Label**'s **(ID)** property to **startLabel** and its **Text** property to **Click Start!**. Notice that the **Command** control appears below the **Label** control. In the Mobile Web Form Designer, each control is placed one after the other, vertically. Changing how the form is rendered by a client can be altered using properties such as **BreakAfter** (discussed momentarily). Changing the value of a property in the designer changes that control's corresponding markup in the ASPX document.

We now add the second form. We set its **(ID)** property to **resultForm** and add a **Label** to it. The **Label**'s **(ID)** property is set to **resultLabel**. We delete the default value (**Label**) for **resultLabel**'s **Text** property in design view, because the **Text** property's value is set programmatically in the code-behind file. When a **Label**'s **Text** property does not contain text, the **Label**'s name is displayed in square brackets in the Mobile Web Form Designer. This text is not displayed at run time. The resulting ASPX page is shown in Fig. 22.10.

6. *Add page logic.* Once the user interface has been designed, C# code can be added to the code-behind file. In this example, lines 46–62 of Fig. 22.2 are added to the code-behind file. When the command button in **startForm** is clicked, method **startCommand_Click** (lines 46–52) is called to handle the **Click** event. The statement within this method sets **resultForm** as the active form, which results in method **resultForm_Activate** (lines 55–62) being called. This method sets and displays the contents of **resultLabel**.

7. *Run the program.*[7] Select **Build > Build Solution** to build the solution. Next, select **File > Browse With....** From the list of browsers on the left side of the dialog, select *Microsoft Mobile Explorer Emulator*, and click **Browse**. The

---

7. Before performing this step, the MME must be installed. This software can be downloaded at **msdn.microsoft.com/downloads/default.asp?url=/downloads/ sample.asp?url=/msdn-files/027/001/706/msdncompositedoc.xml**.

MME window opens and loads the Web page (the ASPX file). Notice that the URL is **http://localhost/Welcome/Welcome.aspx** (Fig. 22.2), indicating that our ASPX file is located within the directory **Welcome**.

After the mobile Web Form is created, the programmer can view it by opening the MME outside Visual Studio .NET and typing the Web page's URL in the emulator's combo box. When testing an ASP .NET application on the same computer, type **http://localhost/***ProjectFolder***/***PageName***.aspx**, where *ProjectFolder* is the folder in which the page resides (usually the name of the project) and *PageName* is the name of the ASP .NET page.

In the next example (Fig. 22.11), we create a tip calculator, which calculates a tip amount based on a dollar amount and a tip percentage. We also demonstrate how to embed a C# script in an ASPX file. The script begins with a **<script>** tag on line 18, wherein we specify the language (via the **Language** attribute) that is used in the script. On lines 21–38, we define method **calculateCommand_Click**, which calculates the tip amount based on the amount and tip percentage information entered by the user. This method is called when the user clicks the **Calculate Tip** button. Users enter information into two **TextBox** controls (lines 61–62 and 75–76). [Note: For simplicity, we do not check the user input for numeric values.]

Fig. 22.10 **Welcome.aspx** after adding two **Label**s and setting their properties.

Below each **TextBox** control, we included a *validation control*. Validation controls examine user input. For example, if users enter incorrect information or omit required information, most applications cannot proceed because the information submitted is not in the proper format or is missing. In this example, we use the ***RequiredFieldVali-dator*** control, which ensures that another control contains data when users attempt to submit the page. In this example, the two **TextBox**es are required to have data because both the tip percentage and the total amount are required to perform the calculation. The first of these validation controls (**tipValidator**) is defined on lines 64–68. The ***Con-trolToValidate*** attribute (line 65) specifies which control is validated. In this case, our validator is set to validate the **TextBox** named **tipTextBox**. If this **TextBox** is empty when the user clicks **Calculate Tip**, the **RequiredFieldValidator** displays the error message specified in its **Text** property (in this case, **Please enter the tip percentage**). The second validator (lines 78–82) behaves in a similar manner, but validates **totalTextBox**. Calling method **calculateCommand_Click** tests the condition **Page.IsValid** on line 24. This condition determines whether the page is *valid* (i.e., errors were not raised by either validator). If the page is valid, the remainder of **calculateCommand_Click** will execute. If the page is not valid (i.e., one or both of the **TextBox**es are empty), then the page reloads and displays one or more error messages.

```
1    <%-- Fig. 22.11: TipCalculator.aspx   --%>
2    <%-- A Web Form that calculates tips. --%>
3
4    <%@ Page language="c#" Codebehind="TipCalculator.aspx.cs"
5        Inherits="TipCalculator.TipCalultor"
6        AutoEventWireup="false" %>
7
8    <%@ Register TagPrefix="mobile"
9        Namespace="System.Web.UI.MobileControls"
10       Assembly="System.Web.Mobile, Version=1.0.3300.0,
Culture=neutral, PublicKeyToken=b03f5f7f11d50a3a" %>
11
12   <meta name="GENERATOR" content="Microsoft Visual Studio 7.0">
13   <meta name="CODE_LANGUAGE" content="C#">
14   <meta name="vs_targetSchema"
15      content="http://schemas.microsoft.com/Mobile/Page">
16
17   <%-- embedded script containing C# code --%>
18   <script runat="server" language="C#">
19
20       // calculate tip
21       protected void calculateCommand_Click(
22          object sender, System.EventArgs e )
23       {
24          if ( Page.IsValid )
25          {
26             decimal tip;
27             string dollarAmount;
28
```

Fig. 22.11 Web Form with embedded C# code. (Part 1 of 4.) (Image courtesy Openwave Systems, Inc.)

```
29              tip = Decimal.Parse( totalTextBox.Text ) *
30                 Decimal.Parse( tipTextBox.Text ) /
31                 ( decimal ) 100;
32
33              // change tip to dollar value
34              dollarAmount = String.Format( "{0:C}", tip );
35              resultLabel.Text = "Tip Amount: " + dollarAmount;
36           }
37
38        } // end calculateCommand_Click
39
40        // clear form
41        protected void clearCommand_Click(
42           object sender, System.EventArgs e )
43        {
44           tipTextBox.Text = "";
45           totalTextBox.Text = "";
46           resultLabel.Text = "";
47
48        } // end clearCommand_Click
49
50     </script>
51
52     <body Xmlns:mobile="http://schemas.microsoft.com/Mobile/WebForm">
53
54        <mobile:Form id="tipCalculatorForm" runat="server">
55
56           <mobile:Label id="instructionLabel1" runat="server"
57              BreakAfter="False">
58              Enter Tip Percentage:
59           </mobile:Label>
60
61           <mobile:TextBox id="tipTextBox" runat="server">
62           </mobile:TextBox>
63
64           <mobile:RequiredFieldValidator id="tipValidator"
65              runat="server" ControlToValidate="tipTextBox"
66              ErrorMessage="RequiredFieldValidator">
67              Please enter the tip percentage
68           </mobile:RequiredFieldValidator>
69
70           <mobile:Label id="instructionLabel2" runat="server"
71              BreakAfter="False">
72              Enter Total Amount:
73           </mobile:Label>
74
75           <mobile:TextBox id="totalTextBox" runat="server">
76           </mobile:TextBox>
77
78           <mobile:RequiredFieldValidator id="totalValidator"
79              runat="server" ControlToValidate="totalTextBox"
80              ErrorMessage="RequiredFieldValidator">
```

Fig. 22.11 Web Form with embedded C# code. (Part 2 of 4.) (Image courtesy Openwave Systems, Inc.)

```
81                Please enter the total amount
82          </mobile:RequiredFieldValidator>
83
84          <mobile:Label id="resultLabel" runat="server">
85          </mobile:Label>
86
87          <mobile:Command id="calculateCommand"
88             OnClick="calculateCommand_Click" runat="server"
89             BreakAfter="False">
90             Calculate Tip
91          </mobile:Command>
92
93          <mobile:Command id="clearCommand" runat="server"
94             OnClick="clearCommand_Click">
95             Clear
96          </mobile:Command>
97
98       </mobile:Form> <%-- end form tipCalculatorForm --%>
99
100  </body>
```

Fig. 22.11 Web Form with embedded C# code. (Part 3 of 4.) (Image courtesy Openwave Systems, Inc.)

Fig. 22.11 Web Form with embedded C# code. (Part 4 of 4.) (Image courtesy Openwave Systems, Inc.)

Once **calculateCommand_Click** calculates the tip amount and displays it, the user has the ability to enter new values. Notice, however, that there are some differences between the way this program renders in the IE browser and on the Openwave™ browser. In later examples, we demonstrate how to write programs that perform different actions, depending on the browser. For example, the **TextBox**es are displayed next to their respective labels in IE, but the Openwave™ browser displays them on separate lines. Controls can be placed on the same line by setting the control's *BreakAfter property* to **False**. The MIT determines if the control can fit on the same line, or if the control must be placed on the next line, by checking the device's screen size. Each device's screen size and other device-specific information, such as support for color graphics and the ability to initiate a phone call, are stored in the **machine.config** file. For example, Fig. 22.12 shows a section of the **machine.config** file that lists the features that MME supports. The markup in Fig. 22.12 indicates that the MME supports HTML markup (line 6) and GIF images (line 7). The **machine.config** file is located in the

C:\WINDOWS\Microsoft.NET\Framework\v1.0.3705\CONFIG

directory. [*Note*: The version number (i.e., **v1.0.3705**) is subject to change.]

```
1   <!-- HTML-oriented capabilities of the HTML MME browsers -->
2   <filter
3      match=".+"
4      with="${httpRequest}">
5      preferredRenderingType  = "html32"
6      preferredRenderingMime  = "text/html"
7      preferredImageMime = "image/gif"
8      supportsImageSubmit = "true"
9      supportsBold = "true"
10     supportsItalic = "true"
11     supportsFontSize = "true"
12     supportsFontName = "true"
13     supportsFontColor = "true"
14     supportsBodyColor = "true"
15     supportsDivAlign = "true"
16     supportsDivNoWrap = "false"
17  </filter>
```

Fig. 22.12 Section of **machine.config** file.

22.4 Advanced Mobile Web Forms Controls

In this section, we introduce a more sophisticated example that plays the popular game of chance called Craps. Craps is a casino game of chance using a pair of dice where a player wins, or loses, based on the roll of the dice. The basic rules of the game are provided as part of the example. Figures 22.13 and 22.14 display the ASPX page and code-behind file, respectively. The ASPX page (Fig. 22.13) contains two forms—one that displays the rules to the user (**rulesForm**) and one provides the game's user interface (**gameForm**). The instructions in **rulesForm** are displayed in a **Label** control.

```
1   <%-- Fig. 22.13: Craps.aspx              --%>
2   <%-- An interactive mobile craps game. --%>
3
4   <%@ Page language="c#" Codebehind="Craps.aspx.cs"
5       Inherits="Craps.CrapsGame" AutoEventWireup="false" %>
6
7   <%@ Register TagPrefix="mobile"
8       Namespace="System.Web.UI.MobileControls"
9       Assembly="System.Web.Mobile, Version=1.0.3300.0,
Culture=neutral, PublicKeyToken=b03f5f7f11d50a3a" %>
10
11  <meta content="Microsoft Visual Studio 7.0" name="GENERATOR">
12  <meta content="C#" name="CODE_LANGUAGE">
13  <meta content="http://schemas.microsoft.com/Mobile/Page"
14     name="vs_targetSchema">
15
16  <body Xmlns:mobile="http://schemas.microsoft.com/Mobile/WebForm">
17
18      <mobile:form id="rulesForm" runat="server">
19
```

Fig. 22.13 ASPX page for mobile Craps program. (Part 1 of 3.)

```
20          <%-- centered Label --%>
21          <mobile:Label id="titleLabel" runat="server"
22             Alignment="Center">
23             --Craps Rules--
24          </mobile:Label>
25
26          <%-- game rules for user --%>
27          <mobile:Label id="rulesLabel" runat="server">
28             A player rolls two dice. Each die has six faces.
29             These faces contain 1, 2, 3, 4, 5 and 6 spots.
30             After the dice have come to rest, the sum of the
31             spots on the two upward faces is calculated.
32             If the sum is 7 or 11 on the first throw,
33             the player wins. If the sum is 2 (snake eyes),
34             3 (trey) or 12 (boxcars) on the first throw
35             (called craps), the player loses
36             (i.e., the house wins). If the sum is 4, 5, 6, 8, 9
37             or 10 on the first throw, then that sum becomes the
38             player's 'point.' To win, you must continue rolling
39             the dice until you make your point. The player loses
40             by rolling a 7 before making the point.
41          </mobile:Label>
42
43          <mobile:Command id="newGameCommand" runat="server">
44             New Game
45          </mobile:Command>
46
47      </mobile:form> <%-- end rulesForm --%>
48
49      <mobile:Form id="gameForm" runat="server">
50
51          <%-- statusLabel displays 'point' or   --%>
52          <%-- message if user won or lost        --%>
53          <mobile:Label id="statusLabel" runat="server">
54          </mobile:Label>
55
56          <%-- Panel object groups a Label and two Images --%>
57          <mobile:Panel id="dicePanel" runat="server">
58             <mobile:Label id="rollValueLabel" runat="server">
59             </mobile:Label>
60
61             <mobile:Image id="firstImage" runat="server"
62                BreakAfter="False">
63             </mobile:Image>
64
65             <mobile:Image id="secondImage" runat="server">
66             </mobile:Image>
67          </mobile:Panel>
68
69          <mobile:Command id="playCommand" runat="server"
70             BreakAfter="False">
71             Play
72          </mobile:Command>
```

Fig. 22.13 ASPX page for mobile Craps program: (Part 2 of 3.)

```
73
74        <mobile:Command id="rollCommand" runat="server"
75           BreakAfter="False">
76           Roll Again
77        </mobile:Command>
78
79        <mobile:Command id="quitCommand" runat="server">
80           Quit
81        </mobile:Command>
82
83     </mobile:Form> <%-- end gameForm --%>
84
85  </body>
```

Fig. 22.13 ASPX page for mobile Craps program. (Part 3 of 3.)

The second form (**gameForm**) is activated when the user begins a new game. Form **gameForm**'s **statusLabel** (line 53) displays information about the current game's status. On lines 57–67, two new controls—*Panel* and *Image*—are introduced. The **Panel** control groups related controls. Setting the **Panel**'s **Visible** property to **false** causes each control on the **Panel** to be hidden. In this example, the **Panel** (**dice-Panel**) contains a **Label** (**rollValueLabel**) and two **Image** controls (**firstImage** and **secondImage**). **Label rollValueLabel** displays the result of the user's roll, and the two **Image** controls display the dice that correspond to the user's roll. Buttons are provided that allow the user to play, roll again or quit (lines 69–81).

Figure 22.14 shows the code-behind file (**Craps.aspx.cs**). This file defines several methods, including **newGameCommand_Click**, **gameForm_Activate**, **playCommand_Click**, **Roll_Click**, **quitCommand_Click** and **RollDice**. Clicking the **New Game** button on the rules page calls method **newGameCommand_Click** (lines 72–80), which sets form **gameForm** (line 75) as the active form and sets **dicePanel**'s **Visible** property (line 78) to **false**.

```
1   // Fig. 22.14: Craps.aspx.cs
2   // The code-behind file for a game of craps.
3
4   using System;
5   using System.Collections;
6   using System.ComponentModel;
7   using System.Data;
8   using System.Drawing;
9   using System.Web;
10  using System.Web.Mobile;
11  using System.Web.SessionState;
12  using System.Web.UI;
13  using System.Web.UI.MobileControls;
14  using System.Web.UI.WebControls;
15  using System.Web.UI.HtmlControls;
16
```

Fig. 22.14 Code-behind file for craps application. (Part 1 of 6.) (Image courtesy Openwave System, Inc.)

```
17   namespace Craps
18   {
19       /// <summary>
20       /// Summary description for CrapsGame.
21       /// </summary>
22       public class CrapsGame :
23           System.Web.UI.MobileControls.MobilePage
24       {
25           // first form
26           protected System.Web.UI.MobileControls.Form rulesForm;
27
28           // controls on rulesForm
29           protected System.Web.UI.MobileControls.Label titleLabel;
30           protected System.Web.UI.MobileControls.Label rulesLabel;
31           protected System.Web.UI.MobileControls.Command
32               newGameCommand;
33
34           // second form
35           protected System.Web.UI.MobileControls.Form gameForm;
36
37           // controls on gameForm
38           protected System.Web.UI.MobileControls.Label statusLabel;
39           protected System.Web.UI.MobileControls.Panel dicePanel;
40           protected System.Web.UI.MobileControls.Image firstImage;
41           protected System.Web.UI.MobileControls.Image secondImage;
42           protected System.Web.UI.MobileControls.Command playCommand;
43           protected System.Web.UI.MobileControls.Command rollCommand;
44           protected System.Web.UI.MobileControls.Command quitCommand;
45           protected System.Web.UI.MobileControls.Label
46               rollValueLabel;
47
48           private void Page_Load( object sender, System.EventArgs e )
49           {
50               // Put user code to initialize the page here
51           }
52
53           // Visual Studio .NET generated code
54
55           // special values
56           enum Names
57           {
58               SNAKE_EYES = 2, TREY = 3,
59               YO_LEVEN = 11, BOX_CARS = 12
60           };
61
62           private void gameForm_Activate(
63               object sender, System.EventArgs e )
64           {
65               // user is given option to start game
66               playCommand.Visible = true;
67               playCommand.Text = "Play";
68               rollCommand.Visible = false;
```

Fig. 22.14 Code-behind file for craps application. (Part 2 of 6.) (Image courtesy Openwave System, Inc.)

```
69                statusLabel.Text = "Press Play to start!";
70           } // end gameForm_Activate
71
72           private void newGameCommand_Click(
73                object sender, System.EventArgs e )
74           {
75                ActiveForm = gameForm;
76
77                // game has not begun, dice not shown
78                dicePanel.Visible = false;
79
80           } // end newGameCommand_Click
81
82           private void playCommand_Click(
83                object sender, System.EventArgs e )
84           {
85                int sum;
86
87                statusLabel.Text = "";
88                sum = RollDice();
89
90                // display dice for this roll, store point
91                dicePanel.Visible = true;
92                Session.Add( "myPoint", sum.ToString() );
93
94                // analyze first roll
95                switch ( sum )
96                {
97
98                   // user has won
99                   case 7:
100                  case ( int ) Names.YO_LEVEN:
101
102                      // game is over; user cannot roll again
103                      rollCommand.Visible = false;
104                      statusLabel.Text = "*YOU WIN!!!*";
105                      playCommand.Text = "Play Again";
106                      break;
107
108                  // user has lost
109                  case ( int ) Names.SNAKE_EYES:
110                  case ( int ) Names.TREY:
111                  case ( int ) Names.BOX_CARS:
112                      rollCommand.Visible = false;
113                      statusLabel.Text ="*SORRY. YOU LOSE.*";
114                      playCommand.Text = "Play Again";
115                      break;
116
117                  // users continue to play if they
118                  // have neither won nor lost
119                  default:
120                      Session[ "myPoint" ] = sum.ToString();
```

Fig. 22.14 Code-behind file for craps application. (Part 3 of 6.) (Image courtesy Openwave System, Inc.)

```
121
122                      statusLabel.Text = "Point is " +
123                         Session[ "myPoint" ] + ".";
124                      playCommand.Visible = false;
125
126                      // user is given option to roll
127                      rollCommand.Visible = true;
128                      break;
129
130              } // end switch
131
132          } // end playCommand_Click
133
134          private void rollCommand_Click(
135              object sender, System.EventArgs e )
136          {
137              int roll;
138              int point =
139                  Int32.Parse( Session[ "myPoint" ].ToString() );
140
141              roll = RollDice();
142
143              // analyze current roll
144              // if both conditions are false, user roll again
145              if ( roll == point )
146              {
147                  statusLabel.Text = "*YOU WIN!!!*";
148                  playCommand.Text = "Play Again";
149                  rollCommand.Visible = false;
150                  playCommand.Visible = true;
151              }
152              else if ( roll == 7 )
153              {
154                  statusLabel.Text = "*SORRY. YOU LOSE.*";
155                  playCommand.Text = "Play Again";
156                  rollCommand.Visible = false;
157                  playCommand.Visible = true;
158              }
159
160          } // end rollCommand_Click
161
162          private void quitCommand_Click(
163              object sender, System.EventArgs e )
164          {
165              ActiveForm = rulesForm;
166
167          } // end quitCommand_Click
168
169          private int RollDice()
170          {
171              int die1, die2, dieSum;
172              Random randomNumber = new Random();
```

Fig. 22.14 Code-behind file for craps application. (Part 4 of 6.) (Image courtesy Openwave System, Inc.)

```
173
174                die1 = 1 + randomNumber.Next( 6 );
175                die2 = 1 + randomNumber.Next( 6 );
176
177                // display dice images
178                firstImage.ImageUrl = "redDie" + die1.ToString() +
179                   ".png";
180                secondImage.ImageUrl = "redDie" + die2.ToString() +
181                   ".png";
182
183                // calculate sum of dice
184                dieSum = die1 + die2;
185                rollValueLabel.Text = "Your roll was " +
186                   dieSum.ToString() + ":";
187
188                return dieSum;
189
190          } // end RollDice
191
192       } // end class CrapsGame
193
194 } // end namespace Craps
```

Fig. 22.14 Code-behind file for craps application. (Part 5 of 6.) (Image courtesy Openwave System, Inc.)

Fig. 22.14 Code-behind file for craps application. (Part 6 of 6.) (Image courtesy Openwave System, Inc.)

When **gameForm** becomes the active form, the **Play** button's **Visible** property is set to **true** and the **Roll Again** button's **Visible** property is set to **false** (i.e., this is the first role and not a "point" situation). When the user clicks the **Play** button, method **playCommand_Click** is called (lines 82–132), to handle the player's initial roll. On line

88, we call method **RollDice** (lines 169–190), which simulates the rolling of two dice by generating two random values in the range of 1 to 6. This method also changes the values in **dicePanel**. On lines 178–181, the images **firstImage** and **secondImage** are set to display the dice images. Notice that we use the **ImageUrl** property and set its value to the location of the image we wish to display. On lines 184–186, we total the dice values and store their sum in **dieSum**. Line 188 returns **dieSum**'s value, which is assigned to variable **sum** on line 88. Line 92 creates the key-value pair to store in our **Session** object. This pair contains the value of the player's point, which can be retrieved using the key **"myPoint"**.

We use a **switch** statement to determine the value of the first roll (lines 95–131). If users roll a 7 or an 11, they win. If users roll a 2, 3 or 12, they lose. Otherwise, the **default** case is executed (lines 119–128). In the **default** case, the user's roll is stored in a **Session** object (line 120) and displayed via **statusLabel**'s **Text** property (lines 122–123). We then hide the **Play** button and show the **Roll Again** button. When users click the **Roll Again** button, method **rollCommand_Click** (defined on lines 134–160) is called to roll the dice again (line 141) and analyze their sum. The player wins if their "point" is rolled (line 145) and loses if a 7 is rolled (line 152). Otherwise, the game continues, and users can roll again or quit playing. Method **quitCommand_Click** (lines 162–167) is called when the **Quit** button is clicked. This method changes the active form to **rulesForm**, the form that displays the rules of the game.

22.5 Example: Deitel Wireless Portal

In this example (Fig. 22.15), we create the Deitel Wireless Portal Web site. This site contains links to many WAP-accessible sites. The links are organized into four categories (news, travel and food, financial, and contact information), each of which is displayed on separate form controls. The ASPX page consists of five forms and one C# script. The first form welcomes users and displays the category headings, while other forms contain the links for each category.

The C# script in this file contains method **contactForm_OnActivate** (lines 19–29), which adds items to **contactList**, a *List* control. The **List** control renders a list of items in a mobile Web page. Each list item is of type *MobileListItem*. The **List** class contains property *Items*, which can be used to **get** and **set** **MobileListItem**s. The **get** accessor returns the items as a *MobileListItemCollection* object. The **MobileListItemCollection** class, unlike the **List** class, provides functionality for manipulating a list of items programmatically. Lines 24–27 call **MobileListItem-Collection** methods *Clear* and *Add* to update **contactList**. Method **Clear** (line 24) removes all items in the list, while method **Add** (lines 25–27) inserts items into the list.

```
1   <%-- Fig. 22.15: Portal1.aspx    --%>
2   <%-- A simple mobile Web portal. --%>
3
4   <%@ Register TagPrefix="mobile"
5       Namespace="System.Web.UI.MobileControls"
6       Assembly="System.Web.Mobile, Version=1.0.3300.0,
Culture=neutral, PublicKeyToken=b03f5f7f11d50a3a" %>
```

Fig. 22.15 Demonstrating **List**s and **Link**s. (Part 1 of 5.) (Image courtesy Openwave System, Inc.) (Courtesy of Screaming Media, Inc.)

```
7   <%@ Page language="c#" Codebehind="Portal1.aspx.cs"
8       Inherits="Portal1.MobileWebForm1"
9       AutoEventWireup="false" %>
10
11  <meta content="Microsoft Visual Studio 7.0" name="GENERATOR">
12  <meta content="C#" name="CODE_LANGUAGE">
13  <meta content="http://schemas.microsoft.com/Mobile/Page"
14     name="vs_targetSchema">
15
16  <script runat="server" language="C#">
17
18    // add items to list
19    private void contactForm_OnActivate( object sender,
20        EventArgs e )
21    {
22       // clear list (from previous executions)
23       // add three phone numbers
24       contactList.Items.Clear();
25       contactList.Items.Add("DWP Sales (555)555-1234");
26       contactList.Items.Add("DWP Tech Support (555)555-2468");
27       contactList.Items.Add("DWP Main (555)555-3696");
28
29    } // end contactForm_OnActivate
30
31  </script>
32
33  <body Xmlns:mobile="http://schemas.microsoft.com/Mobile/WebForm">
34
35     <mobile:Form id="welcomeForm" runat="server">
36
37        <mobile:Label id="welcomeLabel" runat="server">
38           Welcome to the Deitel Wireless Portal!
39        </mobile:Label>
40
41        <%-- when link is clicked users are sent --%>
42        <%-- to URL specified by NavigateUrl      --%>
43
44        <%-- # indicates internal link --%>
45        <mobile:Link id="newsLink" runat="server"
46           NavigateUrl="#newsForm">
47           News
48        </mobile:Link>
49
50        <mobile:Link id="financialLink" runat="server"
51           NavigateUrl="#financialForm">
52           Financial
53        </mobile:Link>
54
55        <mobile:Link id="travelFoodLink" runat="server"
56           NavigateUrl="#travelFoodForm">
57           Travel/Food
58        </mobile:Link>
```

Fig. 22.15 Demonstrating **List**s and **Link**s. (Part 2 of 5.) (Image courtesy Openwave System, Inc.) (Courtesy of Screaming Media, Inc.)

```
59
60      <mobile:Link id="contactLink" runat="server"
61         NavigateUrl="#contactForm">
62         Contact
63      </mobile:Link>
64   </mobile:Form>
65
66   <mobile:Form id="newsForm" runat="server">
67
68      <%-- NavigateUrl contains external link --%>
69      <%-- users are sent to another site      --%>
70      <mobile:Link id="bloombergLink" runat="server"
71         NavigateUrl=
72         "http://www.bloomberg.com/delivery/hdml/home.hdml">
73         Bloomberg
74      </mobile:Link>
75
76      <mobile:Link id="cnetLink" runat="server"
77         NavigateUrl="http://wap.cnet.com/">
78         CNET News
79      </mobile:Link>
80
81      <mobile:Link id="nytLink" runat="server"
82         NavigateUrl="http://www.nytimes.com/wap">
83         New York Times
84      </mobile:Link>
85   </mobile:Form>
86
87   <mobile:Form id="financialForm" runat="server">
88      <mobile:Link id="wsjLink" runat="server"
89         NavigateUrl="http://wap.wsj.com/">
90         Wall Street Journal
91      </mobile:Link>
92
93      <mobile:Link id="finwinLink" runat="server"
94         NavigateUrl="http://finwin.com">
95         FinWin
96      </mobile:Link>
97
98      <mobile:Link id="stockPointLink" runat="server"
99         NavigateUrl=
100        "http://wml.stockpoint.com/index.wml">
101        StockPoint
102     </mobile:Link>
103  </mobile:Form>
104
105  <mobile:Form id="travelFoodForm" runat="server">
106     <mobile:Link id="citiWizLink" runat="server"
107        NavigateUrl="http://wap.citiwiz.com/index.wml">
108        CitiWiz
109     </mobile:Link>
110
```

Fig. 22.15 Demonstrating **List**s and **Link**s. (Part 3 of 5.) (Image courtesy Openwave System, Inc.) (Courtesy of Screaming Media, Inc.)

```
111          <mobile:Link id="testBestLink" runat="server"
112             NavigateUrl="http://wap.10best.com/">
113             10Best
114          </mobile:Link>
115
116          <mobile:Link id="expediaLink" runat="server"
117             NavigateUrl="http://mobile.msn.com/hdml/travel.asp">
118             Expedia
119          </mobile:Link>
120       </mobile:Form>
121
122       <mobile:Form id="contactForm"
123          OnActivate="contactForm_OnActivate" runat="server">
124
125          <mobile:Label id="contactLabel" runat="server">
126             Contact Information
127          </mobile:Label>
128
129          <%-- list object contains phone numbers --%>
130          <mobile:List id="contactList" runat="server">
131          </mobile:List>
132       </mobile:Form>
133
134    </body>
```

Fig. 22.15 Demonstrating **List**s and **Link**s. (Part 4 of 5.) (Image courtesy Openwave System, Inc.) (Courtesy of Screaming Media, Inc.)

Fig. 22.15 Demonstrating **List**s and **Link**s. (Part 5 of 5.) (Image courtesy Openwave System, Inc.) (Courtesy of Screaming Media, Inc.)

Lines 35–64 define form **welcomeForm**, which is the Web site's main menu. This form consists of a **Label** control and four **Link** controls, which create hyperlinks that redirect users to other forms and sites, depending on the value of the **NavigateUrl** property. For example, on line 56 the **NavigateUrl** property is set to **#travelFoodForm**. The **Text** property is set to **Travel/Food**. The Web site displays the value of the **Link** control's **Text** property (**Travel/Food**) as a hyperlink when the example is run. When users click this **Link**, they are redirected to the value specified in the **NavigateUrl** property. In this case, users are redirected to the form **travelFoodForm** (defined in lines 105–120). The pound (**#**) sign in each **NavigateUrl** value denotes that resource is located in the ASPX file. **NavigateUrl** values preceded with a **#** are called *internal links* (sometimes referred to as *page anchors*). Later, we will see that **NavigateUrl** values also can be set to *external links* (i.e., locations outside the ASPX file). External links do not contain the **#** symbol.

Lines 66–120 define the forms that contain different categories of Web links. Each form contains multiple external links. Lines 122–132 define the form **contactForm** that displays the items in the **List** control (defined on line 130).

Many of the links connect to WAP sites when clicked at run time, and thus cannot be displayed in IE. In the next section, we examine how the MIT provides ways to handle device-specific functionality.

22.6 Device-Independent Web Design Using Style Sheets and Templates

In this section, we enhance the Deitel Wireless Portal Web site's look and feel by using additional controls, such as the **AdRotator** control that randomly selects and displays advertisements. We also discuss how to use "templates" and "style sheets" to maximize the capabilities of the incoming device. In this section, we present an important aspect of mobile Web applications development—programming sites to handle requests from disparate devices. We begin by examining the ASPX file (Fig. 22.16) and the files accessed by our application (Figures 22.17 and 22.18), before we move on to discuss the code-behind file (Fig. 22.19).

A **Stylesheet** control is a collection of **Style** elements. Most MIT controls have a **StyleReference** property, which sets the control's font, color, alignment, etc. This property's value is set to the **Name** attribute of the **Style** element it references. **Stylesheet** controls allow the developer to specify the style of the page elements (headers, fonts, colors, etc.) separately from the structure of the document (i.e., mobile tags) and allow developers to target a specific device (called *Device-Specific Rendering*). For example, developers can write code to enrich the display for HTML-based browsers without compromising mobile accessibility. In this chapter, IE and the Openwave™ Mobile browser are used to test the examples. However, IE browsers are capable of displaying higher resolution graphics and more sophisticated Web pages.

 Software Engineering Observation 22.2

Separating structure from content allows greater manageability of a site and makes changing the site's style easier.

```
1   <%-- Fig. 22.16: Portal2.aspx    --%>
2   <%-- A simple mobile Web portal. --%>
3
4   <%@ Register TagPrefix="mobile"
5       Namespace="System.Web.UI.MobileControls"
6       Assembly="System.Web.Mobile, Version=1.0.3300.0,
Culture=neutral, PublicKeyToken=b03f5f7f11d50a3a" %>
7
8   <%@ Page language="c#" Codebehind="Portal2.aspx.cs"
9       Inherits="Portal2.WebPortal"
10      AutoEventWireup="false" %>
11
12  <meta content="Microsoft Visual Studio 7.0" name="GENERATOR">
13  <meta content="C#" name="CODE_LANGUAGE">
14  <meta content="http://schemas.microsoft.com/Mobile/Page"
15      name="vs_targetSchema">
16
17  <body Xmlns:mobile="http://schemas.microsoft.com/Mobile/WebForm">
18
19      <%-- Stylesheet rendered for     --%>
20      <%-- each form that specifies it --%>
21      <mobile:stylesheet id="Stylesheet1" runat="server">
22          <mobile:Style Name="DWPStyles">
23              <DeviceSpecific>
```

Fig. 22.16 Style sheets and templates in a mobile Web Form. (Part 1 of 5.)

```
24
25                    <%-- templates created for HTML browsers --%>
26                    <Choice Filter="isHTML32">
27                       <HeaderTemplate>
28                          <mobile:Image runat="server"
29                             ImageUrl="top.jpg">
30                          </mobile:Image>
31                       </HeaderTemplate>
32                    </Choice>
33
34                    <%-- templates created for other browsers --%>
35                    <Choice>
36                       <HeaderTemplate>
37                          <Mobile:Label runat="server"
38                             StyleReference="Title"
39                             Text="Deitel Wireless Portal" ID="Label1" />
40                       </HeaderTemplate>
41                    </Choice>
42                 </DeviceSpecific>
43              </mobile:Style>
44       </mobile:stylesheet> <%-- end of style sheet --%>
45
46    <%-- opening page showing dwp image --%>
47    <mobile:form id="welcomeForm" runat="server">
48       <mobile:Image id="welcomeImage" runat="server"
49          AlternateText="DeitelWireless"
50          ImageUrl="logo.wbmp">
51          <DeviceSpecific>
52             <Choice Filter="isHTML32" ImageUrl="logocolor.jpg">
53             </Choice>
54          </DeviceSpecific>
55       </mobile:Image>
56
57       <mobile:Link id="enterLink" runat="server"
58          Alignment="Center" NavigateUrl="#mainForm">
59          Enter
60       </mobile:Link>
61    </mobile:form> <%-- end welcomeForm --%>
62
63    <%-- Stylesheet 'DWPStyles' specified --%>
64    <mobile:form id="mainForm" runat="server"
65       StyleReference="DWPStyles">
66
67       <mobile:Link id="newsLink" runat="server"
68          NavigateUrl="#newsForm">
69          News
70       </mobile:Link>
71
72       <mobile:Link id="financialLink" runat="server"
73          NavigateUrl="#financialForm">
74          Financial
75       </mobile:Link>
76
```

Fig. 22.16 Style sheets and templates in a mobile Web Form. (Part 2 of 5.)

```
77              <mobile:Link id="travelFoodLink" runat="server"
78                 NavigateUrl="#travelFoodForm">
79                 Travel/Food
80              </mobile:Link>
81
82              <mobile:Link id="contactLink" runat="server"
83                 NavigateUrl="#contactForm">
84                 Contact
85              </mobile:Link>
86
87              <mobile:Label id="specialsLabel" runat="server"
88                 Font-Bold="True">
89                 Specials:
90              </mobile:Label>
91
92              <mobile:Label id="bookTitleLabel" runat="server"
93                 Font-Italic="True">
94              </mobile:Label>
95
96              <mobile:Label id="descriptionLabel" runat="server">
97              </mobile:Label>
98
99              <mobile:AdRotator id="AdRotator1" runat="server"
100                AdvertisementFile="adBanners.xml"
101                ImageKey="WirelessImageUrl">
102
103                <DeviceSpecific>
104                   <Choice Filter="isMME" ImageKey="JpgImageUrl">
105                   </Choice>
106
107                   <Choice Filter="isHTML32" ImageKey="ImageUrl"
108                      NavigateUrlKey="IENavigateUrl">
109                   </Choice>
110                </DeviceSpecific>
111
112             </mobile:AdRotator>
113
114      </mobile:form> <%-- end mainForm --%>
115
116      <mobile:form id="newsForm" runat="server"
117         StyleReference="DWPStyles">
118
119             <mobile:Link id="bloombergLink" runat="server"
120                NavigateUrl=
121                "http://www.bloomberg.com/delivery/hdml/home.hdml">
122                Bloomberg
123             </mobile:Link>
124
125             <mobile:Link id="cnetLink" runat="server"
126                NavigateUrl="http://wap.cnet.com/">
127                CNET News
128             </mobile:Link>
129
```

Fig. 22.16 Style sheets and templates in a mobile Web Form. (Part 3 of 5.)

```
130          <mobile:Link id="nytLink" runat="server"
131             NavigateUrl="http://www.nytimes.com/wap">
132             New York Times
133          </mobile:Link>
134
135          <mobile:Link id="mainLink1" runat="server"
136             NavigateUrl="#mainForm">
137             Main
138          </mobile:Link>
139
140       </mobile:form> <%-- end newsForm --%>
141
142       <mobile:form id="financialForm" runat="server"
143          StyleReference="DWPStyles">
144
145          <mobile:Link id="wsjLink" runat="server"
146             NavigateUrl="http://wap.wsj.com/">
147             Wall Street Journal
148          </mobile:Link>
149
150          <mobile:Link id="finWinLink" runat="server"
151             NavigateUrl="http://finwin.com">
152             FinWin
153          </mobile:Link>
154
155          <mobile:Link id="stockPointLink" runat="server"
156             NavigateUrl=
157             "http://wml.stockpoint.com/index.wml">
158             StockPoint
159          </mobile:Link>
160
161          <mobile:Link id="mainLink2" runat="server"
162             NavigateUrl="#mainForm">
163             Main
164          </mobile:Link>
165       </mobile:form> <%-- end financialForm --%>
166
167       <mobile:form id="travelFoodForm" runat="server"
168          StyleReference="DWPStyles">
169
170          <mobile:Link id="citiWizLink" runat="server"
171             NavigateUrl="http://wap.citiwiz.com/index.wml">
172             CitiWiz
173          </mobile:Link>
174
175          <mobile:Link id="tenBestLink" runat="server"
176             NavigateUrl="http://wap.10best.com/">
177             10Best
178          </mobile:Link>
179
180          <mobile:Link id="expediaLink" runat="server"
181             NavigateUrl="http://mobile.msn.com/hdml/travel.asp">
182             Expedia
```

Fig. 22.16 Style sheets and templates in a mobile Web Form. (Part 4 of 5.)

```
183            </mobile:Link>
184
185            <mobile:Link id="mainLink3" runat="server"
186               NavigateUrl="#mainForm">
187               Main
188            </mobile:Link>
189
190         </mobile:form> <%-- end travelFoodForm --%>
191
192         <mobile:form id="contactForm" runat="server"
193            StyleReference="DWPStyles">
194
195            <mobile:Label id="contactLabel" runat="server">
196               Contact Information
197            </mobile:Label>
198
199            <%-- list containing three items created --%>
200            <mobile:List id="contactList" runat="server">
201               <Item Value="DWP Sales (555)555-1234"
202                  Text="DWP Sales (555)555-1234">
203               </Item>
204
205               <Item Value="DWP Tech Support (555)555-2468"
206                  Text="DWP Tech Support (555)555-2468">
207               </Item>
208
209               <Item Value="DWP Main (555)555-3696"
210                  Text="DWP Main (555)555-3696">
211               </Item>
212            </mobile:List>
213
214            <mobile:Link id="mainLink4" runat="server"
215               NavigateUrl="#mainForm">
216               Main
217            </mobile:Link>
218         </mobile:form> <%-- end contactForm --%>
219
220   </body>
```

Fig. 22.16 Style sheets and templates in a mobile Web Form. (Part 5 of 5.)

We begin with the ASPX file, shown in Fig. 22.16. Lines 21–44 define a style sheet. Although **Stylesheet** controls can contain multiple **Style** objects, ours contain only one. The **Style** element (lines 22–43) has its **Name** attribute's value set to **DWPStyles**. Forms use the **Name** attribute's value to reference (via the **StyleReference** attribute) the style sheet.

Style DWPStyles contains a **DeviceSpecific** element, used for applications where multiple devices are being targeted. A **DeviceSpecific** element contains one or more **Choice** elements, which provide the display information for a particular device (or a set of devices, based on the capabilities of the incoming device). The **Choice** element contains a **Filter** attribute that is evaluated and compared to the **Filter**s specified within the **DeviceFilters** element of our **Web.config** file (Fig. 22.17) to determine if the microbrowser running the application supports the specified property. Each **filter**

element in **Web.config** contains three attributes: **name**, **compare** and **argument**. The **name** attribute's value is selected by the programmer from a predefined list in the **Web.config** file. The **compare** attribute's value must be one of several predefined browser properties specified in the **machine.config** file (Fig. 22.12). The **argument** attribute is the value of the browser property.

```
1    <?xml version="1.0" encoding="utf-8" ?>
2
3    <configuration>
4       <system.web>
5          <deviceFilters>
6
7             <!-- Markup Languages -->
8             <filter name="isHTML32"
9                compare="PreferredRenderingType"
10               argument="html32" />
11            <filter name="isWML11"
12               compare="PreferredRenderingType"
13               argument="wml11" />
14            <filter name="isCHTML10"
15               compare="PreferredRenderingType"
16               argument="chtml10" />
17
18            <!-- Device Browsers -->
19            <filter name="isGoAmerica"
20               compare="Browser" argument="Go.Web" />
21            <filter name="isMME" compare="Browser"
22               argument="Microsoft Mobile Explorer" />
23            <filter name="isMyPalm" compare="Browser"
24               argument="MyPalm" />
25            <filter name="isPocketIE" compare="Browser"
26               argument="Pocket IE" />
27            <filter name="isUP3x" compare="Type"
28               argument="Phone.com 3.x Browser" />
29            <filter name="isUP4x" compare="Type"
30               argument="Phone.com 4.x Browser" />
31
32            <!-- Specific Devices -->
33            <filter name="isEricssonR380" compare="Type"
34               argument="Ericsson R380" />
35            <filter name="isNokia7110" compare="Type"
36               argument="Nokia 7110" />
37
38            <!-- Device Capabilities -->
39            <filter name="prefersGIF"
40               compare="PreferredImageMIME"
41               argument="image/gif" />
42            <filter name="prefersWBMP"
43               compare="PreferredImageMIME"
44               argument="image/vnd.wap.wbmp" />
45            <filter name="supportsColor" compare="IsColor"
46               argument="true" />
```

Fig. 22.17 Web.config file used for **Portal2.aspx**. (Part 1 of 2.)

```
47              <filter name="supportsCookies" compare="Cookies"
48                 argument="true" />
49              <filter name="supportsJavaScript"
50                 compare="Javascript" argument="true" />
51              <filter name="supportsVoiceCalls"
52                 compare="CanInitiateVoiceCall"
53                 argument="true" />
54
55           </deviceFilters>
56        </system.web>
57     </configuration>
```

Fig. 22.17 Web.config file used for Portal2.aspx. (Part 2 of 2.)

Filter elements describe the microbrowser's properties. These properties allow developers to evaluate the incoming device programmatically. To do this, the developer can call method **HasCapability** (class **MobileCapabilities**), which takes information about a specific **Filter** as an argument and returns **true** if the incoming device supports those capabilities. The element that is chosen is rendered for the user. On lines 26–32, the first **Choice** element is specified. The filter **"isHTML32"** indicates that this element is for HTML browsers and is defined in Fig. 22.17 on lines 8–10. The **name** of this filter (line 8) is used for identification purposes. The **compare** attribute is set to **preferredRenderingType** (line 9), which differentiates between the possible devices. The **argument** attribute sets the value for the device. This value can be anything from a boolean value to a MIME type. In this example, the **Choice** element is selected based on the **preferredRenderingType**. This property represents the image's MIME type that the incoming device supports. The rendering type is set by the **argument** attribute, in this case **html32**. This indicates that the **Choice** with this **Filter** is selected if the incoming device is expecting images with MIME type **html32**. The code that follows (lines 28–30 of Fig. 22.16) displays **top.jpg**, an image format supported by HTML browsers. The Openwave™ Mobile browser cannot display JPEGs, so the contents of the **HeaderTemplate** element (discussed momentarily) located within the default **Choice** element (lines 35–41) are displayed. This **Choice** element is the default choice because it does not contain a **Filter** attribute. For HTML browsers, lines 26–32 execute; for other browsers, lines 35–41 execute.

Notice that within each **Choice** element there is a *templated control*, which contains a set of template elements (e.g., **HeaderTemplate** elements). Templates mark up content for display on incoming devices. We use a set of templates, rather than just one template, to support the variety of devices targeted by this application. However, only one template is applied per targeted device. In this example, we use templates to create a header that is displayed on all devices. For HTML devices (e.g., IE and MME), the header is a full-color image, non-HTML clients display the header as text. Where the content is rendered is determined by the template element type. On lines 27–31, we use the **HeaderTemplate**, which is rendered at the top of a **Form** control or a **List** control. In this template, the image **top.jpg** is displayed. For the default **HeaderTemplate** (lines 36–40), we display the text **Deitel Wireless Portal**. To create content that is displayed at the bottom of a **Form** control or a **List** control, the **FooterTemplate** is used.

Lines 47–61 define form **welcomeForm**, which greets users entering the Web site. This form does not reference style sheet **DWPStyles**. Instead, we use the **Device-**

Specific and **Choice** elements to show that Device-Specific Rendering can be accomplished without a style sheet. If the incoming device is capable of displaying colors, a large, full-color **.jpg** image will be displayed. The default device displays a bitmap version of the company logo. Lines 57–60 provide a **Link** object that redirects the user to form **mainForm**.

Lines 64–114 define form **mainForm**. This form and the remainder of the forms in the document use the **StyleReference** attribute to reference the **DWPStyles** style sheet. Form **mainForm** contains several **Link**s (lines 67–85) and three **Label**s, two of which are used in the **AdRotator1_AdCreated** method to provide a text description of the item being advertised. The **AdRotator** itself is defined on lines 99–112.

The advertisements are stored in the XML file specified in the **AdvertisementFile** property. This file (**AdBanners.xml**) is shown in Fig. 22.18. Information for three different advertisements is marked up. Each advertisement's information is specified within an **Ad** element. Each advertisement has five elements—**ImageUrl**, **WirelessImageUrl**, **NavigateUrl**, **AlternateText** and **Impressions**.

```
1    <?xml version="1.0"?>
2
3    <Advertisements>
4        <Ad>
5            <ImageUrl>banner1.gif</ImageUrl>
6            <WirelessImageUrl>buyMe.wbmp</WirelessImageUrl>
7            <JpgImageUrl>buyMe.jpg</JpgImageUrl>
8            <NavigateUrl></NavigateUrl>
9            <IENavigateUrl>http://www.amazon.com/exec/obidos/ASIN/
013028419X/deitelassociatin/107-7206886-3349351</IENavigateUrl>
10           <AlternateText>banner1Text</AlternateText>
11           <Impressions>80</Impressions>
12       </Ad>
13       <Ad>
14           <ImageUrl>banner2.gif</ImageUrl>
15           <WirelessImageUrl>buyMe.wbmp</WirelessImageUrl>
16           <JpgImageUrl>buyMe.jpg</JpgImageUrl>
17           <NavigateUrl></NavigateUrl>
18           <IENavigateUrl>http://www.amazon.com/exec/obidos/ASIN/
0130284173/deitelassociatin/107-7206886-3349351</IENavigateUrl>
19           <AlternateText>banner2Text</AlternateText>
20           <Impressions>80</Impressions>
21       </Ad>
22       <Ad>
23           <ImageUrl>banner3.gif</ImageUrl>
24           <WirelessImageUrl>buyMe.wbmp</WirelessImageUrl>
25           <JpgImageUrl>buyMe.jpg</JpgImageUrl>
26           <NavigateUrl></NavigateUrl>
27           <IENavigateUrl>http://www.amazon.com/exec/obidos/ASIN/
0130323640/deitelassociatin/107-7206886-3349351</IENavigateUrl>
28           <AlternateText>banner3Text</AlternateText>
29           <Impressions>80</Impressions>
30       </Ad>
31   </Advertisements>
```

Fig. 22.18 AdBanners.xml file used for Portal2.aspx.

Each advertisement in our file can have multiple images associated with it. One of these images is selected based on the capabilities of the incoming device. To specify these capabilities, we again use a **DeviceSpecific** element (lines 103–110 of Fig. 22.16) that contains one or more **Choice** elements. We assign the **Choice** element's **Filter** attribute to specify one of the filters (e.g., **isHTML32**) in our **Web.config** file. In this example, we introduce another attribute—*ImageKey*. We use element *WirelessImageUrl* to reference the image specified by the **ImageKey** attribute. For instance, if the value of **ImageKey** is **JPEGImageUrl**, the image displayed is the one specified in element **JPEGImageUrl**. In this example, the filter we use is **"isMME"** (defined in our **Web.config** file), which is specified on line 104 of Fig. 22.16 and defined on lines 21–22 of Fig. 22.17. If the incoming device is the MME (version 3.0), the image displayed is selected from one of the **WirelessImageUrl** elements in **AdBanners.xml** (lines 6, 15 and 24 of Fig. 22.18). If the incoming device is not the MME, the program examines the next **Choice** element. The default image is used for other microbrowsers, because additional **Choice** elements have not been provided. The default image is specified in the *ImageUrl* element. If the image cannot be displayed for some reason (either we specified an image that is not supported on the current browser or the image cannot be located), text marked up in the **AlternateText** element is displayed in place of the image.

Each advertisement also contains *NavigateUrl* and *Impressions* elements. **NavigateUrl** marks up the location where users are redirected when the advertisement is clicked. In this example, we leave this element empty (i.e., nothing happens if the image is clicked). The **Impressions** element marks up the advertisement's weight. Advertisements with larger weights are displayed more frequently.

Portability Tip 22.2

*When using the **NavigateUrl** element, it is the programmer's responsibility to ensure that the Web site specified by the URL can be rendered on the incoming device.*

Forms **newsForm**, **financialForm** and **travelFoodForm** (lines 116–190) are similar to those used in the previous example, with one important difference—these forms call the **ResolveLinks** method, which determines whether the user is redirected to an HTML site or a WAP site. We discuss method **ResolveLinks** shortly.

Lines 192–218 define the **contactForm** form, which contains a **List** object populated with phone numbers. In this case, the **List** items are added directly in the form instead of in the **<script>** section, as in the last example. All forms contain a **Link** back to the main menu, except for **MainMenu** itself.

Let us now discuss the code-behind file (Fig. 22.19), which contains two methods: **AdRotator1_AdCreated** (lines 80–111) and **ResolveLinks** (lines 114–135). Method **AdRotator1_AdCreated** is an event handler for our **AdRotator**'s *AdCreated* event, which is raised when an advertisement of our **AdRotator** is displayed. This event contains an **AlternateText** property which provides access to the value of the **AlternateText** element in the XML file. Lines 83, 92 and 101 of **AdRotator1_AdCreated** use this property to determine the current advertisement and to set appropriate values to the **Text** properties of **BookTitleLabel** and **Description-Label**. For instance, if the image chosen is that of our *XML How to Program* publication, method **AdRotator1_AdCreated** would display the title of our XML book in **BookTitleLabel**, and information about this specific publication in **DescriptionLabel**.

Method **ResolveLinks**, defined on lines 114–135, is an event handler for the **Activate** events of forms **newsForm**, **financialForm** and **travelFoodForm**. This method is used to determine the destination of a form's links based on the capabilities of an incoming device. Some Web sites, such as **www.finwin.com**, detect the incoming device and return the appropriate markup. Other sites, such as the *Wall Street Journal*, have separate URLs for their wireless sites. To access the *Wall Street Journal* wireless site, users would visit **wap.wsj.com** instead of **www.wsj.com**. **ResolveLinks** determines the capabilities of the incoming device programmatically by using the **MobileCapabilities** class. This class inherits from class *HttpBrowserCapabilities*, which encapsulates information about the current browser. Notice the *Request.Browser* property (line 118), which is part of the *HttpRequest* class and returns an **HttpBrowserCapabilities** object. On lines 116–118, we cast this object to type **MobileCapabilities**, and assign it to our **MobileCapabilities** instance, referenced by **capabilities**. By accessing the *Browser* property of **capabilities**, we can determine if the incoming device is IE. If true, the user is redirected to the appropriate HTML sites.

```
1   // Fig. 22.19: DeitelWirelessPortal2.aspx.cs
2   // Code-behind file for the Deitel Wireless Portal 2.
3
4   using System;
5   using System.Collections;
6   using System.ComponentModel;
7   using System.Data;
8   using System.Drawing;
9   using System.Web;
10  using System.Web.Mobile;
11  using System.Web.SessionState;
12  using System.Web.UI;
13  using System.Web.UI.MobileControls;
14  using System.Web.UI.WebControls;
15  using System.Web.UI.HtmlControls;
16
17  namespace Portal2
18  {
19     public class WebPortal :
20        System.Web.UI.MobileControls.MobilePage
21     {
22        // style sheet
23        protected System.Web.UI.MobileControls.StyleSheet Stylesheet1;
24
25        // welcome form and its controls
26        protected System.Web.UI.MobileControls.Form welcomeForm;
27        protected System.Web.UI.MobileControls.Image welcomeImage;
28        protected System.Web.UI.MobileControls.Link enterLink;
29
30
31        // main form and its controls
32        protected System.Web.UI.MobileControls.Form mainForm;
33        protected System.Web.UI.MobileControls.Link newsLink;
```

Fig. 22.19 Code-behind file for the Deitel Wireless Portal. (Part 1 of 5.)

```
34      protected System.Web.UI.MobileControls.Link financialLink;
35      protected System.Web.UI.MobileControls.Link travelFoodLink;
36      protected System.Web.UI.MobileControls.Link contactLink;
37      protected System.Web.UI.MobileControls.Label specialsLabel;
38      protected System.Web.UI.MobileControls.Label
39         bookTitleLabel;
40      protected System.Web.UI.MobileControls.AdRotator
41         AdRotator1;
42      protected System.Web.UI.MobileControls.Label
43         descriptionLabel;
44
45      // news form and its controls
46      protected System.Web.UI.MobileControls.Form newsForm;
47      protected System.Web.UI.MobileControls.Link bloombergLink;
48      protected System.Web.UI.MobileControls.Link cnetLink;
49      protected System.Web.UI.MobileControls.Link nytLink;
50      protected System.Web.UI.MobileControls.Link mainLink1;
51
52      // financial form and its controls
53      protected System.Web.UI.MobileControls.Form financialForm;
54      protected System.Web.UI.MobileControls.Link wsjLink;
55      protected System.Web.UI.MobileControls.Link finWinLink;
56      protected System.Web.UI.MobileControls.Link stockPointLink;
57      protected System.Web.UI.MobileControls.Link mainLink2;
58
59      // travel/food form and its controls
60      protected System.Web.UI.MobileControls.Form travelFoodForm;
61      protected System.Web.UI.MobileControls.Link citiWizLink;
62      protected System.Web.UI.MobileControls.Link tenBestLink;
63      protected System.Web.UI.MobileControls.Link expediaLink;
64      protected System.Web.UI.MobileControls.Link mainLink3;
65
66      // contacts form and its controls
67      protected System.Web.UI.MobileControls.Form contactForm;
68      protected System.Web.UI.MobileControls.Label contactLabel;
69      protected System.Web.UI.MobileControls.List contactList;
70      protected System.Web.UI.MobileControls.Link mainLink4;
71
72      private void Page_Load( object sender, System.EventArgs e )
73      {
74         // Put user code to initialize the page here
75      }
76
77      // Visual Studio .NET generated code
78
79      // display proper text for current advertisement
80      private void AdRotator1_AdCreated( object sender,
81         System.Web.UI.WebControls.AdCreatedEventArgs e )
82      {
83         if ( e.AlternateText == "banner1Text" )
84         {
85            bookTitleLabel.Text = "e-Business and e-Commerce " +
86               "How To Program:";
```

Fig. 22.19 Code-behind file for the Deitel Wireless Portal. (Part 2 of 5.)

```
 87                     descriptionLabel.Text = "This book carefully " +
 88                         "explains how to program multi-tiered, " +
 89                         "client/server, database-intensive, Web-based," +
 90                         " e-Business and e-Commerce applications.";
 91                  }
 92                  else if ( e.AlternateText == "banner2Text" )
 93                  {
 94                     bookTitleLabel.Text = "XML How To Program:";
 95                     descriptionLabel.Text = "Offers a careful explanation " +
 96                         "of XML-based systems development, for faculty " +
 97                         "students and professionals. Includes " +
 98                         "extensive pedagogic features, including " +
 99                         "Internet resources.";
100                  }
101                  else if ( e.AlternateText == "banner3Text" )
102                  {
103                     bookTitleLabel.Text = "e-Business and e-Commerce " +
104                         "For Managers:";
105                     descriptionLabel.Text = "For all managers, business " +
106                         "owners and others who need a comprehensive " +
107                         "overview of how to build and manage " +
108                         "an e-Business.";
109                  }
110
111              } // end AdRotator1_AdCreated
112
113              // change links for IE browsers
114              private void ResolveLinks( object sender, System.EventArgs e )
115              {
116                  System.Web.Mobile.MobileCapabilities capability =
117                      ( System.Web.Mobile.MobileCapabilities )
118                      Request.Browser;
119
120                  // if the browser name contains "IE", change links
121                  if ( capability.Browser.IndexOf( "IE" ) != -1 )
122                  {
123                     bloombergLink.NavigateUrl =
124                         "http://www.bloomberg.com";
125                     cnetLink.NavigateUrl = "http://www.cnet.com";
126                     nytLink.NavigateUrl = "http://www.nyt.com";
127                     wsjLink.NavigateUrl = "http://www.wsj.com";
128                     stockPointLink.NavigateUrl =
129                         "http://stockpoint.com/";
130                     citiWizLink.NavigateUrl = "http://www.citiwiz.com";
131                     tenBestLink.NavigateUrl = "http://www.10best.com";
132                     expediaLink.NavigateUrl = "http://www.expedia.com";
133                  }
134
135              } // end ResolveLinks
136
137          } // end class WebPortal
138
139      } // end namespace Portal2
```

Fig. 22.19 Code-behind file for the Deitel Wireless Portal. (Part 3 of 5.)

Fig. 22.19 Code-behind file for the Deitel Wireless Portal. (Part 4 of 5.)

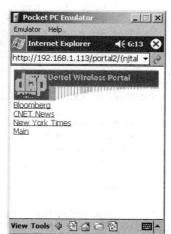

Fig. 22.19 Code-behind file for the Deitel Wireless Portal. (Part 5 of 5.)

22.7 Consuming a Web Service from a Mobile Application

In Chapter 18, ASP .NET and Web Services, we created an airline-reservation example where users can reserve a seat on a flight. In this example, we show how to access the same Web service from a mobile device. The only difference between this example and the example presented in Chapter 18 is the client, which we built using the MIT.

The airline-reservation Web service receives information regarding the type of seat the customer wishes to reserve and then makes a reservation if the seat is available. The logic for the airline reservation Web service has a single **WebMethod—Reserve—** which searches its seat database to locate a seat matching a user's request. If it finds an appropriate seat, **Reserve** updates the database, makes the reservation and returns **true**; otherwise, no reservation is made and the method returns **false**. [*Note*: We do not show the code listing for the Web service here because it is listed in Chapter 18, Web Services.]

Reserve takes two arguments—a **string** representing the desired seat type (i.e., window, middle and aisle) and a **string** representing the desired class type (i.e., economy and first class). If the result of the query is not empty, the application reserves the first seat number that the query returns and **Reserve** returns **true**, indicating that the reservation was successful. If the result of the query is not successful, **Reserve** returns **false**, indicating that no available seats matched the request.

Figure 22.20 presents the ASPX listing for the mobile Web form through which users can select seat types. This page allows users to reserve a seat on the basis of its class and location in a row of seats. The page then uses the airline-reservation Web service to carry out users' requests. If the database request is not successful, the user is instructed to modify the request and try again.

```
1   <%-- Fig. 22.20: Reservation.aspx --%>
2   <%-- Airline Reservation client.        --%>
3   <%@ Page language="c#" Codebehind="Reservation.aspx.cs"
4       Inherits="Reservation.MakeReservation"
5       AutoEventWireup="false" %>
6
7   <%@ Register TagPrefix="mobile"
8       Namespace="System.Web.UI.MobileControls"
9       Assembly="System.Web.Mobile, Version=1.0.3300.0,
Culture=neutral, PublicKeyToken=b03f5f7f11d50a3a" %>
10
11  <meta name="GENERATOR" content="Microsoft Visual Studio 7.0">
12  <meta name="CODE_LANGUAGE" content="C#">
13  <meta name="vs_targetSchema"
14      content="http://schemas.microsoft.com/Mobile/Page">
15
16  <body Xmlns:mobile="http://schemas.microsoft.com/Mobile/WebForm">
17
18      <mobile:Form id="reservationForm" runat="server">
19          <mobile:Label id="instructionLabel" runat="server">
20              Please select the type of seat and class
21              you wish to reserve:
22          </mobile:Label>
23
24          <mobile:Label id="seatLabel" runat="server"
25              Font-Size="Large">
26              Seat:
27          </mobile:Label>
28
```

Fig. 22.20 ASPX page that allows a mobile device to access a Web service. (Part 1 of 2.)

```
29          <mobile:SelectionList id="seatList" runat="server">
30             <Item Value="Aisle" Text="Aisle"></Item>
31             <Item Value="Middle" Text="Middle"></Item>
32             <Item Value="Window" Text="Window"></Item>
33          </mobile:SelectionList>
34
35          <mobile:Label id="classLabel" runat="server"
36             Font-Size="Large">
37             Class:
38          </mobile:Label>
39
40          <mobile:SelectionList id="classList" runat="server">
41             <Item Value="Economy" Text="Economy"></Item>
42             <Item Value="First" Text="First"></Item>
43          </mobile:SelectionList>
44
45          <mobile:Command id="reserveCommand" runat="server">
46             Reserve!
47          </mobile:Command>
48       </mobile:Form>
49
50       <mobile:Form id="confirmationForm" runat="server">
51          <mobile:Label id="confirmationLabel" runat="server">
52          </mobile:Label>
53
54          <mobile:Label id="confirmSeatLabel" runat="server">
55          </mobile:Label>
56
57          <mobile:Label id="confirmClassLabel" runat="server">
58          </mobile:Label>
59       </mobile:Form>
60
61    </body>
```

Fig. 22.20 ASPX page that allows a mobile device to access a Web service. (Part 2 of 2.)

This page defines two *SelectionList* objects, which display a short list of choices, and a **Button**. One **SelectionList** displays all the seat types from which users can select. The second lists the class types. Users click the **Button**, named **reserveButton**, to submit requests after making selections from the **Selection-List**. The code-behind file (Fig. 22.21) contains the event handler for this button.

```
1    // Fig. 22.21: Reservation.aspx.cs
2    // Making a reservation using a Web Service.
3
4    using System;
5    using System.Collections;
6    using System.ComponentModel;
7    using System.Data;
8    using System.Drawing;
```

Fig. 22.21 Code-behind file for mobile Web application that access a Web Service. (Part 1 of 4.)

```
9   using System.Web;
10  using System.Web.Mobile;
11  using System.Web.SessionState;
12  using System.Web.UI;
13  using System.Web.UI.MobileControls;
14  using System.Web.UI.WebControls;
15  using System.Web.UI.HtmlControls;
16
17  namespace Reservation
18  {
19     public class MakeReservation :
20        System.Web.UI.MobileControls.MobilePage
21     {
22        protected System.Web.UI.MobileControls.Label
23           instructionLabel;
24
25        protected System.Web.UI.MobileControls.Label seatLabel;
26        protected System.Web.UI.MobileControls.SelectionList
27           seatList;
28
29        protected System.Web.UI.MobileControls.Label classLabel;
30        protected System.Web.UI.MobileControls.SelectionList
31           classList;
32
33        protected System.Web.UI.MobileControls.Command
34           reserveCommand;
35
36        protected System.Web.UI.MobileControls.Form
37           confirmationForm;
38
39        protected System.Web.UI.MobileControls.Form
40           reservationForm;
41
42        protected System.Web.UI.MobileControls.Label
43           confirmationLabel;
44
45        protected System.Web.UI.MobileControls.Label
46           confirmSeatLabel;
47
48        protected System.Web.UI.MobileControls.Label
49           confirmClassLabel;
50
51        private void Page_Load( object sender, System.EventArgs e )
52        {
53           // Put user code to initialize the page here
54        }
55
56        // Visual Studio .NET generated code
57
58        private localhost.Reservation agent =
59           new localhost.Reservation();
60
```

Fig. 22.21 Code-behind file for mobile Web application that access a Web Service. (Part 2 of 4.)

```
61        private void reserveCommand_Click(
62           object sender, System.EventArgs e )
63        {
64           ActiveForm = confirmationForm;
65
66        } // reserveCommand_Click
67
68        private void confirmationForm_Activate(
69           object sender, System.EventArgs e )
70        {
71           // if WebMethod returned true, signal success
72           if ( agent.Reserve( seatList.Selection.Text,
73              classList.Selection.Text ) )
74           {
75              confirmationLabel.Text = "Your reservation has " +
76                 "been made. Thank You!";
77
78              confirmSeatLabel.Text =
79                 "Seat: " + seatList.Selection.Text;
80
81              confirmClassLabel.Text =
82                 "Class: " + classList.Selection.Text;
83           }
84           else
85           {
86              confirmationLabel.Text = "This seat is not " +
87                 "available, please hit your browser's Back " +
88                 "button and try again.";
89           }
90
91        } //confirmationForm_Activate
92
93     } // end class MakeReservation
94
95  } // end namespace Reservation
```

Fig. 22.21 Code-behind file for mobile Web application that access a Web Service. (Part 3 of 4.)

Fig. 22.21 Code-behind file for mobile Web application that access a Web Service. (Part 4 of 4.)

Lines 58–59 create a **Reservation** object (i.e., an instance of the Web service). When the user clicks **Reserve**, the **reserveCommand_Click** event handler executes, and the page reloads. The event handler (lines 68–91) calls the Web service's **Reserve** method and passes it the selected seat and class type as arguments. If **Reserve** returns

true, the application displays a message thanking the user for making a reservation; otherwise, the user is notified that the type of seat requested is not available, and the user is instructed to try again.

Well, that's it for now. We sincerely hope that you have enjoyed learning with *C# for Experienced Programmers*. As this book went to the presses, we were already at work on *ASP .NET with C# for Experienced Programmers*, a book appropriate for professional developers writing enterprise applications.

22.8 Summary

The Microsoft® Mobile Internet Toolkit (MIT) allows programmers to create mobile Web applications. The MIT extends the functionality of Visual Studio .NET and is a powerful tool that uses the .NET Framework to create Web content for mobile devices using languages such as C# and Visual Basic .NET.

The Wireless Application Protocol (WAP) is a set of communications protocols that are designed to enable wireless devices to access the Internet. The Wireless Markup Language (WML) is the markup language used to describe content for WAP devices. WAP supports WML to deliver wireless content. The MIT supports three main clients—HTML devices, WAP devices and iMode devices. HTML devices are those that display HTML markup, such as Internet Explorer or Pocket PC.

Creating a mobile Web application in Visual Studio .NET generates an ASPX page (with the **.aspx** file extension), which contains the markup for the page's user interface. The business logic for the application can be embedded in the ASPX file as a script or in a code-behind file. The business logic is executed on the Web server.

Mobile Web Form controls (or mobile controls) are the objects used to create mobile applications. Some basic mobile controls include labels and buttons. Every mobile control's start tag has its **runat** attribute set to **"server"** to indicate that the control must be executed on the server.

The MIT determines if multiple controls can fit on the same line by checking the device's screen size. Each device's screen size and other device-specific information, such as support for color graphics or the ability to initiate a phone call, are stored in the **machine.config** file.

A **Stylesheet** control is a collection of **Style** elements. Many MIT controls have a **StyleReference** property, which sets the control's font, color, alignment, etc. **Stylesheet** controls allow the developer to specify the style of the page elements (headers, fonts, colors, etc.) separately from the structure of the document (i.e., mobile tags) and allow developers to target specific devices (called Device-Specific Rendering).

A **DeviceSpecific** element is present when multiple devices are being targeted. A **DeviceSpecific** element contains one or more **Choice** elements. The **Choice** element contains a **Filter** attribute that is evaluated and compared to the **Filter**s specified within the **deviceFilters** element in **Web.config**. Each **filter** element in **Web.config** contains three attributes: **name**, **compare** and **argument**. The **name** value is selected from a predefined list in **Web.config** by the programmer. The **compare** attribute's value must be one of several predefined browser properties specified in **machine.config**. The **argument** attribute is the expected value of the browser property.

22.9 Internet and World Wide Web Resources

msdn.microsoft.com/vstudio/nextgen/technology/mobilewebforms.asp
This site presents an online introduction to mobile Web Forms, as well as other useful links.

www.devx.com
This online information source does not yet contain information about the MIT, but it does offer information on wireless technologies and .NET, including discussions, help and code.

www.w3.org/TR/1998/NOTE-compactHTML-19980209
This site provides detailed information on cHTML and devices that support cHTML.

msdn.microsoft.com/library/default.asp?url=/library/en-us/mwsdk/ html/mwstartpage.asp
This documentation site provides some background information on the MIT, as well as links to documentation on more specific topics, such as information on the MIT's runtime.

www.asp.net/Default.aspx?tabindex=4&tabid=44
This all-purpose ASP .NET site provides links to several downloads and samples using the MIT.

Newsgroups

microsoft.public.dotnet.framework.aspnet.mobile
Questions and answers on several MIT topics are posted frequently on this Microsoft newsgroup. All levels of programmers can communicate and learn from each other.

Operator Precedence Chart

Operators are shown in decreasing order of precedence from top to bottom with each level of precedence separated by a horizontal line.[1]

Operator	Type	Associativity
.	member access	left-to-right
( )	parenthesized expression	
[ ]	element access	
++	post increment	
--	post decrement	
new	object creation	
typeof	typeof	
checked	checked	
unchecked	unchecked	
+	unary plus	left-to-right
-	unary minus	
!	unary	
~	unary	
++	pre-increment	
--	pre-decrement	

Fig. A.1 Operator precedence chart. (Part 1 of 2.)

---

1. This operator-precedence chart is based on Section 7.2.1, *Operator precedence and associativity,* of the C# Language Specification (for more information, visit **msdn.microsoft.com/library/default.asp?url=/library/en-us/csspec/html/CSharpSpec-Start.asp**).

Operator	Type	Associativity
* / %	multiplication division modulus	left-to-right
+ -	addition subtraction	left-to-right
<< >>	shift left shift right	left-to-right
< > <= >= *is*	relational less than relational greater than relational less than or equal to relational greater than or equal to type comparison	left-to-right
== !=	relational is equal to relational is not equal to	left-to-right
&	logical AND	left-to-right
^	logical exclusive OR	left-to-right
|	logical inclusive OR	left-to-right
&&	conditional AND	left-to-right
||	conditional OR	left-to-right
?:	conditional	right-to-left
= *= /= += -= <<= >>= &= ^= |=	assignment multiplication assignment division assignment addition assignment subtraction assignment shift left assignment shift right assignment logical AND assignment logical exclusive OR assignment logical inclusive OR assignment	right-to-left

Fig. A.1   Operator precedence chart. (Part 2 of 2.)

Number Systems

Objectives

- To understand basic number system concepts such as base, positional value and symbol value.
- To understand how to work with numbers represented in the binary, octal and hexadecimal number systems
- To abbreviate binary numbers as octal numbers or hexadecimal numbers.
- To convert octal numbers and hexadecimal numbers to binary numbers.
- To covert back and forth between decimal numbers and their binary, octal and hexadecimal equivalents.
- To understand binary arithmetic and how negative binary numbers are represented using two's complement notation.

Here are only numbers ratified.
William Shakespeare

Nature has some sort of arithmetic-geometrical coordinate system, because nature has all kinds of models. What we experience of nature is in models, and all of nature's models are so beautiful.
It struck me that nature's system must be a real beauty, because in chemistry we find that the associations are always in beautiful whole numbers—there are no fractions.
Richard Buckminster Fuller

Outline

B.1   Introduction

B.2   Abbreviating Binary Numbers as Octal Numbers and Hexadecimal Numbers

B.3   Converting Octal Numbers and Hexadecimal Numbers to Binary Numbers

B.4   Converting from Binary, Octal or Hexadecimal to Decimal

B.5   Converting from Decimal to Binary, Octal or Hexadecimal

B.6   Negative Binary Numbers: Two's Complement Notation

B.7   Summary

B.1 Introduction

In this appendix, we introduce the key number systems that programmers use, especially when they are working on software projects that require close interaction with "machine-level" hardware. Projects like this include operating systems, computer networking software, compilers, database systems, and applications requiring high performance.

When we write an integer such as 227 or –63 in a program, the number is assumed to be in the *decimal (base 10) number system*. The *digits* in the decimal number system are 0, 1, 2, 3, 4, 5, 6, 7, 8, and 9. The lowest digit is 0 and the highest digit is 9—one less than the *base* of 10. Internally, computers use the *binary (base 2) number system*. The binary number system has only two digits, namely 0 and 1. Its lowest digit is 0 and its highest digit is 1—one less than the base of 2. Figure B.1 summarizes the digits used in the binary, octal, decimal and hexadecimal number systems.

As we will see, binary numbers tend to be much longer than their decimal equivalents. Programmers who work in assembly languages and in high-level languages that enable programmers to reach down to the "machine level," find it cumbersome to work with binary numbers. So two other number systems the *octal number system (base 8)* and the *hexadecimal number system (base 16)*—are popular primarily because they make it convenient to abbreviate binary numbers.

In the octal number system, the digits range from 0 to 7. Because both the binary number system and the octal number system have fewer digits than the decimal number system, their digits are the same as the corresponding digits in decimal.

The hexadecimal number system poses a problem because it requires sixteen digits—a lowest digit of 0 and a highest digit with a value equivalent to decimal 15 (one less than the base of 16). By convention, we use the letters A through F to represent the hexadecimal digits corresponding to decimal values 10 through 15. Thus in hexadecimal we can have numbers like 876 consisting solely of decimal-like digits, numbers like 8A55F consisting of digits and letters, and numbers like FFE consisting solely of letters. Occasionally, a hexadecimal number spells a common word such as FACE or FEED—this can appear strange to programmers accustomed to working with numbers. Figure B.2 summarizes each of the number systems.

Each of these number systems uses positional notation—each position in which a digit is written has a different positional value. For example, in the decimal number 937 (the 9, the 3, and the 7 are referred to as symbol values), we say that the 7 is written in the ones position, the 3 is written in the tens position, and the 9 is written in the hundreds position. Notice that each of these positions is a power of the base (base 10), and that these powers begin at 0 and increase by 1 as we move left in the number (Fig. B.3).

For longer decimal numbers, the next positions to the left would be the thousands position (10 to the 3rd power), the ten-thousands position (10 to the 4th power), the hundred-thousands position (10 to the 5th power), the millions position (10 to the 6th power), the ten-millions position (10 to the 7th power) and so on.

In the binary number 101, we say that the rightmost 1 is written in the ones position, the 0 is written in the twos position, and the leftmost 1 is written in the fours position. Notice that each of these positions is a power of the base (base 2), and that these powers begin at 0 and increase by 1 as we move left in the number (Fig. B.4).

For longer binary numbers, the next positions to the left would be the eights position (2 to the 3rd power), the sixteens position (2 to the 4th power), the thirty-twos position (2 to the 5th power), the sixty-fours position (2 to the 6th power), and so on.

In the octal number 425, we say that the 5 is written in the ones position, the 2 is written in the eights position, and the 4 is written in the sixty-fours position. Notice that each of these positions is a power of the base (base 8), and that these powers begin at 0 and increase by 1 as we move left in the number (Fig. B.5).

Binary digit	Octal digit	Decimal digit	Hexadecimal digit
0	0	0	0
1	1	1	1
	2	2	2
	3	3	3
	4	4	4
	5	5	5
	6	6	6
	7	7	7
		8	8
		9	9
			A (decimal value of 10)
			B (decimal value of 11)
			C (decimal value of 12)
			D (decimal value of 13)
			E (decimal value of 14)
			F (decimal value of 15)

Fig. B.1   Digits of the binary, octal, decimal and hexadecimal number systems.

Attribute	Binary	Octal	Decimal	Hexadecimal
Base	2	8	10	16
Lowest digit	0	0	0	0
Highest digit	1	7	9	F

Fig. B.2   Comparison of the binary, octal, decimal and hexadecimal number systems.

Positional values in the decimal number system			
Decimal digit	9	3	7
Position name	Hundreds	Tens	Ones
Positional value	100	10	1
Positional value as a power of the base (10)	10^2	10^1	10^0

Fig. B.3   Positional values in the decimal number system.

For longer octal numbers, the next positions to the left would be the five-hundred-and-twelves position (8 to the 3rd power), the four-thousand-and-ninety-sixes position (8 to the 4th power), the thirty-two-thousand-seven-hundred-and-sixty eights position (8 to the 5th power), and so on.

In the hexadecimal number 3DA, we say that the A is written in the ones position, the D is written in the sixteens position, and the 3 is written in the two-hundred-and-fifty-sixes position. Notice that each of these positions is a power of the base (base 16), and that these powers begin at 0 and increase by 1 as we move left in the number (Fig. B.6).

For longer hexadecimal numbers, the next positions to the left would be the four-thousand-and-ninety-sixes position (16 to the 3rd power), the sixty-five-thousand-five-hundred-and-thirty-six position (16 to the 4th power), and so on.

Positional values in the binary number system			
Binary digit	1	0	1
Position name	Fours	Twos	Ones
Positional value	4	2	1
Positional value as a power of the base (2)	2^2	2^1	2^0

Fig. B.4   Positional values in the binary number system.

Positional values in the octal number system			
Decimal digit	4	2	5
Position name	Sixty-fours	Eights	Ones
Positional value	64	8	1
Positional value as a power of the base (8)	8^2	8^1	8^0

Fig. B.5 Positional values in the octal number system.

Positional values in the hexadecimal number system			
Decimal digit	3	D	A
Position name	Two-hundred-and-fifty-sixes	Sixteens	Ones
Positional value	256	16	1
Positional value as a power of the base (16)	16^2	16^1	16^0

Fig. B.6 Positional values in the hexadecimal number system.

B.2 Abbreviating Binary Numbers as Octal Numbers and Hexadecimal Numbers

The main use for octal and hexadecimal numbers in computing is for abbreviating lengthy binary representations. Figure B.7 highlights the fact that lengthy binary numbers can be expressed concisely in number systems with higher bases than the binary number system.

Decimal number	Binary representation	Octal representation	Hexadecimal representation
0	0	0	0
1	1	1	1
2	10	2	2
3	11	3	3
4	100	4	4
5	101	5	5
6	110	6	6
7	111	7	7

Fig. B.7 Decimal, binary, octal and hexadecimal equivalents. (Part 1 of 2.)

Decimal number	Binary representation	Octal representation	Hexadecimal representation
8	1000	10	8
9	1001	11	9
10	1010	12	A
11	1011	13	B
12	1100	14	C
13	1101	15	D
14	1110	16	E
15	1111	17	F
16	10000	20	10

Fig. B.7   Decimal, binary, octal and hexadecimal equivalents. (Part 2 of 2.)

A particularly important relationship that both the octal number system and the hexadecimal number system have to the binary system is that the bases of octal and hexadecimal (8 and 16 respectively) are powers of the base of the binary number system (base 2). Consider the following 12-digit binary number and its octal and hexadecimal equivalents. See if you can determine how this relationship makes it convenient to abbreviate binary numbers in octal or hexadecimal. The answer follows the numbers.

Binary Number	Octal equivalent	Hexadecimal equivalent
100011010001	4321	8D1

To see how the binary number converts easily to octal, simply break the 12-digit binary number into groups of three consecutive bits each, and write those groups over the corresponding digits of the octal number as follows

100	011	010	001
4	3	2	1

Notice that the octal digit you have written under each group of thee bits corresponds precisely to the octal equivalent of that 3-digit binary number as shown in Fig. B.7.

The same kind of relationship may be observed in converting numbers from binary to hexadecimal. In particular, break the 12-digit binary number into groups of four consecutive bits each and write those groups over the corresponding digits of the hexadecimal number as follows

1000	1101	0001
8	D	1

Notice that the hexadecimal digit you wrote under each group of four bits corresponds precisely to the hexadecimal equivalent of that 4-digit binary number as shown in Fig. B.7.

B.3 Converting Octal Numbers and Hexadecimal Numbers to Binary Numbers

In the previous section, we saw how to convert binary numbers to their octal and hexadecimal equivalents by forming groups of binary digits and simply rewriting these groups as their equivalent octal digit values or hexadecimal digit values. This process may be used in reverse to produce the binary equivalent of a given octal or hexadecimal number.

For example, the octal number 653 is converted to binary simply by writing the 6 as its 3-digit binary equivalent 110, the 5 as its 3-digit binary equivalent 101, and the 3 as its 3-digit binary equivalent 011 to form the 9-digit binary number 110101011.

The hexadecimal number FAD5 is converted to binary simply by writing the F as its 4-digit binary equivalent 1111, the A as its 4-digit binary equivalent 1010, the D as its 4-digit binary equivalent 1101, and the 5 as its 4-digit binary equivalent 0101 to form the 16-digit 1111101011010101.

B.4 Converting from Binary, Octal or Hexadecimal to Decimal

Because we are accustomed to working in decimal, it is often convenient to convert a binary, octal, or hexadecimal number to decimal to get a sense of what the number is "really" worth. Our diagrams in Section B.1 express the positional values in decimal. To convert a number to decimal from another base, multiply the decimal equivalent of each digit by its positional value, and sum these products. For example, the binary number 110101 is converted to decimal 53 as shown in Fig. B.8.

To convert octal 7614 to decimal 3980, we use the same technique, this time using appropriate octal positional values as shown in Fig. B.9.

Converting a binary number to decimal					
Positional values:	32	16	8	4	2	1
Symbol values:	1	1	0	1	0	1
Products:	1*32=32	1*16=16	0*8=0	1*4=4	0*2=0	1*1=1
Sum:	= 32 + 16 + 0 + 4 + 0 + 1 = 53					

Fig. B.8   Converting a binary number to decimal.

Converting an octal number to decimal			
Positional values:	512	64	8	1
Symbol values:	7	6	1	4
Products	7*512=3584	6*64=384	1*8=8	4*1=4
Sum:	= 3584 + 384 + 8 + 4 = 3980			

Fig. B.9   Converting an octal number to decimal.

To convert hexadecimal AD3B to decimal 44347, we use the same technique, this time using appropriate hexadecimal positional values as shown in Fig. B.10.

B.5 Converting from Decimal to Binary, Octal or Hexadecimal

The conversions of the previous section follow naturally from the positional notation conventions. Converting from decimal to binary, octal or hexadecimal also follows these conventions.

Suppose we wish to convert decimal 57 to binary. We begin by writing the positional values of the columns right to left until we reach a column whose positional value is greater than the decimal number. We do not need that column, so we discard it. Thus, we first write:

Positional values:**6432168421**

Then we discard the column with positional value 64 leaving:

Positional values:**321684 2 1**

Next we work from the leftmost column to the right. We divide 32 into 57 and observe that there is one 32 in 57 with a remainder of 25, so we write 1 in the 32 column. We divide 16 into 25 and observe that there is one 16 in 25 with a remainder of 9 and write 1 in the 16 column. We divide 8 into 9 and observe that there is one 8 in 9 with a remainder of 1. The next two columns each produce quotients of zero when their positional values are divided into 1 so we write 0s in the 4 and 2 columns. Finally, 1 into 1 is 1 so we write 1 in the 1 column. This yields:

Positional values:**321684 2 1**
Symbol values:**11 1   0 0 1**

and thus decimal 57 is equivalent to binary 111001.

To convert decimal 103 to octal, we begin by writing the positional values of the columns until we reach a column whose positional value is greater than the decimal number. We do not need that column, so we discard it. Thus, we first write:

Positional values:**5126481**

Then we discard the column with positional value 512, yielding:

Positional values:**6481**

Converting a hexadecimal number to decimal			
Positional values:	4096	256	16	1
Symbol values:	A	D	3	B
Products	A*4096=40960	D*256=3328	3*16=48	B*1=11
Sum:	= 40960 + 3328 + 48 + 11 = 44347			

Fig. B.10 Converting a hexadecimal number to decimal.

Next we work from the leftmost column to the right. We divide 64 into 103 and observe that there is one 64 in 103 with a remainder of 39, so we write 1 in the 64 column. We divide 8 into 39 and observe that there are four 8s in 39 with a remainder of 7 and write 4 in the 8 column. Finally, we divide 1 into 7 and observe that there are seven 1s in 7 with no remainder so we write 7 in the 1 column. This yields:

> Positional values:**6481**
> Symbol values:**14 7**

and thus decimal 103 is equivalent to octal 147.

To convert decimal 375 to hexadecimal, we begin by writing the positional values of the columns until we reach a column whose positional value is greater than the decimal number. We do not need that column, so we discard it. Thus, we first write

> Positional values:**4096256161**

Then we discard the column with positional value 4096, yielding:

> Positional values:**256161**

Next we work from the leftmost column to the right. We divide 256 into 375 and observe that there is one 256 in 375 with a remainder of 119, so we write 1 in the 256 column. We divide 16 into 119 and observe that there are seven 16s in 119 with a remainder of 7 and write 7 in the 16 column. Finally, we divide 1 into 7 and observe that there are seven 1s in 7 with no remainder so we write 7 in the 1 column. This yields:

> Positional values:**256161**
> Symbol values:**17 7**

and thus decimal 375 is equivalent to hexadecimal 177.

B.6 Negative Binary Numbers: Two's Complement Notation

The discussion in this appendix has been focussed on positive numbers. In this section, we explain how computers represent negative numbers using *two's complement notation*. First we explain how the two's complement of a binary number is formed, and then we show why it represents the negative value of the given binary number.

Consider a machine with 32-bit integers. Suppose

```
int number = 13;
```

The 32-bit representation of **number** is

```
00000000 00000000 00000000 00001101
```

To form the negative of **number** we first form its *one's complement* by applying C#'s ^ operator:

```
onesComplement = number ^ 0x7FFFFFFF;
```

Internally, **onesComplement** is now **number** with each of its bits reversed—ones become zeros and zeros become ones as follows:

number:
00000000 00000000 00000000 00001101

onesComplement:
11111111 11111111 11111111 11110010

To form the two's complement of **number**, we simply add one to the one's complement of **number**.

Thus, the two's complement of **number** is

11111111 11111111 11111111 11110011

Now, if this is in fact equal to –13, we should be able to add it to binary 13 and obtain a result of 0. Let us try this:

```
 00000000 00000000 00000000 00001101
+11111111 11111111 11111111 11110011
-------------------------------------
 00000000 00000000 00000000 00000000
```

The carry bit coming out of the leftmost column is discarded, and we indeed get zero as a result. If we add the one's complement of a number to the number, the result would be all ones. The key to getting a result of all zeros is that the twos complement is one more than the one's complement. The addition of one causes each column to add to zero with a carry of one. The carry keeps moving leftward until it is discarded from the leftmost bit, and hence the resulting number is all zeros.

Computers actually perform a subtraction such as

```
x = a - number;
```

by adding the two's complement of **number** to **a** as follows:

```
x = a + ( onesComplement + 1 );
```

Suppose **a** is 27 and **number** is 13 as before. If the two's complement of **number** is actually the negative of **number**, then adding the two's complement of **number** to **a** should produce the result 14. Let us try this:

```
a (i.e., 27)               00000000 00000000 00000000 00011011
+( onesComplement + 1 )   +11111111 11111111 11111111 11110011
                          -------------------------------------
                           00000000 00000000 00000000 00001110
```

which is indeed equal to 14.

B.7 Summary

When programmers write an integer such as 19, 227 or –63 in a C# program, the number is considered to be in the decimal (base-10) number system. The digits in the decimal number system are 0, 1, 2, 3, 4, 5, 6, 7, 8 and 9. The lowest digit is 0 and the highest digit is 9— one less than the base of 10.

Internally, computers use the binary (base-2) number system. The binary number system has only two digits, namely, 0 and 1. Its lowest digit is 0 and its highest digit is 1—

one less than the base of 2. Computers represent negative numbers using two's-complement notation.

The digits of the octal number system (base 8) range from 0 to 7. The hexadecimal number system (base 16) requires 16 digits—a lowest digit of 0 and a highest digit with a value equivalent to decimal 15 (one less than the base of 16). By convention, letters A through F are the hexadecimal digits representing decimal values 10 through 15.

Career Opportunities

Objectives

- To explore the various online career services.
- To examine the advantages and disadvantages of posting and finding jobs online.
- To review the major online career services Web sites available to job seekers.
- To explore the various online services available to employers seeking to build their workforces.

What is the city but the people?
William Shakespeare

A great city is that which has the greatest men and women,
If it be a few ragged huts it is still the greatest city in the
whole world.
Walt Whitman

To understand the true quality of people, you must look into
their minds, and examine their pursuits and aversions.
Marcus Aurelius

The soul is made for action, and cannot rest till it be
employed. Idleness is its rust. Unless it will up and think and
taste and see, all is in vain.
Thomas Traherne

Outline

C.1   Introduction
C.2   Resources for the Job Seeker
C.3   Online Opportunities for Employers
       C.3.1   Posting Jobs Online
       C.3.2   Problems with Recruiting on the Web
       C.3.3   Diversity in the Workplace
C.4   Recruiting Services
C.5   Career Sites
       C.5.1   Comprehensive Career Sites
       C.5.2   Technical Positions
       C.5.3   Wireless Positions
       C.5.4   Contracting Online
       C.5.5   Executive Positions
       C.5.6   Students and Young Professionals
       C.5.7   Other Online Career Services
C.6   Summary
C.7   Internet and World Wide Web Resources

C.1 Introduction

There are approximately 40,000 career-advancement services on the Internet today.[1] These services include large, comprehensive job sites, such as **Monster.com** (see the upcoming **Monster.com** feature), as well as interest-specific job sites such as **Just-JavaJobs.com**. Companies can reduce the amount of time spent searching for qualified employees by building recruiting features on their Web sites or establishing accounts with career sites. This results in a larger pool of qualified applicants, as online services can automatically select and reject resumes based on user-designated criteria. Online interviews, testing services and other resources also expedite the recruiting process.

Applying for a position online is a relatively new method of exploring career opportunities. Online recruiting services streamline the process and allow job seekers to concentrate their energies in careers that are of interest to them. Job seekers can explore opportunities according to geographic location, position, salary or benefits packages.

Job seekers can learn how to write resumes and cover letters, post them online and search through job listings to find the jobs that best suit their needs. *Entry-level positions*, or positions commonly sought by individuals who are entering a specific field or the job market for the first time; contracting positions; executive-level positions and middle-management-level positions are all available on the Web.

Job seekers will find a number of time-saving features when searching for jobs online. These include storing and distributing resumes digitally, e-mail notification of possible positions, salary and relocation calculators, job coaches, self-assessment tools and information on continuing education.

In this appendix, we explore online career services from the employer and employee's perspective. We suggest sites on which applications can be submitted, jobs can be searched and applicants can be reviewed. We also review services that build recruiting pages directly into e-businesses.

C.2 Resources for the Job Seeker

Finding a job online can greatly reduce the amount of time spent applying for a position. Instead of searching through newspapers and mailing resumes, job seekers can request a specific positions in specific industries through search engines. Some sites allow job seekers to setup intelligent agents to find jobs that meet their requirements. Intelligent agents are programs that search and arrange large amounts of data and report answers based on that data. When the agent finds a potential match, it sends it to the job seeker's inbox. Resumes can be stored digitally, customized quickly to meet job requirements and e-mailed instantaneously. A potential candidate also can learn more about a company by visiting its Web site. Most employment sites are free to job seekers. These sites typically generate their revenues by charging employers for posting job opportunities and by selling advertising space on their Web pages (see the **Monster.com** feature).

Career services, such as **FlipDog.com**, search a list of employer job sites to find positions. By searching links to employer Web sites, **FlipDog.com** is able to identify positions from companies of all sizes. This feature enables job seekers to find jobs that employers may not have posted outside the corporation's Web site.

Monster.com

Super Bowl ads and effective marketing have made **Monster.com** one of the most recognizable online brands (see Fig. C.1). In fact, in the 24 hours following Super Bowl XXXIV, 5 million job searches occurred on **Monster.com**.[2] The site allows people looking for jobs to post their resumes, search job listings, read advice and information about the job-search process and take proactive steps to improve their careers. These services are free to job seekers. Employers can post job listings, search resume databases and become featured employers.

Posting a resume at **Monster.com** is simple and free. **Monster.com** has a resume builder that allows users to post a resume to its site in 15–30 minutes. Each user can store up to 5 resumes and cover letters on the **Monster.com** server. Some companies offer their employment applications directly through the **Monster.com** site. **Monster.com** has job postings in every state and all major categories. Users can limit access to their personal identification information. As one of the leading recruiting sites on the Web, **Monster.com** is a good place to begin a job search or to find out more about the search process.

Fig. C.1   Monster.com home page. (Courtesy of **Monster.com.**)

Job seekers can visit **FlipDog.com** and choose, by state, the area in which they are looking for positions. Applicants also can conduct worldwide searches. After a user selects a region, **FlipDog.com** requests the user to choose a job category containing several specific positions. The user's choice causes a list of local employers to appear. The user can specify an employer or request that **FlipDog.com** search the employment databases for jobs offered by all employers (see Fig. C.2).

Other services, such as employment networks, also help job seekers in their search. Sites such as **Vault.com** (see the **Vault.com** feature) and **WetFeet.com** allow job seekers to post questions in designated chat rooms or on electronic bulletin boards about employers and positions.

C.3   Online Opportunities for Employers

Recruiting on the Internet provides several benefits over traditional recruiting. For example, Web recruiting reaches a much larger audience than posting an advertisement in a local newspaper. Given the breadth of the services provided by most online career services Web sites, the cost of posting online can be considerably less than posting positions through traditional means. Even newspapers, which depend greatly on career opportunity advertising, are starting online career sites.[3]

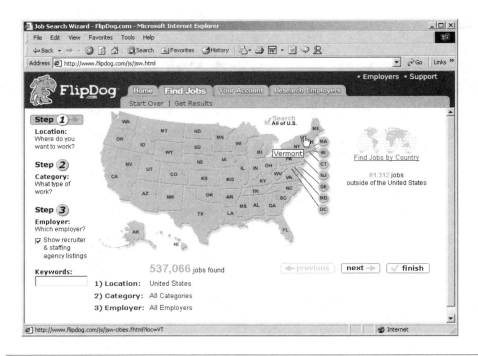

Fig. C.2   **FlipDog.com** job search. (Courtesy of **Flipdog.com**.)

Vault.com: Finding the Right Job on the Web[4]

Vault.com allows potential employees to seek out additional, third-party information for over 3000 companies. By visiting the *Insider Research* page, Web users have access to a profile on the company of their choice, as long as it exists in **Vault.com**'s database. In addition to **Vault.com**'s profile, there is a link to additional commentary by company employees. Most often anonymous, these messages can provide prospective employees with potentially valuable decision-making information. However, users must consider the integrity of the source. For example, a disgruntled employee may leave a posting that is not an accurate representation of the corporate culture of his or her company.

The **Vault.com** *Electronic Watercooler*™ is a message board that allows visitors to post stories, questions and concerns and to advise employees and job seekers. In addition, the site provides e-newsletters and feature stories designed to help job seekers in their search. Individuals seeking information on business, law and graduate schools can also find information on **Vault.com**.

Job-posting and career-advancement services for the job seeker are featured on **Vault.com**. These services include *VaultMatch*, a career service that e-mails job postings as requested, and *Salary Wizard*™, which helps job seekers determine the salary they are worth. Online guides with advice for fulfilling career ambitions are also available.

Vault.com: Finding the Right Job on the Web[4] (Cont.)

Employers can also use the site. *HR Vault*, a feature of **Vault.com**, provides employers with a free job-posting site. It offers career-management advice, employer-to-employee relationship management and recruiting resources.

e-Fact C.1

According to Forrester Research, 33 percent of today's average company's hiring budget goes toward online career services, while the remaining 66 percent is used for traditional recruiting mechanisms. Online use is expected to increase to 42 percent by 2004, while traditional mechanisms may be reduced to 10 percent.[5]

Generally, jobs posted online are viewed by a larger number of job seekers than jobs posted through traditional means. However, it is important not to overlook the benefits of combining online efforts with human-to-human interaction. There are many job seekers who are not yet comfortable with the process of finding a job online. Often, online recruiting is used as a means of freeing up a recruiter's time for the interviewing process and final selection.

e-Fact C.2

Cisco Systems cites a 39 percent reduction in cost-per-hire expenses, and a 60 percent reduction in the time spent hiring.[6]

C.3.1 Posting Jobs Online

When searching for job candidates online, there are many things employers need to consider. The Internet is a valuable tool for recruiting, but one that takes careful planning to acquire the best results. It provides a good supplementary tool, but should not be considered the complete solution for filling positions. Web sites, such as WebHire (**www.webhire.com**), enhance a company's online employment search (see the WebHire feature).

There are a variety of sites that allow employers to post jobs online. Some of these sites require a fee, which generally runs between $100–$200. Postings typically remain on the Web site for 30–60 days. Employers should be careful to post to sites that are most likely to be visited by eligible candidates. As we discovered in the previous section, there are a variety of online career services focused on specific industries, and many of the larger, more comprehensive sites have categorized their databases by job category.

When designing a posting, the recruiter should consider the vast number of postings already on the Web. Defining what makes the job position unique, including information such as benefits and salary, might convince a qualified candidate to further investigate the position (see Fig. C.3).[7]

HotJobs.com career postings are cross-listed on a variety of other sites, thus increasing the number of potential employees who see the job listings. Like **Monster.com** and **jobfind.com**, **HotJobs.com** requires a fee per listing. Employers also have the option of becoming **HotJobs.com** members. Employers can gain access to HotJob's *Private Label Job Boards* (private corporate employment sites), online recruiting technology and online career fairs.

WebHire™[8]

Designed specifically for recruiters and employers, WebHire is a multifaceted service that provides employers with *end-to-end recruiting solutions*. The service offers job-posting services as well as candidate searches. The most comprehensive of the services, *WebHire™ Enterprise*, locates and ranks candidates found through resume-scanning mechanisms. Clients will also receive a report indicating the best resources for their search. Other services available through the *WebHire™ Employment Services Network* include preemployment screening, tools for assessing employees' skill levels and information on compensation packages. An employment law advisor helps organizations design interview questions.

WebHire™ Agent is an intelligent agent that searches for qualified applicants based on job specifications. When WebHire Agent identifies a potential candidate, an e-mail is sent to the candidate to generate interest. WebHire Agent then ranks applicants according to the skills information it gains from the Web search; the information is stored so that new applicants are distinguished from those who have already received an e-mail from the site.

Yahoo!® Resumes, a feature of WebHire, allows recruiters to find potential employees by typing in keywords on the Yahoo! Resumes search engine. Employers can purchase a year's membership to the recruiting solution for a flat fee; there are no per-use charges.

Job Seeker's Criteria

Position (responsibilities)

Salary

Location

Benefits (health, dental, stock options)

Advancement

Time Commitment

Training Opportunities

Tuition Reimbursement

Corporate Culture

Fig. C.3   List of a job seeker's criteria.

Boston Herald *Job Find* (`www.jobfind.com`) also charges employers to post on its site. The initial fee entitles the employer to post up to three listings. Employers have no limitations on the length of their postings.

Other Web sites providing employers with employee recruitment services include **CareerPath.com**, America's Job Bank (**www.ajb.dni.us/employer**), CareerWeb (**www.cweb.com**), **Jobs.com** and **Career.com**.

C.3.2 Problems with Recruiting on the Web

The large number of applicants presents a challenge to both job seekers and employers. On many recruitment sites, matching resumes to positions is conducted by *resume-filtering software*. The software scans a pool of resumes for keywords that match the job description. While this software increases the number of resumes that receive attention, it is not a foolproof system. For example, the resume-filtering software might overlook someone with similar skills to those listed in the job description, or someone whose abilities would enable them to learn the skills required for the position. Digital transmissions can also create problems because certain software platforms are not always acceptable by the recruiting software. This sometimes results in an unformatted transmission, or a failed transmission.

A lack of confidentiality is another disadvantage of online career services. In many cases, a job candidate will want to search for job opportunities anonymously. This reduces the possibility of offending the candidate's current employer. Posting a resume on the Web increases the likelihood that the candidate's employer might come across it when recruiting new employees. The traditional method of mailing resumes and cover letters to potential employers does not impose the same risk.

According to recent studies, the number of individuals researching employment positions through traditional means, such as referrals, newspapers and temporary agencies, far outweighs the number of job seekers researching positions through the Internet.[9] Optimists feel, however, that this disparity is largely due to the early stages of e-business development. Given time, online career services will become more refined in their posting and searching capabilities, decreasing the amount of time it takes for a job seeker to find jobs and employers to fill positions.

C.3.3 Diversity in the Workplace

Every workplace inevitably develops its own culture. Responsibilities, schedules, deadlines and projects all contribute to a working environment. Perhaps the most defining elements of a *corporate culture* are the employees. For example, if all employees were to have the same skills, same backgrounds and the same ideas, the workplace would lack diversity. It also might lack creativity and enthusiasm. One way to increase the dynamics of an organization is to employ people of different backgrounds and cultures.

The Internet hosts demographic-specific sites for employers seeking to increase diversity in the workplace. By recruiting people from different backgrounds, new ideas and perspectives are brought forth, helping businesses meet the needs of a larger, more diverse target audience.[10]

Blackvoices.com and **hirediversity.com** are demographic-specific Web sites. BlackVoices™, which functions primarily as a portal (a site offering news, sports and weather information, as well as Web searches), features job searching capabilities and the ability for prospective employees to post resumes. HireDiversity is divided into several categories, including opportunities for African Americans, Hispanics and women. Other online recruiting services place banner advertisements on ethnic Web sites for companies seeking diverse workforces.

The Diversity Directory (**www.mindexchange.com**) offers international career-searching capabilities. Users selecting the **Diversity** site can find job opportunities, information and additional resources to help them in their career search. The site can be searched according to demographics (African American, Hispanic, alternative lifestyle, etc.) or by subject (employer, position, etc.) via hundreds of links. Featured sites include **BilingualJobs.com**, *Latin World* and *American Society for Female Entrepreneurs.*

Many sites have sections dedicated to job seekers with disabilities. In addition to providing job-searching capabilities, these sites include additional resources, such as equal opportunity documents and message boards. The *National Business and Disability Council (NBDC)* provides employers with integration and accessibility information for employing people with disabilities, and the site also lists opportunities for job seekers.

C.4 Recruiting Services

There are many services on the Internet that help employers match individuals to positions. The time saved by conducting preliminary searches on the Internet can be dedicated to interviewing qualified candidates and making the best matches possible.

Advantage Hiring, Inc. (**www.advantagehiring.com**) provides employers with a resume-screening service. When a prospective employee submits a resume for a particular position, Advantage Hiring, Inc. presents *Net-Interview*™, a small questionnaire to supplement the information presented on the resume. The site also offers *SiteBuilder*, a service that helps employers build an employee recruitment site. An online demonstration can be found at **www.advantagehiring.com**. The demonstration walks the user through the Net-Interview software, as well as a number of other services offered by Advantage Hiring (see Fig. C.4).

Recruitsoft.com is an application service provider (ASP) that offers companies recruiting software on a *pay-per-hire* basis (Recruitsoft receives a commission on hires made via its service). *Recruiter WebTop*™ is the company's online recruiting software. It includes features such as Web-site hosting, an employee-referral program, skill-based resume screening, applicant-tracking capabilities and job-board posting capabilities. A demonstration of Recruiter WebTop's *Corporate Recruiting Solutions* can be found at **www.recruitsoft.com/process**. Other online recruiting services include **Hire.com**, and **Futurestep.com**™.

The Internet also provides employers with a cost-effective means of testing their prospective employees in such categories as decision making, problem solving and personality. Services such *eTest* help to reduce the cost of in-house testing and to make the interview process more effective. Test results, given in paragraph form, present employers with the interested individual's strengths and weaknesses. Based on these results, the report suggests interview methods, such as asking *open-ended questions*, which are questions that require more than a "yes" or "no" response. Sample reports and a free-trial test can be found at **www.etest.net**.

Employers and job seekers can also find career placement exercises at **www.advisorteam.net/User/ktsintro.asp**. Some of these services require a fee. The tests ask several questions regarding the individual's interests and working style. Results help candidates determine the best career for their skills and interests.

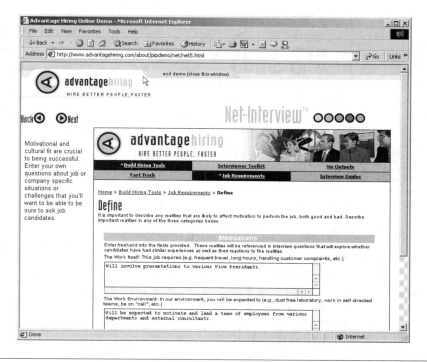

Fig. C.4   Advantage Hiring, Inc.'s Net-Interview™ service. (Courtesy of Advantage Hiring, Inc.)

C.5 Career Sites

Online career sites can be comprehensive or industry specific. In this section, we explore a variety of sites on the Web that accommodate the needs of both the job seeker and the employer. We review sites offering technical positions, free-lancing opportunities and contracting positions.

C.5.1 Comprehensive Career Sites

As mentioned previously, there are many sites on the Web that provide job seekers with career opportunities in multiple fields. **Monster.com** is the largest of these sites, attracting the greatest number of unique visitors per month. Other popular online recruiting sites include **JobsOnline.com**, **HotJobs.com**, **www.jobtrak.com** (a **Monster.com** site) and **Headhunter.net**.

Searching for a job online can be a conducted in a few steps. For example, during an initial visit to **JobsOnline.com**, a user is required to fill out a registration form. The form requests basic information, such as name, address and area of interest. After registering, members can search through job postings according to such criteria as job category, location and the number of days the job has been posted. Contact information is provided for additional communication.

C.5.2 Technical Positions

Technical positions are becoming widely available as the Internet grows more pervasive. Limited job loyalty and high turnover rates in technical positions allow job seekers to find jobs that best suit their needs and skills. Employers are required to rehire continuously to keep positions filled and productivity levels high. The amount of time for an employer to fill a technical position can be greatly reduced by using an industry-specific site. Career sites designed for individuals seeking technical positions are among the most popular online career sites. In this section, we review several sites that offer recruiting and hiring opportunities for technical positions.

e-Fact C.3

It costs a company 25 percent more to hire a new technical employee than it does to pay an already employed individual's salary.[11]

Dice.com (**www.dice.com**) is a recruiting Web site that focuses on technical fields. Company fees are based on the number of jobs the company posts and the frequency with which the postings are updated. Job seekers can post their resumes and search the job database for free. **JustTechJobs.com** directs job seekers toward 39 specific computer technologies for their job search. Language-specific sites include **JustJavaJobs.com**, **JustCJobs.com** and **JustPerlJobs.com**. Hardware, software and communications technology sites are also available. Other technology recruiting sites include **HireAbility.com**, and **HotDispatch.com**.

C.5.3 Wireless Positions

The wireless industry is developing rapidly. According to **WirelessResumes.com**, the number of wireless professionals is 328,000. This number is expected to increase 40 percent each year for the next five years. To accommodate this growth, and the parallel demand for professionals, **WirelessResumes.com** has created an online career site specifically for the purpose of filling wireless jobs (see the **WirelessResumes.com** feature).

WirelessResumes.com: *Filling Wireless Positions*

WirelessResumes.com is an online career site focused specifically on matching wireless professionals with careers in the industry. This narrow focus enables businesses to locate new employees quickly—reducing the time and expense attached to traditional recruiting methods. Similarly, candidates can limit their searches to precisely the job category of interest. Wireless carriers, device manufacturers, WAP and Bluetooth developers, e-commerce companies and application service providers (ASPs) are among those represented on the site.

In addition to searching for jobs and posting a resume, **WirelessResumes.com** provides job seekers with resume writing tips, interviewing techniques, relocation tools and assistance in obtaining a Visa or the completion of other necessary paperwork. Employers can use the site to search candidates and post job opportunities.

The Caradyne Group (**www.pcsjobs.com**), an executive search firm, connects job seekers to employers in the wireless technology field. Interested job seekers must first fill out a "Profile Questionnaire." This information is then entered into The Caradyne Group's database and is automatically matched to an open position in the job seeker's field of expertise. If there are no open positions, a qualified consultant from The Caradyne Group will contact the job seeker for further a interview and discussion.

C.5.4 Contracting Online

The Internet also serves as a forum for job seekers to find employment on a project-by-project basis. *Online contracting services* allow businesses to post positions for which they wish to hire outside resources, and individuals can identify projects that best suit their interests, schedules and skills.

e-Fact C.4

Approximately six percent of America's workforce falls into the category of independent contractor.[12]

Guru.com (**www.guru.com**) is a recruiting site for contract employees. Independent contractors, private consultants and trainers use **guru.com** to find short-term and long-term contract assignments. Tips, articles and advice are available for contractors who wish to learn more about their industry. Other sections of the site teach users how to manage their businesses, buy the best equipment and deal with legal issues. **Guru.com** includes an online store where contractors can buy products associated with small-business management, such as printing services and office supplies. Companies wishing to hire contractors must register with **guru.com**, but individuals seeking contract assignments do not.

Monster.com's Talent Market™ offers online auction-style career services to free agents. Interested users design a profile, listing their qualifications. After establishing a profile, free agents "Go Live" to start the bidding on their services. The bidding lasts for five days during which users can view the incoming bids. At the close of five days, the user can choose the job of his or her choice. The service is free for users, and bidding employers pay a commission on completed transactions.

eLance.com is another site where individuals can find contracting work. Interested applicants can search eLance's database by category, including business, finance and marketing (Fig. C.5). These projects, or *requests for proposals* (RFPs), are posted by companies worldwide. When users find projects for which they feel qualified, they submit bids on the projects. Bids must contain a user's required payment, a statement detailing the user's skills and a feedback rating drawn from other projects on which the user has worked. If a user's bid is accepted, the user is given the project, and the work is conducted over eLance's file-sharing system, enabling both the contractor and the employer to contact one another quickly and easily. For an online demonstration, visit **www.elance.com** and click on the **take a tour...** link.

Other Web sites that provide contractors with projects and information include eWork® Exchange (**www.ework.com**), **MBAFreeAgent.com**, **Aquent.com** and **WorkingSolo.com**.

Fig. C.5   eLance.com request for proposal (RFP) example. (Courtesy of eLance, Inc.)

C.5.5 Executive Positions

In this section, we discuss the advantages and disadvantages of finding an executive position online. Executive career advancement sites usually include many of the features found on comprehensive job-search sites. Searching for an executive position online differs from finding an entry-level position online. The Internet allows individuals to continually survey the job market. However, candidates for executive-level positions must exercise a higher level of caution when determining who is able to view their resume. Applying for an executive position online is an extensive process. As a result of the high level of scrutiny passed on a candidate during the hiring process, the initial criteria presented by an executive level candidate often are more specific than the criteria presented by the first-time job seeker. Executive positions often are difficult to fill, due to the high demands and large amount of experience required for the jobs.

SixFigureJobs (**www.sixfigurejobs.com**) is a recruitment site designed for experienced executives. Resume posting and job searching is free to job seekers. Other sites, including **www.execunet.com**, **Monster.com**'s ChiefMonster™ (**www.chiefmonster.com**) and **www.nationjob.com** are designed for helping executives find positions.

C.5.6 Students and Young Professionals

The Internet provides students and young professionals with tools to get them started in the job market. Individuals still in school and seeking internships, individuals who are just graduating and individuals who have been in the workforce for a few years make up the target market. Additional tools specifically designed for this *demographic* (a population defined by a specific characteristic) are available. For example, journals kept by previous interns provide prospective interns with information regarding what to look for in an internship, what to expect and what to avoid. Many sites will provide information to lead young professionals in the right direction, such as matching positions to their college or university major.

Experience.com is a career services Web site geared toward the younger population. Members can search for positions according to specific criteria, such as geographic location, job category, keywords, commitment (i.e. full time, part time, internship), amount of vacation and amount of travel time. After applicants register, they can send their resumes directly to the companies posted on the site. In addition to the resume, candidates provide a personal statement, a list of applicable skills and their language proficiency. Registered members also receive access to the site's *Job Agent*. Up to three Job Agents can be used by each member. The agents search for available positions, based on the criteria posted by the member. If a match is made, the site contacts the candidate via e-mail.[13,14]

Internships.wetfeet.com helps students find internships. In addition to posting a resume and searching for an internship, students can use the relocation calculator to compare the cost of living in different regions. Tips on building resumes and writing essays are provided. The *City Intern* program provides travel, housing and entertainment guides to interns interviewing or accepting a position in an unfamiliar city, making them feel more at home in a new location.

In addition to its internship locators, undergraduate, graduate, law school, medical school and business school services, the Princeton Review's Web site (**www.review.com**) offers career services to graduating students. While searching for a job, students and young professionals can also read through the site's news reports or even increase their vocabulary by visiting the "word for the day." Other career sites geared toward the younger population include **campuscareercenter.com**, **brassring-campus.com** and **collegegrad.com**.

C.5.7 Other Online Career Services

In addition to Web sites that help users find and post jobs online, there are a number of Web sites that offer features that will enhance searches, prepare users to search online, help applicants design resumes or help users calculate the cost of relocating.

Salary.com helps job seekers gauge their expected income, based on position, level of responsibility and years of experience. The search requires job category, ZIP code and specific job title. Based on this information, the site will return an estimated salary for an individual living in the specified area and employed in the position described. Estimates are returned based on the average level of income for the position.

In addition to helping applicants find employment, **www.careerpower.com** provides individuals with tests that will help them realize their strengths, weaknesses, values, skills and personality traits. Based on the results, which can be up to 10–12 pages per test, users can best decide what job categories they are qualified for and what career choice will be best suited to their personal ambitions. The service is available for a fee.

InterviewSmart™ is another service offered through CareerPower that prepares job seekers of all levels for the interviewing process. The service can be downloaded for a minimal fee or can be used on the Web for free. Both versions are available at **www.career-power.com/CareerPerfect/interviewing.htm#is.start.anchor**.

Additional services will help applicants find positions that meet their unique needs or help them design their resumes to attract the attention of specific employers. **Dog-friendly.com**, organized by geographic location, helps job seekers find opportunities that allow them to bring their pets to work, and **cooljobs.com** is a searchable database of unique job opportunities.

C.6 Summary

The Internet can improve an employer's ability to recruit employees and can help users find career opportunities worldwide. Job seekers can learn how to write a resume and cover letter, post them online and search through job listings to find the jobs that best suit their needs. Employers are able to post jobs that can be searched by an enormous pool of applicants. Job seekers can store and distribute resumes digitally, receive e-mail notification of possible positions, use salary and relocation calculators, consult job coaches and use self-assessment tools when searching for a job on the Web.

There are approximately 40,000 career-advancement services on the Internet today. Finding a job online can greatly reduce the amount of time spent applying for a position. Potential candidates can also learn more about a company by visiting its Web site. Most sites are free to job seekers. These sites typically generate their revenues by charging employers who post their job opportunities and by selling advertising space on their Web pages. On many recruitment sites, the match of a resume to a position is conducted with resume-filtering software. Career sites designed for individuals seeking technical positions are among the most popular online career sites. Online contracting services both allow businesses to post positions for which they wish to hire outside resources, and allow individuals to identify projects that best suit their interests, schedules and skills.

The Internet provides students and young professionals with some of the necessary tools to get them started in the job market. The target market is made up of individuals still in school and seeking internships, individuals who are just graduating and individuals who have been in the workforce for a few years. A number of Web sites offer features that enhance job searches, prepare users to search online, help design applicants' resumes or help users calculate the cost of relocating. Web recruiting reaches a much larger audience than does posting an advertisement in the local newspaper. A variety of sites allow employers to post jobs online. Some of these sites require a fee, which generally runs between $100 and $200. Postings remain on the Web site for approximately 30–60 days.

In designing a job posting, defining what makes a job position unique and including information such as benefits and salary might convince a qualified candidate to investigate the position further. The Internet hosts demographic-specific sites for employers seeking to increase diversity in the workplace. The Internet has provided employers with a cost-effective means of testing their prospective employees in such categories as decision making, problem solving and personality.

C.7 Internet and World Wide Web Resources

Information Technology (IT) Career Sites

www.dice.com

This is a recruiting Web site that focuses on the computer industry.

www.guru.com

This is a recruiting site for contract employees. Independent contractors, private consultants and trainers can use **guru.com** to find short-term and long-term work.

www.hallkinion.com

This is a Web recruiting service for individuals seeking IT positions.

www.techrepublic.com

This site provides employers and job seekers with recruiting capabilities and information regarding developing technology.

www.justcomputerjobs.com

This site serves as a portal with access to language-specific sites, including Java, Perl, C and C++.

www.hotdispatch.com

This forum provides software developers with the opportunity to share projects, discuss code and ask questions.

www.techjobs.bizhosting.com/jobs.htm

This site directs job seekers to links of numerous technological careers listed by location, internet, type of field, etc.

Career Sites

www.careerbuilder.com

A network of career sites, including IT Careers, *USA Today* and MSN, CareerBuilder attracts 3 million unique job seekers per month. The site provides resume-builder and job-searching agents.

www.recruitek.com

This free site caters to jobs seekers, employers and contractors.

www.monster.com

This site, the largest of the online career sites, allows people looking for jobs to post their resumes, search job listings and read advice and information about the job-search process. It also provides a variety of recruitment services for employers.

www.jobsonline.com

Similar to **Monster.com**, this site provides opportunities for job seekers and employers.

www.hotjobs.com

This online recruiting site offers cross-listing possibilities on additional sites.

www.jobfind.com

This job site is an example of locally targeted job-search resources. **JobFind.com** targets the Boston area.

www.flipdog.com

This site allows online job candidates to search for career opportunities. It employs intelligent agents to scour the Web and return jobs matching the candidate's request.

www.cooljobs.com

This site highlights unique job opportunities.

www.inetsupermall.com
This site aids job searchers in creating professional resumes and connecting with employers.

www.wirelessnetworksonline.com
This site helps connect job searchers to careers for which they are qualified.

www.careerweb.com
This site highlights featured employers and jobs and allows job seekers and employers to post and view resumes, respectively.

www.jobsleuth.com
On this site job seekers can fill out a form that indicates their desired field of employment. Job Sleuth™ searches the Internet and returns potential matches to the user's inbox. The service is free.

www.ajb.org
America's Job Bank is an online recruiting service provided through the Department of Labor and the state employment service. Searching for and posting positions on the site are free.

Executive Positions

www.sixfigurejobs.com
This is a recruitment site designed for experienced executives.

www.leadersonline.com
This career services Web site offers confidential job searches for mid-level professionals. Potential job matches are e-mailed to job candidates.

www.ecruitinginc.com
This site is designed to search for employees for executive positions.

Diversity

www.latpro.com
This site is designed for Spanish-speaking and Portuguese-speaking job seekers. In addition to providing resume-posting services, the site enables job seekers to receive matching positions via e-mail. Advice and information services are available.

www.blackvoices.com
This portal site hosts a career center designed to match African American job seekers with job opportunities.

www.hirediversity.com
In addition to services for searching for and posting positions, resume-building and updating services are also available on this site. The site targets a variety of demographics including African Americans, Asian Americans, people with disabilities, women and Latin Americans.

People with Disabilities

www.halftheplanet.com
This site represents people with disabilities. The site is large and includes many different resources and information services. A special section is dedicated to job seekers and employers.

www.wemedia.com
This site is designed to meet the needs of people with disabilities. It includes a section for job seekers and employers.

www.disabilities.com
This site provides users with a host of links to information resources on career opportunities.

www.mindexchange.com
The diversity section of this site provides users with several links to additional resources regarding people with disabilities and employment.

www.usdoj.gov/crt/ada/adahom1.htm
This is the Americans with Disabilities Act home page.

www.abanet.org/publicserv/mental.html
This is the Web site for The Commission on Mental and Physical Disability Law.

janweb.icdi.wvu.edu
The Job Accommodation Web site offers consulting services to employers regarding integration of people with disabilities into the workplace.

General Resources

www.vault.com

This site provides potential employees with "insider information" on over 3000 companies. In addition, job seekers can search through available positions and post and answer questions on the message board.

www.wetfeet.com
Similar to **vault.com**, this site allows visitors to ask questions and receive "insider information" on companies that are hiring.

Special Interest

www.eharvest.com/careers
This Web site provides job seekers interested in agricultural positions with online career services.

www.opportunitynocs.org
This career services site is for both employers and job seekers interested in non-profit opportunities.

www.experience.com
This Web site is designed specifically for young professionals and students seeking full-time, part-time and internship positions.

www.internships.wetfeet.com
Students seeking internships can search job listings on this site. It also features City Intern, to help interns become acquainted with a new location.

www.brassringcampus.com
This site provides college graduates and young professionals with less than five years of experience with job opportunities. Additional features help users buy cars or find apartments.

Online Contracting

www.ework.com
This online recruiting site matches outside contractors with companies needing project specialists. Other services provided through eWork include links to online training sites, benefits packages and payment services and online meeting and management resources.

www.elance.com
Similar to **eWork.com**, eLance matches outside contractors with projects.

www.MBAFreeAgent.com
This site is designed to match MBAs with contracting opportunities.

www.aquent.com
This site provides access to technical contracting positions.

www.WorkingSolo.com
This site helps contractors begin their own projects.

Recruiting Services

www.advantagehiring.com
This site helps employers screen resumes.

www.etest.net
This site provides employers with testing services to assess the strengths and weaknesses of prospective employees. This information can be used for better hiring strategies.

www.hire.com
Hire.com's eRecruiter is an application service provider that helps organizations streamline their Web-recruiting process.

www.futurestep.com
Executives can register confidentially at **Futurestep.com** to be considered for senior executive positions. The site connects registered individuals to positions. It also offers career management services.

www.webhire.com
This site provides employers with end-to-end recruiting solutions.

Wireless Career Resources

www.wirelessresumes.com
This site connects employers and job seekers with resumes that focus on jobs revolving around wireless technology.

www.msua.org/job.htm
This site contains links to numerous wireless job-seeking Web sites.

www.wiwc.org
This site's focus is wireless communication job searching for women.

www.firstsearch.com
At this site a job seeker is able to discover part-time, full-time and salary-based opportunities in the wireless industry.

www.pcsjobs.com
This is the site for The Caradyne Group, which is an executive search firm that focuses on finding job seekers wireless job positions.

www.cnijoblink.com
CNI Career Networks offers confidential, no-charge job placement in the wireless and telecommunications industries.

WORKS CITED

The notation <**www.domain-name.com**> indicates that the citation is for information found at the Web site.

1.   J. Gaskin, "Web Job Sites Face Tough Tasks," *Inter@ctive Week*, 14 August 2000: 50.

2. J. Gaskin, 50.

3. M. Berger, "Jobs Supermarket," *Upside*, November 2000: 224.

4. `<www.vault.com>`.

5. M. Berger, 224.

6. Cisco Advertisement, *The Wall Street Journal,* 19 October 2000: B13.

7. M. Feffer, "Posting Jobs on the Internet," 18 August 2000 `<www.webhire.com/hr/spotlight.asp>`.

8. `<www.webhire.com>`.

9. J. Gaskin, 51.

10. C. Wilde, "Recruiters Discover Diverse Value in Web Sites," *Information Week* 7, February 2000: 144.

11. A.K. Smith, "Charting Your Own Course," *U.S. News and World Report*, 6 November 2000: 58.

12. D. Lewis, "Hired! By the Highest Bidder," *The Boston Globe*, 9 July 2000: G1.

13. `<www.experience.com>`.

14. M. French, "Experience Inc., E-Recruiting for Jobs for College Students," *Mass High Tech*, 7 February–13 February 2000: 29.

Visual Studio .NET Debugger

Objectives

- To understand syntax and logic errors.
- To become familiar with the Visual Studio .NET debugging tools.
- To understand the use of breakpoints to suspend program execution.
- To examine data using expressions in the debugging windows.
- To debug methods and objects.

And often times excusing of a fault
Doth make the fault the worse by the excuse.
William Shakespeare

To err is human, to forgive divine.
Alexander Pope

Outline

D.1   Introduction

D.2   Breakpoints

D.3   Examining Data

D.4   Program Control

D.5   Additional Method Debugging Capabilities

D.6   Additional Class Debugging Capabilities

D.7   Summary

D.1 Introduction

Two types of errors occur during software development: syntax errors and logic errors. Syntax errors (or compilation errors) occur when program statements violate the grammatical rules of a programming language, such as failure to end a statement with a semicolon. When a compiler detects syntax errors, the compiler terminates without building the application. By contrast, logic errors do not prevent programs from compiling or executing, but rather prevent programs from operating as expected.

Syntax errors are easier to fix than are logic errors. Upon detecting a syntax error, the compiler provides the description and line number in the ***Task List*** window (Fig. D.1). This information gives the programmer a "clue" as to how to eliminate the error, so the compiler can create the program. However, logic errors often are more subtle and usually do not inform the user exactly where in the program the error occurred. This appendix overviews both types of errors and details Visual Studio .NET's capabilities for detecting and correcting the these logic errors.

Fig. D.1   Syntax error.

Testing and Debugging Tip D.1

After fixing one error, you may observe that the number of overall errors perceived by the compiler is significantly reduced.

Testing and Debugging Tip D.2

When the compiler reports a syntax error on a particular line, check that line for the syntax error. If the error is not on that line, check the preceding few lines of code for the cause of the syntax error.

Debugging is the process of finding and correcting *logic errors* in applications. Logic errors are more subtle than syntax errors because a program that includes a logic error compiles successfully but does not run as expected. Logic errors often are difficult to debug, because the programmer cannot see the code as it executes. One strategy that novice programmers often use to debug programs is to display program data directly, using message boxes or **Console.WriteLine** statements. For example, the programmer might print the value of a variable when its value changes to determine whether the variable is assigned the correct value. This approach is cumbersome, because programmers must insert a line of code wherever they suspect there might be a problem. Furthermore, once the program has been debugged, the programmer then must remove the extraneous statements, which often can be difficult to distinguish from the original program code.

A *debugger* is software that allows a programmer to analyze program data and trace the flow of program execution while the application runs. A debugger provides capabilities that allow the programmer to suspend program execution, examine and modify variables, call methods without changing the program code and more. In this appendix, we introduce the Visual Studio .NET debugger and several of its debugging tools. [*Note*: A program must compile successfully before it can be used in the debugger.]

D.2 Breakpoints

Breakpoints are a simple but effective debugging tool. A breakpoint is a marker that a programmer places in a code listing. When a program reaches a breakpoint, execution pauses—this allows the programmer to examine the state of the program and ensure that it is working as expected. Figure D.2 is a program that outputs the value of ten factorial (10!),[1] but contains two logic errors—the first iteration of the loop multiplies **x** by **10** instead of multiplying **x** by **9**, and the result of the factorial calculation is multiplied by **0** (so the result is always **0**). We use this program to demonstrate Visual Studio .NET's debugging abilities—using its breakpoint capabilities as our first example.

```
1   // Fig. D.2: DebugExample.cs
2   // Sample program to debug.
3
4   using System;
5
```

Fig. D.2   Debug sample program. (Part 1 of 2.)

---

1. The factorial of **x** (**x**!) is defined as the product of all digits less than or equal to **x** but greater than zero. For example, 10! = 10 * 9 * 8 * 7 * 6 * 5 * 4 * 3 * 2 * 1.

```
6   namespace Debug
7   {
8      class DebugExample
9      {
10        static void Main( string[] args )
11        {
12           int x = 10;
13
14           Console.Write( "The value of " + x + " factorial is: " );
15
16           // loop to determine x factorial, contains logic error
17           for ( int i = x; i >= 0; i-- )
18              x *= i;
19
20           Console.Write( x );
21
22           Console.ReadLine(); // delay program exit
23
24        } // end main
25
26     } // end class DebugExample
27
28   } // end namespace Debug
```

```
The value of 10 factorial is: 0
```

Fig. D.2   Debug sample program. (Part 2 of 2.)

To set breakpoints in Visual Studio, click the gray area to the left of any line of code or right-click a line of code and select **Insert Breakpoint**. A solid red circle appears, indicating that the breakpoint has been set (Fig. D.3). The program execution is suspended when it reaches the line containing the breakpoint.

To enable breakpoints and other debugging features, we must compile the program using the debug configuration (Fig. D.4). Select **Debug** from the configuration toolbar if it is not already selected. Alternatively, select **Build > Configuration Manager** and change the **Active Solution Configuration** to **Debug**.

Breakpoint   Breakpoint tooltip

Fig. D.3   Setting a breakpoint.

Fig. D.4   Debug configuration setting.

Selecting **Debug > Start** compiles the program and begins debugging. When debugging a console application, the console window appears (Fig. D.5), allowing program interaction (input and output). When the debugger reaches the breakpoint (line 18) program execution is suspended, and the IDE becomes the active window. Programmers may need to switch between the IDE and the console window while debugging programs.

Figure D.6 shows the IDE with program execution suspended at the breakpoint. The *yellow arrow* to the left of the statement

```
x *= i;
```

indicates the line at which execution is suspended and that the line contains the next statement to execute. Note that the title bar of the IDE displays **[break]**—this indicates that the IDE is in *break mode* (i.e., the debugger is running). Once the program reaches the breakpoint, a programmer can "hover" with the mouse on a variable (in this case **x** or **i**) in the source code to view the value of that variable in a tooltip as shown in Fig. D.6.

Testing and Debugging Tip D.3

Placing a breakpoint after a loop in a program allows the loop to complete without stopping before the breakpoint is reached.

D.3 Examining Data

Visual Studio .NET includes several debugging windows that allow programmers to examine variables and expressions. All the windows are accessible from the **Debug > Windows** submenu. Some windows are listed only when the IDE is in break mode (also called *debug mode*). The **Watch** window, which is available only in break mode (Fig. D.7), allows programmers to examine the values of related groups of variables and expressions. Visual Studio .NET provides a total of four **Watch** windows.

Fig. D.5   Console application suspended for debugging.

Title bar displays **[break]**

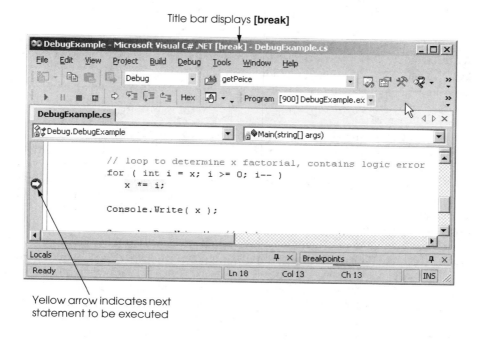

Yellow arrow indicates next
statement to be executed

Fig. D.6   Execution suspended at a breakpoint.

Expressions

Fig. D.7   **Watch** window.

Upon first opening, the **Watch** window will not contain any expressions to evaluate. To examine data, type an expression into the **Name** field. Most valid C# expressions can be entered in the **Name** field, including expressions that contain method calls. Consult the documentation under "**debugger, expressions**" for a full description of valid expressions.

Once an expression is entered, its type and value appear in the **Value** and **Type** fields. The first expression entered is the variable **i**, which has a value of **10** (line 12 assigns the value of **10** to variable **x**, and line 17 assigns the value of **x** to **i**). The **Watch** window also can evaluate more complex arithmetic expressions (e.g., **(i + 3) * 5**). Thus, the **Watch** window provides a convenient way to display various types of program data without modifying code.

By entering the variables and expressions that are relevant to a program's logic error, programmers can trace incorrect values to the source of the error and eliminate it. For example, to debug the program in Fig. D.2, we might enter the expression **i * x** in the **Watch** window. When we reach the breakpoint for the first time, the expression has a value **100** instead of **90**, which indicates a logic error in our program. This occurs because the loop at lines 17–18 started multiplying **x** by **10** as opposed to multiplying by **9**. We subtract **1** from the initial value that the **for** loop assigns to **i** (i.e., change **10** to **9**) to correct the error.

If a **Name** field in the **Watch** window contains a variable name, the variable's value can be modified for debugging purposes. To modify a variable's value, click its value in the **Value** field and enter a new value. Any modified value appears in red.

If an expression is invalid, an error appears in the **Value** field. For example, **Variable-ThatDoesNotExist** is not an identifier used in the program (fourth line in Fig. D.7). Therefore, Visual Studio .NET issues an error message in the **Value** field. To remove an expression, select it and press *Delete*.

Visual Studio also provides the ***Locals***, ***Autos*** and ***This*** windows (Fig. D.8), which are similar to the **Watch** window, except the programmer does not specify their contents. The **Locals** window displays the name and current value for all the variables that have block scope in the method containing the current statement (indicated by the yellow arrow in Fig. D.6). The **Autos** window displays the variables and values of the current statement and the previous statement. Variables can be changed in either window by clicking the appropriate **Value** field and entering a new value. The **This** window displays data that has class scope for an object. If the program is inside a **static** method (such as method **Main** in a console application), the **This** window is empty.

Fig. D.8   **Autos**, **Locals** and **This** windows.

A programmer can evaluate expressions line-by-line in the **Immediate** window (Fig. D.9). To evaluate an expression, a programmer types this expression into the window and presses *Enter*. For example, when a programmer enters `Console.WriteLine(i)` and presses *Enter*, the value of `i` is output to the console window. A developer also can use the assignment operator (`=`) to perform assignments in the **Immediate** window. Notice that the values for `i` and `x` in the **Locals** window contain these updated values.

Testing and Debugging Tip D.4

*Use the **Immediate** window to call a method one time. Placing a method call inside the **Watch** window calls that method every time the program breaks.*

D.4 Program Control

The Visual Studio .NET Debugger give programmers considerable control over the execution of a program. Using breakpoints and program-control commands provided by the debugger, programmers conveniently can analyze the execution of code at any point in a program. This is useful when a program contains multiple calls to methods that are known to execute properly. The **Debug** toolbar contains buttons that provide convenient access for controlling the debugging process (Fig. D.10). To display the **Debug** toolbar, select **View > Toolbars > Debug**.

The debug toolbar in Fig. D.10 controls debugger execution. The ***Restart*** button executes the program from the beginning, pausing at the beginning of the program to allow the programmer to set breakpoints before the program executes again. The ***Continue*** button resumes execution of a suspended program. The ***Stop Debugging*** button ends the debugging session, and the ***Break All*** button allows the programmer to suspend an executing program directly (i.e., without explicitly setting breakpoints). After execution suspends, the yellow arrow appears indicating the next statement to be executed.

Testing and Debugging Tip D.5

*When a program is executing, problems such as infinite loops usually can be interrupted by selecting **Debug > Break All** or by clicking the corresponding button on the toolbar.*

Clicking the ***Show Next Statement*** button places the cursor on the same line as the yellow arrow. This command is useful when a programmer needs to return to the current execution point after setting breakpoints in a program that contains many lines of code.

The ***Step Over*** button executes the next executable statement and advances the yellow arrow to the following line. If the next line of code contains a method call, the method is executed in its entirety as one step. This button allows the user to execute the program one line at a time without seeing the details of every method that is called. This is useful when a program contains multiple calls to methods that are known to execute properly. We discuss the **Step Into** and **Step Out** buttons in the next section.

The **Hex** button toggles the display format of data. If enabled, **Hex** displays data in hexadecimal (base 16) format, rather than displaying data in decimal (base 10) format. Experienced programmers often prefer to read values in hexadecimal format—especially large numbers because hexadecimal number representation is more concise and can be converted easily to binary (base 2) form. For more information about the hexadecimal and decimal number formats, see Appendix B, Number Systems.

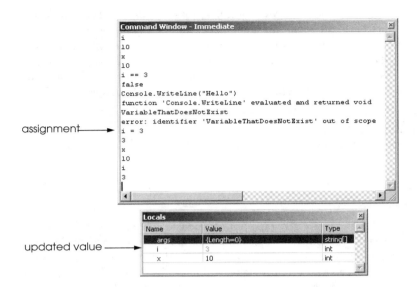

assignment ⟶

updated value ⟶

Fig. D.9   Immediate window.

The **Breakpoints** window displays all the breakpoints set for the program (Fig. D.11). A checkbox appears next to each breakpoint, indicating whether the breakpoint is *active* (checked) or *disabled* (unchecked). Lines with disabled breakpoints contain an unfilled red circle rather than a solid one (Fig. D.12). The debugger does not pause execution at disabled breakpoints.

Fig. D.10   Debug toolbar icons.

Fig. D.11   Breakpoints window.

```
// loop to determine x factorial, contains logic error
for ( int i = x; i >= 0; i-- )
    x *= i;

Console.Write( x );
```

Disabled breakpoint

Fig. D.12 Disabled breakpoint.

Testing and Debugging Tip D.6

Disabled breakpoints allow the programmer to maintain breakpoints in key locations in the program so they can be reactivated when needed. Disabled breakpoints are always visible.

In the **Breakpoints** window (Fig. D.11), the **Condition** field displays the condition that must be satisfied to suspend program execution at that breakpoint. The **Hit Count** field displays the number of times the debugger has stopped at each breakpoint. Double-clicking an item in the **Breakpoints** window moves the cursor to the line containing that breakpoint.

A programmer can add breakpoints to a program by clicking the **New** button in the **Breakpoints** window. This causes a **New Breakpoint** dialog to display (Fig. D.13). The **Function, File, Address** and **Data** tabs allow the programmer to suspend execution at either a method, a line in a particular file, an instruction in memory or when the value of a variable changes. The **Hit Count...** button (Fig. D.14) can be used to specify when the breakpoint should suspend the program (the default is to **always break**). A breakpoint can be set to suspend the program when the hit count reaches a specific number, when the hit count is a multiple of a number or is greater than or equal to a specific number.

The Visual Studio debugger also allows execution to suspend at a breakpoint depending on the value of an expression. Clicking the **Condition...** button opens the **Breakpoint Condition** dialog (Fig. D.15). The **Condition** checkbox indicates whether breakpoint conditions are enabled. The radio buttons determine how the expression in the text box is evaluated. The **is true** radio button pauses execution at the breakpoint whenever the expression is true. The **has changed** radio button causes program execution to suspend when it first encounters the breakpoint and again each time the expression differs from its previous value when the breakpoint is encountered. When the **New Breakpoint** dialog has been closed, the **Breakpoints** window displays the condition and hit count options for the new break point.

Suppose we set **x * i != 0** as the condition for the breakpoint in our loop, with the **has changed** option enabled. (We might choose to do this because the program produces an incorrect output of **0**). Program execution suspends when it first reaches the breakpoint and records that the expression has a value of **true**, because **x * i** is **100** (or **10** if we fixed the earlier logic error). We continue, and the loop decrements **i**. While **i** is between **10** and **1**, the condition's value never changes, and execution is not suspended at that breakpoint. When **i** is **0**, the expression **x * i != 0** is **false**, and execution is suspended. At this point, the programmer identifies the second logic error in our program—the final iteration of the **for** loop multiplies the result by **0**. To return the IDE to design mode, click the **Stop Debugging** button on the **Debug** toolbar.

Function tab   **File** tab   **Address** tab   **Data** tab

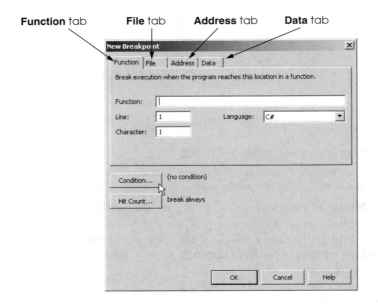

Fig. D.13 **New Breakpoint** dialog.

Fig. D.14 **Breakpoint Hit Count** dialog.

Fig. D.15 **Breakpoint Condition** dialog.

D.5 Additional Method Debugging Capabilities

In programs with many methods, it is often difficult to determine which methods may have been involved in incorrect calculations that resulted in a logic error. To simplify this process, the Visual Studio debugger includes tools for analyzing methods and method calls. We demonstrate some method-debugging tools in the following example (Fig. D.16).

The **Call Stack** window contains the program's *method call stack*, which allows the programmer to determine the exact sequence of calls that lead to the current method and to examine calling methods on the stack. This window allows the programmer to determine the flow of control in the program that resulted in the execution of the current method. For example, a breakpoint is inserted in **MyMethod**, the call stack in (Fig. D.17) indicates that the program called method **Main** first, followed by **MyMethod**.

```
1   // Fig. D.16: MethodDebugExample.cs
2   // Demonstrates debugging methods.
3
4   using System;
5
6   namespace Debug
7   {
8
9      // provides methods for demonstrating
10     // Visual Studio's debug tools
11     class MethodDebug
12     {
13        // entry point for application
14        static void Main( string[] args )
15        {
16           // display MyMethod return values
17           for ( int i = 0; i < 10; i++ )
18              Console.WriteLine( MyMethod( i ) );
19
20           Console.ReadLine();
21        } // end method Main
22
23        // perform calculation
24        static int MyMethod( int x )
25        {
26           return ( x * x ) - ( 3 * x ) + 7;
27        } // end method MyMethod
28
29        // method with logic error
30        static int BadMethod( int x )
31        {
32           return 1 / ( x - x );
33        } // end method BadMethod
34
35     } // end class MethodDebug
36
37   } // end namespace Debug
```

Fig. D.16 Debugging methods.

Most recently called method

Fig. D.17 **Call Stack** window.

Double-clicking any line in the **Call Stack** window displays the next line to be executed in that method. This allows the programmer to determine how the result of each method will affect the calling method's execution. Visual Studio .NET highlights the line in green and displays the tooltip shown in Fig. D.18.

Visual Studio .NET also provides additional program-control buttons for debugging methods. The **Step Over** button executes one statement in a method, then pauses program execution at the following line. Using **Step Over**, if an evaluated statement invokes a method, the method is invoked, and execution stops at the next statement. Using **Step Into**, if a statement invokes a method, control transfers to the method for line-by-line. The **Step Out** button finishes executing the current method and returns control to the line that called the method.

Testing and Debugging Tip D.7

*Use **Step Out** to finish a method that was stepped into accidentally.*

Figure D.19 lists each program-control debug feature, its shortcut key and a description. Experienced programmers often prefer using these shortcut keys to access menu commands.

Fig. D.18 IDE displaying a method's calling point.

Control Button	Shortcut Key	Description
Continue	*F5*	Continues program execution. Execution continues until either a breakpoint is encountered or the program ends (through normal execution).
Stop Debugging	*Shift + F5*	Stops debugging and returns to Visual Studio design mode.
Step Over	*F10*	Advances to next statement, does not step into method calls.
Step Into	*F11*	Executes next statement. If the statement contains a method call, control transfers to the method for line-by-line debugging. If the statement does not contain a method call, **Step Into** behaves like **Step Over**.
Step Out	*Shift + F11*	Finishes executing the current method and suspends program execution in the calling method.

Fig. D.19   Debug program control features.

Programmers can use the **Immediate** window, discussed in Section D.3 for testing method arguments passed to a method (Fig. D.20). Testing the arguments helps determine if a method is functioning properly.

D.6 Additional Class Debugging Capabilities

In most sophisticated C# programs, a large portion of program data is contained in objects. For these purposes, Visual Studio includes class debugging features, which allow programmers to determine the current state of objects used in a program. We demonstrate some class debugging features using the code presented in Fig. D.21. To examine an instance of class **DebugEntry**, we place a breakpoint at line 43, as shown in Fig. D.22. [*Note*: A C# file may contain multiple classes, as is the case with this example.]

Fig. D.20   Using the **Immediate** window to debug methods.

```
1    // Fig. D.21: DebugClass.cs
2    // Console application to demonstrate object debugging.
3
4    using System;
5
6    namespace ClassDebug
7    {
8
9       // creates array containing three different classes
10      public class DebugEntry
11      {
12         public int someInteger = 123;
13         private int[] integerArray = { 74, 101, 102, 102 };
14         private DebugClass debugClass;
15         private Random randomObject;
16         private object[] list = new object[ 3 ];
17
18         // constructor
19         public DebugEntry()
20         {
21            randomObject = new Random();
22            debugClass = new DebugClass( "Hello World",
23               new object() );
24
25            list[ 0 ] = integerArray;
26            list[ 1 ] = debugClass;
27            list[ 2 ] = randomObject;
28         }
29
30         // display values retrieved from three objects
31         public void DisplayValues()
32         {
33            Console.WriteLine( randomObject.Next() );
34            Console.WriteLine( debugClass.SomeString );
35            Console.WriteLine( integerArray[ 0 ] );
36         }
37
38         // main entry point for application
39         [STAThread]
40         public static void Main()
41         {
42            DebugEntry entry = new DebugEntry();
43            entry.DisplayValues();
44         }
45      } // end class DebugEntry
46
47      // demonstrates class debugging
48      public class DebugClass
49      {
50         // private variables
51         private string someString;
52         private object privateObject;
53
```

Fig. D.21   Object debugging example. (Part 1 of 2.)

```
54          // constructor
55          public DebugClass( string stringData,
56             object objectData )
57          {
58             someString = stringData;
59             privateObject = objectData;
60          }
61
62          // accessor property for someString
63          public string SomeString
64          {
65             get
66             {
67                return someString;
68             }
69
70             set
71             {
72                someString = value;
73             }
74          } // end property SomeString
75
76       } // end class DebugClass
77
78    } // end namespace ClassDebug
```

Fig. D.21   Object debugging example. (Part 2 of 2.)

```
// main entry point for application
[STAThread]
public static void Main()
{
    DebugEntry entry = new DebugEntry();
    entry.DisplayValues();
}
```

Fig. D.22   Breakpoint location for class debugging.

To assist class debugging, Visual Studio .NET allows the programmer to expand and view all data members and properties of a class, including **private** members. In any of the three windows (i.e., **Watch**, **Locals**, **Autos** and **This**), a class that has data members is displayed with a plus (**+**) (Fig. D.23). When a programmer clicks the plus box, all the object's data members and their values display. If a member references an object, the object's data members also can be listed by clicking the object's plus box.

Many logic errors are the result of incorrect array calculations. To simplify the identification of such errors, the debugger includes the ability to display all the values in an array. Figure D.24 displays the contents of the **list** array. The object at index **0** is and **int** array, which is expanded to show its contents. Index **1** contains a **DebugClass** object—expanded to show the object's **private** data members, as well as a **public** property. Index **2** contains a **Random** object, defined in the Framework Class Library (FCL).

The Visual Studio debugger contains several other debugging windows, including **Threads**, **Modules**, **Memory**, **Disassembly** and **Registers**. These windows are used by experienced programmers to debug large, complex projects—consult the Visual Studio .NET documentation for more details on these features.

In this appendix, we demonstrated several techniques for debugging programs, methods and classes. The Visual Studio .NET debugger is a powerful tool that allows programmers to build more robust, fault-tolerant programs.

Fig. D.23 Expanded class in **Watch** window.

Fig. D.24 Expanded array in **Watch** window.

D.7 Summary

Debugging is the process of finding logic errors in applications. Syntax errors (or compilation errors) occur when program statements violate the grammatical rules of a programming language and are caught by the compiler. Logic errors occur when a program compiles successfully, but does not run as expected. Debuggers allow programmers to examine a program while it is executing.

A breakpoint is a marker set at a line of code. When a program reaches a breakpoint, execution is suspended. The programmer then can examine the state of the program and ensure that the program is working properly. To set breakpoints, click the gray area to the left of any line of code. Alternatively, right-click a line of code and select **Insert Breakpoint**. The **Breakpoints** window displays all the breakpoints currently set for a program.

Disabled breakpoints allow the programmer to maintain breakpoints in key locations in the program so that they can be used again when needed.

The **Watch** window allows the programmer to examine the values of variables and expressions. To examine data, type a valid C# expression, such as a variable name, into the **Name** field. Once the expression has been entered, its type and value appear in the **Type** and **Value** fields. Variables in the **Watch** window can be modified by the user for testing purposes. To modify a variable's value, click the **Value** field and enter a new value.

The **Locals** window displays the name and current value of all the local variables or objects in the current scope. The **Autos** window displays the variables and objects used in the previous statement and the current statement (indicated by the yellow arrow).

The **Immediate** window is useful for testing arguments passed to a method. This helps determine whether a method is functioning properly. To evaluate an expression in the **Immediate** window, simply type the expression into the window and press *Enter*.

The **Call Stack** window contains the program's method call stack, which allows the programmer to determine the exact sequence of calls that led to the current method and to examine calling methods on the stack.

The **Continue** button resumes execution of a suspended program. The **Stop Debugging** button ends the debugging session. The **Break All** button allows the programmer to place an executing program in break mode. The **Show Next Statement** button places the cursor on the same line as the yellow arrow that indicates the next statement to execute. The **Step Over** button executes the next executable line of code, advances the yellow arrow to the executable line that follows and, finally, pauses program execution. If the executed line of code contains a method call, the method is executed in its entirety as one step. The **Step Into** button executes the next statement. If the statement contains a method call, control transfers to the method for line-by-line debugging. If the statement does not contain a method call, **Step Into** behaves like **Step Over**. The **Step Out** button finishes executing the method and returns control to the line that called the method. The **Hex** button toggles the display format of data. If enabled, **Hex** displays data in a hexadecimal (base-16) form, rather than decimal (base-10) form.

Visual Studio .NET includes class debugging features that allow the programmer to determine the current state of any objects used in a program. To assist class debugging, Visual Studio .NET allows the programmer to expand and view all data members' variables and properties of an object, including those declared `private`.

Generating Documentation in Visual Studio .NET

Objectives

- To introduce Visual Studio .NET's documentation generation tool.
- To introduce XML documentation comments.
- To understand XML documentation tags and their use.
- To generate HTML and XML documentation files.

Outline

E.1   Introduction
E.2   Documentation Comments
E.3   Documenting C# Source Code
E.4   Creating Comment Web Pages
E.5   Creating XML Documentation Files
E.6   Summary

E.1 Introduction

A single programmer can implement most of the programs from this book. However, industrial software is more complex, and each project almost always requires the talent of several programmers. In such projects, communication among programmers is a necessity. When a programmer writes code for a class, programmers from the same group should understand how that class operates. For this reason, each programmer should document specific information on a class, such as the class's role in a system, the functionality that each method provides for the class and the purpose of each class variable. This documentation helps all programmers understand how classes can interoperate, and facilitates modification, use and extension of each class.

To facilitate the creation of documentation for a project, Visual Studio .NET provides the *XML documentation tool*. This tool converts key pieces of information in source code—such as the class's members, the hierarchy to which the class belongs and any other general remarks the programmer wishes to document—to HTML[1] or XML[2] format. The programmer specifies the general remarks to be documented by placing them in special regions in the code, called *XML documentation comments*.

In this appendix, we introduce Visual Studio .NET's documentation capabilities. We begin by discussing the format and structure of the XML documentation comments that the documentation-generation tool uses to create the documentation files. We then show how to generate the documentation through a LIVE-CODE™ example. We recommend reading through Chapters 5–7 before reading this appendix, because the examples presented in this appendix relate to the examples from these chapters.

E.2 Documentation Comments

Before the Visual Studio documentation-generation tool can generate documentation files, the programmer must insert XML documentation comments into the source files. These comments contain the information that the programmer wishes to document. The documentation-generation tool recognizes only single-line comments that begin with three forward slashes (***///***). An example of a simple documentation comment is

---

1. HTML is discussed in Appendices I and J.
2. XML is discussed in Chapter 15.

```
/// <summary>
/// this is a comment
/// </summary>
```

In this comment, the first line begins element **summary**, the second line defines the text that element **summary** contains and the third line closes element **summary**. As we will discuss later in this text, the documentation tool will document only the text within these **summary** tags. All XML declaration comments (excluding the three forward slashes) must contain well-formed XML. Like general comments, the compiler does not translate documentation comments to MSIL (Microsoft Intermediate Language), so they do not become "part of" the program.

Because the documentation tool creates XML files, documentation comments can contain certain types of markup, such as HTML tags and customized XML content. For example, the documentation comment

```
/// <summary>
/// Sorts integer array using <em>MySort</em> algorithm
/// </summary>
```

contains the HTML tags **** and ****. In the generated HTML files, **MySort** appears as *emphasized text* (normally italic).

E.3 Documenting C# Source Code

Figure E.1, Fig. E.2 and Fig. E.3 present a modified version of the **Point**, **Circle** and **CircleTest** classes from Section 9.4 that contains XML documentation comments. In the text that follows the example, we discuss each XML element used in the documentation comments. In Section E.4, we discuss how the documentation tool can generate XML documentation from this file.

```
1   // Fig. E.1: Point.cs
2   // Class Point maintains an X and Y coordinate.
3
4   using System;
5
6   namespace CircleTest
7   {
8      /// <summary>
9      /// Class <c><b>Point</b></c> defines a point as a pair
10     /// of x and y coordinates.
11     /// </summary>
12     public class Point
13     {
14        /// <summary>
15        /// This private member of <c><b>Point</b></c>
16        /// represents the x coordinate.
17        /// </summary>
18        /// <returns> The x coordinate as an integer.</returns>
19        private int x;
```

Fig. E.1   **Point** marked up with XML comments. (Part 1 of 3.)

```
20
21          /// <summary>
22          /// This private member of <c><b>Point</b></c>
23          /// represents the x coordinate.
24          /// </summary>
25          /// <returns> The y coordinate as an integer.</returns>
26      private int y;
27
28          /// <summary>
29          /// Default constructor for class <c><b>Point</b></c>.
30          /// </summary>
31          /// <remarks>
32          /// Sets properties <c><b>X</b></c> and <c><b>Y</b></c> to 0.
33          /// </remarks>
34      public Point()
35      {
36          // implicit call to base-class constructor occurs here
37      }
38
39          /// <summary>
40          /// Constructor for <c><b>Point</b></c> that accepts two
41          /// integers that represent the x- and
42          /// y coordinates of the point.
43          /// </summary>
44          /// <remarks>
45          /// Uses <c><b>X</b></c> and <c><b>Y</b></c>
46          /// properties to set the coordinates of the point,
47          /// <em>not</em> private members <c><b>x</b></c>
48          /// and <c><b>y</b></c>.
49          /// </remarks>
50          /// <param name="xValue">
51          /// The x coordinate of the circle
52          /// </param>
53          /// <param name="yValue">
54          /// The y coordinate of the circle.
55          /// </param>
56      public Point( int xValue, int yValue )
57      {
58          // implicit call to base-class constructor occurs here
59          X = xValue;
60          Y = yValue;
61      }
62
63          /// <summary>
64          /// Provides get and set access to member
65          /// <c><b>x</b></c>.
66          /// </summary>
67          /// <value>
68          /// <c><b>X</b></c> accesses the value of the
69          /// <c><b>x</b></c> data member.
70          /// </value>
71      public int X
72      {
```

Fig. E.1   **Point** marked up with XML comments. (Part 2 of 3.)

```
73          get
74          {
75              return x;
76          }
77
78          set
79          {
80              x = value;
81          }
82      }
83
84      /// <summary>
85      /// Provides get and set access to member
86      /// <c><b>y</b></c>.
87      /// </summary>
88      /// <value>
89      /// <c><b>Y</b></c> accesses the value of the
90      /// <c><b>y</b></c> data member.
91      /// </value>
92      public int Y
93      {
94          get
95          {
96              return y;
97          }
98
99          set
100         {
101             y = value;
102         }
103     }
104
105     /// <summary>
106     /// Converts the <c><b>Point</b></c> to
107     /// <b>string</b> format.
108     /// </summary>
109     /// <returns>
110     /// Returns a string in format:
111     /// [x coordinate, y coordinate].
112     /// </returns>
113     public override string ToString()
114     {
115         return "[" + X + ", " + Y + "]";
116     }
117
118 } // end class Point
119 }
```

Fig. E.1   **Point** marked up with XML comments. (Part 3 of 3.)

```
1   // Fig. E.2: Circle.cs
2   // Class Circle inherits from Point.
```

Fig. E.2   **Circle** class marked up with XML comments. (Part 1 of 4.)

```
3
4    using System;
5
6    namespace CircleTest
7    {
8        /// <summary>
9        /// Class <c><b>Circle</b></c> inherits from class
10       /// <c><b>Point</b></c>. It has an additional member to
11       /// represent the radius, a property that provides access
12       /// to it and method <c><b>Area</b></c> to compute the area
13       /// of the circle.
14       /// </summary>
15       public class Circle : Point
16       {
17           /// <summary>
18           /// This private member of <c><b>Circle</b></c>
19           /// represents the radius.
20           /// </summary>
21           private double radius;
22
23           /// <summary>
24           /// Default constructor for class <c><b>Circle</b></c>.
25           /// </summary>
26           /// <remarks>
27           /// Sets the radius to 0.
28           /// </remarks>
29           public Circle()
30           {
31               // implicit call to base class constructor occurs here
32           }
33
34           /// <summary>
35           /// Constructor for <c>Circle</c> that accepts two integers
36           /// that represent the x- and y-coordinates of the circle
37           /// and a <b>double</b> that represents the radius.
38           /// </summary>
39           /// <remarks>
40           /// Uses property <c><b>Radius</b></c> to set the radius
41           /// of the circle, <em>not</em> private member
42           /// <c><b>radius</b></c>.
43           /// </remarks>
44           /// <param name="xValue">
45           /// The x-coordinate of the circle
46           /// </param>
47           /// <param name="yValue">
48           /// The y-coordinate of the circle.
49           /// </param>
50           /// <param name="radiusValue">
51           /// The radius of the circle.
52           /// </param>
53           public Circle( int xValue, int yValue, double radiusValue )
54               : base( xValue, yValue )
55           {
```

Fig. E.2 Circle class marked up with XML comments. (Part 2 of 4.)

```
56          Radius = radiusValue;
57       }
58
59       /// <summary>
60       /// Provides get and set access to member
61       /// <c><b>radius</b></c>.
62       /// </summary>
63       /// <remarks>
64       /// The <c><b>set</b></c> method ensures
65       /// that <c><b>radius</b></c> is
66       /// <em>not</em> set to a
67       /// negative number.
68       /// </remarks>
69       /// <value>
70       /// <c><b>Radius</b></c> accesses the value of the
71       /// <c><b>radius</b></c> data member.
72       /// </value>
73       public double Radius
74       {
75          get
76          {
77             return radius;
78          }
79
80          set
81          {
82             if ( value >= 0 )
83                radius = value;
84          }
85       }
86
87       /// <summary>
88       /// Computes the diameter of the circle.
89       /// </summary>
90       /// <returns>
91       /// Returns the diameter of the circle.
92       /// </returns>
93       public double Diameter()
94       {
95          return Radius * 2;
96       }
97
98       /// <summary>
99       /// Computes the circumference of the circle.
100      /// </summary>
101      /// <remarks>
102      /// Uses constant <c><b>Math.PI</b></c>
103      /// <see cref="System.Math.PI"/>
104      /// </remarks>
105      /// <returns>
106      /// Returns the circumference of the circle.
107      /// </returns>
```

Fig. E.2   **Circle** class marked up with XML comments. (Part 3 of 4.)

```
108         public double Circumference()
109         {
110             return Math.PI * Diameter();
111         }
112
113         /// <summary>
114         /// Computes the area of the circle.
115         /// </summary>
116         /// <remarks>
117         /// Uses constant <c><b>Math.PI</b></c>
118         /// <see cref="System.Math.PI"/>
119         /// </remarks>
120         /// <returns>
121         /// Returns the area of the circle.
122         /// </returns>
123         public double Area()
124         {
125             return Math.PI * Math.Pow( Radius, 2 );
126         }
127
128         /// <summary>
129         /// Converts the <c><b>Circle</b></c> to
130         /// <b>string</b> format.
131         /// </summary>
132         /// <remarks>
133         /// Overrides <c><b>ToString</b></c> method of base class.
134         /// <see cref="CircleTest.Point.ToString"/>
135         /// </remarks>
136         /// <returns>
137         /// Returns a string that includes the center of the
138         /// circle and its radius.
139         /// </returns>
140         public override string ToString()
141         {
142             return "Center = " + base.ToString() +
143                 "; Radius = " + Radius;
144         }
145
146     } // end class Circle
147 }
```

Fig. E.2 **Circle** class marked up with XML comments. (Part 4 of 4.)

```
1  // Fig. E.3: CircleTest.cs
2  // Manipulating a Circle object.
3
4  using System;
5  using System.Windows.Forms;
6
7  namespace CircleTest
8  {
```

Fig. E.3 **CircleTest** class marked up with XML comments. (Part 1 of 3.)

```
 9     /// <summary>
10     /// Class <c><b>CircleTest</b></c> test the
11     /// <c><b>Point</b></c> and <c><b>Point</b></c> classes.
12     /// </summary>
13     class CircleTest
14     {
15        /// <summary>
16        /// Entry point of application.
17        /// </summary>
18        /// <remarks>
19        /// In this application all command-line arguments
20        /// are ignored.
21        /// </remarks>
22        /// <param name="args">
23        /// Optional arguments to Main.
24        /// </param>
25        static void Main( string[] args )
26        {
27           Circle circle = new Circle( 37, 43, 2.5 );
28
29           // append Circle properties to output
30           string output = "X coordinate is " + circle.X + "\n" +
31              "Y coordinate is " + circle.Y + "\n" +
32              "Radius is " + circle.Radius;
33
34           // set new coordinates and radius
35           circle.X = 2;
36           circle.Y = 2;
37           circle.Radius = 4.25;
38
39           output += "\n\n" +
40              "The new location and radius of circle are " +
41              "\n" + circle + "\n";
42
43           // display Circle's Diameter
44           output += "Diameter is " +
45              String.Format( "{0:F}", circle.Diameter() ) + "\n";
46
47           // display Circle's Circumference
48           output += "Circumference is " +
49              String.Format( "{0:F}", circle.Circumference() ) + "\n";
50
51           // display Circle's Area
52           output += "Area is " +
53              String.Format( "{0:F}", circle.Area() );
54
55           MessageBox.Show( output, "Demonstrating Class Circle" );
56
57        } // end method Main
58
59     } // end class CircleTest
60  }
```

Fig. E.3   **CircleTest** class marked up with XML comments. (Part 2 of 3.)

Fig. E.3 **CircleTest** class marked up with XML comments. (Part 3 of 3.)

XML documentation comments can be placed before a class definition, an interface definition, a constructor or a member (i.e., an instance variable or a reference). The programmer can place a description (i.e., purpose) of the class in element **summary**. The **summary** element can contain as many lines as necessary to provide a description of the class method, properties, members, etc. As we will see in the next section, any content placed in element **summary** will be marked up in a column (labeled **Description**) of an HTML table. An example of a **summary** is shown on lines 8–11 of Fig. E.1 to provide a description of class **Point**. (We also used these tags in Section E.2 when we introduced documentation comments.)

Two elements commonly used to describe methods are **returns** and **param**. Element **returns** contains information on the return value, as illustrated by lines 109–112 of Fig. E.1. Method **ToString** of **Point** returns a formatted **string** that has the point's *x-y* coordinate pair. Similarly, the **param** element contains information on a method's parameters. For example, lines 50–55 of Fig. E.1 associate one **param** element with variable **x**, and another **param** element with variable **y**.

We use **c** XML elements to mark up regions of code in our comments. Line 102 of Fig. E.2 shows the use of the **c** element to specify that **Math.PI** should be marked up as code in the resulting documentation. Notice that the **c** element contains **b** element that places **Math.PI** in boldface type on the Web page.

The **remarks** tag enables programmers to document any "miscellaneous" information or detailed comments. For example, lines 116–119 of Fig. E.2 documents that method **Area** uses the constant **Math.PI**.

The **see** tag (lines 103, 118 and 134 of Fig. E.2) is references another class or member (method, constant, property, etc.). Any member can be referenced by using the fully qualifying name (e.g., **System.Console.ReadLine**). The **value** tag (lines 67–70 and 88–91 of Fig. E.1 and lines 69–72 of Fig. E.2) is used to describe properties. These comments have no effect on the comment Web pages that can be generated.

For more information on these tags and other tags to use, visit the following URI:

```
ms-help://MS.VSCC/MS.MSDNVS/csref/html/
vclrftagsfordocumentationcomments.htm
```

E.4 Creating Comment Web Pages

In this section, we show how Visual Studio .NET can create documentation in Web-page format from source code that contains the XML documentation comments. We demonstrate this feature on the project containing the classes of Fig. E.1, Fig. E.2 and Fig. E.3. After opening this project, select **Tools > Build Comment Web Pages** (Fig. E.4).

The **Build Comment Web Pages** window will appear, enabling the developer to specify the project(s) containing the files that Visual Studio .NET should document (Fig. E.5). If the developer selects **Build for entire Solution**, Visual Studio .NET will document all files in the current solution. If the developer selects **Build for selected Projects**, Visual Studio .NET will document only those files in the project that the developer specifies. In addition, the developer can specify the directory where Visual Studio .NET should store the generated HTML content. If the developer selects **Add to Favorites**, Visual Studio .NET will bookmark this content in the **Favorites** menu of Internet Explorer.

Press **OK** to generate the HTML content. Visual Studio immediately creates and displays the documentation using a style sheet. In our example, the user can view the communication from classes **Circle**, **CircleTest** and **Point** by selecting the desired class in the left-most column. Figure E.6 shows the documentation for class **Circle**.

Note that all member names and **summary** elements in Fig. E.2 have been formatted and placed in **Members** and **Description** columns, respectively (Fig. E.6). Selecting an item from the **Members** column opens an HTML page associated with that item. Figure E.7 shows the HTML page associated with method **Area** of class **Circle**. Notice that the **returns** tags in Fig. E.2 on lines 120–122 mark up the text that is documented as the text placed in the **Description** column.

Fig. E.4   Selecting the **Build Comment Web Pages** from **Tools** menu.

Fig. E.5   Saving a document to a file.

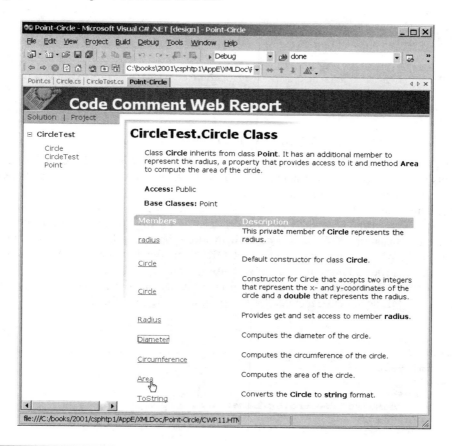

Fig. E.6   HTML documentation of class `Circle`.

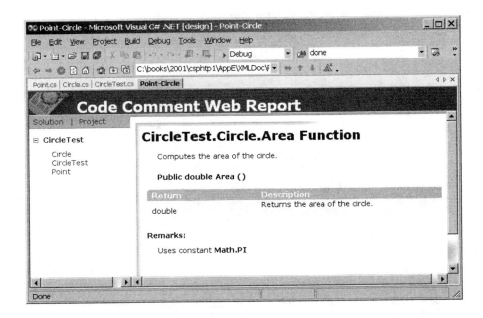

Fig. E.7   HTML documentation of method **Area** method of class **Circle**.

E.5 Creating XML Documentation Files

In this section, we discuss how to generate an XML documentation file that contains all elements in the source code comments. An application then can read such a file and create custom documentation from its information.

To create an XML documentation file for a project, right-click on the project in the **Solution Explorer** and select **Properties**. Select the **Configuration** folder, then the **Build** tab. Change the **XML Documentation File** property to the name of the file that will store the XML documentation and click **OK**. If this file does not exist, Visual Studio will create the file and place it in the **bin/Debug** directory of the current project. Select **Build > Build Solution** to compile the project and create the XML document. Figure E.8 shows the XML document generated for the example in Fig. E.1–Fig. E.3.

```
1   <?xml version="1.0"?>
2   <doc>
3       <assembly>
4           <name>Point-Circle</name>
5       </assembly>
6       <members>
```

Fig. E.8   XML documentation generated by Visual Studio .NET. (Part 1 of 6.)

```
 7
 8          <member name="T:CircleTest.Circle">
 9             <summary>
10                Class <c><b>Circle</b></c> inherits from class
11                <c><b>Point</b></c>. It has an additional member to
12                represent the radius, a property that provides
13                accessto it and method <c><b>Area</b></c> to
14                compute the area of the circle.
15             </summary>
16          </member>
17
18          <member name="T:CircleTest.Point">
19             <summary>
20                Class <c><b>Point</b></c> defines a point as a pair
21                of x and y coordinates.
22             </summary>
23          </member>
24
25          <member name="F:CircleTest.Point.xCoordinate">
26             <summary>
27                This protected member of <c><b>Point</b></c>
28                represents the x coordinate.
29             </summary>
30             <returns> The x coordinate as an integer.</returns>
31          </member>
32
33          <member name="F:CircleTest.Point.yCoordinate">
34             <summary>
35                This protected member of <c><b>Point</b></c>
36                represents the x coordinate.
37             </summary>
38             <returns> The y coordinate as an integer.</returns>
39          </member>
40
41          <member name="M:CircleTest.Point.#ctor">
42             <summary>
43                Default constructor for class <c><b>Point</b></c>.
44             </summary>
45             <remarks>
46                Sets properties <c><b>X</b></c> and <c><b>Y</b></c> to 0.
47             </remarks>
48          </member>
49
50          <member name=
51             "M:CircleTest.Point.#ctor(System.Int32,System.Int32)">
52             <summary>
53                Constructor for <c><b>Point</b></c>
54                that accepts two integers
55                that represent the x and y coordinates of the point.
56             </summary>
57             <remarks>
58                Uses <c><b>X</b></c> and <c><b>Y</b></c>
59                properties to set the coordinates of the point,
```

Fig. E.8   XML documentation generated by Visual Studio .NET. (Part 2 of 6.)

```
60              <em>not</em> private members <c><b>x</b></c>
61              and <c><b>y</b></c>.
62          </remarks>
63          <param name="xValue">
64              The x coordinate of the circle
65          </param>
66          <param name="yValue">
67              The y coordinate of the circle.
68          </param>
69      </member>
70
71      <member name="M:CircleTest.Point.ToString">
72          <summary>
73              Converts the <c><b>Point</b></c> to
74              <b>string</b> format.
75          </summary>
76          <returns>
77              Returns a string in format:
78              [x coordinate, y coordinate].
79          </returns>
80      </member>
81
82      <member name="P:CircleTest.Point.X">
83          <summary>
84              Provides get and set access to member
85              <c><b>x</b></c>.
86          </summary>
87          <value>
88              <c><b>X</b></c> accesses the value of the
89              <c><b>x</b></c> data member.
90          </value>
91      </member>
92
93      <member name="P:CircleTest.Point.Y">
94          <summary>
95              Provides get and set access to member
96              <c><b>y</b></c>.
97          </summary>
98          <value>
99              <c><b>Y</b></c> accesses the value of the
100             <c><b>y</b></c> data member.
101         </value>
102     </member>
103
104     <member name="F:CircleTest.Circle.radius">
105         <summary>
106             This private member of <c><b>Circle</b></c>
107             represents the radius.
108         </summary>
109     </member>
110
111     <member name="M:CircleTest.Circle.#ctor">
112         <summary>
```

Fig. E.8   XML documentation generated by Visual Studio .NET. (Part 3 of 6.)

```
113                           Default constructor for class <c><b>Circle</b></c>.
114                       </summary>
115                       <remarks>
116                           Sets the radius to 0.
117                       </remarks>
118                   </member>
119
120                   <member name="M:CircleTest.Circle.#ctor(System.Int32,
121                       System.Int32,System.Double)">
122                       <summary>
123                           Constructor for <c><b>Circle<b></c> that accepts two
124                           integersthat represent the x and y coordinates of the
125                           circle and a <b>double</b> that represents the radius.
126                       </summary>
127                       <remarks>
128                           Uses property <c><b>Radius</b></c> to set the radius
129                           of the circle, <em>not</em> private member
130                           <c><b>radius</b></c>.
131                       </remarks>
132                       <param name="xValue">
133                           The x coordinate of the circle
134                       </param>
135                       <param name="yValue">
136                           The y coordinate of the circle.
137                       </param>
138                       <param name="radiusValue">
139                            The radius of the circle.
140                       </param>
141                   </member>
142
143                   <member name="M:CircleTest.Circle.Diameter">
144                       <summary>
145                           Computes the diameter of the circle.
146                       </summary>
147                       <returns>
148                           Returns the diameter of the circle.
149                       </returns>
150                   </member>
151
152                   <member name="M:CircleTest.Circle.Circumerence">
153                       <summary>
154                           Computes the circumference of the circle.
155                       </summary>
156                       <remarks>
157                           Uses constant <c><b>Math.PI</b></c>
158                           <see cref="F:System.Math.PI"/>
159                       </remarks>
160                       <returns>
161                           Returns the circumference of the circle.
162                       </returns>
163                   </member>
164
165                   <member name="M:CircleTest.Circle.Area">
```

Fig. E.8   XML documentation generated by Visual Studio .NET. (Part 4 of 6.)

```
166          <summary>
167             Computes the area of the circle.
168          </summary>
169          <remarks>
170             Uses constant <c><b>Math.PI</b></c>
171             <see cref="F:System.Math.PI"/>
172          </remarks>
173          <returns>
174             Returns the area of the circle.
175          </returns>
176       </member>
177
178       <member name="M:CircleTest.Circle.ToString">
179          <summary>
180             Converts the <c><b>Circle</b></c> to
181             <b>string</b> format.
182          </summary>
183          <remarks>
184             Overrides <c><b>ToString</b></c> method of base class.
185             <see cref="!:CircleTest.Point.ToString"/>
186          </remarks>
187          <returns>
188             Returns a string that includes the center of the
189             circle and its radius.
190          </returns>
191       </member>
192
193       <member name="P:CircleTest.Circle.Radius">
194          <summary>
195             Provides get and set access to member
196             <c><b>radius</b></c>.
197          </summary>
198          <remarks>
199             The <c><b>set</b></c> method
200             ensures that <c><b>radius</b></c>
201             is <em>not</em> set to a
202             negative number.
203          </remarks>
204          <value>
205             <c><b>Radius</b></c> accesses the value of the
206             <c><b>radius</b></c> data member.
207          </value>
208       </member>
209
210       <member name="T:CircleTest.CircleTest">
211          <summary>
212             Class <c><b>CircleTest</b></c> inherits from class
213             tests the <c><b>Point</b></c> and
214             <c><b>Point</b></c> classes.
215          </summary>
216       </member>
217
218       <member name="M:CircleTest.CircleTest.Main(System.String[])">
```

Fig. E.8   XML documentation generated by Visual Studio .NET. (Part 5 of 6.)

```
219                <summary>
220                    Entry point of application.
221                </summary>
222                <remarks>
223                    In this application all command-line arguments
224                    are ignored.
225                </remarks>
226                <param name="args">
227                    Optional arguments to Main.
228                </param>
229            </member>
230
231        </members>
232  </doc>
```

Fig. E.8   XML documentation generated by Visual Studio .NET. (Part 6 of 6.)

Notice that only class members are included in the XML file that is generated. Each class member has a **member** element which includes all XML comments for that member. For example, lines 50–69 define a **member** element that contains information on the two-argument **Point** constructor. The **name** attribute of a **member** tag is a **string** that contains information about the name and type of the member. The type is specified by a capital letter: **M** stands for method, **P** for property (or indexer), **E** for event and **T** for type (i.e, class). For a complete listing of these abbreviations, select **Help > Index**; then locate the topic **processing XML files in C#**. In Fig. E.8, line 51 contains the value of the **name** attribute and contains an **M** as the first letter, indicating that line 51 declares a method. (Recall that a constructor is a specialized method.) A colon follows, after which the full name of the method is shown. For this example, it is **Circle-Test.Point.#ctor(System.Int32,System.Int32)**. Because this is a constructor, **#ctor** is used in the fully qualified name. This constructor takes two **int**s, with the parentheses after the name of each member specifying that member's type.

E.6 Summary

A single programmer can implement most of the programs from this book. However, industrial software is more complex, and each project almost always requires the talent of several programmers. In such projects, communication among programmers is a necessity. When a programmer writes code for a class, programmers from the same group should understand how that class operates. For this reason, each programmer should document specific information on a class, such as the class's role in a system, the functionality that each method provides for the class and the purpose of each class variable. The documentation helps all programmers understand how classes can interoperate and facilitates the modification, use and extension of each class.

To aid in the creation of documentation for a project, Visual Studio .NET provides the XML documentation tool. This tool converts key pieces of information in source code—such as the class's members, the hierarchy to which the class belongs and any other general remarks the programmer wishes to document—to HTML or XML format. The programmer specifies the general remarks to be documented by placing them in special regions in the code, called XML documentation comments.

Before the Visual Studio documentation-generation tool can generate documentation files, the programmer must insert XML documentation comments into the source files. These comments contain the information that the programmer wishes to document. The documentation-generation tool recognizes only single-line comments that begin with three forward slashes (**///**).

Once XML documentation comments have been added to a source file, the developer can create comment Web pages via the **Tools > Build Comment Web Pages** option. This opens the **Build Comment Web Pages** window, where the developer specifies the project(s) containing the files that Visual Studio .NET should document. If the developer selects **Build for entire Solution**, Visual Studio .NET will document all files in the current solution. If the developer selects **Build for selected Projects**, Visual Studio .NET will document only those files in the project that the developer specifies. In addition, the developer can specify the directory in which Visual Studio .NET should store the generated HTML content. If the developer selects **Add to Favorites**, Visual Studio .NET will bookmark this content in the **Favorites** menu of Internet Explorer.

Alternatively, the developer has the option to create XML documentation files from their comments. The information in these files can then be formatted by an outside application to create more specialized documentation. To create an XML documentation file for a project, right-click on the project in the **Solution Explorer** and select **Properties**. Select the **Configuration** folder, followed by the **Build** tab. Change the **XML Documentation File** property to the name of the file that will store the XML documentation, and click **OK**.

ASCII Character Set

	0	1	2	3	4	5	6	7	8	9
0	nul	soh	stx	etx	eot	enq	ack	bel	bs	ht
1	nl	vt	ff	cr	so	si	dle	dc1	dc2	dc3
2	dc4	nak	syn	etb	can	em	sub	esc	fs	gs
3	rs	us	sp	!	"	#	$	%	&	`
4	(	)	*	+	,	-	.	/	0	1
5	2	3	4	5	6	7	8	9	:	;
6	<	=	>	?	@	A	B	C	D	E
7	F	G	H	I	J	K	L	M	N	O
8	P	Q	R	S	T	U	V	W	X	Y
9	Z	[	\	]	^	_	'	a	b	c
10	d	e	f	g	h	i	j	k	l	m
11	n	o	p	q	r	s	t	u	v	w
12	x	y	z	{			}	~	del		

Fig. F.1   ASCII character set.

The digits at the left of the table are the left digits of the decimal equivalent (0–127) of the character code, and the digits at the top of the table are the right digits of the character code. For example, the character code for "F" is 70, and the character code for "&" is 38.

Most readers of this book are interested in the ASCII character set used to represent English characters on many computers. The ASCII character set is a subset of the Unicode character set used by C# to represent characters from most of the world's languages. For more information on the Unicode® character set, see Appendix G.

G

Unicode®

Objectives

- To become familiar with Unicode.
- To discuss the mission of the Unicode Consortium.
- To discuss the design basis of Unicode.
- To understand the three Unicode encoding forms: UTF-8, UTF-16 and UTF-32.
- To introduce characters and glyphs.
- To discuss the advantages and disadvantages of using Unicode.
- To provide a brief tour of the Unicode Consortium's Web site.

Outline

G.1   Introduction
G.2   Unicode Transformation Formats
G.3   Characters and Glyphs
G.4   Advantages and Disadvantages of Unicode
G.5   Unicode Consortium's Web Site
G.6   Using Unicode
G.7   Character Ranges
G.8   Summary

G.1 Introduction

The use of inconsistent character *encodings* (i.e., numeric values associated with characters) when developing global software products causes serious problems because computers process information using numbers. For example, the character "a" is converted to a numeric value so that a computer can manipulate that piece of data. Many countries and corporations have developed their own encoding systems that are incompatible with the encoding systems of other countries and corporations. For example, the Microsoft Windows operating system assigns the value 0xC0 to the character "A with a grave accent," while the Apple Macintosh operating system assigns that same value to an upside-down question mark. This results in the misrepresentation and possible corruption of data because the data is not processed as intended.

In the absence of a widely implemented universal character encoding standard, global software developers had to *localize* their products extensively before distribution. Localization includes the language translation and cultural adaptation of content. The process of localization usually includes significant modifications to the source code (such as the conversion of numeric values and the underlying assumptions made by programmers), which results in increased costs and delays releasing the software. For example, some English-speaking programmers might design global software products assuming that a single character can be represented by one byte. However, when those products are localized for Asian markets, the programmer's assumptions are no longer valid; thus, the majority, if not the entirety, of the code needs to be rewritten. Localization is necessary with each release of a version. By the time a software product is localized for a particular market, a newer version, which needs to be localized as well, may be ready for distribution. As a result, it is cumbersome and costly to produce and distribute global software products in a market where there is no universal character encoding standard.

In response to this situation, the *Unicode Standard*, an encoding standard that facilitates the production and distribution of software, was created. The Unicode Standard outlines a specification to produce consistent encoding of the world's characters and *symbols*. Software products that handle text encoded in the Unicode Standard need to be localized, but the localization process is simpler and more efficient because the numeric values need not be converted and the assumptions made by programmers about the character encoding are universal. The Unicode Standard is maintained by a nonprofit organization called the

Unicode Consortium, whose members include Apple, IBM, Microsoft, Oracle, Sun Microsystems, Sybase and many others.

When the Consortium envisioned and developed the Unicode Standard, they wanted an encoding system that was *universal, efficient, uniform* and *unambiguous*. A universal encoding system encompasses all commonly used characters. An efficient encoding system allows text files to be parsed easily. A uniform encoding system assigns fixed values to all characters. An unambiguous encoding system represents a given character in a consistent manner. These four terms are referred to as the Unicode Standard *design basis*.

G.2 Unicode Transformation Formats

Although Unicode incorporates the limited ASCII *character set* (i.e., a collection of characters), it encompasses a more comprehensive character set. In ASCII, each character is represented by a byte containing 0s and 1s. One byte is capable of storing the binary numbers from 0 to 255. Each character is assigned a number between 0 and 255; thus, ASCII-based systems can support only 256 characters, a tiny fraction of the world's characters. Unicode extends the ASCII character set by encoding the vast majority of the world's characters. The Unicode Standard encodes all of those characters in a uniform numerical space from 0 to 10FFFF hexadecimal. An implementation will express these numbers in one of several transformation formats, choosing the one that best fits the particular application at hand.

Three such formats are in use, called *UTF-8, UTF-16* and *UTF-32*, depending on the size of the units—in *bits*—being used. UTF-8, a variable width encoding form, requires one to four bytes to express each Unicode character. UTF-8 data consists of 8-bit bytes (sequences of one, two, three or four bytes depending on the character being encoded) and is well suited for ASCII-based systems when there is a predominance of one-byte characters (ASCII represents characters as one-byte). Currently, UTF-8 is widely implemented in UNIX systems and in databases. [*Note*: Currently, Internet Explorer 6.0 and Netscape Communicator 6 only support UTF-8, so document authors should use UTF-8 for encoding XML and XHTML documents.]

The variable width UTF-16 encoding form expresses Unicode characters in units of 16-bits (i.e., as two adjacent bytes, or a short integer in many machines). Most characters of Unicode are expressed in a single 16-bit unit. However, characters with values above FFFF hexadecimal are expressed with an ordered pair of 16-bit units called *surrogates*. Surrogates are 16-bit integers in the range D800 through DFFF, which are used solely for the purpose of "escaping" into higher numbered characters. Approximately one million characters can be expressed in this manner. Although a surrogate pair requires 32 bits to represent characters, it is space efficient to use these 16-bit units. Surrogates are rare characters in current implementations. Many string-handling implementations are written in terms of UTF-16. [*Note*: Details and sample code for UTF-16 handling are available on the Unicode Consortium Web site at **www.unicode.org**.]

Implementations that require significant use of rare characters or entire scripts encoded above FFFF hexadecimal should use UTF-32, a 32-bit, fixed-width encoding form that usually requires twice as much memory as UTF-16 encoded characters. The major advantage of the fixed-width UTF-32 encoding form is that it expresses all characters uniformly, so it is easy to handle in arrays.

There are few guidelines that state when to use a particular encoding form. The best encoding form to use depends on computer systems and business protocols, not on the data.

Typically, the UTF-8 encoding form should be used where computer systems and business protocols require data to be handled in 8-bit units, particularly in legacy systems being upgraded because it often simplifies changes to existing programs. For this reason, UTF-8 has become the encoding form of choice on the Internet. Likewise, UTF-16 is the encoding form of choice on Microsoft Windows applications. UTF-32 is likely to become more widely used in the future as more characters are encoded with values above FFFF hexadecimal. Also, UTF-32 requires less sophisticated handling than UTF-16 in the presence of surrogate pairs. Figure G.1 shows the different ways in which the three encoding forms handle character encoding.

G.3 Characters and Glyphs

The Unicode Standard consists of *characters*, written components (i.e., alphabetic letters, numerals, punctuation marks, accent marks, etc.) that can be represented by numeric values. Examples of characters include U+0041 LATIN CAPITAL LETTER A. In the first character representation, U+*yyyy* is a *code value*, in which U+ refers to Unicode code values, as opposed to other hexadecimal values. The *yyyy* represents a four-digit hexadecimal number of an encoded character. Code values are bit combinations that represent encoded characters. Characters are represented using *glyphs*, various shapes, fonts and sizes for displaying characters. There are no code values for glyphs in the Unicode Standard. Examples of glyphs are shown in Fig. G.2.

The Unicode Standard encompasses the alphabets, ideographs, syllabaries, punctuation marks, *diacritics*, mathematical operators, etc. that comprise the written languages and scripts of the world. A diacritic is a special mark added to a character to distinguish it from another letter or to indicate an accent (e.g., in Spanish, the tilde "~" above the character "n"). Currently, Unicode provides code values for 94,140 character representations, with more than 880,000 code values reserved for future expansion.

Character	UTF-8	UTF-16	UTF-32
LATIN CAPITAL LETTER A	0x41	0x0041	0x00000041
GREEK CAPITAL LETTER ALPHA	0xCD 0x91	0x0391	0x00000391
CJK UNIFIED IDEOGRAPH-4E95	0xE4 0xBA 0x95	0x4E95	0x00004E95
OLD ITALIC LETTER A	0xF0 0x80 0x83 0x80	0xDC00 0xDF00	0x00010300

Fig. G.1   Correlation between the three encoding forms.

Fig. G.2   Various glyphs of the character A.

G.4 Advantages and Disadvantages of Unicode

The Unicode Standard has several significant advantages that promote its use. One is the impact it has on the performance of the international economy. Unicode standardizes the characters for the world's writing systems to a uniform model that promotes transferring and sharing data. Programs developed using such a schema maintain their accuracy because each character has a single definition (i.e., *a* is always U+0061, % is always U+0025). This enables corporations to manage the high demands of international markets by processing different writing systems at the same time. Also, all characters can be managed in an identical manner, thus avoiding any confusion caused by different character code architectures. Moreover, managing data in a consistent manner eliminates data corruption, because data can be sorted, searched and manipulated using a consistent process.

Another advantage of the Unicode Standard is *portability* (i.e., the ability to execute software on disparate computers or with disparate operating systems). Most operating systems, databases, programming languages and Web browsers currently support, or are planning to support, Unicode. Additionally, Unicode includes more characters than any other character set in common use (although it does not yet include all of the world's characters).

A disadvantage of the Unicode Standard is the amount of memory required by UTF-16 and UTF-32. ASCII character sets are 8 bits in length, so they require less storage than the default 16-bit Unicode character set. However, the *double-byte character set (DBCS)* and the *multi-byte character set (MBCS)* that encode Asian characters (ideographs) require two to four bytes, respectively. In such instances, the UTF-16 or the UTF-32 encoding forms may be used with little hindrance on memory and performance.

G.5 Unicode Consortium's Web Site

If you would like to learn more about the Unicode Standard, visit **www.unicode.org**. This site provides a wealth of information about the Unicode Standard. Currently, the home page is organized into various sections: *New to Unicode*, *General Information*, *The Consortium*, *The Unicode Standard*, *Work in Progress* and *For Members*.

The *New to Unicode* section consists of two subsections: **What is Unicode?** and **How to Use this Site**. The first subsection provides a technical introduction to Unicode by describing design principles, character interpretations and assignments, text processing and Unicode conformance. This subsection is recommended reading for anyone new to Unicode. Also, this subsection provides a list of related links that provide the reader with additional information about Unicode. The **How to Use this Site** subsection contains information about using and navigating the site as well hyperlinks to additional resources.

The *General Information* section contains six subsections: **Where is my Character?**, **Display Problems?**, **Useful Resources**, **Enabled Products**, **Mail Lists** and **Conferences**. The main areas covered in this section include a link to the Unicode code charts (a complete listing of code values) assembled by the Unicode Consortium as well as a detailed outline on how to locate an encoded character in the code chart. Also, the section contains advice on how to configure different operating systems and Web browsers so that the Unicode characters can be viewed properly. Moreover, from this section, the user can navigate to other sites that provide information on various topics such as, fonts, linguistics and other standards such as the *Armenian Standards Page* and the *Chinese GB 18030 Encoding Standard*.

The Consortium section consists of five subsections: **Who we are**, **Our Members**, **How to Join**, **Press Info** and **Contact Us**. This section provides a list of the current Unicode Consortium members as well as information on how to become a member. Privileges for each member type—*full*, *associate*, *specialist* and *individual*—and the fees assessed to each member are listed here.

The Unicode Standard section consists of nine subsections: **Start Here**, **Latest Version**, **Technical Reports**, **Code Charts**, **Unicode Data**, **Updates & Errata**, **Unicode Policies**, **Glossary** and **Technical FAQ**. This section describes the updates applied to the latest version of the Unicode Standard, as well as categorizing all defined encoding. The user can learn how the latest version has been modified to encompass more features and capabilities. For instance, one enhancement of Version 3.2 is that it contains additional encoded characters. Also, if users are unfamiliar with vocabulary terms used by the Unicode Consortium, then they can navigate to the **Glossary** subsection.

The *Work in Progress* section consists of three subsections: **Calendar of Meetings**, **Proposed Characters** and **Submitting Proposals**. This section presents the user with a catalog of the recent characters included into the Unicode Standard scheme as well as those characters being considered for inclusion. If users determine that a character has been overlooked, then they can submit a written proposal for the inclusion of that character. The **Submitting Proposals** subsection contains strict guidelines that must be adhered to when submitting written proposals.

The *For Members* section consists of two subsections: **Member Resources** and **Working Documents**. These subsections are password protected; only consortium members can access these links.

G.6 Using Unicode

Visual Studio .NET uses Unicode UTF-16 encoding to represent all characters. Figure G.3 uses C# to display the text "Welcome to Unicode!" in eight different languages: English, French, German, Japanese, Portuguese, Russian, Spanish and Simplified Chinese. [*Note*: The Unicode Consortium's Web site contains a link to code charts that lists the 16-bit Unicode code values.]

```
1   // Fig. G.3: Unicode.cs
2   // Using unicode encoding
3
4   using System;
5   using System.Drawing;
6   using System.Collections;
7   using System.ComponentModel;
8   using System.Windows.Forms;
9   using System.Data;
10
11  public class Unicode : System.Windows.Forms.Form
12  {
13      internal System.Windows.Forms.Label lblChinese;
14      internal System.Windows.Forms.Label lblSpanish;
15      internal System.Windows.Forms.Label lblRussian;
```

Fig. G.3   Unicode values for multiple languages. (Part 1 of 3.)

```
16      internal System.Windows.Forms.Label lblPortuguese;
17      internal System.Windows.Forms.Label lblJapanese;
18      internal System.Windows.Forms.Label lblGerman;
19      internal System.Windows.Forms.Label lblFrench;
20      internal System.Windows.Forms.Label lblEnglish;
21      private System.ComponentModel.Container components = null;
22
23      // Visual Studio .NET generated code
24
25      // main entry point for the application.
26      [STAThread]
27      static void Main()
28      {
29          Application.Run(new Unicode());
30      }
31
32      private void Unicode_Load(object sender, System.EventArgs e)
33      {
34          // English
35          char[] english = {'\u0057', '\u0065', '\u006C',
36              '\u0063', '\u006F', '\u006D', '\u0065', '\u0020',
37              '\u0074', '\u006F', '\u0020' };
38
39          lblEnglish.Text = new string(english) +
40              "Unicode" + '\u0021';
41
42          // French
43          char[] french = { '\u0042', '\u0069', '\u0065',
44              '\u006E', '\u0076', '\u0065', '\u006E', '\u0075',
45              '\u0065', '\u0020', '\u0061', '\u0075', '\u0020' };
46
47          lblFrench.Text = new string(french) +
48              "Unicode" + '\u0021';
49
50          // German
51          char[] german = {'\u0057', '\u0069', '\u006C',
52              '\u006B', '\u006F', '\u006D', '\u006D', '\u0065',
53              '\u006E', '\u0020', '\u007A', '\u0075', '\u0020'};
54
55          lblGerman.Text =  new string(german) +
56              "Unicode" + '\u0021';
57
58          // Japanese
59          char[] japanese = { '\u3078',  '\u3087', '\u3045',
60              '\u3053', '\u305D', '\u0021'};
61
62          lblJapanese.Text = "Unicode" + new string(japanese);
63
64          // Portuguese
65          char[] portuguese = {'\u0053', '\u0065', '\u006A',
66              '\u0061', '\u0020', '\u0062', '\u0065', '\u006D',
67              '\u0020', '\u0076', '\u0069', '\u006E', '\u0064',
68              '\u006F', '\u0020', '\u0061', '\u0020' };
```

Fig. G.3   Unicode values for multiple languages. (Part 2 of 3.)

```
69
70          lblPortuguese.Text = new string(portuguese) +
71              "Unicode" + '\u0021';
72
73          // Russian
74          char[] russian = {  '\u0414', '\u043E', '\u0431',
75              '\u0440', '\u043E', '\u0020', '\u043F', '\u043E',
76              '\u0436', '\u0430', '\u043B', '\u043E', '\u0432',
77              '\u0430', '\u0442', '\u044A', '\u0020', '\u0432',
78              '\u0020' };
79
80          lblRussian.Text = new string(russian) +
81              "Unicode" + '\u0021';
82
83          // Spanish
84          char[] spanish = {'\u0042', '\u0069', '\u0065',
85              '\u006E', '\u0076', '\u0065', '\u006E', '\u0069',
86              '\u0064', '\u006F', '\u0020', '\u0061', '\u0020' };
87
88          lblSpanish.Text = new string(spanish) +
89              "Unicode" + '\u0021';
90
91          // Simplified Chinese
92          char[] chinese = {'\u6B22', '\u8FCE', '\u4F7F',
93              '\u7528', '\u0020' };
94
95          lblChinese.Text = new string(chinese) +
96              "Unicode" + '\u0021';
97      }  // end method Unicode_Load
98  } // end class Unicode
```

Fig. G.3   Unicode values for multiple languages. (Part 3 of 3.)

Lines 35–37 contain the hexadecimal codes for the English text. The **Code Charts** page on the Unicode Consortium Web site contains a document that lists the code values for the **Basic Latin** *block* (or category), which includes the English alphabet. The hexadecimal codes in lines 35–36 equate to "**Welcome** ". When using Unicode characters in C#, the format **\u***yyyy* is used, where *yyyy* represents the hexadecimal Unicode encoding. For example, the letter "W" (in "Welcome") is denoted by **\u0057**. Line 36 contains the hexadecimal for the *space* character (**\u0020**). The unicode value for the word "**to** " is on line 37. Lines 39–40 create a new string from the character array and append the word "Unicode." "Unicode" is not encoded because it is a registered trademark and has no equivalent translation in most languages. Line 40 also contains the **\u0021** notation for the exclamation mark (**!**).

The remaining welcome messages (lines 43–96) contain the unicode values for the other seven languages. The code values used for the French, German, Portuguese and Spanish text are located in the **Basic Latin** block, the code values used for the Simplified Chinese text are located in the **CJK Unified Ideographs** block, the code values used for the Russian text are located in the **Cyrillic** block and the code values used for the Japanese text are located in the **Hiragana** block.

[*Note*: To render the Asian characters in a Windows application, you may need to install the proper language files on your computer. To do this in Windows 2000, open the **Regional Options** dialog from the **Control Panel** (**Start > Settings > Control Panel**). At the bottom of the **General** tab is a list of languages. Check the **Japanese** and the **Traditional Chinese** checkboxes and press **Apply**. Follow the directions of the install wizard to install the languages. For additional assistance, visit **www.unicode.org/help/display_problems.html**.]

G.7 Character Ranges

The Unicode Standard assigns code values, which range from **0000** (**Basic Latin**) to **E007F** (*Tags*), to the written characters of the world. Currently, there are code values for 94,140 characters. To simplify the search for a character and its associated code value, the Unicode Standard generally groups code values by *script* and function (i.e., Latin characters are grouped in a block, mathematical operators are grouped in another block, etc.). As a rule, a script is a single writing system that is used for multiple languages (e.g., the Latin script is used for English, French, Spanish, etc.) The **Code Charts** page on the Unicode Consortium Web site lists all the defined blocks and their respective code values. Figure G.4 lists some blocks (scripts) from the Web site and their range of code values.

Script	Range of Code Values
Arabic	U+0600–U+06FF
Basic Latin	U+0000–U+007F
Bengali (India)	U+0980–U+09FF
Cherokee (Native America)	U+13A0–U+13FF
CJK Unified Ideographs (East Asia)	U+4E00–U+9FAF
Cyrillic (Russia and Eastern Europe)	U+0400–U+04FF
Ethiopic	U+1200–U+137F
Greek	U+0370–U+03FF
Hangul Jamo (Korea)	U+1100–U+11FF
Hebrew	U+0590–U+05FF
Hiragana (Japan)	U+3040–U+309F

Fig. G.4   Some character ranges. (Part 1 of 2.)

Script	Range of Code Values
Khmer (Cambodia)	U+1780–U+17FF
Lao (Laos)	U+0E80–U+0EFF
Mongolian	U+1800–U+18AF
Myanmar	U+1000–U+109F
Ogham (Ireland)	U+1680–U+169F
Runic (Germany and Scandinavia)	U+16A0–U+16FF
Sinhala (Sri Lanka)	U+0D80–U+0DFF
Telugu (India)	U+0C00–U+0C7F
Thai	U+0E00–U+0E7F

Fig. G.4   Some character ranges. (Part 2 of 2.)

G.8 Summary

Before Unicode, software developers were plagued by the use of inconsistent character encoding (e.g., using numeric values for characters). Most countries and organizations had their own encoding systems, which were incompatible with each other. Without Unicode, localization of global software requires significant modifications to the source code, which results in increased cost and in delays in releasing the product.

The Unicode Consortium developed the Unicode Standard in response to the serious problems created by multiple character encodings and the use of those encodings. The Unicode Standard facilitates the production and distribution of localized software. It outlines a specification for the consistent encoding of the world's characters and symbols. Software products that handle text encoded in the Unicode Standard need to be localized, but the localization process is simpler and more efficient. The Unicode Standard is designed to be universal, efficient, uniform and unambiguous.

A universal encoding system encompasses all commonly used characters; an efficient encoding system parses text files easily; a uniform encoding system assigns fixed values to all characters; and an unambiguous encoding system represents the same character for any given value. Unicode extends the limited ASCII character set to include all the major characters of the world. Unicode makes use of three Unicode Transformation Formats (UTF)—UTF-8, UTF-16 and UTF-32—each of which may be appropriate for use in different contexts. UTF-8 data consists of 8-bit bytes (sequences of one, two, three or four bytes, depending on the character being encoded) and is well suited for ASCII-based systems when there is a predominance of one-byte characters. (ASCII represents characters with one byte.) UTF-8 is a variable-width encoding form that is more compact for text involving mostly Latin characters and ASCII punctuation. UTF-16, the default encoding form of the Unicode Standard, is a variable-width encoding form that uses 16-bit code units instead of bytes. Most characters are represented by a single unit, but some characters require surrogate pairs. Surrogates are 16-bit integers in the range D800 through DFFF and are used solely for the purpose of "escaping" into higher numbered characters. Without surrogate pairs, the UTF-16 encoding form can encompass only 65,000 characters, but with the surrogate pairs, the number is expanded to include over a million characters. UTF-32 is a 32-bit, fixed-width encoding form whose major advantage is that it expresses all characters uniformly, so that they are easy to handle in arrays and other structures.

A character is any written component that can be represented by a numeric value. Characters are represented with glyphs, shapes, fonts and sizes. Code values are bit combinations that represent encoded characters. The Unicode notation for a code value is U+*yyyy*, in which U+ refers to the Unicode code values, as opposed to other hexadecimal values. The *yyyy* represents a four-digit hexadecimal number.

The Unicode Standard has become the default encoding system for XML and any language derived from XML, such as XHTML. The Visual Studio .NET IDE uses UTF-16 encoding to represent all characters. In using Unicode characters in C# code, the entity reference **\u***yyyy* is used, where *yyyy* represents the hexadecimal Unicode encoding.

COM Integration

H.1 Introduction

Initially, applications created for Windows or DOS were designed as single *monolithic executables*—i.e., complete applications packaged as single executable files. However, as software became more complex, developers began to experience difficulties constructing all the necessary components of an application. Furthermore, as the size of applications increased, it became impractical to redistribute an entire application to accommodate each application upgrade or bug fix.

To address these problems, Microsoft incorporated *shared libraries* into Windows, enabling developers to reuse and modularize code. A shared library, or *dynamic link library (DLL)* in Windows, is a file that contains compiled code that an application loads at execution time. The fact that these libraries are loaded at runtime allows developers to modify specific libraries and test the results without rebuilding an entire application. Multiple applications can use a single shared library, which reduces the overall memory requirements for running those applications. The partitioning of programs into small pieces also makes it easier to distribute application upgrades, because only the modified DLLs must be redistributed.

The introduction of shared libraries solved many problems that previously had restricted modularity and code reusability. However, the libraries also raised new concerns. Monolithic applications rarely created version conflicts—if an application vendor fixed a bug in one piece of software, it was unlikely that the upgrade would affect any other software on the system. With the establishment of system-wide shared libraries, a vendor's upgrade or modification of a library could "break" software that used an older version of that library. Often, developers packaged DLLs with their applications to ensure software compatibility. However, the packaged DLLs could overwrite preexisting libraries on users' systems, possibly affecting previously installed software. Problems introduced by shared libraries were so difficult to locate and fix that their effects became known as "DLL hell."

Microsoft developed the *Component Object Model (COM)* in an attempt to expand DLL functionality and correct DLL problems. COM is a specification that controls library versions and backwards compatibility and defines a communication standard among libraries. Microsoft defined the COM specification to be detailed and strict, thus ensuring that COM developers create compatible libraries. Microsoft also implemented the COM architecture on a large scale—virtually all Windows libraries adhere to the COM specification.

When implemented correctly, COM ensures highly organized and reusable libraries, but the specification does have limitations. For example, COM is difficult to program and deploy, because developers must guarantee that new COM components are both compatible with previous versions and correctly registered with the system. If a COM library is placed on a system without proper registration, the component will not be represented correctly in the registry, and applications might be unable to find or use the library.

In the .NET platform, COM components are no longer necessary. Microsoft .NET components retain the benefits of COM while resolving many of its associated problems. Components in .NET maintain all identification information internally—the independence of the component from the Windows Registry ensures correct component identification. Many developers and companies have invested significant resources in the development of COM components, but want to harness the power, organization and functionality of .NET. To facilitate developers' migration from COM to .NET, Microsoft created a set of tools designed to integrate existing COM components into the .NET platform.

H.2 ActiveX Integration

In recent years, ActiveX controls have been popular COM components. C# allows developers to import and use ActiveX controls in Windows Forms applications. We include an ActiveX **LabelScrollbar** control on our Web site which we now use to demonstrate Microsoft's ActiveX integration utility.

To use this control, students first must register the **.OCX** file in the Windows Registry. To register the control, open a **Command Prompt** and invoke the **RegSvr32** utility program which is located in the directory **c:\winnt\system32**. (This path might vary among different computers and Windows versions.) Figure H.1 depicts the successful registration of the **LabelScrollbar** ActiveX control.

Fig. H.1   ActiveX control registration.

Once students register the ActiveX control, they must add it to the Visual Studio IDE's toolbox. To accomplish this, right click the toolbox and select **Customize Toolbox** (Fig. H.2). The **Customize Toolbox** lists all the COM components that are registered on the machine. Select the **Deitel LabelScrollbar .OCX** file to add the **LabelScrollbar** to the toolbox and then click **OK**. When you add the **LabelScrollBar** to your Web form Visual Studio generates libraries **Deitel** and **AxDeitel** and adds them to the references in the **Solution Explorer**. The first reference (**Deitel**) is the *Common Runtime Library proxy*, which allows the programmer to access the ActiveX component's methods and properties from .NET code. The second reference (**AxDeitel**) is the *Windows Forms proxy*, which allows the programmer to add the ActiveX component to a form. In this context a *proxy* is an object which allows .NET code to interact with COM code, we discuss the interaction between .NET and COM in greater detail in the next section. Note that, once the **LabelScrollbar** is added to the toolbox, two DLL files are generated in the **bin** directory of the application: **AxInterop.Deitel.dll** and **Interop.Deitel.dll**.

The first image in Fig. H.3 depicts the IDE toolbox after the **LabelScrollBar** has been added. The second image displays a list of the **LabelScrollBar** control properties, consisting of properties defined in the ActiveX control (i.e., **Min**, **Max**, **SmallChange**, **LargeChange**, and **Value**) and Visual Studio-defined properties (e.g., **Anchor**, **Dock** and **Location**).

To demonstrate **LabelScrollBar**'s functionality, we add three **LabelScrollbar**s to a form (Fig. H.4). These controls enable a user to select RGB values (i.e., red, green and blue) that specify the color of a **PictureBox**.

Fig. H.2   **Customize Toolbox** dialog with an ActiveX control selected.

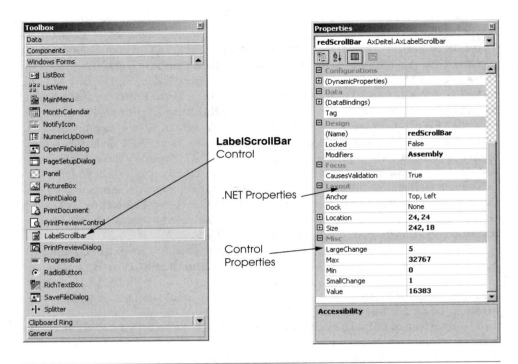

Fig. H.3   IDE's toolbox and **LabelScrollbar** properties.

```
1   // Fig. H.4: LabelScrollbar.cs
2   // demonstrates ActiveX component usage in .NET.
3
4   using System;
5   using System.Drawing;
6   using System.Collections;
7   using System.ComponentModel;
8   using System.Windows.Forms;
9   using AxDeitel;
10
11  namespace FigH_04
12  {
13      // Demonstrates ActiveX LabelScrollBar control
14      public class LabelScrollTest : System.Windows.Forms.Form
15      {
16          private System.Windows.Forms.PictureBox pbColorBox;
17          private AxDeitel.AxLabelScrollbar redScrollBar;
18          private AxDeitel.AxLabelScrollbar greenScrollBar;
19          private AxDeitel.AxLabelScrollbar blueScrollBar;
20
21          /// Required designer variable.
22          private System.ComponentModel.Container components = null;
23
```

Fig. H.4   ActiveX COM control integration in C#. (Part 1 of 3.)

```csharp
24          public LabelScrollTest()
25          {
26             InitializeComponent();
27
28             // setup LabelScrollbar properties
29             SetupRGBTitleScrollbar( redScrollBar );
30             SetupRGBTitleScrollbar( blueScrollBar );
31             SetupRGBTitleScrollbar( greenScrollBar );
32
33             // initialize PictureBox back color
34             pbColorBox.BackColor = Color.FromArgb(
35                redScrollBar.Value, greenScrollBar.Value,
36                blueScrollBar.Value );
37
38          } // end constructor
39
40          // initialize LabelScrollBar properties
41          private void SetupRGBTitleScrollbar(
42             AxLabelScrollbar scrollBar )
43          {
44             scrollBar.Min = 0;            // minimum value
45             scrollBar.Max = 255;          // maximum value
46             scrollBar.LargeChange = 10;   // large change value
47             scrollBar.SmallChange = 1;    // small change value
48
49          } // end method SetupRGBTitleScrollBar
50
51          // Visual Studio .NET generated code
52
53          [STAThread]
54          static void Main()
55          {
56             Application.Run( new LabelScrollTest() );
57          }
58
59          // handles scrollbar changed event
60          private void scrollbar_Change( object sender,
61             System.EventArgs e )
62          {
63             pbColorBox.BackColor = Color.FromArgb(
64                redScrollBar.Value, greenScrollBar.Value,
65                blueScrollBar.Value );
66          } // end method scrollbar_Change
67       } // end class LabelScrollTest
68    } // end namespace FigH_04
```

Fig. H.4   ActiveX COM control integration in C#. (Part 2 of 3.)

Fig. H.4   ActiveX COM control integration in C#. (Part 3 of 3.)

The constructor calls **SetupRGBTitleScrollbar** (lines 41–49), which sets the initial property values of **Min**, **Max**, **LargeChange** and **SmallChange** for each **LabelScrollbar** control. The **Max** property of each **LabelScrollbar** is set to **255**, allowing a color range of over 16 million colors.

The constructor also sets the **PictureBox**'s initial back color (lines 34–36). Lines 60–66 define the event handler for the **LabelScrollbar**'s **change** event. When the user changes the value of a **LabelScrollbar**, the **change** event fires and the **PictureBox**'s background color changes.

H.3 DLL Integration

Visual Studio .NET also supports the integration of COM DLLs. This process is similar to the integration of ActiveX components. To demonstrate how Visual Studio .NET integrates a COM DLL, we have included **deitelvb6addition.dll** on our Web site. This simple library contains function **AdditionFunction**, which takes two arguments, adds them together and returns the result.

The first step in the integration of this COM DLL is to identify the DLL in the Windows Registry with the **RegSvr32** utility as follows:

```
regsvr32 deitelvb6addition.dll
```

After registering the library, add a reference to it in a C# program by right-clicking **References** in the **Solution Explorer** and selecting **Add Reference**. In the **Add Reference** dialog (Fig. H.5), select the **COM** tab. Then, choose **Simple Addition DLL** and click **OK**. A dialog appears, indicating that .NET must generate a *primary interop assembly* (Fig. H.5). Select **Yes** when this dialog appears. The primary interop assembly contains information for all methods and classes contained in the COM library.

In Windows, all components (both .NET and COM) must be accompanied by identification information. This information contains *Globally Unique Identifiers (GUID)* for the component and its internal classes, as well as language-independent descriptions of all classes and types that are defined in the component. These language-independent descriptions help to enable component reuse across multiple programming languages. A GUID consists of a long string of numbers that a computer generates on the basis of the computer's current time, hardware and a random number. The GUID algorithm never generates the same identifier twice; thus, GUIDs enable unique component identification across all computers.

Fig. H.5   Add Reference dialog DLL Selection.

When a COM component is registered, its GUID is stored in the Windows Registry; programs then can use the registry to locate and identify the component. Once a program has located a desired component, it uses the component's *type library* to find and use the library's objects and methods. A *type library* describes all of a COM component's interfaces, types and methods; the type library is included in either the component **.dll** file or in a separate **.tlb** file. The separation of component identifiers (located in the Windows Registry) from the data represented on the disk (the library file) is the source of many problems associated with the COM architecture. By contrast, .NET components avoid these problems by maintaining all identification information internally. When Visual Studio imports a COM component, it creates a file that contains all identification and data-description information internally. Visual Studio obtains the component GUID from the Windows Registry and converts the data description from the type library-format into the .NET assembly format. This processing creates a new DLL file, called a primary interop assembly, which then is placed into the applications **bin** directory.

The primary interop assembly is used by .NET to locate COM methods and to translate component data types between the .NET platform types and COM component types. The translation for each COM component is performed by a *Runtime Callable Wrapper (RCW)*. The RCW is a proxy object created by the .NET runtime from the information in the object's primary interop assembly. The RCW manages the COM object and performs communication between .NET code and the COM object.

Performance Tip H.1

The .NET and COM architectures are fundamentally different in terms of memory manage-ment and object representation. Method calls to COM objects can degrade program perfor-mance because the RCW must convert all data types between the managed (.NET) context and the unmanaged (COM) context.

When we instantiate a COM object in C#, we are actually creating a new instance of the object's RCW. The communication between the RCW and the COM component is entirely transparent, enabling the .NET developer to interact with the COM object as if it were a .NET object.

We created an application (Fig. H.6) demonstrating how to use the **Simple Addition DLL** that we want to integrate into .NET. This program includes three text boxes and a button. After entering an **int** into each of the first two text boxes, the user clicks the **Cal-culate** button, and the program displays the sum of the two **int** in the third text box.

Line 29 creates the RCW **additionObject** for COM component **Deitel_DLL.CAddition**. Lines 55–59 enable the **calculateButton** button if both text boxes contain values, and disable the button if the text boxes are empty. When the user clicks **Calculate**, the button fires the event handler **calculateButton_Click**, which obtains the content of the text boxes and adds the values. The event handler calls COM method **addFunction**, which returns the sum as an **int** (lines 74–75). The result then is displayed in **txtResultBox** (line 77).

In this appendix, we demonstrated the use of COM libraries and ActiveX controls from a .NET application. In addition, we briefly explored the history of COM and the differences between its architecture and that of .NET. After reading this appendix, students should have a basic understanding of COM and should be able to use COM components in .NET appli-cations. To learn more about .NET and COM, consult the Web resources described in Section H.5.

```
1   // Fig. H.6: Addition.cs
2   // Uses a COM component to add two integers.
3
4   using System;
5   using System.Drawing;
6   using System.Collections;
7   using System.ComponentModel;
8   using System.Windows.Forms;
9   using System.Data;
10  using Deitel_DLL;
11
12  namespace Addition
13  {
14     // adds two integers using a COM component
15     public class Addition : System.Windows.Forms.Form
16     {
17        // display labels
18        private System.Windows.Forms.Label SecondLabel;
19        private System.Windows.Forms.Label FirstLabel;
20
```

Fig. H.6   COM DLL component in C#. (Part 1 of 3.)

```
21      // integer text boxes
22      private System.Windows.Forms.TextBox resultBox;
23      private System.Windows.Forms.TextBox firstIntegerBox;
24      private System.Windows.Forms.TextBox secondIntegerBox;
25
26      // calculates addition
27      private System.Windows.Forms.Button calculateButton;
28
29      private CAddition additionObject = new CAddition();
30
31      // Required designer variable.
32      private System.ComponentModel.Container
33         components = null;
34
35      public Addition()
36      {
37         InitializeComponent();
38      }
39
40      // Visual Studio .NET generated code
41
42      // The main entry point for the application.
43      [STAThread]
44      static void Main()
45      {
46         Application.Run( new Addition() );
47      }
48
49      // event handler to enable calculateButton
50      private void integerBox_TextChanged( object sender,
51         System.EventArgs e )
52      {
53         // enable calculate button if both boxes
54         // contain text
55         if ( firstIntegerBox.Text != "" &&
56            secondIntegerBox.Text != "" )
57            calculateButton.Enabled = true;
58         else
59            calculateButton.Enabled = false;
60      } // end method integerBox_TextChanged
61
62      // event handler that displays sum when calculate
63      // is clicked
64      private void calculateButton_Click( object sender,
65         System.EventArgs e )
66      {
67         int firstInteger, secondInteger, total;
68
69         firstInteger = Int32.Parse( firstIntegerBox.Text );
70         secondInteger = Int32.Parse( secondIntegerBox.Text );
71
72         // addition object invokes AddFunction that
73         // returns integer value
```

Fig. H.6   COM DLL component in C#. (Part 2 of 3.)

```
74          total = additionObject.AddFunction( ref firstInteger,
75             ref secondInteger );
76
77          resultBox.Text = total.ToString();
78       } // end method calculateButton_Click
79    } // end class Addition
80 } // end namespace Addition
```

Fig. H.6   COM DLL component in C#. (Part 3 of 3.)

H.4 SUMMARY

Initially, applications created for Windows or DOS were designed as single monolithic executables—entire applications packaged in single executable files. As applications grew larger and more complex, it became impractical for developers to construct and distribute all the necessary components of an application, because doing so would result in longer development times and more costly distribution mechanism. Microsoft incorporated dynamic link libraries (DLLs) into Windows to allow developers to modularize and reuse code. A shared library, or dynamic link library, is a file containing compiled code that an application loads at execution time. Runtime loading allows developers to modify a single library and immediately test the results without rebuilding the entire application. Shared libraries increase the modularity of programs by allowing multiple applications to access a single code library. The partition of programs into smaller "pieces" makes it easier to distribute application upgrades, because only modified DLLs must be redistributed. Often, developers packaged DLLs with their applications to ensure software compatibility. However, the packaged DLLs could overwrite preexisting libraries on users' systems, possibly breaking previously installed software.

The problems introduced by shared libraries were so difficult to locate and fix that their effects became known as "DLL hell." In an attempt to combat "DLL hell," Microsoft developed the Component Object Model (COM), a specification that controls library versions, backwards compatibility and language interoperability. The COM specification, defined by Microsoft, is both detailed and strict, to ensure that COM developers create compatible libraries. Microsoft implemented the COM architecture on a large scale. Today, virtually all Windows libraries adhere to the COM specification. When implemented correctly, COM ensures highly organized and reusable libraries, but it does have limitations. For example,

COM is difficult to program and deploy, because developers must guarantee that new COM components are both compatible with previous versions and registered with the system. Microsoft .NET components retain the benefits of COM while avoiding many of its associated problems. To facilitate developer's migration from COM to .NET, Microsoft created a set of utilities designed to integrate existing COM components into the .NET platform.

Windows components contain Globally Unique Identifiers (GUIDs) for the component and its internal classes, as well as language-independent descriptions of all classes and types that are defined in the component. Language-independent descriptions help enable component reuse across multiple programming languages. A GUID consists of a long string of numbers that a computer generates on the basis of the computer's current time, hardware and a random number. The GUID algorithm never generates the same identifier twice; thus, GUIDs enable unique component identification across all computers. When a COM component is registered, its GUID is stored in the Windows Registry; programs then can use the registry to locate and identify the component. A *type library* describes all of a COM component's interfaces, types and methods; the type library is included either in the component **.dll** file or in a separate **.tlb** file. The separation of component identifiers (located in the Windows Registry) from the data represented on the disk (the library file) is the source of many problems associated with the COM architecture.

.NET reduces component problems by maintaining all identification information internally. A primary interop assembly is used by .NET to locate COM methods and to translate component data types between the .NET platform types and COM component types. The translation for each COM component is performed by a Runtime Callable Wrapper (RCW)—a proxy object created by the .NET runtime from the information in the object's primary interop assembly. The RCW manages the COM object and performs communication between .NET code and the COM object. When we instantiate a COM object in C#, we are actually creating a new instance of the object's RCW. The communication between the RCW and the COM component is entirely transparent, enabling the .NET developer to interact with the COM object as if it were a .NET object.

H.5 Internet and World Wide Web Resources

www.microsoft.com/com
The Microsoft COM Web page provides technical white papers, documentation and developer support. This Web page is an essential resource for COM developers.

www.cs.umd.edu/~pugh/com
This Web site presents a high-level technical overview of the COM architecture.

msdn.microsoft.com/msdnmag/issues/01/08/Interop/Interop.asp
This Web site provides an introduction to integration services provided in .NET. The Web site includes introductory examples and describes .NETs COM Interopability capabilities.

1

Introduction to HyperText Markup Language 4: Part 1

Objectives

- To understand the key components of an HTML document.
- To use basic HTML elements to create World Wide Web pages.
- To add images to your Web pages.
- To understand how to create and use hyperlinks to traverse Web pages.
- To create lists of information.

To read between the lines was easier than to follow the text.
Henry James

Mere colour, unspoiled by meaning, and annulled with definite form, can speak to the soul in a thousand different ways.
Oscar Wilde

High thoughts must have high language.
Aristophanes

I've gradually risen from lower-class background to lower-class foreground.
Marvin Cohen

Outline

I.1   Introduction
I.2   Markup Languages
I.3   Editing HTML
I.4   Common Elements
I.5   Headers
I.6   Linking
I.7   Images
I.8   Special Characters and More Line Breaks
I.9   Unordered Lists
I.10   Nested and Ordered Lists
I.11   Summary
I.12   Internet and World Wide Web Resources

I.1 Introduction

In this appendix we introduce the basics of creating Web pages in HTML. We write many simple Web pages. In Appendix J, Introduction to HyperText Markup Language 4: Part 2, we introduce more sophisticated HTML techniques, such as *tables*, which are particularly useful for structuring information from databases. In this appendix, we do not present any C# programming.

In this appendix, we introduce basic HTML *elements* and *attributes*. A key issue when using HTML is the separation of the *presentation of a document* (i.e., how the document is rendered on the screen by a browser) from the *structure of that document*. In this appendix and in Appendix J, we discuss this issue in depth.

I.2 Markup Languages

HTML is a *markup language*. It is used to format text and information. This "marking up" of information is different from the intent of traditional programming languages, which is to perform actions in a designated order.

In HTML, text is marked up with *elements*, delineated by *tags* that are keywords contained in pairs of angle brackets. For example, the HTML *element* itself, which indicates that we are writing a Web page to be rendered by a browser, begins with the start tag **<html>** and terminates with the end tag **</html>**. These elements format your page in a specified way. Over the course of the next two appendices, we introduce many of the commonly used tags and how to use them.

Good Programming Practice I.1

HTML tags are not case sensitive. However, keeping all the letters in one case improves program readability. Although the choice of case is up to you, we recommend that you write all of your code in lowercase. Writing in lowercase ensures greater compatibility with future markup languages that are designed to be written with only lowercase tags and elements.

Common Programming Error I.1

Forgetting to include end tags for elements that require them is a syntax error and can grossly affect the formatting and look of your page. Unlike conventional programming languages, a syntax error in HTML does not usually cause page display in browsers to fail completely.

I.3 Editing HTML

In this appendix we show how to write HTML in its *source-code form*. We create *HTML documents* using a text editor and store them in files with either the **.html** or **.htm** file name extension. A wide variety of text editors exist. We recommend that you initially use a text editor called Notepad, which is built into Windows. Notepad can be found inside the **Accessories** panel of your **Program** list, inside the **Start** menu. You can also download a free HTML source-code editor called HTML-Kit at **www.chami.com/html-kit**. Unix users can use popular text editors like *vi* or *emacs*.

Good Programming Practice I.2

*Assign names to your files that describe their functionality. This practice can help you identify documents faster. It also helps people who want to link to your page, by giving them an easier-to-remember name for the file. For example, if you are writing an HTML document that will display your products, you might want to call it **products.html**.*

As mentioned previously, errors in conventional programming languages like C, C++ and Visual Basic often prevent the program from running. Errors in HTML markup are usually not fatal. The browser will make its best effort at rendering the page, but will probably not display the page as you intended.

The file name of your *home page* (the first of your HTML pages that a user sees when browsing your Web site) should be **index.html**, because when a browser does not request a specific file in a directory, the normal default Web server response is to return **index.html** (this may be different for your server) if it exists in that directory. For example, if you direct your browser to **www.deitel.com**, the server actually sends the file **www.deitel.com/index.html** to your browser.

I.4 Common Elements

Throughout these HTML appendices, we will present both HTML source code and a sample screen capture of the rendering of that HTML in Internet Explorer. Figure I.1 shows an HTML file that displays one line of text.

Lines 1 and 2

```
<!DOCTYPE HTML PUBLIC "-//W3C//DTD HTML 4.01//EN"
          "http://www.w3.org/TR/html4/strict.dtd">
```

are required in every HTML document and are used to specify the *document type*. The document type specifies which version of HTML is used in the document and can be used with a validation tool, such as the W3C's **validator.w3.org**, to ensure an HTML document conforms to the HTML recommendation. In these examples we create HTML version 4.01 documents. All of the examples in these appendices have been validated through the Web site **validator.w3.org**.

The HTML document begins with the opening **<html>** tag (line 3) and ends with the closing **</html>** tag (line 17).

```
1   <!DOCTYPE HTML PUBLIC "-//W3C//DTD HTML 4.01//EN"
2              "http://www.w3.org/TR/html4/strict.dtd">
3   <html>
4
5   <!-- Fig. I.1: main.html -->
6   <!-- Our first Web page. -->
7
8   <head>
9      <title>C# How to Program - Welcome</title>
10  </head>
11
12  <body>
13
14     <p>Welcome to Our Web Site!</p>
15
16  </body>
17  </html>
```

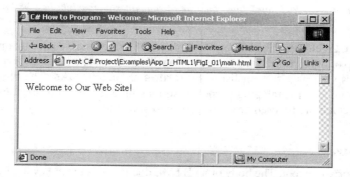

Fig. I.1   Basic HTML file.

Good Programming Practice I.3

Always include the **<html>**...**</html>** *tags in the beginning and end of your HTML document.*

Good Programming Practice I.4

Place comments throughout your code. Comments in HTML are placed inside the **<!--**... **-->** *tags. Comments help other programmers understand the code, assist in debugging and list other useful information that you do not want the browser to render. Comments also help you understand your own code, especially if you have not looked at it for a while.*

We see our first *comments* (i.e., text that documents or describes the HTML markup) on lines 5 and 6

```
<!-- Fig. I.1: main.html -->
<!-- Our first Web page. -->
```

Comments in HTML always begin with **<!--** and end with **-->**. The browser ignores any text and/or tags inside a comment. We place comments at the top of each HTML document giving the figure number, the file name and a brief description of the purpose of the example. In subsequent examples, we also include comments in the markup, especially when we introduce new features.

Every HTML document contains a **head** element, which generally contains information about the document, and a **body** element, which contains the page content. Information in the **head** element is not generally rendered in the display window, but may be made available to the user through other means. Lines 8–10

```
<head>
    <title>C# How to Program - Welcome</title>
</head>
```

show the **head** element section of our Web page. Including a **title** element is required for every HTML document. To include a title in your Web page, enclose your chosen title between the pair of tags **<title>...</title>** in the **head** element.

Good Programming Practice I.5

Use a consistent title-naming convention for all pages on your site. For example, if your site is called "Al's Web Site," then the title of your links page might best be "Al's Web Site - Links." This practice presents a clearer picture to those browsing your site.

The **title** element names your Web page. The title usually appears on the colored bar at the top of the browser window, and also will appear as the text identifying your page if a user adds your page to their list of **Favorites** or **Bookmarks**. The title is also used by search engines for cataloging purposes, so picking a meaningful title can help search engines direct a more focused group of people to your site.

Line 12

```
<body>
```

opens the **body** element. The body of an HTML document is the area where you place the content of your document. This includes text, images, links and forms. We discuss many elements that can be inserted in the **body** element later in this appendix. Remember to include the end **</body>** tag before the closing **</html>** tag.

Various elements enable you to place text in your HTML document. We see the *paragraph element* on line 14

```
<p>Welcome to Our Web Site!</p>
```

All text placed between the **<p>...</p>** tags forms one paragraph. Most Web browsers render paragraphs as set apart from all other material on the page by a line of vertical space both before and after the paragraph. The HTML in line 12 causes Internet Explorer to render the enclosed text as shown in Fig. I.1.

Our code example ends on lines 16 and 17 with

```
</body>
</html>
```

These two tags close the body and HTML sections of the document, respectively. As discussed earlier, the last tag in any HTML document should be **</html>**, which tells the browser that all HTML coding is complete. The closing **</body>** tag is placed before the **</html>** tag because the body section of the document is entirely enclosed by the HTML section. Therefore, the body section must be closed before the HTML section.

I.5 Headers

The six *headers* are used to delineate new sections and subsections of a page. Figure I.2 shows how these elements (**h1** through **h6**) are used. Note that the actual size of the text of each header element is selected by the browser and can vary significantly between browsers.

Good Programming Practice I.6

Adding comments to the right of short HTML lines is a clean-looking way to comment code.

```html
1   <!DOCTYPE HTML PUBLIC "-//W3C//DTD HTML 4.01//EN"
2           "http://www.w3.org/TR/html4/strict.dtd">
3   <html>
4
5   <!-- Fig. I.2: header.html -->
6   <!-- HTML headers.         -->
7
8   <head>
9      <title>C# How to Program - Welcome</title>
10  </head>
11
12  <body>
13
14     <h1>Level 1 Header</h1>      <!-- Level 1 header -->
15     <h2>Level 2 header</h2>      <!-- Level 2 header -->
16     <h3>Level 3 header</h3>      <!-- Level 3 header -->
17     <h4>Level 4 header</h4>      <!-- Level 4 header -->
18     <h5>Level 5 header</h5>      <!-- Level 5 header -->
19     <h6>Level 6 header</h6>      <!-- Level 6 header -->
20
21  </body>
22  </html>
```

Fig. I.2   Header elements **h1** through **h6**.

Line 14

```
<h1>Level 1 Header</h1>
```

introduces the **h1** *header element*, with its start tag **<h1>** and its end tag **</h1>**. Any text to be displayed is placed between the two tags. All six header elements, **h1** through **h6**, follow the same pattern.

Good Programming Practice I.7

Putting a header at the top of every Web page helps those viewing your pages understand what the purpose of each page is.

I.6 Linking

The most important capability of HTML is its ability to create hyperlinks to other documents, making possible a worldwide network of linked documents and information. In HTML, both text and images can act as *anchors* to *link* to other pages on the Web. We introduce anchors and links in Fig. I.3.

The first link can be found on line 19

```
<p><a href = "http://www.yahoo.com">Yahoo</a></p>
```

```
1   <!DOCTYPE HTML PUBLIC "-//W3C//DTD HTML 4.01//EN"
2            "http://www.w3.org/TR/html4/strict.dtd">
3   <html>
4
5   <!-- Fig. I.3: links.html      -->
6   <!-- Introduction to hyperlinks. -->
7
8   <head>
9      <title>C# How to Program - Welcome</title>
10  </head>
11
12  <body>
13
14     <h1>Here are my favorite Internet Search Engines</h1>
15
16     <p><strong>Click on the Search Engine address to go to that
17        page.</strong></p>
18
19     <p><a href = "http://www.yahoo.com">Yahoo</a></p>
20
21     <p><a href = "http://www.altavista.com">AltaVista</a></p>
22
23     <p><a href = "http://www.askjeeves.com">Ask Jeeves</a></p>
24
25     <p><a href = "http://www.webcrawler.com">WebCrawler</a></p>
26
27  </body>
28  </html>
```

Fig. I.3   Linking to other Web pages. (Part 1 of 2.)

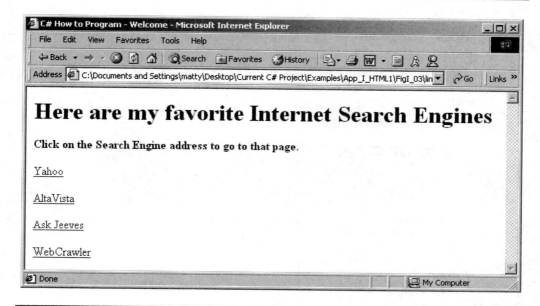

Fig. I.3   Linking to other Web pages. (Part 2 of 2.)

Links are inserted with the **a** *(anchor) element*. The anchor element is unlike the elements we have seen thus far in that it requires certain *attributes* (i.e., markup that provides information about the element) to specify the hyperlink. Attributes are placed inside an element's start tag and consist of a name and a value. The most important attribute for the **a** element is the location to which you would like the anchoring object to be linked. This location can be any resource on the Web, including pages, files and e-mail addresses. To specify the address to link to, add the **href** *attribute* to the anchor element as follows: **<a href = "***address***">**. In this case, the address we are linking to is **http://www.yahoo.com**. The hyperlink (line 19) makes the text **Yahoo** a link to the address specified in **href**.

Anchors can use **mailto** URLs to provide links to e-mail addresses. When someone selects this type of anchored link, most browsers launch the default e-mail program to initiate an e-mail message to the linked address. This type of anchor is demonstrated in Fig. I.4.

```
1  <!DOCTYPE HTML PUBLIC "-//W3C//DTD HTML 4.01//EN"
2           "http://www.w3.org/TR/html4/strict.dtd">
3  <html>
4
5  <!-- Fig. I.4: contact.html   -->
6  <!-- Adding email hyperlinks. -->
7
8  <head>
9     <title>C# How to Program - Welcome</title>
10 </head>
11
```

Fig. I.4   Linking to an e-mail address. (Part 1 of 2.)

```
12    <body>
13
14       <p>My email address is <a href = "mailto:deitel@deitel.com">
15       deitel@deitel.com</a>. Click on the address and your browser
16       will open an email message and address it to me.</p>
17
18    </body>
19    </html>
```

Fig. I.4   Linking to an e-mail address. (Part 2 of 2.)

We see an e-mail link on lines 14 and 15

```
<p>My email address is <a href = "mailto:deitel@deitel.com">
deitel@deitel.com</a>. Click on the address and your browser
```

The form of an e-mail anchor is **<a href = "mailto:***emailaddress***">...</a>**. It is important that this whole attribute, including the **mailto:**, be placed in quotation marks.

I.7 Images

We have thus far dealt exclusively with text. We now show how to incorporate images into Web pages (Fig. I.5).

```
1     <!DOCTYPE HTML PUBLIC "-//W3C//DTD HTML 4.01//EN"
2              "http://www.w3.org/TR/html4/strict.dtd">
3     <html>
4
5     <!-- Fig. I.5: picture.html    -->
6     <!-- Adding images with HTML. -->
7
8     <head>
9        <title>C# How to Program - Welcome</title>
10    </head>
11
```

Fig. I.5   Placing images in HTML files. (Courtesy of Prentice Hall, Inc.) (Part 1 of 2.)

```
12    <body>
13
14       <p><img src = "csphtp.jpg" height = "236" width = "181"
15          alt = "Demonstration of the alt attribute"></p>
16
17    </body>
18    </html>
```

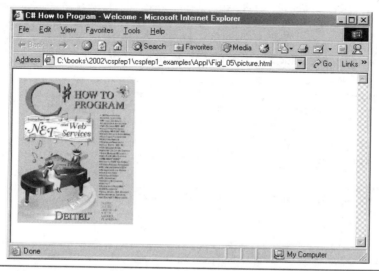

Fig. I.5   Placing images in HTML files. (Courtesy of Prentice Hall, Inc.) (Part 2 of 2.)

The image in this code example is inserted in lines 14 and 15:

```
<p><img src = "csphtp.jpg" height = "236" width = "181"
   alt = "Demonstration of the alt attribute"></p>
```

You specify the location of the image file in the **img** element. This is done by adding the **src = "***location***"** attribute. You can also specify the **height** and **width** of an image, measured in pixels. The term pixel stands for "picture element." Each pixel represents one dot of color on the screen. This image is 181 pixels wide and 236 pixels high.

Good Programming Practice I.8

*Always include the **height** and the **width** of an image inside the **img** tag. When the browser loads the HTML file, it will know immediately how much screen space to give the image and will therefore lay out the page properly, even before it downloads the image.*

Common Programming Error I.2

Entering new dimensions for an image that changes its inherent width-to-height ratio distorts the appearance of the image. For example, if your image is 200 pixels wide and 100 pixels high, you should always make sure that any new dimensions have a 2:1 width-to-height ratio.

The **alt** attribute is required for every **img** element. In Fig. I.5, the value of this attribute is

```
alt = "Demonstration of the alt attribute"
```

Attribute **alt** is provided for browsers that have images turned off or cannot view images (e.g., text-based browsers). The value of the **alt** attribute will appear on-screen in place of the image, giving the user an idea of what was in the image. The **alt** attribute is especially important for making Web pages *accessible* to users with disabilities, as discussed in Chapter 21, Accessibility.

Good Programming Practice I.9

*Include a description of the purpose of every image, using the **alt** attribute in the **img** tag.*

Now that we have discussed placing images on your Web page, we will show you how to transform images into anchors to provide links to other sites on the Internet (Fig. I.6).

```
1   <!DOCTYPE HTML PUBLIC "-//W3C//DTD HTML 4.01//EN"
2              "http://www.w3.org/TR/html4/strict.dtd">
3   <html>
4
5   <!-- Fig. I.6: nav.html              -->
6   <!-- Using images as link anchors. -->
7
8   <head>
9      <title>C# How to Program - Welcome</title>
10  </head>
11
12  <body>
13
14     <p>
15        <a href = "links.html">
16        <img src = "buttons/links.jpg" width = "65" height = "50"
17           alt = "Links Page"></a><br>
18
19        <a href = "list.html">
20        <img src = "buttons/list.jpg" width = "65" height = "50"
21           alt = "List Example Page"></a><br>
22
23        <a href = "contact.html">
24        <img src = "buttons/contact.jpg" width = "65" height = "50"
25           alt = "Contact Page"></a><br>
26
27        <a href = "header.html">
28        <img src = "buttons/header.jpg" width = "65" height = "50"
29           alt = "Header Page"></a><br>
30
31        <a href = "table.html">
32        <img src = "buttons/table.jpg" width = "65" height = "50"
33           alt = "Table Page"></a><br>
34
35        <a href = "form.html">
36        <img src = "buttons/form.jpg" width = "65" height = "50"
37           alt = "Feedback Form"></a><br>
38     </p>
39
```

Fig. I.6   Using images as link anchors. (Part 1 of 2.)

```
40    </body>
41    </html>
```

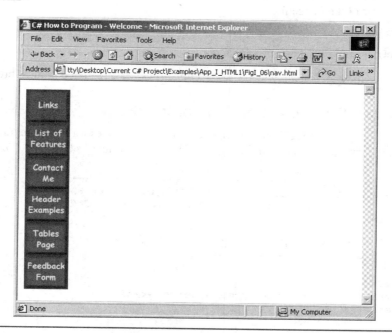

Fig. I.6   Using images as link anchors. (Part 2 of 2.)

We see an image hyperlink in lines 15–17

```
<a href = "links.html">
<img src = "buttons/links.jpg" width = "65" height = "50"
   alt = "Links Page"></a><br>
```

Here we use the **a** element and the **img** element. The anchor works the same way as when it surrounds text; the image becomes an active hyperlink to a location somewhere on the Internet, indicated by the **href** attribute inside the **<a>** tag. Remember to close the anchor element when you want the hyperlink to end.

If you direct your attention to the **src** attribute of the **img** element,

```
src = "buttons/links.jpg"
```

you will see that it is not in the same form as that of the image in the previous example. This is because the image we are using here, **about.jpg**, resides in a subdirectory called **buttons**, which is in the main directory for our site. We have done this so that we can keep all our button graphics in the same place, making them easier to find and edit.

You can always refer to files in different directories simply by putting the directory name in the correct format in the **src** attribute. If, for example, there was a directory inside the **buttons** directory called **images**, and we wanted to put a graphic from that directory onto our page, we would just have to make the source attribute reflect the location of the image: **src = "buttons/images/filename"**.

You can even insert an image from a different Web site into your site (after obtaining permission from the site's owner, of course). Just make the **src** attribute reflect the location and name of the image file.

On line 17

```
alt = "Links Page"></a><br>
```

we introduce the ***br*** *element*, which causes a *line break* to be rendered in most browsers.

I.8 Special Characters and More Line Breaks

In HTML, the old QWERTY typewriter setup no longer suffices for all our textual needs. HTML 4.01 has a provision for inserting special characters and symbols (Fig. I.7).

```
1    <!DOCTYPE HTML PUBLIC "-//W3C//DTD HTML 4.01//EN"
2            "http://www.w3.org/TR/html4/strict.dtd">
3    <html>
4
5    <!-- Fig. I.7: contact.html       -->
6    <!-- Inserting special characters. -->
7
8    <head>
9        <title>C# How to Program - Welcome</title>
10   </head>
11
12   <body>
13
14       <!-- special characters are entered using the form &code; -->
15       <p>My email address is <a href = "mailto:deitel@deitel.com">
16       deitel@deitel.com</a>. Click on the address and your browser
17       will automatically open an email message and address it to my
18       address.</p>
19
20       <hr> <!-- inserts a horizontal rule -->
21
22       <p>All information on this site is <strong>&copy;</strong>
23       Deitel <strong>&amp;</strong> Associates, 2002.</p>
24
25       <!-- text can be struck out with a set of <del>...</del>   -->
26       <!-- tags, it can be set in subscript with <sub>...</sub>, -->
27       <!-- and it can be set into superscript with <sup...</sup> -->
28       <p><del>You may copy up to 3.14 x 10<sup>2</sup> characters
29       worth of information from this site.</del> Just make sure
30       you <sub>do not copy more information</sub> than is allowable.
31       </p>
32
33       <p>No permission is needed if you only need to use <strong>
34       &lt; &frac14;</strong> of the information presented here.</p>
35
36   </body>
37   </html>
```

Fig. I.7   Inserting special characters into HTML. (Part 1 of 2.)

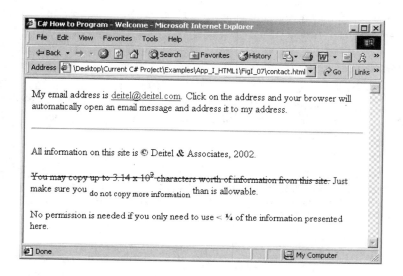

Fig. I.7   Inserting special characters into HTML. (Part 2 of 2.)

There are some *special characters* inserted into the text of lines 22 and 23:

```
<p>All information on this site is <strong>&copy;</strong>
Deitel <strong>&amp;</strong> Associates, 2002.</p>
```

All special characters are inserted in their code form. The format of the code is always **&*code*;**. An example of this is **&**, which inserts an ampersand. Codes are often abbreviated forms of the character (like **amp** for ampersand and **copy** for copyright) and can also be in the form of *hex codes*. (For example, the hex code for an ampersand is 38, so another method of inserting an ampersand is to use **&**.) Please refer to the chart in Appendix M for a listing of special characters and their respective codes.

In lines 28–31, we introduce three new styles.

```
<p><del>You may copy up to 3.14 x 10<sup>2</sup> characters
worth of information from this site.</del> Just make sure
you <sub>do not copy more information</sub> than is allow-
able.
</p>
```

You can indicate text that has been deleted from a document by including it in a **del** element. This could be used as an easy way to communicate revisions of an online document. Many browsers render the **del** element as strike-through text. To turn text into *superscript* (i.e., raised vertically to the top of the line and made smaller) or to turn text into *subscript* (the opposite of superscript, lowers text on a line and makes it smaller), use the **sup** or **sub** element, respectively.

Line 20

```
<hr> <!-- inserts a horizontal rule -->
```

inserts a horizontal rule, indicated by the **\<hr\>** tag. A horizontal rule is rendered by most browsers as a straight line going across the screen horizontally. The **hr** element also inserts a line break directly below it.

I.9 Unordered Lists

Figure I.8 demonstrates displaying text in an *unordered list*. Here, we reuse the HTML file from Fig. I.3, adding an unordered list to enhance the structure of the page. The *unordered list element* **ul** creates a list in which every line begins with a bullet mark in most Web browsers.

```
 1   <!DOCTYPE HTML PUBLIC "-//W3C//DTD HTML 4.01//EN"
 2            "http://www.w3.org/TR/html4/strict.dtd">
 3   <html>
 4
 5   <!-- Fig. I.8: links.html              -->
 6   <!-- Unordered list containing hyperlinks. -->
 7
 8   <head>
 9      <title>C# How to Program - Welcome</title>
10   </head>
11
12   <body>
13
14      <h1>Here are my favorite Internet Search Engines</h1>
15
16
17      <p><strong>Click on the Search Engine address to go to that
18         page.</strong></p>
19
20      <ul>
21         <li>
22            <a href = "http://www.yahoo.com">Yahoo</a>
23         </li>
24
25         <li>
26            <a href = "http://www.altavista.com">AltaVista</a>
27         </li>
28
29         <li>
30            <a href = "http://www.askjeeves.com">Ask Jeeves</a>
31         </li>
32
33         <li>
34            <a href = "http://www.webcrawler.com">WebCrawler</a>
35         </li>
36      </ul>
37
38   </body>
39   </html>
```

Fig. I.8   Unordered lists in HTML. (Part 1 of 2.)

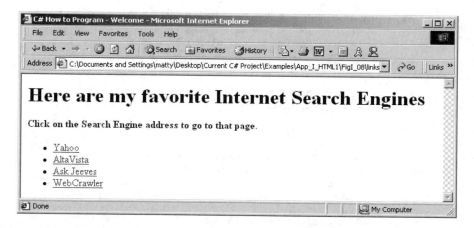

Fig. I.8   Unordered lists in HTML. (Part 2 of 2.)

The first list item appears in lines 21–23

```
<li>
   <a href = "http://www.yahoo.com">Yahoo</a>
</li>
```

Each entry in an unordered list is a *li* (*list item*) element. Most Web browsers render these elements with a line break and a bullet mark at the beginning of the line.

I.10 Nested and Ordered Lists

Figure I.9 demonstrates *nested lists* (i.e., one list inside another list). This feature is useful for displaying information in outline form.

```
1   <!DOCTYPE HTML PUBLIC "-//W3C//DTD HTML 4.01//EN"
2              "http://www.w3.org/TR/html4/strict.dtd">
3   <html>
4
5   <!-- Fig. I.9: list.html                 -->
6   <!-- Advanced Lists: nested and ordered. -->
7
8   <head>
9      <title>C# How to Program - Welcome</title>
10  </head>
11
12  <body>
13
14     <h1>The Best Features of the Internet</h1>
15
16     <ul>
17        <li>You can meet new people from countries around
18           the world.</li>
```

Fig. I.9   Nested and ordered lists in HTML. (Part 1 of 3.)

```
19          <li>You have access to new media as it becomes public:
20
21          <!-- this starts a nested list, which -->
22          <!-- uses a modified bullet. The list -->
23          <!-- ends when you close the <ul> tag -->
24          <ul>
25              <li>New games</li>
26              <li>New applications
27
28                  <!-- another nested list -->
29                  <ul>
30                      <li>For business</li>
31                      <li>For pleasure</li>
32                  </ul> <!-- this ends the double nested list -->
33              </li>
34
35              <li>Around the clock news</li>
36              <li>Search engines</li>
37              <li>Shopping</li>
38              <li>Programming
39
40                  <ul>
41                      <li>C#</li>
42                      <li>Java</li>
43                      <li>HTML</li>
44                      <li>Scripts</li>
45                      <li>New languages</li>
46                  </ul>
47
48              </li>
49
50          </ul> <!-- this ends the first level nested list -->
51      </li>
52
53      <li>Links</li>
54      <li>Keeping in touch with old friends</li>
55      <li>It is the technology of the future!</li>
56
57  </ul>    <!-- this ends the primary unordered list -->
58
59  <h1>My 3 Favorite <em>CEOs</em></h1>
60
61  <!-- ordered lists are constructed in the same way as   -->
62  <!-- unordered lists, except their starting tag is <ol> -->
63  <ol>
64      <li>Lawrence J. Ellison</li>
65      <li>Steve Jobs</li>
66      <li>Michael Dell</li>
67  </ol>
68
69  </body>
70  </html>
```

Fig. I.9   Nested and ordered lists in HTML. (Part 2 of 3.)

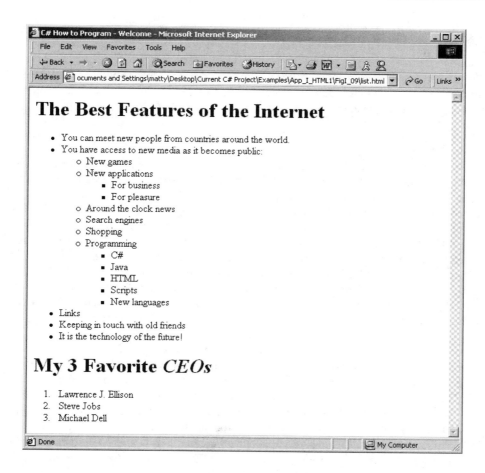

Fig. I.9   Nested and ordered lists in HTML. (Part 3 of 3.)

Our first nested list begins on line 24, and its first element is on 25.

```
<ul>
    <li>New games</li>
```

A nested list is created in the same way as the list in Fig. I.8, except that the nested list is itself contained in a list element. Most Web browsers render nested lists by indenting the list one level and changing the bullet type for the list elements.

Good Programming Practice I.10

Indenting each level of a nested list in your code makes the code easier to edit and debug.

In Fig. I.9, lines 16–57 show a list with three levels of nesting. When nesting lists, be sure to insert the closing **</ul>** tags in the appropriate places. Lines 63–67

```
<ol>
    <li>Lawrence J. Ellison</li>
    <li>Steve Jobs</li>
    <li>Michael Dell</li>
</ol>
```

define an *ordered list* element with the tags **<ol>**...**</ol>**. Most browsers render ordered lists with a sequence number for each list element instead of a bullet. By default, ordered lists use decimal sequence numbers (1, 2, 3, ...).

I.11 Summary

HTML is not a procedural programming language like C, Fortran, Cobol or Pascal. It is a markup language which identifies the elements of a page so that a browser can render the page on the screen. HTML is used to format text and information. This "marking up" of information is different from the intent of traditional programming languages, which is to perform actions in a designated order.

In HTML, text is marked up with elements, delineated by tags that are keywords contained in pairs of angle brackets. HTML documents are created via text editors. All HTML documents stored in files require either the **.htm** or the **.html** file name extension. For most Web servers, the filename of a home page should be **index.html**. When a browser requests a directory, the default Web server response is to return **index.html** if it exists in that directory.

The document type specifies which version of HTML appears in the document and can be used with a validation tool, such as the W3C's **validator.w3.org**, to ensure that an HTML document conforms to the HTML specification. **<html>** tells the browser that everything contained between the opening **<html>** tag and the closing **</html>** tag is HTML. Every HTML file is separated into a header section and a body. Including a title is mandatory for every HTML document. Use the **<title>**...**</title>** tags to do so. They are placed inside the header. The **<body>** tag opens the **body** element. The body of an HTML document is the area where you place all content you would like browsers to display. Headers are a simple form of text formatting that typically increase text size, based on the header's "level" (**h1** through **h6**). Headers are often used to delineate new sections and subsections of a page.

The most important capability of HTML is creating hyperlinks to documents on any server, to form a worldwide network of linked documents and information. Links are inserted with the **a** (anchor) element. To specify the address you would like to link to, add the **href** attribute to the anchor element, with the address as the value of **href**. Anchors can link to e-mail addresses. When someone clicks this type of anchored link, their default e-mail program initiates an e-mail message to the linked address.

You specify the location of an image file with the **src =** "*location*" attribute in the **<img>** tag. You can specify the **height** and **width** of an image, measured in pixels. The **alt** tag is provided for browsers that cannot view pictures or that have images turned off (e.g., text-based browsers). The value of the **alt** attribute will appear on the screen in place of the image, giving the user an idea of what was in the image.

HTML 4.01 has a provision for inserting special characters and symbols. All special characters are inserted in the format of the code, always **&code;**. An example of this is **&**, which inserts an ampersand. Codes are often abbreviated forms of the character (like **amp** for ampersand and **copy** for copyright) and also can be in the form of hex codes. (For example, the hex code for an ampersand is 38, so another method of inserting an ampersand is to use **&**.) The **del** element marks text as deleted, which is rendered with a strike-through by most browsers. To turn text into superscript or subscript, use the **sup** or **sub**element, respectively.

Most visual Web browsers place a bullet mark at the beginning of each element in an unordered list. All entries in an unordered list must be enclosed within **<ul>...</ul>** tags, which open and close the unordered list element. Each entry in an unordered list is contained in an **li** element. You then insert and format any text. Nested lists display information in outline form. A nested list is a list that is contained within an **li** element. Most visual Web browsers indent nested lists one level and change the type of bullet to reflect the nesting. An ordered list (**<ol>...</ol>**) is rendered by most browsers with a sequence number instead of a bullet at the beginning of each list element. By default, ordered lists use decimal sequence numbers (1, 2, 3, ...).

I.12 Internet and World Wide Web Resources

There are many resources available on the World Wide Web that go into more depth on the topics we cover. Visit the following sites for additional information on this appendix's topics:

www.w3.org
The *World Wide Web Consortium* (W3C) is the group that makes HTML recommendations. This Web site holds a variety of information about HTML—on both its history and its present status.

www.w3.org/TR/html401
The *HTML 4.01 Specification* contains all the nuances and fine points in HTML 4.01.

www.w3schools.com/html
The HTML School. This site contains a complete guide to HTML, starting with an introduction to the WWW and ending with advanced HTML features. The site also has a good reference for the features of HTML.

www2.utep.edu/~kross/tutorial
This University of Texas at El Paso site contains another guide to simple HTML programming. The site is helpful for beginners, because it focuses on teaching and gives specific examples.

www.w3scripts.com/html
This site, an offshoot of *W3Schools*, is a repository for examples of code exhibiting all of the features of HTML, from beginner to advanced level.

Introduction to HyperText Markup Language 4: Part 2

Objectives

- To create tables with rows and columns of data.
- To control the display and formatting of tables.
- To create and use forms.
- To create and use image maps to aid hyperlinking.
- To make Web pages accessible to search engines.
- To use the `frameset` element to create more interesting Web pages.

Yea, from the table of my memory
I'll wipe away all trivial fond records.
William Shakespeare

Outline

J.1   Introduction
J.2   Basic HTML Tables
J.3   Intermediate HTML Tables and Formatting
J.4   Basic HTML Forms
J.5   More Complex HTML Forms
J.6   Internal Linking
J.7   Creating and Using Image Maps
J.8   <meta> Tags
J.9   frameset Element
J.10   Nested framesets
J.11   Summary
J.12   Internet and World Wide Web Resources

J.1 Introduction

In Appendix I, Introduction to HyperText Markup Language 4: Part 1, we discussed some basic HTML features. We built several complete Web pages featuring text, hyperlinks, images and such formatting tools as horizontal rules and line breaks.

In this appendix, we discuss more substantial HTML elements and features. We will see how to present information in *tables*. We discuss how to use forms to collect information from people browsing a site. We explain how to use *internal linking* and *image maps* to make pages more navigable. We also discuss how to use *frames* to make navigating Web sites easier. By the end of this appendix, you will be familiar with most commonly used HTML tags and features. You will then be able to create more complex Web sites. In this appendix, we do not present any C# programming.

J.2 Basic HTML Tables

HTML 4.0 *tables* are used to mark up tabular data, such as data stored in a database. The table in Fig. J.1 organizes data into rows and columns.

```
1   <!DOCTYPE HTML PUBLIC "-//W3C//DTD HTML 4.01//EN"
2              "http://www.w3.org/TR/html4/strict.dtd">
3   <html>
4
5   <!-- Fig. J.1: table.html -->
6   <!-- Basic table design.  -->
7
8   <head>
9      <title>C# How to Program - Tables</title>
10  </head>
```

Fig. J.1   HTML table. (Part 1 of 2.)

```
11
12   <body>
13
14      <h1>Table Example Page</h1>
15
16      <!-- the <table> tag opens a new table and lets you -->
17      <!-- put in design options and instructions         -->
18      <table border = "1" width = "40%">
19
20         <!-- use the <caption> tag to summarize the table's -->
21         <!-- contents (this helps the visually impaired)    -->
22         <caption>Here is a small sample table.</caption>
23
24         <!-- The <thead> is the first (non-scrolling)   -->
25         <!-- horizontal section. <th> inserts a header -->
26         <!--  cell and displays bold text              -->
27         <thead>
28            <tr><th>This is the head.</th></tr>
29         </thead>
30
31         <!-- All of your important content goes in the <tbody>. -->
32         <!-- Use this tag to format the entire section          -->
33         <!-- <td> inserts a data cell, with regular text        -->
34         <tbody>
35            <tr><td>This is the body.</td></tr>
36         </tbody>
37
38      </table>
39
40   </body>
41   </html>
```

Fig. J.1   HTML table. (Part 2 of 2.)

All tags and text that apply to the table go inside the **<table>** element, which begins on line 18:

```
<table border = "1" width = "40%">
```

The **border** *attribute* lets you set the width of the table's border in pixels. If you want the border to be invisible, you can specify **border = "0"**. In the table shown in Fig. J.1, the value of the border attribute is set to **1**. The **width** attribute sets the width of the table as either a number of pixels or a percentage of the screen width.

Line 22

```
<caption>Here is a small sample table.</caption>
```

inserts a **caption** element into the table. The text inside the **caption** element is inserted directly above the table in most visual browsers. The caption text is also used to help *text-based browsers* interpret the table data.

Tables can be split into distinct horizontal and vertical sections. The first of these sections, the head area, appears in lines 27–29

```
<thead>
    <tr><th>This is the head.</th></tr>
</thead>
```

Put all header information (for example, the titles of the table and column headers) inside the **thead** element. The **tr**, or *table row element*, is used to create rows of table cells. All of the cells in a row belong in the **<tr>** element for that row.

The smallest unit of the table is the *data cell*. There are two types of data cells, one type—the **th** element—is located in the table header. The other type—the **td** element—is located in the table body. The code example in Fig. J.1 inserts a header cell, using the **th** element. Header cells, which are placed in the **<thead>** element, are suitable for column headings.

The second grouping section, the **tbody** element, appears in lines 34–36

```
<tbody>
    <tr><td>This is the body.</td></tr>
</tbody>
```

Like **thead**, the **tbody** element is used for formatting and grouping purposes. Although there is only one row and one cell (line 35) in the above example, most tables will use **tbody** to group the majority of their content in multiple rows and multiple cells.

Look-and-Feel Observation J.1

Use tables in your HTML pages to mark up tabular data.

Common Programming Error J.1

Forgetting to close any of the elements inside the **table** *element is an error and can distort the table format. Be sure to check that every element is opened and closed in its proper place to make sure that the table is structured as intended.*

J.3 Intermediate HTML Tables and Formatting

In the previous section and code example, we explored the structure of a basic table. In Fig. J.2, we extend our table example with more structural elements and attributes.

```
 1   <!DOCTYPE HTML PUBLIC "-//W3C//DTD HTML 4.01//EN"
 2               "http://www.w3.org/TR/html4/strict.dtd">
 3   <html>
 4
 5   <!-- Fig. J.2: table.html         -->
 6   <!-- Intermediate table design. -->
 7
 8   <head>
 9      <title>C# How to Program - Tables</title>
10   </head>
11
12   <body>
13
14      <h1>Table Example Page</h1>
15
16      <table border = "1">
17         <caption>Here is a more complex sample table.</caption>
18
19         <!-- <colgroup> and <col> are used to format     -->
20         <!-- entire columns at once. SPAN determines how -->
21         <!-- many columns the <col> tag effects.         -->
22         <colgroup>
23            <col align = "right">
24            <col span = "4">
25         </colgroup>
26
27         <thead>
28
29            <!-- rowspans and colspans combine the indicated -->
30            <!-- number of cells vertically or horizontally  -->
31            <tr>
32               <th rowspan = "2">
33                  <img src = "camel.gif" width = "205"
34                     height = "167" alt = "Picture of a camel">
35               </th>
36               <th colspan = "4" valign = "top">
37                  <h1>Camelid comparison</h1><br>
38                  <p>Approximate as of 8/99</p>
39               </th>
40            </tr>
41
42            <tr valign = "bottom">
43               <th># of Humps</th>
44               <th>Indigenous region</th>
45               <th>Spits?</th>
46               <th>Produces Wool?</th>
47            </tr>
48
49         </thead>
50
```

Fig. J.2   Complex HTML table. (Part 1 of 2.)

```
51          <tbody>
52
53            <tr>
54              <th>Camels (bactrian)</th>
55              <td>2</td>
56              <td>Africa/Asia</td>
57              <td rowspan = "2">Llama</td>
58              <td rowspan = "2">Llama</td>
59            </tr>
60
61            <tr>
62              <th>Llamas</th>
63              <td>1</td>
64              <td>Andes Mountains</td>
65            </tr>
66
67          </tbody>
68
69       </table>
70
71    </body>
72 </html>
```

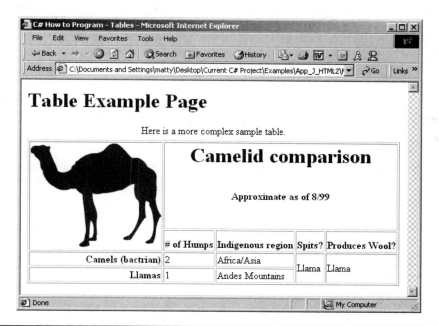

Fig. J.2   Complex HTML table. (Part 2 of 2.)

The table begins on line 16. The **colgroup** *element*, used for grouping columns, is shown on lines 22–25

```
<colgroup>
   <col align = "right">
```

```
     <col span = "4">
  </colgroup>
```

The **colgroup** element can be used to group and format columns. Each **col** element in the **<colgroup>…</colgroup>** tags can format any number of columns (specified with the **span** attribute). Any formatting to be applied to a column or group of columns can be specified in both the **colgroup** and **col** tags. In this case, we align the text inside the leftmost column to the right. Another useful attribute to use here is **width**, which specifies the width of the column.

Most visual Web browsers automatically format data cells to fit the data they contain. However, it is possible to make some data cells larger than others. This effect is accomplished with the **rowspan** and **colspan** attributes, which can be placed inside any data cell element. The value of the attribute specifies the number of rows or columns to be occupied by the cell, respectively. For example, **rowspan = "2"** tells the browser that this data cell will span the area of two vertically adjacent cells. These cells will be joined vertically (and will thus span over two rows). An example of **colspan** appears in line 36,

```
  <th colspan = "4" valign = "top">
```

where the header cell is widened to span four cells.

We also see here an example of vertical alignment formatting. The **valign** attribute accepts the following values: **"top"**, **"middle"**, **"bottom"** and **"baseline"**. All cells in a row whose **valign** attribute is set to **"baseline"** will have the first text line occur on a common baseline. The default vertical alignment in all data and header cells is **valign = "middle"**.

The remaining code in Fig. J.2 demonstrates other uses of the **table** attributes and elements outlined above.

Common Programming Error J.2

*When using **colspan** and **rowspan** in table data cells, consider that the modified cells will cover the areas of other cells. Compensate for this in your code by reducing the number of cells in that row or column. If you do not, the formatting of your table will be distorted, and you could inadvertently create more columns and/or rows than you originally intended.*

J.4 Basic HTML Forms

HTML provides several mechanisms to collect information from people viewing your site; one is the *form* (Fig. J.3).

```
1  <!DOCTYPE HTML PUBLIC "-//W3C//DTD HTML 4.01//EN"
2            "http://www.w3.org/TR/html4/strict.dtd">
3  <html>
4
5  <!-- Fig. J.3: form.html    -->
6  <!-- Form design example 1. -->
7
8  <head>
9     <title>C# How to Program - Tables</title>
10 </head>
```

Fig. J.3   Simple form with hidden fields and a text box. (Part 1 of 2.)

```
11
12   <body>
13
14      <h1>Feedback Form</h1>
15
16      <p>Please fill out this form to help us improve our site.</p>
17
18      <!-- This tag starts the form, gives the method of sending -->
19      <!-- information and the location of form scripts.         -->
20      <!-- Hidden inputs give the server non-visual information  -->
21      <form method = "post" action = "/cgi-bin/formmail">
22
23      <p>
24         <input type = "hidden" name = "recipient"
25            value = "deitel@deitel.com">
26
27         <input type = "hidden" name = "subject"
28            value = "Feedback Form">
29
30         <input type = "hidden" name = "redirect"
31            value = "main.html">
32      </p>
33
34      <!-- <input type = "text"> inserts a text box -->
35      <p><label>Name:
36         <input name = "name" type = "text" size = "25">
37      </label></p>
38
39      <p>
40         <!-- input types "submit" and "reset" insert buttons -->
41         <!-- for submitting or clearing the form's contents  -->
42         <input type = "submit" value = "Submit Your Entries">
43         <input type = "reset" value = "Clear Your Entries">
44      </p>
45
46      </form>
47
48   </body>
49   </html>
```

Fig. J.3   Simple form with hidden fields and a text box. (Part 2 of 2.)

The form begins on line 21

```
<form method = "post" action = "/cgi-bin/formmail">
```

with the **form** element. The **method** attribute indicates the way the information gathered in the form will be sent to the *Web server* for processing. Use **method = "post"** in a form that causes changes to server data, for example when updating a database. The form data will be sent to the server as an *environment variable,* which scripts are able to access. The other possible value, **method = "get"**, should be used when your form does not cause any changes in server-side data, for example when making a database request. The form data from **method = "get"** is appended to the end of the URL (for example, **/cgi-bin/formmail?name=bob&order=5**). Also be aware that **method = "get"** is limited to standard characters and cannot submit any special characters.

A *Web server* is a machine that runs a software package like Microsoft's PWS (Personal Web Server), Microsoft's IIS (Internet Information Server) or Apache. Web servers handle browser requests. When a browser requests a page or file somewhere on a server, the server processes the request and returns an answer to the browser. In this example, the data from the form goes to a CGI (Common Gateway Interface) script, which is a means of interfacing an HTML page with a script (i.e., a program) written in Perl, C, Tcl or other languages. The script then handles the data fed to it by the server and typically returns some information for the user. The **action** attribute in the **form** tag is the URL for this script; in this case, it is a simple script that e-mails form data to an address. Most Internet Service Providers (ISPs) will have a script like this on their site, so you can ask your system administrator how to set up your HTML to use the script correctly.

For this particular script, there are several pieces of information (not seen by the user) needed in the form. Lines 24–31

```
<input type = "hidden" name = "recipient"
   value = "deitel@deitel.com">

<input type = "hidden" name = "subject"
   value = "Feedback Form">

<input type = "hidden" name = "redirect"
   value = "main.html">
```

specify this information using *hidden input elements.* The **input** element is common in forms and always requires the **type** attribute. Two other attributes are **name**, which provides a unique identifier for the **input** element, and **value**, which indicates the value that the **input** element sends to the server upon submission.

As shown above, hidden inputs always have the attribute **type = "hidden"**. The three hidden inputs shown are typical for this kind of CGI script: An e-mail address to which the data will be sent, the subject line of the e-mail and a URL to which the user is redirected after submitting the form.

Good Programming Practice J.1

*Place hidden **input** elements in the beginning of a form, right after the opening **<form>** tag. This makes these elements easier to find and identify.*

The usage of an **input** element is defined by the value of its **type** attribute. We introduce another of these options in lines 35–37:

```
<p><label>Name:
   <input name = "name" type = "text" size = "25">
</label></p>
```

The input *type = "text"* inserts a one-line text box into the form (line 36). A good use of the textual input element is for names or other one-line pieces of information. The **label** element on lines 35–37 provide a description for the **input** element on line 36.

We also use the *size* attribute of the **input** element to specify the width of the text input, measured in characters. You can also set a maximum number of characters that the text input will accept using the **maxlength** attribute.

Good Programming Practice J.2

*When using **input** elements in forms, be sure to leave enough space with the **maxlength** attribute for users to input the pertinent information.*

Common Programming Error J.3

*Forgetting to include a **label** element for each form element is a design error. Without these labels, users will have no way of knowing what the function of individual form elements is.*

There are two types of **input** elements in lines 42–43

```
<input type = "submit" value = "Submit Your Entries">
<input type = "reset" value = "Clear Your Entries">
```

that should be inserted into every form. The *type = "submit"* **input** element allows the user to submit the data entered in the form to the server for processing. Most visual Web browsers place a button in the form that submits the data when clicked. The **value** attribute changes the text displayed on the button (the default value is *"submit"*). The input element *type = "reset"* allows a user to reset all form elements to the default values. This can help the user correct mistakes or simply start over. As with the **submit** input, the **value** attribute of the **reset input** element affects the text of the button on the screen, but does not affect its functionality.

Common Programming Error J.4

*Be sure to close your form code with the **</form>** tag. Neglecting to do so is an error and can affect the functionality of other forms on the same page.*

J.5 More Complex HTML Forms

We introduce additional form input options in Fig. J.4.

```
1   <!DOCTYPE HTML PUBLIC "-//W3C//DTD HTML 4.01//EN"
2            "http://www.w3.org/TR/html4/strict.dtd">
3   <html>
4
5   <!-- Fig. J.4: form.html    -->
6   <!-- Form design example 2. -->
7
8   <head>
9      <title>C# How to Program - Tables</title>
10  </head>
```

Fig. J.4   Form including textareas, password boxes and checkboxes. (Part 1 of 3.)

```
11
12   <body>
13
14      <h1>Feedback Form</h1>
15
16      <p>Please fill out this form to help us improve our site.</p>
17
18      <form method = "post" action = "/cgi-bin/formmail">
19
20         <p>
21            <input type = "hidden" name = "recipient"
22               value = "deitel@deitel.com">
23
24            <input type = "hidden" name = "subject"
25               value = "Feedback Form">
26
27            <input type = "hidden" name = "redirect"
28               value = "main.html">
29         </p>
30
31         <p><label>Name:
32            <input name = "name" type = "text" size = "25">
33         </label></p>
34
35         <!-- <textarea> creates a textbox of the size given -->
36         <p><label>Comments:
37            <textarea name = "comments" rows = "4" cols = "36">
38            </textarea>
39         </label></p>
40
41         <!-- <input type = "password"> inserts textbox whose -->
42         <!-- readout will be in *** not regular characters    -->
43         <p><label>Email Address:
44            <input name = "email" type = "password" size = "25">
45         </label></p>
46
47         <p>
48            <strong>Things you liked:</strong><br>
49
50            <label>Site design
51            <input name = "thingsliked" type = "checkbox"
52               value = "Design"></label>
53
54            <label>Links
55            <input name = "thingsliked" type = "checkbox"
56               value = "Links"></label>
57
58            <label>Ease of use
59            <input name = "thingsliked" type = "checkbox"
60               value = "Ease"></label>
61
62            <label>Images
```

Fig. J.4   Form including textareas, password boxes and checkboxes. (Part 2 of 3.)

```
63            <input name = "thingsliked" type = "checkbox"
64               value = "Images"></label>
65
66            <label>Source code
67            <input name = "thingsliked" type = "checkbox"
68               value = "Code"></label>
69         </p>
70
71         <p>
72            <input type = "submit" value = "Submit Your Entries">
73            <input type = "reset" value = "Clear Your Entries">
74         </p>
75
76      </form>
77
78   </body>
79   </html>
```

Fig. J.4   Form including textareas, password boxes and checkboxes. (Part 3 of 3.)

Lines 37–38

```
<textarea name = "comments" rows = "4" cols = "36">
</textarea>
```

introduce the **textarea** element. The **textarea** element inserts a text box into the form. You specify the size of the box with the **rows** attribute, which sets the number of rows that will appear in the **textarea**. With the **cols** attribute, you specify how wide the **textarea** should be. This **textarea** is four rows of characters tall and 36 characters wide. Any default text that you want to place inside the **textarea** should be contained in the **textarea** element.

The input **type = "password"** (line 44)

```
<input name = "email" type = "password" size = "25">
```

inserts a text box with the indicated size. The password input field provides a way for users to enter information that the user would not want others to be able to read on the screen. In visual browsers, the data the user types into a password input field is shown as asterisks. However, the actual value the user enters is sent to the server. Nonvisual browsers may render this type of input field differently.

Lines 50–68 introduce another type of form element, the checkbox. Every **input** element with **type = "checkbox"** creates a new checkbox item in the form. Checkboxes can be used individually or in groups. Each checkbox in a group should have the same **name** (in this case, **name = "thingsliked"**). This notifies the script handling the form that all of the checkboxes are related to one another.

Common Programming Error J.5

*When your form has several checkboxes with the same **name**, you must make sure that they have different **value**s, or else the script will have no way of distinguishing between them.*

Additional form elements are introduced in Fig. J.5. In this form example, we introduce two new types of input options. The first of these is the *radio button*, introduced in lines 80–97. Inserted into forms with the **input** attribute **type = "radio"**, radio buttons are similar in function and usage to checkboxes. Radio buttons are different in that only one element in the group may be selected at any time. All of the **name** attributes of a group of radio inputs must be the same and all of the **value** attributes different. Insert the attribute **checked** to indicate which radio button you would like selected initially. The **checked** attribute can also be applied to checkboxes.

Common Programming Error J.6

*When you are using a group of radio inputs in a form, forgetting to set the **name** values to the same name will let the user select all the radio buttons at the same time—an undesired result.*

```
1   <!DOCTYPE HTML PUBLIC "-//W3C//DTD HTML 4.01//EN"
2           "http://www.w3.org/TR/html4/strict.dtd">
3   <html>
4
5   <!-- Fig. J.5: form.html    -->
6   <!-- Form design example 3. -->
7
8   <head>
9      <title>C# How to Program - Tables</title>
10  </head>
11
12  <body>
13
14     <h1>Feedback Form</h1>
15
```

Fig. J.5   Form including radio buttons and pulldown lists. (Part 1 of 4.)

```
16        <p>Please fill out this form to help us improve our site.</p>
17
18        <form method = "post" action = "/cgi-bin/formmail">
19
20           <p>
21              <input type = "hidden" name = "recipient"
22                 value = "deitel@deitel.com">
23
24              <input type = "hidden" name = "subject"
25                 value = "Feedback Form">
26
27              <input type = "hidden" name = "redirect"
28                 value = "main.html">
29           </p>
30
31           <p><label>Name:
32              <input name = "name" type = "text" size = "25">
33           </label></p>
34
35           <p><label>Comments:
36              <textarea name = "comments" rows = "4" cols = "36">
37                 </textarea>
38           </label></p>
39
40           <p><label>Email Address:
41              <input name = "email" type = "password" size = "25">
42           </label></p>
43
44           <p>
45              <strong>Things you liked:</strong><br>
46
47              <label>Site design
48                 <input name = "things" type = "checkbox"
49                    value = "Design">
50              </label>
51
52              <label>Links
53                 <input name = "things" type = "checkbox"
54                    value = "Links">
55              </label>
56
57              <label>Ease of use
58                 <input name = "things" type = "checkbox"
59                    value = "Ease">
60              </label>
61
62              <label>Images
63                 <input name = "things" type = "checkbox"
64                    value = "Images">
65              </label>
66
67              <label>Source code
```

Fig. J.5   Form including radio buttons and pulldown lists. (Part 2 of 4.)

```
68              <input name = "things" type = "checkbox"
69                  value = "Code">
70          </label>
71      </p>
72
73      <!-- <input type = "radio"> creates one radio button -->
74      <!-- radio buttons and checkboxes differ in that      -->
75      <!-- only one radio button in group can be selected    -->
76      <p>
77          <strong>How did you get to our site?:</strong><br>
78
79          <label>Search engine
80              <input name = "how get to site" type = "radio"
81                  value = "search engine" checked></label>
82
83          <label>Links from another site
84              <input name = "how get to site" type = "radio"
85                  value = "link"></label>
86
87          <label>Deitel.com Web site
88              <input name = "how get to site" type = "radio"
89                  value = "deitel.com"></label>
90
91          <label>Reference in a book
92              <input name = "how get to site" type = "radio"
93                  value = "book"></label>
94
95          <label>Other
96              <input name = "how get to site" type = "radio"
97                  value = "other"></label>
98
99      </p>
100
101     <!-- <select> tags present drop down menus    -->
102     <!-- with choices indicated by <option> tags -->
103     <p>
104         <label>Rate our site:
105
106         <select name = "rating">
107             <option selected>Amazing:-)</option>
108             <option>10</option>
109             <option>9</option>
110             <option>8</option>
111             <option>7</option>
112             <option>6</option>
113             <option>5</option>
114             <option>4</option>
115             <option>3</option>
116             <option>2</option>
117             <option>1</option>
118             <option>The Pits:-(</option>
119         </select>
120
```

Fig. J.5   Form including radio buttons and pulldown lists. (Part 3 of 4.)

```
121              </label>
122          </p>
123
124          <p>
125              <input type = "submit" value = "Submit Your Entries">
126              <input type = "reset" value = "Clear Your Entries">
127          </p>
128
129      </form>
130
131  </body>
132  </html>
```

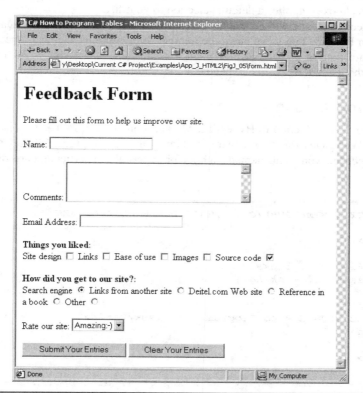

Fig. J.5   Form including radio buttons and pulldown lists. (Part 4 of 4.)

The last type of form input that we introduce here is the **select** element (lines 106–119). This will place a selectable list of items inside your form.

```
<select name = "rating">
    <option selected>Amazing:-)</option>
    <option>10</option>
    <option>9</option>
    <option>8</option>
    <option>7</option>
    <option>6</option>
```

```
<option>5</option>
<option>4</option>
<option>3</option>
<option>2</option>
<option>1</option>
<option>The Pits:-(</option>
</select>
```

This type of form input is created via a **select** element. Inside the opening **<select>** tag, be sure to include the **name** attribute.

To add an item to the list, add to the **select** element an *option* element containing the text to be displayed. The **selected** attribute, like the **checked** attribute for radio buttons and checkboxes, applies a default selection to your list.

The preceding code will generate a pull-down list of options in most visual browsers, as shown in Fig. J.5. You can change the number of list options visible at one time, using the *size* attribute of the **select** element. Use this attribute if you prefer an expanded version of the list to the one-line expandable list.

J.6 Internal Linking

In Appendix I, Introduction to HyperText Markup Language 4: Part 1, we discussed how to link one Web page to another with text and image anchors. Figure J.6 introduces *internal linking*, which lets you create named anchors for hyperlinks to particular parts of an HTML document.

```
1   <!DOCTYPE HTML PUBLIC "-//W3C//DTD HTML 4.01//EN"
2             "http://www.w3.org/TR/html4/strict.dtd">
3   <html>
4
5   <!-- Fig. J.6: links.html -->
6   <!-- Internal linking.     -->
7
8   <head>
9      <title>C# How to Program - Tables</title>
10  </head>
11
12  <body>
13
14     <!-- <a name = ".."></a> makes internal hyperlinks -->
15     <p>
16        <a name = "features"></a>
17     </p>
18
19     <h1>The Best Features of the Internet</h1>
20
21     <!-- internal link's address is "xx.html#linkname" -->
22     <p>
23        <a href = "#ceos">Go to <em>Favorite CEOs</em></a>
24     </p>
25
```

Fig. J.6   Using internal hyperlinks to make your pages more navigable. (Part 1 of 3.)

```
26    <ul>
27        <li>You can meet people from countries around the world.
28        </li>
29
30        <li>You have access to new media as it becomes public:
31
32          <ul>
33              <li>New games</li>
34              <li>New applications
35
36                <ul>
37                    <li>For Business</li>
38                    <li>For Pleasure</li>
39                </ul>
40
41              </li>
42
43              <li>Around the Clock news</li>
44              <li>Search Engines</li>
45              <li>Shopping</li>
46              <li>Programming
47
48                <ul>
49                    <li>HTML</li>
50                    <li>Java</li>
51                    <li>Dynamic HTML</li>
52                    <li>Scripts</li>
53                    <li>New languages</li>
54                </ul>
55
56              </li>
57          </ul>
58
59        </li>
60
61        <li>Links</li>
62        <li>Keeping In touch with old friends</li>
63        <li>It is the technology of the future!</li>
64    </ul>
65
66    <p><a name = "ceos"></a></p>
67
68    <h1>My 3 Favorite <em>CEOs</em></h1>
69
70    <p>
71        <a href = "#features">Go to <em>Favorite Features</em></a>
72    </p>
73
74    <ol>
75        <li>Lawrence J. Ellison</li>
76        <li>Steve Jobs</li>
77        <li>Michael Dell</li>
78    </ol>
```

Fig. J.6   Using internal hyperlinks to make your pages more navigable. (Part 2 of 3.)

```
79
80   </body>
81   </html>
```

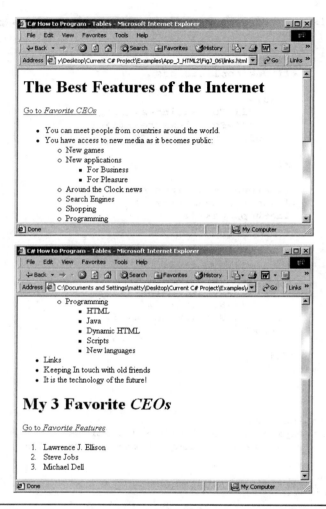

Fig. J.6   Using internal hyperlinks to make your pages more navigable. (Part 3 of 3.)

Lines 15–17

```
<p>
   <a name = "features"></a>
</p>
```

show a named anchor for an internal hyperlink. A named anchor is created via an **a** element with a **name** attribute. Line 15 creates an anchor named **features**. Because the name of the page is **list.html**, the URL of this anchor in the Web page is **list.html#features**. Line 71

```
<a href = "#features">Go to <em>Favorite Features</em></a>
```

shows a hyperlink with the anchor **features** as its target. Selecting this hyperlink in a visual browser would scroll the browser window to the **features** anchor (line 16). Examples of this occur in Fig. J.6, which shows two different screen captures from the same page, each at a different anchor. You can also link to an anchor in another page, using the URL of that location (using the format **href = "page.html#name"**).

Look-and-Feel Observation J.2

Internal hyperlinks are most useful in large HTML files with lots of information. You can link to various points on the page to save the user from having to scroll down and find a specific location.

J.7 Creating and Using Image Maps

We have seen that images can be used as links to other places on your site or elsewhere on the Internet. We now discuss how to create *image maps* (Fig. J.7), which allow you to designate certain sections of the image as *hotspots* and then use these hotspots as links.

All elements of an image map are contained inside the **<map>...</map>** tags. The required attribute for the **map** element is **name** (line 18):

```
<map name = "picture">
```

As we will see, this attribute is needed for referencing purposes. A hotspot on the image is designated with the **area** element. Every **area** element has the following attributes: **href** sets the target for the link on that spot, **shape** and **coords** set the characteristics of the area and **alt** functions just as it does in the **img** element.

```
1   <!DOCTYPE HTML PUBLIC "-//W3C//DTD HTML 4.01//EN"
2              "http://www.w3.org/TR/html4/strict.dtd">
3   <html>
4
5   <!-- Fig. J.7: picture.html          -->
6   <!-- Creating and using imape maps. -->
7
8   <head>
9      <title>C# How to Program - Tables</title>
10  </head>
11
12  <body>
13
14     <p>
15
16     <!-- <map> opens and names image map formatting -->
17     <!-- area and to be referenced later            -->
18     <map name = "picture">
19
20        <!-- "shape = rect" indicates rectangular -->
21        <!-- area, with coordinates of the        -->
22        <!-- upper-left and lower-right corners    -->
```

Fig. J.7   Picture with links anchored to an image map. (Part 1 of 2.)

```
23          <area href = "form.html" shape = "rect"
24             coords = "3, 122, 73, 143"
25             alt = "Go to the feedback form">
26
27          <area href = "contact.html" shape = "rect"
28             coords = "109, 123, 199, 142"
29             alt = "Go to the contact page">
30
31          <area href = "main.html" shape = "rect"
32             coords = "1, 2, 72, 17"
33             alt = "Go to the homepage">
34
35          <area href = "links.html" shape = "rect"
36             coords = "155, 0, 199, 18"
37             alt = "Go to the links page">
38
39          <!-- "shape = polygon" indicates area of -->
40          <!-- cusotmizable shape, with the        -->
41          <!-- coordinates of every vertex listed   -->
42          <area href = "mailto:deitel@deitel.com" shape = "poly"
43          coords = "28, 22, 24, 68, 46, 114, 84, 111, 99, 56, 86, 13"
44             alt = "Email the Deitels">
45
46          <!-- "shape = circle" indicates circular -->
47          <!-- area with center and radius listed   -->
48          <area href = "mailto:deitel@deitel.com" shape = "circle"
49             coords = "146, 66, 42" alt = "Email the Deitels">
50       </map>
51
52       <!-- <img src=... usemap = "#name"> says that   -->
53       <!-- indicated image map will be used with image -->
54       <img src = "deitel.gif" width = "200" height = "144"
55          alt = "Harvey and Paul Deitel" usemap = "#picture">
56       </p>
57
58    </body>
59    </html>
```

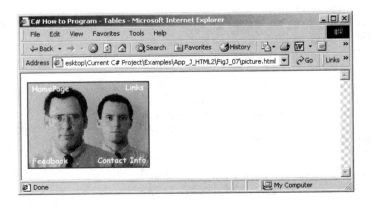

Fig. J.7   Picture with links anchored to an image map. (Part 2 of 2.)

The markup on lines 23–25

```
<area href = "form.html" shape = "rect"
    coords = "3, 122, 73, 143" alt = "Go to the feedback form">
```

causes a *rectangular hotspot* to be drawn around the *coordinates* given in the **coords** element. A coordinate pair consists of two numbers, which are the locations of the point on the *x* and *y* axes. The *x* axis extends horizontally from the upper-left corner, the *y* axis vertically. Every point on an image has a unique *x–y* coordinate. In the case of a rectangular hotspot, the required coordinates are those of the upper-left and lower-right corners of the rectangle. In this case, the upper-left corner of the rectangle is located at 3 on the *x* axis and 122 on the *y* axis, annotated as (*3, 122*). The lower-right corner of the rectangle is at (*73, 143*).

Another map area is in lines 42–44

```
<area href = "mailto:deitel@deitel.com" shape = "poly"
    coords = "28, 22, 24, 68, 46, 114, 84, 111, 99, 56, 86, 13
    alt = "Email the Deitels">
```

In this case, we use the value *poly* for the **shape** attribute. This creates a hotspot in the shape of a polygon, using the coordinates in the **coords** attribute. These coordinates represent each vertex, or corner, of the polygon. The browser will automatically connect these points with lines to form the area of the hotspot.

shape = "circle" is the last shape attribute that is commonly used in image maps. It creates a *circular hotspot*, and requires both the coordinates of the center of the circle and the radius of the circle, in pixels.

To use the image map with an **img** element, you must insert the **usemap = "#***name***"** attribute into the **img** element, where *name* is the value of the **name** attribute in the **map** element. Lines 54–55

```
<img src = "deitel.gif" width = "200" height= "144" alt =
    "Harvey and Paul Deitel" usemap = "#picture">
```

show how the image map **name = "picture"** is applied to the **img** element.

J.8 <meta> Tags

People use search engines to find interesting Web sites. Search engines usually catalog sites by following links from page to page and saving identification and classification information for each page visited. The main HTML element that search engines use to catalog pages is the *meta* tag (Fig. J.8).

A **meta** tag contains two attributes that should always be used. The first of these, *name*, identifies the type of **meta** tag you are including. The *content* attribute provides information the search engine will catalog about your site.

```
1   <!DOCTYPE HTML PUBLIC "-//W3C//DTD HTML 4.01//EN"
2           "http://www.w3.org/TR/html4/strict.dtd">
3   <html>
4
5   <!-- Fig. J.8: main.html        -->
6   <!-- <meta> and <!doctype> tags. -->
```

Fig. J.8   Using **meta** to provide keywords and a description. (Part 1 of 2.)

```
 7
 8   <head>
 9      <!-- <meta> tags give search engines information -->
10      <!-- they need to catalog your site            -->
11      <meta name = "keywords" content = "Webpage, design, HTML,
12         tutorial, personal, help, index, form, contact, feedback,
13         list, links, frame, deitel">
14
15      <meta name = "description" content = "This Web site will help
16         you learn the basics of HTML and Webpage design through the
17         use of interactive examples and instruction.">
18
19      <title>C# How to Program - Tables</title>
20   </head>
21
22   <body>
23
24      <h1>Welcome to Our Web Site!</h1>
25
26      <p>
27         We have designed this site to teach about the wonders of
28         <em>HTML</em>. We have been using <em>HTML</em> since
29         version <strong>2.0</strong>, and we enjoy the features
30         that have been added recently. It seems only a short
31         time ago that we read our first <em>HTML</em> book.
32         Soon you will know about many of the great new
33         features of HTML 4.01.
34      </p>
35
36      <p>Have Fun With the Site!</p>
37
38   </body>
39   </html>
```

Fig. J.8   Using **meta** to provide keywords and a description. (Part 2 of 2.)

Lines 11–13 demonstrate the **meta** tag.

```
<meta name = "keywords" content = "Webpage, design, HTML,
   tutorial, personal, help, index, form, contact, feedback,
   list, links, frame, deitel">
```

The **content** of a **meta** tag with *name = "keywords"* provides search engines with a list of words that describe key aspects of your site. These words are used to match with searches—if someone searches for some of the terms in your **keywords meta** tag, they have a better chance of being notified about your site in the search-engine output. Thus, including **meta** tags and their **content** information will draw more viewers to your site.

The *description* attribute value (lines 15–17)

```
<meta name = "description" content = "This Web site will help
   you learn the basics of HTML and Webpage design through the
   use of interactive examples and instruction.">
```

is quite similar to the **keywords** value. Instead of giving a list of words describing your page, the **content**s of the keywords **meta** element should be a readable 3-to-4-line description of your site, written in sentence form. This description is also used by search engines to catalog and display your site.

Software Engineering Observation J.1

meta elements are not visible to users of the site and must be placed inside the header section of your HTML document.

J.9 frameset Element

All of the Web pages we have designed so far have the ability to link to other pages but can display only one page at a time. Figure J.9 introduces *frames*, which can help you display more than one HTML file at a time. Frames, when used properly, can make your site more readable and usable for your users.

```
1   <!DOCTYPE HTML PUBLIC "-//W3C//DTD HTML 4.01 Frameset//EN"
2           "http://www.w3.org/TR/html4/frameset.dtd">
3   <html>
4
5   <!-- Fig. J.9: index.html -->
6   <!-- HTML Frames I.        -->
7
8   <head>
9      <meta name = "keywords" content = "Webpage, design, HTML,
10         tutorial, personal, help, index, form, contact, feedback,
11         list, links, frame, deitel">
12
13      <meta name = "description" content = "This Web site will help
14         you learn the basics of HTML and Webpage design through the
15         use of interactive examples and instruction.">
16
17      <title>C# How to Program - Tables</title>
18   </head>
19
20   <!-- the <frameset> tag gives dimensions of your frame -->
21   <frameset cols = "110,*">
22
23      <!-- the individual frame elements specify -->
24      <!-- which pages appear in given frames     -->
25      <frame name = "nav" src = "nav.html">
26      <frame name = "main" src = "main.html">
27
28      <noframes>
29         <p>
30            This page uses frames, but your browser
31               does not support them.
32         </p>
33
```

Fig. J.9   Web site using two frames—navigation and content. (Part 1 of 2.)

```
34              <p>
35                 Please, <a href = "nav.html">follow this link to
36                    browse our site without frames</a>.
37              </p>
38          </noframes>
39
40      </frameset>
41      </html>
```

Fig. J.9   Web site using two frames—navigation and content. (Part 2 of 2.)

On lines 1 and 2,

```
<!DOCTYPE HTML PUBLIC "-//W3C//DTD HTML 4.01 Frameset//EN"
            "http://www.w3.org/TR/html4/frameset.dtd">
```

we encounter a new document type. The document type specified here indicates that this HTML document uses frames. You should use this document type whenever you use frames in your HTML document.

The framed page begins with the opening **frameset** tag, on line 21

```
<frameset cols = "110,*">
```

This tag tells the browser that the page contains frames. The **cols** attribute of the opening **frameset** tag gives the layout of the frameset. The value of **cols** (or **rows**, if you will be writing a frameset with a horizontal layout) gives the width of each frame, either in pixels or as a percentage of the screen. In this case, the attribute **cols = "110,*"** tells the browser that there are two frames. The first one extends 110 pixels from the left edge of the screen, and the second frame fills the remainder of the screen (as indicated by the asterisk).

Now that we have defined the page layout, we have to specify what files will make up the frameset. We do this with the *frame* element in lines 25 and 26:

```
<frame name = "nav" src = "nav.html">
<frame name = "main" src = "main.html">
```

In each **frame** element, the **src** attribute gives the URL of the page that will be displayed in the frame. In the preceding example, the first frame (which covers 110 pixels on the left side of the **frameset**) will display the page **nav.html** and has the attribute **name = "nav"**. The second frame will display the page **main.html** and has the attribute **name = "main"**.

The purpose of a **name** attribute in the **frame** element is to identify the frame, enabling hyperlinks in a **frameset** to load in their intended target **frame**. For example,

```
<a href = "links.html" target = "main">
```

would load **links.html** in the frame whose **name** attribute is **"main"**.

A target in an anchor element can also be set to a number of preset values: **target="_blank"** loads the page in a new blank browser window, **target="_self"** loads the page into the same window as the anchor element, **target="_parent"** loads it in the parent **frameset** (i.e., the **frameset** which contains the current frame) and **target="_top"** loads the page into the full browser window (the page loads over the **frameset**).

In lines 28–38 of the code example in Fig. J.9, the **noframes** element displays HTML in those browsers that do not support frames.

Portability Tip J.1

*Not everyone uses a browser that supports frames. Use the **noframes** element inside the **frameset** to direct users to a nonframed version of your site.*

Look-and-Feel Observation J.3

Frames are capable of enhancing your page, but are often misused. Never use frames to accomplish what you could with other, simpler HTML formatting.

J.10 Nested `framesets`

You can use the **frameset** element to create more complex layouts in a framed Web site by nesting **frameset** areas as in Fig. J.10.

The first level of **frameset** tags is on lines 21 and 22

```
<frameset cols = "110,*">
    <frame name = "nav"src = "nav.html">
```

The **frameset** and **frame** elements here are constructed in the same manner as in Fig. J.9. We have one frame that extends over the first 110 pixels, starting at the left edge.

The second (nested) level of the **frameset** element covers only the remaining **frame** area that was not included in the primary **frameset**. Thus, any frames included in the second **frameset** will not include the leftmost 110 pixels of the screen. Lines 26–29 show the second level of **frameset** tags.

```
<frameset rows = "175,*">
   <frame name = "picture" src = "picture.html">
   <frame name = "main" src = "main.html">
</frameset>
```

In this **frameset** area, the first frame extends 175 pixels from the top of the screen, as indicated by the **rows = "175,*"**. Be sure to include the correct number of **frame** elements inside the second **frameset** area. Also, be sure to include a **noframes** element and to close both of the **frameset** areas at the end of the Web page.

```
1    <!DOCTYPE HTML PUBLIC "-//W3C//DTD HTML 4.01 Frameset//EN"
2           "http://www.w3.org/TR/html4/frameset.dtd">
3    <html>
4
5    <!-- Fig. J.10: index.html   -->
6    <!-- HTML frames II.          -->
7
8    <head>
9
10      <meta name = "keywords" content = "Webpage, design, HTML,
11         tutorial, personal, help, index, form, contact, feedback,
12         list, links, frame, deitel">
13
14      <meta name = "description" content = "This Web site will help
15         you learn the basics of HTML and Webpage design through
16         the use of interactive examples and instruction.">
17
18      <title>C# How to Program - Tables</title>
19   </head>
20
21   <frameset cols = "110,*">
22      <frame name = "nav" src = "nav.html">
23
24      <!-- nested framesets are used to change formatting -->
25      <!-- and spacing of frameset as whole               -->
26      <frameset rows = "175,*">
27         <frame name = "picture" src = "picture.html">
28         <frame name = "main" src = "main.html">
29      </frameset>
30
31      <noframes>
32         <p>
33            This page uses frames, but your browser does
34               not support them.
35         </p>
36
37         <p>
38            Please, <a href = "nav.html">follow this link
39               to browse our site without frames</a>.
```

Fig. J.10 Framed Web site with a nested frameset. (Part 1 of 2.)

```
40            </p>
41          </noframes>
42
43        </frameset>
44      </html>
```

Fig. J.10   Framed Web site with a nested frameset. (Part 2 of 2.)

Testing and Debugging Tip J.1

When using nested **frameset** *elements, indent every level of* **frame** *tag. This makes the page clearer and easier to debug.*

Look-and-Feel Observation J.4

Nested **frameset***s can help you create visually pleasing, easy-to-navigate Web sites.*

J.11 Summary

HTML tables organize data into rows and columns. All tags and text that apply to a table go inside the **<table>...</table>** tags. Tables can be split into distinct horizontal and vertical sections. Put all header information (such as table titles and column headers) inside the **<thead>...</thead>** tags. The **tr** (table row) element formats the cells of individual rows. All of the cells in a row belong within the **<tr>...</tr>** tags of that row. The smallest area of the table that we are able to format is the data cell. There are two types of data cells: those located in the header (**<th>...</th>**) and those located in the table body (**<td>...</td>**). Header cells, usually placed in the **<thead>** area, are suitable for titles and column headings. Like **thead**, **tbody** serves formatting and groups information. Most tables use **tbody** to house the majority of their content. **td** table data cells are left aligned by default. **th** cells are centered by default. Just as you can use the **thead** and

tbody elements to format groups of rows on a table, you can use the **colgroup** element to group and format columns. The **colgroup** element is used by setting in its opening tag the number of columns it affects and the formatting it imposes on that group of columns. Each **col** element contained inside the **<colgroup>...</colgroup>** tags can in turn format a specified number of columns.

HTML provides several mechanisms—including the **form**—to collect information from people viewing your site. Use **method = "post"** in a form that causes changes to server data—for example, when updating a database. The **form** data will be sent to the server as an environment variable, which scripts are able to access. The other possible value, **method = "get"**, should be used when your form does not cause any changes in server-side data—for example, when making a database request. The **form** data from **method = "get"** are appended to the end of the URL. The **action** attribute in the **form** tag is the path to a script that processes the **form** data. The input element is common in forms and always requires the **type** attribute. Two other attributes are **name**, which provides a unique identification for the **input**, and **value**, which indicates the value that the **input** element sends to the server upon submission. The input **type = "text"** inserts a one-line text bar into the form. The value of this **input** element and the information that the server sends to you from the **input** is the text that the user types into the text bar. The **type = "submit" input** element places a button in the form that, when clicked, submits data to the server. The **value** attribute of the **submit** input changes the text displayed on the button. The **type = "reset"** input element places a button on the form that, when clicked, will clear all entries the user has entered into the form. The **textarea** element inserts a box into the form. You specify the size of the box (which is scrollable) inside the opening **<textarea>** tag with the **rows** attribute and the **cols** attribute. Data entered in a **type = "password"** input appear on the screen as asterisks. The password is used to submit sensitive information that the user would not want others to be able to read. It is just the browser that displays asterisks—the real **form** data are still submitted to the server. Every **input** element with **type = "checkbox"** creates a new checkbox in the form. Checkboxes can be used individually or in groups. Each checkbox in a group should have the same **name**. Inserted into forms by means of the **input** attribute **type = "radio"**, radio buttons are different from checkboxes in that only one in the group may be selected at any time. All of the **name** attributes of a group of radio inputs must be the same and all of the **value** attributes different. The **select** element places a selectable list of items inside your form. To add an item to the list, insert an **option** element in the **<select>...</select>** area and type what you want the list item to display on the same line. You can change the number of list options visible at one time by including the **size = "***size***"** attribute inside the **<select>** tag. Use this attribute if you prefer an expanded version of the list to the one-line expandable list.

An image map allows you to designate certain sections of the image as hotspots and then use these hotspots as anchors for linking. All elements of an image map are contained inside the **<map>...</map>** tags. The required attribute for the **map** element is **name**. A hotspot on the image is designated with the **area** element. Every **<area>** tag has the following attributes: **href** sets the target for the link on that spot, and **shape** and **coords** set the characteristics of the area and **alt** function, just as they do in **<img>** tags. To use an image map with a graphic on your page, you must insert the **usemap = "#***name***"** attribute into the **img** element, where *name* is the value of the **name** attribute in the **map** element.

The main element that interacts with search engines is the **meta** element. **meta** tags contain two attributes that should always be used. The first of these, **name**, is an identification of the type of **meta** tag you are including. The **content** attribute gives the information the search engine will be cataloging. The **content** of a **meta** tag with **name =** **"keywords"** provides the search engines with a list of words that describe the key aspects of your site. By including **meta** tags and information on their content, you can give precise information about your site to search engines. This will help you draw a more focused audience to your site. The **description** value of the **name** attribute in the **meta** tag should be a three-to-four-line description of your site, written in sentence form. This description is used by the search engine to catalog and display your site. **meta** elements are not visible to users of the site and should be placed inside the header section of your HTML document.

The **frameset** tag tells the browser that the page contains frames. In each **frame** element, the **src** attribute gives the URL of the page that will be displayed in the specified frame. The purpose of a **name** attribute in the **frame** element is to give an identity to that specific frame, which enables hyperlinks in a **frameset** to load their intended **frame**. The **target** attribute in an anchor element is set to the **name** of the **frame** in which the new page should load. Not everyone viewing a page has a browser that can handle frames. You therefore need to include a **noframes** element inside of the **frameset**. You should include regular HTML tags and elements within the **<noframes>...</noframes>** tags. Use this area to direct the user to a nonframed version of the site. By nesting **frameset** elements, you can create more complex layouts.

J.12 Internet and World Wide Web Resources

www.geocities.com/SiliconValley/Orchard/5212
Adam's Advanced HTML Page is geared to those seeking to master the more advanced techniques of HTML. the site includes instructions for creating tables, frames and marquees and discusses other advanced topics.

www.w3scripts.com/html
This site, an offshoot of *W3Schools*, is a repository for examples exhibiting all of the features of HTML, from beginner to advanced.

www.blooberry.com/indexdot/html
Index Dot HTML, The Advance HTML Reference... is a site that has a great directory and a tree-based index of all HTML elements, plus more.

www.neiljohan.com/html/advancedhtml.htm
The *Advanced HTML Guide* gives insights into improving your site, using HTML in ways you might not have thought possible.

Introduction to XHTML: Part 1

Objectives

- To understand important components of XHTML documents.
- To use XHTML to create World Wide Web pages.
- To add images to Web pages.
- To understand how to create and use hyperlinks to navigate Web pages.
- To mark up lists of information.

To read between the lines was easier than to follow the text.
Aristophanes

Outline

K.1   Introduction

K.2   Editing XHTML

K.3   First XHTML Example

K.4   W3C XHTML Validation Service

K.5   Headers

K.6   Linking

K.7   Images

K.8   Special Characters and More Line Breaks

K.9   Unordered Lists

K.10   Nested and Ordered Lists

K.11   Summary

K.12   Internet and World Wide Web Resources

K.1 Introduction

In this appendix, we introduce *XHTML*[1]—the *Extensible HyperText Markup Language*. In the next appendix, Introduction to XHTML: Part 2, we introduce more sophisticated XHTML techniques, such as *tables*, which are particularly useful for structuring information from *databases* (i.e., software that stores structured sets of data). In this appendix, we do not present any C# programming.

Unlike procedural programming languages such as C, Fortran, Cobol and Visual Basic, XHTML is a *markup language* that specifies the format of text that is displayed in a Web browser such as Microsoft's Internet Explorer or Netscape's Communicator.

One key issue when using XHTML[2] is the separation of the *presentation of a document* (i.e., the document's appearance when rendered by a browser) from the *structure of the document's information*. Throughout this appendix and the next, we will discuss this issue in depth.

K.2 Editing XHTML

In this appendix, we write XHTML in its *source-code form*. We create *XHTML documents* by typing them in with a text editor (e.g., *Notepad*, *Wordpad*, *vi* or *emacs*), saving the documents with either an **.html** or **.htm** file-name extension.

---

1. XHTML has replaced the HyperText Markup Language (HTML) as the primary means of describing Web content. XHTML provides more robust, richer and more extensible features than HTML. For more on XHTML/HTML, visit **www.w3.org/markup**.
2. As this book was being submitted to the publisher, XHTML 1.1 became a World Wide Web Consortium (W3C) Recommendation. The XHTML examples presented in this book are based upon the XHTML 1.0 Recommendation, because Internet Explorer 5.5 does not support the full set of XHTML 1.1 features. In the future, Internet Explorer and other browsers will support XHTML 1.1. When this occurs, we will update our Web site (**www.deitel.com**) with XHTML 1.1 examples and information.

Good Programming Practice K.1

Assign documents file names that describe their functionality. This practice can help you identify documents faster. It also helps people who want to link to a page, by giving them an easy-to-remember name. For example, if you are writing an XHTML document that contains product information, you might want to call it **products.html**.

Machines running specialized software called a *Web server* store XHTML documents. Clients (e.g., Web browsers) request specific *resources*, such as the XHTML documents from the Web server. For example, typing **www.deitel.com/books/downloads.htm** into a Web browser's address field requests **downloads.htm** from the Web server running at **www.deitel.com**. This document is located in a directory named **books**.

K.3 First XHTML Example

In this appendix and the next, we present XHTML markup and provide screen captures that show how Internet Explorer renders (i.e., displays) the XHTML. Every XHTML document we show has line numbers for the reader's convenience. These line numbers are not part of the XHTML documents.

Our first example (Fig. K.1) is an XHTML document named **main.html** that displays the message **Welcome to XHTML!** in the browser.

The key line in the program is line 14, which tells the browser to display **Welcome to XHTML!** Now let us consider each line of the program.

Lines 1–3 are required in XHTML documents to conform with proper XHTML syntax. For now, copy and paste these lines into each XHTML document you create. The meaning of these lines is discussed in detail in Chapter 15, Extensible Markup Language (XML).

Lines 5–6 are *XHTML comments*. XHTML document creators insert comments to improve markup readability and describe the content of a document. Comments also help other people read and understand an XHTML document's markup and content. Comments do not cause the browser to perform any action when the user loads the XHTML document into the Web browser to view the document. XHTML comments always start with **<!--** and end with **-->**. Each of our XHTML examples includes comments that specify the figure number and file name and provide a brief description of the example's purpose. Subsequent examples include comments in the markup, especially to highlight new features.

Good Programming Practice K.2

Place comments throughout your markup. Comments help other programmers understand the markup, assist in debugging and list useful information that you do not want the browser to render. Comments also help you understand your own markup when you revisit a document for modifications or updates in the future.

```
1   <?xml version = "1.0"?>
2   <!DOCTYPE html PUBLIC "-//W3C//DTD XHTML 1.0 Strict//EN"
3       "http://www.w3.org/TR/xhtml1/DTD/xhtml1-strict.dtd">
4
5   <!-- Fig. K.1: main.html -->
6   <!-- Our first Web page. -->
7
```

Fig. K.1   First XHTML example. (Part 1 of 2.)

```
8   <html xmlns = "http://www.w3.org/1999/xhtml">
9      <head>
10         <title>C# How to Program - Welcome</title>
11      </head>
12
13      <body>
14         <p>Welcome to XHTML!</p>
15      </body>
16   </html>
```

Fig. K.1   First XHTML example. (Part 2 of 2.)

XHTML markup contains text that represents the content of a document and *elements* that specify a document's structure. Some important elements of an XHTML document include the **html** element, the **head** element and the **body** element. The **html** element encloses the *head section* (represented by the **head** *element*) and the *body section* (represented by the **body** *element*). The head section contains information about the XHTML document, such as the *title* of the document. The head section also can contain special document formatting instructions called *style sheets* and client-side programs called *scripts* for creating dynamic Web pages. The body section contains the page's content that the browser displays when the user visits the Web page.

XHTML documents delimit an element with *start* and *end* tags. A start tag consists of the element name in angle brackets (e.g., **<html>**). An end tag consists of the element name preceded by a **/** in angle brackets (e.g., **</html>**). In this example, lines 8 and 16 define the start and end of the **html** element. Note that the end tag on line 16 has the same name as the start tag, but is preceded by a **/** inside the angle brackets. Many start tags define *attributes* that provide additional information about an element. Browsers can use this additional information to determine how to process the element. Each attribute has a *name* and a *value* separated by an equal sign (**=**). Line 8 specifies a required attribute (**xmlns**) and value (**http://www.w3.org/1999/xhtml**) for the **html** element in an XHTML document. For now, simply copy and paste the **html** element start tag on line 8 into your XHTML documents. We discuss the details of the **html** element's **xmlns** attribute in Chapter 15, Extensible Markup Language (XML).

Common Programming Error K.1

Not enclosing attribute values in either single or double quotes is a syntax error.

Common Programming Error K.2

Using uppercase letters in an XHTML element or attribute name is a syntax error.

An XHTML document divides the **html** element into two sections—head and body. Lines 9–11 define the Web page's head section with a **head** element. Line 10 specifies a **title** element. This is called a *nested element*, because it is enclosed in the **head** element's start and end tags. The **head** element also is a nested element, because it is enclosed in the **html** element's start and end tags. The **title** element describes the Web page. Titles usually appear in the *title bar* at the top of the browser window and also as the text identifying a page when users add the page to their list of **Favorites** or **Bookmarks**, which enable users to return to their favorite sites. Search engines (i.e., sites that allow users to search the Web) also use the **title** for cataloging purposes.

Good Programming Practice K.3

Indenting nested elements emphasizes a document's structure and promotes readability.

Common Programming Error K.3

XHTML does not permit tags to overlap—a nested element's end tag must appear in the document before the enclosing element's end tag. For example, the nested XHTML tags **<head><title>hello</head></title>** *cause a syntax error, because the enclosing* **head** *element's ending* **</head>** *tag appears before the nested* **title** *element's ending* **</title>** *tag.*

Good Programming Practice K.4

Use a consistent **title** *naming convention for all pages on a site. For example, if a site is named "Bailey's Web Site," then the* **title** *of the main page might be "Bailey's Web Site—Links." This practice can help users better understand the Web site's structure.*

Line 13 opens the document's **body** element. The body section of an XHTML document specifies the document's content, which may include text and tags.

Some tags, such as the *paragraph tags* (**<p>** and **</p>**) in line 14, mark up text for display in a browser. All text placed between the **<p>** and **</p>** tags form one paragraph. When the browser renders a paragraph, a blank line usually precedes and follows paragraph text.

This document ends with two closing tags (lines 15–16). These tags close the **body** and **html** elements, respectively. The ending **</html>** tag in an XHTML document informs the browser that the XHTML markup is complete.

To view this example in Internet Explorer, perform the following steps:

1. Copy the Appendix K examples onto your machine (these examples can be downloaded from **www.deitel.com**).

2. Launch Internet Explorer, and select **Open...** from the **File** Menu. This displays the **Open** dialog.

3. Click the **Open** dialog's **Browse...** button to display the **Microsoft Internet Explorer** file dialog.

4. Navigate to the directory containing the Appendix K examples and select the file **main.html**; then, click **Open**.

5. Click **OK** to have Internet Explorer render the document. Other examples are opened in a similar manner.

At this point your browser window should appear similar to the sample screen capture shown in Fig. K.1. (Note that we resized the browser window to save space in the book.)

K.4 W3C XHTML Validation Service

Programming Web-based applications can be complex, and XHTML documents must be written correctly to ensure that browsers process them properly. To promote correctly written documents, the World Wide Web Consortium (W3C) provides a *validation service* (**validator.w3.org**) for checking a document's syntax. Documents can be validated either from a URL that specifies the location of the file or by uploading a file to the site **validator.w3.org/file-upload.html**. Uploading a file copies the file from the user's computer to another computer on the Internet. Figure K.2 shows **main.html** (Fig. K.1) being uploaded for validation. Although the W3C's Web page indicates that the service name is **HTML Validation Service**,[3] the validation service is able to validate the syntax of XHTML documents. All the XHTML examples in this book have been validated successfully through **validator.w3.org**.

By clicking **Browse...**, users can select files on their own computers for upload. After selecting a file, clicking the **Validate this document** button uploads and validates the file. Figure K.3 shows the results of validating **main.html**. This document does not contain any syntax errors. If a document does contain syntax errors, the Validation Service displays error messages describing the errors.

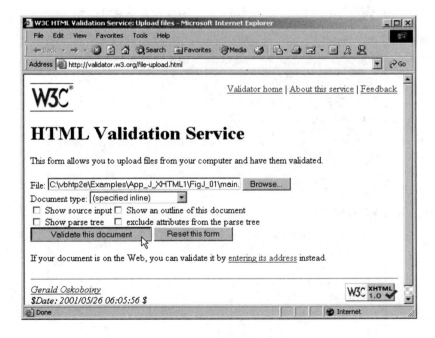

Fig. K.2   Validating an XHTML document. (Courtesy of World Wide Web Consortium (W3C).)

---

3. HTML (HyperText Markup Language) is the predecessor of XHTML designed for marking up Web content. HTML is a deprecated technology.

Testing and Debugging Tip K.1

Use a validation service, such as the W3C HTML Validation Service, to confirm that an XHTML document is correct syntactically.

K.5 Headers

Some text in an XHTML document may be more important than some other. For example, the text in this section is considered more important than a footnote. XHTML provides six *headers*, called *header elements*, for specifying the relative importance of information. Figure K.4 demonstrates these elements (**h1** through **h6**).

Portability Tip K.1

The text size used to display each header element can vary significantly between browsers.

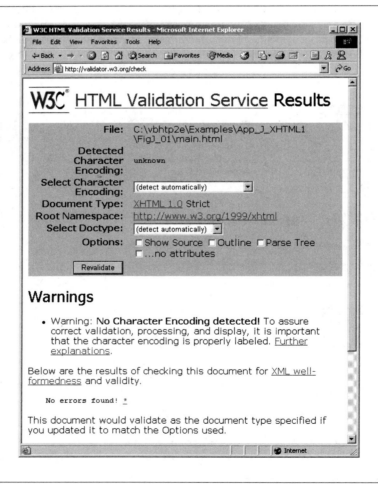

Fig. K.3   XHTML validation results. (Courtesy of World Wide Web Consortium (W3C).)

```
1   <?xml version = "1.0"?>
2   <!DOCTYPE html PUBLIC "-//W3C//DTD XHTML 1.0 Strict//EN"
3       "http://www.w3.org/TR/xhtml1/DTD/xhtml1-strict.dtd">
4
5   <!-- Fig. K.4: header.html -->
6   <!-- XHTML headers.           -->
7
8   <html xmlns = "http://www.w3.org/1999/xhtml">
9       <head>
10          <title>C# How to Program - Welcome</title>
11      </head>
12
13      <body>
14
15          <h1>Level 1 Header</h1>
16          <h2>Level 2 header</h2>
17          <h3>Level 3 header</h3>
18          <h4>Level 4 header</h4>
19          <h5>Level 5 header</h5>
20          <h6>Level 6 header</h6>
21
22      </body>
23  </html>
```

Fig. K.4   Header elements **h1** through **h6**.

Header element **h1** (line 15) is considered the most significant header and is rendered in a larger font than the other five headers (lines 16–20). Each successive header element (i.e., **h2**, **h3**, etc.) is rendered in a smaller font.

Look-and-Feel Observation K.1

Placing a header at the top of every XHTML page helps viewers understand the purpose of each page.

Look-and-Feel Observation K.2

Use larger headers to emphasize more important sections of a Web page.

K.6 Linking

One of the most important XHTML features is the *hyperlink,* which references (or *links* to) other resources, such as XHTML documents and images. In XHTML, both text and images can act as hyperlinks. Web browsers typically underline text hyperlinks and color their text blue by default, so that users can distinguish hyperlinks from plain text. In Fig. K.5, we create text hyperlinks to four different Web sites.

Line 17 introduces the **<strong>** tag. Browsers typically display text marked up with **<strong>** in a bold font.

```
1    <?xml version = "1.0"?>
2    <!DOCTYPE html PUBLIC "-//W3C//DTD XHTML 1.0 Strict//EN"
3        "http://www.w3.org/TR/xhtml1/DTD/xhtml1-strict.dtd">
4
5    <!-- Fig. K.5: links.html         -->
6    <!-- Introduction to hyperlinks. -->
7
8    <html xmlns = "http://www.w3.org/1999/xhtml">
9        <head>
10           <title>C# How to Program - Welcome</title>
11       </head>
12
13       <body>
14
15          <h1>Here are my favorite sites</h1>
16
17          <p><strong>Click a name to go to that page.</strong></p>
18
19          <!-- create four text hyperlinks -->
20          <p>
21              <a href = "http://www.deitel.com">Deitel</a>
22          </p>
23
24          <p>
25              <a href = "http://www.prenhall.com">Prentice Hall</a>
26          </p>
27
28          <p>
29              <a href = "http://www.yahoo.com">Yahoo!</a>
30          </p>
31
32          <p>
33              <a href = "http://www.usatoday.com">USA Today</a>
34          </p>
35
36       </body>
37    </html>
```

Fig. K.5   Linking to other Web pages. (Part 1 of 2.)

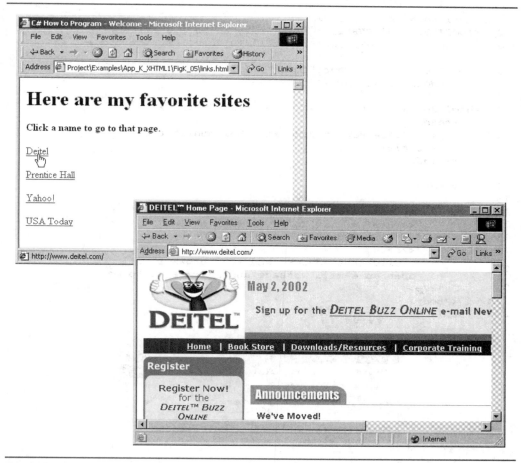

Fig. K.5   Linking to other Web pages. (Part 2 of 2.)

Links are created using the *a* (*anchor*) *element*. Line 21 defines a hyperlink that links the text **Deitel** to the URL assigned to attribute ***href***, which specifies the location of a linked resource, such as a Web page, a file or an e-mail address. This particular anchor element links to a Web page located at **http://www.deitel.com**. When a URL does not indicate a specific document on the Web site, the Web server returns a default Web page. This pages often is called **index.html**; however, most Web servers can be configured to to use any file as the default Web page for the site. (Open **http://www.deitel.com** in one browser window and **http://www.deitel.com/index.html** in a second browser window to confirm that they are identical.) If the Web server cannot locate a requested document, the server returns an error indication to the Web browser and the browser displays an error message to the user.

Anchors can link to e-mail addresses through a ***mailto:*** URL. When someone clicks this type of anchored link, most browsers launch the default e-mail program (e.g., Outlook Express) to enable the user to write an e-mail message to the linked address. Figure K.6 demonstrates this type of anchor.

```
 1   <?xml version = "1.0"?>
 2   <!DOCTYPE html PUBLIC "-//W3C//DTD XHTML 1.0 Strict//EN"
 3      "http://www.w3.org/TR/xhtml1/DTD/xhtml1-strict.dtd">
 4
 5   <!-- Fig. K.6: contact.html     -->
 6   <!-- Adding email hyperlinks. -->
 7
 8   <html xmlns = "http://www.w3.org/1999/xhtml">
 9      <head>
10         <title>C# How to Program - Welcome</title>
11         </title>
12      </head>
13
14      <body>
15
16         <p>My email address is
17            <a href = "mailto:deitel@deitel.com">
18               deitel@deitel.com
19            </a>
20            . Click the address and your browser will
21            open an e-mail message and address it to me.
22         </p>
23      </body>
24   </html>
```

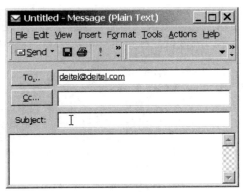

Fig. K.6   Linking to an e-mail address.

Lines 17–19 contain an e-mail link. The form of an e-mail anchor is **<a href = "mailto:***emailaddress***">...</a>**. In this case, we link to the e-mail address **deitel@deitel.com**.

K.7 Images

The examples discussed so far demonstrated how to mark up documents that contain only text. However, most Web pages contain both text and images. In fact, images are an equal and essential part of Web-page design. The two most popular image formats used by Web developers are Graphics Interchange Format (GIF) and Joint Photographic Experts Group (JPEG) images. Users can create images, using specialized pieces of software, such as Adobe PhotoShop Elements and Jasc Paint Shop Pro (**www.jasc.com**). Images may also be acquired from various Web sites, such as **gallery.yahoo.com**. Figure K.7 demonstrates how to incorporate images into Web pages.

Lines 16–17 use an ***img*** element to insert an image in the document. The image file's location is specified with the **img** element's ***src*** attribute. In this case, the image is located in the same directory as this XHTML document, so only the image's file name is required. Optional attributes ***width*** and ***height*** specify the image's width and height, respectively. The document author can scale an image by increasing or decreasing the values of the image **width** and **height** attributes. If these attributes are omitted, the browser uses the image's actual width and height. Images are measured in *pixels* ("picture elements"), which represent dots of color on the screen. The image in Fig. K.7 is **181** pixels wide and **238** pixels high.

```
1   <?xml version = "1.0"?>
2   <!DOCTYPE html PUBLIC "-//W3C//DTD XHTML 1.0 Strict//EN"
3       "http://www.w3.org/TR/xhtml1/DTD/xhtml1-strict.dtd">
4
5   <!-- Fig. K.7: picture.html    -->
6   <!-- Adding images with XHTML. -->
7
8   <html xmlns = "http://www.w3.org/1999/xhtml">
9      <head>
10        <title>C# How to Program - Welcome</title>
11     </head>
12
13     <body>
14
15        <p>
16           <img src = "csphtp.jpg" height = "238" width = "181"
17              alt = "C# How to Program book cover" />
18
19           <img src = "jhtp.jpg" height = "238" width = "181"
20              alt = "Java How to Program book cover" />
21        </p>
22
23     </body>
24  </html>
```

Fig. K.7   Placing images in XHTML files. (Courtesy of Prentice Hall, Inc.) (Part 1 of 2.)

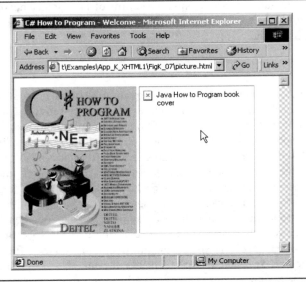

Fig. K.7   Placing images in XHTML files. (Courtesy of Prentice Hall, Inc.) (Part 2 of 2.)

Good Programming Practice K.5

*Always include the **width** and the **height** of an image inside the **<img>** tag. When the browser loads the XHTML file, it will know immediately from these attributes how much screen space to provide for the image and will lay out the page properly, even before it downloads the image.*

Performance Tip K.1

*Including the **width** and **height** attributes in an **<img>** tag will help the browser load and render pages faster.*

Common Programming Error K.4

Entering new dimensions for an image that change its inherent width-to-height ratio distorts the appearance of the image. For example, if your image is 200 pixels wide and 100 pixels high, you should ensure that any new dimensions have a 2:1 width-to-height ratio.

Every **img** element in an XHTML document has an **alt** attribute. If a browser cannot render an image, the browser displays the **alt** attribute's value. A browser might not be able to render an image for several reasons. It might not support images—as is the case with a *text-based browser* (i.e., a browser that can display only text)—or the client may have disabled image viewing to reduce download time. Figure K.7 shows Internet Explorer rendering the **alt** attribute's value when a document references a nonexistent image file (**jhtp.jpg**).

The **alt** attribute is important for creating *accessible* Web pages for users with disabilities, especially those with vision impairments and text-based browsers. Specialized software called *speech synthesizers* often are used by people with disabilities. These software applications "speak" the **alt** attribute's value so that the user knows what the browser is displaying. We discuss accessibility issues in detail in Chapter 21, Accessibility.

Some XHTML elements (called *empty elements*) contain only attributes and do not mark up text (i.e., text is not placed between the start and end tags). Empty elements (e.g., **img**) must be terminated, either by using the *forward slash character* (**/**) inside the closing right angle bracket (**>**) of the start tag or by explicitly including the end tag. When using the forward slash character, we add a space before the forward slash to improve readability (as shown at the ends of lines 17 and 20). Rather than using the forward slash character, lines 19–20 could be written with a closing **</img>** tag as follows:

```
<img src = "jhtp.jpg" height = "238" width = "181"
    alt = "Java How to Program book cover"></img>
```

By using images as hyperlinks, Web developers can create graphical Web pages that link to other resources. In Fig. K.8, we create six different image hyperlinks.

```
1   <?xml version = "1.0"?>
2   <!DOCTYPE html PUBLIC "-//W3C//DTD XHTML 1.0 Strict//EN"
3       "http://www.w3.org/TR/xhtml1/DTD/xhtml1-strict.dtd">
4
5   <!-- Fig. K.8: nav.html                -->
6   <!-- Using images as link anchors. -->
7
8   <html xmlns = "http://www.w3.org/1999/xhtml">
9       <head>
10          <title>C# How to Program - Welcome
11          </title>
12      </head>
13
14      <body>
15
16          <p>
17              <a href = "links.html">
18                  <img src = "buttons/links.jpg" width = "65"
19                      height = "50" alt = "Links Page" />
20              </a><br />
21
22              <a href = "list.html">
23                  <img src = "buttons/list.jpg" width = "65"
24                      height = "50" alt = "List Example Page" />
25              </a><br />
26
27              <a href = "contact.html">
28                  <img src = "buttons/contact.jpg" width = "65"
29                      height = "50" alt = "Contact Page" />
30              </a><br />
31
32              <a href = "header.html">
33                  <img src = "buttons/header.jpg" width = "65"
34                      height = "50" alt = "Header Page" />
35              </a><br />
36
```

Fig. K.8   Using images as link anchors. (Part 1 of 2.)

```
37                    <a href = "table.html">
38                        <img src = "buttons/table.jpg" width = "65"
39                            height = "50" alt = "Table Page" />
40                    </a><br />
41
42                    <a href = "form.html">
43                        <img src = "buttons/form.jpg" width = "65"
44                            height = "50" alt = "Feedback Form" />
45                    </a><br />
46                </p>
47
48            </body>
49        </html>
```

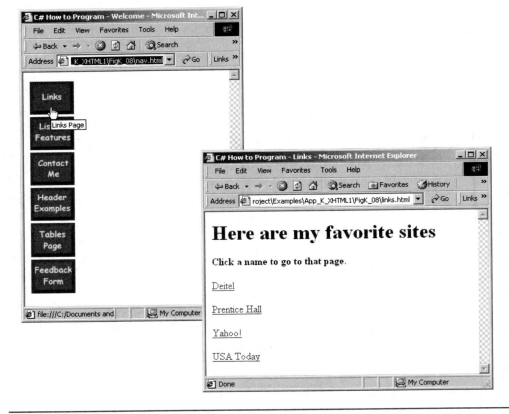

Fig. K.8   Using images as link anchors. (Part 2 of 2.)

Lines 17–20 create an *image hyperlink* by nesting an **img** element within an anchor (**a**) element. The value of the **img** element's **src** attribute value specifies that this image (**links.jpg**) resides in a directory named **buttons**. The **buttons** directory and the XHTML document are in the same directory. Images from other Web documents also can be referenced (after obtaining permission from the document's owner) by setting the **src** attribute to the name and location of the image.

On line 20, we introduce the ***br*** *element*, which most browsers render as a *line break*. Any markup or text following a **br** element is rendered on the next line. Like the **img** element, **br** is an example of an empty element terminated with a forward slash. We add a space before the forward slash to enhance readability.

K.8 Special Characters and More Line Breaks

When marking up text, certain characters or symbols (e.g., **<**) may be difficult to embed directly into an XHTML document. Some keyboards may not provide these symbols, or the presence of these symbols may cause syntax errors. For example, the markup

```
<p>if x < 10 then increment x by 1</p>
```

results in a syntax error, because it uses the less-than character (**<**), which is reserved for start tags and end tags such as **<p>** and **</p>**. XHTML provides *special characters* or *entity references* (in the form **&***code***;**) for representing these characters. We could correct the previous line by writing

```
<p>if x &lt; 10 then increment x by 1</p>
```

which uses the special character **<** for the less-than symbol.

Figure K.9 demonstrates how to use special characters in an XHTML document. For a list of special characters, see Appendix M, HTML/XHTML Special Characters.

```
1   <?xml version = "1.0"?>
2   <!DOCTYPE html PUBLIC "-//W3C//DTD XHTML 1.0 Strict//EN"
3      "http://www.w3.org/TR/xhtml1/DTD/xhtml1-strict.dtd">
4
5   <!-- Fig. K.9: contact2.html       -->
6   <!-- Inserting special characters. -->
7
8   <html xmlns = "http://www.w3.org/1999/xhtml">
9      <head>
10         <title>C# How to Program - Welcome
11         </title>
12      </head>
13
14      <body>
15
16         <!-- special characters are    -->
17         <!-- entered using form &code; -->
18         <p>
19            Click
20            <a href = "mailto:deitel@deitel.com">here
21            </a> to open an e-mail message addressed to
22            deitel@deitel.com.
23         </p>
24
25         <hr /> <!-- inserts a horizontal rule -->
26
```

Fig. K.9   Inserting special characters into XHTML. (Part 1 of 2.)

```
27        <p>All information on this site is <strong>&copy;</strong>
28           Deitel <strong>&amp;</strong> Associates, Inc. 2002.</p>
29
30        <!-- to strike through text use <del> tags      -->
31        <!-- to subscript text use <sub> tags           -->
32        <!-- to superscript text use <sup> tags         -->
33        <!-- these tags are nested inside other tags -->
34        <p><del>You may download 3.14 x 10<sup>2</sup>
35           characters worth of information from this site.</del>
36           Only <sub>one</sub> download per hour is permitted.</p>
37
38        <p>Note: <strong>&lt; &frac14;</strong> of the information
39           presented here is updated daily.</p>
40
41     </body>
42  </html>
```

Fig. K.9   Inserting special characters into XHTML. (Part 2 of 2.)

Lines 27–28 contain other special characters, which are expressed as either word abbreviations (e.g., **amp** for ampersand and **copy** for copyright) or *hexadecimal (hex)* values (e.g., **&** is the hexadecimal representation of **&**). Hexadecimal numbers are base-16 numbers—digits in a hexadecimal number have values from 0 to 15 (a total of 16 different values). The letters A–F represent the hexadecimal digits corresponding to decimal values 10–15. Thus, in hexadecimal notation we can have numbers like 876 consisting solely of decimal-like digits, numbers like DA19F consisting of digits and letters, and numbers like DCB consisting solely of letters. We discuss hexadecimal numbers in detail in Appendix B, Number Systems.

In lines 34–36, we introduce three new elements. Most browsers render the **del** element as strike-through text. With this format, users can easily indicate document revisions. To *superscript* text (i.e., raise text on a line with a decreased font size) or *subscript* text (i.e., lower text on a line with a decreased font size), use the **sup** and **sub** elements, respectively. We also use special characters **<** for a less-than sign and **¼** for the fraction 1/4 (line 38).

In addition to special characters, this document introduces a *horizontal rule*, indicated by the **<hr />** tag in line 25. Most browsers render a horizontal rule as a horizontal line. The **<hr />** tag also inserts a line break above and below the horizontal line.

K.9 Unordered Lists

Up to this point, we have presented basic XHTML elements and attributes for linking to resources, creating headers, using special characters and incorporating images. In this section, we discuss how to organize information on a Web page using lists. In Appendix L, Introduction to XHTML: Part 2, we introduce another feature for organizing information, called a table. Figure K.10 displays text in an *unordered list* (i.e., a list that does not order its items by letter or number). The *unordered list element* **ul** creates a list in which each item begins with a bullet symbol (called a *disc*).

Each entry in an unordered list (element **ul** in line 20) is an **li** (*list item*) element (lines 23, 25, 27 and 29). Most Web browsers render these elements with a line break and a bullet symbol indented from the beginning of the new line.

```
1   <?xml version = "1.0"?>
2   <!DOCTYPE html PUBLIC "-//W3C//DTD XHTML 1.0 Strict//EN"
3       "http://www.w3.org/TR/xhtml1/DTD/xhtml1-strict.dtd">
4
5   <!-- Fig. K.10: links2.html              -->
6   <!-- Unordered list containing hyperlinks. -->
7
8   <html xmlns = "http://www.w3.org/1999/xhtml">
9      <head>
10        <title>C# How to Program - Links</title>
11     </head>
12
13     <body>
14
15        <h1>Here are my favorite sites</h1>
16
17        <p><strong>Click on a name to go to that page.</strong></p>
18
19        <!-- create an unordered list -->
20        <ul>
21
22           <!-- add four list items -->
23           <li><a href = "http://www.deitel.com">Deitel</a></li>
24
25           <li><a href = "http://www.w3.org">W3C</a></li>
26
27           <li><a href = "http://www.yahoo.com">Yahoo!</a></li>
28
29           <li><a href = "http://www.cnn.com">CNN</a></li>
30
31        </ul>
32
```

Fig. K.10   Unordered lists in XHTML. (Part 1 of 2.)

```
33      </body>
34  </html>
```

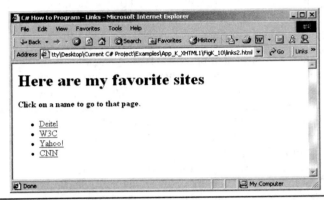

Fig. K.10   Unordered lists in XHTML. (Part 2 of 2.)

K.10 Nested and Ordered Lists

Lists may be nested to represent hierarchical relationships, as in an outline format. Figure K.11 demonstrates nested lists and *ordered lists* (i.e., list that order their items by letter or number).

```
1   <?xml version = "1.0"?>
2   <!DOCTYPE html PUBLIC "-//W3C//DTD XHTML 1.0 Transitional//EN"
3       "http://www.w3.org/TR/xhtml1/DTD/xhtml1-transitional.dtd">
4
5   <!-- Fig. K.11: list.html              -->
6   <!-- Advanced Lists: nested and ordered. -->
7
8   <html xmlns = "http://www.w3.org/1999/xhtml">
9      <head>
10         <title>C# How to Program - Lists</title>
11      </head>
12
13      <body>
14
15         <h1>The Best Features of the Internet</h1>
16
17         <!-- create an unordered list -->
18         <ul>
19            <li>You can meet new people from countries around
20               the world.</li>
21
22            <li>
23               You have access to new media as it becomes public:
24
25               <!-- start nested list, use modified bullets -->
26               <!-- list ends with closing </ul> tag         -->
```

Fig. K.11   Nested and ordered lists in XHTML. (Part 1 of 3.)

```
27                    <ul>
28                       <li>New games</li>
29                       <li>
30                          New applications
31
32                          <!-- ordered nested list -->
33                          <ol type = "I">
34                             <li>For business</li>
35                             <li>For pleasure</li>
36                          </ol>
37
38                       </li>
39
40                       <li>Around the clock news</li>
41                       <li>Search engines</li>
42                       <li>Shopping</li>
43                       <li>
44                          Programming
45
46                          <!-- another nested ordered list -->
47                          <ol type = "a">
48                             <li>XML</li>
49                             <li>Java</li>
50                             <li>XHTML</li>
51                             <li>Scripts</li>
52                             <li>New languages</li>
53                          </ol>
54
55                       </li>
56
57                    </ul> <!-- ends nested list started in line 27 -->
58
59                 </li>
60
61                 <li>Links</li>
62                 <li>Keeping in touch with old friends</li>
63                 <li>It is the technology of the future!</li>
64
65           </ul>    <!-- ends unordered list started in line 18 -->
66
67           <h1>My 3 Favorite <em>CEOs</em></h1>
68
69           <!-- ol elements without type attribute have -->
70           <!-- numeric sequence type (i.e., 1, 2, ...) -->
71           <ol>
72              <li>Lawrence J. Ellison</li>
73              <li>Steve Jobs</li>
74              <li>Michael Dell</li>
75           </ol>
76
77        </body>
78     </html>
```

Fig. K.11   Nested and ordered lists in XHTML. (Part 2 of 3.)

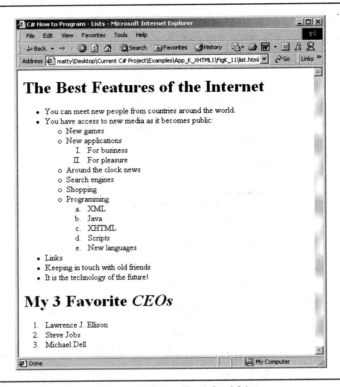

Fig. K.11   Nested and ordered lists in XHTML. (Part 3 of 3.)

The first ordered list begins in line 33. Attribute **type** specifies the *sequence type* (i.e., the set of numbers or letters used in the ordered list). In this case, setting **type** to **"I"** specifies upper-case roman numerals. Line 47 begins the second ordered list and sets attribute **type** to **"a"**, specifying lowercase letters for the list items. The last ordered list (lines 71–75) does not use attribute **type**. By default, the list's items are enumerated from one to three.

A Web browser indents each nested list to indicate a hierarchal relationship. By default, the items in the outermost unordered list (line 18) are preceded by discs. List items nested inside the unordered list of line 18 are preceded by *circles*. Although not demonstrated in this example, subsequent nested list items are preceded by *squares*. Unordered list items may be explicitly set to discs, circles or squares by setting the **ul** element's **type** attribute to **"disc"**, **"circle"** or **"square"**, respectively.

Note: XHTML is based on HTML (HyperText Markup Language)—a legacy technology of the World Wide Web Consortium (W3C). In HTML, it was common to specify the document's content, structure and formatting. Formatting might specify where the browser places an element in a Web page or the fonts and colors used to display an element. The so-called *strict* form of XHTML allows only a document's content and structure to appear in a valid XHTML document, and not that document's formatting. Our first several examples used only the strict form of XHTML. In fact, the purpose of lines 2–3 in each of the examples before Fig. K.11 was to indicate to the browser that each document conformed to the strict XHTML definition. This enables the browser to confirm that the document is valid. There are other XHTML document types as well. This particular example uses the XHTML *transitional* document type, which exists to enable XHTML document creators to use legacy HTML technologies in an XHTML document. In the example, the **type** attribute of the **ol** element (lines 33 and 47) is a legacy HTML technology. Changing lines 2–3 as shown enables us to demonstrate ordered lists with different numbering formats. Normally, such formatting is specified with style sheets. Most examples in this book adhere to strict HTML form.

Testing and Debugging Tip K.2

Most current browsers still attempt to render XHTML documents, even if they are invalid.

K.11 Summary

XHTML (Extensible Hypertext Markup Language) is a markup language for creating Web pages. A key issue in using XHTML is the separation of the presentation of a document (i.e., the document's appearance when rendered by a browser) from the structure of the information in the document. In XHTML, text is marked up with elements, delimited by tags that are names contained in pairs of angle brackets. Some elements may contain additional markup called attributes, which provide further information about the element. A machine that runs a specialized piece of software called a Web server stores XHTML documents. XHTML documents that are syntactically correct are guaranteed to render their elements properly. XHTML documents that contain syntax errors may not display properly. Validation services (e.g., **validator.w3.org**) ensure that an XHTML document is syntactically correct.

Every XHTML document contains a start **<html>** tag and an end **</html>** tag. Comments in XHTML always begin with **<!--** and end with **-->**. The browser ignores all text inside a comment. Every XHTML document has a **head** element, which generally contains information, such as a title, and a **body** element, which contains the content of the page. Information in the **head** element generally is not rendered in the display window, but it may be made available to the user through other means. The **title** element names a Web page. The title usually appears in the colored bar (called the title bar) at the top of the browser window and also appears as the text identifying a page when users add your page to their list of **Favorites** or **Bookmarks**. The body of an XHTML document is the area in which the document's content is placed. The content may include text and tags. All text placed between the **<p>** and **</p>** tags forms one paragraph. XHTML provides six headers (**h1** through **h6**) for specifying the relative importance of information. Header element **h1** is considered the most significant header and is rendered in a larger font than those of the other five headers. Each successive header element (i.e., **h2**, **h3**, etc.) is rendered in a smaller font. Web browsers typically underline text hyperlinks and color them blue by default. The **<strong>** tag renders text in a bold font.

Users can insert links with the **a** (anchor) element. The most important attribute for the **a** element is **href**, which specifies the resource (e.g., page, file or e-mail address) being linked. Anchors can link to an e-mail address, using a **mailto** URL. When someone clicks this type of anchored link, most browsers launch the default e-mail program (e.g., Outlook Express) to initiate an e-mail message to the linked address.

The **img** element's **src** attribute specifies an image's location. Optional attributes **width** and **height** specify the image's width and height, respectively. Images are measured in pixels ("picture elements"), which represent dots of color on the screen. Every **img** element in a valid XHTML document must have an **alt** attribute, which contains text that is displayed if the client cannot render the image. The **alt** attribute makes Web pages more accessible to users with disabilities, especially those with vision impairments.

Some XHTML elements are empty elements, contain only attributes and do not mark up text. Empty elements (e.g., **img**) must be terminated, either by using the forward-slash character (**/**) or by explicitly writing an end tag. The **br** element causes most browsers to render a line break. Any markup or text following a **br** element is rendered on the next line. XHTML provides special characters or entity references (in the form **&***code***;**) for representing characters that cannot be marked up. Most browsers render a horizontal rule, indicated by the **<hr />** tag, as a horizontal line. The **hr** element also inserts a line break above and below the horizontal line.

The unordered list element **ul** creates a list in which each item in the list begins with a bullet symbol (called a disc). Each entry in an unordered list is an **li** (list item) element. Most Web browsers render these elements with a line break and a bullet symbol at the beginning of the line. Lists may be nested to represent hierarchical data relationships. Attribute **type** specifies the sequence type (i.e., the set of numbers or letters used in the ordered list).

K.12 Internet and World Wide Web Resources

www.w3.org/TR/xhtml1
The *XHTML 1.0 Recommendation* contains general information, information on compatibility issues, document type definition information, definitions, terminology and much more relating to XHTML.

www.xhtml.org
XHTML.org provides XHTML development news and links to other XHTML resources, which include books and articles.

www.w3schools.com/xhtml/default.asp
The *XHTML School* provides XHTML quizzes and references. This page also contains links to XHTML syntax, validation and document type definitions.

validator.w3.org
This is the W3C XHTML validation service site.

hotwired.lycos.com/webmonkey/00/50/index2a.html
This site provides an article about XHTML. Key sections of the article overview XHTML and discuss tags, attributes and anchors.

wdvl.com/Authoring/Languages/XML/XHTML
The Web Developers' Virtual Library provides an introduction to XHTML. This site also contains articles, examples and links to other technologies.

www.w3.org/TR/1999/xhtml-modularization-19990406/DTD/doc
The XHTML 1.0 DTD documentation site provides links to DTD documentation for the strict, transitional and frameset document type definitions.

Introduction to XHTML: Part 2

Outline

L.1   Introduction
L.2   Basic XHTML Tables
L.3   Intermediate XHTML Tables and Formatting
L.4   Basic XHTML Forms
L.5   More Complex XHTML Forms
L.6   Internal Linking
L.7   Creating and Using Image Maps
L.8   meta Elements
L.9   frameset Element
L.10 Nested framesets
L.11 Summary
L.12 Internet and World Wide Web Resources

L.1 Introduction

In the previous appendix, we introduced XHTML. We built several complete Web pages featuring text, hyperlinks, images, horizontal rules and line breaks. In this appendix, we discuss more substantial XHTML features, including presentation of information in *tables* and *incorporating forms* for collecting information from a Web-page visitor. We also introduce *internal linking* and *image maps* for enhancing Web-page navigation and *frames* for displaying multiple documents in the browser. By the end of this appendix, you will be familiar with the most commonly used XHTML features and will be able to create more complex Web documents. In this appendix, we do not present any C# programming.

L.2 Basic XHTML Tables

This section presents the XHTML *table*—a frequently used feature that organizes data into rows and columns. Our first example (Fig. L.1) uses a table with six rows and two columns to display price information for fruit.

```
1   <?xml version = "1.0"?>
2   <!DOCTYPE html PUBLIC "-//W3C//DTD XHTML 1.0 Strict//EN"
3      "http://www.w3.org/TR/xhtml1/DTD/xhtml1-strict.dtd">
4
5   <!-- Fig. L.1: table1.html   -->
6   <!-- Creating a basic table. -->
7
8   <html xmlns = "http://www.w3.org/1999/xhtml">
9      <head>
10        <title>A simple XHTML table</title>
11     </head>
12
```

Fig. L.1   XHTML table. (Part 1 of 3.)

```
13      <body>
14
15          <!-- the <table> tag begins table -->
16          <table border = "1" width = "40%"
17              summary = "This table provides information about
18                  the price of fruit">
19
20              <!-- <caption> tag summarizes table's    -->
21              <!-- contents to help visually impaired -->
22              <caption><strong>Price of Fruit</strong></caption>
23
24              <!-- <thead> is first section of table -->
25              <!-- it formats table header area        -->
26              <thead>
27                  <tr> <!-- <tr> inserts one table row -->
28                      <th>Fruit</th> <!-- insert heading cell -->
29                      <th>Price</th>
30                  </tr>
31              </thead>
32
33              <!-- all table content is enclosed within <tbody> -->
34              <tbody>
35                  <tr>
36                      <td>Apple</td> <!-- insert data cell -->
37                      <td>$0.25</td>
38                  </tr>
39
40                  <tr>
41                      <td>Orange</td>
42                      <td>$0.50</td>
43                  </tr>
44
45                  <tr>
46                      <td>Banana</td>
47                      <td>$1.00</td>
48                  </tr>
49
50                  <tr>
51                      <td>Pineapple</td>
52                      <td>$2.00</td>
53                  </tr>
54              </tbody>
55
56              <!-- <tfoot> is last section of table -->
57              <!-- it formats table footer          -->
58              <tfoot>
59                  <tr>
60                      <th>Total</th>
61                      <th>$3.75</th>
62                  </tr>
63              </tfoot>
64
65          </table>
```

Fig. L.1   XHTML table. (Part 2 of 3.)

```
66
67        </body>
68    </html>
```

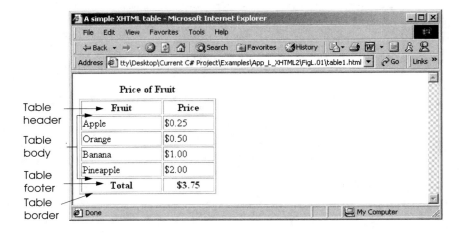

Fig. L.1   XHTML table. (Part 3 of 3.)

Tables are defined with the **table** element. Lines 16–18 specify the start tag for a table element that has several attributes. The **border** attribute specifies the table's border width in pixels. To create a table without a border, set **border** to **"0"**. This example assigns attribute **width "40%"**, to set the table's width to 40 percent of the browser's width. A developer can also set attribute **width** to a specified number of pixels.

Testing and Debugging Tip L.1

Try resizing the browser window to see how the width of the window affects the width of the table.

As its name implies, attribute **summary** (line 17) describes the table's contents. Speech devices use this attribute to make the table more accessible to users with visual impairments. The **caption** element (line 22) describes the table's content and helps text-based browsers interpret the table data. Text inside the **<caption>** tag is rendered above the table by most browsers. Attribute **summary** and element **caption** are two of many XHTML features that make Web pages more accessible to users with disabilities. We discuss accessibility programming in detail in Chapter 21, Accessibility.

A table has three distinct sections—*head*, *body* and *foot*. The head section (or *header cell*) is defined with a **thead** element (lines 26–31), which contains header information, such as column names. Each **tr** element (lines 27–30) defines an individual *table row*. The columns in the head section are defined with **th** elements. Most browsers center text formatted by **th** (table header column) elements and display it in bold. Table header elements are nested inside table row elements.

The body section, or *table body*, contains the table's primary data. The table body (lines 34–54) is defined in a **tbody** element. *Data cells* contain individual pieces of data and are defined with **td** (*table data*) elements.

The foot section (lines 58–63) is defined with a **tfoot** (table foot) element and represents a footer. Text commonly placed in the footer includes calculation results and footnotes. Like other sections, the foot section can contain table rows and each row can contain columns.

L.3 Intermediate XHTML Tables and Formatting

In the previous section, we explored the structure of a basic table. In Fig. L.2, we enhance our discussion of tables by introducing elements and attributes that allow the document author to build more complex tables.

The table begins on line 17. Element **colgroup** (lines 22–27) groups and formats columns. The **col** element (line 26) specifies two attributes in this example. The **align** attribute determines the alignment of text in the column. The **span** attribute determines how many columns the **col** element formats. In this case, we set **align**'s value to **"right"** and **span**'s value to **"1"** to right-align text in the first column (the column containing the picture of the camel in the sample screen capture).

Table cells are sized to fit the data they contain. Document authors can create larger data cells by using attributes **rowspan** and **colspan**. The values assigned to these attributes specify the number of rows or columns occupied by a cell. The **th** element at lines 36–39 uses the attribute **rowspan = "2"** to allow the cell containing the picture of the camel to use two vertically adjacent cells (thus the cell *spans* two rows). The **th** element at lines 42–45 uses the attribute **colspan = "4"** to widen the header cell (containing **Camelid comparison** and **Approximate as of 9/2002**) to span four cells.

```
1   <?xml version = "1.0"?>
2   <!DOCTYPE html PUBLIC "-//W3C//DTD XHTML 1.0 Strict//EN"
3      "http://www.w3.org/TR/xhtml1/DTD/xhtml1-strict.dtd">
4
5   <!-- Fig. L.2: table2.html        -->
6   <!-- Intermediate table design. -->
7
8   <html xmlns = "http://www.w3.org/1999/xhtml">
9      <head>
10         <title>C# How to Program - Tables</title>
11     </head>
12
13     <body>
14
15        <h1>Table Example Page</h1>
16
17        <table border = "1">
18           <caption>Here is a more complex sample table.</caption>
19
20           <!-- <colgroup> and <col> tags are -->
21           <!-- used to format entire columns -->
22           <colgroup>
23
24              <!-- span attribute determines how  -->
25              <!-- many columns <col> tag affects -->
```

Fig. L.2   Complex XHTML table. (Part 1 of 3.)

```
26                  <col align = "right" span = "1" />
27            </colgroup>
28
29            <thead>
30
31                <!-- rowspans and colspans merge specified    -->
32                <!-- number of cells vertically or horizontally   -->
33                <tr>
34
35                   <!-- merge two rows -->
36                   <th rowspan = "2">
37                      <img src = "camel.gif" width = "205"
38                         height = "167" alt = "Picture of a camel" />
39                   </th>
40
41                   <!-- merge four columns -->
42                   <th colspan = "4" valign = "top">
43                      <h1>Camelid comparison</h1><br />
44                      <p>Approximate as of 9/2002</p>
45                   </th>
46                </tr>
47
48                <tr valign = "bottom">
49                   <th># of Humps</th>
50                   <th>Indigenous region</th>
51                   <th>Spits?</th>
52                   <th>Produces Wool?</th>
53                </tr>
54
55            </thead>
56
57            <tbody>
58
59                <tr>
60                   <th>Camels (bactrian)</th>
61                   <td>2</td>
62                   <td>Africa/Asia</td>
63                   <td rowspan = "2">Llama</td>
64                   <td rowspan = "2">Llama</td>
65                </tr>
66
67                <tr>
68                   <th>Llamas</th>
69                   <td>1</td>
70                   <td>Andes Mountains</td>
71                </tr>
72
73            </tbody>
74
75         </table>
76
77      </body>
78   </html>
```

Fig. L.2   Complex XHTML table. (Part 2 of 3.)

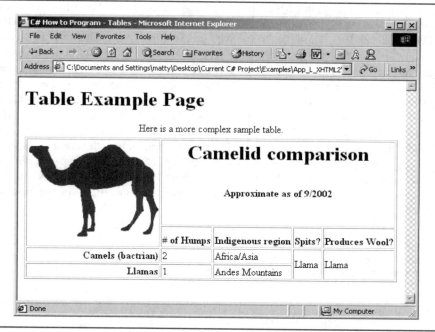

Fig. L.2   Complex XHTML table. (Part 3 of 3.)

 Common Programming Error L.1

*When using **colspan** and **rowspan** to adjust the size of table data cells, keep in mind that the modified cells will occupy more than one column or row; other rows or columns of the table must compensate for the extra rows or columns spanned by individual cells. If you do not, the formatting of your table will be distorted, and you could inadvertently create more columns and rows than you originally intended.*

Line 42 introduces attribute **valign**, which aligns data vertically and may be assigned one of four values—**"top"** aligns data with the top of the cell, **"middle"** vertically centers data (the default for all data and header cells), **"bottom"** aligns data with the bottom of the cell and **"baseline"** ignores the fonts used for the row data and sets the bottom of all text in the row on a common *baseline* (i.e., the horizontal line to which each character in a word is aligned).

L.4 Basic XHTML Forms

When browsing Web sites, users often need to provide information such as e-mail addresses, search keywords and zip codes. XHTML provides a mechanism, called a *form*, for collecting such user information.

Data that users enter on a Web page normally is sent to a Web server that provides access to a site's resources (e.g., XHTML documents or images). These resources are located either on the same machine as the Web server or on a machine that the Web server can access through the network. When a browser requests a Web page or file that is located on a server, the server processes the request and returns the requested resource. A request contains the name and path of the desired resource and the method of communication (called a *protocol*). XHTML documents use the HyperText Transfer Protocol (HTTP).

Figure L.3 sends the form data to the Web server, which passes the form data to a *CGI* (*Common Gateway Interface*) script (i.e., a program) written in Perl, C or some other language. The script processes the data received from the Web server and typically returns information to the Web server. The Web server then sends the information in the form of an XHTML document to the Web browser. [*Note*: This example demonstrates client-side functionality. If the form is submitted (by clicking **Submit Your Entries**), an error occurs.]

Forms can contain visual and non-visual components. Visual components include clickable buttons and other graphical user interface components with which users interact. Non-visual components, called *hidden inputs*, store any data that the document author specifies, such as e-mail addresses and XHTML document file names that act as links. The form begins on line 23 with the *form* element. Attribute *method* specifies how the form's data is sent to the Web server.

```
1   <?xml version = "1.0"?>
2   <!DOCTYPE html PUBLIC "-//W3C//DTD XHTML 1.0 Strict//EN"
3       "http://www.w3.org/TR/xhtml11/DTD/xhtml11-strict.dtd">
4
5   <!-- Fig. L.3: form.html    -->
6   <!-- Form design example 1. -->
7
8   <html xmlns = "http://www.w3.org/1999/xhtml">
9      <head>
10         <title>C# How to Program - Forms</title>
11     </head>
12
13     <body>
14
15        <h1>Feedback Form</h1>
16
17        <p>Please fill out this form to help
18           us improve our site.</p>
19
20        <!-- <form> tag begins form, gives -->
21        <!-- method of sending information -->
22        <!-- and location of form scripts  -->
23        <form method = "post" action = "/cgi-bin/formmail">
24
25           <p>
26
27              <!-- hidden inputs contain non-visual -->
28              <!-- information                      -->
29              <input type = "hidden" name = "recipient"
30                 value = "deitel@deitel.com" />
31
32              <input type = "hidden" name = "subject"
33                 value = "Feedback Form" />
34
```

Fig. L.3   Simple form with hidden fields and a textbox. (Part 1 of 2.)

```
35                  <input type = "hidden" name = "redirect"
36                     value = "main.html" />
37          </p>
38
39          <!-- <input type = "text"> inserts text box -->
40          <p>
41             <label>Name:
42                <input name = "name" type = "text" size = "25"
43                   maxlength = "30" />
44             </label>
45          </p>
46
47          <p>
48
49             <!-- input types "submit" and "reset" -->
50             <!-- insert buttons for submitting   -->
51             <!-- and clearing form's contents    -->
52             <input type = "submit" value =
53                "Submit Your Entries" />
54
55             <input type = "reset" value =
56                "Clear Your Entries" />
57          </p>
58
59       </form>
60
61    </body>
62 </html>
```

Fig. L.3   Simple form with hidden fields and a textbox. (Part 2 of 2.)

Using **method = "post"** appends form data to the browser request, which contains the protocol (i.e., HTTP) and the requested resource's URL. Scripts located on the Web server's computer (or on a computer accessible through the network) can access the form data sent as part of the request. For example, a script may take the form information and update an electronic mailing list. The other possible value, **method = "get"**, appends the form data directly to the end of the URL. For example, the URL **/cgi-bin/formmail** might have the form information **name = bob** appended to it.

The **action** attribute in the **<form>** tag specifies the URL of a script on the Web server; in this case, it specifies a script that e-mails form data to an address. Most Internet Service Providers (ISPs) have a script like this on their site; ask the Web-site system administrator how to set up an XHTML document to use the script correctly.

Lines 29–36 define three **input** elements that specify data to provide to the script that processes the form (also called the *form handler*). These three **input** element have **type** attribute **"hidden"**, which allows the document author to send form data that is not entered by a user to a script.

The three hidden inputs are an e-mail address to which the data will be sent, the e-mail's subject line and a URL where the browser will be redirected after submitting the form. Two other **input** attributes are *name*, which identifies the **input** element, and *value*, which provides the value that will be sent (or posted) to the Web server.

Good Programming Practice L.1

*Place hidden **input** elements at the beginning of a form, immediately after the opening* ***<form>*** *tag. This placement allows document authors to locate hidden **input** elements quickly.*

We introduce another **type** of **input** in lines 38–39. The **"text"** input inserts a *text box* into the form. Users can type data in text boxes. The **label** element (lines 37–40) provides users with information about the **input** element's purpose.

Common Programming Error L.2

*Forgetting to include a **label** element for each form element is a design error. Without these labels, users cannot determine the purpose of individual form elements.*

The **input** element's **size** attribute specifies the number of characters visible in the text box. Optional attribute **maxlength** limits the number of characters input into the text box. In this case, the user is not permitted to type more than **30** characters into the text box.

There are two types of **input** elements in lines 52–56. The **"submit"** input element is a button. When the user presses a **"submit"** button, the browser sends the data in the form to the Web server for processing. The **value** *attribute* sets the text displayed on the button (the default value is **Submit**). The **"reset"** input element allows a user to reset all **form** elements to their default values. The **value** attribute of the **"reset"** input element sets the text displayed on the button (the default value is **Reset**).

L.5 More Complex XHTML Forms

In the previous section, we introduced basic forms. In this section, we introduce elements and attributes for creating more complex forms. Figure L.4 contains a form that solicits user feedback about a Web site.

The **textarea** element (lines 42–44) inserts a multiline text box, called a *textarea*, into the form. The number of rows is specified with the **rows** *attribute* and the number of columns (i.e., characters) is specified with the **cols** *attribute*. In this example, the **textarea** is four rows high and 36 characters wide. To display default text in the text area, place the text between the **<textarea>** and **</textarea>** tags. Default text can be specified in other **input** types, such as textboxes, by using the **value** attribute.

The **"password"** input in lines 52–53 inserts a password box with the specified **size**. A password box allows users to enter sensitive information, such as credit card numbers and passwords, by "masking" the information input with asterisks. The actual value input is sent to the Web server, not the asterisks that mask the input.

Lines 60–78 introduce the *checkbox* **form** element. Checkboxes enable users to select from a set of options. When a user selects a checkbox, a check mark appears in the check box. Otherwise, the checkbox remains empty. Each **"checkbox" input** creates a new checkbox. Checkboxes can be used individually or in groups. Checkboxes that belong to a group are assigned the same **name** (in this case, **"thingsliked"**).

```
1   <?xml version = "1.0"?>
2   <!DOCTYPE html PUBLIC "-//W3C//DTD XHTML 1.0 Strict//EN"
3       "http://www.w3.org/TR/xhtml1/DTD/xhtml1-strict.dtd">
4
5   <!-- Fig. L.4: form2.html    -->
6   <!-- Form design example 2. -->
7
8   <html xmlns = "http://www.w3.org/1999/xhtml">
9       <head>
10          <title>C# How to Program - Forms</title>
11      </head>
12
13      <body>
14
15          <h1>Feedback Form</h1>
16
17          <p>Please fill out this form to help
18              us improve our site.</p>
19
20          <form method = "post" action = "/cgi-bin/formmail">
21
22              <p>
23                  <input type = "hidden" name = "recipient"
24                      value = "deitel@deitel.com" />
25
26                  <input type = "hidden" name = "subject"
27                      value = "Feedback Form" />
28
29                  <input type = "hidden" name = "redirect"
30                      value = "main.html" />
31              </p>
32
33              <p>
34                  <label>Name:
35                      <input name = "name" type = "text" size = "25" />
36                  </label>
37              </p>
38
39              <!-- <textarea> creates multiline textbox -->
40              <p>
41                  <label>Comments:<br />
```

Fig. L.4   Form with textareas, password boxes and checkboxes. (Part 1 of 3.)

```
42                      <textarea name = "comments" rows = "4"
43                         cols = "36">Enter your comments here.
44                      </textarea>
45                   </label></p>
46
47              <!-- <input type = "password"> inserts -->
48              <!-- textbox whose display is masked    -->
49              <!-- with asterisk characters           -->
50              <p>
51                 <label>E-mail Address:
52                    <input name = "email" type = "password"
53                       size = "25" />
54                 </label>
55              </p>
56
57              <p>
58                 <strong>Things you liked:</strong><br />
59
60                 <label>Site design
61                 <input name = "thingsliked" type = "checkbox"
62                    value = "Design" /></label>
63
64                 <label>Links
65                 <input name = "thingsliked" type = "checkbox"
66                    value = "Links" /></label>
67
68                 <label>Ease of use
69                 <input name = "thingsliked" type = "checkbox"
70                    value = "Ease" /></label>
71
72                 <label>Images
73                 <input name = "thingsliked" type = "checkbox"
74                    value = "Images" /></label>
75
76                 <label>Source code
77                 <input name = "thingsliked" type = "checkbox"
78                    value = "Code" /></label>
79              </p>
80
81              <p>
82                 <input type = "submit" value =
83                    "Submit Your Entries" />
84
85                 <input type = "reset" value =
86                    "Clear Your Entries" />
87              </p>
88
89           </form>
90
91        </body>
92     </html>
```

Fig. L.4   Form with textareas, password boxes and checkboxes. (Part 2 of 3.)

Fig. L.4   Form with textareas, password boxes and checkboxes. (Part 3 of 3.)

Common Programming Error L.3

*When your **form** has several checkboxes with the same **name**, you must make sure that they have different **value**s, or the scripts running on the Web server will not be able to distinguish between them.*

We continue our discussion of forms by presenting a third example that introduces several more form elements from which users can make selections (Fig. L.5). In this example, we introduce two new **input** types. The first type is the *radio button* (lines 90–113), specified with type **"radio"**. Radio buttons are similar to checkboxes, except that only one radio button in a group of radio buttons may be selected at any time. All radio buttons in a group have the same **name** attribute; they are distinguished by their different **value** attributes. The attribute–value pair *checked = "checked"* (line 92) indicates which radio button, if any, is selected initially. The **checked** attribute also applies to checkboxes.

```
1    <?xml version = "1.0"?>
2    <!DOCTYPE html PUBLIC "-//W3C//DTD XHTML 1.0 Strict//EN"
3       "http://www.w3.org/TR/xhtml1/DTD/xhtml1-strict.dtd">
4
5    <!-- Fig. L.5: form3.html    -->
6    <!-- Form design example 3. -->
7
8    <html xmlns = "http://www.w3.org/1999/xhtml">
9       <head>
10          <title>C# How to Program - Forms</title>
11       </head>
12
13       <body>
14
15          <h1>Feedback Form</h1>
16
17          <p>Please fill out this form to help
18             us improve our site.</p>
19
20          <form method = "post" action = "/cgi-bin/formmail">
21
22             <p>
23                <input type = "hidden" name = "recipient"
24                   value = "deitel@deitel.com" />
25
26                <input type = "hidden" name = "subject"
27                   value = "Feedback Form" />
28
29                <input type = "hidden" name = "redirect"
30                   value = "main.html" />
31             </p>
32
33             <p>
34                <label>Name:
35                   <input name = "name" type = "text" size = "25" />
36                </label>
37             </p>
38
39             <p>
40                <label>Comments:<br />
41                   <textarea name = "comments" rows = "4"
42                      cols = "36"></textarea>
43                </label>
44             </p>
45
```

Fig. L.5   Form including radio buttons and drop-down lists. (Part 1 of 4.)

```
46          <p>
47            <label>E-mail Address:
48              <input name = "email" type = "password"
49                size = "25" />
50            </label>
51          </p>
52
53          <p>
54            <strong>Things you liked:</strong><br />
55
56            <label>Site design
57              <input name = "thingsliked" type = "checkbox"
58                value = "Design" />
59            </label>
60
61            <label>Links
62              <input name = "thingsliked" type = "checkbox"
63                value = "Links" />
64            </label>
65
66            <label>Ease of use
67              <input name = "thingsliked" type = "checkbox"
68                value = "Ease" />
69            </label>
70
71            <label>Images
72              <input name = "thingsliked" type = "checkbox"
73                value = "Images" />
74            </label>
75
76            <label>Source code
77              <input name = "thingsliked" type = "checkbox"
78                value = "Code" />
79            </label>
80
81          </p>
82
83          <!-- <input type = "radio" /> creates one radio   -->
84          <!-- button. The difference between radio buttons -->
85          <!-- and checkboxes is that only one radio button -->
86          <!-- in a group can be selected.                  -->
87          <p>
88            <strong>How did you get to our site?:</strong><br />
89
90            <label>Search engine
91              <input name = "howtosite" type = "radio"
92                value = "search engine" checked = "checked" />
93            </label>
94
95            <label>Links from another site
96              <input name = "howtosite" type = "radio"
97                value = "link" />
98            </label>
```

Fig. L.5   Form including radio buttons and drop-down lists. (Part 2 of 4.)

```
 99
100                    <label>Deitel.com Web site
101                       <input name = "howtosite" type = "radio"
102                          value = "deitel.com" />
103                    </label>
104
105                    <label>Reference in a book
106                       <input name = "howtosite" type = "radio"
107                          value = "book" />
108                    </label>
109
110                    <label>Other
111                       <input name = "howtosite" type = "radio"
112                          value = "other" />
113                    </label>
114
115            </p>
116
117            <p>
118                <label>Rate our site:
119
120                    <!-- <select> tag presents a drop-down -->
121                    <!-- list with choices indicated by      -->
122                    <!-- <option> tags                        -->
123                    <select name = "rating">
124                       <option selected = "selected">Amazing</option>
125                       <option>10</option>
126                       <option>9</option>
127                       <option>8</option>
128                       <option>7</option>
129                       <option>6</option>
130                       <option>5</option>
131                       <option>4</option>
132                       <option>3</option>
133                       <option>2</option>
134                       <option>1</option>
135                       <option>Awful</option>
136                    </select>
137
138                </label>
139            </p>
140
141            <p>
142                <input type = "submit" value =
143                   "Submit Your Entries" />
144
145                <input type = "reset" value = "Clear Your Entries" />
146            </p>
147
148        </form>
149
150    </body>
151 </html>
```

Fig. L.5   Form including radio buttons and drop-down lists. (Part 3 of 4.)

Fig. L.5   Form including radio buttons and drop-down lists. (Part 4 of 4.)

Common Programming Error L.4

*When using a group of radio buttons in a form, forgetting to set the **name** attributes to the same name lets the user select all of the radio buttons at the same time, which is a logic error.*

The ***select*** element (lines 123–136) provides a drop-down list from which the user can select an item. The **name** attribute identifies the drop-down list. The ***option*** element (lines 124–135) adds items to the drop-down list. The **option** element's ***selected*** attribute specifies which item initially is displayed as the selected item in the **select** element.

L.6 Internal Linking

In Appendix K, we discussed how to hyperlink one Web page to another. Figure L.6 introduces *internal linking*—a mechanism that enables the user to jump between locations in the same document. Internal linking is useful for long documents that contain many sections. Clicking an internal link enables users to find a section without scrolling through the entire document.

```
1    <?xml version = "1.0"?>
2    <!DOCTYPE html PUBLIC "-//W3C//DTD XHTML 1.0 Strict//EN"
3       "http://www.w3.org/TR/xhtml1/DTD/xhtml1-strict.dtd">
4
5    <!-- Fig. L.6: links.html -->
6    <!-- Internal linking.   -->
7
8    <html xmlns = "http://www.w3.org/1999/xhtml">
9       <head>
10          <title>C# How to Program - List</title>
11       </head>
12
13       <body>
14
15          <!-- <a name = ".."></a> creates internal hyperlink -->
16          <p><a name = "features"></a></p>
17
18          <h1>The Best Features of the Internet</h1>
19
20          <!-- address of internal link is "#linkname" -->
21          <p>
22             <a href = "#ceos">Go to <em>Favorite CEOs</em></a>
23          </p>
24
25          <ul>
26             <li>You can meet people from countries
27                around the world.</li>
28
29             <li>You have access to new media as it becomes public:
30
31                <ul>
32                   <li>New games</li>
33                   <li>New applications
```

Fig. L.6   Using internal hyperlinks to make pages more easily navigable. (Part 1 of 3.)

```
34
35                        <ul>
36                            <li>For Business</li>
37                            <li>For Pleasure</li>
38                        </ul>
39
40                    </li>
41
42                    <li>Around the clock news</li>
43                    <li>Search Engines</li>
44                    <li>Shopping</li>
45                    <li>Programming
46
47                        <ul>
48                            <li>XHTML</li>
49                            <li>Java</li>
50                            <li>Dynamic HTML</li>
51                            <li>Scripts</li>
52                            <li>New languages</li>
53                        </ul>
54
55                    </li>
56                </ul>
57
58            </li>
59
60            <li>Links</li>
61            <li>Keeping in touch with old friends</li>
62            <li>It is the technology of the future!</li>
63        </ul>
64
65        <!-- named anchor -->
66        <p><a name = "ceos"></a></p>
67
68        <h1>My 3 Favorite <em>CEOs</em></h1>
69
70        <p>
71
72            <!-- internal hyperlink to features -->
73            <a href = "#features">
74                Go to <em>Favorite Features</em>
75            </a>
76        </p>
77
78        <ol>
79            <li>Lawrence J. Ellison</li>
80            <li>Steve Jobs</li>
81            <li>Michael Dell</li>
82        </ol>
83
84    </body>
85 </html>
```

Fig. L.6   Using internal hyperlinks to make pages more easily navigable. (Part 2 of 3.)

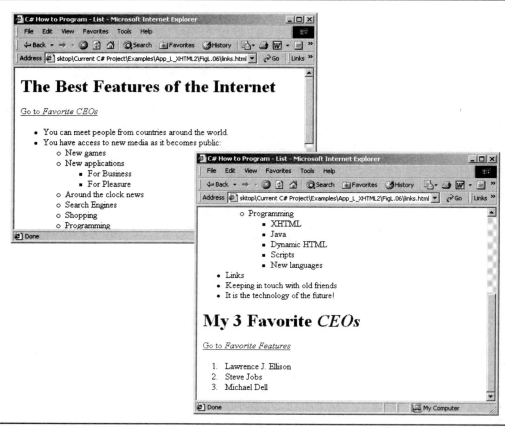

Fig. L.6   Using internal hyperlinks to make pages more easily navigable. (Part 3 of 3.)

Line 16 contains a *named anchor* (called **features**) for an internal hyperlink. To link to this type of anchor inside the same Web page, the href attribute of another anchor element includes the named anchor preceded with a pound sign (as in **#features**). Lines 73–74 contain a hyperlink with the anchor **features** as its target. Selecting this hyperlink in a Web browser scrolls the browser window to the **features** anchor at line 16.

Look-and-Feel Observation L.1

Internal hyperlinks are useful in XHTML documents that contain large amounts of information. Internal links to various sections on the page make it easier for users to navigate the page: They do not have to scroll to find a specific section.

Although not demonstrated in this example, a hyperlink can specify an internal link in another document by specifying the document name followed by a pound sign and the named anchor as in:

> **href** = "page.html#name"

For example, to link to a named anchor called **booklist** in **books.html**, **href** is assigned **"books.html#booklist"**.

L.7 Creating and Using Image Maps

In Appendix K, we demonstrated how images can be used as hyperlinks to link to other resources on the Internet. In this section, we introduce another technique for image linking called the *image map*, which designates certain areas of an image (called *hotspots*) as links. Figure L.7 introduces image maps and hotspots.

```
1   <?xml version = "1.0" ?>
2   <!DOCTYPE html PUBLIC "-//W3C//DTD XHTML 1.0 Strict//EN"
3       "http://www.w3.org/TR/xhtml1/DTD/xhtml1-strict.dtd">
4
5   <!-- Fig. L.7: picture.html         -->
6   <!-- Creating and using image maps. -->
7
8   <html xmlns = "http://www.w3.org/1999/xhtml">
9      <head>
10         <title>C# How to Program - Image Map
11         </title>
12      </head>
13
14      <body>
15
16         <p>
17
18            <!-- <map> tag defines image map -->
19            <map id = "picture">
20
21               <!-- shape = "rect" indicates rectangular  -->
22               <!-- area, with coordinates for upper-left -->
23               <!-- and lower-right corners               -->
24               <area href = "form.html" shape = "rect"
25                  coords = "2,123,54,143"
26                  alt = "Go to the feedback form" />
27
28               <area href = "contact.html" shape = "rect"
29                  coords = "126,122,198,143"
30                  alt = "Go to the contact page" />
31
32               <area href = "main.html" shape = "rect"
33                  coords = "3,7,61,25" alt = "Go to the homepage" />
34
35               <area href = "links.html" shape = "rect"
36                  coords = "168,5,197,25"
37                  alt = "Go to the links page" />
38
39               <!-- value "poly" creates hotspot in shape -->
40               <!-- of polygon, defined by coords         -->
41               <area shape = "poly" alt = "E-mail the Deitels"
42                  coords = "162,25,154,39,158,54,169,51,183,39,161,26"
43                  href = "mailto:deitel@deitel.com" />
44
```

Fig. L.7 Image with links anchored to an image map. (Part 1 of 2.)

```
45                    <!-- shape = "circle" indicates a circular -->
46                    <!-- area with the given center and radius -->
47                    <area href = "mailto:deitel@deitel.com"
48                        shape = "circle" coords = "100,36,33"
49                        alt = "E-mail the Deitels" />
50              </map>
51
52              <!-- <img src =... usemap = "#id"> indicates that -->
53              <!-- specified image map is used with this image  -->
54              <img src = "deitel.gif" width = "200" height = "144"
55                  alt = "Deitel logo" usemap = "#picture" />
56        </p>
57
58      </body>
59    </html>
```

Fig. L.7   Image with links anchored to an image map. (Part 2 of 2.)

Lines 19–50 define an image map via a ***map*** element. Attribute ***id*** (line 19) identifies the image map. If **id** is omitted, the map cannot be referenced by an image. Shortly, we discuss how to reference an image map. Hotspots are defined with ***area*** elements (as shown on lines 24–26). Attribute **href** (line 24) specifies the link's target (i.e., the resource to which to link). Attributes ***shape*** (line 24) and ***coords*** (line 25) specify the hotspot's shape and coordinates, respectively. Attribute **alt** (line 26) provides alternative text for the link.

> **Common Programming Error L.5**
>
> *Not specifying an **id** attribute for a **map** element prevents an **img** element from using the **map**'s **area** elements to define hotspots.*

The markup on lines 24–26 creates a *rectangular hotspot* (**shape = "rect"**) for the *coordinates* specified in the **coords** attribute. A coordinate pair consists of two numbers representing the location of a point on the *x*-axis and the *y*-axis, respectively. The *x*-axis extends horizontally and the *y*-axis extends vertically from the upper-left corner of the image. Every point on an image has a unique *x*–*y* coordinate. For rectangular hotspots, the required coordinates are those of the upper-left and lower-right corners of the rectangle. In this case, the upper-left corner of the rectangle is located at 2 on the *x*-axis and 123 on the *y*-axis, annotated as *(2, 123)*. The lower-right corner of the rectangle is at *(54, 143)*. Coordinates are measured in pixels.

Common Programming Error L.6

Overlapping coordinates of an image map cause the browser to render the first hotspot it encounters for the area.

The map **area** (lines 41–43) assigns the **shape** attribute **"poly"** to create a hotspot in the shape of a polygon, using the coordinates in attribute **coords**. These coordinates represent each *vertex*, or corner, of the polygon. The browser connects these points with lines to form the hotspot's area.

The map **area** (lines 47–49) assigns the **shape** attribute **"circle"** to create a *circular hotspot*. In this case, the **coords** attribute specifies the circle's center coordinates and the circle's radius, in pixels.

To use an image map with an **img** element, the **img** element's **usemap** attribute is assigned the **id** of a **map**. Lines 54–55 reference the image map named **"picture"**. The image map is located within the same document, so internal linking is used.

L.8 meta Elements

People use search engines to find useful Web sites. Search engines usually catalog sites by following links from page to page and saving identification and classification information for each page. One way that search engines catalog pages is by reading the content in each page's **meta** elements, which specify information about a document.

Two important attributes of the **meta** element are **name**, which identifies the type of **meta** element and **content**, which provides the information search engines use to catalog pages. Figure L.8 introduces the **meta** element.

Lines 14–16 demonstrate a **"keywords"** **meta** element. The **content** attribute of such a **meta** element provides search engines with a list of words that describe a page. These words are compared with words in search requests. Thus, including **meta** elements and their **content** information can draw more viewers to your site.

```
1   <?xml version = "1.0"?>
2   <!DOCTYPE html PUBLIC "-//W3C//DTD XHTML 1.0 Strict//EN"
3      "http://www.w3.org/TR/xhtml1/DTD/xhtml1-strict.dtd">
4
5   <!-- Fig. L.8: main.html -->
6   <!-- Using meta tags.     -->
7
8   <html xmlns = "http://www.w3.org/1999/xhtml">
9      <head>
10        <title>C# How to Program - Welcome</title>
11
12        <!-- <meta> tags provide search engines with -->
13        <!-- information used to catalog site         -->
14        <meta name = "keywords" content = "Web page, design,
15           XHTML, tutorial, personal, help, index, form,
16           contact, feedback, list, links, frame, deitel" />
```

Fig. L.8   Using **meta** to provide keywords and a description. (Part 1 of 2.)

```
17
18          <meta name = "description" content = "This Web site will
19              help you learn the basics of XHTML and Web page design
20              through the use of interactive examples and
21              instruction." />
22
23      </head>
24
25      <body>
26
27          <h1>Welcome to Our Web Site!</h1>
28
29          <p>
30              We have designed this site to teach about the wonders
31              of <strong><em>XHTML</em></strong>. <em>XHTML</em> is
32              better equipped than <em>HTML</em> to represent complex
33              data on the Internet. <em>XHTML</em> takes advantage of
34              XML's strict syntax to ensure well-formedness. Soon you
35              will know about many of the great new features of
36              <em>XHTML.</em>
37          </p>
38
39          <p>Have Fun With the Site!</p>
40
41      </body>
42  </html>
```

Fig. L.8   Using **meta** to provide keywords and a description. (Part 2 of 2.)

Lines 18–21 demonstrate a ***"description"* meta** element. The **content** attribute of such a **meta** element provides a three- to four-line description of a site, written in sentence form. Search engines also use this description to catalog your site and sometimes display this information as part of the search results.

Software Engineering Observation L.1

*meta elements are not visible to users and must be placed inside the **head** section of your XHTML document. If **meta** elements are not placed in this section, they will not be read by search engines.*

L.9 frameset Element

All of the Web pages we have presented in this book have the ability to link to other pages, but can display only one page at a time. Figure L.9 uses *frames*, which allow the browser to display more than one XHTML document simultaneously, to display the documents in Fig. L.8 and Fig. L.10.

Most of our prior examples adhered to the strict XHTML document type. This particular example uses the *frameset* document type—a special XHTML document type specifically for framesets. This new document type is specified in lines 2–3 and is required for documents that define framesets.

A document that defines a frameset normally consists of an **html** element that contains a **head** element and a ***frameset*** element. The **<frameset>** tag (line 24) informs the browser that the page contains frames. Attribute *cols* specifies the frameset's column layout. The value of *cols* gives the width of each frame, either in pixels or as a percentage of the browser width. In this case, the attribute **cols = "110,*"** informs the browser that there are two vertical frames. The first frame extends **110** pixels from the left edge of the browser window, and the second frame fills the remainder of the browser width (as indicated by the asterisk). Similarly, **frameset** attribute *rows* can be used to specify the number of rows and the size of each row in a frameset.

```
1   <?xml version = "1.0"?>
2   <!DOCTYPE html PUBLIC "-//W3C//DTD XHTML 1.0 Frameset//EN"
3       "http://www.w3.org/TR/xhtml1/DTD/xhtml1-frameset.dtd">
4
5   <!-- Fig. L.9: index.html -->
6   <!-- XHTML frames I.       -->
7
8   <html xmlns = "http://www.w3.org/1999/xhtml">
9       <head>
10          <title>C# How to Program - Main</title>
11
12          <meta name = "keywords" content = "Webpage, design,
13              XHTML, tutorial, personal, help, index, form,
14              contact, feedback, list, links, frame, deitel" />
15
16          <meta name = "description" content = "This Web site will
17              help you learn the basics of XHTML and Web page design
18              through the use of interactive examples
19              and instruction." />
20
21      </head>
22
23      <!-- <frameset> tag sets frame dimensions -->
24      <frameset cols = "110,*">
25
26          <!-- frame elements specify which pages -->
27          <!-- are loaded into given frame        -->
28          <frame name = "leftframe" src = "nav.html" />
29          <frame name = "main" src = "main.html" />
30
31          <noframes>
32              <p>This page uses frames, but your browser does not
33              support them.</p>
34
35              <p>Please, <a href = "nav.html">follow this link to
36              browse our site without frames</a>.</p>
37          </noframes>
38
39      </frameset>
40  </html>
```

Fig. L.9   Web document containing two frames—navigation and content. (Part 1 of 2.)

Fig. L.9   Web document containing two frames—navigation and content. (Part 2 of 2.)

The documents that will be loaded into the **frameset** are specified with **frame** elements (lines 28–29 in this example). Attribute **src** specifies the URL of the page to display in the frame. Each frame has **name** and **src** attributes. The first frame (which covers **110** pixels on the left side of the **frameset**) is named **leftframe** and displays the page **nav.html** (Fig. L.10). The second frame is named main and displays the page **main.html**.

Attribute **name** identifies a frame, enabling hyperlinks in a **frameset** to specify the **target frame** in which a linked document should display when the user clicks the link. For example,

```
<a href = "links.html" target = "main">
```

loads **links.html** in the frame whose **name** is **"main"**.

Not all browsers support frames. XHTML provides the **noframes** element (lines 31–37) to enable XHTML document designers to specify alternative content for browsers that do not support frames.

Portability Tip L.1

Some browsers do not support frames. Use the **noframes** *element inside a* **frameset** *to direct users to a nonframed version of your site.*

Fig. L.10 is the Web page displayed in the left frame of Fig. L.9. This XHTML document provides the navigation buttons that, when clicked, determine which document is displayed in the right frame.

```
1   <?xml version = "1.0"?>
2   <!DOCTYPE html PUBLIC "-//W3C//DTD XHTML 1.0 Transitional//EN"
3       "http://www.w3.org/TR/xhtml1/DTD/xhtml1-transitional.dtd">
4
5   <!-- Fig. L.10: nav.html          -->
6   <!-- Using images as link anchors. -->
7
8   <html xmlns = "http://www.w3.org/1999/xhtml">
9
10      <head>
11         <title>C# How to Program - Navigation Bar
12         </title>
13      </head>
14
15      <body>
16
17         <p>
18            <a href = "links.html" target = "main">
19               <img src = "buttons/links.jpg" width = "65"
20                  height = "50" alt = "Links Page" />
21            </a><br />
22
23            <a href = "list.html" target = "main">
24               <img src = "buttons/list.jpg" width = "65"
25                  height = "50" alt = "List Example Page" />
26            </a><br />
```

Fig. L.10   XHTML document displayed in the left frame of Fig. L.9. (Part 1 of 2.)

```
27
28          <a href = "contact.html" target = "main">
29             <img src = "buttons/contact.jpg" width = "65"
30                height = "50" alt = "Contact Page" />
31          </a><br />
32
33          <a href = "header.html" target = "main">
34             <img src = "buttons/header.jpg" width = "65"
35                height = "50" alt = "Header Page" />
36          </a><br />
37
38          <a href = "table1.html" target = "main">
39             <img src = "buttons/table.jpg" width = "65"
40                height = "50" alt = "Table Page" />
41          </a><br />
42
43          <a href = "form.html" target = "main">
44             <img src = "buttons/form.jpg" width = "65"
45                height = "50" alt = "Feedback Form" />
46          </a><br />
47       </p>
48
49    </body>
50 </html>
```

Fig. L.10   XHTML document displayed in the left frame of Fig. L.9. (Part 2 of 2.)

Line 29 (Fig. L.9) displays the XHTML page in Fig. L.10. Anchor attribute **target** (line 18 in Fig. L.10) specifies that the linked documents are loaded in frame **main** (line 30 in Fig. L.9). A **target** can be set to a number of preset values: **"_blank"** loads the page into a new browser window, **"_self"** loads the page into the frame in which the anchor element appears and **"_top"** loads the page into the full browser window (i.e., removes the **frameset**).

L.10   Nested `framesets`

You can use the **frameset** element to create more complex layouts in a Web page by nesting **frameset**s, as in Fig. L.11. The nested **frameset** in this example displays the XHTML documents in Fig. L.7, Fig. L.8 and Fig. L.10.

The outer frameset element (lines 23–41) defines two columns. The left frame extends over the first 110 pixels from the left edge of the browser, and the right frame occupies the rest of the window's width. The **frame** element on line 24 specifies that the document **nav.html** (Fig. L.10) will be displayed in the left column.

Lines 28–31 define a nested **frameset** element for the second column of the outer frameset. This **frameset** defines two rows. The first row extends 175 pixels from the top of the browser window, and the second occupies the remainder of the browser window's height, as is indicated by **rows = "175,*"**. The **frame** element at line 29 specifies that the first row of the nested **frameset** will display **picture.html** (Fig. L.7). The **frame** element at line 30 specifies that the second row of the nested **frameset** will display **main.html** (Fig. L.8).

Testing and Debugging Tip L.2

*When using nested **frameset** elements, indent every level of **<frame>** tag. This practice makes the page clearer and easier to debug.*

In this appendix, we presented XHTML for marking up information in tables, creating forms for gathering user input, linking to sections within the same document, using **<meta>** tags and creating frames.

```
1    <?xml version = "1.0"?>
2    <!DOCTYPE html PUBLIC "-//W3C//DTD XHTML 1.0 Frameset//EN"
3       "http://www.w3.org/TR/xhtml1/DTD/xhtml1-frameset.dtd">
4
5    <!-- Fig. L.11: index2.html -->
6    <!-- XHTML frames II.        -->
7
8    <html xmlns = "http://www.w3.org/1999/xhtml">
9       <head>
10          <title>C# How to Program - Main</title>
11
12          <meta name = "keywords" content = "Webpage, design,
13             XHTML, tutorial, personal, help, index, form,
14             contact, feedback, list, links, frame, deitel" />
15
16          <meta name = "description" content = "This Web site will
17             help you learn the basics of XHTML and Web page design
18             through the use of interactive examples
19             and instruction." />
20
21       </head>
22
23       <frameset cols = "110,*">
24          <frame name = "leftframe" src = "nav.html" />
25
26          <!-- nested framesets are used to change -->
27          <!-- formatting and layout of frameset   -->
28          <frameset rows = "175,*">
29             <frame name = "picture" src = "picture.html" />
30             <frame name = "main" src = "main.html" />
31          </frameset>
32
33          <noframes>
34             <p>This page uses frames, but your browser does not
35             support them.</p>
36
37             <p>Please, <a href = "nav.html">follow this link to
38             browse our site without frames</a>.</p>
39          </noframes>
40
41       </frameset>
42    </html>
```

Fig. L.11   Framed Web site with a nested frameset. (Part 1 of 2.)

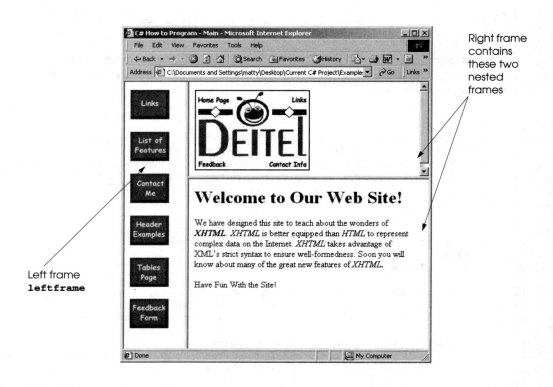

Right frame contains these two nested frames

Left frame **leftframe**

Fig. L.11   Framed Web site with a nested frameset. (Part 2 of 2.)

L.11 Summary

XHTML tables mark up tabular data and are one of the most frequently used features of the language. The **table** element defines an XHTML table. Attribute **border** specifies the table's border width, in pixels. Tables without borders set this attribute to **"0"**. Element **summary** summarizes the table's contents and is used by speech devices to make the table more accessible to users with visual impairments. Element **caption** describes the table's content. The text inside the **<caption>** tag is rendered above the table in most browsers. A table can be split into three distinct sections: the head (**thead**), the body (**tbody**) and the foot (**tfoot**). The head section contains such information as table titles and column headers. The table body contains the primary table data. The table foot contains secondary information, such as footnotes. Element **tr**, or table row, defines individual table rows. Element **th** defines a header cell. Text in **th** elements usually is centered and displayed in bold by most browsers. This element can be present in any section of the table. Data within a row are defined with **td**, or table data, elements. Element **colgroup** groups and formats columns. Each **col** element can format any number of columns (specified with the **span** attribute). The author of the document has the ability to merge data cells with the **rowspan** and **colspan** attributes. The values assigned to these attributes specify the number of rows or columns occupied by the cell. These attributes can be placed inside any data-cell tag.

XHTML provides forms for collecting information from users. Forms contain visual components, such as buttons that users click. Forms may also contain nonvisual components, called hidden inputs, that are used to store any data, such as e-mail addresses and XHTML document file names used for linking. A form begins with the **form** element. Attribute **method** specifies how the form's data are sent to the Web server. The **"text"** input inserts a textbox into the form. Textboxes allow the user to input data. The **input** element's **size** attribute specifies the number of characters visible in the **input** element. Optional attribute **maxlength** limits the number of characters input into a textbox. The **"submit"** input submits the data entered in the form to the Web server for processing. Most Web browsers create a button that submits the data when the form is clicked. The **"reset"** input allows a user to reset all **form** elements to their default values. The **textarea** element inserts a multiline textbox, called a textarea, into a form. The number of rows in the textarea is specified with the **rows** attribute, the number of columns (i.e., characters) with the **cols** attribute. The **"password"** input inserts a password box into a form. A password box allows users to enter sensitive information, such as credit card numbers and passwords, by "masking" the information input with another character. Asterisks are the masking character used for most password boxes. The actual value input, and not the asterisks that mask the input, is sent to the Web server. The checkbox input allows the user to make a selection. When the checkbox is selected, a check mark appears in the checkbox. Otherwise, the checkbox is empty. Checkboxes can be used individually and in groups. Checkboxes that are part of the same group have the same **name**. A radio button is similar in function and use to a checkbox, except that only one radio button in a group can be selected at any time. All radio buttons in a group have the same **name** attribute value, but different attribute **value**s. The **select** input provides a drop-down list of items. The **name** attribute identifies the drop-down list. The **option** element adds items to the drop-down list. The **selected** attribute, like the **checked** attribute for radio buttons and checkboxes, specifies which list item is displayed initially.

Image maps designate certain sections of an image as links. These links are more properly called hotspots. Image maps are defined with **map** elements. Attribute **id** identifies the image map. Hotspots are defined with the **area** element. Attribute **href** specifies the link's target. Attributes **shape** and **coords** specify the hotspot's shape and coordinates, respectively, and **alt** provides alternative text.

One way that search engines catalog pages is by reading the **meta** element's contents. Two important attributes of the **meta** element are **name**, which identifies the type of **meta** element, and **content**, which provides information a search engine uses to catalog a page.

Frames allow the browser to display more than one XHTML document simultaneously. The **frameset** element informs the browser that the page contains frames. Not all browsers support frames. XHTML provides the **noframes** element to specify alternative content for browsers that do not support frames.

L.12 Internet and World Wide Web Resources

courses.e-survey.net.au/xhtml/index.html
The *Web Page Design—XHTML* site provides descriptions and examples for various XHTML features, such as links, tables, frames and forms. Users can e-mail questions or comments to the Web Page Design support staff.

www.vbxml.com/xhtml/articles/xhtml_tables
The *VBXML.com* Web site contains a tutorial on creating XHTML tables.

www.webreference.com/xml/reference/xhtml.html
This Web page contains a list of the frequently used XHTML tags, such as header tags, table tags, frame tags and form tags. It also provides a description of each tag.

HTML/XHTML
Special Characters

The table of Fig. M.1 shows many commonly used HTML/XHTML special characters—called *character entity references* by the World Wide Web Consortium. For a complete list of character entity references, see the site

www.w3.org/TR/REC-html40/sgml/entities.html

Character	HTML/XHTML encoding	Character	HTML/XHTML encoding
non-breaking space	` `	ê	`&#234;`
§	`&#167;`	ì	`&#236;`
©	`&#169;`	í	`&#237;`
®	`&#174;`	î	`&#238;`
1/4	`&#188;`	ñ	`&#241;`
1/2	`&#189;`	ò	`&#242;`
3/4	`&#190;`	ó	`&#243;`
à	`&#224;`	ô	`&#244;`
á	`&#225;`	õ	`&#245;`
â	`&#226;`	÷	`&#247;`
ã	`&#227;`	ù	`&#249;`
å	`&#229;`	ú	`&#250;`
ç	`&#231;`	û	`&#251;`
è	`&#232;`	•	`&#8226;`

Fig. M.1 HTML/XHTML special characters.

Character	HTML/XHTML encoding	Character	HTML/XHTML encoding
é	é	™	™

Fig. M.1   HTML/XHTML special characters.

HTML/XHTML Colors

Colors may be specified by using a standard name (such as **aqua**) or a hexadecimal RGB value (such as **#00FFFF** for **aqua**). Of the six hexadecimal digits in an RGB value, the first two represent the amount of red in the color, the middle two represent the amount of green in the color, and the last two represent the amount of blue in the color. For example, **black** is the absence of color and is defined by **#000000**, whereas **white** is the maximum amount of red, green and blue and is defined by **#FFFFFF**. Pure **red** is **#FF0000**, pure green (which is called **lime**) is **#00FF00** and pure **blue** is **#0000FF**. Note that **green** is defined as **#008000**. Figure N.1 contains the HTML/XHTML standard color set. Figure N.2 contains the HTML/XHTML extended color set.

Color name	Value	Color name	Value
aqua	#00FFFF	navy	#000080
black	#000000	olive	#808000
blue	#0000FF	purple	#800080
fuchsia	#FF00FF	red	#FF0000
gray	#808080	silver	#C0C0C0
green	#008000	teal	#008080
lime	#00FF00	yellow	#FFFF00
maroon	#800000	white	#FFFFFF

Fig. N.1   HTML/XHTML standard colors and hexadecimal RGB values.

Color name	Value	Color name	Value
aliceblue	#F0F8FF	deeppink	#FF1493
antiquewhite	#FAEBD7	deepskyblue	#00BFFF
aquamarine	#7FFFD4	dimgray	#696969
azure	#F0FFFF	dodgerblue	#1E90FF
beige	#F5F5DC	firebrick	#B22222
bisque	#FFE4C4	floralwhite	#FFFAF0
blanchedalmond	#FFEBCD	forestgreen	#228B22
blueviolet	#8A2BE2	gainsboro	#DCDCDC
brown	#A52A2A	ghostwhite	#F8F8FF
burlywood	#DEB887	gold	#FFD700
cadetblue	#5F9EA0	goldenrod	#DAA520
chartreuse	#7FFF00	greenyellow	#ADFF2F
chocolate	#D2691E	honeydew	#F0FFF0
coral	#FF7F50	hotpink	#FF69B4
cornflowerblue	#6495ED	indianred	#CD5C5C
cornsilk	#FFF8DC	indigo	#4B0082
crimson	#DC1436	ivory	#FFFFF0
cyan	#00FFFF	khaki	#F0E68C
darkblue	#00008B	lavender	#E6E6FA
darkcyan	#008B8B	lavenderblush	#FFF0F5
darkgoldenrod	#B8860B	lawngreen	#7CFC00
darkgray	#A9A9A9	lemonchiffon	#FFFACD
darkgreen	#006400	lightblue	#ADD8E6
darkkhaki	#BDB76B	lightcoral	#F08080
darkmagenta	#8B008B	lightcyan	#E0FFFF
darkolivegreen	#556B2F	lightgoldenrodyellow	#FAFAD2
darkorange	#FF8C00	lightgreen	#90EE90
darkorchid	#9932CC	lightgrey	#D3D3D3
darkred	#8B0000	lightpink	#FFB6C1
darksalmon	#E9967A	lightsalmon	#FFA07A
darkseagreen	#8FBC8F	lightseagreen	#20B2AA
darkslateblue	#483D8B	lightskyblue	#87CEFA
darkslategray	#2F4F4F	lightslategray	#778899
darkturquoise	#00CED1	lightsteelblue	#B0C4DE
darkviolet	#9400D3	lightyellow	#FFFFE0

Fig. N.2   HTML/XHTML extended colors and hexadecimal RGB values. (Part 1 of 2.)

Color name	Value	Color name	Value
limegreen	#32CD32	mediumblue	#0000CD
mediumpurple	#9370DB	mediumorchid	#BA55D3
mediumseagreen	#3CB371	plum	#DDA0DD
mediumslateblue	#7B68EE	powderblue	#B0E0E6
mediumspringgreen	#00FA9A	rosybrown	#BC8F8F
mediumturquoise	#48D1CC	royalblue	#4169E1
mediumvioletred	#C71585	saddlebrown	#8B4513
midnightblue	#191970	salmon	#FA8072
mintcream	#F5FFFA	sandybrown	#F4A460
mistyrose	#FFE4E1	seagreen	#2E8B57
moccasin	#FFE4B5	seashell	#FFF5EE
navajowhite	#FFDEAD	sienna	#A0522D
oldlace	#FDF5E6	skyblue	#87CEEB
olivedrab	#6B8E23	slateblue	#6A5ACD
orange	#FFA500	slategray	#708090
orangered	#FF4500	snow	#FFFAFA
orchid	#DA70D6	springgreen	#00FF7F
palegoldenrod	#EEE8AA	steelblue	#4682B4
palegreen	#98FB98	tan	#D2B48C
paleturquoise	#AFEEEE	thistle	#D8BFD8
palevioletred	#DB7093	tomato	#FF6347
papayawhip	#FFEFD5	turquoise	#40E0D0
peachpuff	#FFDAB9	violet	#EE82EE
peru	#CD853F	wheat	#F5DEB3
pink	#FFC0CB	whitesmoke	#F5F5F5
mediumaquamarine	#66CDAA	yellowgreen	#9ACD32

Fig. N.2   HTML/XHTML extended colors and hexadecimal RGB values. (Part 2 of 2.)

Bit Manipulation

Objectives

- To understand the concept of bit manipulation.
- To use bitwise operators.
- To use class **BitArray** to perform bit manipulation.

Outline

O.1   Introduction

O.2   Bit Manipulation and the Bitwise Operators

O.3   Class `BitArray`

O.4   Summary

O.1 Introduction

In this appendix, we present an extensive discussion of bit manipulation and the *bitwise operators* that enable it. We also discuss class **BitArray**, from which we create objects useful for manipulating sets of bits.

O.2 Bit Manipulation and the Bitwise Operators

C# provides extensive bit-manipulation capabilities for programmers who must work at the "bits-and-bytes" level. Operating systems, test-equipment software, networking software and many other kinds of software require that programmers communicate "directly with the hardware." In this section and the next, we discuss C#'s bit-manipulation capabilities. After introducing C#'s bitwise operators, we demonstrate the use of the operators in live-code examples.

Computers represent data internally as sequences of bits. Arithmetic Logic Units (ALUs), Central Processing Units (CPUs) and other pieces of hardware in a computer process data as bits or groups of bits. Each bit can assume either the value **0** or the value **1**. On all systems, a sequence of 8 bits forms a *byte*—the standard storage unit for a variable of type **byte**. Other data types require larger numbers of bytes for storage. The bitwise operators manipulate the bits of integral operands (i.e., **sbyte**, **byte**, **char**, **short**, **ushort**, **int**, **uint**, **long** and **ulong**).

Note that the discussion of bitwise operators in this section illustrates the binary representations of the integer operands. For a detailed explanation of the binary (also called base-2) number system, see Appendix B, Number Systems.

The operators *bitwise AND* (**&**), *bitwise inclusive OR* (**|**) and *bitwise exclusive OR* (**^**) operate similarly to their logical counterparts, except that the bitwise versions operate on the level of bits. The bitwise AND operator sets each bit in the result to 1 if the corresponding bits in both operands are 1 (Fig. O.2). The bitwise inclusive OR operator sets each bit in the result to 1 if the corresponding bits in either (or both) operand(s) are 1 (Fig. O.3). The bitwise exclusive OR operator sets each bit in the result to 1 if the corresponding bit in exactly one operand is 1 (Fig. O.4). Exclusive OR is also known as *XOR*.

The *left-shift* (**<<**) operator shifts the bits of its left operand to the left by the number of bits specified in its right operand. The *right-shift* (**>>**) operator shifts the bits in its left operand to the right by the number of bits specified in its right operand. If the left operand is negative, **1**s are shifted in from the left, whereas, if the left operand is positive **0**s are shifted in from the left. The bitwise *complement* (**~**) operator sets all **0** bits in its operand to **1** and all **1** bits to **0** in the result; this process sometimes is referred to as "taking the *one's complement* of the value." A detailed discussion of each bitwise operator appears in the examples that follow. The bitwise operators and their functions are summarized in Fig. O.1.

Operator	Name	Description
&	bitwise AND	Each bit in the result is set to **1** if the corresponding bits in the two operands are both **1**. Otherwise, the bit is set to **0**.
|	bitwise inclusive OR	Each bit in the result is set to **1** if at least one of the corresponding bits in the two operands is **1**. Otherwise, the bit is set to **0**.
^	bitwise exclusive OR	Each bit in the result is set to **1** if exactly one of the corresponding bits in the two operands is **1**. Otherwise, the bit is set to **0**.
<<	left shift	Shifts the bits of the first operand to the left by the number of bits specified by the second operand; fill from the right with **0** bits.
>>	right shift	Shifts the bits of the first operand to the right by the number of bits specified by the second operand. If the first operand is negative, **1**s are shifted in from the left; otherwise, **0**s are shifted in from the left.
~	complement	All **0** bits are set to **1**, and all **1** bits are set to **0**.

Fig. O.1　Bitwise operators.

Bit 1	Bit 2	Bit 1 & Bit 2
0	0	0
1	0	0
0	1	0
1	1	1

Fig. O.2　Results of combining two bits with the bitwise AND operator (**&**).

Bit 1	Bit 2	Bit 1 | Bit 2
0	0	0
1	0	1
0	1	1
1	1	1

Fig. O.3　Results of combining two bits with the bitwise inclusive OR operator (**|**).

Bit 1	Bit 2	Bit 1 ^ Bit 2
0	0	0
1	0	1
0	1	1
1	1	0

Fig. O.4   Results of combining two bits with the bitwise exclusive OR operator (^).

When using the bitwise operators, it is useful to display values in their binary representations to illustrate the effects of these operators. In Fig. O.5, integers are displayed in their binary representations as groups of eight bits each. Method **GetBits** (lines 67–91) of class **PrintBits** uses the bitwise AND operator (line 79) to combine variable **number** with variable **displayMask**. Often, the bitwise AND operator is used with a *mask* operand—an integer value with specific bits set to **1**. Masks hide some bits in a value and select other bits. **GetBits** assigns mask variable **displayMask** the value **1 << 31** (**10000000 00000000 00000000 00000000**). The left-shift operator shifts the value **1** from the low-order (rightmost) bit to the high-order (leftmost) bit in **displayMask** and fills in **0** bits from the right. Because the second operand is 31, 31 bits (each is **0**) are filled in from the right. The word "fill" in this context, means that we add a bit to the right end, and delete one from the left end. Every time we add a **0** to the right end, we remove the bit at the left end.

The statement on line 79 determines whether a **1** or a **0** should be appended to **StringBuilder output** for the leftmost bit of variable **number**. For this example, assume that **number** contains **11111** (**00000000 00000000 00101011 01100111**). When **number** and **displayMask** are combined using **&**, all the bits except the high-order bit in variable **number** are "masked off" (hidden), because any bit "ANDed" with **0** yields **0**. If the leftmost bit is **0**, **number & displayMask** evaluates to **0**, and **0** is appended; otherwise, **1** is appended. Line 83 then left shifts variable **val** one bit with the expression **number <<= 1**. (This is equivalent to **number = number << 1**.) These steps are repeated for each bit in variable **number**. At the end of method **GetBits**, line 89 converts the **StringBuilder** to a **string** and returns it from the method.

```
1   // Fig. O.5: PrintBits.cs
2   // Printing the bits that constitute an integer.
3
4   using System;
5   using System.Drawing;
6   using System.Collections;
7   using System.ComponentModel;
8   using System.Windows.Forms;
9   using System.Data;
10  using System.Text;
11
12
```

Fig. O.5   Displaying the bit representation of an integer. (Part 1 of 3.)

```
13   // displays bit representation of user input
14   public class PrintBits : System.Windows.Forms.Form
15   {
16      private System.Windows.Forms.Label promptLabel;
17      private System.Windows.Forms.Label viewLabel;
18
19      // for user input
20      private System.Windows.Forms.TextBox inputTextBox;
21
22      // bit representation displayed here
23      private System.Windows.Forms.Label displayLabel;
24
25      private System.ComponentModel.Container components = null;
26
27      // default constructor
28      public PrintBits()
29      {
30         InitializeComponent();
31      }
32
33      // Visual Studio .NET generated code
34
35      [STAThread]
36      static void Main()
37      {
38         Application.Run( new PrintBits() );
39      }
40
41      // process integer when user presses Enter
42      private void inputTextBox_KeyDown(
43         object sender, System.Windows.Forms.KeyEventArgs e )
44      {
45         // if user pressed Enter
46         if ( e.KeyCode == Keys.Enter )
47         {
48            // test whether user enetered an integer
49            try
50            {
51               displayLabel.Text = GetBits(
52                  Convert.ToInt32( inputTextBox.Text ) );
53            }
54
55            // if value is not integer, exception is thrown
56            catch ( FormatException )
57            {
58               MessageBox.Show( "Please Enter an Integer",
59                  "Error", MessageBoxButtons.OK,
60                  MessageBoxIcon.Error );
61            }
62         }
63
64      } // end method inputTextBox_KeyDown
65
```

Fig. O.5   Displaying the bit representation of an integer. (Part 2 of 3.)

```
66      // convert integer to its bit representation
67      public string GetBits( int number )
68      {
69         int displayMask = 1 << 31;
70
71         StringBuilder output = new StringBuilder();
72
73         // get each bit, add space every 8 bits
74         // for display formatting
75         for ( int c = 1; c <= 32; c++ )
76         {
77            // append 0 or 1 depending on result of masking
78            output.Append(
79               ( number & displayMask ) == 0 ? "0" : "1" );
80
81            // shift left so that mask will find bit of
82            // next digit during next iteration of loop
83            number <<= 1;
84
85            if ( c % 8 == 0 )
86               output.Append( " " );
87         }
88
89         return output.ToString();
90
91      } // end method GetBits
92
93   } // end class PrintBits
```

Fig. O.5   Displaying the bit representation of an integer. (Part 3 of 3.)

Common Programming Error 22.2
Using the logical AND operator (&&) in place of the bitwise AND operator (&) is a common programming error.

Common Programming Error 22.3
Using the logical OR operator (||) in place of the bitwise inclusive OR operator (|) is a common programming error.

The program in Fig. O.6 demonstrates the bitwise AND operator, the bitwise inclusive OR operator, the bitwise exclusive OR operator and the bitwise complement operator. The program uses method **GetBits**, which returns a **string** which contains the bit representation of its integer argument. Users enter values into **TextBox**es and press the button corresponding to the operation they would like to test. The program displays the result in both integer and bit representations.

```
1    // Fig. O.6: BitOperations.cs
2    // A class that demonstrates miscellaneous bit operations
3
4    using System;
5    using System.Drawing;
6    using System.Collections;
7    using System.ComponentModel;
8    using System.Windows.Forms;
9    using System.Data;
10   using System.Text;
11
12   // allows user to test bit operators
13   public class BitOperations : System.Windows.Forms.Form
14   {
15       private System.Windows.Forms.Label promptLabel;
16       private System.Windows.Forms.Label representationLabel;
17       private System.Windows.Forms.Label value1Label;
18       private System.Windows.Forms.Label value2Label;
19       private System.Windows.Forms.Label resultLabel;
20
21       // display bit reprentations
22       private System.Windows.Forms.Label bit1Label;
23       private System.Windows.Forms.Label bit2Label;
24       private System.Windows.Forms.Label resultBitLabel;
25
26       // allow user to perform bit operations
27       private System.Windows.Forms.Button andButton;
28       private System.Windows.Forms.Button inclusiveOrButton;
29       private System.Windows.Forms.Button exclusiveOrButton;
30       private System.Windows.Forms.Button complementButton;
31
32       // user inputs two integers
33       private System.Windows.Forms.TextBox bit1TextBox;
34       private System.Windows.Forms.TextBox bit2TextBox;
35
36       private System.Windows.Forms.TextBox resultTextBox;
37
38       private int value1, value2;
39
40       private System.ComponentModel.Container components = null;
41
42       // default constructor
43       public BitOperations()
44       {
45           InitializeComponent();
46       }
47
48       // Visual Studio .NET generated code
49
50       [STAThread]
51       static void Main()
52       {
```

Fig. O.6   Demonstrating the bitwise AND, bitwise inclusive OR, bitwise exclusive OR and bitwise complement operators. (Part 1 of 4.)

```
53          Application.Run( new BitOperations() );
54       }
55
56       // AND
57       private void andButton_Click(
58          object sender, System.EventArgs e )
59       {
60          SetFields();
61
62          // update resultTextBox
63          resultTextBox.Text =
64             string.Format( "{0}", value1 & value2 );
65
66          resultBitLabel.Text = GetBits( value1 & value2 );
67       }
68
69       // inclusive OR
70       private void inclusiveOrButton_Click(
71          object sender, System.EventArgs e )
72       {
73          SetFields();
74
75          // update resultTextBox
76          resultTextBox.Text =
77             string.Format( "{0}", value1 | value2 );
78          resultBitLabel.Text = GetBits( value1 | value2 );
79       }
80
81       // exclusive OR
82       private void exclusiveOrButton_Click(
83          object sender, System.EventArgs e )
84       {
85          SetFields();
86
87          // update resultTextBox
88          resultTextBox.Text =
89             string.Format( "{0}", value1 ^ value2 );
90          resultBitLabel.Text = GetBits( value1 ^ value2 );
91       }
92
93       // complement of first integer
94       private void complementButton_Click(
95          object sender, System.EventArgs e )
96       {
97          value1 = Convert.ToInt32( bit1TextBox.Text );
98          bit1Label.Text = GetBits( value1 );
99
100         // update resultTextBox
101         resultTextBox.Text = string.Format( "{0}", ~value1 );
102         resultBitLabel.Text = GetBits( ~value1 );
103      }
104
```

Fig. O.6   Demonstrating the bitwise AND, bitwise inclusive OR, bitwise exclusive OR and bitwise complement operators. (Part 2 of 4.)

```
105        // convert integer to its bit representation
106        private string GetBits( int number )
107        {
108            int displayMask = 1 << 31;
109
110            StringBuilder output = new StringBuilder();
111
112            // get each bit, add space every 8 bits
113            // for display formatting
114            for ( int c = 1; c <= 32; c++ )
115            {
116                // append 0 or 1 depending on the result of masking
117                output.Append(
118                    ( number & displayMask ) == 0 ? "0" : "1" );
119
120                // shift left so that mask will find bit of
121                // next digit in the next iteration of loop
122                number <<= 1;
123
124                if ( c % 8 == 0 )
125                    output.Append( " " );
126            }
127
128            return output.ToString();
129
130        } // end method GetBits
131
132        // set fields of Form
133        private void SetFields()
134        {
135            // retrieve input values
136            value1 = Convert.ToInt32( bit1TextBox.Text );
137            value2 = Convert.ToInt32( bit2TextBox.Text );
138
139            // set labels to display bit representations of integers
140            bit1Label.Text = GetBits( value1 );
141            bit2Label.Text = GetBits( value2 );
142        }
143
144    } // end class BitOperations
```

Fig. O.6   Demonstrating the bitwise AND, bitwise inclusive OR, bitwise exclusive OR and bitwise complement operators. (Part 3 of 4.)

Fig. O.6   Demonstrating the bitwise AND, bitwise inclusive OR, bitwise exclusive OR and bitwise complement operators. (Part 4 of 4.)

The first output window of Fig. O.6 shows the results of combining the value **17** and the value **20** using the bitwise AND operator (**&**); the result is **16**. The second output window shows the results of combining the value **17** and the value **20** using the bitwise OR operator; the result is **21**. The third output shows the results of combining the value **17** and the value **20** using the exclusive OR operator; the result is **5**. The fourth output window shows the results of taking the one's complement of the value **17**. The result is **-18**.

The program in Fig. O.7 demonstrates the use of the left-shift operator (**<<**) and the right-shift operator (**>>**). Method **GetBits** returns a **string** containing the bit representation of an integer value passed to it as an argument. When users enter an integer in a **TextBox** and press *Enter*, the program displays the bit representation of the specified integer in a **Label**.

```
1   // Fig. O.7: BitShift.cs
2   // Demonstrates bitshift operators.
3
4   using System;
5   using System.Drawing;
6   using System.Collections;
7   using System.ComponentModel;
8   using System.Windows.Forms;
9   using System.Data;
10  using System.Text;
11
12  // shifts bits to the right or left
13  public class BitShift : System.Windows.Forms.Form
14  {
15     private System.Windows.Forms.Label inputLabel;
16
17     // accepts user input
18     private System.Windows.Forms.TextBox inputTextBox;
19
20     // displays integer in bits
21     private System.Windows.Forms.Label displayLabel;
22     private System.Windows.Forms.Button rightButton;
23     private System.Windows.Forms.Button leftButton;
24
25     private System.ComponentModel.Container components = null;
26
27     // default constructor
28     public BitShift()
29     {
30        InitializeComponent();
31     }
32
33     // Visual Studio .NET generated code
34
35     [STAThread]
36     static void Main()
37     {
38        Application.Run( new BitShift() );
39     }
40
41     // process user input
42     private void inputTextBox_KeyDown(
43        object sender, System.Windows.Forms.KeyEventArgs e )
44     {
45        if ( e.KeyCode == Keys.Enter )
46           displayLabel.Text =
47              GetBits( Convert.ToInt32( inputTextBox.Text ) );
48     }
49
50     // do left shift
51     private void leftButton_Click(
52        object sender, System.EventArgs e )
53     {
```

Fig. O.7   Using the bitshift operators. (Part 1 of 3.)

```
54          // retrieve user input
55          int number = Convert.ToInt32( inputTextBox.Text );
56
57          // do left shift operation
58          number <<= 1;
59
60          // convert to integer and display in textbox
61          inputTextBox.Text = number.ToString();
62
63          // display bits in label
64          displayLabel.Text = GetBits( number );
65       }
66
67    // do right shift
68    private void rightButton_Click(
69       object sender, System.EventArgs e )
70    {
71          // retrieve user input
72          int number = Convert.ToInt32( inputTextBox.Text );
73
74          // do right shift operation
75          number >>= 1;
76
77          // convert to integer and display in textbox
78          inputTextBox.Text = number.ToString();
79
80          // display bits in label
81          displayLabel.Text = GetBits( number );
82       }
83
84    // convert integer to its bit representation
85    private string GetBits( int number )
86    {
87          int displayMask = 1 << 31;
88
89          StringBuilder output = new StringBuilder();
90
91          // get each bit, add space every 8 bits
92          // for display formatting
93          for ( int c = 1; c <= 32; c++ )
94          {
95             // append a 0 or 1 depending on the result of masking
96             output.Append(
97                ( number & displayMask ) == 0 ? "0" : "1" );
98
99             // shift left so that mask will find bit of
100            // next digit during next iteration of loop
101            number <<= 1;
102
103            if ( c % 8 == 0 )
104               output.Append( " " );
105         }
106
```

Fig. O.7   Using the bitshift operators. (Part 2 of 3.)

```
107          return output.ToString();
108
109     } // end method GetBits
110
111 } // end class BitShift
```

Fig. O.7   Using the bitshift operators. (Part 3 of 3.)

Each shift operator has its own button on the application's GUI. As a user clicks each button, the bits in the integer shift left or right by one bit. The **TextBox** and **Label** display the new integer value and new bit representation, respectively.

The left-shift operator (**<<**) shifts the bits of its left operand to the left by the number of bits specified in its right operand. The rightmost bits are replaced with **0**s; **1**s shifted off the left are lost. The first two output windows in Fig. O.7 demonstrate the left-shift operator. To produce the output, the user entered the value 23 and clicked the left-shift button, resulting in the value **46**.

The right-shift operator (**>>**) shifts the bits of its left operand to the right by the number of bits specified in its right operand. **0**s replace vacated bits on the left side if the number is positive, and **1**s replace the vacated bits if the number is negative. Any **1**s shifted off the right are lost. The third and fourth output windows depict the result of shifting **184** to the right once.

Each bitwise operator (except the bitwise complement operator) has a corresponding assignment operator. Figure O.8 describes these *bitwise assignment operators*, which are used in a manner similar to the arithmetic assignment operators introduced in Chapter 3.

Bitwise assignment operators	
&=	Bitwise AND assignment operator.
|=	Bitwise inclusive OR assignment operator.
^=	Bitwise exclusive OR assignment operator.

Fig. O.8   Bitwise assignment operators. (Part 1 of 2.)

Bitwise assignment operators	
`<<=`	Left-shift assignment operator.
`>>=`	Right-shift assignment operator.

Fig. O.8   Bitwise assignment operators. (Part 2 of 2.)

O.3 Class `BitArray`

Class **BitArray** facilitates the creation and manipulation of *bit sets*, which programmers often use to represent a set of *boolean flags*. A boolean flag is a variable that keeps track of a certain boolean decision. **BitArray**s are resizable dynamically—more bits can be added once a **BitArray** object is created, causing the object to grow to accommodate the additional bits.

Class **BitArray** provides several constructors, one of which accepts an **int** as an argument. The **int** specifies the number of bits that the **BitArray** represents, all of which are initially set to **false**.

Method *Set* of **BitArray** can change the value of an individual bit; it accepts the index of the bit to change and its new **bool** value. Class **BitArray** also includes an indexer that allows us to get and set individual bit values. The indexer returns **true** if the specified bit is on (i.e., the bit has value 1) and returns **false** otherwise (i.e., the bit has value 0 or "off").

Class **BitArray** method *And* performs a bitwise AND between two **BitArray**s and returns the **BitArray** result of the operation. Methods *Or* and *Xor* perform bitwise inclusive OR and bitwise exclusive OR operations, respectively. Class **BitArray** also provides a *Length* property, which returns the number of elements in the **BitArray**.

Figure O.9 implements the *Sieve of Eratosthenes*, which is a technique for finding prime numbers. A prime number is an integer that is divisible evenly only by itself and one. The Sieve of Eratosthenes operates as follows:

> *a) Create an array with all elements initialized to 1 (true). Array elements with prime subscripts remain 1. All other array elements eventually are set to 0.*
>
> *b) Starting with array subscript 2 (subscript 1 must not be prime), every time an array element is found with a value of 1, loop through the remainder of the array and set to 0 every element whose subscript is a multiple of the subscript for the element with value 1. For example, for array subscript 2, all elements after 2 in the array that are multiples of 2 are set to 0 (subscripts 4, 6, 8, 10, etc.); for array subscript 3, all elements after 3 in the array that are multiples of 3 are set to 0 (subscripts 6, 9, 12, 15, etc.); and so on.*

At the end of this process, the subscripts of the array elements that are one are prime numbers. The list of prime numbers can then be displayed by locating and printing these subscripts.

```
1   // Fig. O.9: BitArrayTest.cs
2   // Demonstrates BitArray class.
3
```

Fig. O.9   Sieve of Eratosthenes. (Part 1 of 3.)

```
 4   using System;
 5   using System.Drawing;
 6   using System.Collections;
 7   using System.ComponentModel;
 8   using System.Windows.Forms;
 9   using System.Data;
10
11   // implements Sieve of Eratosthenes
12   public class BitArrayTest : System.Windows.Forms.Form
13   {
14      private System.Windows.Forms.Label promptLabel;
15
16      // user inputs integer
17      private System.Windows.Forms.TextBox inputTextBox;
18
19      // display prime numbers
20      private System.Windows.Forms.TextBox outputTextBox;
21
22      // displays whether input integer is prime
23      private System.Windows.Forms.Label displayLabel;
24
25      private BitArray sieve;
26
27      private System.ComponentModel.Container components = null;
28
29      // default constructor
30      public BitArrayTest()
31      {
32         InitializeComponent();
33
34         // create BitArray and set all bits to true
35         sieve = new BitArray( 1024 );
36         sieve.SetAll( true );
37
38         int finalBit = ( int ) Math.Sqrt( sieve.Length );
39
40         // perform sieve operation
41         for ( int i = 2; i < finalBit; i++ )
42            if ( sieve.Get( i ) )
43               for ( int j = 2 * i; j < sieve.Length; j += i )
44                  sieve.Set( j, false );
45
46         int counter = 0;
47
48         // display prime numbers
49         for ( int i = 2; i < sieve.Length; i++ )
50            if ( sieve.Get( i ) )
51               outputTextBox.Text += i +
52                  ( ++counter % 7 == 0 ? "\r\n" : "    " );
53      }
54
55      // Visual Studio .NET generated code
56
```

Fig. O.9   Sieve of Eratosthenes. (Part 2 of 3.)

```
57        [STAThread]
58        static void Main()
59        {
60            Application.Run( new BitArrayTest() );
61        }
62
63        private void inputTextBox_KeyDown(
64            object sender, System.Windows.Forms.KeyEventArgs e )
65        {
66            // if user pressed Enter
67            if ( e.KeyCode == Keys.Enter )
68            {
69                int number = Convert.ToInt32( inputTextBox.Text );
70
71                // if sieve is true at index of integer
72                // input by user, then number is prime
73                if ( sieve.Get( number ) )
74                    displayLabel.Text = number + " is a prime number";
75                else
76                    displayLabel.Text =
77                        number + " is not a prime number";
78            }
79        } // end method inputTextBox_KeyDown
80
81  } // end class BitArrayTest
```

Fig. O.9   Sieve of Eratosthenes. (Part 3 of 3.)

We use a **BitArray** to implement the algorithm. The program displays the prime numbers in the range 1–1023 in a **TextBox**. The program also provides a **TextBox** in which users can type any number from 1–1023 to determine whether that number is prime. (In which case, it displays a message indicating that the number is prime.)

The statement on line 35 creates a **BitArray** of **1024** bits. **BitArray** method **SetAll** sets all the bits to **true** on line 36; then, lines 41–44 determine all prime numbers occurring between 1 and 1023. The integer **finalBit** determines when the algorithm is complete.

When the user inputs a number and presses *Enter*, line 73 tests whether the input number is prime. This line uses the **Get** method of class **BitArray**, which takes a number and returns the value of that bit in the array. Lines 74 and 76 print an appropriate response.

O.4 Summary

Computers represent data internally as sequences of bits. Each bit can assume the value **0** or the value **1**. On all systems, a sequence of 8 bits forms a byte—the standard storage unit for a variable of type **byte**. Other data types require larger numbers of bytes for storage. The bitwise AND operator sets each bit in the result to **1** if the corresponding bits in both operands are **1**. The bitwise inclusive-OR operator sets each bit in the result to **1** if the corresponding bit in either or both operands is **1**. The bitwise exclusive-OR operator sets each bit in the result to **1** if the corresponding bit in exactly one operand is **1**. Exclusive OR is also known as XOR.

The left-shift (**<<**) operator shifts the bits of its left operand to the left by the number of bits specified in its right operand. The right-shift (**>>**) operator shifts the bits in its left operand to the right by the number of bits specified in its right operand. If the left operand is negative, **1**s are shifted in from the left, whereas if the left operand is positive, **0**s are shifted in from the left. The bitwise complement (**~**) operator sets all **0** bits in its operand to **1** in the result and sets all **1** bits to **0** in the result; this process is sometimes referred to as "taking the one's complement of the value." Often, the bitwise AND operator is used with a mask operand—an integer value with specific bits set to **1**. Masks hide some bits in a value and select other bits. Each bitwise operator (except the bitwise complement operator) has a corresponding assignment operator.

Class **BitArray** facilitates the creation and manipulation of bit sets, which programmers often use to represent a set of boolean flags. A boolean flag is a variable that keeps track of a certain boolean decision. **BitArray**s are resizable dynamically—more bits can be added once a **BitArray** object is created, causing the object to grow to accommodate the additional bits. Method **Set** of **BitArray** can change the value of an individual bit—it accepts the index of the bit to change and the **bool** value to which the bit should change. **BitArray** method **And** performs a bitwise AND between two **BitArray**s and returns the **BitArray** that is the result of performing this operation. Methods **Or** and **Xor** perform bitwise inclusive OR and bitwise exclusive OR, respectively. **BitArray** method **SetAll** sets all the bits in the **BitArray** to **true**.

Crystal Reports® for Visual Studio .NET

P.1 Introduction

All industries collect and maintain data relevant to their businesses. For example, manufacturing companies maintain information about inventories and production, retail shops record sales, health care organizations maintain patient records and publishers track book sales and inventories. However, just storing data is not enough: Managers must use these data to make informed business decisions. Information must be properly organized, easily accessible and shared among various individuals, departments and affiliates. This facilitates data analysis that can reveal business-critical information, such as sales trends or potential inventory shortages. To make this possible, developers have used reporting software—a key tool enabling the presentation of stored data sources.

Crystal Reports® was first released in 1992 as a Windows-based report writer, and Microsoft adopted Crystal Reports as the standard for Visual Basic in 1993.[1] Visual Studio .NET now integrates a special edition of Crystal Reports, further tying Crystal Reports to all .NET programming languages, including C#, and to Windows and Web development. This appendix presents the resources that *Crystal Decisions*, the company that produces Crystal Reports, offers on its Web site, and overviews Crystal Report's unique functionality and features in Visual Studio .NET.

P.2 Crystal Reports Web Site Resources

Crystal Decisions offers resources to developers working in Visual Studio .NET at their Web site, **www.crystaldecisions.com/net**. The site updates the changes in Visual Studio .NET versions in English, Simplified Chinese, Traditional Chinese, French, German, Italian, Japanese, Korean and Spanish. Crystal Decisions also provides technical support for Crystal Reports C# developers via e-mail or phone. The site offers walk-

---

1. "Company History," **<www.crystaldecisions.com/about/ourcompany/ history.asp>**.

throughs, an online newsletter, a multimedia product demo, discussion groups, a developer's zone and an overview of Crystal Reports in Visual Studio .NET.

P.3 Crystal Reports and Visual Studio .NET

Developers working in Visual Studio .NET's integrated development environment (IDE) can create and integrate reports in their applications using Crystal Reports software. The Visual Studio .NET edition Crystal Reports provides powerful capabilities to developers. Features of Crystal Reports for Visual Studio .NET include an API (application programming interface) that allows developers to control how reports are cached on servers—setting timeouts, restrictions, etc. Developers can create reports in multiple languages, because Crystal Reports now fully supports Unicode data types. The reports that are created can be viewed in many file formats. A user can convert a report to Microsoft Word, Adobe's Portable Document Format (PDF), HyperText Markup Language (HTML) and others so that report information can be distributed easily and used in a wide variety of documentation. Figure P.1 displays a sample Crystal Report exported to a PDF document. Any Crystal Report created in Visual Studio .NET can become an embedded resource for use in Windows and Web applications and Web services. This section overviews the initial stages of creating reports as well as some more advanced capabilities.

Fig. P.1   Crystal Report sample in PDF form. (Courtesy Crystal Decisions -
www.crystaldecisions.com.)

To aid Visual Studio .NET developers design reports, Crystal Reports provides a *Report Expert*. Experts are similar to "templates" and "wizards"—they guide users through the creation of a variety of reports while handling the details of how the report is created, so the user need not be concerned with them. The available Experts create several types of reports, including standard, form-letter, form, cross-tab, subreport, mail label and drill-down reports (Fig. P.2). Figure P.3 illustrates the **Standard Report Expert** interface.

Fig. P.2   Report expert choices. (Courtesy Crystal Decisions - **www.crystaldecisions.com**.)

Fig. P.3   Expert formatting menu choices. (Courtesy Crystal Decisions - **www.crystaldecisions.com**.)

Crystal Reports for Visual Studio .NET is comprised of several components. Once a report is set up, either manually or by using an Expert, developers use the Crystal Reports Designer in Visual Studio .NET to modify, add and format objects and fields, as well as to format the report layout and manipulate the report design (Fig. P.4). The Designer then generates RPT files (**.rpt** is the file extension for a Crystal Report). These RPT files are processed by the Crystal Reports engine, which delivers the report output to one of two Crystal Report viewers—a Windows Forms viewer control or a Web Forms viewer control, depending on the type of application the developer specifies. The viewers then present the formatted information to the user.

Walkthroughs illustrating the new functionality are available on the Crystal Decisions Web site at **www.crystaldecisions.com/netzone**. The walkthroughs include integrating and viewing Web reports through Windows applications, creating interactive reports in Web applications, exposing Crystal Reports through Web services and reporting from ActiveX Data Objects (ADO) .NET data.[2] (For a detailed discussion of ADO .NET and other database tools, see Chapter 16, Database, SQL and ADO .NET.) This section overviews the functionality of some of the Web applications and Web services walkthroughs.

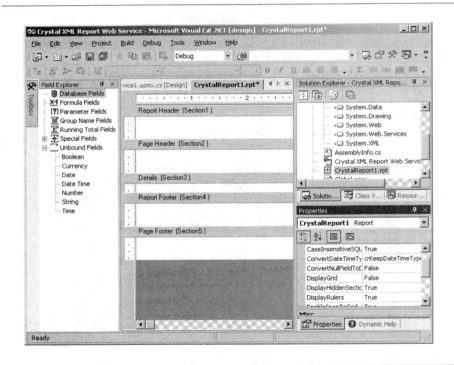

Fig. P.4   Crystal Reports designer interface. (Courtesy Crystal Decisions - **www.crystaldecisions.com**.)

2. The walkthroughs on the Crystal Decisions Web site were tested using C# in Visual Studio .NET, but a developer should be able to use the walkthroughs with any language supported by Visual Studio .NET.

P.3.1 Crystal Reports in Web Applications

Using Crystal Reports for Visual Studio .NET, a developer can integrate highly interactive Crystal Reports into a Web page. ASP .NET technology integrated into Visual Studio .NET enables interactivity by producing cross-platform, dynamic Web applications. We discuss these technologies in detail in Chapter 17, ASP .NET, Web Forms and Web Controls.

Web Forms consist of HTML files with embedded Web Controls and code-behind files that contain programming logic. Crystal Reports provides a Web Forms Report Viewer, which is a Web Form that hosts the report. When a client accesses such a Web Form, the event handler can update and format information in the report and send the report to the user.[3]

A walkthrough on the Crystal Decision's Web site instructs a programmer how to enable Web page interactivity and how to use ASP .NET and its controls. In the walkthrough, the user accesses information about countries by first entering a country name in the text box. When the user submits the information, the country name is passed to the Web forms viewer control and the report is updated—the Web forms page updates the report in HTML and sends it to the client browser.

P.3.2 Crystal Reports and Web Services

Any Crystal Report created in C# can be published as an "XML Report Web Service" using Crystal Reports for Visual Studio (Fig. P.5). A Web service provides methods that are accessible over the Internet to any application, independent of programming language or platform.

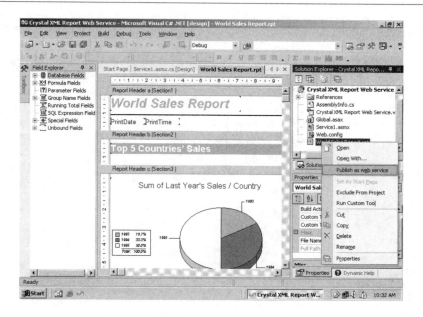

Fig. P.5 Crystal Report being published as Web service. (Courtesy Crystal Decisions - **www.crystaldecisions.com**.)

---

3. "Interactivity and Reports in Web Applications," *Crystal Reports for Visual Studio .NET.* **<www.crystaldecisions.com/netzone>**.

An XML Report Web service would be an excellent vehicle with which business partners could access specific report information. Crystal Decisions provides a walkthrough to overview the steps to familiarize the user with implementing a report as a Web service. (We discuss Web services in detail in Chapter 18, ASP .NET and Web Services.)

When a Crystal report is published as an XML Report Web service, Visual Studio .NET generates a DLL file that contains the report, and an XML file. Both files are published to a Web server so that a client can access the report. The XML-based Simple Object Access Protocol (SOAP) message passes the data to and from the Web service.

When a developer uses Visual Studio .NET to create and publish the Web service, the developer can bind the service either to a Windows or to a Web application to display the data returned from the Web service. The walkthrough details how to create and generate the Web service, bind the service to either a Windows or Web viewer and how to build the client application that will view the service.[4]

---

4. "Exposing Reports as Web Services," *Crystal Reports for Visual Studio .NET.* **<www.crystal-decisions.com/netzone>**.

Bibliography

Albahari, B., P. Drayton and B. Merrill. *C# Essentials, Second Edition*. Cambridge, MA: O'Reilly & Associates, 2002.

Anderson, R., A. Homer, R. Howard and D. Sussman. *A Preview of Active Server Pages+*. Birmingham, UK: Wrox Press, 2000.

Anderson, R., B. Francis, A. Homer, R. Howard, D. Sussman and K. Watson. *ASP .NET*. Chicago, IL: Wrox Press, Inc., 2001.

Archer, T. *Inside C#, Second Edition*. Redmond, WA: Microsoft Press, 2002.

Blaha, M. R., W. J. Premerlani and J. E. Rumbaugh. "Relational Database Design Using an Object-Oriented Methodology." *Communications of the ACM*. Vol. 31, No. 4, April 1988, 414–427.

Carr, D. F. "Dave Winer: The President of Userland and SOAP Co-Creator Surveys the Changing Scene." *Internet World*. March 2001, 53–58.

Carr, D. "Hitting a High Note." *Internet World*. March 2001, 71.

Carr, D. "Slippery SOAP." *Internet World*. March 2001, 72–74.

Chappel, D. "A Standard for Web Services: SOAP vs. ebXML." *Application Development Trends*, February 2001, 17.

Chappel, D. "Coming Soon: The Biggest Platform Ever." *Application Development Trends Magazine*, May 2001, 15.

Codd, E. F. "A Relational Model of Data for Large Shared Data Banks." *Communications of the ACM*, June 1970.

Codd, E. F. "Fatal Flaws in SQL." *Datamation*, Vol. 34, No. 16, August 15, 1988, 45–48.

Codd, E. F. "Further Normalization of the Data Base Relational Model." *Courant Computer Science Symposia*, Vol. 6, *Data Base Systems*. Upper Saddle River, N.J.: Prentice Hall, 1972.

Conard, J., P. Dengler, B. Francis, J. Glynn, B. Harvey, B. Hollis, R. Ramachandran, J. Schenken, S. Short and C. Ullman. *Introducing .NET*. Birmingham, UK: Wrox Press, 2001.

Correia, E. J. "Visual Studio .NET to Speak in Tongues." *Software Development Times*, April 2001, 12.

Appleman, D. *Moving to VB .NET: Strategies, Concepts, and Code*. Berkeley, CA: Apress Publishing, 2001.

Date, C. J. *An Introduction to Database Systems, Seventh Edition*. Reading, MA: Addison-Wesley Publishing, 2000.

Davydov, M. "The Road to the Future of Web Services." *Intelligent Enterprise*. May 2001, 50–52.

Deitel, H. M. *Operating Systems, Second Edition*. Reading, MA: Addison Wesley Publishing, 1990.

Deitel, H. M. and Deitel, P. J. *Java How To Program, Fourth Edition*. Upper Saddle River, NJ: Prentice Hall, 2001

Deitel, H. M., Deitel, P. J. and T. R. Nieto. *Visual Basic 6 How To Program*. Upper Saddle River, NJ: Prentice Hall, 1999.

Deitel, H. M., P. J. Deitel, T. R. Nieto, T. M. Lin and P. Sadhu. *XML How To Program*. Upper Saddle River, NJ: Prentice Hall, 2001

Dejong, J. "Microsoft's Clout Drives Web Services." *Software Development Times*, March 2001, 29, 31.

Dejong, J. "One-Stop Shopping: A Favored Method." *Software Development Times*, February 2001, 20.

Dejong, J. "Raising the Bar." *Software Development Times*, March 2001, 29–30.

Erlanger. L. "Dissecting .NET." *Internet World*, March 2001, 30–36.

Erlanger. L. ".NET Services." *Internet World*, March 2001, 47.

Esposito, D. "Data Grid In-Place Editing." *MSDN Magazine*, June 2001, 37–45.

Esposito, D. "Server-Side ASP .NET Data Binding: Part 2: Customizing the Data Grid Control." *MSDN Magazine*, April 2001, 33–45.

Finlay, D. "GoXML Native Database Clusters Data, Reduces Seek Time." *Software Development Times*, March 2001, 5.

Finlay, D. "New York Prepares for .NET Conference." *Software Development Times*, June 2001, 23.

Finlay, D. "UDDI Works on Classification, Taxonomy Issues." *Software Development Times*, March 2001, 3.

Fontana, J. "What You Get in .NET." *Network World*, April 2001, 75.

Galli, P. and R. Holland. ".NET Taking Shape, But Developers Still Wary." *eWeek*, June 2001, pages 9, 13.

Gillen, A. "Sun's Answer to .NET." *EntMag*, March 2001, 38.

Gillen, A. "What a Year It's Been." *EntMag*, December 2000, 54.

Gladwin, L. C. "Microsoft, eBay Strike Web Services Deal." *Computer World*, March 2001, 22.

Grimes, R. "Make COM Programming a Breeze with New Feature in Visual Studio .NET." *MSDN Magazine*, April 2001, 48–62.

Gunnerson, E. *A Programmer's Introduction to C#: Second Edition*. New York, NY: Apress, 2001.

Harvey, B., S. Robinson, J. Templeman and K. Watson. *C# Programming With the Public Beta*. Birmingham, UK: Wrox Press, 2000.

Holland, R. "Microsoft Scales Back VB Changes." *eWeek*, April 2001, 16.

Holland, R. "Tools Case Transition to .NET Platform." *eWeek*, March 2001, 21.

Hulme, G, V. "XML Specification May Ease PKI Integration." *Information Week*, December 2000, 38.

Hutchinson, J. "Can't Fit Another Byte." *Network Computing*, March 2001, 14.

Jepson, B. "Applying .NET to Web Services." *Web Techniques*, May 2001, 49–54.

Jones, B. *Sams Teach Yourself C# in 21 Days*. Indianapolis, IN: Sams Publishing, 2002.

Karney. J. ".NET Devices." *Internet World*, March 2001, 49–50.

Kiely, D. "Doing .NET In Internet Time." *Information Week*, December 2000, 137–138, 142–144, 148.

Kirtland, M. "The Programmable Web: Web Services Provides Building Blocks for the Microsoft .NET Framework." *MSDN Magazine*, September 2000 `<msdn.microsoft.com/ msdnmag/issues/0900/WebPlatform/WebPlatform.asp>`.

Levitt, J. "Plug-And-Play Redefined." *Information Week*, April 2001, 63–68.

McCright, J. S. and D. Callaghan. "Lotus Pushes Domino Services." *eWeek*, June 2001, 14.

Michaelis, M. and P. Spokas. *C# Developer's Headstart*. New York, NY: Osbourne/McGraw-Hill, 2001.

"Microsoft Chimes in with New C Sharp Programming Language." Xephon Web site. June 30, 2000 `<www.xephon.com/news/00063019.html>`.

Microsoft Corporation, *Microsoft C# Language Specifications*. Redmond, VA: Microsoft Press, 2001.

Microsoft Developer Network Documentation. Visual Studio .NET CD-ROM, 2001.

Microsoft Developer Network Library. .NET Framework SDK. Microsoft Web site `<msdn.microsoft.com/library/default.asp>`.

Moran, B. "Questions, Answers, and Tips." *SQL Server Magazine*, April 2001, 19–20.

MySQL Manual. MySQL Web site `<www.mysql.com/doc/>`.

Oracle Technology Network Documentation. Oracle Web site. `<otn.oracle.com/docs/content.html>`.

Otey, M. "Me Too .NET." *SQL Server Magazine*. April 2001, 7.

Papa, J. "Revisiting the Ad-Hoc Data Display Web Application." *MSDN Magazine*, June 2001, 27–33.

Powell, R. and R. Weeks. *C# and the .NET Framework: The C++ Perspective*. Indianapolis, IN: Sams Publishing, 2002.

Pratschner, S. "Simplifying Deployment and Solving DLL Hell with the .NET Framework." *MSDN Library*, September 2000 `<msdn.microsoft.com/library/techart/dplywithnet.htm>`.

Prosise, J. "Wicked Code." *MSDN Magazine*, April 2001, 121–127.

Relational Technology, *INGRES Overview*. Alameda, CA: Relational Technology, 1988.

Ricadela, A. "IBM Readies XML Middleware." *Information Week*, December 2000, 155.

Ricadela, A. and P. McDougall. "eBay Deal Helps Microsoft Sell .NET Strategy." *Information Week*, March 2001, 33.

Richter, J. "An Introduction to Delegates." *MSDN Magazine*, April 2001, 107–111.

Richter, J. "Delegates, Part 2." *MSDN Magazine*, June 2001, 133–139.

Rizzo, T. "Let's Talk Web Services." *Internet World*, April 2001, 4–5.

Rizzo, T. "Moving to Square One." *Internet World*, March 2001, 4–5.

Robinson, S., O. Cornes, J. Glynn, B. Harvey, C. McQueen, J. Moemeka, C. Nagel, M. Skinner and K. Watson. *Professional C#, Second Edition*. Birmingham, UK: Wrox Press, 2002.

Rollman, R. "XML Q & A." *SQL Server Magazine*, April 2001, 57–58.

Rubinstein, D. "Suit Settled, Acrimony Remains." *Software Development Times*, February 2001, 1, 8.

Rubinstein, D. "Play It Again, XML." *Software Development Times*, March 2001, 12.

Scott, G. "Adjusting to Adversity." *EntMag*, March 2001, 38.

Scott, G. "Putting on the Breaks." *EntMag*, December 2000, 54.

Sells, C. "Managed Extensions Bring .NET CLR Support to C++." *MSDN Magazine*. July 2001, 115–122.

Seltzer, L. "Standards and .NET." *Internet World*, March 2001, 75–76.

Shohoud, Y. "Tracing, Logging, and Threading Made Easy with .NET." *MSDN Magazine*, July 2001, 60–72.

Sliwa, C. "Microsoft Backs Off Changes to VB .NET." *Computer World*, April 2001, 14.

Songini, Marc. "Despite Tough Times, Novell Users Remain Upbeat." *Computer World*, March 2001, 22.

Spencer, K. "Cleaning House." *SQL Server Magazine*, April 2001, 61–62.

Spencer, K. "Windows Forms in Visual Basic .NET." *MSDN Magazine*, April 2001, 25–45.

Stonebraker, M. "Operating System Support for Database Management." *Communications of the ACM*, Vol. 24, No. 7, July 1981, 412–418.

Surveyor. J. ".NET Framework." *Internet World*, March 2001, 43–44.

Tapang, C. C. "New Definition Languages Expose Your COM Objects to SOAP Clients." *MSDN Magazine*, April 2001, 85–89.

Thai, T. and H. Q. Lam. *.NET Framework Essentials*. Cambridge, MA: O'Reilly & Associates, Inc., 2002.

Troelsen, A. *C# and the .NET Platform*. New York, NY: Apress, 2001.

Utley, C. *A Programmer's Introduction to Visual Basic .NET*. Indianapolis, IN: Sams Publishing, 2001.

Visual Studio .NET ADO .NET Overview. Microsoft Developers Network Web site `<msdn.microsoft.com/vstudio/nextgen/technology/adoplusdefault.asp>`.

Ward, K. "Microsoft Attempts to Demystify .NET." *EntMag*, December 2000, 1.

Waymire, R. "Answers from Microsoft." *SQL Server Magazine*, April 2001, 71–72.

Whitney, R. "XML for Analysis." *SQL Server Magazine*, April 2001, 63–66.

Wille, C. *Presenting C#*. Indianapolis, IN: Sams Publishing, 2000.

Winston, A. "A Distributed Database Primer." *UNIX World*, April 1988, 54–63.

Zeichick, A. "Microsoft Serious About Web Services." *Software Development Times*, March 2001, 3.

Index

Symbols

`--` (predecrement/postdecrement operator) 67, 68
`!` (logical NOT) 84, 85
`!=` (is not equal to) 53
`"` (double quotation) 45, 48
`""` 662
`#` used for internal links 1087
`#endregion` 90, 91
`#region` 90, 91
`%` (modulus operator) 52, 53
`%=` (modulus assignment operator) 67
`&` (bitwise AND) 1312, 1313, 1316
`&` (boolean logical AND) 84, 88
`&` (menu access shortcut) 360, 361
`&&` (logical AND) 84
`&=` (bitwise AND assignment operator) 1323
`&amp;` 1215
`&copy;` 1215
`&frac14;` 1268
`&lt;` 1267, 1268
(GUI) graphical user interface 317
`*` SQL wildcard character 722
`*/` (end a multiline comment) 43
`*=` (multiplication assignment operator) 67
`+` operator 53, 477
`++` (preincrement/postincrement operator) 67

`+=` (addition assignment operator) 67
`//` (single-line comment) 43
`/=` (division assignment operator) 67
`;` (empty statement) 51
`;` (statement terminator) 45
`<` (is-less-than operator) 53
`<%@Page...%>` directive 763
`<%@Register...%>` directive 824
`<<` (left-shift operator) 1312, 1313, 1314, 1320
`<<=` (left-shift assignment operator) 1324
`<=` (is-less-than-or-equal-to operator) 53
`<>` angle brackets 658
`<?` and `?>` delimiters 696
`<see>` tag 1169
`=` (assignment operator) 56, 67
`-=` (subtraction assignment operator) 67
`==` (comparison operator) 53
`==` comparison operator 468
`>` (is-greater-than operator) 53
`>=` (is-greater-than-or-equal-to operator) 53
`>>` (right-shift operator) 1312, 1313, 1320
`>>=` (right-shift assignment operator) 1324

`?` regular expression metacharacter 588
`?` SQL wildcard character 722
`?:` (ternary conditional operator) 63, 68
`[]` (brackets) 122
`\` separator character 583
`\'` escape sequence 49
`\\` escape sequence 49
`\n` escape sequence 48
`\r` escape sequence 48
`\t` escape sequence 48
`\u`*yyyy* unicode format 1187
`^` (bitwise exclusive OR) 1312, 1313, 1316, 1324
`^` (boolean logical exclusive OR) 84
`^=` (bitwise exclusive OR assignment operator) 1323
`_` (underscore) 44
`{` (left brace) 44, 45, 64
`|` (bitwise inclusive OR) 1312, 1313, 1316, 1324
`|` (boolean logical inclusive OR) 84
`|=` (bitwise inclusive OR assignment operator) 1323
`||` (logical OR) 84
`}` (right brace) 44, 45, 64
`~` (bitwise complement operator) 1312, 1313, 1316

A

A binary search tree containing 12 values 965

a element 1209, 1213, 1261, 1266

A graphical representation of a binary tree 965

A graphical representation of the **InsertAtBack** operation 954

A graphical representation of the **InsertAtFront** operation 954

A graphical representation of the **RemoveFromBack** operation 956

A graphical representation of the **RemoveFromFront** operation 955

A portion of a **Shape** class hierarchy 197

A property of structure **Color** 515

abbreviating an assignment expression 67

Abort method of class **Thread** 426

AbortRetryIgnore member of enumeration **MessageBoxButtons** 74

AboutBox method of class **AxMediaPlayer** 562

absolute positioning 772

abstract base class 239

abstract class 239, 240, 250, 251, 264

Abstract class **Employee** definition 251

abstract data type (ADT) 12, 139

abstract derived class 251

abstract method 239, 250, 251

Abstract **Shape** base class 241

abstraction 194

AcceptButton property 320

AcceptSocket method of class **TcpListener** 908

AcceptsReturn property 331

access method 142

access shared data 440

access shortcut 360

accessibility 1007, 1039, 1041, 1048, 1052, 1053, 1055

accessibility aids in Visual Studio .NET 1007, 1008

Accessibility Wizard 1041, 1044, 1048

Accessibility Wizard initialization option 1042

Accessibility Wizard mouse cursor adjustment tool 1044

AccessibilityDescription property of class **Control** 1020

AccessibilityName property of class **Control** 1020

AccessibleDescription property of class **Control** 1015

AccessibleName property of class **Control** 1015

AccessibleRole enumeration 1016

AccessibleRole property of class **Control** 1016

Accessing and displaying a database's data 735

Accessing **private** class members from client code generates syntax errors 148

accessing shared memory without synchronization 434

action 45, 182

action attribute 1037, 1284

action oriented 139

Activation property of class **ListView** 391

active 1062

Active Accessibility 1039

active form 1062

Active Server Pages (ASP) .NET 7, 15

active window 319

ActiveLinkColor property of class **LinkLabel** 369

ActiveMdiChild property of class **Form** 405

ActiveX 1192

ActiveX COM control integration in C# 1194

ActiveX control 18, 1193

ActiveX DLL 18

Acts designed to ensure Internet access for people with disabilities 1004

Ad attribute 783

Ad element 1095

Ada programming language 424

AdBanners.xml file used for **Portal2.aspx** 1095

AdCreated event 1096

add custom control to a form 421

Add member of enumeration **MenuMerge** 406

Add method 548, 691

Add method of class **ArrayList** 868, 985, 989

Add method of class **Hashtable** 893, 1000

Add method of class **MobileListItemCollection** 1083

Add method of class **TreeNodeCollection** 387

Add method of **Columns** collection 822

Add Reference dialog 50

Add Reference dialog DLL Selection 1197

Add Tab menu item 398

Add User Control... option in Visual Studio .NET 418

Add Windows Form... option in Visual Studio .NET 405

Adding a new label to the form 38

adding a proxy class for a Web service 857

Adding a reference to an assembly in Visual Studio .NET 50

adding a Web service reference to a project 857

adding **Web References** in Visual Studio 857

addition assignment operator (**+=**) 67

AddLine method of class **GraphicsPath** 541

AddressBook.cs 744

Adjusting up window element size 1043

ADO .NET 15, 711, 734, 755

AdRotator class 780, 781

AdRotator class demonstrated on a Web form 781

AdRotator control 1088

AdRotator.aspx 781

AdRotator.aspx.cs 782

AdRotatorInformation.xml 783

ADT (abstract data type) 12, 139

advanced accessibility settings in Microsoft Internet Explorer 6.0 1053

Advanced Research Projects Agency (ARPA) 2

Advantage Hiring, Inc. 1130

AdvertisementFile property 1095

AdvertisementFile
property of class **AdRota-tor** 781
AdvertisementFile used in
AdRotator example 783
advertisment 796
AfterSelect event of class
TreeView 387
Agent.cs 568
aggregation 147
airline reservation Web service
878
airline Web Service in design view
880
Alignment property 38
allocating arrays 124
allocating memory 125
Allowed implicit conversions 107
AllowPaging property 836
AllowPaging property of a
DataGrid control 836
AllowSorting property of
windows form designer 836
alphabetic icon 32
alphabetizing 468
alt attribute 17, 1007, 1211,
1264
Alt key 353, 360
Alt property 356
<alt> tag 1053
AlternateText element 1095
ALU (arithmetic and logic unit)
1312
America's Job Bank 1128
American Society for Female
Entrepreneurs 1130
American Standard Code for
Information Interchange
(ASCII) 17
ampersand (**&**) 1215
Analysis.cs 65
ancestor node 665
anchor 1208, 1213
anchor control 328
Anchor property 329
anchoring a control 328
Anchoring demonstration 328
AND 732, 733
AND boolean logical operator (**&**)
84
AND logical operator (**&&**) 84
And method of class **BitArray**
1324
angle bracket (**<>**) 658, 1203
animated character 14
animation 513

animation of a series of images
546
answer element 1038
Apache 1230
API (application programming
interface) 511
APL progamming language 7
Append method of class
StringBuilder 484, 485
Append methods of class
StringBuilder 485
AppendFormat method of class
StringBuilder 485, 487
AppendText method of class
File 583
Apple Computer, Inc. 1182
Application class 367
application programming
interface (API) 511
application service provider (ASP)
1130
Application that writes an XML
representation of a
DataSet to a file 752
application tracing 836
Application with accessibility
features 1016
Application.Exit method
367, 377
ApplicationException
class 294
Aquent.com 1133
arc angle 530
arc method 530
Arc-method demonstration 531
area element 1241, 1296
ARGB values 514
argument 45, 99, 103
argument attribute of a
devicefilter 1093,
1094, 1107
ArgumentOutOfRangeEx-ception 466, 477, 488,
989
arithmetic and logic unit (ALU)
1312
Arithmetic assignment operators
67
arithmetic calculation 52
arithmetic operator 52
arithmetic overflow 285, 286
ARPA (Advanced Research
Projects Agency) 2
ARPAnet 2, 3
ArrangeIcons value in **Lay-outMdi** enumeration 408

array 12, 98
Array class 981
array elements of primitive data
types passed call-by-value
126
array indexer (**[]**) 122
array is an object 123
array of a nonprimitive data type
124
array of arrays 132
array of primitive data types 124
array subscript operator, **[]** 989
ArrayList class 548, 868, 869,
981, 984, 989
ArrayListTest.cs 985
ArrayReferenceTest.cs
127
arrays are C# objects 138
arrays as object 126
arrays passed call-by-reference
126
article.xml 657
article.xml displayed by
Internet Explorer 660
ASC (ascending order) 700, 723,
725
ascent 524
ASCII (American Standard Code
for Information Interchange)
1182
ASCII character, test for 356
ASCX code for the header 824
ASCX file 824
ASMX file 845
ASMX file rendered in Internet
Explorer 845
ASMX page 847
ASP (Active Server Pages) .NET 7
ASP .NET comment 763
ASP .NET server controls 758
ASP.NET Web service project
type 855
ASP.NET_SessionId cookie
805
ASPX file 758, 1060, 1107
.aspx file extension 758
ASPX file for the guest book
application 816
ASPX file that allows a user to
select an author from a drop-down list 830
ASPX file that presents a list of
programming languages 798
ASPX file that takes ticket
information 880

ASPX listing for the guest book page 816
ASPX page for mobile Craps program 1075
ASPX page that allows a mobile device to access a Web service 1102
ASPX page that displays book information 803
ASPX page that displays the Web server's time 762
ASPX page with tracing turned off 837
assembly 49, 187
Assembly attribute 1061
Assembly **TimeLibrary** contains class **Time3** 184
Assembly **TimeLibrary** used from class **AssemblyTest** 188
<assign> tag 1032
assign element 1038
assign value to a variable 56
Assigning derived-class references to base-class references 234
assignment operator (**=**) 54, 56, 67
assignment statement 56
associate left to right 58, 68
associate right to left 52, 58, 68
associativity of operators 52, 68, 122
asterisk (*****) 719, 1299
asterisk (*****) indicating multiplication 52
asterisk (*****) occurence indicator 684
asterisk character in XSLT 699
asynchronous event 286
ATTLIST 685
attribute 89, 661, 1209
attribute of an element 1255
audio clip 424
audio-video interleave (AVI) 559
Aural Style Sheet 1055
AuralCSS 1040
authorISBN table of **books** database 712, 713, 714
authorization 830
Authors table of **books** database 712
Authors.aspx 830
Authors.aspx.cs 832
auto-hide 31
AutoEventWireup attribute of ASP.NET page 763

auto-hide 31
auto-hide, disable 31
automatic garbage collection 425
Autos window 1148
AutoScroll property 337
AVI (audio-video interleave) 559
AxAgent control 568, 575
AxMediaPlayer class 561

B

B property of structure **Color** 516
B2B 844
BackColor property 37, 327
background color 37
BackgroundImage property 327
backslash (****) 48
Ballmer, Steve 10
bandwidth 3, 544
594
base 2 number system 1312
base case(s) 117
base class 89, 193, 194, 196
base-class constructor 198
base-class constructor call syntax 215
base-class default constructor 198
Base class for GUIs in our file-processing applications 594
base-class method is overridden in a derived class 216
base-class **Private** member 197
base-class reference 235, 236
baseline 1281
behavior 89, 138
Berkeley System Distribution (BSD) 9
Berners-Lee, Tim 3
BilingualJobs.com 1130
binary digit 579
binary number system 1312
binary operator 52, 56, 85
binary representation 1312, 1314
binary search tree 965, 971, 972
binary tree 942, 965, 972
binary tree sort 972
BinaryFormatter class 582, 604
BinaryReader class 629, 917
BinarySearch method of class **Array** 983
BinarySearch method of class **ArrayList** 990
BinaryTreeLibrary.cs 966, 974

BinaryWriter class 917
Bind method of class **Socket** 907
binding a server to a port 907
bit (size of unit) 579, 1182, 1312
bit manipulation 579, 1312
bit mask 1314
bit representation of an integer 1314
bit set 1324
BitArray class 981, 1312, 1324, 1326
BitArray indexer 1324
BitArrayTest.cs 1324
Bitmap class 540
BitOperations.cs 1317
bits-and-bytes level 1312
BitShift.cs 1321
bitwise AND (**&**) 1312, 1313, 1316
bitwise AND assignment operator (**&=**) 1323
bitwise assignment operator 1323
bitwise complement operator (**~**) 1312, 1313, 1316
bitwise exclusive OR (**^**) 1312, 1313, 1316, 1324
bitwise exclusive OR assignment operator (**^=**) 1323
bitwise inclusive OR (**|**) 1312, 1313, 1316, 1324
bitwise inclusive OR assignment operator (**|=**) 1323
bitwise operators 343, 1312, 1313, 1314, 1323
BizTalk 15, 662
BizTalk Framework 703
BizTalk markup using an offer Schema 703
BizTalk Schema Library 703
BizTalk Server (BTS) 703
BizTalk Terminologies 703
biztalkmarkup.xml 703
Black static property of structure **Color** 515
Blackjack 865
Blackjack game that uses **Blackjack** Web service 869
Blackjack Web service 865
Blackjack.cs 869
BlackjackService.asmx.cs 865
Blackvoices.com 1129
block 64, 105, 908
block element 1032, 1037
block for input/output 428

block scope 114, 147
blocked state 427
Blue static property of
  structure **Color** 515
Bluetooth 1132
body 44
body element 824, 1206, 1255,
  1256
body of a class definition 44, 141
body of the **if** structure 53
body of the method definition 45
body of the **while** structure 64
body section 1255
Bold member of enumeration
  FontStyle 523
Bold property of class **Font** 522
book.xdr 689
book.xml 688, 690
book.xsd 690
books database 712
books database table
  relationships 718
bookxdrfail.xml 694
bookxsd.xml 690
bookxsdfail.xml 694
bool primitive data type 63, 106
bool promotions 107
bool values 87
boolean decision 1324
boolean flag 1324
boolean logical AND operator (**&**)
  84
boolean logical exclusive OR
  operator (**^**) 84
boolean logical inclusive OR
  operator (**|**) 84
border = "0" 1225
border attribute 1225, 1278
Boss class inherits from class
  Employee 252
bottom tier 761
BounceKeys 1046
boundary of control 417
bounding rectangle 528, 530
bounding rectangle for an oval 530
br (line break) element 1214,
  1267
braces (**{** and **}**) 64, 70, 81, 104
braces not required in **case**s 79
brackets (**[]**) 122
braille display 1007, 1040
braille keyboard 1039
Brassringcampus.com 1135
Break All button 1149
break program 1149
break statement 11, 77, 81

<break> tag 1032
BreakAfter property 1074
breakpoint 1144
breakpoint condition 1151
breakpoint hit count 1151
breakpoint, active 1150
breakpoint, disabled 1150
breakpoint, set 1145
Breakpoints window 1150
BreakTest.cs 81
brick-and-mortar store 796
Browser property 1097
browser request 1230, 1281
Brush class 511, 516, 527
BSD (Berkeley System
  Distribution) 9
BTS (BizTalk Server) 703
Bubble sort using delegates 273
Bubble-sort **Form** application 274
BubbleSortForm.cs 274
buffer 434
buffer empty 434
BufferedStream class 582
buffering 14
Build menu 27, 42
Build Solution option 42
building-block approach 6
built-in array capabilities 981
built-in data type 55, 182
Business letter DTD 684
business logic 762
business rule 762
business-to-business (B2B) 844
button 24, 50, 51, 318
Button class 330
button label 330
Button properties and events
  332
Buttons for message dialogs 73
byte 580, 1312
byte offset 617
byte primitive data type 106,
  1312
byte promotions 107

C
C formatting character 76
C programming language 1204,
  1253
C-style comment 43
C# keywords 62
C# Language Specification 295
C# primitive data types 106
C# program for examination-
  results problem 65

C# programming language 7, 9,
  662
C#'s view of a file of *n* bytes 582
C#'s view of an *n*-byte file 582
C++ programming language 1204
C++-style single-line comment 43
cache 734
Calculating compound interest
  with **for** 72
Calculating factorials with a
  recursive method 118
call element 1038
Call Stack 303, 1153
call-by-reference 126
call-by-value 126
called method 99
caller 99
callerID attribute 1038
calling method 99
CallXML 17, 1033
callxml element 1033, 1038
CallXML example that reads three
  ISBN values 1035
CallXML **hangup** element 1033
CampusCareerCenter.com
  1135
CancelButton property 320
Candidate Recommendation 4
capacity of a collection 984
Capacity property of class **Ar-
  rayList** 984
Capacity property of class
  ArrayList 990
Capacity property of class
  StringBuilder 482
caption element 1024, 1278
Card class 494
Card dealing and shuffling
  simulation 495
card games 494
Card.cs 494
Career.com 1128
CareerPath.com 1128
CareerWeb 1128
carriage return 48
carry bit 1120
Cascade value in **LayoutMdi**
  enumeration 408
Cascading Style Sheets (CSS) 4,
  17
case-sensitive language 44, 1203
case statement 76, 79
CAST eReader 1021
cast operation 235
cast operator 74, 108
catch all exception types 288

catch block (or handler) 288,
    292, 296
categorized icon 32
CCircle5 class inherits from
    class **CPoint3** and
    overrides a finalizer method
    224
CDATA flag 685
Center for Applied Special
    Technology 1021, 1056
Centering the text in the label 39
CERN (the European
    Organization for Nuclear
    Research) 3
CGI (Common Gateway
    Interface) 1230
CGI script 1230, 1284
changes in server-side data 1230
Changing a property in the code-
    view editor 93
Changing a property value at
    execution time 95
Changing property **BackColor**
    37
Char array 466
char primitive data type 106
char promotions 107
Char structure 463, 491
Char.IsDigit method 491
Char.IsLetter method 491
Char.IsLetterOrDigit
    method 491
Char.IsLower method 493
Char.IsPunctuation
    method 493
Char.IsSymbol method 493
Char.IsUpper method 493
Char.IsWhiteSpace method
    493
Char.ToLower method 493
Char.ToUpper method 493
Char's **static** character-
    testing methods and case-
    conversion methods 491
character 580, 1183
character class 499
Character classes 499
character constant 463
character entity reference 18
character set 580, 1182
character string 45
Characters property of class
    AxAgent 574
CharMethods.cs 491
checkbox 318, 330, 340, 1231,
    1285

CheckBox class 340
checkbox label 340
CheckBox properties and events
    340
CheckBoxes property of class
    ListView 391
CheckBoxes property of class
    TreeView 386
CheckBoxTest.cs 341
checked attribute 1234, 1288
Checked constant 340
checked context 312
checked operator 312
Checked property 340, 344
Checked property of class
    MenuItem 362
Checked property of class
    TreeNode 387
CheckedChanged event 341,
    344
CheckedIndices property of
    class **CheckedListBox**
    378
CheckedItems property of
    class **CheckedListBox**
    378
CheckedListBox and a
    ListBox used in a program
    to display a user selection
    379
CheckedListBox and **List-
    Box** used in a program to
    display a user selection 379
CheckedListBox class 359,
    372, 377
CheckedListBox properties,
    methods and events 378
CheckedListBoxTest.cs
    379
CheckState property 340
CheckStateChanged event
    341
Chemical Markup Language
    (CML) 15
Chess-game code 551
ChessGame.cs 551
ChiefMonster™ 1134
Child class for MDI
    demonstration 412
child element 659, 661, 965
child node 385, 665
child window minimized 406
Child.cs 412
choice element of **form** tag
    1031

choice element of **menu** tag
    1031
<Choice> tag 1092, 1095, 1107
<choice> tag 1032
cHTML (compact HyperText
    Markup Language) 1059,
    1060
cHTML content 1059
circle 1272
Circle class contains an *x-y*
    coordinate and a radius 201
Circle class marked up with
    XML comments 1164
Circle class that inherits from
    class **Point** 232
Circle2 class that inherits from
    class **Point** 205
Circle2 class that inherits from
    class **Point2** 244
Circle3 class that inherits from
    class **Point2** 209
Circle3 class that inherits from
    class **Point3** 268
Circle3.cs 268
Circle4 class that inherits from
    class **Point3** but does not
    use **protected** data 214
Circle5 class inherits from
    class **Point3** and overrides
    a finalizer method 224
CircleTest class marked up
    with XML comments 1167
CircleTest demonstrates class
    Circle functionality 204
CircleTest3 demonstrates
    class **Circle3**
    functionality 210
CircleTest4 demonstrates
    class **Circle4**
    functionality 216
circular buffer 449, 460
circular hotspot 1243, 1297
CircularBuffer.cs 450
CityWeather.cs 887
class 5, 12, 44, 139
Class **Control** layout properties
    329
Class **Control** properties and
    methods 327
class definition 44, 55, 141, 1169
Class **FrmInheritance**, which
    inherits from class **Form**,
    contains a button (**Learn
    More**) 413

Class **FrmVisualTest**, which inherits from class **VisualForm.FrmInheritance**, contains an additional button 415

class hierarchy 230, 239

class keyword 44, 89

class library 6, 194

class name 44

class scope 114, 147

class-scope variable hidden by method-scope variable 147

class that stores equation information 895

class that stores weather information about a city 887

Class View (Visual Studio .NET) 189

Classes that derive from class **Brush** 516

classes to implement abstract data types 182

classwide information 168

clear element 1038

Clear method of class **Array** 984

Clear method of class **ArrayList** 985

Clear method of class **MobileListItemCollection** 1083

Clear method of class **TreeNodeCollection** 387

Clear method of **DataSet** 744

Clear method of **Hashtable** 1000

clearDigits element 1038, 1039

click a button 330

Click event 1062

Click event of class **MenuItem** 361, 363

Clicker 4 1051

clicking the mouse 24

client 181

client interacting with server and Web server. Step 2: The HTTP response, **HTTP/1.0 200 OK** 760

Client portion of a client/server stream-socket connection 913

client tier 762

Client.cs 889, 913, 931

client/server chat 910

ClipRectangle property of class **PaintEventArgs** 416, 417

clock 418

ClockUserControl.cs 418

close a file 610

Close button icon 42

Close method of class **Form** 320

Close method of class **Socket** 908, 918

Close method of class **StreamReader** 610

Close method of class **TcpClient** 909, 910

closed polygon 534

CloseFigure method of class **GraphicsPath** 541

closing a project 27

CLR (Common Language Runtime) 9

CLS (Common Language Specification) 9

CML (Chemical Markup Language) 15

CNN.com 796

COBOL (COmmon Business Oriented Language) 8, 1253

Code generated by the IDE for **lblWelcome** 91

code reuse 981

code value 1183

code-behind file 758, 824, 1060, 1107

Code-behind file for a mobile application that displays a welcome message 1062

Code-behind file for a page that displays the Web server's time 764

Code-behind file for a page that updates the time every minute 764

Code-behind file for craps application 1077

Code-behind file for mobile Web application that access a Web Service 1103

Code-behind file for page demonstrating the **AdRotator** class 782

Code-behind file for the guest book application 818

Code-behind file for the log in page for authors application 825

Code-behind file for the page that allows a user to choose an author 832

code-behind file for the reservation page 881

Code-behind file for the word generator page 788

code-behind file for **WebForm1.aspx** generated by Visual Studio .NET 773, 1068

code-behind file in Web services 845

Code-behind file that writes cookies to the client 800

coercion of arguments 106

col element 1228, 1279

colgroup element 1227, 1228, 1279

Collapse method of class **TreeNode** 387

collapse node 385

collapsed code 89

collapsing a tree 30

Collect method of **GC** 172, 227

collection 981

collection class 981

Collegegrads.com 1135

collision detection 548

color constant 515

color manipulation 513

Color methods and properties 515

Color property of class **ColorDialog** 519

Color structure 512, 514

Color structure members 515

Color structure **static** constants and their RGB values 515

ColorDialog class 519

ColorDialog used to change background and text color 519

cols attribute 1233, 1246, 1284, 1299

colspan attribute 1228, 1279

column 711, 712, 1223

column heading 1225

column number 720

Columns collection 822

COM (Component Object Model) 18, 1191, 1193

COM component 18, 1192

COM limitation 1192

combo box 50, 51

ComboBox class 318, 359, 380
ComboBox demonstration 381
ComboBox properties and events 381
ComboBox used to draw a selected shape 382
ComboBoxTest.cs 382
comma-separated list of arguments 56, 70, 99, 104
command-and-control system 424
Command control 1061
command prompt 23
command window 23
Commands property of interface 575
comment (**//**) 43, 1205, 1254
Comment constant of enumeration **XmlNode-Type** 667
comments in HTML 1205
commercial application 579
CommissionWorker class inherits from class **Employee** 253
Common Form properties and events 320
Common Gateway Interface (CGI) 1230, 1282
Common Language Runtime (CLR) 9, 295, 309
Common Language Specification (CLS) 9
Common Programming Error 6
Common Runtime Library proxy 1193
compact HyperText Markup Language (cHTML) 1059, 1060
compare attribute of a **devicefilter** 1093, 1094, 1107
CompareTo method of **IComparable** 974
CompareTo method of structure **Char** 494
compilation error 1143
compile, debug setting 1145
Compiler error messages generated from overloaded methods 122
compiler optimization 249
compiling 942
complex curve 541
complex number class 277
complex type 691
ComplexNumber.cs 277

complexType element 691
component 319
Component Object Model (COM) 18, 1191, 1193
Component Pascal progamming language 8
Components and controls for Windows Forms 319
composition 147, 161, 194, 196
comprehensive job sites 1123
Concat method of class **String** 477
Concat static method 478
concatenation of **string**s 56
concrete class 239
concurrency 424
concurrent producer and consumer threads 440
concurrent programming 424
concurrent threads 440
condition 53
condition variable 447
conditional AND 85
conditional expression 63, 143
conditional operator (**?:**) 63, 68, 84
conditional OR operator 85
conference element 1039
Confusing the equality operator **==** with the assignment operator **=** 54
Connect method of class **TcpListener** 909
connect to a database 735
connected lines 534
connection 907
connection attempt 909
connection between client and server terminates 910
Connection property of **Ole-DbCommand** 742
connection to a server 909, 937
connectionless service 907
connectionless transmission with datagrams 919, 939
connection-oriented, streams-based transmission 919, 939
consistent state 146, 154
console application 23
Console class 45, 582
console window 23, 439, 448
Console windows with tabs and without tabs 1014
Console.ReadLine method 56

Console.WriteLine method 45
const and **readonly** class member demonstration 174
const keyword 12, 125, 126, 173
const variable 79
constant 79, 173
constant integral value 76
constant variable 125, 126
constituent controls 417
constrained version of a linked list 956
constructor 142, 149, 227, 1169
consume method 434
consumer 448
consumer thread 434
consuming a Web service 849
contact.html 1209, 1214, 1262, 1267
container 318, 320
Container class for chess pieces 549
container elements 659
Contains method of class **ArrayList** 985, 990
Contains method of class **Stack** 994
ContainsKey method of **Hashtable** 1000
content attribute of **meta** element 689, 764, 1297
context-sensitive help 34
continue statement in a **for** structure 11, 81, 82, 83
ContinueTest.cs 83
control 11, 25, 30, 317, 319
control boundary 417
Control class 326, 417
control layout 28
control layout and properties 326
Control property 356
control structure 62
control variable 69, 70
controlling expression 76
control-structure nesting 62
control-structure stacking 62
ControlToValidate attribute 1071
ControlToValidate property of class **RegularExpressionValidator** 788
converge on a base case 117
Convert class of namespace **System** 106

Converting a binary number to
    decimal 1117
Converting a hexadecimal number
    to decimal 1118
Converting an octal number to
    decimal 1117
cookie 796, 797, 798, 805
    deletion 797
    domain 806
    expiration 797
    expiration date 797
    Expires property 797
    header 797
CookieContainer class 868,
    869
Cookies being read from a client in
    an ASP .NET application
    804
Cookies getting created in an ASP
    .NET Web application 800
Cookies property of **Request**
    class 805
Cookies recieved in an ASP .NET
    Web application 804
Cooljobs.com 1136
coordinate system 512, 513
coordinates (0, 0) 512
coords element 1243, 1296
Copy method of class **Array** 981
Copy method of class **File** 583
copy of an argument 110
CopyTo method of class **String**
    466
CORDA Technologies 1007
corporate culture 1126, 1129
count attribute if **prompt**
    element 1031
Count property of class
    ArrayList 990
Count property of **Hashtable**
    1000
counter-controlled repetition 69
counter variable 77
Counter-controlled repetition with
    the **for** structure 69
Counts property of **HttpSes-**
    sionState class 812, 815
Create and write to a sequential-
    access file 599
Create method of class **File**
    583
create new classes from existing
    class definitions 141
Create New Web dialog 1065
CreateDirectory method of
    class **Directory** 584

CreateInstance method of
    class **Array** 984
CreateRandomAccess-
    File.cs 621
CreateSequentialAc-
    cessFile.cs 599
CreateText method of class
    File 583
creating a child form to be added
    to an MDI form 405
Creating a **Mobile Web Appli-**
    cation in Visual Studio
    .NET 1065
Creating a new Windows
    application 35
Creating a **Panel** with scrollbars
    338
Creating an ASP .NET Web
    Application in Visual Studio
    769
creating comment Web pages
    1170
creating data types 182
Creating files for random-access
    file-processing applications
    621
Credit-inquiry program 610
CreditInquiry.cs 610
Crystal Decisions 1328
Crystal Reports 19, 1328
Crystal Reports Designer 1331
CSS (Cascading Style Sheets) 4,
    17, 1025
CSS2 1025
Ctrl key 353
Current property of
    IEnumerator 990
current time 418
CurrentPageIndex property
    836
CurrentPageIndex property
    of a **DataGrid** control 836
CurrentThread static
    Thread property 428
CurrentValue event of class
    CheckedListBox 379
Curriculum progamming language
    8
cursor 45
curve 541
Custom 420
custom control 416, 417
Custom control added to a **Form**
    421
Custom control added to the **Tool-**
    Box 420

Custom control creation 417, 420
customization 797
customize an application 30
Customize Toolbox 1193
Customize Toolbox dialog
    selecting an ActiveX control
    1193
Customize Toolbox... option in
    Visual Studio .NET 419
customize Visual Studio .NET 25,
    28
customizing the **Toolbox** 559
CustomValidator class 824,
    829
Cyan static property of
    structure **Color** 515
cylinder 245
Cylinder class inherits from
    class **Circle4** and
    overrides method **Area** 218
Cylinder2 class inherits from
    class **Circle2** 245
Cylinder3 class inherits class
    Circle3 270
Cylinder3.cs 270

D

D formatting character 76
DarkBlue static property of
    structure **Color** 523
DarkGray static property of
    structure **Color** 515
Dash member of enumeration
    DashStyle 541
DashCap enumeration 541
DashCap property of class **Pen**
    541
DashStyle enumeration 541
DashStyle property of class
    Pen 541
data abstraction 182
data entry 50
data hiding 142
data hierarchy 580, 581
data in support of actions 182
data independence 4
data manipulation 543
data member 139, 149
Data menu 28
data representation of an abstract
    data type 182
data structure 16, 98, 142, 942
data tier 761
database 710, 1203, 1253

Database information input into a
     DataGrid 832
database management system
     (DBMS) 581, 710
database table 711
datagram 919
DataGrid class 735, 742
DataGrid control 822, 836
DataSet class 734, 752
DataSource property of a **Da-
     taGrid** control 822
DataTable class 822
data-type attribute 699
date and time 418
Date class encapsulates day,
     month and year information
     162
DateTime structure 418
DBCS (double byte character set)
     1184
DBMS (database management
     system) 581
DB2 710
Dead thread state 426
deadlock 433, 434
debug configuration setting 1145
Debug menu 27, 1146
Debug sample program 1144
Debug toolbar 1149
DebugClass.cs 1156
DebugExample.cs 1144
debugger 1144
debugging 836, 1143, 1205, 1254
Debugging methods 1153
debugging, begin 1146
debugging, call stack 1153
debugging, step into 1154
debugging, step out 1154
debugging, step over 1149
decendant node 665
decimal digit 580
decimal primitive data type 73,
     106
decimal promotions 107
decision symbol 53
DeckOfCards.cs 495
declaration 55, 64, 104
declaration space of a class 114
declaring arrays 124
decrement expression 70
decrement operator (**--**) 67, 68
default constructor 149, 198
default font 523
default namespace 664, 665
Default namespaces
     demonstration 664

default package 145
default properties 91
default setting 1048
default sorting order is ascending
     723
default statement 76
defaultnamespace.xml 664
Definitions of **TreeNode** and
     Tree for a binary search
     tree 966
degree 530
deitel:BooksType 691
deitel@deitel.com xli
Deitel™ Buzz Online e-mail
     newsletter 21
del element 1268
delegate 272
Delegate class 273
delegate reference 325
delegate, create new 326
DELETE FROM 719, 733
Delete method of class
     Directory 584
Delete method of class **File**
     583
DELETE statement 733
DeleteCommand property of
     OleDbAdapter 742
DeleteDialog.cs 652
deletion 945
delimit 658
Demomstrating the **ArrayList**
     class 985
Demonstrating keyboard events
     355
Demonstrating **List**s and **Link**s
     1083
Demonstrating order in which
     constructors and destructors
     are called 226
demonstrating **ref** and **out**
     parameters 110, 298
Demonstrating the bitwise AND,
     bitwise inclusive OR,
     bitwise exclusive OR and
     bitwise complement
     operators 1317
Demonstrating the linked list 951
Demonstrating the logical
     operators 86
Demonstrating window auto-hide
     31
Demonstrating XML namespaces
     662

Demonstration of methods that
     draw lines, rectangles and
     ellipses 528
dequeue operation of queue 183,
     961
derived class 89, 193, 194, 196
DESC 723, 724
Description column 1170
Description property of a
     WebMethod attribute 855
Description property of a
     WebService attribute 854
deselected state 343
Deserialize method of class
     BinaryFormatter 604
design mode 41, 42, 1066
Design mode of Mobile Web
     Form designer 1067
Design mode of the Mobile Web
     Form designer 1066
Design mode of Web Form
     designer 771
design units 522
design view of a Web service 856
destructor 168
destructor method 168
Details of **Click** event 325
Device-Specific Rendering 1088,
     1107
<DeviceSpecific> tag 1092,
     1094, 1107
diacritic 1183
dialog 25, 47, 51
Dice.com 1132
direct-access files 616
direct base class 193
directive in ASP .NET page 763
Directory class 350
Directory class methods
     (partial list) 584
DirectoryInfo class 397, 583
DISCO (Discovery file) 858,
     1269, 1272
.disco file extension 859
disconnected 734
discovery (DISCO) files 858,
     1269, 1272
disk I/O completion 286
disk space 944
dismiss (hide) a dialog 51
Display Color Settings 1043
Display member of
     enumeration
     GraphicsUnit 522
display output 47
Display Settings 1041

displaying a line of text 45
displaying a phrase 43
Displaying multiple lines in a
    dialog 48
Displaying the bit representation
    of an integer 1314
DisplayLogoForm.cs 544
DisplayQueryResults.cs
    742
distributed computing 844
diversity 1130
divide-and-conquer approach 11,
    98
divide by zero 292
DivideByZeroException
    class 292
DivideByZeroTest.cs 289
division assignment operator (**/=**)
    67
division by zero is undefined 182
D-link 1007
DLL (dynamic link library) 12,
    1191, 1193, 1197, 1198
.dll file 1197
"DLL hell" 1191
DNS (domain name server) 759
DNS lookup 759
do/while repetition structure 11,
    62, 80
dock control 328
Dock property 329
docking a control 328
docking demonstration 329
DockPadding property 329
Document member of
    enumeration **Graphic-**
    sUnit 522
Document Object Model (DOM)
    665
document type 763, 1204
Document Type Definition (DTD)
    683, 684, 686
Dogfriendly.com 1136
DOM (Document Object Model)
    665
DOM parser 665
DOM structure of an XML
    document illustrated by a
    class 669
domain name server (DNS) 759
Domain property of **Http-**
    Cookie class 806
dot (**.**) operator 50, 147, 169, 197
double 73
double-byte character set (DBCS)
    1184

Double class 310
double-clicking 24
double primitive data type 106
double promotions 107
double quotes (**""**) 45, 48, 662
double-selection structure 62
double-subscripted array 131
Double-subscripted array with
    three rows and four columns
    131
DoWhileLoop.cs 80
down arrow 28, 37
drag 32
drag and drop 321
draw on control 417
draw shapes 511
DrawArc method of class
    Graphics 531
DrawArcs.cs 531
DrawEllipse method of class
    Graphics 385, 528
drawing a line 527
drawing a rectangle 527
drawing an oval 527
DrawLine method of class
    Graphics 528, 534
DrawPie method of class
    Graphics 385, 531
DrawPolygon method of class
    Graphics 534
DrawPolygons.cs 534
DrawRectangle method of
    class **Graphics** 385, 527,
    528
DrawShapes.cs 538
DrawStarsForm.cs 541
DrawString method of class
    Graphics 519, 523
drop-down list 318, 380
DropDown style for **ComboBox**
    382
DropDownList class 824
DropDownList style for
    ComboBox 382
DropDownStyle property of
    class **ComboBox** 381, 382
DTD (Document Type Definition)
    683, 686
.dtd file extension 686
DTD for a business letter 684
DTD repository 689
duplicate elimination 973
duplicate of datagram 919
dynamic data structures 942
dynamic help 33
Dynamic Help window 33

dynamic link library (**.dll**) 49
dynamic link library (DLL) 12,
    184, 187, 1191, 1193, 1197,
    1198
dynamic memory allocation 944,
    945

E

E formatting character 76
e-mail (electronic mail) 2
EagleEyes 1040
EBNF (Extended Backus-Naur
    Form) grammar 684
echo a packet back to a client 919
ECMA (European Computer
    Manufacturer's Association)
    9
ECMAScript 786
Edit menu 27
Edit menu in Internet Explorer 50
editable list 382
efficient (Unicode design basis)
    1182
Eiffel progamming language 8
eights position 1113
eLance.com 1133
electronic devices with two stable
    states 579
ELEMENT 684
element 122, 658, 691, 1203
Element constant of
    enumeration **XmlNode-**
    Type 666
element type declaration 684
ElementType 689
eliminate resource leak 296
Ellipse bounded by a rectangle
    530
eltOnly attribute 689
emacs text editor 1204, 1253
Emacspeak 1007
e-mail (electronic mail) 2, 908,
    1263
e-mail anchor 1210, 1263
embedded parentheses 52
employee 237
Employee class encapsulates
    employee name, birthday
    and hire date 163
EmployeesTest class tests the
    Employee class hierarchy
    259
empty **case** 79
empty element 662, 1265, 1267
EMPTY keyword 685

empty statement (**;**) 57, 81
Enabled property 327
Enabled property of a **trace**
    element 837
EnabledViewState attribute
    763
EnableSession property of a
    WebMethod attribute 867
EnableSessionState
    attribute 763
encapsulate 138
encapsulation 249
encoding 1181
encoding declaration 1033
encoding scheme 18
encrypt 829
end-of-file marker 581
end of session message 1034,
    1037
end tag 658, 1255
EndElement constant of
    enumeration **XmlNode-**
    Type 667
#endregion 90, 91
EndsWith method of class
    String 471
Enlarged icons in the development
    window 1009
Enlarging icons using the **Cus-**
    tomize feature 1009
enqueue operation of queue 183,
    961
EnsureCapacity method of
    class **StringBuilder**
    482
Enter method of class **Monitor**
    432, 440, 447, 448, 459
entity
    & 685
    < 685
entity reference 685, 1267
entry point 146
entry point of a program 44, 47
entry point of control structure 62
entry-level position 1123
enumeration 340
<enumerate> tag 1032
enumerator 990
environment variable 1230
Equality and relational operators
    53
"equals equals" (the **==** operator)
    54
Equals method of class **String**
    468
Equation.cs 895

Error 74
error handling 56
error-processing code 287
Error property of class **Con-**
    sole 581
ErrorMessage property 787
    in a Web Form 829
escape character 732
escape sequence **\n** 48
European Computer
    Manufacturer's Association
    (ECMA) 9
Event 323
event 13, 100, 321
event argument 323
event driven 321
event-driven process 514
event-driven programming xl
event handler 100, 1037
event handler, create 323
event handler, documentation 323
event handler, register 325
event handler, remove 326
Event-handling model using
    delegates 321
event handling model 321
event icon 32
event multicasting 326
events at an interval 418
Events section of the **Properties**
    window 322
Events window in Visual
    Studio.NET 322
eWork® Exchange 1133
Examples
    A binary search tree
        containing 12 values 965
    A graphical representation of a
        binary tree 965
    A graphical representation of
        the **InsertAtBack**
        operation 954
    A graphical representation of
        the **InsertAtFront**
        operation 954
    A graphical representation of
        the **RemoveFromBack**
        operation 956
    A graphical representation of
        the **RemoveFromFront**
        operation 955
    A picture with links anchored
        to an image map 1241
    A portion of a **Shape** class
        hierarchy 197

Abstract class **Employee**
    definition 251
Abstract **Shape** base class
    241
Accessing and displaying a
    database's data 735
Accessing **private** class
    members from client code
    generates syntax errors 148
ActiveX COM control
    integration in C# 1194
Acts designed to ensure
    Internet access for people
    with disabilities 1004
AdBanners.xml file used
    for **Portal2.aspx** 1095
Add Reference dialog 50
Adding a new label to the form
    38
AddressBook.cs 744
AdRotator class
    demonstrated on a Web form
    781
AdRotator.aspx 781
AdRotator.aspx.cs 782
AdRotatorInforma-
    tion.xml 783
AdvertisementFile used
    in **AdRotator** example 783
Agent.cs 568
Airline Reservation Web
    service 878
An illustration of font metrics
    525
Analysis.cs 65
Anchoring demonstration 328
Animation of a series of
    images 546
Append methods of class
    StringBuilder 485
Application that writes an
    XML representation of a
    DataSet to a file 752
Application with accessibility
    features 1016
Arc-method demonstration
    531
ArrayListTest.cs 985
ArrayReference-
    Test.cs 127
Article.xml displayed by
    Internet Explorer 660
ASCX code for the header 824
ASPX file for the guest book
    application 816

ASPX file that allows a user to select an author from a drop-down list 830

ASPX file that presents a list of programming languages 798

ASPX file that takes ticket information 880

ASPX listing for the guest book page 816

ASPX page for mobile Craps program 1075

ASPX page that allows a mobile device to access a Web service 1102

ASPX page that displays book information 803

ASPX page that displays the Web server's time 762

ASPX page with tracing turned off 837

Assembly **TimeLibrary** used from class **AssemblyTest** 188

Authors table of **books** database 712

Authors.aspx 830

Authors.aspx.cs 832

BankUI.cs 594

Base class for GUIs in our file-processing applications 594

Binary search tree 972

BinaryTreeLibrary.cs 966, 974

BitArrayTest.cs 1324

BitOperations.cs 1317

BitShift.cs 1321

BizTalk markup using an offer Schema 703

BizTalk terminologies 703

biztalkmarkup.xml 703

Blackjack game that uses **Blackjack** Web service 869

Blackjack Web service 865

Blackjack.cs 869

BlackjackService.asmx.cs 865

book.xsd 690

bookxdrfail.xml 694

bookxsd.xml 690

bookxsdfail.xml 694

Boss class inherits from class **Employee** 252

break statement in a **for** structure 81

BreakTest.cs 81

Bubble sort using delegates 273

Bubble-sort **Form** application 274

BubbleSortForm.cs 274

Business letter DTD 684

Button properties and events 332

Buttons for message dialogs 73

C# program for examination-results problem 65

C#'s view of an n-byte file 582

Calculating compound interest with **for** 72

Calculating factorials with a recursive method 118

CallXML elements 1038

CallXML example that reads three ISBN values 1035

Card class 494

Card dealing and shuffling simulation 495

Card.cs 494

Centering the text in the label 39

Changing a property in the code-view editor 93

Char's **static** character-testing methods and case-conversion methods 491

Character classes 499

CharMethods.cs 491

CheckBox properties and events 340

CheckBoxTest.cs 341

CheckedListBox and **ListBox** used in a program to display a user selection 379

CheckedListBox properties, methods and events 378

CheckedListBox-Test.cs 379

Chess-game code 551

ChessGame.cs 551

ChessPiece.cs 549

Child class for MDI demonstration 412

Child.cs 412

Circle class contains an x-y coordinate and a radius 201

Circle class marked up with XML comments 1164

Circle class that inherits from class **Point** 232

Circle2 class that inherits from class **Point** 205

Circle2 class that inherits from class **Point2** 244

Circle3 class that inherits from class **Point2** 209

Circle3 class that inherits from class **Point3** 268

Circle3.cs 268

Circle4 class that inherits from class **Point3** but does not use **protected** data 214

Circle5 class inherits from class **Point4** and overrides a finalizer method 224

CircleTest class marked up with XML comments 1167

CircleTest demonstrates class **Circle** functionality 204

CircleTest3 demonstrates class **Circle3** functionality 210

CircleTest4 demonstrates class **Circle4** functionality 216

CircularBuffer.cs 450

CityWeather.cs 887

Class **Control** layout properties 329

Class **Control** properties and methods 327

Class **FrmInheritance**, which inherits from class **Form**, contains a button (**Learn More**) 413

Class **FrmVisualTest**, which inherits from class **VisualForm.FrmInheritance**, contains an additional button 415

Class that stores equation information 895

Class that stores weather information about a city 887

Classes that derive from class **Brush** 516

Client portion of a client/server stream-socket connection 913

Client.cs 889, 913, 931

ClockUserControl.cs
418
Code generated by the IDE for
lblWelcome 91
Code-behind file for a mobile
application that displays a
welcome message 1062
Code-behind file for a page
that displays the Web
server's time 764
Code-behind file for craps
application 1077
Code-behind file for mobile
Web application that access a
Web Service 1103
Code-behind file for page
demonstrating the **AdRotator** class 782
Code-behind file for the guest
book application 818
Code-behind file for the log in
page for authors application
825
Code-behind file for the page
that allows a user to choose
an author 832
Code-behind file for the
reservation page 881
Code-behind file for the word
generator page 788
code-behind file for
WebForm1.aspx
generated by Visual Studio
.NET 1068
Code-behind file that writes
cookies to the client 800
Color 515
Color structure members 515
ColorDialog used to
change background and text
color 519
COM DLL component in C#
1198
ComboBox demonstration
381
ComboBox properties and
events 381
ComboBox used to draw a
selected shape 382
ComboBoxTest.cs 382
CommissionWorker class
inherits from class
Employee 253
Common Form properties and
events 320
Complex XHTML table 1279

ComplexNumber.cs 277
Components and controls for
Windows Forms 319
Concat static method
478
Console windows with tabs
and without tabs 1014
const and **readonly** class
member demonstration 174
contact.html 1209, 1214,
1262, 1267
Container class for chess
pieces 549
continue statement in a
for structure 11, 81, 82, 83
ContinueTest.cs 83
Cookies being created in an
ASP .NET Web application
800
Cookies being read from a
client in an ASP .NET
application 804
Cookies recieved in an ASP
.NET Web application 804
Counter-controlled repetition
with the **for** structure 69
Create and write to a
sequential-access file 599
**CreateRandomAccess-
File.cs** 621
**CreateSequentialAc-
cessFile.cs** 599
Creating a **Mobile Web Ap-
plication** in Visual Studio
.NET 1065
Creating a new Windows
application 35
Creating a **Panel** with
scrollbars 338
Creating files for random-
access file-processing
applications 621
Credit-inquiry program 610
CreditInquiry.cs 610
Custom control added to a
Form 421
Custom control added to the
ToolBox 420
Custom control creation 417
Custom-control creation 420
Cylinder class inherits
from class **Circle4** and
overrides method **Area** 218
Cylinder2 class inherits
from class **Circle2** 245

Cylinder3 class inherits
class **Circle3** 270
Cylinder3.cs 270
Data hierarchy 581
Database information input
into a DataGrid 832
Date class encapsulates day,
month and year information
162
Debug sample program 1144
DebugClass.cs 1156
DebugExample.cs 1144
Debugging methods 1153
DeckOfCards.cs 495
Default namespaces
demonstration 664
DeleteDialog.cs 652
DeleteDialogForm class
enables users to remove
records from files in
transaction-processor case
study 652
Demonstrating keyboard
events 355
Demonstrating **List**s and
Links 1083
Demonstrating order in which
constructors and destructors
are called 226
Demonstrating **ref** and **out**
parameters 110, 298
Demonstrating that **finally**
blocks always execute 298
Demonstrating the bitwise
AND, bitwise inclusive OR,
bitwise exclusive OR and
bitwise complement
operators 1317
Demonstrating the linked list
951
Demonstrating the logical
operators 86
Demonstrating window auto-
hide 31
Demonstrating XML
namespaces 662
Demonstration of methods that
draw lines, rectangles and
ellipses 528
Design mode of the Mobile
Web Form designer 1066
Details of **Click** event 325
Directory class methods
(partial list) 584
Displaying multiple lines in a
dialog 48

Displaying the bit representation of an integer 1314
DisplayLogoForm.cs 544
DisplayQueryRe-sults.cs 742
DivideByZeroTest.cs 289
do/while repetition structure 80
docking demonstration 329
DOM structure of an XML document illustrated by a class 669
DoWhileLoop.cs 80
DrawArcs.cs 531
DrawPolygons.cs 534
DrawShapes.cs 538
DrawStarsForm.cs 541
DTD for a business letter 684
Dynamic Help window 33
Ellipse bounded by a rectangle 530
Employee class encapsulates employee name, birthday and hire date 163
EmployeesTest class tests the **Employee** class hierarchy 259
Enlarged icons in the development window 1009
Enlarging icons using the **Customize** feature 1009
Equality and relational operators 53
Equation.cs 895
Event-handling model using delegates 321
Events section of the **Properties** window 322
Exception handlers for **FormatException** and **DivideByZeroException** 289
Exception properties and demonstrating stack unwinding 304
Execute SQL statements on a database 742
Execution of the **Welcome1** program 47
Expanded and checked menus 360
File class methods (partial list) 583

FileSearch.cs 588
FileTest.cs 584
First program in C# 43
Font class read-only properties 522
Font window 39
FontFamily class used to obtain font-metric information 525
FontFamily methods that return font-metric information 525
Fonts and **FontStyle**s 523
ForCounter.cs 69
Form including radio buttons and drop-down lists 1288
Form including textareas, password boxes and checkboxes 1231
Form with sizing handles 36, 37
form.html 1282
form2.html 1285
form3.html 1288
Framed Web site with a nested frameset 1248, 1303
GDI+ coordinate system. Units are measured in pixels 513
Generator.asmx.cs 897
Generator.aspx 786
Generator.aspx.cs 788
Generator.html 793
GetHashCode method demonstration 472
Graphical representation of a linked list 945
Graphics methods for drawing arcs 531
Graphics methods for drawing polygons 534
Graphics methods that draw lines, rectangles and ovals 528
GroupBox properties 337
GroupBoxPanelExample.cs 338
Handling a divide-by-zero exception 289
HashtableTest.cs 996
Header elements **h1** through **h6** 1207, 1259
header.html 1207, 1259
hello.xml 1033
Home page written in VoiceXML 1026

HourlyWorker class inherits from class **Employee** 257
HTML and ECMAScript sent to the client browser 793
HTML documentation of class **Circle** 1171
HTML documentation of method **Area** method of class **Circle** 1172
HTML mode of Mobile Web Form designer 1067
HTML/XHTML extended colors and hexadecimal RGB values 1309
HTML/XHTML special characters 1307
HTML/XHTML standard colors and hexadecimal RGB values 1308
HugeInteger Web service 849
HugeInteger.asmx.cs 849
Icons for message dialogs 74
IDE in run mode, with the running application in the foreground 42
IDE showing program code for a simple program 89
Image Collection Editor window for an **ImageList** component 392
Image resizing 544
Image with links anchored to an image map 1295
ImageHeader.ascx 824
Important methods of class **HttpCookie** 806
index.html 1299
index2.html 1303
Indexers provide subscripted access to an object's members 176
Inheritance examples 195, 196
Inheritance hierarchy for university **CommunityMembers** 196
Initializing arrays in three different ways 124
Initializing multidimensional arrays 133
Inserting and aligning the picture box 40
Inserting special characters into HTML 1214

Inserting special characters
into XHTML 1267
Interfaces2Test.cs
271
InterfacesTest.cs 264
isbn.xml 1035
IShape interface provides
methods **Area** and **Volume**
and property **Name** 266
Keyboard events, delegates
and event arguments 354
KeyDemo.cs 355
Label in position with its
Text property set 38
Label properties 331
**LabelTextBoxButton-
Test.cs** 332
letter.xml 660
letter2.xml 685
**LinesRectanglesOv-
als.cs** 528
LinkedListLibrary.cs
947
Linking to an e-mail address
1262, 1209
Linking to other Web pages
1208, 1260
LinkLabel properties and
events 369
LinkLabels used to link to a
folder, a Web page and an
application 370
LinkLabelTest.cs 370
links.html 1208, 1216,
1260, 1292
List of **Form** events 324
list.html 1217, 1270
ListBox and
CheckedListBox on a
form 373
ListBox on an ASPX page
803
ListBox properties, methods
and events 373
ListBox used in a program
to add, remove and clear
items 375
ListBoxTest.cs 375
Listing for **namespace.xml**
662
ListTest.cs 951
ListView displaying files
and folders 393
ListView properties and
events 391
ListViewTest.cs 393

Log in Web Form 822
Login.aspx 822
Login.aspx.cs 825
LogoAnimator.cs 546
main.html 1205, 1254,
1297
main.vxml 1026
MainMenu and **MenuItem**
properties and events 362
Manipulating the **Anchor**
property of a control 329
Math tutor application 900
MDI parent and MDI child
events and properties 405
MDI parent window and MDI
child windows 404
MDI parent-window class 409
MdiLayout enumeration
values 408
MediaPlayerTest.cs
559
MenuItem property **MdiL-
ist** example 407
Menus used for changing text
font and color 363
MenuTest.cs 363
**MethodDebugExam-
ple.cs** 1153
Microsoft Agent
demonstration 568
Microsoft Schema file that
contains structure to which
bookxdr.xml conforms.
689
Minimized and maximized
child windows 406
Miscellaneous **String**
methods **Replace**,
ToLower, **ToUpper**, **Trim**
and **ToString** 479
Modifying a database 744
Mouse events, delegates and
event arguments 351
Multiple forms in a mobile
Web Form page 1060
nav.html 1212, 1265, 1301
**NegativeNumberExcep-
tion.cs** 309
Nested and ordered lists in
HTML 1217
Nested and ordered lists in
XHTML 1270
New Project dialog 26
New **Text** property value
reflected in design mode 94
NewDialog.cs 649

NewDialogForm class
enables users to create
records in transaction-
processor case study 649
News article formatted with
XML 657
Numeric formatting characters
76
Object debugging example
1156
Operators **checked** and **un-
checked**, and handling
arithmetic overflow 313
OptionPage.aspx.cs
800
Options supplied on an ASPX
page 798, 806
OptionsPage.aspx 798,
806
OptionsPage.aspx.cs
808
Overflow.cs 313
Overloaded constructor
demonstration 152
Overloaded constructors
provide flexible object-
initialization options 150
Painter.cs 352
Panel properties 337
Passing an array reference by
value and by reference 127
PathNavigator.cs 676
Paths used to draw stars on a
form 541
Peedy calculating the total 568
Peedy flying animation 565
Peedy introducing himself
when the window opens 563
Peedy recounting the order
567
Peedy repeating the user's
request for anchovies as an
additional topping 567
Peedy repeating the user's
request for Seattle-style pizza
566
Peedy waiting for speech input
566
Peedy's reaction when he is
clicked 564
Person class implements
IAge interface 262
Picture with links anchored to
an image map 1241
picture.html 1210, 1263,
1295

PictureBox properties and events 349

PictureBoxTest.cs 349

PieceWorker class inherits from class **Employee** 255

Placing images in HTML files 1210

Placing images in XHTML files 1263

Point class represents an *x-y* coordinate pair 198, 231

Point marked up with XML comments 1162

Point2 class inherits from abstract class **Shape** 242

Point2 class represents an *x-y* coordinate pair as **protected** data 207

Point2 class represents an *x-y* coordinate pair as **protected** data 207

Point3 class implements interface **IShape** 267

Point3 class uses properties to manipulate its **private** data 212

Point3.cs 267

Point4 base class contains constructors and finalizer 222

PointTest class demonstrates class **Point** functionality 200

Polygon-drawing demonstration 534

Positive and negative arc angles 531

Precedence and associativity chart 87

Precedence of arithmetic operators 53

PrintBits.cs 1314

Producer and consumer threads accessing a circular buffer 450

Producer and consumer threads accessing a shared object with synchronization 440

Producer and consumer threads accessing a shared object with syncronization 440

Producer and consumer threads accessing a shared object without synchronization 435

Producer and consumer threads accessing a shared object without syncronization 435

Program that demonstrates class **Array** 982

Program to display hidden text in a password box 332

Programmer-defined control that displays the current time 418

Project properties dialog 420

Properties demonstration for class **Time3** 158

Properties of class **Control** related to accessibility 1015

Properties window 32, 39

Properties.cs 304

Publication page of Deitel and Associates' VoiceXML page 1028

publications.vxml 1028

Quantifiers used regular expressions 502

QueueInheritanceLibrary.cs 962

QueueTest.cs 963

RadioButton properties and events 344

RadioButtonsTest.cs 344

Random-access file with fixed-length records 617

RandomAccessRecord.cs 617

Reading records from random-access files sequentially 629

Reading sequential-access files 606

ReadRandomAccessFile.cs 629

ReadSequentialAccessFile.cs 606

Receiving temperature and weather data from a Web service 889

RecommendationsPage.aspx 803, 812

RecommendationsPage.aspx.cs 804

Record for random-access file-processing applications 617

Record for sequential-access file-processing applications 596

Record.cs 596

Record-transaction class for the transaction-processor case study 634

Regex methods **Replace** and **Split** 507

Regex methods **Replace** and **Split** 507

RegexMatches.cs 499

RegexSubstitution.cs 507

Regular expression used to determine file types 588

Regular expressions checking birthdays 499

Relational-database structure of an **Employee** table 711

Removing tabs from Visual Studio environment 1013

Reservation.asmx.cs 878

Sample data for the program of Fig. 17.9 605

Sample Internet Explorer window with GUI components 318

Saving a document to a file 1171

Schema-validation example 692

Scoping example 115

SDI and MDI forms 404

Searching for characters and substrings in **String**s 473

section of **machine.config** file 1075

Selecting the **Build Comment Web Pages** from **Tools** menu 1170

Self-referential class objects linked together 944

Server portion of a client/server stream-socket connection 910

Server side of client/server Tic-Tac-Toe program 925

Server.cs 910, 919

Server-side portion of connectionless client/server computing 919

Session data read by an ASP .NET Web application to provide recommendations for the user 813

Session information displayed in a **ListBox** 812

Sessions are created for each user in an ASP .NET Web application 808

Sessions created for each user in an ASP .NET Web application 808

Setting the form's **Text** property 36

Setting the project location 35

Shapes drawn on a form 538

ShowColors.cs 516

Sieve of Eratosthenes 1324

Simple Class Library 188

Simple event-handling example using visual programming 323

Simple form with hidden fields and a text box 1282

Simple program as it executes 34

SimpleEventExample.cs 323

SOAP Request for the **HugeInteger** Web service 848

Solution Explorer window 29

Some basic GUI components 318

Some common escape sequences 48

Some methods of class **ArrayList** 985

sorting.xsl 697

sports.xml 682

SQL query keywords 719

SquareRootTest.cs 310

StackComposition class encapsulates functionality of class **List** 960

StackCompositionLibrary.cs 960

StackInheritance extends class **Lis** 957

StackInheritanceLibrary.cs 957

StackInheritanceTest.cs 958

StackTest.cs 991

Start Page in Visual Studio .NET 24

StartDialog.cs 639

StartDialogForm class enables users to access dialog boxes associated with various transactions 639

StartsWith and **EndsWith** methods 471

static member demonstration 171

static members are accessible to all objects of a clas 170

Static method **Concat** 478

String constructors 465

String indexer, **Length** properties and **CopyTo** method 466

String methods **Replace**, **ToLower**, **ToUpper** and **Trim** 479

String methods **Replace**, **ToLower**, **ToUpper**, **Trim** and **ToString** 479

String test to determine equality 469

StringBuilder class constructors 481

StringBuilder size manipulation 483

StringBuilder text insertion and removal 488

StringBuilder text replacement 489

StringBuilder's **AppendFormat** method 486

StringBuilderAppend.cs 485

StringBuilderAppendFormat.cs 486

StringBuilderConstructor.cs 481

StringBuilderFeatures.cs 483

StringBuilderInsertRemove.cs 488

StringBuilderReplace.cs 489

StringCompare.cs 469

StringConstructor.cs 465

StringHashCode.cs 472

StringIndexMethods.cs 473

StringMethods.cs 466

StringMiscellaneous2.cs 479

StringStartEnd.cs 471

Stylesheets and templates in a Mobile Web Form 1088

SubConcatenation.cs 478

SubString.cs 476

Substrings generated from **String**s 476

SwitchTest.cs 77

Synchronized.cs 440

Syntax error generated from overloaded methods 122

System.Drawing namespace's classes and structures 512

Tabbed pages in Visual Studio .NET 398

TabControl properties and events 399

TabControl used to display various font settings 400

TabControl with **TabPages** example 399

Table optimized for screen reading using attribute **headers** 1022

table1.html 1276

table2.html 1279

TableDisplay.cs 735

TabPages added to a **TabControl** 399

TemperatureServer Web service 884

TemperatureServer.asmx.cs 884

Test2 demonstrates polymorphism in Point-Circle-Cylinder hierarchy 247

Test3 uses interfaces to demonstrate polymorphism in Point-Circle-Cylinder hierarchy 271

Testing class **Cylinder** 220

TextBox properties and events 331

TextToSpeech.cs 1016

The result of changing a property value at execution time 95

this reference demonstration 167

this reference used implicitly and explicitly to enable an object to manipulate its own data and invoke its own methods 166

Thread life cycle 426

Thread-priority scheduling 429

thread-priority scheduling 429

Threads sleeping and printing 429

ThreadTester.cs 429

TicketReservation.aspx 880

TicketReservation.aspx.cs 881

Time1 abstract data type represents the time in 24-hour format 140

Time1.cs 140

TipCalculator.aspx 1071

Toolbox window 30

Tool-tip demonstration 28

Transaction.cs 634

TransactionProcessor.cs 638

TransactionProcessorForm class runs the transaction-processor application 638

TransformTest.cs 700

Tree structure for Fig. 18.1 665

Tree.cs 263

TreeNode Editor 388

TreeNode properties and methods 387

TreeTest.java 970

TreeTestLibrary.cs 978

TreeView displaying a sample tree 386

TreeView properties and events 386

TreeView used to display directories 388

TreeViewDirectoryStructureTest.cs 388

Tutor.cs 900

Unordered lists in HTML 1216

Unordered lists in XHTML 1269

Unsynchronized.cs 435

UpdateDialog.cs 644

User-defined exception classes 310

Using **<meta>** and **<DOCTYPE>** 1243

Using a default namespace 664

Using a **PictureBox** to display images 349

Using an abstract data type 144

Using **CheckBox**es to change font styles 341

Using class **StackInheritance** 958

Using **GroupBox**es and **Panel**s to arrange **Button**s 338

Using images as link anchors 1212, 1265

Using inheritance to create a queue 963

Using internal hyperlinks to make your pages more navigable 1238, 1292

Using **meta** to provide keywords and a description 1297

Using operator overloading 280

Using overloaded methods 120

Using **RadioButton**s to set message-window options 344

Using the **foreach** structure with an array 135

Using the **HugeInteger** Web service 859

Using the mouse to draw on a form 352

Using the **Properties** window to set a property value 92

Using the **Stack** class 991

UsingArray.cs 982

UsingExceptions.cs 298

UsingFontMetrics.cs 525

UsingFonts.cs 523

UsingForeach.cs 135

UsingHugeIntegerService.cs 859

UsingMDI.cs 409

UsingTabs.cs 400

Validate.cs 502

Validating user information using regular expressions 502

ValidationTest.cs 692

Validators used in a Web Form that generates possible letter combinations from a phone number 786

Viewing the tracing information for a project 838

Visual Inheritance through the Form Designer 415

Visual Studio .NET creating and linking a virtual directory for the **Welcome** project folder 1065

Visual Studio .NET environment after a new project has been created 26

Visual Studio .NET menu bar 27

Visual Studio .NET menu bar summary 27

Visual Studio .NET **Menu Designer** 361

VisualInheritance.cs 413

VisualInheritanceTest.cs 415

VoiceXML tags 1032

Web controls demonstration 776

Web Form with embedded C# code 1071

Web service that generates random equations 897

Web site using two frames: navigational and content 1245, 1299

Web.config file used for **Portal2.aspx** 1093

WebControls.aspx 776

WebTime.aspx 762

WebTime.aspx.cs 764

WebTime.html 767

Welcome.aspx 816, 1060

Welcome.aspx after adding two **Label**s and setting their properties 1070

Welcome.aspx.cs 818, 1062

Welcome1.cs 43

Welcome4.cs 48

Windows Form Designer generated code expanded 90

Windows Form Designer generated code reflecting new property values 92

Windows Media Player demonstration 559

withheaders.html 1022

withoutheaders.html 1021

**WriteRandomAccess-
File.cs** 624

Writing records to random-
access files 624

XHTML document displayed
in the left frame of Fig. 5.9
1301

XHTML table 1276

XHTML table without
accessibility modifications
1021

XML document containing
book information 696

XML document referencing its
associated DTD 685

XML document that conforms
to W3C XML Schema 690

XML document that describes
various sports 682

XML document that does not
conform to XSD schema 694

XML documentation
generated by Visual Studio
.NET 1172

XML file containing **AdRotator** information 783

XML file that does not
conform to the Schema in
Fig. 18.17 694

XML namespaces
demonstration 662

XML to mark up a business
letter 660

XML used to mark up an
article 657

XML Validator displaying an
error message 688

XML Validator used to
validate an XML document
687

XmlDom.cs 669

XmlNodeReader used to
iterate through an XML
document 666

XmlReaderTest.cs 666

XMLWriter.cs 752

XPath expressions and
descriptions 683

XPathNavigator class
used to navigate selected
nodes 676

XSD Schema document to
which **bookxsd.xml**
conforms 690

XSL document that transforms
sorting.xml into
XHTML. 697

XSL style sheet applied to an
XML document 700

exception 13, 285

Exception class 288, 294, 297,
303

exception handler 285, 288, 292,
294

Exception handlers for **FormatException** and **Di-
videByZeroException**
289

Exception library class 13

Exception properties and
demonstrating stack
unwinding 304

exception thrown within a
SyncBlock 459

Exclamation 74

.exe extension 49

Execute SQL statements on a
database 742

ExecuteNonQuery method of
OleDbCommand 752

Execution of the **Welcome1**
program 47

execution stack 956

exhausting memory 119

Exists method of class
Directory 584

Exit method of class
Application 367, 377

Exit method of class **Environment** 918

Exit method of class **Monitor**
432, 440, 448, 449, 459

exit point of control structure 62

<exit> tag 1032

Expand method of class **TreeN-
ode** 387

expand node 385

expand tree 30

ExpandAll method of class
TreeNode 387

Expanded and checked menus 360

expanded code 90

Experience.com 1135

Expires property of a cookie
797

Expires property of **Http-
Cookie** class 806

explicit conversion 73, 106

explicit relationships between data
659

exponentiation operator 74

expose a method 855

exposing a Web service method
844

expression 1147

Extended Backus-Naur Form
(EBNF) grammar 684, 688

extensibility 4

Extensible HyperText Markup
Language (XHTML) 4, 15,
18, 1253

extensible language 144

Extensible Markup Language
(XML) 4, 10, 845

Extensible Stylesheet Language
(XSL) 662, 695

Extensible Stylesheet Language
Transformation (XSLT) 15

external DTD 686

external help 34

external link 1087

Extra Keyboard Help 1047

F

F formatting character 76

F1 help key 34

factorial 117

fall through 79

falsity 53

fault-tolerant program 285

favorites 1170, 1178

FCL (Framework Class Library)
5, 9, 10, 99, 183

field 139, 580, 711, 712

FIFO (first-in, first-out) 182

file 580

file as a collection of bytes 580

File class methods (partial list)
583

File menu 27, 50

file-position 610

file-position pointer 610

file processing 579

file synchronization 8

FileAccess enumeration 604

FileName property of class
AxMediaPlayer 561

file-processing programs 582

files 579

FileSearch.cs 588

FileStream class 582, 603, 609

FileTest.cs 584

Fill method of class **Graphics**
543

Fill method of
    OleDbAdapter 742
<filled> tag 1032
FillEllipse method of class
    Graphics 385, 528
FillPie method of class
    Graphics 385, 531
FillPolygon method of class
    Graphics 534
FillRectangle method of class
    Graphics 385, 519, 527,
    528
filter 33
Filter property 1092, 1096,
    1107
Finalize method 222
finalizer 168
finally block 288, 296
find 27
firewall 848
First program in C# 43
first-in, first-out (FIFO) data
    structure 182, 183, 961
FirstNode property of class
    TreeNode 387
five-pointed star 541
fixed-length records 616
FlipDog.com 1124
float 73
float primitive data type 106,
    109
float promotions 107
FlowLayout 772
Focus method 319, 327
Focused property 327
font 512, 522
Font class 512, 523
Font class read-only properties
    522
font control 522
font descent 524
font height 524
font leading 524
font manipulation 513
font metrics 524, 525
font name 523
Font property 38, 327, 342
font size 38, 523
font style 38, 341, 523
Font window 38, 39
FontFamily class 512, 525
FontFamily class used to
    obtain font-metric
    information 525

FontFamily methods that
    return font-metric
    information 525
FontFamily property of class
    Font 522
Fonts and **FontStyle**s 523
FontStyle enumeration 523
FooterTemplate 1094
for repetition structure 11, 62,
    69, 70, 71, 74
for structure header 70
ForCounter.cs 69
foreach repetition structure 62
foreach structure 12
ForeColor property 327
foreign key 718
form 27, 318, 1223, 1228, 1276,
    1281
Form array 792
form background color 37
Form class 89, 320
Form Close method 320
Form control 1094
form element 1031, 1032, 1230,
    1282
Form including textareas,
    password boxes and
    checkboxes 1231
form input 1238
Form properties and events 320
Form property **IsMdiCon-
    tainer** 404
form title bar 36
Form with sizing handles 36
format attribute 1039
Format menu 28
Format method of **String** 143
format specifications 143
format specifier 75
format string 143, 487
FormatException class 291,
    292
formatting character 75
forms 830
forms authentication 829
FormsAuthentication class
    829
Fortran (FORmula TRANslator)
    progamming language 8,
    1253
forward slash (**/**) 658, 1265
ForwardDiagonal member of
    enumeration **LinearGra-
    dientMode** 540
frame 1024, 1245, 1298
frame element 1247, 1301

Framed Web site with a nested
    frameset 1248, 1303
frameset document type 1298
frameset element 1246, 1247
Framework Class Library (FCL)
    5, 9, 10, 99, 183
Freedom Scientific 1038
FROM 719, 723, 724, 725, 727
FromArgb method of structure
    Color 515
FromImage method of class
    Graphics 540
FromName method 515
FullName property 397
FullPath property of class
    TreeNode 387
fully qualified name 727
function 44
Futurestep.com 1130

G

G formatting character 76
G property of structure **Color** 516
gallery.yahoo.com 1263
garbage collection 167, 425
garbage collector 167, 222, 466
garbage-collector thread 425
GC class 172
GDI+ (Graphics Device
    Interface+) 14, 511
GDI+ coordinate system 513
general path 541
Generator.asmx.cs 897
Generator.aspx 786
Generator.aspx.cs 788
Generator.html 793
Genie Microsoft Agent character
    562
get accessor 148, 154, 155, 157,
    158
Get method of class **BitArray**
    1326
get request type 1038, 1283
Get Started section of Visual
    Studio .NET 24
GetCellAscent method of
    class **FontFamily** 525
GetCellDescent method of
    class **FontFamily** 525
GetCreationTime method of
    class **Directory** 584
GetCreationTime method of
    class **File** 583
GetCurrentDirectory
    method 350

getDigits element 1037
GetDirectories method of class **Directory** 390, 584
GetDirectories method of class **DirectoryInfo** 397
GetEmHeight method of class **FontFamily** 525
GetEnumerator method of **ArrayList** 990
GetEnumerator method of **Hashtable** 1000
GetFiles method of class **Directory** 584
GetFiles method of class **DirectoryInfo** 397
GetHashCode method demonstration 472
GetHashCode method of class **Object** 996
GetHashCode of class **String** 472
GetItemChecked method of class **CheckedListBox** 378
GetLastAccessTime method of class **Directory** 584
GetLastAccessTime method of class **File** 583
GetLastWriteTime method of class **Directory** 584
GetLastWriteTime method of class **File** 583
GetLineSpacing method of class **FontFamily** 525
GetNodeCount method of class **TreeNode** 387
GetSelected method of class **ListBox** 374
GetStream method of class **Socket** 909
GetXml method of **DataSet** 752
global scope 114
global variable 169, 1034
Globally Unique Identifier (GUID) 1196
glyph 1183
Goldfarb, Charles 707
Good Programming Practice 6
goto statement 1038
<goto> tag 1032
<grammar> tag 1032
Graphical representation of a linked list 945

graphical user interface (GUI) 13, 27, 49, 317
Graphics class 382, 511, 513, 523, 527, 540, 541, 543
graphics context 513
Graphics Device Interface+ (GDI+) 14, 511
Graphics Interchange Format (GIF) 1263
Graphics methods for drawing arcs 531
Graphics methods for drawing polygons 534
Graphics methods that draw lines, rectangles and ovals 528
Graphics property of class **PaintEventArgs** 417
GraphicsPath class 541
GraphicsUnit structure 522
Gray static property of structure **Color** 515
"grayed-out" 327
greedy quantifier 501
Green static property of structure **Color** 515
GridLayout 772
GridLayout and **FlowLayout** illustration 774
GROUP BY 719
group of related fields 580
GroupBox 337
GroupBox Controls property 337
GroupBox properties 337
GroupBox properties and events 337
GroupBoxPanelExample.cs 338
guest book 815
Guest-book application GUI 816
GUI (graphical user interface) 13, 27, 49
GUI component 49, 317, 318
GUI event handling 155
GUID (Globally Unique Identifier) 1196
Gunning Fog Index 1008, 1056

H

h1 header element 1207, 1208, 1258
h6 header element 1207, 1258
handle event 322
handling errors 56

"has-a" relationship 194
HasCapability method of class **MobileCapabilities** 1094
hash code 472
hash table 472
Hashtable class 893, 981, 995
HashtableTest.cs 996
Haskell progamming language 8
HatchBrush class 516, 537
HatchStyle enumeration 516
head 942, 1255
head element 763, 1206, 1255
head of a queue 961
head section 1255
header 1207, 1258
header cell 1225, 1278
header element 1258
header.html 1207, 1259
headers attribute 1022, 1024
headers element 17
HeaderTemplate 1094
Headhunter.net 1131
height attribute 1211, 1263, 1264
Height property of class **Font** 522
Hejlsberg, Anders 9
Hello World CallXML example 1033
Help menu 28, 33
help, context-sensitive 34
help, dynamic 33
help, external 34
help, internal 34
helper method 142, 972
Henter-Joyce 1038, 1056
hex code 1215
hexadecimal value 1268
hidden
　element 796
　field 796
hidden input elements 1230
hide an internal data representation 183
Hide method of class **Form** 320, 327
hiding implementation 99, 147, 181
hierarchy 659
hierarchy diagram 195
hierarchy of shapes 237
high-order bit 1314
Highest ThreadPriority enumeration member 427
Hire.com 1130

HireAbility.com 1132
Hirediversity.com 1129
hit count 1151
Hoare, C. A. R. 432
home page 1204
Home Page Reader (HPR) 1008
Home page written in VoiceXML 1026
horizontal coordinate 512
horizontal rule 18, 1269
horizontal tab 48
host 759
hostname 759
hot key 360
HotDispatch.com 1132
HotJobs.com 1127, 1131
hotspot 1241, 1295
hotwired.lycos.com/ webmonkey/00/50/ index2a.html 1274
HourlyWorker class inherits from class **Employee** 257
HPR (Home Page Reader) 1008
hr element 1216, 1269
href attribute 1209, 1213, 1241, 1261, 1294
.htm (html file extension) 1204
.html (html file name extension) 1204
.html (XHTML file name extension) 1253
HTML (HyperText Markup Language) 3, 15, 758, 759, 1060, 1203, 1253
   form 797, 815
   HTML element 824
HTML and ECMAScript sent to the client browser 793
HTML comment 1205
HTML control 775
HTML device 1059, 1107
HTML document 18
HTML documentation of class **Circle** 1171
HTML documentation of method **Area** method of class **Circle** 1172
html element 763, 1255
HTML frame 18
HTML-Kit 1204
HTML list 18
HTML mode of Mobile Web Form designer 1067
HTML mode of Web Form designer 772
HTML recommendation 1204

HTML source code 1204
HTML table 18
HTML tag 759, 1203
HTML/XHTML extended colors and hexadecimal RGB values 1309
HTML/XHTML special characters 1307
HTML/XHTML standard colors and hexadecimal RGB values 1308
HTTP (HyperText Transfer Protocol) 759, 1038
HTTP being used with firewalls 848
HTTP GET request 846
HTTP header 761
HTTP method 760
HTTP POST request 846
HTTP transaction 760
http://www.w3.org/ 2001/XMLSchema URI 691
HttpBrowserCapabilities class 1097
HttpCookie class 803, 805, 806
   Domain property 806
   Expires property 806
   Name property 805, 806
   Path property 806
   Secure property 806
   Value property 805, 806
HttpCookie properties 806
HttpCookieCollection 805
HttpRequest class 1097
HttpSession class 812
   SessionID property 812
HttpSessionState class 806, 808, 811, 812, 815
   Counts property 812, 815
   IsNewSession property 812
   IsReadOnly property 812
   Keys property 812, 815
   SessionID property 812
   Timeout property 812
HttpSessionState properties 812
HugeInteger Web service 849
HugeInteger.asmx.cs 849
hyperlink 759, 1208, 1213, 1260
HyperText Markup Language (HTML) 3, 15, 758, 759, 1060, 1253
HyperText Transfer Protocol (HTTP) 759

I
I/O completion 428
IAgentCtlCharacter interface 568, 574, 575
IAgentCtlUserInput interface 576
IBM Corporation 1182
IComparable interface 973, 974
IComponent interface 319
icon 28
Icons for message dialogs 74
id attribute of a mobile control 1061
IDE (integrated development environment) 9, 11, 13, 23
IDE in run mode, with the running application in the foreground 42
IDE showing program code for a simple program 89
IDE's toolbox and **LabelScrollbar** properties 1194
identifier 44
IDictionaryEnumerator interface 1000
IE (Internet Explorer) 25, 317, 370, 659, 1253, 1264
IEEE 754 floating-point 106
IEnumerator interface 990, 1000
if selection structure 53, 56, 61, 63
<if> tag (**<if>…</if>**) 1032
if/else selection structure 11, 61, 63
IIS (Internet Information Services) 759
image anchor 1238
Image Collection Editor 391
Image Collection Editor window for an **ImageList** component 392
Image control 1077
image hyperlink 1213, 1266
image map 18, 1241, 1243, 1296
Image property 40, 349
ImageHeader.ascx 824
ImageIndex property of class **ListViewItem** 391
ImageIndex property of class **TreeNode** 387
ImageKey attribute 1096
ImageList class 391

ImageList collection 386
ImageList property of class
 TabControl 399
ImageList property of class
 TreeView 386
images in Web pages 1210, 1263
ImageUrl attribute 783
ImageUrl element 1095, 1096
img element 17, 1007, 1213,
 1243, 1263, 1264, 1266
Immediate window 1149
immutable **String** 466
iMode device 1059, 1107
implement an interface 266
implementation 139, 147
implementation-dependent code
 147
implementation of a class hidden
 from its clients 146
implicit conversion 73, 106
implicitly **sealed** method 249
#IMPLIED flag 685
Important methods of class **HttpCookie** 806
Impressions attribute 783
Impressions element 1095,
 1096
In property of class **Console**
 581
Inch member of enumeration
 GraphicsUnit 522
Inclusive Technology 1051
incoming device 1060
Increment and decrement
 operators 68
increment and decrement
 operators 68
increment expression 70, 82
incrementation of a **for** structure
 71
indefinite postponement 428
indentation techniques 45
Indenting each level of a nested
 list in code 1219
Indeterminate constant 340
Index event of class
 CheckedListBox 379
Index property of class **Menu-
Item** 362
index.html 1204
indexer 466
indexer for class **Hashtable**
 893
indexer property 175

Indexers provide subscripted
 access to an object's
 members 176
IndexOf method of class **Array**
 984
IndexOf method of class
 ArrayList 985, 990
IndexOf method of class
 String 473, 476
IndexOfAny method of class
 String 473
**IndexOutOfRangeExcep-
tion** class 294
indirect base class 195
infinite loop 70, 119, 924
infinite recursion 119
infinity symbol 718
Information 74
information hiding 138, 139, 181,
 249
information parameter 658
information tier 761
Informix 710
inherit from class **Control** 417
inherit from Windows Form
 control 417
inherit interface 239
inheritance 139, 141, 147, 193,
 196, 227, 230, 266
Inheritance examples 195
inheritance hierarchy 195, 240
Inheritance hierarchy for
 university **Communi-
tyMember**s 196
inheritance with exceptions 294
Inherits attribute 1060
Inherits attribute of ASP .NET
 page 763
Init event 766
initial set of classes 139
initialization at the beginning of
 each repetition 66
initialize instance variables 146
initializer list 125, 132
initializers 149
initializing arrays 123, 124
Initializing arrays in three
 different ways 124
initializing double-subscripted
 arrays in declarations 132
Initializing multidimensional
 arrays 133
inlining code 249
inner block 114
INNER JOIN 719, 727

InnerException property of
 Exception 303, 307
innermost pair of parentheses 52
inorder traversal of a binary tree
 966
input 27
input data from the keyboard 318
input element 1230, 1231, 1284
input/output 582
input/output blocking 428
input/output request 427
INRIA (Institut National de
 Recherche en Informatique
 et Automatique) 4
insert an item into a container
 object 142
INSERT INTO 719, 731
Insert method of class **Array-
List** 985
Insert Separator option 361
INSERT statement 731
InsertCommand property of
 OleDbAdapter 742
Inserting and aligning the picture
 box 40
inserting separators in a menu 361
insertion point 945
instance of a built-in type 139
instance of a user-defined type 139
instance variable 141, 149, 154,
 165, 198, 201, 1169
"instant-access" application 616
instantiate (or create) objects 139
Institut National de Recherche en
 Informatique et
 Automatique (INRIA) 4
int primitive data type 55, 106
int promotions 107
integer mathematics 182
integer value 55
integral data type 109, 312
integrated development
 environment (IDE) 9, 11, 23
intelligent agent 1124
IntelliSense 93
interactions among objects 182
interactive animated character 14,
 562
interface 140, 148, 261, 262, 265,
 266, 711
interface definition 1169
interface keyword 261
Interfaces2Test.cs 271
InterfacesTest.cs 264
internal data representation 183
internal help 34

internal hyperlink 18, 1238, 1241, 1292, 1294
internal link 1087
internal member access modifier 197
Internet 2, 3
Internet Explorer (IE) 25, 317, 370, 659, 1253, 1264
Internet Explorer window 50
Internet Information Services (IIS) 759
Internet Protocol (IP) 3
Internet Protocol Addresses (IP Address) 907
Internet Service Provider (ISP) 1230, 1284
Internshipprograms.com 1135
Interrupt method of class **Thread** 427
Interval property of class **Timer** 418
InterviewSmart™ 1136
intranet 5
Invalidate method of class **Control** 514
InvalidCastException 235, 236
InvalidOperationException 994
Invoke 846
invoking a method 99
invoking a method of a Web service from a Web browser 847
IP (Internet Protocol) address 3, 759, 907
IPAddress class 909
IPEndPoint class 909
"is-a" relationship 194, 235, 238, 266
IsAccessible property of class **Control** 1016, 1020
isbn attribute 699
IsDigit method of class **Char** 491
IsEmptyElement Property of XmlNodeReader 672
IShape interface provides methods **Area** and **Volume** and property **Name** 266
isHTML32 filter 1094
IsLetter method of class **Char** 491
IsLetterOrDigit method of class **Char** 491

IsLower method of class **Char** 493
IsMdiChild property of class **Form** 405
IsMdiContainer property of class **Form** 404, 405
IsNewSession property of **HttpSessionState** class 812
ISP (Internet Service Provider) 1230, 1284
IsPostBack property of class **Page** 792
IsPunctuation method of class **Char** 493
IsReadOnly property of **HttpSessionState** class 812
IsSymbol method of class **Char** 493
IsUpper method of class **Char** 493
IsValid property of **Page** object 1071
IsValid property of **ServerValidateEventArgs** class 829
IsWhiteSpace method of class **Char** 493
Italic member of enumeration **FontStyle** 523
Italic property of class **Font** 522
ItemActivate event of class **ListView** 392
ItemCheck event of class **CheckedListBox** 378
ItemCheckEventArgs event of class **CheckedListBox** 379
Items property of class **ComboBox** 381
Items property of class **List** 1083
Items property of class **ListBox** 373
Items property of class **ListView** 392
ItemSize property of class **TabControl** 399
iteration 69
iteration of a loop 70, 82
iterative 119
iterator 241, 990
iterator class 241

J

J# progamming language 8
jagged array 130, 132
Java Development Kit (Java SDK 1.3) 1026
JAWS (Job Access with Sound) 1038, 1056
jobfind.com 1127
Jobs.com 1128
JobsOnline.com 1131
Join method of class **Thread** 427, 460
joining tables 718
Joint Photographic Experts Group (JPEG) 1263
JScript .NET 8
JSML 1055
JustCJobs.com 1132
JustComputerJobs.com 1132
JustJavaJobs.com 1123, 1132

K

Keio University 4
key code 356
key data 356
key event 353, 354
key value 356, 973
key, modifier 353
keyboard 317
Keyboard events, delegates and event arguments 354
KeyDemo.cs 355
KeyDown event 354
KeyEventArgs properties 354
KeyPress event 354
KeyPressEventArgs properties 354
Keys property of **HttpSessionState** class 812, 815
KeyUp event 354
keyword 44, 62
Koenig, Andrew 285

L

label 37, 38, 50, 51, 317, 318, 330
Label class 330
Label control 1061
Label in position with its **Text** property set 38
Label properties 331
labels in a **switch** structure 76

LabelTextBoxButton-
   Test.cs 332
Language attribute 1060
language attribute 763
language attribute of a
   <script> tag 1070
language independence 10
language interoperability 10
LargeImageList property of
   class **ListView** 391
LastChild property of **XmlN-**
   ode 673, 675
last-in, first-out (LIFO) data
   structure 956
LastIndexOf method of class
   Array 984
LastIndexOf method of class
   String 473, 476
LastIndexOfAny method of
   class **String** 473
last-in-first-out (LIFO) 181
LastNode property of class
   TreeNode 387
Latin World 1130
layout control 28, 326
layout windows 28
LayoutMdi enumeration values
   408
LayoutMdi method of class
   Form 405, 408
LayoutMdi.ArrangeIcons
   408
LayoutMdi.Cascade 408
LayoutMdi.TileHorizon-
   tal 408
LayoutMdi.TileVertical
   408
lazy quantifier 501
leaf node in a binary search tree
   965, 971
left brace (**{**) 44, 45
left child 965
left-shift assignment operator
   (**<<=**) 1324
left-shift operator (**<<**) 1312,
   1313, 1314, 1320
left subtree 965, 971
Length property of class
   BitArray 1324
Length property of class
   String 466, 467
Length property of class
   StringBuilder 482
letter 580
letter.dtd 684
letter.xml 660

letter2.xml 685
level of nesting 1219
lexicographical comparison 468
<li> (list item) tag 1217, 1269
LIFO (last-in, first-out) 181
LIKE 722, 723, 725
line 511
linear collection 944
linear data structure 964
LinearGradientBrush class
   516, 537, 540
LinearGradientMode
   enumeration 540
linearized 1021
LinesRectanglesOv-
   als.cs 528
link 944, 965
Link control 1087
link element in VoiceXML 1032
link for a self-referential class 943
link one Web page to another 1238
<link> tag 1032
LinkArea property of class
   LinkLabel 369
LinkBehavior property of
   class **LinkLabel** 369
LinkButton 836
LinkClicked event of class
   LinkLabel 368, 370
LinkColor property of class
   LinkLabel 369
linked document 1208
linked list 16, 142, 241, 942, 944,
   945
linked list in sorted order 945
LinkedListLibrary.cs 947
LinkLabel class 359, 368
LinkLabel properties and
   events 369
LinkLabel used to link to a
   folder, a Web page and an
   application 370
LinkLabels 370
LinkLabels used to link to a
   folder, a Web page and an
   application 370
LinkLabelTest.cs 370
Links property of class **Lin-**
   kLabel 369
links.html 1208, 1216, 1260
links2.html 1269
LinkVisited property of class
   LinkLabel 369
list 318
List control 1083, 1094, 1096
List of **Form** events 324

list, editable 382
list.html 1217, 1270
ListBox and **CheckedList-**
   Box on a form 373
ListBox class 359, 372
ListBox on an ASPX page 803
ListBox properties, methods
   and events 373
ListBox used in a program to
   add, remove and clear items
   375
ListBox Web control 812
ListBoxTest.cs 375
Listing for **namespace.xml**
   662
ListTest.cs 951
ListView class 391
ListView displaying files and
   folders 393
ListView properties and events
   391
ListViewTest.cs 393
literal **String** objects 464
live-code approach xl
Load event 320
Load method of **XMLDocument**
   668
Load method of **XslTrans-**
   form 700
local dialog 1031
local variable 99, 114
local variable of a method 114,
   147, 165
localhost 1065
localhost 918
localization 1181
localization setting 75
Locals window 1148
local-variable declaration space
   114
Location property 329
lock keyword 433, 447, 448, 458
locking objects 432
Log in Web Form 822
logging feature 1034
logic element 1037
logic error 56, 1144
logical AND operator (**&&**) 84, 85
logical exclusive OR 85
logical negation (**!**) 84, 85
logical NOT operator (**!**) 84, 85
logical operator 84
logical OR operator (**| |**) 84, 85
logical XOR 85
Login.aspx 822
Login.aspx.cs 825

loginUrl 830
546
long primitive data type 106
long promotions 107
long-term retention of data 579
longdesc attribute 1007
Look-and-Feel Observation 6
loop body 70, 80
loop-continuation condition 69,
     70, 77, 80, 82
loopback IP address 918
low-order bit 1314
lowercase 44
lowercase letter 44
Lowest ThreadPriority
     enumeration member 427
Lynx 1024

M

m-by-*n* array 131
machine.config file 1074,
     1107
Magenta static property of
     structure **Color** 515
magnetic disk 579
magnetic tape 579
mailto: URL 1210, 1261
Main method 44, 47, 55, 69, 419
Main thread of execution 428
main.html 1205, 1254
MainMenu and **MenuItem**
     properties and events 362
MainMenu class 360, 361
MainMenu properties 362
MainMenu properties and events
     362
maintainability 942
maintenance of software 6
manipulating array elements 124
Manipulating the **Anchor**
     property of a control 329
many-to-many relationship 719
map element 1241, 1296
marked for garbage collection 169
markup 759
markup language 18, 1203, 1253
Massachusetts Institute of
     Technology (MIT) 4
match 697
Match class 463, 499, 502
match the selection criteria 720
MatchCollection class 499
Math class 75, 898
math tutor application 900
Math.Sqrt method 106

mathematical formula 657
Mathematical Markup Language
     (MathML) 15
MathML (Mathematical Markup
     Language) 15
maxDigits attribute 1037
MaxDropDownItems property
     of class **ComboBox** 380,
     381
MaximumSize property 330
maxlength attribute 1231,
     1284
maxOccurs attribute 689, 691
maxTime attribute 1037, 1038
MaxValue constant of **Int32**
     312
MBAFreeAgent.com 1133
MBCS (multi-byte character set)
     1184
MDI (multiple document
     interface) 13, 403
MDI form 405
MDI parent and MDI child events
     and properties 405
MDI parent window and MDI
     child windows 404
MDI parent-window class 409
MDI title bar 405
MdiChildActivate event of
     class **Form** 405
MdiChildren property of class
     Form 405
MdiLayout enumeration 408
MdiList property of class
     MenuItem 407
MdiParent property of class
     Form 405
MediaPlayerTest.cs 559
member 1169
member access modifier 141
member access modifier
     private 142
member access modifier **public**
     141
member access operator 197
member tag 1177
Members column 1170
memory consumption 981
memory leak 167, 295
MemoryStream class 582
menu 27, 50, 317, 359
menu access shortcut 360
menu access shortcut, create 361
menu bar 50, 51, 317
menu bar in Visual Studio .NET
     27

Menu Designer in Visual Studio
     .NET 360
menu item 360
menu separator 361
<menu> tag 1031, 1032
menu, ellipsis convention 361
MenuItem properties 362
MenuItem property **MdiList**
     example 407
MenuItems property of class
     MainMenu 362
MenuItems property of class
     MenuItem 362
MenuMerge enumeration 406
MenuMerge.Add 406
MenuMerge.MergeItems 406
MenuMerge.Remove 406
MenuMerge.Replace 406
Menus used for changing text font
     and color 363
Menus used to change text font
     and color 363
MenuTest.cs 363
Mercury programming language 8
Merge records from Tables 726
MergeItems member of
     enumeration **MenuMerge**
     406
MergeOrder property of class
     MenuItem 362, 406
MergeType property of class
     MenuItem 362, 406
Merlin **Microsoft Agent**
     character 562
Message 307
message box 1144
Message property of class
     Exception 293, 297, 303
MessageBox class 11, 47, 50
MessageBoxButtons class 73
**MessageBoxButtons.Abor
     tRetryIgnore** 74
MessageBoxButtons.OK 73
**MessageBoxButtons.OK-
     Cancel** 73
**MessageBoxButtons.
     RetryCancel** 73
**MessageBoxButtons.Yes-
     No** 73
**MessageBoxButtons.Yes-
     NoCancel** 73
MessageBoxIcon class 73
MessageBoxIcon.Error 74
**MessageBoxIcon.
     Exclamation** 74

MessageBoxIcon.
Information 74
MessageBoxIcon.
Question 74
meta element 764, 1243, 1245,
    1297, 1298
method 44
method = "get" 1230, 1283
method = "post" 1230, 1283
method attribute 1038, 1230,
    1282
method body 105
method call 99
method call stack 303
method definition 45
method **Factorial** 117
method header 104
method overloading 72, 119
method-call operator 103
MethodDebugExample.cs
    1153
microbrowser 1058
Microsoft 1182
Microsoft Agent 14, 562, 568
Microsoft Agent Character Editor
    562
Microsoft Agent Control 2.0
    568
Microsoft Agent demonstration
    568
Microsoft Intermediate Language
    (MSIL) 9, 47
Microsoft Internet Explorer
    accessibility options 1052
Microsoft Linguistic Sound
    Editing Tool 562
Microsoft **Magnifier** 1041
Microsoft Mobile Explorer
    Emulator (MME) 1069
Microsoft **Narrator** 1048, 1051
Microsoft .NET 7
Microsoft **On-Screen Key-**
    board 1051, 1052
Microsoft SansSerif font 523
Microsoft Schema file that
    contains structure to which
    bookxdr.xml conforms.
    689
Microsoft Serif font 523
Microsoft SQL Server 710
Microsoft Windows 95/98 23
Microsoft Windows NT/2000 23
microsoft.public.dot-
    net.framework.asp-
    net.mobile newsgroup
    1108

Microsoft® Mobile Internet
    Toolkit (MIT) 1058, 1107
middle tier 762
MIDI (Musical Instrument Digital
    Interface) 559
Millimeter member of
    enumeration **Graphic-**
    sUnit 522
MIME (Multipurpose Internet
    Mail Extensions) 761, 797
minimized and maximized child
    window 406
Minimized and maximized child
    windows 406
MinimumSize property 330
minOccurs attribute 689, 691
minus sign (-) 659
MIT (Massachusetts Institute of
    Technology) 4
MIT (Microsoft Mobile Internet
    Toolkit) 1058, 1107
MIT (Mobile Internet Toolkit) 17
mixed-type expression 107
mobile control 1061, 1107
Mobile Internet Toolkit (MIT) 17
mobile tag prefix 1061
Mobile Web Application
    project type 1065
Mobile Web Form control 1061,
    1107
Mobile Web Form Designer 1066
Mobile Web Forms group in the
    Toolbox 1069
MobileCapabilities class
    1094, 1097
MobileListItem class 1083
MobileListItemCollec-
    tion class 1083
modal dialog 598
mode attribute 830
model attribute 689
modifier key 353
modify a variable at run time 1148
Modifying a database 744
modulus assignment operator (**%=**)
    67
modulus operator (**%**) 52
Monitor class 425, 427, 428,
    432, 440, 447, 448
monolithic excecutable 1191
Monster.com 1123, 1127,
    1131, 1133
More Windows... option in
    Visual Studio .NET 407
Motion Pictures Experts Group
    (MPEG) 559

mouse 317
Mouse Button Settings 1048
mouse click 351
mouse cursor 1043
mouse event 351
Mouse events, delegates and event
    arguments 351
mouse move 351
mouse pointer 28, 31
mouse press 351
Mouse Speed dialog 1049
mouse, drag 32
MouseDown event 351
MouseEventArgs class 351
MouseEventArgs properties
    351
MouseHover event 351, 1016
MouseKeys 1047
MouseLeave event 351
MouseMove event 351
MouseUp event 351
Move method of class
    Directory 584
Move method of class **File** 583
MoveNext of **IEnumerator**
    990
MoveTo method of interface
    IAgentCtlCharacter
    576
MPEG format 559
MS-DOS prompt 23
mscorlib.dll 49
MSDN documentation 73
msdn.microsoft.com/
    downloads/samples/
    Internet/xml/
    xml_validator/sam-
    ple.asp 686
msdn.microsoft.com/li-
    brary/de-
    fault.asp?url=/
    library/en-us/mws-
    dk/html/mw-
    startpage.asp 1108
msdn.microsoft.com/
    vstudio/device/mit-
    devices.asp 1059
msdn.microsoft.com/
    vstudio/nextgen/
    technology/mo-
    bilewebforms.asp
    1108
MSIL (Microsoft Intermediate
    Language) 9, 47
MSN.com 796
msxml parser 659

multi-tier application 761
multi-byte character set (MBCS) 1184
multicast delegate 273
multicast event 321, 326
MulticastDelegate class 273, 321
MultiColumn property of class **ListBox** 373
multidimensional array 98, 130
MultiExtended value of **SelectionMode** 372
multilevel priority queue 427
MultiLine property of class **TabControl** 331, 399
multimedia 559
multiple document interface (MDI) 13, 403
Multiple forms in a mobile Web Form page 1060
multiple inheritance 193
multiple-subscripted array 130, 131
multiple-line comment (**/* */**) 43
multiple-selection structure 62, 76
multiplication assignment operator (***=**) 67
Multipurpose Internet Mail Extensions (MIME) 761, 797
MultiSelect property of class **ListView** 391, 392
MultiSimple value of **SelectionMode** 372
multithread safe 946
multithreading 13, 424
Musical Instrument Digital Interface (MIDI) 559
mutual exclusion 343
mutually exclusive options 343
MySQL 710

N

N formatting character 76
n-tier application 761
name attribute 691, 1230, 1284
name attribute of a **device-filter** 1093, 1094, 1107
name attribute of a **Style** 1092
name attribute of **member** tag 1177
name attribute of **meta** element 764
name node-set function 699
name of an attribute 1255

Name property of class **Font** 335, 522
Name property of **HttpCookie** class 805, 806
Name property of structure **Color** 519
named constant 125
namespace 44, 47, 141, 145, 662
Namespace attribute 1061
namespace keyword 184
namespace prefix 662, 665
namespace prefix **xsd** 691
Namespace property of a **WebService** attribute 854
namespace.xml 662
NamespaceURI 674
naming collision 184, 662
NaN constant of class **Double** 310
Narrator reading **Notepad** text 1051
narrowing conversion 106
nav.html 1212, 1265
NavigateUrl attribute 783
NavigateUrl element 1095, 1096
NavigateUrl property 1087
navigation bar 824
navigational frame 1245, 1299
negative arc angles 531
negative infinity 292
NegativeNumberException.cs 309
nested tags 1247
nested block 114
nested element 658, 1256
nested **for** loop 132, 134
nested **frameset** element 1249, 1302, 1303
nested list 1217, 1219, 1270
nested parentheses 52
.NET initiative 7
.NET-compliant language 10
.NET component 1192
.NET Framework 9, 99
.NET Framework Class Library 44, 99, 424
.NET Language 7
.NET platform 7
Netscape Communicator 1253
network address 907
network message arrival 286
networking 579
NetworkStream class 909
new operator 123, 144, 167, 944, 981

New Project dialog 26
new project in Visual Studio .NET 27
New **Text** property value reflected in design mode 94
NewDialog.cs 649
NewDialogForm class enables users to create records in transaction-processor case study 649
newline character (**\n**) 48
News article formatted with XML 657
NewValue event of class **CheckedListBox** 379
next attribute of **choice** element 1031
Next method of class **Random** 899
NextNode property of class **TreeNode** 387
no-argument constructor 149, 152
node 385
node, child 385
node, expand and collapse 385
node, parent 385
node, root 385
Nodes property of class **TreeNode** 387
Nodes property of class **TreeView** 386
node-set function 699
noframes element 1247, 1248, 1301
None value of **SelectionMode** 372
nonlinear data structures 944
non-primitive data type array 126
nonvalidating XML parser 683
NOT operator (logical) 84, 85
not-selected state 343
Notepad text editor 368, 1204, 1253
noun 5
Now property of structure **DateTime** 418
null reference 943
NullReferenceException 294
Number systems Appendix 1111
numeric formatting characters 75

O

Oberon programming language 7
object 5, 138, 139

object-based programming (OBP) xl, 139
Object Browser (Visual Studio .NET) 189
Object class 141, 248, 472
Object debugging example 1156
object of a derived class 230
object of a derived class is instantiated 221
object orientation 138
object oriented 139
object-oriented programming (OOP) xl, 5, 139, 193, 230
object passed by reference 139
object primitive data type 106
object speak 138
object think 138
object-oriented programming 662
objects constructed "inside out" 227
OBP (object-based programming) 139
occurence indicator 684
Ocularis 1040
.OCX file 1192, 1193
off-by-one error 70
OK button on a dialog 51
OK member of enumeration **MessageBoxButtons** 73
OKCancel member of enumeration **MessageBoxButtons** 73
ol (ordered list) tag 1220
OleDbCommand class 734
OleDbConnection class 734
OleDbDataAdapter class 734
OleDbDataReader class 735, 829
one-dimensional array 130
one-to-many relationship 718
One value of **SelectionMode** 372
one's complement (~) 1119, 1312, 1320
ones position 1113
onHangup element 1037
OnInit method 766
online contracting service 1133
online guest book 815
online recruiting 1125
onMaxSilence element 1037
OnPaint method from class **Control** 416, 417, 513
On-Screen Keyboard 1051
onTermDigit element 1037

OOP (object-oriented programming) xl, 5, 139, 193, 230
Open method of class **File** 583
open technology 657
opened 582
OpenFileDialog class 605, 610
opening a project 27
OpenRead method of class **File** 583
OpenRead method of class **WebClient** 887
OpenText method of class **File** 583
OpenWrite method of class **File** 583
operand 56
operations of an abstract data type 182
operator = 56
operator == 57
operator keyword 279
operator overloading 277
operator precedence 52
operator precedence chart 17
Operator precedence chart Appendix 1109
Operators **checked** and **unchecked**, and handling arithmetic overflow 313
optical disk 579
optimization 75
OptionPage.aspx.cs 800
Options supplied on an ASPX page 798, 806
OptionsPage.aspx 798, 806
OptionsPage.aspx.cs 808
Or method of class **BitArray** 1324
OR operator (boolean logical exclusive) 84
OR operator (boolean logical inclusive) 84
OR operator (logical) 84
Oracle 710
Oracle Corporation 1182
Orange static property of structure **Color** 515
order attribute 700
ORDER BY 719, 723, 724, 725
Order in which constructors and destructors are called 226
ordered 711
ordered list 1270, 1272
ordered list element 1220

ordering of records 719
out keyword 110
out-of-line transfer of control 250
out-of-range array subscript 286, 294
Out property of class **Console** 581
outer block 114
OutOfMemoryException 944
output 27, 45, 48
output cursor 45
output directory 419
output file 419
overflow 286, 312
Overflow.cs 313
OverflowException class 312
overload resolution 120
overloaded constructor 149
Overloaded constructor demonstration 152
Overloaded constructors provide flexible object-initialization options 150
overloaded method 120
overloading 119, 216
overridden 194
override keyword 240
Oz programming language 7

P

p (paragraph) element 1206, 1256
P formatting character 76
packet 907
page anchor 1087
Page class 766, 792, 808
  Session property 808
  trace property 837
page content 1206
Page directive 1060
page layout software 463
page tracing 836
Page.IsValid 1071
Page_Unload method 767
<%@Page...%> directive 763
PageIndexChange event 836
PageIndexChange event for a **DataGrid** control 836
pageLayout property of ASP.NET page 772
PagerStyle property 836
PagerStyle property of a **DataGrid** control 836
PageSize property 836

PageSize property of a **Data-Grid** control 836
Paint 397
Paint Shop Pro 1263
Painter.cs 352
PaintEventArgs class 416, 513
PaintEventArgs properties 417
palette 37
panel 318
Panel class 337, 512
Panel control 1077
Panel Controls property 337
Panel properties 337
Panel properties and events 337
panel with scrollbars 338
parallelogram 194
param tag 1169
parameter 99, 103
parameter-list 104
parent element 659
parent menu 360
parent node 385, 665, 965
parentheses **( )** 52
parentheses "on the same level" 53
Parse method of class **Int32** 56
parsed character data 685
parser 659, 664
Pascal programming language 8
pass-by-reference 110
pass-by-value 110
Passing an array reference by value and by reference 127
passing an array to a method 126
password box 1231, 1285
password textbox 330
PasswordChar property of **TextBox** class 330, 331
paste 27
Path property of **HttpCookie** class 806
path to a resource 759
PathGradientBrush class 537
PathNavigator.cs 676
Paths used to draw stars on a form 541
pattern matching 722
pattern of **1**s and **0**s 580
payroll system 237, 580
#PCDATA flag 685
Peedy calculating the total 568
Peedy flying animation 565
Peedy introducing himself when the window opens 563

Peedy recounting the order 567
Peedy repeating the user's request for anchovies as an additional topping 567
Peedy repeating the user's request for Seattle-style pizza 566
Peedy the Parrot Microsoft Agent character 562
Peedy waiting for speech input 566
Peedy's reaction when he is clicked 564
Peek method of class **Stack** 994
Pen class 511, 515, 527
percent sign (**%**) is the modulus operator 52
Performance Tip 6
Perl progamming language 8
permission settings 392
persistent data 579
persistent information 796
Person class implements **IAge** interface 262
personalization 796
PhotoShop Elements 1263
PhysicalApplication-Path property of **Request** class 815
picture box 39, 349
picture.html 1210, 1263
PictureBox class 349, 408
PictureBox properties and events 349
PictureBoxTest.cs 349
PieceWorker class inherits from class **Employee** 255
pin a window 31
pin icon 31
Pink static property of structure **Color** 515
pixel 1263
Pixel member of enumeration **GraphicsUnit** 522
platform independence 10
play element 1039
Play method of interface **IAgentCtlCharacter** 574
playback, choppy 425
player thread 425
plus sign (**+**) 659
plus sign (**+**) occurence indicator 684
Point class represents an *x-y* coordinate pair 198, 231

Point marked up with XML comments 1162
point-of-sale system 616
Point structure 512
Point2 class inherits from abstract class **Shape** 242
Point2 class represents an *x-y* coordinate pair as **protected** data 207
Point3 class implements interface **IShape** 267
Point3 class uses properties to manipulate its **private** data 212
Point3.cs 267
Point4 base class contains constructors and finalizer 222
PointTest class demonstrates class **Point** functionality 200
Polygon-drawing demonstration 534
polymorphic processing of related errors 294
polymorphic programming 237, 241
polymorphic screen manager 238
polymorphism 12, 79, 139, 228, 230, 235, 238, 240, 250
pool of threads 909
Pop method of class **Stack** 990, 991
pop stack operation 956
popping off a stack 181
port number 907, 908
portability 10, 1184
Portability Tip 6
portable 657
porting 10
position number 122
positional notation 1113
Positional value 1114
Positional values in the decimal number system 1114
Positive and negative arc angles 531
positive infinity 292
post request type 1038, 1283
postback 792
postdecrement 67, 68, 71
postincrement 67, 71
postorder traversal of a binary tree 966
Pow method of class **Math** 74, 898

Precedence and associativity chart 87

Precedence and associativity of the operators discussed so far in this book 68, 123

precedence chart 52

precedence chart Appendix 1109

precedence of arithmetic operators 53, 68, 122

precedence rule 52

predecrement 67, 68

predicate method 142, 946

preferredRenderingType browser property 1094

preincrement 67, 71

preorder traversal of a binary tree 966

prepackaged data structures 981

presentation logic 762

presentation of a document 1203, 1253

previous statement, variable in 1148

PrevNode property of class **TreeNode** 387

primary interop assembly 1196

primary key 711, 718

prime number 1324

primitive (or built-in) data type 107, 109

primitive data type 55

Princeton Review 1135

print a line of text 45

print spooling 961

PrintBits.cs 1314

printing a project 27

Priority property of class **Thread** 428

privacy invasion 796

privacy protection 796

private member access modifier 141, 142, 148, 154

Private members of a base class 196

procedural programming language 5, 139

Process class 369

processing instruction 696

processing instruction target 696

processing instruction value 696

produce method 434

producer 448

producer and consumer threads accessing a circular buffer 450

producer and consumer threads accessing a shared object with synchronization 440

producer and consumer threads accessing a shared object without synchronization 435

producer thread 434

producer/consumer relationship 434

program control 23

program development 23

program development process 182

program execution stack 956

Program that demonstrates class **Array** 982

Program to display hidden text in a password box 332

program, break execution 1149

program, suspend 1144

programmer-defined class 44

Programmer-defined control that displays the current time 418

programmer-defined method 99

programmer-defined type 139

project 25

Project menu of Visual Studio 140

Project menu of Visual Studio .NET 27

Project properties dialog 420

project, Windows control library 419

promote 73

promotion 73, 796

prompt 56

prompt element in VoiceXML 1031

<prompt> tag 1032

Properties demonstration for class **Time3** 158

Properties of class **Control** related to accessibility 1015

Properties window 31, 32, 36, 39, 91, 772, 1068

Properties window on a Web Page 837

Properties.cs 304

property 31

property definition 148

property for a form or control 31

property of an object 5, 11

Proposed Recommendation 4

Protected 197

protection attribute 830

proxy 1193

proxy class for Web services 849, 857

pseudocode 63, 64

pseudocode **if/else** structure 63

pseudocode statement 64

public interface 142

public keyword 252

public member access modifier 141, 142

public member of a derived class 196

public method 143

public operation encapsulated in an object 147

public service 142

public static members 169

Publication 1028

Publication page of Deitel and Associates' VoiceXML page 1028

publishers table of **books** database 712, 713

publishing a Web service 849

Pulse method of class **Monitor** 427, 433, 440

Pulse method of **Monitor** 448

PulseAll method of class **Monitor** 427, 433

Push method of class **Stack** 990

push stack operation 956

pushing into a stack 181

PWS (Personal Web Server) 1230

Python progamming language 8

Q

quantifier 501

Quantifiers used in regular expressions 502

Quantifiers used regular expressions 502

quantum 427

quantum expiration 426

query 710, 712

query a database 735

Question 74

question mark (**?**) occurence indicator 684

queue 16, 142, 182, 942, 961

Queue class 981

QueueInheritance extends class **List** 962

QueueInheritanceLibrary.cs 962

QueueTest.cs 963

R

R formatting character 76

R property of structure **Color** 515

RAD (rapid application development) 9, 13, 183

radio 1234, 1288

radio button 330, 343

radio button group 343

radio buttons, using with **TabPage** 403

RadioButton class 340, 343

RadioButton properties and events 344

RadioButtonsTest.cs 344

RadioCheck property of class **MenuItem** 362, 368

random-access file 14, 579, 616, 629, 649

Random class 899

random number generation 494

Random-access file with fixed-length records 617

RandomAccessRecord.cs 617

rapid application development (RAD) 9, 13, 183

RCW (Runtime Callable Wrapper) 1197

RDBMS (relational database management system) 761

RDK (Redistribution Kit) 1039

Read method 694

Read method of class **Console** 582

Read method of class **NetworkStream** 909

read-only text 330

readability 1008, 1056, 1254

ReadByte method of class **NetworkStream** 909

Reading records from random-access files sequentially 629

ReadLine method of class **Console** 56, 582

readonly keyword 12, 173

ReadOnly property 331

ReadSequentialAccessFile.cs 606

ReadString method of class **BinaryReader** 918

ReadXml method of **DataSet** 752

Ready thread state 426

receive a connection 917

receive data from a server 918

Receive method of class **Socket** 908

Receive method of class **UdpClient** 919, 924

ReceiveFrom method of class **Socket** 908

receiving an array through a method call 126

receiving temperature and weather data from a Web service 889

reclaim memory 172

reclaiming dynamically allocated memory 425

recognizing clients 796

RecommendationsPage 813

RecommendationsPage.aspx 803, 812

RecommendationsPage.aspx.cs 804, 813

record 580, 711, 717

Record for random-access file-processing applications 617

Record for sequential-access file-processing applications 596

record key 580, 616

record set 712

record size 616

Record.cs 596

recordAudio element 1039

Record-transaction class for the transaction-processor case study 634

Recruitsoft.com 1130

Rectangle structure 511, 512, 528, 540

rectangular array 130

rectangular hotspot 1243, 1296

recursion 391

recursion step 117

recursive call 117

recursive method 11, 117, 118

recursive method **Factorial** 117

red circle, solid 1145, 1150

Red static property of structure **Color** 515

Redistribution Kit (RDK) 1039

ref keyword 110

reference 1169

reference manipulation 942

reference to a new object 144

reference type 109

referring to a base-class object with a base-class reference 236

referring to a base-class object with a derived-class reference 237

referring to a derived-class object with a base-class reference 237

referring to a derived-class object with a derived-class reference 237

Regex class 463, 499, 500

Regex methods **Replace** and **Split** 507

RegexMatches.cs 499

RegexSubstitution.cs 507

#region 90, 91

region of code 90

regional invalidation 548

Register directive 1061

register event handler 325

<%@Register...%> directive 824

Registering an ActiveX control 1192

RegSvr32 utility 1192, 1196

regular expression 587

Regular expression used to determine file types 588

Regular expressions checking birthdays 499

Regular member of enumeration **FontStyle** 523

"reinventing the wheel" 44

relational database 710

relational database management system (RDBMS) 761

relational database model 711

relational database table 711

Relational-database structure of an **Employee** table 711

relative positioning 772

release a lock 447, 448

release resource 296

release the lock 459

remarks tag 1169

remote machine 844

Remote Procedure Call (RPC) 844

Remove member of enumeration **MenuMerge** 406

Remove method of class **ArrayList** 985, 989

Remove method of class **StringBuilder** 488

Remove method of class **TreeNodeCollection** 387

Remove method of **Hashtable** 1000

Remove method of **TreeNode-Collection** 671

RemoveAt method of class **ArrayList** 985

RemoveRange method of class **ArrayList** 985

Removing tabs from Visual Studio environment 1013

renaming code files in Visual Studio .NET 47

renders 761

repetition control structure 62, 64

repetition structure 11

Replace member of enumeration **MenuMerge** 406

Replace method of class **Regex** 507, 508

Replace method of class **String** 478, 479

Replace method of class **StringBuilder** 489

Report Expert 1330

Request class 815

Cookies property 805

PhysicalApplication-Path property 815

request for proposal 1133

Request object 792, 805

Request.Browser 1097

RequiredFieldValidator class 788

RequiredFieldValidator control 1071

Reservation.asmx.cs 878

reserved word 44

reserving memory 123

Reset of **IEnumerator** 990

resolution 512

resource leak 167, 287, 295

Response.Write 836

Restart button 1149

result of an uncaught exception 288

result set 712, 720

result tree 695

Results of combining two bits with the bitwise AND operator (**&**) 1313

Results of combining two bits with the bitwise exclusive OR operator (**^**) 1314

Results of combining two bits with the bitwise inclusive OR operator (**|**) 1313

results of invoking a Web service method from a Web browser 847

resume 1124, 1129

Resume method of class **Thread** 427

resume-filtering software 1129

resumption model of exception handling 288

rethrow an exception 302

RetryCancel member of enumeration **MessageBoxButtons** 73

return statement 103, 104, 105, 117

return-value-type 104

returning an object from a Web-service method 899

returns tag 1169, 1170

reusability 942

reusable component 194

reusable software component 5, 6, 30, 184

reuse 44

Reverse method of class **Array** 984

RGB values 514, 515

right brace (**}**) 44, 45

right child 965

right-shift assignment operator (**>>=**) 1324

right-shift operator (**>>**) 1312, 1313, 1320

right subtree 965, 972

RightToLeft property of class **MainMenu** 362

Robby the Robot Microsoft Agent character 562

robust application 56, 285

root element 658, 686

root node 385, 665, 965

root node, create 385

RotateTransform method of class **Graphics** 543

Round member of enumeration **DashCap** 541

round-robin 427

row 711

rows attribute (**textarea**) 1233, 1284

rows to be retrieved 719

rowspan attribute (**tr**) 1228, 1279

RPC (Remote Procedure Call) 844

RPG progamming language 8

Rule of Entity Integrity 717, 718

Rule of Referential Integrity 718

rules of operator precedence 52

Run command in Windows 369

run element 1038

Run menu 42

run mode 41

run-time exception 294

runat attribute 1061, 1107

Runnable thread state 426

running an application 369

Running thread state 426, 429

Runtime Callable Wrapper (RCW) 1197

runtime logic error 56

S

Salary.com 1135 605

Sample Internet Explorer window with GUI components 318

SaveFileDialog class 598

Saving a document to a file 1171

sbyte primitive data type 106

sbyte promotions 107

scalar quantities 126

scalars 126

scheduling 427

Schema 683, 687

schema element 691

schema repository 689

Schemas property of **XmlSchemaCollection** 694

Schema-validation example 692

Scheme progamming language 8

scope 147

scope (block) 114

scope (class) 114

scope (global) 114

scope of a variable 70

scope of an identifier 114

Scoping example 115

screen cursor 48

screen-manager program 238

screen reader 1007, 1020, 1038, 1048, 1053

script 1188, 1255

<script> tag 1070

scroll key 1062

scrollbar 317, 318

scrollbar and window border size dialog 1042

scrollbar in panel 338
SDI (single document interface) 403
SDI and MDI forms 404
SDK (Software Development Kit) 1039
sealed 249
search engine 1206, 1243, 1256, 1297
searching 942
Searching for characters and substrings in **String**s 473
searching technique 98
secondary storage device 579
section of **machine.config** file 1075
sector 531
Secure property of **Http-Cookie** class 806
secure protocol 806
SeekOrigin enumeration 628
SeekOrigin.Begin constant 628
SELECT 712, 719, 720, 721, 722, 723, 724, 725, 727
select 712, 719
select all fields from a table 720
Select Case logic 237
SelectCommand property of **OleDbAdapter** 742
selected attribute 1292
selected state 343
SelectedImageIndex property of class **Tree-Node** 387
SelectedIndex property of class **ComboBox** 381
SelectedIndex property of class **ListBox** 373
SelectedIndex property of class **TabControl** 400
SelectedIndexChanged event of class **ComboBox** 381
SelectedIndexChanged event of class **ListBox** 374
SelectedIndexChanged event of class **TabControl** 400
SelectedIndices property of class **ListBox** 373
SelectedItem property of class **ComboBox** 381
SelectedItem property of class **ListBox** 373

SelectedItem property of class **ListView** 392
SelectedNode property of class **TreeView** 387
SelectedTab property of class **TabControl** 400
selecting 24
Selecting the **Build Comment Web Pages** from **Tools** menu 1170
selection control structure 11, 61, 62
selection criteria 720
SelectionMode enumeration 372
SelectionMode property of class **CheckedListBox** 378
SelectionMode property of class **ListBox** 372, 373
SelectionMode.MultiExtended 372
SelectionMode.MultiSimple 372
SelectionMode.None 372
SelectionMode.One 372
self-referential class 942, 944
Self-referential class objects linked together 944
Self-referential object 943
semicolon (**;**) 45, 55, 57
send data to a server 918
Send method of class **Socket** 908
Send method of class **UdpClient** 919, 924
sendEvent element 1038
SendTo method of class **Socket** 908
separator bar 361
separator, menu 361
sequence 964
sequence element 691
sequence of items 944
sequence structure 11
sequence type 1272
sequential-access file 579, 581, 598, 616, 649
sequential execution 61
sequential file 14
Serializable attribute 593
SerializationException 606
Serialize method of class **BinaryFormatter** 604

serialized object 593
server Internet address 918
server port number 918
Server portion of a client/server stream-socket connection 910
Server side of client/server Tic-Tac-Toe program 925
Server.cs 910, 919
Server-side portion of connectionless client/server computing 919
ServerValidate event of **CustomValidator** class 824, 829
ServerValidateEventArgs class 829
IsValid property 829
Value property 829
service 147
service description for a Web service 845, 846
session 1033
session attribute 1038
Session data read by an ASP .NET Web application to provide recommendations for the user 813
session ID 796
Session information displayed in a **ListBox** 812
session item 811
Session property of **Page** class 808
session tracking 796
sessionID 1033
SessionID property of **HttpSessionState** class 812
Sessions are created for each user in an ASP .NET Web application 808
session-tracking 797
set accessor 148, 154, 155, 157, 158
Set Automatic Timeouts 1048, 1049
SET keyword 732
Set method of class **BitArray** 1324
SetAll method of class **BitArray** 1326
setAttribute method of interface **HttpSession** 811

SetAuthCookie method of
   FormAuthenication
   class 829
SetDataBinding method of
   DataGrid 742
Setting the form's **Text** property
   36
Setting the project location 35
SGML (Standard Generalized
   Markup Language) 3, 15
shape class hierarchy 196, 197
Shapes 538
Shapes drawn on a form 538
shared buffer 434, 448
shared library 1191
shared memory 434
Shared Source CLI (Common
   Language Infrastructure) 9
Shared Source Common
   Language Infrastructure
   (CLI) 9
Shift key 353
Shift property 356
short primitive data type 106
short promotions 107
short-circuit evaluation 85
shortcut key 360, 1011
Shortcut key creation 1013
Shortcut property of class
   MenuItem 362
shortcuts with the **&** symbol 360
Show method 327
Show method of class **Form** 405,
   412
Show method of class **Message-**
   Box 50, 72
Show method of interface
   IAgentCtlCharacter
   574
Show Next Statement button
   1149
Show of class **Form** 320
ShowColors.cs 516
ShowDialog method of class
   OpenFileDialog 605,
   610
ShowDialog method of class
   SaveFileDialog 598
ShowShortcut property of
   class **MenuItem** 363
ShowSounds 1045, 1047
sibling 965
sibling node 385, 665
side effect 85
Sieve of Eratosthenes 1324
signature 120, 121, 216

Simple class library 188
Simple event-handling example
   using visual programming
   323
Simple Object Access Protocol
   (SOAP) 5, 10, 844, 846
Simple program as it executes 34
Simple style for **ComboBox** 382
SimpleEventExample.cs
   323
single-clicking with left mouse
   button 24
single document interface (SDI)
   403
single-entry/single-exit control
   structure 62
single inheritance 193
single-line comment 43
single-quote character (**' s**) 662
single-selection structure 62
single-subscripted array 130, 131
singlecast delegate 273
single-quote character 722
SixFigureJobs 1134
size attribute (**input**) 1231,
   1284
Size property of class **Font** 330,
   522
SizeInPoints property of
   class **Font** 522
SizeMode property 349
sizing handle 36
sizing handle, disabled 36
sizing handle, enabled 36
Sleep method of class **Thread**
   427, 428, 439
sleeping thread 428
SmallImageList property of
   class **ListView** 392
Smalltalk programming language
   8
SMIL (Synchronized Multimedia
   Integration Language) 15,
   1040
SOAP (Simple Object Access
   Protocol) 5, 10, 844, 846
SOAP envelope 848
SOAP request 848
SOAP Request for the **HugeIn-**
   teger Web service 848
socket 906
Socket class 917
soft key 1062
software component 8
Software Development Kit (SDK)
   1039

Software Engineering
   Observation 6
software reusability 6, 147, 184,
   193
solid arc 531
solid polygon 534
solid rectangle 528
SolidBrush class 519, 523, 527
solution 25
Solution Explorer after adding
   a Web reference to a project
   859
Solution Explorer in Visual
   Studio .NET 29, 412
Solution Explorer window 29,
   1196
Solution Explorer window for
   project **WebTime** 770
solution, debug setting 1145
Some basic GUI components 318
Some common escape sequences
   48
Some methods of class **Array-**
   List 985
Sort method of class **Array** 981
Sort method of class
   ArrayList 985
Sort property 836
Sort property in **DataView**
   class 836
sorted array 946
Sorted property of class **Com-**
   boBox 381
Sorted property of class **List-**
   Box 373
SortedList class 981
sorting 942
sorting technique 98
sorting.xml 696
sorting.xsl 697
SoundSentry 1044
source code 1170
source-code form 1204, 1253
source tree 695
span attribute 764, 1279
spawning 908
special character 464, 1215, 1230,
   1267, 1268
special symbol 580
speech device 1278
speech recognition 14, 1040, 1056
speech recognition engine 562
speech synthesis 14, 1040, 1056
speech synthesizer 1040, 1264
split a statement 51

Split method of class **Regex** 507, 508

spooling 961

sports.xml 682

SQL (Structured Query Language) 710, 712, 719

SQL keywords 719

SQL query keywords 719

SQL statement 712

SqlDataReader class 735

Sqrt method of class **Math** 106, 310

square 194, 1272

square brackets in a query 720

SquareRootTest.cs 310

src attribute (**img**) 1213, 1263, 1266

Src file 824

stack 16, 142, 181, 956

stack 956

Stack class 981, 990

stack unwinding 289, 304

StackComposition class encapsulates functionality of class **List** 960

StackCompositionLibrary.cs 960

StackInheritance extends class **List** 957

StackInheritanceLibrary.cs 957

StackInheritanceTest.cs 958

StackTest.cs 991

StackTrace property of **Exception** 303, 304, 307

standard character 1230

standard error 582

Standard Generalized Markup Language (SGML) 3, 15

standard input 581

Standard ML language 8

standard output object 45, 582

standard reusable component 194

standard time format 145

start a multiline comment (**/***) 43

Start button 42

Start method of class **Process** 369

Start method of class **TcpListener** 908

Start method of class **Thread** 426, 431

Start Page 24

Start Page in Visual Studio .NET 24

start tag 431, 658, 661, 1255

StartDialog.cs 639

StartDialogForm class enables users to access dialog boxes associated with various transactions 639

Started thread state 426, 448

starting angle 530

StartsWith and **EndsWith** methods 471

StartsWith method of class **String** 471

startup project 29

starvation 428

state button 340

stateless protocol 796

statement 45

static constructor 168

static entities 98

static keyword 168, 169, 172, 173

static member demonstration 171

static members are accessible to all objects of a clas 170

static method 50

static method cannot access non-**static** class members 169

Static method **Concat** 478

static variable 169

Step Into button 1154

Step Out button 1154

Step Over button 1149

StickyKeys 1045

Stop Debugging button 1149, 1151

Stopped thread state 426, 427

straight line 541

Stream class 582

stream input/output 579

stream of bytes 581

stream socket 924

StreamReader class 582

streams 907

streams-based transmission 919, 939

StreamWriter class 582

Strikeout member of enumeration **FontStyle** 523

Strikeout property of class **Font** 522

string 14, 45

String class 143, 252, 253, 463

String Collection Editor in Visual Studio .NET 374

string concatenation 56

string constant 464

String constructors 465

string formatting characters 76

String indexer 468

String indexer, **Length** properties and **CopyTo** method 466

String Length property, the **CopyTo** method and **StrReverse** function 466

string literal 45, 464

String methods **Replace**, **ToLower**, **ToUpper**, **Trim** and **ToString** 479

string of characters 45

string primitive data type 56, 106

String test to determine equality 469

String testing for equality 469

StringBuilder class 14, 463, 481

StringBuilder class constructors 481

StringBuilder size manipulation 483

StringBuilder text insertion and removal 488

StringBuilder text replacement 489

StringBuilder's **AppendFormat** method 486

StringBuilderAppend.cs 485

StringBuilderAppendFormat.cs 486

StringBuilderConstructor.cs 481

StringBuilderFeatures.cs 483

StringBuilderInsertRemove.cs 488

StringBuilderReplace.cs 489

StringCompare.cs 469

StringConstructor.cs 465

StringHashCode.cs 472

StringIndexMethods.cs 473

StringMethods.cs 466

StringMiscellaneous2.cs 479

StringStartEnd.cs 471

strong element 1260
strongly typed language 109
Stroustrup, Bjarne 285
struct keyword 491
structure 491
structured programming xl, 11, 83, 182
Structured Query Language (SQL) 710, 712, 719
<Style> tag 1088, 1107
style sheet 659, 1052, 1088, 1107, 1255
StyleReference property 1088, 1107
Stylesheets and templates in a Mobile Web Form 1088
sub element 1215, 1268
sub-initializer list 132
subclass 89
SubConcatenation.cs 478
<subdialog> tag 1032
submenu 360
submit attribute 1038
submit data to a server 1231
submit input 1231
subscript 122, 131, 1215, 1268
Substring method of class **String** 476
SubString.cs 476
Substrings generated from **String**s 476
subtraction assignment operator (**-=**) 67
Success property of **Match** 501
sum function 700
summary attribute 1024, 1278
summary tag 1169
Sun Microsystems, Inc. 1182
sup element 1268
superclass 89
superscript 1215, 1268
suspend a program 1144
Suspend method of class **Thread** 427
Suspended thread state 427
sweep 530
switch logic 79
switch selection structure 11, 61, 76, 77
SwitchTest.cs 77
Sybase, Inc. 710, 1182
symbol 1181
SyncBlock 432, 447
synchronization 432, 434, 440
synchronized 946

Synchronized Multimedia Integration Language (SMIL) 1040
Synchronized.cs 440
synchronous error 286
syntax error 45, 47
syntax error in HTML 1204
system caret 1053
SYSTEM flag 686
System namespace 44, 141, 463
system service 908
System.Collections namespace 956, 981
System.Data namespace 734
System.Data.OleDb namespace 734
System.Data.Sqlclient namespace 734
System.Drawing namespace 511, 512, 538
System.Draw-ing.Drawing2D namespace 511, 541
System.GC.WaitForPend-ingFinalizers method 172
System.IO namespace 582
System.Net namespace 869
System.Runtime.Serial-ization.Format-ters.Binary namespace 604
System.Text namespace 463
System.Text.RegularEx-pressions namespace 463, 499
System.Threading namespace 424
System.Web namespace 766
System.Web.Mobile assembly 1061
System.Web.Security namespace 829
System.Web.UI namespace 766
System.Web.UI.Mobile-Controls namespace 1062
System.Web.UI.WebCon-trols namespace 766
System.Windows.Forms 49
System.Windows.Forms namespace 47, 49, 89, 320
System.Xml namespace 665
System.Xml.Xsl namespace 700

SystemException class 294, 309

T

tab 48
tab order 1015
tab stop 48, 1015
Tabbed pages in Visual Studio .NET 398
tabbed window 27
TabControl class 398
TabControl properties and events 399
TabControl used to display various font settings 400
TabControl with **TabPage**s example 399
TabControl, adding a **TabPage** 399
TabCount property of class **TabControl** 400
TabIndex property of class **Control** 327, 1020
table 711, 1021, 1022, 1203, 1223, 1253
table body 1278
table column 711
table data 1278
table element 131, 1224, 1278
table head element 1278
table in which record will be updated 732, 733
table of values 130
Table optimized for screen reading using attribute **headers** 1022
table row 1278
TableDisplay.cs 735
TabPage class 398
TabPage, add to **TabControl** 398
TabPage, using radio buttons 403
TabPages added to a **TabCon-trol** 399
TabPages added to a **TabCon-trol** 399
TabPages property of class **TabControl** 400
TabStop property 327
TabStop property of class **Con-trol** 1020
tabular format 124
tag 759, 1203
tag name 824

tag prefix 764, 1061

TagPrefix attribute 1061

tail of a queue 961

target = "_blank" 1302

target = "_self" 1302

target = "_top" 1302

target ="_blank" 1247

target ="_parent" 1247

target ="_self" 1247

target ="_top" 1247

targetNamespace attribute 691

targetSessions attribute 1039

Task List window 1143

tbody (table body) element 1225, 1278

TCP (Transmission Control Protocol) 907

TCP/IP (Transmission Control Protocol/Internet Protocol) 3

TcpClient class 909

TcpListener class 907, 908

td element 1278

telephone system 919

TemperatureServer Web service 884

TemperatureServer.asmx.cs 884

TempFileCollection class 670

template element 1094

templated control 1094

temporary data storage 579

termDigits attribute 1037, 1039

terminating right brace (**}**) of a block 114

termination housekeeping 168

termination model of exception handling 288

ternary operator (**?:**) 63

Test2 demonstrates polymorphism in Point-Circle-Cylinder hierarchy 247

Test3 uses interfaces to demonstrate polymorphism in Point-Circle-Cylinder hierarchy 271

Testing and Debugging Tip 6

Testing class **Cylinder** 220

text 562

text-based browser 1264

text box 1284

Text constant of enumeration **XmlNodeType** 667

text editor 463, 1204, 1253

text element 1033, 1037

text file 665

Text property 37, 327, 335

Text property of class **LinkLabel** 369

Text property of class **MenuItem** 363

Text property of class **TreeNode** 387

TextAlign property 327

textarea 1231

textarea element 1233, 1284, 1285

text-based browser 1212, 1225

TextBox class 317, 318, 330

TextBox control 1070

TextBox properties and events 331

TextChanged event 331

TextReader class 582

text-to-speech (TTS) 1015, 1033, 1048

text-to-speech engine 562

TextToSpeech.cs 1016

TextureBrush class 516, 537, 541

TextWriter class 582

tfoot (table foot) element 1279

th (table header column) element 1022, 1278

The Diversity Directory 1130

The National Business and Disability Council (NBDC) 1130

thead (table head) tag 1225, 1278

this keyword 165, 169

this reference demonstration 167

this reference used implicitly and explicitly to enable an object to manipulate its own data and invoke its own methods 166

Thread class 425, 917

Thread life cycle 426

thread life cycle 426

thread of execution 424

Thread-priority scheduling 429

thread-priority scheduling 429

thread scheduling 439

thread state 425

thread state *Dead* 426

thread state *Ready* 426

thread state *Runnable* 426

thread state *Running* 426, 429

thread state *Started* 426

thread state *Stopped* 426, 427

thread state *Suspended* 427

thread state *Unstarted* 426

thread state *WaitSleepJoin* 427, 428, 433

thread synchronization 432

ThreadAbortException 426

ThreadPriority enumeration 427, 428

threads sleeping and printing 429

ThreadStart delegate 426, 429, 432

ThreadTester.cs 429

three-dimensional application 543

Three-tier architecture 761

throw an exception 288, 292

throw point 288, 303

throw statement 297

Tick event of class **Timer** 418, 548

TicketReservation.aspx 880

TicketReservation.aspx.cs 881

Tic-Tac-Toe 924

tightly packed binary tree 973

TileHorizontal value in **LayoutMdi** enumeration 408

TileVertical value in **LayoutMdi** enumeration 408

time and date 418

Time1 abstract data type represents the time in 24-hour format 140

Time1.cs 140

timeout 1048

timeout attribute of **prompt** element 1032

Timeout property of **HttpSessionState** class 812

timer 418

Timer class 546

timeslicing 427

TipCalculator.aspx 1071

title bar 27, 36, 42, 1256

title bar, MDI parent and child 405

title element 699, 759, 1024, 1206, 1256

title of a document 1255

title-bar string 72

titles table of **books** database 712, 715
.tlb file 1197
ToggleKeys 1046
ToInt32 method of **Convert** 291, 292
ToLongTimeString method of structure **ToLong-TimeString** 418
ToLower method of class **Char** 493
ToLower method of class **String** 478, 479
toolbar 28
toolbar icon 28
Toolbox 772, 1068
Toolbox window 30
Tools menu 28
tooltip 28, 783
Tool-tip demonstration 28
top tier 762
ToString method of class **Decimal** 260
ToString method of class **String** 307, 480
ToString method of class **StringBuilder** 482, 484
ToString method of **Object** 199
ToUpper method of class **Char** 493
ToUpper method of class **String** 478, 479
tr (table row) element 1225, 1278
Trace class 837
  Warn method 837
  Write property 837
trace element in a **Web.config** file 837
Trace property 16
trace property of **Page** class 837
trace.axd file 837
TraceContext class 837
tracing 836
Tracing enabled on a page 838
Tracing information for a project 838
track 1040
tracking customers 796
transaction-processing system 616
Transaction.cs 634
TransactionProcessor.cs 638

TransactionProcessorForm class runs the transaction-processor application 638
transfer of control 61
Transform method of **XslTransform** 700
TransformTest.cs 700
TranslateTransform method of class **Graphics** 541
Transmission Control Protocol/Internet Protocol (TCP/IP) 3
trapezoid 194
traverse a tree 972
tree 16, 385, 964
tree structure 659
Tree structure for **article.xml** 665
Tree structure for Fig. 18.1 665
Tree.cs 263
TreeNode class 387
TreeNode Editor 388
TreeNode Editor in Visual Studio .NET 385
TreeNode properties and methods 387
TreeTest.cs 970, 978
TreeView 359
TreeView class 385
TreeView displaying a sample tree 386
TreeView properties and events 386
TreeView used to display directories 388
TreeViewDirectoryStructureTest.cs 388
trigger an event 318
Trim method of class **String** 478
trim method of **string** 676
TrimToSize method of class **ArrayList** 985, 990
truth 53
try block 288, 292
try block expires 288
TTS (text-to-speech) engine 1033
Tutor.cs 900
two-dimensional arrays 131
two-dimensional data structure 964
two-dimensional shape 511
two's complement 1120
twos position 1113
type = "hidden" 1230

type = "password" 1234
type = "radio" 1234
type = "reset" 1231
type = "submit" 1231
type = "text" 1231
type attribute 691, 1230, 1272, 1284
Type class 1020
typesetting system 463

U

U+$yyyy$ (Unicode notational convention) 1183
UDDI (Universal Description, Discovery, and Integration) 858
UDP 907
UdpClient class 919
uint primitive data type 106
uint promotions 107
ul element 1269
ulong primitive data type 106
ulong promotions 107
unambiguous (Unicode design basis) 1182
unary operator 74, 85
UnauthorizedAccessException class 390
unbounded value 691
Unchecked constant 340
unchecked context 312
unchecked operator 312
Underline member of enumeration **FontStyle** 523
Underline property of class **Font** 522
underscore (_) 44
undo 27
uneditable text or icons 318
Unicode 18, 106, 110
Unicode character 580
Unicode character set 464
Unicode Consortium 1182
Unicode Standard design basis 1181, 1182
Uniform Resource Identifier (URI) 663
unique class name 184
Univac 1108 2
universal (Unicode design principle) 1182
universal data access 8
Universal Description, Discovery, and Integration (UDDI) 858

Universal Resource Locator (URL) 663

universal time format 141, 143, 145

Unload event 767

unmanaged resource 767

unordered list element (**ul**) 1216, 1217, 1269

Unstarted thread state 426

Unsynchronized.cs 435

UPDATE 719, 732

UPDATE query 877

UpdateCommand property of **OleDbAdapter** 742

UpdateDialog.cs 644

updating a database 1230

upper-left corner of a GUI component 512

uppercase 44

URI (Uniform Resource Identifier) 663

URL (Uniform Resource Locator) 759, 796

URL (Universal Resource Locator) 663

usemap attribute 1297

UseMnemonic property of class **LinkLabel** 369

user agent 1007, 1053

user control 824

User Datagram Protocol (UDP) 907

user-defined method 99

user-defined type 139

user interface 762

UserControl class 417

user-defined exception class 308

userInput of class **_AgentEvents_CommandEvent** 576

ushort primitive data type 106

ushort promotions 107

Using a **PictureBox** to display images 349

Using an abstract data type 144

Using **CheckBox**es to change font styles 341

Using class **StackInheritance** 958

Using default namespaces 664

using directive 44, 49

Using **GroupBox**es and **Panel**s to arrange **Button**s 338

Using inheritance to create a queue 963

Using internal hyperlinks to make pages more navigable 1238, 1292

Using **meta** to provide keywords and a description 1297

using operator overloading 280

Using overloaded methods 120

using parentheses to force the order of evaluation 52

Using **RadioButton**s to set message-window options 344

Using **string** indexer, **Length** property and **CopyTo** method 466

using temperature and weather data 889

Using the **foreach** structure with an array 135

using the **HugeInteger** Web service 859

Using the mouse to draw on a form 352

Using the **Properties** window to set a property value 92

Using the **Stack** class 991

UsingArray.cs 982

UsingExceptions.cs 298

UsingFontMetrics.cs 525

UsingFonts.cs 523

UsingForeach.cs 135

UsingHugeIntegerService.cs 859

UsingMDI.cs 409

UsingTabs.cs 400

UTF-8 1182

UTF-16 1182

UTF-32 1182

utility method 142

\u*yyyy* Unicode format 1187

V

valid 683

valid identifier 44

valid page 1071

Validate.cs 502

Validating user information using regular expressions 502

validating XML parser 683

validation control 1071

validation service 1257

ValidationExpression property of class **RegularExpressionValidator** 788

ValidationTest.cs 692

validator 785

validator.w3.org 1204, 1257, 1274

validator.w3.org/file-upload.html 1257

Validators used in a Web Form that generates possible letter combinations from a phone number 786

validity 684

validity checking 154

valign = "middle" 1228

valign attribute (**th**) 1228, 1281

value attribute 1038, 1039, 1230, 1231, 1284

value of an attribute 1255

Value property of **HttpCookie** class 805, 806

Value property of **ServerValidateEventArgs** class 829

value tag 1169

value types 109

VALUES 731

ValueType class 491

<var> tag (**<var>…</var>**) 1032

var attribute 1037, 1038

variable 55, 139

variable reference 68

variable scope 70

variable, in previous statement 1148

variable, modify at run time 1148

Vault.com 1126

version 697

version attribute of **xml** declaration 1033

version parameter of **xml** tag 658

vertex 1297

vertical alignment formatting 1228

vertical coordinate 512

vi text editor 1204, 1253

ViaVoice 1007, 1025

video clip 424

View menu in Internet Explorer 27, 50

View property of class **ListView** 392

Viewing the tracing information for a project 838

__VIEWSTATE hidden input 795

ViewStateEnabled attribute 795

virtual directory 759

virtual key code 356

Visible property 327

VisitedLinkColor property of class **LinkLabel** 369

Visual Basic .NET 8

Visual C++ .NET 8, 10

Visual Inheritance through the Form Designer 415

visual programming 11, 320

Visual Studio .NET 11, 23

Visual Studio .NET Class View 189

Visual Studio .NET creating and linking a virtual directory for the **Welcome** project folder 1065

Visual Studio .NET Debugger 17

Visual Studio .NET environment after a new project has been created 26

Visual Studio .NET-generated console application 46, 335

Visual Studio .NET menu bar 27

Visual Studio .NET menu bar summary 27

Visual Studio .NET **Menu Designer** 361

Visual Studio .NET Object Browser 189

Visual Studio accessibility guidelines 1008

Visual Studio creating and linking a virtual directory for the **WebTime** project folder 770

VisualInheritance.cs 413

VisualInheritanceTest.cs 415

vocabulary 662

Voice Server SDK 1.0 1026

Voice settings window 1051

voice synthesis 1025

VoiceXML 15, 17, 1025, 1026, 1031, 1040, 1055

VoiceXML tags 1032

void return-value-type 104

Voxeo (**www.voxeo.com**) 1033, 1034

Voxeo Account Manager 1034

.vsdisco file extension 859

<vxml> tag 1032

W

W3C (World Wide Web Consortium) 4, 16, 707, 1055, 1272

W3C host 4

W3C Recommendation 4, 690, 1253

W3C XML Schema 687

WAI (Web Accessiblity Initiative) 16, 1006

WAI Quick Tip 1006

wait element 433, 1039

Wait method of class **Monitor** 427, 440, 447, 448

WaitForPendingFinalizers method of class **GC** 172

waiting line 942

waiting thread 448

WaitSleepJoin thread state 427, 428, 433

walk the list 955

WAP (Wireless Application Protocol) 1058, 1107, 1132

WAP browser 1059

WAP device 1059, 1107

Warn method of **Trace** class 837

WAV file format 559

Web 18

Web Accessibility Initiative (WAI) 16, 1055

Web-based application development 758

Web Content Accessibility Guidelines 1.0 1006, 1008, 1021, 1025

Web Content Accessibility Guidelines 2.0 (Working Draft) 1006

Web control 15, 758

Web controls commonly used in ASP.NET applications 775

Web controls demonstration 776

Web Form 15, 758, 797, 808, 836

    Properties window 837

Web Form page 758

Web Form with embedded C# code 1071

Web Forms menu in the **Toolbox** 771

Web reference 857

Web reference selection and description 858

Web server 759, 908, 1230, 1254, 1281

Web server/Client interaction. Step 1: The **GET** request, **GET /books/downloads.htm HTTP/1.0** 760

Web service xxxix, 7, 16, 844

Web Service Description Language (WSDL) 845

Web-service method 844

Web service that generates random equations 897

Web Services 183

Web site using two frames: navigational and content 1245, 1299

Web user control 824

Web.config file 1092, 1096, 1107

Web.config file used for **Portal2.aspx** 1093

Web.config namespace 829, 837

WebClient class 887

WebControl class 766

WebControls.aspx 776

WebHire 1127

WebMethod attribute 844, 846, 855

WebService attribute 854

WebService class 855

WebTime.aspx 762

WebTime.aspx.cs 764

WebTime.html 767

Welcome.aspx 816, 1060

Welcome.aspx after adding two **Label**s and setting their properties 1070

Welcome.aspx.cs 818, 1062

Welcome1.cs 43

Welcome2.cs 48

well-formed document 683

WHERE 719, 720, 721, 722, 723, 725, 732, 733

while repetition structure 11, 62, 64

White static property of structure **Color** 515

whitespace character 45, 480, 499

widening conversion 106

widget 317

width attribute 1211, 1263, 1264, 1278

width of text input 1231

width-to-height ratio 1264, 1211

Wiltamuth, Scott 9

window auto-hide 31

window gadget 317
window layout 28
Window menu 28
window tab 27
Windows 2000 17
Windows 95/98 23
Windows application 23, 25
Windows control library 419
Windows Control Library
    project 593
Windows Explorer 370
Windows Form 13, 318
Windows Form Designer
    generated code expanded 90
Windows Form Designer
    generated code reflecting
    new property values 92
Windows Forms proxy 1193
Windows Media Player 559
Windows Media Player
    demonstration 559
Windows NT/2000 23
Windows Registry 1192
Windows Wave file format
    (WAV) 559
WinForms 318
wire format 846
wire protocol 846
Wireless Application Protocol
    (WAP) 1058, 1132
wireless device 1058, 1107
wireless Internet 1058
Wireless Markup Language
    (WML) 1058, 1059, 1060,
    1107
WirelessImageUrl element
    1095, 1096
WirelessResumes.com 1132
WML 1058, 1107
WML (Wireless Markup
    Language) 1059, 1060
word character 499
word processor 463, 473
Wordpad 1253
Working Draft 4
WorkingSolo.com 1133
World Wide Web (WWW) 3, 16,
    317, 424
World Wide Web Consortium
    (W3C) 4, 16, 657, 707, 1055
Write method of class **Binary-**
    Writer 918
Write method of class **Console**
    56, 582
Write method of class **Net-**
    workStream 909

Write property of **Trace** class
    837
WriteByte method of class
    NetworkStream 909
WriteLine method 1144
WriteLine method of class
    Console 45, 582
WriteRandomAccess-
    File.cs 624
WriteXml method of **DataSet**
    752
Writing records to random-access
    files 624
WSDL (Web Service Description
    Language) 845
WWW (World Wide Web) 3, 16
www.advantagehir-
    ing.com 1130
www.advisorteam.net/
    AT/User/kcs.asp 1130
www.asp.net/De-
    fault.aspx?tabin-
    dex=4&tabid=44 1108
www.biztalk.com 705
www.careerpower.com 1135
www.chami.com/html-kit
    1204
www.chiefmonster.com
    1134
www.deitel.com xl, xli, 21,
    1204, 1261
www.devx.com 1108
www.etest.net 1130
www.ework.com 1133
www.execunet.com 1134
www.jasc.com 1263
www.jobfind.com 1128
www.jobtrak.com 1131
www.microsoft.com 21
www.microsoft.com/net 8,
    21
www.mindexchange.com
    1130
www.nationjob.com 1134
www.netvalley.com/in-
    tval.html 21
www.prenhall.com/dei-
    tel xli, 21
www.recruitsoft.com/
    process 1130
www.review.com 1135
www.sixfigurejobs.com
    1134
www.unicode.org 1184
www.voxeo.com (Voxeo)
    1033, 1034

www.w3.org 4, 21
www.w3.org/2000/10/
    XMLSchema 691
www.w3.org/markup 1253
www.w3.org/TR/1998/
    NOTE-compactHTML-
    19980209 1108
www.w3.org/TR/xhtml1
    1274
www.w3.org/XML/Schema
    690
www.w3.org/XML/Sche-
    ma.html 686
www.w3schools.com/xht-
    ml/default.asp 1274
www.webhire.com 1127
www.xhtml.org 1274
www.yahoo.com 1209

X

x-axis 512
x-coordinate 512
X formatting character 76
Xalan XSLT processor 695
XBRL (Extensible Business
    Reporting Language) 15
Xerces parser 659
XHTML (Extensible HyperText
    Markup Language) 4, 15, 17,
    1253
XHTML comment 1254
XHTML form 1281
XHTML Recommendation 1055,
    1274
XHTML table without
    accessibility modifications
    1021
XML (Extensible Markup
    Language) 4, 10, 15, 657,
    845, 1058
XML comment 1161
XML declaration 658
XML document containing book
    information 696
XML document referencing its
    associated DTD 685
XML document that conforms to a
    Microsoft Schema document
    688
XML document that conforms to
    W3C XML Schema 690
XML document that describes
    various sports 682
XML document that does not
    conform to XSD schema 694

XML documentation 1162
XML documentation comment
    1161
XML documentation generated by
    Visual Studio .NET 1172
XML file containing **AdRotator**
    information 783
.xml file extension 659
XML file that does not conform to
    the Schema in Fig. 18.17 694
XML GL (XML Guidelines) 1025
XML Guidelines (XML GL) 1025
xml namespace 662
XML namespaces demonstration
    662
XML node 659, 665
XML parser 659
XML processors 659
XML root 659
XML Schema 15, 662, 688, 690
XML serialization 894
XML tag 658
XML to mark up a business letter
    660
XML used to mark up an article
    657
XML Validator 686
XML Validator displaying an
    error message 688
XML Validator used to validate an
    XML document 687
XML vocabulary 5
XML.com 707
XML.org 707
XML4J parser 659
XML-Data Reduced 688
XmlDeclaration constant of
    enumeration **XmlNode-
    Type** 667
XmlDom.cs 669
XmlNodeReader class 666
XmlNodeReader used to iterate
    through an XML document
    666
XmlNodeType enumeration 667
xmlns attribute 663, 665
XmlReader class 666
XmlReaderTest.cs 666
XmlValidatingReader class
    691
XMLWriter.cs 752
Xor method of class **BitArray**
    1312, 1324
XPath expression 675, 676, 706
XPath expressions and
    descriptions 683

XPathNavigator class used to
    navigate selected nodes 676
XPathNodeIterator Class
    676
.xsd extension 690
XSD Schema document to which
    bookxsd.xml conforms.
    690
xsd:date 691
xsd:double 691
xsd:int 691
xsd:string 691
xsd:time 691
XSL (Extensible Stylesheet
    Language) 662, 695
XSL document that transforms
    sorting.xml into
    XHTML 697
XSL specification 707
XSL style sheet applied to an
    XML document 700
XSL variable 700
xsl:template 697
XSLT (Extensible Stylesheet
    Language Transformation)
    15
XSLT processor 695
XsltArgumentList class 700
XslTransform class 700
x-y coordinate 1243, 1297

Y

y-axis 512
y-coordinate 512
Yahoo! 1128
yellow 514
yellow arrow 1146
Yellow static property of
    structure **Color** 515
YesNo member of enumeration
    MessageBoxButtons 73
YesNoCancel member of
    enumeration **Message-
    BoxButtons** 73

Z

zero-based counting 126
zeroth element 122

The DEITEL™
Suite of Products...

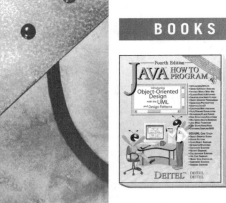

Java™ How to Program Fourth Edition

BOOK / CD-ROM

©2002, 1546 pp., paper
(0-13-034151-7)

The world's best-selling Java text is now even better! The Fourth Edition of *Java How to Program* includes a new focus on object-oriented design with the UML, design patterns, full-color program listings and figures and the most up-to-date Java coverage available.

Readers will discover key topics in Java programming, such as graphical user interface components, exception handling, multithreading, multimedia, files and streams, networking, data structures and more. In addition, a new chapter on design patterns explains frequently recurring architectural patterns—information that can help save designers considerable time when building large systems.

The highly detailed optional case study focuses on object-oriented design with the UML and presents fully implemented working Java code.

Updated throughout, the text includes new and revised discussions on topics such as Swing, graphics and socket- and packet-based networking. Three introductory chapters heavily emphasize problem solving and programming skills. The chapters on RMI, JDBC™, servlets and JavaBeans have been moved to *Advanced Java 2 Platform How to Program*, where they are now covered in much greater depth. (See *Advanced Java 2 Platform How to Program* below.)

Advanced Java™ 2 Platform How to Program

BOOK / CD-ROM

©2002, 1811 pp., paper
(0-13-089560-1)

Expanding on the world's best-selling Java textbook—*Java How to Program*—*Advanced Java 2 Platform How To Program* presents advanced Java topics for developing sophisticated, user-friendly GUIs; significant, scalable enterprise applications; wireless applications and distributed systems. Primarily based on Java 2 Enterprise Edition (J2EE), this textbook integrates technologies such as XML, JavaBeans, security, Java Database Connectivity (JDBC), JavaServer Pages (JSP), servlets, Remote Method Invocation (RMI), Enterprise JavaBeans™ (EJB) and design patterns into a production-quality system that allows developers to benefit from the leverage and platform independence Java 2 Enterprise Edition provides. The book also features the development of a complete, end-to-end e-business solution using advanced Java technologies. Additional topics include Swing, Java 2D and 3D, XML, design patterns, CORBA, Jini™, JavaSpaces™, Jiro™, Java Management Extensions (JMX) and Peer-to-Peer networking with an introduction to JXTA. This textbook also introduces the Java 2 Micro Edition (J2ME™) for building applications for handheld and wireless devices using MIDP and MIDlets. Wireless technologies covered include WAP, WML and i-mode.

C# How to Program

BOOK / CD-ROM

©2002, 1568 pp., paper
(0-13-062221-4)

An exciting new addition to the How to Program series, *C# How to Program* provides a comprehensive introduction to Microsoft's new object-oriented language. C# builds on the skills already mastered by countless C++ and Java programmers, enabling them to create powerful Web applications and components—ranging from XML-based Web services on Microsoft's .NET platform to middle-tier business objects and system-level applications. *C# How to Program* begins with a strong foundation in the introductory and intermediate programming principles students will need in industry. It then explores such essential topics as object-oriented programming and exception handling. Graphical user interfaces are extensively covered, giving readers the tools to build compelling and fully interactive programs. Internet technologies such as XML, ADO .NET and Web services are also covered as well as topics including regular expressions, multithreading, networking, databases, files and data structures.

Also coming soon in the Deitels' .NET Series:

• *Visual C++ .NET How to Program*

programming concepts that yield visible or audible results in Web pages and Web-based applications. This book discusses effective Web-based design, server- and client-side scripting, multitier Web-based applications development, ActiveX® controls and electronic commerce essentials. This book offers an alternative to traditional programming courses using markup languages (such as XHTML, Dynamic HTML and XML) and scripting languages (such as JavaScript, VBScript, Perl/CGI, Python and PHP) to teach the fundamentals of programming "wrapped in the metaphor of the Web."

Updated material on **www.deitel.com** and **www.prenhall.com/deitel** provides additional resources for instructors who want to cover Microsoft® or non-Microsoft technologies. The Web site includes an extensive treatment of Netscape® 6 and alternate versions of the code from the Dynamic HTML chapters that will work with non-Microsoft environments as well.

Wireless Internet & Mobile Business How to Program

©2002, 1292 pp., paper
(0-13-062226-5)

While the rapid expansion of wireless technologies, such as cell phones, pagers and personal digital assistants (PDAs), offers many new opportunities for businesses and programmers, it also presents numerous challenges related to issues such as security and standardization. This book offers a thorough treatment of both the management and technical aspects of this growing area, including coverage of current practices and future trends. The first half explores the business issues surrounding wireless technology and mobile business, including an overview of existing and developing communication technologies and the application of business principles to wireless devices. It also discusses location-based services and location-identifying technologies, a topic that is revisited throughout the book. Wireless payment, security, legal and social issues, international communications and more are also discussed. The book then turns to programming for the wireless Internet, exploring topics such as WAP (including 2.0), WML, WMLScript, XML, XHTML™, wireless Java programming (J2ME)™, Web Clipping and more. Other topics covered include career resources, wireless marketing, accessibility, Palm™, PocketPC, Windows CE,

i-mode, Bluetooth, MIDP, MIDlets, ASP, Microsoft .NET Mobile Framework, BREW™, multimedia, Flash™ and VBScript.

Python How to Program

BOOK / CD-ROM

©2002, 1376 pp., paper
(0-13-092361-3)

This exciting new book provides a comprehensive introduction to Python— a powerful object-oriente programming language with clear syntax and th ability to bring together various technologies quickl and easily. This book covers introductory-programming techniques and more advanced topics such as graphical user interfaces, databases, wireless Internet programming, networking, security, process management, multithreading, XHTML, CSS, PSP and multimedia. Readers will learn principles that are applicable to both systems development an Web programming. The book features the consisten and applied pedagogy that the *How to Program Series* is known for, including the Deitels' signatur LIVE-CODE™ Approach, with thousands of lines o code in hundreds of working programs; hundreds of valuable programming tips identified with icons throughout the text; an extensive set of exercises projects and case studies; two-color four-way synta coloring and much more.

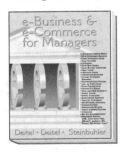

e-Business & e-Commerce for Managers

©2001, 794 pp., cloth
(0-13-032364-0)

This comprehensive overview of building and managing e-businesses explores topics such as the decision to bring a business online, choosing a business model, accepting payments, marketing strategies and security, as well as many other importa issues (such as career resources). The book feature Web resources and online demonstrations that supplement the text and direct readers to additiona materials. The book also includes an appendix tha develops a complete Web-based shopping-cart app cation using HTML, JavaScript, VBScript, Active Server Pages, ADO, SQL, HTTP, XML and XSL. Plus, company-specific sections provide "real-world examples of the concepts presented in the book.

XML How to Program

`BOOK / CD-ROM`

©2001, 934 pp., paper (0-13-028417-3)

This book is a comprehensive guide to programming in XML. It teaches how to use XML to create customized tags and includes chapters that address standard custom-markup languages for science and technology, multimedia, commerce and many other fields. Concise introductions to Java, JavaServer Pages, VBScript, Active Server Pages and Perl/CGI provide readers with the essentials of these programming languages and server-side development technologies to enable them to work effectively with XML. The book also covers cutting-edge topics such as XSL, DOM™ and SAX, plus a real-world e-commerce case study and a complete chapter on Web accessibility that addresses Voice XML. It includes tips such as Common Programming Errors, Software Engineering Observations, Portability Tips and Debugging Hints. Other topics covered include XHTML, CSS, DTD, schema, parsers, XPath, XLink, namespaces, XBase, XInclude, XPointer, XSLT, XSL Formatting Objects, JavaServer Pages, XForms, topic maps, X3D, MathML, OpenMath, CML, BML, CDF, RDF, SVG, Cocoon, WML, XBRL and BizTalk™ and SOAP™ Web resources.

Perl How to Program

`BOOK / CD-ROM`

©2001, 1057 pp., paper (0-13-028418-1)

This comprehensive guide to Perl programming emphasizes the use of the Common Gateway Interface (CGI) with Perl to create powerful, dynamic multi-tier Web-based client/server applications. The book begins with a clear and careful introduction to programming concepts at a level suitable for beginners, and proceeds through advanced topics such as references and complex data structures. Key Perl topics such as regular expressions and string manipulation are covered in detail. The authors address important and topical issues such as object-oriented programming, the Perl database interface (DBI), graphics and security. Also included is a treatment of XML, a bonus chapter introducing the Python programming language, supplemental material on career resources and a complete chapter on Web accessibility. The text includes tips such as Common Programming Errors, Software Engineering Observations, Portability Tips and Debugging Hints.

e-Business & e-Commerce How to Program

`BOOK / CD-ROM`

©2001, 1254 pp., paper (0-13-028419-X)

This innovative book explores programming technologies for developing Web-based e-business and e-commerce solutions, and covers e-business and e-commerce models and business issues. Readers learn a full range of options, from "build-your-own" to turnkey solutions. The book examines scores of the top e-businesses (examples include Amazon, eBay, Priceline, Travelocity, etc.), explaining the technical details of building successful e-business and e-commerce sites and their underlying business premises. Learn how to implement the dominant e-commerce models—shopping carts, auctions, name-your-own-price, comparison shopping and bots/ intelligent agents—by using markup languages (HTML, Dynamic HTML and XML), scripting languages (JavaScript, VBScript and Perl), server-side technologies (Active Server Pages and Perl/CGI) and database (SQL and ADO), security and online payment technologies. Updates are regularly posted to www.deitel.com and the book includes a CD-ROM with software tools, source code and live links.

www.deitel.com/newsletter/subscribe.html

Complete Training Courses

Each complete package includes the corresponding *How to Program Series* book and interactive multimedia CD-ROM Cyber Classroom. *Complete Training Courses* are perfect for anyone interested Web and e-commerce programming. They are affordable resources for college students and professionals learning programming for the first time or reinforcing their knowledge.

Each *Complete Training Course* is compatible with Windows 95, Windows 98, Windows NT and Windows 2000 and includes the following features:

Intuitive Browser-Based Interface

You'll love the *Complete Training Courses'* new browser-based interface, designed to be easy and accessible to anyone who's ever used a Web browser. Every *Complete Training Course* features the full text, illustrations and program listings of its corresponding *How to Program* book—all in full color—with full-text searching and hyperlinking.

Further Enhancements to the Deitels' Signature LIVE-CODE™ Approach

Every code sample from the main text can be found in the interactive, multimedia, CD-ROM based *Cyber Classrooms* included in the *Complete Training Courses*. Syntax coloring of code is included for the *How to Program* books that are published in full color. Even the recent two-color and one-color books use effective multi-way syntax shading. The *Cyber Classroom* products always are in full color.

Audio Annotations

Hours of detailed, expert audio descriptions of thousands of lines of code help reinforce concepts.

Easily Executable Code

With one click of the mouse, you can execute the code or save it to your hard drive to manipulate using the programming environment of your choice. With selected *Complete Training Courses*, you can also load all of the code into a development environment such as Microsoft® Visual C++™, enabling you to modify and execute the programs with ease.

Abundant Self-Assessment Material

Practice exams test your understanding with hundreds of test questions and answers in addition to those found in the main text. Hundreds of self-review questions, all with answers, are drawn from the text; as are hundreds of programming exercises, half with answers.

www.phptr.com/phptrinteractiv

Deitel & Associates, Inc. has partnered with Prentice Hall's parent company, Pearson PLC, and its information technology Web site, InformIT.com, to launch the Deitel InformIT kiosk at www.InformIT.com/deite The Deitel InformIT kiosk contains information on the continuum of Deitel products, including:

- **Free informational articles**
- **Deitel e-Matter**
- **Books and e-Books**
- **Web-based training**

- **Instructor-led training by Deitel & Associates**
- *Complete Training Courses/Cyber Classrooms*

Deitel & Associates is also contributing to two separate weekly InformIT e-mail newsletters.

The first is the InformIT promotional newsletter, which features weekly specials and discounts on Pearson publications. Each week a new Deitel™ product is featured along with information about our corporate instructor-led training courses and the opportunity to read about upcoming issues of our own e-mail newsletter, the DEITEL™ BUZZ ONLINE.

The second newsletter is the InformIT editorial newsletter, which contains approximately 50 new articles per week on various IT topics, including programming, advanced computing, networking, security, databases, creative media, business, Web development, software engineering, operating systems and more. Deitel & Associates contributes 2-3 articles per week pulled from our extensive existing content base or material being created during our research and development process.

Both of these publications are sent to over 750,000 registered users worldwide (for opt-in registration, visit www.InformIT.com).

Cyber Classrooms, Web-Based Training and Course Management Systems

DEITEL is committed to continuous research and development in e-Learning.

We are pleased to announce that we have incorporated examples of Web-based training, including a five-way Macromedia® Flash™ animation of a for loop in Java™, into the *Java 2 Multimedia Cyber Classroom, 4/e* (which is included in *The Complete Java 2 Training Course, 4/e*). Our instructional

designers and Flash animation team are developing additiona simulations that demonstrate key programming concepts.

We are enhancing the Multimedia Cyber Classroom product to include more audio, pre- and post-assessment question and Web-based labs with solutions for the benefit of professor and students alike. In addition, our Multimedia Cyber Classroom products, currently available in CD-ROM format, are being ported to Pearson's CourseCompass course-management system—*a powerful e-platform for teaching and learning.* Many Deitel materials are available in WebCT, Blackboard and CourseCompass formats for colleges, and will soon be available for various corporate learning management systems.

Sign up now for the new *DEITEL™ Buzz Online* newsletter at:

Future Publications

Here are some new titles we are considering for 2002/2003 release:

Computer Science Series: *Operating Systems 3/e, Data Structures in C++, Data Structures in Java, Theory and Principles of Database Systems.*

Database Series: *Oracle, SQL Server, MySQL.*

Internet and Web Programming Series: *Open Source Software Development: Apache, Linux, MySQL and PHP.*

Programming Series: *Flash™.*

.NET Programming Series: *ADO .NET with Visual Basic .NET, ASP .NET with Visual Basic .NET, ADO .NET with C#, ASP .NET with C#.*

Object Technology Series: *OOAD with the UML, Design Patterns, Java™ and XML.*

Advanced Java™ Series: *JDBC, Java 2 Enterprise Edition, Java Media Framework (JMF), Java Security and Java Cryptography (JCE), Java Servlets, Java2D and Java3D, JavaServer Pages™ (JSP), JINI and Java 2 Micro Edition™ (J2ME).*

DEITEL™ BUZZ ONLINE Newsletter

The Deitel and Associates, Inc. free opt-in newsletter includes:

- Updates and commentary on industry trends and developments
- Resources and links to articles from our published books and upcoming publications.
- Information on the Deitel publishing plans, including future publications and product-release schedules
- Support for instructors
- Resources for students
- Information on Deitel Corporate Training

To sign up for the Deitel™ Buzz Online newsletter, visit `www.deitel.com /newsletter/subscribe.html`.

E-Books

We are committed to providing our content in traditional print formats and in emerging electronic formats, such as e-books, to fulfill our customers' needs. Our R&D teams are currently exploring many leading-edge solutions.

Visit `www.deitel.com` and read the DEITEL™ BUZZ ONLINE for periodic updates.

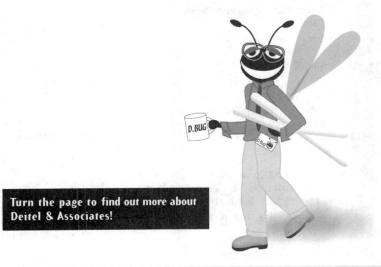

Turn the page to find out more about Deitel & Associates!